E. C. KRUSE

THE BIBLICAL ILLUSTRATOR
EXODUS

THE

BIBLICAL ILLUSTRATOR

BY
JOSEPH S. EXELL

EXODUS

BAKER BOOK HOUSE
GRAND RAPIDS 6, MICHIGAN
1962

Library of Congress Catalog Card Number: 54-11086

First Printing, July 1955
Second Printing, September 1958
Third Printing, May 1962

PHOTOLITHOPRINTED BY CUSHING - MALLOY, INC.
ANN ARBOR, MICHIGAN, UNITED STATES OF AMERICA
1962

INTRODUCTION TO THE BOOK OF EXODUS.

EXODUS: A SEQUEL TO GENESIS.—This, the second part of the Pentateuch, is a sequel to Genesis; it is joined on to Genesis by the conjunction *and*, and bears a remarkable resemblance to it. In Genesis, the earth rises out of darkness into light; in Exodus, Israel emerges out of the darkness of Egyptian bondage into light and liberty. The beginning of Genesis speaks of intestine struggles which preceded the creation of the earth in its present state; such, also, was the condition of Israel, "without form and void," before the Exodus. At the Creation the earth was brought forth out of the water, on the face of which the Spirit moved. And surely it was not without a meaning that the great leader of Israel, its mediator and lawgiver, the type of Christ Himself, Moses, was drawn out of the water, and thence received his name. Surely it was not without a meaning that Israel, whose children had been merged in water (as the prior earth was), rose to new life out of the waters of the Red Sea, over which the Spirit brooded in the cloud, and "they were baptized unto Moses in the cloud and in the sea." In Genesis the earth is born, by the Spirit, out of the water; in Exodus, Israel is born anew by the Spirit out of the water; and both these are figures of the new birth in Christ by water and the Spirit. Here is an inner analogy between Genesis and Exodus, and this treatment of the two great subjects bespeaks an unity of authorship. It bespeaks the presence also of the Divine Mind, guiding the hand of the writer. (*Bishop Christopher Wordsworth.*) Exodus is not the full counterpart of Genesis. That venerable document is matched in grandeur of scope not even by the rest of the Pentateuch, but only by the remainder of the volume of revelation. It opens with a creation, of which man forms the prominent object; the Old Testament closes with the anticipation of a new creation (Isa. lxv. 17), in which also man will hold the conspicuous place; and the New Testament records the atoning obedience of Christ, and the quickening work of the Holy Ghost, as the guarantee and earnest of that new creation, the consummation of which it again announces to the Church (2 Pet. iii. 13). Genesis also touches upon the history of the whole race of man, and even after the call of Abraham traces the peaceful intercourse subsisting between the chosen family and the rest of mankind. Exodus marks the full-grown antagonism between the chosen nation and the heathen world, records the violent separation between the two, and then confines itself mainly to the history of the party that remained in communion with God. Its distinguishing event, the Exodus, is accordingly the prototype of that great event in the experience of the individual, in which he comes out from the bondage of the flesh into the freedom of the Spirit, as well as of those great occasions in the history of the Church in which it reasserts its spiritual life and liberty, and passes with all the determination of new-born principle from the wilful service of sin into the conscientious obedience of holiness. This coming out is a process continually going on during the history of the Church until all have come out, and the doomed world is given over to everlasting destruction. It is the manner of Scripture to signalize the primary event in any given series as a lesson and example to all future generations. In Genesis are recorded all kinds of origins or births, and, among others, the birth of Isaac, the seed of promise. In Exodus is recounted the deliberate action of the new-born, in coming out of the land of bondage. The wilderness between this land and the land of promise, the troubles, temptations, and failings of such a state of life, the giving of the Law to a new-born and emancipated people, the setting up of the ordinances of a holy religion, are all typical events, prefiguring others of a like nature, but of still grander and grander import. They do not stand alone on memory's tablet, but embody a principle of constant value, which comes out in a series of analogous events in the course of human affairs. They are standing monuments in the great field of the past, written in legible characters on the page of history for the instruction of coming days. The scope of the Book of Exodus, however, is not to be limited to the mere fortunes of the chosen people. Even if it stood alone, its communications could not be confined to so narrow an area. It details a certain stage of that momentous process, by which the covenant of God with man is to be upheld, and its benefits secured for a growing proportion of our fallen race, until at length the main body at least of all kindreds and tongues returns to God. (*Professor J. G. Murphy.*)

DESCRIPTION OF THE BOOK.—Recollection, "remembrance," of the great original works of God in creation and redemption is the appropriate appointed means of originating and sustaining, in the heart and life of men, that righteousness, and peace, and joy in the Holy Ghost which constitute His true kingdom in individuals and in communities. The Pentateuch, as the instrument of God in that recollection of the Beginnings, is thus evermore in a fontal relation to the true new life of mankind in the Creator and Redeemer. And the vast importance of Exodus begins to appear when it is seen to be, thus, the central vitally essential part of a whole, whose importance is so vast as a feeder of that life which is unseen and eternal. For Exodus is not only a continuation of the narrative in Genesis on to the last three Books of Moses. Our translators, when they make the V, at the opening of this book, to be, not " and," as in Lev. i. 1, but " now " mean that here there is something more than simply continuation of the narrative. And, in fact, there is here a decisively new reach of the stream. It is not merely, as when the Nile rushes down its cataract from Ethiopia, a sudden transition into a new manner of movement, amid new surroundings. It is as if a new and mighty river had sprung out of a smitten rock, or poured down from heaven in effusion Pentecostal. For instance, on the face of the movement there is that very great new thing, the first appearance among mankind of a visible kingdom of God; a kingdom destined to unfold into that Christendom which is the only real civilization of the peoples in human history. And at the heart af the movement, as the very life and soul of it all, there is the new supernatural revelation of God now, for the first time since the Flood, going forth to mankind as a public instruction which is gospel preaching (Heb. iv. 2). It is accompanied by the first appearance of credential evidence of miracles and prophecy. And in especial, that revelation takes the practical form of an actual supernatural redemption and consecration ; in the accomplishment of which there are brought into view, for the instruction of mankind in all nations through all ages, those principles of the kingdom of God, regarding His character, and moral government, and gracious purposes towards mankind, which are the *principia* of the only true religion that is ever to live upon the earth. These are main, plain, unquestionable characteristics of the Book. The first part of it, the redemption from Egypt, has a place like that of the Gospels in the New Testament Scripture ; and the second part of it, regarding the consecration in Sinai, has a place like that of the Acts of the Apostles, along with the Epistles to the Hebrews, to the Galatians, and to the Romans. What greater thing could be said in illustration of the importance of it? In some obvious respects, it is the most fundamentally important book ever given to mankind. And the study of it is essential to a real and scholarly acquaintance with the history of man. (*J. Macgregor, D.D.*)

DIVISIONS OF THE BOOK.—The Book consists of two distinct portions. The former (chap. i.-xix.) gives a detailed account of the circumstances under which the deliverance of the Israelites was accomplished. The second (chap. xx.-xl.) describes the giving of the Law, and the institutions which completed the organization of the people as "a kingdom of priests, and an holy nation." These two portions are unlike in style and structure, as might be expected from the difference of their subject-matter; but their mutual bearings and interdependence are evident, and leave no doubt as to the substantial unity of the Book. The historical portion owes all its significance and interest to the promulgation of God's will in the law. The institutions of the Law could not, humanly speaking, have been established or permanently maintained but for the deliverance which the historical portion records. (*Canon F. C. Cook.*) The first part of Exodus is predominantly historical; the second essentially legislative or dogmatical; but yet the former contains three important *laws;* and the latter, the *history* of a flagrant breach, on the part of Israel, of the promises made concerning the faithful observance of the Law, the erection of the holy Tabernacle, and the consecration of Aaron and his descendants. (*M. M. Kalisch, Ph.D.*)

MOSAIC AUTHORSHIP.—1. One argument is drawn from the representation of the personal character and qualifications of Moses. In its most important features it is such as could never have been produced by a writer collecting the traditional reminiscences or legends of a later age : not such even as might have been drawn by a younger contemporary. To posterity, to Israelites of his own time, Moses was simply the greatest of men; but it is evident that the writer of this Book was unconscious of the personal greatness of the chief actor. He was indeed thoroughly aware of the greatness of his mission, and consequently of the greatness of the position, which was recognized at last by the Egyptians (see chap. xi. 3) ; but as to his personal qualifications, the points which strike him most forcibly are the deficiencies of natural gifts and powers, and the defects of character, which he is scrupulously careful to record, together with the rebukes and penalties which they brought upon him, and the obstacles which they opposed to his work. Such a representation is perfectly intelligible, as proceeding from Moses himself; but what in him was humility would have been obtuseness in an annalist, such as never is found in the accounts of other great men, nor in the notices of Moses in later Books. 2. This Book could not have been written by any man who had not passed many years in Egypt, and who had not also a thorough knowledge, such as could only be acquired by personal observation, of the Sinaitic Peninsula. But it is improbable that any Israelite between the time of Moses and Jeremiah could have possessed either of these qualifications; it is not credible, or even possible, that any should have combined both. 3. A weighty argument is drawn from the accounts of the miracles, by which Moses was expressly bidden to attest his mission, and by which he was enabled to accomplish the deliverance of his people. They are such as no later writer living in Palestine could have invented for Egypt. From beginning to end no miracle is recorded which does not strike the mind by its peculiar suitableness to the place, time, and circumstances under which it was wrought. The plagues are each and all Egyptian; and the modes by which the people's wants are supplied in the Sinaitic Peninsula recall to our minds the natural condition of such a journey in such a country. 4. The portion of the Book which follows the account of the departure from Egypt has characteristics marked with equal distinctness, and bearing with no less force upon the question of authorship. It is not merely that the length of each division of the journey, the numerous halting places, are distinctly marked; for, although such notices could not possibly have been invented, or procured at any later period by a dweller in Palestine, the fact might be accounted for by the supposition that some ancient records of the journey had been preserved by written or oral tradition; but the chapters which belong either to the early sojourn of Moses, or to the wanderings of the Israelites, are pervaded by a peculiar tone, a local colouring, an atmosphere, so to speak, of the desert, which has made itself felt by all those who have explored the country. And this fact is the more striking when we bear in mind that, although the great general features of the Peninsula, the grouping of its arid heights and the direction of its innumerable wadys are permanent, still changes of vast and scarcely calculable importance in matters which personally affect the traveller and modify his impressions, have taken place since the time of Moses. At present one great difficulty felt by all travellers is the insufficiency of the resources of the Peninsula to support such a host as that which is described in the narrative; a difficulty not wholly removed by the acceptance of the accounts of Providential interventions, which appear to have been not permanent, but limited to special occasions. But facts can be adduced which confirm, and indeed go far beyond, the conjectures of travellers, who have pointed out that the supply of water, and the general fertility of the district, must have been very different before the process of denudation, which has been going on for ages, and is now in active progress, had commenced. We have now proofs from inscriptions coeval with the pyramids, both in Egypt and in the Peninsula, that under the Pharaohs of the third to the eighteenth dynasty, ages before Moses, and up to his time, the whole district was occupied by a population whose resources and numbers must have been considerable, since they were able to resist the forces of the Egyptians, who sent large armies in repeated but unsuccessful attempts to subjugate the Peninsula. Their principal object, however, was effected, since they established permanent settlements at Sarbet el Khadim, and at Mughara, to work the copper-mines. These settlements were under the command of officers of high rank, and are proved by monuments and inscriptions to have been of an extent which implies the existence of considerable resources in the immediate neighbourhood. Taking summarily the points in this part of the argument, we find the following coincidences between the narrative and accounts of travellers. Absence of water where no sources now exist, abundance of water where fountains are still found, and indications of a far more copious supply in former ages; tracts, occupying the same time in the journey, in which food could not be found; and in some districts a natural production similar to manna, most abundant in rainy seasons (such as several notices show the season of the Exodus to have been), but not sufficient for nourishment, nor fit for large consumption, without such modifications in character and quantity as are attributed in the narrative to a Divine intervention. We have the presence of Nomad hordes, and an attack made by them precisely in the district, and under the circumstances when their presence and attack might be expected. We have a route which the late exploration of the Peninsula shows to have been probably determined by conditions agreeing with incidental notices in the history; and when we come to the chapters in which the central event in the history of Israel—the delivery of God's Law—is recorded, we find localities and scenery which travellers concur in declaring to be such as fully correspond to the exigencies of the narrative, and which, in some accounts (remarkable at once for scientific accuracy and graphic power), are described in terms which show they correspond, so far as mere outward accessories can correspond, to the grandeur of the manifestation. In addition to the positive arguments thus adduced, a negative argument at least equally conclusive demands attention. No history or composition in existence, which is known to have been written long after the events which it describes, is without internal indications of its later origin; contemporary documents may be interwoven with it, and great pains taken in ages of literary refinement and artifice to disguise its character; but even when anachronisms and errors of detail are avoided, which is seldom, if ever, effectually done, the genuine touch of antiquity is invariably and inevitably absent. Whether we look at the general tone of this narrative, the style equally remarkable for artlessness and power, or at the innumerable points of contact with external facts capable of exact determination, we are impressed by the weight of this internal evidence, supported, as it has been shown to be, by the unbroken and unvarying tradition of the nation to whom the narrative was addressed, and by whom it was held too sacred not to be preserved from wilful mutilation or interpolation. 5. Another argument is drawn from the account of the Tabernacle. The following facts are demonstrated : (1) In form, structure, and materials the Tabernacle belongs altogether to the wilderness. The wood used in the structure is found there in abundance The skins and other native materials belong equally to the locality. The metals—bronze, silver, and gold—were those which the Israelites knew, and doubtless brought with them from Egypt. The names of many of the materials and implements used were Egyptian. The arts required for the construction of the Tabernacle, and for all its accessories, were precisely those for which the Egyptians had been remarkable for ages—such as artizans who had lived under the influence of Egyptian civilization would naturally have learned. (2) The peculiar way in which the history of the erection of the Tabernacle is recorded suggests another argument, which has not received due attention. Two separate accounts are given. In the first Moses relates the instructions which he received, in the second he describes the accomplishment of the work. Nothing would be less in accordance with the natural order of an history written at a later period than this double account. It has been represented as an argument for a double authorship, as though two sets of documents had been carelessly or superstitiously adopted by a compiler. It is, however, fully accounted for by the obvious hypothesis that each part of the narrative was written at the time, and on the occasion, to which it immediately refers. When Moses received these instructions he wrote a full account of them for the information of the people. This was on all accounts probable and necessary: among other obvious reasons, it was necessary in order that the people might learn exactly what amount of materials and what amount of work would be required of them. When, again, he had executed his task, it was equally proper, and doubtless also in accordance with the habits of a people keen and jealous in the management of their affairs, and at no time free from tendencies to suspicion, that he should give a formal account of every detail in its execution—a proof, to such as might call for proof, that all their precious offerings had been devoted to the purpose; and, what was of far more importance, that the Divine instructions had been completely and literally obeyed. (*Canon F. C. Cook.*)

CHARACTER OF THE EXODUS MOVEMENT.—1. In its inward spiritual nature the movement was one of faith in God. Though "exodus" be a common word for exit or departure, it has come to have an appropriate special meaning in reference to such a movement as that in question was. And we may profitably here for a little consider what is meant by such an exodus? (See in Seeley's "Expansion of England.") A true exodus is not a mere migration of a people, such as we read of in the history of primæval Celts and Germans, occasioning so much uneasiness and trouble to "civilized" Romans and others. Such a movement might be merely blind instinct, like that of bees in swarming ; or it might be merely the result of some—so to speak—mechanical pressure, from within or from without. Again, those colonizing movements of individuals, through which new nationalities are coming to be formed in the British empire, differ from a true exodus in their motive impulse and spirit, as going to market on business differs from going to church for worship of God. But one of the Pilgrim Fathers of America said that they had gone thither across the ocean "to serve God." And there he expressed the true spirit of an exodus. It is a migration for the purpose of serving God. Such was the purpose of Israel's departure from Egypt. Even the three days' leave of absence, which was all they asked at first (chap. v. 3), was for an act of high service to "the God of the Hebrews." The Egyptians no doubt (chap. i. 10) understood whither this was purposely tending. And (chap. iv. 18, 29–31 ; cf. iii, 12) the Israelites themselves, from their first thought about the movement, had thought of it as one for final abandonment of Egypt, "to serve God" in the promised land. Their movement not only was religious, it was religion : religion was not a means, but the end ; as in temple-building, religion, which is the end of the work (finis operis), ought also to be (finis operantis) the end in view of the worker. Now such was the character of Israel's movement Canaanward. When we look close into the history, we perceive that the Hebrews were in large measure not in the true spirit of the movement (Heb. iii. 12). Among them there was much of ungodly selfish worldliness (Heb. iii. 9) ; so that in the end they as a people perished in the wilderness through unbelief (Heb. iii. 16–18). Yet a nation entered Canaan. And they were not all unbelievers who died in the wilderness ;—Miriam, for instance, and Aaron, and Moses. Even at the worst (cf. 1 Kings xix. 18 and xx. 41), there may have been in Israel as large a proportion of Calebs and Joshuas (Isa. i. 9) as would have sufficed to prevent the destruction of Sodom. What we seek to see in this movement is its characteristic impulse, the spirit of its true life. And that, no doubt, is faith in the living God, as revealed supernaturally, in positive covenant promises of redemption. Such had been the distinctive nature of Abraham's life on earth (Gen. xv. 6). And it continued to be the characteristic of his covenant seed (Rom. iv. 3, 11). The people cried to God. They followed Moses, because they believed that he was Jehovah's messenger. They went through the Red Sea, looking for salvation in Abraham's God Almighty. "By faith" they passed the Red Sea; and "by faith" the walls of Jericho fell down (Heb. xi. 29, 30). Such was the distinctive nature of the movement from first to last. Not only the history shows this ; this is what the history shows. 2. It was a movement into brotherhood of man. On the face of it, it was into nationality of social condition. At the original settlement in Goshen (chap. i. 1–5), the sons of Israel were passing from the simply domestic condition under patriarchy, into the distinctly tribal. As their numbers grew into national dimensions, the continued influence of patriarchy, as an ideal, still kept the separate tribes in a unity of outward connection, as of Swiss cantons under the Hapsburgs. But the unity, which at last found its full expression in the nation full and independent, had its true root, or living foundation, in a constitution that is not of nature—the new constitution of redeeming grace, which (chap. xix. 6) makes the nation to be Theocracy, holy to the Lord, and of which the citizens are to be a brotherhood, united in the common bond of a filial relationship to God (chap. iv. 22, 23). This idea is involved in the nature of a spiritual patriarchate, such as Abraham's was. The noble custom of adoption (chap. xii. 48, 49) made statutory in Egypt at the foundation of Israel's national existence, provided for expanded application of the idea, for blessing unto all the families of the earth (Gen. xii. 3). But what we clearly see in Exodus is the realization of the idea in the foundation of the Israelitish kingdom of God. It was a nation, arranging into compact order (chap. xiii. 18, xiv. 8), that formed at the Red Sea, to pass on to the trysting-place (chap. iii. 12) of Covenant with God. And it was a nation (chap. xix. 6), specifically a Theocracy, or kingdom of God, that in that covenant was vested with title to Canaan. (*J. Macgregor, D.D.*)

Moses and his mission.—1. Survey him, first, mentally. His was an organizing mind; recall how he took a nation, or rather horde of ignorant bondmen, and moulded them in his own lifetime into a compact and vigorous nationality; or how he took the elements of theology and morality and jurisprudence and sociology, and organized them into that majestic series of institutes which we style after his own name, the Mosaic Code. Again, his was an expressive mind: recall how, notwithstanding his modest disclaimer of the gift of eloquence, he was Jehovah's greatest prophet, mighty in his words as well as in his works, chanting in nobler strains than Homer ever sang his triumphal ode, his patriarchal hymn, his dying songs. Again, his was a prophetic mind: endowed with extraordinary range of vision, his mental eye pierced immensely beyond the limits of contemporary ken, surveying as from the observatory of his own Pisgah height of prophecy the far-off Promised Land, wherein he discerned the vast outlines of a profound theology, an exquisite morality, a beneficent jurisprudence, a perfected society. Again, his was a practical mind: while prophetically descrying in the far off distances of time stupendous orbs and nebulæ of truths hidden from all eyes but his own, he at the same time remained in this tiny world of ours, distinguishing the minutest duties and subtilest distinctions, beholding in the microscopic world of daily life a universe as vast as that which broadened before his telescopic sweep, legislating alike broadly for all human time and minutely for all human space, with one hand, if I may venture to say it, weighing the mountains in scales, and with the other hand counting the small dust of the balance. Once more, his was a constructive mind: instead of wasting his mental forces in ill-timed attempts to overthrow existing bad institutions, he ennobled his great gifts by a supreme effort to build up a new human society, constructing out of the very ruins of the past the everlasting temple of the future. In brief, if ever there was a man who could be strictly called a genius, that man was Moses. 2. And now survey him morally. He was, indeed, a saintly character, a prodigy of goodness. Not that he was faultless. His naturally impetuous temperament brought him more than once into serious trouble, as in the affair of the Egyptian homicide, and the smiting of the rock of Meribah. But it is to the infinite credit of Moses that he sought to overcome this constitutional infirmity of temper, and succeeded in getting his powers into placid balance, in his very patience winning and possessing his soul. Sympathetic, as when he entered into the woes of his enslaved countrymen in Egypt; self-denying, as when he refused to be longer called the son of Pharaoh's daughter; conscientious, as when he chose rather to be evil entreated with the people of God, than to enjoy the pleasures of sin for a season; discriminating, as when he accounted the reproach of Christ greater riches than the treasures of Egypt; far-sighted, as when he looked beyond unto the recompense of reward; enduring, as when he saw Him who is invisible; brave, as when he confronted Menephtha's court, and Israel's tumultuous demands; stately, as when he wielded the sword of outraged authority; patient, as when he endured in gratitude, insolence, and rebellion; magnanimous, as when he offered to die in place of his apostate people; lowly, as when his face shone with Jehovah's glory, and he knew it not; trustful, as when he climbed lonely Abarim to die: Moses was indeed religion's great saint. Brave as Achilles, without Achilles' petulance; heroic as Hercules, without Hercules' savagery; judicial as Minos, without Minos' gloom; constructive as Vulcan, without Vulcan's grotesqueness; wise as Mercury, without Mercury's strategy: eloquent as Apollo, without Apollo's deceit; patient as Prometheus, without Prometheus' stoicism; devout as Numa, without Numa's superstition; imperial as Jupiter, without Jupiter's weakness:—Moses was indeed history's ideal character. Verily, there hath not risen in all humanity a prophet like unto Moses, whom Jehovah knew face to face. 3. Having thus glanced at the outlines of Moses' unique career and the outlines of Moses' unique personality, let us now glance at the outlines of Moses' unique mission. That mission was manifold. First: It was a part of Moses' mission to outline a theology, or doctrine of religion. Thus, while the surrounding nations were worshipping a plurality of gods, Moses proclaimed that there is but one God, a God who is self-existent, eternal, unchangeable, spiritual, true, just, holy, gracious, merciful, long-suffering, in a word, infinitely perfect. Again, it was a part of Moses' mission to outline a morality or doctrine of character. While the morality of the surrounding nations was debased by gross misconceptions and positive vices, Moses proclaimed a morality that was exquisite in its distinctions, just in its dealings, brotherly in its spirit. Again, it was a part of Moses' mission to outline a jurisprudence or doctrine of state. While the surrounding nations were governed by irresponsible monarchs, whose caprices made and unmade laws, Moses proclaimed a commonwealth, over which ruled no human king, whose citizens were peers, whose officers were elective. Again, it was a part of Moses' mission to outline a sociology or doctrine of man. While the surrounding nations regarded each other with distrust and hate, repelling all immigration which did not follow in the retinue of conquest, Moses proclaimed the brotherhood of mankind inviting, it is true, all men to become Jews, but in order that all men might become cosmopolites. Again, it was a part of Moses' mission to outline a ritual or doctrine of worship. While the surrounding nations were worshipping their own images and ceremonies and sacrifices and priests as being the end of religion, Moses proclaimed a liturgy as being the means of religion, bidding his people discern in the ritual of the Tabernacle a type of the worship in the temple not made with hands. Once more, and in summary, it was the mission of Moses to outline a Theocracy, or doctrine of God-rule. While every other nation regarded itself as its own law and end, Moses proclaimed that the Hebrew people was divinely raised up to be a means to an end, namely this, to serve as the symbol and prophecy of the universal and everlasting Church, or Jehovah's kingdom on earth. Thus the mission of Moses was the mightiest mission ever assigned to statesmen, reformer, philanthropist, or theologian. And nobly did Moses fulfil his mighty mission. How nobly he fulfilled it is proved by the fact that, although more than three thousand years have passed since Moses lived, his code is still the basis of modern theology, modern morality, modern jurisprudence, modern sociology, modern worship : in a single word, modern civilization. The world has outgrown the Analects of Confucius, the Vedas of Brahm, the Soutras of Boodh, the Zendavesta of Zoroaster, the Koran of Mohammed, even the Positivism of Comte. But the world has not outgrown the institutes of Moses. The lawgiver of Sinai is to this day history's commanding figure, all that is worthy of the name of civilization sitting reverently at his feet. And how, let me ask in passing, do you account for all this ? For, considering his circumstances, the character and work of Moses was a positive moral anachronism. Remember for example, that he framed his civil code some two thousand years before Justinian collected his Pandects, a thousand years before the Twelve Tables were suspended in the Roman Forum, eight hundred years before Solon legislated for Athens ; remember also that Moses himself lived in a time of profound moral apostasy, fifteen hundred years before the Divine Man taught us how to live. Can you account for this striking anachronism in any better way than by accepting the Scriptural statement that Jehovah was wont to speak unto His prophet Moses face to face, not in dark speeches, but as a man speaketh unto his friend ? 4. Having thus glanced at the outlines of Moses' unique career and character and mission, let us now glance at some of the lessons suggested by Moses' unique personality. And, first, a lesson of Divine adjustment. The story of Moses illustrates in a striking way the truth that God ever adjusts men to crises. For example : When the wickedness of men had become so great that Jehovah determined to sweep him from the earth, he raised up Noah to become the second father of the race; again, when the second humanity had relapsed into heathenism, and a great character was needed to restore the kingdom of God on earth, Jehovah raised up Abraham to become the father of the faithful; again, when Moses had completed his legislative mission, and a soldier was needed to conquer the Promised Land, Jehovah raised up the martial Joshua to succeed the peaceful Moses. Secondly : A lesson of Divine providence. Recall how the infant Moses was saved ; he was not saved by a miracle or anything extraordinary in itself ; he was saved by a sympathetic woman's natural instinct. Thirdly : A lesson of Divine warning. If any one of all the hosts of Israel had the right to enter the Promised Land, it was, we would have thought, their emancipator and lawgiver and prophet. Nevertheless, saintly though he was, he was not allowed to enter it. And we know the reason : it was because the Children of Israel had angered him at the waters of Meribah, by rebelling against him, and provoking him, so that he spake unadvisedly with his lips. Beware, then, oh friends, of what you call little sins ; for they may cost you the promised Canaan. (*G. D. Boardman, D.D.*)

THE MAGICIANS OF EGYPT.—The magicians of Egypt did in like manner with their enchantments. In *like* manner, but in unlike, too. Of course, men can imitate God and God's doings in a great many ways, because man himself has an imitated relationship to God, and is endowed with powers like to those which God has and uses. Indeed, the direct path to all our possible growth, progress, and ennoblement lies in that line and effort of imitating God. We may do what He doeth and as He doeth in many things. Possibly human beings may accomplish works and effect results which other human beings inspecting and pronouncing on shall be perplexed to decide whether to refer them to God or to men. But there is this one rule of right and wisdom always to be rigidly obeyed. Whenever man attempts to imitate God in method or means, in acts or devices, he must do the work with a view to the same purposes as those for which God works. We may imitate God in what He does merely for our enjoyment, our pleasure, to amuse us, or to add to our means of happiness. We may make musical instruments to imitate the music of the air, the sea, the bird, the happy, gleeful child, or the harmonious strains of heaven's own choir. We may make flowers of wax or paint them on the canvas. We may chisel the marble into human forms. We may draw on the canvas the lineaments of the human features, landscapes of field, meadow, valley, or mountain, or scenes of sky and ocean. We may make the sun do our painting for us. We may use all our skill and inventiveness, which are, in fact, but God's own workings, to copy, adorn, or imitate His doings. Yet none of these things is it right or safe for us to do, in order to beguile or deceive our fellow-men, to cheat their senses in order to pervert their understandings, to play on their credulity and make them superstitious, to tell them pious fables in the service of religion, or ever to mislead them by false imitations in means or effects of the ways in which Divine power can alone honestly work. The moment the purpose of deception or of artful effect is introduced into any imitative work of men folly and mischief follow with their train. But, notwithstanding all the enlightenment and all the prevailing credulity of our times and communities, imitations and counterfeits for the sake of deception abound and multiply with infinite ingenuity and variety in all the affairs of human life. It is difficult, indeed, to say of any honest work or product of God or of men that there is no sham imitation, no adulterated specimen, no false semblance of it, palmed upon the world. Some wise and humane persons who are aware of the extent of this deception in medical practice, and of the number and sacrifices of its victims, have suggested the expediency of procuring the enactment by the legislature of a very severe law against such triflers with the miseries and the credulity of their fellow-creatures. But it is very doubtful whether legislation on the subject would be either wise or effective. And over how many of the shops and warehouses and manufactories of our busy world might be inscribed as a motto designating the character of the tricks and frauds practised in them the old, frank Bible sentence! "And the magicians of Egypt, they also did in like manner with their enchantments." All God's products are honest ones. All His materials are what they purport to be. He does indeed please our senses with a few illusory phenomena, such as the ocean mirage, the rainbow, the double moon, and the falling star, which is no star. But He never makes wool out of cotton, nor coffee out of beans, nor sugar out of sand. The magicians do those things. Yet it would be a nobler comfort if we could get back to the original honest basis and show of things as they come from the hand of God. Oh that things were and that people were what they pretend to be! Veneering, varnish, lacquer, imitation, play just as demoralizing arts upon us as we do with them. No one can substitute sham for reality in anything outside of him without doing the same by something inside of him. So sometimes we feel an immense craving to get back to nature in everything, to get out of the hands of the magicians with all their tricks and shams, and to be able to say devoutly of all that addresses our senses or our hearts, "This is from the finger of God." But, whenever we draw a moral from the Sacred Book, we are bound to lead it up to its highest application. The especial work of God is that which serves the agency and produces the fruits of true religion. Yet the magicians come in here to try the art of imitations both as to means and effects. We want now the real thing, the work of God, the truth as it is in Jesus, the power of God unto salvation to every one that believeth. We must look sharply at all our devices and methods, all our appliances and plannings. We must commit religious work to religious men and women, and to religious means: we must use no arts in it, and accept no substitutes for it. There have been eras and intervals recurring in the history of Christendom, of marked revivals, quickenings and deepenings and strong reactings of the power of religion. And there have been imitated semblances of these things, promises or hopes of them, not realized tokens mistaken for them, cries of "Lo, here!" "Lo, there!" It is "the finger of God" which in all things marks truth and reality, whatever the magicians may do with their enchantments. (*G. E. Ellis, D.D.*)

THE BIBLICAL ILLUSTRATOR.

EXODUS.

CHAPTER I.

VERS. 1–5. **The children of Israel which came into Egypt.**—*Israel in Egypt:*—
I. A RETROSPECTIVE VIEW. 1. These verses lead us back to the time when Jacob
came with his family to Egypt. (1) It was a time of great distress from famine in
Canaan. (2) It was a crisis-time in the history of the chosen family (Gen. xlv.
17–28 ; xlvi. 1–4). (3) It was a time of great encouragement from what had been
disclosed in Joseph's history. 2. These verses summarize the history of the
children of Israel from the time of Jacob's emigration to Egypt till the bondage
of the Israelites—about 115 years. (1) This was a time of great happiness and
prosperity for the Israelites. (a) The entire period, from the call of Abraham to
the Exodus, was 430 years. (b) Up to the descent into Egypt, a period of 215 years,
the family had increased to only "seventy souls." (c) From the going down to
Egypt to the Exodus—215 years—the 70 had multiplied to 600,000 males, giving
a population of nearly 2,000,000. II. THE CHANGE OF ADMINISTRATION (ver. 8).
Not merely another, but a "new" king, implying a change of dynasty.
Now, probably, commenced the rule of the "shepherd kings." 2. The
phrase, "who knew not Joseph," suggests the prestige of Joseph's name to
the former Pharaohs. A good man's influence dies not with the death of
his body. III. THE CHANGE OF GOVERNMENT POLICY (vers. 9–14). 1. The
nature of this change. From being a fostering government to being cruel and
repressive. Unwise policy, because suicidal. 2. The reason for this change (ver.
10). 3. The result of this change (ver. 12). (1) Such a result is according to God's
law of nations. Working classes always more fruitful than others. (2) Such a
result was according to God's covenant law. Lessons : 1. God's children in Egypt
a type of God's children in the world. 2. The policy of the new king a type of the
godlessness, selfishness, and inhumanity of those who work from a worldly standpoint. 3. The frustration of this policy a type of God's overruling power. (*D. C.
Hughes, M.A.*)   *God's knowledge of man's domestic life :*—I. HE KNOWS THE
CHILDREN OF THE FAMILY. "Reuben, Simeon," &c. 1. He knows the character of
each. 2. He knows the friendly relations, or otherwise, existing between them, and
the intentions of each. II. HE WATCHES THE JOURNEYING OF THE FAMILY—"which
came," &c. Do not journey into Egypt without an indication of the Divine will.
All family changes should be under the instruction of heaven. This insures safety,
protection, development—though sometimes discipline. III. HE MARKS THE DEATH
OF THE FAMILY (ver. 6). (*J. S. Exell, M.A.*)   *Israel in Egypt :*—With Israel in
Egypt begins a new era in the world's progress. Biography becomes history.
Instead of individuals or a tribe, God has now a nation with which to work. He
has undertaken a vast purpose. This people—united by common parentage,
common faith, and common hope—He is to weld still more compactly by fellowship
in disaster and deliverance into a nation which shall be the miracle of history, as
intensely and persistently individual as its founder. With this nation He enters
into covenant and, through its faith and experience, reveals to the world the one
holy God, and brings in its Redeemer. Such a mission costs ; its apostles must
suffer. Yet this relief intervenes : personal blessing is not lost in national pains.
The strong word covering this process is discipline : the development of character
and efficiency under rigorous conditions. The first element is—I. FAITH ; taking

as real what cannot be seen, accepting as sure what has not come to pass. Seemingly, this fruit of heaven cannot grow on earthly soil unless it be wet with tears. II. The second word of blessing is DISENTANGLEMENT. The hope of the ages lay in freeing Israel, not from Egypt, but from what Egypt represents. Heathenism is a bitter and bloody thing. But heathenism filled the world outside the chosen nation. Only stern guidance could lead away from it, for over its deformities were spread distortions of natural needs and blandishments of sanctioned lust. God can accomplish vast things with a soul wholly consecrated to Him; but how rarely He finds such a soul, except as He leads it through affliction to make it loose its hold on all but Him! III. With this even partially gained, comes that strong word EFFICIENCY. The nation which was Jacob the Supplanter passes its Peniel and becomes Israel the Prince of God, having power with God and men. Into its hands are put the direction of earth's history and the hope of its redemption. The distresses of those early generations are as the straining and rending of the crust or the grinding march of glaciers, unsparing but beneficent, preparing a fertile soil on which at last men shall dwell safely, lifting thankful hands to heaven. (*C. M. Southgate.*) *Egypt a type of the world :*—Sodom is associated in our minds with wickedness only, though no doubt it was a great place in its day; but Egypt stands out before us as a fuller and more adequate type of the world, with her glory as well as her shame. And from Israel's relation to Egypt we may learn two great lessons: one of counsel how to use the world, the other of warning against abusing it. From God's purpose in regard to Israel let us learn that just as Egypt was necessary as a school for His chosen people, so the world ought to be a school for us. We are not to despise its greatness. No word of contempt for Egypt's greatness is found in the sacred records. The nation was intended to learn, and did acquire, many useful arts which were of much service to them afterwards in the Land of Promise. Moses, the chosen of God, was learned in all the wisdom of the Egyptians, and was thereby qualified for the great work for which he was called. In these examples we may see how to use this world, making it a school to prepare us for our inheritance and the work the Lord may have for us there to do. On the other hand, let us beware of so yielding to the seductions of this evil world as to lose our hold of God, and His covenant, and so incur the certainty of forfeiting our eternal birthright and becoming the world's slaves, helping perhaps to rear its mighty monuments, with the prospect possibly of having our names engraved in stone among the ruins of some buried city, but without the prospect of having them written "among the living in Jerusalem," the eternal city of God. Earth's great ones belong to the dead past; but heaven's great ones have their portion in a glorious future. (*J. M. Gibson, D.D.*) *Making history :*—We are making history when we least think of it. That which seems a little matter to us may be a link in a chain that binds the ages. What we do to-day or to-morrow is done for all time. It cannot be undone. It and all its countless results must stand entailed to the latest generations; and we are to have honour or shame according as our part is now performed. The poor boy who drives the horse along a canal tow-path may think it makes little difference whether he does that work well or poorly. But forty years after, when he is in nomination for the presidency of a great nation, he will find that men go back to his boyhood story to learn whether he was faithful in that which was least, as proof that he would be faithful also in that which is much. There is no keeping out of history. We have got to be there. The only safe way of standing well in history is by doing well in all things. You are just now going to Boston, or to New York, or to Chicago, or to Savannah, or to London—will the record of your spirit and conduct as you go there read well ten years hence, or a hundred? That depends on what your spirit and conduct are at the present time. And if you stay at home your place in history—in God's record of history—is just as sure as if you went to Egypt or to the Holy Land. That record is making up to-day : "Now, these are the names of the children of ——, which came into ——, or, which stayed at ——." If you want a record which shall redound to your honour, and of which your children's children shall be proud, you have no time to lose in getting things straight for it. (*H. C. Trumbull.*)

Ver. 6. **Joseph died, and all his brethren.**—*The death of a whole family :*—I. IT WAS A VERY LARGE FAMILY. II. IT WAS A VERY DIVERSIFIED FAMILY. 1. They were diversified in their sympathies. 2. They were diversified in social position. III. IT WAS A VERY TRIED FAMILY. IV. IT WAS A VERY INFLUENTIAL FAMILY. V. IT WAS A

VERY RELIGIOUSLY PRIVILEGED FAMILY. Lessons: 1. A rebuke to family pride.
2. A warning against seeking satisfaction in family joys. 3. A lesson as to
the right use of family relationships. Live together as those who must
die. 4. Some strong reasons for expecting family meetings after death.
(1) Such different characters cannot admit exactly the same fate. Extinction is either too good for the sinner, or else a strange reward for the saint.
(2) Family affection seems too strong to be thus quenched. (*U. R. Thomas.*)
The universal characteristic :—The succession of generations among the children of
men has been, from Homer downwards, likened to that of the leaves among the trees
of the forest. The foliage of one summer, withering gradually away, and strewing
the earth with its wrecks, has its place supplied by the exuberance of the following
spring. But there is one point in which the analogy does not hold,—there is one
difference between the race of leaves and the race of men : between the leaves of
successive summers an interval of desolation intervenes, and " the bare and wintry
woods " emphatically mark the passage from one season to another. But there is
no such pause in the succession of the generations of men. Insensibly they melt
and shade into one another : an old man dies, and a child is born ; daily and hourly
there is a death and a birth ; and imperceptibly, by slow degrees, the actors in life's
busy scene are changed. Hence the full force of this thought—" One generation
passeth away, and another generation cometh "—is not ordinarily felt. The first
view of this verse that occurs to us is its striking significance and force as a commentary on the history of which it so abruptly and emphatically announces the
close. The previous narrative presents to us a busy scene—an animated picture ;
and here, as if by one single stroke, all is reduced to a blank. It is as if having
gazed on ocean when it bears on its broad bosom a gallant and well-manned fleet—
bending gracefully to its rising winds, and triumphantly stemming its swelling
waves—you looked out again, and at the very next glance beheld the wide waste of
waters reposing in dark and horrid peace over the deep-buried wrecks of the recent
storm. " And all that generation " : How startling a force is there in this awful
brevity, this compression and abridgment—the names and histories of millions
brought within the compass of so brief a statement of a single fact concerning them
—that they all died ! Surely it seems as if the Lord intended by this bill of mortality for a whole race, which His own Spirit has framed, to stamp as with a
character of utter mockery and insignificance the most momentous distinctions and
interests of time ; these all being engulfed and swallowed up in the general doom of
death, which ushers in the one distinction of eternity. I. Let us ponder the
announcement AS IT RESPECTS THE INDIVIDUAL—" Joseph died." His trials, with
their many aggravations—his triumphs, with all their glories—were alike brief and
evanescent ; and his eventful career ended, as the obscurest and most common-
place lifetime must end—for " Joseph died." Joseph is at home, the idol of a fond
parent. Ah ! dote not, thou venerable sire, on thy fair and dutiful child. Remember
how soon it may be said of him, and how certainly it must be said of him, that
" Joseph died." Joseph is in trouble—betrayed, persecuted, distressed, a prisoner,
a slave. But let him not be disquieted above measure. It is but a little while,
and it shall be said of him that " Joseph died." Joseph is exalted—he is high in
wealth, in honour, and in power. But why should all his glory and his joy elate
him ? It will be nothing to him soon—when it comes to be said of him that
" Joseph died." Ah ! there is but one of Joseph's many distinctions, whether of
character or of fortune, that does not shrivel beside this stern announcement. The
simplicity of his trust in God, the steadfastness of his adherence to truth and holiness, the favour of Heaven, his charity out of a pure heart and a good conscience
and faith unfeigned—these will stand the shock of collision with this record of his
decease. II. " AND ALL HIS BRETHREN." They too all died, and the vicissitudes of
their family history came to an end in the silent tomb. " Joseph died, and all his
brethren." Ah ! how intimately should this reflection have knit them together in
unity of interest, of affection, and of aim ! The tie of a common origin is scarcely
stronger or closer than the tie of a common doom. The friend, the beloved
brother who has gone, has acquired, by his death, new value in your esteem—a
new and sacred claim to your regard. Now for the first time you discover how dear
he should have been, how dear he was, to your hearts—dearer far than you had ever
thought. How fondly do you dwell on all his attractions and excellencies ! How
frivolous are all former causes of misunderstanding, all excuses for indifference,
now seen to be ! And whither are they gone ? And what are their views now, and
what their feelings, on the matters which formed the subject of their familiar inter-

course here? Are they united in the region of blessedness above? Or is there a fearful separation, and are there some of their number on the other side of the great gulf? III. "AND ALL THAT GENERATION." The tide of mortality rolls on in a wider stream. It sweeps into the one vast ocean of eternity all the members of a family—all the families of a race. The distinctions alike of individuals and of households are lost. Every landmark is laid low. Some are gone in tender years of childhood, unconscious of life's sins and sufferings—some in grey-headed age, weighed down by many troubles. Some have perished by the hand of violence—some by natural decay. And another generation now fills the stage—a generation that, in all its vast circle of families, can produce not one individual to link it with the buried race on whose ashes it is treading. On a smaller scale, you have experienced something of what we now describe. In the sad season of bereavement, how have you felt your pain embittered by the contrast between death reigning in your heart and home, and bustling life going on all around! In the prospect, too, of your own departure, does not this thought form an element of the dreariness of death, that when you are gone, and laid in the silent tomb, others will arise that knew not you?—your removal will scarce occasion even a momentary interruption in the onward course and incessant hurry of affairs, and your loss will be but as that of a drop of water from the tide that rolls on in its career as mighty and as majestical as ever. But here, it is a whole generation, with all its families, that is engulfed in one unmeasured tomb! And lo! the earth is still all astir with the same activities, all gay with the same pomps and pageantries, all engrossed with the same vanities and follies, and, alas! the same sins also, that have been beguiling and disappointing the successive races of its inhabitants since the world began! And there is another common lot— another general history—another universal characteristic: "After death, the judgment." Joseph rises again, "and all his brethren, and all that generation." And they all stand before the judgment-seat. There is union then. The small and the great are there; the servant and his master—all are brought together. But for what? What a solemn contrast have we here! Death unites after separation : the judgment unites in order to separation. Death, closing the drama of time, lets the ample curtain fall upon its whole scenery and all its actors. The judgment, opening the drama of eternity, discloses scenery and actors once more entire. (*R. S. Candlish, D.D.*) *Death :*—I. DEATH REMOVES THE MOST USEFUL MEN—" Joseph." 1. He had instructed his brethren. 2. He had enriched his father. 3. He had saved his nation. 4. He had taught the world an eternal lesson. II. DEATH REMOVES THE LARGEST FAMILIES—" All his brethren." III. DEATH REMOVES THE PROUDEST NATIONS. 1. Pitiable. 2. Irremediable. 3. Admonitory. (*J. S. Exell, M.A.*) *Death's disciplinary power :*—God deprives the Church of her comfort and stay—1. That she may gain the power of self-reliance. 2. That she may show her ability to be independent of all human instrumentalities. 3. That she may move into the exigencies of the future. (*Ibid.*) *Death common to all :*—In one of Nathaniel Hawthorne's note-books there is a remark as to qualifying men by some common quality or circumstance that should bring together people the most unlike in other respects, and make a brotherhood and sisterhood of them. "First by their sorrows; for instance, whenever there are any, whether in fair mansion or hotel, who are mourning the loss of friends. Secondly, all who have the same maladies, whether they lie under damask canopies, or on straw pallets, or in the wards of hospitals. Then proceed to generalize and classify all the world together, as none can claim other exemption from either sorrow, sin, or disease; and if they could, yet death, like a great parent, comes and sweeps them all through one darksome portal—all his children." (*H. O. Mackey.*) *Death admonitory :*—There is a bird peculiar to Ireland, called the cock of the wood, remarkable for the fine flesh and folly thereof. All the difficulty to kill them, is to find them out, otherwise a mean marksman may easily despatch them. They fly in woods in flocks, and if one of them be shot, the rest remove not but to the next bough, or tree at the farthest, and there stand staring at the shooter, till the whole covey be destroyed; yet as foolish as this bird is, it is wise enough to be the emblem of the wisest man in the point of mortality. Death sweeps away one, and one, and one, here one, and there another, and all the rest remain no whit moved, or minding of it, till at last a whole generation is consumed and brought to nothing. (*J. Spencer.*) *Death's impartiality :*—Death levels the highest mountains with the lowest valleys. He mows down the fairest lilies as well as the foulest thistles. The robes of illustrious princes and the rags of homely peasants are both laid aside in the wardrobe of the grave. (*Archbp. Secker.*) *Meditate on death :*—There was a motto on the walls of the Delphian Temple, ascribed to Chilo, one of the seven wise men of Greece—"Consider the end." *Death levels all distinctions :*—As trees growing in the wood are known—some by difference of their trunks, and some by the properties of their branches, leaves, flowers, and fruits ; but this knowledge is had of them only whilst they stand, grow, and are not consumed; for if they be committed to the fire, and are turned into ashes, they cannot be known. It is impossible that, when the ashes of divers kinds of trees are mingled together, the tall pine should be discerned from the great oak, or the mighty poplar from a low shrub, or any one tree from another; even so men, whilst they live in the wood of this world, are known—some by the stock of their ancestors, some by the flourishing leaves of their words and eloquence, some in the flowers of beauty, and some in the shrub of honesty, many by their savage ignorance, and some by their kindness ; but when death doth bring them into dust, and has mixed all together, then their ashes cannot be known—then there is no difference between the mighty princes of the world and the poor souls that are not accounted of. (*Cawdray.*)

Vers. 7–22. **The children of Israel were fruitful.**—*The increase of the Church :*— I. NOTWITHSTANDING THE REMOVAL OF ITS CHIEF OFFICER (ver. 6). Joseph dead; his influence gone; his counsel inaccessible. To-day the Church loses her chief officers, but it still grows. II. NOTWITHSTANDING THE DECADE OF THE GENERATION (ver. 6). So to-day men die, but the Church, by making new converts, multiplies her progeny to an almost incredible extent. III. NOTWITHSTANDING THE PERSECUTION TO WHICH IT WAS SUBJECTED (ver. 11). The Church can never be put down by force. The Infinite Power is on her side. This is more than all that can be against her. IV. NOTWITHSTANDING THE ARTIFICES BY WHICH IT WAS SOUGHT TO BE BETRAYED (vers. 15–22). So the Church has been in danger through the treachery of the outside world, and through the daring cruelty of meddlesome men. Still it grows. May it soon fill the world, as the Israelites did Egypt ! All Church increase is from God ; not from men, not from means. God has promised to multiply the Church. (*J. S. Exell, M.A.*) *Increase by God's blessing :*—1. The death of fathers cannot hinder God's increase of the Church's children. They decrease and these increase under God. 2. God's promises for His Church's increase cannot fall to the ground. He doth fulfil them. 3. Fruitfulness, abundant increase, multiplication excessive, and strength, are the Church's blessing from God. 4. God works wonderfully to fulfil His promise of increasing His people. 5. The land of enemies is made by God a nursery for the increase of His Church. 6. God's blessing makes His Israel to fill Egypt, the Church to fill the world. (*G. Hughes, B.D.*) *A large population, and what it led to :*— I. A LARGE POPULATION IS OF GREAT ADVANTAGE TO A NATION. 1. It gives an impulse to civilization. 2. It augments the force of the national prowess. 3. It invests the nation with importance in the estimation of surrounding kingdoms. II. A LARGE POPULATION SOMETIMES EXCITES THE SUSPICION AND ENVY OF NEIGHBOURING KINGS. 1. Pharaoh was jealous of the numerical growth of Israel. 2. He was suspicious of what might befall his country in future exigencies. III. THIS SUSPICION FREQUENTLY LEADS KINGS TO PRACTISE THE MOST ABJECT SLAVERY. 1. It was cunning. 2. It was unjust. 3. It was painful. 4. It was apparently productive of gain. But what was gained in public buildings was lost in sensitiveness of conscience, force of manhood, and worth of character. Slavery involves a loss of all that is noble in human nature, and it leads to murder (ver. 22). IV. SLAVERY IS AN INCOMPETENT METHOD OF CONQUEST. 1. Because it does not gain the sympathy of the people it conquers. 2. Because it arouses the indignation of those who are subject to its cruelties. 3. It does not save a ruler from the calamity he seeks to avert. (*J. S. Exell, M.A.*) *A large population :*—The larger the population of a nation, the greater are its capabilities of sympathy, mutual dependency, and help, and oftentimes the greater difficulty in its right government. (*Ibid.*) *Oppression and growth :*—1. There are three aspects in which the oppression of Israel in Egypt may be viewed. It was the fulfilment of God's own word ; it was education ; it was a type. 1. The covenant with Abraham had included the prediction of four hundred years of oppression in a strange land. The fulfilment is reached through the fears and cruel policy of Pharaoh. The Bible decisively upholds the view that not in Israel alone, but everywhere, the movements of nations, as the incidents of individual lives, are directed by God. To it the most important thing about Egypt and the mighty Rameses was that he and it were the instruments for carrying out God's designs in reference to Israel. Has not history verified the view ? Who cares about anything else in that reign in comparison with its relation to the slaves in

Goshen? 2. The oppression was, further, education. We can say nothing certainly as to the teaching which Israel received in science, art, letters, or religion. Some debts, no doubt, accrued in all these departments. Probably the alphabet itself was acquired by them, and some tinge of acquaintance was made by a few with other parts of the early blossoming Egyptian civilization. But the oppression taught them better things than these. Pressure consolidates. Common sorrows are wonderful quickeners of national feeling. The heavier the blows, the closer grained the produce of the forge. Not increase of numbers only, but tough knit conscious-ness of their unity, was needed for their future. They acquired some beginnings of that extraordinary persistency of national life which has characterized them ever since, in these bitter days. Note further, they learned endurance, without which the education of a nation, as of a man, is defective. The knowledge of God's covenant with Abraham would in some degree be preserved, and it taught them that their affliction was part of the Divine plan for them. So they would learn—at least the best of them would—to look for the better things following which the covenant held forth, and would be able to see some gleam of the dawn even in the thickest darkness. " If winter comes, can spring be far behind ? " The evil foretold and accomplished is turned into prophecy of the good foretold and yet unseen. 3. The growth of Israel under its oppression. The pressure which was intended to crush only condensed. " The more they afflicted them, the more they . . . grew." So the foiled oppressors glared at them with a mixture of awe and loathing, for both feelings are implied in the words rendered " were grieved." It is the history of the nation in a nutshell. The same marvellous tenacity of life, the same power of baffling oppression and thriving under it, have been their dower ever since, and continue so yet. The powers that oppress them fill the world with their noise for awhile, and pass away like a dream ; they abide. For every tree felled, a hundred saplings spring up. What does it mean? and how comes it ? The only answer is that God preserves them for a better deliverance from a worse bondage, and as His witnesses in their humiliation, as they were His in their prosperity. The fable of the one of their race who bade Christ march on to Calvary is true concerning them. They are doomed to live and to wander till they shall recognize Him for their Messiah. That growth is a truth for God's Church, too. The world has never crushed by persecuting. There is a wholesome obsti-nacy and chivalry in human nature which rallies adherents to a persecuted cause. Truth is most powerful when her back is at the wall. Times of oppression are times of growth, as a hundred examples from the apostles' days down to the story of the gospel in Madagascar prove. The world's favour does more harm than its enmity. Its kisses are poisonous ; its blows do no hurt. (*A. Maclaren, D.D.*) *Fruitfulness of Israelites in Egypt :*—Some commentators resort to natural causes to account for this amazing increase. A modern writer declares that " the females in Egypt, as well among the human race as among animals, surpass all others in fruitfulness." But we prefer to ascribe the matter to Divine intervention. The blessing of Jehovah was now signally conferred upon the people. God " increased His people greatly, and made them stronger than their enemies " (Psa. cv. 24). The word that after a long delay came to Israel, the third patriarch, was now fulfilled (Gen. xxxv. 11). Though the performance of God's promises is sometimes slow, yet it is always sure. It was when the Israelites lost the benefit of the pro-tection of Joseph that God made their numbers their defence, and they became better able than they had been to shift for themselves. If God continue our friends and relations to us while we most need them, and remove them when they can be better spared, let us own that He is wise, and not complain that He is hard upon us. (*A. Nevin, D.D.*) *Ancestry numerically regarded :*—The number of a man's ancestors doubles in every generation as his descent is traced upward. In the first generation he reckons only two ancestors, his father and mother. In the second generation the two are converted into four, since he had two grandfathers and two grandmothers. But each of these four had two parents, and thus in the third generation there are found to be eight ancestors ; that is, eight great-grandparents. In the fourth generation the number of ancestors is sixteen ; in the fifth, thirty-two ; in the sixth, sixty-four ; in the seventh 128. In the tenth it has risen to 1,024 ; in the twentieth it becomes 1,048,576 ; in the thirtieth no fewer than 1,073,741,834. To ascend no higher than the twenty-fourth generation we reach the sum of 16,777,216, which is a great deal more than all of the inhabitants of Great Britain when that generation was in existence. For if we reckon a generation at thirty-three years, twenty-four of such will carry us back 792 years, or to A.D. 1093, when

William the Conqueror had been sleeping in his grave at Caen only six years, and his son William II., surnamed Rufus, was reigning over the land. At that time the total number of the inhabitants of England could have been little more than two millions, the amount at which it is estimated during the reign of the Conqueror. It was only one-eighth of a nineteenth-century man's ancestors if the normal ratio of progression, as just shown by a simple process of arithmetic, had received no check, and if it had not been bounded by the limits of the population of the country. Since the result of the law of progression, had there been room for its expansion, would have been eight times the actual population, by so much the more is it certain that the lines of every Englishman's ancestry run up to every man and every woman in the reign of William I., from the king and queen downward, who left descendants in the island, and whose progeny has not died there. (*Popular Science Monthly.*)   *Successful colonists :*—Englishmen are not the only successful colonists ; and the credit, if any, of exterminating aborigines they are entitled to share with insects. Let us take the case of the Australian bee. The Australian bee is about the size of a fly, and without any sting; but the English bee has been so successfully introduced as to be now abundant in a wild state in the bush, spreading all over the Australian continent, and yielding large quantities of honey, which it deposits in the hollows of trees ; the immense quantities of honey-yielding flowers afford an abundant supply of material. The foreign bee is fast driving away the aboriginal insect as the European is exterminating the black from the settled districts, so that the Australian bee is now very scarce. (*Scientific Illustrations and Symbols.*)   **A new king.**—*Change of government :*—1. God's blessing on His Church is the cause that worldly rulers consult against it. 2. Blessings from God and oppositions from worldly powers usually are connected. 3. Changes of kings and governments may bring changes on the Church's state. 4. New and strange rulers are set up, when new and strange things are to be in the Church. 5. God suffers such to rise up, and orders them to His praise. 6. All God's goodness by His instruments to the world are apt to be committed to oblivion and ignorance. 7. Ignorance and oblivion of God's mercies by His Church causeth wicked rulers to persecute them. (*G. Hughes, B.D.*)   *Egypt's new king :*—I. HE WAS OUT OF SYMPATHY WITH THE PURPOSE AND PROVIDENCE OF GOD. II. HE WAS OUT OF SYMPATHY WITH THE CONDUCT OF HIS PREDECESSORS. III. HE WAS ENVIOUS IN HIS DISPOSITION. Envious men generally bring on themselves the evils of which they suspect the innocent to be guilty. IV. HE WAS CUNNING IN HIS ARRANGEMENTS. Policy a bad basis for a throne. It invites suspicion, alienates respect, leads to ruin. V. HE WAS CRUEL IN HIS REQUIREMENTS. VI. HE WAS THWARTED IN HIS PROJECT. Mere power cannot always command obedience. It is sometimes defeated by weakness. Heaven is on the side of the oppressed. (*J. S. Exell, M.A.*)   *The vicissitudes of power :*—The vicissitudes of power—1. Are independent of past services. 2. Are independent of moral character. 3. Are frequently dependent upon the arbitrary caprice of a despotic king. (*Ibid.*)   *A bad king will make a wicked people :*—1. He will influence the weak by his splendour. 2. Terrify the timid by his power. 3. Gain the servile by his flattery. 4. Gain the simple by his cunning. 5. Sometimes gain the good by his deception. (*Ibid.*)   *Like ruler, like people :*—If the mountains overflow with waters, the valleys are the better ; and if the head be full of ill-humours, the whole body fares the worse. The actions of rulers are most commonly rules for the people's actions, and their example passeth as current as their coin. The common people are like tempered wax, easily receiving impressions from the seals of great men's vices ; they care not to sin by prescription and damn themselves with authority. And it is the unhappy privilege of greatness to warrant, by example, others' as well as its own sins, whilst the unadvised take up crimes on trust and perish by credit. (*J. Harding.*)   *The king that knew not Joseph :*— It is said Joseph was not " known " by this dynasty. This is a strong expression, used to denote the perfect obscurity into which this good and great man had fallen ; or rather, the contempt in which this benefactor and true patriot was held by those who were unable to appreciate him. It was not that Joseph's character had waned in beauty ; it was not that his intellect had lost its sagacity ; but the new dynasty wished to pursue a course of action and conduct inconsistent with that purity, integrity, and candour which Joseph had counselled ; and therefore he was cast off. Less worthy men were taken in his place. But what occurred to Joseph is just what befalls Christians still, in proportion as their Christianity ceases to be latent. We are told by an apostle that the world knoweth us not, because it knew Christ not. 1. The reason why the world does not appreciate the Christian character is that the Christian lives a higher life. He is, in proportion as he is a Christian, influenced by motives and hopes, and guided by laws and a sense of a presence, which an unconverted, worldly man, such as was the new king of Egypt who knew not Joseph, cannot at all understand. 2. Another reason why the world does not appreciate the Christian now is that it judges a Christian by itself, and thinks that he must be at heart, notwithstanding all his pretences, what it is. The world loves sin, delights in it. And when the world meets with a man who professes to have laid his ambition at the foot of the Cross, and whose thirst for power is the noble thirst of doing good, it will say, " This sounds very fine, but we do not believe it. The only difference between you and us is that we do not pretend to these things, and that you do; for behind the curtain you practise what we practise, and are exactly what we are." Therefore the world hates the Christian, not simply for his Christianity, but because it cannot conceive such a man to be any other than a thorough hypocrite. (*J. Cumming, D.D.*) *A king's ignorance:*—I. WHO WAS THIS MAN? 1. Exiled for many years. 2. Belonged to an alien dynasty. 3. May simply mean that he refused to know Joseph. II. WHY DID HE REIGN? To carry out the promise of God. 1. God does not always use the same methods. Brought Israel into Egypt by prosperity; took them out by adversity. 2. God had to prepare the way for His work. III. WHAT HAS HE TO DO WITH US? 1. He shows us how human wisdom overreaches itself. His policy only brought about the very object he wished to avoid. 2. He shows us the abuse of privileges. He might have known Joseph. Ignorance is no excuse for those who ought to know. (*Homilist.*) *Emptiness of fame:*—The readiness with which the populace forgets its vaunted idols has ever been a favourite topic with third-rate moralists. A surviving friend of William Pitt was convinced of the emptiness of fame by seeing the greatest statesman of the age completely forgotten in ten days. Queen Elizabeth's passage into oblivion was even more rapid, for, according to an eminent historical authority, she " was as much forgot in four days as if she had never existed." To be sure in such cases the oblivion has been short-lived. Posterity has amply remedied the brief injustice of contemporary opinion, (*Christian Journal.*) *Oblivion and neglect:*—It is a memorable example, amongst many others that we have, of William the Conqueror's successor, who being unhappily killed, as he was hunting in the New Forest, all his nobles and courtiers forsook him, only some few that remained laid his body in a collier's cart, which being drawn with one silly lean beast through very foul and filthy way, the cart broke, and there lay the spectacle of worldly glory, both pitifully gored and all bemired. Now, if this were the portion of so mighty a prince, whom immediately before so glorious a troop attended, what then must others of meaner rank expect and look for, but only with death's closing up of their eyes to have all their friends excluded, and no sooner gone but to be as suddenly forgotten. Hence it is that oblivion and neglect are the two handmaids of death. (*J. Spencer.*) **Let us deal wisely.**—*Wrong councils:*—Kings ought to know better than to convene councils to oppose the intentions of God. Such conduct is— 1. Daring. 2. Reprehensible. 3. Ruinous. 4. Ineffectual. (*J. S. Exell, M.A.*) *The end and design of the council:*—1. To prevent the numerical increase of Israel. 2. To enfeeble the military power of Israel. 3. To detain the Israelites in permanent bondage. (*Ibid.*) *Persecution of God's people for hypothetical offences:*—Hypothetical offences have generally been the ground of the persecution of the people of God. It has rarely been for a crime proved, but generally for a crime possible. And this dynasty, in the exercise of what it thought a very far-reaching diplomacy, but really a very wild and foolish hallucination, determined to persecute, and gradually crush, the children of Israel. The result proved that the wisdom of man is folly with God. Whatever is undertaken that has no sanction from God, never will have any real or permanent success before men. But attempt anything, however wise it looks, or talented it appears, yet if it be not inspired by principle, it is a rope of sand—it must fall to pieces. Let us, therefore, ever feel that we never can do wisely, unless we do well, and that the highest principle is ever the purest and best policy. The dynasty that succeeded the ancient Pharaoh did not know this. They thought they could extirpate God's people. They might as well have tried to extirpate the sun from the firmament, or the fruits and trees of the earth; for the everlasting arms are around all them that love and fear God; and they are an immortal people who are the sons and daughters of the Most High. The Egyptians found here that the more they afflicted them, the more they multiplied. (*J. Cumming, D.D.*) *A perversion of language:*—The *wisdom* here proposed to be employed was the wisdom of the serpent; but with men of reprobate minds, governed solely by the corrupt spirit of this world, whatever measures tend to promote their own interests and circumvent their opponents, is dignified by the epithet *wise*, though it be found, when judged by a purer standard, to be in reality nothing less than the very policy of hell. (*G. Bush.*)   *Pharaoh's sceptical reasoning :*—All Pharaoh's reasoning was that of a heart that had never learnt to take God into its calculations. He could accurately recount the various contingencies of human affairs, the multiplying of the people, the falling out of war, the joining with the enemy, their escape out of the land, but it never once occurred to him that God could have anything whatever to do in the matter. Had he only thought of this, it would have upset his entire reasoning. Ever thus is it with the reasonings of man's sceptical mind. God is shut out, and their truth and consistency depend upon His being kept out. The death-blow to all scepticism and infidelity is the introduction of God into the scene. Till He is seen, they may strut up and down upon the stage with an amazing show of wisdom and plausibility, but the moment the eye catches even the faintest glimpse of that blessed One whose

"Hand unseen
Doth turn and guide the great machine,"

they are stripped of their cloak, and disclosed in all their nakedness and deformity. (*A. Nevin, D.D.*)   *Jealousy of autocrats :*—Autocrats, whether elected or usurping, are all more or less jealous. The female autocrat is in some respects worse than the male. Two queen bees will not live together in the same hive. And indeed, as soon as a young queen-bee is about to lay her eggs, she is anxious to destroy all the royal pupæ which still exist in the hive. When she has become a mother, she attacks one after the other the cells which still contain females. She may be seen to throw herself with fury upon the first cell she comes to. She tears an opening in it large enough for her to introduce her sting. When she has stung the female which it contains, she withdraws to attack another. Man is not much behind these jealous insects. Among certain tribes of Ethiopians the first care of the newly crowned chief is to put in prison all his brothers, so as to prevent wars by pretenders to the throne. And even among more civilized nations the records are numerous of the mean and petty tricks and cruelties adopted by kings and queens for disposing of any possible rivals. (*Scientific Illustrations and Symbols.*)   **The more they multiplied.**—*Moral growth proportionate to affliction :*—1. This is true of individual moral character. 2. This is especially true in the development of the Church. (*J. S. Exell, M.A.*)   *Why does persecution and trial operate thus ?*—1. To manifest the love of God towards His Church. 2. To manifest the power of God over His enemies. 3. To fulfil the promise of God made to the good. 4. To manifest His providence towards the Church. 5. To strike terror into the hearts of tyrants. 6. To manifest the divinity of truth, and pure moral character. (*Ibid.*)   *The Egyptians were grieved :*—1. Because their plots were a failure. 2. Because their cruelty was unavailing. 3. Because they had exasperated an enemy they could not subdue. . . . Half the grief of the world is occasioned by the failure of wicked and cruel purposes. (*Ibid.*)   *Persecution fertilising :*—"The blood of the martyrs is the seed of the Church." Persecuting the Church is but like casting manure upon the ground. It for a while covers the plants, and seems to destroy them; but it makes the earth more fertile, and the plants more numerous and vigorous. (*J. Orton.*)   *Strange increase:*—How diverse were the barbarities and kinds of death inflicted on the Christian confessors ! The more they were slain, the more rapidly spread the faith; in place of one sprang up a hundred. When a great multitude had been put to death one at court said to the king, "The number of them increaseth, instead of, as thou thinkest, diminishing." "How can that be?" exclaimed the king. "But yesterday," replied the courtier, "thou didst put such-and-such a one to death, and lo ! there were converted double that number; and the people say that a man appeared to the confessors from heaven, strengthening them in their last moments." Whereupon the king himself was converted. (*The Apology of Al Kindy,* A.D. 830.)   *Prosperity under persecutions :*—Whatever has been done by enemies in rage or in recklessness, God has always met it calmly and quietly. He has shown Himself ready for every emergency. And He has not only baffled and utterly defeated all the inventions of wicked men, but He has turned their strange devices to good account, for the development of His own sovereign purposes. I. IN THE CASE OF ISRAEL, it did seem to be a deep-laid plot, very politic and crafty indeed, that as the kings of Egypt, themselves of an alien race, had subdued the Egyptians, they should prevent the other alien race, the Israelites, from conquering them. Instead of murdering them wholesale, it did seem a wise though a cruel thing to make them slaves; to divide them up and down the country; to appoint them to the most menial work in the land, that they might be crushed down and their spirits become so base that they would not dare to rebel. Thus we may suppose it was hoped that their physical strength would be so relaxed, and their circumstances so reduced, that the clan would soon be insignificant if not utterly extinct. But God met and overruled this policy in various ways. "The more they afflicted them, the more they multiplied." The glory of God shines forth conspicuously in the use to which He turned the persecutions they endured. The severe treatment they had to bear from the enemy became to them a salutary discipline. In order to cut loose the bonds that bound them to Egypt, the sharp knife of affliction must be used; and Pharaoh, though he knew it not, was God's instrument in weaning them from the Egyptian world, and helping them as His Church to take up their separate place in the wilderness, and receive the portion which God had appointed for them. Once more—and here you may see the wisdom of God—the very means which Pharaoh devised for the effectual crushing of the people—the destruction of the male children—became the direct, nay, the Divine provision for educating a deliverer for them. II. Let us now carry the same thought a stage farther, and take a brief survey of THE HISTORY OF THE CHILDREN OF GOD. The like means will appear in manifold operation. Men meditate mischief, but it miserably miscarries. God grants protection to the persecuted, and provides an escape from the most perilous exposure. Full often the darkest conspiracy is brought to the direst confusion. Persecution has evidently aided the increase of the Church by the scattering abroad of earnest teachers. We are very apt to get hived—too many of us together—and our very love of one another renders it difficult to part us and scatter us about. Persecution therefore is permitted to scatter the hive of the Church into various swarms, and each of these swarms begins to make honey. We are all like the salt if we be true Christians, and the proper place for the salt is not massed in a box, but scattered by handfuls over the flesh which it is to preserve. Moreover, persecution helps to keep up the separation between the Church and the world. When I heard of a young man that, after he joined the Church, those in his workshop met him at once with loud laughter and reproached him with bitter scorn, I was thankful, because now he could not take up the same position with themselves. He was a marked man: they who knew him discovered that there was such a thing as Christianity, and such a one as an earnest defender of it. Again, persecution in the Christian Church acts like a winnowing fan to the heaps gathered on the threshing-floor. Persecution has a further beneficial use in the Church of God, and it is this. It may be that the members of the Church want it. The Roman who professed that he would like to have a window in his bosom, that everybody might see his heart, would have wished, I should think, before long for a shutter to that window; yet it is no slight stimulus to a man's own circumspection for him to know that he is observed by unfriendly eyes. Our life ought to be such as will bear criticism. And this persecution has a further usefulness. Often does it happen that the enmity of the world drives the Christian nearer to his God. III. And now I close this address by just very briefly hinting that THIS GREAT GENERAL TRUTH APPLIES TO ALL BELIEVERS; but I will make a practical use of it. Are you passing through great trials? Very well then, to meet them I pray that God's grace may give you greater faith; and if your trials increase more and more, so may your strength increase. You will be acting after God's manner, guided by His wisdom, if you seek to get more faith out of more trial, for that trial does strengthen faith, through Divine grace, experience teaches us, and as we make full proof of the faithfulness of God, our courage, once apt to waver, is confirmed. (*C. H. Spurgeon.*) *How to defeat the devil :*—Always take revenge on Satan if he defeats you, by trying to do ten times more good than you did before. It is in some such way that a dear brother now preaching the gospel, whom God has blessed with a very considerable measure of success, may trace the opening of his career to a circumstance that occurred to myself. Sitting in my pulpit one evening, in a country village, where I had to preach, my text slipped from my memory, and with the text seemed to go all that I had thought to speak upon it. A rare thing to happen to me; but I sat utterly confounded. I could find nothing to say. With strong crying I lifted up my soul to God to pour out again within my soul of the living water that it might gush forth from me for others; and I accompanied my prayer with a vow that if Satan's enmity thus had brought me low, I would take so many fresh men whom I might meet with during the week, and train them for the ministry, so that with their hands and tongues I would avenge myself on the Philistines. The brother I have alluded to came to me the next morning. I accepted him at once as one whom God had sent, and I helped him, and others after him, to prepare for the service, and to go forth in the Saviour's name to preach the gospel of the grace of God. Often when we fear we are defeated, we ought to say, "I will do all the more. Instead of dropping from this work, now will I make a general levy, and a sacred conscription upon all the powers of my soul, and I will gather up all the strength I ever had in reserve, and make from this moment a tremendous life-long effort to overcome the powers of darkness, and win for Christ fresh trophies of victory." After this fashion you will have an easier time of it, for if you do more good the more you are tempted, Satan will not so often tempt you. When he knows that all the more you are afflicted so much the more you multiply, very likely he will find it wiser to let you alone, or try you in some other method than that of direct and overt opposition. So whenever you have a trial, take it as a favour; whenever God holds in one hand the rod of affliction, He has a favour in the other hand; He never strikes a child of His but He has some tender blessing in store. If He visits you with unwonted affliction, you will have unusual delight; the Lord will open new windows for you, and show His beauty as He shows it not to others. According as your tribulations abound, so also shall your consolations abound in Christ Jesus. (*Ibid.*)   *Egypt, the house of bondage to God's people :*—I. THE CHARACTER OF EGYPT, AND HER INFLU-ENCE ON HER CHILDREN. 1. Egypt was distinguished as the abode of a peculiarly easy and luxurious life. In Egypt, as in the world, there was all that could lay the soul to sleep under its vine and fig-tree, and reduce it to the level of the brutes which the Egyptian worshipped as more wise and wonderful than man. This easiness of the terms of life is fatal to the noblest elements in man. Look at Naples. No heroism can be extracted from the Lazzaroni. Give the fellow a bit of bread, a slice of melon, and a drink of sour wine, and he will lie all day long on the quays, basking in the sun and the glorious air; and what cares he if empires rise or totter to their fall? Egypt was the Naples of the old world; wealth, luxury, elaborate refinement, of a kind not inconsistent with gross-ness; but no moral earnestness, no manhood, no life. Nature wooed man to her lap in Egypt and won him, bathing him in luxurious pleasures—Egypt was the world. 2. Moreover, Egypt was cut off very much from all the political and intellectual activity in which Babylon was compelled to share. She could "live to herself and die to herself," as was not possible for Babylon. She could play away her strength and her life in wanton pleasures at her will. Egypt is the image of the wanton world herein. It was full of the wisdom of this world, the wisdom of the under-standing, which prostitutes itself easily to the uses of a sensual and earthly life. II. THE EXPERIENCE OF GOD'S CHILDREN THERE—its influence on a people conscious that they had a soul to be saved. 1. They went down to Egypt with the fairest prospect—certainty of sustenance, and promise of wealth, honour, and power. They were to settle in Goshen; better, richer land than the bare hills which would be their only home in Canaan, whose rich valleys would be mainly occupied by the native inhabitants—land in every way suited to yield pasture to their flocks. So the world woos us. We are born in it, God placed us here, God gave us these keen senses, these imperious appetites, and the means of their fullest indulgence; and why should we tighten the rein? See you no new reason why Egypt, when the patriarchs dwelt there, was a fit and full image of "the world"? 2. They had not lived there long, before, rich and fruitful as was the land, they began to find their life a bondage. Egypt was strange to them. They could not amalgamate with the inhabitants. The Egyptians came to feel it; alienation sprang up and bitterness. Egypt laid chains on them to keep them in her service, while they groaned and writhed, and sighed to be gone—to be free. And rich as the world's pastures may be, propitious as may be its kings, the soul of man grows uneasy in its abodes. There are moments of utter heart-sickness amidst plenty and luxury, such as a sick child of the mountains knows, tossing on a purple bed of state : "Oh, for one breath of the sunny breezes, one glance at the shadows sweeping over the brown moorlands ; one breath, one vision, would give me new life." The very prosperity makes the soul conscious of its fetters. 3. The moment comes, in every experience, when the bondage becomes too grevious to be borne; when the spirit cries out and wrestles for deliverance, and the iron, blood-rusted, enters the very heart. The men became conscious of their higher vocation, and wept and pleaded more earnestly ; and their tyrants yoked them more tightly, and loaded them more heavily; till, like Job, they cursed God's light and hated life, in bitterness of soul. And the soul in its Egypt, the world, drinks deep of this experience. The moment comes when it wakes up and says, "I am a slave"; "I am a beast"; "I will shake off this yoke"; "I will be free." Then begins a battle-agony; a strife for life and immortality—the end either a final, eternal relapse into captivity, or an exodus into the wilderness and to heaven. Let the soul fight its own battles, and the most heroic struggles shall not save it. Let it follow the Captain of Salvation, and gird on the armour of God, and death and hell shall not spoil it. (*J. B. Brown, B.A.*) *The taskmasters of the world :*—1. Sin is a taskmaster. 2. The rich are often taskmasters. 3. The ambitious are often taskmasters. These taskmasters are—(1) Authoritative: "They did set over thee." (2) Painful: "To afflict thee." (3) Inconsiderate: "Burdens." (*J. S. Exell, M.A.*) *That God allowed His people thus to be enslaved and afflicted :*—1. A mystery. 2. A problem. 3. A punishment. 4. A discipline. (*Ibid.*) *Suffering and strength :*—One thing experience teaches, that life brings no benediction for those who take it easily. The harvest cannot be reaped until the soil has been deeply ploughed and freely harrowed. "Learn to suffer and be strong," says the poet; and certain it is that without suffering there can be no strength. Not, indeed, that suffering is or makes strength, but that it evokes the latent power, and rouses into action the energies that would have otherwise lain ingloriously supine. The discipline of life is a necessary prelude to the victory of life; and all that is finest, purest, and noblest in human nature is called forth by the presence of want, disappointment, pain, opposition, and injustice. Difficulties can be conquered only by decision; obstacles can be removed only by arduous effort. These test our manhood, and at the same time confirm our self-control. (*W. H. D. Adams.*) *Life maintained by struggling :*— You lament that your life is one constant struggle; that, having obtained what you tried hard to secure, your whole strength is now required in order to retain it; and that your necessities impose on you the further obligation of additional exertions. It is so; but do not repine. As a rule, the maintenance of life is everywhere conditional on struggling. It is not only so with men and animals. It is so even in the vegetable world. You struggle with obstacles; but the very trees have to do the same. Observe them; take heart and grow strong. M. Louis Figuier says that the manner in which roots succeed in overcoming obstacles has always been a subject of surprise to the observer. The roots of trees and shrubs, when cramped or hindered in their progress, have been observed to exhibit considerable mechanical force, throwing down walls or splitting rocks, and in other cases clinging together in bunches or spreading out their fibres over a prodigious space, in order to follow the course of a rivulet with its friendly moisture. Who has not seen with admiration how roots will adapt themselves to the special circumstances of the soil, dividing their filaments in a soil fit for them almost to infinity, elsewhere abandoning a sterile soil to seek one farther off which is favourable to them; and as the ground was wide or less hard, wet or dry, heavy or light, sandy or stony, varying their shapes accordingly? Here are wonderful energy, and illustrations of the way in which existence may be maintained by constant action. (*Scientific Illustrations and Symbols.*) *Use of adversity:*—The springs at the base of the Alpine Mountains are fullest and freshest when the summer sun has dried and parched the verdure in the valleys below. The heat that has burned the arid plains has melted mountain glacier and snow, and increased the volume of the mountain streams. Thus, when adversity has dried the springs of earthly comfort and hope, God's great springs of salvation and love flow freshest and fullest to gladden the heart. (*Irish Congregational Magazine.*) *Moulding influences of life :*—The steel that has suffered most is the best steel. It has been in the furnace again and again; it has been on the anvil; it has been tight in the jaws of the vice; it has felt the teeth of the rasp; it has been ground by emery; it has been heated and hammered and filed until it does not know itself, and it comes out a splendid knife. And if men only knew it, what are called their "misfortunes" are God's best blessings, for they are the moulding influences which give them shapeliness and edge, and durability, and power. (*H. W. Beecher.*) *The advantage of afflictions :*—Stars shine brightest in the darkest night; torches are better for the beating; grapes come not to the proof till they come to the press; spices smell sweetest when pounded; young trees root the faster for shaking; vines are the better for bleeding; gold looks the brighter for scouring; glow-worms glisten best in the dark; juniper smells sweetest in the fire; pomander becomes most fragrant for chafing; the palm-tree proves the better for pressing; camomile, the more you tread it, the more you spread it. Such is the condition of all God's children, they are then most triumphant when most tempted; most glorious when most afflicted; most in the favour of God when least in man's; as their conflicts, so their conquests; as their tribulations, so their triumphs; true salamanders, that live best in the furnace of persecution, so that heavy afflictions are the best benefactors to heavenly affections. (*J. Spencer.*) *The university of hard knocks :*—A great deal of useless sympathy is in this day expended upon those who start in life without social or monetary help. Those are most to be congratulated who have at the beginning a rough tussel with circumstances. John Ruskin sets it down as one of his calamities that in early life he "had nothing to endure." A petted and dandled childhood makes a weak and insipid man. You say that the Ruskin just quoted disproves the theory. No. He is showing in a dejected, splenetic, and irritated old age the need of the early cudgelling of adversity. He seems fretting himself to death. A little experience of the hardship of life would have helped to make him gratefully happy now. No brawn of character without compulsory exertion. The men who sit strong in their social, financial, and political elevations are those who did their own climbing. Misfortune is a rough nurse, but she raises giants. Let our young people, instead of succumbing to the influences that would keep them back and down, take them as the parallel bars, and dumb-bells, and weights of a gymnasium, by which they are to get muscle for the strife. Consent not to beg your way to fortune, but achieve it. God is always on the side of the man who does his best. God helps the man who tries to overcome difficulties. (*Dr. Talmage.*) *Graces multiply by affliction :* —Graces multiply by afflictions, as the saints did by persecutions. (*T. Adams.*) *Beneficial effects of affliction :*—The walnut tree is most fruitful when most beaten. Fish thrive best in cold and salt waters. The most plentiful summer follows upon the hardest winter. (*J. Trapp.*) *Injuries overruled :*—Though your attempt to destroy a man's position may fail to accomplish that object, it may be productive of serious injury to him. Yet, fortunately for him, that very injury may afterwards bring forth good results. His friends may rally round him; his resources may be added to through the medium of the sympathetic; or he may be so acted on as to put forth power from within which develops new graces and fresh vigour. You injure a tree, and you will discover reparation is at work even there. The wheel of your cart, for instance, grazes the trunk, or the root of the tree is wounded by your passing ploughshare; the result is an adventitious bud comes. Wherever you see those adventitious buds which come without any order, you may recollect that their formation is frequently thus produced by the irritation caused by injury. You cut down the heads of a group of forest trees ; you have not destroyed them. Like the men you have injured, they live to tell the tale. The pollarded dwarf remains to declare what the forest tree would have become but for you. Even the date of your attack can be ascertained; for the stunted group will cover themselves with branches all of the same age and strength, which will exhibit to the sky the evidence of the story: Injured these all are ; yes, but not destroyed. (*Scientific Illustrations and Symbols.*) *Affliction and growth :*—Bunyan's figure of Satan pouring water on the fire to extinguish it, and it all the while waxing brighter and hotter because the unseen Christ was pouring oil upon it, illustrates the prosperity of God's people in affliction. "The more they afflicted them, the more they grew." When a fire attains a certain heat and volume, to pour water upon it is only to add fuel. The water, suddenly changed to its component gases, feeds, instead of extinguishing, the flame. So God changes the evil inflicted upon His people into an upbuilding and sanctifying power. (*H. C. Trumbull.*)   **They made their lives bitter with hard bondage.**— *The bondage of sin :*—I. THE BONDAGE AS AN ILLUSTRATION OF SIN. "Whosoever committeth sin is the servant of sin." 1. The unnaturalness of this bondage. Men were fitted to serve God, not Satan. All their powers are perverted, misused, and reversed, when they are in courses of disobedience, and rebellion. "Right" means "straight," and "wrong" means "wrung." 2. The severity of this bondage. No taskmaster for men has ever been found more brutal than a brutal man. The devil has no despot out of hell more despotic than sinners to place over sinners. When villains get villains in their power, how they do persist in lashing them into further villainy and vice! 3. The injustice of this bondage. Satan never remembers favours bestowed. One may give himself, body, soul, and spirit to the devil, and no fidelity will win him the least consideration. Injustice is the rule in sin, it never in any case has exceptions. The prince of evil simply uses his devotees all the worse because of their servility and patience. 4. The destructiveness of this bondage of sin. The wanton waste of all that makes life worth a struggle by persistent courses of sin is familiar to every thoughtful observer. Wickedness never builds up; it always pulls down. Once in the heat of a public discussion some infidels challenged an immediate reply to what they called their arguments. A plain woman arose in the audience; she proceeded to relate how her husband had been dissipated and unkind; she had prayed for him, and he had become a praying man and a good father; years of comfort and of peace had they now dwelt together in the love of each other and the fear of God. "So much," she continued, "has my religion done for me. Will you kindly state now what your religion has done for you in the same time?" Done? unbelief does not do anything, it undoes. II. And now with so sorrowful a showing as this bondage has to make, it seems surprising to find that the Israelites were counselled to "remember" it. WHY SHOULD THEY RECALL SUCH HUMILIATION? 1. Such reminiscences promote humility. Spiritual pride is as dangerous as a vice. What have we that God's mercy has not bestowed upon us? Why boast we over each other? Recollect that "the Lord hath taken you, and brought you forth out of the iron furnace, even out of Egypt, to be unto Him a people of inheritance, as ye are this day." To Him we owe everything we are. 2. Such a remembrance quickens our considerate charity for others. Our disposition is to condemn and denounce the degeneracies of the times in which we live. Wherein are people worse now than we ourselves were once? How do we know what we might have been if it had not been for the arrest of our rebellion by the power of the Holy Ghost? Once, as a drunken man reeled past his door, John Newton exclaimed: "But for the grace of God, there goes John Newton!" (*C. S. Robinson, D.D.*) *Embittering the lives of others:*—It is no credit to Pharaoh that God overruled his oppression of the Israelites to their advantage. For his course there is nothing but guilt and shame. He who makes another life bitter has got the bitterness of that life to answer for, whatever good may come to his victim through the blessing of God. It is a terrible thing—a shameful thing also—to make another's life bitter. Yet there are boys and girls who are making their mothers' lives bitter; and there are husbands who are making the lives of their wives bitter; and there are parents who are making their children's lives bitter. Is no one's life made bitter by your course? Is there no danger of bitterness of life to any one through your conduct—or your purposed action? Weigh well these questions; for they involve much to you. Pharaoh is dead; there is no danger of his making our lives bitter with hard bondage. But the devil is not dead; and there is danger of our being in hard bondage to him. Pharaoh's bondage was overruled for good to those who were under it. The devil's bondage is harder than Pharaoh's, and no good ever comes of it to its subjects. It were better for us to have died under the hardest bondage of Pharaoh than to live on under the devil's easiest bondage. (*H. C. Trumbull.*) *Pharaoh's cruel policy:*—It is worth notice that the king holds council with his people, and evidently carries them with him in his policy. The Egyptians had more than their share of the characteristic ancient hatred and dread of foreigners, and here they are ready to second any harsh treatment of these intruders, whom three hundred years have amalgamated. Observe, too, that the cruel policy of Pharaoh is policy, and that only. No crime is alleged; no passion of hate actuates the cold-blooded proposal. It is simply a piece of state-craft, perfectly cool, and therefore indicating all the more heartlessness. Calculated cruelty is worse than impulsive cruelty. Like some drinks, it is more nauseous cold than hot. No doubt the question what to do with a powerful subject race, on a threatened frontier, who were suspected of kindred and possible alliance with the enemy on the other side of the boundary, was a difficult one. Rameses must have thought of Goshen and the Israelites much as we may fancy Prince Bismarck thinks of Alsace. He was afraid to let them become more powerful, and he was loath to lose them. Whether they stayed or went, they were equally formidable. High policy, therefore, which, in Old Egypt, and in other lands and ages nearer home, has too often meant undisguised selfishness and cynical cruelty, required that the peaceful happiness of a whole nation should be ruthlessly sacrificed; and the calm Pharaoh, whose unimpassioned, callous face we can still see on the monuments, laid his plans as unmoved as if he had been arranging for the diminution of the vermin in the palace walls. What a picture of these God-defying, man-despising, ancient monarchies is here! What would he have thought if any of his counsellors had suggested, "Try kindness"? The idea of attaching subject peoples by common interests, and golden bonds of benefit, had to wait millenniums to be born. It is not too widely spread yet. (*A. Maclaren, D.D.*) *The despotism of sin:*—I. IT COMMENCES BY SUGGESTING A SMALL

TRIBUTE TO THE SINNER. It wins us by the hope of a good investment—whereby we may secure wealth, prosperity, fame. A false hope; a deceptive promise. Sin is cunning; has many counsellors; many agencies. You are no match for it. II. IT SUCCEEDS IN GETTING THE SINNER COMPLETELY WITHIN ITS POWER. 1. Sin gets the sinner under its rule. 2. Sin makes the sinner subject to its counsel. 3. Sin makes the sinner responsible to its authority. III. IT ULTIMATELY IMPOSES UPON THE SINNER AN IN-TOLERABLE SERVITUDE. 1. The servitude of a bitter life. Destroys friendly companionships, breaks up family comfort. 2. The servitude of hard work. Unprofitableness and folly of sin. 3. The servitude is degrading. Brings men from respect to derision—from plenty to beggary—from moral rulership to servitude. *(J. S. Exell, M.A.)* *The spiritual bondage of men:*—I. AN ENTIRE AND UNIVERSAL BONDAGE. No merciful limit nor mitigation (see 2 Tim. ii. 26; 2 Pet. ii. 19; John viii. 34; Rom. v. 18, Rom. iii. 23; Gal. iii. 22). 1. It extends to all mankind. 2. The slavery of the individual is as complete and total, as that of the species is universal. (1) Understanding depraved. (2) Will perverted. (3) Affections depraved. II. A SEVERE AND CRUEL BONDAGE. No mastery can be found more pitiless than that of the unhallowed affections and passions which rule the mind, until the Almighty Redeemer breaks the yoke, and sets the captive free from the law of sin and death. III. A HELPLESS BONDAGE. 1. The oppressor of the soul abounds too greatly in power and resources to dread any resistance from a victim so helpless. Our strength for combat against such an enemy is perfect weakness. 2. In addition to his own power Satan has established a close alliance with every appetite and affection of our nature. Morally unable to deliver ourselves. Hope in God alone. Seek His aid through prayer. *(R. P. Buddicom, M.A.)* *The sufferings of Israel were rendered more intense:* — 1. As a punishment for their idolatry. 2. To inspire within them a deep hatred toward Egypt, so that through their perils in the wilderness they might not wish to return thither. 3. That the prospect of Canaan might animate and refresh their souls. 4. That after such excessive and unpaid labour they might fairly spoil the Egyptians on their departure. 5. That they might be aroused to earnest prayer for deliverance. 6. That the power and mercy of God might be more forcibly displayed in their freedom. Here is a true picture of tyranny: 1. Its rigour increases with failure. 2. It becomes more impious as it is in evident opposition to the Divine providence. 3. It discards all the claims of humanity. 4. It ends in its own defeat and overthrow. *(J. S. Exell, M.A.)* *The bondage:*—Situated as they were within the bounds of a foreign kingdom, at first naturally jealous, and then openly hostile towards them, it is not difficult to account for the kind of treatment inflicted on them, viewing the position they occupied merely in its worldly relations and interests. But what account can we give of it in its religious aspect—as an arrangement settled and ordained on the part of God? Why should He have ordered such a state of matters concerning His chosen seed? For the Egyptians— "though their hearts thought not so"—were but instruments in His hands, to bring to pass what the Lord had long before announced to Abraham as certainly to take place (Gen. xv. 13). 1. Considered in this higher point of view, the first light in which it naturally presents itself is that of a doom or punishment, from which, as interested in the mercy of God, they needed redemption. For the aspect of intense suffering, which is latterly assumed, could only be regarded as an act of retribution for their past unfaithfulness and sins. (1) It first of all clearly demonstrated, that, apart from the covenant of God, the state and prospects of those heirs of promise were in no respect better than those of other men—in some respects it seemed to be the worse with them. They were equally far off from the inheritance, being in a state of hopeless alienation from it; they had drunk into the foul and abominable pollutions of the land of their present sojourn, which were utterly at variance with an interest in the promised blessing; and they bore upon them the yoke of a galling bondage, at once the consequence and the sign of their spiritual degradation. They differed for the better only in having a part in the covenant of God. (2) Therefore, secondly, whatever this covenant secured for them of promised good, they must have owed entirely to Divine grace. (3) Hence, finally, the promise of the inheritance could be made good in their experience only by the special kindness and interposition of God, vindicating the truth of His own faithful word, and in order to this, executing in their behalf a work of redemption. While the inheritance was sure, because the title to it stood in the mercy and faithfulness of God, they had of necessity to be redeemed before they could actually possess it. 2. It formed an essential part of the preparation which they needed for occupying the inheritance. (1) It was necessary by some means to have a desire awakened in their bosoms towards Canaan, for the pleasantness of their habitation had become a snare to them. The affliction of Israel in Egypt is a testimony to the truth, common to all times, that the kingdom of God must be entered through tribulation. The tribulation may be ever so varied in its character and circumstances ; but in some form it must be experienced, in order to prevent the mind from becoming wedded to temporal enjoyments, and to kindle in it a sincere desire for the better part, which is reserved in heaven for the heirs of salvation. Hence it is so peculiarly hard for those who are living in the midst of fulness and prosperity to enter into the kingdom of God. And hence, also, must so many trying dispensations be sent even to those who have entered the kingdom, to wean them from earthly things, and constrain them to seek for their home and portion in heaven. (2) But if we look once more to the Israelites, we shall see that something besides longing desire for Canaan was needed to prepare them for what was in prospect. For that land, though presented to their hopes as a land flowing with milk and honey, was not to be by any means a region of inactive repose, where everything was to be done for them, and they had only to take their rest, and feast themselves with the abundance of peace. There was much to be done, as well as much to be enjoyed ; and they could neither have fulfilled, in regard to other nations, the elevated destiny to which they were appointed, as the lamp and witness of heaven, nor reaped in their own experience the large measure of good which was laid up in store for themselves, unless they had been prepared by a peculiar training of vigorous action, and even compulsive labour, to make the proper use of all their advantages. (*P. Fairbairn, D.D.*)   *The bondage of sin :*—Throughout the Scriptures the circumstances of Israel in Egypt are referred to as typical of the servitude under which the sinner is held. There is more than guilt in wickedness. It would indeed be bad enough, even if that were all, but there is slavery besides. Our Lord Himself says, " Whosoever committeth sin is the slave of sin " ; and there are no taskmasters so exacting as a man's own lusts. Look at the drunkard ! See how his vile appetite rules him ! It makes him barter every comfort he possesses for strong drink. It lays him helpless on the snowy street in the bitter winter's cold. It sends him headlong down the staircase, to the injury of his body and the danger of his life. If a slaveholder were to abuse a slave as the drunkard maltreats himself, humanity would hiss him from his place, and denounce him as a barbarian. And yet the inebriate does it to himself, and tries to sing the while the refrain of the song which ends, " We never, never shall be slaves." The same thing is true of sensuality. Go search the hospitals of this city ; look at the wretched victims of their own lusts who fill the wards, and then say if man's inhumanity to himself be not, in some aspects of it, infinitely more terrible than his oppression of his neighbours. Visit our prisons, and see how avarice, fashion, frivolity, and the love of standing well with their companions, have held multitudes in their grip, forcing them—nay, I will not say forcing them, for they sin wilfully—but leading them to dishonesty day by day, until at last the inner servitude gives place to an external imprisonment. The setting of slaves to make bricks without straw is nothing to the drudgery and the danger—as of one standing on the crater's edge—that dishonesty brings upon a man when once it has him in its power. And it is the same with every kind of sin. But this slavery need not be perpetual, for the Great Emancipator has come. (*W. M. Taylor, D.D.*)   *Egypt opposed to Israel :*—It is no new thing for Egypt to be unkind and cruel to Israel. Israelites and Egyptians are of contrary dispositions and inclinations ; the delight of one is the abomination of the other. Besides, it is the duty of Israel to depart out of Egypt. Israel is in Egypt in respect of abode, not of desire. Egypt is not Israel's rest. If Egypt were a house of hospitality, it would more dangerously and strongly detain the Israelites, than in being a house of bondage. The thoughts of Canaan would be but slight and seldom if Egypt were pleasant. It is good that Egyptians should hate us, that so they may not hurt us. When the world is most kind, it is most corrupting ; and when it smiles most, it seduces most. Were it not for the bondage in Egypt, the food and idols of Egypt would be too much beloved. Blessed be God, who will by the former wean us from the latter ; and will not let us have the one without the other : far better that Egypt should oppress us than we oppose God. (*W. Jenkyn.*)   *The bondage of sin :*—Vice, as it groweth in age, so it improveth in stature and strength ; from a puny child it soon waxeth a lusty stripling, then riseth to a sturdy man, and after a while becomes a massy giant whom we shall scarce dare to encounter, whom we shall be very hardly able to vanquish; especially seeing that, as it groweth taller and stouter, so we shall dwindle and become more impotent, for it feedeth upon our vitals and thriveth by our decay; it waxeth mighty by stripping us of our best forces, by enfeebling our reason, by preventing our will, by corrupting our temper, by debasing our courage, by seducing all our appetites and passions to a treacherous compliance with itself; every day our mind growing more blind, our will more restive, our spirit more faint, our appetites more fierce, our passions more headstrong and untameable. The power and empire of sin do strangely by degrees encroach, and continually get ground upon us till it has quite subdued and enthralled us. First we learn to bear it, then we come to like it; by and by we contract a friendship with it; then we dote on it; at last we become enslaved to it in a bondage which we shall hardly be able or willing to shake off. (*Isaac Barrow.*) *Darkest before the dawn :*—" Fear not to go down into Egypt; for I will there make of thee a great nation " (Gen. xlvi. 3). Look down, thou sainted patriarch! see what has here become of thy posterity, increased now fourteen thousand fold; nay, see, Thou God of Abraham, what has become of Thine inheritance, how they have watched and prayed in vain! " The Lord hath forsaken, the Lord hath forgotten! " And this continues, not for years, but centuries, each year of which seems in itself a century! " Verily, Thou art a God that hidest Thyself! " With such a scene of sorrow in his view, the most unfortunate among us well may cease complaint; and he who has to some extent learned to observe God's dealings in His providence, may have himself already marked how, in the present case, an old-established law in God's government is set before us in the form of a most touching incident: the Lord ofttimes makes everything as dark as they can possibly become, just that thereafter and thereby the light may shine more brilliantly. Ishmael must faint beneath the shrubs ere Hagar shall be told about the well. Joseph must even be left to sigh, not merely in his slavery, but in imprisonment and deep oblivion, ere he is raised to his high dignity. The host of the Assyrians must stand before Jerusalem's gates ere they are smitten by the angel of the Lord. The prophet Jeremiah must be let sink down into the miry pit, ere he is placed upon a rock. Did not a violent persecution of the Christians precede the triumph of the gospel? In the night of mediæval times, must not star after star set ere the Reformation dawn arose? Yes; is not Israel's history in this respect also the history of God's own people in succeeding times, even in the present day? They suffer persecution, are oppressed, ill-treated, and opposed through a mistaken policy; all kinds of force are often used for their restraint under the sacred name of liberty; yet still they stand, and take deep root, and grow, expecting better times will come in spite of these fierce hurricanes. Nay, verily, the Lord has not forgotten to be gracious, though He sometimes seems to hide His face; nor does He cease to rule the world, though He delays to interpose. The Father watches and preserves his child amidst the fiercest fires of persecution; and although the furnace of the trial through which he comes be heated seven times more than usual, every degree of heat is counted, measured, regulated by the Lord Himself. Though He permits injustice, and even lets it grow to an extraordinary height, He yet employs it for a purpose that may well command our adoration and regard—the purifying and the perfecting of those who are His own. (*J. J. Van Oosterzee, D.D.*) *The bitter lives:*— I. GOD'S BLESSING MAKES FRUITFUL. 1. The promise to Abraham (Gen. xvii. 2–8). 2. The number of the Israelites in Egypt (vers. 9, 10). II. Note the MISTAKES COMMITTED THROUGH PREJUDICE. 1. The Egyptians hated and spurned the Israelites; therefore, ultimately, lost the blessing of their presence. 2. Statesmanship fails in placing policy before principle. 3. Cruelty begot enmity; kindness would have won. III. SELFISHNESS SOON FORGETS PAST FAVOURS. A new ruler disregarded the claims of Joseph's seed. This world works for present and prospective favours. IV. Here is A TYPE OF THE GROWTH OF SIN. The Israelites came into the best part of Egypt; first pleasant, then doubtful, then oppressed, then finally enslaved. 1. Sin yields bitter fruit. 2. We have taskmasters in our habit. 3. Life becomes a burden: sorrows of servitude. V. Note the REASON FOR THIS AFFLICTION. 1. They were becoming idolatrous (Josh. xxiv. 14; Ezek. xx. 5–8). 2. Bitterness now would help to prevent return to Egypt. 3. We sometimes find sorrow here that we may look above. VI. GOD'S FAVOUR HERE CONTRASTED WITH MAN'S OPPOSITION. Pharaoh failed; the Israelites multiplied. VII. AFFLICTION HELPS US. 1. As afflicted, so they grew. 2. Christ purgeth us for more fruit. 3. Self-denial is the path to power. (*Dr. Fowler.*) *The mummy of Rameses the Great:*—After the verification by the Khedive of the outer winding-sheet of the mummy in the sight of the other illustrious personages, the initial wrapping was removed, and there was disclosed a band of stuff or strong cloth rolled all around the body; next to this was a second envelope sewed up and kept in place by narrow bands at some distance each from each; then came two thicknesses of small bandages; and then a new winding-sheet of linen, reaching from the head to the feet. Upon this a figure representing the goddess Nut, more than a yard in length, had been drawn in red and white colour, as prescribed by the ritual for the dead. Beneath this amulet there was found one more bandage; when that was removed, a piece of linen alone remained, and this was spotted with the bituminous matter used by the embalmers; so at last it was evident that Rameses the Great was close by—under his shroud. Think of the historic changes which have passed over the world since that linen cloth was put around the form of the king. Think what civilization stood facing an old era like his. A single clip of the scissors, and the king was fully disclosed. The head is long and small in proportion to the body. The top of the skull is quite bare. On the temple there are a few sparse hairs, but at the poll the hair is quite thick, forming smooth, straight locks about two inches in length. White at the time of death, they have been dyed a light yellow by the spices used in embalmment. The forehead is low and narrow; the brow-ridge prominent; the eyebrows are thick and white; the eyes are small and close together; the nose is long, thin, arched like the noses of the Bourbons; the temples are sunken; the cheek-bones very prominent; the ears round, standing far out from the head, and pierced, like those of a woman, for the wearing of ear-rings; the jawbone is massive and strong; the chin very prominent; the mouth small but thick-lipped; the teeth worn and very brittle, but white and well preserved. The moustache and beard are thin. They seem to have been kept shaven during life, but were probably allowed to grow during the king's last illness; or they may have grown after death. The hairs are white, like those of the head and eyebrows, but are harsh and bristly, and a tenth of an inch in length. The skin is of earthy brown, splotched with black. Finally, it may be said the face of the mummy gives a fair idea of the face of the living king. The expression is unintellectual, perhaps slightly animal; but, even under mummification, there is plainly to be seen an air of sovereign majesty, of resolve, and of pride. The rest of the body is as well preserved as the head; but, in consequence of the reduction of the tissues, its external aspect is less life-like. He was over six feet in height. The chest is broad; the shoulders are square; the arms are crossed upon the breast; the hands are small and dyed with henna. The legs and thighs are fleshless; the feet are long, slender, somewhat flat-soled, and dyed, like the hands, with henna. The corpse is that of an old man, but of a vigorous and robust old man. . . . The man was an incarnation of selfishness. To him there was but one being in the universe for whom he needed to care one groat; only a single will was to be consulted, only a single man's comfort was to be sought; he himself was the sole centre of all things. Man's strength, and woman's honour, life, wealth, time, and ease of other men, went for his personal glorification. And now the world looks at him, and gives him his due, in the light of the charities and decencies God commands. What do we mean when we speak of " a hard man "? One of the visitors who saw that mummy unrolled, a cool, quiet German, wrote afterwards this clause of description : " The expression of the features is that of a man of decided, almost tyrannical character." That ought to be so. This is the despot who ordered that the tally of bricks should remain undiminished, while his slaves should have to forage for their own necessity of straw. He was " a hard man." Is any one of us hard? Do we need to be kings in order to have that name? Can one be hard upon his clerks, his journeymen, his neighbours, in so far as he has power? So, again, does " a man of decided, almost tyrannical character " fashion and fix his character in the expression of his features? Do you recognize " a hard man " by his looks, when you set eyes upon him in ordinary life? Will one's disposition grow on him, until it shows itself in his forehead, his lips, his chin, the poise of his proud head? As years pass, are your features growing heavier and colder? Furthermore, is it on the body alone that character makes an impression? Is it possible that, even unconsciously to ourselves, soul as well as body is becoming indurate and chilly? Is money forcing features on our inner life and being? As we rise in life, do we grow interested in others; unselfish, gentle, forbearing in our judgments, or stiff, and rigid, and violent, and impatient of others' successes? And finally, if character thus perpetuates itself in the soul as well as on the body, is there anything disclosed to us of the world to come which will avail to change the destiny we have fashioned? On the day royal Rameses was buried, they wrapped his aged bald head in cerements, and covered him in the shadows. He comes up now after some awful centuries of silence, and he looks just as he used to look. It is likely his soul has not grown different either. We know nothing about his future. It is ours that concerns us. What is going to change any lineament of soul in the mysterious Hereafter? (*C. S. Robinson, D.D.*) **If it be a son, then ye shall kill him.**—*High social position used for the furtherance of a wicked purpose:*—I. SOMETIMES HIGH SOCIAL POSITION EXERTS ITS AUTHORITY FOR THE ACCOMPLISHMENT OF A WICKED AND CRUEL PURPOSE. 1. The king commands the murder of the male children of the Israelites. Diabolical massacre of innocents. Abuse and degradation of regal power. 2. He seeks to accomplish this by bringing the innocent into a participation of his murderous deed. Tyrants are generally cowards. II. WHEN HIGH SOCIAL AUTHORITY IS USED TO FURTHER A WICKED DESIGN, WE ARE JUSTIFIED IN OPPOSING ITS EFFORT. 1. We are not to do wrong because a king commands it. To oppose murder, when advocated by a king, and when it could be accomplished unknown—or, if known, gain applause of nations—is—(1) heroic; (2) benevolent; (3) divinely rewardable; (4) duty of all who fear God. 2. Such opposition must embody the true principle of piety. The midwives feared God more than they feared the king. 3. Such opposition will secure for us the Divine protection. III. FOR SUCH OPPOSITION WE SHALL BE DIVINELY REWARDED (vers. 20, 21). (*J. S. Exell, M.A.*) *Why were the males to be put to death?*—1. Because they were the most capable of insurrection and war. 2. Because the Israelitish women were fairer than the Egyptian, and so might be kept for the purposes of lust. 3. Because the Israelitish women were industrious in spinning and needlework, and so were kept for service. (*Ibid.*) *Pharaoh's murderous intentions :*—His plan was a quiet one. I dread the quietness of murderers. When murderers lay their heads together, and fall into soft whispers, their whispers are more awful than the roar of cannon or the crash of thunder. The king's plan was to murder the male child the instant it was born. The thing could easily be done. A thumb pressed on the throat would do it. A hand covering the external organs of respiration for a few moments would be sufficient. This was his simple plan of beating back the manhood of the dreaded nation. He was going to do it very simply. Oh, the simplicity of murderers is more intricate than any elaboration of complexity on the part of innocent men ! There was to be no external demonstration of violence—no unsheathing of swords—no clash of arms on the field of battle ; the nation was to be sapped very quietly. Sirs ! Murder is murder, whether it is done quietly or with tumult and thunder. Beware of silent manslaughter ! Beware of quiet murder ! Nothing sublimer than butchery struck the mind of this idiot king. Thoughts of culture and kindness never flashed into the dungeon of his soul. He had no idea of the omnipotence of love. He knew not of the power of that government which is founded on the intelligence and affection of the common people. Annihilation was his fierce remedy There is a profound lesson here. If a king fears children, there must be great power in children ; if the tyrant begins with the children, the good man should begin with them too. (*J. Parker, D.D.*) **The midwives feared God.**—*Pharaoh's evil intention frustrated by God:*—1. Tyrants' commands are sometimes crossed by God's good hand. 2. The true fear of God, from faith in Him, will make weakest creatures abstain from sin. 3. The name of the only God is powerful to support against the word of mightiest kings. 4. God's fear will make men disobey kings, that they may obey God. 5. The fear of God will make souls do good, though commanded by men to do evil. 6. Life preservers discover regard to God, and not bloody injurious life destroyers. 7. God makes them save life whom men appoint to destroy it. 8. The good hand of God doth keep the males or best helps of the Church's peace, whom persecutors would kill (ver. 17). (*G. Hughes, B.D.*) *Beneficent influence of the fear of God :*—They who fear God are superior to all other fear. When our notion of authority terminates upon the visible and temporary, we become the victims of fickle circumstances ; when that notion rises to the unseen and eternal, we enjoy rest amid the tumult of all that is merely outward and therefore perishing. Take history through and through, and it will be found that the men and women who have most devoutly and honestly feared God have done most to defend and save the countries in which they lived. They have made little noise ; they have got up no open-air demonstrations ; they have done little or nothing in the way of banners and trumpets, and have had no skill in getting up torchlight meetings ; but their influence has silently penetrated the national life, and secured for the land the loving and mighty care of God. Where the spiritual life is profound and real, the social and political influence is correspondingly vital and beneficent. All the great workers in society are not at the front. A hidden work is continually going on ; the people in the shade are strengthening the social foundation. There is another history beside that which is written in the columns of the daily newspaper. Every country has heroes and heroines uncanonised. (*J. Parker, D.D.*)   *A definition of the fear of God :*—Fear of God is that holy disposition or gracious habit formed in the soul by the Holy Spirit, whereby we are inclined to obey all God's commands; and evidences itself by—1. A dread of His displeasure. 2. Desire of His favour. 3. Regard for His excellences. 4. Submission to His will. 5. Gratitude for His benefits. 6. Conscientious obedience to His commands. (*C. Buck.*)   *Civilizing influence of the fear of God :*—A weary day had been passed in visiting a wretched neighbourhood. Its scenes were sad, sickening, repulsive. Famine, fever, want, squalid nakedness, moral and physical impurities, drunkenness, death, and the devil were all reigning there. Those only who have known the sinking of heart which the miseries of such scenes produce, especially when aggravated by a close and tainted atmosphere, can imagine the grateful surprise with which, on opening a door, we stepped into a comfortable apartment. Its whitewashed walls were hung around with prints, the household furniture shone like a looking-glass, and a bright fire was dancing merrily over a clean hearth-stone. It was an oasis in the desert. And we well remember, ere question was asked or answered, of saying to ourselves, " Surely the fear of God is in this place ; this must be the house of a church-going family." It proved to be so. Yet it was a home where abject poverty might have been expected and excused. A blind man dwelt there. (*T. Guthrie, D.D.*)   *The fear of God :*—Learn a life-lesson from the monument to Lord Lawrence in Westminster Abbey. Of all the memorials there, you will not find one that gives a nobler thought. Simply his name, and the date of his death, and these words ; " He feared man so little, because he feared God so much." Here is one great secret of victory. Walk ever in the fear of God. Set God ever before you. Let your prayer be that of the Rugby boy, John Laing Bickersteth, found locked up in his desk after his death : " O God, give me courage that I may fear none but Thee." (*Great Thoughts.*)   *Obedience to conscience :*— Lord Erskine, when at the bar, was remarkable for the fearlessness with which he contended against the Bench. In a contest he had with Lord Kenyon he explained the rule and conduct at the bar in the following terms :—" It was," said he, " the first command and counsel of my youth always to do what my conscience told me to be my duty, and leave the consequences to God. I have hitherto followed it, and have no reason to complain that any obedience to it has been even a temporal sacrifice; I have found it, on the contrary, the road to prosperity and wealth, and I shall point it out as such to my children." (*W. Baxendale.*)   *Excellency of the fear of God :*—It hath been an usual observation, that when the king's porter stood at the gate and suffered none to come in without examination what he would have, that then the king was within; but when the porter was absent, and the gates open to receive all that came, then it was an argument of the king's absence. So in a Christian, such is the excellency of the fear of God, that when it is present, as a porter shutting the doors of the senses, that they see not, hear not what they list, it is an argument the lord of that house, even God Himself, is within ; and when this fear is away, a free entrance is given to all the most dissolute desires, so that it is an infallible demonstration of God's removal from such a soul. (*J. Spencer.*) *Fear of God a safeguard :*—If we fear God, we need know no other fear. That Divine fear, like the space which the American settler burns around him as a defence against the prairie fire, clears a circle, within which we are absolutely safe. The old necromancists believed that if a man was master of himself he enjoyed complete immunity from all danger ; if his will was firmly set, the powers of evil could not harm him; he could defy a host of devils raging around. Against the malice of human and infernal power, the citadel of a man's heart that is set upon God is impregnable. (*Dr. Hugh Macmillan.*)   *The best service :*—He who serves God, serves a good master. He who truly serves God is courageous and heroic. Here are two humble women who despise the patronage of a crown, and set a king's edict at defiance. There is no bravery equal to the bravery that is moral. It makes the weakest a conqueror, and lifts up the lowest to pluck the palm of victory. A short-sighted policy would have said, "Please Pharaoh " ; a true heart said, " Please God." Pharaoh had much to give. He held honours in his hand. He could deal out gold and silver. He could give a name among the Egyptians. What of it ! God could turn his honours into shame, and send the canker on his gold.

Serve God! Well tended is that fold which God watches. Pharaoh may frown, but his frowns will be unseen and unregarded amid the light of an approving heaven! (*J. Parker, D.D.*) **Cast into the river.**—*The last edict of a tyrant king :*—I. IT WAS PUBLIC IN ITS PROCLAMATION. How men advance from one degree of sin to another. II. IT WAS CRUEL IN ITS REQUIREMENTS. Why should a tyrant king fear the infant sons of Israel? He knew they would be his enemies in the future if spared. Young life is the hope of the Church and the terror of despots. (*J. S. Exell, M.A.*) *Progress in sin :*—There is a woful gradation in sin. As mariners, setting sail, lose sight of the shore, then of the houses, then of the steeples, and then of the mountains and land; and as those who are waylaid by a consumption first lose vigour, then appetite, and then colour; thus it is that sin hath its woful gradations. None decline to the worst at first, but go from one degree of turpitude to another, until the very climax is reached. *The climax of cruelty :*—If we glance once more at the different means which Pharaoh devised for the oppression and diminution of the Hebrews, we find that they imply the following climax of severity and cruelty : he first endeavoured to break their energy by labour and hardship (vers. 11–14), then to effect their diminution by killing the newborn male children through the midwives (vers. 15, 16); and when neither of these plans had the desired result—the former in consequence of the unusual robustness of the Hebrew women, the latter owing to the piety and compassion of the midwives—he tried to execute his design by drowning the young children (ver. 22); which last device was in two respects more audacious and impious than the second: first, because he now, laying aside all shame, showed publicly his despotism against a harmless foreign tribe, which relied on the hospitality solemnly promised to them ; and, secondly, because now the whole people were let loose against the Hebrews ; spying and informing was made an act of loyalty, and compassion stamped as high-treason. (*M. M. Kalisch, Ph.D.*) *Increasing power of sin :*— When once a man has done a wrong thing it has an awful power of attracting him and making him hunger to do it again. Every evil that I do may, indeed, for a moment create in me a revulsion of conscience, but stronger than that revulsion of conscience it exercises a fascination over me which it is hard to resist. It is a great deal easier to find a man who has never done a wrong thing than to find a man who has only done it once. If the wall of the dyke is sound it will keep the water out, but if there is the tiniest hole in it, it will all come in. So the evil that you do asserts its power over you ; it has a fierce, longing desire after you, and it gets you into its clutches. Beware of the first evils, for, as sure as you are living, the first step will make the second seem to become necessary. The first drop will be followed by a bigger second, and the second, at a shorter interval, by a more copious third, until the drops become a shower, and the shower becomes a deluge. The course of evil is ever wider and deeper, and more tumultuous. The little sins get in at the window and open the front door for the big housebreakers. One smooths the path for the other. All sin has an awful power of perpetuating and increasing itself. As the prophet says in his awful vision of the doleful creatures that make their sport in the desolate city, "None of them shall want her mate. The wild beasts of the desert shall meet with the wild beasts of the islands." Every sin tells upon character, and makes the repetition of itself more and more easy. "None is barren among them." And all sin is linked together in a slimy tangle, like a field of seaweed, so that the man once caught in its oozy fingers is almost sure to drown. (*A. Maclaren, D.D.*)

CHAPTER II.

VERS. 1–4. **An ark of bulrushes.**—*The birth of Moses :*—I. As OCCURRING OF NOBLE PARENTAGE. 1. They were of moderate social position. 2. They were of strong parental affection. 3. They were of good religious character. Happy the child that is linked to the providence of God by a mother's faith! Faith in God is the preserving influence of a threatened life—physically, morally, eternally. II. As HAPPENING IN PERILOUS TIMES. 1. When his nation was in a condition of servitude. That this servitude was severe, exacting, grievous, disastrous, murderous, is evident from the last chapter. 2. When a cruel edict was in force against the young. III.

As INVOLVING MOMENTOUS ISSUES. 1. Issues relating to the lives of individuals. The birth of Moses made Miriam a watcher, gave her an introduction to a king's daughter, and has given immortality to her name. It brought Aaron into historical prominence. 2. Issues involving the freedom of an enslaved people. 3. Issues relating to the destiny of a proud nation. IV. As EXHIBITING THE INVENTIVENESS OF MATERNAL LOVE. 1. In that she devised a scheme for the safety of her child. The mother was more clever than the tyrant king and his accomplices. Tyranny is too calculating to be clever. Maternal love is quick and spontaneous in thought. V. As ELUDING THE EDICT OF A CRUEL KING. The mother of Moses was justified in eluding this edict, because it was unjust, murderous; it did violence to family affection, to the laws of citizenship, and to the joyful anticipation of men. (*J. S. Exell, M.A.*) *The infancy of Moses :*—1. His concealment. 2. His rescue. 3. His restoration. (*Caleb Morris.*) *Lessons :*—1. Providence is preparing good, while wickedness is working evil to the Church. 2. Lines, tribes, and persons are appointed by God, by whom He will work good to His people. 3. In the desolations of the Church's seed, God will have His to marry and continue it. 4. Tribes cursed for their desert, may be made instrumental of good by grace. 5. Choice and taking in marriage should be under Providence, free, and rational (ver. 1). 6. The greatest instruments of the Church's good God ordereth to being in the common way of man. 7. God ordereth, in His wisdom, instruments of salvation to be born in times of distinction. 8. No policies or cruelties of man can hinder God from sending saviours to His Church (ver. 2). (*G. Hughes, B.D.*) *The ark of bulrushes :*—I. THE GOODLY CHILD—Moses. 1. Its birth. (1) In an evil time. The edict of Pharaoh, like the sword of Damocles, over its head. God takes care that men needed for His work in evil times shall be born in them—Wickliffe, Luther. (2) Of an oppressed people and humble origin. Great men often of lowly extraction. 2. Its appearance—"Goodly." Beautiful, not only to a mother's eyes, but really so. Its beauty appealed to the mother, as its tears to the princess. 3. The excitement caused by its birth. Babes usually welcomed. Here were fear and sorrow and perplexity. This Divine gift becomes a trial, through the wickedness of man. Sin turns blessings into curses, and joy into sorrow. II. THE ANXIOUS MOTHER—Jochebed. 1. Her first feelings. Touched by the rare loveliness of her child. Bravely resolves to evade the decree. She had another son—Aaron—now three years of age (chap. vii. 7); but could not spare one. 2. Her careful concealment. For three months she contrived to preserve her secret from the Egyptians. Anxiously thinking what she might presently do. 3. Her ingenious device. Concealment no longer possible. She will trust God rather than Pharaoh. III. THE OBEDIENT DAUGHTER — Miriam. 1. Her obedience. The blessing of obedient children. Trusted by the mother. The elder should care for, and watch over, the younger. 2. Her surprise. The princess and her retinue appear. She attentively watches. The ark discovered, brought out, and opened. Her anxiety. She approaches. 3. Her thoughtfulness. She is quick-witted. Sees compassion in the princess's face. Shall she fetch a nurse? Of the Hebrew women? 4. Her great joy. Her brother saved. Her return home. Perhaps the mother was praying for the child. Jochebed's surprise and gratitude and joy. A great result grew out of her obedience (1 Pet. i. 14; Eph. vi. 1; Col. iii. 20). IV. THE COMPASSIONATE PRINCESS. Kindness in the house of Pharaoh! "Out of the strong sweetness." Children not always to be judged by their parents. Eli's sons were not godly (1 Sam. ii. 12). Pharaoh's daughter not cruel, as her father. Moved by an infant's tears, she at once comprehends the history of the child. Resolves to adopt it. Providential use of compassion, maternal solicitude, filial obedience, infantile beauty and helplessness. "All things work together for good." Learn— 1. To prize a mother's love, and return it. 2. To imitate Miriam's obedience and sisterly affection. 3. Not to judge of children by their parents. 4. To admire the wisdom of Providence. 5. "Unto us a child is born, unto us a son is given "— Jesus. (*J. C. Gray.*) *The cradle on the waters :*—I. THE POWER OF YOUNG LIFE TO ENDURE HARDSHIP. Codling of children is foolish, unhealthy. II. THE USE THAT ONE MEMBER OF A FAMILY MAY BE TO ANOTHER. Services which seem trifling may prove far-reaching in effect. Miriam thus helped to bring about the freedom of her nation. III. THE PATHETIC INFLUENCE OF A BABE'S TEARS. Touching tokens of sorrow, weakness, helplessness. Potent, inviting help. Many are moved by the sight of personal grief who look unmoved upon a national calamity. IV. THE SENSITIVE CONSCIENCE OF A TYRANT'S DAUGHTER. (*J. S. Exell, M.A.*) *The babe in the bulrushes :*—I. Let us CONSIDER THE PERILS WHICH SURROUNDED THIS PUR-

POSEFUL LIFE, WHICH WAS RESCUED IN SUCH A REMARKABLE MANNER. 1. For one thing, it was the life of an infant child. Infancy alone is more than enough to extinguish such a diminutive glimmer of existence; just leave him where he is a little longer, and you will never hear of that child's going up into Mount Sinai. There is only the side of a slight basket between him and swift drowning; one rush of the waves through a crevice, and the march through the wilderness will never be made. 2. Observe also this was the life of a proscribed child. 3. And then observe that this was the life of an outcast child. He had no friends. His mother had already hidden him until concealment was dangerous. II. Let us TRY TO FIND SOME SUGGESTIONS AS TO MODERN LIFE AND DUTY. There Moses lay, before he was called Moses, or had any right to be—an infant, proscribed, outcast child! You pity him; so do I pity him, with all my heart. Still, I will tell you frankly what I pity more by far, and I trust to better purpose. There are hundreds of sons and daughters of misery drifting out upon a stream of vice, which the Nile river, with all its murkiness and its monsters, cannot parallel for an exposure of peril— a river of depraved humanity, hurrying on before it everything stainless and promising into the darkness of destiny behind the cloud. It was a woman who ultimately brought up this babe from the bulrush ark. Women know how to save children better than men do. The spirit in which all this work must be done is that of faith. There is a sense of possibility in every child's constitution, and this is what gives a loftier value to it than that which is possessed by any other creature of the living God. A child owns in it what a diamond has not: a child can grow, and a diamond cannot. They say it takes a million of years, more or less, to make a big diamond; but the biggest of diamonds has a past only, and the smallest of children has a limitless future. Faith and works are what seemed once to disturb the balance of a man whose business it was to write an epistle in the New Testament. See what a vivid illustration this has in the story here before us. Jochebed had absolute faith; so had Amram; and so had Miriam for all we know. But it would have done no good to fall down and go to crying, nor to sit down and quote the promises, nor to be trampled down and give up the baby. Jochebed told Amram to get her some of the toughest rushes he could find, and he went and did it; then she awaked Moses, and wrapped him in the most comfortable way she could for an outing; then she took some pitch and bitumen, and told Miriam a patient story as to how she was to watch her brother. The word "ark" is found only in this instance, and in that not altogether unlike it in the case of Noah; only in these two places has the inspired Word of God employed it. There was the same principle at stake in both experiences—Noah believed God, and then made his "ark"; Amram and Jochebed believed God, and then made their "ark." And I can readily imagine that these pious parents got their first notion of the plan to save the baby out of the story of Noah; and so they used, whenever they spoke of it, to employ the same name. At any rate, it has a lesson for every one of us. Trust God, always trust God; then do all within your power to help on the purpose you prayerfully hope He is about to undertake for you. Make the best ark you can; place it in the river at the safest spot you can find; leave it there; then trust God. The main point is, venturesomeness is the highest element of belief in our Father in heaven. (*C. S. Robinson, D.D.*)   *The mother of Moses :*—I. THE MOTHER'S LOVE OF THE CHILD. Divine. Providential. II. THE MOTHER'S INGENUITY. Danger risked. Ample reward. III. THE MOTHER'S HEROISM. A sacrifice of love. (*J. O. Davies.*)   *The mother remained at home, showing*—1. The dignity of her faith—she could wait away from the scene of trial. 2. Her supreme hope in God—the issue was to be Divine. 3. Her happy confidence in her little daughter—children do their work better when they feel that they are trusted with it entirely. (*J. S. Exell, M.A.*)   *The beautiful ministry of a youthful life :*— 1. Loving. 2. Cautious. 3. Obedient. 4. Reflective. 5. Courteous. 6. Successful. (*Ibid.*)   *The faith of Moses' parents :*—We shall study the history of Moses without the key if we overlook the point made by the writer to the Hebrews (chap. xi. 23). "By faith," &c. Faith in God made them fearless of Egypt's cruel king. It may sometimes happen that profound interest in a babe of apparently rare promise shall run in a very low and selfish channel, suggesting how much he may do to comfort their own hearts, or to build up the glory of their house or of their name; but when, by a heavenly faith, it takes hold of useful work for God, when it prompts to a special consecration of all the possibilities of his future to the kingdom of Christ, it is morally sublime. Such seems to have been the faith of the parents of the child Moses. How their faith prompted ingenious methods of concealments; how it wrought in harmony with God's wise providence, not only to preserve the life of this consecrated child, but to give him a place in the heart of Pharaoh's daughter, and thus open to his growing mind all the wealth of Egypt's culture and wisdom, we learn somewhat from this story. (*H. Cowles, D.D.*) *Moses and Christ :*—Moses and Christ stand together in the same supernatural scheme; they are in the line of the same Divine purpose; they work together, though in different ways, towards the same end. Although they occupy far distant ages, and live under completely different conditions, they largely undergo the same experiences, conform to the same laws, confront the same difficulties, and manifest the same spirit. In many cases the events of their lives actually and literally correspond, and in many more it only needs that the veil of outward manifestation be lifted to see that in spirit they are one. And this not by accident, but by design. The plan of God is a complete whole. That Moses, the founder of the preparatory dispensation, should be pre-eminently like Him who was to fulfil it, is most natural; that he should, in his measure, set Him forth, is what we might expect (see Deut. xviii. 15; John v. 46). To point out that likeness, and, at the same time, mark the contrasts, is the work upon which we enter. We shall study Moses in the light of Christ. Like two rivers, at one time we shall see the two lives to flow together in the same channel—the same quiet flowing, the same tortuous course, the same cataracts in each; but anon they divide, and pursue each a separate bed, only to meet again far away beyond. 1. We take the two lives at their beginnings. The time of each is most significant. The age in each case was charged with expectancy. Both were periods of bondage, and bondage crying out for a deliverer. Both were born to be emancipators. But the one birth is not like the other. The source of the one river is at our feet; the source of the other is like Egypt's own mysterious Nile—far, far away in a land of mystery, and where mortals have never trodden. 2. The two deliverers are alike again in this—that they owe nothing of their greatness to their parents. Amram and Joseph, Jochebed and Mary, stand upon the ordinary level of mankind. God is not bound down to evolution. He can raise up a Moses from the slave huts of Egypt; He can send forth His Christ from the peasantry of Galilee. 3. They start together from obscurity and poverty and adversity. 4. Both children are born to great issues, and both must meet, therefore, that opposition with which goodness is ever assailed. It would seem that the birth of any soul having great moral capabilities arouses the opposition of the powers of darkness. Fable and legend have recognized this, and have made their heroes pass through extraordinary dangers whilst only children. Romulus and Remus, cast away to die, were nursed by a wolf, and thus lived to build the foundations of Rome and the Roman Empire. Cyrus, the founder of the Medo-Persian monarchy, was said to have been thrown out into the wilderness, and to have been adopted by a shepherd's wife, whose own babe was dead. Our own King Arthur, too, passed a similar peril. Doubtless these are no more than legends, confused echoes possibly from the story of Moses itself; but they serve to show us how mankind has ever recognized that lives destined to be great are met by hardship and opposition. Moses and Christ are one in this. 5. The likeness of the two births is not, however, completed until we notice the special providences of God, by which they are delivered from their enemies. What are the edicts of Pharaoh or the swords of Herod against the purposes of the Most High? Who are kings and princes, that they should withstand the Lord? What are all the combinations of evil, and all the plots of the devil, against His will, who ruleth over all? (*H. Wonnacott.*) *The bulrush :*—The bulrush is the papyrus, or paper-reed, of the ancients. It grows in marshy places, and was once most abundant on the banks of the Nile; but now that the river has been opened to commerce, it has disappeared, save in a few unfrequented spots. It is described as having "an angular stem from three to six feet high, though occasionally it grows to the height of fourteen feet; it has no leaves; the flowers are in very small spikelets, which grow in thread-like, flowering branchlets, which form a bushy crown to each stem." It was used for many purposes by the Egyptians—as, for example, for shoes, baskets, vessels of different sorts, and boats; but it was especially valuable as furnishing the material corresponding to our paper, on which written communication could be made. To obtain this last fibre, the course exterior rind was taken off, and then with a needle the thin concentric layers of the inner cuticle, sometimes to the number of twenty to a single plant, were removed. These were afterward joined together with a mixture of flour, paste, and glue; and a similar layer of strips being laid crosswise in order to strengthen the fabric, the whole sheet was subjected to pressure, dried in the sun, beaten with a mallet, and polished with ivory. When completed and written over, the sheets were united into one, and rolled on a slender wooden cylinder. Thus was formed a book, and the description of the process gives the etymology and primal significance of our own word "volume." (*W. M. Taylor, D.D.*) *Children in need of preserving mercy* :—The spot is traditionally said to be the Isle of Rodak, near old Cairo. In contrasting the perils which surrounded the infancy of Moses with the security and comfort with which we can rear our own offspring, we have abundant grounds of gratitude. Yet it should not be forgotten that whatever care we may exercise for our little ones, or whatever guardianship we may afford them, they as really require the preserving mercy of heaven when reposing in their cradles or sporting in our parlours as did Moses when enclosed in his ark of bulrushes and exposed to the waves or the ravenous tenants of the Nile. (*A. Nevin, D.D.*) *Training of children* :—What if God should place in your hand a diamond, and tell you to inscribe on it a sentence which should be read at the last day, and be shown then as an index of your own thoughts and feelings ? What care, what caution, would you exercise in the selection. Now, this is what God has done. He has placed before you the immortal minds of your children, more imperishable than the diamond, on which you are about to inscribe every day and every hour by your instructions, by your spirit, or by your example, something which will remain, and be exhibited for or against you at the judgment day. (*Dr. Payson.*) *Parental instruction best* :—Even as a plant will sooner take nourishment and thrive better in the soil where it first grew and sprung up than in any other ground, because it liketh its own soil best ; so, likewise, children will sooner take instruction and good nurture from their parents, whom they best like, and from whom they have their being, than from any other. (*Cawdray.*) *Divine ordering of events* :—The mother had done her part. The rushes, the slime, and the pitch were her prudent preparations ; and the great God has been at the same time preparing *His* materials, and arranging *His* instruments. He causes everything to concur, not by miraculous influence, but by the simple and natural operation of second causes, to bring about the issue designed in His counsels from everlasting. (*G. Bush, D.D.*) *God's providence in our family life* :—The phrase "special providence," is liable to be misunderstood. The teaching of this book is not that God overrules some things more than others, but that He is in all alike, and is as really in the falling of a sparrow as the revolution of an empire. God was as truly in the removal of the little ones that were taken away as He was in the saving of Amram's son ; and there were lessons of love and warning from the one, no less than of love and encouragement from the other. Nay more, God is in the daily events of our households precisely as He was in those of the family of the tribe of Levi long ago. The births and the bereavements ; the prosperity and the adversity ; the joys and the sorrows of our homes, are all under His supervision. He is guiding us when we know it not ; and His plan of our lives, if we will only yield ourselves to His guidance, will one day round itself into completeness and beauty. (*W. M. Taylor, D.D.*) *The events of life under a Divine providence* :—When Druyse, the gunsmith, invented the needle-gun, which decided the battle of Sadowa, was it a mere accident ? When a farmer's boy showed Blucher a short cut by which he could bring his army up soon enough to decide Waterloo for England, was it a mere accident ? When the Protestants were besieged at Bezors, and a drunken drummer came in at midnight and rang the alarm bell, not knowing what he was doing, but waking up the host in time to fight their enemies that moment arriving, was it an accident ? When, in the Irish rebellion, a starving mother, flying with her starving child, sank down and fainted on a rock in the night, and her hand fell on a warm bottle of milk, did that just happen so ? God is either in the affairs of men or our religion is worth nothing at all, and you had better take it away from us, and instead of this Bible, which teaches the doctrine, give us a secular book, and let us, as the famous Mr. Fox, the Member of Parliament, in his last hour, cry out : "Read me the eighth book of Virgil." Oh my friends ; let us rouse up to an appreciation of the fact that all the affairs of our life are under a King's command, and under a Father's watch. (*T. De Witt Talmage.*) *The minute providence of God* : —You must have been struck, as you read these opening verses of the biography of the greatest of Old Testament worthies, with their simplicity and truth-likeness. There is no mention of prodigies such as those which were said to attend the birth of Cyrus, and such as mythology delighted to tell concerning Romulus and Remus. It is a plain unvarnished story. There is no word of any miracle. The incidents are such as, allowing for the difference between ancient and modern life, might have happened among ourselves. And yet see how they fit into each other, altogether irrespective of, and indeed independent of, human calculation. Had it been the case of a single fortunate occurrence, we might have talked of chance; but the coalition of so many acts of so many agents indicates design. When you come to a great railway junction, at which trains arrive from north and south and west, in time to be united to another that is just starting for the east, and you see the connection made, nobody talks of a happy coincidence. There was a presiding mind guiding the time of the arrival of the train in each case, so that the junction was reached by all at the required moment. Now, at the birth and preservation of Moses, one feels himself standing at the meeting-place of many separate trains of events, all of which coalesce to save the life of the child, and to put him in the way of securing the very best education which the world could then furnish. (*W. M. Taylor, D.D.*) His sister:—*Miriam :*—I. How she trusted in God. In Hebrews xi. we read that by faith Moses was hid of his parents. It was chiefly the doing of his mother and Miriam. Amram probably had little hand in it, as he had to work night and day, making bricks without straw under the lash of ruffian slave-drivers. Now Miriam could not have so shared her mother's confidence, if she had not also shared her mother's faith. And her faith was great, for it outlived great trials. As she was a very quick-witted girl she must have had many a deep thought. The hands of Providence were strangely crossed. But her faith did not fail. Oh girl, great is thy faith, for thou trustest in Jehovah, though He seemeth to be slaying thee and thine. How she condemns many girls who are content to live without God! II. How she loved her family. She had real daughterly and sisterly feeling; she was true to her family, helping her mother all she could, entering into her plan and making it a success, risking her own life to save her brother's. It is not the cleverness nor the success, but the spirit of her act which you should think upon. What a help and a comfort she must have been to her sorely-tried mother! Faith in God made her thoughtful and feeling-hearted, and great sorrows drew out her sweetest, strongest sympathy with her poor parents. She loved her folk more than she feared Pharaoh. In that level land Pharaoh's pyramids and palaces were the only mountains; how very small she must have felt when she stood near them! And how awful and mighty Pharaoh must have seemed to her! Yet she was not afraid of the king's commandment. Hers was the true love which makes the weak strong, the timid brave, and the simple wise; which betters what is best in boy and girl, and works wonders for others' good. It made Miriam the saviour of Moses. It gave her great presence of mind, that is, the rare power of doing at once in a moment of danger the very thing that needs to be done. As a pointsman by a single timely jerk puts a whole train on the right line, so she by a single hint turned the sympathy of the princess into the right channel, and moulded it into action before it cooled down. No girl ever did greater service to her family and her kind. And she did it not by aiming at some great thing, but by forgetting self and doing her work at home in the right spirit. Cultivate the heavenly beauty of Miriam's conduct. What is true and good is beautiful with an everlasting beauty: disease cannot mar, death cannot destroy it. In girls nothing is uglier than the lack of love at home. It is bad enough in a boy, but it makes a girl simply hideous. For girls have been formed by God to soften and sweeten life, and we are shocked when they poison the fountains at home. III. How Miriam remained steadfast. We left Miriam with Pharaoh's daughter; and we meet her again, about eighty years afterwards, on the shore of the Red Sea (chap. xv. 20). Miriam was more than one hundred and twenty years old when she died, yet with only one exception, so far as we know, she stood firm in God's service. IV. How she fell at Hazeroth. Oh Miriam, how art thou fallen from heaven, thou beautiful star of the morning! The time came when Miriam must give place to Zipporah, Moses' wife, "an Ethiopian woman" (Num. xii.). Miriam would naturally feel that her share in the saving of Moses gave her special claims upon him. Her envy was stirred, and she spake against Moses. Two things made her sin worse. She pretended that zeal for religion was her motive, and so gained Aaron over to her side (ver. 2). And then Moses was the meekest of men; and her anger should have melted at his meekness. You may wonder that I have praised for steadfastness one who had such a sad fall. But a character is fixed not by an act or two, but by the habits of years. I remember standing for the first time on the bridge of a far-famed river. Just under me there was a backward eddy, and a stiff breeze was also rippling the surface backwards. I was quite deceived: I fancied that the stream flowed in the direction of the eddy and the ripples. When I walked along the bank I smiled at my mistake. I should do Miriam a great wrong did I judge her by that act; for it was the one backward eddy, the one backward rippling in the on-rushing current of a good life. Now, what exactly was Miriam's sin? Was it not selfishness bursting out into envy and jealousy? Her selfishness took a very common form; for it filled her with ill-will against a new-comer into the family by marriage—that Ethiopian woman! How natural! yet how ugly! If one could see the soul of an envious girl, as the blessed angels see it, it would shock us as much as Miriam's leprosy shocked all beholders. Let the love of God in Christ fill and flood your soul; and then it will absorb and change your self-love, as the ocean absorbed and changed the brook; and all your selfish grumblings will disappear in the peace of God that passeth all understanding. (*J. Wells.*)   *The watching sister :*—Society needs watchers as well as workers. Had we been passing the spot at which the sister of Moses took up her position of observation, we might have condemned her as an idler standing there and doing nothing! We should be careful of our condemnation, seeing how little we know of the reality of any case. In doing nothing, the girl was in reality doing everything. If she had done more, she would have done less. There is a silent ministry as well as a ministry of thunder. Mark the cunning of love! The watcher stood afar off. Had she stood quite close at hand, she would have defeated the very object of her watching. She was to do her work without the slightest appearance of doing it. Truly there is a great art in love, and in all good ministry. There are wise master-builders, and also builders who are very foolish. Sometimes we must look without staring; we must speak without making a noise; we must be artful without dissimulation, and hide under the calmest exterior the most urgent and tumultuous emotion. (*J. Parker, D.D.*)   *Miriam's tact :*—"Stood afar off"! Mark that. There is tact in everything. Had she gone too near, she might have been suspected. Eagerness would have defeated itself. Our watching must not be obtrusive, officious, demonstrative, and formal. We are not policemen, but friends. We are not spies, but brothers and sisters. We must watch as though we were not watching. We must serve as though we were not serving. There is a way of giving a gift which makes it heavy and burdensome to the receiver; there is a way of doing it which makes the simplest offering a treasure. Sometimes we increase each other's sorrow in the very act of attempting to diminish it. (*Ibid.*)   *A devoted sister :*—Caroline Herschel was the devoted helper of her brother, Sir Wm. Herschel. Her only joy was to share in his labours and help to his successes. She lived for years in the radiance of genius; sharing its toils and privileges. After her brother's death she was honoured by various scientific societies in many ways. But these she regarded as tributes to her brother, rather than the reward of her own efforts. (*H. O. Mackey.*)   *Sisters and brothers :*—"Go home," some one might have said to Miriam. "Why risk yourself out there alone on the banks of the Nile, breathing the miasma and in danger of being attacked of wild beast or ruffian; go home!" No; Miriam, the sister, most lovingly watched and bravely defended Moses, the brother. Is he worthy her care and courage? Oh, yes; the sixty centuries of the world's history have never had so much involved in the arrival of any ship at any port as in the landing of that papyrus boat caulked with bitumen. Its one passenger was to be a none-such in history. Lawyer, statesman, politician, legislator, organiser, conqueror, deliverer. Oh, was not Miriam, the sister of Moses, doing a good thing, an important thing, a glorious thing, when she watched the boat woven of river plants and made watertight with asphaltum, carrying its one passenger? Did she not put all the ages of time and of a coming eternity under obligation, when she defended her helpless brother from the perils aquatic, reptilian, and ravenous? What a garland for faithful sisterhood! For how many a lawgiver, hero, deliverer, and saint are the world and the Church indebted to a watchful, loving, faithful, godly sister? God knows how many of our Greek lexicons and how much of our schooling was paid for by money that would otherwise have gone for the replenishing of a sister's wardrobe. While the brother sailed off for a resounding sphere, the sister watched him from the banks of self-denial. Miriam was the oldest of the family, Moses and Aaron, her brothers, are younger. Oh, the power of the elder sister to help decide the brother's character for usefulness and for heaven! She can keep off from her brother more evils than Miriam could have driven back water-fowl or crocodile from the ark of bulrushes. The older sister decides the direction in which the cradle-boat shall sail. By gentleness, by good sense, by Christian principle she can turn it towards the palace, not of a wicked Pharaoh, but of a holy God; and a brighter princess than Thermutis shall lift him out of peril, even religion, whose ways are ways of pleasantness, and all her paths are peace. Let sisters not begrudge the time and care bestowed on a brother. It is hard to believe that any boy that you know so well as your brother can ever turn out anything very useful. Well, he may not be a Moses. There is only one of that kind needed for six thousand years. But I tell you what your brother will be—either a blessing or a curse to society, and a candidate for happiness or wretchedness. Whatever you do for your brother will come back to you again. If you set him an ill-natured, censorious, unaccommodating example, it will recoil upon you from his own irritated and despoiled nature. If you, by patience with all his infirmities and by nobility of character, dwell with him in the few years of your companionship, you will have your counsels reflected back upon you some day by his splendour of behaviour in some crisis where he would have failed but for you. (*Dr. Talmage.*)   *Weak links useful :*—And you, again, the weak and little ones, will you still fancy you may well be quite passed by, when Miriam's case proclaims to you how needful even the weak link is to join the other links into one chain, and how God can avail Himself even of a child deemed insignificant in the promotion of our human bliss and joy? (*J. J. Van Oosterzee, D.D.*)

Vers. 5, 6. **This is one of the Hebrews' children.**—*The princess and the orphan :*— I. THE CLAIMS OF THE ORPHAN. 1. The first claim on her compassion was the claim of infancy. "She saw the child." That sentence contains an argument. It was an appeal to the woman's heart. Rank, caste, nationality, all melted before the great fact of womanhood. This feeling was spontaneous. She did not feel compassion because it was her duty, but because it was her nature. God has provided for humanity by a plan more infallible than system, by implanting feeling in our nature. 2. Consider the degradation of the child's origin. "Hebrews' children." The exclusiveness of the Egyptian social system was as strong as that of the Hindoo—slave—enemy—to be slain. Princess brought up with these ideas. She was animated by His Spirit who came to raise the abject, to break the bond of the oppressor. 3. The last reason we find for this claim was its unprotected state. It wept ; those tears told of a conscious want—the felt want of a mother's arms. II. THE ORPHAN'S EDUCATION. 1. It was a suggestion from another. This woman brought up in luxury—had warm feelings—not knowing how to do good—was told by another. Results of this training : 1. Intellectually. He learned to ask "Why" "the bush is not consumed." 2. In the moral part of his character we notice his hatred of injustice. (*F. W. Robertson, M.A.*)   *The child :*—1. The moment of its degradation. 2. The moment of its sadness. 3. The moment of its hope. 4. The moment of its unknown future. 5. The moment of a mother's recompense. (*J. S. Exell, M.A.*)   *God rules :*—1. Providence sometimes raises the poor out of the dust to set them among princes (Psa. cxiii. 7, 8), to make men know that the heavens do rule. 2. Those whom God designs for great services He finds ways to qualify and prepare beforehand. The fact of the princess disobeying her father's command in adopting the child, so far from being a difficulty, as some have made it, is the very impress of truth itself. If there is a thing too strong for man's laws, it is a woman's heart. Witness Antigone burying her brother. (*A. Nevin, D.D.*)   *Womanly compassion of Pharaoh's daughter :*—The sweet picture of womanly compassion in Pharaoh's daughter is full of suggestions. Her name is handed down by one tradition as "Merris," and "Meri" has been found as the appellation of a princess of the period. A rabbinical authority calls her "Bithiah," that is, "Daughter of Jehovah"; by which was, no doubt, intended to imply that she became in some sense a proselyte. This may have been only an inference from her protection of Moses. There is a singular and very obscure passage in 1 Chron. iv. 17, 18, relating the genealogy of a certain Mered, who seems to have had two wives, one "the Jewess," the other "Bithiah, the daughter of Pharaoh." We know no more about him or her, but Keil thinks that Mered probably "lived before the Exodus"; but it can scarcely be that the "daughter of Pharaoh," his wife, is our princess, and that she actually became a "daughter of Jehovah," and, like her adopted child, refused royal dignity and preferred reproach. In any case, the legend of her name is a tender and beautiful way of putting the belief that in her "there was some good thing towards the God of Israel." But, passing from that, how the true woman's heart changes languid curiosity into tenderness, and how compassion conquers pride of race and station, as well as regard for her father's edict, as soon as the infant's cry, which touches every good woman's feelings, falls on her ear ! "One touch of nature makes the whole world kin." All the centuries are as nothing; the strange garb, the stranger mental and spiritual dress, fade, and we have here a mere woman, affected as every true sister of hers to-day would be by the helpless wailing. God has put that instinct there. Alas that it ever should be choked by frivolity or pride, and frozen by indifference and self-indulgence! Gentle souls spring up in unfavourable soil. Rameses was a strange father for such a daughter. How came this dove in the vulture's cage? Her sweet pity beside his cold craft and cruelty is like the lamb couching by the lion. Note, too, that gentlest pity makes the gentlest brave. She sees the child is a Hebrew. Her quick wit understands why it has been exposed, and she takes its part, and the part of the poor weeping parents, whom she can fancy, against the savage law. No doubt, as the Egyptologists tell us, the princesses of the royal house had separate households and abundant liberty of action. Still, it was bold to override the strict commands of such a monarch. But it was not self-willed sense of power, but the beautiful daring of a compassionate woman to which God committed the execution of His purposes. And that is a force which has much like work trusted to it in modern society too. Our great cities swarm with children exposed to a worse fate than the baby among the flags. Legislation and official charity have far too rough hands and too clumsy ways to lift the little life out of the coffer, and to dry the tears. We must look to Christian women to take a leaf out of "Bithiah's" book. First, they should use their eyes to see the facts, and not be so busy about their own luxury and comfort that they pass the poor pitch-covered box unnoticed. Then they should let the pitiful call touch their heart, and not steel themselves in indifference or ease. Then they should conquer prejudices of race, pride of station, fear of lowering themselves, loathing, or contempt. And then they should yield to the impulses of their compassion, and never mind what difficulties or opponents may stand in the way of their saving the children. If Christian women knew their obligations and their power, and lived up to them as bravely as this Egyptian princess, there would be fewer little ones flung out to be eaten by crocodiles, and many a poor child, who is now abandoned from infancy to the devil, would be rescued to grow up a servant of God. She, there by the Nile waters, in her gracious pity and prompt wisdom is the type of what Christian womanhood, and, indeed, the whole Christian community, should be in relation to child life. (*A. Maclaren, D.D.*) *God's providential care of children :*—I remember reading a story of a baby—a wee child—that travelled by railroad. Away whirled the coach very fast; but it soon knocked against something, and all were thrown out—men, women, mothers, and babes, some were pitched here, some there; heads were broken, hands cut off. In the midst of the confusion, a voice was heard crying—"Where is my baby? Oh! my dear baby! I cannot find him anywhere. Did nobody see my sweet baby? What shall I do?" One man lost his leg, another his hand, another his eye; but the mother did not mind them, but was going about, wringing her hands, and crying, "Where is my baby?" After much search for it, and for a great while in vain, at length a man went over to a place where there was a bandbox, he took up the bandbox, and what do you think he found under it? The baby, fast asleep! Now, if God takes care of babies, surely He would take care of all little children. *Womanly compassion :*—Of what infinite value to society is that tenderness, compassion, and benevolence which the Almighty has mercifully impressed on the female heart. It is a woman's exclusive gift; it is the foundation of all her virtues; the mainspring of her usefulness. Let her then daily consider the awful responsibility of such a gift; let her consider it as amongst her most valuable possessions; and solely employ it for the benefit of her fellow-creatures; and more especially for the nursing, training, and educating the young of her own species: let her give her heart, her tenderness, her compassion, to the infant orphan and the deserted child; let her, in humble imitation of her great Master, become a teacher of the ignorant, and an instructor of babes; and let her, like Him, fold in her arms the lovely emblems of those beings that form the kingdom of heaven. Let her, with active zeal, bring little children to Christ, that He may bless them; and though, under her fostering care no great legislator, prince, or prophet may arise, a superior reward will await her labours: that which is promised to those who save a soul from death. It will be her peculiar and happy lot to rear good Christians and useful members of society; and above all, blessed spirits for eternal happiness in the communion of saints made perfect. (*Mrs. King.*) *Providentially preserved :*—Sir Thomas Gresham, who built the Royal Exchange in London, was the son of a poor woman, who, while he was an infant, abandoned him in a field. By the providence of God, however, the chirping of a grasshopper attracted a boy to the spot where the child lay; and his life was by this means preserved. (*W. Baxendale.*) *Royal compassion:*—Some years ago, her Majesty the Queen came to open a new wing of the London Hospital. For some days previously nothing else was talked about in the papers and on the streets but Her Majesty's intended visit. There was a little orphan child lying in one of the wards of the hospital, and she, too, had heard that the Queen was coming. She said to the nurse, " Do you think the Queen will come and see me?" "I am afraid not, darling," said her nurse, " she will have so many people to see and so much to do." " But, I should so much like to see her," pleaded the little patient, " I should be so much better if I saw her "; and day after day the poor child was expressing her anxiety to see her Majesty. When the Queen came, the governor told her Majesty, and the Queen, with her large kindly heart and motherly instincts, said, " I should like to see that dear child. Would you just take me to the ward?" and Queen Victoria was conducted to the bedside of the orphan girl. The little thing thought it was one of the women come in the crowd to see the opening of the hospital, and said, " Do you think the Queen will come and see me? I should like to see the Queen." "I am the Queen," said her visitor. "I heard you were anxious to see me. I hope you will be so much better now;" and she stroked down her fevered, wasted, pale brow, gave some money to the nurse to get some nice things for the child, and went her way. The child said, "I am ever so much better now that I have seen the Queen." *God's purpose accomplished by unexpected agencies:*—The wheels in a clock or a watch move contrary one to another, some one way, some another, yet all serve the intent of the workman, to show the time, or to make the clock to strike. So in the world, the providence of God may seem to run cross to His promises. One man takes this way, another runs that way; good men go one way, wicked men another; yet all in conclusion accomplish the will and centre in the purpose of God, the great Creator of all things. *The Gentiles useful in the deliverance of Israel:*—In the fact that the deliverer of Israel from the power of Egypt was himself first delivered by the daughter of the king of Egypt, we find the same interweaving of the history of Israel with that of the Gentiles already observed in the history of Joseph; and we may now regard it as a law, that the preference shown to Israel when it was selected as the chosen seed on whom the blessings were first bestowed, was to be counterbalanced by the fact that the salvation of Israel could not be fully effected without the intervention of the Gentiles. (*M. Baumgarten, D.D.*) *The value of first thoughts:*—All done in a moment, as it were! Such are the rapid changes in lives which are intended to express some great meaning and purpose of God. They are cast down, but not destroyed; persecuted, but not forsaken! From the action of Pharaoh's daughter we learn that first thoughts are, where generous impulses are concerned, the only thoughts worth trusting. Sometimes we reason that second thoughts are best; in a certain class of cases this reasoning may be substantially correct, but, where the heart is moved to do some noble and heroic thing, the first thought should be accepted as an inspiration from God, and carried out without self-consultation or social fear. Those who are accustomed to seek contribution or service for the cause of God, of course know well what it is to encounter the imprudent prudence which says, "I must think about it." Where the work is good, don't think about it; do it, and then think. When a person goes to a place of business, and turns an article over and over, and looks at it with hesitation, and finally says, "I will call again," the master of the establishment says in his heart, "Never!" If Pharaoh's daughter had considered the subject, the probability is that Moses would have been left on the Nile or under it; but she accepted her motherly love as a Divine guide, and saved the life of the child. (*J. Parker, D.D.*) *The unconscious element in life:*—Pharaoh's daughter little knew what she was doing. And do any of us know what we are doing? Is there not something behind the very plainest transaction which, after all, may be the shadow of the Divine hand? You throw a penny to a poor child in the street; that penny may buy an orange to moisten the lips of his poor mother, dying in an unknown garret. (*Ibid.*) *God's way of working:*—Israel's deliverer is brought up on Pharaoh's bread. This is God's method of executing His purposes. He restrains the wrath of man, and causes the remainder to praise Him. He sets a watch upon His enemies. He puts His hook in the jaws of leviathan. He suddenly violates the security of the wicked, and shows kings that they reckon badly who reckon without Him. (*Ibid.*)

Ver. 9. **Take this child away, and nurse it for me.**—*Care for children:*—I. To

NONE IS GOD'S COMMENDATION VOUCHSAFED MORE FULLY THAN TO THOSE WHO LOVE CHILDREN FOR CHRIST'S SAKE. The presence of childhood represents and brings back our own. Children confide in those around them with a sweet and simple faith. They obey from affection, not fear. And so our Father in heaven would have His children trust Him, casting all our care upon Him, for He careth for us. II. CHILDREN TEACH US REVERENCE AS WELL AS FAITH. They listen with a solemn awe when we talk to them of God. They tread softly, and speak with bated breath in His holy place. III. CHILDREN TEACH US TO BE KIND, PITIFUL, AND TENDER-HEARTED. They cannot bear to witness pain. They do all they can to soothe. Have we these sorrowful sympathies? IV. If the love of Christ is in our hearts, it should constrain us to DO OUR VERY BEST, THOUGHTFULLY, PRAYERFULLY, GENEROUSLY, TO PRESERVE IN THE CHILDREN AND TO RESTORE IN OURSELVES THAT WHICH MADE THEM SO PRECIOUS IN HIS SIGHT, AND makes them so like Him now—like Him in their innocence, their sweet humility, their love. (*Dean Hole.*) *The providence of God in relation to the young :—*I. AS RESCUING THEM FROM THE PERIL OF UNHAPPY CIRCUMSTANCES. 1. Moses was rescued from murder—in the Egyptian palace he was safe. 2. Moses was rescued from slavery—in the Egyptian palace he was free. II. AS ENSURING AN EDUCATION NÉCESSARY TO FIT THEM FOR THEIR FUTURE ENGAGEMENTS. 1. As the son of Pharaoh's daughter, Moses had the opportunity of a good scholastic education. 2. As the son of Pharaoh's daughter he would be prepared to undertake the freedom of his nation. III. AS EMPLOYING THE MOST UNLIKELY AGENCY. The tyrant's daughter was the means of rescuing Moses from peril, and of educating him for his future calling. Unlikely means—1. Because her father had issued an edict for the death of all Israelitish children. 2. Because it appeared unlikely that a royal daughter should wish to adopt the son of an Israelite. IV. AS EMPLOYING THE MOST EFFICIENT INSTRUMENTALITY. 1. The mother of the boy—who could better teach him the wrongs of his country than she—that hundreds had suffered the fate he had managed to escape—the slavery of his people—the tyranny of the king. She instructed him during the earliest days of his youth—her instruction would therefore be enduring—hence he would go to the Egyptian court with a knowledge of his country's woe—and of his father's God. 2. The daughter of the king. V. AS REQUIRING THE UTMOST HUMAN EFFORT POSSIBLE. 1. His mother did the best for Moses that she could. 2. His mother was judicious in her conduct towards Moses. VI. AS PERFECTLY CONSISTENT WITH THE FREE AGENCY OF INDIVIDUALS. (*J. S. Exell, M.A.*) *The training of children :—*I. THE FIRST QUALIFICATION FOR THE TRAINING OF CHILDREN IS THE LOVE OF CHILDREN. The hard heart in which the merriment of childhood kindles no sunshine and wakens no music, is no more fit for the resting and growing place of an infant, than the sands of the desert are fit for the planting of a vineyard or the sowing of a wheatfield. II. The second grand essential to the right training of children, is to receive them as SACRED TRUSTS FROM GOD TO BE NURSED FOR HIM. Whence do we think the child comes to us? What do we desire it to be, in its relation to ourselves, and to the world, and to God? A mere doll, to be dressed for the gratification of our vanity? A mere pet animal, to be fed and fondled for our amusement? A mere competitor in the race of life, to struggle for a little while after its pleasures, honours, and riches, and then pass away for ever? Or do we regard it as a being of unbounded susceptibilities, and destined to eternity, which God has committed to us to train for His glory and the enjoyment of Himself for ever? When this simple but sublime thought, that a human soul has been committed to us to be trained for God, has once possessed us, it will ally itself with our love for children working itself out without effort, and almost without thought into our daily conduct. III. A third essential to the right training of children is THE REQUIREMENT OF UNANSWERING OBEDIENCE. The best answer to a child's, "Why must I do this, or abstain from that?" is "Because your father or mother requires it." If further explanations are to be given, they should come after as a reward for obedience, and not before, as its condition. The habit of unanswering obedience is easily established, and when once fixed is permanent. And it should be further remembered that this requirement of unanswering obedience is saturated and sweetened through and through by the love of children. It is exalted and lifted above the impulses of selfish petulance and passion, by a sense of the Divine trust committed to us. IV. Parents ought DILIGENTLY TO CULTIVATE AND WIN THE ABSOLUTE CONFIDENCE AND AFFECTION OF THEIR CHILDREN. So, as years roll on, authority will broaden out into loving companionship, and obedience become a delightful conformity to the wishes of those who are dearer than themselves. Tempered and guided by the principles already announced, this plan will succeed. I do not say there will be no exceptional cases. There is a mystery in the heredity of evil and in the working of iniquity which seems at times to defy all general rules. Let parents understand this: that their children may attain the highest ends of life without wealth, without social distinction, and even without the higher forms of secular education; but they cannot inherit the richest blessings of the family relation, without being thoroughly in love with their father and mother, as the representatives and appointed agents of God, who says, "Take this child and nurse it for Me, and I will give thee thy wages." (*H. J. Van Dyke, D.D.*) *The education of Moses :*—There from a mother's lips he learned the story of the great forefather Abraham, his call, and God's covenant with him and his seed; the meaning of the mark of circumcision in his flesh, and the duties to which it bound him; the Divine unity and holiness; the worship and service that is the Creator's due; was made tenderly alive to the wrongs and sufferings of his people; was taught patriotism and piety, and prepared to become in due time the vindicator of Israel's freedom and faith. (*R. A. Hallam, D.D.*) *The education of Moses :*—1. See how much in the making up of the leader of His chosen people God makes of secular instruction—what ample provision God made for it in his equipment for his arduous and difficult task. The Scriptures give no countenance to ignorance. The world has knowledge to impart which the Church may gladly accept. The Church is in many ways beholden to the world. Egypt was largely a benefactor to Moses and to the Israelitish people. Nothing that Egypt had imparted would be without its use in such a task. God did not despise it as a means, but subsidized it, and brought all its resources and influences to bear in making for Himself the man who was to lift His Church from a tribe into a nation, from slavery to independence. Though He could have communicated all these qualifications to Moses by a direct gift, He did not, but chose to bestow them upon him by means. To despise secular knowledge, and think that we are better Christians for being destitute of worldly lore, is fanatacism, and not piety. Civilization is the ally of religion and not its foe. Intelligence strengthens godliness, and does not lower or injure it. 2. Finally, see the value of early and specially of maternal influence, in its bearing on the religious character and life. What a power both of impulsion and of resistance it had in the case of Moses! By this means Jochebed against fearful odds was successful, more than a match for them. An obscure woman, with no more than ordinary attainments, of a proscribed race, acting in a capacity little better than menial, she was too much for all Egypt's sages, and scholars, and priests, and nobles and rulers. There were two things that gave her great advantage in the contest. She got the start of them. She worked by the law of love. Before any Egyptian influence could reach the child, she had possession of his ear and of his heart. What an encouragement is here to all mothers, to all parents! How much greater things they may be labouring for than they contemplate or foresee. (*Ibid.*) *Infancy of Moses :*—I. THE DUTY ENJOINED. 1. The object—"This child." (1) What it may become. Philosopher, warrior, statesman, philanthropist, &c. (2) What it must become. A responsible moral agent. 2. The duty—"Nurse it." This includes—(1) Attention to physical wants. (2) Cultivation of mental faculties. (3) Religious instruction. II. THE REWARD PROMISED— "And I will pay thee thy wages." You may be rewarded—1. By seeing your efforts crowned with success. 2. You shall at any rate possess the consciousness of the Divine favour. 3. You shall leave your children with composure when you come to die. 4. You shall stand before them with confidence in the judgment day. (1) Let pious parents be encouraged in the way of duty. 2. Let negligent parents consider the cruelty of their conduct, and the bitter consequences which must result from it. (*J. Burns, D.D.*) *God's method of raising up souls for His service :*—I. GOD GIVES AND SENDS THEM AS THEY ARE NEEDED. II. THAT THEY MAY BE FULLY TRAINED AND PREPARED FOR THEIR WORK, THEY ARE "MADE LIKE UNTO THEIR BRETHREN." III. THE VERY FAMILY AND PEOPLE THAT SOUGHT TO DESTROY ISRAEL ARE MADE INSTRUMENTAL IN NOURISHING AND REARING THE DELIVERER OF ISRAEL AND THE AVENGER OF HIS BRETHREN'S WRONGS. Injustice and cruelty are made to avenge themselves in the end. IV. IN THE RAISING UP OF THE MAN MOSES WE HAVE A MOST INSTRUCTIVE EXEMPLIFICATION OF THE DOCTRINE AND WORKING OF THE DIVINE PROVIDENCE. V. IN PHARAOH'S DAUGHTER, AND THE PART SHE TAKES, WE HAVE THE PROOF THAT HUMAN NATURE, THE HUMAN HEART, IS ONE; AND THAT ALL CLASSES OF MANKIND, ALL NATIONS, ARE DESTINED TO BECOME ONE IN GOD'S GREAT SAVING PLAN. (*Pulpit Analyst.*) *The power of a mother's love :*—1. To control its impulse. 2. To school its utterance. 3. To make self-denial for the good of her child. 4. To enter into the method of Providence concerning the future of her boy. (*J. S. Exell, M.A.*) *A beautiful pattern of self-control:*—1. Not arising from indifference. 2. Not arising from hard-heartedness. 3. But arising from the calm indwelling of faith. (*Ibid.*)   *This mother a model nurse:*—1. Because she taught her son to have sympathy with the slave. 2. Because she taught him to despise injustice (ver. 12). 3. Because she taught him the folly of anger (ver. 13). 4. Because she taught him to defend the weak (ver. 17). (*Ibid.*)   *A mother the best nurse:*—1. Because she has truest sympathy with the circumstances of the child's life. 2. Because she is more truly concerned for the right development of its moral character. 3. Because then she will have gladdening memories of its infancy and childhood. (*Ibid.*) *Bringing up in the faith:*—"How can an outward action, or ceremony, like the baptism of water, alter the inward state and affect the real course of life?" It can do it just as the Egyptian princess, by one gesture of her arm and one command from her lips, does in fact raise a new-born infant from the slave's cabin to the fellowship of monarchs. It is no miraculous or talismanic transformation. There is no violent revolution of the secret forces or moral circulations of the soul. But the child is set into new relations, and out of those new relations flow, as naturally as the stream through a new channel cut in the hills, new habitudes, new dispositions, a new life, a new heart, a new destiny. Observe that there is nothing here which insures the child's safety: nothing that precludes the possibility of his falling back again, if he chooses, into bondage; nothing that compels him to stay in his Lord's house or in any way overrules his liberty—the awful liberty to apostatize into guilt and perdition. Now we pass on to another question. What will it be to nourish your child for Christ? 1. In the first place, it will be to keep in your own heart a constant feeling of the charge laid upon you in the child's spiritual nature. The power of this feeling will be manifested not only in express words and direct actions, but in countless and daily signs of your faith which the child is sure to understand. The unconscious part of education, especially of the education of the soul, is always, probably, the more important part, yet the least considered. In other words, what we are tells more on a child, in the long run, than what we say. Every father or mother is not only either for Christ or against Him in the house— but they are perpetually, inevitably, helping to set out and enlist their offspring for Him or against Him. 2. Again, those parents nourish the child for Christ, who, after they have presented him in holy baptism, take care not to contradict the vow they have there made by a systematic indoctrination of him into ideas and fashions which Christ abhors. They do not come here to give him up by a ceremony to his Maker, and then begin steadily to baptize him themselves into the bitter and polluted spirit of this world. 3. Turn to a more positive and attractive aspect of your obligation. You are to nourish your child into a familiar knowledge of his personal membership in Christ and his sonship in Christ's kingdom. Two other things must accompany this work; the one as a help, the other as a hope, but both of them powers, indispensable to your success. 1. The child is to be nourished with the habitual practice of intercessory prayer. Whatever you may fail of in your knowledge, or your earthly providing, or your power of religious influence otherwise, have hope in your intercessions. 2. And therefore, finally, take this child away and nourish him for Christ with the expectation of a blessing. That expectation is to be not only a comfort to you on the way, but one of the spiritual forces with which you are to prevail. This Lord, who has lent you the little one, not only loves the importunities of His people; He delights in their largest confidences. (*Bp. F. D. Huntington.*)   *The children of the poor, the charge of the Church:*—I. First, let us look at THE CLASS OF CHILDREN WHO ARE SPECIALLY COMMITTED TO OUR CARE AND CONCERN. It seems a truth sufficiently obvious from analogy, that the strong ought to take care of the weak, and the rich ought peculiarly to regard the poor. 1. God especially regards the poor. 2. The souls of the poor are as valuable as the rich. 3. God has selected from among the poor many of the most eminent characters both in the Church and in the world. II. Now let us glance at another point of the doctrine, and that is—THE TRAINING WE ARE TO GIVE THEM. "Take this child, and nurse it for Me." We are to nurse them and train them for God. Here I would lay great emphasis. Education is an engine of great moral power. It enlarges the mind; it ennobles the individual; it furnishes him with a fund of enjoyment; it capacitates him for usefulness; it directs his energies to proper objects. But let it be well and thoroughly understood that if education be not founded on religious and on scriptural principles, you put a weapon into the hand of an individual to do more evil—to do it secretly and effectually. You render him a more expert agent to fight against God and to oppose the reign of holiness. III. But there is another point which ought to be touched upon : and that is—THE REWARD WE MAY EXPECT. "I will give thee thy wages." Not "apples of gold"; not "pictures of silver"; not honours that shall adorn our brows, achieved by the victories of the noble and the wiles of the great. Not literal "wages." But still there is a reward; good, and blessed and large. And what is this reward? Wages far higher than money can bring. Is there no reward in doing good? No reward, that "when the ear hears you, then it blesses you; and when the eye sees you, it bears witness to you"? No reward, to see those dear children growing up to fill important stations in life by your instrumentality? No reward, to reflect that you have been turning many in your generation to serve God, and to serve their generation? No reward, to think that you are acting out true patriotism, and training children who shall serve their country and bless the age in which they live? But especially, is there no reward, when the Master, whose glance is life and "whose favour is better than life," shall at the last day say, "Inasmuch as ye have done it," &c. (*J. Sherman.*)   *The training of children for God:*—God speaks to every parent, teacher, pastor, with every child He puts into their care. I. So He speaks to the parent with A DEFINITE AND INDIVIDUAL CHARGE. He says not : "Take some child," but, This one take and train. There is no question here as to which out of the many is to be the object of your care. How that definiteness enhances the solemnity of the charge! It is the very charge you would have chosen, too. The tie of nature is a stronger one than you can make with bands of gold or fetters of brass, and when that tie receives the strengthening sanction of God's approval, it is the most enduring thing in all the world. God has organized, and He sanctions, the family and its sweet bonds. II. For in these words of Pharaoh's daughter, taken as the King's own word to us, we find THE SECRET OF THE TRAINING OF THE CHILD. "Nurse it for Me." Not for yourself are you to train this child entrusted to your care. It was not given for your amusement or your service. Nor may you train them for themselves, as though the world was made for them and all their business was to please themselves with it. The only right and worthy object of our labours for the children, and it should be an aim clearly before us, is to bring them up for God. We surely cannot do it unless it be our definite purpose. Train it not for, but in, Christian faith and love and obedience, and teach it always to live to please the Lord that bought us. The New Testament teaching is like the Old : based on the same principles, uttered in similar form—"And ye fathers, provoke not your children to wrath : but bring them up in the nurture and admonition of the Lord." III. And so we shall receive THE REWARD. "I will give thee thy wages." It was the daughter of the king who promised thus to Moses' mother. It is the King Himself who gives His word to us. He pays us for taking care not of our children, but of His. Here is the worst mistake of all, if we do not recognize them as God's children and we as only nurses in His employ. The promise is as definite as the charge. "I will pay thee." It is the faithful parent or the faithful teacher who will be rewarded. (*G. M. Boynton.*) *Children to be educated for God:*—I. WHAT IS IMPLIED IN EDUCATING CHILDREN FOR GOD. 1. A realizing, heartfelt conviction that they are His property, His children, rather than ours; and that He commits them for a time to our care, merely for the purpose of education, as we place children under the care of human instructors for the same purpose. 2. A cordial and solemn dedication or surrender of them to Him, to be His for ever. 3. We must do all that we do for them from right motives. 4. If we would educate our children for God, we must educate them for His service. (1) This implies that we pay more attention to the soul than to the body. (2) It implies that we pay more attention to the heart or disposition than to the mind. (3) It implies that we educate them for eternity rather than for time; for a future world—rather than for this. II. THE REWARD WHICH HE GIVES TO THOSE WHO PERFORM THIS DUTY ARIGHT. This reward consists—1. In the pleasure which attends every attempt to educate children for God. 2. Another part of the reward which God bestows on those who educate their children for Him, is the happiness which they enjoy when they see their labours crowned with success. (*E. Payson, D.D.*)   *On the Christian education of children:*—What are the wages of fidelity in the important work of the Christian education of children? 1. In the first place, then, a part of the reward of fidelity in religiously educating your children consists in the pleasure of the work. It is an innocent, an interesting, and an honourable occupation. 2. There enters into the reward of religiously educating children, the pleasure which arises from doing good to society. 3. There is high honour in co-operating with God, and great happiness in conforming to the intentions of His providence. 4. The good of his children is what every parent purposes to himself, as the object, perhaps, of his fondest desire, as the motive to all his parental conduct. And herein is a large part of the wages of fidelity in religiously educating them, that thereby their great good in this life will be most effectually promoted. It is a perilous and unhappy world into which you introduce them. And yet the misfortune is, that in education respect is more generally had to its pleasures than its sorrows, to its honours than its snares. The great question concerning your offspring is, where in it shall wisdom be found, and where is the place of satisfaction? Look around you. See in what path they shall be most likely to find peace. Examine the claims of wealth, of honour, of rank, of power, of pleasure. Turn to religion. Institute a comparison between her claims and theirs. Inquire which of them has most efficacy to quell the passions, which are the parents of evil; to soothe the sorrows, which are the offspring of our condition; to open sources of happiness at which the weary spirit may always be refreshed; and to take the barbs from the arrows of death? Such a comparison will assuredly produce a result in favour of a Christian education. 5. The faithful parent has a recompense for his care in the religious education of his children, in the greater security of his own happiness. It is through the child that the heart of a parent is most vulnerable. The hour comes when your children shall stand around you, and you will perceive that you are leaving them without you in this evil world. What can mitigate this anguish of death? What but to be able to say of them, when you cast on them your final look, " I am going unto my Father, and their Father; and to my God, and their God." They will honour me in their lives when I shall be gone. The Almighty is their Friend and He will protect them. 6. But not in this life is the reward of the faithful in any case complete. By far the largest part of the " wages," which God, in His mercy, has promised to any of their good works, is reserved to be given them in the great day of the final consummation. (*Bp. Dehon.*) *Permanence of early impressions :*—A farmer decided to remove an old beech-tree which grew on his farm. The wood-cutter noticed on the bark of the tree some curious marks looking like the letters J. L., roughly cut, and below them some ornamental design. After the tree had been cut down and was being separated into lengths he was startled to find on the hard dry wood at the core of the tree, directly opposite the place on the bark where he had noticed the marks, the clearly cut letters J. L., on a dark background, and below them an anchor. On inquiries being made, it was found that the letters were the initials of a sailor named John Leland, who, in an idle hour, had cut them on the beech-tree when it was young. There were thirty-seven rings between the letters and the bark of the tree, and the woodsman said that each ring represented one year's growth of the tree. He inferred that the letters must have been cut in the year 1853, and his belief was confirmed when he learned that it was in that year that the sailor had spent some time in that neighbourhood. Thus the inscription had not only remained in the place where it was cut at the first, but as each year added to the growth of the tree, the letters still appeared on the surface, scarcely legible there, it is true, but perfectly clear at the core. It is so with human character. Many an old man, in spite of the rough usage of the world and the scar of time and trouble, bears upon his walk and conversation the marks of the handwriting which in his youth God put in his heart. *Care of children :*—A florist, who was so absorbed with his " cuttings " that he did not hear until twice spoken to, apologized, saying, " I beg your pardon, but you see one must put his whole mind on these young things, if he would have them do well; and I cannot bear that one should die on my hands, for I should almost feel as if I had murdered it."

Ver. 10. **She called his name Moses.**—*Moses trained in Egypt—a lesson in providence :*—The great lesson of this incident, as of so much before, is the presence of God's wonderful providence, working out its designs by all the play of human motives. In accordance with a law, often seen in His dealings, it was needful that the deliverer should come from the heart of the system from which he was to set his brethren free. The same principle which sent Saul of Tarsus to be trained at the feet of Gamaliel, and made Luther a monk in the Augustinian convent at Erfurt, planted Moses in Pharaoh's palace and taught him the wisdom of Egypt, against which he was to contend. It was a strange irony of Providence which put him so close to the throne which he was to shake. For his future work he needed to be lifted above his people, and to be familiar with the Egyptian court as well as with Egyptian learning. If he was to hate and to war against idolatry, and to rescue an unwilling people from it, he must know the rottenness of the system, and must have lived close enough to it to know what went on behind the scenes, and how foully it smelled when near. He would gain influence over his countrymen by his connection with Pharaoh, whilst his very separation from them would at once prevent his spirit from being broken by oppression, and would give him a keener sympathy with his people than if he had himself been crushed by oppression. His culture, heathen as it was, supplied the material on which the Divine Spirit worked. God fashioned the vessel, and then filled it. Education is not the antagonist of inspiration. For the most part, the men whom God has used for His highest service have been trained in all the wisdom of their age. When it has been piled up into an altar, "then the fire of the Lord" falls. Our story teaches us that God's chosen instruments are immortal till their work is done. No matter how forlorn may seem their outlook, how small the probabilities in their favour, how opposite the gaol may seem the road He leads them, He watches them. Around that frail ark, half lost among the reeds, is cast the impregnable shield of His purpose. All things serve that will. The current in the full river, the lie of the flags that stop it from being borne down, the hour of the princess's bath, the direction of her idle glance, the cry of the child at the right moment, the impulse welling up in her heart, the swift resolve, the innocent diplomacy of the sister, the shelter of the happy mother's breast, the safety of the palace—all these and a hundred more trivial and unrelated things are spun into the strong cable wherewith God draws slowly but surely His secret purpose into act. So ever His children are secure as long as He has work for them; and His mighty plan strides on to its accomplishment over all the barriers that men can raise. (*A. Maclaren, D.D.*) *Birth and training of Moses :*—I. THE WONDERFUL CLEARNESS OF BIBLE PORTRAITS. Some of the pictures of the men whom the world has united in calling masters are well-nigh indistinguishable. They are like an old manuscript which you must study out word by word. II. THE SUPERIOR DIGNITY AND GLORY OF THE HUMAN LIFE. Where now is the city Cain builded? What about the civil movements of that far-off day? its political revolutions? Who cares any thing about them? Learn from this, that it is human life fashioned by the Divine Artificer, and in His own image, which is the noblest thing altogether in this world. III. THE BIRTH AND TRAINING OF MOSES. 1. The time of the birth. Pharaoh's Joseph had gone. His bones only were now in Egypt—a poor part of any man. "Every son that is born of the Hebrews ye shall cast into the river." And so Moses was doomed before he was born. "From his mother's womb to the waters of the Nile, ' ran the decree. And Moses did go to the Nile, but in God's way—not in Pharaoh's—as we shall see. 2. The goodliness, the beauty of the child. An infant child. Is there anything more beautiful? Look at its little hands. Can any sculptor match them? Behold the light of its eyes. Does any flower of earth open up with such a glory? Look upon the rose, the lily, the violet, as they first open their eyes upon this world. Ah! there is no such light in any of them. A man is far gone—a woman farther—when the child which comes to them—the immortal clasp of their two hearts—is not beautiful in their sight. Earth has no honour so great as the parentage of an immortal; heaven no higher dignity. But in Moses' case beauty was to reach unto an end nobler than itself. It was to fill the mother's heart with a subtler strategy, with a bolder daring. It was to fascinate the eyes of a princess. It was to work the deliverance of a mighty nation. So beauty, when not abused, ever beyond itself reaches unto a nobler end. And this beauty of the sunset, of the landscape and the flower, fruits in the human life. It emphasizes purity, it lifts up towards God. Ah, mothers! be not so anxious to keep your child from the looking-glass as to teach her that she holds a noble gift from God in that face, in that form, of hers. 3. The exposed and endangered condition of the babe. For a while the mother hid him; hid him from the eyes of Pharaoh and his minions. But the powers that be have many eyes. "And when she could no longer hide him, she took for him an ark of bulrushes, and daubed it with slime and with pitch, and put the child therein, and she laid it in the flags by the river's brink." Did ever mother launch such a craft before? Ay, often. Every day they do it. Every day, every hour, some mother is committing her child to the currents of this world, than which the waters of the Nile were not more cruel. Think of harlotry, the painted devil. Think of intemperance, the destroying fiend. Think of dishonour, the consuming fire. Are not these worse than all the crocodiles that ever opened jaw in river of earth? And yet must they do it! Upon the angry surface of this world's danger must mothers launch their hopes; their only consolation being—God is strong, and a Father to defend. I can imagine the mother of Moses weaving her little ark of bulrushes. Love makes her hands to be full of skill as ever shipbuilder's were. So mothers now. The ark which they make is the covenant with their God; its lining, the world-resisting element of a mother's prayers; and then with eyes that cannot see for tears, and with heart-strings breaking, they push forth their little craft—their heart's hope—their world. And now may God defend the boy, for the mother may not—cannot longer. IV. THE TRAINING OF MOSES. Note the elements of this. 1. He had his mother. Sure I am, if Pharaoh's daughter could have glanced into that home just then, she would have thought that she had happened upon a most excellent nurse. "Very affectionate, surely," she would have said, "and I hope she has judgment." Yes, princess; never fear. Your nurse has excellent judgment, too. Her strange love will make her very wise. This was the first element of Moses' training. A human life, like any other life, needs training. And for this work there is no one like the mother. Interest makes her wise. Love makes her unwearying. Were the Israelites accustomed to point to that "hated throne"? If so, all this story would filter through a mother's heart into the mind of the growing child. She would tell it him as he lay upon her lap. She would sing it to him as she rocked him to sleep. Talk it to him as he played about the house. The sympathetic instinct between mother and child would be a syphon, through which, with every hour of the day, would flow the story of Israel's bitter wrong. And did the promise of the God of Abraham, of Isaac, and Jacob linger in the darkened minds of their enslaved descendants, keeping hope alive there, and the expectation of deliverance? If so, with this hope the mother would feed the mind and fill the heart of her growing boy. With the word freedom, she would daily stir his ambition. 2. His home in the palace of Pharaoh. "And the child grew, and she brought him unto Pharaoh's daughter, and he became her son." He was to break the chains of slavery, not to be bound by them. Therefore he must be lifted up to the greatness of his work. Two most necessary elements of preparation he gained by going into the home of the Pharaoh. The first was knowledge. Moses, we read, was learned in all the wisdom of the Egyptians. And this he got as the adopted son of Pharaoh's daughter. Good impulses, a noble spirit, is not enough. Knowledge is power, and necessary power, save when God works by miracles. Therefore Moses was homed in the palace. He goes to study the throne which he is yet to shake. Out of Pharaoh's armoury he will gird himself for the coming contest with Pharaoh. His residence at court would serve to impress him with the immense power with which the Hebrews contended, and the heel of which was upon their necks. And yet he must know this, or he will not be prepared for his work. 3. The desert. "He that believeth shall not make haste." So he that worketh for God shall not make haste. These forty years had taught him something. His first failure had taught him something. So had his desert life, in which he had been alone with God. Moses at eighty years of age, in his own estimation, was not nearly so much of a man as at forty. So of all growing men always. There are many now in the world, not yet out of their teens, who are a deal wiser and mightier, and fitter to cope with error and wrong, than they will be twenty years hence; that is, provided they keep on growing these twenty years. But God has a school ready for such (that is, if they are worth the schooling), and one which they will not be long in entering. It is the school of mistakes—of failure; the school in which many a man spells out this lesson, "What a big fool I was!" This was the training which God now gives to Moses. He allows him, in the impulse of youth, to strike a blow, and then gives him forty years in the desert to meditate upon its folly. In conclusion, note some of the great lessons which our subject teaches. 1. We learn how low, oftentimes, God permits the true cause to sink. The world has often seen the last stronghold of human rights defended by the might of one solitary arm. So it was here. Yes, Israel's hope floated in the little ark of bulrushes among the flags upon the river's brink. And yet Israel's cause was safe enough. With faith in God, we need never fear. Suppose there is left but one human life for defence. God and such a one are always a majority. 2. We learn the measureless importance of one single human life. God often throws into the balance of the moral world a single life, to keep it even. Think of this, ye teachers, and count no life committed to your care common or unclean. 3. The grand work of man-building. This is what God, the Great Architect, is for ever engaged in. It is that which some—yes, all of us, are called to do. Time itself, with all its centuries, is only one of many hands engaged in this sublime work. Everything else in this world, all sorrow, all joy, all wars, all peace, all slavery, all liberty, all learning, all art, is only so much scaffolding. The slavery of the Hebrews; the cruel despotism of Pharaoh; the mother's love and the mother's fear; the princess, the Nile; ay, even the bulrushes which grew by its brink—all these were used of God in building up His servant, the man Moses. Up, up, upward unto God, rises the immortal man. His are the glory and power of an endless life. 4. We learn how easy it is for God to fashion a human life to suit His purpose. "To the Nile with it," shouts Pharaoh from his throne. "To the Nile," responds the power of Egypt. "Yes," says God, "to the Nile; but from it too; from it, unto a home, unto the palace, unto the headship of a mighty nation, unto Sinai, unto Pisgah." In the very palace of the Pharaohs, God nurses a life for the overthrow of the Pharaohs. With such delightful facility does God model and mould human life. (*S. S. Mitchell, D.D.*) *Moses:*—I. THE CHILD OF POVERTY. You and I will draw near and look upon this strange nest and nestling. He was a foundling, that is, a child left by its parents and found by some passer-by. His name means water-saved. I knew a foundling who was called Horace Nelson, because he was found, one winter morning, on Glasgow Green near Nelson's monument. He was named from the monument, which was not harder than his mother's heart; and so Moses was named from the water out of which he was drawn. Each seemed to be nobody's child; and so the one was named as the child of the water, and the other as the child of the monument. That slave's child in the ark seems the poorest of the poor. Left as a prey to flood and famine, to crocodiles and vultures, was ever poor child in sadder plight? Yet his fame now fills the world as the man of men next to the Messias, the Conqueror of Pharaoh, the Leader of Israel, and the Giver of the Law to all mankind. At Moses' cradle learn never to scorn a poor child because he is poor. Often the child of poverty has, like Moses, stood before kings, and proved himself kinglier than they. Let not the poor be discouraged; let not the rich be proud. But it is very sinful as well as very senseless to despise the poor. God never does so. Before leaving it, take another look at Moses' cradle. Ah, the baby's beauty makes us glad! 'Tis the human face divine. He is "a goodly child"; "exceeding fair"; he has an heavenly beauty. I have come to know hundreds of our poorest children, and have often been struck with their beauty, which shone through all their hardships. What fine powers of body and mind and heart many of them have! What cleverness! what wit! what kindly feeling! In their beautiful eyes you may notice the beamings of a promising soul. Indeed, I have sometimes wondered whether God's bounty had not endowed them so richly with these better gifts in order to make up for the want of what money can buy. Imitate Pharaoh's daughter whom you bless and admire. Turn not proudly or coldly away from the forsaken child. II. THE CHILD OF PROVIDENCE. God's providence is God's forethought, or foresight; His kind care over us in all things. I wish you would think about the wonders of providence. Take an instance from your school books. This nineteenth century has been shaped by the battle of Waterloo. And God did it all with a few drops of rain. The rain on the night before the battle made the clayey soil slippery, so that the French could not get their guns forward till the sun had dried the ground. But for the rain, Napoleon would probably have won. God's providence brings about the greatest things by means of the smallest. The dangers around the child Moses were very great. The Nile might drown him; the sun by day or the moon by night might smite him; the crocodiles were around, and the vultures above him; there seemed no hope for the darling boy. The dangers around the most favoured children are perhaps as great, though not so easily seen. Believe firmly, then, that God is on earth as well as in heaven, and that His hand is in small things no less than in great. And think how much you owe to His fatherly providence. Your mother may have done all a mother could, your Miriam may have watched over you, but it was God's providence that placed you in the ark of safety which has carried you on to this good hour. And you should thank Him also for unseen and unknown deliverances. The whole web of your life is woven with mercies. III. THE CHILD OF GRACE. Grace saved him from his greatest dangers. Through the palace a dark river ran, drowning men's souls in perdition. Vices more deadly than the crocodiles were rife around him. He found plagues in Pharaoh's court more frightful than any he afterwards sent into it. I imagine that no youth ever had greater temptations than Moses (Heb. xi. 24). His character was formed by that choice: his blessed life was a harvest from that one seed. The choice you make between Christ and the world, makes you. Notice that Moses' choice was most reasonable, though to the Egyptians it seemed sheer madness. Moses' was also a joyous choice. Think not that he was the most wretched youth in Egypt when he forsook Egypt's gods. Ah, no. His choice would pain him in many ways; but then he had the deep satisfaction of having done what was right. He had better joys than the Egyptians dreamt of. And he must have made in his boyhood this choice which he publicly confessed as soon as he came of age. Like him, choose Christ in youth, and declare your choice. You gather fresh flowers for your friends; and will you offer Christ only an old withered flower, that has lost all its beauty and perfume? (*J. Wells.*)　　*Child-growth:*—Physically—mentally—morally. 1. Important to families—leaving home. 2. Interesting to strangers—princess. 3. Important to nations—Egypt. (*J. S. Exell, M.A.*)　　*Child-nomenclature:*—1. Perpetuating the memory of a cruel edict. 2. Perpetuating the memory of a loving mother. 3. Perpetuating the memory of a kindly providence. 4. Perpetuating the memory of a compassionate stranger. Home life exchanged for palace life. (1) It would be at first unwelcome—stranger. (2) It would gradually become a temptation—its gaiety. (3) It would forcefully become a discipline. (*Ibid.*)　　*Adoption by royalty:*—Suppose that you were to see the child of a beggar in the streets, or the child of a criminal in prison, and it so happened that the emperor of Russia or the queen of England were to see this little unfortunate creature and exclaim, " I will adopt it as my own," and were to have it taken to a palace, clad in rich dresses, fed at the royal table, brought up under the royal care, and even prepared for a throne. " Oh," you would think, " what a change of life! what happiness for this child!" And if it were an angel, or an archangel, or a seraph that adopted it, in order to make it, if it were possible, an angel that should never die; that would be a thousand times more glorious still. Think, now, what it is to become a child of God; and this is, nevertheless, what all of us may become by faith in Jesus Christ. What wonderful glory! what marvellous happiness! Thus St. John exclaims, " Behold what manner of love the Father hath bestowed upon us, that we should be called the sons of God." And it is by faith that we become the children of God. " For ye are all the children of God by faith in Christ Jesus." (*Prof. Gaussen.*)　　*Moses' education in Egypt:*—The adopted son of the daughter of an Egyptian king *must* have been trained in all the wisdom of Egypt. This is also in harmony with the tradition reported by Manetho, which makes Moses a priest of Heliopolis, and therefore presupposes a priestly education. It was precisely this education in the wisdom of the Egyptians, which was the ultimate design of God in all the leadings of His providence, not only with reference to the boy, but, we might say, to the whole of Israel. For it was in order to appropriate the wisdom and culture of Egypt, and to take possession of them as a human basis for Divine instruction and direction, that Jacob's family left the land of their father's pilgrimage, and their descendants' hope and promise. But the guidance and fate of the whole of Israel were at this time concentrated in Moses. As Joseph's elevation to the post of grand vizier of Egypt placed him in a position to provide for his father's house in the time of famine, so was Moses fitted by the Egyptian training received at Pharaoh's court to become the leader and lawgiver of his people. (*M. Baumgarten, D.D.*)　　*Moses' choice:*—There can be no doubt that the foster-son of the king's daughter, the highly-gifted and well-educated youth, had the most brilliant course open before him in the Egyptian state. Had he desired it, he would most likely have been able to rise like Joseph to the highest honours. But affairs were very different now. Moses could not enter on such a course as this without sacrificing his nation, his convictions, his hopes, his faith, and his vocation. But that he neither would, nor durst, nor could. (*J. H. Kurtz, D.D.*)　　*An incident expressed in a name:*—Admiral *Bythesea*, V.C., C.B., who has just retired after having for many years been the Consulting Naval Officer to the Government of India, was picked up as an infant far out at sea, lashed to a bale of goods. A lady—presumably his mother—was with him, but she was dead, and there was no evidence of any kind by which the name of the waif could be traced. The officers of the man-of-war which picked up the poor little infant did all they could to find out his relations, and, finding all their attempts futile, they determined to adopt the child, to whom they gave the name of "*By the Sea.*" He was sent to a naval school, and when old enough joined the navy. By a happy coincidence the first ship in which he served was the one which had saved his life as an infant. He took to his profession, and during the Crimean war distinguished himself at the Island of Wardo, where he earned the Victoria Cross and the decoration of C.B. Later on his services in India gave him the Companionship of the order of the Indian Empire, and he now retires from the service with the rank of admiral—a consummation little dreamed of by the kind-hearted officers who rescued and educated him.

Vers. 11, 12. **He slew the Egyptian.**—*The oppressor slain; or a wrong way of reproving injury :*—I. THERE ARE MANY INSTANCES OF CRUEL OPPRESSION IN THE WORLD. 1. There is oppression in the commercial life of men. The rich smite the poor— the fortunate the unfortunate—the defrauder the honest tradesman. 2. There is oppression in the social life of men. The haughty frown upon the humble. 3. There is oppression in the political life of men. There is the oppression of an unjust king—of a politic statesman—of an unruly crowd—of an unrighteous edict. 4. There is oppression in the Church life of men. The man of little religion wishes to dictate to and perplex those who are more devout than himself. II. IT IS THE DUTY OF A GOOD AND PATRIOTIC MAN TO OPPOSE THESE MANIFESTATIONS OF OPPRESSION. 1. Because he should have sympathy with the burdens of the oppressed. 2. Because he should recognize the brotherhood of men. 3. Because he should recognize the claim of nationality. III. THAT A GOOD MAN MUST BE CAREFUL AS TO THE SPIRIT AND MANNER IN WHICH HE RESENTS OPPRESSION, OR HE MAY BE AS CRUEL AS THOSE WHOM HE REPROVES. 1. His conscience told him that he was doing wrong. 2. The spirit and manner in which the oppressor should be reproved. (1) Boldly. (2) Firmly. (3) Sometimes kindly. (4) Make him feel the wrong of his conduct. (*J. S. Exell, M.A.*) *Retributive justice :*—Look at retributive justice in man in three aspects. I. As EXCITED. "He spied an Egyptian," &c. It was always there, working no doubt silently, and in many ways, but now it broke into flame. The moral outrage he witnessed roused him, &c. II. As RESTRAINED. "He looked this way," &c. The sight of a child will so frighten the nocturnal desperado that it will paralyze his arms and drive him panic-struck from the scene. Man keeps man in check. A wise and beneficent arrangement. It is a power, however, that has its limits. It should never prevent us from doing right. III. As FREE. "When he saw there was no man, he slew," &c. Were the retributive instincts of human nature left entirely unrestrained the earth would become a pandemonium. (*Homilist.*) *Lessons :*—1. Maturity of years and parts God appoints unto the instruments of deliverance. 2. Providence orders objects to be seen to move instruments unto their work. 3. Sight of pressures and injuries upon the Church must move helpers to compassion. 4. Single injuries done to any member of the Church may occasion just revenge. (*G. Hughes, B.D.*) *Strife, intervention, and flight of Moses :*— I. STRIFE. 1. Between the Egyptian and Hebrew. The Egyptian was smiting the Hebrew. Whipping him to his work, or punishing him for doing less than his allotted task. Cruel, tyrannical. The strong and protected, persecuted the weak and defenceless. Pride of power. Official meanness. Domineering spirit and conduct. 2. Between Hebrew and Hebrew. This is a worse feature of strife. Fellow bondsmen increasing each other's sufferings. Children of one family-striving. II. INTERVENTION. 1. The person. Moses. Adopted son of Pharaoh's daughter. Learned. Mighty in deeds and words. Honour, title, wealth before him. 2. His patriotic feelings. Did not abandon his nationality. "Not ashamed to call them brethren." 3. Slays the Egyptian. Unjustifiable conduct. "Vengeance is mine, I will repay, saith the Lord." Yet it was an heroic act, under the peculiar circum- stances. The first blow for freedom. 4. Concealment. Hides the body. 5. Second intervention. Not to kill, but to expostulate. 6. Repudiation of Moses by his brethren. Jesus was despised and rejected, "came to His own, and His own received Him not." III. FLIGHT OF MOSES. 1. The reason. Pharaoh sought to slay him. Moses, dwelling in the palace, would soon hear of this design. His friends—perhaps the princess if living—would inform him. 2. The course of his flight. Over ground to be presently traversed by the Israelites. A long and solitary journey. His thoughts by the way. 3. Incidents of the end. The well's mouth. How many incidents have occurred at the mouth of wells ! The sheperdesses and the boors. Moses' courage and politeness. The Christian should be a true gentleman. The reward of chivalry and politeness. Kind words and deeds easy. Defence of the weak a mark of true nobleness. Moses a real nobleman. Christ mighty to save the weak ; and willing. LEARN—1. The meanness of taking a base advantage. 2. The strong should be helpers of the weak. 3. Jesus, a prophet like unto Moses, raised up to be our peacemaker and deliverer. (*J. C. Gray.*) *Moses' sympathy with his brethren :*—Strong was the temptation that beset Moses. He had a fair oppor- tunity (as we say) to make his fortune, and to have been serviceable to Israel too, with his nterest at court, and yet he obtained a glorious victory by faith. He esteemed it greater honour and advantage to be a son of Abraham than an adopted child of the royal family. He had a tender concern for his poor brethren in bondage, with whom (though he might easily have avoided it) he chose to suffer affliction ; he looked on their burdens as one that not only pitied them, but was resolved to venture with them, and, if necessary, to venture for them. We must not be satisfied with wishing well to, doing service for, or speaking kindly on behalf of the people of God. We ought to be fully identified with them, no matter how despised or reproached they may be. It is, in a measure, an agreeable thing to a benevolent and generous spirit to patronize Christianity, but it is a wholly different thing to be identified with Christians, or to suffer with Christ. A patron is one thing, a martyr is quite another. This distinction is apparent throughout the entire book of God. Obadiah took care of God's witnesses, but Elijah was a witness for God. Darius was so attached to Daniel that he lost a night's rest on his account, but Daniel spent that selfsame night in the lion's den, as a witness for the truth of God. Nicodemus ventured to speak a word for Christ, but a more matured discipleship would have led him to identify himself with Christ. (*A. Nevin, D.D.*) *Brotherly sympathy :* —Prior to the return of Mr. Henson, the original of "Uncle Tom," to America in 1851, he was invited to a dinner party in the lordly mansion of one of our city merchants ; and when seated at a table covered with the most tempting viands, and surrounded with every comfort and luxury which affluence could provide, he was so overpowered with the remembrance of his former misery and degradation that he rose from the table, feeling that he could not partake of a single morsel of the sumptuous banquet. His generous host went after him, and asked whether he was taken unwell, or whether he would like some other kind of dishes. "Oh no," was the touching and pathetic response of this good old man, "I am well enough ; but, oh ! how could I sit down to such a luxurious feast as this when I think of my poor brother at this moment a wretched, miserable, outcast slave, with perhaps scarcely a crust of bread or a glass of water to appease the cravings of nature?" (*John Lobb.*) *Blood thicker than water :*—Commodore Tatnall was in command of the United States squadron in the East Indies, and, as a neutral, witnessed the desperate fight near Pekin between the English and Chinese fleets. Seeing his old friend, Sir James Hope, hard pressed and in need of help, he manned his barge, and went through a tremendous fire to the flag-ship. Offering his services, surprise was expressed at his action. His reply was, "Blood is thicker than water." (*H. O. Mackey.*) *Sympathy with burden bearers :*—Napoleon, at St. Helena, was once walking with a lady, when a man came up with a load on his back. The lady kept her side of the path, and was ready to assert her precedence of sex ; but Napoleon gently waved her on one side, saying, "Respect the burden, madam." You constantly see men and women behave to each other in a way which shows that they do not "respect the burden," whatever the burden is. Sometimes the burden is an actual visible load ; sometimes it is cold and raggedness ; sometimes it is hunger ; sometimes it is grief, or illness. And how far, pray, are we to push the kind of chivalry which "respects the burden"? As far as the love of God will go with us. A great distance ; it is a long way to the foot of the rainbow. (*Good Words.*) *Some people will never look on the burdens of their brethren :*—1. They pretend not to see them. 2. They have no sympathy with them. 3. They fear lest their purse, or energy should be taxed. 4. They miss the luxury of relieving them. (*J. S. Exell, M.A.*) *The inquiring look of conscience :*—1. It was anxious. 2. It was suspicious. 3. It was troubled. 4. It was perplexed. 5. It was mistaken. (*Ibid.*) *The inquiring look of conscience :*—1. Gives a moment for reflection. 2. Indicates the moral evil of the deed. 3. Suspects an unhappy issue from the deed. (*Ibid.*) *Hidden sin :* —"He slew the Egyptian, and hid him in the sand." I. Hidden by fallacy. "The Egyptian." He was cruel—unjust ; had I not a right to kill him? Moses might reason thus to convince himself. A man must bury sin out of the sight of his own conscience, before he can be happy—by false argument or true. II. Hidden by folly. "In the sand." 1. Would leave traces of his deed. 2. The dead body would be easily discovered. So all our efforts to bury sin are equally futile. God sees it. He can lead men to its grave. Sin leaves traces. It is better not to be under the necessity of making the soul into a grave, or any spot of life into a tomb. If we do, there will sure to come a resurrection. A man who is going to commit sin, requires to have all his wits about him. (*Ibid.*) *The upward look best :*—This action teaches a deep practical lesson to all the servants of God. There are two things by which it is superinduced : namely, the fear of man's wrath, and the hope of man's favour. The servant of the living God should neither regard the one nor the other. What avails the wrath or favour of a poor mortal, to one who holds the Divine commission, and enjoys the Divine presence? It is, in the judgment of such an one, less than the small dust of the balance. Divine intelligence will ever lead us to look upward and onward. Whenever we look around to shun a mortal's frown or catch his smile, we may rest assured there is something wrong; we are off the proper ground of Divine service. (*C. H. Mackintosh.*)   *The chivalry of Moses:* —This is one of the first recorded acts of the meekest of men! Do not let us be hard upon him! The impulse was right. There must be men in society who can strike, and who need to strike but once. Let it be understood that this, after all, was but the lowest form of heroism—it was a boy's resentment—it was a youth's untempered chivalry. One can imagine a boy reading this story, and feeling himself called upon to strike everybody who is doing something which displeases him. There is a raw heroism; an animal courage; a rude, barbaric idea of righteousness. We applaud Moses, but it is his method rather than his method which is approved. Every man should burn with indignation when he sees oppression. In this instance it must be clearly understood that the case was one of oppressive strength as against down-trodden weakness. This was not a fight between one man and another; the Egyptian and the Hebrew were not fairly pitted in battle: the Egyptian was smiting the Hebrew—the Hebrew in all probability bending over his labour, doing the best in his power, and yet suffering the lash of the tyrant. It was under such circumstances as these that Moses struck in the cause of human justice. In this fiery protest against wrong, in this blow of ungoverned temper against a hoary and pitiless despotism, see somewhat of the tender sympathy that was in Jochebed embodied in a form natural to the impetuosity of youth. Little did Moses know what he did when he smote the nameless Egyptian. In smiting that one man, in reality he struck Pharaoh himself, and every succeeding tyrant! (*J. Parker, D.D.*)   *Moses' rash haste:*—We may not shut our eyes to the fact that but for his lack of self-restraint Moses might have become an earlier benefactor to the people whom he desired to liberate. He was running before he had been sent; and he discovered by the result that neither was he as yet competent to be the leader of the people, nor were the people ready to rise at his call. There is a long distance often between the formation of a purpose and the right opportunity for its execution; and we should not always regard promptitude as wise. The providential indicators of duty are the call within us, and the willingness of those whom we would benefit, to receive our blessing; and if either of these is absent, we should pause. Above all, we should not allow the passion of a moment to throw us off our guard and lead us into sin, for we may be sure that in the end it will only retard our enterprise and remove us from the sphere of our activities. The ripening of a purpose is not always the mark of the presence of an opportunity. "Raw-haste" is always "half-sister to delay"; and wrong-doing can never help forward, directly at least (however God may afterward overrule it), a good cause. (*W. M. Taylor, D.D.*)   *The prince and the serfs:*—Many years ago, there was a little boy named Alexander. He was the son of Nicholas, Emperor of Russia, in whose empire there were many millions of poor people, called serfs. These were kept in a state much resembling slavery, and were sold with the lands on which they lived. Many of them were poor and wretched; some few were prosperous and wealthy; but all were under the control of the lords on whose territories they dwelt. One day, Nicholas noticed that little Alexander looked very sad and thoughtful, and asked him of what he was thinking. "Of the poor serfs," replied the little boy; "and, when I become emperor, I will emancipate them." This reply startled the emperor and his courtiers; for they were very much opposed to all such plans for improvement of the condition of the poor. They asked little Alexander how he came to think of doing this, and what led him to feel so interested for the serfs. He replied, "From reading the Scriptures, and hearing them enforced, which teach that all men are brothers." The emperor said very little to his boy on the subject, and it was hoped that the influences and opinions which prevailed in the royal court would gradually correct the boyish notions of the young prince; but this expectation was vain. The early impressions of the little boy grew deeper and stronger; and when at last the great Nicholas died, and Alexander was placed upon his father's throne, he called the wise statesmen of the land to his councils, and a plan of emancipation was formed; and the imperial decree went forth, which abolished serfdom throughout all the Russian empire. It is in this way that God works wonders by the power of His Word. The great fact, that God has "made of one blood all nations of men for to dwell on all the face of the earth," lodged like an incorruptible seed in the heart of the young prince, and growing with his growth, and strengthening with his strength; at last budded and blossomed, and brought forth the fruit or blessing for millions of the human race.

Vers. 13, 14. **Two men of the Hebrews strove together.**—*Moses' championship of the right :*—In the first instance we might have thought that in taking part with the Hebrew against the Egyptian, Moses was but yielding to a clannish feeling. It was race against race, not right against wrong. In the second instance, however, that conclusion is shown to be incorrect. We now come to a strife between two Hebrews, both of whom were suffering under the same galling bondage. How did the youthful Moses deport himself under such circumstances ? Did he take part with the strong against the weak ? Did he even take part with the weak against the strong ? Distinctly the case was not one determined by the mere disparity of the combatants. To the mind of Moses the question was altogether a moral one. When he spoke, he addressed the man who did the wrong ; that man might have been either the weaker or the stronger. The one question with Moses turned upon injustice and dishonourableness. Do we not here once more see traces of his mother's training ? yet we thought that the home life of Moses was a life unrecorded ! Read the mother in the boy ; discover the home training in the public life. Men's behaviour is but the outcome of the nurture they have received at home. Moses did not say, You are both Hebrews, and therefore you may fight out your own quarrel : nor did he say, The controversies of other men are nothing to me ; they who began the quarrel must end it. Moses saw that the conditions of life had a moral basis ; in every quarrel as between right and wrong he had a share, because every honourable-minded man is a trustee of social justice and common fair play. We have nothing to do with the petty quarrels which fret society, but we certainly have to do with every controversy, social, imperial, or international, which violates human right, and impairs the claims of Divine honour. We must all fight for the right : we feel safer by so much as we know that there are amongst us men who will not be silent in the presence of wrong, and will lift up a testimony in the name of righteousness, though there be none to cheer them with one word of encouragement. (*J. Parker, D.D.*) *The Hebrew quarrel :*—1. Multiplied their enemies. 2. Weakened Israel. 3. Banished Moses. Divisions defeat the Church. Moses, as—1. A judge dooming his enemies. 2. A peacemaker among his countrymen. (*Dr. Fowler.*) *Lessons :*— 1. Daily and successive is the care of God's saving instruments to His oppressed Church. 2. God's faithful instruments leave courtly pleasures to visit God's afflicted frequently. 3. In visiting for good the oppressed Church, sad contentions may appear among the members. 4. It is an observable evil by overseers, to see Church members striving together. 5. Duels in the Church and among its members are sad things to record. 6. Men called of God must interpose and curb the injurious and offending parties. 7. Smiting of neighbours and brethren is a sin sharply reprovable in the Church (ver. 13). 8. Injurious and offending parties are apt to recoil against rulers upon reproof. 9. Wickedness makes men question any authority of God, that would suppress them. 10. Sin will not endure to be suppressed by power; but will rage against it. 11. It is the artifice of malefactors to recriminate powers for escaping themselves. 12. Zealous avengers of God's oppressed may be terrified sometimes with the criminations of the wicked. (*G. Hughes, B.D.*) *A good man's interference with a quarrel :*—I. IT IS THE DUTY OF GOOD MEN TO TRY TO SUBDUE ANY QUARRELS THEY MAY BE CALLED TO WITNESS. 1. Because they recognize the common grief of men. The suffering of humanity an argument for friendliness. 2. Because they recognize the claim arising from the brotherhood of men. 3. Because they ought to be superior to the passion of strife. II. IN THIS ENDEAVOUR GOOD MEN SHOULD MAKE MORAL CONSIDERATIONS THE BASIS OF THEIR APPEAL TO THE QUARRELSOME. 1. Not favouritism. 2. Not greater physical strength. Christianity must aid weakness when associated with rectitude. 3. Not hope of reward. A satisfied conscience is brighter and more enduring than gold. III. GOOD MEN, IN TRYING TO SUBDUE THE QUARRELS OF OTHERS, OFTEN GET LITTLE THANKS, AND MAY INVOLVE THEMSELVES IN TROUBLE. "Who made thee," &c. 1. They imagined that Moses assumed unrightful authority. 2. They reminded Moses of, and taunted him with, past sin. It requires a blameless life to rebuke evil. 3. The heroic interference of Moses lacked moral continuity. His own sin made him a coward. 4. Moses incurred the hatred of Pharaoh. Through endeavouring to stay this quarrel, he lost position and comfort ; but it was the means of putting him on the track of Divinely-imposed duty, which would win him world-wide renown. (*J. S. Exell, M.A.*) *Wherefore smitest thou thy fellow ?*—Apply this question—1. To the domestic circle. 2. To society at large. 3. To the Church. (*Ibid.*) *Some find reason for their conduct:*—1. In revenge. 2. In impulse. 3. Necessity. (*Ibid.*) *Discouragement:*—The best friends of the Church often meet with the most discouragement. 1. Their authority is rejected. 2. They are not understood. 3. Their safety is endangered. 4. The welfare of the Church is imperilled. (*Ibid.*) *The good man must not be turned aside from duty by circumstances:*—1. Moses was not offended by this treatment. 2. He did not give up in despair. 3. He worked out the training of his boyhood. 4. He worked out the providence of God. 5. He worked out the dictates of his conscience. (*Ibid.*) *Discord and strife:*—In the ringing of bells, whilst every one keeps his due time and order, what a sweet and harmonious sound they make! All the neighbouring villages are cheered with the sound of them; but when once they jar and check each other, either jangling together or striking preposterously, how harsh and unpleasing is that noise. So that as we testify our public rejoicings by an orderly and well-timed peal, when we would signify the town is on fire, we ring the bells backward in a confused manner. It is just thus in the Church. When every one knows his station, authority, and keeps his due rank, there is melodious concert of comfort and contentment; but when either states or persons will be clashing with each other, the discord is grievous and prejudicial. (*J. Hall.*) *Results of physical degradation:*—The Israelites had sunk into brute insensibility under oppression. It is a remarkable fact we cannot too earnestly reflect on, always and everywhere true, that extreme physical degradation dulls the intellect, and destroys moral sensibility. Some persons complain, that the very poorest classes of the community, who live in underground cellars and upper garrets, are unthankful. But it is because we are undutiful. Physical degradation has a most pernicious effect upon the moral, spiritual, and intellectual feelings of mankind. It brutalizes and barbarizes. I believe that our missions, with all their value—our city missionaries and our Scripture readers, doing a most noble work—are here vastly obstructed in their work. I believe a great physical and social amelioration in poor men's homes must be made, before a substantial moral and spiritual one begins in their hearts. We must raise the masses above the level of the brutes, before we can raise them to the level of Christians. You must make them men, before you can make them, by the grace of God, Christians. (*J. Cumming, D.D.*)

Ver. 15. **He sat down by a well.**—*The meditations of a perplexed soul:*—I. They occurred at an important crisis in the life of Moses. "But Moses fled from the face of Pharaoh." 1. Moses had vacated a good home. 2. Moses had incurred the anger of Pharaoh. II. They afford an opportunity for determining on a new course of life. III. They are soon interrupted by a call to new activities (ver. 17). IV. They were indulged in a very favourable place. The well in olden time, a fine scene for rest and contemplation. Christ, when He was tired, sat on a well. His rest was broken by the advent of a woman, whom He ultimately led to Himself in contrition of heart. (*J. S. Exell, M.A.*) *Moses' flight:*—1. Criminations of God's servants are soon carried to the ears of persecutors. 2. Persecutor's ears are open to receive all reports against God's people. 3. Fame of any evil against God's servants stirs up violent men to pursue them. 4. The death of God's instruments for His Church's good is the aim of bloody enemies. 5. God provides Midian to save what Egypt would destroy. 6. God is pleased to change court enjoyments for a poor well, to refresh His weary saints (ver. 15). (*G. Hughes, B.D.*)

Vers. 16–22. **Moses was content to dwell with the man.**—*The reward of a kindly action:*—I. The hospitality of a kind family (ver. 20). 1. This hospitality was much needed by Moses. 2. This hospitality was prompted by parental inquiry. A good and considerate father often turns his home into a sanctuary for the servants of God. By welcoming an heroic stranger to it, he may bring himself into harmony with great histories, and sublime providences. II. Employment for every-day life. When a young man is thus welcomed by a kind family he must expect to share their work, as also their food. The study of Moses in Egypt had not raised him above hard work. III. A wife (ver. 21). A man who will defend a woman is worthy of a wife. The greatest and most important events of our lives depend upon little deeds of kindness. IV. Another advance in the intention of Divine providence. Moses has finished his education of the palace. He now commences that of the desert. (*J. S. Exell, M.A.*) *Moses in Midian:*—1. We see here, first, activity presented to us as an indispensable and effective element in education. This is the great lesson taught by Moses in Midian. Head knowledge Moses had obtained in Egypt; hand work he was to practise in Midian. He was already learned in all Egypt's wisdom; he was now to be a participant in all Midian's labour. The latter was needful to give the former robustness, practical force, and substantial usefulness. In Egypt he was a student, in Midian a worker; and in the combination of the two he became a man of wonderful heroism, and high executive power. Egypt could not do this for him. It could instruct him, it could polish him; it did. Remaining in Egypt he might have been a man of elegant leisure; or with his literary resources, have lived among books, and become, perhaps, puffed up with knowledge, or bewildered with speculation. Idle learning is apt to come to that. In Midian his business was to do, to turn his knowledge into skill, make it practical. We need knowledge; we cannot have too much of it, if it be genuine. But we must ground action upon it. We are to be workers, doers in some line of useful activity, if we would fulfil the end of our being. Neither the ignorant worker nor the indolent scholar is the man for this world, but the intelligent and instructed doer, whose brains prompt his hands, and whose hands second his brains. 2. Again, Moses in Midian is to us a pattern of a wise conformity. He did not stand aloof from the people among whom he lived in a proud superciliousness or an offensive singularity; nor did he waste his time in an idle regretting of the past, and an uncomfortable repining at the unpleasant change of his condition. He made the best of the state into which God's providence had called him, and so was neither odious nor unhappy in it. Our Lord was much of a conformist in His time, and the Pharisees called Him a "friend of publicans and sinners." He was their friend, but not in the Pharisees' sense. And what He practised He recommended. He said to His disciples, "When ye enter into a house, salute it," " and in the same house abide, eating such things as they set before you." So, too, the great apostle, St. Paul, tells us that he " was made all things unto all men," and says, " To the Jews I became as a Jew that I might gain the Jews; to them that are without law as without law, that I might gain them that are without law." This is worldly wisdom, and it is religious wisdom too. We are not to rebel against our circumstances, not to dwell upon lost good. 3. Finally, we see in Moses in Midian the example of a wise patience. Forty years elapsed during which his great undertaking was in abeyance, and gave no signs of an approaching resumption. He knew that "to everything there is a season, and a time to every purpose under heaven," and that " it is not for us to know the times and the seasons which the Father hath put in His own power." He had nothing to do but to wait, and he did wait, and uncomplainingly. How different is this from the course of many reformers, patriots, philanthropists, of whom, like some of old, it may well be said, " I have not sent them, yet they ran: I have not spoken unto them, yet they prophesied"; whose haste outruns the dilatory motion of the chariot of God, and whose eagerness chides God's delay by devices of their own, and headstrong enterprises and efforts, on which God has never promised His blessing, nor have they asked it. Good things we have purposed, good things we have hoped for, do not come as rapidly as our impetuous wishes are fain to anticipate. " Tarry thou the Lord's leisure; be strong, and He shall comfort thine heart; and put thou thy trust in the Lord." (*R. A. Hallam, D.D.*) *Discipline needed after faith :*—" But," you will say, " when once the right choice has been made, and the decisive step is taken, there was surely no necessity at least for painful disappointment." Say not so; for surely it was just in this way that the character of Moses was refined. It is quite possible that, at the first, a man may be a true believer, and remain, alas! weak, vain, proud, arrogant. Such was the case with Moses when you see him summoned to avenge the wrongs of Israel. He has firm faith in God and in His promises; his feelings and affections are no longer bound to Egypt; and there can be little doubt, or none, concerning his sincerity : but he is sadly wanting in humility. Moses is conscious of a special destiny for something great, but thinks he is the man that can the least be spared in any case. His is a merely carnal zeal to save his fellow-Israelites, as is quite evident from the great failure that befell his first attempt; for his heart, a prey to his own folly, is the sport and plaything, now of pride and arrogance, and now of fear and cowardice. He will, he can, he shall do just as he thinks right; but God is not yet willing. God shall certainly perform His will through Moses, but not through a Moses such as this. The darling of the whole Egyptian world still stands too high; he must descend a step or two before he can be used to serve Him who hates lofty looks, be they of friends or foes. Moses has made great progress in

Egyptian wisdom ; but he is as yet quite unaware that, in the wisdom of the Holy Ghost, while he is nothing, God is everything. Although his heart is right, his will is not sufficiently subdued ; he still counts far too much both on his own strength and the gratitude of men ; his old man yet must needs be slain, as he slew the Egyptian. Therefore the Lord Himself assails him now, and seems in this quite as unmerciful as he had been to the oppressor of his brethren. In the first Israelite to whom he showed himself as a deliverer, he must be made to see, as in a glass, the nation's meanness and ingratitude, that he may learn to do all for the sake of God, but nothing for the sake of man ; and that he never may presume to say, " My hand hath led out Israel." Moses' first action lets us see what he shall afterwards be able for, when God's grace shall have wholly filled and purified his manly soul ; just as the husbandman perceives, in the strong crop of weeds, the promise of good harvest, when the ground shall have been cleared of tares, and sown with wheat. But harrowing and ploughing, that break down the hardest clods,—such are the operations specially attended to by Him who is the heavenly Husbandman, when, in His wisdom, He proposes to lay out a field that is particularly fine ; and disappointment to our dearest and legitimate, perhaps, indeed, our most praiseworthy plans, forms the deep furrow drawn across us, that the heavenly seed may afterwards be sown. Christians ! do not forget that God is constantly employing such a means for cleansing these our hearts from that impurity which brings Him so much pain, and us so much disgrace. Have you formed fine ideals of the good that you will do for the promotion of your neighbour's happiness ? It shall not be, says God ; you still rely too much on your own strength, expecting far too little from the Lord, who must do all. Have you been sketching out a golden future for yourself ? God blows on your designs some time or other, right before your eyes, that, with a broken but a humble heart, you may exclaim, " I know, O Lord, that the way of man is not in himself ! " Have you been really so foolish as, unthinking, to rely on human love and gratitude ? God, in some rude and startling way, opens your eyes, that, fleeing in your terror from the falling idol, you may fall down at the feet of the true God—nay, sink into your heavenly Father's arms ! (*J. J. Van Oosterzee, D.D.*) *A large family :*—1. Of sacred station. 2. Of womanly influence. 3. Of industrious activity. (*J. S. Exell, M.A.*) *Domestic toil :*—1. The employment of true womanhood. 2. The test of true womanhood. 3. The glory of true womanhood. (*Ibid.*) *Two classes of men are typified by the conduct of these shepherds, and Moses :*—The former—1. Oppose the honest. 2. Persecute the industrious. 3. Hinder the diligent. The latter—1. Co-operate with the weak. 2. Sympathize with the persecuted. 3. Defend the imperilled. 4. Win the victory. 5. Receive hospitality. (*Ibid.*) *Why is it that ye have left the man ?*—This question may be asked in reference to the world's philanthropists, preachers, who are striving to defend the weak. 1. Is it because you do not understand him ? 2. Is it because you do not believe in him ? 3. Is it because you are selfish ? 4. Is it because you have not been taught better ? 5. Fetch him to your home as soon as possible. (*Ibid.*) *A contented resident :*—1. A wondrous sight—accustomed to a palace. 2. A happy sight—pastoral toil. 3. A scarce sight—men are restless. He was content— 1. With his daily companionships. 2. With his daily occupation. 3. With the scene of his residence. 4. With his matrimonial alliance. (*Ibid.*) *A pilgrim life the best for preachers :*—1. Good for their health. 2. Good for their moral training. 3. Good for their moral usefulness. 4. Good for the enlargement of their social friendships. (*Ibid.*) *A friend of the oppressed commended :*—A young lad came from school late, and with a flushed countenance. His mother inquired into the cause. A number of thoughtless and wicked boys were teasing a child of a helpless widow, in order to provoke those bursts of imbecile passion for which she was remarkable. Contrary to expectation, the widow remained unmoved, merely hastening her footsteps and those of her little daughter. This led the boys to increase their efforts, till they inflicted positive injury on the child. John, the lad alluded to above, remonstrated, and finally fought one of the boys in defence of the widow's child. He went home with the widow, and received her thanks. He then set out for home, but was doubtful how his conduct would be viewed by his mother. She had taught him to avoid all broils. He stated the case to her, and received her warm commendation for his sympathy with the oppressed, and his bravery in their defence. That commendation made him for life the generous and fearless friend and defender of the oppressed. (*Wesleyan S. S. Magazine.*) *An extended visit :*— The Countess of Huntingdon once told Mr. Toplady, the author of " Rock of Ages," that when she visited Dr. Watts on one occasion he thus accosted her : " Madam, your ladyship is come to see me on a very memorable day." " Why so remarkable "? she asked. " This day thirty years," he replied, " I came hither to the house of my good friend Sir Thomas Abney, intending to spend but one single week under his friendly roof ; and I have extended my visit to the length of exactly thirty years." " Sir," added Lady Abney, " what you have termed a long thirty years' visit, I consider as the shortest my family ever received." *Alone with God :*—Nothing can possibly make up for the lack of secret communion with God, or the training and discipline of His school. " All the wisdom of the Egyptians" would not have qualified Moses for his future path. He might have taken out his degree in the school of man, and yet have to learn his alphabet in the school of God. Mere human wisdom and learning, how valuable soever in themselves, can never constitute any one a servant of God, nor equip him for any department of Divine service. Such things may qualify unrenewed nature to figure before the world ; but the man whom God will use most must be endowed with widely-different qualifications— such qualifications as can alone be found in the deep and hallowed retirement of the Lord's presence. All God's servants have been made to know and experience the truth of these statements. Moses at Horeb, Elijah at Cherith, Ezekiel at Chebar, Paul in Arabia, and John at Patmos, are all striking examples of the immense practical importance of being alone with God. And when we look at the Divine Servant, we find that the time He spent in private was nearly ten times as long as that which He spent in public. He, though perfect in understanding and in will, spent nearly thirty years in the obscurity of a carpenter's house at Nazareth, ere He made His appearance in public. And, even when he had entered upon His public career, how oft did He retreat from the gaze of men, to enjoy the sweet and sacred retirement of the Divine presence ! Now we may feel disposed to ask, how could the urgent demand for workmen ever be met, if all need such protracted training, in secret, ere they come forth to their work ? This is the Master's care— not ours. He can provide the workmen, and He can train them also. That is not man's work. God alone can provide and prepare a true minister. Nor is it a question with Him as to the length of time needful for the education of such an one. We know how He could educate him in a moment, if it were His will to do so. One thing is evident, namely, that God has had all His servants very much alone with Himself, both before and after their entrance upon their public work ; nor will any one ever get on without this. The absence of secret training and discipline will, necessarily, leave us barren, superficial, and theoretic. (*C. H. Mackintosh.*) *Solitary discipline :*—There was much in the solitude of his shepherd life that would stimulate him to devout meditation. Here amidst " the sleep that is among the lovely hills," he communed with himself, with nature, and with God ; facing for himself those " obstinate questionings " which continually arise when one seeks to fathom the mysteries of being. A very different university was this from that at which he studied among the worshippers of the sun at Heliopolis ; yet more helpful to him even than the education which he had received in Egypt, would be his musings upon the mountain sides, as he rose from the thunder-riven peaks to Him who before the mountains were brought forth is, from everlasting to everlasting, God. Like the Scottish boy, who in the intervals of his shepherd life mapped out for himself with beads the distances of the stars, and designated himself " God Almighty's scholar," Moses was now under the special tuition of the Lord. His books were the silent stars and giant hills ; the shrubs that grew at his feet, and the flocks that went on beside him, browsing on the grass ; and often and often would he pore lovingly over the pages of man's first Bible—Nature. But most frequently, perhaps, he would look within and try to read himself ; and after awhile there was to come to him the vision which would open to him as a scroll " the marvel of the everlasting will." (*William M. Taylor, D.D.*) *A new training school :*—The flight of Moses from Egypt introduced him into a new training school. At Pharaoh's court he had learned much that was required to fit him for his vocation, as the deliverer and leader of Israel, as the mediator of the ancient covenant and founder of the theocracy, and also as a prophet and lawgiver. But his education there had been of a very partial character. He had learned to rule, but not to serve, and the latter was as necessary, if not more so than the former. He possessed the fiery zeal of youth, but not the circumspection, the patience, or the firmness of age. A consciousness of his vocation had been aroused within him when in Egypt ; but it was mixed with selfishness, pride, and ambition, with headstrong zeal, but yet with a pusillanimity which was soon daunted. He did not understand the art of being still and enduring, of waiting and listening for the direction of God, an art so indispensable for all who labour in the kingdom of God. In the school of Egyptian wisdom his mind had been enriched with all the treasures of man's wisdom, but his heart was still the rebellious unbelieving heart of the natural man, and therefore but little adapted for the reception of Divine wisdom, and by no means fitted for performing the works of God. And even the habit of sifting and selecting, of pondering and testing, acquired by a man of learning and experience, must certainly have been far from securing anything like the mature wisdom and steadfastness demanded by his vocation. All this he had yet to acquire. Persecution and afflic- tion, want and exile, nature and solitude, were now to be his tutors, and complete his education, before he entered upon the duties of his Divine vocation. (*J. H. Kurtz, D.D.*) *Moses' domestic life in Midian:*—The house of the Midianitish priest was, doubtless, a severe but salutary school of humiliation and affliction, of want and self-denial, to the spoiled foster-son of the king's daughter. We can understand this, if we merely picture to ourselves the contrast between the luxury of the court and the toil connected with a shepherd's life in the desert. But we have good ground for supposing that his present situation was trying and humiliat- ing in other respects also. His marriage does not seem to have been a happy one, and his position in the house of his father-in-law was apparently somewhat subordinate and servile. (*Ibid.*) *Zipporah.*—*Character of Zipporah:*—Zipporah is represented as a querulous, self-willed, and passionate woman, who sets her own will in opposi- tion to that of her husband, who will not trouble herself about his religious convic- tions, and, even when his life is evidently in danger, does not conceal the reluctance with which she agrees to submit, in order to save him. We might be astonished to find that a man of so much force of character as Moses possessed, could ever suffer this female government. But the circumstances in which he was placed suffi- ciently explain them. He had arrived there poor and helpless, as a man who was flying from pursuit. A fortunate combination of circumstances led to his receiving the Emir's daughter as his wife. It is true he could not pay the usual dowry. But the remarkable antecedents of his life, his superior mental endowments, his manly beauty, and other things, may have been regarded at first by his chosen bride and her relations as an adequate compensation for its omission. But if the character of Zipporah were such as we may conclude it to have been from chap. iv. 24 sqq., we can very well imagine that she soon began to despise all these, and made her husband feel that he was only eating the bread of charity in her father's house. Nor does he seem to have been admitted to any very intimate terms with his father- in-law; at least we might be led to this conclusion by the reserve with which he communicated to Jethro his intended departure, and the little confidence which he displayed (chap. iv. 18). Thus he was, and continued to be, a foreigner among the Midianites; kept in the background and misunderstood, even by those who were related to him by the closest ties. And if this was his condition, the sorrows arising from his exile, and his homeless and forlorn condition, must have been doubly, yea trebly severe. Under circumstances such as these, his attachment to his people, and his longing to rejoin them, instead of cooling, would grow stronger and stronger. There is something very expressive in this respect in the names which he gave to the sons who were born to him during his exile (ver. 22; xviii. 3, 4). They enable us to look deeply into the state of his mind at that time, for (as so frequently happened) he incorporated in them the strongest feelings and desires of his heart. (*Ibid.*)

Vers. 23–25. **Sighed by reason of the bondage.**—*The bondage of the Israelites :*— The Israelites were to be a witnessing nation—a nation in which the worship of the true God was to be maintained, while other nations were sunk in idolatry ; and the revelation which God gave of Himself preserved, while all the world was sunk in grossest darkness ; and the humane principles of the Divine law, not only taught, but practised, in a world where injustice and violence and cruelty were rampant. And it requires no very acute or penetrating discernment to perceive how their ex- perience under the Egyptian bondage was likely to conduce to the fulfilment of their mission. I. It was an illustration to them of THE TREATMENT WHICH THE CHURCH MIGHT EXPECT FROM THE WORLD, FITTED TO PROMOTE IN THEM THE ISOLATION which it was necessary they should maintain. Egypt was the world in its best state. They saw in her an illustration of what the intellect and muscle of man may ac- complish when his heart is alienated from God. She was a learned and powerful nation, great in war and advanced in art. The Israelites were thus brought in con- tact with the world in its best and most attractive form, and thereby taught, by bitter experience, what treatment they might expect from the world, and what relation to it it behoved them to sustain. II. In another way their bondage experience would tend to the same result, BY PROMOTING THAT MUTUAL SYMPATHY WHICH IS THE NECESSARY BOND OF NATIONAL LIFE. Great troubles and great deliverances shared in common have the effect of fusing into one body those who before were only an aggregate of individuals without any uniting tie. III. But there was yet another end to be served by their bondage—THE TEACHING AND PRACTICE OF THE HUMANE PRINCIPLES OF THE DIVINE LAW, IN THE FACE OF THE OPPRESSION and violence and cruelty which were then prevalent throughout the world. (*W. Landels, D.D.*) *The king dying, the people suffering, God reigning :*—L. THE KING DYING. 1. He was despotic in his rule. Unmoved by human suffering. 2. He was vindictive in his temper. 3. He was altogether out of sympathy with the providential arrangements of God. And now he dies. The despot meets with the conqueror. He must appear before the God whose authority he has tried to dethrone. The folly—woe—eternal ruin of sin. II. THE PEOPLE SUFFERING. 1, Their suffering was tyrannic. Freedom lost. Spirit broken. 2. Their suffering was intense. "Sighed." 3. Their suffering was long continued. 4. Their suffering appealed to the Infinite. Suffering should link our souls to God. It should be an inspiration to prayer. III. GOD REIGNING. 1. God reigns, though kings die. Wisdom of trusting only in the Infinite. 2. God reigns, though men suffer. Realize the Divine Rulership. 3. God reigns in harmony with His covenant made with the good. The Divine will is not capricious, but benevolent in design, and continuous in operation. Let every nation and family have a covenant with God. Lessons: 1. Do not despond in times of affliction. 2. Afflictions are designed to bring us into harmony with the requirements of God's covenant for our good. 3. It is the purpose of God to work the freedom and welfare of men. (*J. S. Exell, M.A.*)   *Lessons :*—1. Oppressors may die, and yet persecution not die with them. 2. Cries to heaven are often extorted from God's persecuted children. 3. If men want freedom, they cannot do better than direct their attention to God. (*Ibid.*)   *Death indiscriminating :*—Death is so dim-sighted and so blundering-footed that he staggers across Axminster tapestry as though it were a bare floor, and sees no difference between the fluttering rags of a tatterdemalion and a conqueror's gonfalon. Side by side we must all come down. No first class, second class, or third class in death or the grave. Death goes into the house at Gad's Hill, and he says, "I want that novelist." Death goes into Windsor Castle, and he says, "I want Victoria's consort." Death goes into Ford's Theatre, at Washington, and says, "I want that President." Death goes on the Zulu battle-field, and says, "I want that French Prince Imperial." Death goes into the marble palace at Madrid, and says, "Give me Queen Mercedes." Death goes into the almshouse, and says, "Give me that pauper." Death comes to the Tay Bridge, and says, "Discharge into my cold bosom all those passengers." Alike! Alike! By embalmment, by sculptured sarcophagus, by pyramidal grandeur, by epitaphal commemoration, by mere intoxicated "wake" or grander cathedral dirge, we may seem to give a caste to the dead, but it is soon over. I took out my memorandum-book and lead-pencil in Westminster Abbey a few weeks ago, and I copied a verse that it would interest you to hear:—

> "Think how many royal bones
> Sleep within these heaps of stones;
> Here they lie—had realms and lands—
> Who now want strength to stir their hands."

(*T. De Witt Talmage.*)   God heard.—*The bitter cry of Israel heard :*—I. SALVATION BEGINS WITH A SIGH. Until a sinner is weary of sin, it is of no use to bring the tidings of redemption to him. II. GOD HEARS THE GROANINGS OF POOR SINNERS. Psa. xviii. 6; xxxiv. 6; lxxvii. 1; Joel ii. 32; John vi. 37. III. HE SEES OUR AFFLICTIONS AND KNOWS OUR SORROWS. IV. HE REMEMBERS HIS COVENANT.   (*G. F. Pentecost, D.D.*) *God remembered, remembers :*—At last they remembered God and His promises. They thought of their ingratitude towards Him and towards Moses, and they began to sigh after God. This was what God was waiting for in order to show them mercy. He was waiting for their humiliation, their return to Him, their aversion to Egypt, their fervent prayers. It is to this frame of mind that God wishes to bring His children when He corrects them, and leaves them for a time in the hands of the wicked. You will find immediately afterwards, in the following verses, four expressions, which describe the goodness of God towards this unhappy people. "God heard their groaning; and God remembered His covenant with Abraham, with Isaac, and with Jacob. And God looked upon the children of Israel, and God had respect unto them." Remark that the name of God is repeated four times in these verses, as if to express with greater force the free grace and sovereignty of His merciful dealings with the Israelites. It was not because of their merits that He had pity upon them, any more than it is because of ours that He sends His gospel to us who have broken His law, neglected Him, and insulted Him by our ingratitude. But to us He calls, and says, "Come unto Me, that ye may have eternal life." (*Prof. Gaussen.*)　　*God hears the cry of His suffering children :*— My little boy has three calls. He opens the study door and calls, "Papa." I pay no attention to him because I know it is merely to attract notice. Again he comes throwing the study door open, and running in, he calls, "Papa, look here, I have something to show you." I know by his call that he is really in earnest, and I turn to share in his joy. He has still another call; when he is in the garden he may meet with an accident; in a quick and distressed voice he calls, "Papa." I know by the call that my child is in trouble, and I am out of the house in an instant, and by my boy's side, doing what I can to help him. In like manner God deals with us. We sometimes call to Him, scarcely meaning anything by our call, and never looking for or expecting a reply. Then, again, we wish to call the Lord's attention to some unexpected joy or pleasure which we have received. He listens to us because He delights to share in all that concerns us. But, dear friends, how quickly the Lord will come to the call of one in distress! He knows all the different calls of His children, and specially those in trouble, for has He not promised, "Call upon Me in the day of trouble, and I will deliver thee." (*D. L. Moody.*)

CHAPTER III.

Vers. 1–6. **A flame of fire out of the midst of a bush.**—*Moses at the burning bush :*— I. The story of Moses is the story, at first, of failure. Two great streams of influences moulded his life—the one drawn from the Egyptian surroundings of his early days, and the other drunk in with his mother's milk and his mother's teaching. On the one side he had before him the revelation of the world in its majesty and power, brute energy and magnificence, massive purpose and force, and splendid genius, with a kind of weird and magical faith in the dim powers of the unseen—those speechless-eyed deities of Egypt looking for ever into his face; and, along with these, a rugged sense of the responsibility of human life. And then, from the Hebrew side, another strain of thought. There came belief in the governing providence of God; there was belief in something more than might and majesty of force, and brute power; something like a belief that the weak might yet become strong—for the early history of that people was the history of the individual, or of the tribe waiting, not for his power upon the tokens of brute force, but waiting, rather, for his power upon the evolution of their history under the providence of God. But where he expected amongst people of his kin to find aspirations after better things, and responsiveness to his own spirit, he met only with chillness, coldness, and refusal to follow. Then came his exile in Midian—an exile from all his early dreams and hopes, an exile from the splendid position he had in Egypt, an exile from the future which glowed before him, and an exile, too, from the confidence he had that there was the power capable of lifting the hearts of his people and making them fit to strike a blow for freedom. II. Look, now, at the vision which restored him to faith and energy. 1. A revelation of permanence. The bush was not consumed; it held its own life amidst the devouring flame. Moses' feeling was one of suffering from that which, after all, is so common an experience of life—from the temptation to cry, "Vanity of vanities, all is vanity." It was something at such a moment to find that the revelation was to him one of permanence, where everything had slipped from his grasp. A while ago young dreams were his; a while ago, in his manhood, a noble purpose was his; and now all is gone, the temptation is to sit down and take a cynical attitude, and say, with a world where all things change, and where nothing abides, the safest and the wisest course is to laugh at existence, and take up either the language of despair, which wails out vanity of vanities, or the easy cynicism which treats life as a joke. But to the man in that state came a revelation of permanence. In the midst of all this change of things there is something which abides. Do not believe the answer to the cry of your heart, that all things perish, that the powers of decay touch everything in your life. There is in the unconsumed bush, there is in the change and policy of the world, an element of permanence. 2. A revelation of purity. "The place whereon thou standest is holy ground." In our first thought we think of permanence in material things. We see intellectual and moral things pass away and the materials remain; but the revelation of faith, the revelation of God, the revelation of all noble impulses of men, is everlastingly this: it is in the elements of purity that the powers of permanence are concerned. Mark you that the revelation given to Moses was not simply of the burning bush. Thrust thine hand into thy bosom; and he thrust it in, and drew it out leprous. Thrust thine hand into thy bosom again; and he did so, and drew it out clean. What significance is here to remind him that the cause of his failure lay not in the want of high purpose and high moral methods! The failure was not the failure of Moses' purpose, it was not the failure of his high hopes; there was permanent power, possibly, but there was a leprous stain within the breast of the patriot, and he understood it so; for when at last his dream was nearly accomplished, and he had led the people out from beneath the tryannies of the Pharaohs, and had planted them in the wilderness, then he drew from the throne of God that real law, that holy code, and he gave it to them graven as the image of eternity upon permanent stone, and said this is the law of the longevity of the people; these ten commandments, engrafted into the people's life, made part of their aspirations, part of their feelings, part of their intellectual powers, part of their whole social life, will guarantee their permanence. It shall be your life if ye will observe to do these things. The vision had taught him that permanence was to be found in purity. 3. A revelation of personal power and love. Behind the purity is a personal God. We might pause a moment and say, Why is this? If I have this moral law, and if the possession of this righteous strength gives permanence, why this personal God behind? The answer is simple. You and I may think there is energy in law; but, after all, law is merely a name given to certain causes and effects and sequences. There is no inspiration necessary in law. To tell Moses, indeed, that here this people could live, that there was no reason why Israel should die, that the element of permanence might be there if only the element of righteousness was there, would be to mock Moses, who might have said, "All my patriotic hopes are gone; here I get the answer of permanence, but I do not get the guarantee of it. I get no inspiration as to whether any one cares." Lo! the answer is given: "God cares; these people that seemed God forsaken, have yet God as their God; righteousness is not a dead letter, righteousness is an expression of a living will, and an expression of a living will will moulding human life to achieve some great and final thing." Thus he began to see that he was not struggling merely against the nerveless hearts of men, but living and loving hearts were co-operating with his, and the aspirations which had dawned within his breast were not simply his own weak thought, but were the answers back to the purposes of God; for in the best sense it is true that the aspirations of man are the aspirations of God; and when you realize that, then you begin to see how needed is the guarantee which Moses asked, "Give me strength; what am I that I should go?" Because He is the God of Abraham, the God of Isaac, and the God of Jacob—the God of this people who seemed to be no people; therefore their resurrection is possible. III. THE REVELATION WAS NOT FOR MOSES ALONE. You remember the scene in "Alton Locke," where the poet would go to the Southern Pacific, and there find inspiration for his song, and a shrewd Scotchman took him into the slums of a great city, where the squalor and dinginess of life existed, and said to him that the poet sees poetry everywhere—the poetry is there if you will turn your poet's eye upon it. So also is religion. There is in every common bush the light of God, and only those who see it draw off their shoes. It is the old story again. God is near, God is in this place, and we knew it not. You may say that the vision, and that faith which the life which has surrounded you, has slowly dimmed and numbed, and you say, "There is no revelation for me; my heart, my mind, is a wilderness now; there were little fruits and flowers in the garden of my early life, and I hoped to dedicate my life, and consecrate my services, to God—perhaps as a minister of His Church, perhaps in a high calling in the State; but now I have grown confused with new and strange thoughts, that rise sirocco-like; new things have swept away the old, and have left me no verdure and flowers in their place; I am in a wilderness, and there is no revelation of fire for me." Pardon me, there is. Alter your views. Do you never feel a sense of dissatisfaction? did ever cross your mind the law of self-condemnation, and have you not said, "I meant to make more of my life in this place of study, and meant to have worked for a purpose; and now I am dissatisfied? Where I meant to be a living agent, I have only become an idle dreamer. I look back upon a wasted and unprofitable life, and say, Woe is me! all the bright, hopeful views have gone, and my life is like a shipwrecked thing." Is not that pain, which is the witness of your failure, the fire of God? He lets it burn, that it may burn away the base thing, and that you may see in the voice of noble discontent the possibility of stepping up once more to the dream of your early life, and by the strength of God achieving it. But we forget to turn aside to see the great sights about us. Give your hearts leisure sometimes to meet with God, and God will meet with you. Give your souls the opportunity of letting the light of God's vision shine sometimes with a possibility of reflection upon your own life, and the fire will glow, and the bush will burn, and the revelation will begin. (Bp. Boyd Carpenter.) *The vision and the voice:*—I. The vision. 1. The vision was miraculous. 2. Moses had this vision when he was in solitude. 3. It was symbolic—(1) Of Israel in Egypt. (2) Of the Church in the world. (3) Of the truth of the gospel. (4) Of ourselves, who have the religious life within us. II. The voice. 1. It revealed the majesty and grandeur of God. 2. It revealed the special providence of the great God—the God of Abraham, Isaac, and Jacob. 3. It proclaimed the faithfulness of God. 4. It demanded reverence. (T. Jones.) *Moses at the bush:*—This narrative is a chain of glorious wonders. We see here—I. An old man called to go out on the great errand of his life. The education of Moses for the great mission of his life lasted eighty years. God never sends forth fruit until the season is fitted for the fruit, and the fruit for the season; when the hour was ready for the man, and the man for the hour, then God sent forth Moses. II. The burning bush from which that call was sounded. 1. This was a sign to indicate the peculiar presence of God. 2. It was also a symbol of His people, eminently adapted to encourage the prophet in undertaking their cause. III. The angel who uttered this call. We see at the first glance that He is Divine; we next learn that He is an angel; we further find, from a chain of Scripture proofs, that He is Christ. IV. The covenant under which the angel gave him his commission. It was the same covenant that had been given to Abraham, Isaac, and Jacob. V. The angel's name. That name asserts—1. His real existence. 2. His underived existence. 3. His independent existence. 4. His eternity. VI. The effect to be wrought by the remembrance of His name. 1. It was intended to inspire profoundest reverence for the Being to whom it belongs. 2. It reveals the infinite sufficiency of a Christian's portion. 3. It gives encouragement to evangelical enterprise. (C. Stanford, D.D.) *Moses' education and life-work:*—I. How was the earlier history of Moses an education for the great work of his life? In order to free his people from their bondage, Moses needed sympathy and faith; and the Bible gives us three phases of his life, wonderfully adapted to educate him in these qualities. 1. His education in the Egyptian court. 2. His attempt to convince the people of their brotherhood. 3. His flight into the wilderness. II. How did this vision explain to Moses the work of his life? 1. The vision of God prepared him for the work of his life. It showed him the everlastingness of God, and his own unworthiness to do God's work. But the voice upheld him amid the overwhelming sense of his nothingness, and made him feel his vocation. 2. The vision of God gave endurance in fulfilling that work. Even should his work seem to fail, he had a grasp on eternity which would keep him strong and true. (E. L. Hull, B.A.) *The Divine call and its sign:*—I. The call of the chosen leader. Moses was already a believing man, walking in favour and fellowship with God, and in sympathy with his down-trodden people. We must carefully distinguish between Moses' decision for God, and God's disclosure of duty to Moses. The one took place in his early manhood; the other was deferred till the threshold of old age, when God gave the charge of the story before us, and the servant's self-denying choice was rewarded by the sovereign's honourable commission. The two experiences differ, you see, as conversion from service, as personal consecration from official appointment, as entrance on a life of holiness from entrance on a life of work. 1. And here comes our first lesson—a lesson for all who, like Moses, await God's call—the lesson, namely, of faith and of self-restraint. Are we struck with the fact that of the hundred and twenty years assigned to Moses, eighty were spent in preparation, and only forty in work? But it is God's way. What seems a time of uselessness as regards the world may be a time of probation as regards yourself. And the time of probation, if quietly endured and conscientiously improved, may issue, ere God has done with you, in a work of deliverance on the earth, whose concentration, rapidity, and success may amply explain the preceding delay. 2. Take a second lesson at this point in passing—a lesson of diligence. I know not how God means to meet and to summon you, if, as in Moses' case, He has special service in store for you; but I am sure of this, that revelations of special service are given only in the midst of conscientious application to ordinary duty. 3. Learn here yet a third truth—a lesson of constant watchfulness. For though Moses was at the time unexpectant, he was not upon that account heedless. His mind was in sympathy with the spiritual and eternal, and his eye was kept open to discern it. Be sure that, for all his industry in his worldly calling, the mood of Moses was such that no indication or hint could escape him from the world that is unseen and Divine. And let us take that spirit along with us, if, like Moses, we would find the lights and the beacons of God on our path—a spirit of devout and careful attention, of inquiry, and of vigilant thought. 4. The lesson of reverence is needed too. While the secret of the Lord is for those that seek Him, it is also for those that fear Him. 5. Holy diffidence. Much of the best work with which the Church has been served has been rendered by men who, like Moses, were at first overcome by the thought of it, and would fain have drawn back had Providence permitted. Take the example of the great pioneer of the Church in Scotland—the leader of its glorious exodus from the superstition and tyranny of popery to the heritage which God had prepared for it, in the light wherewith His Spirit illumines, and the liberty wherewith His truth makes free. When Knox was called to the pastorate of the church of St. Andrews, and the first step was disclosed to him of a road that led onwards to service and fame, we read that a strange thing happened. The audience were gathered, the service was proceeded with, the wish of the people was announced by the officiating minister, and echoed back as he spoke by the cries of the people themselves. But when Knox rose to speak in return, he broke down into tears, left the meeting-place abruptly, and enclosed himself in the privacy of his house; "and from that day," as the chronicler tells of him, "till the day he presented himself to preach, his countenance and behaviour did sufficiently declare the grief and the trouble of his heart, for no man saw any sign of mirth from him, neither had he pleasure to accompany any man for days together." Such feelings of diffidence and misgiving will a true man feel whensoever he is honoured with special service; nor, if he is wise, will he seek to repress it. II. THE REVELATION OF THE CHANGELESS GOD. Nothing will establish the Church, nothing will support and encourage its leaders in times of trial such as those through which Israel was passing, like the thought of the changelessness of God, and in especial the changelessness and eternity of His love, of which trials, however grievous, and temptations, however scorching, form only a brief and a passing phase. The processes God employs may be many, but the principle He acts on is one. The manifestations He makes of Himself may be various, but the character that underlies them is the same. (*W. A. Gray.*) *Man in relation to mystery* :—I. THAT SOMETIMES MEN MEET WITH MYSTERY IN THE PURSUIT OF THEIR DAILY CALLING. 1. This vision was unexpected. 2. This vision was educational. II. THAT SOMETIMES MYSTERY IS ASSOCIATED WITH THINGS OF A VERY ORDINARY CHARACTER. "A bush." The smallest, the most trivial, the apparently unmeaning things, events of life, are full of mystery, contain a heavenly presence, a Divine voice, will teach a reflective spirit, will become an impulse to a higher life—avocation. The bushes of life are full of mystery. The world is a great secret—is vocal with messages of freedom to listening souls. III. THAT MYSTERY SHOULD BE INVESTIGATED WITH THE UTMOST DEVOTION OF SOUL. "Put off thy shoes from off thy feet." 1. There must be devotion in opposition to levity. 2. There must be devotion in opposition to curiosity. Why this devotion? (1) Because mystery is holy. (2) Because mystery is authoritative. It commands us to take off our shoes. Its authority is Divine; will be recognized by true manhood. IV. THAT SOMETIMES GOOD MEN ARE FAVOURED WITH A GRAND UNFOLDING OF MYSTERY. "I am the God," &c. 1. God observes the conduct of men in relation to mystery. "And the Lord saw that he turned aside to see." What a subduing, inspiring thought, that God knows all the efforts of our souls in their investigation of mystery. 2. God speaks to men who are anxious to investigate mystery. "God called to him out of the midst of the bush." God speaks—allows us to investigate.

3. God reveals Himself as the great solution of all mystery. (*J. S. Exell, M.A.*) *Desert revelations:*—I. LET US CONTEMPLATE THE ELEMENT OF WONDER IN THE HISTORY. 1. This was the crowning preparation and call of Moses for his life's work. 2. This was to be the beginning of a new stage in the life and history of the chosen people, and of the history of the Divine unfolding. II. SOME OF THE ELEMENTS OF WONDER HERE ARE OLD. 1. The Angel Jehovah was not a created Being. The designation is evidently used in a special sense, because, He speaks as God Himself and receives Divine homage. Here it means the Divine as self-revealing; the Infinite bringing Himself into relations of knowledge with a limited and finite creature, and into relations of covenanted grace and mercy. It is God to whom we can get near, understand, grasp, love, serve, obey. 2. The Angel Jehovah was God of the fathers. But He was revealed to them as El Shaddai, God Almighty. 3. But what He had been to the fathers He still was. The fathers' God! The God of our dead! The sanctities of home life go into and along with our religion. 4. There was still another old element in the wonder; and that was the Fire. This was the same element which appeared amid and upon the cherubic symbols, darting hither and thither like flashing sword in the sunshine at the gate of Eden, and which we read of as "the Presence," the faces of Jehovah; and as "the glory of the Lord." III. BUT TO THE WONDER WHICH WAS OLD THERE WERE ELEMENTS ADDED WHICH ARE NEW. God reveals Himself here under a new name. An old word is vitalized with a new meaning, and is laid at the foundation of a dispensation. He will be known in all the Mosaic times and institutions, not as El Shaddai, but as Jehovah, "I am that I am." He is the one self-existent, unchangeable, ever-living God of ages. From everlasting to everlasting God. But the name is adopted and comes into use, specially in relation to the deliverance from Egypt and the constitution of the nation. So it means, the Sovereign Ruler and Ordainer of the Ages, who has become a Righteous Deliverer and Redeemer. (*W. H. Davison, D.D.*)   *The burning bush :—* 1. Observe the substance of the figure. Not a fine tall tree, a cedar or a cypress, but a bush—a mere bush. Such is the image of the Church—poor and humble. It was at one time in the ark, and there was a wicked Ham, at another in the family of Abraham, and there was a mocking Ishmael. It was now in Egypt, consisting of slaves and brickmakers. Jesus had not where to lay His head, His followers were the common people, His apostles were fishermen. 2. Observe the condition of the bush. It burned with fire. Fire denotes suffering. Christians must have tribulation in the world. They are never to consider "fiery trials" as strange things. Of how many can God say, "I have chosen thee in the furnace of affliction"? 3. Mark the bush's preservation. The bush was not consumed. Sometimes the Church has burned in the fire of persecution, and sometimes of derision. But with what result? Whilst kingdoms and empires have passed away, and not a wreck of them is left but some vestiges in ruins, lingering in monumental mockery of the boasts of men, the Church still stands, as she is destined ever to do, in the light and strength of her omnipotent and faithful Lord. And this is as true of every individual believer as of the whole Church collectively. (*A. Nevins, D.D.*)   *The bush as an emblem :—* Some also see in this bush an emblem of—1. The awfulness of God's offended justice (Deut. iv. 21; Mal. iii. 2). 2. The incarnation and sufferings of Christ, the bush representing His human nature (Isa. liii. 2), the flame of fire shadowing forth His Divine nature (Deut. iv. 24), and the union of the flame with the bush denoting the union of the Divine with the human nature. 3. Those dreadful sufferings by which sin should be expiated—Christ enduring the fierce flames of the wrath of God, yet not consumed (Heb. ix. 28). (*Ibid.*)   *Was this a great sight ?—*1. It was the great I AM who exhibited it. 2. It afforded a bright gleam of hope to Israel, that their bondage was nearly over (vers. 7, 8). In order to see this great sight, we must turn aside—1. From the world (1 John ii. 15; 2 Cor. vi. 17). 2. Carnal reasoning (1 Cor. ii. 14; John iii. 9). 3. All known sin (Eph. iv. 17, 18; 2 Pet. i. 9). (*Ibid.*) *The God of Moses:*—Here we have an account of God's disclosure of Himself to Moses; we have that which is the root out of which Moses' whole conception of God and His government grew. Laying aside all preconceptions and prejudices, let us see what sort of a portrait this chapter gives us: 1. It shows us a self-revealing God; a God who discloses Himself to the human race, and communicates with them. 2. This God is one who is not indifferent to the woes and sufferings of His people. 3. He is a God of deliverance. 4. In working out this deliverance, He chooses human and imperfect instruments. 5. The very name by which God at once reveals and conceals Himself suggests the similitude between the Old Testament and the New Testament revelations. "I am," says Jehovah to Moses; "you must trust

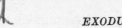

Me and walk by faith in My assurance, and not in an intellectual comprehension of My character and My purposes." "I am," says Christ to Philip; "you must trust in Me, and walk by your faith in Me: not by an understanding of what the Father is who hath sent Me, or a comprehension of what the Father purposes to accomplish in and by you." In a sense the Egyptian inscription, the Athenian altar, and Herbert Spencer's definition are true; God is the Unknown and Unknowable. The intellect tries in vain to draw aside the veil; but love and sympathy pass behind it. Philosophy in vain endeavours to analyse and interpret mother-love; but the child in simplicity and faith reposes on it. The God of Moses and the God of the twelve disciples are alike in this—that They are the incomprehensible "I am"; to be loved, trusted, obeyed, rested on, but never to be measured, fathomed and understood. Sometimes from my hill-side home among the Highlands of the Hudson I see, fifty miles away, obscured by haze and overhanging clouds, and partially veiled, perhaps, in mist or rain, the distant outline of the Catskill range; and then the veil is drawn aside, the turbaned mist is lifted off their foreheads, and that which before was dim and indistinct stands out against the dark background of sky in clear, intelligible outline, yet leaving all the dress of grey rock and green tree and foaming cataract, and dark gloom, and flitting sunshine breaking through the trees, to the imagination; for at best it is only an outline I can see. So in the Old Testament I look upon the outline of my God veiled in cloud; in the New Testament the cloud is lifted, the mist is cleared away, and through an atmosphere like that of the most perfect October day I look on the same outline, distinct and beautiful against a heavenly background: and still it is but an outline that I see of the mystery and majesty of the nature I shall never know, never be able even to explore, until I stand in His presence and am invited to know Him even as I am known. (*Lyman Abbott, D.D.*) *Moses and the burning bush; or, a picture of a true student and the Bible :—* 1. That God's purposes are punctual in their accomplishment (see Gen. xv.). The clock of time had now struck the four hundred years, and God forthwith began to redeem His pledge. 2. That God's purposes, in relation to our world, are generally accomplished by the agency of man. 3. That the men whom God employs for the carrying out of His purposes, He qualifies by a special revelation. 4. That this special revelation which He vouchsafes, is frequently symbolical in its character. All nature is a symbol. Truth in symbol is palpable, attractive, impressive. The burning bush was a symbol. But what did it symbolize? God's presence. I. OBSERVE MOSES DIRECTING HIS EARNEST ATTENTION TO THE DIVINE REVELATION. 1. Moses directs his attention to it, under an impression of its greatness. 2. Moses directs his attention to it, in order to ascertain its import. It is ever so with a true student of the Bible. He will seek to find out "the reason of things." II. OBSERVE MOSES HOLDING INTERCOURSE WITH GOD THROUGH THE DIVINE REVELATION. 1. God's communications depended upon his attention. Only he who looks and inquires, hears in the Bible the voice of God. 2. God's communications were consciously personal to him. 3. God's communications were directive and elevating. III. OBSERVE MOSES REALIZING THE PROFOUNDEST IMPRESSIONS THROUGH THE DIVINE REVELATION. "Hid his face," &c. 1. These impressions are peculiarly becoming in sinful intelligences. The Bible is designed to produce reverence for God. 2. These impressions are necessary to qualify men for God's work. 3. These impressions are consonant with the highest dignity and enjoyment. He that is consciously least is always greatest. (*Homilist.*) *The burning bush :*—I. THE LOCALITY. How many noted Scriptural events took place on mountains! 1. It seems as if they were above the common herd of man. 2. They are difficult of access. All religious duties must be connected with difficulty. 3. They were mostly places of solitude. II. THE SPOT. A bush. 1. Its insignificance. 2. Its incongruity. What apparent connection between God and a bush? 3. Its intrinsic worthlessness. III. THE PHENOMENON. 1. The bush burned with fire. God's glory appeared in it, humble as it was. 2. The bush, though burning, was not consumed. (*Ibid.*) *Moses encouraged by the burning bush :*—Some would have us learn, that it is God's glory makes the Church beautiful, and gives the poor bush its excellence and power; others, that the burning fire represents the afflictions to which we are subject as Christians, which exist, but do not consume the soul. We may, indeed, profitably extract any such lessons; they all help us on our way. But I think the appearance was only intended to encourage Moses. He was sent forth to go to Pharaoh, but complained of his own inability. God showed him that it was not the power of the instrument that was to prevail, but the influence of the Spirit which animated it; even as it was not the bush which was remarkable, but the fire which dwelt in it.

(*Ibid.*) *The burning bush; or, the Church in the world:*—Remember also, that you may attain the end of your being in any place; that you may adorn with moral beauty the very humblest sphere; that you may confer upon your position greater dignity than any position could possibly confer upon you. When we read the histories of the world's brightest characters, we seem to forget altogether the social ranks to which they belonged; the dazzling brightness of their heroism, their valour, their truth, makes their outward surroundings of no account; the one prominent fact which forces itself upon our attention is, that they acquitted themselves like men, and won the admiration of all succeeding ages. Who ever stops to reflect that John Bunyan was a tinker; that Paul the apostle was a tent-maker; that Jesus of Nazareth was a carpenter's son? Be it ours, therefore, not to murmur at our circumstances, but to make the most of whatever circumstances in which we may be placed. Let us learn from this scene how to conduct ourselves in God's presence. Of course, God is present everywhere, our conduct should therefore be an habitual recognition of this solemn fact. Still there are times and places in which we come into God's special presence. When we open God's book, and meditate upon its contents, and endeavour to profit in the study of it, His presence breathes in every page, and speaks words of mercy, warning, and encouragement to our souls. Ah! my friends, it makes one sad to think, how men can treat their Bible as if it were mere trash; how men can repeat their prayers, as if they were useless forms; how men can hear the gospel, as if it were a worthless tale! I. THE CHURCH IN THE MIDST OF THE WORLD. The primary reference in the text is to the Jewish Church in Egypt. There is an uncompromising antagonism, an eternal conflict, between the Church and the world. And the Church being comparitively small in number, engages in this conflict at great odds. Hence it frequently seems as if she must be eventually overcome. The spirit of this world is in direct opposition to the principles which the Church is commissioned to hold forth. The morality which it propagates is a standing protest against the world's most cherished notions. Is it likely that such teaching as this should provoke no opposition? It has provoked opposition of the strongest, keenest, deadliest kind. I shall not detain you with any account of the horrible persecutions which the Church has passed through during the last eighteen centuries of its history. But in spite of all, the Church has proved itself invincible; though persecuted, it has not been cast down; though burned with fire, it has not been consumed. Nay, we can say even more. The very trials to which the Church has been exposed, have only helped to develop its powers, to widen its influence, to make it what it is at the present day. The bush has been set on fire. True. But what then? The fire itself has been for its benefit; fanned into a mighty conflagration, it has shone all the more brilliantly in the midst of the world's darkness. II. GOD IN THE MIDST OF THE CHURCH. The glory which appeared in the bush is a fit emblem of God's presence in the Church—His life-giving presence—His protecting presence—His conquering presence. God is in the heart of every true member of the Church, God is the source of his spiritual life, God is the secret of his spiritual power. God's presence is the Church's chief defence. It is not strange that she has been so firm, so immovable, so enduring, when we consider the mighty Being, whose power has protected her. "The Lord of hosts is with us; the God of Jacob is our refuge." But this great fact—this ever-abiding presence of God in the Church —suggests a still more precious thought; for it is a guarantee for the Church's future; its future safety, its future triumphs, its future glory. (*D. Rowlands, B.A.*) *The burning bush:*—Moses was not engaged in any unworthy work, or any career of sin. He was tending the flock of his father-in-law, and he led the flock to the backside of the desert, and came to the mountain of God. Here, perhaps, he had been often before, but as he led the flock along that familiar track, suddenly there came to him, in the calm and quiet of that lonely place, this wonderful revelation of the Lord, which became a point of departure in Moses' own heart and history, and in the history of the people of God. So, I say, that which makes life worth living is this—we will come to the point at once—the great glory of our life is that God comes into it and reveals His presence; that God opens our eyes to see that there is more in the world than simply our daily calling, our flock of sheep, and our temporal interests; that life is more than a day's work, no matter how diligently and conscientiously performed, and a night's sleep. God, the personal God, is here to greet our own eyes with the kindling glory of the manifestation of His own presence. He will change our life, its whole current, its whole outcome. And I would like at the outset to waken up an expectation in those who are rather apt to think that the day is gone by for them either to expect or to receive such visions and revelations of the Lord. My friends, Moses was an old man when this took place. Therefore let not those growing old, either in years or in cares, give in or sink down. Many a long day and year Moses had trudged about this very region, when suddenly one year, one day, one hour, one particular moment, he lifted up his eyes, and, as we all know now, Lo! there was God. In the midst of all the ordinary humdrum and routine of life I see something. There is a glimmer, a something extraordinary somewhere, sometime, and I open my eyes. I was often there before, and saw nothing; but now there is a gleam, a light, an Epiphany. My very soul is engaged, led on, and on, and on, until the end of it is God as man speaking to me, lifting up my life by the grappling-hooks of His own purposes, and using and glorifying it and me for ever and ever. I want to show, for example, that you might have had a man, another shepherd, and that man might have been going on for seventy or eighty years of age like Moses, and he never would have seen this revelation. He would have got so down to the level of a shepherd's life and a shepherd's experience that when he saw the bush burning he would have got some natural explanation for it, and passed on. It would have come too late in the day for him to say, "That is worth looking at. It is a little extra blush on that bush; but it cannot be a fire, it is only an extra glow of the sunlight on the furze. I do not think I ever saw it just so before, though." Meantime the sheep give a bleat, and he turns his face away, and on he goes. Oh, it is hard to waken up some of us! We are so unlike Moses. No; old as he was, he was as curious as a bairn. He had still the faculty to open his eyes and see wonderful sights, and clap his hands, and wonder what they were. May God take away the oldness of some of us, and give us the freshness of youth! It will be the beginning of salvation. Open your eyes! The world is not done, and you are not done. Your days are only in the beginning, and if you only get your eyes open to see what is here, they will never close again. When once God shows Himself to us in Christ, we, at last, have our eyes open. Curiosity! a human thing;—and God pulled Moses by that little thread—curiosity. And this great chain cable came after it—faith, clear, strong faith in a personal God, speaking to him, and giving him a personal message and mission. "And Moses said, I will now turn aside, and see this great sight, why the bush is not burnt." Now, turn aside; get off the track, oh man; step out of your way; turn aside. Go, go, go along this new course; it is not far to go. Do not sit still and let things go past. It is a wonderful world; it is a wonderful church; all life is just bursting with wonder, if you will only turn aside. But not everybody sees the burning. Everybody sees the bush. It is only Moses that becomes aware of the "glory on the grass"; "the silence that is in the starry sky"; "the sleep that is among the lonely hills." The world is more than mud or atoms brought together fortuitously, or in any other way. The world is a burning bush. It is so far earth—solid, material. I can handle it, and become a man of science, and say, "What is in it?" And, God help me, I can become so much a mere scientist as only to see the bush and leaves and berries, and the shape of the leaves and the shape of the stem, and tell you how it grew, and then say, "There is no flame." Just so; there is a way of looking at that bush, man—a way of looking at the bush that puts out its light, or your light, which is the same thing. There could have been a kind of man come tramping along here with the sheep, and with one single look he would have quenched that flame; and the same damnable thing may be in you and me. We may look at nature, and look at our own bodies, and look at Christ in the Bible; and look at the Bible itself, with such a blank look and stare of unbelief that God withdraws Himself, and never comes back. Never! There is a way of looking, a trick in the eye, that is an abomination to God, and He simply withdraws. Everything is a burning bush. Nature is such a burning bush. Nature is full of the supernatural, everywhere ready to burst forth, but you must not push forward, but stand back if you wish to see it. The more we push in irreverently, the more it flies from us. Our own bodies—a burning bush! Have you ever thought of that? Here is the physical, the material, the natural, but in it and on it the immaterial, the spiritual, in a true sense, the metaphysical. Streaming out of it, and above it, and beyond it, is that which lifts itself up from the mass of blood and brain and bone, and says, "I, I am." Then, again, here is a burning bush for you—the Bible. So much of it natural: the boards, and that means the binder; the print, and that means the printer; the thoughts, and that means the thinker—like any other book. Like any other book, but, God be praised, more than any other book. For the glory, the voice, the "Thus saith the Lord," comes out from this, that comes from no other book. Such a burning bush is the Church of Christ, and I speak not now of her survival of fiery trials. Now, a congregation, a Church, either in the large sense or the sectional sense of the word, is just like any other corporation or society. It has its laws and purposes, and there is so much in it of man's planning and guiding and ordering. Yet a Church is not a mere guild like any other; a corporation of people like any other gathering. No, no, no! It is like them as that bush is like any other bush; but, man, there is a glory in it, there is a wonder in it! The Lord is in this place. "In all places—all places—where I record My name, there will I come, and I will bless them." "Oh, Thou that dwellest in Thy Church, shine forth." For some of us it is becoming only a bush, an institution like any other. And I see coming to us Christ Himself as a burning bush. There He lies, a baby, like your own, my good woman; but, unlike your own, there is a glory, there is a flame. Wherever you come across Him, as babe, or as boy, or as man, or as crucified, there is the flame, there is the extra superadded something, and that something is the eternal and uncreated Godhead. Worship Him, wherever you meet Him, from Bethlehem right on to the cross, on to the glory. Worship Him—God in human flesh. Turn aside and see this great sight: why human nature can exhibit this mystery—why the bush is not burnt. But further, all this came to Moses, humanly speaking, this wonderful revelation, because of reverence. "Draw not nigh hither: put off thy shoes from off thy feet, for the place whereon thou standest is holy ground." He was near enough. I can quite well understand that very likely no man more than Moses would feel, "Oh, I would like to see this great sight, and get to the bottom of it." But he could not, and we should not. God has set bounds to the inquiries of the human spirit, not cramping bounds, but wise and safe ones. So with many other difficulties. How am I at once body and spirit? But I am warned by this, that many men who have gone into that question in order to find out about it have put out their eyes. They come back from the examination of the human frame, from wonder upon wonder, they come back and say, "We have found no spirit, no breath of God; all that has no warrant from our researches." Out you go with your researches! And they go to this Bible and say, "It is a very wonderful Book, and we have examined it in the spirit of frank, candid, and fearless inquiry. We have not scoffed at the Book, nor scorned it; we have examined it in the spirit of frank and fearless inquiry, and we find the glory is gone." It is just so. There is only one method—the reverent; and one result—and that is to know God better and bow down flatter before Him. You cannot take away the hyphen that holds the "burning" and the "bush" together. When even Moses would have gone forward to see why, he was kept back, and his thoughts turned in more profitable directions. So you are forbidden to go nearer; you are near enough to see and to know and to bow down and to give an intelligent, whole-hearted adoration and worship of obedience. And any spirit that enters into you and me, and makes me go beyond the point where Moses had to pull up, is a dangerous spirit, alike in method and result. (*J. McNeill.*) *The call of Moses:*—I. THE OCCASION OF THE CALL. 1. Solitude. 2. God is watching a man. 3. God doesn't call until the man turns aside to see. II. THE SOURCE OF THE CALL. A bramble that does not burn away. III. RESULTS OF THE CALL. 1. Reverent self-surrender. 2. Transformation of life. (*E. Judson.*) *The manifestation of God:*—I. THE MANIFESTATION OF GOD IN THE PURITY OF ITS NATURE. 1. Purity is essential to the being of God. 2. Purity is essential to the government of God. 3. Purity is essential to the worship of God. II. THE MANIFESTATION OF GOD IN THE SEVERITY OF ITS OPERATION—"the bush was burned with fire." Every impurity must be consumed, and every obstacle to the kingdom of God must be destroyed. This severity is evident—1. In the chastisements of the godly, and—2. In the utter destruction of the impenitent. III. THE MANIFESTATION OF GOD IN ITS GRACIOUS INTENTION—"and the bush was not consumed." 1. God in Christ is a Saviour. 2. The operations of the Holy Spirit purify the soul, but do not destroy the man. (*British Weekly.*) *The burning bush:*—I. THE CIRCUMSTANCES IN WHICH MOSES WAS, WHEN THE LORD APPEARED TO HIM. In desert. Keeping sheep. What a contrast to his employments in youth! Yet probably this was the happiest part of his life. Time for reflection and for poetical musings. II. THE NATURE OF THE APPEARANCE. 1. The emblem in which the Church was held forth—"Bush." If numbers and splendour are the mark of a true Church as its properties, where should we find for many ages the Church of God? Seldom in the Old Testament, never in the New. The Church of God was once enclosed in the ark; at this time it consisted of a number of slaves and brickmakers. 2. The condition in which it was found. "Burning with fire." Grievously oppressed and persecuted. 3. Its preservation.

" Not consumed." The blood of the martyrs has ever been the seed of the Church. 4. The cause of this security. The angel of the Lord was in the midst of it. III. THE ATTENTION IT AWAKENED. Let us, like Moses, turn aside, and contemplate His revelations. IV. GOD'S PROHIBITION, OR RATHER, REGULATION. A check on curiosity. Be satisfied with the facts of Christianity, without the philosophy of them. Be content with the use of things, rather than attempt to dive into their nature and their qualities. Take the religious controversies, which have occupied so much time, and which have injured so many fine tempers; and what have they commonly turned to, but things too deep for human reasoning to fathom, too lofty to be soared to without presumption, or too insignificant to merit regard? V. GOD'S ADDRESS. All along, from the beginning, God has shown favour to some for the sake of others. Under the law He was called—" The God of Abraham, Isaac, and Jacob ": because the covenant made with them was for Israel : in him they were blessed, and for his sake they received all things. But now the covenant made for the spiritual Israel, was made with a far more glorious character; it was set up from everlasting—from the beginning, ere the earth was. His name is Jesus: it is in Him that we are accepted; it is in Him that we are blessed with all spiritual blessings in heavenly places ; it is for His sake that we receive all things. And therefore, while of old His style was, " The God of Abraham, Isaac, and Jacob," it is now, under the gospel, " The God and Father of our Lord Jesus Christ." There are two things derivable from this address of God, when He says, " I am the God of Abraham, Isaac, and Jacob." The first is, that unquestionably, therefore, Moses had some knowledge of a future state. He does not say, He was " the God of Abraham, Isaac, and Jacob "; but, " I am the God of Abraham, Isaac, and Jacob " ; their spirits are with Me now; their renewed bodies shall be, by and by, as certainly as they are now in the dust. You observe, also, that God sustains His relationship to those of your connections, who are gone before. VI. Let us observe THE IMPRESSION MADE UPON MOSES. " And Moses hid his face ; for he was afraid to look upon God." 1. Here you see, first, that Divine manifestation always produces self-diffidence and abasement. 2. You see, also, how little we can physically bear. " Flesh and blood cannot inherit the kingdom of God " ; the splendour would be too much for the eye, the sounds too much for the ear ; the poor frame would break down under that " far more exceeding and eternal weight of glory." (*W. Jay.*) *God's Bible not consumed :*—This book, do you see it ? Not a leaf, not a word, not a letter of it, but has been burned ten thousand times—on parchment, papyrus, and paper ; in many a language and many a land it has fed the furnace and lit the fire. It has been piled by thousands and thousands at a time in huge bonfires, and offered amid the yells of triumphant crowds, a holocaust to gods of wood and to the triple-crowned idol of the papal throne ! " The bush has burned with fire." " But the bush was not consumed." This Book is ubiquitous ; never a land under heaven that has it not, never a language among men that does not contain it. Paganism, I tell you, has had it trampled into dirt by beasts ; popery has burnt it at the hands of the common hangman; sceptical science has branded and seared it as with hot iron; infidelity has torn it into shreds; and atheism, of the modern type, has besmeared its pages with mud and filth whose fumes are insupportable—but the bush is not consumed ! Lo ! the bush burned with fire. But the blessed Saviour declares that " the servant shall be as his Lord." What has been done to Him in the world, He says, shall be done to you also, Christian believer. Then the burning bush is a lively image of the Christian too. Now I desire to leave one final thought with you. Why did not the fire burn the bush ? Because the Lord was in it. He had made it His temporary dwelling-place. Why did not the fire burn the Christ ? Through wrath and rage of man and devil, through cross, and death, and hell, He passed unscathed. Why ? Because of the Divine in Him. Because the bush of that clay temple of humanity was the tabernacle in which dwelt the Deity. Why has not the fierce, horrible, and perpetual fires of persecution and testing succeeded in destroying the Christian Church ? Because God is in it. In it the tabernacle of God is with men. Christ walks amid the golden candlesticks ; the Father dwells where His name is recorded, and the very life-breath of the Church is the living Spirit of God. (*J. J. Wray.*) *The burning bush :*—I. AN EMBLEM. 1. This bush had God in the midst of it (ver. 4), and the Church has God in the midst of her (Psa. xlvi. 5). 2. This bush, burning in the night, gave a great light in the wilderness ; and the Church of God gives a great light in this dark world. 3. The bush burns, but is unburnt. The Church suffers, but still survives. II. A MIRACLE. The first miracle we read of was wrought upon fire. Fire had been more worshipped than any of the elements of nature: from the Moloch of the Ammonites to the Juggernaut of the Hindoos, no idol has had such crowded temples or costly offerings. God struck His first blow at the favourite idol. " He will not give His honour to another, nor His glory to graven images." " He will not have a rival—He cannot have an equal." All the miracles of Egypt were wrought against idolatry. Each was a blow struck at some favourite idol. In Babylon another blow was struck at fire, in the case of the three Hebrew youths. III. A MAGNET. " I will draw near and see," &c. Since the fall, man has ever been more alive to the gratification of his curiosity than the welfare of his soul. Plain truths, though big with importance to him, he neglects; but mysteries in nature, providence, and revelation, he industriously pries into. IV. A MONITOR. It is true, that now we are not ordered to keep at a distance, but draw near; instead of timidity, there is to be boldness; instead of a burning bush a throne of grace; and instead of a God upon whose face we cannot look, there is an incarnate God upon whose face we can look. Yet this monitor teaches us this most important truth—that we can come to God acceptably, only when we come in His own way; and God's way is through Christ, " with reverence and godly fear." (*T. Macconnell.*) *The burning bush:*—I. THE LEARNED SHEPHERD. 1. Humility. From a palace he stoops to this lowly life. 2. Patience. For forty years he thus laboured. 3. Fidelity. Led his father-in-law's flock. Involved seeking out the best pasturage: folding, and guarding, &c. A good servant in his own house, before God made him a master in Israel. "Faithful in little," &c. II. THE GREAT SIGHT. 1. Where it appeared. In the wilderness. God there also. 2. When it appeared. In the time of Israel's sorrow, and Moses' toil. 3. Wherefore it appeared. (1) Because the day of deliverance was near. (2) To instruct the mind of Moses, and excite his curiosity. (3) To represent the state of the Israelites. A Church in the furnace of affliction. The bush not consumed, though the fire was hot. Israel flourishing in trial. It was not only a " wonder," but a " sign." A great sight, but not merely a something to look at and investigate; but also to learn from. III. THE PRESENT GOD. He dwelt in the bush (Mark xii. 26; Luke xx. 37; Acts vii. 35; Deut. xxxiii. 16). God in the bush showed His relation to His people. 1. With them in trouble. 2. Sustains them in trouble. 3. With them a source of instruction. Learn—1. To cultivate high qualities in lowly callings. 2. Seek our comfort in affliction from an ever-present God. (*J. C. Gray.*) *The burning bush:*—1. As an emblem it instructs. 2. As a miracle it astonishes. 3. As a magnet it attracts. 4. As a monitor it warns. (*J. S. Exell, M.A.*) *A great sight:*—1. Occasioned by a Divine agency. 2. Illumined by a Divine presence. 3. Given for a Divine purpose. (*Ibid.*) *Great sights:*—1. Desired by the world. 2. Sought by the pleasure-seeker. 3. Found only by the Christian. 4. The inspiration of a good life. (*Ibid.*) *The moral preparation and condition necessary for the beholding of heavenly visions:*—1. We must turn aside from the gaiety of the world. 2. From the futility of merely human reasonings. 3. From the commission of moral evil in daily life. 4. From following the instruction of incompetent teachers. 5. They are largely dependent upon our personal willingness of soul—God speaks to all men who reverently turn aside to hear Him. (*Ibid.*) *God calls truth-seekers by name:*—"Moses,"— Nathaniel. 1. To indicate His delight in them. 2. His favour toward them. 3. His hope of them. 4. To prepare them for further revelations. (*Ibid.*) *The name of a good man vocal on the lips of God:*—1. An honour. 2. A destiny. 3. A prophecy. 4. A vocation. (*Ibid.*) *The truth-seeker's response:*—1. His personality. 2. His place. 3. His willingness. We should always respond to the calls of heaven. (*Ibid.*) *The soul's turning aside to see often leads to visions of God:*—1. In His Book. 2. In His works. 3. In His providences. 4. In His Church and sanctuary. (*Ibid.*) *Soul visions:*—1. Obtained by prayer. 2. Refreshing to the soul. 3. Strengthening to manhood. 4. Related to human suffering. (*Ibid.*) *The neighbourhood of Horeb:*—The southern end of the peninsula of Sinai, to which the sacred narrative now takes us, consists of a confused mass of peaks (the highest above 9,000 feet), some of dark green porphyry, but mostly red granite of different hues, which is broken by strips of sand or gravel, intersected by wádies or glens, which are the beds of winter torrents, and dotted here and there with green spots, chiefly due to perennial fountains. The great central group among these mountains is that of Horeb, and one special height in it Sinai, the "mount of God." Strangely enough, it is just here amidst this awful desolateness that the most fertile places in "the wilderness" are also found. Even in our days part of this plateau is quite green. Hither the Bedouin drive their flocks when summer has parched all the lower districts. Fruit-trees grow in rich luxuriance in its valleys, and "the neigh-bourhood is the best watered in the whole peninsula, running streams being found in no less than four of the adjacent valleys." It was thither that Moses, probably in the early summer, drove Reuel's flock for pasturage and water. Behind him, to the east, lay the desert; before him rose in awful grandeur the mountain of God. The stillness of this place is unbroken; its desolateness only relieved by the variety of colouring in the dark green or the red mountain peaks, some of which "shine in the sunlight like burnished copper." The atmosphere is such that the most distant outlines stand out clearly defined, and the faintest sound falls distinctly on the ear. All at once truly a "strange sight" presented itself. On a solitary crag, or in some sequestered valley, one of those spiked, gnarled, thorny acacia trees, which form so conspicuous a feature in the wádies of "the desert," of which indeed they are "the only timber tree of any size," stood enwrapped in fire, and yet "the bush was not consumed." (A. Edersheim, D.D.) The bush and the fire:—In the brier we have a symbol of the people of Israel. From this time till the cursing of the fig-tree, which had no fruit on it but only leaves, the chosen people of God are frequently and variously referred to under the figure of a bush or tree. Here they are repre-sented as a low, contemptible brier, in contradistinction to the tall majestic trees, which proudly rear their heads to the clouds, and are gazed at and admired by the world. Hence the brier was symbolical of Israel, as a people despised by the world. The fire is always used in the Scriptures as a symbol of Divine holiness. And this is the case here; for the record expressly says that the presence of God was made known in the fire. The burning brier, therefore, was a symbol of the community of God, in which the holiness of God had its abode. The brier was burning in the fire, but it was not consumed, although from its nature it deserved to be consumed, and could easily be so. It was a miracle that it was not consumed. And thus was it also a miracle of mercy, that the holiness of God could dwell in a sinful community without consuming it. But in the midst of the thorns of the natural life of the community there was hidden a noble, imperishable germ, namely, the seed of the promise, which Jehovah Himself had prepared. It could not, indeed, be set free without the pain of burning, but by that burning it was made holy and pure. There was also another fact of great importance represented by this symbol, viz., that the fire of Divine holiness, which burned in Israel, without consuming it, served also as an outward defence. Hitherto, every one who passed by might ridicule, injure or trample on the insignificant bush, but henceforth whoever touched it would burn his own fingers. (J. H. Kurtz, D.D.) A beautiful conjunction of the natural and supernatural:—A bush burned into a sanctuary! Though the heavens cannot con-tain the Great One, yet He hides Himself under every flower, and makes the broken heart of man His chosen dwelling-place. So great, yet so condescending; infinite in glory, yet infinite in gentleness. Wherever we are, there are gates through nature into the Divine. Every bush will teach the reverent student something of God. The lilies are teachers, so are the stars, so are all things great and small in this wondrous museum, the universe! In this case it was not the whole mountain that burned with fire; such a spectacle we should have considered worthy of the majesty of God; it was only the bush that burned: so condescendingly does God accommodate Himself to the weakness of man. The whole mountain burning would have dismayed the lonely shepherd; he who might have been overwhelmed by a blazing mountain was attracted by a burning bush. (J. Parker, D.D.) Honest vocations:—Forty years was Moses a courtier, and forty years after that a shepherd. That great men may not be ashamed of honest vocations, the greatest that ever were have been content to take up with mean trades. The contempt of honest calling in those which are well born argues pride without wit. There can be no fitter disposition for a leader of God's people than constancy in his undertakings, without either weariness or change. He that hath true worth in himself and fami-liarity with God finds more pleasure in the deserts of Midian than others can do in the palace of kings. While he is tending his sheep God appears unto him. God never graces the idle with his visions. (Bishop Hall.) Solitude a preparation for service:—Writing of his father, Nathaniel Hawthorne, Julian Hawthorne says: "The knights-errant of old watched their armour previous to embarking on their enterprise; the young Indian chiefs were made to undergo a period of solitude and fasting before being admitted to full standing. Bunyan wrote his book in Bedford jail; and Hawthorne, in Salem, withdrew himself from the face of man, and medi-tated for twelve lonely years upon humanity. He came forth a great original writer. He was destined to do a great work, and to that end were needed, not only his native abilities, but an exceptional initiation, or forty days in the wilderness." (*H. O. Mackey.*) *Usefully employed :—*Satan loves to meet men idle. God delights to honour diligence and fidelity. (*William Jay.*) *Exile profitings :—*James Douglas, son of the banished Earl of Angus, afterwards well known by the title of Earl of Morton, lurked during the exile of his family in the north of Scotland, under the assumed name of James Innes, otherwise James the Grieve (*i.e.*, Reve or Bailiff). "And as he bore the name," says Godscroft, "so did he also execute the office of a grieve or overseer of the lands and rents, the corn and cattle, of him with whom he lived." From the habits of frugality and observation which he acquired in his humble situation, the historian traces that intimate acquaintance with popular character which enabled him to rise so high in the State, and that honourable economy by which he repaired and established the shattered estates of Angus and Morton. (*Sir Walter Scott.*) **Put off thy shoes.**—*Reverence :—*I. THE ESSENCE OF REVERENCE LIES IN OUR FORMING A TRUE ESTIMATE OF OUR PLACE AMONG THE POWERS AROUND US, AND SO UNDERSTANDING ARIGHT AND HABITUALLY FEELING WHAT IS OUR RELATION TO THEM. Now, to do this —1. We must apprehend something of the mystery of life in ourselves and in others. 2. We must recognize the distinction of the different grades of being in those in whom life is, and seek to find and to keep our own due place in that mighty and marvellous scale of existences. II. WE MUST BOW DOWN BEFORE HIM WHO IS THE FOUNTAIN OF ALL LIFE, THE LIFE OF ALL WHO LIVE. This adoration of the soul before Him is the central point of the grace of reverence, and its influence pervades and adjusts all our other relations, both towards Himself and towards the other creatures of His hand. III. It is a question of the deepest moment to us all HOW, IN AN AGE ONE SPECIAL TEMPTATION OF WHICH IS CLEARLY TO LOSE ITS REVERENCE, THE GIFT CAN BE KEPT QUICK AND LIVING IN OURSELVES. 1. The first step must be the keeping guard against whatever tends to irreverence. All that professedly robs life of its mystery does this. So, even more directly, does all that robs revelation of its awfulness. Receiving God's Word as God's Word, striving to do it, striving to overcome temptations to doubt, not by crushing them out, but by turning them into occasions of prayer and of adoration, these efforts, and such as these, will keep us in an irreverent age from the great loss of irreverence. 2. Above all, we must pray for reverence as the gift of God ; for such prayer not only draws down a certain answer, but even by its own action tends to put our spirits in the frame of reverence. (*Bp. S. Wilberforce.*) *Access to God :—*1 Accesses by honest hearts to the place of God's appearing may be rash. 2. Such hasty and unadvised accesses, God forbids unto His servants. 3. Due preparations must be made by creatures in their accesses to God. 4. Places have been and may be relatively holy, for God's appearance in them. 5. So far to use them holily as in reference to God's presence is the duty of all (ver. 5). (*G. Hughes, B.D.*) *The reception of the Christian mysteries :—* Here is an intimation, that clearness of intellect is not that upon which mainly depends the right perception of God's revelation of Himself. Moral fitness, rather than subtilty of intellect, is needed for receiving rightly this revelation of Himself. This, indeed, is but what we might reasonably expect ; for as the Christian revelation, by its own profession, is not a mere intellectual abstraction, but in its nature and foundations is essentially moral, the evidence on which it rests cannot, as in abstract science, be addressed purely to the intellect. To receive it rightly, the will must assent to it no less than the understanding ; a pure and teachable spirit is the main distinction of that temper in which we should approach the mysteries of the Christian revelation. I. From this, then, it follows, first, THAT MAN IS RESPONSIBLE FOR HIS BELIEF ;—responsible, that is, just as he is for any other branch of moral conduct : that it is, indeed, a part of his trial, and a great one, whether he will believe : that, as a right belief is the only source of moral purity, so a wrong belief, where a true revelation is offered to us, is the undoubted fruit of moral evil : and hence, that as in all other parts of his probation, it is out of the power of fallen man by his own might and strength to do that which is right, so especially is it out of his power to believe ; but that, as in all other parts of his probation, so too in this, obedience is within the power of redeemed man, through that blessed help of God's most Holy Spirit which will not be withheld from those who seek for it. II. And this leads us on to the second part of our inquiry ; for to be thoroughly convinced of the certainty of this connection, is one of the first means of maintaining a fit temper for receiving these great mysteries. So long as we in any degree deem of them as of subjects into which we are to obtain a peculiar insight by our own reasonings, WE SHALL FIND IT IMPOSSIBLE TO REPRESS THAT PRIDE OF INTELLECT, WHICH, WHILST IT FLATTERS US WITH APPARENT DISCOVERIES, DOES, IN FACT, MOST EFFECTUALLY SHUT OUT

THE LIGHT OF TRUTH. We must be content to be learners, not discoverers, in the school of faith; receiving a revelation, not reasoning out conclusions : and this temper we cannot maintain, unless we come into God's presence remembering that, so far only as He gives us to know Him can we know aright ; for that we need perfect purity to see Him as He is, and that we are compassed about with infirmity. Then only when the thought of His holiness and of our corruption bows us to the earth, shall we receive His teaching with the simplicity of children; fixing on the ground those eyes which were ready to gaze too rashly at the wonders of His presence, and be ready, indeed, to " put off our shoes from our feet," feeling that " the place whereon we stand is holy ground." To this conviction, moreover, we should join a constant watchfulness, lest allowed sin in any form, lest boldness of spirit, or slothfulness in our use of holy things, impair the reverence of our souls. To these means must be added further as perhaps the greatest instrument of all for preserving the unsullied clearness of a reverend faith, that we be deep and constant students of God's holy Word. We need not fear, with Bishop Andrewes, to speak of " the Word as one of those arteries which convey the Spirit to us." In a two-fold way does the faithful study of the Scripture, by increasing in us the gift of the Holy Ghost, secure our receiving rightly the mysteries of God : first, since it is the especial province of the Spirit to reveal these mysteries, those will the most surely grow in light who grow in grace ; they who the most humbly seek His teaching will be the most surely led on into all truth. There is a " teaching of the Spirit " ; we may, as children, give up ourselves to Him, and humbly trust He will enlighten us. And then, secondly, besides the increase of this direct teaching, we are thus made the fitter recipients of His instruction ; for since, as we saw before, the due reception of these mysteries depends more on moral than on intellectual fitness, they who by a growth in grace are growing in holiness, are indeed taking the surest way to purge the eyes of their understanding, so that they may see without speck or dimness what the Lord has revealed of Himself (Psa. cxix. 99, 100). (*Bp. S. Wilberforce.*) *Reverence in God's presence :—* The impression that God is here, ought ever to have a solemnizing effect upon our minds, and repress everything like carelessness, listlessness, or levity. Had we a proper sense of the Divine majesty resting upon our spirits, would it be possible that we could give way to that profane heedlessness of mind which often steals over us ? Would one short hour's attendance betray us into slumber ? Would a crowd of worldly or sensual thoughts intrude into our minds ? Could the eye find leisure to roam over the assembly, and upon the dress or deportment of others ? Could a scornful or simpering countenance by significant smiles communicate its contemptuous or frivolous emotions to another? Assuredly not. (*G. Bush.*) *Holy ground :* —This admonition may be understood in various ways. I. AS A CHECK TO VAIN CURIOSITY. Let us be satisfied, in religious matters, with what the Holy Spirit has made plain. II. AS AN INCENTIVE TO HUMILITY IN THE PRESENCE OF GOD. We should offer outward tokens of respect and reverence when we come to worship in His holy house. III. AS A PROOF OF THE SANCTITY OF GOD'S PRESENCE. All places set apart for the worship of God are " holy ground," God will be sanctified in all that come near Him. (*Preacher's Analyst.*) *Lessons :*—1. All ground is holy which has been consecrated by valour, virtue, piety, or love. The island of Erromanga, where Williams died ; the banks of Avon and of Doon, where the two greatest bards of England and Scotland were born; the patriot-fields of Marathon, Morgarten, and Bannockburn ; the moors of Drumclog and Airsmoss, where the Covenanters fought and fell ; the peaks of Lochnagar and Ben Cruachan ; the bald and sovereign head of Mont Blanc ; these, and ten thousand such spots as these, are holy ground ; and if men do not, like Moses at the bush, put off their shoes while standing there, yet may they uncover their heads, and feel that in doing reverence to the great of old and to the works of nature, they are doing homage to something which has in it a large portion of the Divine, which is Godlike, although not God. 2. Let us, in a figure, put off our shoes as we draw near, even here, unto God. Let us strip ourselves of the high buskins of pride, of the light sock of indifference and idle mirth, of the luxurious slippers of sensual sin, and of the hard shoes of rude presumption; and let us, with naked and trembling feet, and with covered face, but, at the same time, with all holy boldness and filial love, in the sanctuary and at the Lord's table, the presence of that God who is " a consuming fire." 3. What an overpowering reflection is that, of us all having one day to draw in a very close degree near to the presence of God. Conceive a mortal, although winged being, after long wandering through the universe, caught in a current too mighty for his pinions, and which he feels is hurrying him into the very heart of the burning sun! Conceive his horror as he sees the orb becoming larger and larger, and feels it becoming hotter and hotter; and how in vain he struggles to turn upon his way, and shun that ocean of fire which is to consume him. But on, on, on, he is precipitated, and the imagination shrinks back as she sees the contact and hears the shriek of the extinguished wretch. Thus may a guilty soul after death feel itself approaching its Maker; resisting the attraction, but resisting in vain, drawn ruthlessly within the circle of that eye of fire, and exclaiming as it sinks in terror, "It is a fearful thing to fall into the hands of the living God." But even the saint shudders sometimes at the thought of meeting a Being so tremendous, and would on his death-bed shudder more, did not at one time a merciful stupor deaden his sensibilities, and were it not that at another the thought of God is swallowed up in the image of Christ. (*G. Gilfillan.*) *Holy ground:*—All places are holy, but some are especially so:—1. Because they are hallowed by the supreme residence of God. 2. By happy memories. 3. By holy friendships. 4. By moral conquest. (*J. S. Exell, M.A.*) *The humility and reverence of an accepted worshipper:*—It has been said that God is everywhere present, and therefore should everywhere be honoured alike; it has been said, that the mind and the heart are everything, and that the posture of the body is nothing. In opposition to these refined speculations of modern days, it were sufficient to hold up the authority and command of the Word of God. But we may properly remark, in addition to this, that though the Almighty is everywhere present, He may be present at some times and in some places, in a peculiar manner. Our blessed Lord Himself has declared, "Where two or three are gathered together in My name, there am I in the midst of them." It is again contended, that the mind and the affections may be equally lifted up to God in any posture; sitting or lying down, as well as kneeling: and to a certain extent this remark may be perfectly true. If the mind and affections be equally interested in the two cases; if the devotion be equally pure and the obedience equally sincere, then the acceptance of the service may be equal. But how can the obedience in these two cases be equally complete and sincere, when we know that God has enjoined, in His holy Word, a reverent posture of devotion—a posture, which we find all good men, in all ages, scrupulously observing? A carelessness of posture is an act of positive disobedience. Nor is it easy to believe, that the feelings of devotion are equally pious and sincere. Does not nature herself, when the soul is overwhelmed, teach us to humble and prostrate the body? There may be, in many instances, sufficient reasons for declining this bodily service; there may be infirmity, there may be other reasons; but where there are not, such service would seem to be indispensable to the devout and accepted worshipper. Let me not appear to be countenancing the practices of those, whose religion chiefly consists in outward form: let it not be supposed, that any corporeal homage is of the smallest avail, unless it proceed from an earnest and a pious heart: so far otherwise, that to bow down unmeaningly in the presence of the Lord, is an act of insufferable hypocrisy. Yet we must not, from such abuses as these, draw arguments against a positive duty; we must not conclude, as some are perverse enough to do, that every outward appearance and form are hypocritical. Such a conclusion is not only weak, but wicked. "Keep thy foot when thou goest to the house of God": be jealous of thy ways; be narrowly attentive to thy demeanour; be watchful of the affections and imaginations of thy heart: thou goest for a holy and mighty purpose, see that it be answered; see that thou be accepted in thy deed; see that thou return with a blessing on thy head. (*J. Slade, M.A.*) *Value of reverence:*—All that delicate perception of what is due from man to man upon which the high-bred courtesy of life depends, is closely linked to a reverential spirit. Society, when robbed by irreverence of the shrinking consideration for others which a sense of the mystery of redeemed life within them can alone make real, has already lapsed half-way to barbarism. Man becomes ready to sacrifice man in the chase for wealth, or honour, or pleasure, or power; and class grows to be parted fatally from class, by the selfish enjoyment of those who possess, and the selfish discontent of those who lack what they see others have. Family life, too, suffers the same wrong; its tender kindliness cannot long survive the death of reverence. And all this, observe, reaches far beyond the surface of mere manners. For it affects all those exertions and sacrifices for others which require a high ideal standard to call them out; it leads men to be contented with poor and immediate results measurable by the direct gain or loss of money, pleasure, or power. It dwarfs, too, almost all the actings of the intellect. In such a state of society the highest art can scarcely more exist than verdure without dew, or life without an atmosphere.

Science, too, will soon feel the loss, for no one ever penetrated deeply into nature's secrets unless a deep reverence for that which he explored taught him to be of a humble spirit—made him a true learner, and not a self-conceited theorist—kept him ready to follow out hints, and to lift the veil which God has cast over even His natural works with a hand which almost trembled under a sense of the mightiness of the mysteries it was revealing. But pre-eminently is this true as to the reception of God's revelation of Himself. For here above all is the receptive faculty injured by the lack of reverence. As to this the ancient voice which broke the silence of the mount of Horeb sounds yet in the ear of every man who would turn aside to see the awful sight, " Put off thy shoes from off thy feet, for the place whereon thou standest is holy ground." The humility, the patience, the docility, without which there can be no clear intuition into the mystery of God's nature and ways, cannot survive in the irreverent heart. The scorner is, in God's Word, but another word for the atheist. (*Bp. S. Wilberforce.*) *The earth holy ground:*—1. The whole earth is holy ground, because here God's perfections are everywhere so conspicuously displayed. Wherever I go or stay, I will think that Jesus has lived upon the earth, and that nowhere, in thought or in deed, can I sin where it is not holy ground. Besides, in the lives of every single one of us have there been holy experiences, and we have single spots on the earth's surface, which make for us the whole earth holy. Either that place is most holy to us where we first saw the light, or where our ancestors dwell or have dwelt, or where the years of our childhood glided joyously by; can we see it again, visit it, without tears in our eyes and thanks in our hearts; without looking up to heaven? Is not that place holy to us, where the most important earthly relations were formed; where we found a partner for life in marriage? Is not that place holy to us, where we experienced some good fortune we had longed for, sent to us by the Giver of all good ; deliverance from danger, the safe return of relatives and friends? Alone wandered Jacob through a wild pathless waste. In weariness and grief he closed his eyes. But how completely was he comforted by the vision of that ladder let down from heaven, and of his Lord speaking to him in accents of blessing! Holy to him was that place! And should not that place be holy to us where the Lord, faithful, earnest, ay, severe, appeared to us in the purifying flame of affliction? These places we think of, as though the events connected with them happened of themselves. Shall we not remember that God is over all, and that He is near in joy and sorrow; in danger, which He allows, but out of which He delivers us? If we do this, earth will more and more become to us holy ground, the very gate of heaven ; and more and more holy will be our lives from the constant feeling of God's nearness and presence. 2. The earth is holy ground, because God is worshipped upon it. As God revealed Himself to man from the beginning, there never has been a period when some of His creatures, however small the number, have not known and worshipped Him aright. The patriarchs builded altars to Him and called on His holy name. Few and small, at first, were these streams of the knowledge and the worship of God. Behold, how mightily He has extended them ! And the time will come, He confidently awaits it, when the knowledge of the Lord will fill the earth, as the waters fill the sea. Perfect in heaven stands the Kingdom of God, to which our race after a long pilgrimage will attain. But because of our high destination holy is the earth on which we have journeyed thither. And is not our fatherland holy ground? Yes, so we proclaim it : and that without comparing it with any other land. Yes, ye children, holy is your home, because of the edifying life of your parents. Yes, ye residents of this city, there is within the enclosure of your own walls, outside of the churches where God is worshipped, many a spot, upon which He approvingly smiles. Look, then, at this : this earth on which you dwell and walk, is a holy place. It is so because of the worship of God; because of the faith and piety which have been displayed upon it. Recognize this fact, and let it inspire you with fervent enthusiasm, or with wholesome reverence; this earth can be made holy or profane by yourselves. 3. The earth is holy ground, because of what daily transpires upon it, and because of what will yet transpire upon it, intimately linking it to the world of spirits. What is more frequent than birth and death? Not less holy than birth is death itself. (*J. E Rankin.*) *From curiosity to reverence:*—Many a man has been led through the gate of curiosity into the sanctuary of reverence. Moses purposed but to see a wonderful sight in nature, little dreaming that he was standing as it were face to face with God. Blessed are they who have an eye for the startling, the sublime, and the beautiful in nature, for they shall see many sights which will fill them with glad amazement. Every sight of God is a " great sight "; the sights become little to us because we view them without feeling or holy expectation. It was when the Lord saw that Moses turned aside to see that He called unto him and mentioned him by name. This is indeed a great law. If men would turn aside to see, God would surely speak to them. But we do not do this. We pass by all the great sights of nature with comparative indifference, certainly, as a general rule, without reverence. The sea wants to speak to us, but we listen not to its sounding voice; the stars are calling to us, but we shut them out; the seasons come round to tell their tale, but we are pre-occupied with trifling engagements. We must bring so much with us if we would put ourselves into healthful communion with nature: we must bring the seeing eye, the hearing ear, and the understanding heart: we must, at all events, be disposed to see and hear, and God will honour the disposition with more than expected blessing. (*J. Parker, D.D.*) *Religious awe:*—Curiosity must not become familiarity. The difference between the creature and the Creator must always be infinite. Is not *all* ground holy? Is not God everywhere? Certainly so; yet it hath pleased God to mark special lines and special places as peculiarly holy. We are not to treat all places alike. Every successful appeal to man's reverence redeems him from vulgarity. When a man loses his sense of religious awe, he has exhausted the supreme fountain of spiritual joy. He then measures everything by himself: he is to himself as God, and from the point of self-idolatry he will speedily sink to the point of self-despair. It is only the good man who can be satisfied from himself, and this is only because goodness has its very root in God. (*Ibid.*) *Cultivate reverence:*—Cultivate the spirit of reverence. For ours is an age of iconoclasm, overthrowing ancestral traditions, dethroning venerable beliefs, making the sacred common, dissolving the sacramental in the physical equation of correspondence with environment; in brief, shattering the very instinct of homage. And this is peril indeed! For, as Emerson says, " No greater calamity can befall a nation than its loss of worship." Bad as heathenism is, irreligion is worse. Better superstition than atheism. Young man, believe me; no man is ever so great as when he kneels. Be it yours to have the same lowly reverence which so beautifully marked such illustrious scientists as a Galen, who regarded his professional life as " a religious hymn in honour of the Creator"; a Copernicus, on whose tombstone, in St. John's of Frauenburg, is the following epitaph: " Not the grace bestowed on Paul do I ask, not the favour shown to Peter do I crave; but that which Thou didst grant the robber on the cross do I implore"; a Kepler, who concludes his treatise entitled " Harmony of the Worlds" thus: " I thank Thee, my Creator and Lord, that Thou hast given me this joy in Thy creation, this delight in the works of Thy hands; I have shown the excellency of Thy works unto men, so far as my finite mind was able to comprehend Thy infinity; if I have said aught unworthy of Thee, or aught in which I have sought my own glory, graciously forgive it "; a Newton, who never mentioned the name of Deity without uncovering his head. (*G. D. Boardman.*) *Reverence:*—When a boy in Princeton College, it was my inestimable privilege to be the pupil-assistant of Professor Joseph Henry, the illustrious Christian scientist, in his original experiments. When for the first time electric signals were sent from point to point, the earth itself being used for the return current, Professor Henry put me at one end of the circuit, while he stood directing the experiments at the other. I can well remember the wonderful care with which he arranged all his principal experiments; when he approached the solution the experiment was repeated and repeated over and over again, and all its variable conditions altered and recombined in every form. Then often, when the testing moment came, that eminent scientist would raise his hand in adoring reverence, and call upon me to uncover my head and worship in silence, " Because," he said, " God is here. I am about to ask God a question." (*A. Hodge.*) *Lowering the standard of reverence:*—It is very easy to lower our standard of reverence for anything. We have only to speak of it habitually in a light way. There is nothing like it to take the life out of the most precious texts of Scripture. We may repent of such a sin with bitter weeping, but those words can never be to us again what they were before. We may have cut down a bridge we shall some day vainly long to cross. A gentleman of keen wit used often to point his remarks with some apt quotation from the Bible. A friend who greatly admired him was present in his last hours, and asked with deep sympathy what was the future outlook. " Very gloomy, indeed," was his response. Surprised and deeply pained, he hastened to quote some precious promises suited to the solemn hour. " I have spoiled them all for myself," was his answer. " There is not one but is associated with some jest." His light went out in darkness, though his name was on the church roll. What a lesson is here for all who are willing to be taught by it!

Lay it to heart. (*Christian Age.*)   *Unclogged feet :*—Put off thy shoes of sensuality, and other sins. Affections are the feet of the soul; keep them unclogged. (*J. Trapp.*)

Ver. 6. **I am the God of thy father.**—*The ancestral God our God:*—This declaration was made in order to assure Moses that even in the present oppressed state of his nation in Egypt, the Most High had not forgotten them, or His relation to them as a God in covenant. This would be an unspeakable consolation to Moses, to find himself addressed by that God of whose appearances and promises to his fathers he had often heard, and to know that His heart was as kindly affected to him as it ever had been to his venerated ancestors. How comforting beyond measure to the Christian, in his more favoured moments, to be assured that the God of all the good who have ever lived is *his* God, and equally pledged by His covenant faithfulness, to show to him the same loving-kindness that He showed to them! (*G. Bush.*)   *The Divine revelation:*—The Divine Being here reveals Himself as— 1. The God of individual men. 2. The God of families. 3. The God of the immortal good. (*J. S. Exell, M.A.*)   *The God of Abraham, Isaac, and Jacob :*— He is thus the God of generations, the God of individuals, and the God of the whole human family. There is something inexpressibly beautiful in the idea that God is the God of the father, and of the son, and of all their descendants; thus the one God makes humanity into one family. (*J. Parker, D.D.*)

Ver. 7. **I have surely seen the affliction of My people.**—*God's people—the Jews: their history, and their affliction :*—Quite apart from its religious significance, there is no other historical phenomenon that is to be compared for a moment in interest with this ever-growing wonder of the Jewish race. The light falls clearly and steadily on its history from first to last. The whole connected story lies before us like a mighty river, which from some high mountain summit you can trace from its fountain to the ocean. I. THE HISTORY OF THIS PEOPLE IS THUS THE HISTORY OF MANKIND IN ITS CENTRAL SEATS OF POWER. It brings with it living reminiscences of the remotest past. In order to understand how strange a phenomenon is this indomitable vitality of the race—a race without a home or a country—compare their history with that of the numberless tribes of other races who have been either migratory or settled. Excepting the Arabs, also Abraham's descendants, all the other settled contemporary races around Palestine have either died out completely, as the ancient people of Tyre, Edom, Assyria, Babylon, Egypt; or, if migratory, they have been lost and absorbed after a few centuries. The bond that has held the Jews apart from other nations, and yet together, has been their common religion, their common historical glory. When all Eastern Asia held evil to be incurable, and eternal, and Divine, the race of Abraham held that evil was "but for a moment," and that God's goodness and justice alone were eternal; and it is they who have taught this lesson to the nations of the modern world. II. Notice, next, THE TRAGIC SIDE OF THIS WONDERFUL NATIONAL HISTORY. The honour of being the intellectual and spiritual leaders of the world for four thousand years has been paid for by four thousand years of national martyrdom and humiliation. The terrific penalties announced at the beginning for failure in their national vocation amidst the great nations of the ancient world, have been exacted to the letter. The so-called Christian nations have made their lives for nearly fifteen hundred years one prolonged Egyptian bondage. New Testament Christianity has at last taught us English, at least, to love the nation to whom we owe such priceless blessings. We believe that the time is hastening on when Christ will return to avenge the quarrel of Israel, and to end "the times of the Gentiles" by the restoration of the scattered nation to its old central position in a renovated world. (*E. White.*)   *Of Israel's salvation:*—I. GOD IS BEFOREHAND WITH HIS SALVATION. It is not so much that God has prepared salvation for us, as that He has prepared us for salvation. Salvation was laid up in Christ before sin entered into the world. So that when sin did enter in—and there was need—God brought it forth. There is great comfort and assurance in this truth. II. GOD DOES NOT ALWAYS ANSWER OUR PRAYERS IMMEDIATELY, OR FROM THE SPOT WHERE OUR PRAYERS ARE MADE. Let us pour out our prayers, and leave them with God. If they fall within His gracious covenant of salvation, they will receive the answer in due time, and as quickly as it is possible for us to receive and bear it. III. GOD'S MESSAGE TO MOSES. 1. There is compassion and mercy with the Lord. Salvation proceeds from His love and grace. 2. Notice that He says—"I am come down to deliver them." (1) He has not sent another, but has come Himself.

In Christ. (2) God has not left it for us to reach up to Him, but has in mercy bowed the heavens, and come down to us. We frequently hear people talking about getting up to God. Not long ago, a lady told me that she was "trying to get through nature up to nature's God." This may do for sentiment; but it is not a possible way to reach God. It is true that the "invisible things of Him, . . . even His eternal power and Godhead," are seen by the things that are; but this is not to get to God. To know that there is a God in the universe who is eternally powerful —is not to know Him as a Saviour. It does not help me out of the bondage of sin, or into peace and joy, to know that God is almighty. I must know that He is gracious, and that He receiveth sinners, before I can be at peace. Nay, in fact, I cannot get to Him; He must come to me. 3. God told Moses that He was going to do three things for Israel. (1) To deliver them. (2) To bring them up. (3) To give them a better land. (*G. F. Pentecost, D.D.*) *A picture of human sorrow :*— I. GOD KNOWS THE SORROWS TO WHICH HIS PEOPLE ARE EXPOSED. 1. Because of the relationship He sustains to them. "My people." (1) It indicates ownership. (2) Endearment. (3) Astonishment. The choicest of God's saints in circumstances of great trial. A problem the next world will better solve. 2. Because His omniscient eye is upon them. He sees their trials. 3. Because they are in the habit of making known their sorrows to Him by prayer. II. THAT AT THE PROPER TIME GOD WILL DELIVER HIS PEOPLE FROM SORROW (ver. 8). 1. Sometimes after it has been long continued. 2. Sometimes when least expected. 3. Sometimes by agencies once despised. III. GOD USES HUMAN INSTRUMENTALITIES IN THE DELIVERANCE OF HIS PEOPLE FROM SORROWS. 1. Prepared by life's discipline. 2. Encouraged by heaven's vision. 3. Called by God's voice. (*J. S. Exell, M.A.*) "*My people* " :—1. Therefore we must love Him. 2. Therefore we must serve Him. 3. Therefore we must aid His Church. (*Ibid.*) *God's cognizance of His people's afflictions :*—How interesting is this fact, that God takes cognizance of the afflictions of His people; of one as of many; of great and small! One sometimes is puzzled to determine whether God appears greatest when He rides on the whirlwind and directs the storm, speaks in the thunder, and manifests His glory in the lightning, or when he descends to minister every pulse to the minutest microscopic insect, or to notice the pains, the sorrows, and the sufferings of the humblest and the lowliest of the human family. I have no doubt that God's greatness is more magnificently revealed by the microscope, than it is by the telescope; in creation and in providence in little things, than in great things; and that He appears arrayed in a richer glory when His fatherly hand lays its healing touch upon a broken heart, than when that hand launches the thunderbolt, or gives their commissions to the angels of the sky. God's people could not suffer in the brick-yards of Egypt, without drawing down the sympathies, as they shared in the cognizance, of the Lord God of Abraham. (*J. Cumming, D.D.*) *Three things to be remembered :*—1. God had seen the affliction of the Israelites. Alas! it seemed to them as though they were not seen by any one. God sees all. "The eyes of the Lord are in every place." 2. He had heard their cry. The Israelites had begun to entreat for mercy; and, notwithstanding their ignorance, wickedness, and idolatry, the Lord was pleased to hear them. 3. He knew their sorrows; not only He saw and heard, but He knew all, much better than men did, and He pitied their misery. Yes, God sees the affliction and hears the cry of His creatures who are suffering. Do not forget this when you are in sorrow. (*Prof. Gaussen.*) "*I know their sorrows* " :—It is wonderful what a provision is made by Deity for human "sorrow." The First Blessed Person in the Trinity is as a Father. A loving Father; a Father, too, most when He chastens most. And the Second is co-equal. A Brother. "A Man of sorrows," who is "acquainted with our griefs." And the Third, co-equal still, is a Comforter. "Father "—"Brother "—"Comforter." What eloquence does it give to the Voice of the wilderness, "I know their sorrows." We should lay great stress on the "I." It is a conclusive I. No one can say that "I" as He says it,—not father, or mother, or dearest friend. It is "I "—alone in the universe—"know your sorrows." I who made the "sorrows"; I who made you; I who can balance the burden and the strength; I to whom all ears are open and all secrets disclosed. But there are sorrows *and* sorrows. There are selfish "sorrows," which cannot bear to be seen in happiness, and rather like to make others sad. There are "sorrows" of sheer formality, which come and go with the seasons. There are "sorrows" of mere vexations and mortified pride, which come for any little thing. There are morbid "sorrows," which mope about in solitude. There are defiant "sorrows," which put away all sympathy, and refuse to be comforted.

There are idle " sorrows," which lead to no action ; barren because there is no root. And there are sorrows " which have an actual sin, and sin lives in that " sorrow." And there are " sorrows " which call themselves contrite, but have no penitence ; they are merely nature's fears. And there are hardened " sorrows," putting away God, grieving the Holy Ghost, and working death ! And God " knows " these sorrows, and His eye detects them in a moment—all their hollowness and all their hypocrisy. (*J. Vaughan, M.A.*) *God's knowledge of His people's sorrows :*— Our nature yearns for sympathy. I. How CHEERING IS THE ANNOUNCEMENT OF THE TEXT. 1. It is not a mere man who says this, but God—the Creator, the Lord of life and death, the Redeemer, the Comforter. 2. When we remember that the Speaker is the Omnipresent and Omniscient God, we remember also that His knowledge is something more than man's mere knowledge of the fact. He sees the beginning and the end of an event at once ; He knows all about our sorrows—whence they came, how, when, why. 3. It greatly raises our thoughts of God's condescension if we consider who these people were, and what their sorrows. (1) They were God's people ; but in men's eyes they were but a poor band of slaves, toiling day and night under hard taskmasters. (2) Their sorrows were those which poverty and hard labour bring. 4. As God knew His people's sorrows then, so He knows ours now, however infinitely various they may be—however great, however small— whether of body, mind, or soul. The Lord Jesus knows by experience, toil, fatigue, pain, weeping, anxiety, desolation. II. LESSONS OF COMFORT. 1. If our Lord knows our sorrows thus intimately, we may go and lay the whole before Him, assured of sympathy (Matt. xiv. 12). 2. If our Lord knows our sorrows, we may be sure that these sorrows are well ordered. 3. If our Lord knows our sorrows, we may be sure that He will help us in due time, and that although He seem to tarry long, He only tarries for our good. III. LESSONS OF INSTRUCTION. 1. If God, who is love and power, knows our sorrows and permits them, though He does not willingly afflict, He must mean something by them ; there is a voice in them which we should listen to. Let us ask, what does my heavenly Father mean by this affliction ? What sins most beset me ? What graces are most lacking in me ? 2. By afflicting us, our Father means not only to correct our shortcomings, but to purify our faith. 3. God tries our patience by sorrow, for the example of others. How does the sight of a Christian sufferer cheer and strengthen his fellow-travellers on the Christian course ! Let us take care that, in our time of suffering, we glorify God by our—(1) Calmness, (2) Confidence, (3) Patience, (4) Thankfulness. 4. Not only may our suffering affliction be a blessing to others as an example, but as calling forth their sympathy and love. (*S. P. C. K. Sermons.*) *The Divine care and presence :*—I. INFINITE SYMPATHY. Often adversity leads us into a spirit of carelessness and unbelief. In our impatience we cannot wait for the Lord. The history of Israel says—"Leave all to God ; He will order and provide." II. SEASONABLE INTERVENTION. Often God waits to teach us our own helplessness before interposing; but " the salvation of the righteous is of the Lord." " When the fulness of time was come," &c. III. ABUNDANT BENEFACTION. Christ is a greater Moses, through whom we are not only delivered from the punishment of sin, but sanctified also as " a peculiar people," and made " meet for the inheritance," &c. Our conversion is merely the turning-point. Heaven is the goal, and God is with us all the way. (*J. C. McLachlan, M.A.*) *" I know their sorrows ":*—I. THE PERSON. 1. He can help. Fulness of resource. 2. He will help. Whole scheme of salvation based on this. 3. He delights to help. Sympathy, the natural outcome of God's heart. II. THE KNOWLEDGE. 1. It is certain. He cannot be deceived, or mistaken. What a consolation for afflicted ! 2. It is unlimited. God knows *all* sorrows. 3. It is compassionate. Touched with feeling of our infirmity. III. THE SORROW. 1. It may be long continued. Delay disciplines. 2. It may be deeply oppressive. 3. It may be widely experienced. "I know their sorrows." (1) Therefore do not complain. (2) Therefore wait His time for deliverance. (3) Therefore seek His grace. (*J. S. Exell, M.A.*) *God can always hear :*—A poor old deaf man resided in Fife. He was visited by his minister shortly after coming to his pulpit. The minister said he would often call and see him ; but time went on, and he did not visit him again until two years after, when, happening to go through the street where the deaf man was living, he saw his wife at the door, and could therefore do no other than inquire for her husband. " Weel, Margaret, how is Tammas ? " " None the better o' you," was the rather curt reply. " How ! how ! Margaret ? " inquired the minister. " Oh, ye promised twa year syne to ca' and pray once a fortnight wi' him, an' ye hae ne'er darkened the door sin' syne." " Weel, weel, Margaret, don't be so short; I thought it was not so necessary to call and pray with Tammas, for he is sae deaf ye ken he canna hear me." "But, sir," said the woman, with a rising dignity of manner, "the Lord's no deaf!" And it is to be supposed the minister felt the power of her reproof.

Ver. 8. **I am come down to deliver them.**—*The world's sorrow and Christ's redemption :*—1. Christ came down from heaven. 2. Christ came at the call of the world's sorrow. 3. Christ came to achieve the world's moral freedom. 4. Christ came to destroy the kingship of sin.. 5. Christ came to lead men into happiness. 6. Christ came to awaken holy agencies for the spiritual welfare of the race. (*J. S. Exell, M.A.*) *Jehovah resents the oppression of the Church :*—1. Surely. 2. Speedily. 3. Continually. 4. Retributively. (*Ibid.*)   "*I am come down*" :—God is said to descend. 1. In accommodation to a human form of speech. 2. To show judgment on the wicked (Gen. xviii). 3. Perhaps to indicate the situation of Egypt, which was a low country. 4. To indicate some notable event about to follow. Babel. (*Ibid.*)   "*To bring them up out of that land*":—1. Of bad rulership. 2. Of wicked companionship. 3. Of hostile religious influences. 4. Of servile bondage. 5. There are many countries in the world where it is dangerous for God's people to reside. (*Ibid.*)   "*Unto a good land, and a large*":—1. Canaan was large compared with Goshen. 2. God exchanges the situations of His people for their good. 3. God does not intend His people to remain long the slaves of any earthly power. 4. The spiritual Israel will in eternity enter into the fulness of these words. (*Ibid.*) "*The Canaanites and the Hittites*":—A disinherited people :—1. Disinherited by God, as the Supreme Disposer of all territory. 2. As under a special curse. 3. As guilty of unrepented sin. 4. A warning for nations to-day. (*Ibid.*)   *The Divine resolution :*—Here the absolute, free, unconditional grace of the God of Abraham, and the God of Abraham's seed, shines forth in all its native brightness, unhindered by the "ifs" and "buts," the vows, resolutions, and conditions of man's legal spirit. God had come down to display Himself, in sovereign grace, to do the whole work of salvation, to accomplish His promise made to Abraham, and repeated to Isaac and Jacob. He had not come down to see if, indeed, the subjects of His promise were in such a condition as to merit His salvation. It was sufficient for Him that they needed it. He was not attracted by their excellencies or their virtues. It was not on the ground of aught that was good in them, either seen or foreseen, that He was about to visit them, for He knew what was in them. In one word, we have the true ground of His gracious acting set before us in the words, " I am the God of Abraham," and "I have seen the affliction of My people." These words reveal a great fundamental principle in the ways of God. It is on the ground of what He is, that He ever acts. " I AM," secures all for " My people." Assuredly He was not going to leave His people amid the brick-kilns of Egypt, and under the lash of Pharaoh's taskmasters. They were His people, and He would act toward them in a manner worthy of Himself. Nothing should hinder the public display of His relationship with those for whom His eternal purpose had secured the land of Canaan. He had come down to deliver them ; and the combined power of earth and hell could not hold them in captivity one hour beyond His appointed time. He might and did use Egypt as a school, and Pharaoh as a schoolmaster ; but when the needed work was accomplished, both the school and the schoolmaster were set aside, and His people were brought forth with a high hand and an outstretched arm. (*C. H. Mackintosh.*)

Ver. 10. **I will send thee unto Pharaoh.**—*The calling of a great deliverer :*—I. His call was rendered necessary by intense national suffering (ver. 7). 1. The sufferings to which the Israelites were exposed. (1) Politically they were prisoners. (2) Socially they were bondmen. (3) Commercially they were ruined. (4) Religiously they were degenerate. 2. The Divine attention to the sufferings of the Israelites. God has deep sympathy with the sorrowful. (1) God sees the pain of the oppressed. (2) God hears the cry of the oppressed. (3) God relieves the pain of the oppressed. II. He was called to his mission by the immediate agency of God (ver. 10). 1. His free agency was consulted. Such a call is—(1) Honourable. (2) Responsible. 2. His adaptability was considered. Social considerations are subordinate. A shepherd may be called to accomplish the freedom of Israel. Hence the Divine call to human souls is—(1) Emphatic. (2) Judicious. (3) Hopeful. III. He was definitely made acquainted with the mission he had to undertake (ver. 10). 1. He was to pay a visit to royalty. 2. He was to achieve the freedom of Israel. God forewarns him of the difficulties, that they may not surprise or overwhelm. This arrangement is—(1) Merciful. (2) Considerate. (3) Accommodated to our weakness. IV. IN THE PERFORMANCE OF HIS MISSION HE WAS ANIMATED BY THE HIGHEST HOPES (ver. 8). 1. He anticipated the freedom of Israel. 2. He anticipated conquest in the event of war. 3. He anticipated residence in a land of beauty and fertility. God always animates those engaged in great service by great hopes. Lessons: 1. That God knows how to prepare men to become the deliverers of the good. 2. That a Divine call is requisite for the mission of life. 3. That human sorrow is pathetic and powerful in its appeal to God. (*J. S. Exell, M.A.*) *The mission of Moses; or, the qualification for a Divine work :*—I. GOD ELEVATES THE RACE BY THE INSTRUMENTALITY OF INDIVIDUAL MEN. 1. It serves to promote in man the principle of self-helpfulness. 2. It serves to promote social unity. II. GOD SPECIALLY QUALIFIES THE MAN HE EMPLOYS TO ELEVATE THE RACE. 1. By a special manifestation of Himself. 2. By impressing him with the divinity of his mission. 3. By assuring him of His co-operation. 4. By making him sensible of his own insufficiency. 5. By providing him with a coadjutor to supplement his deficiencies. (*Homilist.*) *The call of Moses :*—I. THE MANNER OF THE CALL. 1. Remarkable for its suddenness. 2. Remarkable for its mysteriousness. 3. Remarkable for its manifestation of God. (1) His holiness. (2) His faithfulness. II. THE REASON OF THE CALL. 1. The severity of the affliction of God's people. 2. The cry of God's people, which had come up into the ears of God. III. THE PURPOSE OF THE CALL. 1. The deliverance of His people from the task-master. 2. The fulfilment of the Divine covenant with Abraham, Isaac, and Jacob. IV. THE ENCOURAGEMENT TO OBEY THE CALL. The personal presence of God. V. THE NAME OF HIM WHO ISSUED THE CALL. 1. The revelation of this name was called out by a significant question of Moses. 2. The significance of the name. (1) It represents the personality, eternity, and supremacy of God. (2) It represents an authority and sovereignty that even Pharaoh cannot gainsay. Lessons: 1. We learn God's deep and practical interest in His people. 2. We learn that God is a hearer and an answerer of prayer. 3. We learn God's wisdom in calling His servants. 4. We learn the all-sufficiency of the Divine encouragement to every worker. (*D. C. Hughes, M.A.*) *God's choice of instruments :*—God chooses the humblest instruments. He passes by the tempest, and waters the fields and gardens with His imperceptible dew. He passes by the great elephant, and bestows the hues of sapphire and amethyst upon the tiny humming-bird. He passes by the lofty pines and huge elm tree, and lavishes blossom and perfume on the violet. All history teaches the same truth. Moses was the son of a poor Levite; Gideon was a thresher; David was a shepherd boy; Amos was a herdsman; the apostles were obscure and unlearned; Zwingle was a shepherd; Melancthon, the great theologian of the Reformation, was an armourer; Luther was the child of a poor miner; Fuller was a farm servant; Carey, the originator of the plan of translating the Bible into the language of the millions of Hindustan, was a shoemaker; Morrison, who translated the Bible into the Chinese language, was a last-maker; Dr. Milne was a herd-boy; Adam Clarke was the son of Irish cotters; John Foster was a weaver; Jay, of Bath, was a herdsman. (*Christian Age.*) *The call of Moses :*— I. THE PREPARATIONS FOR THE CALL. His miraculous escape in infancy; his careful training in the court of Pharaoh; his knowledge of governments, men, armies, religious rites; his silent years of obscurity, watching the leisure of the seasons as they came and went, the slow movements of the stars; the care of God for the helpless creatures over which he was a shepherd; the home-life—all these were a part of the call. His soul ripened. II. THE CALL ITSELF. A greater one was never issued to mortal man. The only greater one was assigned to that Prophet like unto Moses who, in the fulness of time, came to lead the world out of a worse than Egyptian bondage through the death of the cross. III. THE HESITATION OF MOSES AT THE GREAT SUMMONS. He was perfectly honest before God. And it is because he was so honest that we can understand him and get our lessons from him at this turning-point in his career. We would not lose the picture of this great man—this chosen vessel of God—hesitating, confessing his cowardly feelings, and trying to hide away from duty. The response from Jehovah was as sudden as the command, and it was a complete satisfaction for all the real and imaginary troubles in the situation : "Certainly I will be with thee." IV. Lastly, if we seek further PRACTICAL LESSONS from this part of sacred history, we shall be led to ask why the Bible makes so much of the calls its chief characters received to their office. Was it merely to prove the genuineness of their commission ? They proved that by their works done in the name of God. Was it to show the power of Him who can call out children to Abraham from the stones and cause things that are not to be as those that are? Not this alone, but rather to make us feel that we may be receiving calls to His service, though we disregard them, and that, if we live near Him, life may at any time take on a new form and character. (*E. N. Packard.*)   *The deliverer and his commission:*—The personal history of the deliverer and his commission, viewed in reference to the higher dispensation of the Gospel, exhibits the following principles, on which it will be unnecessary to offer any lengthened illustration.   1. The time for the deliverer appearing and entering on the mighty work given him to do, as it should be the one fittest for the purpose, so it must be the one chosen and fixed by God.   It might seem long in coming to many, whose hearts groaned beneath the yoke of the adversary; and they might sometimes have been disposed, if they had been able, to hasten forward its arrival.   But the Lord knew best when it should take place, and with unerring precision determined it beforehand.   Hence we read of Christ's appearance having occurred "in due time," or "in the fulness of time."   2. The Deliverer, when He comes, must arise within the Church itself.   With her is the covenant of God; and she alone is the mother of the victorious seed, that destroys the destroyer.   3. Yet the deliverance, even in its earlier stages, when existing only in the personal history of the deliverer, is not altogether independent of the world.   The blessing of Israel was interwoven with acts of kindness derived from the heathen; and the child Moses, with whom their very existence as a nation and all its coming glory was bound up, owed his preservation to a member of Pharaoh's house, and in that house found a fit asylum and nursing-place.   Thus the earth "helped the woman," as it has often done since.   In the history even of the Author and Finisher of our faith, the history of redemption links itself closely to the history of the world.   4. Still the deliverer, as to his person, his preparation, his gifts and calling, is peculiarly of God.   That such a person as Moses was provided for the Church in the hour of her extremity, was entirely the result of God's covenant with Abraham; and the whole circumstances connected with his preparation for the work, as well as the commission given him to undertake it, and the supernatural endowments fitting him for its execution, manifestly bespoke the special and gracious interposition of heaven.   But the same holds true in each particular, and is still more illustriously displayed in Christ. (*P. Fairbairn, D.D.*)   *Preparation for the ministry:*—I. A HUMAN MINISTRY FOR A DIVINE SALVATION.   The mother in the nursery, or at the bedside of her children; the father, by his godly life, as well as by direct instruction; the merchant among his clerks and salesmen; the employer among his employés; the mistress among her servants: all these have opportunities for the exercise of the ministry of grace.   Other means besides the public ministry, or the direct dealing of the Christian worker, are used of God to bring His people up out of the land of bondage into His kingdom of life and light.   A thousand silent and cumulative influences may be amongst the agencies that end in the conversion of every soul.   II. THIS MINISTRY IS NOT SELF-APPOINTED.   "I will send thee."   In all our service we should bear in mind that we are to go in God's name, by His appointment to do His work and not our own: otherwise the work will be a miserable failure, and the name of God will be blasphemed.   III. THE NATURE OF THE COMMISSION.   "I will *send.*"   The Lord calls all His people to go forth into this world with a testimony and witness from Him.   What the Lord needs now, as at the beginning, is that His disciples should go everywhere preaching Jesus and the Resurrection.   When the Spirit works freely in believers, then are many more disciples made.   IV. MOSES WAS TO GO DOWN TO WHERE THE PEOPLE WERE.   Now, mark that when God bade Moses to go down He did not tell him to build a pulpit on the border of Egypt, and cry, "Come!"   I heard of a minister who was asked to go and see a man who was anxious about his soul.   He replied, "He knows where I live.   If he wants my help or counsel, let him come to me.   If he is in earnest, he will."   I should have said to him, "If you are in earnest about your Master's work, and know the meaning of the commission under which you hold your office, you will go to him."   Do not forget that our commission is to "go." (*G. F. Pentecost, D.D.*)   *The Divine call to service:*—1. It is persuasive—"come."   2. It is immediate—"now."   3. It is logical—"therefore." (*J. S. Exell, M.A.*)   "*I will send thee unto Pharaoh*":—1. A vocation.   2. A preparation.   3. A commission. (*Ibid.*)   *A God-given task:*—1. Arduous in its requirement.   2. Responsible in its exercise.   3. Glorious in its issue.   4. Unique in its character. (*Ibid.*)   Notes:—1. God's call—is instant, and suffers no delay.   2. Though God needs no man, He calls some for the help of His people.   3. Such as God calls, He sends to bring about deliverance. 4. The mission of God may be of the poorest man to the greatest potentate. 5. God's command is enough to empower the weakest man for the strongest work. (*Ibid.*) *The principle of mediation in God's dealings with men :*— In the eighth verse God says, "I am come down to deliver them out of the hand of the Egyptians"; and in the tenth verse He says, "I will send thee unto Pharaoh." Is there not a discrepancy here ? If God Himself came down to do a work, why did He not go and do it personally ? One word from Himself would surely have done more for the cause which He had espoused than all the words which the most gifted of His creatures could have used. Looking at this incident as standing alone, it does undoubtedly appear most remarkable that God did not personally execute what He had personally conceived. The thinking was His, so was the love ; all the spiritual side of the case belonged exclusively to God ; yet He calls a shepherd, a lonely and unfriended man, to work out—with painful elaboration, and through a long series of bewildering disappointments—the purpose which it seems He Himself might have accomplished with a word. We find, however, that the instance is by no means an isolated one. Throughout the whole scheme of the Divine government of the human family, we find the principle of mediation. God speaks to man through man. Undoubtedly, this is mysterious. To our imperfect understanding, it would seem that the direct personal revelation of His presence and glory would instantly secure the results which are so desirable, and yet so doubtful. It is here that faith must lead us. Moreover, this principle of individual selection in the matter of all great ministries, is in keeping with the principle which embodies in a single germ the greatest forests. It is enough that God gives the one acorn, man must plant it and develop its productiveness. God works from the one to the many. (*J. Parker, D.D.*) **That thou mayest bring forth My people.**—*The typical character of Moses considered, as the deliverer, mediator, lawgiver, and guide of Israel :*—I. MOSES TYPICAL OF CHRIST AS A DELIVERER. 1. When we were dead in sin, God prepared a Deliverer. 2. Only one Deliverer for the whole race. 3. A Man, like unto His brethren. 4. Moses, like Christ, made no common sacrifice to fulfil the duty with which God had charged him: II. In no point of view is the character of Moses more venerable, or himself more illustrious as a type of our blessed Lord, than when we regard in him THE APPOINTED MEDIATOR BETWEEN GOD AND ISRAEL. Moses was qualified for this office—by cordial love—meekness—long suffering—disinterestedness—ever-watchful zeal ; so God could have no interest with men except through Christ, who is far more qualified for the office of mediator than Moses. III. In attempting to estimate the character of Moses as a type of Christ, we must by no means neglect to regard him in his office of LAWGIVER TO ISRAEL. It was necessary that some mode of government should be given to them. This was given by the Most High—through Moses. So, in the mournful captivity of the soul, the lust of the flesh, and the pride of life, oppose the will of God ; and the fallen creature becomes a fatal law unto himself. Even when the condemnation of impiety is removed, and the fetters with which it bound all the passions, and faculties, and principles of the mind are broken, the liberated bond-servant needs a revelation of the Word of God by which his conduct may be governed. Christ a law-giver— assisted at the formation of the law—can best explain it—best enforce it. IV. Consider his typical character, as [THE LEADER AND GUIDE OF ISRAEL. Ye may have fled from Egypt ; but are ye beyond the reach of temptation ? Have ye passed through all the wilderness of sin and seduction ? Have ye triumphed over all your enemies, and received your allotted portion in the habitations of eternal rest and glory ? Ye have not. A difficult pilgrimage is before you : but infinite mercy has not left you to wander alone. Your Conductor fully knows the way to that blessedness whither ye are endeavouring to follow Him. Ignorant as ye are, He can give you knowledge—feeble, He can support you—faint, He can refresh you. Lessons : 1. Be persuaded that the gospel is worthy of all acceptation. 2. But if worldly and unholy affections still oppose the influence of that gospel over your hearts, yield not tamely to the slavery they would impose, until ye are provided with an answer to the awful question, How shall we escape, if we neglect so great salvation ? 3. It will naturally be asked, Thou that teachest another, teachest thou not thyself ? While therefore the ministers of religion are endeavouring to make others wise unto salvation, they may read in this history a rebuke to their own unbelief and timidity. (*R. P. Buddicom, M.A.*) *Leaders :*—1. Leaders we must have. To be a leader one must have courage. Not without reason did Sir Walter Scott say : "It appears to me that what is least forgiven in a man of any mark and likelihood is want of that quality called pluck. All the fine qualities of genius cannot make amends for it." Boldness is demanded by the very nature of the case. He who never moves till every one else is moving may be an excellent companion or follower; but a leader he is not. He who would lead must go before, must be in advance. 2. But courage must have some basis; and this basis is found largely in convictions. He who would lead must have not opinions alone but convictions. He must have before him some definite result to be reached, and a fixed conception of the manner in which the end is to be gained. And all this must not be a surmise, but an assurance. We cannot lead people with a perhaps. Usually, in proportion to the positiveness of one's convictions will be his courage in obeying them. If one's aims, methods, convictions are elevated and noble, so much the better ; but convictions he must have, if he would be a leader, and he must hold them with a tenacity that death alone can unloose. 3. One of the convictions that go to make up leadership is a belief that things ought to be done, that they can be done, that they must be done ; or, in other words, faith. There must be faith in a cause, faith in one's self, in one's destiny, in man ; or, rather, there must be a faith in what God is able and desirous to do for man and through man. To say " nothing can be done " is to say " God can do nothing." This despair is not only totally unchristian, it is fatal to leadership. " I can't " is powerless, or potent only for evil. " I can do all things through Christ which strengtheneth me " conducts to victory. 4. Out of faith comes progressiveness. To have no aspiration beyond holding things just where they are —or, perhaps, pushing them back an inch or two—this is fatal. But there is inspiration in the thought of achieving something that has not been done before, of treading heights unattained hitherto. The brakeman is very well in his way. But he is not the conductor. He cannot start the train. 5. For leadership there must be sympathy—a knowledge of men, of their feelings, of their desires, hopes, and fears, prejudices, &c. And for leadership there must be unselfishness. Many other qualities are needed that a man may lead wisely, successfully. These seem to me indispensable that he may lead at all.

Ver. 11. **Who am I?**—*Ministerial timidity :*—I. IT IS SOMETIMES OCCASIONED BY UNDUE AND DEPRECIATING THOUGHTS OF SELF. 1. By undue thought of our social position. 2. By undue thought of our intellectual weakness. 3. By undue thought of our moral inability. II. IT IS SOMETIMES OCCASIONED BY AN UNDUE ESTIMATION OF THE DIFFICULTIES OF THE WORK. 1. This may arise from the depressing experiences of youth. 2. This may arise from the removal of friendly aids. III. IT IS SOMETIMES OCCASIONED BY OUR NOT APPRECIATING, AS WE OUGHT, THE DIVINE PRESENCE AND HELP. 1. The Divine presence is our guide. 2. The Divine presence is our sustaining influence. 3. The Divine presence is our victory. IV. IT SHOULD BE REMOVED BY THE HOPES WITH WHICH IT IS ANIMATED. 1. By the hope of achieving the freedom of a vast nation. 2. By the hope of leading a vast nation into the land of promise. Moses was to lead the Israelites into Canaan: (1) Fertile. (2) Abundance. (3) Beauty. So, the minister of Christ has to lead men to heaven— this is the hope by which he is animated—and ought to subdue all timidity—and inspire him with holy joy. (*J. S. Exell, M.A.*) *Notes :*—1. God may sometimes be denied by the best of men in their infirmity. 2. The best souls are apt to have the lowest thoughts of themselves for God's work. 3. Visible difficulties in the Church may dishearten men to work. 4. The power of Egyptian oppressors may startle weak instruments of deliverance. 5. The redemption of men from the house of bondage is a startling fact. (*Ibid.*) *The power of increasing age :*—1. To change the views. 2. To calm the temper. 3. To humble the soul. (*Ibid.*) *Work greater than self :*—No wonder that he so inquired. The message seemed to be much greater than the messenger. He works best who magnifies his office. Preachers, and all ministers of good, should see their work to be greater than themselves if they would work at the highest point of energy. Let a man suppose his work to be easy, to be unworthy of his talents, and he will not achieve much success. (*J. Parker, D.D.*) *A Divine commission :*—I. GOOD MEN OFTEN WANT GREATER CONFIDENCE IN THE SERVICE OF GOD. 1. Distrust may arise from an honest conviction of personal unfitness. The most suitable workers are often the most diffident. Great talkers are little workers. 2. Distrust may arise from a false impression of opposing difficulties. Our estimate of what we can accomplish should be measured by our determination and love. 3. Distrust may arise from a positive relapse of religious fervour. Love inspires zeal. II. GOOD MEN OFTEN WANT SPECIAL ENCOURAGEMENT IN THE SERVICE OF GOD. 1. God encourages His servants by the assurance of His presence. He will give—(1) Strength for every conflict; (2)

Wisdom for every emergency; (3) Protection from every danger. 2. God encourages His servants by the assurance of ultimate success. III. GOOD MEN OFTEN REQUIRE MINUTE INSTRUCTION IN THE SERVICE OF GOD. When Moses determined to go to the Israelites, he anticipated the difficulties that would arise. They would want proof of his Divine commission, and he asks, "What shall I say unto them?" 1. We should inquire of God respecting our secular engagements. Why am I engaged in this work, and not in some other? What is the object for which I work? What is the influence of my work upon my life? What is the spirit in which I work? 2. We should inquire of God respecting our intellectual tendencies. This is an age of intellectual unrest. Old theories are discarded, and old doctrines thrown aside. Am I wandering from the old paths? Am I resting on the true foundation? 3. We should inquire of God respecting our religious progress. Spiritual life necessitates spiritual growth. Our progress may be slow and imperceptible, but it must advance or perish. Are we going forward in the Divine life? Is faith stronger? is love deeper? is zeal more intense? IV. GOOD MEN OFTEN RECEIVED DIVINE AUTHORITY FOR THE SERVICE OF GOD. 1. What evidence had Moses of his Divine commission? It was attested by a miraculous call. 2. What evidence had the Israelites of his Divine commission? It was attested by a miraculous power. (*J. T. Woodhouse.*)   *Moses' self-distrust:*—These words indicate humility, not fear. Among the grounds which he alleges for his hesitation, in no instance is there any allusion to personal danger; what he feared was failure owing to incompetency, especially in the power of expression. This shrinking from self-assertion is the quality which seems to be specially intimated by the word rendered "meek" in Numb. xii. 3. (*Canon Cook.*)   *False humility :*—Some people in studying this passage in the life of Moses will praise his humility. His pleas were all on the ground of personal unworthiness or unfitness for the great work. But let us not be deceived. That "humility" is not to be commended that shrinks from any duty which God commands. At Baalbec, in a quarry, lies a magnificent block, almost detached and ready for transportation. It was undoubtedly intended to be placed with its fellows in the wall which supported the Temple of the Sun. So large, so grand, it is a failure, because it never filled the place for which it was hewn. Like failures are many human lives. Who can tell how many men lie among the wastes and ruins of life, that God designed to fill grand places, but that, when called, refused to go? They folded their talents away in the napkins of supposed humility, of self-distrust, or of indolence or disobedience, and buried them in the earth. For ever they will lie in the quarries, pale ghosts of glorious "might have beens," while the places in God's temple which they were meant to fill remain for ever vacant. We can only make our lives successful by promptly, joyfully, and unhesitatingly accepting every call of our Master to His service, by putting ourselves utterly into His hands to be used anywhere, in any way, in any work, for any end, as He may direct. (*The Westminster Teacher.*)

Ver. 12. **Certainly I will be with thee.**—*The guarantee of success :*—Take this assurance as applying to the whole service of sanctified life, and it entitles us to draw four practical inferences. I. "Certainly I will be with thee."—THEN MAN IS SERVANT, NOT MASTER. He should know his place, or he can never keep it. As servant, he should—1. Constantly consult his Master. 2. Constantly speak in the name of his Master. 3. Constantly be jealous of the honour of his Master. II. "Certainly I will be with thee."—THEN THE WORK MUST SUCCEED. What is the guarantee of success? 1. Not human cleverness; ministers may be clever, so may churches, &c.; we may have learned sermons, able sermons, ingenious sermons, &c. 2. Not skilful organisation. Cards, bazaars, registers, circulars, &c., all useless as ends. 3. The word of the Lord is the guarantee of success. "The mouth of the Lord hath spoken it." "My word shall not return unto Me void." III. "Certainly I will be with thee."—THEN THE SERVANT IS TO BE RECEIVED FOR THE MASTER'S SAKE. "He that receiveth you receiveth Me, and he that receiveth Me receiveth Him that sent Me." The true minister carries a blessing with him. The Romans were to receive Phœbe in the Lord. What a lesson to ministers—they are representatives of God! IV. "Certainly I will be with thee."—THEN THERE NEED BE NO LACK OF GRACE OR POWER. "If any man lack wisdom," &c. "Lo, I am with you alway," &c. "Ye have not because ye ask not, or because ye ask amiss." The servants may take counsel of one another, but not to the interruption of continuous and trustful prayer to the Master. 1. God is with His servants for their comfort. 2. For their guidance. 3. For their safety. Application: Notice—1. The individuality of the promise, "I will be with thee"—with the one man. 2. The emphasis of the promise—"Certainly." Who is with us in our life-ministry? (*J. Parker, D.D.*) *The Divine companionship realised by the good in the service of the Christian life:*—I. IT WAS CONSIDERATE. Promise made when most needed—at time of weakness. II. IT WAS EMPHATIC. Leaving no room for doubt. III. IT WAS SYMPATHETIC. "With thee." Not I will follow thee—not I will go before thee—not I will be near thee—but with thee—as a companion to cheer thy soul; as a friend—to give thee counsel; as a God—to make thee victorious. How can a mission fail when God is with the worker? (*J. S. Exell, M.A.*) *God's presence with His ministers:*—The mission of Moses resembles that of every Christian minister, in that—I. HE WAS SENT TO HIS BRETHREN. II. WHEN HE WENT TO THEM, HE FOUND THEM IN A STATE OF BONDAGE AND OPPRESSION; their spirits crushed, their minds degraded. III. HE FOUND THAT HE ONLY PROVOKED THEM BY HIS ENDEAVOURS TO DELIVER THEM. IV. PROMISES WERE GIVEN TO SUPPORT HIM UNDER HIS DISAPPOINTMENTS. View the promise in the way of—1. Encouragement. God will be with every minister—(1) As a guide; (2) To strengthen and support him under trial; (3) To comfort and console him. 2. Caution. While each pastor rests on the consolation of this privilege, he must not forget the call to watchfulness and holiness which is inseparably connected with it. (*H. Raikes, M.A.*) *God is with His ministers:*—When I first entered the ministry, twenty years ago, I was filled with an enthusiasm that was as fresh as it was inexperienced in the work of winning souls. I felt sure, when I began to preach, that all the world would hear and be converted. The gospel was so simple; the news so good; the grace of Christ so precious—that I could think of nothing else but that my hearers would at once give themselves to Christ. I was under the impression that the reason people were not converted in greater numbers was that the preachers did not make the gospel simple and plain. This I supposed that I could do. Alas, I was as ignorant as Moses when he made his first attempt to save his brethren. I did not know what the bondage was, though I myself had been delivered. I did not realize the darkness of the unrenewed mind, the enmity of the unrenewed heart. I did not know the strength of the chain with which Satan has bound souls. But, like Melancthon, who had a similar thought, I found that "old Adam was stronger than young Pentecost"; and I confess that to this hour, though I have been in the work for twenty years, I never sit down by the side of an unconverted man, woman, or child, to attempt to lead them to Christ, without a certain sense of fear. My insufficiency always comes before me when I think of what is involved in this work. To persuade a man to reform his life, to give up certain sins and hurtful lusts, is comparatively easy : but to convert a sinner to God is difficult work indeed; and without the aid of the Divine Spirit it is impossible for man to effect it. What answer have we to give to this honest shrinking from a difficult work? Let us hear how God answered Moses: "Certainly I will be with thee." As though He had said, "Why, Moses, you did not expect that I was going to send you down to Egypt alone, to deliver My people? Have you forgotten that I said *I* had come down to deliver? You indeed are to be My instrument; but I will be with you to make you mighty, and to bring the apparently impossible work to pass." This puts the work in a new light. If God goes with us to the work, then can we undertake anything. When Jesus said, " Go ye into all the world, and make disciples of all nations," He did not forget to say, " Lo, I am with you alway." (*G.F. Pentecost, D.D.*) *The invisible but ever-present God:*—God thus puts Himself apparently into a secondary position. Moses is to stand at the front, and, so far as publicity is concerned, to incur the whole responsibility of the proposed movement. It was easy for Moses to say that he was prompted of God to make certain representations to Israel and Pharaoh, but how were they to be convinced that Moses was servant and not master? This is the difficulty of all the highest service of life, namely, that the spiritual is invisible, and yet omnipotent; public attention is fixed upon the human agent, and professions of spiritual inspiration and impulse are treated with distrust, if not with contempt, by the most of mankind. It is the invisible Christ who is with the Church. Were He present manifestly, it is supposed that greater results would accrue from Christian service; but the supposition must be mistaken, inasmuch as He to whom such service is infinitely dearer than it ever can be to ourselves has determined the manner of Christian evangelisation. What, then, is the great duty and privilege of the Church? It is to realize the presence and influence of the Invisible. The Church is actually to see the Unseen. There is another vision beside the vision of the body; faith itself is sight ; and where faith is complete, there is a consciousness of God's presence throughout our life and service which amounts to a distinct vision of God's personal presence and government. (*J. Parker, D.D.*) *The spirit of destiny :*—Moses has been, as it were, audibly and visibly called to service and invested with authority. A keen pleasure would seem to attach to experiences of that kind. Surely it was a blessed thing to speak face to face with God, and to go straight away from the communing to do the work which had been prescribed. The directness of the interview, the absence of all second causes and instrumentalities, has about it a solemnity which profoundly affects the heart. But is my destiny less Divine because it has been revealed to me under conditions which seem to separate widely between the Creator and the creature? Has God only one method of working in revealing to a man what that man's work in life is intended to be? We do not always see the fountain; sometimes we have to be content to drink at the stream. The danger is lest we imagine the stream created itself, forgetting in our irreligion and folly that the stream is impossible apart from the fountain. A man is sometimes awakened to his destiny by his fellow-men. In other cases a man's destiny seems to be determined by what he calls his circumstances or his environment. But why this wide and circuitous way of putting the case to the mind? We do not depose God by mistaking the origin of our action; we do but show the poorness of our own judgment, or the want of justice which impoverishes our lives of their best qualities. Every man should put to himself the question—What is my destiny? What does God mean me to be and do in the world? (*Ibid.*) *The presence of God :*—In the early days of the Theological Seminary at Alleghany, it was often in great need of money. Once, in a time of extremity, the Rev. Dr. Francis Herron, President of the Board of Directors, the Rev. Dr. Elisha P. Swift, also a director, and Rev. Jos. Patterson, met to devise some way of relief. With all their faith, the first-mentioned brethren were greatly dejected, "We have no one to help us," said one of them. "No one!" replied Mr. Patterson, warmly: "Why! I know of a thousand here." The two looked astonished. He continued, "Is not Dr. Herron a cipher? is not Dr. Swift a cipher? am not I a cipher? But Jesus Christ is surely One. And if we put one before three ciphers, does it not make a thousand?" They took new courage, went to that One who is able to help, and did not pray in vain. *Christ's presence promised :*—Chrysostom beautifully says, for our comfort: "I have a pledge from Christ—have His note of hand—which is my support, my refuge and haven; and though the world should rage, to this security I cling. How reads it? 'Lo, I am with you alway, even unto the end of the world.' If Christ be with me, what shall I fear? If He is mine, all the powers of earth to me are nothing more than a spider's web."

Ver. 13. **What shall I say unto them ?**—*Ministerial difficulties to be anticipated, and how to overcome them :*—I. MINISTERS MUST ANTICIPATE DIFFICULTIES IN THE PERFORMANCE OF THEIR LIFE-MISSION. 1. Arising from prejudice in reference to the man. 2. Arising from scepticism in reference to the truth. 3. Arising from lethargy in reference to the mission. II. TO OVERCOME THESE DIFFICULTIES MINISTERS MUST SEEK DIRECTION FROM GOD. 1. Divine recognition of ministerial difficulty. He will not reject any who seek His aid. 2. Divine sympathy with ministerial difficulty. (1) Manifested by the gift of heavenly vision (ver. 2). (2) Manifested by the gift of needful instruction (vers. 15–17). (3) Manifested by the gift of holy companionship (ver. 12). Such a manifestation of Divine sympathy ought to inspire every minister with spirit and fortitude for his work. They that are for him, are more than all that can be against him. (*J. S. Exell, M.A.*) *Why did Moses ask the name of God ?*—1. Not to instruct his ignorance. He had not forgotten God in Egypt. 2. Not to gratify his curiosity. 3. But to satisfy Israel. Error has many gods, he therefore wanted to know how he might prove to the enslaved nation that he came in the name of the True One. (*Ibid.*) *Lessons :*— 1. It is good for a minister to know on whose business he is going. 2. God's answer to one objection oftentimes begets another in His servants. 3. Dissatisfaction of men about God's instruments is very probable. 4. God's servants very reasonably expect that He will clear up all doubt as to His name, and their duty. (*Ibid.*) "*What shall I say unto them ?*"—*a question for the pulpit :*—I. SHALL I SAY UNTO THEM TRUTHS THAT ARE IN HARMONY WITH THEIR DEPRAVED CONDITION? No; ministers are not to preach doctrines in harmony with the depraved tastes of men—but to awaken them from their sin, by the proclamation of the Divine name and freedom. II. SHALL I GIVE THEM AN ARGUMENTATIVE DISCOURSE? It would be necessary for Moses to convince the Israelites that he was divinely commissioned—

and the chief use that a minister can make of logic is to prove the divinity of his call to the ministry. III. SHALL I GIVE THEM A SENSATIONAL DISCOURSE? Had Moses done this he might have aroused a wave of feeling, but it would soon have subsided into calm. The freedom of the nation would not have been achieved in this way. The sensational preachers of the world are not doing the most towards the moral freedom of the race. IV. SHALL I SAY UNTO THEM HOW CLEVER I AM? Moses had humbled himself before God. And men humble before God are generally so before their fellows. Ministers should not make a display of their learning—such conduct will never accomplish the freedom of souls. V. SHALL I TELL THEM ABOUT THE CROSS OF JESUS? "Yes," replies the penitent sinner; "that is what I want." "Yes," replies the aged believer; "that is the charm of my soul." Preach the Cross as the emancipation of the world. Not ourselves, but Christ Jesus the Lord. (*Ibid.*)   *What to preach :*—I remember being asked by the late Dr. McLeod, who was head physician in one of the Government asylums, if I would preach to some of the inmates. "What kind of men are they?" I inquired. "Oh, mostly sailors; and if you accept the invitation to preach to them, you must make up your mind to stand a good knock or two, perhaps even a blow in the face; but if you wish to make friends with them, you must take no notice of it." "I am not a bit afraid of them," I replied; "if they be sailors I shall speak to them as sailors, and I am sure they will not touch me.". I went and spoke to them. There was no attempt to molest me, but many of the poor fellows came up to me afterwards and thanked me for what I said. Some declared that what they liked about me was that I spoke to them as sailors. No one who had ever spoken to them before had done so. Their former visitors had seemed to believe all that they were told, that they were kings, dukes, and earls, but I had spoken to them as sailors, to their true selves, and though insane, they felt that I was speaking the truth. Similarly we must speak to sinners as being just what they are. (*Christian Herald.*) *God-directed speaking :*—A man in America died, who had long been renowned for wickedness. His intellectual abilities were of no mean order; his property was considerable, and he had belonged to a family of good position. By the practice of every kind of dissipation he had achieved an evil notoriety, and gloried in being considered the most fascinating and dangerous *roué* in the country. This being so, his associates resolved upon giving him a funeral worthy of his reputation. As one means of ensuring this, they invited one of the most eminent Presbyterian ministers in the region to deliver the funeral discourse. To the surprise of many, after some little hesitation, he consented. On the day and at the hour appointed the country church was crowded to overflowing by an assembly composed of the relatives, friends, and companions of the deceased, together with a mixed multitude drawn from far and near by curiosity to hear what such a minister could find to say of such a man. Punctual to the moment, the tall form of the clergyman ascended the pulpit, and the service began. There was first the reading of the Scriptures. Then followed a prayer, subdued and tender, for the family and relatives of the deceased. But the announcement of the text fell upon the assembly like a clap of thunder. It was from Luke xvi. 23: "And in hell he lifted up his eyes, being in torments." The sermon was a most pungent and powerful exhibition of the character, course, and end of a wicked man. It held the assembly spellbound to the very last word; but there was in it not a single direct allusion to the person whose obsequies they had come there to celebrate. In silence and in deep solemnity the congregation dispersed after the service was finished. Some were indignant, but any attempt to excite odium against the preacher was a failure. It was generally thought that in what he had done he was governed by a sense of duty. He was said to have stated afterwards that when he was invited to preach on that occasion he had determined to decline, but, in answer to prayer, received a message which he believed to be from God—"Go—and preach the preaching that I bid thee." (*Ibid.*)   *God's servants report God's words :*—Words spoken on your own account, without reference to your Lord, will fall to the ground. When the footman goes to the door to answer a caller, he asks his master what he has to say, and he repeats what his master tells him. You and I are waiting-servants in the house of God, and we are to report what our God would have us speak. The Lord gives the soul-saving message, and clothes it with power: He gives it to a certain order of people, and under certain conditions. (*C. H. Spurgeon.*)   *Moses' difficulty :*—If Moses had been rejected forty years before, what resistance and what objections might he not expect then? And when he should speak to them of the God of their fathers, and should say to them, "I have seen Him; He has spoken to me, He has made promises to me, He has sent me to you," would they believe him, would they listen to him, would they understand him? It was thus that the apostles of Jesus Christ, when they went to gather together the people of God amid idolaters, had to encounter two classes of enemies; on the one hand, the emperors of Rome, the rich and powerful priests of the old religions, who had their gods, Jupiter, Mars, Mercury, and many more; on the other hand, the nations whom they were sent to convert : there was the gieatest difficulty. Read the Acts of the Apostles, and you will readily perceive that the apostles' impediments and persecutions came from the people more than from the emperors and the great men of the world. But do you fully understand the objection that Moses expected from the unbelief of the people? The Israelites had probably become idolaters by living among the Egyptians, who worshipped a great number of gods, each of which had its name, as Ammon, Isis, Osiris, Apis. They shall say to me, What is His name? Is He truly the God of our fathers? Has He said so to thee? We do not see Him ; He has forsaken us. (*Prof. Gaussen.*)   *A necessary inquiry:*—Before going on any of life's great errands, we should know *who* has sent us, and *what* is the business on which we proceed. Inquiries of this kind will lead to a true apprehension of our position, and in not a few cases to a reversion of our daily course. What are you living for? You are hurrying and whirling forward at a tremendous rate, your brain teems upon conceptions, your hand hardly knows a moment's rest, you pursue the bubble, you jostle and compete and envy, you flatter and are flattered, you hoard and you dispense. What does it all mean? Who sketched the map by which you regulate your pilgrimage? What account can you give of yourself to those who ask the name of your guiding spirit? Take the subject in the light of every-day affairs, and the singular absurdity of not knowing on whose business you are engaged will instantly appear. You meet a traveller who is professedly engaged in business; you ask him what is his business, and he cannot answer ; you ask him whose interests he represents, and no reply is forthcoming; you ask him whither he is bound, and he returns the inquiry with a look of vacancy ;—to what conclusion can you come respecting such a person? You instantly feel that the man is a child, and that the child has gone astray. The same thing holds true in the deeper and vaster concerns of life; and he who is wisely and profoundly anxious to know on what basis he is proceeding in commercial transactions, should look beyond the mere detail, and face the great question—upon what principle is my intellectual, emotional, moral, and spiritual life proceeding? Oh man, be persuaded for a moment to tarry in thy impetuous course, and cross-examine thine own heart! Don't be deluded by the whirl and thunder and tempest of an outer life; mistake not commotion for progress, enthusiasm for regeneration, self-applause for the benediction of heaven! (*J. Parker, D.D.*)

Ver. 14. **I AM hath sent me unto you.**—*Immutable authority :*—I. Moses on entering upon a great mission naturally inquires the CONDITIONS upon which he proceeds. II. In the REVELATION made to Moses, "I AM hath sent me unto you," we have being distinguished from manifestation. "I AM" is the summary of Being. III. The ANSWER which Moses received from Almighty God was an immutable authority for the greatest of missions. Only let us be sure that we are doing God's errand, and Pharaoh and Cæsar, and all names of material power, will fall before us, never again to rise. (*J. Parker, D.D.*)   The great "*I AM*":—I. God is the INCOMPREHENSIBLE One, and yet is revealed in His intercourse with men. The conviction of His unsearch-ableness lies at the root of all reverence and awe. Before the "I AM that I AM" our spirits lie in deepest adoration, and rise into loftiest aspiration. But we need equally the other side. We need a God revealed in the essential features of His character ; and it is in His dealings with men who feared and loved Him that He has made Himself known. II. God is the INDEPENDENT AND ABSOLUTE One, and yet He enters into covenant and most definite relationships with men. He is the God of Abraham, Isaac, and Jacob. III. God is the ETERNAL One, and yet the God of dying men. Every moment that we have of fellowship with the Eternal God assures us that for us there is no death. IV. God is the UNCHANGEABLE One, yet the God of men of all different types and temperaments. The same Lord over all. Take these three patriarchs, so closely related in blood—Abraham, Isaac, Jacob. How different they were! Yet God was the God of all three, for they all agreed in being seekers of God. (*J. Leckie, D.D.*)   The great "*I AM*":—The first thought, perhaps, of all which lies wrapped in these two grand comprehensive words, "I

AM," is mystery. Our best worship is in silence, and our truest wisdom when we confess without confession. " It is too high for me, I cannot attain unto it." The utmost conception of the most exalted intellect of the most heaven-taught man is only a faint approximation thereto. " I AM." It still lies in the future of a far-off beatitude—"Blessed are the pure in heart for they shall see God." But where do these glimpses lie of the great I AM; and how can we now know Him at all? I believe, first, in nature. The wonderful organization and marvellous system of nature, in the world I live in. Next I look for it in the Holy Word which He has given to me with the impress of His mind and being. But more in that Spirit which dwells in me and which is the reflection of the nature and a very part of the life and the essence of God. Thirdly, and better still in Him, His own dear Son, " the brightness of His glory and the express image of His person," and who claims to Himself that very name (John viii. 58). No created thing could ever say with truth, "I am." God alone has no other origin but Himself. He depends upon nothing ; His life is essential life ; all life, from all eternity past to all eternity yet to come. He is "I AM." Therefore because He is the I AM, all is present time with God. It is the present tense ever. The consequences are tremendous. All our past sins, all our past mercies, all our past promises and vows, all our past life, and all the life that is yet to come, it is all the present moment with God, in all its freshness and clearness and distinctness at this moment—" I AM." Hence the absolute and perfect unchangeableness ! Or take another instance in that great name " I AM." All life, which is life indeed, must emanate from Him. He is the life. And there is another view which we may take of these two grand words, " I AM." God does not say what He is. He leaves that to us. We must fill in the blank. " I am whatever you make Me. If you disbelieve Me, if you think little of Me, I am a just God, a holy God, a jealous God, an avenging God, a strict God, a punishing God ; I shall by no means spare the guilty, I am a consuming fire. If you are a penitent sinner, if you have left Me and are coming back to Me, if you are sorry for what you have done, if you have grieved Me, and now wish to please Me, I am a forgiving God, full of mercy and compassion, of great pity, passing by transgression and sin more than any one asketh. I am love. If you are really My child, poor, weak, unworthy, sinful though you are, yet still My child, striving to please Me, earnest to serve Me, desiring more and more to see Me and be with Me, telling Me everything in your little heart, trusting Me, loving Me, I am your own dear loving faithful Father ; I am yours and you are Mine to the very end. I have loved you and chosen you from all eternity, and I never change. Though I do sometimes hide Myself, yet behind the cloud *I am*, I AM, I AM. I am thine, and thou art Mine, for ever and ever ! " (*J. Vaughan, M.A.*) *The Divine name :*—I. As ONLY REVEALED BY THE DIVINE BEING HIMSELF. II. AS ONLY PARTIALLY UNDERSTOOD BY THE GRANDEST INTELLECTS. III. As SUFFICIENTLY COMPREHENDED FOR THE PRACTICAL SERVICE OF THE CHRISTIAN LIFE. We know enough of God to give strength, responsibility, hope, to our Christian work and life. (*J. S. Exell, M.A.*) *The name of the Lord :*—The answer is twofold. It repeats the idea that He is the God of their father ; but it connects that with the idea that He is Jehovah. I. THE ETERNAL NAME. " God said unto Moses, I AM THAT I AM. Say unto the children of Israel, I AM hath sent me unto you." The word is that from which Jehovah comes. It expresses the idea of existence. In announcing Himself by this name the Divine Being excludes all notion of any commencement or termination of His existence, or that He is indebted for it to any other. It is self-existence, necessary existence ; His non-existence is an impossibility and cannot be entertained. Jesus Christ " the same yesterday, and to-day, and for ever." " The Alpha and the Omega, the first and the last." " He who was, and is, and is to come." Perhaps the most helpful conception we have of permanence is given by the spectacle of the lofty mountains which stand unmoved and unchanged for centuries and millenniums. We call them the everlasting hills. But He was before the mountains, and will continue His undying existence when they have disappeared in the final dissolution. II. THE ABIDING RELATIONSHIP. " The Lord God of your fathers, the God of Abraham, the God of Isaac, and the God of Jacob." The two names are closely connected, because He could not be the one God of successive generations if He were not Jehovah—the Everlasting. 1. You will mark that He is not only Jehovah, God in Himself, as He cannot but be; He is the God of the persons here mentioned. Think what a great thing it is that He should be the God of any one ! Think what a blessedness and a glory it is to have His almightiness on your side ; His love your resting-place ; His throne your refuge in distress ; His unchanging faithfulness your abiding confidence. 2. Next, observe that He was the God of each of the persons named. God knows how to be the God of all His people however they differ from each other in those subtle shades of character which, like the features of the face, distinguish one man from another. 3. Then observe, further, He was the God of their successive generations. This thought is valuable in connection with the idea that God still has a people. The spiritual seed of Abraham. Also that the children of godly parents should value the blessing of having their father's God. Fear to forfeit it. 4. Nor must we overlook the important use the Great Teacher made of the statement in our text. Argument for resurrection and immortality in Matt. xxii. 24–32. III. THE PERMANENT NAME. God's eternity contrasts with our brief life : warrants our confidence in Him : suggests the blessedness of those who are interested in Him. (*John Rawlinson.*) *God's name of Himself :*—I. PERSONALITY—"I." 1. We attach three ideas to personality. (1) Essential distinctness. (2) Individual consciousness. (3) Spontaneity. 2. God's personality—(1) Explains the unity of the universe. (2) Meets the aspirations of human nature. II. SELF-EXISTENCE—"I AM." 1. The independent amidst dependent beings. 2. The Unchangeable amidst a changing universe. III. Unsearchableness—"I AM that I AM." 1. Mystery is essential to Deity. 2. Mystery is a want of human nature. Stirs intellect, wakes wonder, inspires reverent awe of souls. (*Homilist.*)   "*I AM*" :—I. THE HIGHEST INQUIRY OF MAN AS A MORAL AGENT. 1. This inquiry is most reasonable. 2. This inquiry is most urgent. II. THE HIGHEST REVELATION TO MAN AS A MORAL STUDENT. "I AM—" what? The Fountain of all life, the Foundation of all virtue, the Source of all blessedness, the Cause, the Means, and the End of all things in the universe but sin. 1. This is the revelation that man as a thinker craves for. 2. This is the revelation which the gospel gives. III. THE HIGHEST AUTHORITY OF MAN AS A MORAL WORKER. Lessons : 1. God is. The grandest fact in the universe. 2. God is an absolute personality. 3. God deals with individual men. "Hath sent *me.*" 4. God makes man His messenger to men. (*Ibid.*)   *The minister sent by God :*—I. THE DIVINE EXISTENCE. "I AM." He who is, and who will be what He is. II. THE MINISTRY A DIVINE INSTITUTION. "I AM hath sent me unto you." This creates the relation of pastor and people. III. MUTUAL DUTIES OF PASTOR AND PEOPLE. 1. The duty of the pastor. (1) He must preach the gospel in its purity and simplicity. (2) He must administer the ordinances. (3) He must maintain a wholesome discipline in the Church. 2. The duty of the people. (1) Sympathy ; (2) Love ; (3) Obedience ; (4) Co-operation ; (5) Prayer for their minister. (*J. W. Ray.*)   *The immutability of God :*—I. THAT JEHOVAH IS UNCHANGEABLE IS PROVED FROM WHAT WE KNOW OF HIS OTHER ATTRIBUTES. We are assured, for example, that He is infinite in goodness, infinite in knowledge, infinite in power. The simple inquiry before us is, Are these attributes subject to change? Now, change in any being implies increase, or diminution, or entire removal of certain properties. To suppose any attribute of God to cease entirely, is to suppose that He ceases to be God. Change, then, if it occurs at all, must imply either increase or diminution of His perfections. On this principle, it is easy to see that the least change in the degree of His power, for example, must make Him more than almighty, or less than almighty ; the least change in His knowledge must make Him more than omniscient, or less than omniscient ; in other words, the least change in a perfect and infinite being is inconceivable. II. THAT JEHOVAH IS UNCHANGEABLE IS PROVED FROM EXPLICIT AND REPEATED DECLARATIONS OF THE BIBLE. (See Mal. iii. 6 ; Tit. i. 2 ; James i. 17 ; Psa. cii. 27). The inferences resulting from the truth thus established are so important as to demand the remaining time that can be allotted to this discourse. 1. All conceptions of God which apply time and succession to His existence, are erroneous. "One day is with the Lord as a thousand years, and a thousand years as one day." He is no older than He was from eternity. Age is a relative term : it implies beginning ; but God is eternal. It implies change ; but God is unchangeable. Time is the measure of created existence ; but God is uncreated. Hence, the diversity of views which we have of the same thing at different times, results from the imperfection of our knowledge. Change of opinion implies liability to mistake. Increase of knowledge implies past ignorance ; decrease of knowledge implies present ignorance. But neither of these can apply to Him whose "understanding is infinite." 2. God has no new purposes. This follows, by unquestionable inference, from His immutability. Whatever was His purpose from eternity is His purpose now : and whatever is His purpose now, was His purpose from eternity. Two things then are certain. (1) That God is unchangeable. (2) That God has purposes. The inference is perfectly conclusive that these purposes are eternal. This argument cannot be evaded. It has the clearness of demonstration. 3. The certainty of final salvation to true believers is a reasonable doctrine, grounded on the immutable truth of God, as implied in the promises of the new covenant. These promises of the unchanging God must be fulfilled. 4. When God is said to repent, it implies no change in His character or purpose. 5. The immutability of God is no discouragement to prayer, but the best ground of encouragement. If Jehovah were fickle, like earthly monarchs, then, indeed, it would be vain to pray. The answer of prayer implies no change in the mind of God. 6. The unchangeable perfection of God is a doctrine full of comfort to His people. This world, with all its concerns, bears the stamp of mutability. Amid these scenes of fluctuation, is there no object then in heaven or earth that is unchanging? Yes, one; God is unchanging. Here is stability. 7. The immutability of God is a doctrine full of terror to His enemies. (*E. Potter, D.D.*) *God, the great "I AM" :*—If I say "I am," I say what is not true of me. I must say "I am something—I am a man, I am bad, or I am good, or I am an Englishman, I am a soldier, I am a sailor, I am a clergyman"—and then I shall say what is true of me. But God alone can say "I AM" without saying anything more. And why? Because God alone *is*. Everybody and everything else in the world *becomes* : but God *is*. We are all becoming something from our birth to our death—changing continually and becoming something different from what we were a minute before; first of all we were created and made, and so became men ; and since that we have been every moment changing, becoming older, becoming wiser, or alas! foolisher; becoming stronger or weaker; becoming better or worse. Even our bodies are changing and becoming different day by day. But God never changes or becomes anything different from what He is now. What He is, that He was, and ever will be. Many heathen men have known that there was one eternal God, and that *God is*. But they did not know that God Himself had said so ; and that made them anxious, puzzled, almost desperate, so that the wiser they were, the unhappier they were. For what use is it merely knowing that *God is*? The question for poor human creatures is, "But what sort of a being is God?" Is He far off? Does He care nothing about us? Does He let the world go its own way, right or wrong? Is He proud and careless? A Self-glorifying Deity whose mercy is not over all His works, or even over any of them? And the glory of the Bible, the power of God revealed in the Bible, is, that it answers the question, and says, "God does care for men, God does see men, God is not far off from any one of us. Ay, God speaks to men—God spoke to Moses and said, not "God is," but "I AM." God in sundry times and divers manners spoke to our fathers by the prophets and said, "I AM." But more—Moses said, "I AM hath sent me." God does not merely love us, and yet leave us to ourselves. He sends after us. He sends to us. But again: "I AM hath sent me unto you." Unto whom? Who was Moses sent to? To the Children of Israel in Egypt. And what sort of people were they? Were they wise and learned? On the contrary, they were stupid, ignorant, and brutish. Were they pious and godly? On the contrary, they were worshipping the foolish idols of the Egyptians—so fond of idolatry that they must needs make a golden calf and worship it. Then why did God take such trouble for them? Why did God care for them, and help them, and work wonders for them? Why? Exactly because they were so bad. Just because they were so bad, His goodness yearned over them all the more, and longed to make them good. Just because they were so unclean and brutish, His holiness longed all the more to cleanse them. Because they were so stupid and ignorant, His wisdom longed to make them wise. Because they were so miserable, His pity yearned over them, as a father over a child fallen into danger. Because they were sick, they had all the more need of a physician. Because they were lost, there was all the more reason for seeking and saving them. Because they were utterly weak, God desired all the more to put His strength into them, that His strength might be made perfect in weakness. (*C. Kingsley, M.A.*) *God's memorial name :*—I. In this memorial name of God WE ARE TAUGHT HIS LOFTY EXISTENCE. "I AM that I AM" is a name synonymous in meaning with Jehovah. This name includes within its vast extent of signification all past, present and future existence and duration. 1. Self-existence is a Divine attribute. 2. Eternity necessarily follows from His self-existence. 3. His proprietorship springs from the fact of His existence. II. THE REVELATION OF THIS MEMORIAL NAME TO MOSES HAD PURPOSE. It was a crisis in the history of Moses, and also of that of Israel in Egypt. 1. One purpose it served was to strengthen Moses in executing his work. 2. Another purpose was to check idolatrous practices. 3. It taught Moses the safety of the people. 4. The revelation of this name in connection with the people's ancestry shows that they were the heirs of immortality. 5. The revelation of this name indicated victory. (*J. H. Hill.*) *The greatness and glory of God :*—The creature is nothing in comparison with God ; all the glory, perfection, and excellency of the whole world do not amount to the value of a unit in regard of God's attributes ; join ever so many of them together, they cannot make one in number ; they are nothing in His regard, and less than nothing. All created beings must utterly vanish out of sight when we think of God. As the sun does not annihilate the stars, and make them nothing, yet it annihilates their appearances to our sight ; some are of the first magnitude, some of the second, some of the third, but in the daytime all are alike, all are darkened by the sun's glory : so it is here, there are degrees of perfection and excellency, if we compare one creature with another, but let once the glorious brightness of God shine upon the soul, and in that light all their differences are unobserved. Angels, men, worms, they are all nothing, less than nothing, to be set up against God. This magnificent title " I AM," darkens all, as if nothing elsewhere. (*T. Manton, D.D.*)

Ver. 15. **The Lord God of your fathers, the God of Abraham, the God of Isaac.** —*The God of the generations :*—Men are always influenced more or less by the power of great names. This appears in every sphere of life, social, scientific, political, literary, religious. The name of a wise, heroic, or philanthropic, or notably godly man, is a perpetual fountain of inspiration—a well-spring of living water from which we gather stimulus, courage, power to be and to do. The sound of it stirs the pulses of our better life. But no names in any country, or among any people, have wielded a mightier power than these three mentioned in the text exerted over the minds and history of the Jews. Abraham, Isaac, and Jacob stood forth in every succeeding age in increasing lustre, unshadowed even by the memories of other noble names, such as Moses, Daniel, Solomon, Elijah, Isaiah. Appeal to them was always effective when all other means of rousing the national heart failed. I. IT ANNOUNCES GOD'S RELATION TO INDIVIDUAL LIFE. " I am the God of Abraham, Isaac, and Jacob." Here there is a sublime fact upon which our minds can lay hold. The statement is not vague or unsubstantial, but tells us that the great God has to do with men, and holds a distinct personal relation towards each of them. Perhaps we have been too apt to attempt to satisfy ourselves with impalpable generalities, and to talk of God as the God of Creation, from whose fulness of life and omnipotence of energy the universe has derived its existence. In like manner we employ what may be termed His official titles to represent Him to our thought. He is the King of kings, the Ruler, the Governor of the nations. But the hearts of men crave a more intimate knowledge of God than these ideas can possibly convey. We cannot satisfy ourselves with abstractions. Official titles never command our affection. What we want is not a revelation that only declares God's universal dealings with humanity, but His personal interest in individual men. And we see that thus early in the history of the race this revelation is clearly made. Nay, from the first and earliest declaration of God's relation to the world, this is unhesitatingly announced. All the beautiful stories of Divine intercourse with men contained in the Book of Genesis are recorded to teach us that God has not been satisfied with a merely general and official relationship to men, but that He has ever had regard to the personal wants, the personal struggles, the personal sins, the personal joys and sorrows, the personal lives and deaths of each man, woman, and child born into this world. " I am the Lord thy God " ; and our response is, " This God is our God. He will be our guide even unto death." " The Lord is my shepherd, I shall not want." More clearly still is this revelation made in the New Testament—that carries the truth further, and by Jesus Christ we are shown that God has the most intimate relation with human souls. Indeed, the very use of the word " Father " implies this personal relationship. It is impossible for a true father to regard and treat the members of his family in a general indiscriminate manner—looking upon them in the mass, and not as individuals—that were to destroy the very meaning and beauty of family life. But the father knows that he has a distinct love for each member. Thus our Lord teaches us the particular and special and personal nature of the relationship of God to us. We are not lost in the mass, as one in a crowd for whom no one cares, and whom no one would miss. " I am the God of Abraham, the God of Isaac, and the God of Jacob." Connected with this is another thought worthy of notice. It is that God here expresses His relation to persons of distinct and differing characters. Perhaps no three men were more unlike than this father, son, and grandson. Look at Abraham, the bold, brave, generous, trusting chief, a dweller in tents, at home in the desert. Compare him with the quiet, meditative, ease-loving, simple-minded Isaac, somewhat fond of savoury living, who succeeded him. There is as much unlikeness as could possibly exist between father and son. Take, again, Jacob, the cunning, adroit, ingenious, selfish, money-loving, physically timid—a man who probably had more brains than either of his predecessors, but who was made to be a politician, a statesman, to whose active, contriving spirit, sitting at home, or roving in the desert, would be alike uncongenial. There we have three men totally distinct in character, yet the declaration is made—"I am the God of Abraham, Isaac, and Jacob." Surely there is meaning in this, and it is that God cares equally for, and is as truly related to, one kind of disposition and character as another. Ah! there is exquisite beauty and comfort in the tenderly-expressed words of John concerning Christ—"Now Jesus loved Martha, and her sister, and Lazarus." Three varieties of character, but all beloved. If all this be true, what need of our nature is left unsatisfied? If this be true, who is there will not feel that his life, so specially the subject of God's thought, is therefore a grander, nobler, and, withal, a more responsible thing? Who will depreciate his own proud worth? Who will bemoan his lot, thinking with envy of others better circumstanced? II. IT ANNOUNCES GOD'S RELATION TO SUCCESSIVE GENERATIONS. These three men represented an unbroken succession of three generations, running into one another, yet in a measure distinct. May we not learn from these facts that God is not a God of seasons and partialities, but that He belongs to all the successive generations as they move across the world to the silence of the grave? There is no break in His thoughtful care or in the manifestations of His love. He does not appear at one age and disappear at another, at one time show Himself peculiarly concerned with human welfare, at another time altogether indifferent about the joys and sorrows, the sins and the cravings of men. In such a Being as that we could neither trust nor believe. There is no intermission. God's intercourse with men is never broken off. This intercourse may assume different forms. What is suited to one age may be altogether unsuited to the next. At one time His revelations may be such as the senses can testify to; He may instruct men in His mind and will through the medium of miracles, flashing symbols of omnipotence before their eyes; at other times He may reveal Himself in a person, in a human life, as we believe He did in Christ Jesus our Lord. At others, all visions may disappear; no miracle shall startle the world into wondering awe. God is not tied to methods. He may and does employ all at one time or another in order to convince men of His nearness to them and interest in their life. "The God of the Hebrews is not our God." That is the sum of much of the unbelief of the day. The cry is for palpable evidence. Palpable evidence! Why, we have abundance of it on all sides. Miracles! There is no need of them. Why, the very researches of our scientific men are doing away with the necessity for miracles, for they are demonstrating by their discoveries that the world is full of order, of beauty, of marvellous contrivances that must be the work of mind. Here are the proofs of Divine existence, Divine working, Divine wisdom and bounty and power. To believe He is not as much the God of this generation as of any in all the long past, is to cut to the very root of all true faith and trust in Him, is to regard Him as partial, as doing more for one people than for another equally in need of His revelation of power and love; it is to throw us back for our faith in God upon dead history, which can never create or nourish into a living hope the trust of human souls. We may say that the age of supernatural displays of mere power is passed, but we are called upon to rise from the merely materialistic and tangible, and to realise God in the hallowed and invisible communion of the Spirit. The God of the father is to be the God of the son and the grandson by legitimate, unhindered succession, and those who come after can speak of "the God of our fathers." That there is no reason against it in the will and purposes of the Divine Being Himself we have seen. He is willing to bless and enrich each and all, without choice or favouritism. But in how few cases in the family life is He recognized from one generation to another. Here I bring the matter direct home to your hearts. I know I must be speaking to some who are thinking of pious parents. You have a godly father or mother, or perhaps both. What of yourself? Are you continuing the succession? The name you bear has been associated with godliness in one or two generations past. Is it to be separated in your time? What will your children say of you? Will they be able to pray to the God of their parents? (*W. Braden.*)

Ver. 16. **Gather the elders.**—*The wisdom of gathering the few; or the considerateness of the Divine Being in reference to the mission of His servants :*—I. THIS WOULD BE THE MOST EFFECTIVE METHOD OF ENLIGHTENING THE MIND OF THE NATION IN REFERENCE TO THE DIVINE INTENTION. 1. This afforded Moses a good opportunity for personal explanations. 2. It was a good precaution against the ignorance and fanaticism of the common people. The more agencies a man can bring into his life-work the better. II. IT WOULD BE THE MOST EFFECTIVE METHOD OF GAINING THE SYMPATHY OF THE NATION. All great workers should be judicious in their movement. III. IT WOULD THUS BE THE MOST EFFECTIVE METHOD OF WORKING OUT THE DIVINE PROJECT IN REFERENCE TO THE NATION. 1. How considerate of the Divine Being to give Moses this idea of working ! Many men will not listen to the Divine instructions. This is the occasion of the great failure of so much religious energy. 2. How numerous are the agencies put in motion for the performance of Divine projects. God is the source of all commissions for the moral good of man. 3. All great workers may find a pattern here. Not to trust their new and Divine enterprises to the tide of popular opinion—storms may gather—may be wrecked. Launch them first on the more tranquil waters of the few—afterwards they will be more likely to weather the national gale. (*J. S. Exell, M.A.*)

Ver. 17. **A land flowing with milk and honey.**—*An inferior motive for a religious life :*—I. SOME PEOPLE ARE RELIGIOUS BECAUSE THEY HOPE THEREBY TO BE SAVED FROM AFFLICTION. " I will bring you out of the affliction of Egypt." 1. They hope to escape the affliction of a bad name. 2. They hope to escape the affliction of a retributive providence. 3. They hope to escape the affliction of moral punishment from God. II. OTHER PEOPLE ARE RELIGIOUS BECAUSE THEY HOPE THEREBY TO BETTER THEIR CONDITION, AND GAIN GREATER ENJOYMENT. " Unto a land flowing with milk and honey. "—1. Because they imagine religion will free them from slavery. 2. Because they imagine religion will give them an advantage over their enemies. 3. Because they imagine religion will give them rich possession. III. THAT WHILE THE LAND FLOWING WITH MILK AND HONEY MAY BE ONE MOTIVE FOR A RELIGIOUS LIFE, THE SUPERIOR IS LOVE TO GOD AND MORAL FREEDOM. (*J. S. Exell, M.A.*) *The resolution of Divine mercy :*—1. Awakens instruments to convey its message. 2. Prepares Churches to welcome its tidings. 3: The giving of a new impulse to history. (*Ibid.*) *The encouragement God gives to Christian workers :*—1. Divine aid in the work. 2. Bright hope in their future. 3. Glad success in their toil. (*Ibid.*) *A happy residence :*—1. A land of plenty. 2. A land of beauty. 3. A land of promise. 4. A land of freedom. 5. A land of rest. 6. A land typal of heaven. (*Ibid.*)

Ver. 18. **Let us go, we beseech thee, three days' journey.**—*A moderate request :*—This request seems at first to be put in a politic form, as if to secure a favourable answer. This, however, was quite unnecessary, since the Almighty was about to bring His people out of Egypt by a strong hand. It is merely expressed in a style of reserve and moderation. It was not requisite to reveal to Pharaoh, who was in a hostile mood, all the intentions of God concerning His people. Hence Pharaoh is merely informed that the God of the Hebrews has met with them ; and their request is limited to the first step to be taken in obedience to His will. A three days' journey is mentioned, simply because this would take them clear out of Egypt, one day being employed in setting out, one in marching, and the third in coming to a resting-place. And a sacrifice is added, because this is the first act of obedience. The former involves their departure out of Egypt, the latter commences the perfect service of God. This is exactly the mode in which God trains His people. The immediate duty and the immediate blessing are set before them, and these are pregnant with all farther and higher duties and blessings. So He deals with Pharaoh. But there is not only reserve, but moderation in the request. It makes the smallest demand consistent with actually leaving, and assigns the highest reason for taking this step, namely, the command of God. By sedulously avoiding every thing harsh and extravagant in its terms, it affords the least possible occasion for Pharaoh to harden his heart, and dismiss the petitioners with an obstinate refusal. At the same time it is a bold and open assertion of liberty. If the people had formed a secret plot to escape from the land of their bondage, we should have been slow to condemn, if not prompt to applaud. But this is not the Lord's way. If Pharaoh had condescended to ask at once, " Who shall go ? Will your wives and children go ? Will your cattle and your other moveables be taken with you " ? he would have received, as he eventually did, a ready and candid reply. But such questions were in reality superfluous. Pharaoh was well aware that bondsmen who had marched three days out of the land of the oppressor, with their families and goods, would not return without compulsion. (*J. G. Murphy, LL.D.*)

Vers. 19–22. **I am sure the king of Egypt will not let you go.**—*The Divine knowledge of the success or otherwise of ministerial work :*—I. THAT GOD IS THOROUGHLY ACQUAINTED WITH THE MORAL OBSTINACY OF MEN. 1. There are many people who act like Pharaoh in relation to the commands of God. God knows such people. Their names are vocal on His lips. He tells His servants about them. He indicates judgments in reference to them. Such people are almost beyond the reach of ministerial influence. The minister is not altogether responsible for the success of his mission. He cannot force men to be good. 2. In all the commissions of human life God recognises the free agency of the wicked. Is it not a mystery that man has the ability to oppose the will of God? 3. We may inquire into the utility of employing Christian agency where the result will be ineffectual. To leave impenitent sinners without excuse. II. THAT GOD IS THOROUGHLY ACQUAINTED WITH THE METHOD HE WILL PURSUE IN REFERENCE TO THE MORALLY OBSTINATE. 1. God deals with the morally obstinate after the method of a consecutive plan. First, He prepares the messenger to visit and teach them; then gives him the message; then tells him how to make it known; then smites in judgments, successive, severe. Thus God does not deal with the morally obstinate according to the impulse of the moment—fitfully, incidentally, but according to a harmonious, merciful, self-consistent plan—a plan that will admit of the repentance and faith of the sinner. 2. God sometimes meets the morally obstinate with demonstrations of His power. "I will stretch out," &c. III. THAT GOD CAN THWART THE INTENTION OF THE MORALLY OBSTINATE BY THEIR OWN WICKEDNESS, AND BY THE CONDUCT OF THEIR COMRADES (ver. 22). (*J. S. Exell, M.A.*)

CHAPTER IV.

VER. 1. **But, behold, they will not believe me.**—*Moses' temptation to shrink from the contest :*—Our duty to our Lord in this world requires that we should do somewhat more than live a life of obedience to Him. Our obedience must be acknowledged obedience. We must never be loth to say, "Whose we are, and Whom we serve." We may read this lesson writ large in the history of God's sending Moses to deliver His people. Moses went through a trial on Mount Horeb, the exact opposite of the trial of Christ. I. MOSES WAS TEMPTED TO DECLINE THE CONTEST with the world altogether, to shrink from action and from prominence, when God called him. Christ was tempted to take the world by storm, to overwhelm it with conviction. II. MOSES WAS FULL OF SYMPATHY FOR THE POOR, full of a desire to see God's ancient promises realized; but when the time came, and God said, "Now go," then, for the first time, it flashed upon Moses that he was unfit to carry out what he had so aspired to be trusted with. His eighty years of life had been given him that in its vast experience he might learn that God was all, man was nothing. He had very nearly learned it in truth; the crust or chrysalis of self was very nearly ready to drop off; it needed just this interview with God to rid him of it entirely. He had seen the miraculous powers with which he had been endowed, but he had not fully understood them, and therefore his will was pausing still. III. THE VOICE OF GOD WITHIN HIM AND WITHOUT HIM WAXED MORE IMPERIOUS. God sternly pointed out that such eloquence as he longed for was but a secondary qualification. "Thy brother, I know that he can speak well"; the legislator need not be the orator. There is not one of us who ever complained to God of insufficient strength without finding his complaint answered either by ministration of grace or disappearance of difficulties. IV. WHAT INTERESTS TREMBLED IN THE BALANCE while Moses was debating! It is not for ourselves only that we shall be responsible if we debate till the time is gone. (*Archbishop Benson.*) *God's call and man's duty :*—I. GOD PROPOSES GREAT THINGS TO MEN. In proportion as any call in life is great, let the heart pause and consider whether its very greatness is not a proof of its divinity. II. WE ARE NOT TO LOOK AT WHAT WE ARE, but at what God is. When He calls, He qualifies for the work

III. WHAT IS RIGHT IN ITSELF MAY BE PERVERTED AND ABUSED. Timidity is right in itself; but when pushed into cowardice, it is wrong. Self-distrust is right in itself; but if it degenerates into atheism, then it is the plague and destruction of the soul. IV. GOD'S CALL TO FAITH IS THE GREATEST CALL TO HIS UNIVERSE. Our duty is to go forward to the unknown and the invisible, and live by faith. (*J. Parker, D.D.*) *The mission of Moses :*—I. THE NATURE OF THE MISSION. 1. Its difficulty and danger. 2. It was divinely appointed. II. MOSES WAS TRAINED SPECIALLY FOR IT. 1. The school of providence. 2. Our need of discipline. III. MOSES WAS SUFFICIENTLY EQUIPPED. The rod. 1. The use of little things. 2. The use of present means. Use "what is in thy hand." IV. MOSES SHRANK FROM HIS MISSION. Modesty and self-distrust generally go with true greatness and exalted virtue. (*P. S. Henson, D.D.*) *The lament of the pulpit :*—I. THE PREACHER HAS FREQUENTLY TO LAMENT THE SCEPTICISM OF HIS CONGREGATION. Practical unbelief. II. THE PREACHER HAS FREQUENTLY TO LAMENT THE INATTENTION OF HIS CONGREGATION. Nothing worse than disobedience to the messages of God. III. THE PREACHER HAS FREQUENTLY TO LAMENT THE QUERULOUS SPIRIT OF HIS CONGREGATION. They question inspiration, preparation, qualification of teacher. And often in unkind, factious spirit. Should rather welcome him as from God, sent to achieve their moral freedom. IV. THAT THIS CONDUCT ON THE PART OF CONGREGATIONS HAS A MOST DEPRESSING INFLUENCE ON THE MINDS OF MINISTERS. He needs the attention, sympathy, prayers, help of those whom he seeks to free from the tyranny of sin. He has enough to contend with external hindrances, with the opposition of Pharaoh, without having added to it that of the slave whose fetter he seeks to break. (*J. S. Exell, M.A.*) *Why did Moses imagine that the Israelites would not believe him?*—1. Because he knew that they were a stiff-necked people. 2. Because he considered himself of insufficient authority to command their respect. 3. Because the power and tyranny of Pharaoh would deter them from believing him. 4. Because they would think it unlikely that God, who had never been seen by man, should appear to him. (*Ibid.*) *Human distrust :*— Human distrust is a difficulty which every preacher, teacher, and holy labourer has to encounter. All great movements are carried by consent of parties. God Himself cannot re-establish moral order without the concurrence of the powers that have rebelled against His rule. After all, the spiritual labourer has less to do with the unbelief of his hearers than with the instruction and authority of God. We have to ascertain what God the Lord would have us to say, and then to speak it simply and lovingly, whether men will hear or whether they will forbear. The preacher must prepare himself for having doubts thrown upon his authority; and he must take care that his answer to such doubts be as complete as the authority itself. God alone can give the true answer to human doubt. We are not to encounter scepticism with merely ingenious replies and clever arguments, but in the power and grace of the living God. (*J. Parker, D.D.*) *Ministerial duty in spite of discouragement :*— Dr. Stevens narrates how an eminent minister was very much depressed by the unbelief of his congregation, and how his spirit of depression was shaken off. He dreamed that he was working with a pick-axe on the top of a basaltic rock, which remained non-riven in spite of repeated strokes of his arm of muscle. When about to give up in despair, a stranger of solemn and dignified demeanour appeared on the scene, who reminded him that as a servant he was bound to go on whether the rock yielded or not. "Work is your duty; leave the results to God," were the last words of his strange visitor. The result was that the discouraged pastor resumed his work, and was abundantly rewarded by "the shattering of the rock of unbelief and indifference" among his flock. *Frailty invested with divinity :*—If we pause for a moment and consider the almost insurmountable difficulties which stood in the way of Israel's redemption from Egypt, we can readily appreciate the hesitation on the part of Moses before undertaking this herculean task. Egypt at that time was one of the most powerful of nations. It was not that Egypt desired simply to hold Israel in subjection, that such a strict and powerful sovereignty was exercised; but the Israelites had become the servants, the slaves of the Egyptians, and as such were almost necessary to the vigour of the nation. Besides, four centuries of oppression had left their deep and degrading mark upon the children of Israel. They had become in a measure satisfied with their condition. Hope had taken to itself wings. Ambition had died within them. There native fire and energy had wasted away. To redeem a people who do not care to be redeemed, to set free a nation which is content with captivity, is a work well-nigh impossible. And then, to add to the difficulty of the case, supposing even that they were free, where will they go? Their own land, the land promised to their father Abraham, is already occupied. Warlike tribes have come down from the north and strongly entrenched themselves within its borders. " Who and what am I," said Moses, " that I should go upon this great mission ? What proofs can I bring to assure the people that I am come from God ? They will not believe my word, and they will ask, Where is the God of our fathers and what is His name ? What sign have I to convince them ? What power have I to display " ? At length God answers, What is that in thy hand ? And he said a rod. He was told to cast it upon the ground, when all at once it became a writhing serpent. You will notice all through the Scriptures in the dealings of God with His people, that in almost every instance He proceeds upon the principle contained in our text. When any great work is to be done, when any special mission is to be undertaken, God does not bring down to the accomplishment of His purpose strange or wonderful agencies, but He rather takes the simple things that lie about common life, and makes them achieve the Divine will. God seems to take the most exquisite pleasure in clothing human frailty with Divine strength and beauty, and imparting to the most ordinary and trivial things, heavenly meaning and significance. Indeed, God's constant purpose seems to have been to unite this world with another one, to blend this life with a life infinitely higher and grander. Life is robbed of all its harmony, all its grace, all its impressiveness if we ever allow it to become separated from the Divine and the eternal, and the little boat which is unswung from the davits and carried off by a huge billow from its place on the ocean steamer, is no more helpless as it rolls in the trough of the sea, and is no more pitiable in its desolation, than the life which is adrift from God out upon the great waters of human experience and distress. To many life is a weary drudgery all the way from the cradle to the grave. It is nothing but work and eat and sleep. Once in a great while there is a little change, but not often. The great bulk of life is a sad monotony, and millions look forward to the quiet and rest of the grave. And why are these people in this dismal plight ? Simply because their life is not connected with the Divine life, because this world is not made a part of the heavenly world, and like a car which has become detached from the swift express and flung out upon a siding, it stands helpless and forsaken in the dark and dismal night. Suppose that here are three plates of common glass a foot square, an eighth or a quarter of an inch in thickness, and suppose that they are given to three men to dispose of them as they please. One takes his and he covers it with black enamel, and on the ebonized surface he paints a human face, or some lovely flowers. Another takes his and he spreads upon it a solution of quicksilver and it becomes a mirror throwing back to the beholder his own face and expression. But the third takes his to the best room in his house, he inserts it in the window which has the most commanding view, and then carefully removing all the dust and finger-marks, he looks through its open substance and sees the skies in their morning beauty, the fields in living green or glistening white, and thus brings heaven and earth within the circle of that room. Now these are the ways in which most of us live. We take our life and we enamel or ebonize it. We make it opaque. We cannot see through it to anything that lies beyond ; and though we paint it, and try to adorn it, yet we in no wise remove the mystery ; the darkness in the sad background which even the flowers will not hide away. Some use the coating of mercury, and make their life nothing but a mirror which reflects themselves. Self is the image ever rising before their eyes. But the wise man makes this life simply a transparency through which he can see the life of God. There are three forms of power by which the machinery of clocks is kept in motion. The first and the one of the oldest date is that of the weight suspended upon a chain or rope. The bulk and heaviness of the weight was always in proportion to the size of the clock, and the wheels were literally driven by the sheer force of the big weights as they slowly descended. The second is that of the spring, the band of steel coiled within its cylinder spending its strength in expansion, and forcing the wheels to revolve in its great desire to get free. The third is that of electricity, where the current is carried along the wire from the central battery. Silently, but almost irresistibly, the mysterious force operates upon the machinery, ensuring an accuracy and faithfulness which can be gained in no other way. And in these we have illustrations of how human life is carried on. Many of us go by weight. We are dragged down by heaviness and toil, and compelled by the demands of circumstances to go our weary round. Others go through by the sheer force of their own energy. They have power and strength in themselves to propel them around the dial-plate of common existence, and in this way they fulfil the measure of their days. But some have an electric current. The wires of their thought are in connection with the great battery of God. Life to them is not a mere drag. Life to them is not merely an expenditure of vital force. Life to them means heavenly communion, Divine fellowship, holy enjoyment, and the days of their pilgrimage are accomplished in simple dependence upon the Almighty will. Now, what seems to be the very plain, the very obvious meaning of this rod? Is it not this: that the most common things within our possession, and under our control, can be so wrought upon by Divine influence, and so charged with Divine power, as to accomplish the most strange and glorious results? St. Paul tells us in the Epistle to the Corinthians that God has a strange choice in the selection of His instrumentalities: "Not many wise men after the flesh, not many mighty, not many noble are called: but God hath chosen the foolish things of the world to confound the wise." And if you will go down the lines of history you will see that God has carried out this principle in its integrity. And this ought not to strike us as either strange or remarkable, because we do just the same ourselves. We take the most common things that we can find, and we unite them with other things until we finally develop the most potential forces of our time. A few gallons of water, a few pieces of coal are enough to send the mad steam hissing through the pipes, eager to turn yon giant engine, or send the train of cars thundering along the line. A few drops of vitriol, a few pieces of prepared zinc, a single thread of wire, and lo, the electric force flashes as light around our world. A few grains of charcoal and sulphur mixed with nitre are sufficient to give us the dreadful gunpowder which sends iron giants swinging in the air that beat into ruin walls and parapets of stone. We take the most common rods that Nature has in her hand, and we breathe upon them, and they become instinct with life; we give them of our genius and our strength; we lift them up out of their low estate. We take the iron and the coal from the mines, we dig out the metals that are in the hills, we dignify them and ennoble them until at length they become our most valued agents and servants. But we must always remember that the rod of itself will be valueless unless it have with it the presence and favour of God. Of what worth was the mere rod which Moses held in his hand that day as he stood before the burning bush? In all probability it was only the shepherd's crook which he used while attending the flocks of Jethro. The rod itself was almost of no value whatever. And so exactly with our life. Before we can be really useful, before we can accomplish any great work, before we can live up to the measure of our power, we must first of all meet with God. We must stand before the burning bush; we must listen to the Divine voice; we must receive the heavenly commission; we must accept the Divine command. Until this is done our life is nothing but a rod—a rod without any special use or intrinsic value, and which will one day break in our hands, and be cast into the fire and be destroyed. Look how this is illustrated: What is that in thy hand? "A sling," said David. "It is enough; go up against the giant"; and the great Goliath fell before the shepherd-boy. What is that in thy hand? "A sword," answered Jonathan. "It is enough," and the brave youth, followed by his armour-bearer, goes up against an army, and the Philistines are defeated by these twain. What is that in thy hand? "A piece of parchment," answered Luther. It is enough, and he proceeds to nail his famous protest upon the doors of the Roman Church and the era of the Reformation broke upon darkened Europe. What is that in thy hand? "A pen," said Bunyan, as he spoke from under the arches of Bedford jail. It is enough, and he wrote the story of the "Pilgrim's Progress," which will live while the world endures. Men and women, with common, simple things about them, have heard the voice of God, and doing just what their hand found to do, they made their life memorable in the history of the Church and accomplished the Divine will. What is that in your hand? "Only a rod," answers the mother from beside the cradle, the workman standing at the bench, the clerk behind the counter, the man of business at his desk. Only a rod, and is that all? Oh, there is something of far greater value than you now suppose. Ask that honest farmer in a few weeks from now standing in the open furrows, what is that in his hand, and he will answer, only a few grains of seed. But is that all? Far from it. Those grains of seed contain the germs of the great harvest which will fill our lands with plenty, and crowd the threshing-floors with abundance. Then say not "Only a rod." There is no such word as "only" about human life. Every part of it is invested with mysterious grandeur and possibility. We cannot tell how far the most simple thing will reach. A word dropped from our lips, a hand clasped within ours, something apparently trifling done and then forgotten, will go on long after we have passed away, and a life which throws its shadows all down eternity cannot have anything but which is of value. (*J. W. Johnston.*)

Vers. 2–5. **What is that in thine hand?**—*A trivial possession:*—I. GOD FREQUENTLY MAKES INQUIRY ABOUT THE MOST TRIVIAL POSSESSIONS OF MEN. 1. Have they been honourably gained? 2. Are they being put to their proper use? 3. Are they in a line with Divine power? II. GOD FREQUENTLY MAKES THE MOST TRIVIAL POSSESSIONS OF MEN TEACH GREAT TRUTHS. 1. This shows the Divine adaptability to the circumstances of men. 2. This shows the Divine wisdom in making insignificant things teach Divine truth. 3. This shows the Divine simplicity of the plans and purposes of Heaven. III. THAT THE MOST TRIVIAL POSSESSIONS ARE USEFUL TO OTHERS AS WELL AS THOSE TO WHOM THEY BELONG. IV. THAT THE MOST TRIVIAL POSSESSIONS OF MEN PROVE, AFTER ALL, THE MOST USEFUL, and ought therefore to awaken human gratitude. (*Ibid.*) *A rod:*—1. The subject of Divine inquiry. 2. The token of a shepherd's office. 3. The symbol of a leader's power. 4. The prophecy of a nation's freedom. (*Ibid.*) *The rod:*—When God installed Moses into his great trust, He gave him a wand or staff of office as its badge. But it was not the baton of a general nor the sceptre of a king. It was only the shepherd's rod. In Moses' hand it became what no jewelled crosier ever has been or will be. This stick was to be not only the ensign of his power, but its instrument. And in this simplicity, indeed, lay its special fitness for its office; because all men who looked upon it could see that its power was not in itself, not inherent; not in the rod, but effectual only by a self-imposed law of God's action, and conditioned in its success upon His fidelity to His own rule. In this, as afterwards of the yet humbler symbol of the cross,—in this, the symbol of his simplicity, of his exile, of his lowliness, the world was to be conquered. 1. I remark in regard to this rod, that it had no natural aptitude for its work. There was nothing in its natural qualities to distinguish it from any other rod, and its appointment to be Moses' staff of office and instrument of miracle wrought in it no physical change whatever. It was still mere wood. Sufficient force would break it. A sharp tool would cut it. And it was according to the analogy of His ways: and so St. Paul broadly states it. "Base things of the world, and things which are despised, hath God chosen, yea, and things which are not, to bring to nought things that are." It is God's way to do great things by weak means. That is the Divine philosophy of action, the opposite of man's. 2. Notice, again, that God in doing His great works does not need any instruments, but uses them simply of His own sovereign will; and this appears in their obvious inadequacy in themselves to the results which they, nevertheless, produce. Moses was not indispensable to God, nor his rod to Moses, but by God's determination. If we look at our Lord's miracles when He was upon earth, we shall see this truth strikingly illustrated. In the variety of their methods they are so exhibited as at once to show His independence of all means, and His sovereign power in appointing and employing them. So this wonder-working rod of Moses answered simply the purpose of forming a visible link between the Divine will and the effect that was produced. The rod did not do the miracle, but a Power that worked by it; and that showed itself able to dispense with it by employing in its work an instrument so manifestly incapable of contributing anything to the proposed result. A word brings Lazarus from the grave; a touch of the bier awakens the widow's son. And thus we come to the philosophy of means in the system of grace. They are visible signs of God's working, such signs as cannot work except as God works in them; and to us they are tests of obedience and trials of faith. There is nothing quite so irrational as rationalism. To obey God is the most rational of things. And to stand arguing and questioning about a thing, debating its propriety and efficacy when God has told us to do it, is eminently irrational. Moses might have stood and said, This wooden stick cannot divide the waters, or turn the dust to flies, or make the heavens dark, or draw water out of a rock; and he would have said nothing but the truth. And yet, if Moses had thrown away his rod, he could never have invented anything else that would have done these things, and the things would have remained undone. There is a supernatural working in the world that the world does not take knowledge of. And it works by a class of instrumentalities that the world regards as childish and impotent. The reliance some people place upon them it counts superstition, and derides as futile and delusive. To expect any benefit from them they consider irrational. The measure of their belief is their reason. So they eliminate all miracle from the Scriptures, and all that is supernatural from the Church of God; and out of the poor residue they construct what they call rational Christianity, and a very mean Christianity it is. And so they illustrate very well the apostle's saying, " Professing themselves wise, they became fools." And there are too many Christians who, without going such lengths, are quite too ready to criticise God's appointments, and either hold them of light obligation, or greatly underrate their value and efficacy. But there is a supernatural element in the Church of Christ, and God in it works invisibly by means. " Water," say they, " cannot cleanse the soul, nor bread and wine nourish it. The touch of a prelate can have no power to convey the influences of the Spirit to ministers in Ordination, or to lay people in Confirmation." Men may see that the ten commandments are right and salutary, and may observe them on that account. Their reason pronounces them proper, and therefore they regard them. They would regard them if they had found them in the Koran, or the Books of Confucius. There is much of this sort of virtue, and it is respectable and useful to its possessor and to society. But it is not obedience, it is not religion. Faith does not underlie it. The love of God is not its life. Moses took his rod in his hand and with it he did wonders. He believed in it, because he believed in God, and in God's assignment of it to him as an instrument of power. And then it was an instrument of power, a wonder staff, before which impediments vanished and foes fled away. (*R. A. Hallam, D.D.*) *A talk with children—" What is that in thine hand? "*—This was a question which astonished Moses. It was a surprising thing to him that God should think anything of a shepherd's crook. It would not have astonished him to hear God speak about sceptres, but that He should call special attention to an old rod that he had carried as a shepherd a thousand times was more than he could have ever expected. But God now began to show Moses that he could turn that rod to higher use than he had ever done hitherto. There are many things put into the hands of little children the full use of which they do not yet know. 1. For instance, when at first you are taught to write a pen is placed in your hand. What an amount of trouble you have before you learn even how to hold that pen! For a long time you do not exactly know how to hold the gift that is given you; and for a still longer time you little know what use you may yet make of it. When the apostle Paul was a boy in school, and had to learn how to use the stylus, or pen, he little knew what use he would be able to make of his pen in writing his Epistles. So with regard to the apostle John. So also with reference to John Bunyan. When he was at school, a poor boy, he was not taught much, since he was only to be a tinker. But a pen was put into his hand, and it is wonderful what use he made of it in later years in writing the " Pilgrim's Progress." Who knows? perhaps there is a child here to-day who has only just learnt how to use the pen, and yet thousands may yet thank God for what he will write. 2. Again, some of you have recently been on a journey by train. Had you looked at the engine before you started you might have seen a man laying hold of a handle, or lever. You might well have asked him, " What is that in thine hand? " Had you done so, he would have replied, " This is the lever by which I have power over the engine and make it to go fast or slow, or by which I stop it." Thus, by holding just that little piece of iron, the engine-driver is perfect master of that huge and powerful engine. 3. Again, you go with your father to a telegraph office. He wants to send a message to America. The clerk looks at the message and lays hold of a small handle by which he sends those words along the cable through the depths of the Atlantic Ocean, and they are read in a few seconds in New York. 4. Again, in times of war, when ships draw near a port, you may find a man in a small room, or shed, who watches until a ship comes to a certain point. He then touches a little button and the ship is blown up in an instant. There is a connection between that little button and a mine of explosives which is hidden in the water beneath the ship; and although that mine may be many miles away from that little telegraph office, a touch of the button by a man's hand at once explodes the mine and works terrible destruction. When an Arab baby-boy is born, his parents put a little ant into his right hand, and closing the hand upon it say, " May the child be as busy and clever as the little ant." That is the best wish they can utter for their children. But we would put something better than an ant in your little hands. We would have you hold firmly the Bible, and remember all that it tells you of the Saviour's love. We would have you study prayerfully that Book, and live according to its teaching. (*D. Davies.*)   *Work for all :*—The subject that I desire to bring before your attention is that of appointed instrumentality. God accomplishes the purposes of His grace by instrumentality. Blessed are they who are enabled to give themselves up with all that they have and all that they are to be employed in the Lord's service. We are not employed to be writers of God's revealed will, nor to be leaders of God's people, nor to be in other respects what Moses was. But he was a pattern to believers in Christ, as far as instrumentality went, in the work to which he was called. I. Now consider PREPARA-

TION FOR USEFULNESS. In the case of Moses we see very remarkably a course of preparation going forward for many years, both as respects the dealing of God's providence with him, and also as respects the blessing of God's grace bestowed upon him. II. But this brings me now to the second particular, namely, ENCOURAGEMENT IN GOD'S SERVICE AS HIS INSTRUMENTS. You will observe our text brings Moses before us, after all this lengthened preparation and when God was calling him to begin his work, as one who was making excuses and objections. As if he had said, "Well, but what good can I do? There is no use in my going on this errand; I am not fit for it." If you read the remaining part of this chapter, you will see that this conviction of his mind was expressed again and again. And here we may observe, by the way, that there is such a thing as false humility. Humility, when it is genuine, the work of God's Spirit, cannot be overprized. But there may be what looks like humility that is not the fruit of God's Spirit. If God calls me or you to any particular service, and we think that we are very humble and say, "No, I cannot attempt that service, I am not fit for it," this is false humility, because God never gives work without giving strength and wisdom to do it. God never brings a trial upon us without providing grace to enable us to bear the trial; so that believers in Christ may say, under all circumstances, "All is well." But without dwelling further upon this, the point I wish to notice is, how God removed Moses' objection. "The Lord said unto him, What is that in thine hand? And he said, A rod. And the Lord said, Cast it on the ground." He did so, and then the circumstances occurred which you will read in the following verses. Observe, Moses had but a simple rod in his hand when he came to that point in his history on which the Lord was telling him to enter upon the special work for which he had been prepared. And yet if Moses' heart were right with God, he had that in his hand which might be useful in God's service, though it was only a rod. Man's wisdom is here utterly at fault. If man had been asked, "Now, what means should be used in order to deliver out of the iron bondage of a powerful monarch a nation such as Israel?" man would have formed some plan by which an army might be raised, and furnished with suitable weapons of war, and a suitable opportunity taken in order to throw off the yoke of Pharaoh's government and rule. But here was Moses, God's instrument, and he had neither sword, nor spear, nor army; he had a simple rod, a shepherd's rod in his hand. Observe, God does not require of Moses, when He tells him to go to His work, that which Moses has not. He does not require of Moses sword, and spear, and shield, and armies, in order to go forth to be a deliverer of Israel. The question is not to him, "What canst thou do? Canst thou obtain those who will go forth under thy command to fight a battle of loyalty and for liberty? Canst thou get together ammunition and other things which they will need for their warfare"? Moses might have then said with truth he could not engage in the work. But all that God said to him was, "Moses, what is that in thine hand?"—not, "What canst thou get?" but, "What hast thou got?" Now, we learn from this, that God can use any instrument which He pleases for His work, and that those are altogether wrong who suppose that they are not called upon to do anything in the service of God because, perhaps, they are not distinguished as others of their fellow-creatures—have not so much money, not so much influence, not so great learning, not so much time on their hands, and so on. It is not to be looked at in this way, as if God demanded of us that which we have not, but simply that He requires of us that which we have. Observe, next, the Lord said unto Moses, "Cast it on the ground"; and upon its being cast on the ground, the rod, we are told, "became a serpent." Afterwards he was told to put forth his hand, and "it became a rod in his hand." God, by this double miracle, laid hold of that rod of Moses as His rod; it was no longer the rod of Moses only; it was the rod of God. (*W. Cadman, M.A.*) *What is that in thine hand?*—I. A QUESTION FOR MOSES. Well—what had he? A rod. That is, as I suppose, a shepherd's crook: a stout sapling, curved at one end, to help him in caring for his flock. But how could this help him in caring for Israel? Who can turn it into a talisman to draw their hearts to him? It is enough to tell of the Being and the power and the skill of the Creator; but not enough to prove a Divine commission. There was need of some further revelation—and this further revelation was not withheld. What was Moses told to do with the rod? "Cast it on the ground"; as though God had said, "*You* can do nothing with it, see what *I* can do." "And it became a serpent." Now here we are confronted with the supernatural, the miraculous; for there is no natural evolution of vegetable out of animal, or animal out of vegetable. God can do it—and do it quite as easily as He can bring the sturdy staff out of the feeble bud; but it is not in His ordinary course of action. He will only resort to it when some extraordinary end is in view. But was there not a lesson in this miracle? Was it not a symbol of the great things God was about to do? II. A QUESTION FOR CHRISTIANS. 1. Is there not work for every one of us?—and work not unlike that to which Moses was called. The state of the world at large is described in this volume under many figures, very sad and very affecting; and one of the saddest and most affecting is that of slavery. Slaves of appetite—slaves of covetousness—slaves of fashion: we hear their sighs—their groans, sometimes. For the lust of the flesh, and the lust of the eyes, and the pride of life are hard taskmasters; they will give their bondsmen no rest or peace: there is no slavery like that of sin! And therefore the cry of the gospel is— "Emancipation!" "If the Son shall make you free, ye shall be free indeed." 2. But what good can we hope to do? There are as many difficulties in our way as in the way of Moses. Our fellow-men are so accustomed to slavery that they won't believe in freedom. Ay—and they are so accustomed to all kinds of folly and imposture that they won't believe that our message comes from God. How then can we succeed? Now comes the question of the text, "What is that in thine hand"? What power of influence has God given you? Now see whether that power may not be used for Him. "Oh, but," you say, "my influence is a very insignificant thing"! And so is a shepherd's crook. But see what a shepherd's crook became in the hand of Moses; and remember that God may "choose weak things to confound the mighty, and foolish things to confound the wise." 3. And so the question comes to us—"What is that in thine hand?" Not—what would you like to have there, or hope to have there? but—what have you? Be it the three hundred pence, or be it the two mites—use it for God, and see what God will make of it! Certainly nothing will recommend the gospel to those around us like the personal exertion of those who advocate it. (*F. Tucker, B.A.*)   *Great things from small:*—God often does His greatest works by the humblest means. The great forces of nature are not the earthquake which tumbles cities into ruins. This power passes in a moment; the soft silent light, the warm summer rain, the stars whose voice is not heard—these are the majestic mighty forces which fill the earth with riches, and control the worlds which constitute the wide universe of God. So in Providence. Not the great Church organization, excellent and proper as it is. Martin Luther, a poor monk who had difficulty in getting bread to eat, shook the world; Linnæus, with eight shillings in his pocket, began to study botany; Columbus had no grand steamer to carry him across the wide Atlantic. He wearied his life, and at last got from the rulers of his time a reluctant permission to embark with a hundred and fifty men only, and in three small ships. The founders of the United States of America were humble pious men. The Pilgrim Fathers sought only a place to rest the soles of their feet where they could worship God in peace. The founders of Christianity were fishermen. Christ Himself the Carpenter, the Nazarene, despised and crucified, was the wisdom and the power of God. For, did He not say—"I, if I be lifted up, will draw all men unto Me"? So in the text—"What is that in thine hand? A rod"—the emblem, the tool of his daily work. With this Moses was to do mighty deeds. Rabbinical tradition has it that Moses was an excellent shepherd. He followed a lamb across the wilderness, plucked it with his rod from a precipice amid the rocks, and carried it in his bosom; whereupon God said—"Let us make this Moses the shepherd of Israel." He, a stranger, a fugitive, a humble shepherd, becomes the lawgiver, the leader, the deliverer of his people. The lesson of the text is plain. God still meets every man, and asks the old question—"What is that in thine hand?" Is it the tool of an ordinary trade?—with that God will be served. The artisan where he is, in his humble workshop, by using the rod which is in his hand, the merchant in his business, are in the place where they are now; all are called upon to do service. Few have rank, or wealth, or power, or eloquence. Let those illustrious few use their ten talents; but let us, the obscure millions, use the simple duties of life—the rod that is in our hand. A smile, like a little rushlight, may cheer a sick man tossing on his bed. Happiness-givers are the true representatives of Christ; to shed abroad in home and social circles the joy and the charity of Christ is the true work of Christ's followers; and in this blessed happiness-giving all, exalted and lowly, may alike engage. (*J. Cameron Lees, D.D.*)   *Splendid instruments not necessary:*—A rod: probably the shepherd's crook, the symbol of his present condition. Among the Arabs a long staff with a curved head, varying from three to six feet in length, is used for this purpose. This rod was made the subject of a double miracle. From the story of Moses' rod the poets invented fables of the thyrsus of Bacchus and the caducæus of Mercury. Homer represents Mercury as taking his rod to work miracles, precisely in the same way as God commanded Moses to take his. God takes the weakest instruments to accomplish His mightiest ends. "A rod," "a ram's horn," "a cake of barley meal," "an earthen pitcher," "a shepherd's sling," anything, in short, when used of God, will do His appointed work. Men imagine that splendid ends can only be reached by splendid means, but such is not God's way. He can use a crawling worm as well as a scorching sun, a gourd as well as a vehement east wind. (*A. Nevin, D.D.*) *The rod as a symbol:*—The staff was the shepherd's crook, with which he had hitherto conducted the flock of Jethro. Hence it represented his vocation as a shepherd. This he was to throw away, *i.e.*, he was to give up his calling and follow a new one. But the staff which he had thrown away became a serpent, and Moses fled before it. His vocation hitherto had been a poor and despised one; but it was also quiet, peaceful, and free from danger. When this was given up, he was to be exposed to dangers of such magnitude, that even his life would be threatened. Moses could foresee all this, and hence the obstinacy with which he refused to enter upon his new vocation. But at the word of God he laid hold of the snake, and it became a staff in his hand once more. This showed that, by the power of God, he would be able to overcome the dangers that would surround him, when he relinquished his present calling. By overpowering the snake he recovered his staff, but it was no longer his staff; it was the rod of God (ver. 20), and with the staff thus altered he was to perform the work entrusted to him (ver. 17). It was still a shepherd's staff, and his new vocation was a shepherd's calling. From being a shepherd of Jethro's sheep he was to become the shepherd of God's sheep, the leader and lawgiver of the people of God. And he became so, by overcoming the dangers which intervened between these two different employments. We must also observe, that this was the rod with which he was to bring the plagues upon Egypt; and therefore it was the retributory counterpart to the rod with which the Egyptian taskmasters had beaten the Israelites (ver. 14). As soon, then, as Moses appeared before the people and performed this sign, it showed them, first, that the dangers to which the mission of Moses would expose them—dangers which they soon experienced (chap. v.)—would be overcome; and secondly, that the staff of shepherd and ruler, with which Moses was to lead and govern them, was not assumed without authority, but given to him by God, and therefore the question could not be asked, as it was before, "Who made thee a prince and a judge over us?" (chap. ii. 14). He afterwards performed the same miracle in the presence of Pharaoh (chap. vii. 10, &c.). (*J. H. Kurtz, D.D.*)   *The symbol of a consecrated life:*—I believe the rod cast down, and taken up again, typifies the entire consecration of the Christian's life to God. The rod was the ordinary sign and instrument of Moses' daily occupation. That cast down, and taken up, became filled with power; and by it he proved to Israel and to Pharaoh that he had seen Jehovah. We are commanded in 1 Cor. vii. 24 to abide in the calling "wherein we are called." I suppose we may understand from this that we do not need to change our station and calling (supposing it to be an honest one) in order to serve God. Are we shepherds, carpenters, merchants, lawyers, doctors, teachers, servants, or what not, we may serve God in that calling quite as efficiently as in any other. So He can, and will, make you mighty in the use of your calling, be it what it may, high or low, learned or mechanical, the calling of a master or a servant, a mistress or a maid. Only cast it down at the feet of Jesus, in humble and holy consecration; and then take it up again to use it and pursue it for Him. What God needs to-day in this world is a host of men and women, in every walk of life, who are living for God, and serving Him in their calling, using it as a means of illustrating God's righteousness. He wants some merchants to do business for Him, that the world may know what God's thought of righteousness in trade is. The banker may serve God in the same way. The medical man has a calling in which he may leave the testimony of God's tenderness in the sick room; and by his ministry of healing exercised on the body he has an opportunity, such as is afforded to no other man in the world, to point his patients to the great Physician and Healer of souls. As it is, alas that so many Christian physicians fail to cast down their rods at the feet of Christ! The lawyer at the bar, and the judge on the bench, may be God's witnesses in their profession. The teacher with the children (a most difficult position) may also cast his or her rod down. The governess, the nurse, and the mother may be consecrated to God for those to whom God has sent them, or whom He has given them. The servant in the house—both the maid-servant and the man-servant—every one, in his or her place, may throw down the rod of their calling at the feet of Jesus, and take it up again in power.   (*G. F. Pentecost, D.D.*)

Vers. 6, 7. Leprous as snow.—*Leprosy as emblematical of doubt:*—I. THAT AS LEPROSY WAS THE WORST DISEASE THAT COULD HAVE BEEN PERMITTED TO THE HAND OF MOSES, SO DOUBT OF THE DIVINE WORD IS THE MOST HURTFUL THAT CAN OVERTAKE THE HUMAN MIND. 1. Both are small in their commencements. 2. Both are progressive in their developments. 3. Both are gloomy in their forebodings. 4. Both are isolating in their tendency. 5. Both are paralysing in their influence. 6. Both are deadly in their result. II. THAT AS LEPROSY COMES UPON MEN UNEXPECTEDLY, SO DOES DOUBT UPON THE HUMAN MIND. The germ of scepticism often remains long concealed in the human mind; its workings are subtle, and we know not what will be the extent of its future harvest. III. THAT AS LEPROSY COULD ONLY BE REMOVED BY THE DIVINE TOUCH, SO HUMAN DOUBT CAN ONLY BE REMOVED BY COMMUNION WITH GOD. (*J. S. Exell, M.A.*)   *Various suppositions as to the meaning of this miracle:*—1. Some give it a moral signification—as that the leprous hand of Moses showeth the works of the law that justifieth not. 2. Some give it a mystical signification—that the leprous hand of the synagogue of the Jews was cast off as the leprous person out of the house, and the hand restored betokeneth the Gentile Church adopted instead of the Jewish. 3. Some refer it to Christ, that He being the Hand, that is, the power of His Father, by taking our nature upon Him, became as it were leprous, that is, deformed, by His sufferings and passion, but by His resurrection and ascension His glory appeareth. 4. Some give it an historical signification—by the leprous hand they understand the miserable state of the Hebrews in the time of their cruel servitude, who in their deliverance received their former liberty. 5. Some think that the leprous hand signifieth the pollutions of Egypt, wherewith Israel was defiled, who being delivered were restored to the true worship of God. 6. That the first sending of Moses to the Israelites brought upon them more cruel treatment, but his after ministry brought them joy and deliverance. 7. That the hand being the instrument of working, betokeneth the ministry and authority of Moses, and that God would use a weak instrument to effect His will, Moses having lived a long time in banishment seemed a thing leprous and vile, yet God should in this His service make him a glorious vessel and instrument. 8. That as the leprosy is only cured by God, so their deliverance was only God's work, and to humble Moses by the remembrance of his own infirmity. 9. As far as the intrinsic significancy of the sign is concerned, it was evidently calculated to teach that whatever is new, vigorous, vital, and flourishing, may at once be withered at the word of Omnipotence; and again with equal facility restored to its pristine condition. (*Ibid.*)   *Ability for God's service:*—1. Human hands weak and unfit for service. 2. Sanctified power is only attained from God. 3. Hence the worker must be humble, but not impotent or paralytic in hand. (*Ibid.*)   *Soul-instruction:*—I. AS UNDERTAKEN BY A DIVINE TEACHER. There are lessons for every man to learn, which heaven only can teach. II. AS EMPLOYING THE MOST ·IMPRESSIVE SYMBOLISM. The Divine teaching is always suggestive, never exhaustive. III. AS OCCUPYING BUT A SHORT SPACE OF TIME. An eternal lesson may be learnt in a moment. IV. AS PREPARING FOR IMPORTANT DUTY. Divine instruction is never aimless. Designed not merely to make men clever, but to give them the power of moral emancipation. (*Ibid.*)   *The leprous hand restored:*—That which happened to the hand of Moses was a picture of what had happened, and was still to happen, to the people of Israel. By going down to Egypt, the Israelites had been preserved from the injurious influence of Canaanitish customs. Through the favour of the first Pharaohs, Egypt was undoubtedly a hiding-place, in which the family of Jacob had been cherished and preserved, when it was distressed both in body and mind. But there had been a change in both the men and the times, and Israel was enslaved, despised, and held in abomination in the land of Egypt. When Israel departed from Egypt, he was like a homeless leper. But Jehovah led him once more to a hiding-place, where he was cleansed from the leprosy which he had·brought with him from Egypt, and where he was set apart as a holy people and a priestly nation (chap. xix. 6). It is very easy to explain why this sign was not exhibited before Pharaoh as well as the others (chap. vii.). The thing signified was of too internal and spiritual a nature, it was too closely connected with the counsel of God concerning His people to be appropriately displayed to Pharaoh. (*J. H. Kurtz, D.D.*)

Vers. 8, 9. They will believe the voice of the latter sign.—*The paralysis of* *doubt :*—A man needs not to be a thorough unbeliever, overtly renouncing all allegiance to revealed truth, in order to become useless in the pulpit and religiously powerless in society. He needs only to put a note of interrogation after some of the articles of his creed. That is enough, without absolutely erasing them. The hesitant is as impotent for spiritual good as the heretic. The man who is shooting for the Queen's cup may as well attempt to hold his rifle with a paralysed arm as take aim with a trembling hand. That tremor will be fatal to success in hitting the mark. Truth uttered questioningly and apologetically will prove an arrow of conviction to no man's soul. This, it seems to me, rather than absolute and pronounced infidelity, is the bane and weakness of the age. It pervades the pulpit and the pew. From the former, doctrines may be still propounded with logical accuracy, with great precision of definition, with much beauty and felicity of illustration, but with not enough of conviction to drive them forcibly home. The rifle is a beautiful piece of mechanism, but there is something amiss with the powder. (*J. Halsey.*) *The Divine treatment of human doubt :*—I. THE DIVINE BEING RECOGNIZES THE PROBABILITY THAT MEN WILL NOT WELCOME THE TRUTH UPON ITS FIRST PRESENTATION TO THEM. Yet the message proclaimed by Moses was—1. Adapted to their condition Announcing freedom. The tendency of all unbelief is to intensify slavery of moral nature. 2. Wonderfully simple. 3. Divinely authenticated. Miracles will not convince a sceptic. II. THE DIVINE BEING MERCIFULLY MAKES PROVISION FOR THE CONVICTION AND PERSUASION OF MEN in reference to the reality of the truth proclaimed, notwithstanding their confirmed unbelief. This method of treatment is—1. Considerate. Every facility given for complete investigation. 2. Merciful. Sign after sign. 3. Condescending. III. THE PERSISTENT UNBELIEF OF MEN IS LIKELY TO AWAKEN EVIDENCES OF TRUTH INDICATIVE OF THE DIVINE DISPLEASURE (ver. 9). 1. Evidences that recall past sorrows. Reminding of murder of children in river. 2. Evidences prophetic of future woe. Indicating a strange and unhappy change in their condition, if they embraced not the message of Moses. (*J. S. Exell, M.A.*) *The voice of the first sign :*—1. It speaks of the thraldom of man. 2. It speaks of the inability of man to liberate himself therefrom. 3. It speaks of the agency that God has provided for the freedom of man. 4. It speaks of the strange unwillingness of man to credit the tidings of freedom. (*Ibid.*)   *Miracles :*—1. Miracles at first may miss their end, and not persuade men to faith. 2. Second miracles may do that which the first failed to effect. 3. God's word and promise alone can make miracles themselves effectual means of faith. 4. Miracles have voices which should command faith and obedience. (*Ibid.*)   *Ministers exposed to unbelief :*—That a true minister, notwithstanding—1. His call. 2. His spiritual preparation. 3. His knowledge of the Divine name. 4. His supreme moral power, and—5. Intimate communion with God—is exposed to the unbelief of those whom he seeks to benefit. (*Ibid.*)   *The obstinacy of unbelief :*—It will reject the truth. 1. In opposition to the word of him by whom it is brought. 2. In opposition to the Divine power by which it is accompanied. 3. In opposition to the benevolent design it contemplates. 4. In opposition to accumulative demonstration. (*Ibid.*) *The folly of rejecting the gospel of emancipation :*—One can hardly conceive a poor wayworn wretch, as he lies on the arid waste, panting with blackened lips and swollen tongue, striking the kind traveller's flask from his hand, and spilling the precious water among the blistering sands. The slave boy—now an African bishop —exulted gleefully when a British cruiser snapped the fetters from his youthful limbs and bore him to free Liberia. Can folly surpass that insensate madness which makes the sinner spurn the clear, cool, crystal drops of life, and perversely traverse the wilds of sin ? Can madness outrival that supreme folly which leads the hapless bondsman of sin to hug the chains of condemnation, and obstinately kiss the fetters of wrath ?

Vers. 10-13. **O my Lord, I am not eloquent.**—*The objections made to religious service :*—I. THESE OBJECTIONS WERE MADE AFTER GOD HAD GIVEN HIM A FULL INSIGHT INTO THE NATURE OF THE SERVICE REQUIRED. 1. The insight given into the nature of this service was infallible. 2. It was forceful. 3. It was sympathetic. II. THESE OBJECTIONS FREQUENTLY ARISE FROM AN UNDUE CONSCIOUSNESS OF SELF. 1. From a consciousness of natural infirmity. This ought to inspire within them a more thorough determination to seek Divine help. Silence is often more eloquent and valuable than speech. 2. From a supposition of moral incapacity. The call of God is calculated to educate all the sublime tendencies of the soul, and renders men fit for the toil allotted to them. 3. That, rather than self, God must be the supreme idea of the soul when about to enter upon religious service. Our hearts should be a temple in which every act of service should be rendered to the Infinite. III. THESE OBJECTIONS DO NOT SUFFICIENTLY REGARD THE EFFICACY OF THE DIVINE HELP THAT IS PROMISED IN THE SERVICE. " Now therefore go, and I will be with thy mouth, and teach thee what thou shalt say." 1. The Divine help is adapted to our natural infirmity. It is far better to have God joined to our infirmity, than to have the eloquent tongue without Him. Thus there are times when an infirmity may be an inestimable advantage to a Christian worker. 2. The Divine help is adapted to our full requirement. God did not merely promise to aid the speech of Moses, but also to teach him what he should say. So in the Christian service of to-day, good men are not merely aided in the line of their natural infirmity, but also along the entire line of their requirement. IV. THESE OBJECTIONS ARE A REFLECTION ON THE PROPRIETY OF THE DIVINE SELECTION FOR THE SERVICE. " And the Lord said unto him, who hath made man's mouth," &c. 1. This method of conduct is ungrateful. 2. Irreverent. V. THESE OBJECTIONS DO NOT SUFFICIENTLY RECOGNIZE THE DIGNITY AND HONOUR THE SERVICE WILL COMMAND. 1. There was the honour of achieving the freedom of a vast nation. 2. There was the honour of conquering a tyrant king. 3. There was the honour of becoming the lawgiver of the world. VI. THESE OBJECTIONS ARE LIABLE TO AWAKEN THE DIVINE DISPLEASURE. . " And the anger of the Lord was kindled against Moses." 1. This anger may be manifested in our removal from the service. 2. This anger may be manifested by the positive infliction of penalty. 3. This anger may occasion our eternal moral ruin. Learn: 1. Good men ought to know better than to object to the service of God. 2. That in the service of God men find the highest reward. 3. That in the service of God men attain the truest immortality. (*J. S. Exell, M.A.*) *Uselessness of mere words :—* I am tormented with the desire of writing better than I can. I am tormented, say I, with the desire of preaching better than I can. But I have no wish to make fine, pretty sermons. Prettiness is well enough when prettiness is in place. I like to see a pretty child, a pretty flower ; but in sermons, prettiness is out of place. To my ear, it would be anything but commendation, should it be said to me, " You have given us a pretty sermon." If I were put upon trial for my life, and my advocate should amuse the jury with tropes and figures, or bury his arguments beneath a profusion of flowers of his rhetoric, I would say to him, " Tut, man, you care more for your vanity, than for my hanging. Put yourself in my place—speak in view of the gallows—and you will tell your story plainly and earnestly." I have no objections to a lady winding a sword with ribbons, and studding it with roses as she presents it to her hero-lover ; but in the hour of battle he will tear away the ornaments, and use the naked edge on the enemy. (*Robert Hall.*) *The art of the orator undesirable in a preacher :*—Hipponicus, intending to dedicate a costly statue, was advised by a friend to employ Policletus, a famous workman, in the making of it ; but he, being anxious that his great expense should be the admiration of all men, said that " he would not make use of a workman whose art would be more regarded than his own cost." When in preaching the great truths of gospel salvation the enticing words which man's wisdom teacheth are so much sought out that the art of the orator is more regarded by the hearers than the value of the truth spoken, it is no wonder that the Lord refuses to grant His blessing. He will have it seen that the excellency of the power lies not in our speech, but in His gospel. (*C. H. Spurgeon.*) *Eloquence :*—"I am not eloquent." I. THEN TRUE ELOQUENCE MAY HAVE ITS USE. 1. To explain Divine truth. 2. To inspire men with the thought of freedom. 3. To manifest the perfection of the gift of speech. II. THEN DO NOT CONDEMN MEN WHO ARE. III. THEN DO NOT ENVY THOSE WHO ARE ACKNOWLEDGED TO BE SO. If we have not eloquence, we have some other equally valuable talent in its place. IV, THEN THE LORD CAN USE A FEEBLE INSTRUMENTALITY. This will enhance the Divine glory. V. THEN WORDS ARE NOT THE CHIEF CONDITIONS OF SERVICE. Ideas, thoughts, emotions, and spiritual influences, occupy a more prominent place. VI. THEN DO NOT GRUMBLE, BUT SEEK THE DIVINE AID IN YOUR INFIRMITY. He will help and bless work done for Him. (*J. S. Exell, M.A.*) *Slowness of speech :*—I. AN INFIRMITY. II. A DISCRETION. III. A DISCIPLINE. (*Ibid.*) *Why was Moses not gifted with eloquence ?*—It might certainly be asked with propriety, why Moses, who was singled out by Providence as the great medium for bringing the wisdom of heaven down to the earth, for ever substituting Divine truth instead of human error, and who was gifted with such uncommon perfection of the mind and intellect, was denied the power of eloquence, apparently so indispensable for his extraordinary vocation. But it was an act of the sublime wisdom of the Almighty to withhold from Moses just the gift of persuasion, lest it should appear that he owed the triumph over the obstinacy of Pharaoh and the disbelief of the Israelites, not to the miracles of God and the intrinsic worth of the Law, but to the artifices and subtleties of oratory, which too often procure, even to fallacies and sophisms, an ephemeral victory. It was wisely designed that the power of God should the more gloriously shine through a humble and imperfect instrument. This is a remarkable and deeply interesting difference between the legislator of Israel and the founders of almost all other religions, to whom, uniformly, no quality is ascribed in a higher degree than the gift of eloquence. (*M. M. Kalisch, Ph.D.*)   *Self-consciousness :*—Moses has now descended from the high level of the argument, and narrowed the case into one of mere human personality. He has forgotten the promise, "Certainly I will be with thee." The moment we get away from Divine promise and forget great principles, we narrow all controversy and degrade all service. Self-consciousness is the ruin of all vocations. Let a man look into himself, and measure his work by himself, and the movement of his life will be downward and exhaustive. Let him look away from himself to the Inspirer of his life, and the Divine reward of his labours, and he will not so much as see the difficulties which may stand ever so thickly in his way. Think of Moses turning his great mission into a question which involved his own eloquence! All such reasoning admits of being turned round upon the speaker as a charge of foolish, if not of profane, vanity. See how the argument stands : "I am not eloquent, and therefore the mission cannot succeed in my hands," is equivalent to saying, "I am an eloquent man, and therefore, this undertaking must be crowned with signal success." The work had nothing whatever to do with the eloquence or ineloquence of Moses. It was not to be measured or determined by his personal gifts : the moment, therefore, that he turned to his individual talents, he lost sight of the great end which he was called instrumentally to accomplish. (*J. Parker, D.D.*)   *Fluency in speech :*—Moses was a thinker rather than a speaker. Fluency was not his forte. He saw too much in a moment to be able to give utterance to it all at once ; and so his lack of readiness in the use of language was the result of the richness of his thought, rather than of its poverty. When the bottle is full, its contents flow out less freely by far than when it is two parts empty. So, very often, the fluency of one speaker is due to the fact that he sees only one side of a subject ; while the hesitancy of another is the consequence of his taking in at a glance all the bearings of his theme, and of his desire to say nothing on it that will imperil other great principles with which it is really, but not to all minds visibly, connected. (*W. M. Taylor, D.D.*)   **I will be with thy mouth.**—*Natural infirmities in relation to moral service :*—I. THAT GOD DOES NOT ALWAYS SEE FIT TO REMOVE NATURAL INFIRMITIES FROM THOSE WHO ARE COMMISSIONED TO IMPORTANT SERVICE. 1. They keep us humble. 2. They remind us of God. 3. They prompt us to prayer. II. THAT GOD RENDERS NATURAL IMPEDIMENTS EFFECTIVE TO THE CLEAR MANIFESTATION OF HIS POWER AND GLORY. 1. Should win our submission. 2. Should gain our confidence. 3. Should inspire our praise. III. THAT GOD SO FAR COMPASSIONATES OUR NATURAL INFIRMITIES AS TO RELIEVE THEM BY CONGENIAL AND EFFICIENT HELP. 1. Fraternal. 2. Adapted to need. 3. Constant. (*J. S. Exell, M.A.*)   *The Divine Creatorship :*—I. SHOULD SILENCE THE VOICE OF COMPLAINT UNDER NATURAL INFIRMITIES. II. SHOULD BECOME AN ARGUMENT FOR THE READY PERFORMANCE OF ANY MISSION ON WHICH WE MAY BE DIVINELY SENT. III. SHOULD LEAD US REVERENTLY TO ACKNOWLEDGE THE SOVEREIGNTY OF GOD IN THE VARIED ALLOTMENTS OF LIFE. (*Ibid.*)   *Lessons :*—I. THE DIVINE COMMISSION. II. THE DIVINE COMPANIONSHIP. III. THE DIVINE INSTRUCTION. (*Ibid.*)   *Speech, or dumbness, from God :*—I. LANGUAGE IS OF DIVINE ORIGINAL. You may have been accustomed to consider it just as natural to man to speak as to walk ; but this is a mistake. A child left to itself may learn to walk, but a child left to itself would never learn to speak ; it would utter sounds, but it would never connect sounds with thoughts—it would never, that is, learn to express certain thoughts by certain sounds. It might invent some jargon of its own, but as to anything which should at all resemble even the elements of a language, and a system of sounds by which everything around us should be classified and defined, you will never think that this could be found in the accidental babblings of infancy ; and however you may seek to account upon natural principles for the origin of language, we still venture to say, that unless you receive the Mosaic account of the Creation, there is no phenomenon so hopelessly inexplicable as language. Unless it be supposed that God formed man at first, and gave him the organs of speech, ay, and then taught him their use, and furnished him with words by which ideas should be expressed, language is the most unintelligible of prodigies; and you may search the universe and find nothing which you may not account for without God, if you can shut out His agency from the introduction of speech. And there is scriptural evidence of the fact, that God taught man language, or that the language first spoken was Divine in its origin. You will observe, that so soon as man was created God spake unto him; and thus the first use of words was to communicate the thoughts of God. But the thoughts of God must have been communicated in the words of God, and man could not have understood God's words, unless he had been first taught them of God; so that when on the very outset of human existence you find conversation held between man and his Maker, you are forced to conclude, that since on no supposition could man in such a brief space have invented a language, the employed language must have been Divine, and Adam must have received from God the earliest intimations of speech. II. EVERY CASE OF INABILITY TO SPEAK IS OF DIVINE APPOINTMENT. God has meted out to us our every endowment, whether of body or of mind; we are indebted for nothing to chance, for everything to Providence; and though it were beside our purpose to inquire into the reasons which may induce God to deny to one man the sense of sight, and to another the sense of hearing, we are as much bound to recognise His appointment in these bodily defects as in the splendid gifts of a capacious memory, a rich imagination and a sound judgment, which procure for their possessor admiration and influence. And when there shall come the grand clearing up of the mysteries and discrepancies of the present dispensation, we nothing doubt that the Almighty will show that there was a design to be answered by every deformed limb, and every sightless eyeball, and every speechless tongue, and that in regard both to the individual himself and to numbers with whom he stood associated, there has been a distinct reference to the noblest and most glorious of ends, in the closing up of the inlets of the senses, or in the yielding the members to disease or contraction. The deaf and dumb child shall be proved to have acted a part in the furtherance of the purposes of God, which it could never have performed, had it delighted its parents by hearkening to their counsels and pouring forth the music of its speech; the blind man and the cripple shall be shown to have been so placed in their pilgrimage through life, that they should have been decidedly disadvantaged, the one by sight, the other by strength. "Who maketh," then, "the dumb, or deaf, or the seeing or the blind? have not I the Lord?" Thine, O God, is the allowing upon earth the melancholy assemblage of those who seem but fractions of men; but wise and good, though unsearchable and past finding out, are all Thy ways and all Thy permissions. III. And there are two INFERENCES which you should draw from the facts thus established, and which we would press with all earnestness on your attention. 1. You discern, first of all, the extreme sinfulness of looking slightingly or with contempt on those who are afflicted with any bodily defect or deformity. Ridicule in such case, however disguised and softened down, is ridicule of an appointment of God; and to despise in the least degree a man because he possesses not the full measure of senses and powers, is to revile the Creator, who alone ordered the abstraction. 2. If we are indebted to God for every sense and every faculty, are we not laid under a mighty obligation to present our bodies a living sacrifice to our Maker? (*H. Melvill, B.D.*) *Gifts other than eloquence an element in leadership :*—Probably Moses stammered, as he said he was slow of speech; and was not fluent in speaking, notwithstanding all his learning. A man may be a philosopher, a statesman, may have a clear head and a strong will, a solid judgment and a great mind, and yet be destitute of any talent for speaking. It was the same with St. Paul (see 1 Cor. ii. 1–4; 2 Cor. x. 10), who was so full of wisdom and zeal and love, but had no eloquence. (*Prof. Gaussen.*) *Inspiration better than education :*—Speaking of art-training, Mr. Ruskin says: "Until a man has passed through a course of academy studentship, and can draw in an improved manner with French chalk, and knows foreshortening, and perspective, and something of anatomy, we do not think he can possibly be an artist. What is worse, we are very apt to think that we can make him an artist by teaching him anatomy, and how to draw with French chalk: whereas the real gift in him is utterly independent of all such accomplishments." So the highest powers of the teacher or preacher, the power of interpreting the Scriptures with spiritual insight, of moving the hearers to earnest worship and decision, may exist with or without the culture of the schools. Learned Pharisees are impotent failures compared with a rough fisherman Peter anointed with the Holy Ghost. Inspiration is more than education. (*H. O. Mackey.*) *Strength not always appropriate :*—Professor Tyndall states as a most remarkable fact, that the waves which have up to this time been most effectual in shaking asunder the atoms of compound molecules are those of least mechanical power. "Billows," he instructively adds, "are incompetent to produce effects which are easily produced by ripples." It is so with us. Often the greatest of us cannot do things that the smallest and weakest can. God sends power from on high to them, and it should be our prayer that God will endue us with power from on high that we may do His work, even though we be the weakest and humblest of His servants. *God can make use of poor material:*—The meek Moses lost sight of the fact that God does not of necessity require good material. The paper manufacturer is not nice in the choice of his materials. He does not, writes Arnot, reject a torn or filthy piece as unfit for his purpose. All come alike to him; for he knows what he can make of them. The filthy rags can be made serviceable. So God needed not a man highly endowed with mental gifts and intellectual energies, with commanding presence and persuasive eloquence. His providence and grace could prepare Moses for his mission. *God's biddings are enablings:*—The missionary John Williams once said that there were two little words which were able to make the most lofty mountains melt: "Try" and "Trust." Moses had yet to learn the use of these words. God taught him. The sailor has to be taught that he must not look on the dark and troubled waters, but at the clear blue heavens where shines the pole-star. Moses was gazing at the surging sea of Egyptian wrath, and God taught him to direct his gaze heavenward; then to try and trust, for greater is He that is with you than all that be against you. As an early Christian writer enjoins, let us not forget—as Moses did at first—that all God's biddings are enablings, and that it is for us not to ask the reason but to obey.

Ver. 13. **Send, I pray Thee, by the hand of him whom Thou wilt send.**—*An evasion of spiritual work:*—I. MOSES RECOGNIZED THE NECESSITY THAT THE WORK SHOULD BE ACCOMPLISHED. II. HE MANIFESTED A DISPOSITION TO SHRINK FROM ACHIEVING THE WORK HIMSELF. III. HE EXPRESSED A DESIRE THAT SOME OTHER PERSON SHOULD BE CALLED TO, AND ENTRUSTED WITH, THE WORK. IV. HE WAS IN DANGER OF LOSING THE HONOUR OF THE WORK TO WHICH HE WAS CALLED. (*J. S. Exell, M.A.*) *The joy of being used by God:*—I have a letter from a dear Christian lady in this city who refused to speak to an inquirer when I asked her to, on the ground that she could not talk to an inquirer. The next day she was deeply humiliated to think that she had refused to speak to an anxious soul; and the question even of her own acceptance with God came up for discussion in her own mind. "Can I be a child of God, if I am not willing to speak to an anxious soul about Jesus?" She was led by this to cast herself down in consecration to God to be used of Him in any way, and especially in speaking to the anxious. Here is an extract from a letter just received. "I am constrained to tell you that He allowed me on Sunday night, for the first time, the intense joy of helping to lead a dear soul to Himself. Oh, the rest, and joy, and peace to my own heart, is more than tongue can tell! To think that after being His child for seventeen years, and being cold and useless all that wasted time, He should then be so loving and gracious as to use me, such a worthless cumberer. Oh, it is wonderful! Praise His dear name." Dear friend, would you not like to have a similar experience? (*G. F. Pentecost, D.D.*) *The inventiveness of reluctance:*—Man excusing himself from duty is a familiar picture. It is not a picture indeed; it is a personal experience. How inventive we are in finding excuses for not doing the will of God! How falsely modest we can become! depreciating ourselves, and putting ourselves before God in a light in which we could never consent to be put before society by the criticism of others. Is not this a revelation of the human heart to itself? We only want to walk in paths that are made beautiful with flowers, and to wander by streams that lull us by their own tranquillity. Nerve, and pluck, and force we seem to have lost. In place of the inventiveness of love we have the inventiveness of reluctance or distaste. It should be our supreme delight to find reasons for co-operating with God, and to fortify ourselves by such interpretations of circumstances as will plainly show us that we are in the right battle, fighting on the right side, and wielding the right weapon. The possibility of self-deception is one of the most solemn of all subjects. I cannot question the sincerity of Moses in enumerating and massing all the difficulties of his side of the case. He meant every word that he said. It is not enough to be sincere; we must have intelligence and conscience enlightened and enlarged. Mistakes are made about this matter of sincerity; the thing forgotten being that sincerity is nothing in itself, everything depending upon the motive by which it is actuated and the object towards which it is directed. The Church is to-day afflicted with the spirit of self-excusing :—it cannot give, because of the depression of the times; it cannot go upon its mighty errands, because of its dainty delicateness; it cannot engage in active beneficence, because its charity should begin at home; it cannot enter into ardent controversy, because it prefers the comfort of inaction. Churches should not tell lies to themselves. The first great thing to be done is for a man to be faithful to his own heart, to look himself boldly in the face, and speak the clear truth emphatically to his own consciousness. (*J. Parker, D.D.*)

Vers. 14–17. **He shall be thy spokesman.**—*Mutual aid in religious work :*—
I. THAT SOMETIMES GREAT MEN ARE CALLED TO UNDERTAKE A WORK AGAINST THE PERFORMANCE OF WHICH THEY IMAGINE THEMSELVES TO HAVE A NATURAL IMPEDIMENT. 1. Men should be certain that their so-called impediment will be a real hindrance in the service to which they are sent. In these days, when people are called to work, they at once refer to their infirmity and unfitness for it; but their real infirmity is not so much their slowness of speech, as their unbelief, and unwillingness to follow the Divine command. They have not the moral courage to encounter difficulty. 2. But we admit that sometimes men are called to religious work, against the performance of which they have a true natural impediment. And why this apparent anomaly? (1) It is because with the command He gives the moral energy necessary for its execution. He gives the timid man the stimulus of the vision. He gives him the inspiration of a miracle. (2) Its design is to educate man on the side of his weakness. (3) It is to render the mission all the more triumphant when accomplished. It is the distinguishing glory of Christianity that it makes provision for the victory of the weak, who have within their souls the grace of God. II. THAT AT SUCH TIMES GOOD MEN REQUIRE THE AID OF OTHERS WHOSE TALENTS COMPENSATE FOR THEIR INFIRMITIES. 1. This help was adapted to the infirmity of Moses. "Is not Aaron the Levite thy brother? I know that he can speak well." So there are a variety of gifts and talents in the Church. The one is the complement of the other. 2. This help was arranged by the Providence of God. "And also, behold, he cometh forth to meet thee." (1) As to the time of meeting. (2) As to the place of meeting. (3) As to the purpose of meeting. 3. This help was founded upon, and rendered welcome by, family relationship. "Thy brother." III. THAT SUCH CO-OPERATION RENDERS RELIGIOUS WORK MUCH MORE JUBILANT AND SUCCESSFUL. 1. It is happy. It is adapted to our weak condition of faith. 2. It is sympathetic. 3. It is hopeful. (*J. S. Exell, M.A.*)   *Moses and Aaron:*—
I. THE CERTIFICATED AMBASSADOR. Moses. 1. His hesitation. Caused by—(1) His own meekness. Had not a high opinion of himself. (2) His knowledge of the people he was sent to deliver, and also of the oppressor. He had not forgotten their rejection of him. 2. His certificate. Power to work sundry miracles is given. 3. His unbelief. Moses seems, at this time, to rely too much on human qualities. His lack of eloquence, he thinks, will be a great hindrance. II. THE GRACIOUS COMPENSATION. Moses and Aaron the complement of each other. The man of words and the man of action. Human qualities are mercifully distributed. No one man perfect. Each needs the help and talents of others. Providence designs that men should not be independent of one another. "Two heads better than one." Opposites often found in one family. Moses and Aaron—brothers. Different qualities and talents in a household to be used, and combined, for the service of God. Let none envy the gifts of others, but cultivate his own. III. THE BROTHERS' MEETING. 1. In the wilderness. Place of brotherly meeting a garden in the desert of life. How great the joy of meeting each other where all around is paradise, and no separation or toil in prospect. 2. Marked by affection. They "kissed" each other. Mutual respect and love. 3. Their intercourse. Chief matter in hand was Moses's commission. Aaron, the elder, cheerfully takes the second place. Is indebted for even that to the humility of Moses. They journey on together, and at once address themselves to their work. Learn—1. God's witnesses are witnessed to. Seals to their ministry. 2. Humbly to regard ourselves, but do any work to which Providence calls us. 3. Rejoice in others' powers, and cheerfully unite for common ends. 4. Thank God for our meeting on earth, and prepare for the better one. 5. Christ, our elder Brother,

meets us in the wilderness, salutes us with the kiss of love, and goes with us to all our holy labours. (*J. C. Gray.*)   *Mutual service:*—In the valley of Chamounix there stands a very interesting monument; it presents two figures—Saussure, the great scientist, and Balmat, the guide, who was the very first to stand on the summit of Mont Blanc.   Saussure on the summit of the mighty mountain could do what the poor guide could not do, he could observe the structure of the rocks, take observations of barometrical variations, note the intensity of the solar rays, the mode of formation of clouds, and he could describe the superb scenery unfolded to his view with the feeling of an artist and the pen of a poet.   Balmat could do nothing of all this but had it not been for his skill and daring, Saussure had never scaled the glorious height.   So on the monument both are immortalized, the lowly guide, the famous philosopher, for by their mutuality they triun p'ied and gave mankind a new world of science and poetry.   So it ever is in the Church.   In Christian fellowship all souls serve one another.   (*W. L. Watkinson.*)   *Life and service interdependent:*—In the great honey industries of South California the bees play a most important and valuable part.   But they cannot pierce the skins of the apricots until the lady-bug has made a hole for them.   It must have been an accidental thing at the outset, the first bee joining a lady-bug at her feast of apricot, but they have now become necessary to the honey-crop of the district.   All life and service is interdependent —Timothy is necessary to Paul; the least essential to the great.   (*H. O. Mackey.*) *The Divine anger:*—1. Often righteously provoked.   2. Often gentle in its reproof.   3. Truly benevolent in its disposition.   (*J. S. Exell, M.A.*)   *I know that he can speak well:*—I. Then God takes knowledge of the varied talents of men.   II. Then God will hold men responsible for their talents.   III. Then the talents of men cannot be better employed than in the service of the Church. (*Ibid.*)   *Christian workers more ready to rely on man than on God:*—We have noted the timidity and hesitation of Moses, notwithstanding the varied promises and assurances with which Divine grace had furnished him.   And now, although there was nothing gained in the way of real power, although there was no more virtue or efficacy in one mouth than in another, although it was Moses, after all, who was to speak unto Aaron, yet Moses was quite ready to go when assured of the presence and co-operation of a poor feeble mortal like himself, whereas he could not go when assured again and again that Jehovah would be with him.   How his case, like a mirror, reflects our own hearts!   We are more ready to trust anything than the living God.   How deeply should it humble us before the Lord that, though we move along with bold decision when we possess the countenance and support of a poor frail mortal like ourselves, yet we falter, hesitate, and demur when we have the light of the Master's countenance and the strength of His omnipotent arm to support us.   (*A. Nevin, D.D.*)

Ver. 18. **Let me go, I pray thee.**—*A true recognition of filial duty :*—I. It consists in a true recognition of parental authority.   1. Moses was animated by honesty.   2. Moses was related by marriage.   3. Moses was obliged by kindness.   II. It is compatible with silence in reference to the inner experiences of our spiritual life and work.   Moses only asked the consent of his father-in-law to visit his brethren in Egypt; he did not name the primary object of his journey.   This was quite consistent, under the circumstances, with a true recognition of filial duty.   1. Silence is not necessarily cunning.   2. Silence may be discreet.   3. Silence may be self-protective.   Many toils of Christian workers have been brought to nought by the lack of precautionary measures on the part of those who have been entrusted with them.   III. It should awaken kindly and judicious parental consideration and response.   "And Jethro said to Moses, Go in peace."   1. Sometimes the request should be granted.   2. Always goodwill should be expressed.   "Go in peace."   3. Supremely should self be forgotten.   (*J. S. Exell, M.A.*)   *The compulsion of service :*—This case of Moses reminds us that our best lifework is that on which we enter under a feeling that it is absolutely essential that we should do it.   Moses tried in every way to put away from him the office to which God called him.   But still it came back upon him.   He felt that he must go ; and when that irrepressible *must* shaped itself in his soul, he went, and carried all before him.   It is the irrepressible in a man that makes him great.   So long as the work he undertakes is performed because he must do something, there is nothing remarkable either about him or about it ; but when he enters upon it because it is something that *he must do,* then prepare yourself for something noble.   Is it not just in this that the quality which we call genius peculiarly resides ?   If a man thinks that he would like to write in verse, or to paint something, or to make a speech, or what not, his work will never be heard of.   But if there is in him a song which insists on singing itself out, or a painting which will not let him rest until he has put it on the canvas, or a truth, the utterance of which he cannot hold back, then he is sure to be at length a poet, an artist, or an orator.   That was a wise old minister who, on being consulted by a youth who desired to become a preacher of the gospel, said to him, " Young man, don't become a minister if you can help it."   It is the man who cannot help being a preacher who will be most effective always in the pulpit. The work which we can help doing is not for us.   If Moses could have successfully excused himself, he would have been no fit man for the great crusade on which he entered.   But it was because, in spite of all his reluctance, there was within him the overmastering sense that God had called him to be Israel's deliverer that he was at length so successful.   Ah ! have we not here the cause of so many failures in moral and religious enterprises ?   The men who have inaugurated them have done so for personal *éclat* or pecuniary profit, and not because of this inner compulsion.   (*W. M. Taylor, D.D.*)   *Domestic sympathy in duty :*—Moses tells Jethro of his commission from Jehovah, and asks permission to carry out the Lord's will.   This request is at once granted.   It is most encouraging to be thus cordially seconded by those of our own house in our purpose to serve the Lord, whether in public or private ministry.   We also, whether we are called into the public or private service of God, ought to communicate with those of our own household.   My advice is always to a young convert, to go at once to those at home, to whom they naturally owe confidence, and tell them what the Lord has done for them, and that He has called them to service.   If it is son or daughter, go to mother or father ; if it is wife or husband, then to husband or wife.   Seek not to keep your conversion, or your consecration to God, a secret from those of your own household.   It sometimes happens that one must stand alone in one's house.   This is often very hard to do.   Once Paul was compelled to stand alone. " At my first answer no man stood with me, but all forsook me: . . . notwithstanding the Lord stood with me, and strengthened me."   This we can always count on ; and no one is alone with whom the Lord stands.   I once knew a husband and wife, each of whom, afraid of the other, had sought the Lord in one of our meetings, apart from the other, each being afraid that the other would ridicule.   They had both of them been open and scoffing unbelievers.   Now both had found the Lord ; but each was afraid to confess it to the other, and yet each of them noticed a change in the other.   At last the wife summoned courage to tell her husband that she had been so burdened with a sense of her sin, that, having no rest, she had sought the Lord and found Him.   To her unspeakable joy the husband caught her in his arms, and confessed the same for himself to her.   Let us always first go home and tell our friends how great things the Lord hath done for us, and saved our souls ; and then shall we have a free course to serve the Lord.   Otherwise our hands will be tied ; and we shall be hindered in every way from faithful service.   I think there will always be some one at home who will be glad that we have met with the Lord ; either for the first time, or in a way that means an entire consecration to Him and His service.   And as Jethro said to Moses, so will they say to us: " Go in peace."   (*G. F. Pentecost, D.D.*)

Ver. 19. **All the men are dead which sought thy life.**—*The death of enemies :*— 1. In a world like this, the greater the man the more enemies he will have.   2. Death in this world is constantly sweeping away our enemies as well as friends. I. The death of our enemies should RESTRAIN RESENTMENT.   Were it not wrong to return evil for evil, to revile those who revile us, it would scarcely be wise.   While we are preparing our retaliating machinery, death is doing his work with them. Our blows will scarcely reach them before they fall, and then, when they are gone, they can do us no harm.   But if we have retaliated, the memory of the retaliation will give us pain.   II. The death of our enemies should STIMULATE US TO OVERCOME EVIL BY GOOD.   The sublimest conquest is not that which will crush the body or wound the feelings, but that which will subdue the enmity and win the hostile soul to friendship and love.   (*Homilist.*)   *The Divine precaution for the safety of Christian workers :*—I.   IT IS SOMETIMES MANIFESTED BY REMOVING GOOD MEN AND GREAT WORKERS FROM DANGEROUS ASSOCIATIONS.   1. Christian workers are sometimes removed from the pride of high society.   2. Christian workers are sometimes removed from the contamination of great sin. 3. Christian workers are sometimes removed from the pedantry of great learning. 4. Christian workers are sometimes removed from physical evil. II. IT IS SOMETIMES MANIFESTED BY INFORMING GOOD MEN AND GREAT WORKERS OF·THE REMOVAL OF DANGER. Time aids the enterprises of heaven. Death subdues the hatred and passion of men. III. THE DIVINE PRE-CAUTION DOES NOT ALLOW AN ABANDONMENT OF THE WORK COMMITTED TO THE GOOD. (*J. S. Exell, M.A.*) *Death of enemies :*—Hearing a whole choir of birds chirping merrily together, my curiosity was excited to inquire into the occasion of their convocation and merriment, when I quickly perceived a dead hawk in the bush, about which they made such a noise, seeming to triumph at the death of an enemy. I could not blame them for singing the knell of one who, like a cannibal, was wont to feed upon their living bodies, tearing them limb from limb, and scaring them with his frightful appearance. Over this bird, which was so formidable when alive, the most timid wren or titmouse did not now fear to chirp and hop. This occurrence brought to my mind the case of tyrants and oppressors. When living, they are the terror of mankind ; but when dead, they are the objects of general contempt and scorn. " When the wicked perish, there is shouting " (Prov. xi. 10).

Ver. 20. **Returned to the land of Egypt.**—*The journey to Egypt :*—I. THAT A GOOD MAN JOURNEYING ON THE SERVICE OF GOD SHOULD TAKE HIS FAMILY WITH HIM. Never go on any good errand without your family; teach the youthful feet to walk in obedience to God. II. THAT A GOOD MAN JOURNEYING ON THE SERVICE OF GOD SHOULD TAKE HIS ROD WITH HIM. Never go on a journey of moral service without God. Especially if you are a minister of the gospel, take the rod on your journey to Egypt. 1. It will keep you humble. It will remind you of your humble occupation in the desert, when you are tempted to pride, in the great service to which God has called you. Every Christian worker needs to have something within his soul to inspire humility. 2. It will make you happy. When you are desponding and sad, when the work does not open up to your effort as you would wish, the rod will remind you of the vision at the bush, and of the miracles wrought at the commencement of the mission. The reason why there are so many unhappy workers in the Church, is because they have left the rod at home. 3. It will make you powerful. With this rod Moses was to work miracles. So if Christian workers had the rod of God in their hand, they would be able to show to the world much more effectively than they do, the holy tokens of their mission. (*J. S. Exell, M.A.*)

Ver. 21. **See that thou do all these wonders before Pharaoh.**—*Moses before Pharaoh :*—Israel was under the sovereign control of the King of Egypt. He had property in them. Moses in the name of the Lord suddenly asked Pharaoh to give Israel their freedom. He was startled. He did not acknowledge the Lord. A political petition was presented to him, and he dealt with it on political grounds. It was not a spiritual question which was proposed to Pharaoh. It was exclusively a political question. It was therefore within this sphere that the Divine action was taken, and that action is fitly described in the text as a hardening of Pharaoh's heart. The question will then arise, what the meaning of that hardening was, and what useful results accrued from a process which appears to us to be so mysterious. The hardening of Pharaoh's heart, as involving the development of a merely political scheme, may amount in effect to no more than this, " I will delay the process, this request shall not be granted at once; and I will prolong the process in order that I may bring out lessons for Pharaoh himself, for the children of Israel, and for mankind at large ; were Pharaoh to let the children of Israel escape from him at once, the result would be mischievous to themselves ; therefore in mercy, not in anger, I will harden Pharaoh's heart." So far, the question is not a moral one, except in the degree in which all questions have more or less of a moral bearing. It has been supposed by some that in the case of this exercise of Divine sovereignty, the sum total of Pharaoh's wickedness was increased. Not so. There is the greatest difference between wickedness being localized and wickedness being increased. As the history proceeds, we see that the political situation enlarges itself into a spiritual problem. Pharaoh made a promise to Moses, which he did not keep. Thus he hardened his own heart. Applying these lessons to ourselves as sinners, I have now to teach that Jesus Christ tasted death for every man, and that whosoever will may avail himself of the blessings secured by the mediation of the Saviour. If any man excuses himself on the ground that God has hardened his heart, that man is trusting to an excuse in the most solemn affairs of his being which he would not for a moment tolerate in the region of his family life or commercial relations. We must not be sensible in ordinary affairs and insane in higher concerns. Were a servant to tell her mistress that she is fated to be unclean in her habits, that mistress would instantly and justly treat her with angry contempt. Were a clerk to tell a banker that he was fated to come late every morning, and go away early every afternoon, the statement would be received as a proof of selfishness or insanity. Were a travelling companion to tell you to make no attempt to be in time for the steamboat or train, because if you were fated to catch it there would be no fear of your losing it, you would treat his suggestion as it deserved to be treated. Yet men who can act in a common-sense manner in all such little affairs, sometimes profess that they will not make any attempt in a religious direction, because they believe in the doctrine of predestination or fatalism. Wicked and slothful servants, they shall be condemned out of their own mouth! "Come unto Me, all ye that labour and are heavy laden, and I will give you rest." "Whosoever will, let him come." "Him that cometh to Me, I will in no wise cast out." "How often would I have gathered you, as a hen doth gather her brood under her wings, and ye would not!" In presence of such statements as these, it must be the very consummation of blasphemy to turn round upon God and say, "I wanted to be saved, but Thou didst harden my heart and condemn me to hell." (*J. Parker, D.D.*)

Vers. 22, 23. **Israel is My son, even My firstborn.**—*The primogeniture of the good :*—I. THAT THE GOOD HAVE A DIVINE FATHER. 1. He is merciful to the children. 2. He vindicates the children from their foes. II. THAT THE GOOD HAVE HEAVENLY PRIVILEGES. As the sons of God. 1. They have the privilege of high birth. Only they who are the subjects of this new birth know the privileges it confers upon them. Nor can the meanest ancestry of earth be excluded therefrom. 2. They have the privilege of good moral culture. In God's family all the children are well disciplined. This culture of our moral nature is designed to fit us more thoroughly for the high relationship into which we are called, that we may be responsive to all its duties, and in harmony with its sacred destinies. III. THAT THE GOOD HAVE INSPIRING HOPES. 1. The hope of a happy death. 2. The hope of a vast inheritance. 3. The hope of a sublime future. Christians are the sons of God. Lessons : 1. Live worthy of your great Parent. 2. Act worthy of your noble ancestry. 3. Embrace your glorious privileges. 4. Let nothing dim your bright hopes. (*J. S. Exell, M.A.*) **Let My son go, that he may serve Me.**— *The Divine intention in the moral freedom of man :*—I. THAT GOD HAS A DEFINITE PURPOSE IN THE MORAL FREEDOM OF MEN. His great aim is to bring men from the tyranny of passion, pride, covetousness and self, into the freedom of a tranquil, humble, and self-denying service. Hence the Divine preparation that is given to the varied agencies that are to achieve this freedom. II. THAT THE PURPOSE OF GOD IN THE MORAL FREEDOM OF MEN IS THAT THEY SHOULD SERVE HIM. 1. That we should serve Him in our business. 2. That we should serve Him in our social life. 3. That we should serve Him with all our energies. Why should we serve Him ? (1) Because we are His sons. (2) Because of the freedom He has wrought for us. (*Ibid.*) *The great Emancipator :*—I. Let us endeavour to fix our thoughts upon THE VOICE OF GOD, which was a real power to bring up His people out of Egypt. That voice was threefold ; asserting His proprietorship in them, demanding their freedom, and ordaining their destiny. II. Now here was THE VOICE OF MAN. What a come-down it seems to be. "Thou shalt say unto Pharaoh, Thus saith the Lord, Let My son go." Why did not the Lord say it Himself ? Why did He need to pick up a Moses and send him to say it ? Well, had the Lord said it Himself to Pharaoh, it would have been very startling, and Pharaoh must have yielded ultimately to the Divine fiat : but do you not see the deeper marvel in the milder proceeding, when Jehovah, as it were, hides His power and cloaks it in weakness ? Instead of appealing to Pharaoh with that voice which breaks the cedars of Lebanon, and makes the hinds to calve, He speaks to him by one who was slow of speech and of a stammering tongue. Now, if God's voice can vanquish Pharaoh when it masks itself behind the feebleness of a stammering Moses, it will be more glorious than it would have been if it had used no instrumentality whatever. Go on with steady perseverance. Be ye sure of this, ye shall not labour in vain or spend your strength for naught. Are you still slow of speech? Nevertheless, go on. Have you been rebuked and rebuffed? Have you had little else than defeat? This is the way to success. You shall macadamize the road with the rough flints of your failure. Toil on and believe on. Be steadfast in your confidence, for with a high hand and an outstretched arm the Lord will fetch out His own elect, and He will fetch some of them out by you. III. Our last word is upon THE POWER OF GOD. Without the power of God the voice of man would have been an utter failure. What effect was produced by the voice of Moses? Went there not forth with it a power which plagued Pharaoh? It filled the sinful land of Egypt with plagues. So men that preach God's gospel with God's power fill the world with plagues. What will occur by and by? Why, the oppressor will be glad to part with his bondsmen. It sometimes happens that the ungodly become themselves very glad to get rid of God's chosen people, whom they are prone to persecute. "Their melancholy ill comports with our liveliness," so they say. A lady who joined this Church some years ago, moving in the higher circles of society, said to me, "I was quite willing to continue my acquaintance with my friends, but I found they gave me the cold shoulder, and did not want me." Just so. It is a great mercy when the Egyptians say, "Get ye gone," and when they are ready to give you jewels of silver and jewels of gold to get rid of you. The Lord wants His people to come right out and to be separate; He knows how by the simple utterance of the gospel to put such a division between His people and those who are not His people, that even the ungodly shall begin to say, "Get you gone; we want to have nothing further to do with you." Glory be to God when such a thing as that happens. (*C. H. Spurgeon.*)   *A Divine threat:*—1. Claims attention.   2. Certain of execution. 3. Stern in requirement.   (*J. S. Exell, M.A.*)

Vers. 24–26. **Zipporah took a sharp stone.**—*Neglected duty a hindrance to the performance of religious work :*—I. MOSES HAD NEGLECTED THE DUTY OF CIRCUMCISING HIS SON.   II. THAT THIS NEGLECT OF DUTY INTRODUCED AN EXPERIENCE OF PAIN INTO HIS LIFE.   III. THAT THIS NEGLECT OF DUTY ENDANGERED THE PERFORMANCE OF HIS RELIGIOUS WORK. Many a Christian worker is rendered feeble to-day by the sin of his past life. Let us beware how we imperil the freedom of men, and the work of God, by our own neglect. Freedom from sin is the great essential to the success of Christian work.   IV. THAT THE NEGLECT OF THIS DUTY WAS MOST FOOLISH, AS IT HAD AFTER ALL TO BE PERFORMED. Men will have to face their neglected duties again, if not for performance in this world, yet for judgment in the next. (*J. S. Exell, M.A.*)   *The Divine purpose of a strange event :*—I. TAKE THE FACT JUST AS STATED (ver. 24).   1. The very terms are confessedly startling. The Lord seeking and trying to kill! But His fatherly heart withheld His arm.   2. The character of the sufferer makes it still more remarkable. To cut short such a life as that of Moses—how strange!   3. Considerations of time and circumstances only deepen the wonder. God had just spoken to Moses as a friend, and expressly engaged him for an exceptionally important work.   4. The prominence and emphasis given to the record complicates the mystery. It is God speaking to all generations on things belonging to their peace.   II. CAUSE AND PURPOSE OF SO STRANGE A DISPENSATION.   1. Moses' compliance with Egyptian custom of circumcising only adults.   2. So long as he discarded the national seal or sign of the covenant made with Abraham, he was essentially unfit to take the place of recognized champion and deliverer of God's people.   3. His position was that of a rebel, determined not to submit to an ordinance acknowledged to be Divine. God would sooner "kill" Moses than allow him to enter on a work in a state of hardened impenitence.   III. IMMEDIATE RESULTS. Moses yielded, and God "let him go."   1. Though up to that moment there seemed no hope of escape, the instant there was confession on one side, there came forgiveness on the other.   2. Henceforth there is not simply a change, but a marked improvement in his entire spirit and character.   IV. CONSEQUENT BLESSINGS AND BLESSEDNESS.   1. The disease was instantly arrested.   2. Thereon followed another token for good, to cheer and to strengthen his heart (vers. 27–29).   3. In further evidence of complete reconciliation, think of the wonderful and unparalleled success with which the mission was crowned.   CONCLUSION.   1. To such as are in vigorous health, the moral is—boast not thyself of to-morrow.   2. To such as may recently have passed through heavy affliction, it suggests the wisdom of much earnest self-scrutiny.   3. Of the large class of almost Christians, "not far from the kingdom of God," it asks with special solemnity— "Why halt ye between two opinions?"   4. To those of us who call ourselves Christians, and profess to be aiming at public usefulness, its unmistakable voice is—"They should be clean that bear the vessels of the sanctuary." Sins unforsaken, however secret, or however deplored, are sins unforgiven. (*H. Griffith.*) *Lessons:*—1. After greatest encouragements may bitter discoveries be made from God to His servants. 2. In the way of obedience, God's servants may meet with the sharpest temptations. 3. The place intended for rest by us may be turned into a place of trouble by God. The inn. 4. Jehovah Himself may meet His dearest servants as an adversary. 5. God may seek to kill, when He purposeth not to kill His servants. 6. It is some sad defects in God's servants that put Him upon such attempts (ver. 24). (*G. Hughes, B.D.*) *The circumcision at the inn:*—1. That a law, the fitness and utility of which we cannot discover by our natural reason, is more a test of the spirit of obedience than a moral requirement that commends itself to our judgment as good and proper; because our compliance with the latter may be but a compliment to our own intelligence, and not at all an act of deference to the Divine authority. Of what use is circumcision to the child? Or what good can it do to apply a little water to a child's face? Surely, the guilt of neglecting such rites as these, if there be any, must be very small. It is not of small account that ourselves and our children should be in the Church of God, and have, by covenant with God, a part in its rich privileges and blessings. And God can surely appoint His own form of entrance into it, and His own mark of membership in it. To neglect these rites is trampling on God's love, and spurning His favours; and though He may not now, as in old time, visit our offence with physical disease or other visible inflictions, He will surely not hold us guiltless. 2. Sickness, or danger of death in some form, is here sent as a reminder of a past neglect of duty. Is not this often its office? 3. But it is far better, surely, to forestall such medicinal sufferings by a voluntary revision of our lives, and a voluntary supplying of those things that are wanting, by a remedying of neglects as far as it can be done, a supplying of deficiencies as far as opportunity is given us. (*R. A. Hallam, D.D.*) *Another meeting with the Lord:*—I. IF WE GIVE OURSELVES TO THE LORD IN CONSECRATION, WE MAY BE SURE THAT BEFORE WE GET FAIRLY TO OUR WORK WE MUST REPAIR ANY OF THE WASTE PLACES IN OUR LIVES THAT ARE APPARENT. And if we have overlooked any, we may expect that the Lord will meet us with a drawn sword, and hold us prisoners to Himself, until we make the crooked thing straight. Every person who has sought to walk in the consecrated way has found out the truth that "judgment must begin at the house of God." In other words, if we are to bring other people out of Egyptian bondage, we must show in ourselves that we ourselves are delivered. How can a man bring another up out of the bondage of strong drink, if he is indulging in that drink himself? How can a man or woman lead another out of the Egyptian world of pleasure and self-indulgence, if they are living in pleasure themselves? One has said, "If you want to lift a soul out of the pit you must first get a good solid footing out of the pit yourself." II. THERE IS A STILL DEEPER MEANING IN THIS TRANSACTION. So soon as the rite of circumcision was complied with, in the person of the son of Moses (who, I must think, stands for himself in this case, because it was a denial of the truth on his part to have allowed the rite to lapse in that son, as much so as to have neglected it in his own body), "the Lord let him go." "So, the Lord let him go," is significant. We are made free, in meeting the Lord and fulfilling His will. It will be seen that the drawn sword was, after all, the sword of life. For in fighting against our uncircumcised flesh the Lord is fighting against the death that is in us. He never slays, but to make alive. And if we accept His judgment against ourselves and die to the flesh, by being crucified with Christ, behold, we live! (*G. F. Pentecost, D.D.*) *Lessons from the incident at the inn:*—1. That God takes notice of and is much displeased with the sins of His own people, and that the putting away of their sins is indispensably necessary to the removal of the Divine judgments. 2. That no circumstances of prudence or convenience can ever with propriety be urged as an excuse for neglecting a clearly commanded duty, especially the observance of sacramental ordinances. 3. That he who is to be the interpreter of the law to others ought in all points to be blameless, and in all things conformed to the law himself. 4. That when God has procured the proper respect to His revealed will, the controversy between Him and the offender is at an end; the object of His government being not so much to avenge Himself as to amend the criminal. (*G. Bush.*) *Results of neglect:*—There is no need that the man in a skiff amid Niagara's rapids should row toward the cataract; resting on his oars is quite enough to send him over the awful verge. It is the neglected wheel that capsizes the vehicle, and maims for life the passengers. It is the neglected leak that sinks the ship. It is the neglected field that yields briers instead of bread. It is the neglected spark near the magazine whose tremendous explosion sends its hundreds of mangled wretches into eternity. The neglect of an officer to throw up a rocket on a certain night caused the fall of Antwerp, and postponed the deliverance of Holland for twenty or more years. The neglect of a sentinel to give an alarm hindered the fall of Sebastopol, and resulted in the loss of many thousand lives. *He who would lead others into obedience must himself be exemplary :*—Moses had, perhaps, yielded to the importunities of his Midianitish wife in this matter; she may have been tempted to think that it was a very slight thing after all. But he must learn to know no one but God, when duty is in the case; and in the very outset of his ministry, he must have it impressed upon his heart that nothing is little which God has thought it important enough to command. There is a temptation to be encountered at the beginning of every enterprise; and according as we meet that, we demonstrate our fitness or unfitness for entering upon the undertaking. When you are starting out on some new and noble work, with aspirations kindled at some flaming bush of Divine revelation to your soul, " be not high-minded, but fear." Look for some test to be administered to you just then, and look for it in no great affair, but rather in some such common thing as the getting of your daily bread, or in some such domestic matter as the government of your children; for by these God may be determining your fitness for the work you covet; and if you fail in the trial, there will come no second probation. (*W. M. Taylor, D.D.*) *Circumcision among the Egyptians :*—The Egyptians, according to Herodotus, Strabo, and other writers, practised circumcision. " This custom," says the former, " can be traced both in Egypt and Ethiopia to the remotest antiquity " (l. ii. c. 104). At what age it was performed by the Egyptians is uncertain; but it is worthy of remark that the Arabians circumcised their children when they were thirteen years old, because the founder of their nation, Ishmael, was circumcised at that age (Gen. xvii. 23). The Midianites, though descended also from Abraham by Keturah, omitted it, and this explains the reluctance of Zipporah to perform the rite upon her son. To save her husband's life, however, she consented to it, and herself performed the operation, using for the purpose a sharp stone, or knife of flint, which, as Herodotus tells us, was preferred to steel for purposes connected with religion, and especially for making cuttings or incisions in the human person (Herod. ii. 86). Specimens of these knives, both broad and narrow, have been found in the tombs at Thebes, where they were used in the preparation and embalming of mummies, and may be seen in collections of Egyptian antiquities. (*T. S. Millington.*)

Ver. 27. **Go into the wilderness to meet Moses.**—*Family relationships :*—I. THE BROTHERHOOD AND AFFECTION SUBSISTING BETWEEN THE DIFFERENT MEMBERS OF GOD'S FAMILY. This is twofold. God's people stand in a twofold relation to one another, as— (1) natural and—(2) spiritual men. II. Notice THE BREACHES OF INTERCOURSE BROUGHT ABOUT IN THIS WORLD BETWEEN THOSE MEMBERS OF GOD'S FAMILY WHO HAVE SEEN AND KNOWN ONE ANOTHER IN THE FLESH. 1. Many interruptions of intercourse are brought about by providential arrangements. 2. All direct communication between brethren in the Lord is cut off by death. III. Consider THE NEED OF AND CONSEQUENT YEARNING AFTER EACH OTHER'S SOCIETY AND ASSISTANCE WHICH, WHILE PARTED, THE MEMBERS OF GOD'S FAMILY EXPERIENCE. The need is based upon, and flows from, their spiritual constitution in one body. We are, in the design of God, constituent parts of a whole, and we are continually evincing our consciousness of this truth. IV. Consider THE BLISSFUL REUNION OF THE SUNDERED MEMBERS OF GOD'S FAMILY IN THE REALMS OF GLORY. There shall be a day when all the yearnings of the Christian's heart after the society of his brethren shall be satisfied to the full, when his joy shall receive its entire complement in his recognition of and intercommunication with those whom he has known and loved in the Lord. (*Dean Goulburn.*)   *Moses and Aaron :*—I. GOD BROUGHT THE LEADERS TOGETHER. A strange place for their meeting, and a strange scene. II. GOD BROUGHT HIS LEADERS TO HIS PEOPLE. God may be obliged to prepare His leaders as well as His people. Moses was not ready for his work until he was eighty years old. How much of God's work may be waiting for His leaders ! Pray for leaders set apart in the Mount of God; but pray, too, for elders to gather about them. And pray again for a people ready to be led. Everything must stay until so much is attained,—a consecrated ministry, a consecrated eldership, a consecrated church. III. GOD BROUGHT HIS LEADERS BEFORE PHARAOH. God's enemies must be subdued if they reject the Divine message. But first He will thoroughly apply gentle methods. (*G. R. Leavitt.*) *Moses and Aaron:*—I. AARON'S COMMISSION. 1. Its reason suggestive to the reluctant servant (vers. 1–14). 2. The fact suggestive of the Divine condescension and forbearance. II. AARON'S OBEDIENCE. 1. Prompt. 2. Sincere. III. MOSES AND AARON CARRYING OUT THE DIVINE COMMAND. 1. They observed their respective places. 2. Their reception by the people (ver. 31). IV. THE INTERVIEW BETWEEN MOSES, AARON, AND PHARAOH. 1. The reasonableness of the request. 2. The unreasonableness and haughtiness of the reply. Lessons: 1. To analyze the Divine motive, in the use of all these human instrumentalities, is fraught with most helpful and instructive suggestions. 2. The unwisdom of hesitancy, in accepting a clearly-indicated call of God, is here seen. 3. The modesty and judiciousness with which the request of Moses and Aaron was couched, suggest the carefulness which soul-winners should exercise. 4. In the haughtiness of Pharaoh we discover the preliminary step to his fall. (*D. C. Hughes, M.A.*) *Lessons:*—1. God joineth His seconds to His firsts, as He seeth need for redemption of His Church. 2. The same Jehovah only fits and calls His first and second instruments for His works. All from God. 3. God may call the elder after the younger brother, and subject him. 4. God can bring brethren together which were as lost one to another. 5. Motion and place and work, God points out to His instruments of salvation. 6. God makes the deserts places for deliverers to meet in for His Church's good. 7. God's call to meeting of instruments is to teach them their respective work. 8. Hearts which God toucheth are ready for obedience to God's call. 9. The mount of God, and God in the mount, is best for His servants to meet about His work. 10. Nature and grace teach men to give signs of love and loyalty to God's substitutes below (ver. 27). 11. It is just for supreme powers to open their commissions from God to inferiors. 12. God's words alone are to be declared, which He speaks to His servants, and are to be spoken by them. 13. Mission and commission of God's ministers must appear both from God. 14. God's wonderful works as well as gracious works must be showed at His command. 15. Joint ambassadors of the Church's deliverance need to know God's words and works (ver. 28). (*G. Hughes, B.D.*) *The two brothers:*—I. AS EDUCATED BY DIFFERENT METHODS. II. AS MEETING AFTER A LONG SEPARATION. 1. The meeting was providential. 2. The meeting had a moral and national significance. 3. The meeting was welcome to the brothers. III. AS UNITING IN A GRAND ENTERPRISE. Brothers should unitedly place themselves in a line with the providence of God. IV. AS ENTERING UPON AN IMPORTANT FUTURE. All the casual meetings of life are important in their bearing upon present work and future destiny. V. AS REFLECTING COMMENDATION UPON THEIR FAMILY. Sons honour their parents when they undertake an enterprise for the good of men. Brothers cannot be better united than in the cause of God. (*J. S. Exell, M.A.*) *The meeting of two brothers:*—I. IT WAS IN A STRANGE PLACE. Some men are only brotherly before the crowd, in privacy or solitude they are social despots. The wilderness will test our affection. II. IT WAS CHARACTERIZED BY WARMTH OF AFFECTION. They kissed each other. Brothers do not often act thus in these days. They think it unmanly to do so. The age is cold at heart. It is a token of courage as well as love that a brother will thus greet his brother. But let the kiss be accompanied by kindly attentions, otherwise it is a mockery. III. IT WAS THE OCCASION FOR RELIGIOUS TALK AND CONSULTATION. No better topic than this. (*Ibid.*) *Christian brothers:*—1. Called by God to work. 2. Joined by God in work. 3. Conversing together about work. 4. Learning their respective work. (*Ibid.*) *Providential arrangements:*—But admire the manner in which God governs the things of this world and of His Church. When it pleases Him to save a soul, or call a servant, He causes all persons and all events to work together for this end, and in a way already determined. As a skilful general sends each division of his army, without the knowledge of the others, to assemble on the same field of battle, so the Lord sends His servants who are fighting the good fight, to the place and at the time where they ought to meet. It was thus that He sent Peter to Cornelius, Ananias to Paul, Philip to the eunuch. It is thus that in our time He sends missionaries to heathen lands. It was thus that He caused Farel and Calvin to meet at Geneva, that they might help each other, and form a friendship that lasted during their lives, and greatly contributed to the success of their work. How this thought enlightens, strengthens, comforts, and rejoices those who are engaged serving God. (*Prof. Gaussen.*) *The two brothers:*—The history of Moses and Aaron appearing together at the court of Pharaoh, the one working miracles and the other as his spokesman, may have given rise to the traditions of the Greeks and Romans, in which Jupiter and Mercury, both of them Egyptian deities worshipped at Hammon and Thoth, are described visiting the earth in a similar relationship. The latter was represented with the caduceus, a rod twisted about with serpents, and was the god of speech or eloquence. To such traditions the saying of the people of Lystra may be referred, when Paul had healed the cripple (Acts xiv. 11). (*T. S. Millington.*) *Moses and Aaron; or, the use of association:*—True greatness is modest. It is a false greatness that magnifies its own powers, and disparages the strength of opposing forces. One of the penalties of greatness is isolation. It removes the man from common aids and sympathies, and sets him by himself. Greatness is lonely. This isolation Moses was beginning to feel, while the task before him grew awful, and swelled into a frightful magnitude. Solitude, and that isolation which is worse than solitude—separation from the insight and sympathy of men around us—is weakening. Moses grew weak and drew back. Thinkers are not always speakers, nor speakers thinkers. Nay, thought in its very striving after accuracy and exactness, is apt to be a hindrance of fluency. Moses could think and act, but he could not speak. He was a greater man than his brother, but his brother was a better speaker. He could excogitate the ideas, and his brother could put them into words for him. God is economical in His bestowments, and seldom heaps His manifold favours on one man. Cromwell, whether a good or a bad man, was certainly a great man; yet out of his tangled utterances it was hard to come at his meaning. Here, then, the want was supplied, and with it, as appears in the subsequent history, a much broader surface of want besides; for God is, " able to do exceeding abundantly above all that we ask or think," and is "wont to give more than either we desire or deserve." The abundance of His mercy will not be kept within the narrow bounds our mean conceptions set to it. Moses, in the guise of an Egyptian, and as the son of Pharaoh's daughter, had learned to recognize and love his brother Aaron under Amram's roof; they had been nurtured for uses of which neither of them dreamed. How much of this provision for a secret future is there in the lives of men. What important effects to the end of life may flow from the seemingly casual associations and intimacies of childhood! This companionship at once delivered Moses from his solitude, the isolation of peculiarity, by raising up for him a co-worker, to stand with him on the same elevated plane above the mass of the people, and aid him in bearing cares on which none but one so commissioned might presume to intrude. Here, then, was unity with subordination, and harmony with distribution and diversity; and thus the apparatus of action for the great enterprise was complete. See here the good of association. See how it raised Moses out of the ague of despondency that overtook him when the object of his long desire had at last come within his grasp; how it warmed his powers into resolute endeavour, and shed a benign influence upon his subsequent labours and sufferings. So "Jonathan, Saul's son arose, and went to David in the wood, and strengthened his hand in God." So, too, our blessed Lord thought of this principle and acted upon it, and stamped it with the seal of His infallible wisdom, when He sent out His disciples two by two, making but six missions, where an earthly wisdom would have thought it better economy to make twelve. And the great St. Paul had always with him Barnabas, or Mark, or Luke, or Gaius, or Epaphroditus in his missionary travels and labours. Let us remember that in the Divine household we are knit together into one fellowship, and are to learn to be mutually considerate and helpful, and " bear each other's burdens," as " every one members one of another." God's work, our work, will be done more easily, pleasantly, effectually. See here, too, the good of subordination. Aaron was always with Moses, his shadow or second self; but Moses always was head. If both had been heads the machinery would not have worked so kindly, smoothly, and comfortably. Nothing does well with two heads. (*R. A. Hallam, D.D.*)

Vers. 29, 30. **Gathered together all the elders.**—*The first interview of Moses and Aaron with the elders of Israel, and the welcome they received :*—I. THEY ACTED UPON THE DIVINE SUGGESTION. All Christian work should be undertaken according to the Divine suggestion, and in harmony with the Divine will. God generally tells men how to work as well as what to do. If we were left to mark out our own methods of toil, we should often involve both ourselves and the enterprise entrusted to us in great danger. II. THEY SPAKE ACCORDING TO THE DIVINE DICTATION. Great workers require to be taught by God. In this consists their safety and success. A man who speaks to the world the messages of God will always be listened to. III. THEY

SUCCEEDED ACCORDING TO DIVINE INTIMATION. Thus Moses and Aaron awakened— 1. Faith. 2. Hope. 3. Devotion—of Israel. Moses had previously said that Israel would not believe him. We mistake our missions. We cannot form an estimate of success. If we act and speak according to the instruction of God we must succeed. (*J. S. Exell, M.A.*) Lessons :—1. Declaring of God's will is suitably united to the assembling of His people. 2. God's spokesmen made by Him are fittest to declare his mind to His people. 3. The words of Jehovah only, which He hath spoken to His servants, must be given to His assembly. 4. God may give His mind more immediately to one servant than to another (to Moses). 5. God's stupendous works must be done, as well as His words spoken, to His people. 6. God's congregation are the first subject to whom His words and works are sent. (*G. Hughes, B.D.*) The gathering of the elders :—The gathering of the " elders " of the children of Israel may point to no more than a family and tribal organization which was not known or used by the Egyptians for the purposes of government, but only used among the Israelites themselves for their religious and ritual teaching. But it would be contrary to most oriental experience to suppose so. It has been the custom of most eastern rulers, as of the Turks to-day, to recognize all proper governmental organizations among a subject people. It was even a large part of the wisdom of the politic Romans. The general government, indeed, extends its power to the individual, and is not slow to do so. But it is both convenient to have an opportunity for the " respondeat superior " principle in law to work, and politic to have thus a hold upon the more generous feelings of the subject classes. The heads of the subject, tribe, or people are made responsible for, collection (or at least the payment) of tribute, and for the preservation of a certain law and order, and are the ready subjects of extortion on very slight pretences. On the other hand, their brethren of inferior order take pride in them, and serve them, and through them the general government, with much less driving. A pretty fair example of this in modern times can be seen in the Turkish recognition of the various religious bodies within its domains. Perhaps it is the best of modern illustrations. (*Prof. Isaac H. Hall.*)

Ver. 31. **The people believed.**—Lessons :—1. The people's faith should closely follow upon God's word ministered, and by His works confirmed. A good connec- tion. 2. Where God promiseth success to His ministers in the faith of others, there they shall believe (chap. iii. 18). 3. All professed believers, receive not God's word with the same faith. 4. Hearing is the usual sense of bringing in faith and the fruits of it. 5. God's gracious visitation of His Church, and providential sight of its afflictions, is very good to be heard by them. 6. Such hearing of God's visiting love and redeeming providence must affect God's Israel. 7. Faith working by this sense stirs up souls to suitable returns unto God. 8. The humblest and sincerest worship in body and spirit is the most suitable return to God for His redemption. (*G. Hughes, B.D.*) Human and Divine attitudes :—I. THE ATTI- TUDES PREDICATED OF THE PEOPLE. 1. Their belief. 2. Their reverence. 3. Their devotion. II. THE ATTITUDES PREDICATED OF GOD. 1. He saw the affliction of Israel. 2. Visited Israel. (*J. S. Exell, M.A.*) Faith easy when in the line of *desire* :—People are a great deal more apt to receive a message as from God when it is in the line of their own longings. The Israelites were quick to receive from God a promise of relief from Egyptian brick-making, readier to worship than when they wanted water or meat on the desert and failed to find it ready at hand for them. And they were very much like the rest of us in all this. How we should bow our heads and worship if the one inner longing of our hearts at this moment were granted to us, or even promised of God, all of a sudden! But how is it while God keeps back from us that which we long for, and we know that He is prompted to His course by both wisdom and love? Do we bow our heads and worship, all the same? Well, we bow our heads ; but not always to worship. (*H. C. Trumbull.*) Confidence in God :—The Roman noblemen could give no greater proof of their confidence in their city and army, than when they bought the land on which their Carthaginian enemies were encamped around the city. And we can give no greater proof of our confidence in God, than by trusting Him in the land which our enemies, darkness and sickness and trouble, seem to possess, and acting as if He were their master, and mightier than they all. (*W. Baxendale.*) The believing people :— I. GOD ALWAYS FURNISHES SUFFICIENT EVIDENCE TO JUSTIFY BELIEF. Moses was a stranger to the people ; Aaron doubtless well known. He had a welcome message —deliverance. Miracles in outward form : miracles typical in character : rod changed to a serpent and back, Moses changed from a shepherd to a ruler; cleansing of leprosy, the purifying of the human for Divine use. II. HEARING PRECEDES BELIEVING. God sent Aaron to speak. Ministers sent to preach. III. THE ISRAELITES MANIFEST THEIR FAITH PUBLICLY. We must confess Christ in token of faith. IV. GOD PREPARES THE WAY FOR THE RECEPTION OF HIS TRUTH. Aaron called to meet Moses. God's Spirit precedes and accompanies the truth we utter. V. FAITH SECURES DELIVERANCE. By it the Israelites secured theirs. So must we by ours. It is unto us according to our faith. (*Dr. Fowler.*) *Bowed heads :—* 1. Some heads are bowed with business cares. During the last four years many homes have been broken, and others sadly reduced, not so much through men's own folly, as from the long and serious depression in trade. 2. Some heads are bowed with sorrow over sinful children. That never-fading picture of the Prodigal Son, painted by a master hand, is often too truly representative of our own families. Young men, think of all the pain and anguish you cause for those dear parents by your lives of sin. 3. Some heads are bowed with bereavement. To many of us there have come dark days of sorrow and pain. Roses have withered in our domestic gardens; buds have been nipped before they had time to bloom; lights we loved have gone out. (*Charles Leach.*)

CHAPTER V.

VER. 1. **Let My people go.**—*The deliverance of God's people :*—The history of the deliverance of God's people from the bondage of Egypt, their pilgrimage through the wilderness, and their ultimate settlement in the Land of Promise, bears a striking analogy to the history of the human soul. I. The words "Let My people go," regarded as spoken concerning human souls, may be said TO CONTAIN IN THEMSELVES THE WHOLE GOSPEL HISTORY OF OUR REDEMPTION. Even the small word " My " is emphatic. 1. We are God's people; not Satan's people. When God claims us we should remember that He claims His own, and that we are bound to support His claim. 2. The summons to let the people of God go implies a bondage from which they are to be delivered. That which forms the basis of Holy Scripture is the fact that man committed sin. He rebelled against his Maker, and became the slave of one to whom he owed no obedience. 3. If the words " Let My people go " imply the existence of slavery, they still more emphatically imply the way and the promise of redemption. The Gospel of Christ, as preached throughout the whole world, is just this—" Let My people go." II. THE WHOLE SYSTEM OF ORDINANCES AND SACRAMENTS, in which we find ourselves by God's providence, like the system of ordinances and sacrifices which was given to Israel when they came out of Egypt, ARE INTENDED TO INSURE AND PERFECT AND TURN TO THE BEST ACCOUNT THE LIBERTY WHICH THE LORD HAS GIVEN US, for the soul of man may not be content with emancipation once and for all. III. THE CONSIDERATION OF WHAT JESUS CHRIST HAS DONE FOR US IS THE CHIEF MEANS OF MOVING OUR HEARTS TO SEEK THAT LIBERTY WHICH GOD DESIGNS US ALL TO POSSESS. (*Bp. Harvey Goodwin.*) *Freedom to serve God :*—I. Perfect freedom is not the thing demanded of Pharaoh, nor is this the prize of their high calling held out before the eyes of the Israelites. To serve God is the perfect freedom held out : to change masters, to be rid of him who had no claim to their allegiance, and to be permitted without hindrance to serve Him who was indeed their Lord and their God. This was the boon offered to the children of Israel, and demanded on their account by Moses as the ambassador of God. II. This feature in the deliverance of the Israelites is worthy of special notice, when we regard it as typical of the deliverance from sin and the bondage of the devil, which our heavenly Father is willing to effect for each of us. "Let My people go,"—not that they may be free from a master, BUT THAT THEY MAY SERVE ; let them go, because they have been redeemed by Christ, and are not their own, but His. The deliverance from sin which God works for His people is, in fact, a change from one service to another : a change from service to sin, which is perfect bondage, to service to God, which is perfect freedom. III. THE BLESSEDNESS OF THE SERVICE OF GOD IS NOT ESTIMATED AS IT OUGHT TO BE ; men in these days are too like the children of Israel, who seemed to think that they had conferred a favour on Moses by following his guidance, and that the least reverse would be a sufficient excuse to justify them in going back again to Egypt. There is nothing in their conduct more strange or more blamable than in the conduct of men calling themselves Christians, who do not perceive that in the earnest discharge of God's service is their highest happiness as well as their principal duty and most blessed privilege. (*Ibid.*) *Lessons :*—1. God's ambassadors must proceed orderly in delivering their message —first to Israel, secondly to Pharaoh. 2. Order of persons as well as time is observable by God's servants. 3. The poorest persons under God's authority may press into the presence of the proudest kings. 4. God's ambassadors must speak and declare His will to the greatest potentates. 5. God's messengers must go in His authority and vouch His name. 6. The true way of making out God unto man is concretely not abstractly. Every nation acknowledgeth God, but not Israel's God. 7. The true God hath a peculiar people whom He owneth in the world. 8. The will of God is to have His people set free from all that hinders them from Him. 9. The end of all redemption is that God's people should serve Him. 10. The true service of God is a festival living to Him. 11. Such feasting with God is better in the wilderness than in Egypt. 12. All such feasting, sacrificing, and worship must terminate in Jehovah. (*G. Hughes, B.D.*)   *Moses before Pharaoh :*—1. The sense of his high commission enabled him to discharge the duty it laid upon him with dignity and boldness. The sinking of heart that had seized him upon its first announcement had passed away ; and in its place had come "the spirit of power, and of love, and of a sound mind." 2. Aaron was with him ; but the relation he sustained to the work is marked, as it is throughout the narrative, by the order of the names, Moses and Aaron—never Aaron and Moses—a companion, an associate, but only as a helper, a support, a spokesman, though Aaron was the elder. There are chords in our nature that vibrate mysteriously to another's touch, a magnetism that works by laws imperfectly understood, by which the presence and sympathy of a companion, silent though it be, and without visible action, braces and enlivens the heart ; and that, though the disparity be so great that the inferior who cares for us can only think as we think, and feel as we feel, without any contribution of useful counsel or active succour. "At my first answer," says St. Paul, "no man stood with me, but all men forsook me." Let us not say that we cannot help our friend because we are inferior and of small resources. It is too often but the cover of cowardice or coldness of heart. He that knows the magic there is in a look, a touch, or a word, to alleviate and quicken a pained or fainting soul, feels the falsehood. Nor let us, in our height of pride and self-sufficiency, despise the "fellowship of kindred minds" because they are below us, and, it may be, without manifest strength to aid. A little child's sympathy is not to be despised. Moses' commission was sole, but Aaron's presence facilitated its execution. There is a wonderful power in company. 3. What Moses first asked of Pharaoh for his people, then, was a religious privilege—liberty to go out into the wild country beyond the bounds of Goshen, and worship God ; sacrifice to that great Being in whom their fathers had trusted, but whose image, we may well believe, had grown dim among them during their long period of depression and enslavement. Moses was a religious reformer. The revival of truth, faith, and loyalty to Jehovah, lay at the bottom of all the other great things he was to do for them. The feast in the wilderness was preliminary to all that was to follow, to stand as the frontispiece of that series of wonderful events in which their deliverance was to be accomplished, the prologue of the great drama of their entrance upon national life. 4. To Pharaoh, in this call, there was a test of faith, and of that obedience in which all real faith finds its true expression. God came forth from His obscurity and spoke to him. Would he hear that voice, recognize it as the voice of Him who is "King of kings"? In humanity there is a chord that ever vibrates to God's touch, and an ear that hears His voice. It was the call of God's mercy to Pharaoh, Jehovah's coming near to him to do him good. Alas! he "knew not the time of his visitation." But if the heart of Pharaoh towards God was tested by this call, so was his heart towards man. It was an appeal to his humanity. 5. See the wisdom of acting in great matters with judgment, moderation, and patience. Many a good design has been ruined by abruptness, haste, and grasping greed. Moses did not succeed in his embassy, but he adopted fit and judicious methods to obtain success ; and if they failed to secure their object. it was simply because they encountered an opposition that no power or skill could overcome. The eagerness that will have all at once, loses all. The impatience that will reach the goal at a single bound, never reaches it. To have asked the immediate emancipation of the Israelites would have been manifestly useless. 6. Finally, beware of striving against God. It can end in nothing but destruction. Its gains are losses, its successes 'its most ruinous failures. (*R. A.*

Hallam, D.D.)   *Reasons for sending Moses and Aaron :*—Why did God send Moses and Aaron to Pharaoh, when He could have destroyed Him with a stroke, and have wrought the freedom of Israel? 1. That God's power might appear in showing His wonders. 2. That the Israelites might see the great care God had over them. 3. To exercise their patience, not being delivered at once. 4. To leave Pharaoh without excuse. (*J. S. Exell, M.A.*)   *A proclamation of God :*—1. His name. 2. His authority. 3. His regard for His people. 4. His desire for the freedom of man. (*Ibid.*)   *The freedom of men :*—1. Earnestly desired. 2. Effectively undertaken. 3. Divinely approved. 4. Successfully achieved. (*Ibid.*)   *A Divine challenge :*— The slavery of Israel in Egypt was hopeless slavery; they could not get free unless God interfered and worked miracles on their behalf. And the slavery of the sinner to his sin is equally hopeless; he could never be free, unless a mind that is infinitely greater than he can ever command shall come to his assistance and help. What a blessed circumstance it is, then, for those poor chosen children of God, who are still in bondage, that the Lord has power to say, and then power to carry out what He has said—" Thus saith the Lord, let My people go, that they may serve Me." I. THE FULNESS OF THE SENTENCE. "Thus saith the Lord, let My people go, that they may serve Me." I don't doubt but what there are some of God's people who have not any idea they are His people. The demand was not made to Pharaoh, "Make their tasks less heavy; make the whip less cruel; put kinder taskmasters over them." No, but, "Let them go free." Christ did not come into the world merely to make our sin more tolerable, but to deliver us right away from it. He did not come to make our lusts less mighty; but to put all these things far away from His people, and work out a full and complete deliverance. Again, you will mark, it says, "Let My people go." It says nothing about their coming back again. Once gone, they are gone for ever. II. THE RIGHTNESS OF IT. The voice of justice, and pity, and mercy, cries to death, and hell, and sin, "Let My people go free—Satan, keep thine own if thou wilt, but let My people go free, for they are Mine. This people have I created for Myself; they shall show forth My praise. Let My people go free, for I have bought them with My precious blood. Thou hast not bought them, nor hast thou made them: thou hast no right to them; let My people go free." All this is our comfort about poor sinners, and we hope that some of them, though they don't know it, are God's people. III. THE REPETITION OF THIS SENTENCE. Observe now, as Pharaoh would not give up the people, the sentence had to be repeated again, and again, until at last God would bear it no longer, but brought down on him one tremendous blow. He smote the firstborn of Egypt, the chief of all their strength, and then He led forth His people like sheep by the hands of Moses and Aaron. In like manner this sentence of God has to be repeated many times in your experience and mine, "Thus, saith the Lord, let My people go free," and if you are not quite free yet, don't despair; God will repeat that sentence till at last you shall be brought forth with silver and gold, and there shall not be a feeble thought in all your soul; you shall go forth with gladness and with joy; you shall enter into Canaan at last, up yonder where His throne is glittering now in glorious light, that angel eyes cannot bear. It is no wonder then, if it is to be repeated in our experience, that the Church of Christ must keep on repeating it in the world as God's message. Go, missionary, to India, and say to Juggernaut, and Kalee, and Brahma, and Vishnu, "Thus saith the Lord, let My people go free." Go, ye servants of the Lord, to China, speak to the followers of Confucius, and say, "Thus saith the Lord, let My people go free." Go ye to the gates of the harlot city, even Rome, and say, "Thus saith the Lord, let My people go, that they may serve Me." Think not though you die that your message will die with you. 'Tis for Moses to say, "Thus saith the Lord," and if he be driven from Pharaoh's sight, the "Thus saith the Lord" still stands, though His servant fall. Yes, brothers and sisters, the whole Church must keep on throughout every age, crying, "Thus saith the Lord, let My people go." IV. THE OMNIPOTENCE OF THE COMMAND. Sin is a Pharaoh, but God is Jehovah. Your sins are hard; you cannot overcome them of yourself, but God can. There is hope yet; let that hope arouse you to action. Say to your soul to-night, "I am not in hell, though I might have been. I am still on praying ground and pleading terms, and now, God helping me, I will begin to think." And when you begin to think you will begin to be blessed. (*C. H. Spurgeon.*)   *God's people :*— I. WHO ARE THESE WHOM GOD CALLS "MY PEOPLE"? 1. They are a distinct and separate race. The people of God are not those who agree with each other as to certain theories—in these things they may be sundered far as the poles. It is not that they come together on certain particular occasions and observe the same ceremonies. No ceremonies however ancient, however solemn, however significant, however faithfully observed can make us His people. The distinction is one of birth. It is a difference of nature. Born of God, begotten of God, they are the children of God. Within them is the very Spirit of God whereby they cry " Abba Father." 2. They are created of God by a distinct and wholly supernatural act. The children of a new life—of the resurrection. And out of that relationship to God come a thousand new relationships. There is a new authority which is ever supreme—there is a new nature, with new hopes, and new desires; and new needs; and new aspirations; and new delights; a nature which can find its only satisfaction in Him in whom it found its source; there is a new relationship to all things. Born of God, they look further; they soar higher; they find more. II. But if these are His people, WHY DOES HE SUFFER THEM TO BE HERE? Forsaken, wronged— has God forgotten to be gracious? Who shall deliver them out of the hand of Pharaoh? 1. That they may know that I am the Lord—this is the key to it all. They are led into the wilderness where there is neither bread nor water, that they may learn to look up to God for their help : so they are hemmed in by all possible evils in Egypt, that they may see the greatness and might of their God in their deliverance. The mightier the nation that oppressed them, the greater the glory of their deliverance. The more hopeless their condition, and the more hopeless the people, so much more room was there for God to show forth His mighty arm. The greatness of life—its breadth and depth, its expanse like heaven above us, its solidity like the earth beneath us—is exactly according to our knowledge of our God. And the deep peace and rest—the blessedness and satisfaction—these too come only from knowing Him. We are most indebted—not to those things for which it is easiest to give thanks, but to those from which we have shrunk, and which set us wondering, fearing, perhaps even doubting. The reaper is a happy man, and poets sing and artists paint the scene of harvest home. But the keen frosts that break the clods, and the patient ploughman plodding wearily behind the share with which he cleaves the soil in chill winter winds and under cheerless skies—these are apt to be forgotten and unthanked. And yet what should the reaper bring if the plough-man went not forth? " My people." God sends them to school that they may learn to know Him. 2. Learn further that wherever His people are led, they can never get where God cannot help them. Be sure of that. Whatever clouds gather they cannot hide His child in the darkness. No circumstances can ever shut us out from His help. 3. The Lord knoweth them that are His. He leadeth them in a way that they know not, but He knoweth the way. Fear not: we too may sing—" He leadeth us in a right way to bring us to a city of habitation." 4. Notice yet another characteristic of His people. See Israel come forth from Egypt. Every man, every woman, every child bows his head beneath a doorpost on which is sprinkled the blood—each one passes between the side posts whereon is the crimson stain. They are the redeemed of the Lord—My people—ransomed by a great price. The people of God find their deliverance in the power of the Cross. (*M. G. Pearse.*)   *Moses and Aaron before Pharaoh :*—We never heard of an insurrection against a tyrannical government, deliberately planned, for which there was not aggregated some sort of preparation in armies and munitions of war. So we inquire in this instance, What was the number of Israel's troops now on their belligerent way to beseige the capital of Egypt? Only one organized battalion, consisting of these two old men! What were the arms they carried? These were altogether seven weapons in detail. Any one can count them at his pleasure : one shepherd's crook, called a "rod," one tremendous name in the Hebrew language, four promises, and a miracle. These were expected to revolutionize Egypt. I. INADEQUACY OF CONSPICUOUS RESOURCES IS NO ARGUMENT AGAINST SUCCESS, WHEN GOD IN PERSON HAS SENT HIS SERVANTS FORTH TO DO HIS ERRAND. II. THE ALMIGHTY GOD HAS NEVER LET GO HIS HOLD UPON ANY INDIVIDUAL OF THE HUMAN RACE, FOR ALL THE SPITEFUL REBELLION SOME MEN HAVE SHOWN. III. IT IS OF THE UTMOST IMPORTANCE THAT INTELLIGENT PEOPLE SHOULD HAVE A SAFE CREED. Undoubtedly Pharaoh is very much in earnest. He does not "know" Jehovah; he knows the deities he has been educated to worship. But if we only wait a little longer, and read the story of the exodus clear through to the crossing of the Red Sea, we shall find out whether it made any difference to Pharaoh what he believed in that moment when he defied Jehovah! IV. SEE HOW CLEARLY THE ALL-WISE GOD WORKS UP TO SIMPLE ISSUES WITH EVERY WILFUL TRANSGRESSOR BEFORE HE CASTS HIM UTTERLY OUT. There is only one question which confronts any man, no matter how many are the forms in which it may be put : Will you, or will you not, obey God? V. THOSE WHO SEEK TO HELP

THEIR FELLOW-MEN IN THIS WORLD MUST EXPECT MISJUDGMENT. VI. So we reach our final lesson : THE NATURAL AND FIRST RESULT OF STIRRING UP SIN IS TO AGGRAVATE ITS VIOLENCE. Satan hates to lose his slaves. The heart is desperately wicked, and seems to grow more malignant than before. "It is always darkest just before day." This does not happen so ; it is the Divine rule. (*C. S. Robinson, D.D.*) *Divine condescension to Pharaoh :*—At the outset, we observe the more than dutiful manner in which Israel was directed to act towards Pharaoh. Absolutely speaking, Pharaoh had no right to detain the people in Egypt. Their fathers had avowedly come not to settle, but temporarily " to sojourn," and on that understanding they had been received. And now they were not only wrongfully oppressed, but unrighteously detained. It was infinite condescension to Pharaoh's weakness, on the part of God, not to insist from the first upon the immediate and entire dismissal of Israel. Less could not have been asked than was demanded of Pharaoh, nor could obedience have been made more easy. Assuredly such a man was ripe for the judgment of hardening ; just as, on the other hand, if he had at the first yielded obedience to the Divine will, he would surely have been prepared to receive a further revelation of His will, and grace to submit to it. And so God in His mercy always deals with man. "He that is faithful in that which is least, is faithful also in much: and he that is unjust in the least, is unjust also in much." The demands of God are intended to try what is in us. It was so in the case of Adam's obedience, of Abraham's sacrifice, and now of Pharaoh ; only that in the latter case, as in the promise to spare Sodom if even ten righteous men were found among its wicked inhabitants, the Divine forbearance went to the utmost verge of condescension. (*A. Edersheim, D.D.*) *Divine authority for the message :*—On one occasion when Whitefield was preaching, an old man fell asleep, and some of the audience became listless. Suddenly changing his manner, Whitefield broke forth in an altered tone, declaring that He had not come to speak in his own name, otherwise they might lean on their elbows and go to sleep. "No ; I have come to you in the name of the Lord of Hosts, and I must and will be heard." The sleeper started wide awake; the hearers were stripped of their apathy at once; and every word of the sermon was attended to. It was thus that Moses addressed Pharaoh; and it is thus all witness for God should address the listeners—with authority. **Hold a feast unto Me.**—*The first attempt at a religious service :*—I. THAT THIS FIRST ATTEMPT AT A RELIGIOUS SERVICE WAS MADE RESPONSIVE TO THE CALL, AND IN HARMONY WITH THE WILL, OF GOD. 1. Thus there was a great necessity that the work now attempted by Moses and Aaron should be accomplished. 2. Moses and Aaron were the right men to undertake this work. In the first place, Moses had been directly called by God to do it ; also Aaron had been providentially conducted to this sphere of work. In this we see the different methods by which God enjoins work upon good men. Then, again, Moses and Aaron had been Divinely prepared for their work. Men are prepared in different ways. Solitude prepares one man ; publicity will prepare another—the preparation must be in harmony with the temperament of the man, and the work that he has to perform. The Church requires to think less of results, and more of the methods by which they are to be attained. 3. Moses and Aaron undertook this work in the proper spirit. II. THAT OUR FIRST ATTEMPT AT RELIGIOUS SERVICE IS OFTEN MET BY OPEN PROFANITY AND IGNORANCE. 1. Moses and Aaron were met by a manifestation of ignorance. 2. They were met by deep profanity. 3. They were met by unwarrantable pride. III. THAT OUR FIRST ATTEMPT AT SERVICE IS OFTEN MISUNDERSTOOD, AND ITS MOTIVE MALIGNED. 1. Pharaoh was not sensitive to the claims of duty. 2. Pharaoh was not a disinterested interpreter of the claims urged upon him. IV. THAT SOMETIMES OUR FIRST ATTEMPT AT RELIGIOUS SERVICE APPEARS TO BE MORE PRODUCTIVE OF HARM THAN GOOD, AND TO HAVE THE VERY OPPOSITE EFFECT TO THAT DESIGNED. Lessons : 1. Begin at once some enterprise for the moral freedom of humanity, 2. If in the first attempt at service you meet with difficulty and rejection, do not be dismayed. 3. That you must be finally successful in your efforts. (1) For they are appointed by God. (2) You are upheld by heaven. (3) You have the sympathy of all good men. (*J. S. Exell, M.A.*)

Ver. 2. **Who is the Lord that I should obey His voice ?**—*Pharaoh's question answered :*—If we would know God as He is, we should neither take our own idea nor adopt the world's estimates, but see Him as He has revealed Himself in His Word, especially in the Gospel which began to be spoken by His Son, the only Teacher competent to instruct us here. 1. God is One, indeed, who will punish sin, &c. As a Holy God, He hates it ; and, as a Just God, He will "by no means clear the guilty," &c. 2. But, at the same time, He is One who would rather not, and who will not unless He must. Judgment is His strange work, and He "would have all men to be saved and to come to a knowledge of the truth." 3. One, too, so averse to punish that He "spared not His own Son," &c. Abraham could give no higher proof of his love to God than by his willingness to offer up his son, his only son, Isaac. "God so loved," &c. 4. One, too, who, in addition to giving His Son, strives with men by His Word, ordinances, Spirit, Providence, to dispose them to accept that Son and find peace and joy in believing. 5. One, again, who has filled His Word with warnings to arouse, invitations to attract, directions to instruct, promises to encourage, &c. 6. One, too, who has thrown the door of hope wide open to all, and imposed no impossible, or even difficult, condition in the case of any. 7. One, in fine, who can say, "What more could I have done for My vineyard that I have not done in it?" One whose plan, provision and proffer of salvation is such that if any fail of its privileges, they can but blame themselves. This is the Lord! Not only our Creator (that itself should summon our service; see Psalm c.), nor only our Preserver (living by His bounty, should we not live by His bidding, too?); but also our Redeemer: the God and Father of our Lord Jesus Christ. Surely, then, if there be any voice, we should obey, it is His. That voice, further, is the voice of One who knows us; knows our frame, knows what suits us, knows what will contribute to our well-being. His commands are so far from being arbitrary that in the very keeping of them there is great reward; and, following the course they indicate, we shall ever have growing reason to say, "The lines are fallen unto me in pleasant places"; while, on the other hand, all experience, as well as revelation, declares, "the way of transgressors is hard." The sinner flies from God's voice, thinking it a voice of anger; whereas, did he but stop and listen, he would "wonder at the gracious words that proceed out of His mouth." Only let us "acquaint ourselves with Him, and we shall be at peace, and good shall thereby come to us." But if we follow after lying vanities, we forsake our own mercies. (*David Jamison, B.A.*)　　*Lessons:*—1. Proud imperious spirits are hasty to reply roughly upon God's messengers. 2. Idolaters are apt to despise God in the true revelation of Him. 3. Hardened souls vent their contempt upon God Himself more than on His Church. 4. Contempt of Jehovah suffers not men to hear His voice. 5. Disobedience to God ushers in oppression to His people. 6. Scorners of God can never come to the right knowledge of God or acknowledgment of Him. 7. Wicked wretches glory in the contempt of knowing God. 8. Denial of knowing God denieth all good commanded for His people. (*G. Hughes, B.D.*)　　*God entitled to an obedience:*—I. WE OUGHT TO OBEY GOD, BECAUSE HE IS THE BENEVOLENT CREATOR OF THE UNIVERSE. II. WE ARE BOUND TO OBEY GOD, BECAUSE HE IS THE CONSTANT PRESERVER OF THE CREATURES OF HIS POWER. III. WE ARE UNDER YET GREATER OBLIGATIONS TO OBEY GOD, BECAUSE HE IS THE PERFECT GOVERNOR OF THE UNIVERSE. IV. WE ARE OBLIGATED IN THE HIGHEST DEGREE TO OBEY GOD, BECAUSE HE IS THE MERCIFUL REDEEMER OF SINNERS. (*C. Coffin, D.D.*)　　*God's claim on our obedience:*—I. SOME PARTICULARS RELATIVE TO GOD'S VOICE. 1. The persons to whom He speaks—Mankind. (1) His favourite creatures. (2) Ignorant creatures. (3) Improvable creatures. 2. The means by which He speaks. (1) His works. (a) Of creation. (b) Of providence. (2) His Word. 3. What He says to us. He speaks to us variously, according to our various states, as sinful, submissive, and reclaimed creatures. As sinful creatures, who transgress His laws, He speaks to us in the language of reproof; charging us with rebellion (Isa. i. 1, 2); and ingratitude (Deut. xxxii. 6); and in the language of warning; showing us that we are rejected by Him (Prov. xv. 8, 26); under His curse (Gal. iii. 10); and under the sentence of eternal death (Ezek. xviii. 20; Rom. vi. 21). As submissive creatures, who desire to obey Him, He speaks to us in the language of kind authority (Isa. lv. 6, 7; Matt. xi. 28, 29); of encouragement (Isa. i. 16–18); and of caution against delay (Psa. xcv. 7, 8). As reclaimed creatures, restored to His favour and service, He speaks to us in the language of instruction (Mic. vi. 8; Tit. ii. 12); and in the language of consolation, (Isa. xl. 1; Psa. lxxxiv. 11). 4. With what design He speaks. This is to engage our obedience. His works teach us to glorify Him as God (Rom. i. 21). His Word requires practical piety as man's indispensable duty (1 Sam. xv. 22; Matt. vii. 21; James i. 22, 25). The obedience thus required must be prompt, without delay (Job. xxii. 21). Universal, without defect (Psa. cxix. 6). Persevering, without intermission (Rom. ii. 7); and humble, without arrogance. It must be humbly ascribed to Divine grace (Isa. xxvi. 12); humbly presented through Christ for acceptance (1 Pet. ii. 5); and humbly as unprofitable at best (Luke xvii. 10). Such being the obedience which God requires, let us consider—II. HIS CLAIMS ON OUR OBEDIENCE TO HIS VOICE. These will appear by answering the inquiry here instituted—" Who is the Lord? " &c. 1. He is our indisputable Proprietor. 2. He is our acknowledged Sovereign. 3. He is our best Friend, and kindest Benefactor. 4. He is the Disposer of our eternal destiny. (1) Omniscient. (2) Just. (3) Powerful. (*Sketches of Sermons.*) *Pharaoh's impious interrogation :*—I. GOD HAS SPOKEN TO MANKIND. II. WHY AND HOW YOU SHOULD HEAR. 1. Why. (1) Because of His right in and over you. (2) Because of His condescension to you. (3) Because of the design of His speaking —your present and eternal welfare. 2. How. With awe, sacred attentions, holy anxiety. III. THE IMPIETY AND FOLLY OF REFUSING TO HEAR THE VOICE OF GOD. 1. It is a flagrant contempt of God. 2. It is open rebellion against authority. 3. It must be eventually ruinous to the sinner. (*J. Burns, D.D.*)   *Scorners of God :*— 1. They hear not His voice. 2. They perceive not His revelations. 3. They recognize not His claims. 4. They insult His servants. 5. They enslave His people. 6. They are obstinate in their denials. (*J. S. Exell, M.A.*)   *Pharaoh fighting against God :*—A certain king used to wander about in disguise. Once he fell into a quarrel, and was getting rather roughly handled. But as soon as his assailant knew that he was pummeling the king, he dropped on his knees, asking for mercy. It is a good thing to know against whom we are fighting. Pharaoh did not realize that. When Job came to see that he was fighting against God, he said, "Behold, I am vile. . . . I will lay mine hand upon mine mouth." *" I know not the Lord "* —*agnosticism of the heart and will :*—A kind of agnosticism more prevalent than agnosticism of a scientific kind. There is an agnosticism of the heart ; there is an agnosticism of the will. Men reason foolishly about this not knowing. Men imagine that because they know not the Lord, the Lord knows not them. There is a vital distinction. We do not extinguish the sun by closing our eyes. If men will not inquire for God in a spirit worthy of such an inquiry, they can never know God. Pharaoh's no-knowledge was avowed in a tone of defiance. It was not an intellectual ignorance, but a spirit of moral denial. Pharaoh practically made himself god by denying the true God. This is the natural result of all atheism. Atheism cannot be a mere negative ; if it pretend to intelligence it must, in some degree, involve the Godhead of the being who presumes to deny God ; the greatest difficulty is with people who know the Lord, and do not obey Him. If they who professedly know the Lord, would carry out His will in daily obedience and sacrifice of the heart, their lives would constitute the most powerful of all arguments. (*J. Parker, D.D.*)   *Dangerous ignorance :*—He says he does not know Jehovah ; he does not recognize His authority or admit His claims. His soul is full of practical unbelief in God—a fact which commonly lies at the bottom of all the hardening of sinners' hearts in every age. Pharaoh did not at first contemplate crossing swords and measuring strong arms with the Almighty God. If he had taken this view of the case he might have paused a while to consider. So it usually is with sinners. Unbelief in God conduces to launch them upon this terrible conflict. Once committed, they become more hardened ; one sin leads on to more sinning till sin becomes incurable—shall we say it ?—an uncontrollable madness. (*H. Cowles, D.D.*) *" Who is the Lord ? "*—This is—1. The language of independence. " Who is the Lord ? " I am the lord of Egypt, &c. 2. Of decided opposition ; a setting up of his will against that of Jehovah ; "Who is the Lord that I should obey Him ? " 3. Of contemptuous rejection of Divine authority. He says, " Let My people go " ; but I say, I will not. 4. Of insolent defiance, braving all terrors. Are we not struck with horror at the impiety of Pharaoh's answer to the message of Jehovah? But what, if in this congregation, there be a man or woman in whose heart the same principle of rebellion reigns ! 1. I address myself first to the young—" My son, give Me thine heart." Now what is the answer of many ? is your heart either divided, or altogether devoted to worldly pursuits and gratifications? if so then the principle, if not the words of Pharaoh is yours. 2. I would address those who are more advanced in life. Ye men of business, I have a message to you. Let me ask you if, on account of worldly gain, you do not sometimes violate your conscience ? Then is not your language, " Who is the Lord " ? I must mind my business first, I know not the Lord, neither will I let my gains go. (*George Breay, B.A.*) *Pharaoh's ignorance self-imposed :*—We may think that this would be of course the language of a heathen king, of one who was not in the covenant. The Scripture does not teach us so. We are told that the Lord spoke to Laban and to Abimelech, and that they understood His voice. When Joseph told Pharaoh who was reigning in his day, that the Lord had sent him his dream, and had interpreted it, he believed the message and acted accordingly. It is never assumed in any part of Scripture that God is not declaring Himself to heathens, or that heathens may not own Him. We shall find precisely the opposite doctrine in the Old Testament as in the New. When then this Pharaoh said, "Who is the Lord, that I should obey His voice?" we are to understand that he had brought himself into a condition of ignorance and darkness, which did not belong to him in consequence of his position, or of any natural disadvantages. He had come to regard himself as the Lord, his will as the will which all things were to obey; therefore he said inevitably, "Who is the Lord?' He had lost the sense of a righteous government and order in the world; he had come to believe in tricks and lies; he had come to think men were the mere creatures and slaves of natural agencies. Had God no voice for such a man, or for the priests and the people whom he represented, and whose feelings were the counterparts of his? We shall find that He had. (*F. D. Maurice, M.A.*)

Ver. 3. **Let us go, we pray thee, three days' journey.**—*Lessons :*—1. God's ambassadors must not forsake His message, upon man's denial. 2. Further arguments must press God's message, when the proposal is not enough. 3. The God of the Hebrews must be owned by them, though despised by Pharaoh. 4. Relation unto God, and call from Him necessitates souls to follow His commands. 5. Although God command powers, yet it beseemeth His people to entreat them. 6. To go at God's call, and serve Him only after His will must be insisted on by His. 7. Small desires of the Church for God, leave powers on earth inexcusable in denying. 8. To sacrifice to God and to feast with Him are synonymous. 9. Entreaties from powers to serve God for averting His judgments is reasonable. 10. Pestilence and sword are God's judgments exacting the neglect of His service. 11. These plagues are incident on all that neglect God, but much more on them that forbid others to serve Him. 12. The fear of these judgments should awe souls from slighting His message to them. (*G. Hughes, B.D.*) *It is right to recognize the danger of disobedience to God :*—"Let us go . . . lest He fall upon us with pestilence, or with the sword." It is right to have in mind the fact that God will punish us if we refuse to do as He tells us to. It may answer for other people to talk about needing no other motive to well doing than love; but you and I are not always influenced by love alone. If we knew to-day that we could do wrong with entire impunity—do a little wrong, I mean, a pet wrong, a wrong that no one would know anything about, and that wouldn't seem to harm anybody very much any way—could do it without any suffering or any punishment; do you think we should be just as strong for the right as now, while we know that the disclosure and the punishment of sin is sure? Well, even if you and I think so, God doesn't take that view of it. God threatens as well as entreats. He holds up the danger of punishment for sin, as well as the rewards of loving and serving Him trustfully; and God doesn't make any mistake in so doing. (*S. S. Times.*)

Ver. 4. **Get you unto your burdens.**—*Wrong judgment :*—Good men are often wrongly judged:—1. In respect to their motives. 2. Actions. 3. Writings. (*J. S. Exell, M.A.*) *The claims of religion :*—You will observe that God gave a command, and Pharaoh refused either to obey the command, or to pay anything like respect unto it. I. LET US CONSIDER WHAT IT IS THAT GOD REQUIRES. In the case of Israel we see that He requires what I may sum up in three particulars. 1. He requires that they should acknowledge Him publicly as their God; that is the first principle. "Let My people go, that they may hold," &c. 2. He requires of Israel that there should be a marked acceptance of His way of reconciliation. "Let us go and sacrifice unto the Lord our God." From the very first when man sinned, there was God's revealed way by which the sinner must come near to Him; and, therefore, the feast that was to be held unto Jehovah, was a feast that was to be founded upon sacrifice. 3. God requires that everything else should give way and yield to the discharge of these required duties. They were to go at once to Pharaoh, and ask his permission to go and obey God's commands, and to sacrifice unto Him as their Lord. They were not to be withheld from doing this by their knowledge of Pharaoh's tyrannical disposition. They were not to be withheld by the remembrance of their worldly duties, or of the hardships and the toils connected with these duties. Now is there anything peculiar to Israel and to God's requirements of Israel in all this? Do we not see, underlying this narrative, a principle which is universally applicable to all those to whom God's message comes? What doth the Lord require of us, to whom the word of this salvation is sent? Does He not demand of us acknowledgment, acceptance of His salvation, and immediate decision? II. But now WHAT DOES MAN THINK OF THE REQUIREMENTS OF GOD? Let us answer this question by referring to the case of Pharaoh. Pharaoh said, "Ye be idle; therefore ye say, let us go and do sacrifice to the Lord. Therefore now go and work." And then again, "Who is the Lord, that I should obey His voice to let Israel go? I know not the Lord, neither will I let Israel go." And again, "Let more work be laid upon the men, that they may labour therein, and let them not regard vain words." What is the meaning of this language? May I not render it truly, but simply, when I say that in Pharaoh's mind there was an opinion that there was no need of so much religion? "Let them go and work"; there was no need of going to sacrifice to the Lord their God. And then when he heard God's threatenings to those who neglected His commands, how did Pharaoh feel then? He maintains that there is no danger in neglecting the supposed commands of God in this matter. He thinks them vain words, all about God's threatenings to those who do not acknowledge Him, and who do not accept His terms of reconciliation. "All these are vain words, pay no attention to them, go and work." That was Pharaoh's way of thinking. And then, further, he thought that there was no sincerity in those who professed to want to worship God. "Ye are idle; therefore ye cry, Let us go and sacrifice. You do not mean to go and sacrifice; you do not want to go and sacrifice; it is your idleness, your hypocrisy." So that you will observe Pharaoh thought thus of God's requirements; first, that there was no need of them; secondly, that there was no danger in neglecting them; and thirdly, that those who professed did not intend to worship, they did not mean what they said. Now is Pharaoh at all singular in the ideas which are thus attributed to him? Is it not still the case that an unconverted man acts in the same way as Pharaoh acted? And then when Pharaoh is reminded of the awful language in which God speaks to those who neglect His requirements, and His judgments against those who know not the Lord, and who obey not the gospel of the Lord Jesus Christ, what does Pharaoh, and what do unconverted men now say, but that in their opinion all these are vain words? Pharaoh thought they were vain words; and so do men now. (*W. Cadman, M.A.*) *Egyptian bondage in the metropolis :*—I. Now, dark as this picture is, I do not hesitate to say that it is FAITHFULLY REPRODUCED AT THE PRESENT TIME. You may see the same thing any day in this metropolis. The bondsmen, whose lives are now made bitter with hard bondage, are the artizans who make the garments you now have on; the men, the women, the children, who minister to your fashions and your luxuries; the shopmen and shopwomen who wait on your convenience, the industrial classes in general, by whose toil this country is rich and luxurious, who are forced to spend the marrow of their strength, and make their lives short and bitter, in providing superfluities for others. The Pharaoh at whose bidding all this is done is the spirit of commerce, that lust of filthy lucre, that morbid and unbridled zeal of competition, which reigns supreme over so large a portion of the world of business. II. Let us therefore inquire WHETHER ANY REMEDY CAN BE APPLIED TO THESE GREAT AND SORE EVILS? Can we individually or collectively do anything towards delivering our brethren from these oppressions and wrongs? Now, it appears to me that there is but one perfect and thorough remedy, and that is the dethronement of the Pharaoh who tyrannizes so cruelly over his subjects; I mean the overthrow of that vicious commercial spirit which has enslaved the great mass of the public. If this were done, if every one traded in a fair and legitimate manner, if every one dealt by others as he would wish to be dealt by himself, if no one entered into the arena of dishonest and ruinous competition, if every employer were as determined to give fair wages to his workpeople, as to secure a fair profit to himself; if these principles were universal, then oppressions would cease in our midst, and our courts and alleys would be the abodes of happiness. But this is not to be yet. The evil and the good will be mingled together until the harvest, which is the end of the world. We can only hope at present for improvements and palliatives. Now—1. With respect to shopkeepers, much evil might be remedied if all the members of each several trade would meet together and bind themselves by a mutual covenant not to keep their shops open beyond a certain reasonable hour. 2. To shop-assistants and operatives, I would suggest that the members of each trade or establishment might with great propriety express their opinions on the subject in a manly and temperate spirit to their employers. 3. And now to the large class of persons who are ordinary purchasers—the public in general—I would say, it is in supplying your wants or conveniences, that all this competition, and oppression, and cruelty is engendered. Much good might be effected by a determination on the part of purchasers never to buy after a certain reasonable hour. III. THE RESTRICTING OF THE HOURS OF LABOUR WITHIN JUST AND REASONABLE LIMITS WOULD BE THE CAUSE OF IMMENSE BENEFIT NOT ONLY TO THE LABOURING MAN, BUT TO ALL CLASSES. I believe that the employers would be gainers even in a money point of view by the improvements now advocated. The men would work with more spirit and energy, because they would feel that they were men, because they would be in a much higher physical condition than when they were overtasked; they would labour with more cheerfulness and good will; the work would be done more skilfully, because with more sustained attention. There would be less drunkenness amongst the men, because in the intervals of labour they would feel less exhausted and have less craving for stimulus. Then, again, the public would be gainers. They would be better served; articles of commerce would not be cheaper possibly, but they would be better in quality, and therefore really cheaper in the end. Moreover, the country would be a gainer, by having a strong, energetic, and numerous race of labouring men, in the stead of the present pale, jaded, and dyspeptic race. Lastly, the Church of Christ would gain many members. There is scarcely any greater hindrance to the progress of religion amongst our industrial classes than this Egyptian system of overtasking the strength. How can that man give due attention to his religious duties on Sunday who is exhausted and prostrate by a week of excessive toil? (*J. Tagg, M.A.*) *Folly of unwise exaction:*—The llama, or guanaco (*Auchenia llama*), is found among the recesses of the Andes. In the silver mines his utility is very great, as he frequently carries the metal from the mines in places where the declivities are so steep that neither asses nor mules can keep their footing. The burden carried by this useful animal, the camel of the New World, should not exceed from one hundred to one hundred and twenty-five pounds. If the load be too heavy he lies down, and no force or persuasion will induce him to resume his journey until the excess be removed. Thus he teaches us the unwisdom of endeavouring to exact too much from those who are willing to serve us well. (*Scientific Illustrations.*) *Pharaoh's complaint:*—That complaint has been made by a good many interested employers since the days of Pharaoh. "How these evangelists do hinder trade"! "What a clog on business this revival is!" "How much money these missionary causes do divert from the shopkeepers!" "This Sunday-go-to-meeting notion takes the profits off of the menagerie; or of the agricultural fair!" "These thanksgivings and fast-days interfere wretchedly with steady work!" "Why can't things go on regular, week in and week out, without any bother about religion?" This is the way the Pharaoh class looks at attention to God's service. But is it the right way? (*S. S. Times.*)

Vers. 7–12. **Ye shall no more give the people straw.**—*Requiring the impossible:*— I. THAT THERE ARE SOME PEOPLE IN SOCIETY WHO STRIVE TO MAKE THOSE UNDER THEM DO THE IMPOSSIBLE. Pharaoh tried to make the Israelites do the impossible, when he commanded them to make bricks without providing them with straw. This demand of tyranny is heard to-day, in our large factories, and amongst our agricultural population. 1. All require men to do the impossible who wish them to work beyond their capabilities. (1) Physical strength. (2) Intellectual ability. (3) Moral energy. 2. All require men to do the impossible who wish them to work beyond their opportunity. Every man must have time, and a proper time to do his work. He must not be expected to do two things at once. 3. Contemplate the method employed to get men to do the impossible. These methods are various. Some will condescend to flattery and cant to get men to do that for which they are wholly unadapted. Others will use force and persecution. (1) They set taskmasters over us. To watch our conduct. To inspect our work. To augment our burden. To darken our sorrow. (2) They abuse us. They say we are idle, and that even after we have made the best attempt within our power to fall in with their unjust demands. (3) They mock our religious sentiment. "Therefore, ye say, let us go and do sacrifice unto the Lord." They impeach our religious motives. These, then, are the ways and methods in which we are treated, when tyrants endeavour to compel us to do the impossible. (4) Some people will attempt to accomplish the impossible. It will involve you in utter failure and distress at last, when you will get no sympathy from those who urged you to it. II. THAT THE PEOPLE WHO STRIVE TO MAKE THOSE UNDER THEM DO THE IMPOSSIBLE ARE THROWING SOCIETY INTO AN ATTITUDE OF PAIN AND COMPLAINT. "Then the officers of the Children of Israel came and cried unto Pharaoh, saying, wherefore dealest thou thus with thy servants." 1. The requirement of the impossible tends to throw society into an attitude of pain. National happiness is to a very large extent the outcome of a free and sympathetic employment of the working classes. 2. The requirement of the impossible tends to throw society into an attitude of complaint. III. THAT THE PEOPLE WHO STRIVE TO MAKE THOSE UNDER THEM DO THE IMPOSSIBLE, AND WHO THROW SOCIETY INTO AN ATTITUDE OF PAIN ARE BUT LITTLE AFFECTED BY THE WOE THEY OCCASION, AND GENERALLY RESENT ANY MENTION OF IT TO THEM. "Go therefore now, and work; for there shall no straw be given you, yet shall ye deliver the tale of bricks." 1. Notwithstanding the outcry of the oppressed, the tyrant demands renewed work. "Go therefore now, and work." 2. Notwithstanding the outcry of the oppressed, the tyrant adheres to his cruel measures. "There shall no straw be given you." 3. Notwithstanding the outcry of the oppressed, the tyrant mocks their woe, and treats them with contempt. Lessons: 1. Never require the impossible. 2. Never attempt the impossible. 3. Adapt methods to ends. 4. Cultivate kindly dispositions toward your employers. (*J. S. Exell, M.A.*) *Lacking the essential:*—Writing on the treatment of his brother, General A. S. Johnston, Mr. W. P. Johnston says: "His command was imperial in extent, and his powers and discretion as large as the theory of the Confederate Government permitted. He lacked nothing except men, munitions of war, and the means of obtaining them! He had the right to ask for anything, and the State executives had the power to withhold everything." (*H. O. Mackey.*) *Strawless bricks:*—I. AN ILLUSTRATION OF THE PAINFUL AGGRAVATIONS OF THE LOT OF THE TOILERS OF EVERY AGE. II. AN ILLUSTRATION OF THE UNSATISFACTORY EFFORTS OF MEN SEEKING FOR HAPPINESS APART FROM RELIGION. III. AN ILLUSTRATION OF THE POWERLESSNESS OF ALL RELIGIOUS SYSTEMS NOT POSSESSED OF A LIVING CHRIST. IV. AN ILLUSTRATION OF FUTILE ENDEAVOURS TO ATTAIN CHRISTIAN PEACE WITHOUT EXERCISING LIVING FAITH. (*F. Hastings.*) *The world and Satan opposed to the Christian's spiritual progress:*—"If thou come to serve the Lord," saith the wisdom of the Son of Sirach, "prepare thy soul for temptation." Have you listened to the gracious pleading of the Spirit of God, in sincere anxiety for a complete and eternal deliverance? You will meet with hindrances, one of the first will arise from those who make a mock at sin, who deride the privileges and duties of pure and undefiled religion. I. THE PREJUDICES OF THE CARELESS AND WORLDLY AGAINST SINCERE AND VITAL GODLINESS. 1. It is regarded as the dream and vision of a heated and enthusiastic imagination. 2. It is regarded as inconsistent with a proper attention to the duties of active life. II. ANOTHER TEMPTATION WHICH SATAN EMPLOYS TO OPPOSE AN ENTIRE DEVOTION OF THE HEART TO GOD, IS BY EXAGGERATING THE IMPORTANCE OF WORLDLY PURSUITS. "Let there be more work laid upon the men." What shall it profit a man if he shall gain the whole world, if he shall lose his own soul? A double caution may be deduced: 1. To those who would hinder the spiritual freedom of others whom they may control or influence; as Pharaoh would have impeded the political deliverance of Israel. You may settle from Scripture and prayer whether the resolutions and desires you oppose arise from the inspiration of God, or the imagination of men. Woe to him that striveth with his Maker. 2. You who are thus hindered, remember that Scripture addresses you with a cautionary voice Be not slothful in business. (*J. R. Buddicom.*) *The burdens increased:*—Note that—I. BENEFACTORS MAY EXPECT MISREPRESENTATION. Moses was censured; Christ rejected by His own. The enemy will slander. Our hope is in working only for God. II. SIN ASKS TO BE LET ALONE. Pharaoh blamed Moses; Ahab blamed Elijah; the Jews blamed the disciples. III. SIN BECOMES MORE TERRIBLE WITH AGE. Pharaoh grew more exacting, and the people weaker; he answers prayers with falsehoods and insults. Sin toys with youth, but scourges manhood. IV. ALL APPEAL MUST BE MADE TO GOD. Moses turned to God; he did not censure the elders. V. IT IS DARKEST JUST BEFORE DAY. Sin grows worse till it breaks down. It threatens in order to drown conscience. (*Dr. Fowler.*) *Sin more tyrannical when men would escape from it:*—When Moses demanded from Pharaoh the liberation of the Hebrews, the tyrant increased their burdens; and in like manner, when the soul rises to expel evil from its domain, it then for the first time discovers the full bitterness of its bondage. Its earliest impulse thereon is to blame the truth which awakened it to a sense of its degradation, for causing the misery which it only revealed. The preacher is accounted cruel when he has been only faithful; and his hearer accuses him of personal malice when he has been only holding up a mirror wherein the angry one caught a glimpse of himself. But all these are hopeful signs. They are, indeed, when rightly regarded and fostered, the prophecies of a coming conversion. The docile slave, who is contented with his condition, is petted and made much of by his master; but if he tries to run away, he is immediately put into fetters. So, when we are roused to battle with sin, it is then that, most of all, we feel its power. Satan does his worst on the soul just as he is about to be expelled from its possession. (*W. M. Taylor, D.D.*) *Means necessary to work :*—I. THAT MAN CANNOT ACCOMPLISH WORK WITHOUT MEANS. A man cannot write a book without intellect, or build a church without money, or save souls without intimate communion with God. Folly to make the attempt. II. THAT ONE MAN HAS OFTEN THE POWER TO INTERCEPT THE MEANS BY WHICH ANOTHER MAN WORKS. III. THAT WHEN MEN ARE ROBBED OF THEIR MEANS OF WORK, THEY ARE THROWN INTO GREAT STRAITS. IV. ANY MAN WHO INTERCEPTS THE WORK OF ANOTHER TAKES A FEARFUL RESPONSIBILITY UPON HIMSELF. (*J. S. Exell, M.A.*) *The Church cast upon her own resources :*— I. THAT THE CHURCH IS OFTEN CAST UPON HER OWN RESOURCES. Times of dark depression. II. THAT WHEN HUMAN AID IS THUS WITHDRAWN, MEN EXPECT FROM THE CHURCH THE SAME AMOUNT OF WORK THAT SHE ACCOMPLISHED BEFORE. III. THAT WHEN THE CHURCH DOES NOT ACCOMPLISH HER WORK AS FULLY AND SPEEDILY UNDER THESE DIFFICULT CIRCUMSTANCES, SHE IS PERSECUTED AND SLANDERED BY THE WORLD. (*Ibid.*) *The discipline of failure :*—The intervention of Moses in behalf of his people was not, at first, attended with happy results. The people themselves were abject and spiritless, and Pharaoh was stubborn and unyielding. The condition of the Hebrews grew worse instead of better. And yet, it was but passing through a stage as helpful to its ultimate success as any other. Great enterprises are wont to encounter such checks in their initial stages. The worm that is to be a butterfly must go into the condition of a chrysalis, and lie motionless, and seemingly dead. The seed that is to be a plant must " fall into the ground and die." Men want the rapid, the grand, and noticeable ; and the " kingdom of heaven cometh not with observation." Men desire deliverance, but they do not like the process of deliverance. Yet such checks are tests of character, trials of men's faith and earnestness. Moses did not despair of a cause because it had met with a reverse. He believed that the cause was God's. He believed in himself as God's instrument to make it victorious. Now I have said that this sort of discipline is common ; and doubtless it is needful and salutary. A defeat at the outset, duly used, is the security of an augmented success. Yet, at no age is the trial that is ever repeating itself, though it be with diminished force, an unprofitable subject of contemplation—the trial of an over-sanguine expectation followed by painful and disheartening failure. Such an one, starting with a full, strong confidence in his own sincerity and earnestness, looks for large and speedy results. "The strong man armed keepeth his house, and his goods are in safety." He looks at him over the ramparts with placid contempt. And now comes the hour of despondency. His ministry is a failure. He is nothing ; he can do nothing. Men will not heed his message. "The trial of your faith is more precious than of gold that perisheth." Try it again. "Thou shalt see greater things than these." "God will help thee, and that right early." "And thou shalt come again with joy, and bring thy sheaves with thee." (*R. A. Hallam, D.D.*)

Vers. 15, 16. **Wherefore dealest thou thus.**—*Lessons:*—1. Oppressed souls cannot but complain of cruel and unjust smitings ; blows make cries. 2. Addresses for relief are fittest from the afflicted to the highest power oppressing. 3. Access and cries and sad speeches are forced from oppressed to oppressors. 4. The execution by instruments is justly charged upon their lords. 5. True servants may justly expostulate about hard dealings from their rulers. 6. Unreasonable exactions will force afflicted ones to expostulate with powers oppressing them (ver. 15). 7. To give no straw and to command bricks is a most unreasonable exaction. 8. To punish innocent servants when others sin is a most unjust oppression. 9. Such sad dealings make God's servants sometimes to complain to earthly powers (ver. 16). (*G. Hughes, B.D.*) *Reasons required for moral conduct:*—I. THERE ARE TIMES WHEN MEN ARE REQUIRED TO GIVE REASONS FOR THEIR METHOD OF MORAL CONDUCT. Public opinion often calls a man to its tribunal. Sometimes men are the questioners. Sometimes God is the Questioner. II. IT IS HIGHLY IMPORTANT THAT EVERY MAN SHOULD BE ABLE TO ALLEGE HEAVENLY PRINCIPLES AND MOTIVES AS THE BASIS OF HIS CONDUCT. Love to God and man is the only true and loyal principle and motive of human action, and only will sustain the scrutiny of infinite rectitude. III. THAT A MAN

WHO CAN ALLEGE HEAVENLY PRINCIPLES AS THE BASIS OF HIS CONDUCT WILL BE SAFE AT ANY TRIBUNAL TO WHICH HE MAY BE CALLED. 1. He will be safe at the tribunal of his own conscience. 2. He will be safe at the tribunal of God's Book. 3. He will be safe at the tribunal of public opinion. 4. He will be safe at the final tribunal of the universe. (*J. S. Exell, M.A.*) *The expostulations of the slave*:—I. THEY EXPOSTULATE THAT THE MEANS NECESSARY TO THE ACCOMPLISHMENT OF THEIR DAILY WORK WERE WITHHELD. "There is no straw given to thy servants." II. THEY EXPOSTULATE THAT THEY WERE BRUTALLY TREATED. "Thy servants are beaten." III. THEY EXPOSTULATE THAT THEY WERE NOT MORALLY CULPABLE IN THEIR NEGLECT OF WORK. "The fault is in thine own people." (*Ibid.*) *The tyrant*:—1. Unreasonable in his demands. 2. Cruel in his resentment. 3. Mistaken in his judgment of guilt. (*Ibid.*) *The true object of blame*:—Gotthold had a little dog, which, when placed before a mirror, became instantly enraged, and barked at its own image. He remarked on the occasion: In general, a mirror serves as an excitement to self-love, whereas it stimulates this dog to anger against itself. The animal cannot conceive that the figure it sees is only its own reflection, but fancies that it is a strange dog, and therefore will not suffer it to approach its master. This may remind us of an infirmity of our depraved hearts. We often complain of others, and take offence at the things they do against us, without reflecting that, for the most part, the blame lies with ourselves.

Vers. 20, 21. **Ye have made our savour to be abhorred.**—*Lessons*:—1. Sense of evil from tyrants may make the oppressed fall foul with their best friends. 2. Providence orders His servants sometimes to meet with friends after sad usage by oppressors. 3. Ministers of salvation wait to meet God's afflicted, when they looked not after them. 4. Instruments of deliverance may desire a good egress of the oppressed from tyrants, and not find it (ver. 20). 5. Sense overcharged with oppression may make men reproach God and curse His ministers. 6. Unbelieving souls are ready to set God against His own word, and instruments sent by Him. 7. Hasty unbelievers under cross providences are ready to charge the cause upon God's ministers. 8. It is the lot of God's instruments of life, to be charged to be causes of death, by foolish souls. 9. Such unreasonable charges are recorded to the shame of such brutish creatures (ver. 21). (*G. Hughes, B.D.*) *Ministers blamed*:—There was no other to lay the blame upon; and so they charge their trouble upon Moses and Aaron. "If you had not come we should have plodded along in our bondage, bearing it as best we could; but you came and raised our hopes, not only to dash them down, but to make our already hard lot more bitter and unbearable." They were angry, apparently not with Pharaoh, but with God's ministers. I have heard it said, that most sinners who have been aroused out of the sleep and death of sin "wake up mad." Indeed, I am quite sure that this is often the case. I remember the case of a man who came to me at one of our meetings in America. He was in the greatest distress of mind, fairly frantic with the conviction of sin, and with the terror of conscience working mightily under the law. At the same time he was bitterly angry with Mr. Moody, who had preceded me in those meetings, and also with me. With a terrible oath he said: "I wish to God you and Moody had never come to this city, and begun these—— Gospel meetings. Before you came and began to preach I had no trouble. I used to go to church regularly on Sunday morning; but I was not troubled about my sins. What a fool I was ever to come into this rink! I have had no peace day or night since I first heard Moody preach. And you have been making it worse. You talk of peace and joy; but you have turned my soul into a perfect hell. I cannot stay away from the meetings; and to come to them only makes me worse. You promise salvation; and I only find torment. I wish to God you would clear out and leave the city; and then perhaps I could get back my old peace. If this is religion, I am sure I do not want any of it." And thus he raved and tore about like a madman. The devil was giving him a great tearing; and he could not distinguish between what the devil and his sin were doing in him, and the grace that was even then loosing him. Let us not be discouraged or surprised if the first effect of our preaching, or labour with souls, seems to make matters worse. "I am a lost soul," cried George Whitefield's brother, one day, while sitting at table with Lady Huntingdon, his brother, and some other earnest Christians who were talking of the things of the Kingdom. "Thank God for that," cried Lady Huntingdon; "for now I am sure the Lord has begun a good work in you." Conviction of sin, and the struggle of the old man to get out of the grip of God's law, are not pleasant experiences; but they precede conversion. (*G. F. Pentecost, D.D.*)

Vers. 22, 23. **Why is it that Thou hast sent me ?**— *The sorrows of Christian service :*—There is a tone of unspeakable sadness in this complaint of Moses. He had been crossed in his aims, his Divinely-inspired hopes had received an unexpected reverse, and all his plans for liberating Israel lay in ruins. It was a bitter moment, and every one who knows anything of the vicissitudes of Christian work will be able to enter into his feelings on this occasion. There come times to every earnest labourer in God's service, when his efforts seem fruitless, and he gets downcast. There are so many unforeseen contingencies to interrupt our work, that it is beyond our power to provide against them. This portion of the Great Law-giver's history will picture to us the sorrows of Christian service arising from—I. OPPOSITION. It may seem strange that any opposition at all should have to be encountered in the prosecution of God's work; yet it has been so in every age, especially when its success affected any of the worldly interests that men hold dear. The reformer, the patriot, the philanthropist, the man who strives to battle with injustice, and to leave the world better than he found it, may always lay their account for opposition. Such is human nature, that it may be taken for granted that those whose vested interests are to be touched will resist change. Pharaoh may, in this respect, be taken as a type of the enemies of philanthropic and Christian work. As Moses and Aaron had to contend with the selfishness of the Egyptian king, so, when our popular leaders have sought the emancipation and elevation of their fellow-men, their efforts have been thwarted by the cupidity of some time-serving official, or the prejudice of some petty aristocrat. Luther had arrayed against him all the forces of Charles V. as well as the emissaries of the Pope. Calvin had to remonstrate with the king of France in favour of religious liberty for his oppressed subjects. Savonarola manfully resisted the tyranny of the Medicean rule in Florence, and paid the penalty with his life. William of Orange contended successfully for the liberation of the Netherlands from the Pharaoh of Papal domination. Instances without number might be adduced from history illustrative of the opposition encountered in the long struggle for human rights. There was a high-handed Pharaoh ever ready to step in and say, This is not for the good of the people, and I will not let it be done. Nor need we be at all surprised at this, when we reflect that One greater than all the philanthropists, reformers, and martyrs, had to endure the contradiction of men in the discharge of the noblest mission the world has ever known. The Lord Jesus came to proclaim principles which, if acted out, would put an end to injustice and oppression. He was opposed on every hand, and so will it be with all who follow in His steps. If you oppose the evil of the world, the world will oppose you. If you resist oppression, the oppressor will resist you. Moses, from the moment he struck at Pharaoh, had trouble to his dying day, but he emancipated a nation and left an undying name. Let no opposition, then, deter you from the right. II. MISREPRE-SENTATION. This additional sorrow was experienced by Moses when the King of Egypt met his demand for the release of Israel by insinuating that his action was prompted by selfish ambition. " Why do ye, Moses and Aaron, let (or hinder) the people from their work ? " As if he had said, The people are content, if you would only let them alone. You are stirring up this agitation for your own interest. Indolence lies at the bottom of the movement. " Ye are idle, ye are idle." From this absurd charge it is obvious in what light Pharaoh regarded the whole question. He looked at it from the side of self-interest. He was not accustomed to look at the moral side of things. He judged every one by his own low moral standard. Now, in all this, have we not a picture of what is going on every day round about us ? Some noble soul, stung at the sight of oppression and injustice, raises his voice in protest from no other motive than to see justice done. The oppressor, smarting under the rebuke, cries out in impotent rage, What have you got to do with it ? Why do you hinder the people from their work ? You are agitating for some selfish purpose. " Ye are idle, ye are idle." You are interfering. Attend to your own affairs. Such is the style of argument which the philanthropist and Christian worker have oftentimes to face. They have to appeal to men destitute of religious feeling, who recognize no interest higher than their pocket. There own motives are of the earth earthy, and they judge others accordingly. One regrets that there is need for this style of remark, but the spirit here condemned is still prevalent among us. I have known a devoted evangelist well-nigh crushed in spirit on having the taunt flung in his face, that he was engaging in Christian work for a living. Such insinuations are a sore annoyance to the sensitive labourer, and well if he can bear them for conscience sake. III. INGRATITUDE. Another discouragement which the Christian worker has often to face, arises from the ingratitude of those whom he seeks to serve. One would have thought they would have enthusiastically hailed him as their deliverer; but, instead of that, they flung back his efforts into his face, and ungratefully taunted him with making their condition more bitter than it had been. They said, Ye have put a sword into Pharaoh's hands to slay us. But how true is all this of Christian work still. The effort to break away from old surroundings originates new pains, and the blame of the new pains is apt to be laid at the door of the man who suggested the change. It is impossible to break off from a long-established evil custom or practice without a painful wrench. It is impossible to deliver a sinner from the consequences of his sins without making disagreeable revelations to him of the wickedness of his heart, which often increases his pains a thousand-fold. The attempt to make things better has often the tendency to make them worse for the time being. And this is a great source of discouragement to the worker. It may cost the drunkard many a pang to throw aside his cups; but he must not reproach the man who led him to see the evils of intemperance. A physician is not cruel because he probes a wound deeply and pains the patient; and he would be an ungrateful patient who would reproach the physician for an operation, however painful, which saved his life. The man who aims at permanent good need not therefore be surprised if he incurs temporary reproach. In the early days of Christianity, the apostles were called men who turned the world upside down. IV. FAILURE. This is another experience for which the Christian worker has to lay his account; and it would be the saddest of all if the failure was final. But it is not final, it is temporary, and only apparent. What we call failure may arise from our—1. Impatience to see results. From the very nature of the work, results do not readily manifest themselves. In manual labour we see the results of our exertions, and can measure our progress from time to time. Take the building of a house. The mason sees the edifice gradually rising before his eyes, and can calculate more or less exactly the time when it will be finished. But in Christian work it is altogether different. You cannot measure results. You have different kind of material to deal with, material that does not readily lend itself to a physical test. You cannot apply the moral test as you can the physical. It is true you may see fruits in changed lives and improved morals, the redress of grievances and the establishment of purer laws; but all that takes time, and the man who laid the foundation of the improvement seldom sees its completion. Now, it is this which makes us so impatient, that we are apt to misunderstand the slowness of the progress. We do not see the improvement we expected, and we draw a wrong conclusion and call it failure. 2. Inability to interpret God's method of working. In Christian work we have not only to lament our lack of results, but in many cases present appearances are positively against us. This, too, gives our services the impression of failure. Had Moses been able to interpret the meaning of events, he would have seen that the increased burdens were the first indication of success, for if Pharaoh had not dreaded that his power was drawing to an end, he would not have demanded more work. It is not easy to acquiesce when things are going against us. Few indeed can look below the surface and read events aright, and this lack of discernment accounts for many of the fancied difficulties of Christian service. (*D. Merson, M.A.*) *Christian workers: their difficulties and discouragements :*—I. THAT CHRISTIAN WORKERS HAVE FREQUENTLY TO CONTEND WITH THE OBSTINACY AND RIDICULE OF MEN IN HIGH POSITIONS. We imagine that ridicule is almost the severest trial the Christian worker has to endure. Thus we see that it is not the Divine plan to shield men from the ridicule and insult incurred by their effort of moral service, but rather to give grace that they may endure as serving Him who is invisible. II. THAT CHRISTIAN WORKERS HAVE FREQUENTLY TO CONTEND WITH THE DISCOURAGEMENT OF A FIRST DEFEAT, AND APPARENT FAILURE. Never be disheartened by apparent failure, it may be but the shutting of a door, which will open wide upon your next approach. III. THAT CHRISTIAN WORKERS HAVE FREQUENTLY TO CONTEND WITH THE MISAPPREHENSION OF THOSE WHOM THEY SEEK TO BENEFIT. IV. THAT CHRISTIAN WORKERS HAVE FREQUENTLY TO CONTEND WITH THEIR OWN MISCONCEPTION OF THE DIVINE METHOD OF WORKING, AND THEIR INABILITY TO RIGHTLY INTERPRET THE MEANING OF EVENTS IN RELATION THERETO. Lessons: 1. Not to be discouraged by apparent failures in Christian service. 2. Not to yield to the scorn of the mighty in our attempt to improve the moral condition of men. 3. To interpret the reproach of the slave in the light of his augmented slavery, and not to be dismayed by it. 4. To prayerfully study daily events so as to find God's purposes of freedom developing themselves therein. (*J. S. Exell, M.A.*) *The apparent failure of Christian service :*—I. OUR SURPRISE THAT CHRISTIAN SERVICE SHOULD BE A FAILURE. It is a matter of surprise—1. Because the workers had been Divinely sent, and prepared for their toil. They had been instructed by vision. They had been enriched by life's discipline. They had gathered impulse from holy communion with heaven. They were invested with the power to work miracles. They were given the message which they were to deliver unto Pharaoh. We cannot but wonder at this failure. 2. Because the workers had received all the accompaniments necessary to their toil. They did not go a warfare in their own charges. All the resources of heaven went with them. 3. Because the workers had arisen to a moral fortitude needful to the work. Once they were cowardly, and shrank from the mission, but their cowardice had broken unto heroism ; their tremor was removed by the promise of God. Hence we should have expected them to have succeeded at once, as a brave soul is never far from victory. II. OUR SORROW THAT CHRISTIAN SERVICE SHOULD BE A FAILURE. It is a matter of sorrow, because—1. The tyrant is unpunished. 2. The slave is unfreed. 3. The workers are disappointed. III. OUR HOPE THAT THE FAILURE OF CHRISTIAN SERVICE WILL NOT BE ULTIMATE. 1. Because the Divine call will be vindicated. 2. Because service for the good of men cannot ultimately fail. Lessons : 1. Do not be alarmed at the temporary failure of Christian work. 2. The apparent failure of Christian work answers some wise purposes. 3. Those who occasion the temporary failure of Christian work are liable to the retribution of heaven. 4. Let Christian workers hold on to the word and promise of God. (*Ibid.*)   *Lessons :*—1. Unjust incriminations from God's people may make the ministers of God quail and recede from their duty. 2. God's faithful instruments though they do retreat of weakness, yet it is unto the Lord. 3. God's faithful ones under pressures may charge God foolishly for doing evil to His people. 4. In such workings of flesh, the Spirit may humbly expostulate with God by prayer. 5. Sad events in ministering may make God's servants question their mission. 6. In such questioning, souls may humbly deprecate the frustration of their ministry (ver. 22). 7. The evil doings of men may turn His servants sometimes to expostulate with God. 8. Wicked men will do worse and worse notwithstanding God's instruments come and speak in His name. 9. Evil instruments may be permitted of God to oppress, and He not at all deliver. (*G. Hughes, B.D.*)   *Perseverance rewarded :*—I once heard a gentleman say that he remembered the making of the railway between Manchester and Liverpool, and it was constructed over ground which at first seemed to say that no line could ever be made. The soil was of a soft, peaty character, and it almost appeared as if no line could be constructed. However, they threw in oceans of stuff, of rubbish of all kinds, and gradually their perseverance was rewarded, for the foundation grew firmer and firmer, the line was built, and now you cannot go over a stronger bit of road on any line in the kingdom. And may it not be so in the cause of missions? Do not let us be in a hurry with regard to results. We may seem to be doing little or nothing, and the morass is as deep as ever. Our work may appear to be fruitless, but in reality we are laying the foundation, and driving deep the piles which prepare the basis for urgent and enduring Christian work and a highway for the Gospel. *The challenge of circumstances :*—All along the history of humanity there are great epochs, where some upward step marks a new era of civilization, such as the invention of the printing press. Yet the environing circumstances did not encourage such inventions. Every adventurer into the realms of the unfamiliar met at once with opposition. It was a square issue with such men whether their inward light or their outward environment was to prevail; and the greater the opposition the firmer their determination. Had Livingstone surrendered to circumstances, he would have remained a factory hand all his life ; it was because he defied his surroundings and conquered them that he rose to eminence. It is a doctrine of fatalism that we are what our forefathers, our climate, and other influences have made us. One might say : "How can I be better? I am a child of godless parents, surrounded by thoughtless people, driven by business, wordly minded—such is the atmosphere in which I live." But such was the atmosphere in which John Lawrence, Governor-General of India, found himself when he first trod the streets of Ca'cutta. He set his face like a flint against luxury, intrigue, profligacy. He took up the challenge of circumstances. With indomitable will he fought, crushing mutiny to-day and righting an injustice to-morrow, until his patient heroism won him the title of the Saviour of India. (*Great Thoughts.*) *Human shortsightedness :*—With every fresh movement of God's grace in the inner life, fresh difficulties and questions are raised. If we will bring these before the Lord, though it should be with the expression of trembling and grief, yet are they not to be regarded as signs of unbelief, but rather of the struggles and contests of faith; and the Lord is patient toward the doubtings of human shortsightedness. (*Otto Von Gerlach, D.D.*) *Success and failure :*—Not unfrequently our first essays at service are encouraging: otherwise we might turn back. But we must be prepared to meet with discouragements further along; as we shall see that Moses did. It is hard to tell, upon the whole, which is the most profitable to the Christian worker—success, or failure. No doubt, both are useful; and in such proportion as God adjusts, they are exactly suited to our need. All failure would so discourage us, that we should turn back from the work; whereas if we never had anything but success, we should become proud and self-sufficient. Discouragements are useful in keeping us humbled and low before God, in a spirit of dependence and prayer; while successes inspire and stimulate us in the work, and give us boldness to go forward in new and more difficult enterprises. I recently met Miss Macpherson, who is doing so much for the poor waifs in London; and she told me of her early trials in getting her work started. At first she felt quite equal to it; and so sure was she that others would see it in the same light that she did, that when she went to solicit money from some of the wealthy merchants of London, with which to build her Home, she had no doubt of an immediate response. She was greatly staggered and discouraged when she found that her expected patrons kindly and politely held themselves excused. This discouragement drove her to her knees; and there she found strength in God. Presently the money came to her from other directions, and in answer to her prayers; and was really of more use to her than if she had obtained it in her own way. And now her success in rescuing children, and finding good homes for them in Canada, is so great, that she is all enthusiasm. She affords an admirable example of what a single-handed woman can do who goes down into Egypt to bring up the little ones. (*G. F. Pentecost, D.D.*)   *God's work not estimated according to apparent results :*—A missionary in China was greatly depressed by the carelessness of his hearers. One day the words of Isa. liii. 1 came to his mind as sent from above, and they were followed by a dream. He thought he was standing near a rocky boulder, and trying with all his might to break it with a sledge-hammer; but blow after blow had no effect—there was no impression made. At length he heard a voice, which said, " Never mind, go on; I will pay you all the same, whether you break it or not." So he went on doing the work that was given him, and was content. (*W. Baxendale.*)

CHAPTER VI.

VER. 1. **Now shalt thou see what I will do.**—*God's reply to the prayer of a disappointed worker:*—I. THIS REPLY TO THE PRAYER OF MOSES INTIMATED THAT GOD WOULD BRING THE TRUE RESULT OF HIS MISSION MORE THOROUGHLY WITHIN THE COGNIZANCE OF HIS SENSES. " And the Lord said unto Moses, Now shalt thou see what I will do to Pharaoh." 1. The mission had hitherto been a great tax upon the faith of Moses. The first repulse made him cry out for the visible and the tangible. 2. Now the mission is lowered to the sensuous vision of Moses. II. THIS REPLY TO THE PRAYER OF MOSES VINDICATED HIS CONDUCT AGAINST THE RECENT INSINUATIONS AND REPROACH OF THE ISRAELITES. Men often take a wrong view of our conduct. God always takes the right view. He knows when His servants are doing what He tells them. He sends them messages of approval for so doing. This vindication—1. Would reassure Moses in his work. 2. Would clear his conscience from all condemnation. 3. Would enable him to interpret his apparent failure. III. THIS REPLY TO THE PRAYER OF MOSES INDICATED HOW THOROUGHLY THE WORK ANNOUNCED BY GOD SHOULD BE ACCOMPLISHED. " For with a strong hand shall he let them go, and with a strong hand shall he drive them out of his land." 1. This shows how wicked men are, under the providence of God, brought to do that which they had once resolutely refused. The sinner knoweth not the future, or he would act with greater wisdom in the present. 2. God makes these revelations in response to prayer, that He may reanimate the dispirited worker. IV. IN REPLY TO THE PRAYER

OF MOSES, GOD VOUCHSAFES A NEW AND SUBLIME REVELATION OF HIS CHARACTER. 1. A sublime revelation of His name. 2. A comforting reference to His covenant. 3. A pathetic reference to the sorrow of Israel. Lessons: 1. That God speaks to disappointed souls in prayer. 2. That the Divine communings with a disappointed soul have an uplifting tendency. 3. That God deals compassionately with the weakness of Christian workers. (*J. S. Exell, M.A.*) *God's long restrained wrath* :—When the ice on the great American rivers is broken up, it is sometimes obstructed in its course towards the sea by a log of wood, or something else, that arrests it. But then, as block after block of ice accumulates, the waters above increase in volume and weight, till their force, with mighty crash, sweeps away all the mass. And so the wrath of God, though long restrained by His love and mercy, sweeps away the incorrigible sinner to perdition. (*H. R. Burton.*) *Conditions of successful work for God* :—1. Faith in God, and honest conviction that God will do as He says He will. 2. Courage to ,do what faith declares. God doesn't use cowards or faint-hearted men to do much for Him. He told Joshua to be of good courage. 3. Perseverance. Keep right on in the place God gives you to work for Him. Many men fail right on the eve of battle. The best silver mine in England was worked for a long time by a man who became discouraged just before it yielded the richest ingots of choicest silver, and he sold out for a song and lost a princely fortune. Keep at it. Get others to help, and work and plod and win success. 4. Enthusiasm is a valuable element, and one that most men need. Too many are afraid of enthusiasm, but all of us need to put more fire and feeling in what we do for the Lord. (*D. L. Moody.*) *The judgments of God upon wicked men* :—I. THAT GOD SENDS SEVERE JUDGMENTS ON MEN WHO REJECT HIS COMMANDS. " Now shalt thou see what I will do to Pharaoh." 1. Notwithstanding his kingship. 2. Notwithstanding his obstinacy. 3. Notwithstanding his despotism. II. THAT THESE JUDGMENTS ARE OFTEN WITNESSED BY CHRISTIAN PEOPLE. " Now shalt thou see." 1. They are seen clearly. 2. Retributively. 3. Solemnly. (*J. S. Exell, M.A.*) *God's everlasting "shalls"* :—It is a great thing to get hold of one of God's everlasting "shalls." For when God says a thing shall be done, who shall hinder ? When God says " shall," you may be sure that He is stirring up His strength and making bare His mighty arm, to do mighty and terrible things in righteousness. Just read through this chapter, and note how Jehovah asserts Himself—" I am the Lord " ; " I have remembered My covenant " ; " I will bring you out from under the burdens of Egypt " ; " I will rid you of their bondage " ; " I will redeem you with a stretched-out arm " ; " I will take you to Me for a people " ; " I will bring you into the land concerning which I did swear to give it to Abraham, and I will give it to you " ; " I am the Lord." All this is very refreshing and encouraging to me. It must have been so to Moses, as he stood there and listened to these strong and blessed words. And so I learn from such words this lesson : when I am discouraged or cast down either about my own salvation, or about the work of the Lord—to turn to the blessed Scriptures and search through the pages, and read over and over again the strong, sure words of God. They sound like bugle-blasts to me, calling me to faith and service. So may the strong words of God reassure any fainting heart ! Be sure that He will not be untrue to even the least of the promises He has made to you ; but will fulfil them all most gloriously. These promises are like the cakes baked for Elijah, in the strength of which he went for forty days. Only we may eat them fresh every day if we are so disposed. (*G. F. Pentecost, D.D.*)

Vers. 2–3. **I am the Lord.**—*Duty to Jehovah* :—Consider the meaning of our duty to God ; the great truth that we have such a duty ; and how it comes about that we have it. I. DUTY IS SOMETHING WHICH IS DUE FROM ONE TO ANOTHER : something which ought to be given, or ought to be done ; not a thing which is given or done under compulsion, under the influence of fear, extorted by force, not even a free gift or offering ; quite different from this ; if a thing is a duty, it must be done because it is right to do it and wrong to omit it. II. The words of the text are, as it were, the sign manual whereby Almighty God, in His dealings with His ancient people the Children of Israel, CLAIMED FROM THEM THE PERFORMANCE OF THAT DUTY WHICH THEY OWED TO HIM. The words which gave validity to an Israelitish law merely rehearsed the fact that He who gave the law was Jehovah ; and nothing more was added, because nothing more remained to be said. III. NOTICE THE PRINCIPLES UPON WHICH OUR DUTY TO GOD DEPENDS. 1. There is a relationship, a close vital connection between God and man, which does not exist between God and any other of His creatures ; man is in a very high sense " the Son of God," so that it is inconceivable that the true aims and purposes of God and man can be distinct. Man being made in God's image, ought to do God's will. 2. Our duty to God depends also on the ground of election. God deals with us now as with His Church in former days; it is still a Church of election. We, to whom God sends His commands, are still rightly described as redeemed out of the house of our bondage; and if the redemption of Israel out of Egypt be nothing better than the faintest type and shadow of the redemption of mankind out of the power of the devil, how much greater is the appeal which is made to us on the ground of that deliverance which Jesus Christ has wrought out. (*Bp. Harvey Goodwin.*)

Vers. 4, 5. **I have also established My covenant with them.**—*A true pattern of gospel redemption:*—I. THAT GOSPEL REDEMPTION COMES TO THE SOUL AFTER A PERIOD OF MORAL BONDAGE AND DISTRESS. 1. It finds the soul in a condition of moral bondage. "Whom the Egyptians keep in bondage." It is the bondage of sin. It has been long continued, through many years of our lives. It has been degrading. It has been fruitless to ourselves. Almost hopeless. 2. It finds the soul in a condition of anxious grief. "I have also heard the groaning," &c. Tears of repentance. Cries for pardon. 3. It is generally preceded by some Christian agency. Aim of ministry to awaken desire for moral freedom. II. THAT GOSPEL REDEMPTION COMES TO THE SOUL BY VIRTUE OF A DIVINE COVENANT AND PROMISE. "I have remembered," &c. 1. God through Christ has made a covenant of salvation with all who trust in the atonement. 2. By virtue of this covenant, all contrite and believing souls may find rest in and pardon from God. 3. This covenant is—(1) Unique. (2) Merciful. (3) Of long standing. III. THAT GOSPEL REDEMPTION BRINGS THE SOUL INTO HOLY AND RESPONSIBLE RELATIONSHIP TO GOD. "And I will take you to Me for a people, and I will be to you a God" (ver. 7). 1. It constitutes the soul a Divine possession. 2. It places the soul under the peculiar guardianship of the Infinite. IV. THAT GOSPEL REDEMPTION LEADS THE FAITHFUL INTO THE INHERITANCE OF CANAAN. What a change! All things are yours. (*J. S. Exell, M.A.*) *Reasons for human redemption:*—I. THE BURDEN OF MAN IS A REASON FOR HUMAN REDEMPTION. No human hand, but Christ alone, can remove it. II. THE LORDSHIP OF CHRIST IS A REASON FOR HUMAN REDEMPTION. He only could fulfil violated law; forgive past neglect; and enable us to keep it in future. III. THE COVENANT OF GOD IS A REASON FOR HUMAN REDEMPTION. (*Ibid.*) *God's covenant to His people:*—1. Stated. 2. Settled. 3. Kept. 4. Happy. 5. Restful.

Vers. 6–8. **I will bring you out.**—*The guarantee:*—1. God is able to deliver His people. 2. God is able to lead His people. 3. God is able to bring His people home. I. REDEMPTION IS POSSIBLE, ALTHOUGH THE DIFFICULTIES ARE GREAT, BECAUSE GOD IS ITS AUTHOR. On the Divine side—1. Satisfaction to the throne in the obedience of Christ; and on the human side—2. The sanctification of man through the blood of Jesus. II. THE MAGNITUDE OF REDEMPTION IS LESS THAN THE DIVINE RESOURCES. God is able to supply—1. Strength; 2. Patience; and—3. Preservation for the journey. III. GOD CAN FULFIL ALL PROSPECTIVE DESIRES IN HEAVEN. (*British Weekly.*) *Israel and Pharaoh : types of the new and old man:*—I. ISRAEL'S POSITION IN EGYPT. One of great and increasing trial. Iron bondage, occasioned instrumentally by cruelty and jealousy of Pharaoh. Ordained of God to wean them from Egypt, and make them long for promised land. II. THE JUDGMENT ON EGYPT. Real contest between kingdom of light and kingdom of darkness. Satan has supernatural power; and in order to deceive Pharaoh, and harden his heart, he gave the magicians power, as far as he could (for there is a limit to his power), to work miracles of deception in imitation of miracles of truth. A miracle does not necessarily prove a man comes from God; but only that he is connected with some higher power—one of two kingdoms. It is the morality of the miracle, and the holiness of the doctrine it is meant to attest, that proves it to be from God. III. THE BEARING OF THESE ON THE CHRISTIAN'S LIFE. See Rom. vii. 9, 24: State of awakened soul; old man and new, with conflict between them; new man often oppressed, old man often dominant though under judgment. (*G. Wagner.*) *A stretched out arm:*—The significance of this figure, "a stretched-out arm," must have been well understood by the Israelites. The deities of the Egyptians were represented with outstretched arms, as symbols of irresistible might. In the hieroglyphics which may yet be seen upon the obelisk at Heliopolis, and with which the Children of Israel must have been familiar, two outstretched arms occur as part of the title of one of the kings, Osirtasen Racheperka, with this meaning, "Osirtasen, the sun, is might!" God's outstretched arm, therefore, is opposed to the king's; and He adds, "I will take you to Me for a people, and I will be to you a God; and ye shall know that I am the Lord your God, which bringeth you out from under the burden of the Egyptians." Moses must also have bethought him of the promise made to him upon the mountains: "See, I have made thee a god to Pharaoh": his outstretched arm was now endued with "might"; it was the instrument by which many of the plagues were brought upon the land, and by which at last Pharaoh and his host were overwhelmed. (*T. S. Millington.*)

Ver. 9. **They hearkened not unto Moses for anguish of spirit.**—*Physical destitution stifling spiritul life :*—A permanent principle of our nature, and a distinctive feature of the Divine government are here embodied in an example. We shall endeavour to explain the historic incident, and to apply the spiritual lesson. I. THE FACT WHICH EMBODIES THE PRINCIPLE. It consists of three parts—1. The message addressed to Israel: "Moses so spake unto the children of Israel." In that message, whether you regard its Author, its bearer, or its nature, everything tended to entice; nothing to repel them. Its Author was the God of Abraham, of Isaac, and of Jacob; its bearer was Moses, a man who for their sakes had sacrificed his position among the princes of Pharaoh, and taken refuge in a desert; its nature was hope to the desponding and freedom to the enslaved. The time, too, seemed fit: when the bondage had become unbearable, word is sent that the bondage is almost done. 2. Their neglect of the message: "They hearkened not unto Moses." It was a spark of fire that fell, but it fell on wetted wood, and kindled therefore no flame. They said nothing against it, but they let it alone. 3. Examine now the specific reason of their apathy. The cause of their indifference to liberty was the extreme severity of their bondage. They hearkened not "for anguish of spirit and for cruel bondage." Here is a paradox: the slavery is excessively severe, and therefore the slave does not care for freedom. Broken hearts have lost their spring, and cannot bound from the bottom of the pit at the call of a deliverer. Great need does not, alone, produce great exertion. The hopeless, helpless captive steadily refuses to stir, lest the chain by the movement should saw deeper into his flesh. II. THE PRINCIPLE EMBODIED IN THE FACT. These things happened to them in order that their history might be a type for us. 1. The message. To us, as to them, it is a message of mercy. Specifically, it proclaims deliverance to the captive. God recognizes all mankind as slaves, and sends an offer of freedom. Christ is the Messenger of the covenant. A greater than Moses is here, publishing a greater salvation. Through the lamb slain is the deliverance wrought. The death of Christ is the death of death. 2. Such is the proposal; but it is not heeded. Comparatively few disbelieve the message or revile the messenger. They simply pay no heed. 3. The reason of this neglect. A carnal mind, which is enmity against God. At one time prosperity, at another adversity, becomes the immediate occasion to an evil heart of departing from the living God. At present we are called to investigate only one class of these occasions or causes of neglect. Anguish of spirit and cruel bondage still make many captives hug their chains, and refuse to hear the voice which invites them to glorious liberty. The lesson here parts into two branches, one pointing to our neighbour's neglect, and another to our own. (1) The first lesson teaches the duty of Christ's disciples to a careless neighbourhood. Abject poverty in these favoured lands exacts a heavier task than Pharaoh from a more numerous host than the Hebrews in Egypt. Self-sacrificing, laborious effort to improve the temporal condition of the poor is a species of revival much needed in the Church of Christ. Of course I do not counsel donations of money or food to the vicious, instead of reproof and instruction: I claim the union of the two. (2) The second lesson applies more directly to ourselves. Anguish of spirit, whether it comes from God's hand in the form of personal affliction, or from man's hand in the form of unjust oppression, may become the occasion of neglecting the salvation of Christ. Beware of neglecting your spiritual state and interests while you are well, in the expectation that distress when it comes will make you religious. There is no truth in nature more certain than this, that the time of health and happiness is the best time for cleaving to Christ and making our calling and election sure. Then it could be best done, if men would then do it. Beware lest you be letting the best time slip past, and the worst time draw on, while you are not saved! It is true that God in sovereign mercy often uses affliction to bring us to Christ; but He does so because we would not come to Christ at an earlier and better time. The mind may be heavenly without "sore bondage," and earthly with it. If you beckon the

Spirit off till affliction come, affliction may come without the Spirit. There is no "anguish of spirit" in "the just made perfect," and yet they are like flames of fire in the keenness of their love to the Lord that bought them. They are happiest who give their bright days to Christ; for when the dark days come, the Light of Life continues to shine within their hearts. (*W. Arnot, D.D.*) *To the saddest of the sad :*—Little words often contain great meanings. It is often the case with that monosyllable "so." In the present instance we must lay stress upon it and read the text thus—"Moses spake *so* unto the Children of Israel." That is, he said what God told him to say. He did not invent his message. He was simply a repeater of the Divine message. As he received it, *so* he spake it. Now, the message Moses brought was rejected, and he knew why it was rejected. He could see the reason. The people were in such bondage, they were so unhappy and hopeless, that what he spake seemed to them to be as idle words. There are hundreds of reasons why men reject the gospel. Amongst all the reasons, however, that I ever heard, that with which I have the most sympathy, is this one—that some cannot receive Christ because they are so full of anguish, that they cannot find strength enough of mind to entertain a hope that by any possibility salvation can come to them. I. And first, will you notice that what Moses brought to these people was glad tidings. IT WAS A FREE AND FULL GOSPEL MESSAGE. To them it was the gospel of salvation from a cruel bondage, the gospel of hope, the gospel of glorious promise. It was a very admirable type and metaphorical description of what the gospel is to us. Moses' word to them was singularly clear, cheering, and comforting; but they could not receive it. II. We come now to note that IT WAS RECEIVED WITH UNBELIEF CAUSED BY ANGUISH OF HEART. We can quite understand what that meant. Let us look into the case. 1. They could not now receive this gospel because they had at first caught at it, and had been disappointed. They limited the great and infinite God to minutes and days; and so, as they found themselves at first getting into a worse case than before, they said to Moses, deliberately, "Let us alone, that we may serve the Egyptians." They did as good as say— You have done us no good; indeed, you have increased our miseries; and we cannot believe in you or accept your message as really from God, seeing it has caused us a terrible increase of our sufferings. Grace may truly and effectually come to a heart, and for a while cause no joy, no peace; but the reverse. Yet press on; be of good courage. Wait hopefully. The God who begins in darkness will end in light. 2. The inability of Israel to believe the message of Moses arose also from the fact that they were earthbound by heavy oppression : the mere struggle to exist exhausted all their energy, and destroyed all their hope. If you have such a struggle for existence here, you should seek that higher, nobler, better life, which would give you, even in penury and want, a joy and a comfort to which you are a stranger now. 3. But, worst of all, there are some who seem as if they could not lay hold on Christ because their sense of sin has become so intolerable, and the wretchedness which follows upon conviction has become so fearful, that they have grown almost to be contentedly despairing. A man who has begun to be numbed with cold, cries to his comrades, "Leave me to sleep myself to death"; and thus do despairing ones ask to be left in their misery. Dear soul, we cannot, we dare not, thus desert you. III. The message was at first not received by Israel by reason of their anguish of soul, but IT WAS TRUE FOR ALL THAT, AND THE LORD MADE IT SO. 1. The first thing the Lord did to prove His persevering grace was to commission Moses again (ver. 1; chap. vii. 2). So the Lord God, in everlasting mercy, says to His minister, "You have to preach the gospel again to them. Again proclaim My grace." 2. But the Lord did more than that for Israel. As these people had not listened to Moses, He called Moses and Aaron to Him, and He renewed their charge. It is a grand point when the Lord lays the conversion of men on the hearts of His ministers, and makes them feel that they must win souls. Moses was bound to bring out Israel. 'But there is Pharaoh." Pharaoh is included in the Divine charge. They have to beat Pharaoh into submission. " But these Children of Israel will not obey." The Lord put them in the charge: did you not observe the words, " He gave them a charge unto the Children of Israel, and unto Pharaoh"? Moses and Aaron, you have to bring Israel out, Pharaoh is to let them go, and Israel is to go willingly. God has issued His royal decree, and be you sure it will stand. 3. I cannot help admiring the next thing that God did when He told His servant what to do. The Lord began to count the heads of those whom He would redeem out of bondage. You see the rest of the chapter is occupied with the children of Reuben, and the children of Simeon, and the children of Levi. God seemed to say, "Pharaoh, let

My people go!" "I will not," said the despot. Straightway the Lord goes right down into the brick-town where the poor slaves are at work, and He makes out a list of all of them, to show that He means to set free. So many there of Simeon. So many here of Reuben. So many here of Levi. The Lord is counting them. Moreover He numbers their cattle, for He declares, "There shall not an hoof be left behind." Men say, "It is of no use counting your chickens before they are hatched"; but when it comes to God's counting those whom He means to deliver, it is another matter; for He knows what will be done, because He determines to do it, and He is almighty. He knows what is to come of the gospel, and He knows whom He means to bless. (*C. H. Spurgeon.*)   *Men content to remain in bondage :—* When Moses came to the Hebrews to deliver them from bondage, they distrusted his commission, and begged to be let alone that they might serve the Egyptians. And so it happens when Christ, the Divine Emancipator, comes to men who have long worn the inherited chain of bondage to sin. They have become so habituated to the hopes, the desires, the pleasures and expectations of a worldly life, that they give no heed to Him who offers to break their chain and bring them forth into glorious and immortal liberty. I have seen the caged eagle beating vainly against the iron bars of his prison, his plumes soiled and torn, his strong wings drooping, the light of his glorious eye dimmed, the pulse of his proud heart panting in vain for conflict with the careering clouds and the mountain blast; and I thought it a pitiable sight to see that kingly bird subjected to such bondage, just to be gazed at by the curious crowd. And I have seen the proud denizen of the air rejoicing in the freedom of his mountain home, basking in the noon's broad light, balancing with motionless wings in the high vault of heaven, or rushing forth like the thunderbolt to meet the clouds on the pathway of the blast; and I thought that that wild and cloud-cleaving bird would choose death, could the choice be his, rather than give up his free and joyous life to drag out a weary bondage in a narrow and stifling cage. And yet I have seen a greater and sadder contrast than that. I have seen men, made in the image of the living God, endowed with the glorious and fearful gift of immortality, capable of becoming co-equal companions with archangels, consenting to be caged and fenced around and fettered down by customs and cares and pleasures and pursuits, that only bind them to earth, make them slaves of things they despise, and answer their noblest aspirations with disappointment. (*D. Marsh, D.D.*) *Ready for deliverance :—*Imagine some poor shipwrecked mariner cast ashore upon a lonely island in mid-ocean. The gallant vessel which had been his home upon the deep went down with all its precious freight before the fury of the storm. His fellow-voyagers all perished in the terrible conflict with the winds and the waves. He alone was cast alive on shore, to suffer more than the bitterness of death in sorrowing for his lost companions, and in longing for a return to his far-distant home. The climate of the island is perpetual summer. Everything needed to sustain life springs from the earth without cultivation. Flowers blossom and fruits ripen through all the year. The forests are full of singing birds. But to the lonely shipwrecked mariner this seeming paradise is a prison. He longs for his distant home beyond the melancholy main. The first thing in the morning and the last at evening he climbs the rocky height overlooking the sea, to search round the whole horizon for some friendly ship coming to deliver him from his watery prison. And when at last he sees a white sail hanging in the far horizon and growing larger as it approaches, it looks to him as if it were the white wing of an angel flying to his rescue. With eager and frantic joy he makes every possible signal to arrest the attention of the coming ship. And when his signals are answered, and a boat is lowered to take him on board, he is ready to rush into the waves and swim out to meet his deliverers before they reach the land. Yet all his joy is excited by the hope of return to an earthly home, where he must still be exposed to pain and sorrow and death. This earth is an island in the infinite ocean of space. It has abundance of riches, and pleasures, and occupations for a few—much toil, and work, and suffering for many—and it must be a temporary resting-place for all. But it has no home for the soul. The ship of salvation is sent to take us to the land of rest. Shall we not look often and eagerly for its coming? And when it appears shall we not be ready and willing to go? Shall we try so to accustom ourselves to the ways of living on this island waste of earth that we shall be unfitted to live in a land where there is no death? (*Ibid.*)

Vers. 10–13. **Go in, speak unto Pharaoh.**—*The successive services of the Christian life :*—I. That the successive services of the Christian life are required not-

WITHSTANDING THE APPARENT FAILURE OF PAST EFFORTS (ver. 10, 11). 1. This service must be continued by Moses and Aaron because the command of God has not yet been executed. 2. This service must be continued by Moses and Aaron because their duty has not been accomplished. 3. This service must be continued by Moses and Aaron because the slaves must be freed. 4. We find Moses and Aaron were sent on exactly the same work as before. There is much waste of effort in the Church, because men are so restless and changeful in their toils. We need determination, concentration, and patience in our effort to free the slave. Failure is no excuse for fickleness in Christian service. II. THAT THE SUCCESSIVE SERVICES OF THE CHRISTIAN LIFE ARE MORE DIFFICULT IN THEIR REQUIREMENTS. The first injunction given to Moses was to call the elders of Israel together that he might communicate to them the Divine will in reference to their nation. Now he is told to go direct to Pharaoh. The language of the 12th verse shows that Moses regarded the service as increased in rigour. 1. This increased rigour of service is surprising. Must the scholar who has failed in the alphabet be put to the declensions of service? 2. This increased rigour of service is disheartening. 3. This increased rigour of service is a discipline. Increased work has often made a bad workman into a good one. It has increased his responsibility. It has awakened him to reflection. III. THAT THE SUCCESSIVE SERVICES OF THE CHRISTIAN LIFE SOMETIMES AWAKEN THE EXPOSTULATIONS OF MEN (ver. 12). 1. These expostulations make mention of natural infirmities. " Who am of uncircumcised lips." It is unnecessary that men should inform God of their natural impediments to religious service. He knows them. He is acquainted with those whom He sends on His errands, with their weakness and strength. If He calls, it is yours to obey. 2. These expostulations make mention of past difficulties and failure. " Behold, the Children of Israel have not hearkened unto me." 3. These expostulations are presumptuous. Lessons : 1. Not to shrink from the successive services of the Christian life. 2. To leave all the moral work of our life to the choice of God. 3. Not to imperil our welfare by expostulation with the providence of heaven. 4. To concentrate our energies patiently on one Christian enterprise. (*J. S. Exell, M.A.*) *Perseverance :* —Johnson tells us that " all the performances of human art, at which we look with praise and wonder, are instances of the resistless force of perseverance ; it is by this that the quarry becomes a pyramid, and that distant countries are united by canals. If a man were to compare the effect of a single stroke of the pickaxe, or of one impression of the spade with the general design or the last result, he would be overwhelmed by the sense of their disproportion ; yet those petty operations incessantly continued, in time surmount the greatest difficulties, and mountains are levelled and oceans bounded by the slender force of human beings." The great Freetrader's motto was that of the needle, " I go through." Having given himself to the cause, he was not the man to desert it ; undismayed by reproach and laughter, and undaunted by the tremendous power of his opponents, he pushed on in his arduous task, clearing the way foot by foot by dint of dogged resolution and unflagging energy. (*C. H. Spurgeon.*)

Vers. 14–27. **These be the heads of their fathers' houses.**—*The genealogy of the Church :*—I. THAT IT WAS, HUMANLY SPEAKING, OF VERY UNPRETENTIOUS ORIGIN. II. THAT IT WAS, MORALLY SPEAKING, OF A VERY MISCELLANEOUS CHARACTER. We have names in this list of very varied moral worth. Some noted for their piety, others remarkable for their profanity. The Church has now a mixed genealogy. All down through the ages the tares and wheat have been growing together, and they will do so until the harvest, which is the end of the world. The miscellaneous character of the Church is accounted for—1. By the diversified temperaments of men. 2. By the diversified thinkings of men. 3. By the diversified character of men. 4. By the diversified alliances of men. III. THAT IT WAS, SOCIALLY SPEAKING, OF VERY GREAT INFLUENCE. It had a great political influence. The Jewish nation was for a long time a theocracy. God was its king. Heaven was its parliament. The priests were of supreme influence in the nation. The community was eminently religious in idea and sentiment. Hence, from the names here recorded there comes out a great stream of social, moral, and political influence upon humanity to-day. (*J. S. Exell, M.A.*) *Lessons :*—1. Order in genealogy is useful to give right understanding of the Church's line. 2. Heads of families in the Church have been too prone to mingle themselves in strange marriages (ver. 15). (*G. Hughes, B.D.*) *A panoramic glance at history :*—I. WE SEE THE MASS OF LIVES THAT ARE CROWDED INTO A BRIEF ERA. The ages soon empty their contents into eternity. II. WE SEE HOW

THE MINUTE DETAILS OF INDIVIDUAL LIFE ARE LOST IN THE AGGREGATE OF HISTORY. The heroes' battles are forgotten. The remembrance of our great calamities is no more. The life of the greatest king is summed up into a sentence on the page of the world's history. III. WE SEE THE GREAT EFFORT OF LIFE TO CULMINATE IN, AND GIVE PROMINENCE TO, THE BIRTH OF ITS HEROES AND EMANCIPATORS. The whole of these lives were preparatory to the lives of Moses and Aaron. All before them were introductory. There is a gradual process in life. Life is ever trying to find emphatic expression in the conduct of the good. History makes this apparent. IV. WE SEE HERE THAT INDIVIDUAL LIVES DERIVE THEIR GREATNESS FROM THE CALL OF GOD TO SERVICE, RATHER THAN FROM SOCIAL CONSIDERATIONS. (*J. S. Exell, M.A.*) *The genealogical table :*—We have here a genealogy of those two great patriots, Moses and Aaron, to show that they were Israelites, bone of their bone, and flesh of their flesh, whom they were sent to deliver, raised up unto them of their brethren, as Christ also should be, who was to be the Prophet and Priest, the Redeemer and Law-giver, of the people of Israel, and whose genealogy also was to be carefully preserved. The heads of the houses of three of the tribes are here named. Reuben, Simeon, and Levi are thus dignified here because they three were left under marks of infamy by their dying father ; and Moses would put this peculiar honour upon them to magnify God's mercy in their repentance and remission, as a pattern to them that should afterward believe : the two first seem to be mentioned only for the sake of Levi, from whom Moses and Aaron descended, and all the priests of the Jewish Church. (*M. Henry.*)

CHAPTER VII.

VERS. 1, 2. I have made thee a god to Pharaoh.—*The moral position in which some men stand to others :*—God made Moses to be a god to Pharaoh, and Aaron to be a prophet. There are many good and noble men in the world to-day, who are gods, the instructors and rulers, of their fellow-creatures. I. THIS EXALTED MORAL POSITION IS THE RESULT OF DIVINE ALLOTMENT. "And the Lord said unto Moses, see, I have made thee a god to Pharaoh." II. THIS EXALTED MORAL POSITION INVOLVES ARDUOUS WORK AND TERRIBLE RESPONSIBILITY. 1. The true gods of society have some-thing more to do than to amuse it. The bearing of their efforts has reference to souls, to man's life in its relation to the Infinite. A man whose highest aim is to excite the merriment of society, is too far removed from divinity to be mistaken for a god. 2. The true gods of society find their employment in communicating to men the messages of God. They come to teach us ; to awaken us ; to enable us to fulfil the will of God. Hence their work is arduous and responsible. III. THIS EXALTED MORAL POSITION IS MOST EFFICIENTLY EMPLOYED IN SEEKING THE FREEDOM OF MEN. But for the slavery of Israel Moses would not have been a god unto Pharaoh. The position is the outcome of a condition of things it ought to remove. It is not for self-aggrandizement. It is to give men the freedom of a Divine salva-tion. (*J. S. Exell, M.A.*)

Vers. 3, 4. I will harden Pharaoh's heart, and multiply My signs and My wonders.—*The struggle between God's will and Pharaoh's :*—The text brings before us the two great results which God forewarned Moses would rise from the struggle between His will and Pharaoh's. On the one hand, the tyranny was to be gradually overthrown by the sublime manifestations of the power of the Lord ; on the other, the heart of Pharaoh himself was to be gradually hardened in the conflict with the Lord. I. WHY WAS THE OVERTHROW OF PHARAOH'S TYRANNY THROUGH THE MIRACLES OF MOSES SO GRADUAL ? Why did not God, by one overwhelming miracle, crush for ever the power of the king ? 1. It was not God's purpose to terrify Pharaoh into submission. He treats men as voluntary creatures, and endeavours, by appealing to all that is highest in their natures, to lead them into submission. 2. In his determination to keep Israel in slavery, Pharaoh had two supports—his confidence in his own power, and the flatteries of the magicians. Through both these sources the miracles appealed to the very heart of the man. 3. The miracles appealed to Pharaoh through the noblest thing he had left—his own sense of religion. When the sacred river became blood, and the light turned to darkness, and the lightning gleamed before him, he must have felt that the hidden God of nature was speaking to him. Not until he had been warned and appealed to in the most powerful manner did the final judgment come. II. WE ARE TOLD THAT THE HEART OF PHARAOH WAS HARDENED BY THE MIRACLES WHICH OVERTHREW HIS PURPOSE. What does this mean? One of the most terrible facts in the world is the battle between God's will and man's. In Pharaoh we see an iron will manifesting itself in tremendous resistance, the results of which were the hardening and the overthrow. There are three possible explanations of the hardening of Pharaoh's heart. 1. It may be attributed entirely to the Divine sovereignty. But this explanation is opposed to the letter of Scripture. We read that Pharaoh hardened his heart. 2. We may attribute it wholly to Pharaoh himself. But the Bible says distinctly, "The Lord hardened Pharaoh's heart." 3. We may combine the two statements, and thus we shall get at the truth. It is true that the Lord hardened Pharaoh, and true also that Pharaoh hardened himself. (*E. L. Hull, B.A.*) *Hardening of conscience:*—It is a very terrible thing to let conscience begin to grow hard, for it soon chills into northern iron and steel. It is like the freezing of a pond. The first film of ice is scarcely perceptible; keep the water stirring and you will prevent the frost from hardening it; but once let it film over and remain quiet, the glaze thickens over the surface, and it thickens still, and at last it is so firm that a waggon might be drawn over the solid ice. So with conscience, it films over gradually, until at last it becomes hard and unfeeling, and is not crushed even with ponderous loads of iniquity. (*C. H. Spurgeon.*)   *Seven characteristics of Pharaoh:*— I. IGNORANT (chap. v. 2). II. DISOBEDIENT (chap. v. 2). III. UNBELIEVING (chap. v. 9). IV. FOOLISH (chap. viii. 10). V. HARDENED (chap. viii. 15). VI. PRIVILEGED (chap. ix. 1). VII. LOST (chap. xiv. 26–28). (*C. Inglis.*) *Judicial hardness of heart inflicted by God:*—I. I shall give some GENERAL OBSERVATIONS from the story; for in the story of Pharaoh we have the exact platform of a hard heart. 1. Between the hard heart and God there is an actual contest who shall have the better. The parties contesting are God and Pharaoh. 2. The sin that hardened Pharaoh, and put him upon this contest, was covetousness and interest of State. 3. This contest on Pharaoh's part is managed with slightings and contempt of God; on God's part, with mercy and condescension. 4. The first plague on Pharaoh's heart is delusion. Moses worketh miracles, turneth Aaron's rod into a serpent, rivers into blood, bringeth frogs, and the magicians still do the same; God permitteth these magical impostures, to leave Pharaoh in his wilful error. 5. God was not wanting to give Pharaoh sufficient means of conviction. The magicians turned their rods into serpents, but "Aaron's rod swallowed up their rods" (ver. 12); which showeth God's super-eminent power. 6. Observe, in one of the plagues Israel might have stolen away, whether Pharaoh would or no (chap. x. 22, 23): but God had more miracles to be done. When He hath to do with a hard heart, He will not steal out of the field, but go away with honour and triumph. This was to be a public instance, and for intimation to the world (1 Sam. vi. 6). The Philistines took warning by it, and it will be our condemnation if we do not. 7. In all these plagues I observe that Pharaoh now and then had his devout pangs. In a hard heart there may be some relentings, but no true repentance. 8. In process of time his hardness turns into rage and downright malice (chap. x. 28). Men first slight the truth, and then are hardened against it, and then come to persecute it. A river, when it hath been long kept up, swelleth and beareth down the bank and rampire; so do wicked men rage when their consciences cannot withstand the light, and their hearts will not yield to it. 9. At length Pharaoh is willing to let them go. After much ado God may get something from a hard heart; but it is no sooner given but retracted; like fire struck out of a flint, it is hardly got, and quickly gone (Hosea vi. 4). 10. The last news that we hear of hardening Pharaoh's heart was a little before his destruction (chap. xiv. 8). Hardness of heart will not leave us till it hath wrought our full and final destruction. Never any were hardened but to their own ruin. II. How GOD HARDENS. 1. Negatively. (1) God infuseth no hardness and sin as he infuseth grace. All influences from heaven are sweet and good, not sour. Evil cannot come from the Father of lights. God enforceth no man to do evil. (2) God doth not excite the inward propension to sin; that is Satan's work. 2. Affirmatively. (1) By desertion, taking away the restraints of grace, whereby He lets them loose to their own hearts (Psa. lxxxi. 12). Man, in regard to his inclinations to sin, is like a greyhound held by a slip or collar; when the hare is in sight, take away the slip, and the greyhound runneth violently after the hare, according to his inbred disposition.   Men are held in by the restraints of grace, which, when removed, they are left to their own swing, and run into all excess of riot.   (2) By tradition.   He delivereth them up to the power of Satan, who worketh upon the corrupt nature of man, and hardeneth it ; he stirreth him up as the executioner of God's curse ; as the evil spirit had leave to seduce Ahab (1 Kings xxii. 21, 22).   (3) There is an active providence which deposeth and propoundeth such objects as, meeting with a wicked heart, maketh it more hard.   God maketh the best things the wicked enjoy to turn to the fall and destruction of those that have them.   In what a sad case are wicked men left by God !   Mercies corrupt them, and corrections enrage them ; as unsavoury herbs, the more they are pounded, the more they stink.   As all things work together for good to them that love God, so all things work for the worst to the wicked and impenitent.   Providences and ordinances ; we read of them that wrest the scriptures to their own destruction (2 Peter iii. 16).   Some are condemned to worldly happiness ; by ease and abundance of prosperity they are entangled : " The prosperity of fools shall destroy them " (Prov. i. 32) ; as brute creatures, when in good plight, grow fierce and man-keen. If we will find the sin, God will find the occasion. (*T. Manton, D.D.*)   *A hardened heart :*—God hardened Pharaoh's heart by submitting to him those truths, arguments, and evidences which he ought to have accepted, but the rejection of which recoiled upon himself, and hardened the heart they did not convince.   Everybody knows, in the present day, that if you listen, Sunday after Sunday, to great truths, and, Sunday after Sunday, reject them, you grow in your capacity of repulsion and ability to reject them, and the more hardened you become ; and thus, the preaching of the gospel that was meant to melt, will be the occasion of hardening your heart —not because God hates you, but because you reject the gospel.   The sun itself melts some substances, whilst, from the nature of the substances, it hardens others. You must not think that God stands in the way of your salvation.   There is nothing between the greatest sinner and instant salvation, but his own unwillingness to lean on the Saviour, and be saved. (*J. Cumming, D.D.*)   *The punishment of unbelief :*—The gospel is " the savour of life unto life, and of death unto death," as one and the same savour is to some creatures refreshing, to others poisonous. But that the gospel is unto death, is not a part of its original intention, but a consequence of perverse unbelief ; but when this takes place, that it is unto death comes as a punishment from God.   Thus the expression "hardening " presupposes an earlier condition, when the heart was susceptible, but which ceased in consequence of the misuse, of Divine revelations and gifts.   As Pharaoh hardens himself, so God hardens him at the same time. (*Otto von Gerlach, D.D.*) *Heart-hardening :*—1. Both the expressions employed and the facts themselves lead to the conclusion, that hardening can only take place where there is a conflict between human freedom and Divine grace.   2. Again, it follows from the notion of hardening, that it can only result from a conscious and obstinate resistance to the will of God.   It cannot take place where there is either ignorance or error.   So long as a man has not been fully convinced that he is resisting the power and will of God, there remains a possibility that as soon as the conviction of this is brought home to his mind, his heart may be changed, and so long as there is still a possibility of his conversion, he cannot be said to be really hardened.   The commencement of hardening is really hardening itself, for it contains the whole process of hardening potentially within itself.   This furnishes us with two new criteria of hardening ; (1) before it commences, there is already in existence a certain moral condition, which only needs to be called into activity to become positive hardness ; and (2) as soon as it has actually entered upon the very first stage, the completion of the hardening may be regarded as certain.   In what relation, then, does God stand to the hardening of the heart ?   Certainly His part is not limited to mere permission. Hengstenberg has proved that this is utterly inadmissible on doctrinal grounds ; and an impartial examination of the Scriptural record will show that it is exegetically inadmissible here.   No.   God desires the hardening, and, therefore, self-hardening is always at the same time hardening through God.   The moral condition, which we have pointed out as the pre-requisite of hardening the soil from which it springs, is a man's own fault, the result of the free determination of his own will. But it is not without the co-operation of God that this moral condition becomes actual hardness.   Up to a certain point the will of God operates on a man in the form of mercy drawing to himself, He desires his salvation ; but henceforth the mercy is changed into judicial wrath, and desires his condemnation.   The will of God (as the will of the Creator), when contrasted with the will of man (as the will of the creature), is from the outset irresistible and overpowering. But yet the will of man is able to resist the will of God, since God has created him for freedom, self-control, and responsibility; and thus when the human will has taken an ungodly direction and persists in it, the Divine will necessarily gives way. Hence, the human will is at the same time dependent on the Divine will, and independent of it. The solution of this contradiction is to be found in the fact, that the will of God is not an inflexibly rigid thing, but something living, and that it maintains a different bearing towards a man's obedience, from that which it assumes towards his stubborn resistance. In itself it never changes, whatever the circumstances may be; but in relation to a creature, endowed with freedom, the manifestation of this will differs according to the different attitudes assumed by the freedom of the creature. In itself it is exactly the same will which blesses the obedient and con-demns the impenitent—there has been no change in its nature, but only in its operations—just as the heat of the sun which causes one tree to bloom is precisely the same as that by which another is withered. As there are two states of the human will—obedience and disobedience—so are there two corresponding states of the Divine will, mercy and wrath, and the twofold effects of these are a blessing and a curse. (*J. H. Kurtz, D.D.*)   *Lessons :*—1. First and foremost, we learn the insufficiency of even the most astounding miracles to subdue the rebellious will, to change the heart, or to subject a man unto God. Our blessed Lord Himself has said of a somewhat analogous case, that men would not believe even though one rose from the dead. And His statement has been only too amply veri-fied in the history of the world since His own resurrection. Religion is matter of the heart, and no intellectual conviction, without the agency of the Holy Spirit, affects the inmost springs of our lives. 2. A more terrible exhibition of the daring of human pride, the confidence of worldly power, and the deceitfulness of sin, than that presented by the history of this Pharaoh can scarcely be conceived. And yet the lesson seems to have been overlooked by too many! Not only sacred history, but possibly our own experience, may furnish instances of similar tendencies; and in the depths of his own soul each believer must have felt his danger in this respect, for "the heart is deceitful above all things, and desperately wicked." 3. Lastly, resistance to God must assuredly end in fearful judgment. Each conviction sup-pressed, each admonition stifled, each loving offer rejected, tends towards increasing spiritual insensibility, and that in which it ends. It is wisdom and safety to watch for the blessed influences of God's Spirit, and to throw open our hearts to the sunlight of His grace. (*A. Edersheim, D.D.*)   *Providence penal :*—In accordance with a vow a Hindu once bandaged up his eyes so tightly that not a single ray of light could enter them. So he continued for years. At last, when his vow was completed, he threw off his bandage, but only to find that through disuse he had completely lost his sight. In one sense, he had deprived himself of sight; in another, God had de-prived him of it. So it was with Pharaoh's spiritual sight. Then comes the warn-ing of consequences. It is very pleasant to go floating down the river toward the rapids. The current is so gentle that one can easily regain the bank. But remain in that current, in spite of all warnings, just one moment too long, and you and your boat will go over the falls. (*S. S. Times.*)

Ver. 5. **The Egyptians shall know that I am the Lord.**—*A knowledge of God :*—I. That the worst of men will one day have to recognize the reality of the Divine existence. "And the Egyptians shall know," &c. 1. Men of bad moral cha-racter shall know this. 2. Men of sceptical dispositions shall know this. II. That they will be brought to a recognition of the Divine existence by severe judgments. 1. Some men will listen to the voice of reason. The Egyptians would not. 2. Such will learn the existence of God by judgment. III. That the existence of God is a guarantee for the safety of the good. "And bring out," &c., from moral and temporal bondage into Canaan, of peace and quiet. (*J. S. Exell, M.A.*)   *The plagues :*—1. These plagues are arranged in regular order, and gradually advance from the external to the internal, and from the mediate to the immediate hand of God. They are in number ten, which is one of the numbers denoting perfection. They are divided first into nine and one, the last one standing clearly apart from all the others in the awful shriek of woe which it draws forth from every Egyptian home. The nine are arranged in threes. In the first of each three the warning is given to Pharaoh in the morning (ver. 15; chaps. viii. 20; ix. 13). In the first and second of each three the plague is announced beforehand (chaps. viii. 1; ix. 1; x. 1); in the third not (chaps. viii. 16; ix. 8; x. 21). At the third the magicians of Pharaoh acknowledge the finger of God (chap. viii. 19), at the sixth they cannot stand before Moses (chap. ix. 11), and at the ninth Pharaoh refuses to see the face of Moses any more (chap. x. 28). In the first three Aaron uses the rod, in the second three it is not mentioned, in the third three Moses uses it, though in the last of them only his hand is mentioned. All these marks of order lie on the face of the narrative, and point to a deeper order of nature and reason out of which they spring. 2. The plagues were characterized by increasing severity, a method of procedure to which we see an analogy in the warnings which the providential government of the world often puts before the sinner. 3. These plagues were of a miraculous character. As such the historian obviously intends us to regard them, and they are elsewhere spoken of as the "wonders" which God wrought in the land of Ham (Psa. cv. 27), as His miracles in Egypt (Psa. cvi. 7), and as His signs and prodigies which He sent into the midst of Egypt (Psa. cxxxv. 9). It is only under this aspect that we can accept the narrative as historical. 4. That the immediate design of these inflictions was the delivering of the Israelites from their cruel bondage lies on the surface of the narrative, but with this other ends were contemplated. The manifestation of God's own glory was here, as in all His works, the highest object in view, and this required that the powers of Egyptian idolatry, with which the interest of Satan was at that time peculiarly identified, should be brought into the conflict and manifestly confounded. For this reason it was that nearly every miracle performed by Moses had relation to some object of idolatrous worship among the Egyptians (see chap. xii. 12). For this reason, also, it was that the first wonders wrought had such distinct reference to the exploits of the magicians, who were the wonder-workers connected with that gigantic system of idolatry, and the main instruments of its support and credit in the world. They were thus naturally drawn, as well as Pharaoh, into the contest, and became, along with him, the visible heads and representatives of the "spiritual wickedness" of Egypt. And since they refused to own the supremacy and accede to the demands of Jehovah, or witnessing that first, and as it may be called harmless, triumph of His power over theirs—since they resolved, as the adversaries of God's and the instruments of Satan's interest in the world, to prolong the contest, there remained no alternative but to visit the land with a series of judgments, such as might clearly prove the utter impotence of its fancied deities to protect their votaries from the might and vengeance of the living God. (*A. Nevin, D.D.*) *The variety of the plagues :*—The diversity and various sorts of those plagues—each sorer than other. The first and second were upon the water, the third and fourth were upon the earth, the five next were upon the air, and the tenth falls upon the firstborn of men, insomuch that their punishment was absolute, not only as to the number of the plagues, which was a number of perfection, but more especially in respect of their nature, matter, and manner, all various and exquisite. For—I. THEY WERE PLAGUED BY ALL KIND OF CREATURES. 1. By all the elements; as water, earth, air and fire. 2. By sundry animals; as frogs, lice, caterpillars, flies, and locusts. 3. By men ; as Moses and Aaron were instruments in God's hand. 4. By the angels who ministered those plagues, both the evil angels (Psa. lxxviii. 44), whom He sent among them, and the good that were employed in destroying their firstborn (chap. xii. 3, &c.), yea, by the very stars, who all combined against them—with the sun and moon—in suspending their light from that land—during the three days' darkness—as all ashamed to look upon such sinful inhabitants thereof, &c. II. THEY WERE PLAGUED IN ALL THINGS WHEREIN THEY MOST DELIGHTED. 1. In all manner of their luscious and delicious fruit, by its being universally blasted or devoured, &c. 2. In their goodliest cattle—some of which they worshipped—all destroyed by murrain, &c. 3. In their River Nilus, which they adored, and for which end, it is supposed, Pharaoh was going down to pay his homage to that idol, when God bade Moses go meet him in the morning (ver. 15). This is intimated in Ezek. xxix. 3, 9, where they are twitted twice for idolizing it, but God made it loathsome to them (ver. 18). 4. In the fish, which was their daily and delicate diet (Numb. xi. 5), for the flesh of many beasts they, out of superstition, would not eat of, as abominable (chap. viii. 26). All the fish died when their water was turned into blood (ver. 21). 5. In their bodies, wherein they greatly prided themselves, but the boils God smote them which spoiled all their beauties in their well-built bodies. 6. In their children, when in every house there was a dead corpse, and that not of a slave or servant, but of their firstborn. All these were the idols of Egypt (chap. xii. 12; Zeph. ii. 11). III. THEY WERE PLAGUED IN ALL THEIR SENSES. 1. In their seeing; for they lost all sight when the plague of darkness took away their light for three days, unless it were horrible sights mentioned in Apocrypha (Wisdom xvii. 6, 7). However, their comfort of seeing they lost. 2. In their hearing. Oh, what a consternation! Dread and terror seized upon them when God uttered His terrible voice in those frightful thunders in the plague of hail, when fire ran along upon the ground, yet did not melt the hailstones (chap. ix. 23). This must be supernatural, and therefore the more dreadful, which might make them think that God was come to rain hell-fire out of heaven upon them as He had done, before this, upon wicked Sodom (Gen. xix.). How did this voice of the Lord break the cedars, &c. (Psa. xxix. 5, 6, &c.), yea, every tree of the field (chap. ix. 25). 3. In their smelling, both by the stench of the frogs (chap. viii. 14), which might mind them of their sin that made them stink before God, and likewise by the stinking rotten matter that ran out of those ulcers wherewith they were smitten (chap. ix. 9–11). As they had oppressed God's people with furnace work in making brick, so the ashes of that furnace became burning boils that break forth into putrid running sores, &c. 4. In their tasting, both by the waters turned into blood, because in them they had shed the blood of the male Hebrew children. These bloody men had blood to drink, for they were worthy (Rev. xvi. 6). Their River Nilus they used to boast of to the Grecians, saying, in mockery to them, "If God should forget to rain, they might chance to perish for it." The rain, they thought, was of God, but not their river (Ezek. xxix. 3, 9), therefore, to confute them in their confidence, as God threatens to dry it up (Isa. xix. 5, 6), so here to bereave them of all the comfortable use of it; they now loathed to drink of it (vers. 18–20). God cursed their blessings (Mal. ii. 2), and also by their thirst thereby procured. Drinking such bloody water did rather torture their taste than please their palate, or quench their thirst. 5. In their touching or feeling, by their dolorous shooting pangs in their body, when the sin of their souls broke forth into sores of their bodies, which pained them so, that, as they could not now sleep in a whole skin, so they gnawed their own tongues for pain. This was superadded to the bitings of flies, wasps, flying-serpents, &c., whereby some might be stung to death (Psa. lxxviii. 45), and the magicians themselves, who had so insolently imitated Moses, the devil being God's ape, were branded with those boils to detect their contumacy. Besides, also, the frogs ravaging upon their bodies so irresistibly, &c., must needs be very offensive to their sense of touching. IV. Lastly, as if all this had been too little to fill up the measure of their plagues and punishments, Pharaoh and all his forces, that hitherto had escaped, were all drawn blindfold into the noose, by fair way, weather, &c., and then were drowned in the Red Sea (chap. xiv. 8, 9, 21, 24, 28). (*C. Ness.*)

Ver. 6. **So did they.**—*Obedience to God :*—I. IT MUST BE RENDERED BY THE SERVANTS OF GOD. "Moses and Aaron." All men who are called to moral service by God must obey Him. 1. Because He gives them their commands. 2. Because He gives them the power to do so. 3. Because He rewards obedience. II. IT MUST BE CO-EXTENSIVE WITH THEIR MISSION. 1. It must be entire. 2. It must be cheerful. 3. It must be holy. III. IT WILL RENDER THEIR MISSION EFFECTIVE—1. Because it will lead to the best mode of service. 2. Because God will delight to honour it. The Divine commands: (1) Rightfully given. (2) To be faithfully executed. (3) To be diligently obeyed. To be supremely regarded. (*J. S. Exell, M.A.*)

Ver. 7. **Fourscore years old.**—*Age of Moses and Aaron :*—Their ages would have an important bearing toward the work of these two men. I. THEIR AGES WOULD INDICATE THAT THEY WERE NOT LIKELY TO BE MISLED BY THE ENTHUSIASM OF YOUTH. The world is slow to take young men into its confidence. It soon smiles at their visions, and laughs at their enthusiastic hopes. II. THEIR AGES WOULD BE LIKELY TO COMMAND THE RESPECT OF THOSE WITH WHOM THEY HAD TO DO. The world wants men of tried energy and long experience to achieve its moral emancipation ; men in whom hot passion has calmed into a settled force. III. THEIR AGES WOULD BE AN INCENTIVE TO FIDELITY, AS THEY HAD SPENT THE YOUNGER PART OF LIFE, AND WOULD BE FORCEFULLY REMINDED OF THE FUTURE. (*J. S. Exell, M.A.*)   *Delay in entering upon work of life :*—Let us learn not to be impatient for the discovery of our true life-work. Moses was eighty years old before he entered upon that noble career by which he became the emancipator and educator of his nation. Two-thirds of his days were gone before he really touched that which was his great, distinctive, and peculiar labour, and his enterprise was all the more gloriously accomplished by reason of the delay. Nor is this a solitary instance. The Lord Jesus Himself lived thirty years, during most of which He was in training for a public ministry, which lasted only two-and-forty months. John Knox never entered a pulpit until he was over forty years of age; and much of the fire and energy of his preaching was owing to the fact that the flame had been so long pent up within his breast. Havelock was a dreary while a mere lieutenant, held back by the iniquitous system of purchase, which was so long in vogue in the English army; but, as it happened, that was only a life-long apprenticeship, by which he was enabled all the more efficiently to become, at length, the saviour of the Indian Empire. So let no one chafe and fret over the delay which seems evermore to keep him from doing anything to purpose for the world and his Lord. The opportunity will come in its own season. It does come, sooner or later, to every man; and it is well if, when at length he hears the voice calling, "Moses! Moses!" he is ready with the answer, "Here am I." For while I would comfort you with the assurance that the hour will come, I do not mean that you should be idle until it strikes. No; for if you adopt such a plan, the certainty is that you will not hear its stroke, or that you will not be ready to begin at its call. The true principle is to do with your might that which is lying at your hand day by day, in the firm conviction that you are thereby training yourself into fitness for your future vocation. (*W. H. Taylor, D.D.*)

Vers. 11, 12. **They also did in like manner with their enchantments.**—*Moses and the magicians:*—I. Moses divinely warned of Pharaoh's demand for a supernatural credential. When men profess to bring a message from God, they should be prepared to substantiate it by satisfactory evidence. II. Moses divinely sustained in meeting the demand. 1. God will never forsake those who go forth to implicitly work His will. 2. God often permits His enemies to temporarily triumph. III. Moses commanded to appeal again to Pharaoh (vers. 14–17). 1. God's knowledge of the human heart. 2. God's knowledge of the purposes and plans of men. 3. God's recognition of free agency, and its correlative responsibility. 4. God deals with men on the basis of their moral freedom, and according to their constitutional nature. Lessons: 1. Here we have a type of the conflict of ages. (1) In its spirit. (2) In its aims. (3) In its result. 2. The side to which we lean, and for which we fight, shows the party to which we really belong. (*D. C. Hughes, M.A.*) *Lessons:*—1. Miracles from God will not persuade wicked hearts to believe. 2. Unbelieving sinners are apt to call in all instruments of Satan to gainsay God. 3. Providence hath of old suffered wisdom to be abused to sorcery and pernicious acts (ver. 11). 4. God hath suffered creatures by Satan's help to do some like things to His miracles. 5. Under God's permission Satan may work strange changes in creatures, but no miracles. 6. God's true miracles devour all lying wonders of Satan (ver. 12). 7. Wicked hearts harden themselves by lying wonders against God, and therefore are hardened by Him. 8. The fruit of such hardening is rebellion against God's word and will. 9. God's word is made good in all the disobedience of the wicked foretold (ver. 13). (*G. Hughes, B.D.*) *Man's effort to repudiate the message of God by an imitation of its miraculous credentials:*—I. That man has a right to expect that any special revelation from God should be accompanied by infallible and unimpeachable credentials (ver. 9). 1. We require these credentials to vindicate the authority of the speaker. The Bible contains the evidences of its Divine origin on its own pages, for on every page we see the miracle repeated, the rod is turned into a serpent. And the miracles which the book contains, and the miracle which it is in itself, are sufficient token to the honest mind that it comes from God. This evidence is equal to the case. It leaves disobedience without excuse. 2. We require these credentials to vindicate the credibility of the speaker. God would never give men power to work a miracle to authenticate a lie. The miracle not only demonstrated the authority of these men, but also the unimpeachable honesty and verity of their statements. And so men take the Bible to-day; they perhaps say that in general terms the book has come from God, and has His authority, and yet how many question the verity of its contents. They call one part of the message a myth, another part a fable, until, indeed, there is very little remaining as true. 3. That God anticipates these requests on the part of man, and provides His messengers with the needed credentials. Any one who rejects the claims of the Bible, rejects the highest proof, the most reliable evidence; hence his condemnation will be awful as that of the rebellious king. 4. The spirit in which these credentials should be investigated and received—(1) Thoughtfully. (2) Devoutly. (3) Never sceptically. (4) Remember that the messengers of God can only offer the credentials divinely permitted to them. II. THAT MEN HAVE RECOURSE TO MANY DEVICES TO WEAKEN AND NULLIFY THE CREDENTIALS WHICH ARE PRESENTED TO THEM IN TOKEN AND SUPPORT OF A DIVINE MESSAGE AND CLAIM. "Then Pharaoh also called the wise men and the sorcerers: now the magicians of Egypt, they also did in like manner with their enchantments." 1. We find that men in the investigation of a Divine message are not satisfied with the evidence they themselves propose. A sceptical mind will not yield even when it has attained evidence for the truth of its own seeking. It is most criminal in its unbelief. 2. We find that men in the investigation of a Divine message often seek others to supply them with sceptical arguments they are not clever enough to produce themselves. 3. We find that men endeavour to confirm their comrades in scepticism by imitating the credentials of the messengers of God. But in vain. The truth-seeker can distinguish between the productions of the two ; he never mistakes the enchantment of the Egyptian for the miracle of Moses. 4. That the men who endeavour to confirm their comrades in scepticism respecting the Divine credentials are subject to the truth. The rods of the Egyptian magicians were swallowed up by Aaron's rod. III. THAT THE MEN WHO REJECT THE CREDENTIALS OF DIVINE MESSENGERS COMMENCE A CONFLICT WHICH WILL BE PRODUCTIVE OF GREAT WOE AND OF FINAL OVERTHROW TO THEM. " And He hardened Pharaoh's heart that he hearkened not unto them ; as the Lord had said." Lessons : 1. That the messengers of God can always produce Divine credentials. 2. That Divine credentials are often rejected by men of high social position. 3. That a continued rejection of Divine credentials will end in destruction. 4. That the servants of God are often perplexed by the conduct of men in rejecting Divine claims. (J. S. Exell, M.A.) Imitation of the good :—The mode in which the magicians " withstood Moses " (see 2 Tim. iii. 1-9) was simply by imitating, so far as they were able, whatever he did. From this we learn the solemn truth that the most Satanic resistance to God's testimony in the world is offered by those who, though they imitate the effects of the truth, have but " the form of godliness," and "deny the power thereof." Persons of this class can do the same things, adopt the same habits and forms, use the same phraseology, profess the same opinions, as others. How needful to understand this ! How important to remember that "as Jannes and Jambres withstood Moses," so do those self-loving, world-seeking, pleasure-hunting professors "resist the truth !" They would not be without "a form of godliness " ; but while adopting "the form," because it is customary, they hate "the power," because it involves self-denial. "The power " of godliness involves the recognition of God's claims, the implanting of His kingdom in the heart, and the consequent exhibition thereof in the whole life and character; but the formalist knows nothing of this, nor does he desire to know it. He does not want his lusts subdued, his pleasures interfered with, his passions curbed, his affections governed, his heart purified. He wants just as much religion as will enable him " to make the best of both worlds." (A. Nevin, D.D.) Egyptian magicians :—They must have possessed a knowledge of nature beyond that of their countrymen, who had sufficient experience of the utility of such knowledge to reverence teachers endued with any rare portion of it. The magicians must have considered this knowledge as Divine ; and have come more and more to regard the different powers of nature and the different objects in which these powers were exhibited, as themselves Divine. They will have been politicians as well as naturalists, ready to employ their lore and the mastery which it gave them over the things of the earth, to uphold the authority of the monarch, or to promote his plans. They will therefore have fallen into a scheme of trick and dissimulation, which would have been ineffectual and impossible if there had not been some truths lying at the root of it; and some real assurance in their own minds both of those truths and of their own capacities. It is this mixture of faith with insincerity—of actual knowledge with the assumption of knowledge, of genuine power with the desire to make the power felt and worshipped, a readiness therefore to abuse it to low grovelling purposes—which we have to recognize in the impostures of all subsequent ages, and to which we are here introduced in one of its primitive manifestations. It was most natural for a politic monarch to wish that a body of strangers, who were doing little good in a certain portion of his land, should be made slaves, and so become agents in carrying out what seemed to him magnificent projects. It was most natural that a body of politic priests—disliking these strangers, for the traditions and customs which separated them from their influence—should readily co-operate with him in that plan, or should be the first suggesters of it. It is equally natural that his Egyptian subjects should sympathize with the design, and should feel that they were raised in the degradation of another race. But it was impossible that king, priests, and people, should effect this seemingly sage and national purpose, without forging new chains for themselves, without losing some perceptions of a moral order in the world and a moral Ruler of it, which had been implied in their government and worship, and which Joseph's arrangements had drawn out; it was impossible but that with the loss of this feeling, they should sink further and further into natural and animal worship. (*F. D. Maurice, M.A.*) **Aaron's rod swallowed up their rods.**—*The power of Aaron's rod :*—I. Let us turn aside to see this great sight—the Divine triumphant over the diabolical: the spiritual subduing the natural—AARON'S ROD SWALLOWING ALL ITS RIVALS. 1. Let us take the case of the awakened sinner. That man was, a few days ago, as worldly, as carnal, as stolid, as he well could be. If any one should propose to make that man heavenly-minded, the common observer would say, "Impossible! As in old Roman walls, the cement has become so strong, that the stone is no longer a separate piece, but has become a part of the wall itself —so this man is cemented to the world, he cannot be separated from it. You must break him in pieces with the hammer of death; you cannot separate him in any other way from the cares of life." Ah, but Aaron's rod shall swallow up this rod. The man listens to the Word; the truth comes with power into his soul; the Holy Ghost has entered him; and the next day, though he goes to his business, he finds no true contentment in it, for he pants after the living God. Now, his spirit pleads its needs, and outstrips the body in the contest for its warmest love. He spurns the trifles of a day: he seeks the jewels of eternity. Grace has won the day, and the worldling seeks the world to come. 2. The same fact, with equal distinctness, is to be observed in the individual when he becomes a believer in Jesus Christ; his faith destroys all other confidences. 3. The same fact is very manifest after faith in all who truly love the Saviour. They who love Christ aright, love no one in comparison with Him. 4. You will notice this in the man who makes his delight in the Lord Jesus. He who makes his delight in Christ after a true sort, will discover that this delight swallows up all other delights. 5. Yet more is it so in a man who is devoted to God's service. The service of God swallows up everything else when the man is truly God's servant. When a man gets fully possessed with an enthusiastic love for Jesus, difficulties to him become only things to be surmounted, dangers become honours, sacrifices pleasures, sufferings delights, weariness rest. II. WE NOW DRAW AN INFERENCE. If it be so, that wherever true religion—the finger of God—comes into a man, it becomes a consuming passion, till the zeal of God's house eats the man up. Then there are many persons who profess religion, who cannot have found the right thing. Those who are mean, miserly, and miserable in the cause of Christ, whose only expenditure is upon self, and whose main object is gain, what can we say of them? Why, that they look upon religion as some great farmers do upon their little off-hand farms. They think it is well to have a little religion; they can turn to it for amusement sometimes, just to ease them a little of their cares; besides, it may be very well, after having had all in this world, to try to get something in the next. They are moral and decent in all ways; they can pray very nicely in prayer-meetings, yet they never dream of consecrating their secular employments unto God. Aaron's rod, in their case, has never swallowed up their rods. III. Now, I will GIVE SOME REASONS WHY I PUT THE SERVICE OF GOD SO PROMINENT, AND THINK THAT AARON'S ROD OUGHT TO SWALLOW UP ALL OTHER RODS. What does the great gospel revelation discover to us? Does it not show us an awful danger, and one only way of escape from it? Does not our religion also reveal to us the joyous reward of another world? It opens to us yonder pearly gates, and bids us gaze on angels and glorified spirits. By hell, and by heaven, therefore, I do entreat you, let Aaron's rod swallow up all other rods; and let love and faith in Jesus be the master passion of your soul. Moreover, do we not learn in our holy faith of a love unexampled? Where was there love such as that which brought the Prince of Glory down to the gates of death, and made Him pass the portals amid shame and scoffing? Shall such love as this have half our hearts? (*C. H. Spurgeon.*)

Vers. 14–25. **They shall be turned to blood.**—*The river which was turned into blood :*—I. THE RIVER. Has received various names. "The river of Egypt" (Gen. xv. 18); "Sihor" (Job xiii. 3); "Shihor" (1 Chron. xiii. 5). Diodorus Siculus says: "The Nile was first called Egypt." Best and longest known by the term Nile, which is derived from the Arabic words Nil, which means "blue," and Nileh, which means "indigo." Designated, therefore, "the dark blue river," on account of its waters assuming at times that appearance. 1. Its sources. These are three "branches." The White River, which is the western branch, and takes its rise in the Mountains of the Moon; the Blue River, which is the central branch, and rises in the highlands of the Galla country, south of Abyssinia; the Black River, which is the eastern branch, and rises in the Mountains of Laska. These three required to make the Nile what it is. Owes its abundance and majesty to each of them. Learn the necessity and the advantage of combined efforts in doing good. 2. Its course. Referring here not to the flow of the three rivers just named and their various tributaries; but coming down to the confluence of the last of these, the Nile runs in a directly northern course to a distance of 1,150 miles. During all this way it receives no permanent streams, although in the rainy season it is often swollen by torrents from the mountains which lie between it and the Red Sea. Fifteen miles below Cairo it divides into two arms. One of these runs into the Mediterranean Sea below Rosetta, the other flows into it near Damietta. The whole extent of the river from its farthest source is 3,300 miles. Has been pursuing this course for the last 6,000 years. As deep and broad as ever. Why? For the same reason that the rays of the sun are as numerous and powerful as at first. He who has supplied the sun with light has supplied the Nile with water. How thankful we should be to Him. 3. Its uses. It has helped to form the clouds. The sun has visited it every day; has received from it some of the human family in various forms. Above all it has been, and continues to be, the life of Egypt. II. The river changed. As at the marriage-feast of Cana in Galilee, the waters in the water-pots blushed into wine, because the Lord willed the transformation; so the waters of the Nile blushed into blood for the same reason. The locomotive in the hands of the driver, the ship and the pilot, the horse and the rider; all the elements of nature much more under God. He can do with every one of them just as He pleases. This, great comfort to all that love Him. They are safe, for nothing can harm them, contrary to His mind respecting them. This should deeply impress those who do not love Him. May be conquered at any moment by the lightning, the wind, or the water. III. The river changed for three reasons. 1. It was changed on account of idolatry. The Egyptians reverenced the Nile; boasted that it made them independent of the rain; believed that all their gods, particularly Vulcan, were born on its banks. In honour of it observed rites, ceremonies, and celebrated festivals. 2. It was changed that the priests of Egypt might be deeply impressed. Nothing which the priests more abhorred than blood. If the slightest stain of blood had been on their persons, even on their sandals or garments, they would have thought themselves deeply polluted. How terrified they must have been when they saw that "there was blood throughout all the land of Egypt." God meant this, that they might begin to think of Him, and turn from their dumb idols to Him. Events, as well as words, are teachers. May we listen at all times to truth. 3. It was changed to show that God is all-powerful. (*A. McAuslane, D.D.*) *The river turned into blood; or, man's chief pleasure and pride made the medium of Divine retribution :*—I. That Divine retributions are sent when other and merciful measures have failed to accomplish the purpose of God in man. II. Divine retributions often consist in making the source of man's truest pleasure the cause of his greatest misery. 1. Sometimes the religious notions of men are made the medium of retributive pain. 2. Sometimes the commercial enterprises of men are made the medium of retributive pain. He who might have been prosperous, had he obeyed the behest of God, is ruined by his folly. 3. Sometimes all the spheres of a man's life are made the medium of retributive pain. If a man gets wrong with God, it affects the entirety of his life. Moral questions penetrate into every realm and department of being, and affect the whole of them, either gladly or wofully, all being dependant upon the attitude of the soul toward the Eternal. Hence it is wise for men to obey the command of God if they would be prosperous. 4. Thus we see how easily and completely God can make human life a retribution to the evil doer. He can turn our glory into shame. III. That the Divine retributions are extensive in their effect, and are operative before the impotent presence of the socially great. "And Moses and Aaron did," &c. 1. This Divine retribution extended throughout all the land of Egypt. 2. This Divine retribution, in the act of infliction, was witnessed by Pharaoh, and he was unable to prevent it. IV. That the Divine retributions are not always effectual to the subjugation of the wicked heart. "And the magicians of Egypt did so with their enchantments," &c. "And Pharaoh turned," &c. 1. The hardihood of a disobedient soul. 2. The resistance of a tyrannic will. 3. The effort of men to mitigate the retribution of God. "All the Egyptians digged," &c. Vain effort. V. THAT THE DIVINE RETRIBUTION SOMETIMES EVOKES PRESUMPTIVE CONDUCT ON THE PART OF THE WICKED. Lessons: 1. That Divine retributions are often merited by men. 2. That God can soon turn our joy into pain. 3. That obedience is the wisdom of man. (*J. S. Exell, M.A.*) *Opportunity in Christian service :*—I. THAT THERE ARE FAVOURABLE TIMES AT WHICH TO APPROACH MEN WITH THE MESSAGES OF GOD. "Get thee unto Pharaoh in the morning." II. THAT THERE ARE FAVOURABLE PLACES IN WHICH TO APPROACH MEN WITH THE MESSAGES OF GOD. "And thou shalt stand," &c. III. THAT THE SERVANTS OF GOD ARE OFTEN DIVINELY INSTRUCTED AS TO THE BEST OPPORTUNITY OF CHRISTIAN SERVICE. "Get thee unto Pharaoh in the morning." By a deep conviction, by a holy impression, and by keen moral vision, God unfolds to good men the most favourable opportunity in which to declare His message to the wicked. (*Ibid.*) *The river changed into blood :*—I. THAT GOD CAN CHANGE THE SCENE OF LIFE INTO DEATH. II. THAT GOD CAN CHANGE USEFUL THINGS INTO USELESS. All life dependent on His will. III. THAT GOD CAN CHANGE BEAUTIFUL THINGS INTO LOATHSOME. (*Ibid.*) *Superstitions respecting the Nile :*—One of its names was Hapi, or Apis, which is the same as the sacred bull. There is extant a hymn to the Nile, written about the time of the Exodus, beginning thus—"Hail, O Nile, thou comest forth over this land, thou comest in peace, giving life to Egypt, O hidden God !" Plutarch, following the jargon of the priests, calls the Nile "the Father and Saviour of Egypt" (Symp. 8, 8); and affirms, "There is nothing so much honoured among the Egyptians as the river Nile." Even the fish and reptiles which it nourished, and the very reeds and flowers which grew in it, were held sacred. About midsummer every year a great festival was celebrated throughout the country in honour of the Nile. Men and women assembled from all parts of the country in the towns of their respective Nomes; grand festivities were proclaimed, and the religious solemnities which then took place were accompanied with feasting, dancing, and a general rejoicing. A wooden image of the river god was carried by the priests through the villages in solemn procession, appropriate hymns were sung, and the blessings of the anticipated inundation were invoked. By the miraculous change of the waters into blood, a practical rebuke was given to these superstitions. This sacred and beautiful river, the benefactor and preserver of their country, this birthplace of their chief gods, this abode of their lesser deities, this source of all their prosperity, this centre of all their devotion, is turned to blood : the waters stink ; the canals and pools, the vessels of wood and vessels of stone, which were replenished from the river, all are alike polluted. (*T. S. Millington.*)

CHAPTER VIII.

VERS. 1–14. **The frogs came up.**—*The procession of frogs :*—I. THE CREATURES THAT WERE TO COME. The frogs of Egypt distinguished for five things. Their ash colour dotted with green spots ; changed their colour when alarmed ; small ; crawled like toads ; made a singular, some say an "abominable" noise, both under the water and on the land. II. THE PLACES TO WHICH THE CREATURES DID COME. III. THE POWER WHICH CAUSED THE CREATURES TO COME. As the changing of the Nile showed that all the elements of nature were under the control of God, so the coming of the frogs to the land of Egypt proved that the animal parts of creation were under His control. IV. THE PURPOSES FOR WHICH THE CREATURES CAME. 1. On account of pride (ver. 2). God still abhors pride, and ever will. Can chastise the proud in a similar way. Can send disease to the pretty face ; take away the idols, money, dress, friends ; weakness to either body or mind ; death to the unbroken circle. "Walk humbly with thy God." 2. On account of superstition. Because the rising of the sun made wild beasts retire, the Egyptians looked on them as emblems of the sun's power. Because the croaking of frogs helped travellers in a desert to discover waters, the Egyptians held them in some reverence. Regarded the frog also as sacred to the Nymphs and Muses. Called attendants upon the deities of streams and fountains. To correct this wrong and extravagant notion about frogs, the Lord sent them over all the land. We should be careful about the objects we love and hate, esteem and disesteem, revere and abhor. V. THE KING'S RE-

QUEST TO HAVE THE CREATURES REMOVED GRANTED. (*A. McAuslane, D.D.*) *Lessons :—*
1. Where the first judgment moveth not, the second may make sinners yield. 2. Vengeance makes wicked men call for God's messengers who have despised them. 3. God's judgments may work scornful oppressors to intreat the despised ministers of God. 4. Jehovah's judgments may and will make proudest potentates to acknowledge Him. 5. In the confession of the wicked God only can take away their judgments. 6. Wicked oppressors themselves do acknowledge that mercy from Jehovah cometh by the prayer of His. 7. Under sense of judgment persecutors may promise liberty of persons and consciences to the Church. 8. Such forced promises are seldom made good by such oppressors (ver. 8). (*G. Hughes, B.D.*) *The plague of frogs ; or, the socially great smitten with the supremely contemptible :* —I. THAT THE SOCIALLY GREAT SOMETIMES PROVOKE THE JUDGMENTS OF GOD. 1. That the socially great provoke the judgments of God by rejecting His claims. 2. By slighting His servants. 3. By rejecting His credentials of truth and duty. II. THAT THE SOCIALLY GREAT HAVE NO MEANS WHEREBY TO RESIST THE JUDGMENTS OF GOD. 1. This judgment was afflictive, loathsome, extensive, irresistible. 2. This judgment yields not to social position, wealth, authority, force. III. THAT THE SOCIALLY GREAT OFTEN INVOLVE OTHERS LESS GUILTY IN THE RETRIBUTION THEY INVITE. IV. THAT THE SOCIALLY GREAT ARE ALWAYS SURROUNDED BY THOSE WHO ARE WILLING TO STRENGTHEN THEM IN OPPOSITION TO THE DIVINE CLAIMS. Lessons : 1. That the socially great ought to be in sympathy with the requirements of God. 2. That the socially great ought to know better than provoke the wrath of the Great King. 3. That social position will not avert the retributions of God. (*J. S. Exell, M.A.*) *Superstitions respecting frogs :*—There is no doubt that frogs were in Egypt the objects of some kind of superstitious regard. It is difficult to say whether they were most reverenced or feared, but, either as good agents or evil, they were numbered among the sacred animals of the Egyptians. The magicians used them in their divinations, and pretended to foretell future events by the changes and swellings which these creatures undergo. Frogs were supposed to be generated from the mud of the river. A frog sitting upon the sacred lotus was symbolical of the return of the Nile to its bed after the inundations. The name Chrur, which seems to have been derived from the sound of its croaking, was also used, with only a slight variation, Hhrur, to denote the Nile descending. Seated upon a date-stone, with a young palm-leaf rising from its back, it was a type of man in embryo. The importance attached to the frog in some parts of Egypt is further apparent from its having been embalmed and honoured with burial in the tombs of Thebes ; and from its frequent appearance upon the monuments and inscriptions. Among the former is the god Pthah, having the head of a frog, and representing the creative power of the deity; there is also a frog-headed goddess named Heka, who was worshipped in the district of Sah, as the wife of Chnum, the god of the cataracts, and to whose favour the annual overflow of the Nile, with all the benefits which followed, was ascribed. Plutarch says the frog was an emblem of the sun, and that the brazen palm tree at Delphi, sacred to Apollo or Osiris, had a great number of frogs engraved upon its base. In hieroglyphics the frog is an emblem of fecundity, an idea which arose naturally from its connection with the river. As the wealth and prosperity of Egypt depended upon the annual overflowing of the Nile, it is not surprising that the people of that land, who seem in every possible instance to have worshipped and served the creature more than the Creator, should have ascribed peculiar honour to the frogs, which abounded most in the time of the inundations ; they may have regarded them as in some sense the authors of their benefits, or rather as beneficent agents sent forth by their sacred river to assist and direct its fertilizing process. But it is probable that the sacred character of these animals was attributable, in some parts of Egypt at least, to the fears entertained for them by the Egyptians, as spirits of evil. There are even now in Africa tribes of ignorant heathen, worshippers of devils, who bow down before the most hideous images they can invent or fashion, and call upon them with abject supplications, in order to propitiate their fetish, and to turn aside the evils he might bring upon them. St. John, in the book of Revelation, represents the frog as an evil spirit ; and his emblems were generally derived from symbolical ideas which prevailed of old (Rev. xvi. 13). Such probably were the frogs which the magicians of Egypt brought forth in opposition to Moses, spirits of devils. Satan, who had greater license and a wider range in those dark times and places than he has now, sent out his demons in this form, at the call of his false prophets, to confirm the Egyptians in their rebellion against God ; and "the magicians did so with their enchantments, and

brought up frogs upon the land of Egypt" (Exod. viii. 7). Whether the Egyptians looked upon these reptiles as benefactors, or dreaded them as ministers of evil, the wonderful plague with which they were now afflicted was a judgment against them for their miserable superstition, and a sign which they could scarcely fail to understand. Fond as they were of a multitude of deities, here were more than they could wish for or endure. David says: "He sent frogs among them, which destroyed them" (Psa. lxxviii. 45) : it was not a mere inconvenience, therefore, but a real punishment; yet we may suppose the Egyptians would not venture to kill or even to resist their sacred tormentors. So terrible and wide-spread was the evil, that we find traces of it in the oldest historians, whose accounts, being derived only from tradition, are inaccurate as to place and people, but founded, we may suppose, upon the realities which are here recorded. Diodorus tells us of "a people called Autariats, who were forced by frogs bred in the clouds, which poured down upon them instead of rain, to forsake their country" (l. iii. c. 30); Pliny tells a similar story of the inhabitants of a district in Gaul. The fact that the frogs of Egypt were sent upon the people by God's command would naturally lead to the idea of their descent from the clouds; while the exodus, both of Israelites and Egyptians, which followed soon afterwards, might give occasion to the story that the people were driven out of their country by the plague. (*T. S. Millington.*) **To-morrow.—** *To-morrow* (for close of year):—We have arrived at another milestone on the journey of life. How many more we have to pass before we reach our journey's end we cannot say; for, unlike the milestones by the roadside, which not only tell the traveller how far he has travelled but how much farther off his destination is; our passing years are milestones which only point backwards. In the face of this terrible uncertainty, then, how foolish it is to echo the word of Pharaoh and say, "To-morrow." 1. In postponing the day of salvation, we are postponing our own happiness. Think of the madness of Pharaoh, enduring another night of the frogs when he could obtain instant release from them. And yet he was no more mad than the sinner is who postpones his salvation from day to day. His sins are more numerous and nauseous than the frogs of Egypt. They swarm everywhere; they leave their slime upon everything; they spawn in the dark corners of his heart; he is plagued with them, and can get no peace. 2. In this procrastination we are flying in the face of God's clearest warnings. Ten times over God's warnings were repeated to Pharaoh before the final destruction came; but even this is not the limit of His longsuffering to usward. His warnings are often uttered a hundred times over to us before the final crash. Yet many pay no heed to them. They are startled for a while, and give a passing thought to their souls, only to sweep away such thoughts in worldliness again, and cry "To-morrow! I will think of this to-morrow." A traveller from India thus relates some of the experiences of his voyage:—"Flocks of greedy albatrosses and cape-pigeons crowded around the ship's stern. A hook was baited with fat, and upwards of a dozen albatrosses rushed at it instantly; and as one after another was being hauled on deck, the remainder, regardless alike of the struggles of the captured and the vociferations of the crew, kept swimming about the stern. Not even the birds which were indifferently hooked, and made their escape, desisted from seizing the bait a second time." Poor, foolish birds, to disregard the death-struggles of so many of their companions and their own experience of the sharpness of the hook! Poor, foolish men, to disregard more terrible warnings still, to procrastinate in spite of the sudden destruction of so many of their companions in the ways of sin and the sharp trials that God has sent to urge them to escape the like destruction! 3. In putting off the great question of salvation till to-morrow, we forget that to-morrow will in all probability see us harder-hearted than to-day. Pharaoh was softened while he was plague-stricken. He seemed even near becoming a worshipper of the true God, for he said to Moses, "Intreat the Lord for me." But when the warning was past, and the morrow came, he relapsed into his old hard-hearted enmity towards God; all the harder for his temporary softening. Transient impressions are terribly dangerous. If you take the red-hot metal and plunge it into cold water, you make it harder than it was before. So it was with the heart of Pharaoh; so it is with our hearts too. (*G. A. Sowter, M.A.*) *The folly of delaying till to-morrow :—*"To-morrow!" has been the cry for years. Serious intentions enough have been formed; but serious intentions, formed only to be forgotten, are but paving a religious way to hell. A sea captain tells how he fell in with the *Central America* on the very evening when she went down. He relates how that, having hailed her, Captain Hernden replied, "I am sinking!" "Had you not better send your passengers on board of us?" said the captain. "Will you stand by me till morning?" was Captain Hernden's reply. "I'll try," said the captain; "but had you not better send your passengers on board at once?" "Stand by me till morning!" was the only answer. The captain did his utmost to stand by the ill-fated ship, but 'mid the darkness of the night and the force of the tempest he saw the *Central America* no more, and subsequently received information apprised him that within an hour of that time she went down in the wild Atlantic. What a pity that poor Captain Hernden *would* put off till the next day that which might have been done that night. But though he doubtless had, to him, some sufficient reason for the course he pursued, that cannot be said of those who neglect the great salvation.

Ver. 15. **When Pharaoh saw that there was respite, he hardened his heart.**— *The hardening nature and awful consequences of sin :*—I. I observe, that when God issues out His terrible threatenings against sinners, HE IS WONT TO SUSPEND OR STAY THE FULL EXECUTION OF HIS SENTENCE, AND GIVE THEM MANY AN INTERVAL FOR REPENTANCE. A criminal shut up in the condemned cell, is said to be respited when, by a royal grant, his punishment is put off from the day appointed. This practice in the administration of human laws, may serve the purpose of illustrating the dispensations of Providence, or the dealings of God with men. The stubborn rebel is often admonished ere he meets the stern arrest of justice; and the guilty soul is often respited before the sentence is carried into execution. It seems to me, that this precedure of the great Judge in the mysterious ways of Providence is a bright display of mercy, blended even with the tokens of His displeasure. Each interval between successive warnings and judgments is a space given for repentance. But the final term of forbearance is not far distant; and with some of you it may be now the very last reprieve. II. I observe, THAT IT PROVES A STATE OF MOST DREADFUL DEPRAVITY, WHEN MEN TAKE OCCASION, FROM THE VERY COMPASSIONS AND MERCIES OF GOD, TO HARDEN THEMSELVES IN SIN. The goodness of God is designed to lead you to repentance; but if you either do not know, or will not consider this, then the most lovely and attractive of all the Divine perfections is shamefully abused and contemned by you. But can you hope to escape? Is it possible to evade the eye of Omniscience, or resist the hand of Omnipotence? Where can you find an asylum for your souls, when the only Refuge which God has prepared, is scorned and set at nought? III. I observe, THAT GOD PERFECTLY KNOWS ALL THE DEEDS OF WICKED MEN BEFORE THEY ARE DONE, AND ALL THEIR DESIGNS BEFORE THEY ARE CONCEIVED. IV. Do you now ask, WHAT ARE THE SIGNS BY WHICH IT MAY BE KNOWN, THAT ANY MAN IS GIVEN UP TO HARDNESS OF HEART? 1. It is a dark sign that the heart is desperately hardened, when men sin on knowingly and deliberately. A crime is deeply aggravated, which is committed with the full consent of the will, in defiance of the clearest dictates of the understanding and the conscience. 2. It is a dark sign that the heart is desperately hardened, when men hate and shun those who faithfully warn and reprove them, and affectionately labour to reclaim them. 3. It is a dark sign that the heart is desperately hardened, when the very intervals and opportunities which mercy gives for repentance, are perverted to the purpose of adding sin to sin. Are there not some of you, who have been brought under the scourge of God's afflicting hand? Remember, it is written, "He that being often reproved hardeneth his neck, shall be suddenly destroyed, and that without remedy." (*John Thornton.*) *Constrained repentance :*—The constrained and pretended penitence of Pharaoh, with the compassion and prayer of Moses, teach us valuable lessons. The penitence of Pharaoh shows us that we ought not to put off our repentance until the hour of sickness, trial, and death; for the seeming conversions which take place at such times may be hypocritical and short-lived, like that of Pharaoh. Is this sincere? The sick man thinks that it is; but if he recover will he not be the same as before? Will he not forget, as Pharaoh did, his promises, humiliation, confessions of sin, and seeming conversion? From the example of Moses we may also obtain important instruction. He had, truly, very many reasons for not putting much faith in the word of the king. Pharaoh had already shown much pride, obstinacy, and deceit; nevertheless, Moses did not repulse him; he knew that God can convert a soul even at the last hour. Pharaoh made promises, and "charity hopeth all things." It is God alone who can judge the heart. We ought, therefore, always to be ready to console, and help with our prayers, even persons who have been most hostile, opposed, and contemptuous to us. There was a worthy pastor of the Canton de Vaud in Switzerland, who, during a time of persecution, had to suffer much because he preached the gospel faithfully. He was even obliged to leave his parish, and to go and settle in another. Some time afterwards, one of the men who had behaved most wickedly to him was converted to the Lord. He immediately determined to go to his former pastor to tell him this good news. " How surprised he will be," thought he as he walked along. He arrived at the village; he rung the bell at the minister's house; the pastor himself opened the door. " I am come to tell you that I am converted; I, who have done you so much harm." " I am not astonished at it," answered the pastor, " for I have prayed for you all these seven years." (*Prof. Gaussen.*)   *Sin interrupted, not forsaken :*—Though the course of sin may be repelled for a season by the dispensation of the law, yet the spring and fountain of it is not dried up thereby. Though it withdraws and hides itself for a season, it is but to shift out of a storm, and then to return again. As a traveller in his way meeting with a violent storm of thunder and rain, immediately turns out of his way to some house or tree for his shelter, but yet this causes him not to give over his journey, as soon as the storm is over he returns to his way and progress again; so it is with men in bondage unto sin. They are in a course of pursuing their lusts; the law meets with them in a storm of thunder and lightning from heaven, terrifies and hinders them in their way. This turns them for a season out of their course; they will run to prayer or amendment of life, for some shelter from the storm of wrath which is feared coming upon their consciences. But is their course stopped? are their principles altered? Not at all; so soon as the storm is over, so that they begin to wear out that sense and the terror that was upon them, they return to their former course in the service of sin again. This was the state with Pharaoh once and again. In such seasons sin is not conquered, but diverted. When it seems to fall under the power of the law, indeed it is only turned into a new channel; it is not dried up. If you go and set a dam against the streams of a river, so that you suffer no water to pass in the old course and channel, but it breaks out another way, and turns all its streams in a new course, you will not say you have dried up that river, though some that come and look into the old channel may think, perhaps, that the waters are utterly gone. So is it in this case. The streams of sin, it may be, run in open sensuality and profaneness, in drunkenness and vicious-ness; the preaching of the law sets a dam against these causes; conscience is terrified, and the man dares not walk in the ways wherein he has been formerly engaged. His companions in sin, not finding him in his old ways, begin to laugh at him, as one that is converted and growing precise; professors themselves begin to be persuaded that the work of God is upon his heart, because they see his old streams dried up; but if there has been only a work of the law upon him, there in a dam put to his course, but the spring of sin is not dried up, only the streams of it are turned another way. It may be the man is fallen upon other more secret or more spiritual sins; or if he be beat from them also, the whole strength of lust and sin will take up its residence in self-righteousness, and pour out thereby as filthy streams as in any other way whatever. So that, notwithstanding the whole work of the law upon the souls of men, indwelling sin will keep alive in them still. (*J. Owen, D.D.*)   *Hypocritical profession :*—As a horse that is good at hand, but nought at length, so is the hypocrite; free and fiery for a spurt, but he jades and tires in a journey. The faith, repentance, reformation, obedience, joy, sorrow, zeal, and other graces and affections of hypocrites, have their first motion and issue from false and erroneous grounds, as shame, fear, hope, and such respects. And it thence comes to pass that, where these respects cease to give them motion, the graces themselves can no more stand than a house can stand when the foundation is taken from under it. The boy that goes to his book no longer than the master holds the rod over him; the master's back once turned, away goes the book, and he to play: so is it with the hypocrite. Take away the rod from Pharaoh; and he will be old Pharaoh still. Now, then, here is a wide difference between the hypocrite and the godly man: the one does all by fits and starts, by sudden motions and flashes; whereas the other goes on fairly and soberly in a settled, constant, regular course of humiliation and obedience. (*Bp. Sanderson.*)   *False repentance :*—Many per-sons who appear to repent, are like sailors who throw their goods overboard in a storm, and wish for them again as soon as it becomes calm.   *Mercy mistaken for weakness :*—How easy it is to mistake mercy for weakness! This was Pharaoh's mistake. The moment the Lord lifted His heavy hand from the Egyptian king, Pharaoh began to forget his oath, and vow, and promise, and to harden his heart, —saying, in effect, " He can do no more; the God of the Israelites has exhausted Himself; now that He has removed His hand He has confessed His weakness rather than demonstrated His pity." We are committing the same mistake every day :

whilst the plague is in the house we are ready to do anything to get rid of it! we will say prayers morning, noon and night, and send for the holy man who has been anointed as God's minister, and will read nothing but solid and most impressive books, listen to no frivolous conversation, and touch nothing that could dissipate or enfeeble the mind. How long will the plague be removed before the elasticity will return to the man and the old self reassert its sovereignty? Not a day need pass. We begin to feel that the worst is past : we say it is darkest before it is dawn, " hope springs eternal in the human breast "; and so easily do we fall back into the old swing between self-indulgence and nominal homage to God. We think we have felt all the Lord can do, and we say, "His sword is no longer ; it cannot reach us now that we have removed away this little distance from its range ; now and here we may do what we please, and judgment cannot fall upon us." Thus we play old Pharaoh's part day by day. He is a mirror in which we may see ourselves. There is nothing mysterious in this part of the solemn reading. However we may endeavour to escape from the line when it becomes supernatural or romantic, we are brought swiftly and surely back to it when we see these repetitions of obduracy and these renewed challenges of Divine anger and judgment. (*J. Parker, D.D.*) *Transient repentance :*—Manton says, " Many a time a brabble falleth out between a man and his lusts ; but he delayeth, and all cometh to nothing. In a heat we bid a naughty servant begone ; but he lingereth and before the next morning all is cool and quiet, and he is again in favour." Ungodly men have their quarrels with their favourite sins on various accounts, but these are like children's pets with one another, soon over because they come of passion, and not from principle. An unholy person will fall out with sin because it has injured his health or his credit, or has brought him into difficulty with his neighbours ; but when these temporary results are ended he falls in love again with the same iniquity. Thus we have seen the drunkard loathing his cups when his eyes were red and his head was aching ; but ere the sun went down the quarrel was ended, and he and Bacchus were rolling in the gutter together. (*" Flowers from a Puritan's Garden."*) *False repentance :*— Pharaoh's professions of repentance and promises of amendment were like those of the child under the rod of chastisement, they were designed to mitigate the infliction, and when the punishment was over they went for nothing. Now, this is always the case when fear alone predominates over the soul. Ah ! how much of our penitence is like this of Pharaoh ; how many are saints on a sick-bed, but as wicked as ever when they recover ! During an epidemic of cholera in the village where I first laboured as a minister, the churches were filled to overflowing by suppliants who had never before entered them ; but when it had passed, they relapsed into worse carelessness than ever : and there may be some here to-night who, when they were dangerously ill, or when they were laying a dear little one's body in the grave, vowed to God that they would yield themselves to Him ; while now they are as far from His service as ever. Let me beseech such hardened ones to beware. (*W. M. Taylor, D.D.*) *Tests of sincerity in repentance :*—Lorenzo de Medici lies dying in the city of Florence : in the terrors of death he has sent for the one man who never had yielded to his threats or caresses—the brave Savonarola. Lorenzo confesses that he has heavy on his soul three crimes : the cruel sack of Volterra, the theft of the public dower of young girls, by which many were driven to a wicked life, and the blood shed after the conspiracy of Pazzi. He is greatly agitated, and Savonarola, to keep him quiet, keeps repeating, "God is merciful," "God is good." "But," he added, "there is need of three things." "And what are they, father?" "First, you must have a great and living faith in the mercy of God." "This I have—the greatest." "Second, you must restore that which you have wrongfully taken, or require your children to restore it for you." Lorenzo looked surprised and troubled ; but he forces himself to compliance, and nods his head in sign of assent. Then Savonarola rises to his feet, and stands over the dying prince. "Last, you must give back their liberties to the people of Florence." Lorenzo, summoning up all his remaining strength, disdainfully turns his back, and, without uttering another word, Savonarola departs without giving him absolution.

Vers. 16–19. **That it may become lice.**—*The plague of lice :*—I. THE PLAGUE ITSELF. 1. This punishment was sent without any previous warning. 2. This plague was inflicted by a very small insect. 3. This plague could not be imitated by the magicians. This rendered Pharaoh's refusal to humble himself all the more unpardonable. II. ITS TEACHING. 1. Its infliction produced no real good. How soon the human mind becomes accustomed to novelties, even of the most extraordinary character. So the fallen soul becomes naturalized to the paths of sin and the lessons of God's judgment. 2. Observe the resources of God. The least thing in His hand can become an instrument of torment. 3. How foolish, then, and how mad, to resist the will of this Divine Being! (*Homilist.*) *Lessons :*— 1. The devil will try his utmost to counterwork God. 2. The devil is impotent upon the least check from God. 3. God's power sets on His judgments when the power of Satan fails (ver. 18). 4. The devil's instruments are forced at last to say they are against God, and He against them. 5. God's finger or the least of His power makes the devil and his instruments fail. 6. Innate unbelief loves to be kept up by liars, but will not yield when they fail. 7. Treble hardening comes on the wicked by treble judgments. 8. God's word faileth not which He hath spoken of the sin and judgment of wicked persecutors (ver. 19). (*G. Hughes, B.D.*) *The plague of lice ; or, an enforced recognition of a Supreme Power in the dire retributions of human life :*—I. THAT MEN ARE SLOW TO RECOGNIZE THE SUPREME POWER IN THE RETRIBUTIONS OF LIFE. 1. Because they have not right views of the character of God. 2. Because they have not a due consciousness of sin and its demerit. II. THAT WICKED MEN ARE MADE BY CONTINUOUS RETRIBUTIONS ULTIMATELY TO RECOGNIZE THE SUPREME POWER AGAINST THEM. " Then the magicians said unto Pharaoh, This is the finger of God." God sometimes plagues men until they acknowledge Him. The events of life are charged with retributions which cannot be hidden by the art of the sorcerer. III. THAT WHEN WICKED MEN ARE MADE TO ACKNOWLEDGE THE SUPREME POWER IN THE RETRIBUTIONS OF LIFE THEY MAY NEVERTHELESS CONTINUE IN OPEN OPPOSITION TO IT. " And Pharaoh's heart was hardened." Lessons: 1. That the retributions of life are designed to lead men to the performance of moral duty. 2. That there are many deceptions calculated to blind men to the hand of God in the events of life. 3. That wicked men are not able to contend with God, and are at times brought to acknowledge His supremacy. (*J. S. Exell, M.A.*) *Dangerous dust :*—Dangerous dust in the air is circulated by the elevated railways in New York. A member of the staff of *The Scientific American* hung a magnet under the track of the elevated road, and when a few minutes later he took it down it was coated with minute particulars of iron dust. This dust, he said, is the cause of many severe cases of eye troubles. The swift passing trains grind off showers of iron particles, which often fall or are blown into the eyes of pedestrians. The microscope shows, that the particles are of innumerable shapes, and they usually have jagged fringes, and many of them have barbs like a fish hook. When lodged in the eye they cannot be attracted therefrom with a magnet, but a gouge-shaped instrument the size of a sewing needle had been devised for the purpose. This peculiarity of the dust resembles that of moral evil. It is in the air, and when once it finds a lodgment in the human heart it cannot be withdrawn without difficulty and suffering. This is the of finger God .—" Like Phidias, who in his image carved his own name, there is God engraven upon every creature." Not in characters of human writing is it written, but in the character of the work. Phidias needed not to have written the word PHIDIAS in so many letters, for the master's hand had a cunning of its own which none could counterfeit. An instructed person had only to look at a statue and say at once, " Phidias did this, for no other hand could have chiselled such a countenance "; and believers have only to look either at creation, providence, or the Divine Word, and they will cry instinctively, " This is the finger of God." Yet, alas, man has great powers of wilful blindness, and these are aided by the powers of darkness, so that, being both blind and in the dark, man is unable to see his God, though His presence is as clear as that of the sun in the heavens. (*C. H. Spurgeon.*) *The limit of false religion :*—Human religions can go to a certain point in good works, especially if they have borrowed their systems and copied their charities from the teachings of Christ, which most of them have done. But beyond a certain point they cannot go. It has been observed that the magicians could not bring living things out of the dust of the ground, as Moses did. And a false religion cannot bring life out of death, as the gospel does. Morality and certain good works it can conjure up ; but spiritual life it cannot produce. Atheism, in the form of scientific materialism, may point to some notable and heroic disciple, such as Professor Clifford, who died without fear, steadfast in his faith that death was the end of him ; but it cannot enable a man to die as Stephen and Paul died. It is not unworthy of our passing thought that the scientific magicians of our day, who are saying, " Who is the Lord ? " have tried very hard to generate a living thing out of the dust ; but they have as utterly and signally failed as the magicians did in the days of Moses. We may confidently keep a good courage in these days, when the scientific and religious magicians are trying to discredit the Word of God with their enchantments. Be sure that if the conflict is pushed far enough they will come to signal grief. In the end God will give glorious victory to those who stand by His truth, and who continue to cast their rods down in the face of an unbelieving world. (*G. F. Pentecost, D.D.*)

Vers. 20-24. **Swarms of flies.**—*The plague of flies; or, an exceptional method of the Divine administration in the affairs of this life :*—I. IT IS A GENERAL RULE OF THE DIVINE ADMINISTRATION THAT THE GOOD AND BAD SHALL ALIKE PARTICIPATE IN THE PAINFUL DISPENSATIONS OF THIS PROBATIONARY LIFE. 1. Because both are guilty of sin. 2. Because both need correction and improvement. 3. Because life is a probation and a discipline. II. IT IS AN EXCEPTIONAL METHOD OF THE DIVINE ADMINISTRATION TO EXEMPT THE GOOD FROM THE TRIALS AND RETRIBUTIONS OF THIS LIFE. "And I will put a division between My people and thy people." 1. Thus we see that there are times in this life when moral character gives exemption from severe retribution. This is the honour God places upon true moral goodness. In this way He occasionally shows His approval of it. Piety shields the house. It will protect a nation from the plague of God. 2. Thus we see that there are times in this life when God manifests to men His care for the good. 3. Thus we see that there are times in this life when God gives men a prophecy of the social equity in the world to come. Then Egypt will be ever separate from Goshen in character, as in retribution and reward. Heaven will adjust the moral relations of the universe. Lessons : 1. That continued sin must be visited by continued retribution. 2. That the providence of God is over the good to save them from pain. 3. That the wicked must see the worth of goodness. (*J. S. Exell, M.A.*)   *God's retributive resources:*—I once knew a good woman who had three children, and the youngest was her pet. And it died, and said she, " Now God has done all that He can do." But a little after another was burnt to death, and then she said, " I see God can do more yet." Soon after the other fell into a boiler of water, and was scalded to death. Says she, " God can do more yet." Afterwards her husband died, and then she said, " Now God has done all things well." If she had said this before, she would have had her husband and two children alive; but God must bring His work to pass. He afflicts us for our good. (*Matthew Wilks.*)   *Flies in Egypt :*—Egypt has always suffered more or less severely in hot weather from the various sorts of flies which arise from the marshy lands. " The most numerous and troublesome among the insects which infest these countries," says Sonnini, " are flies, which cruelly torment both men and animals. It is impossible to form a just idea of their obstinate perseverance when they wish to fasten upon any particular part of the body, as when they are driven away they return and settle again in the same moment, and their pertinacity tires out the most patient sufferer. They particularly delight in fastening upon the corners of the eyes and the edges of the eyelids, to which tender parts they are attracted by a slight humidity." Mr. Lane says—" In spring, summer, and autumn, flies are so abundant as to be extremely annoying during the daytime, and mosquitoes are troublesome at night, unless a curtain be made use of to keep them away, and often in the day." Herodotus also makes mention of the flies of Egypt, and describes the nets with which the inhabitants protected themselves against them. In winter, however, these insects are rarely troublesome, and Pharaoh may have thought that the threat of such a plague was but little likely to be fulfilled. For the same reason the miraculous character of the visitation, when it came, was the more readily acknowledged. (*T. S. Millington.*)   *Increased penalties :*—At sea, when the enemy's ship is sighted in full flight, a gun loaded with powder only is fired by the pursuer to bring the fugitive to. When this fails, the cannon is charged with a ball, but is designedly fired so as not to strike the vessel, in the hope of inducing it to furl the sails. But when this attempt has failed, then the captain of the pursuer orders the gun to be fired straight at the ship attempting to escape. It may be that many shots have taken effect in her rigging and hull before she ceases her flight. Such, too, is the forbearance of God. The first miracle of Moses was harmless—the second came nearer home, in expectation of the stubborn despot's compliance.   *Various kinds of flies in this plague :*—The flies of this plague were evidently of a formidable kind, and very grievous. The Psalmist says—" He sent flies among them, which devoured them " (Psa. lxxviii. 45). There is a kind of beetle common in Egypt which is very destructive, inflicting painful bites, and consuming all sorts of materials. The mosquito also, which is a terrible nuisance in all hot climates, and especially in the vicinity of rivers, answers to this description ; and the house-fly, which swarms in Egypt, carries corruption, and not unfrequently infectious disease, wherever it alights.   It is probable, however, that the flies of this plague were of various kinds, including the above and many others, for David says again " He spake the word, and there came all manner of flies," or " divers sorts of flies " (Psa. cv. 31).   The marginal reading gives a similar description, " a mixture of noisome beasts."   There is no reason, therefore, for supposing that the plague was limited to any one species ; on the contrary, as the flies were everywhere, upon the people and in their houses, on the ground and in the air, and in all the land of Egypt, it appears almost certain that they were of different habits, and therefore of different species.   There were flies that devoured, and flies that stung ; flies that corrupted, and flies that hovered whirring in the air ; flies upon men, inflaming their eyelids and blinding them, and flies upon the cattle ; there were beetles that crawled upon the ground, and perhaps also bees, and wasps, and hornets, pursuing the people fiercely.   It is doubtful whether some kind of flies were not among the sacred insects of the Egyptians.   Some of them have been preserved, perhaps accidentally, in the mummy cloths, and some few, among which are the house-fly, the wasp, and the butterfly, are represented in paintings on the monuments and walls.   To make the miracle more evident, these pests, while vexing the Egyptians almost beyond endurance, giving them no rest either by night or day, were not suffered to approach the Israelites.   " In the land of Goshen were no flies."   (*T. S. Millington.*)

Vers. 25–32. **It is not meet so to do.**—*The impossibility of compromise in a religious life:*—I. THAT THERE CAN BE NO COMPROMISE IN CHRISTIAN MORALITY.   " And Moses said, It is not meet to do so."   1. Because they do not like to give up their sins. 2. Because they will not summon resolution enough to break the force of old and continued habit.   II. THAT THERE CAN BE NO COMPROMISE IN CHRISTIAN WORSHIP. " We will go three days' journey into the wilderness, and sacrifice to the Lord our God, as He shall command us."   It is not enough to worship God ; we must worship Him in the manner He has made known.   Men should not place themselves in temptation by going to unhallowed sanctuaries.   1. Christian worship must not be compromised by idolatry.   2. Christian worship must not be compromised by levity.   Prayer must be the dominant impulse of the soul.   III. THAT THE SERVANTS OF GOD MUST REJECT ALL ATTEMPTS AT RELIGIOUS COMPROMISE.   1. Because religious compromise brings contempt upon the Christian life.   2. Because religious compromise brings contempt upon Christian worship.   (*J. S. Exell, M.A.*)   *It is not meet so to do:*—I. THE IMPOSSIBILITY OF MAINTAINING A SECRET OR HIDDEN CHRISTIAN LIFE.   The life of Christ in the soul will come out in real manifestation and in public recognition of God.   In the first place, the very initial demand of Christ upon His disciples is to confess Him before men, and to take up the cross and come after Him daily.   There is no such thing as a private and concealed faith allowed or alluded to in the Scriptures.   Christianity is no secret organization, but a life that openly and boldly declares itself.   Besides, the very fact that Christianity is a life in the soul makes it impossible to keep it a secret.   A tree might just as well say, " Can I not be a real living tree without giving forth buds and leaves in the springtime ? " or a rose, " Can I not be a rose without bursting into leaf, and in due time sending forth my flowers in their sweetness to rejoice the eye and delight the smell of man ? "   A prominent fruit merchant in one of our New England cities was converted at one of our meetings, and he determined to keep the fact secret.   He was ashamed to confess Christ before his companions, among whom he had been a very profane and godless man.   His special and besetting sin was an awful habit of the wildest profanity, which used to burst out of his mouth at the least provocation to his quick and passionate temper.   Some of his *employés* told me that when he came to the warehouse, where his fruit was sorted and stored after being received from the ships, he would swear and curse at such a rate that they all dreaded his coming.   And especially was this so if a cargo of oranges or bananas turned out badly.   The next morning after he had decided to give himself to Christ he went down to his receiving store.   A large cargo of oranges had been received the day before, and the men were engaged in opening and sorting them. They were dreading his appearance, well knowing that the condition the fruit was in would excite his wrath to the uttermost.   Well, he came in, and without a word he looked over the oranges.   To the astonishment of his men, he said to them pleasantly, " Well, boys, this is rather a bad lot, to be sure.   Just sort them over, and make the best of them. I suppose it can't be helped." Now, that man did not exactly confess Christ in so many words, but the absence of certain expressions from his conversation, and the presence of a new spirit, revealed the fact that he had seen Jesus. At once the men came to the conclusion as to what had happened. They were not wrong. One of them told me the occurrence the next day. That night I related this incident. I did not know the man by sight, and was not sure that he was present; but at the close of the meeting the merchant sprang to his feet and confessed that he was the man; and he there and then publicly confessed Jesus Christ as his Saviour. You see he could not hide the fact from those round about him, nor could he keep from confessing it. II. A MAN CANNOT BE A CHRISTIAN AND WORSHIP GOD IN THE LAND WITHOUT OFFENDING THE WORLD. A gentleman in Boston was converted at one of Mr. Moody's meetings. He purposed keeping it a secret. He belonged to a wealthy and aristocratic family and circle, among whom it was fashionable to sneer at evangelical religion, and at that time especially at Mr. Moody and the great work going on in that city. Shortly afterwards this gentleman was guest at a large dinner-party. In course of the dinner, the tabernacle meetings and Mr. Moody came up for discussion and ridicule. From bad they went to worse, and began to sneer at Jesus and His cross. By and by, when he could bear it no longer, he arose in his place, trembling with embarrassment, yet courageous in purpose, and said, addressing his host: "I do not wish to seem rude; but I cannot be true to myself or to my God, and let this conversation go on any longer. I beg to say that Mr. Moody, though I am personally unknown to him, is my friend; and in that same old 'tabernacle' which is the object of your ridicule, and in one of those meetings which you hold in such contempt, he was the means of awakening me to a true knowledge of my condition before God, and of leading me to Christ, whom I believe to be the very Son of God—and through the merits of His blood I am trusting for forgiveness and eternal life. I cannot let the conversation go on without at least confessing so much. And not wishing to disturb the freedom of your party, or restrain you by my presence, I beg leave of my kind host to retire from this table." III. "WE WILL GO THREE DAYS' JOURNEY INTO THE WILDERNESS." Israel could not worship God in the land, because God had commanded them to go out of the land. "Three days' journey into the wilderness." Where is that? Surely it must teach us that the Christian's place is in resurrection with the Lord. From the cross to the resurrection was three days. "If ye then be risen with Christ, seek those things which are above" (Col. iii. 1). (*G. F. Pentecost, D.D.*) *Not very far away:*—Alas, how many who have named the name of Christ have never gone very far away from the "former things." In the world they are not known as Christians, and are only known as Christians in the church by the fact that their names are on the church roll or parish register as having been baptized and confirmed. It must be apparent to any thoughtful person that any half-and-half position with reference to Christ and His salvation is not only an inconsistent, but a very unhappy, one. I. "NOT VERY FAR AWAY" IS INCONSISTENT WITH THE FIRST LAW OF CHRISTIAN LIFE, which demands that we shall break with this world. "For our citizenship is in heaven" (Phil. iii. 20). "The whole world lieth in the evil one" (1 John v. 19); and to abide in the world is to take up quarters on Satan's ground. Besides, the very object that Moses had in going down to Egypt was to bring the people up out of that land into a good land and large. How could they ever reach Canaan if they consented not to go "very far away"? And how shall we be separated from this present evil world if we, as confessors of Christ, insist on lingering about the borders of the old life? II. "NOT VERY FAR AWAY" IS ENTIRELY INCOMPATIBLE WITH A HAPPY CHRISTIAN LIFE. In the times of the old border wars between the Scots and the English, the people living in the border counties had a most wretched time of it. First the Scots would come pouring down into the northern counties of England, and devastate and destroy there; and then the English would invade the southern counties of Scotland, and desolation and death would be their portion. So it is with the border-Christians. The Word of God catches them in the world, and pricks and cuts without healing; and if they are only a little way in the kingdom they are thoroughly exposed to the temptations and buffetings of Satan. With the back to the world and face to Christ, ever marching forward, is the only way of peace and happiness. III. "NOT VERY FAR AWAY" IS A DANGEROUS PLACE TO BE IN. I once heard of a little girl who fell out of bed during the night. The mother heard the child's fall and cry, and ran to her little one. After she had picked her up and somewhat pacified her, she asked the little girl, "How did you come to fall out, my dear?" The child replied, "Oh, I suppose I went to sleep too near to the edge of the bed where I fell out," and then, quickly correcting her statement, said, "No, I mean I went to sleep too near to the place where I got in." That was the real truth of it. There are a great many persons who profess conversion; but they do not get very far into the kingdom; and then they go to sleep, and when they fall out the real reason is that they did not get far enough in. "Not far away" is a most dangerous compromise to consent to. IV. "NOT VERY FAR AWAY" IS A POSITION FROM WHICH GOD CAN CHOOSE NO WORKERS. I am very free to say that God can make little or no use of a worldly half-and-half Christian. In the first place, the world has no confidence in a Christian who is hand-and-glove with it, while at the same time professing to have found something infinitely better, and to have been saved from the world. In the second place, a half-and-half Christian cannot do with "all his might" what God would give him to do. Consecration and service go necessarily together; and no consecrated life can be maintained on the edge of the world or on the edge of the Church. (*Ibid.*) *Exhortation to the newly awakened:*—The old life—so far as that old life is associated with old companions and with practices which are evil—must be abandoned. It does not mean that you are to turn hermit or nun; but in spirit and practice you belong to another commonwealth. But the Christian in the world is to be as distinct from it as the Gulf Stream is from the ocean through which it flows. Christian and Great-Heart passed through Vanity Fair, but they were not citizens of that place. You are not to turn your back in pharisaical self-righteousness upon your old friends; but henceforth you can only have to do with them on the basis of your out-and-out loyalty to Christ. If you can go with them and take Christ with you to their feasts and pleasures, then go; but if the condition of your going is that you leave your Master behind you, then of course you are not to go: you cannot. Be true to the Master, and your worldly associates will spare you any pains on the point. They will adjust themselves to you, or, rather, from you, until the moment comes when they want a true friend, a guide and helper in some spiritual crisis, and they will come to you, passing by those Christians (?) who are "serving God in the land." (*Ibid.*)

CHAPTER IX.

VERS. 1-7. **The hand of the Lord is upon thy cattle.**—*The suffering that comes upon the brute creation in consequence of the sin of man:*—I. THAT WICKED MEN OFTEN ACT IN REFERENCE TO THE CLAIMS OF GOD IN SUCH A MANNER AS TO PROVOKE HIS JUDGMENTS. II. THAT MEN WHO THUS REJECT THE CLAIMS OF GOD OFTEN INVOLVE THE BRUTE CREATION IN PAIN AND WOE. III. THAT THE MEN WHO THUS INVOLVE THE BRUTE CREATION IN PAIN AND SUFFERING ARE OFTEN UNMOVED BY THE DEVASTATION THEY OCCASION. "And the heart of Pharaoh was hardened." Lessons: 1. That the retribution of sin does not end with those who occasion it. 2. That the brute world is affected by the conduct of man. 3. That men should endeavour to banish pain from the universe by attention to the commands of heaven. (*J. S. Exell, M.A.*)   *Another blow at Egyptian idolatry:*—By the former plagues their religious ceremonies had been interrupted and their sacred abominations defiled : but now their chief deities are attacked. In Goshen, where the cattle are but cattle, they remain untouched: "Of the cattle of the children of Israel there died not one" (ver. 6); but in all other parts of the country, where they are reverenced as gods, the plague is upon them, and they die. Osiris, the saviour, cannot save even the brute in which his own soul is supposed to dwell ; Apis and Mnevis, the ram of Ammon, the sheep of Sais, and the goat of Mendes, perish together. Hence Moses reminds the Israelites afterwards, "Upon their gods also the Lord executed judgments" (Numb. xxxiii. 4); and Jethro, when he had heard from Moses the history of all that God had done in Egypt, confessed, "Now I know that the Lord is greater than all gods; for in the thing wherein they dealt proudly, He was above them" (chap. xviii. 11). (*T. S. Millington.*)   *Calf-worship in modern times:*—There are some traces of this calf-worship to be observed even in our own days. The Hindus still pay reverence to the ox as a sacred animal. One particular kind of cattle, having a hump upon the shoulders, is consecrated to Siva, as the Egyptian bull was to Osiris; they are caressed and pampered by the people; they roam at large, and may destroy the most valuable crops with impunity; none dare lay hands upon them; they are everywhere treated with respect. (*Ibid.*)

Vers. 8–12. **A boil breaking forth with blains.**—*Lessons :* 1. Upon former warnings despised, God falls suddenly on the wicked with vengeance unawares. 2. Though God can plague His enemies without instruments, yet sometimes He will use them. 3. God gives command out of the ashes to bring fiery plagues on the wicked sometimes at His pleasure. 4. Hands full of ashes are to note full measure of vengeance on God's enemies. 5. Signal actions (as here the sprinkling ashes) God sometimes useth for men to see and fear. 6. God can make ashes dust, and dust boils, to plague His enemies. 7. God foretells His servants that His command obeyed shall not be in vain. 8. Man and beast are joined together in plagues when sinners are not warned by smiting beasts alone. 9. God giveth out threatenings of judgment for manner and measure as He will. 10. The botch or blain on Egypt is a memorable plague. God appropriates it (ver. 9). (*G. Hughes, B.D.*)   *Lessons :* 1. Experience of the devil's helplessness against God will not persuade the wicked to desist from him. 2. God's boil shall come upon these wicked instruments, do the devil what he can against it. 3. All Satan's instruments are vanquished at the appearance of God's plague (ver. 11). 4. The great God observes and judgeth to obduration sinners who harden themselves against His judgments. 5. Obduration from God's giving men up to their own lusts makes them more to stop their ears and turn their hearts from His word. 6. God's foreseeing and foresaying order (or limit) the issues of rebellion in the wicked against Himself (ver. 12). (*Ibid.*)   *The physical suffering brought upon men by sin :*—I. THAT THERE IS MUCH PHYSICAL SUFFERING BROUGHT UPON MEN BY SIN AND DISOBEDIENCE. Moral considerations are at the basis of health. The body is influenced by the moods of the soul. Piety is restorative. It gives eternal life. II. THAT THE PHYSICAL SUFFERING CONSEQUENT UPON SIN COMES UPON MEN INDEPENDENT OF THEIR SOCIAL POSITION OR OF THEIR SCIENTIFIC ATTAINMENTS. The king, the magicians, and all the people of Egypt were smitten by the pestilence. None were exempt. 1. Hence we see that social position does not exempt men from the physical suffering consequent upon sin. 2. Hence we see that scientific attainment does not exempt men from the physical suffering consequent upon sin. The boils were upon the magicians. III. THAT THE PHYSICAL SUFFERING CONSEQUENT UPON SIN DOES NOT ALWAYS LEAD TO MORAL REFORMATION. Lessons : 1. That God permits suffering to come upon wicked men to reprove and correct their moral character. 2. That the laws of physical manhood are in harmony with true well-being of the soul. 3. That pain should lead us to review the meaning of our lives. (*J. S. Exell, M.A.*)   *The insignificant commencement of great calamities :*—I. THAT GREAT CALAMITIES ARE OFTEN INSIGNIFICANT IN THEIR COMMENCEMENT. All causes are potent to great effects. A trivial ailment may work death. A little misunderstanding may break up a Church. A little sin may ruin a soul. II. THAT GREAT CALAMITIES ARE OFTEN MYSTERIOUS IN THEIR INFLICTION. It is astonishing how apparently trivial causes are influential to such great results. Men are at a loss to explain how little sins are so far-reaching in their effects. It must be recognized as the wondrous ordination of God, and as the efficient law of moral life, designed to keep men right. III. THAT GREAT CALAMITIES ARE OFTEN IRREPRESSIBLE IN THEIR PROGRESS. When the judgments of God are abroad in the earth, and when little causes are working out their punitive issue in the lives of men and nations, they cannot be restrained by pride or power. (*Ibid.*)   *The helplessness of wicked men in the hour of Divine retribution :*—I. THEY ARE HELPLESS BECAUSE THEY HAVE NOT THE ABILITY TO AVERT THE RETRIBUTIONS OF GOD. Sin ever makes men helpless. II. THEY ARE HELPLESS BECAUSE THEY HAVE NOT THE COURAGE TO ENDURE THE RETRIBUTIONS OF GOD. Sin makes men cowardly. Hell cannot inspire the wicked heart with courage in the hour of trial. III. THEY ARE HELPLESS BECAUSE THEY LACK THOSE MORAL QUALITIES WHICH ALONE CAN AID MEN IN THE HOUR OF RETRIBUTION. Lessons : 1. That though men have experience of Satan's inability to help them in their trouble consequent upon sin, they will not desist from it. 2. That all Satan's instruments are vanquished by the plague of God. (*Ibid.*)   *A type of corrupt souls :*—Let this incident lead us to think how great will be the anguish and confusion of wicked men and persecutors when the Lord Jesus Christ shall come again to earth, and when the light of God shall shine upon them. Then the corruption of their unconverted souls will openly appear, and they will not dare to show themselves before the holy angels, and before the redeemed, who are covered with the robe of Christ's righteousness. Only imagine what would become of any of us if for every evil thought, every wicked word, every falsehood, every slander, every angry word, an ulcer or a boil were to appear on our faces? If it were to happen to us, for example, as to Miriam, the sister of Moses, who, as the punishment of her pride and angry words to her brother, became all at once a leper white as snow, that is to say, covered with a disgusting disease. How horrible we should seem if all the pollutions of our souls were to appear outwardly on our bodies! It is well for us to think occasionally of such things, to examine the sins of our hearts, to humble ourselves before God, and to feel more deeply the need of being washed in the blood of Christ, which "cleanseth from all sin." It is our Lord Jesus Christ alone who can present to Himself His Church (that is, the assembly of His redeemed people) glorious and pure, "not having spot or wrinkle, or any such thing, but holy and without blemish." (*Prof. Gaussen.*)

Vers. 13–16. **To show in thee My power.** — *The plagues of Egypt :* —I. CHARACTERISTICS. 1. Wonders. Filled men with astonishment and awe. 2. Signs. Instructive. Showed the power and anger of Jehovah. "This, the finger," &c. 3. Punitive also. They punished the oppressor, while they opened the doors of the house of bondage. 4. Emblematical of the mission and career of Moses. Thunders of Sinai resounded through them all. 5. Various. Attacked both nature and man; animate and inanimate objects; mineral, vegetable, and animal kingdoms. 6. Numerous. Ten. Indeed more, for there was the undoing as well as the doing. II. PURPOSE. 1. To overthrow the deities of Egypt. Jehovah the only true God—Lord of lords. 2. To punish the oppressor. Those who long years had made the life of Israel bitter, now taste a worse bitterness than they had inflicted. 3. To confound the pride of Pharaoh. Though he was master in the land. Had need to be taught that there was One by whom kings rule. 4. To effect the deliverance of the captives. They gradually paved the way, and ultimately secured this. III. EFFECT. 1. Upon Pharaoh. Hardened his heart. In proportion as he set himself against the manifest will of God. So even the glorious gospel of the blessed God is, to some men, the savour of death unto death. At last even Pharaoh's resistance was broken. 2. Upon the Egyptians. They were gradually subdued, till at length they entreated Pharaoh to let Israel go, as earnestly as ever Moses and Aaron did. 3. Upon Israel. They had dwelt secure while these terrors were abroad. God had hidden them in the chambers of His love and mercy. Their confidence restored. They organize their flight. They see the time is at hand. And at last wait for the final word. Learn—1. To stand in awe of the great God and sin not. 2. To admire the resources of infinite wisdom and power. 3. To take heed lest the gospel be a source of condemnation. 4. To expect no miracles, but turn to the sure word of prophecy. 5. To rejoice in our great deliverer, Jesus Christ. (*J. C. Gray.*) *The Divine name as manifested in the history of a wicked and rebellious soul :* —I. FROM THE HISTORY OF PHARAOH WE SEE THAT IT IS NOT THE WAY OF GOD TO REMOVE A WICKED SOUL BY THE IMMEDIATE STROKE OF POWER. The mercy of the Divine name is declared in the prolonged life of the sinner. II. FROM THE HISTORY OF PHARAOH, WE SEE THAT IT IS THE WAY OF GOD TO SURROUND THE WICKED SOUL BY MANY MINISTRIES OF SALVATION. III. FROM THE HISTORY OF PHARAOH, WE SEE THAT IT IS THE WAY OF GOD TO FOLLOW THE WICKED SOUL WITH CONTINUED JUDG-MENTS. The sorrows of the wicked are not fortuitous or casual, but divinely arranged and continuous. Hence in the life of the sinner is seen the power of the Divine hand. Lessons: 1. That God permits wicked men to live in the universe, notwithstanding the continued rebellion against Him. 2. That a life of sin is a life of judgment. 3. That the sovereignty, mercy, power, and justice of God are seen in His dealings with men. (*J. S. Exell, M.A.*) *God to be recognized in the events of life :* —In listening to a great organ, played by the hand of a master, there is often an undertone that controls the whole piece. Sometimes it is scarcely audible, and a careless listener would miss it altogether. The lighter play goes on, ebbing and flowing, rising and sinking, now softly gliding on the gentler stops, and now swelling out to the full power of the great organ. But amid all the changes and transpositions this undertone may be heard, steadily pursuing its own thought. The careless listener thinks the lighter play the main thing; but he that can appreciate musical ideas, as well as sounds, follows the quiet undertone of the piece, and finds in it the leading thought of the artist. So men see the outward events of life, the actions, the words, the wars, famines, sins; but underneath all God is carrying out His own plans, and compelling all outward things to aid the music He would make in this world. (*Christian Age.*)   *Why Pharaoh was exalted :*— The words do not mean that the Almighty had created Pharaoh for this purpose; but that He had exalted him to worldly distinction, and preserved him alive, when the pestilence was ready to destroy, that he might serve as a beacon to warn the obstinate and rebellious in after times. It is a fearful thought, that God may allow us to reach positions of influence and authority, towards which our own selfish ambition has drawn us ; and all this not for the purpose of imparting a blessing, but really for the manifesting a judgment, or for the display of His omnipotence. (*J. H. Norton, D.D.*)   *Reprobation :*—I. I am to show THAT GOD DID DESTROY PHARAOH. The Deity threatened to cut him off from the earth, which plainly implied something more than barely putting an end to his life. Had He permitted him to die by old age, or by sickness, or even by what is commonly called accident, we should have had no right to conclude from the manner of his dying that he was really destroyed. But there were two circumstances attending his death, which may be justly considered as denoting his destruction. He was cut off in the midst of his wickedness. And another is, that he died by the immediate hand of Divine justice. As God opened the Red Sea in mercy to Israel, so He shut it again in judgment to Pharaoh, whom He had threatened to destroy. II. I am to show THAT GOD RAISED UP PHARAOH TO FIT HIM FOR DESTRUCTION. God worketh all things after the counsel of His own will. He never does anything without a previous design. If He destroyed Pharaoh in the manner which has been represented, there can be no doubt but that He previously intended to destroy him in such a manner. But the Divine declarations supersede the necessity of reasoning upon this head. God made known, from time to time, His purpose of destroying Pharaoh. Now, if we look into the history of God's conduct towards Pharaoh, we shall find that He used all the proper and necessary means to form him a vessel of wrath, and fit him for that miserable end to which he was appointed. 1. He raised him up from nothing into being. He gave him a rational and immortal existence. 2. He raised him up to the throne of Egypt. In this splendid situation he was surrounded with everything that could please his taste, flatter his vanity, and inflame his ambition. And this was a natural and necessary step to prepare him for his final fate. For it is a Divine maxim, that "pride goeth before destruction, and a haughty spirit before a fall." 3. God not only raised Pharaoh to the pinnacle of human glory, but also removed from him outward restraints. Besides giving him the power of an unlimited monarch, was virtually setting him above all legal influence and control. But besides this, God removed Moses from his presence and kingdom, who was learned in all the wisdom of Egypt, and thoroughly acquainted with all the arts and intrigues of a court. 4. God endured this vessel of wrath with much long-suffering and forbearance. Instead of treating him according to his deserts, He waited long to be gracious. He used a variety of means to bring him to repentance. But mercies, as well as judgments, conspired to increase his stupidity and hardness of heart, which prepared him for a more unexpected and more aggravated doom. 5. God hardened his heart. All other methods, without this, would have failed of fitting him for destruction. It is now time to make it appear, if possible—III. THAT GOD IS TO BE JUSTIFIED IN HIS TREATMENT OF PHARAOH. We must proceed upon the supposition that God did treat him in the manner which has been represented; and especially that He did, among other things, actually harden his heart. 1. That better judges than we can pretend to be, have approved of God's treatment of Pharaoh. We find his own testimony in favour of God and against himself. "Pharaoh sent and called for Moses and Aaron, and said unto them, I have sinned this time; the Lord is righteous, and I and my people are wicked." This Pharaoh said after God had raised him up, after He had taken off restraints from his mind, after He had sent severe judgments upon him, after He had hardened his heart, and after He had told him that He had raised him up to destroy him. By this time Pharaoh was nearly ripened for ruin, and properly prepared to judge whether God had injured him, or whether he had injured God. And he freely acknowledges that he was wicked, and had injured God, and that God was righteous, and had never injured him. 2. The sovereignty and justice of God allowed Him to treat Pharaoh in the manner which has just been described. The Deity had a sovereign right to bring Pharaoh into existence, to give him the powers and faculties of a moral agent, to place him at the head of a kingdom, and to operate upon his heart in the same manner in which He operates upon the hearts of other men. And when Pharaoh, under such circumstances, became extremely haughty, cruel, malevolent and obstinate, He had a right, in point of justice, to cut him off from the earth, and send him to endless perdition. (*N. Emmons, D.D.*) *Pharaoh raised up :*—From all we can find out from a careful comparison of what Moses wrote with what Paul added in his letter (Rom. ix. 15–18), it would appear that a paraphrase like this might represent the truth : '' I selected thee for a strong and illustrious example of human insolence in power, its capabilities for wickedness, and the certainty of its final doom ; and this I did in order that I might prove My own supremacy over the creatures of My hand, and thus declare My name in all the ages of the world.'' 1. Observe here that this king was perfectly intelligent concerning what Jehovah asked of him : '' Let My people go, that they may serve Me.'' That was the demand. Does any one say he could not let them go, if he tried ? It was a simple measure of political economy ; he would lose an unreckoned number of valuable slaves. So he made up his mind that the conflict must come on ; he would not let them go. But there was in the struggle more than mere political economy ; from the beginning it is an undenied fact that he knew it was God with whom he was contending ; he was bracing himself for a fight which meant life or death. Why, then, did Menephtah take his stand in defiance of all ? The real reason must be found in his wish to try his gods against Israel's God ; the issue, at first only economic, at last became only spiritual. Those who exercise their sympathy so extensively about this monstrous despot, steeped in conceit and superstition, and who claim that he was treated unfairly and had no chance, ought not to forget that Menephtah was permitted to choose his own forms of contending with Moses. Their weapons were miracles, and the orders of the Hebrew leader were issued in such slow details that for a while the king was able with his magicians to meet the demands of a very respectable rebellion in show. But enough of this. 2. It is more to the point now that we enter on an explanation of this expression about Pharaoh's being '' raised up '' as an exhibition of God's power and supremacy. For years of injustice in administration of the government, of tyranny in treatment of the Israelite working-people, and of superstitious idolatry in his worship, it is clear that Menephtah had been known and read of all men. Just then it pleased God to teach Israel, His chosen people, a lesson of dependence upon Himself ; He determined to show His complete and irresistible supremacy over any one and every one else who was in a position to defy Him. The government of Israel was a theocracy : that is to say, God in person was the King of it, and Moses was the earthly representative before the people. He therefore needed a conspicuous antagonist. Menephtah was chosen. God might have selected the king of the Philistine nation or the Amorite ; it is likely both were as bad as Pharaoh. What He did do was to choose this king of Egypt, the descendant of some awful generations of miscreant tyrants—himself as wicked as the worst. This king, Menephtah, the Lord took when he was at the height of his power. He kept him alive ; He endured his defiance ; He preserved a balance in His mind so that he should not go insane ; He gave him an unbroken season of health ; He guarded against any useless or unhelpful insurrection in his realm ; He patiently bore with his blasphemy. Then, as the conflict grew more malignant, instead of cutting this rebel off in the midst of his daring impiety, God kept giving him more and harder disciplines—all calculated, mind you, to do him good, if he would only accept and improve them to good ; thus kindling anew his passions with fresh fuel. The purpose seems to have been just to draw this one man out, to exhaust his tremendous powers and capabilities to the very utmost, so as to have the Hebrews understand that no king, not even at the highest conception of force and tyranny, was or could be a match for the great Jehovah who was their King and their God. In this sense Pharaoh was ''raised up,'' so as to become a recognized sinner for times and races in the unborn future, a shining shame before the world. 3. '' As he loved cursing, so let it come unto him ; as he delighted not in blessing, so let it be far from him.'' Menephtah does not stand alone in history, by any means. Cain, Saul, the king of Israel, Sihon, Belshazzar, Judas Iscariot, had a similar trial of human will against the Divine. These men were conspicuous ; not all men are as much so ; but all have the same human nature. Indeed, most of us are distinctly conscious of being perfectly unconstrained in all of our moral decisions. We should say, each one of us, if the inquiry were raised, that there never was a moment in all this man's career in which if he had turned and repented, he might not have been saved, no matter how far on in his guilt he might have advanced : so it seems now to ourselves. There is a theological doctrine called reprobation ; the truth appears to be that at some period in the controversy with a human soul, God does judicially withdraw His Spirit, and then there is a solemn crisis reached for the experience of hardness ; it looks as if a man could not repent, could not be saved, beyond that line of defiance and despair. Now, everything the Lord does to save a good man, if done to this reprobate, only makes him worse. How can that be helped ? The free will is kept up, and the sovereignty does not yield. There is no defence, so far as can be discovered, against the power of an unrighteous man to make a vicious perversion of God's most generous dealings. 4. There is a reprobation before death. The sentiment is not accurately true as some persons sing it : it is not always sure that "while the lamp holds out to burn, the vilest sinner may return." For in his heart there may be a hardness that will hinder him for ever from coming to ask for a pardon through Jesus Christ, and that is essential. After this point is reached, however, God goes right on doing as He did before. God never does anything to any soul with the intention of hardening it. He never "raises up " any man for the sake of casting him down again into hell. He has a right to choose as much as we have in any case. He chose Moses instead of Menephtah, and Israel instead of Egypt ; He had mercy on whom He would have mercy. The ancient Thracian emblem of the Deity was a sun with three of its broadest beams proceeding from it : of these, one rested upon a sea of ice and was melting it ; another, on a cliff of rock, and was causing it to flow ; the third, on a dead man's body, and was rousing it to life. Now, just imagine each one of these, or any one of these, was so free-willed as to be able, and so spiteful as to wish, to resist, so a new chill went into the ice, and a fresh hardness into the rock, and a deeper corruption sunk into the dead body ; would the warmth-giving and life-giving sun be to blame, if it still went on shining as before? (*C. S. Robinson, D.D.*)

Ver. 17. **As yet exaltest thou thyself.**—*A self-exalted man :*—I. THAT A SELF-EXALTED MAN OFTEN TREATS WITH CONTEMPT THE CLAIMS OF DUTY. II. THAT A SELF-EXALTED MAN OFTEN TREATS WITH CONTEMPT THE PEOPLE OF GOD. III. THAT A SELF-EXALTED MAN IS OFTEN HUMILIATED BY THE SAD DISCIPLINE OF LIFE. Self-conceit is self-destruction. (*J. S. Exell, M.A.*) *The plague of hail threatened ; or, attention to the word of God the condition of safety in the final judgment of life :*—I. THAT THERE IS A GREAT AND AWFUL JUDGMENT THREATENED UPON MAN IN THE FUTURE. Time known only to God. Enough that fact is certain. II. THAT THERE IS A SHELTER PROVIDED FROM THE FINAL JUDGMENT OF THE FUTURE. 1. Divinely made known. 2. Mercifully sufficient. 3. Gratefully welcomed. III. THAT ONLY THOSE WHO HEED THE WARNING OF GOD, AND AVAIL THEMSELVES OF THE SHELTER PROVIDED, WILL BE SAFE IN THE FINAL JUDGMENT OF LIFE. IV. THAT MANY, THROUGH UNBELIEF, OR THROUGH NEGLECT OF THE WORD OF GOD, WILL PERISH IN THE FINAL JUDGMENT OF LIFE. Lessons : 1. Believe in the judgment to come. 2. Believe in the mercy of Christ. 3. Flee from the wrath to come. (*Ibid.*) *Minding what God says :*— The text describes two classes, viz., those that feared the word of the Lord, and those that "set not their hearts " to it. Here is a very distinct parable in history for our use and instruction. We may note—I. THE DIVINE WARNING. 1. It was "the word of Jehovah." It was sent through a specially commissioned messenger. 2. It was a word of mercy. The Lord willeth not the death of a sinner. 3. It was a word of threatening. But the threat was only against those whose wilful disobedience would merit judgment. II. THE DIFFERENT WAYS IN WHICH IT WAS REGARDED. 1. Wholesome fear. This fear was a fruit of faith. A feeble spark of faith, perhaps, but enough to stimulate action. 2. Careless neglect. Prov. xiv. 16, gives well the contrast of the two classes. This " carnal security " a very common source of spiritual danger. III. THE DEFINITE APPLICATION TO OURSELVES. God has sent His word to us, full of mingled promises and warnings, declarations of mercy and judgment. Are we taking heed thereto? By startling events, by secret stirrings of conscience, by the Bible, by His special messengers, "the ministers of Christ and stewards of the mysteries of God," God speaks. Do we listen? or do we, listless, if not openly scornful, let the utterance be to us as an idle tale? The gospel of Christ, as proclaimed to men, offers a refuge from God's just wrath against sinful man. If we refuse, we shall be worthy of worse punishment than heathen who have never heard, and it shall be more tolerable for them in the day of judgment than for us. Before the hailstorm of judgment come, let us " set our heart to " the word of the Lord ; so shall we be safe in the evil day. (*W. Saumarez Smith, B.D.*)

Vers. 18–26. **The hail shall come down upon them.**—*Brought home :*—I. GOD IS THE TRUE HOME OF THE SOUL. Everything the soul needs is to be found in Him : nowhere else. Here is inviolable security, and everlasting peace. II. CHRIST HAS COME TO BRING US HOME TO GOD. III. THE ETERNAL BLESSEDNESS OF ALL WHO ARE BROUGHT HOME TO GOD BY CHRIST. This is seen in two ways. 1. By what is escaped. "The hail." God's judgments. We have all been solemnly warned. The voice of God cries " gather," (ver. 19). If we slight the call, our blood be upon our own heads ! (Heb. xii. 25). 2. By what is enjoyed (ver. 26). The security of the children of Israel in Goshen, while the storm raged so terribly all around them, touchingly represents the peace of God's people in time and in eternity (Isa. xxxii. 18). IV. The subject suggests SOLEMN QUESTIONS. 1. Where art thou? In the field, exposed, and defenceless, or, at home? 2. Dost thou fear God? (ver. 20, 21). True fear leads to obedience. But many are heedless of counsel and warning, and God's judgments are put " out of sight " (Psa. x. 5). 3. What are you doing to bring others home? If we believe in " the wrath to come," we cannot rest in inaction. (*W. Forsyth, M.A.*) *Lessons :*—1. Human faith of God's threatenings may make men fear and tremble at God's word. Human it may be called in respect of the principle, though the testimony on which it was grounded were Divine. 2. Such fear may make men careful to shun temporal judgments. 3. Wicked men, through fear, may flee from temporal plagues but not eternal (ver. 20). 4. Among wicked men some may refuse human faith which some embrace. 5. Unbelief will not suffer men to lay any of God's words to heart. 6. Regardless of God's threatenings, maketh men leave them and theirs to vengeance (ver. 21). (*G. Hughes, B.D.*) *Lessons :*—1. God's warnings of judgments being not regarded, He quickly gives the word for execution. 2. To encourage faith, God calleth His servants to assist in working vengeance. 3. God makes use of signals to induce judgments sometimes by the hand of His instruments. 4. God's word maketh such signs effectual that they may be feared. 5. God's word creates hail for vengeance, as sometimes in mercy. 6. Man and beast, herbs and all to the utmost extent, are subjected to God's hail at His command (ver. 22). (*Ibid.*) *Salutary fears :*— Threatened judgments test men. Some are more susceptible to the presence of God than others. I. THESE MEN FEARED GOD'S THREATENED JUDGMENT. Fear often arises from faith in God's word. Fear is the alarum of the soul. It is often the first emotion in a new life. It often brings in love, "as the needle draws in the thread." II. THEIR FEAR LED TO APPROPRIATE ACTION. They prepared for the coming storm. There is shelter for all in Christ, and in Him alone. III. THEIR FEAR LED TO WELCOME SAFETY. Obedience brought its reward. Men's property would be safer if they had greater respect for the word of God. (*J. S. Exell, M.A.*) *Belief of the word of God :*—1. Makes men tremble. 2. Makes men wise. 3 Makes men safe. 4. Makes men singular. (*Ibid.*) *Disregard of God :*—1. Ruinous. 2. Presumptuous. 3. Foolish. 4. Common. 5. Inexcusable. (*Ibid.*) *God's command over the elements :*—I. THAT THE MATERIAL UNIVERSE IS GIFTED WITH NUMEROUS AND CONTRARY AGENCIES AND ELEMENTS. 1. The elements of nature called into exercise by this plague were numerous. There was rain, hail, fire and thunder. 2. The elements of nature called into existence by this plague were contrary. The rain was contrary to the fire. There are very opposite elements in the great universe around us ; yet all exist in harmony. One element counteracts and yet co-operates with another. The elements of nature blend in one glorious ministry for man ; though sin often turns them into messengers of justice. 3. The elements of nature called into existence by this plague were emphatic. When the elements of the material universe are arrayed against man they are emphatic in their message. The thunder speaks in loud voice. It has a message to the soul. There is a moral significance in the storm. II. THAT GOD HAS COMPLETE CONTROL OVER ALL THE ELEMENTS OF THE MATERIAL UNIVERSE. 1. So that He can commission His servants to use them according to His will. 2. So that He can make them rebuke the sin of man. He can arm the universe against a wicked soul. 3. God can prevent them from working injury to the good. The heathen imagined that divers Gods were over divers things ; some ruling the air, some the fire, some the water, some the mountains, and some the plains. But God here demonstrates to the Egyptians His complete authority over the whole of nature. This truth is consoling to the good. III. THAT THE MATERIAL PROSPERITY OF A NATION IS GREAT

DEPENDENT UPON THE ELEMENTS OF NATURE, AND THAT THEREFORE GOD ALONE CAN GIVE TRUE PROSPERITY TO A PEOPLE. 1. The fields and gardens of Egypt were ruined. 2. The flax and barley of Egypt were ruined. Egypt was from early times the granary of the world (Gen. xli. 57). And thus we see how the prosperity of a nation is dependent upon the natural government of God in the material world. Let rulers remember this. And let not the people forget it. Sin is a curse to any nation. National righteousness is national prosperity and elevation. Lessons: 1. That the material universe is under the rule of God. 2. That the good are Divinely protected in danger. 3. The national prosperity is the gift of heaven. (Ibid.)　The plague of hail:—A plague of hail, with lightning and thunder, must have been far more awful and portentous in Egypt than in any other country; for there rain was almost unknown, thunderstorms were of rare occurrence, and lightning, when it appeared, was generally of a harmless kind. Modern travellers, indeed, speak of snowstorms, and of thunder and lightning happening occasionally in lower Egypt; but such phenomena appear to have been almost unknown in earlier times. Herodotus says—"During the reign of Psammenitus, Egypt beheld a most remarkable prodigy. There was rain at the Egyptian Thebes, a circumstance which never happened before, and which, as the Thebans themselves assert, has never occurred since. In the higher parts of Egypt it never rains; but at that period it rained in distinct drops" (l. 3, c. 10). Plutarch also observes that "In Egypt no moisture of the air is ever condensed into showers" (de facie, c. 25). Pococke mentions a storm of hail followed by rain in the province of Arsinoe, which "the natives were so far from considering as a blessing, that they observed rain was productive of scarcity, and that the inundation of the Nile alone was serviceable." The Egyptians were much given to the observance of all unusual phenomena, and looked upon them as portentous. According to Herodotus, "Whenever any unusual circumstance occurs they commit the particulars of it to writing, and mark the events which follow" (l. 2, c. 38). If "distinct drops of rain" were regarded as a prodigy worthy of being thus recorded, what must have been the effect of a storm like this, when the hail fell with sufficient violence to destroy both man and beast, and the fire also ran along the ground? "The Egyptians," says Diodorus, "denominated fire Hephaistos, esteeming it a mighty deity, which contributed largely towards the generation and ultimate perfection of beings" (l. 1, c. 1). According to Lucian, "The Persians sacrifice to fire and the Egyptians to water" (de Jove trag. c. 24). Porphyry says—"Even to this day, at the opening of the temple of Serapis, the worship is made by fire and water, for they reverence water and fire above all the elements." These deities now came down upon Egypt with destruction and terror; the very gods in which they trusted turned against them. (T. S. Millington.)　Folly of disregarding warning:—Foolhardiness is not bravery! it is wicked waste of life. At one of the naval engagements between the Federal and Confederate forces, the officer in charge kept ordering the men at the ship's guns to "Look out!" and when a shot came bursting near them to "Lie down!" Most of them obeyed; but some, either from a spirit of bravado or a belief in the doctrine of fatalism, disregarded, saying it was useless to dodge a cannon-ball, and they would chance the risks. By and by a shot came, glanced on the gun, taking off the gunner's cap and the heads of three of the young men who defied the order. It came with a hissing sound, three sharp spats and a heavy report told their sad fate. (H. O. Mackey.)　A warning disregarded:—A gentleman was travelling in Italy in the summer months. As he left Rome he was warned of the danger of sleeping at Baccano. He was told to travel all night rather than stop at that place, as a malignant fever prevailed there. He arrived there about bed-time. The air was balmy and the accommodation inviting. He concluded to stop for the night. Those whose interests would be promoted by his doing so told him there was no danger. He rose in the morning and proceeded on his journey. Some days after he had reached Florence the fever developed itself, and he was soon in his grave. Sinners are warned of the consequences of sinful acts. They are persuaded to disregard the warning. They sin, and the threatened consequences do not immediately appear. They think they shall escape; but ere long God's immutable law overtakes them, and they perish. "The soul that sinneth, it shall die." Safe amidst danger:—A walk along our New York streets has an occasional surprise for the man who keeps his eyes open. Not often, however, does he meet one so pleasant as that which greeted the eye of a pedestrian hurrying along a block near the North River. A brilliant scarlet spot in the cobble stone pavement constantly trodden by horses' feet, and worn by wheels of ice waggons, ash carts and heavy business trucks, drew the passer to a nearer look; and, behold, there, from the scorching sand of a crevice in the pavement had sprung up a thin stem of the portulaca; a single flower had opened its scarlet petals, and was lifting its orange tinted stamens to the sun. There seemed not one chance in a million that the tender plant could have escaped the crushing hoofs and wheels and the tools of the workmen at that moment repairing the pavement; yet there was the lovely blossom, and there at sunset it folded its tiny wings to sleep. Could one fail to learn a lesson of implicit trust in an ever-watchful Father above? *God's regard for His own:*—Miss Gordon Cumming tells the following thrilling story of a Chinese convert at Oiong, whose piety had obtained for him the sobriquet of " Praise the Lord." Miss Cumming says : " A fire broke out in one of the streets of the town, and at first it was not expected to reach as far as where ' Praise the Lord ' lived. As it spread, however, it neared the street where his house stood, and it was evident to the onlookers that all the buildings were doomed. His heathen neighbours hastily collected all their idols, and placed them as a barricade against the approaching flames. The zealous old Christian, seizing his mattock, and swinging it round him, soon reduced the gods of wood and clay to a mass of fragments. Then, having denounced the folly which could trust in senseless images, he lifted up his hands to heaven, and in the hearing of the already wildly excited mob he called upon the great Creator, the true God, his heavenly Father, to save the homes of himself and his neighbours from the threatening fire. It was not the first time that he had proved the promise, ' While they are yet speaking I will hear,' and now he looked for an immediate answer, which would show to the heathen that the God who could stay the fire was the true God. Nor was he disappointed; almost before they could note any physical reason for the change the flames seemed blown back upon themselves—the wind had suddenly veered round, and though many of the houses close by had been scorched, those of the old man and his neighbours escaped unharmed, and the marvelling crowd saw the conflagration recede as swiftly as it had approached." *The flax and barley of Egypt :*— Herodotus says—" The manufacture of linen is peculiar to the Colchians and the Egyptians. The linen which comes from Colchis, the Greeks call Sardonian; the linen of Egypt, Egyptian " (l. 2, c. 105). Pliny's account of it is—" The flax of Egypt, though the least strong of all as a tissue, is that from which the greatest profits are derived. There is no tissue known that is superior to those made from the thread of the Egyptian xylon, either for whiteness and softness, or dressing; the most esteemed vestments worn by the priests of Egypt are made by it " (Hist. Nat. l. 19, c. 2). Pliny mentions four varieties of flax, and first among them the Tanaitic, growing in the lower district of Egypt, Zoan, which was the seat of Pharaoh's government. The destruction of the flax deprived the people of the material for their chief manufacture, and put a stop to the trade which they carried on with neighbouring nations, who sent their treasure into the country to pay for it. The ruin of the barley was equally injurious. Egypt appears to have been from a very early period the granary of the world. Thither Abraham went down to sojourn when the land in which he dwelt was visited with famine ; and thither the sons of Jacob, under similar necessity, naturally turned for help. (*T. S. Millington.*)

Vers. 27, 28. **I have sinned.**—*Pharaoh's " I have sinned " :*—There are no more beautiful words ever spoken on this earth—none to which an angel listens more complacently—none which wing their way more surely to heaven—none which more surely enter into the ears of the Lord God of Sabaoth—than those three—so personal, so true, so simple, and so full, " I have sinned." They occur nine times in the Bible ; and of the nine we may except two. For where they stand—in the seventh chapter of Micah—they are the language, not of an individual, but of a Church. And the prodigal's use of them is, of course, not matter of fact or history; but only part of a parable. There remain, therefore, seven ; seven persons of whom it is written that they said, " I have sinned." It may surprise some of you to know that, of those seven, four are utterly hollow and worthless ; in God's scales, wanting, unreal, and unprofitable. It is a humbling and teaching fact that in three only—of the seven instances in which persons are recorded in the Scriptures to have said, " I have sinned," was the confession true, and the repentance valid. I. At what time God's hardening of Pharaoh's heart began, it is impossible exactly to determine. But evidently from the first it was judicial. A common story. A sin indulged till the man is given over to his sin ; and then the sin made its own punishment. It is not that if you repent you would not be forgiven ; but it is that you reduce your heart to such a state that it places repentance out of your reach. You become like Esau. Esau, after he sold his birthright, never repented, nor wished to repent. He wished his father to repent, though he himself did not repent. Pharaoh could say, "I have sinned," and never felt it,—because his heart was "hard." Many of you are very young, and you have tender hearts. Take care; take care of that dew of your spiritual birth—lest it be brushed away! If you love the world, you will be "hardened." You say, "I will repent of my worldliness." You cannot. Your worldliness will have left you too "hard" to repent. II. What, then, was Pharaoh's "I have sinned"? Where did it tend? 1. It was a mere hasty impulse. There was no thought in it; no careful dealing with his own soul; no depth. 2. The moving principle was nothing but fear. He was agitated—greatly agitated—only agitated. Now, fear may be, and probably must be, a part of real repentance. I do not despise fear. Fear is a sign of penitence. Fear is a very good thing. But I doubt whether there was ever a real repentance that was promoted by fear only. 3. Pharaoh's thoughts were directed far too much to man. It was not the "against Thee, Thee only, I have sinned." He never went straight to God. Hence his confession was not thorough. III. And here comes the solemn thought—for comfort or for fear—in everything that is true, there is a germ, and God sees and recognizes, at once, the germ. It may not have expanded. Perhaps the person—who has it—may not live long enough for it to be expanded in this world. But God knows that it can expand, and that it would expand. God judges by that germ. If it is not—that germ of love and holiness—the rest all goes for nothing. But if it be there—God accepts all for that germ. (*J. Vaughan, M.A.*) *The transient repentance of a wicked soul:*—I. That moods of transient repentance are sometimes awakened by the retributive judgments of God. The penitence of the hypocrite; not a godly sorrow. Induced by the infliction of punishment, rather than by the gentle convictions of the Divine Spirit. True repentance will have reference to God and to the violated law, rather than to self-comfort and immunity from pain. II. That in moods of transient repentance men call for the ministers of God whom they have previously despised. Ministers must be forbearing toward their people, and embrace any opportunity of leading them to the mercy of God. But the repentance that sends for the minister under the impulse of fear, will be likely to dismiss him when the plague is removed. It is well to heed the voice of the servants of God before the hour of retribution. III. That in moods of transient repentance men make promises they will never perform. We should remember in joy the vows made in sorrow, in health, those made in sickness, and then painful discipline will become happy and glorious. IV. That in moods of transient repentance men will acknowledge that prayer to God for mercy is their only method of help. V. That in moods of transient repentance men sometimes obtain the removal of the judgments of God. Token of mercy. Discipline of love to lead to duty. Lessons:—1. That trials are calculated to lead the soul to repentance. 2. That under trials the repentance of men may be transient. 3. That the mercy of God is rich to the proudest sinner. 4. That the servants of God should be helpful to penitent souls. (1) By fidelity. (2) By sympathy. (3) By prayer. (*J. S. Exell, M.A.*) *Repentance inspired by fear:*—I. That repentance inspired by fear is experienced by men of the proudest moral character. This shows the all-conquering power of the truth, in that it can subdue the tyrant-heart. It also shows the mercy of God, in that the most degenerate life is blessed with the refreshing mood of repentance. No heart is utterly destitute of better feelings. II. That repentance inspired by fear anxiously seeks the aid of the servants of God. III. That repentance inspired by fear is just in its condemnation of self, and in its acknowledgment of sin. There are times when confession is a necessity of the soul. When sin is as a fire, which must burn through all subterfuges and manifest itself to the public eye. Hence open confession of sin is not an infallible token of repentance; it may be the outcome of necessity or of terror. IV. That repentance inspired by fear is just in its vindication of the Divine character. Repentance is not to be gauged by the utterance of the lips. V. That repentance inspired by fear promises future obedience to the claims of God. (*Ibid.*) *Repentings and relapsings:*—I. The theistic constitution of the soul. 1. It shows a primitive belief in the existence of God. 2. It shows a primitive belief in the providential government of God. II. The unnaturalness of our spiritual existence. III. The unreliableness of death-bed confessions. Genuine repentance for sin is not the fear of misery, but the relentings of love. **IV. The supreme interest of every man.** (*Homilist.*) *Sense of guilt :*—I. Under its influence man FEELS HUMBLED. II. Under its influence man RESPECTS GODLINESS. III. Under its influence man VINDICATES THE ALMIGHTY. (*Ibid.*) *I have sinned :*—1. A good confession. 2. A simple confession. 3. A faithful confession. 4. A welcome confession. 5. Sometimes an unreal confession. (*J. S. Exell, M.A.*) *The Lord is righteous :*—1. Then admire His administration. 2. Then worship His glory. 3. Then fear His justice. 4. Then vindicate His operations. 5. Then make known His praise. (*Ibid.*) *A wicked people and a wicked monarch :*—1. Sad. 2. Afflicted. 3. Repentant. (*Ibid.*) *Intreat the Lord :*—1. For He hears prayer. 2. For He has respect to the good. 3. For wicked men need Divine help. 4. For He is merciful. (*Ibid.*) *The confession of Pharaoh :*—I. THE RESEMBLANCE OF THE CONFESSION BEFORE US TO THE LANGUAGE OF TRUE CONTRITION, IS CLOSE. 1. It was open, made not to a partizan or friend in the secrecy of retirement, but to Moses and Aaron in public ; to the very man whose presence was likely to fill the sinner with the greatest shame, and to require of him the most mortifying concessions. 2. It was accompanied also with a sense of guilt, and that not confined to one transgression only, but extending to the general conduct of himself and his subjects. 3. It is remarkable too that, like David, he considered his guilt as an offence against God. 4. But this was not all. The confession of Pharaoh included in it an acknowledgment of the justice of God in inflicting these judgments. They were great and heavy, but he does not complain of their severity. He complains only of his own sins, which had so justly drawn them on his head. "The Lord," he says, "is righteous, and I and my people are wicked." 5. There were also some good resolutions connected with the confession of Pharaoh. II. PHARAOH WAS NOT A PENITENT, THOUGH HE BORE SO STRONG A RESEMBLANCE TO ONE. His confession was sincere, but it was not godly. It resembled the language of true repentance, but at the same time it differed essentially from it. 1. In attempting to trace this difference, we may observe that it was a forced confession, extorted from him by the suffering he endured, and the fear of still heavier judgments. The point to be ascertained is not what kind of men we are in affliction or in sickness, in the house of God or in the society of His servants ; but what is the frame of our minds when these excitements are withdrawn? What are we in retirement? What are we in our families? What are we in daily intercourse with the world? 2. The confession of Pharaoh differed from a true confession in this respect also—it was unaccompanied with humiliation before God. He repeatedly besought Moses and Aaron to entreat for him, but he disdained to bend the knee himself. He trembled at the judgments of the Lord, but though they laid waste his country and cut off his first-born, he still refused to humble himself before Him. This spirit of independence is the bane and curse of our fallen nature. The very essence of our depravity consists in it. We will not have God to reign over us. Judgments can terrify, but they cannot humble us. 3. The confession of Pharaoh was defective also in another respect—it was not succeeded by an entire renunciation of sin. The true penitent does not ask, "How far may I indulge my lusts, and yet be safe? How much love may I have for the world and yet escape condemnation?" but, "What right hand have I yet to cut off? What right eye have I yet to pluck out? What lurking sin still remains to be discovered and overcome?" 4. But even if the confession of Pharaoh had not been defective in these things, there was yet another point of difference between it and a genuine confession, and that a most important and ruinous difference—it was not habitual and lasting. The convictions from which it sprung were as temporary as the judgments which gave rise to them, so that he who feared and trembled one hour, hardened his heart the next. Repentance is not an act, it is a habit ; not a duty to be performed once in a man's life, and then to be thought of no more ; it is to be our daily work, our hourly employment. III. Such was the confession of Pharaoh. THE LESSONS IT TEACHES ARE OBVIOUS. 1. It shows us, first, the great need we have of self-examination. We may have confessed our sins from our heart ; but has that heart been humbled, lowly, obedient? Instead of going about to establish our own righteousness, are we submitting ourselves to the righteousness of God? Are we praying, as well as trembling? 2. This shows us also the extreme depravity of the human heart. We need the transforming power, the effectual working, of the Holy Ghost. We must seek repentance as a gift of mercy at the throne of God. 3. We may see, further, the folly of trusting in convictions. Remorse is not penitence. Conviction is not conversion. Fear is not grace. 4. But while we are reminded of the folly of trusting in convictions, we are at the same time taught the guilt and danger of stifling them. They cannot save the soul, but they are designed to make us feel our need of salvation, and to lead us for it to the great Saviour of the lost. 5. There is yet another lesson to be learned from this subject. It seems indeed, on the first view, to speak to us only of the depravity of man and the awful justice of God, but to what subject of medita- tion can we turn, which does not remind us of the Divine mercy? A hardened Pharaoh, as well as a weeping Peter, declares to us, that the guilty will never seek pardon in vain. (*C. Bradley, M.A.*)

Vers. 29, 30. **I know that ye will not yet fear the Lord God.**—*Lessons :*—1. Gracious souls are willing to yield to vilest persecutors to help them though they deceive them. 2. Time and place convenient, God's servants take to answer the desires of the wicked. 3. Heart and hand do God's saints lay out in prayer to God for their enemies. 4. Under God's revelation his ministers may assure the wicked of His mercies. 5. Such discoveries are made to wicked men that they might acknowledge His propriety and sovereignty over all (ver. 29). 6. Though God's servants know how the wicked will afterward behave themselves, yet they may pray for them. 7. God doth foretell by His servants sometimes the incorrigibility of the wicked under judgment and mercy. 8. Wicked men may tremble under vengeance, but never fear the Lord God when it is removed (ver. 30). (*G. Hughes, B.D.*) *Wise ministerial treatment of an obstinate sinner :*—I. THAT THE TRUE MINISTER IS WILLING TO RENDER HELP TO THE VILEST PERSECUTOR IN THE HOUR OF IMAGINED REPENTANCE. Moses did not remain away from Pharaoh in the hour of his penitence. He did not treat him with contempt, as unworthy of further effort. He went to him at once. Ministers are never justified in leaving even the vilest men to themselves in their time of perplexity. They should visit them and render them all the aid in their power. The hypocrite must never be forsaken by the servant of God. II. THAT THE TRUE MINISTER WILL PRAY FOR THE MOST OBSTINATE SINNER IN THE HOUR OF DISTRESS. "As soon as I am gone out of the city, I will spread abroad my hands unto the Lord." 1. The prayer will be offered in private. "Out of the city." Solitude is favourable to prayer. The minister should seek solitude. It is well for him to go outside of the city to meditate and to pray about obstinate men. 2. It will be offered with earnestness. "I will spread abroad my hands unto the Lord." The ministers of God should employ their hands and hearts in prayer to heaven for the souls of wicked men. III. THAT THE TRUE MINISTER MAY ASSURE THE MOST OBSTINATE SINNER OF THE MERCY OF GOD TOWARD HIM. A contrite heart shall not hear the thunder of retributive judgment. IV. THAT THE TRUE MINISTER MUST ASSERT THE UNBENDING SOVEREIGNTY OF GOD TO THE MOST OBSTI- NATE SINNER. V. THAT THE TRUE MINISTER WILL DEAL FAITHFULLY WITH THE MOST OBSTINATE SINNER WHO MAY MANIFEST TOKENS OF REPENTANCE. Lessons: 1. That ministers are often perplexed as to the best method of conduct toward obstinate sinners. 2. They must pray for them. 3. They must be faithful to them. (*J. S. Exell, M.A.*) *The earth is the Lord's :*—1. Then admire its beauty. 2. Then participate in its bounty. 3. Then tread it reverently. 4. Then use it generously. (*Ibid.*) *I know that ye will not fear the Lord God :*—1. Because your mind is dark. 2. Because your heart is hard. 3. Because your conscience is seared. 4. Because your will is rebellious. 5. Because your sin is a pleasure. (*Ibid.*)

Vers. 34, 35. **He sinned yet more.**—*Lessons :*—1. Sense of judgment and mercy without faith worketh more evil in sinners against God. 2. Mercies may prove occasions of hardening unto wicked souls ; but no causes of their sin. 3. Wicked powers by unbelief harden themselves and others (ver. 34). 4. God sets on harden- ing when sinners choose to be stubborn against God. 5. Breach of promise with God is nothing with sinners. 6. God's foretelling of sinners ways aggravates that sin abundantly (ver. 35). (*G. Hughes, B.D.*) *Pharaoh's conduct after the storm :*—I. PHARAOH'S CONDUCT IS OFTEN RESEMBLED BY MEN OF OUR DAY. Men's views of themselves and life change as the dark clouds roll away, and the sun breaks forth to gild their path again. This has become proverbial. II. PHARAOH'S CONDUCT REVEALS THAT HIS HEART HAD BEEN UNCHANGED. Afflictions do change some sinners into saints. They have come out of the storm new men. But it often produces no radical change. It does not change the heart. Love only awakens permanent resistance to sin. III. PHARAOH'S CONDUCT MANIFESTED THE BASEST IN- GRATITUDE. Sin is always lamentable, but more so in the face of Divine mercy. Such insensibility to mercy is sure to bring another judgment. IV. PHARAOH'S

CONDUCT WAS MOST PRESUMPTUOUS. V. PHARAOH'S CONDUCT SHOWS THE AMOUNT OF DEPRAVITY THAT MAY LURK IN A HUMAN HEART. Our only safety is in humiliating ourselves before the Lord, and seeking for His grace to overcome our own stubbornness and sins. (*W. Lilley.*)   *The cessation of penitential sorrow :*—1. When calamity removed. 2. When mercy bestowed. 3. When gratitude expected. (*J. S. Exell, M.A.*)   *Repentance under judgments :*—One day, visiting a prison chaplain, the Rev. W. Harness asked him whether his ministry had been attended with success. "With very little, I grieve to say," was the reply. "A short time since I thought I had brought to a better state of mind a man who had attempted to murder a woman and had been condemned to death. He showed great signs of contrition after the sentence was passed upon him, and I thought I could observe the dawnings of grace upon the soul. I gave him a Bible, and he was most assiduous in the study of it, frequently quoting passages from it which he said convinced him of the heinousness of his offence. The man gave altogether such a promise of reformation, and of a change of heart and life, that I exerted myself to the utmost, and obtained for him such a commutation of his sentence as would enable him soon to begin the world again, and, as I hoped, with a happier result. I called to inform him of my success. His gratitude knew no bounds; he said I was his preserver—his deliverer. 'And here,' he added, as he grasped my hand in parting, 'here is your Bible; I may as well return it to you, for I hope I shall never want it again.'"

CHAPTER X.

VERS. 1, 2. **Show these My signs.**—*How God hardened Pharaoh's heart :*—I. BY A MANIFESTATION OF RICH MERCY, WHICH OUGHT TO HAVE MELTED THE HEART OF THE KING. II. BY A MANIFESTATION OF GREAT POWER, WHICH OUGHT TO HAVE SUBDUED THE HEART OF THE KING. III. BY A MANIFESTATION OF SEVERE JUSTICE, WHICH MIGHT HAVE REBUKED THE HEART OF THE KING. IV. BY SENDING HIS SERVANTS TO INFLUENCE THE HEART OF THE KING TO THE RIGHT. God did not harden Pharaoh's heart by a sovereign decree, so that he could not obey His command; but by ministries appropriate to salvation, calculated to induce obedience—the constant neglect of which was the efficient cause of this sad moral result. Lessons: 1. That man has the ability to resist the saving ministries of heaven. 2. That when man resists the saving ministries of heaven he becomes hard in heart. 3. That hardness of heart is itself a natural judgment from God. 4. That hardness of heart will finally work its own ruin. (*J. S. Exell, M.A.*)   *God sends His minister to hardened souls :*—1. Often. 2. Mercifully. 3. Uselessly. 4. Significantly. 5. Disastrously. (*Ibid.*)   *Hardened sinners :*—1. In companies. 2. Patterns of judgments. 3. Tokens of indignation. 4. The cause of plagues. 5. The curse of the world. 6. Still followed by the minister of God. (*Ibid.*)   *The signs of God to the generations of the future:*—I. THAT GOD IS SUPREME OVER THE KINGDOM OF NATURE. Science places the natural universe under the command of man. This is the Divine ordination. But man's power over nature is derived; God's is underived and independent. Hence—1. He can inflict pain on the wicked. 2. He can protect the good from harm. 3. He can send famine or plenty. II. THAT GOD IS SUPREME OVER THE CUNNING AND POWER OF THE DEVIL. The magicians of Egypt were agents of the devil. They were inspired by him in their opposition to Moses and Aaron. They were aided by his cunning. Their defeat was his defeat also. 1. God can deliver men from the power of the devil. 2. God can destroy the works of the devil. 3. God can frustrate the designs of the devil. Teach this blessed truth and glorious fact to the youthful: that the good agencies of the universe are more potent than the bad. This will lead youthhood to confide in God. III. THAT GOODNESS IS HAPPINESS, AND THAT CONFLICT WITH GOD IS THE MISERY OF MAN. Lessons: 1. That in the lives of individuals we have signs of God. 2. That all the signs of God in human life are to be carefully noted and taught to the young. 3. That all the signs of life are evidence of the Divine supremacy. (*Ibid.*)   *The ministry of sin :*—God makes Pharaoh "to stand" for the benefit of Israel, and in them for the benefit of humanity. It was for Pharaoh in the first instance to resist Divine light and grace, and oppress Israel; it was then for God

to economise the tyrant and his wrath. The conduct of the Egyptian king served
—I. To REVEAL GOD. "That ye may know how that I am the Lord." Pharaoh's
perverseness revealed all the more fully — 1. The Divine love. 2. The Divine
righteousness. 3. The Divine power. II. To FURTHER THE INTERESTS OF ISRAEL.
God overrules sin to high and happy issues. (*W. L. Watkinson.*) · *Transmitting
the knowledge of the true God :*—I. JEHOVAH MADE HIMSELF KNOWN TO THE ISRAELITES
IN EGYPT AS THE ONLY TRUE GOD BY SIGNS. His wondrous acts revealed His
supremacy. Christ is the fullest revelation of the true God. II. THAT THIS KNOW-
LEDGE IS TO BE TRANSMITTED FROM GENERATION TO GENERATION. Parental influence
the most potent in telling of God's acts. No lips teach like the lips of loving
authority. Some parents neglect this solemn duty. Ever ready to speak about
worldly enterprises, the acts of great men, their own ; but they are silent about
God's. Such neglect is ruinous to their children and dishonouring to God. III.
IN THE TRANSMISSION OF THE KNOWLEDGE OF THE TRUE GOD IS THE HOPE OF THE
WORLD. Wherever the knowledge of the true God prevails, righteousness and peace
are found. Idolatry has ever been the bane of mankind. A false conception of
God debases. (*J. S. Exell, M.A.*) *By signs :*—1. Showing the woe of sin. 2.
The folly of human malice. 3. The justice of God. 4. The safety of the Church.
(*Ibid.*) *The signs :*—1. Their nature. 2. Their locality. 3. Their design.
(*Ibid.*) *The Divine supremacy :*—1. Rejected by the proud. 2. Received by the
good. 3. Revealed by the works of God. 4. To be acknowledged by all. (*Ibid.*)
The plagues :—So, allowing all that may be called romantic, supernatural, to fall off
from this story of the plagues, there remains all that God wanted to remain—three
things :—First, the assertion of the Divine right in life. God cannot be turned out
of His own creation ; He must assert His claim, and urge it, and redeem it. The
second thing that remains is the incontestable fact of human opposition to Divine
voices. Divine voices call to right, to purity, to nobleness, to love, to brotherhood ;
and every day we resist these voices, and assert rebellious claims. The third thing
that remains is the inevitable issue. We cannot fight God and win. "It is hard
for thee to kick against the pricks." Why smite with feeble fist the infinite granite
of the infinite strength ? Who will lose ? The certain result will be the overthrow
of the sinner : the drowning of every Pharaoh who hardens himself against the
Divine will and voice. Now that I come to think of it, have not all these plagues
followed my own obstinacy and hardness of heart in relation to things Divine?
We speak of the plagues of Egypt as though they began and ended in that distant
land, and we regard them now as part of an exciting historical romance. I will
think otherwise of them. The local incident and the local colour may be dispensed
with, but the supreme fact in my own consciousness is that God always follows my
obstinacy with plagues. Dangers are rightly used when they move us to bolder prayer;
losses are turned into gains when they lift our lives in an upward direction; disease
is the beginning of health when it leads the sufferer to the Father's house. Pharaoh
had his plagues, many and awful ; and every life has its penal or chastening visita-
tions, which for the present are full of agony and bitterness, but which may be so
used as to become the beginning of new liberties and brighter joys. (*J. Parker,
D.D.*) *God's judgments :*—Lay a book open before a child, or one that cannot
read ; he may stare and gaze upon it, but he can make no use of it at all, because
he understandeth nothing in it ; yet bring it to one that can read, and understandeth
the language that is written in it, he will read you many stories and instructions out
of it ; it is dumb and silent to the one, but speaketh to, and talketh with, the other.
In like manner it is with God's judgments, as St. Augustine well applies it ; all
sorts of men see them, but few are able aright to read them or to understand them
what they say ; every judgment of God is a real sermon of reformation and repentance. (*J. Spencer.*)

Vers. 3–6. **To-morrow will I bring the locusts.**—*Humiliation before God :*—"How
long wilt thou refuse to humble thyself before Me ?" I. I SHALL SHOW OUR NEED OF
HUMILIATION BEFORE GOD. 1. Let us inquire how we have acted toward God. As
our Creator, our Governor, our Benefactor. 2. Let us inquire how we have acted
toward our Lord Jesus Christ. Was made flesh. Died for us. 3. Let us inquire
how we have acted toward the Holy Spirit. Rebelled, vexed, grieved, quenched.
II. I SHALL SHOW WHEREIN TRUE HUMILIATION CONSISTS. 1. In confession of our
sin before God. Fully and unreservedly. With deep and ingenuous sorrow. 2.
In believing application to God through Christ for pardon of our sin. 3. In
renouncing our sins and commencing a course of obedience to God. III. I SHALL

SHOW THE EVILS OF DELAYING TRUE HUMILIATION BEFORE GOD. 1. The guilt (Rom. ii. 4, 5). 2. The folly. Stronger than He? 3. The danger. Pharaoh. Manasseh. (1) Repentance is never too late. (2) Repentance is never too soon. (*G. Brooks.*) *The delay of soul humility :*—I. IN WHAT DOES SOUL-HUMILITY CONSIST? 1. It does not consist in mournful verbal utterances. A humble word may conceal a proud spirit. 2. Nor in outward manifestations of repentance. 3. It is rather evinced in calm resignation to the will of God as revealed in His Word, and as made known in the conscience by the Holy Spirit. II. HOW IS SOUL-HUMILITY TO BE OBTAINED? 1. By having a clear conception of the will of God and of the beauty of truth. 2. By allowing the varied discipline of life its due effect upon the soul. Pain ought to humble a man, reminding him of his mortality. 3. By submitting to the gentle influences of the Holy Spirit. III. WHY IS SOUL-HUMILITY SO LONG DELAYED? 1. Because men will not give up their sins. Humility is the outcome of purity. 2. Because men will not yield to the claims of God. 3. Because men are rendered proud by exalted social position. 4. Men can give no reason for the delay of soul-humility. Humility is the richest and best ornament of the soul, and no good excuse can be assigned for neglecting to wear it. This ornament is but seldom seen in this vaunting age. It is welcome to the eye of heaven. Lessons: 1. Soul-humility should be manifested by man. 2. God's ministers should enforce it. 3. God's people should cultivate it. 4. Its absence cannot be excused. (*J. S. Exell, M.A.*) *The plague of locusts threatened :*—I. IT WAS THREATENED IN CASE THAT PHARAOH WOULD NOT GIVE THE ISRAELITES THE FREEDOM DEMANDED BY GOD (ver. 4). The good have in God a stern Defender. II. THAT SOME MEN ARE MUCH MORE SENSITIVE TO THE THREATENINGS OF GOD THAN OTHERS (ver. 7). III. THAT DIVINE THREATENINGS MUST MAKE MINISTERS FAITHFUL IN THE DISCHARGE OF THEIR DUTY (ver. 9). Denounce all attempts at moral compromise. (*Ibid.*) *To-morrow :*—1. A judgment. 2. A mystery. 3. A crisis. 4. An anxiety. 5. A hope. (*Ibid.*) *If thou refuse :*—1. Then man can refuse to obey God. 2. Then man can dare the judgments of God. 3. Then man takes a great responsibility upon himself. (*Ibid.*) *The locusts :*—1. Very grievous. 2. Darkening the light. 3. Devouring the fruit. 4. Entering the houses. (*Ibid.*) *Good men should leave sinners when they have declared the message of God :*—1. As a reproof. 2. As a contempt. 3. As a prophecy. 4. As a relief. (*Ibid.*) *Locust-scaring gods :*—The Egyptians, in common with other nations whose ideas of religion were derived originally from Egypt, had particular deities to whom they appealed for help in times of particular necessity. There is reason to believe that they had gods to whom they looked for protection against locusts as well as against flies and vermin. Strabo, speaking of certain gods whose titles were derived from insignificant objects, says : "The inhabitants of Mount Œta worshipped Hercules under the title of Hercules Cornopion, because he had delivered them from locusts. So the Erythræans, who live near Melius, worship Hercules Ipoctonus, because he destroyed the *ipes*, or worms, which are destructive to vines : for this pest is found everywhere except in the country of the Erythræans. The Rhodians have in their island a temple of Apollo Erythibius, so called from *erysibe* (mildew), which they call *erythibe*. Among the Æolians in Asia one of their months is called Pornopion, for this name the Bœotians give to *parnopes* (locusts), and sacrifices are performed to Apollo Pornopion." The locust was esteemed sacred in Greece, and the Athenians wore golden cicadæ, or grasshoppers, in their hair, to denote the antiquity of their race, as αὐτόχθονες, "of the land itself," or aborigines. Early historians tell us that the Greeks came originally from Egypt; Cecrops, the first king of Attica, was from Sais; Cadmus, from Thebes; and Danäus and Lynceus, with their colonies, from Chemnis. The locust-scarers of Greece and Asia were, therefore, in all probability, gods of the Egyptians in time of Pharaoh, and were put to shame, with the rest of their deities, by this unprecedented and miraculous visitation. Thus the winds from the four corners of heaven obey the command of Jehovah. As far as man is concerned, nothing is more uncertain, nothing more absolutely beyond control : "the wind bloweth were it listeth, and thou hearest the sound thereof, but canst not tell whence it cometh or whither it goeth" (John iii. 8). But God directeth it under the whole heaven; He calleth it, "Awake, O north wind, and come thou south" (Cant. iv. 16); "He gathereth the wind in His fists" (Prov. xxx. 4); "He bringeth it out of His treasuries" (Psa. cxxxv. 7). At God's command the east wind brought the locusts, in twenty-four hours, from the uttermost parts of the east, collecting them, it may be, from the far-off deserts of Arabia and Persia; and at God's command the west wind carried them away again, as far as the Red Sea. There they all fell down and perished. "I am tossed up and down as the locust " (Psa. cix. 23), says David. These creatures were tossed up and down by the wind wherever God would send them. He had used them as His scourge, an instrument of punishment, in which He could have no pleasure; and when their ungrateful task was done, He drowned them in the sea. To those same depths the infatuated king who refused to be warned by the chastisement was presently to follow them, and with his miserable people, in their turn, to perish. (*T. S. Millington.*)

Ver. 7. **Knowest thou not yet that Egypt is destroyed?**—*Lessons :*—1. Threatening from God may touch hearts of servants and not of rulers. 2. God useth king's own servants to move them, when His ministers can avail nothing. 3. Fear of plagues may move wicked ones to yield, where the fear of God is not. 4. It is usual for wicked men to charge God's servants to be snares, when their sins make them. 5. When God makes His servants ministers of wrath, the wicked are willing to be rid of them. 6. Idolatrous persecutors may tolerate God's Church to serve Him, when vengeance forces them. 7. Experience of destruction past, and fear of more to come, may cause enemies to move for the Church's liberty. 8. Persecuting powers are apt to be stupid and willingly ignorant of such destructions. (*G. Hughes, B.D.*) *A remonstrance against sin :*—I. ADDRESSED BY INFERIORS TO THEIR SUPERIORS. 1. Bold. 2. Wise. 3. Needed. II. INSPIRED BY A DEEP FEELING OF TERROR. It is well for men under any circumstances to cry out against moral evil. III. INFLUENTIAL FOR TEMPORARY GOOD. Some men are apparently more accessible to the advice of their comrades than they are to the commands of heaven. The wicked servant may preach the gospel to his despotic master. IV. ULTIMATELY DISREGARDED. Lessons:—1. Remonstrate with the sinner. 2. Show him the folly and woe of sin. 3. You are not responsible for the result of such a remonstrance. (*J. S. Exell, M.A.*) *Pharaoh's mad ignorance :*—"Knowest thou not yet that Egypt is destroyed? " was the plea of Pharaoh's servants before the locusts came. No; he knew it not; he would not know it. Even now, with the scene of utter desolation everywhere around him, with the fields scorched and barren, and the naked trees stretching out their white and shattered boughs like ghastly skeletons, with even the walls of his houses and the furniture of his chambers marked by the gnawings of those "very grievous locusts," with all these terrible witnesses before his eyes, Pharaoh knew it not. (*T. S. Millington.*)

Vers. 8, 9. **We will go with our young and with our old.**—*Lessons :*—1. Upon importunity of men wicked powers may be moved to recall and treat further with God's ministers when His own word is slighted by them. 2. Upon carnal considerations powers may license the Church to serve its God. 3. Such wicked powers bound their grants of liberty with provisos destructive to God's will (ver. 8). (*G. Hughes, B.D.*) *Lessons :*—1. Captious questions from the wicked are answered with plain answers by God's servants. 2. Faithfulness to God will not suffer His servants to hide His mind to the wicked. 3. God's instruments have encouragement from Him to deliver His demands to greatest powers. 4. Little ones as well as great must be carried along with the Church of God to their rest. 5. The Church's portion in this life as to outward estate God is pleased to have free as well as themselves, that they may comfortably serve Him therewith. 6. The Church's work after redemption is to serve Jehovah, or keep a feast to Him (ver. 9). (*Ibid.*) *Renewed opportunities of moral good :*—"And Moses and Aaron were brought again unto Pharaoh." I. CONSEQUENT UPON THE FAITHFUL REBUKE OF FRIENDS. II. THROUGH CONTACT WITH A HOLY MAN. III. MAY BE LEFT UNUSED THROUGH THE PERVERSENESS OF THE SOUL. (*J. S. Exell, M.A.*) *The children must be rescued :*—But particularly observe the subject of dispute. Concerning whom did it arise? Concerning boys and girls—little children. Pharaoh did not wish them to accompany their parents to hold a feast unto the Lord; he required that they should remain at home as hostages. Moses refused. Well, there are often similar disputes in our time between the devil and the servants of God concerning you. The devil causes worldly men to say, like Pharaoh, "Why should you trouble children with religion, they are too young yet? How can they understand the Bible, since I, who am a grown-up man, and perhaps a learned man, do not understand it? They can take no pleasure in it; it is too serious for them, since for my part I find it a weariness. At their age it becomes them to play, and not to study deeply. Let them enjoy their diversions; let them amuse themselves on the Sunday." Thus the prince of this world, the great Pharaoh of the darkness of this world, would wish to keep you as hostages in error, and ensnare your parents also. If your house were on fire, what would you think of a person who should say to your father, " Go out as quickly as you can, but leave your children in bed " ? Or if you were at school, or an apprentice to a trade, what would you think of a man who should say to your father, " Your son has a holiday, but do not let him come home to be with you, for he is at an age to amuse himself. Do not teach him to love you, and to obey you, for that would weary him." Ah! dear children, you have as much need as we have to escape the wrath to come, and to love God. Ask from Him grace to love Him. The prayer of a child who seeks a new heart for the sake of Jesus Christ always ascends to heaven. (*Prof. Gaussen.*)

Vers. 10, 11. **Driven out from Pharaoh's presence.**—*Driving away the servants of God:*—1. It is to drive away a good friend. 2. It is to drive away a faithful monitor. 3. It is to drive away a real benefactor. 4. It is to drive away an angel of God. (*J. S. Exell, M.A.*) *The threats of the wicked:*—I. EVIL MEN OFTEN SEEK TO RETARD GOD'S SERVANTS IN THEIR WORKS BY THREATS. But in vain. God sustains all whom He sends. No opposition, however virulent, can retard them from doing His work. They may be weak and few, but He is their strength. II. THAT THE THREATS OF EVIL MEN NEED NOT BE FEARED. Nothing can really harm God's servants. They may have to suffer, but suffering will be turned into triumphant joy. Like the saintly Rutherford, they will find that their enemies have only set them to reside for a while in one of God's palaces. Real evil cannot befall them. III. THAT THE EVIL THREATENED MENACES THE THREATENER. As Luther said concerning the potentates of his day, who did not remember the overruling might of God in their projects: "Our Lord God says unto them: For whom do ye hold Me? for a cypher? Do I set here above in vain, and to no purpose? You shall know that I will twist your accounts about finely, and make them all false reckonings." So it was with Pharaoh when he threatened Moses and Aaron. (*W. O. Lilly.*) *The imperiousness of unbelief:*—I. IN ITS RELUCTANCE TO GRANT CONCESSIONS. II. IN ITS IRRITABLE IMPATIENCE IN LISTENING TO THE VOICE OF REASON. III. IN ITS IGNOMINIOUS TREATMENT OF RELIGIOUS TEACHERS. (*G. Barlow.*)

Vers. 12–15. **The locusts went up.**—*The plague of locusts; or, the residue of human comfort and enjoyment destroyed by the retribution of God:*—It has been observed that the plagues of Egypt, as they succeeded each other, were characterized with increasing severity. This one appears an exception to the rule. But only on first sight. The very name of locust was a terror to the Egyptians. They were an awful infliction (Joel i. 6–12). I. THAT SOMETIMES THE RETRIBUTIONS OF GOD LEAVE A RESIDUE OF COMFORT TO THE LIVES OF MEN. It is so in bereavement; if the wife is taken, the child is left. It is so in business; if the capital is lost, it may be the reputation is saved. It is so in personal attributes; if one sense grows dim, another remains yet more active. If the flax and barley are destroyed, the wheat and the rye are left. This is more than is deserved. It is merciful. But it is the kind way of heaven. II. THAT UPON CONTINUED SIN THE RESIDUE OF HUMAN COMFORT MAY BE ENTIRELY REMOVED BY THE RETRIBUTIVE ANGER OF GOD. III. THAT UPON CONTINUED SIN THE REMAINING COMFORTS OF MAN MAY BE DESTROYED BY THE CO-OPERATION OF PRIMARY AND SECONDARY CAUSES. "And the Lord brought an east wind upon the land all that day and all that night; and when it was morning, the east wind brought the locusts." The sceptic may say that the east wind alone brought the locusts upon his green things; but this is unreasonable and atheistical. Men in these days have too much Scripture knowledge to regard nature as the origin of their trouble. God commissions the wind that works desolation upon the hope of the wicked. (*J. S. Exell, M.A.*)

Vers. 16–19. **Intreat the Lord your God.**—*Lessons:*—1. God's hasty judgments may work hasty passions in sinners, though no repentance. 2. Vengeance may make persecutors call in God's servants for help as hastily as they drove them out. 3. Double confession of sin may hypocrites make under plagues, yet not in truth. 4. Proud persecutors may be forced to confess their guilt against men as well as against God (chap. v. 16). 5. Hypocritical oppressors may desire forgiveness of God's people under plagues, as if they would sin no more. 6. Wicked persecutors under judgment are earnest with God's servants to intercede earnestly for them.

7. It is only death which wicked sinners deprecate. 8. Hypocrites pretend upon deliverance from death, as if they would sin no more, or desire no more mercy (ver. 17). (G. Hughes, B.D.) A false repentance:—I. IT PROCEEDS FROM THE IMPULSE OF THE MOMENT, AND NOT FROM CONSCIENTIOUS CONVICTION. II. IT IS MARKED BY SELFISH TERROR, AND NOT BY A GODLY SORROW FOR SIN. III. IT CRAVES FORGIVENESS OF AN IMMEDIATE OFFENCE, RATHER THAN A THOROUGH CLEANSING OF THE HEART. IV. IT CONFIDES IN THE INTERCESSION OF A FELLOW-MORTAL, RATHER THAN IN THE PERSONAL HUMBLING OF THE SOUL BEFORE GOD. Christ is the only Mediator. V. IT REGARDS GOD MORE AS A TERRIBLE DEITY WHOSE WRATH IS TO BE APPEASED, THAN AS THE INFINITE FATHER WHOSE LOVE IS BETTER THAN LIFE. VI. IT EXPRESSES A PROMISE OF AMENDMENT WHICH IS FALSIFIED BY PREVIOUS DISSEMBLINGS. Lessons: 1. To be sure that our repentance is genuine. 2. To bring forth fruit meet for repentance in daily conduct. 3. Not to pass a hasty judgment on the repentance of men. Half the Revivalists of the day would have called Pharaoh a true convert; time tests conversion. (J. S. Exell, M.A.) Pharaoh's imperfect repentances:—Dear children, when any one confesses with sincerity, "I have sinned"; when he says this to God, and not merely to man, be sure that he is never rejected. But let us observe what was wanting in the repentance of Pharaoh. 1. Belief in God. He called Him the Lord your God. He spoke of Him as of a stranger. Now, it is impossible that any person or child can love the Lord until he feels himself reconciled to Him by faith, until he can call Him the Lord my God. 2. Pharaoh had humbled himself before men, rather than before God. 3. He besought the prayers of others, instead of praying for himself. 4. He asked the forgiveness of the servants of God, instead of seeking pardon from God Himself. If he had said, like David, "I acknowledge my sin unto the Lord," he might have added like him, "And Thou forgavest the iniquity of my sin." 5. Pharaoh did not concern himself about the salvation of his soul. He intreated, not that he might be delivered from sin, but only that "this death" should be taken away from him; he did not think of eternity, but only of the plague under which he was suffering. 6. Lastly, remark that the king still cherished secret designs in his heart; his submission was not unreserved. We have begun as it were to repent; but as long as we are not willing to renounce all, to follow Jesus, our repentance is of no avail. Pharaoh said, "Go ye, serve the Lord, only let your flocks and herds be stayed." His heart was not yet submissive, thus his repentance was vain. (Prof. Gaussen.)

Ver. 20. **The Lord hardened Pharaoh's heart.**—Pharaoh's will and God's:—I. The simplest and most patient study of that portion of the Book of Exodus which refers to the Egyptian plagues will lead us to this conclusion, that Moses is the witness for a Divine eternal law, and the witness against every kind of king-craft or priest-craft which breaks this law, or substitutes any devices of man's power or wit in place of it. Moses protested against the deceits and impostures of the magicians, precisely because he protested for the living and eternal Lord. It is a special token of honesty and veracity that Moses records the success of the magicians in several of their experiments. We might fairly have discredited the story as partial and unlikely, if there had been no such admission. Even the most flagrant chicanery is not always disappointed, and in nine cases out of ten, fact and fraud are curiously dovetailed into one another. If you will not do homage to the one, you will not detect the other. II. Do not the words, "God hardened Pharaoh's heart," distinctly describe God as the Author of something in man which is pronounced to be utterly wrong? Is He not said to have foreseen Pharaoh's sin, and not only to have foreseen, but to have produced it? The will of God was an altogether good will, and therefore Pharaoh's will—which was a bad will, a proud self-will—strove against it, and was lashed into fury by meeting with that which was contrary to itself. These words of Scripture are most necessary to us, for the purpose of making us understand the awful contradiction which there may be between the will of a man and the will of his Creator; how that contradiction may be aggravated by what seemed to be means for its cure, and how it may be cured. However hard our hearts may be, the Divine Spirit of grace and discipline can subdue even all things to Himself. (F. D. Maurice, M.A.) The hardening of Pharaoh's heart:—I. THE REALITY OF THE HUMAN WILL, and consequently of responsibility, IS ATTACHED ON DIFFERENT SIDES: HERE ON PHYSIOLOGICAL, AND THERE ON HISTORICAL GROUNDS. We are told that facts connected with the human will admit of exact calculation and prediction, according to what is termed the law of averages, and that consequently the doctrine of free-will, which was never capable of proof, must be displaced by a doctrine recognizing the certainty of human action. To this we answer : 1. The belief that man has the power to choose is so far from wanting proof, that it has all the force which universal consent can give it. 2. This average, which is supposed to rule the will like a rod of iron, is itself most variable. It yields under the hand like tempered clay. That which our will is now acting upon, which varies in different countries because the will of man has made different laws there, cannot be conclusive against the doctrine of free-will. II. THE WORDS OF THE TEXT ARE NOT WITHOUT THEIR WARNING. They mean that God, who punishes sin with death, sometimes punishes sin with sin. When man has repelled the voice of conscience, and the warning of his Bible, and the entreaties of friends, then grace is withdrawn from him, and sin puts on a judicial character, and is at once sin and punishment. (*Abp. Thomson.*)　　*The hardening of the heart :*—" The Lord hardened Pharaoh's heart " is a very remarkable and startling expression, and it is repeated in this history no fewer than ten times. It is startling, for it seems at first sight as if it ascribed the sin of that wicked man to Almighty God. But a little thought will show that it is very far from meaning this. 1. In other places the hardening is attributed to Pharaoh himself. God gives bad men a mysterious power to change their hearts and minds continually for the worse, by their own wicked ways ; so that in the end they cannot believe or repent. It is their own doing, because they bring it on themselves by their sin, and it is God's doing because it is the just punishment which His law has made the effect of their sin. 2. God knew beforehand that the heart of Pharaoh was such that not even miracles would overcome his obstinacy, and knowing this, He determined to deal with him in a manner which ought to have softened and amended him, but which, according to his perverse way of taking it, only hardened him more and more. 3. The taking off of God's hand, after each successive plague, had the effect of hardening Pharaoh's heart more completely. He repents of his own repentance, and wishes he had not given way so far to God's messengers. 4. Pharaoh, like other wicked kings, had no want of evil subjects to encourage him. He had magicians who counterfeited God's miracles, and servants who, on every occasion, were ready to harden their hearts with him. Such is Pharaoh's case ; beginning in heathenish ignorance, but forced by warning after warning to become aware of the truth. Every warning was a chance given him to soften his heart, but he went on hardening it, and so perished. (*Plain Sermons by Contributors to the " Tracts for the Times.*") *Hardening influence of sin :*—Look but upon a youth when he comes first to be an apprentice to some artificer, or handicraft trade, his hand is tender, and no sooner is he set to work but it blisters, so that he is much pained thereby ; but when he hath continued some time at work, then his hand hardens, and he goes on without any grievance at all. It is just thus with a sinner : before he be accustomed to an evil way, conscience is tender and full of remorse, like a queasy stomach, ready to kick at the least thing that is offensive. Oh, but a continued custom, and making a trade of sin, that's it that makes the conscience to be hard and brawny, able to feel nothing! As it is in a smith's forge, a dog that comes newly in, cannot endure the fiery sparks to fly about his ears ; but being once used to it, he sleeps securely ; so let wicked men be long used to the devil's workhouse, to be slaves and vassals to sin, the sparks of hell-fire may fly about them, and the fire of hell flash upon their souls, yet never trouble them, never disturb them at all; and all this ariseth from a continued custom in a course of evil. (*J. Spencer.*)

Vers. 21–23. **Darkness over the land of Egypt.**—*Lessons :*—1. God falls upon sinners without warning where they deal falsely with Him. 2. The same signal God may command for several uses. 3. God's word determines the end unto which all signals are appointed. 4. Men's hands lifted up to heaven God may make use of to bring evils on the earth. 5. It is God's word to make a kingdom the land of darkness. 6. Palpable darkness is a judgment of God's own making (ver. 21). (*G. Hughes, B.D.*)　　*Lessons :*—1. Obedience to God's signal commands must be given by His servants. 2. Signal obedience by God's ministers is not in vain. God giveth the effect. 3. Horrid darkness can God send upon souls darkened through sin. 4. Egyptian darkness is God's exemplary vengeance to the world. 5. The place and duration of darkness are at God's appointment (ver. 22). 6. Dismal darkness is that which takes from men the use of sense and motion. 7. Chains of darkness can God make to hold fast sinners in prison. 8. God executes His judgments on the world with discrimination to His people. 9. Egypt's darkness is

Israel's light (ver. 23). (*Ibid.*) *The plague of darkness ; or, a type of the sad moral condition of unregenerate humanity :*—I. THAT UNREGENERATE HUMANITY IS IN A CONDITION OF MORAL DARKNESS. 1. Ignorant—of God as Father, Christ as Saviour, Holy Ghost as Comforter, and glories of moral universe. 2. Miserable. Groping in darkness to an awful destiny of woe. 3. In danger. Under condemnation of Heaven. II. THAT UNREGENERATE HUMANITY IS IN MORAL DARKNESS THROUGH SIN. No light but from the Cross. III. THAT UNRENEWED HUMANITY IS IN GREAT STRAITS THROUGH, AND HAS NO ARTIFICIAL ALLEVIATION OF, ITS MORAL DARKNESS. 1. The moral vision of humanity is impeded. 2. The moral activity of humanity is suspended. Soul-darkness can only be removed by Christ. Lessons : 1. To seek to relieve the woe of those who sit in darkness and in the shadow of death. 2. To see the effect of sin. 3. To seek light from the Cross of Christ. (*J. S. Exell, M.A.*) *Light in the dwellings of the good :*—I. IN THE DWELLINGS OF THE GOOD THERE IS THE LIGHT OF REVEALED TRUTH. II. IN THE DWELLINGS OF THE GOOD THERE IS THE LIGHT OF PROVIDENTIAL GUIDANCE. III. IN THE DWELLINGS OF THE GOOD THERE IS THE LIGHT OF MORAL CHARACTER. (*Ibid.*) *Home light :*—The true Israel shall have light in their dwellings. Light in the heart brings light in the home. I. THERE IS SUPERNATURAL LIGHT IN THE DWELLINGS OF GOD'S PEOPLE. There is a light brighter than the light of the sun. God's people dwell in it. The light of the glory of God has shone in upon them. No creations of worldly wisdom, wealth, or philosophy can give this heavenly light. II. THAT THIS LIGHT IS THE SOURCE OF MANIFOLD BLESSINGS. Comfort under trial; strength in weakness; peace in disquietude; lessons of resignation, patience, and fortitude: sanctification of affliction; sympathy with the suffering members of the household; preservation in calamitous times; sustaining trust in God under perplexing circumstances; hope of eternal felicity. III. THAT THIS LIGHT IS A FOREGLEAMING OF THAT GLORY WHICH WILL BE ENJOYED BY GOD'S PEOPLE FOR EVER. God's love in Christ is the light of every true Israelite's dwelling on earth, and that is the light of heaven. Christian homes ought to be " spangles of celestial brightness on this darksome earth." The light here is sometimes dimmed. Heaven is its native sphere. It suffers there no eclipse. Our vision too will be clearer. (*Ibid.*) *Light and darkness; or, the Church and the world :*—I. EGYPT IN ITS DARKNESS WAS A TYPE OF THE WORLD. It was so also in other particulars. In its tyrannical dominion by the despotical Pharaoh;—in its diversified idolatry ; but particularly in the darkness which enshrouded it. 1. Darkness is an emblem of ignorance and error, and the world is involved in these. 2. Darkness is an emblem of guilt, and the world is involved in this. 3. Darkness is an emblem of peril, and in this the world is involved. It is to be the scene of the Divine vengeance. It is to be renovated by fire (2 Pet. iii. 10). 4. Darkness is the emblem of misery, and in this the world is involved. Now the misery of the men of the world arises from three things. (1) From the accusations of guilt, the cause of their condemnation. (2) From the unsatisfying nature of their portion. They want happiness, but cannot find it. (3) Their gloomy fears as to the future. II. THE ISRAELITES WITH LIGHT IN THEIR DWELLINGS WERE A TYPE OF THE CHURCH. 1. They have the light of saving knowledge. 2. They have the light of the Divine approbation. 3. They have the light of holiness. In applying this subject we behold the contrast between those who are of the world and the people of God, in several conditions of life. (1) See them in adversity. The wicked have an addition of darkness. No solace,—no ray to cheer them ; hence how often they sink into despair and rush into eternity. The Christian feels, but he recognizes God's hand. (2) See them in sickness. No light. Painful, restless, and an overwhelming anxiety, The sick chamber is as dark as Egypt. But the righteous have light in their dwellings. The serene countenance, the pious resignation, the cheering hope, show the difference. (3) See them in death. With the wicked it is a leap in the dark. But the righteous have light in death—often the celestial beams of glory. (*J. Burns, D.D.*) *The plague of darkness :*— Darkness may have been produced by a deprivation of sight. The sun may have risen and set as usual upon the land, yet the eyes of all the Egyptians being closed and blinded, no ray of light could reach them ; this, if it were attended with pain in the organs of vision, might be properly described as " darkness to be felt." The men of Sodom were stricken with blindness for their sin. The great host which came to take Elisha were smitten with blindness. Moses, in Deuteronomy, where he threatens the people with the botch of Egypt, reminding them of the plague of boils and blains, says immediately afterwards, alluding, probably, to this plague, " The Lord shall smite thee with blindness and thou shalt grope at noonday as the blind gropeth in darkness" (Deut. xxviii. 27–29). Blindness was the punishment inflicted upon Elymas the sorcerer; and these Egyptians were famous for their sorceries. The darkness may therefore have been of this kind, a painful but temporary loss of eyesight. Darkness, such as is here described, may have been occasioned by a thick cloud resting upon the earth, and pervading all the lower regions of the atmosphere: this would enfold the people so as " to be felt," and would intercept the sun's rays effectually by its density. God is often described as manifesting His displeasure in a cloud. Joel speaks of the day of God's vengeance as " a day of darkness and of gloominess, a day of clouds and of thick darkness" (Joel ii. 2) ; and Zephaniah employs nearly the same language (Zeph. i. 15). The pillar that went before the Israelites, and gave them light, was to the Egyptians " a cloud and darkness" (chap. xiv. 20). Such a cloud would be even more terrible in Egypt, sunny Egypt, than in other countries; for there, as we have already seen, the sky is almost always clear, and heavy rains unknown. But in any place, and under any conditions, it must have been full of horror and misery. Nothing could represent this more forcibly than the short sentence, "Neither rose any from his place for three days." It was an horror of great darkness; it rested on them like a pall; they knew not what dangers might be around them, what judgment was next to happen. If there be any truth in the traditions of the Jews on this subject, there were yet greater alarms under this canopy of darkness, this palpable obscurity, than any which would naturally arise out of the physical infliction. Darkness is a type of Satan's kingdom; and Satan had some liberty in Egypt to walk up and down upon the land, and to go to and fro in it. The Jewish Rabbis tell us that the devil and his angels were let loose during these three dreadful days ; that they had a wider range and greater liberty than usual for working mischief. They describe these evil spirits going among the wretched people, glued to their seats as they were with terror ; frightening them with fearful apparitions; piercing their ears with hideous shrieks and groans; driving them almost to madness with the intensity of their fears ; making their flesh creep, and the hair of their head to stand on end. Such a climax seems to be referred to by the Psalmist, " He cast upon them the fierceness of His anger, wrath, and indignation and trouble, by sending evil angels among them " (Psa. lxxviii. 49). The sun was, during the continuance of the plague of darkness, blotted out from the Egyptian sky : either their chief God had forsaken them, and turned against his vicegerent upon earth, or the God of Moses had prevailed against them both. In the intensity of their darkness, unrelieved by any artificial light, the people would bethink themselves of the brilliant illumination they had been in the habit of making in honour of their god, as described by Herodotus, " At the sacrifice solemnized at Sais the assembly is held by night : they suspend before their houses in the open air lamps, which are filled with oil mixed with salt : a wick floats on the top, which will burn all night : the feast is called the feast of lamps. Such of the Egyptians as do not attend the ceremony burn lamps in like manner before their houses, so that on this night, not Sais only, but all Egypt is illuminated. A religious motive is assigned for the festival itself, and for the illumination by which it is distinguished " (Herod. ii. 62). Night, being supposed to divide the empire of the heavens with day, received also its share of Divine honours. Darkness existed before light; and therefore darkness was revered as the most ancient of all deities. Among the verses usually ascribed to Orpheus is a hymn addressed to Night, beginning—" Night, parent of gods and men ! " (Hymn. ad Noct. v. 1.) Plutarch says —" The Egyptians reverence the blind mouse, because they consider darkness to be more ancient than light" (Sympos. l. 4. qu. 5). Thus, again, the vanity of the religious practices of Egypt was plainly shown. Where were now their gods ? Let them pray to the sun ; let them intreat their lord and king Osiris ; he would not look on them, nor give them one ray of his comfort. Let them implore the darkness ; it would not listen to them, nor depart from them. The Israelites, on the contrary, who had never, as a nation, bowed the knee to these creatures, nor had been attracted by their glory to give them the homage due to God alone, were filled with light and warmth. The Lord of heaven and earth sent down his blessing upon their houses, singling them out wherever they might be, and made even the darkness to be light about them. And now, perhaps, they would better understand the worth and excellency of that daily gift of God which men enjoy too generally without much thought of Him whose word created and whose mercy sends it. Looking upon the walls of blackness which were drawn around the houses of the Egyptians, they would learn to prize the glorious light and sunshine which still prevailed in all their dwellings : they would compare their own condition, even as slaves and bondsmen, with the misery of those who had their habitations in the fairest palaces of Egypt—fair no longer now, but dark and desolate; and so they would doubtless look upward with gratitude to their almighty God, and confess the security and happiness of those who trust in Him. (*T. S. Millington.*) *Light in darkness :*—" The happiest child I ever saw," said Bishop Ryle, " was a little girl whom I once met travelling in a railway carriage. She was eight years old, and she was quite blind. She had never been able to see at all. She had never seen the sun, and the stars, and the sky, and the grass, and the flowers, and the trees, and the birds, and all those pleasant things which we see every day of our lives; but still she was quite happy. She was by herself, poor little thing. She had no friends or relations to take care of her, but she was quite happy and con-tent. She said, when she got into the carriage: ' Tell me how many people there are in the carriage, for I am quite blind, and can see nothing.' A gentleman asked her if she was not afraid. ' No,' she said; 'I have travelled before, and I trust in God, and people are always very good to me.' But I soon found out the reason why she was so happy. She loved Jesus Christ, and Jesus Christ loved her; she had sought Jesus Christ, and she had found Him." *Darkness a cause of terror :*— Arago mentions that in the eclipse of 1842, at Perpignan, a dog which was kept from food for twenty-four hours was thrown some bread just before the " totality " of the eclipse began. The dog seized the loaf, begun to devour it ravenously, and then, as the darkness came on, dropped it. Not until the sun burst forth again did the poor creature return to its food. A party of courtiers of Louis XV., too, were once gathered around Cassini to witness an eclipse from the terrace of the Paris observatory, and were laughing at the populace, whose cries were heard as the light began to fade, when, as the unnatural gloom came quickly on, silence fell on them too, the panic terror striking through their laughter. (*H. O. Mackey.*) *Light in darkness :*—God couldn't arrange it more beautiful," said a poor old blind man, as he sat in the chimney-corner of his cottage. " Arrange what ? " said the visitor. " Why, I'm as blind as a mole, but I can hear well; and my old woman there," pointing to his wife in the other corner, " is as deaf as a post, but she can see well. Could God Almighty a' done it better? " This blind, bright saint could certainly see beauty in God's arrangements where it never would have been suspected by on-lookers. It need hardly be said that sightless J. revels in the light where mere sight-seers would grumble at the darkness. His natural blindness seems to have given a quick, keen perception of his spiritual sight. " No walls around me now," he says; " I'm never hemmed in. It's all brightness. Bless'e, I'd ten times sooner be as I be, than have my sight, and not see my Saviour ! " He is—speaking after the manner of men—at poverty's door, yet he has luxurious faith; and, in truth, his bare home is hard by the jewelled walls of the pearly-gated city. Listen to his thankful, contented talk: " They allows the old woman and me two shillings and ninepence, and two loaves, and we can manage on that; and what more do we want ? " (*Sword and Trowel.*)

Vers. 24–26. **Thou must give us also sacrifices.**—*Lessons :*—1. God's instruments of redemption seek not only liberty of persons, but of means, to serve Him. 2. Due worship and true sacrifice to God are the scope of all God's redeemed (ver. 25). 3. God's ministers must be resolute for all, and not bate a jot of what God requires. Not a hoof. 4. All the exactions of God's instruments must be aimed at God's service truly. 5. God's servants know not themselves, but depend upon His dis-covery for what they must offer to Him (ver. 26). (*G. Hughes, B.D.*) *The reluctance with which men yield a complete obedience to the imperative claims of God :*—I. The FACT OF THIS RELUCTANCE ON THE PART OF MAN TO YIELD COMPLETE OBEDIENCE TO THE CLAIMS OF GOD. 1. This reluctance is seen in the judgments that are sent to over-come it. 2. This reluctance is seen in the mercy that is despised. 3. This reluc-tance is seen in the faithful ministries that are rejected. 4. That men resist these judgments, &c., is complete evidence of their great reluctance to surrender all for Him. (1) This reluctance is a matter of revelation. (2) This reluctance is a matter of history. (3) This reluctance is a matter of experience. II. The REASONS OF THIS RELUCTANCE ON THE PART OF MAN TO YIELD COMPLETE OBEDIENCE TO THE CLAIMS OF GOD. These reasons are obvious. 1. Depravity of nature. 2. Pride of heart. 3. Selfishness of motive. 4. Obstinacy of will. III. The FOLLY OF THIS RELUC-TANCE ON THE PART OF MAN TO YIELD COMPLETE OBEDIENCE TO THE CLAIMS OF GOD. 1. Because it provokes painful judgments. 2. Because it is useless to contend with God. 3. Because final overthrow is its certain outcome. Lessons: 1. That man will consent to any terms rather than yield a complete submission to the will of God. 2. That God will only be satisfied by an entire surrender to His will. (*J. S. Exell, M.A.*) *The way in which men endeavour to compromise the service of God :—* I. THAT MEN ENDEAVOUR TO COMPROMISE THE SERVICE OF GOD BY NOMINAL ALLEGIANCE. II. THAT MEN ENDEAVOUR TO COMPROMISE THE SERVICE OF GOD BY AN OCCASIONAL PERFORMANCE OF DUTY. III. THAT MEN ENDEAVOUR TO COMPROMISE THE SERVICE OF GOD BY A PUBLIC PROFESSION OF IT ACCOMPANIED WITH PRIVATE RESERVATIONS. IV. THAT MEN ENDEAVOUR TO COMPROMISE THE SERVICE OF GOD BY EXCLUDING IT FROM THEIR WORLDLY PURSUITS. Lessons : 1. That men must not compromise the service of God. 2. That ministers must warn men against compromising the service of God. (*Ibid.*) *The picture of an unregenerate soul :—*I. IT IS OPPOSED TO THE SERVICE OF GOD. II. IT IS LOATH TO PART WITH ITS EVIL POSSESSIONS. III. IT IS SLOW TO HEED THE VOICE OF THE SERVANTS OF TRUTH. (*Ibid.*) *Compromise; or, wealth left behind in Egypt :—*" Only let your flocks and herds be stayed." How many souls are caught in this snare ! They have left their business, their work, their worldly interests, down in Egypt. They cannot be " very far away " in such case, for they must needs go down to Egypt to attend to their possessions. " Lay not up for yourselves treasures upon earth "; " Make not provision for the flesh, to fulfil the lusts thereof " (Matt. iv. 9; Rom. xiii. 14). These are words that need to be considered in connection with this last snare of Satan. I think when Satan sees a Christian go out of Egypt with all his flocks and herds, he has no hope of getting him back again. So he makes a last stand here : " Keep your business and your religion separate. Give yourself to God; but do not consecrate your property." Now, will you just take a look at the state of the Christian world to-day. Look at the wealth of Christians in London, and in New York, and over the whole world. How they have piled it up—thousands upon thousands, heaps upon heaps ! And where is it? Surely in Egypt. It is not held in sacred stewardship for the Lord. It is used for the most part to gratify " the lust of the flesh," " the lust of the eye," and " the pride of life." Look, I pray, at the magnificence of the residences, the costliness of the furniture, and the expensiveness and luxury of the equipage. Go into the houses of the wealthy Egyptian Christians, and behold the splendour and costliness of their entertainments ! See the crowds of Egyptians gathered there to enjoy the feasts and pleasures that are provided by God's people with the proceeds of the flocks and herds that should be used in His service. Again, look at the condition of the Lord's work the world over. Consider the fewness of the number of missionaries who are abroad ! Note how from every direction the cry comes up for help ! There are men and women who are waiting to give themselves to the work—to forsake home and country, and go to the darkest spots of heathendom ; but there are not the men and the women who are ready to spare from their hoards the money to send and support them. If the flocks and herds were out of Egypt, and really given over to the Lord to be used in His service, the world could and would be evangelized in less than five years. (*G. F. Pentecost, D.D.*) **Not an hoof be left behind.**—*Full redemption :*—Now, it seems to me, that this grand quarrel of old is but a picture of God's continual contest with the powers of darkness. Evil is hard in dying ; it will not readily be overcome. But this is the demand of God, and to the last will He have it. " All My people "; the whole of, every one of them, and all that My people have possessed, all shall come out of the land of Egypt. Christ will have the whole ; He will not be contented with a part, and this He vows to accomplish. " Not an hoof shall be left behind." I. First, then, Christ will have THE WHOLE MAN. In His people whom He has purchased with His blood He will reign without a rival. No sin is to be spared ; no service shunned ; no power unconsecrated. II. This is equally true of THE WHOLE CHURCH as of the whole man—" Not an hoof shall be left behind." When I come to the matter of redemption it seems to me that whatever Christ's design was in dying, that design cannot be frustrated, nor by any means disappointed. All that His heavenly Father gave Him shall come to Him. III. Jesus Christ will not only have all of a man, and all the men He bought, but He will have AIL THAT EVER BELONGED TO ALL THESE MEN. That is to say, all that Adam lost Christ will win back, and that without the diminution of a single jot or tittle. Not an inch of Paradise shall be given up, nor even a handful of its dust resigned. Christ will have all, or else He will have none. IV. CHRIST WILL HAVE THE WHOLE EARTH. (*C. H. Spurgeon.*) *All or none; or, compromise refused :*—This was the Divine policy of " No surrender," and I plead for it with you. Satan says, " Do not use your property for God. Do not use your talents and your abilities ; especially do not use your money for the Lord Jesus. Keep that for yourself. You will want it one of these days, perhaps. Keep it for your own enjoyment. Live to God in other things, but, as to that, live to yourself." Now, a genuine Christian says, "When I gave myself to the Lord I gave Him everything I had. From the crown of my head to the soul of my foot I am the Lord's. He bids me provide things honest in the sight of all men, and care for my household; and so I shall; but yet I am not my own, for I am bought with a price; and therefore it becomes me to feel that everything I have, or ever shall have, is a dedicated thing, and belongs unto the Lord, that I may use it as His steward, not as if it were mine, but at His discretion and at His bidding. I cannot leave my substance to be the devil's. That must come with me, and must be all my Lord's, for His it is even as I am." (*Ibid.*) *Every hoof to be brought out:*—God's will is that we should be completely set free. This will be accomplished. Repeated conflicts first. I. THE TRUTH SUGGESTED THAT OUR DELIVERANCE WILL BE COMPLETE. 1. Our natures will be entirely freed from the thraldom of sin. Every power of body, mind, and soul will ultimately escape from the dominion of evil. 2. Our families shall be saved. 3. The whole Church shall be saved. II. THE ENCOURAGEMENT THAT MAY BE DERIVED FROM THIS TRUTH. We need encouragement. The bondage is often bitter, and hope fails. The enslavers powerful and the chains strong. But a deliverance, complete, triumphant, and eternal, is sure. This ought to lead us— 1. To live in the expectation of perfect freedom from all evil. 2. To continue to strive, believe, and pray for it. 3. To pray and labour zealously for the salvation of our families. 4. To sympathize with and aid the weak and lowly in the Church. (*W. O. Lilley.*) **We know not with what we must serve the Lord until we come thither.**—*Going forth to serve God:*—I. SOME THINGS ARE UNCERTAIN IN THE FUTURE. 1. The continuance of our life on earth. 2. The new circumstances in which we shall be placed. 3. The particular duties which will be required of us. II. SOME THINGS ARE CERTAIN IN THE FUTURE. 1. The obligation of service. 2. Special opportunities of service. 3. Adequate directions for services. III. SOME THINGS ARE NECESSARY FOR THE FUTURE. 1. Diligent preparation of heart. 2. Humble dependence on God. 3. Hopeful anticipation of better things to come. (*B. Dale, M.A.*) *The Lord's stewards:*—I. The teaching is that NOT A PART, BUT THE WHOLE, OF OUR POSSESSIONS MUST GO OUT OF EGYPT WITH US. "There shall not an hoof be left behind." Is that so with you? Are you conscious that all your possessions are solemnly consecrated to the Lord, withdrawn from all Egyptian unrighteousness and sinful self-indulgence? Or are you using your wealth as any other worldly man might use it? II. Notice, THAT IT IS MORE THAN TAKING WEALTH ON TO RELIGIOUS GROUND. Is is distinctly taking it out for the purpose of serving the Lord. Not that the Lord is to have a portion; but that it is all held at His call, for, says Moses, "We know not with what we must serve the Lord." It may be that He will want few, it may be that He will want many sacrifices. We must hold all subject to His call. This is a high standard to hold up before us; but it is without question the true one. I do not believe God grudges to His children any comfort which may be had out of wealth honestly and righteously won from the world; but without doubt the Lord does insist that the necessities of His service must first be met, before we can indulge ourselves. How far we must allow ourselves to go in self-provision is a question that can be easily settled by the man or woman who is honestly out-and-out—spirit, soul, body, and property— for the Lord. (*G. F. Pentecost, D.D.*)

Vers. 28, 29. **I will see thy face no more.**—*Pharaoh and Moses; or, contrasted characters:*—I. IN THIS WORLD OFTEN THE WORST OF MEN COME IN CONTACT WITH THE BEST OF MEN. 1. Pharaoh, an idolater, the greatest of tyrants, a signal monument of God's displeasure; Moses, a true worshipper of the true and living God, the meekest of men, an object of God's highest favour. 2. Such opposite characters as these come in contact in families, in schools, in political and social circles. II. IT IS POSSIBLE THAT THE WORST OF MEN MAY COME IN CONTACT WITH THE BEST WITHOUT BEING AT ALL BENEFITED. 1. Think of the noble example which Moses set before Pharaoh. (1) Disinterestedness. (2) Meekness. (3) Holiness. 2. Think of the important truths which Moses taught Pharaoh. (1) The existence of one true God alone. (2) That this world is under God's control. (3) That Pharaoh was accountable to God. (4) That God was ready to forgive those who had rebelled against Him. III. WHEN THE WORST OF MEN COME IN CONTACT WITH THE BEST WITHOUT BEING BENEFITED THE PARTING IS DEEPLY AFFECTING. (*J. G. Roberts.*)

The intercourse of life:—I. THAT GOOD MEN ARE OFTEN BROUGHT INTO CONTACT WITH BAD MEN. 1. Irrespective of moral character. 2. Irrespective of mental temperament. 3. Irrespective of social position. And why? 1. That men may be imbued with the ideas of a common manhood. 2. That class prejudices may be destroyed. 3. That charity may be developed. 4. That life may become a unity. II. THAT WHEN GOOD MEN ARE BROUGHT INTO CONTACT WITH BAD MEN THE MEETING SHOULD BE EDUCATIONAL TO BOTH. 1. The companionship of the good should be influential to the moral improvement of the bad. 2. The companionship of the bad should inspire the good with feelings of gratitude and humility. Good men might have been far otherwise. III. THAT WHEN GOOD MEN ARE BROUGHT INTO CONTACT WITH BAD MEN THE MEETING IS NOT ALWAYS VALUED AS IT OUGHT TO BE, AND ITS OPPORTUNITY FOR GOOD IS OFTEN UNIMPROVED. Lessons: 1. That a good life is a heavenly ministry. 2. That good men should seek to influence the bad aright. 3. That good men may learn lessons from wicked lines. (*J. S. Exell, M.A.*) *The way in which hardened sinners treat the messengers of God:*—1. With contempt. 2. With threatenings of evil. 3. With banishment. (*Ibid.*) *The way in which messengers of God treat hardened sinners:*—1. They scorn their taunts. 2. They impart to the language of the wicked a deeper significance than was intended. 3. They are courageous. 4. They bid them a sad farewell. (*Ibid.*) *Persistent obstinacy:*—The obstinacy of Pharaoh appears odious to us; but, alas! the same obstinacy is found in all sinners. It is seldom we meet with those who openly say, "I will not be converted, I will do nothing for God, I mock Him, I brave Him, I defy Him." They do not use language such as this, but yet they cherish some secret sin. Among the wicked boys who are unfortunately to be found in most large towns, you will scarcely meet one, even let him perhaps be a thief, who would not say, "I do not wish to die an enemy of God"; but, then, in the meantime he cherishes his sin. What is still more sad, we sometimes hear even serious persons say, "I wish to do the will of God, but cannot cure myself of this fault; it is stronger than I. I do not wish to lose my soul, I wish to obey the commands of God; but I cannot give up the society which is called bad, I cannot give up such and such a habit which I am told is a sinful one, I cannot make those sacrifices which I am told are necessary; I will not do it." And it is thus that people trifle with eternity! Let us take heed; we must give ourselves to God—wholly and without reserve. He will have no divided service. (*Prof. Gaussen.*) *Moses' reply to Pharaoh:*—Remark the solemn and terrible reply of Moses, "Thou hast spoken well, I will see thy face again no more." To understand the meaning of this answer we must remark that it does not finish with this verse, but that it has a continuation in the succeeding chapter. It contains a terrible threat to those who despise and reject the word of God. This was to be the last time that Pharaoh should hear the voice of the man of God, who had so often warned him and prayed for him. For him no more time was to be given. It was finished; the measure of his iniquities was filled up; the wrath of God was to come upon him to the uttermost. "Then Moses went out from Pharaoh in great anger." There is such a thing as holy anger, for the Bible says, "Be ye angry, and sin not; let not the sun go down upon your wrath." Our Lord Himself was indignant with the buyers and sellers in the Temple. And He was "much displeased" with His disciples when they rebuked those who brought young children to Him. He looked round about with anger on those who wished to hinder Him from curing a man on the Sabbath day. The anger of Moses was caused by the obstinacy and ingratitude of Pharaoh, and by the insulting manner in which he braved his Creator and his Judge. The meaning of his terrible reply was this, "Thou hast rejected the word of God; the word of God rejects thee. Thou dost not choose any more to see the face of the servant of the Lord, who has come ten times to warn thee in His name. Well, thou shalt see his face no more. The word of God has been brought to thee, but the word of God will leave thee. The grace of God has been offered thee; thou hast despised it, therefore now will the grace of God leave thee. Thou hast chosen to ruin thyself, therefore thou wilt ruin thyself." How terrible is this! We must all die. Death is very formidable: it is very sad and solemn when we mourn for others; but there is a remedy for this sorrow in a loving Saviour, and in the knowledge that there is a home where all the children of God shall meet each other again. What is really much more terrible than death is this sentence, "Thou shalt see My face no more." (*Ibid.*)

CHAPTER XI.

VER. 1. **One plague more.**—*One more plague :*—I. HEAVEN WILL TERRIBLY PLAGUE THE SINNER. And the one plague more to come upon the impenitent sinner will be awful, it will be just; it will be the natural outcome of a wicked life, and will be inflicted by God. II. IT SHOWS THAT HEAVEN HAS A GREAT RESOURCE OF PLAGUES WITH WHICH TO TORMENT THE SINNER. The material universe, in its every realm, is the resource of heaven for the plaguing of men. Men ask how God can punish the sinner in the world to come. He will not be at a loss for one plague more whereby to torment the finally impenitent. How foolish of man to provoke the anger of God! III. IT SHOWS THAT HEAVEN GIVES AMPLE WARNING OF THE PLAGUES IT WILL INFLICT UPON THE SINNER. Men do not walk ignorantly to hell. IV. IT SHOWS THAT HEAVEN HAS A MERCIFUL INTENTION EVEN IN THE INFLICTION OF ITS PLAGUES. It designed the moral submission of Pharaoh by the threatened plague, and also the freedom of Israel. And so God plagues men that He may save them, and those whom they hold in the dire bondage of moral evil. (*J. S. Exell, M.A.*)   *One effort more :*—The old astronomer with his trusty glass is searching the heavens for a star, "a lost star," he says. "It ought to be there!" he murmers, looking along the jewelled lines of some constellation. Not finding his diamond, he shakes his head, and is about to give up the search. "Just one trial more!" he murmers. He directs his glass towards the sky, and lo, there it is! Out of the dark depths of space flashes the pure, bright face of the lost star. "Found!" he cries. "It was one effort more that did it." Yes, it is true in nature and in the world of grace that it is the one effort more that often restores to its orbit the lost star. It was the one more reaching out of the world of Christian sympathy that by a friendly tap and a kindly word arrested a drunkard and gave to temperance a star orator, Gough. A Sunday-school teacher touches on the shoulder and kindly asks a young man about his soul, and this one effort more of the Church of God brought Dwight L. Moody to the Saviour. *God uses varied instruments :*—One day, seeing some men in a field, I made my way to them, and found they were cutting up the trunk of an old tree. I said, "That is slow work ; why do you not split it asunder with the beetle and wedges"? "Ah, this wood is so cross-grained and stubborn that it requires something sharper than wedges to get it to pieces." "Yes," I replied ; "and that is the way God is obliged to deal with obstinate, cross-grained sinners ; if they will not yield to one of His instruments, you may depend on it He will make use of another." (*G. Grigg.*)

Vers. 4–10. **All the firstborn in the land of Egypt shall die.**—*The last plague threatened :*—It was to be.—I. SOLEMN in its advent. "About midnight." II. FATAL in its issue. "All the firstborn . . . shall die." III. COMPREHENSIVE in its design. "From the firstborn of Pharaoh," &c. IV. HEARTRENDING in its cry. "None like it." V. DISCRIMINATING in its infliction. "The Lord doth put a difference," &c. Piety is the best protection against woe. (*J. S. Exell, M.A.*) *A contrast :*—1. The wicked crying—the good quiet. 2. The wicked dead—the good living. 3. The wicked frightened—the good peaceful. 4. The wicked helpless—the good protected. (*Ibid.*) *Separating the precious from the vile :*—I. THE DIFFERENCE. 1 Eternal. 2. Most ancient. Ordained of God from before foundation of world. 3. Vital. An essential distinction of nature between righteous and wicked. 4. This difference in nature is followed by a difference in God's judicial treatment of the two classes. 5. This distinction is carried out in providence. To the righteous man every providence is a blessing. To the sinner all things work together for evil. 6. This difference will come out more distinctly on the judgment day. II. WHERE IS THIS DIFFERENCE SEEN? 1. In the Temple. 2. In the whole life. 3. In time of temptation. 4. In the hour of death. III. WHY SHOULD THIS DIFFERENCE BE SEEN? Put your finger on any prosperous page in the Church's history, and I will find a little marginal note reading thus : "In this age men could readily see where the Church began and where the world ended." Never were there good times when the Church and the world were joined in marriage with one another. But though this were sufficient argument for keeping the Church and the world distinct, there are many others. The more the Church is distinct from the world in her acts and in her maxims, the more true is her testimony for Christ, and the more potent is her witness against sin. We are sent into this world to testify against evils ; but if we dabble in them ourselves, where is our testimony? If we ourselves be found faulty, we are false witnesses ; we are not sent of God ; our testimony is of none effect. (*C. H. Spurgeon.*)

The Church and the world :—Originally there was "no difference" between the Egyptians and Israel; both were descended from one source, both were tainted with sin. So too, originally, there was no difference between the Church and the world. St. Paul enforces this (1) as between Jew and Gentile (Rom. x. 12); (2) as between individual members of the human family (Rom. iii 22). Consider—I. THE NATURE OF THE DIFFERENCE. There can be no doubt but there was a difference—that the Lord " put " one—between the Egyptians and Israel, and " that the Lord doth put " one between the world and the Church. What is this difference? God's choice. He chose Israel, He did not choose the Egyptians; He has chosen the Church, He has not chosen the world. Herein lies the " difference "; and because it is not a visible or even, in itself, a demonstrable one, the world now, as the Egyptians then, decline to believe in it, and a sign becomes in some sense necessary. II. THE REASON FOR THE DIFFERENCE. Not merit on Israel's part, or sin on Egypt's part; but—1. God's love for Israel's fathers (Deut. iv. 37). 2. God's oath (based upon God's love) to Israel's fathers (Deut. vii. 7, 8). So the Church was chosen because God loved her; though why God loved her, or how He loved her, in a certain sense we cannot tell. III. THE SIGN OF THE DIFFERENCE. As said above, Pharaoh declined to believe in the difference, or, whilst tacitly acknowledging it, refused to act in accordance with it. A sign was given, in order that he might "know how that the Lord doth put a difference between the Egyptians and Israel." That sign consisted in the triumphant exodus of Israel without casualty of any kind, as contrasted with the family distress and national disaster which were about to happen to the Egyptians. Observe that the deliverance was a sign of the difference, not the difference itself. So salvation, in the ordinary but very partial sense of deliverance from future punishment, will be but a " sign " and a consequence of the choice which God has already made, of the " difference " which the Lord has already " put"; a choice and a " difference " about the existence of which the world is sceptical, but the reality of which all will be forced to acknowledge when the sign is given. (*E. Armstrong Hall, M.A.*) *The importance of the firstborn :*—The importance of the firstborn may be thus explained: the firstborn naturally enjoyed both precedence and pre-eminence over the rest, he was the firstling of his father's strength (Gen. xlix. 3), the first-fruit of his mother. As the firstborn, he stood at the head of the others, and was destined to be the chief of whatever family might be formed by the succeeding births. As he stood at the head of the whole he represented the entire nation of the Egyptians. Hence the power which slew all the firstborn in Egypt was exhibited as a power which could slay all that were born then, and, in the slaughter of the whole of the firstborn, the entire body of the people were ideally slain. (*J. H. Kurtz, D.D.*) *The Church and the world :*—I. THE NATURE OF THE DIFFERENCE. 1. Not a difference of understanding. 2. Not a difference of physical development. 3. Not even a difference in moral nature. The Israelites were quite as prone to evil, lust, sin, idolatry, as the Egyptians. 4. The difference was that God chose Israel to be His people, He took them for His own, hedged them by special regulations, laws, discipline. So He has chosen the Church. II. THE REASONS FOR THE DIFFERENCE. 1. That God might have a faithful people even in this world of sin. 2. That Christ might not die in vain. 3. That God might fulfil His promise to the patriarchs. III. THE SIGN OF THE DIFFERENCE. Deliverance from the sin and bondage of the world. (*Homilist.*) **Get thee out, and all the people that follow thee.** *A people's efforts for freedom successful :*—We learn from Professor Bischoff that the steam of a hot spring at Aix-la-Chapelle, although its temperature is only from 133° to 167° F., has converted the surface of some blocks of black marble into a doughy mass. He conceives, therefore, that steam in the bowels of the earth, having a temperature equal to or even greater than the melting point of lava, and, having an elasticity of which even Papin's digester can give but a faint idea, may convert rocks into liquid matter. These wonderful facts might suggest useful thoughts to the despots of the world. Despotism interdicts the expression of political convictions, and seeks to bury them under the adamantean weight of oppressive decrees and colossal cruelty. But it is an unerring moral law that the warm aspirations of a virtuous people shall —like the subtle subterranean gases—arise to freedom, and, despite all impediments, dissolve in due time even the hard and hoary foundations of injustice. (*Scientific Illustrations.*)

CHAPTER XII.

VERS. 1, 2. **The beginning of months.**—*A new start :*—I. The idea of a new start is NATURALLY ATTRACTIVE TO ALL OF US. We are fatigued, we are dissatisfied, and justly so, with the time past of our lives. We long for a gift of amnesty and oblivion. II. THERE ARE SENSES IN WHICH THIS IS IMPOSSIBLE. The continuity of life cannot be broken. There is a continuity, a unity, an identity, which annihilation only could destroy. III. " The beginning of months" is made so by an exodus. REDEMPTION IS THE GROUNDWORK OF THE NEW LIFE. If there is in any of us a real desire for change, we must plant our feet firmly on redemption. IV. When we get out of Egypt, we must remember THAT THERE IS STILL SINAI IN FRONT, WITH ITS THUNDERINGS AND VOICES. We have to be schooled by processes not joyous but grievous. These processes cannot be hurried, they must take time. Here we must expect everything that is changeful, and unresting, and unreposeful, within as without. But He who has promised will perform. He who has redeemed will save. He who took charge will also bring through. (*Dean Vaughan.*)   *The first month of the year :*—I. THE FIRST MONTH OF THE YEAR IS A GOOD TIME FOR RELIGIOUS CONTEMPLATION AND DEVOTION. Then the flight of time, the events of life, and the mortality of man, may all furnish topics for reflection. Then especially should the Passover be celebrated, the blood of Christ anew be sprinkled on the soul; and in this spirit of trust in the Saviour should the year begin. II. THE FIRST MONTH OF THE YEAR IS EVENTFUL IN THE HISTORY OF INDIVIDUAL AND COLLECTIVE LIFE. How many souls, awakened by the circumstances of life, have been led to the Cross at this solemn period? What we are then, we are likely to remain throughout the year; we then get an impulse for good or evil which will affect our moral character to the end. The first month is the keynote of the year's moral life. It is the rough sketch of the soul's life for the year. We should therefore seek to observe it unto the Lord. III. THE FIRST MONTH OF THE YEAR IS IMPORTANT IN ITS RELATION TO THE COMMERCIAL PROSPECTS OF MEN. The new year may mark the advent of new energy, or it may witness the continuance of the old indolence. Lessons: 1. That the ordering of months and of years is of God. 2. That the first month must remind us of the advent of the Saviour. 3. That the first month must be consecrated by true devotion. 4. That the Church must pay some attention to the calendar of the Christian year. 5. That God usually by His ministers makes known His mind to His Church. (*J. S. Exell, M.A.*)   *The beginning of months :*— I want to bring to your mind this fact, that, just as the people of Israel when God gave them the Passover had a complete shifting and changing of all their dates, and began their year on quite a different day, so when God gives to His people to eat the spiritual passover there takes place in their chronology a very wonderful change. Saved men and women date from the dawn of their true life; not from their first birthday, but from the day wherein they were born again of the Spirit of God, and entered into the knowledge and enjoyment of spiritual things. I. First, then, let us DESCRIBE THIS REMARKABLE EVENT, which was henceforth to stand at the head of the Jewish year, and, indeed, at the commencement of all Israelitish chronology. 1. 1. This event was an act of salvation by blood. The law demands death— " The soul that sinneth it shall die." Christ, my Lord, has died in my stead : as it is written, " Who His own self bare our sins in His own body on the tree." Such a sacrifice is more than even the most rigorous law could demand. " Christ our Passover is sacrificed for us." " Christ hath redeemed us from the curse of the law, being made a curse for us." Therefore do we sit securely within doors, desiring no guard without to drive away the destroyer; for, when God sees the blood of Jesus He will pass over us. 2. Secondly, that night they received refreshment from the lamb. Being saved by its blood, the believing households sat down and fed upon the lamb. It was a solemn feast, a meal of mingled hope and mystery. Do you remember when first you fed upon Christ, when your hungry spirit enjoyed the first morsel of that food of the soul? It was dainty fare, was it not? 3. The third event was the purification of their houses from leaven, for that was to go in a most important way side by side with the sprinkling of the blood and the eating of the lamb. You cannot feed on Christ and at the same time hold a lie in your right hand by vain confidence in yourself, or by love of sin. Self and sin must go. This month is the beginning of months, the first month of the year to us, when the Spirit of truth purges out the spirit of falsehood. 4. A fourth point in the Passover is not to be forgotten. On the Passover night there came, as the result of the former things, a wonderful, glorious, and mighty deliverance. " This month," &c. II. Now, secondly, I want to MENTION THE VARIETIES OF ITS RECURRENCE among us at this day. 1. The first recurrence is of course on the personal salvation of each one of us. The whole of this chapter was transacted in your heart and mine when first we knew the Lord. 2. But then it happens again in a certain sense when the man's house is saved. Remember, this was a family business. A family begins to live in the highest sense when, as a family, without exception, it has all been redeemed, all sprinkled with the blood, all made to feed on Jesus, all purged from sin, and all set at liberty to go out of the domains of sin, bound for the kingdom. 3. Extend the thought—it was not only a family ordinance, but it was for all the tribes of Israel. There were many families, but in every house the passover was sacrificed. Would it not be a grand thing if you that employ large numbers of men should ever be able to gather all together and hopefully say, " I trust that all these understand the sprinkling of the blood, and all feed upon Christ." III. And now I come to SHOW IN WHAT LIGHT THIS DATE IS TO BE REGARDED, if it has occurred to us in the senses I have mentioned. Primarily, if it has occurred in the first sense to us personally : what about it then ? 1. Why the day in which we first knew the Saviour as the Paschal Lamb should always be the most honourable day that has ever dawned upon us. Prize the work of grace beyond all the treasures of Egypt. 2. This date is to be regarded as the beginning of life. Let your conversion be the burial of the old existence, and as for that which follows after, take care that you make it real life, worthy of the grace which has quickened you. 3. Our life, beginning as it does at our spiritual pass-over, and at our feeding upon Christ, we ought always to regard our conversion as a festival and remember it with praise. (*C. H. Spurgeon.*) *The beginning of days :*—If you have no such spiritual new year's day, now is a good time to secure one. Says old Thomas Fuller : " Lord, I do discover a fallacy, whereby I have long deceived myself, which is this : I have desired to begin my amendment from my birthday, or from the first day of the year, or from some eminent festival, that so my repentance might bear some remarkable date. But when those days were come, I have adjourned my amendment to some other time. Thus, whilst I could not agree with myself when to start, I have almost lost the running of the race. I am resolved thus to befool myself no longer. I see no day like to-day. . . , Grant, therefore, that to-day I may hear Thy voice. And if this day be remarkable in itself for nothing else, give me to make it memorable in my soul; thereupon, by Thy assistance, beginning the reformation of my life." Let this day be the beginning of months, the first month of the year to you. (*H. C. Trumbull.*) *The lessons of time :*—1. Time gives birth to actions. 2. God ordains that certain periods of life shall determine others (Luke xix. 44). 3. There is an extension of man's trial. One chance more. 4. Procrastination ends destructively. Not only thief of time, but also hardener of men's hearts. 5. Time will end. 6. The issues of time will last for ever. (*British Weekly.*) *Turning over a new leaf :*—The time has come for turning over a new leaf. As the town clock struck midnight of the last day of the old year divers and sundry resolutions which had lain dormant a long time, waiting for the New Year to ring its chimes, came forth into new life. They had long had an existence, these new resolutions had, for in reality they are not new at all, but quite venerable ; for on the first of January of many a past year they have been brought to the surface. And so the new leaf has been turned over, and on its virgin pages these new resolutions have been written, and, alas ! not inscribed for the first time. Were they not written on the new leaf on the first of January, just a year ago, and the New Year's day before that, and can you not go back, and back, and back, till you come to your childhood and the time when you first began to turn over a new leaf ? These new leaves that we are always turning over—how they accuse us ! We write on the newly turned page that we will do many duties which we have left undone—many duties in the home, the church—many duties to our friends, our neighbours, duties to God and to ourselves ; and how long is it before there comes a little January gust and blows the leaf back again ? and then all goes on pretty much as before. The trouble with this matter of leaf-turning, of making good resolutions only to break them, is two-fold. 1. The effort is not made in good faith—it is more a whim than a solemn purpose put into action, and so it is we have altogether too much regard to times and seasons, and too little to the imperative demand of to-day. Conscience is a court whose fiat is to be obeyed not on New Year's day, or Christmas, or on a birth-day, but now—on the instant. A man who defers to execute a right resolution till some particular day has arrived will be pretty sure not to carry it out at all. 2. Then the second difficulty is that we rely too much upon our own will and too little upon God's help. No man can change his own nature or reform himself. He can do much, if he but will, in the direction of carrying out a good resolution ; but the real efficient reliance must be God. (*Christian Age.*)

Vers. 3, 4. **If the household be too little for the lamb.**—*Too little for the lamb :*— I. THE TEXT REMINDS US OF A PRIMARY PRIVILEGE. 1. That each man of Israel ate the passover for himself; " every man according to his eating." So do we feed upon Jesus, each one as his appetite, capacity, and strength enable him to do. 2. But this same delicious fare should be enjoyed by all the family—" a lamb for an house." Oh, that each of the parents and all the children and servants may be partakers of Christ ! II. THE TEXT IS SILENT AS TO A CERTAIN CONTINGENCY. 1. The lamb was never too little for the family ; and assuredly the Lord Jesus was never too little even for the largest family, nor for the most sinful persons. 2. There is no reason to stint our prayers for fear we ask too much. 3. Nor to stay our labours because the Lord Jesus cannot give us strength enough, or grace enough. 4. Nor to restrain our hopes of salvation for the whole family, because of some supposed narrowness in the purpose, provision, or willingness of the Lord to bless. III. THE TEXT MENTIONS A POSSIBILITY, AND PROVIDES FOR IT. 1. One family is certainly too small a reward for Jesus—too little for the Lamb. 2. One family is too little to render Him all the praise, worship, service, and love which He deserves. 3. One family is too little to do all the work of proclaiming the Lamb of God, maintaining the truth, visiting the Church, winning the world. Therefore let us call in the neighbour next unto our house. (1) Our next neighbour has the first claim upon us. (2) He is the most easy to reach, and by each calling his next neighbour all will be reached. (3) He is the most likely person to be influenced by us. At any rate this is the rule, and we are to obey it (see Luke xxiv. 47 ; John i. 41 ; Neh. iii. 28). If our neighbour does not come when invited, we are not responsible ; but if he perished because we did not invite him, blood-guiltiness would be upon us (Ezek. xxxiii. 8). IV. The whole subject suggests THOUGHTS UPON NEIGHBOURLY FELLOWSHIP IN THE GOSPEL. 1. It is good for individuals and families to grow out of selfishness, and to seek the good of a wide circle. 2. It is a blessed thing when the centre of our society is " the Lamb." 3. Innumerable blessings already flow to us from the friendships which have sprung out of our union in Jesus. 4. Our care for one another in Christ helps to realize the unity of the one body, even as the common eating of the passover proclaimed and assisted the solidarity of the people of Israel as one nation. This spiritual union is a high privilege. 5. Thoroughly carried out, heaven will thus be foreshadowed upon earth, for there love to Jesus and love to one another is found in every heart. (*C. H. Spurgeon.*) *Sharing religion with others :*—There are some things which can be shared with our neighbours, and some which cannot, in the religious life. In securing the " means of grace " we can go halves with our next-door neighbours; but not so in the great fact of personal salvation. We can join with a neighbour in taking a pew in church, or in getting a waggon to carry us to church, or in subscribing for a religious paper—and paying for it too; but we can share no neighbour's seat in heaven; his team will never carry us there; the truths which benefit him from the weekly paper do not, because of their gain to him, do us any good. And if our next-door neighbour's family is a household of faith, that doesn't make ours so. The members of his family may be saved and ours lost. Neighbourliness is commanded and commended of God; but God doesn't want you to leave your salvation in the hands of your next-door neighbour. The blood above your neighbour's door-post will not save your household from death. (*H. C. Trumbull.*)

Ver. 12. **Against all the gods of Egypt I will execute judgment.**—*The Lord God of gods :*—When, in Deuteronomy x. 17, Moses says, " The Lord your God is God of gods," and when, in Joshua xxii. 22, the people exclaim, " The Lord God of gods, the Lord God of gods, He knoweth "—what do the words mean? Are there other " gods " than Jehovah? It is likely this inquiry will come up in the mind of almost any student of the Bible when he is reading the account of the ten plagues. The question is hard to discuss; but two considerations can be offered for help, and then we can reach the conclusion. 1. One is this : the entire record, unless a most elastic ingenuity of exposition be employed, seems to say that the contests delineated in the exciting chapters which record the deliverance from bondage and the establishment of Israel was between supernatural powers, rather than between ordinary human antagonists. Pharaoh accepted the gauntlet thrown down by Moses as a defiance to his gods, and, with a courage worthy of a better cause, took it up cheerfully in their name. So the conflict proceeds. The nations stand silently and solemnly by while these tremendous antagonistic forces are employed in the royal abodes, and are aroused only afterwards when the pressure outside begins to be felt. The close of the narrative teaches us that they were perfectly intelligent from the beginning in the conceptions they had of what was going on. Pharaoh finally confesses openly the defeat of his gods when he says humbly to Moses, " Go then, serve Jehovah ; and bless me also ! " And with a like acknowledgment the Israelites ascribe all the glory of their deliverance to God. They do not behave as if they owed even a decent gratitude to Moses or Aaron. 2. We must put with this consideration a second: these so-called " gods " of the Egyptians are spoken of constantly as if they were not mere dumb idols, nor even mere ideal creations of human imagination ; the language could have hardly been stronger if it had meant to leave the impression that they were living existences— beings possessed of life and intelligence and will and some power (see Deut. xxxii. 16, 17 ; 1 Cor. x. 20 ; Psa. lxvi. 4, 5). For some mysterious reason of His own, the sovereign Monarch of the universe has accepted an antagonism between the powers of evil and the powers of good in this world ; and for nearly six thousand years Satan His creature has been waging battle openly amid the sublime agencies of nature with Jesus Christ His Son. We feel as if we must assume real antagonists when we read Moses' own words in Numbers xxxiii. 4 : " The Egyptians buried all their firstborn, which the Lord had smitten among them ; upon their gods also the Lord executed judgment." 3. Thus, then, we reach our conclusion at which all along we have been aiming. Were Pharaoh's gods real gods? How was Jehovah the " God of gods "? And what does our text mean, " Against all the gods of Egypt will I execute judgment"? We ask you to recapitulate in your own minds the delineation made concerning the three cycles of miracles grouped around the three personages who stood on a certain occasion on the Mount of Transfiguration, Jesus Christ, Moses, and Elijah, each the bringer of a dispensation of revealed truth for men's salvation, the law, the prophets, and the gospel. It is sufficient to say, here at the start, that this same onset of demoniacal forces is disclosed in each of these cases, and a recognition made of the fact that the old fight with Satan was renewed, the old fight which began in the Garden of Eden. Demoniacal possession is found in these same three cycles of time, and nowhere else in the history of the Old Testament or the New. This, then, is what is intended when we say that this was a contest between Immanuel and Satan, a positive resumption of the war from the instant when " the seed of the woman " began to bruise the serpent's head. So, when we return to the story we are studying, we are bold to say that this whole contest between Moses and Menephtah was really the sublime and awful conflict between Immanuel and Satan for the slavery, on the one side, for the salvation, on the other, of the race of human souls whom the Almighty had originally made in His own image. Several most welcome explanations, therefore, meet us just here. 1. One is concerning the abrupt cessation of performances, on the part of Pharaoh's magicians, when they exclaimed, " This is the finger of God." They knew that the resistance was virtually over. We may even imagine that these people had sometimes been surprised already at what actually seemed their own power. Then there is a second explanation furnished by this disclosure. 2. We know now why this history has such an evangelical spirit attributed to it when references are made in the New Testament. Read over again, in the light of such an understanding of God's true purpose, the story which the author of the Epistle to the Hebrews gives concerning Moses' choice in his early career ; see how singular is the motive ascribed to him : He took his stand as a believer in Jehovah Jesus as his Redeemer—"By faith Moses," &c. The New Testament writer identifies the two dispensations as the same. Israel was the Church, Jehovah was Jesus ; so Moses became a Christian. 3. In the same way the allusions made to the incidents of the later history become intelligible. You recall the terrible trouble from the fiery serpents ; put with that now the exhortation of the apostle Paul : " Neither let us tempt Christ, as some of them also tempted, and were destroyed of serpents." He here says that Christ was the one who was tempted in that murmuring ; it was Christ who was leading Israel through the wilderness. There never has been but one Church, but one Leader of God's elect, but one Redeemer, but one way in which to be saved. (*C. S. Robinson, D.D.*) *Past redemption point:*—On the bank of the Niagara River, where the rapids begin to swell and swirl most desperately, preparatory to their final plunge, is a sign-board which bears a most startling legend. "Past Redemption Point," it reads. To read it even when one feels the soil firm beneath his feet sends a shiver of horror through one's soul as he looks off upon the turbulent water and realizes the full significance of the sign. The one who gets into those boiling rapids and passes that point, cannot retrace his way, cannot pull to shore, cannot be rescued by friends. Past redemption point! How many men despise the warnings God sends, and pass the last stage at which they could arrest their evil way, and too late they find they have passed redemption point!

Ver. 13. **I will pass over you.**—*The Passover :*—Our interest in the Passover, as in most of the other institutions of the Levitical economy, consists in its relationship to higher institutions, and to a more hallowed provision; it consists in the prefiguration by them of our Surety and Saviour, who is at once the Surety and Saviour of universal man. There are three points in the analogy to be considered. I. We, like the Children of Israel aforetime, are in circumstances of sorrow. 1. They were in bondage. We also have been brought under bondage to sin, and our yoke is harder than theirs, for ours is heart-slavery, the iron has entered into our soul. 2. The Israelites were in circumstances of peril. The Lord was about to execute in their sight His strange work of judgment. The transgressions of our race, the sins which we commit, expose us to consequences far more imminent, and far more terrible. II. For us, as for the Children of Israel of old, there is a remedy provided. The great doctrine of Atonement is here brought before us. By the blood of Jesus, seen by Divine justice sprinkled upon our hearts, wrath is warded off from us, and everlasting salvation is secured. The Cross is the meeting-place of God's mercy for the sinner. III. As there is such a remedy there can be no other. For us as for them there is but one way of escape. "There is no other name under heaven given among men whereby we must be saved." (*W. M. Punshon, D.D.*) *The blood of the Lamb :*—The blood of the slain lamb a type of that shed on Calvary. 1. The blood of salvation; 2. Of substitution; 3. Of sprinkling (useless unless applied); 4. Of separation. (*D. Macmillan.*) *Man's deliverance :*— I. This method of deliverance involved a sacrifice of innocent life. II. This method of deliverance transcended human invention. III. This method of deliverance proved completely efficient. IV. This method of deliverance for its application required practical trust in God. V. This method of deliverance formed a memorable era in the history of the Jews. (*Homilist.*) *The Passover :*—I. The Passover celebrates a deliverance wrought in fulfilment of a divine pledge. The baseness of man does not make void the righteousness of God. II. The Passover festival was the beginning of a new and noble national life. It was the initiatory rite of a peculiar people. An eminent historian, with no theological interest, has compared it to the great feast at the beginning of the French revolution, which was to inaugurate the new age of fraternity. The suggestion is profound and pertinent. It was a national feast. It was to be a perpetual witness to them that the Highest had seen the affliction of His people, and had come down to deliver them; that He had established an intercourse with them which was to endure from age to age. Its full meaning was not, and could not, then be taken in; but they did know that it was the bond of a sacred union between the redeemed nation and Him who had redeemed it; that it was the sign of their acceptance of Him as Ruler and King instead of the Egyptian prince. During our own Civil War, when it had become evident on both sides that it was to be a life-and-death struggle, a proclamation, called the Emancipation Proclamation, was issued by the President, setting free some three or four millions of slaves. That proclamation had no immediate effect whatever upon the actual character of those whom it most concerned. It made them neither better nor worse. A quarter-century has passed away, and multitudes of them are still unchanged. They remain degraded, superstitious, ignorant; and yet you can say to them what you could not say to their fathers. They are free men. The Passover feast has been eaten. A life of liberty, with all its obligations and opportunities, is upon them; upon them whether they will or no; upon them for better or worse. III. The Jewish festival has become a Christian sacrament. The paschal lamb was not only to be sacrificed; it was also to be eaten. Thus we are to keep the feast; thus we are to show a continuous participation in His sacrificial life and death. Crucified and risen with Him, we perpetuate the sacrifice in ourselves. (*E. B. Mason, D.D.*)

The paschal lamb :—I. THE PASCHAL LAMB ITSELF. A beautiful type of the Lord Jesus—the perfect, spotless Saviour. II. ITS CONNECTION WITH, AND APPLICATION TO, ISRAEL. 1. A substitute (see Matt. xx. 28). Christ suffered that we might live with Him and in Him. 2. Blood to be applied, as well as shed. Exercise of faith. 3. Flesh to be eaten. Christ the daily food of the believer's soul. III. THE MANNER IN WHICH ISRAEL WAS TO EAT OF IT. 1. With bitter herbs : repentance. When we feed on the Lamb of God, we must not forget what we have been, and what we are. We must remember our sins—worldliness, contentedness without God, impatience, and murmurings. 2. With unleavened bread (1 Cor. v. 7, 8). 3. With loins girded. Travellers—pilgrims and strangers on earth. Look on scenes and occupations of world as on those which belong to wilderness, not home. At end of journey stands a continuing city, the heavenly Jerusalem. March on. (*G. Wagner.*) *The Passover* (A Good Friday Sermon) :—I. I ASK YOU TO OBSERVE THE PROVISION WHICH GOD MADE IN THE PASSOVER FOR THE SAFETY OF HIS PEOPLE. The dykes of Holland, which shut out the roaring ocean from the fertile fields, and the levees of the Mississippi guiding a mighty river in its course, have more than once been cut. But he who thus enchains the fierce spirit of the flood is apt to find himself in the pathway of its devastation. So can no man cut through the great principles of right and truth without opening sluice ways of destruction for himself. Reckless injustice, cruel oppression, will sooner or later overthrow the very man who has thus wronged his fellow. And nations may equally beware of breaching the barriers of Divine judgment. The water will find out the hiding-place of a guilty people. France reaps to-day the ripening harvest of her martyred Albigenses and her bloody St. Bartholomew. The stroke had fallen with relentless impartiality " from the firstborn of Pharaoh, who sat on his throne, to the firstborn of the captive in the dungeon." There was no distinction in the common and overwhelming calamity. So intertwined were Egypt and Israel. The slave was dependent upon his master, as the vine is upon the oak ; but that very dependence only the more entirely involved the one in the calamity of the other. When death was on the wing of the pestilence, no power short of a miracle could separate the child of Jacob from the firstborn of Egypt. But a miracle did God work, a miracle so peculiar in its character that not one of all Israel's thousands died with the sons of the oppressor. But their deliverance was due to no foresight of their own. The soldier who cuts his way out of the encircling hosts of the enemy, the pilot who safely threads the mazes of the dangerous channel, the statesman who foils the blows and parries the thrusts of his country's enemies on the battle-field of diplomatic controversy, can each point to the skill and prudence with which his web of plans was woven, and glory in his success. But when Israel was saved from the destruction of Egypt's firstborn, no one of all their mighty host could say, " I saw the danger, and by my wisdom provided deliverance." The whole method of safety for God's people was one that originated with God Himself. No man would ever have thought of it, or, if he had, would have had any confidence in its success. It is a lamb slain, through which the Lord would guard each household of Israel from Egyptian condemnation. In one word, it was a sacrifice that alone could stand between the firstborn and the destroyer. Oh, when the Lamb is slain, when the sacrifice is made, when the Son of God hangs bleeding on the Cross, wilt thou wait till the shadowy wing of the death-angel darkens thy door, dreaming that thou hast some better way than God's to save thy soul from righteous condemnation ? II. WHAT WAS THE ISRAELITE TO DO TO AVAIL HIMSELF OF THE SACRIFICE WHICH GOD HAD THUS PROVIDED ? Perched on a grey crag, like the nest where the eagle rears her young, Quebec looked down in proud security upon the St. Lawrence flowing to the sea. With muffled oars and bated breath, beneath the mantle of midnight, an English army floated with the ebb ti de down the stream, and lay hidden at the base of the frowning heights. Inaccessible as the fortress seemed, a path had been discovered. A way there unquestionably was by which the precipice could be scaled. But to avail themselves of that approach, to make use of their discovery, was a task so perilous, a venture so begirt with difficulty and danger, that none but heroes ever would have tried. So did God reveal to the Israelite a path by which he could save his household from the dread visitation of the angel of death. The sacrifice was slain. The paschal lamb lay bleeding its life away. But how was the Hebrew householder to use the sacrifice ? Here was the road to safety, but was it not some mighty effort, some gigantic labour, some costly addition to the sacrifice which would make it a defence in the mysterious visitation of the fast-approaching night ? How through this pathway could the heights of security be gained ? In one word, when God had done His share in the provision of the offering, what was man to do to apply its protection to himself? There is a Divine answer to that question: "Ye shall take a bunch of hyssop, and dip it into the blood that is in the basin, and strike the lintel and the two side-posts with the blood; and the blood shall be for a token upon the houses where ye are, and when I see the blood I will pass over you, and the plague shall not be upon you to destroy you when I smite the land of Egypt." And this is all! No mighty struggles to make the sacrifice more costly. No pompous rites to render it more acceptable. Nothing in the world but sprinkling a few drops of the blood upon the doorway of the dwelling. And even that was no work; it was simply an acceptance of God's work. It was precisely equivalent to saying, "I cannot devise any way of defence to ward off the dread visitation from my dwelling: but I trust God's way." Oh ye who are waiting on the brink of decision for Christ, I pray you hear this precious truth! I tell you, if you only knew what a glorious thing it is that a lost sinner can be saved just by accepting Jesus, you would not leave this church till His precious blood upon your soul bore witness to your salvation. Twenty years ago a venturesome whale-ship, driven from her course, found a deserted brig drifting among the ice-floes of the polar sea. Deserted by her crew, her rudder guided by no human hand, she had sailed, like the ship of the "Ancient Mariner," into that silent sea. Her gallant discoverers brought their prize through untold perils into port. But the tidings spread that the staunch ship, which for well nigh two years had sailed among the frozen horrors of the northern seas, without a living soul within her open sides, was one of an English fleet that the British Government had sent to rescue the heroic Franklin. Then it was that our country did a beautiful, as well as noble act. Our government fitted up the vessel in every minutest detail. From stem to stern her old aspect was restored. On the deck, in her cabin, not an article was lacking to render her complete. And then, with grateful courtesy, the costly gift was sent across the ocean and given back, a freewill offering to the Government of England. The glory of the deed belonged to America alone. No British seaman had helped to save her. Not a farthing of English money had aided in her restoration. Even in her voyage across the Atlantic, the crew that manned, the officers that commanded, her were of our own country's navy. For England there remained nothing to do. She could only accept the salvation of her vessel as a free and generous gift. Oh type of God's work for man; image of the simplicity of man's accepting faith! Brother, your soul has long been like a ship abandoned to the seas. God's mercy alone has kept it so long afloat. Drifting amidst icebergs, tossed on a heaving sea, it is a miracle of Providence that it has not sunk beneath the depths. And now God would save it. He would rescue it from danger. He would restore its long-lost peace, its heavenly hope, its shattered purity, and give it back to you redeemed and for ever saved. But God will do it all. He will not give His glory to another. He will not let you add one solitary item to redeeming love, or pay one farthing for the blessings of salvation. There is absolutely nothing for you to do but to accept the gift. And this is faith. Oh take Him at His word! (*Bp. Cheney.*) *The blood:*—I. First, then, THE BLOOD ITSELF. In the case of the Israelites it was the blood of the paschal lamb. In our case it is the blood of the Lamb of God, which taketh away the sins of the world. 1. The blood of which I have solemnly to speak is, first of all, the blood of a Divinely appointed victim. This indeed is one of the underlying ground-works of the Christian's hope. We can rely upon Jesus Christ's acceptance by His Father, because His Father ordained Him to be our Saviour from before the foundation of the world. 2. Christ Jesus, too, like the lamb, was not only a divinely appointed victim, but He was spotless. Had there been one sin in Christ, He had not been capable of being our Saviour; but He was without spot or blemish—without original sin, without any practical transgression. 3. But some will say, "Whence has the blood of Christ such power to save?" My reply is, not only because God appointed that blood, and because it was the blood of an innocent and spotless being, but because Christ Himself was God. 4. Once more; the blood of which we speak to-day, is blood once shed for many for the remission of sin. The paschal lamb was killed every year; but now Christ hath appeared to take away sin by the offering up of Himself, and there is now no more mention of sin, for Christ once for all hath put away sin, by the offering of Himself. He is a complete Saviour, full of grace for an empty sinner. 5. And yet I must add one more thought, and then leave this point. The blood of Jesus Christ is blood that hath been accepted. II. THE EFFICACY OF THIS BLOOD. "When I see the blood I will pass over you." 1. The blood of Christ hath such a Divine power to save, that nothing but it can ever save the soul. 2. This blood is not simply the only thing that can save, but it must save alone. Put anything with the blood of Christ, and you are lost; trust to anything else with this, and you perish. 3. Yet again we may say of the blood of Christ, it is all-sufficient. There is no case which the blood of Christ cannot meet; there is no sin which it cannot wash away. 4. The blood of Christ saves surely. If we have that blood upon us we must be saved, or else we are to suppose a God unfaithful and a God unkind; in fact, a God transformed from everything that is God-like into everything that is base. 5. And yet again, he that hath this blood sprinkled upon him is saved completely. Not the hair of the head of an Israelite was disturbed by the destroying angel. They were completely saved, so he that believeth in the blood is saved from all things. III. THE ONE CONDITION. "What," says one, "do you preach a conditional salvation?" Yes, I do, there is the one condition. "Where I see the blood I will pass over you." What a blessed condition! it does not say, when *you* see the blood, but when *I* see it. Thine eye of faith may be so dim, that thou canst not see the blood of Christ. Ay, but God's eye is not dim; He can see it, yea, He must see it; for Christ in heaven is always presenting His blood before His Father's face. IV. And now, lastly, WHAT IS THE LESSON? The lesson of the text is to the Christian this: Christian, take care that thou dost always remember, that nothing but the blood of Christ can save thee. (*C. H. Spurgeon.*)   *The sacred love-token:*—I. "The blood shall be to you for a token"—A DISTINGUISHING TOKEN. A bloodless gospel is a lifeless gospel. 1. Our sin deserves death. 2. We believe in substitution. Christ died, "the just for the unjust." 3. We believe that we died in Jesus. 4. Believing this, we next come to the conclusion that we are safe. II. The blood was AN ASSURING TOKEN. 1. The token of suffering. 2. Death. (1) The Lamb of God. (2) A finished sacrifice. III. A MOST SIGNIFICANT TOKEN. 1. Redemption. 2. The Lord's property. 3. Acceptance. 4. Perfect safety. IV. A LOVE-TOKEN. 1. Ancient love. 2. Intense love. 3. Mighty love. 4. Wise all-seeing love. 5. Unlimited love. V. A RECOGNITION TOKEN. 1. The man who has this token is known to the angels as one of the heirs of salvation to whom they minister. 2. The devil also knows that mark, and, as soon as he sees it, he begins to assail the man who bears it, seeking in all sorts of ways to destroy him. 3. This blood-mark is known among the saints themselves, and has a wonderful power for creating and fostering mutual love. 4. Best of all, the Lord knows this token too. A Primitive Methodist brother, when he was in a meeting where a friend could not pray, cried out, "Plead the blood, brother!" and the advice was wise. (*Ibid.*)   *The institution of the Passover:*—I. THE CIRCUMSTANCES UNDER WHICH THE PASSOVER WAS INSTITUTED. 1. It was instituted under perilous circumstances. 2. It was instituted under exceptional circumstances. 3. It was instituted under painful circumstances. And so the Cross of Christ was instituted under circumstances morally dangerous, morally exceptional, and morally painful, but under circumstances which rendered it most welcome to the true Israel. II. THE PROCEEDINGS BY WHICH THE PASSOVER WAS CHARACTERISED. 1. A lamb was slain in the houses of the Israelites. 2. The blood of the Lamb thus slain was sprinkled on the upper door-post of the houses of the Israelites. 3. The slain lamb was eaten by the Israelites in an attitude of pilgrimage and haste. And so the soul must appropriate Christ; it must cultivate an attitude of moral haste, and it must be mindful of its pilgrim condition, if it is to be saved by Him. III. THE RESULTS BY WHICH THE PASSOVER WAS FOLLOWED. 1. After the celebration of the Passover the Israelites were safe. 2. They were free. 3. They were joyous. Lessons: 1. That every household should have an interest in the Lamb slain from the foundation of the world. 2. That to experience the saving benefit of Christ's death the soul must personally receive Him. 3. That Christ as dying is the only hope of the soul. 4. That Christ died for all. (*J. S. Exell, M.A.*)   *The Passover illustrative of atoning work of Christ:*—I. IN THE VICTIM IT PROVIDES (John i. 29). II. IN THE SACRIFICE IT REQUIRES. "Without shedding of blood there is no remission." III. IN THE DUTY IT ENJOINS (ver. 7). The blood of Christ is the only protection of the soul, and must be sprinkled as well as shed (Rom. v. 11). The soul must make a personal appropriation of Christ. To know Christ will profit little. We must feast on Him by faith. IV. IN THE SPIRIT IT DEMANDS (ver. 22). The bunch of hyssop signifies faith and humility. David said, "Wash me with hyssop, and I shall be clean" (Psa. li. 7). Hyssop is a lowly herb growing in rocky places. In the reception of Christ the soul must be humble. 1. The paschal lamb was also to be eaten with unleavened bread and with bitter herbs (ver. 8). Here we have shadowed forth the need of repentance and sincerity. And if the soul is to receive Christ, it must be with a contrite heart and with a deep sense of demerit. 2. The paschal lamb was to be eaten in the attitude of haste (ver. 11). The loins must be girded, the feet must be shod, the hands must hold the staff. The redeemed soul must sit loose to earthly things. The good are pilgrims in the world; they must be ready to go to Canaan. V. In the peril it averts (ver. 13). An emblem of the dangers averted from men by a believing interest in the atonement of Jesus Christ. They are delivered from the power of the second death. They escape the stroke of the destroying angel. Their safety is welcome and happy. VI. In the extent it contemplates. By a proper observance of the Passover all Israel would be preserved from the blow of the destroying angel, not one soul excepted. And so by application to the atonement of Jesus Christ the whole world may receive an eternal salvation from the awful penalties of sin. Lessons: 1. That Christ crucified is the only hope of moral safety. 2. That Christ appropriated is the only refuge of the soul. 3. That Christ must be received by repentance and faith. (*Ibid.*) *The blood-marked house:*—The grand central truth of all the objective truths here is shadowed forth in that blood of the spotless lamb shed and sprinkled on the door-posts. It has a deep, mysterious meaning, and finds its interpretation in the history of Calvary and the Cross, far onward yet, even fifteen hundred years, in the history. The blood-marked house is but representative of every soul tenement on earth, the dweller in which—made alive to the impending doom by the voice that cries from Sinai, "Whosoever sinneth, him will I blot out from My book," and by the voice crying from the depths within—hath fled from under the dark thundercloud of wrath, to Him who was lifted up on the Cross. This blood is not only the central idea of this, but of all the revelations of God. The whole gospel, is, in fact, summed up just here—"When I see the blood I will pass over." Blood! blood! this is the one cry of the gospel—the Alpha and the Omega of the gospel. All hope of the Divine favour—all strength to resist and conquer sin—all power of a holy life comes from this blood. Is man redeemed? It is because "we have redemption through His blood." Are any ransomed from sin? "Not by corruptible ransom of silver and gold" are they purchased, "but by the precious blood of Christ as of a lamb without spot." Are these justified? "Being justified by His blood." Are these cleansed and made holy? "His blood cleanseth from all sin." Are they, as strangers and wanderers from God, restored? "Ye who sometimes were afar off are now made nigh by the blood of Christ." Have they access to the Father's presence in prayer? It is because the High Priest hath gone before "sprinkling the blood." Are they arrayed in spotless robes to appear at the court of the Great King? "They have washed, &c., in the blood of the Lamb." Are sinners cast off at last to eternal death? It is because "they have trampled under foot the blood of the Son of God." Thus in the gospel revelation, all mercy, compassion, and grace of God have their ground in that blood. All conviction of sin, all holy desire in the soul, as well as all hope and trust in the Holy Ghost, come from that blood. (*C. S. Robinson, D.D.*) *Christ our Passover:*— Let us for once use the story as an illustration of evangelical faith as an instrument in attaining salvation under the gospel. In its analysis we are all agreed that saving faith has three elements—knowledge, assent, and trust. Now, we study these in turn. I. In the first place, the security of the Children of Israel on that awful night lay partly in the intelligent knowledge they possessed of the prescribed means of escape from the destroying angel. Four things were taught them—1. It was not the announcement of Moses which made this blood of a slain lamb the sign of deliverance from the plague, but the appointment of God Himself. The essential truth taught here is, that the crucifixion of Christ had no inherent value in itself which could atone for sin; it was the covenant of redemption that gave it its value. 2. It was not the shedding of the lamb's blood which should avail to save them, but the sprinkling of it on the door. Every soul must accept the atonement on God's terms. 3. It was not consciousness of security within, but evidence of obedience without, which would settle the fact of deliverance in every instance. It ought to be a help to sinners to know that God does not go over the past life of those who come to Him, as if on inquisition after their iniquities great or small, when once they plead the merits of His Son as their Redeemer. The vilest become clean in His sight when Christ is wholly accepted. The angel of Divine justice looks only upon the marks which show obedience and substitution. 4. It was reserved to God Himself to judge of the evidence of true and believing surrender to His commands. "When I see the blood, I will pass over you." II. These four things were taught to the people on that remembered night, and constituted their necessary intelligence; from this it is easy to pass on and inquire after the second element of saving faith, ASSENT, illustrated here in the story. 1. See how such a conception rebukes a feeling of indifference in the heart of any sinner. 2. See how this history rebukes a captious spirit making petulant objection to the sovereignty of God. 3. See how this incident rebukes the mistake of trying to be a Christian out of sight. No one is wise in attempting to obey God in secret, when it is written down plainly that part of the command is that we obey Him in public. So the Scripture says, "With the heart man believeth unto righteousness; and with the mouth confession is made unto salvation." 4. See how this history rebukes all delay in the duty of obeying God. What if the Israelites one after another put off the preparation of the lamb for the Passover? What good was there in waiting? How strange it would have been for any one to say, "I want more conviction," or for any one to plead, "I am not really so badly off as this assumes"; or for one to say, "My neighbours are so inconsistent that I cannot endure them"! If a duty is to be done, why does not each man do his duty now? This is what is meant by assent as an element of saving faith. III. There remains only the third element of faith mentioned in the beginning—TRUST. Think of that family just the half-hour before midnight. The lamb lies there; the basin with its bunch of hyssop stained in it is close beside; the doorway is wet with the blood. They have done all their duty just as God bade them; that was all they could do. Now they wait; that waiting is trust—the trust we are talking about. It is the feeling within one's heart which says, "Thus I have tried to do honestly all that the Lord asked at my hands; He told me to bend my will, make my prayer, take my Saviour, and after that leave all the rest to Him; there now I stand and wait." (*Ibid.*) *The Egyptian and the Israelite:*—I. In the history of the Exodus, Egypt and Israel, the opposed nationalities, represent TWO DIFFERENT ESTATES OF THE HUMAN LIFE—the earthly and the spiritual. These opposite estates are presented in eternal contrast throughout the pages of Holy Writ. In the Revelation of St. John the Divine the mystical Babylon represents that earthly, perishable, debased life which is here represented by Egypt; and the everlasting destiny of the spiritual life is represented by the New Jerusalem. The same antithesis is expressed by St. Paul in the fifteenth chapter of his First Epistle to the Corinthians. The apostle contrasts the earthly and the spiritual in the forms of the personal human life, out of which the national and the civil life have their origin: "There is a natural body, and there is a spiritual body." So also in his Epistle to the Ephesians, the opposed states of life typified by Egypt and Israel, Babylon and New Jerusalem, derived from the first Adam and the Second Adam, are contrasted in the words, "That ye put off concerning the former conversation the old man, which is corrupt according to the deceitful lusts; and be renewed in the spirit of your mind; and that ye put on the new man, which after God is created in righteousness and true holiness." The history of the Exodus does not merely narrate facts that occurred in a bygone, distant age. It is also an ever-contemporary history of the struggle of human life going on in every age. The slavery, oppression, debasement, and misery of Israel in Egypt represent to us the bondage, the discontent, and unrest of the human spirit enchained, degraded, and debased by the forces of the carnal and worldly life. The lusts and the passions that goad the human being into the debasing works of vice are task-masters that afflict with sore burdens. Man's eternal inability to find rest and blessedness in the slavery of the sensual and worldly life, is expressed in the words, "The Children of Israel sighed by reason of the bondage, and they cried, and their cry came up unto God, by reason of their bondage." The march out of the Egyptian bondage towards the confines of the land flowing with milk and honey, in order to stand before the Lord in "the mountain of His inheritance," is the great historical parable, composed in the providence of God to represent the progress of the human soul out of the sensual life into the spiritual—out of the low life of the earthly level into the communion of the most high life of God. The Divine voice of the Eternal Love, speaking through the Church, is for ever summoning man to travel towards the land of nobleness and freedom: "When Israel was a child then I loved him, and called My son out of Egypt." The means which God employed to relax the grasp of the tyrant, are the same which He still employs from age to age. The human soul, enslaved by the overmastering forces of the flesh and the world, cannot escape from its bondage without the aid of a power from above. How does God aid the soul to break its chains? He sends trials, sorrows, sicknesses, disappointments. The plagues are not sent in vain. In the hour of each visitation the tyrant grasp of the flesh and of the world upon the spiritual will is weakened, and the claims of spiritual truth are acknowledged. Old habits are not broken by a single chastening. This passage describes, with exact spiritual accuracy, the nature of the final visitation that carries conviction to the oft-hardened, unyielding soul. What, then, are the leading features of the visitation as here set before us? The manifestation of God's presence; the gloom of a night unlit, save by the flashes of the angelic sword; the slaughter of Egypt's best and choicest lives: the exposure of the vanity and weakness of Egypt's creature gods. The all-pervading presence of God was now to be realized in the Egyptian kingdom, according to the words, "I will pass through the land of Egypt." These words express the truth that God was about to compel those who had been living "without God in the world" to realize the power and majesty of His presence. The godless man, living through long years under the government of hard, tyrannical, untrained self-will, ignores the presence of God: "The wicked, through the pride of his countenance, will not seek after God; God is not in all his thoughts." When man has lived long without God in the world, lived the sensual, worldly life of Egypt, what power can enable him to realize the presence of the Invisible Lord, and to recognize in the passing hours the form of His Majesty? Nothing less than some overpowering shock that shakes to its very foundations the fabric of his life-habits, and convulses all the recesses of his being. Such a convulsion is here represented in the words, "I will pass through the land of Egypt this night." The times in which God reveals the terrors of His presence to the sensual, worldly natures, are times of darkness. To the children of Egypt the countenance of God comes in the night of trouble, sickness, and dissolution. In the bright day of health, activity, and wealth, the Egyptian soul realizes not the nearness of God. This night is for ever falling upon the land of Egypt. The prospects of the sensual worldly life are for ever subject to the coming of the darkness. There is not a household in all the land of Egypt that does not, sooner or later, feel the growing darkness of the night of trial settling upon it. But another element in the power of the visitation that carries conviction, is the destruction of "the firstborn." In Holy Writ this expression has a secondary and wider significance. It is used to denote all that is foremost in value and strength. Hence the destruction of all the firstborn of Egypt represents the eternal truth, that the choicest and strongest existences of the earthly and natural life are doomed to change and dissolution. The day of visitation is also a day in which the powerlessness of the Egyptian gods is demonstrated: "Against all the gods of Egypt I will execute judgment." The men of the world and the men of the flesh exalt some of the creatures into the throne that should be occupied by God. Thus does God for ever work out the emancipation of chosen souls. If the natural life were for ever undarkened by affliction; unchastened by bereavement; unrebuked by the overthrow of its idols, then the human spirit would never escape out of the tyrannous bondage of sensuality and gross worldliness, never rise into the mountain of God's inheritance. II. THE ISRAELITE LIVES ARE SAVED FROM THE POWER OF THE DESTROYER. In the hour when the plagues oppressed the life of Egypt, Israel was delivered from the destroying power of the visitation: "I will pass over you, and the plague shall not be upon you to destroy you." Although placed in the midst of the same objective circumstances, Israel and Egypt realized different effects from them. The land in which both sojourned was the same land; but for one people it was a land overrun by the plague of darkness at the very hour when the other people walked in the light. This miracle, accomplished historically in the contrasted destinies of the two typical nations, is repeated spiritually in the experience of all the souls that bear in themselves the two different types of human character, the earthly image of Egypt and the spiritual image of Israel. The land of our sojourning is still subject to the plague of darkness. For instance, the great mystery of human suffering is a problem which casts abroad a "darkness which may be felt." Why do pain, want, and agony exist? To the sensual and worldly man the question is one for which no answer is to be found. As the darkness of Egypt is for ever recurring, so also is the light of Israel. The very same trials which are inexplicably gloomy to the unspiritual man, are intelligible in their purpose, and full of light to the Christian soul. To the question, What is the purpose of suffering? he is taught to answer, that pains and agonies are means of spiritual discipline for perfecting strength and beauty of character. The eternal Light of the world was shining in the Divine-human soul of Jesus Christ, at the very hour when He voluntarily passed under the visitation of the power of darkness, as the Captain of our salvation, to be made perfect by suffering. So for the members of His Body, the souls united to Him, the promise is fulfilled: "He that followeth Me shall not walk in darkness, but shall have the light of life." As the hour which was dark to the Egyptian was bright to the Israelite, so the sword that smote the firstborn of the earthly race passed by the children of the chosen. This miracle, also, is for ever repeated. But for the Christian, the "firstborn," the chief, most cherished object of His being, is the hidden Divine life of Christ in the soul. In the atoning death and resurrection of Jesus, we behold the fulfilment of that eternal spiritual law, which gives safety to the firstborn of Israel. For us men and for our redemption He mortified the natural life, and sacrificed it upon the cross. To the earthly soul, in that self-sacrifice unto death the God·man seemed to have yielded the chief treasure, the "firstborn object of preservation, to the destroying sword. But on the morning of the third day, it became manifest that the true Firstborn was not the life laid down upon the Cross, but the risen life that had survived the sword of the Destroying Angel in the night of Calvary, and come forth in safety and triumph out of the hour of gloom, and out of the pains of death, "because it was not possible that He should be holden of it." So also in all the living members of Christ this destiny is for ever being accomplished anew. The Christian never loses his cherished treasure, the "firstborn" of his heart. Why? Because in the voluntary self-sacrifice of his own natural will he has given up the natural earthly "firstborn," in order to receive him again in a risen, restored form, ensured against the destroying sword. He who belongs to the moral common- wealth of Egypt, and knows no higher laws in the regulation of his inward life than those of natural flesh and blood, will lose the dearest firstborn of his being. He who is enrolled in the commonwealth of Israel, as a living member of Christ, having inscribed on his heart the laws of the spiritual kingdom, has received that "firstborn" of the Eternal Life, who will be found unscathed in the darker hour when the Destroying Angel passes through the land : "He that loseth his life for My sake shall find it." The plague can only be escaped by the spiritual franchise of Israel. They who give their hearts to the external treasures of the sensual and temporal life, will find their firstborn smitten down in the day of visitation. II. THE TOKEN OF THE COVENANT THAT MARKS THE HABITATIONS OF ISRAEL. "The blood shall be to you for a token upon the houses where ye are; and when I see the blood, I will pass over you." The Destroying Angel, according to the eternal order of God, passed harmlessly by the blood-sprinkled houses, and was not authorized to use His sword against the lives of any that presented that token. Throughout Holy Writ the saving efficacy of bloodshed in sacrifice according to God's commandment is declared. "Almost all things are by the law purged with blood; and without shedding of blood is no remission." So in this passage, the power that redeems human nature from slavery and ruin is represented as dwelling in the blood : "When I see the blood I will pass over you." But let us ask again, What is the connection between salvation through blood and the mystery of love? The hidden attribute of love can only be communicated to man by outward expression. The true expression of love is sacrifice. The most precious sacrifice expresses the strongest love. In order to give expression to infinite love, a sacrifice of infinite value was required. Man knows of no treasure equal in value to the gift of life. "The life of the flesh is in the blood." Thus the shedding of the Divine-human blood was the expression of that love which "is the fulfilment of the law." Therefore the power that redeems man from Egypt, and neutralizes all the influences that tend to debase and enslave his nature, is the power of Divine Love working in his being through the presence of the Holy Spirit, that came into humanity as the consequence of that infinite self-sacrifice on Calvary of Him, concerning whom the appointed witness testified, "Behold the Lamb of God, which taketh away the sin of the world." But we must bear in mind that the blood of the sacrificed life was sprinkled upon the habitations of Israel. What is the truth that we are to learn from that? The power of the Divine Love must influence the forms of our earthly human life. The means of grace in the Church are ordained for the purpose of bringing us under the saving power of the Cross of Christ. The highest of these means is the Holy Communion of the Body and Blood of Christ. We must live the life of earnest Christian activity : "Thus shall ye eat it; with your loins girded." We must live in the desire of spiritual progress, earnestly preparing our- selves "to walk henceforth in His most holy ways." We must try to live above the world, in the consciousness that we are hastening on towards another scene of existence : "Ye shall eat it in haste." If we are crucified with Christ, and living the risen life in Him, the tokens of the saving power will be evident in all the habits of our being. The signs of the grace of God that bringeth salvation are for ever the same. They who are marked by them "live soberly, righteously, and godly in this present world." The sobriety that enables us to control our own inward life, is one of the effects of the atoning blood. The sensual, the proud, the self-indulgent man has in the character of his life no sign of the spirit of self-sacrifice. (*H. T. Edwards, M.A.*)   *Christ, our Passover:*—I. First of all, THE NEED FOR THE BLOOD. And upon this we need to be very earnest, and to have a very clear conception. We must not put it on one side, as being a minor consideration. In that time, when Jehovah shall make an inquisition for sin, and shall search out iniquity, and shall set secret sins in the light of His countenance, then we shall feel, if we do not feel now, that there is a needs-be for the blood of Jesus Christ. But, brethren, we need to keep this before us. But think not that in the last day it will be as at this time—that each household shall give its contribution in redemption of its firstborn. Think not that the judgment is to come to households or to families. Be very clear upon that point: it is to come to you; and every one must give an account of himself unto his God. II. Now I pass on with a joyous step to the next point—THE NATURE OF THE BLOOD. Notice here what our figure implies, by teaching, first, wherein is the efficacy of the blood; and, secondly, wherein it is not. 1. You will see that the great efficacy of this blood is that it is *the* blood—not any blood, but the appointed blood. Supposing any one had been so foolish, on that day to which our text refers, as to say, "I will not sprinkle the lamb's blood, but the bullock's, or some other animal's blood, on the door-post"—what would have been the result? It would not have been the appointed blood that was to save. The efficacy of the blood was that it was appointed. Jesus Christ came not of Himself, but was sent by His Father. I hear some one say, "How shall I be sure that God will accept the blood of Christ?" Why, He hath appointed it, and surely if it is His own appointing He will not disown what He hath done Himself; and if He hath appointed the blood to be the means whereby you are to be passed over, rest assured that what He hath fixed He will stand to. 2. And then, again, you will perceive that from this Lamb's blood there is an idea of innocence and of purity. Christ stood not only the innocent Man, but He stood the righteous Man—having lived a life of righteousness, and having wrought in His own flesh and blood a righteousness such as the world hath never seen, and never shall see the like again. We therefore glory this night in the purity of the blood of Jesus Christ. 3. Then, too, you will see that this blood was substitutionary blood. It was blood that had been shed in the place and stead of the family upon whose door-post it was put. Here thou canst see, if Christ died for thee, God, in justice, cannot demand the victim twice, the offering twice—first of all thy substitute, and then thee. That were injustice. He hath received the offering at the hands of the substitute, and therefore thou canst say there is no condemnation for us who are in Christ Jesus, who walk not after the flesh, but after the Spirit. These are the three things in which the type agrees with the antitype. Now we pass to something in which they differ. The type was the blood of a lamb, but He who comes is the blood of a man. Any one who has ever seriously thought upon the subject must have discovered what the apostle Peter so clearly revealed afterwards, that it is impossible for the blood of bulls or of goats to take away sin. But when we come to behold the blood of the perfect Man, then we see that there is something which can remove sin. The blood of bulls and goats could not do it; but the blood of God's own Son in human flesh can do it. And now to that which, after all, is the leading characteristic of this blood, by which we expect to be passed over. It is Divine in its nature, or rather Divine in its value. This, then, is the nature of the blood—appointed by God the Father, perfectly pure, substituted for us, blood of man with the value of Deity—that is the nature of the blood, seeing which, God says He will pass us over. III. Then, thirdly, we come to THE APPLI-CATION OF THAT BLOOD. Yes, I allow that that blood was applied by the man to the door-post, but it was only so applied as he was influenced by a solemn power. It was done by the man himself for the family—I mean the head of the household representing the household—but that was because he was influenced so to do, by sovereign power and sovereign grace. If ever you are saved, you will not be saved in spite of yourself, but you will be saved by being made willing in the day of His power. There is no getting out of human responsibility. There is no getting away from the fact that there are Divine commands. There are Divine promises, but they are linked with Divine commands. There is the promise that will enable you to keep the command, but bear in mind that *you* will have to put on the blood, though it will be by the sweet constraint and sovereign power of grace. IV. And now we must pass on to THE EFFECT OF THE APPLICATION OF BLOOD. We know how God passed through and smote of every household of Egypt the firstborn, but not one died in Israel. Oh, if you could have known the agony some doubtless were in as they sat in their houses that night waiting for the midnight hour to strike— all awake—strong and healthy—not one sick one was found amongst them—not having retired to rest because they needed it not, but all feasting, and yet listening —eating in haste because they wanted to listen as well as because they wanted soon to depart—listening to the death-shrieks of those who were smitten by the angel passing by—wondering whether the angel would come there or not. At last the angel comes, and passes on. Oh, I could think of that till it thrills through me! Did the angel sweep his wing through the air with a perceptible sound, or was all silent till the shriek of death rose again? What it was like I know not; but I think it must have been—oh, it must have been an awful hour to the children of Israel, though it was a gladsome one to their souls! Perhaps at that time there were anxious inquirers too, saying, " Oh, but *we* cannot see the blood." Ah, but the angel can ; the promise is not, " When *you* see the blood I will pass over you," but, " When *I* see the blood." And I dare say there was somewhat of trembling and anxiety lest the blood should not have been put on rightly, or lest something should have been omitted. I have no doubt they did not feel perfectly secure till the angel had passed by, and they were safe, secure, and passed over. And so it happens with the Christian. Though he may have believed in Christ there will come times when he will be inclined to say, " I cannot see the blood," and when he will be very downcast lest death should come to him then, and he should not be quite secure. So then, there may be fear, and trembling, and doubting, and yet perfect security. But still I am certain of this—God would have us to be sure of it and to trust Him. And yet I feel this also, He would have us not to be high-minded, but to fear ; for He says, " Let him that thinketh he standeth take heed lest he fall." Therefore the effect of the application of this blood is this—it is certain you will be passed over, but at the same time you must not be too high-minded—still trusting the blood—never forgetting that you may deceive yourself.

V. And now just to put TWO OR THREE POSSIBLE CASES WHERE THIS BLOOD SHALL NOT BE APPLIED. I go to the entrance of a solitary Israelitish house, and see there are signs of mourning about it. I enter, and I find the mother with the corpse of her firstborn child upon her knees. She is crying, " O my son, my son, would God I had died for thee, O Absalom, my son, my son!" I say, " How is it that death should have smitten him down? Did you not put the blood upon the doorpost? No, you did not, or he would not have been killed. I see no blood upon the door-post—how is this?" " Oh, I never heard of such a thing as blood—I did not know of it." " Oh!" says one, " did no man care for my soul? I never heard of the message of mercy till it was too late, and we never were told that death was coming, nor of salvation from the wrath to come, and we have perished for lack of knowledge." Now, I put it seriously to you, and after the manner of men, of course : Are there not souls lost in the same way now? Are not the heathen crying out perpetually? Does not a wail from the uttermost parts of the earth penetrate the air? Now, let us pass on to another cause. I come to another house, and I find them wailing. I say, " How is this?" The head of the household says, " Oh, my boy, my boy! I was passing by, and I heard an elder saying something to the people ; I went still further, and heard another elder of Israel saying something to a great crowd ; but I went on. I did not know what was going on, for I had just bought a yoke of oxen, and was going to prove them— or purchased a piece of land—and I was so occupied with these things that I did not think to listen. My whole heart was engrossed and engaged upon these things, and I did not think about the plague ; and now see the result. Death has come, and we have been struck down in this way." Ah, how many of you will be struck down in the same way! God's servants have been preaching about faith, and the wrath to come ; but you have been too busy to trouble your minds with such things. I will suppose another case. I say, " How is this, my man? You are perfectly aware of it, I know, because Elder So-and-so took care to tell you of it." " Yes, I am without excuse, I admit ; but you know, sir, I thought to-morrow would have done quite as well as to-day, and so I put it off till to-morrow, and so now my boy is gone." Oh, delay not, for delays are dangerous—procrasti-nation is the thief of time. I could go on giving instances of persons who are thus lost ; let me give one more and I have done. I go to a house and I see death there. " What!" I say, " another case of delusion? Whose is the mistake here?

I see the lamb, I believe you have been feasting—I see preparations for the pass-over, and yet there is death. How is this?" "Well, sir," they reply, "we thought of everything, but we forgot the blood." Ah, many will have at the last day Christianity, but no Christ—they will have everything but the blood. They will say, "Lord, Lord," but He shall say, "I never knew you; ye never knew Me; ye may have spoken My words, but you never had Me in your hearts." It is not Christianity in its most perfect form, or most sanctimonious garb, or most earnest, zealous efforts before the world—it is not Christianity at all that saves, but Jesus Christ, and Jesus Christ alone. (*J. A. Spurgeon.*) *The Passover in Egypt and its typical significance:*—1. The first feature which strikes us is, that the rite was of Divine appointment. This significant Hebrew ceremony would never have been thought of by an Israelite himself. It would have been the last thing that would have suggested itself, on the concluding night of bondage, to kill one of the members of their flock and sprinkle door-post and lintel with its blood. The method of the great Divine Expiation for the sins of the world was pre-eminently God's devising. What human mind would ever have formulated such an idea as that the Eternal would send to this apostate earth of ours the Prince of Life and Lord of Glory, in order to effect, through a death of self-surrender and suffering, the emancipation and final salvation of His people? 2. Let us note, next, the name and nature of the appointed victim—a lamb. The animal of all others that seems to suggest the idea of innocence and meekness. In the lion's whelp, with all its playfulness, there is early discerned the incipient fierceness of untamable years. It seems to us a poor reason which some have given for the selection of the paschal offering, that it was what could most readily be furnished by the shepherds of Goshen from their herds. Let us see, rather, in this first simple element in the typical significance, what the writer of an after age calls, "the meekness and gentleness of Christ." 3. As a further expansion of this thought, the selected paschal lamb was to be "without blemish." Plague-mark or disease or infirmity dare not attach to it. No animal would be accepted with torn fleece or broken limb. Christ was "a Lamb without blemish and without spot." He "offered Himself without spot to God." As one flaw or vein in the marble fatally damages the sculptor's work; as one speck in the lens of microscope or telescope destroys its use and demands a recasting; as one leak would inevitably submerge the noblest vessel that ever rode the waters; so, one leak in the Mighty Ark of Mercy would have been fatal to His qualifications as a ransom for the guilty. Blessed be His name, the Lamb "slain for us" was "holy, harmless, undefiled, and separate from sinners." What a host of witnesses conspired on earth to testify to His immaculate purity! 4. The paschal lamb was not only without blemish, but "a male of the first year"; that is to say, had attained its full growth. It was the choicest of the fold. It was, in its lowly way, the type of absolute perfection. Behold again, a yet additional attestation to the all-perfect Sacrifice! It surely adds to the touching thought of His death, that it was just when the adorable Saviour had attained all that was complete as the Ideal of humanity, that "He was taken out of the land of the living." The Heavenly Flower was cut down, not when in early incipient bud, but in amplest blossom. The pure white Lily bowed its head, not when the latent beauty was undeveloped, but when it had fully revealed its "calyx of gold." The Divine Tree of Life succumbed to the axe, not in the early spring when its branches were unclothed and the fruit unformed; neither in late autumn, with the leaves prematurely seared—but in the full summer of its glory; when every bough was laden with verdure and hanging with richest clusters. The magnificent Temple fell, not when half upreared, nor yet when toil and suffering had left their lines and furrows on the gleaming marble; but rather, just when the top stone had been brought forth with shouting, and the cry arose, "Grace, grace unto it!" 5. The paschal lamb was separated from the flock and kept alive four days. This formed a further Divine injunction, as you will find by reference to the detailed instructions in the opening of the chapter from which our text is taken (vers. 3, 6). Christ, as we have already seen, was designated for His atoning work and sacrifice in the counsels of the Father from the foundation of the world. 6. The paschal lamb—after being presented "on the fourteenth day of the first month, at full moon, between the evenings"—was slain. Here is the foundation truth of the gospel: "the sprinkling of the blood of Jesus Christ." Yes, the "sprinkling"; for observe, that under the varying forms of observance in earlier and later Jewish times, this expressive action was rigidly preserved. Not enough for you or for me is the slaying of the Lamb: in other words, the mere historical fact that the Divine-human Victim died. The Israelite might have piled buttress on buttress, pyramid on pyramid, to effect exclusion. He might have strengthened his dwelling with bars of brass and pillars of iron, lintels and door-posts of cunning workmanship. The Destroyer's weapon would have cleft them in sunder. "Neither is there salvation in any other." The work of Jesus must stand alone in all its solitary grandeur and sufficiency. "When I see the blood"—"the blood," says God—"I will pass over you." The final injunction to the Hebrews regarding their offering; viz., that after the carcass, of the victim was "roast with fires," it was to be eaten: the whole was to be eaten, nothing was to be left. What, among others, is one great spiritual lesson here inculcated? That it is not enough to rest satisfied with the initial act of pardon and forgiveness through the blood of the Cross. Christ must not only be looked to by simple faith, but in His own expressive but much misunderstood and misinterpreted words and simile, "Verily, verily, I say unto you, Except" (in a lofty, spiritual sense) "ye eat the flesh and drink the blood of the Son of God, ye have no life in you." (*J. R. Macduff, D.D.*)   *The protecting blood:*—There is a legend that on that night of the Exodus a young Jewish maiden —the firstborn of the family—was so troubled on her sick-bed that she could not sleep. "Father," she anxiously inquired, "are you sure that the blood is there?" He replied that he had ordered it to be sprinkled on the lintel. The restless girl will not be satisfied until her father has taken her up and carried her to the door to see for herself; and lo! the blood is not there! The order had been neglected, and before midnight the father makes haste to put on his door the sacred token of protection. The legend may be false; but it teaches a very weighty and solemn admonition to every sinful soul who may be near eternity and is not yet sheltered under the atonement of Jesus Christ. (*T. L. Cuyler.*)   *Christ's expiation:*— "In what way can the death of Christ, considered as a sacrifice of expiation, be conceived to operate to the remission of sins?" Archbishop Magee replies: "To this the Christian answer is, 'I know not, nor does it concern me to know, in what manner the sacrifice of Christ is connected with the forgiveness of sins; it is enough that this is declared by God to be the medium through which my salvation is effected. I pretend not to dive into the counsels of the Almighty. I submit to His wisdom.'"   *The blood as a remedy:*—A very useful lesson is taught in the following striking incident: "One night I found," says a minister, "at a meeting, two lads of sixteen years of age sitting in a corner with their open Bibles. One had already been conversing with me; I had noticed the other in an anxious state. 'Well, Johnny,' I said, 'what are you and George doing here?' 'I am trying to clear up his doubts,' said Johnny. 'What does he doubt?' 'His interest in Christ.' 'Well, what are you doing?' 'I am pointing him to the blood.' 'But is he not looking there already?' 'Perhaps he is, but I'm telling him to look till it grows on him.'" Ah, that is what we want; to look at the remedy till it so grows as to annihilate guilt; to look at Christ and heaven till they so grow upon us as to outshine and eclipse the world. To look at the pattern He has set us till it grows in glory, and we grow through the power of the Spirit more "into the same image"! (*J. Cox.*)   *Blessed protection:*—On board a British man-of-war there was but one Bible among seven hundred men. This belonged to a pious sailor who had made a good use of it. He had read it to his comrades, and, by God's blessings on his labours, a little band of praying men was formed that numbered thirteen. One day this ship was going into battle. Just before the fight began, these thirteen men met together to spend a few moments in prayer. They committed themselves to God's care, not expecting to meet again in this world. Their ship was in the thickest of the fight. All around them men were stricken down by death. Two of these men were stationed with three others in charge of one of the guns. The other three men were killed by a single cannon-ball, but there in safety stood the two praying men. They had agreed that when the battle was over those who might still be alive should meet if possible. They met soon after, and what was their joy to find the whole thirteen were there. Not one of them had even been wounded. What a blessed shelter it was that protected those men of prayer! (*R. Newton.*)

Ver. 14. **A feast to the Lord throughout your generations.**—*Analogy between the Jewish Passover and the Lord's Supper:*—I. The Jewish institution was commemorative; so is the Lord's Supper. 1. It was a "memorial" of a deliverance from the most cruel bondage. 2. It was a "memorial" of a deliverance from the most cruel bondage by the sacrifice of an innocent victim. 3. It was a "memorial" of a deliverance wrought by the sovereign compassion of God (chap. iii. 7, 8). II. THE JEWISH INSTITUTION WAS SOCIAL ; SO IS THE LORD'S SUPPER. 1. Here all feel that they are in the same moral condition. 2. Here all feel that they are dependent on the same Redeemer for salvation. 3. Here all feel that they are members of the same family and destined for the same house. III. THE JEWISH INSTITUTION WAS BINDING ; SO IS THE LORD'S SUPPER. 1. It is binding on all. 2. It is binding on all perpetually. (*Homilist.*)   *The Passover :*—I. THE PREPARATION FOR THE PASSOVER. 1. Divinely commanded. 2. The Passover a new era. 3. Details explicitly given. (1) Indicating the importance of having a "Thus saith the Lord" for every ordinance religiously observed. (2) Indicating the importance of observing every Divine ordinance as divinely ordained. (3) In the case of the Israelites, to deviate from the prescribed form would indicate insubordination. (4) The lamb is Divinely declared a type of Christ (1 Cor. v. 17). (5) The lamb being "kept up" from the tenth to the fourteenth may be a type of the time when the promise of Christ was given in Eden, and of His crucifixion on Calvary. II. THE BLOOD OF THE PASSOVER. 1. The disposition to be made of it. 2. The purpose. (1) A sign for the angel of death to exempt the house thus marked. (2) This sign thus became the ground of peace and security to the Israelites. (3) This was also a sign that this exemption, peace, and security, were not of works, but wholly of grace. (4) The application to the believer, covered by the precious blood of Jesus (1 John i. 7 ; 1 Pet. i. 18-20 ; 1 Cor. v. 7, 8 ; Rom. iii. 24, 25). III. EATING THE PASSOVER. Its typical significance. Lessons : 1. The Old Testament seems typical of the New Testament. 2. Doctrine and practice vividly portrayed. (*D. C. Hughes, M.A.*) *Eastertide memories :*—1. It is a day that reminds us of the deep sympathy of mind with nature. The springtime of the year has many meanings for us all. The face of the earth is renewed ; and in imitation of it we renew our dress and the face of our homes. And for thoughtful and sensitive minds, doubtless the lesson goes very deep and very far ; they feel the gentle hint that old dust and cobwebs should be swept out of the mind, and that they should seek for a fresh stock of impressions to carry the work of imagination cheerfully on. 2. We are reminded of our part in the lot of humanity. A long history seems to close ; a new one opens on us Easter Day. We derive the name of Easter from an ancient heathen goddess, Ostera, worshipped by our ancestors. A thousand years ago, her priestesses on Easter eve washed their faces in clear springs : it was a kind of sacrament in her worship. Then, too, the Easter fires were kindled on many a height, as the name Osterberg, which often occurs in Germany, reminds us. The Easter water and the Easter fire had substantially one tendency and one efficacy—to cleanse from evil, to drive away evil spirits, to bring blessing to the hearth and home, to the fields and the toil of the husbandman. How far and wide the notion of a purgation, in the most comprehensive sense, of the doing away with the old and a new beginning, has extended through the world ! We may begin our inquiries in the East of London, where the Jews make a thorough cleansing of the house and of the utensils against the Passover season. With the old leaven let malice and wickedness go out of the heart, and let it recover its unleavened state of sincerity and truth. Corresponding customs to those of the Jews are practised among peoples in all parts of the world, and there is not a tribe of black or brown men from whom we may not learn something edifying for ourselves. At a feast of first-fruits of a tribe of North American Indians, they provide themselves with new clothes, new pots and pans ; they collect all their worn-out clothes and other despicable things, sweep and cleanse their houses, squares, and the whole town of their filth, which, with all the remaining grain and other old provisions, they cast together into one common heap, and consume it with fire. After having fasted for three days, all the fire in the town is extinguished. During the fast they abstain from the gratification of every passion and appetite whatever. A general amnesty is proclaimed ; all malefactors may return to their towns. On the fourth morning the high priest, by rubbing dry wood together, produces new fire in the public square, whence every habitation in the town is supplied with the new and pure flame. Then there is feasting and rejoicing, and on the following days they receive visits from their friends of neighbouring towns, who have in like manner purified and prepared themselves. A man of genius, in describing these things, says, "I have scarcely heard of a truer sacrament—*i.e.*, an outward and visible sign of an inward and spiritual grace—than this, and I have no doubt that they were originally inspired from heaven to do thus, though they have no Biblical record of the revelation." 3. But this feast reminds us of deeper things—of things that never were, nor could be, learned from nature—of the hope of humanity, of triumph over death. If we look at the imagery and traditions of the nations, there is evidence of an overwhelming persuasion that the soul has a life distinct from the body, and that the soul will live again. One strong belief was, when the body was consumed on the funeral pyre, the human burden, as a Roman poet calls it, was cast away, mortality ceased, and higher life began. The phœnix bird, which arose from out of the ashes, was one of the symbolic images in which antiquity found this thought expressed. In another way we may see the same belief forming the very basis of worship. And at the great feasts of the year, such as Eastertide, the first thing was to bring offerings to the spirits of the departed, solemnly to commemorate them, and to unite with them in the social feast. What made those high days so peculiarly solemn, was the thought that the ancestral spirits had come back from the viewless regions to hold communion with their living posterity, and to impart to them a fresh blessing. And here, again, at the head of this belief, is something sweet and sound. If we let the heart's logic have its way with us, we shall hold that the life of humanity is continuous and unbroken, and that they who have gathered with us in the house of God in times gone by return from time to time to visit us in our lingering exile from bliss, and, it may be, secretly to inspire us to follow their faith and to attain whither they have attained. (*E. Johnson, M.A.*) *The Passover :*—I. OBEDIENCE. Lamb to be killed, prepared, eaten. None to be left till morning. Eaten in a certain form and manner. Christ, the Lamb, slain for us, to be received as a whole. His yoke, His cross, as well as His crown. Example. Redeemer. Righteousness. II. FAITH. More reasonable that they should shed the blood of their enemies than of the lamb, and use the sword than the knife. Spreading fire and slaughter. More reasonable, apparently, to help and trust themselves than confide in a word spoken, and a few drops of blood on the door-post. Our faith, and Jesus the Lamb. III. HUMILIATION. Eaten with bitter herbs. Penitential recollections. They prevented mere carnal delight in the feast. Our bitter herbs: remembrance of sin; of our condition; of our prospects, &c. IV. DELIVERANCE. Last night in Egypt. The blood sprinkled. The destroying angel. Door of every Israelite's home opens, and the family comes out. The escape. Learn : 1. That God gives songs in the night. "In darkest shades, if Thou appear." 2. That Christ our Passover was slain for us (1 Cor. v. 7). 3. That we should receive Him with all humility, obedience, and faith. 4. That trusting in Him, we shall have a great deliverance. (*J. C. Gray.*) *A laudable custom :*—Rev. Joseph Sortain, the eloquent Brighton preacher, was of Huguenot extraction. He always observed the custom of his persecuted ancestors of reading the twenty-third Psalm at family worship on Saturday evening. When sometimes asked by guests why he had a special portion of Scripture for that evening, he would reply, "It was the custom of my Huguenot forefathers, and I wish to gain inspiration for my Sunday's duties by the associations it calls up." (*J. Tinling.*)

Vers. 15–19. **The feast of unleavened bread.**—*The feast of unleavened bread ; or, the ordinances of God, and the manner in which they should be observed.* The feast of unleavened bread was a distinct ordinance from the Passover, though following immediately upon it. At this feast the Israelites were to eat unleavened bread ; probably to commemorate the fact that they had left Egypt in such haste that they had no opportunity to leaven their dough, and were consequently obliged to eat unleavened cakes. It would also remind them of the power of God in bringing them out of Egypt when they were without provision for their journey, and it would teach them a lesson of trust in the Divine providence. This feast was an ordinance of God. We observe in reference to it—I. THAT THE ORDINANCES OF GOD ARE CLEARLY MADE KNOWN AND ENJOINED UPON MAN. 1. Divinely authorized. 2. Morally beneficial. 3. Wofully neglected. This neglect is prevalent; it is fearful; it is inexcusable ; it is morally injurious ; it will ultimately meet with its due punishment. II. THAT THE ORDINANCES OF GOD ARE TO BE OBSERVED IN A SPIRIT AND TEMPER FREE FROM SIN. 1. In a spirit free from hypocrisy. 2. In a spirit free from malice and bitterness. 3. The home-life must be in sympathy with God's ordinances. What we are at home we shall be in the ordinances of God. The home-life and the ordinary worship are inseparable ; they are part of the same service, and must be pure. III. THAT THE ORDINANCES OF GOD ARE TO BE OBSERVED WITH SOLEMNITY AND PROPRIETY OF MORAL CONDUCT AND DEMEANOUR. IV. THAT THOSE WHO PROFANE THE ORDINANCES OF GOD ARE UNWORTHY OF THEM,

AND SHOULD BE DENIED THE PRIVILEGE OF THEM. "That soul shall be cut off frcm Israel." Lessons: 1. That there are in connection with the Church of God many ordinances to be observed by men. 2. That these ordinances should be observed with due solemnity and appropriate conduct. 3. That neglect of these ordinances is disobedience to the command of God. (*J. S. Exell, M.A.*)

Vers. 21–23. **Strike the lintel and the two side posts with the blood.**— *Three great truths taught by the Passover* :—I. THE UNIVERSALITY OF CONDEMNATION. Israelite and Egyptian are brought under one common charge of guilt, and there they all stand, "condemned already." II. The great truth of SUBSTITUTION. The lamb instead of the firstborn. "Behold the Lamb of God," &c. III. The third truth taught is APPROPRIATION. The Israelite would not have been safe if he had merely killed the lamb; he had to sprinkle its blood on the lintel and on the two side posts. When we repose our confidence in the Person of Christ, we have taken the bunch of hyssop and dipped it in the blood, and from that moment we are safe. (*W. Hay Aitken, M.A.*) *Christ, our Passover* :—I. The first thing is this, that SALVATION THEN AND NOW IS FREEDOM FROM IMPENDING DOOM. Let us revive that essential idea of our most holy faith in all our hearts and minds. The times greatly need it. As there hung over Egypt that night the awful threat of God's descending wrath, so let my soul and yours never forget there hangs over this city the threat of impending vengeance. And just because of that, a motive which worked that night upon the hearts of Israelites, and ought to work upon our hearts now, was, and should be, the element and moving principle of fear. Let me reassert this: let me iterate and reiterate it — that fear is a legitimate motive in salvation. Perhaps the Israelites on that occasion were immediately drawn by loving obedience to obey what God had spoken. If so, they were different from you and me. I rather think that while some temperaments would just quietly and unquestioningly yield whenever Moses declared the mind and heart of God, as to what was coming of doom, and as to how salvation was to be secured, others would question ; others would be reluctant ; others would be very like ourselves. But we do hope that, no matter how they felt "rubbed the wrong way" (if you will allow the familiar expression), they had sense enough, whether drawn by love or driven by fear, to sprinkle that blood and get in under its shelter in time, and stay there. Ah, yes, it is said to be unphilosophical, that if you do not draw men with love, you will never drive them by fear. Men are moved by fear every day. Why did you go and insure your house last week? Was it not through fear? Why did you insure your life last week, even though the doctor told you that there was nothing wrong with you? Was it not from fear? Grand men, large broad-browed men, are men who are moved by fear. Methinks Noah was a grand, broad-browed man, and "Noah, moved by fear, prepared him an ark for the saving of his house." It was fear as well as love that clenched every bolt in it. So never go away and boast, my friend, that you have such a big intellect that fear will not move you. This is a real legitimate element in salvation. God works upon it. He plays upon that heart-string by His Word and by His Spirit. He did it then in that night in Egypt. II. Now, I should like to say, further, re-stating some simple but essential elements of gospel revelation regarding sin and salvation, that SALVATION WAS OF GOD'S DEVISING. It was altogether a matter of revelation. Nothing was left to man but bare obedience of mind and hand and foot. Mark that I do not say that God spoke irrationally ; I do not say that God simply came and overmastered them with despotic tyrannical power, but I do say that God came forth out of His secret place that memorable night, and Himself devised the plan of salvation. God Himself devised such a plan that no soul needed to be lost if that soul simply believed and obeyed. It was all of God, it was all of grace; so still. III. I wish to say, further, that on this night of this divinely appointed salvation, when it was received and obeyed, there were one or two THINGS WHICH WOULD SURELY STRIKE THE RECIPIENTS, AND THOSE WHO WERE OBEDIENT TO THIS HEAVENLY REVELATION. "Draw out a lamb," says Moses, speaking for God, "draw out a lamb and kill it, and take its blood and sprinkle it on the lintel and on the two side posts." Every Israelitish father who killed the lamb, not simply with a knife and with his hand, but whose mind and heart were working behind the knife, must surely have had this thought borne upon him—"If I am not to die, something is to die." Substitution. Oh, let me ring it out ! "For me, for me," was bound to ring in his ears with every gurgling of that lapping blood. That again is the heart of salvation, for you and for me. If I am to go free, this innocent thing has to part with its very life's blood. "By His stripes we are healed." Bless God for this substitutionary salvation. Then this salvation on that night in Egypt, and this night for you and me, was not only substitutionary, but another very simple idea I would like to revive in your hearts and minds, and it is this: it was after all a matter of simple obedience. "Take the blood." It was not enough that it was sprinkled by every Israelitish father or head of a household who represented them all. Every Israelitish father had to take that bunch of hyssop and dip it in the blood, and strike it on the lintel and pass in, he and his household, just as he was told. And there is an element, therefore, in salvation that is illustrated there. What is faith? It is a simple literal bowing of the soul in abject obedience. And, again, it comes out, contrariwise, that the very essence of unbelief now is not a want of understanding, but a want of obedience. There is a moral taint in unbelief. Now, come away to another evening away down the stream of time for centuries; and again it is becoming dark, and there is a darkness deeper than the darkness of the darkening sky. The darkness and blackness of sin, and of all time, are gathering round about that hill called Calvary. Now, watch that Saviour Christ. See that innocent holy Man, holy as a lamb, without blemish and without spot. See the soldier as he thrusts that spear into His side, and out there come blood and water. And, remember this: there is the last blood that shall ever be shed for human sins. "There remaineth no more sacrifice for sin, but a certain fearful looking for of judgment and fiery indignation that shall devour the adversaries." "Take you a bunch of hyssop, and strike the lintel and the two side posts." God actually condescending to tell a man how to sprinkle the blood! He left no loop-hole by which a man might be lost if he wanted to be saved himself, and to save his wife and his children. If lost, you will be inexcusable. What was the hyssop? Well, so far as I can gather from Scripture, it was a very common plant. You remember that when the range of Solomon's botanical knowledge is being indicated, it is said that Solomon spoke of trees from the hyssop that grows out of the wall to the cedar that is in Lebanon. What a poor salvation if God had said, "Take a sprig of cedar." What an easy salvation it was when He said, "Take a bunch of hyssop" —that kind of coarse grass, I suppose, that would grow out of any dyke-back— just like the grass that grew out of the thatch of your mother's house away in the country long ago—a thing so simple; do you not see that everybody could get at it? Instinctively the father's hand went for it, and used it. There is a something in the powers of your soul and mine that is common and handy, and is continually in use in this work-a-day life of ours. It is continually in use like the bunch of hyssop. And what is that? It is faith. Believe me, faith is as common as the hyssop that sprang out of the wall. With all the rack and ruin that sin has made it is here. Now, what you have to do is this. Take that faith, that confidence that you are exercising in brother-man and sister-woman every day—it is the very cement of society—society would tumble into chaos without it—take that faith of yours and give it a new direction. Give it an operation which it never had before. "Believe in the Lord Jesus Christ, and thou shalt be saved." Faith is common, natural, reasonable, sublime. You put it to its highest power, its loftiest use, when it is turned to trust God in the word that He has spoken, and in the love that He has displayed on Calvary. IV. And the last word I have to say is this—the last word in the text, "TAKE THE BUNCH OF HYSSOP, AND DIP IT IN THE BLOOD, AND LET NONE OF YOU GO OUT OF THE DOOR OF HIS HOUSE UNTIL THE MORNING." I hear to-day, and so do you, about "development," and "growth"; and what we hear about them gets wearisome, does it not? There was very little development that night. "Let none of you go out of the door of his house until the morning." Go in, and stay in, if you would be saved. That is to say, there was to be no advance, and absolutely no development from the simplicity of faith. That which they had begun to do saved them only as they kept it up. Human nature is the same all the world over, whether you are in Egypt or in London; and I can imagine a young Israelite, a young fellow just like ourselves, full of flesh and blood, full of natural go and glow and enthusiasm, feeling it a little irksome as the evening wore on, and as the night darkened down; and feeling that it was rather an ignoble, inglorious position to be huddled in there like sheep, with that word over them, "Let none of you go out of the door of his house until the morning." And to be saved in this simple way by the blood-red mark which they did not see, but which, being outside, could be seen by the Destroying Angel as He passed. And I should not wonder, as the Israelites and the Egyptians were not separated one from another, if the Egyptians were all round about the Israelites; and I should not wonder if some young Egyptians came round about these blood-streaked houses and cried, with scoffs and jokes, "Come out! Come out!" and laughed and said, "What are you doing in there? There is no judgment. There was never such a fine night in Egypt. Come out! Come out!" Was not that hard to bear? Is not that taunt in our ears yet—"Come out, you stupid believers!" And I can imagine a young Israelite chafing and getting restless as the night wore on, and there came no sign of this doom, and no sign of this judgment; I can imagine him shaking himself, and saying, "I will assert my manhood. This may do for the old people"; and he is going over to the door, but his father rises, and with a voice like thunder says, "Unhand that door! Back for your life!" And he was right if he did. He was right. The Egyptians might laugh that night, and the young, restless, hot-headed Israelites might have a little trouble, but nobody laughed in the morning. And you and I, children of faith, believers in God and in God's Christ who died for sin, just for a little while have to stand the laugh, and I admit that it is against our pride. By the grace of God, and in the obedience of faith, let me charge you, hold on, my brother, as you began. Let us keep together, we who belong to "the household of faith." How that expression receives its illustration from this story. Let us keep together. Let us encourage ourselves to stay in doors until the morning. Some of you, God bless you, will not have long to wait. God bless all white and whitening heads in this assembly; you will not have long to wait. "Now is the time of your salvation nearer than when you believed." For you the morning cometh. (*J. McNeill.*) *Anxiety in reference to salvation :*—There is among the Hebrews a legend of two sisters who that night had, with the rest of their household, gone into their dwellings. One of them stood all ready to depart, and began quietly eating her portion of the roast body of the lamb (a type of the soul feeding on Christ), her mind at perfect peace and rest. The other was walking about the dwelling, full of terrible fear lest the Destroying Angel should penetrate therein. This one reproached her sister for being so careless and confident, and finally asked her how it was that she could be so full of assurance when the angel of death and judgment was abroad in the land. The reply was, "Why, sister, the blood has been sprinkled; and we have God's word that when He sees the blood, He will pass over us. Now I have no right to doubt God's word. I believe He will keep His word. If I were in doubt about the blood having been shed; or if I doubted either the integrity or ability of God in connection with His word, I should be uneasy. But, as I do not question the fact that the blood has been shed, and as I believe that God will be true to His word, I cannot but be at peace." They were both equally safe; but one was at peace, while the other was not. Or, as we should say now: one had assurance; and the other was full of doubts. But if the doubting one had believed what God said, she could not have been in distress. It is even so now. Those believers who make the finished work of Christ the ground of their hope, and are resting simply and sincerely on His Word, are at peace; while those who are trying to find peace in themselves, in their frames and feelings, are never at rest. It is the Blood of Jesus that makes us safe; it is the Word of God concerning blood that makes us sure. (*J. Parker, D.D.*)

Vers. 24, 25. **Ye shall keep this service.**—*Celebration of the Passover :*—I. IN THIS INCIDENT WE HAVE A CLEAR RECOGNITION OF THE PRINCIPLE OF VICARIOUS SUFFERING. It is seen in the birth of the infant, in the history of the family circle, in the events of everyday life, but supremely in the Cross of Christ. In the Cross of Christ it is seen in its highest embodiment, in its truest meaning, and in its most glorious possibility. There is the innocent dying for the guilty, the God-man suffering for the race. II. IN THIS INCIDENT WE HAVE A CLEAR RECOGNITION OF THE NEED OF FALLING IN WITH ALL THE- REQUIREMENTS OF THE GREAT SCHEME OF SALVATION. The method whereby the Israelites were to be protected from the stroke of the Destroying Angel was Divinely originated, clearly revealed, and imperative in requirement. The sinner must be saved in God's way, and not after his own. He may reason about the peculiarity of the method of salvation; he may think that other means will be more effective to the end desired; but if he at last is found out of the Divine way of safety, he will inevitably be lost. The blood of Christ sprinkled on the heart is the only sign the Destroying Angel will recognize and regard as the token of safety. III. IN THIS INCIDENT WE HAVE A CLEAR RECOGNITION OF THE FACT THAT THE DIVINE METHOD OF SALVATION WILL AVERT THE MOST

AWFUL PERIL. The trustful soul shall not be hurt by the second death. IV. IN THIS INCIDENT WE HAVE A CLEAR RECOGNITION OF THE FACT THAT THE EFFICACY OF THE DIVINE METHOD OF SALVATION SHOULD BE ASSOCIATED WITH PUBLIC RELIGIOUS ORDINANCES (ver. 24). V. IN THIS INCIDENT WE HAVE A CLEAR RECOGNITION OF THE FACT THAT THE GOOD SHOULD BE ABLE TO GIVE AN INTELLIGENT EXPLANATION OF THEIR MORAL SAFETY (ver. 27). (*J. S. Exell, M.A.*) *The need of an intelligent apprehension of the service and worship of God:*—I. IT IS NECESSARY IN ORDER TO THE TRUE PERFORMANCE OF RELIGIOUS SERVICE AND WORSHIP. II. IT IS NECESSARY IN ORDER TO THE TRUE PERFORMANCE OF PARENTAL DUTY AND INSTRUCTION. III. IT IS NECESSARY IN ORDER TO REFUTE AND SILENCE THE SCEPTICAL REASONINGS OF MEN. (*Ibid.*) *The blood of sprinkling and the children :*—I. THE IMPORTANCE ATTACHED TO THE BLOOD OF SACRIFICE is here made very plain. 1. It became and remained the national mark. 2. It was also the saving token. 3. It was rendered as conspicuous as possible. 4. It was made very dear to the people themselves by the fact that they trusted in it in the most implicit manner. 5. The paschal bloodshedding was to be had in perpetual remembrance. 6. This sprinkling of the blood was to be an all-pervading memory. II. THE INSTITUTION THAT WAS CONNECTED WITH THE REMEMBRANCE OF THE PASSOVER. Inquiry should be excited respecting spiritual things in the minds of children. The doctrine of the expiatory sacrifice is a gospel for the youngest. (*C. H. Spurgeon.*) *Children should be taught the doctrine of the Cross :*—It is well to explain to children the ordinance of the Lord's Supper, for this shows forth the death of Christ in symbol. I regret that children do not oftener see this ordinance. Baptism and the Lord's Supper should both be placed in view of the rising generation, that they may then ask us, " What mean ye by this? " Now, the Lord's Supper is a perennial gospel sermon, and it turns mainly upon the sacrifice for sin. You may banish the doctrine of the Atonement from the pulpit, but it will always live in the Church through the Lord's Supper. You cannot explain that broken bread and that cup filled with the fruit of the vine, without reference to the Lord's atoning death. You cannot explain " the communion of the body of Christ" without bringing in, in some form or other, the death of Jesus in our place and stead. Let your little ones, then, see the Lord's Supper, and let them be told most clearly what it sets forth. Tell them who it was that suffered, and why. And when attention is excited upon the best of themes, let us be ready to explain the great transaction by which God is just, and yet sinners are justified. Children can well understand the doctrine of the expiatory sacrifice ; it was meant to be a gospel for the youngest. The gospel of substitution is a simplicity, though it is a mystery. We ought not to be content until our little ones know and trust in their finished Sacrifice. This is essential knowledge, and the key to all other spiritual teaching. With all their gettings may they get an understanding of this, and they will have the foundation rightly laid. This will necessitate your teaching the child his need of a Saviour. You must not hold back from this needful task. Do not flatter the child with delusive rubbish about his nature being good and needing to be developed. Tell him he must be born again. Don't bolster him up with the fancy of his own innocence, but show him his sin. Mention the childish sins to which he is prone, and pray the Holy Spirit to work conviction in his heart and conscience. (*Ibid.*)

Ver. 28. **Did as the Lord had commanded.**—*Worship and obedience :*—1. Worship of God in faith, humility, and integrity is the fittest way of expressing thanks to him. 2. God's revelation of grace in providences and ordinances deserve praise from His people. 3. Worship of God and obedience to Him are well coupled (ver. 27). 4. Dispatch in obedience is very requisite in God's Israel. 5. Sons of Israel are fit to give worship and obedience, and Jehovah only to receive it. 6. Obedience and worship must be regulated by God's Word only. 7. As God gives to ministers, so the Church must receive, and do exactly. (*G. Hughes, B.D.*)

Vers. 29, 30. **A great cry in Egypt.**—*The death of the firstborn of Egypt :*—I. WE SEE HERE THAT GOD'S VENGEANCE IS AS CERTAINLY EXECUTED UPON THE REBELLIOUS AS IT IS THREATENED. Men cannot elude the stroke of heaven. II. WE SEE HERE THAT GOD'S VENGEANCE IS UPON ALL SINNERS, NO MATTER WHAT THEIR SOCIAL POSITION, WHETHER KING OR BEGGAR. He takes the rich from their wealth, the poor from their misery ; and perhaps in the next life the relations of men may be inverted— the poor man may be the prince, and the prince the slave in the dungeon. III. WE SEE HERE THAT GOD'S VENGEANCE COMES UPON SINNERS WHEN THEY LEAST EXPECT IT, AND IN

THEIR MOMENTS OF FANCIED SECURITY. The darkness cannot hide from Him. We know not what will be in the approaching night. IV. WE SEE HERE THAT GOD'S VENGEANCE MAY MAKE THE MOST OBSTINATE SINNERS YIELD TO THE DEMANDS OF HEAVEN. It is well to avoid the penalties of sin, though this is the very lowest motive for obedience to the will of heaven. The submission of Pharaoh 1. It was immediate upon the plague. 2. It was complete in its obedience. 3. It was comprehensive in its injunction. 4. It was welcomed by the Egyptians. (*J. S. Exell, M.A.*) *"Not a house where there was not one dead"* :—I. WE SHALL NOTICE SOME OF THE PARTICULARS DETAILED IN THIS REMARKABLE HISTORY. It is of no utility we read it, if it be not with care for our instruction. 1. Evidently there was a Divine design in this event. All events are of Providence, and not a single death takes place, however man seeks to shun it, without its concurrence. But in this case, God obviously determined on giving palpable proof of His hand, that the blindest of the Egyptians should be able to see and own it. (1) There was method in the dispensation. (2) The time was remarkable. (3) There was no death in any of the families of the Israelites. 2. Let us ascertain what was the design of God in this peculiar visitation of the Egyptians. He may bear long in patience with the unjust and cruel, but not always, and the lingering stroke will fall the more heavily at last. II. WHEN GOD RESOLVES ON PUNISHING THE REBELLIOUS, IT IS IMPOSSIBLE TO STAY HIS HAND. 1. How sudden was the infliction! No sign was given to the rebellious of this particular calamity; for they had been furnished with signs which they had not properly regarded. 2. What may we suppose were the contemplations and feelings of the Israelites during these solemn proceedings? No doubt they had often been tempted to think hardly of Providence that had given them such evil things, and the Egyptians their good things of wealth and prosperity, at their cost. Now what a reverse! "He is not unrighteous who taketh vengeance." III. THE SCENES OF MORTALITY, STILL SO COMMON IN OUR WORLD, OUGHT TO PRODUCE IN US A DISPOSITION TO THINK OF OUR OWN APPROACHING DISSOLUTION. Let two things be well considered. 1. A sense of the transitory nature of earthly scenes unquestionably is most necessary as a preparation and stimulus to seek the salvation of the soul. 2 What is it to be prepared for death? There is no other question equal in importance to this. You must see and feel yourself a lost sinner without Christ as your Saviour. (*Essex Remembrancer.*) *The marks of spiritual death* :—1. The first mark of spiritual death which I shall mention is that of living in any open and acknowledged sin; such as profane swearing, sabbath breaking, drunkenness, adultery, covetousness, and such like. 2. Another mark of spiritual death is a dependence in whole or in part upon ourselves for salvation. One of the first acts of the Spirit of God upon the heart is to convince men of sin. 3. A third mark of this state is, when under the preaching of the gospel, no change takes place in the life or conversation. 4. Another mark of this state is, a practical preference of the creature to the Creator, or of self to God. When the soul is quickened by the Holy Spirit, it makes God its chief happiness. 5. Another mark of those who are spiritually dead is, living without private and secret prayer. (*J. H. Stewart, M.A.*) *A king's bereavement* :—Henry I., on his return from Normandy, was accompanied by a crowd of nobles and his son William. The white ship in which the prince embarked lingered behind the rest of the royal fleet, while the young nobles, excited with wine, hung over the ship's side taunting the priest who came to give the customary benediction. At last the guards of the king's treasure pressed the vessel's departure, and, driven by the arms of fifty rowers, it swept swiftly out to sea. All at once the ship's side struck on a rock at the mouth of the harbour, and in an instant it sank beneath the waves. One terrible cry, ringing through the stillness of the night, was heard by the royal fleet, but it was not until the morning that the fatal news reached the king. He fell unconscious to the ground and rose never to smile again! (*H. O. Mackey.*) *A father's grief* :—On the death of his only son, the famous Edmund Burke wrote as follows: "The storm has gone over me, and I lie like one of those old oaks which the late hurricane has scattered around me. I am stripped of all my honour. I am torn up by the roots, and lie prostrate on the earth. I am alone." (*J. Tinling, B.A.*) *The last plague, and the deliverance of the Israelites* :— Two questions naturally arise here: Why in this judgment upon the life of man should precisely the firstborn have been slain? and if the judgment was for the overthrow of the adversary and the redemption of Israel, why should a special provision have been required to save Israel also from the plague? 1. In regard to the first of these points, there can be no doubt that the slaying of the firstborn of Egypt had respect to the relation of Israel to Jehovah: "Israel," said God, "is

My son, My firstborn : if thou refuse to let him go, I will slay thy son, thy firstborn "
(chap. iv. 22, 23). But in what sense could Israel be called God's firstborn son?
Something more is plainly indicated by the expression, though no more is very
commonly found in it, than that Israel was peculiarly dear to God, had a sort of
firstborn's interest in His regard. It implies this, no doubt, but it also goes deeper,
and points to the Divine origin of Israel as the seed of promise ; in their birth the
offspring of grace, as contradistinguished from nature. As the firstborn in God's
elect family is to be spared and rescued, so the firstborn in the house of the enemy,
the beginning of his increase, and the heir of his substance, must be destroyed : the
one a proof that the whole family were appointed to life and blessing ; the other, in
like manner, a proof that all who were aliens from God's covenant of grace, equally
deserved, and should certainly in due time inherit, the evils of perdition. 2. In
regard to the other question which concerns Israel's liability to the judgment which
fell upon Egypt, this arose from Israel's natural relation to the world, just as their
redemption was secured by their spiritual relation to God. For, whether viewed in
their individual or in their collective capacity, they were in themselves of Egypt :
collectively, a part of the nation, without any separate and independent existence of
their own, vassals of the enemy, and inhabitants of His doomed territory ;
individually, also, partakers of the guilt and corruption of Egypt. It is the mercy
and grace alone of God's covenant which makes them to differ from those around
them ; and, therefore, to show that while, as children of the covenant, the plague
should not come nigh them, not a hair of their head should perish, they still were
in themselves no better than others, and had nothing whereof to boast, it was, at
the same time, provided that their exemption from judgment should be secured only
by the blood of atonement. (P. Fairbairn, D.D.)   A picture of the wrath to
come :—Is this a dreadful picture ? Yet it is but a type of what must be—a shadow
merely of the wrath to come to all the unsprinkled souls' tenements in eternity. Ye
that affect to think so lightly of death and eternity ! see here this shadow and gather
the elementary ideas of what shall be, from what has been already, under the
government of God. Standing, in imagination, amid these complicated horrors in
Egypt—the groans of the dying, mingling with the shrieks of the living, throughout
a whole empire—all earthly pomp and power levelled to mingle its unavailing cries
with the lowest and meanest in a common woe,—here see what it is for God to
" whet His glittering sword and His hand to take hold on vengeance." (S. Robinson,
D.D.)   God's direct interference :—It is to be observed that in this last plague God
is represented as descending in His own Person. It is no longer the man Moses,
standing as a mediator between the king of Egypt and the King of kings. God
Himself awakes to judgment ; He hath girt His sword upon His thigh, and is come
down ;—" Thus saith the Lord, About midnight will I go out into the midst of
Egypt " (chap. xi. 4). This solemn assurance, though it might well strike terror
into the hearts of the miserable Egyptians, would encourage and confirm the
Israelites. What God had undertaken could not fail, could not miscarry. The
course of Moses' policy with Pharaoh hitherto had brought them no deliverance,
but some increase of their sufferings, and many disappointments. Now they might
feel assured that the promised rescue was at hand. The God of their fathers has
given over the Egyptians appointed unto death, and is gathering the Israelites
together for safety and release. Through the fall of Egypt salvation is come unto
Israel ; and the judgment which slays the one people is ordained as a type of mercy
and redemption for the other, to be commemorated evermore. If God made use of
natural means in a supernatural manner, as in the case of the locusts, and generally
of the other plagues, the miracle would not, on that account, be less miraculous.
But there are circumstances in the account of this plague which distinguish it from
any known or specific form of disease. The firstborn only were smitten ; these were
singled out in every family with unerring precision, the houses of the Israelites,
wherever the blood of the lamb was sprinkled on the door-posts being passed over.
The death of all those thousands, both of man and beast, took place at the same
instant—" at midnight." Every one of these extraordinary events had been foretold
by Moses. Whatever explanations modern scepticism may suggest, they were
admitted without hesitation both by the Egyptians and the Jews to be the Lord's
doing, and marvellous in their eyes. The God whom they knew not had come among
them, and made His presence felt : they stood face to face with their Creator. Fear
fell upon them, and a horrible dread overwhelmed them ; their flesh trembled for
fear of Him, and they were afraid of His judgments. The sins of the parents
were now visited upon the children : the seed of evildoers was cut off. Slaughter

was prepared for the children, for the iniquity of their fathers. Is God unrighteous, then, that taketh vengeance? No; this is an act of retribution. The Egyptians had slain the children of the Israelites, casting their infants into the river. Now the affliction is turned upon themselves; the delight of their eyes is taken from them; all their firstborn are dead, from the firstborn of Pharaoh that sat upon his throne, unto the firstborn of the captive that was in his dungeon. (*T. S. Millington.*) *Midnight terror :*—A Southern lady, writing of the early days of the war in America, says—" The fear of an uprising of the blacks was most powerful with us at night. The notes of the whip-poor-wills in the sweet-gum swamp near the stable, the mutterings of a distant thunderstorm, even the rustle of the night wind in the oaks that shaded my window, filled me with nameless dread. In the daytime it seemed impossible to associate suspicion with those familiar tawny or sable faces that surrounded us. We had seen them for so many years smiling or saddening with the family joys or sorrows: they were so guileless, patient, and satisfied. What subtle influence was at work that should transform them into tigers thirsting for our blood? But when evening came again, the ghost that refused to be laid was again at one's elbow. Rusty bolts were drawn and rusty fire-arms loaded. A watch was set where never before had eye or ear been lent to such a service." (*H. O. Mackey.*)

Vers. 33, 35. **The Egyptians were urgent upon the people that they might send them out of the land.**—*Hastened out of Egypt :*—1. Note the reason of this urgency. Fear lest death overtake them all. 2. Note the utter selfishness of the motive. No true repentance in it. 3. Urgency is fitting when there is imminent danger. 4. There is the greatest need of urgency in every sinner's case. Doom and death are at hand. (*Homiletic Review.*)　　*The Israelites going out of Egyptian bondage; or, the freedom of the Church :*—I. That the Israelites were given their freedom by those who had long oppressed them; and so the Church shall be freed by those who have long enslaved it. II. That the Israelites, in availing themselves of their freedom, had to make many temporary shifts; and so the Church, in stepping into liberty, will have to encounter many perplexities. III. That the Israelites, going into freedom, took with them all the wealth they could get from the Egyptians; and so the Church, in entering upon its liberty, should avail itself of all the valuables it can obtain from the world. (*J. S. Exell, M.A.*)　　**Borrowed from the Egyptians.**— *Borrowing from the enemy :*—I remember, when visiting Denmark some twenty years ago, I learned a little incident in the history of a great Danish admiral. On one occasion, when commanding a little sloop—it was before he was admiral—he had the audacity to engage an English frigate in battle. They both fired away, but after a little time the captain of the frigate noticed that the firing from the sloop ceased. A flag of truce was hoisted; a boat was lowered, and the Danish captain came alongside. Addressing his opponent, he said, " Sir, our powder is all done, and we have come to borrow some from you! " The devil has been using money against the cause of God for many years; let us take it from him, and turn his guns against himself. (*Dr. Sinclair Patterson.*)

Vers. 37–39. **Journeyed from Rameses.**—*The setting forth of the Israelites from Egypt :*—1. The sons of Israel, or Church of God, are in a moving state below. 2. From countries and cities with habitations, God leads His people sometimes to pitch in booths. 3. The number of the seed of God's visible Church is great and multiplied according to His word. 4. Men, women, and children, God numbers with His Church or Israel (ver. 37). 5. Providence so ordering, all sorts of people may join themselves to God's Church, though not in truth. 6. God's Word fails not in giving His Church great substance when He seeth it good (ver. 38). 7. Liberty from Egypt is Israel's good portion with unleavened cakes. 8. Sufficiency and contentation God giveth His people in their straits. 9. In working liberty for His Church, God may put them upon some hardship. 10. God sometimes prevents the providence of His Church for themselves, that He may provide for them (ver. 39). (*G. Hughes, B.D.*)　　**A mixed multitude went up also.**—*The nominal followers of the Christian Church; the motives by which they are actuated, and the perplexities by which they are tested :*—I. THE MOTIVES BY WHICH THE NOMINAL ADHERENTS OF THE CHRISTIAN CHURCH ARE ANIMATED. 1. They are acquainted and impressed with the history of the Church, and hence are induced to follow it. 2. They have an inner conviction that the Church is right, and hence they are sometimes led to follow it. 3. They are associated by family ties with those who are real members of the Christian Church, and hence they are induced to follow it. 4. They are troubled by ideas of the retributive providence of God, and so are induced to seek shelter in the Church. 5. They have an idea that it is socially correct to be allied to the Church, and therefore are induced to follow it. 6. They always follow the multitude. II. THE PERPLEXITIES BY WHICH THE NOMINAL ADHERENTS OF THE CHRISTIAN CHURCH ARE TESTED. We read elsewhere that " the mixed multitude that was among the Israelites fell a lusting " (Num. xi. 4). Their unhallowed desires were not gratified. Their deliverance had not been so glorious as they had imagined. Trial was before them, and they rebelled against the first privations of the wilderness. And so it is, nominal members of the Christian Church are soon tested, and they often yield to the trying conditions of the pilgrim Church life. 1 The nominal members of the Church are tested by the outward circumstances of the Church. 2. They are tested by the pilgrim difficulties of the Church. 3. They are tested by the pilgrim requirements of the Church. (*J. S. Exell, M.A.*) *The character and conduct of the mixed multitude :* —I. THE CHARACTER OF THIS MIXED MULTITUDE. Some, perhaps, were mere idolaters; others had outwardly renounced their superstitions. Some might be connected in marriage with the sons or daughters of Israel ; for such are mentioned : and some, perhaps, were a thoughtless rabble, whom curiosity had called from their homes, that they might go three days' journey with the people, to sacrifice to the Lord in the wilderness. 1. With such a view of the mixed multitude, we may reasonably imagine that they had a very imperfect knowledge of the God of Israel. 2. This mixed multitude had been induced to follow Israel, probably because they had seen the miraculous interpositions of God in behalf of His people, and wished to partake of them. 3. Others, again, had probably accompanied the Israelites in unreflecting carelessness, without anticipating the difficulties and trials before them. 4. The mixed multitude seem never to have entirely united themselves to the community of Israel. II. THEIR CONDUCT IN THE HOUR OF TEMPTATION. The passage in the book of Numbers informs us that they fell a lusting. We know not the peculiar nature of the trials to which they were exposed ; but we find them soon yielding to the power of temptation, and the love of sin. 1. They speedily became discontented with their condition. 2. The inspired penman speaks no more of this mixed multitude; and therefore we are justified in supposing that they who escaped the fire of the Lord, quitted the camp of Israel, and returned to Egypt. In that mixed multitude which throng around the Church of the living God, and profess communion with it, there are, I fear, not a few who sin after the similitude of the transgression committed in the wilderness. (*C. H. Spurgeon.*) *Lessons :*—I. THAT PROFESSION IS NOT NECESSARILY TRUE RELIGION. II. THAT TRIALS ARE NECESSARY PROOF OF FAITH AND LOVE. III. THAT EVIL COMMUNICATIONS CORRUPT GOOD MANNERS. (*R. P. Buddicom.*) *The mixed multitude :*—I. THE EMISSARIES OF SATAN. In all ages there have been these corrupters of the truth in the Church, who have bred schisms of all kinds, " creeping into houses," and " leading captive silly women "; and, as they have gained power and position, becoming more bold in the propagandism of error, both in doctrine and form. II. THE HYPOCRITES. Worldly men come into the Church for the purpose of making " gain of godliness," and using religion as a " cloak of covetousness." I remember very well, when I was a young man, going away from home into a newer part of our country with a view of making my fortune. I was advised by a respectable business man to " connect myself with the most popular church in the town," as a means of " getting on," and securing the recognition and help of the best people. Soon after I became a pastor, I overheard a merchant talking to a young man, and endeavouring to persuade him to join the church ; he used as an argument the fact that when he came to that village a young man, that was the first thing he had done ; and he affirmed that it was " the best stroke of business he had ever done." He attributed his success in life to that fact. And no doubt the hypocrite was right. Verily he had his reward. III. THE FORMALISTS. By these I mean those who are more or less apprehensive of the future, and somewhat troubled about their sins, and who take to the formalism of Christianity as a means of security against the possible dangers of another world. They know nothing of Christ and His salvation ; are strangers to conversion and regeneration : but seize upon the forms and ceremonies of religion as being all that is needful. Among this number may be classed a vast number who have fled for refuge to the " Church " in serious earnest, but who are at best the merest parasites, or semi-parisites. They have no life in themselves, but are clinging to persons or things from whom or from which they fancy they can draw life for themselves. Poor souls! did they only flee to Christ, and be joined to Him, they would indeed be saved; but, as it now is, they are mere Egyptians who are in the midst of the camp of Israel without the mark or sign of blood upon them. IV. THE SELF-DECEIVED. (*G. F. Pentecost, D.D.*) *Mixed multitudes :*—People looking on will judge everything according to their own quality. You cannot get bad people to form good judgments. You cannot persuade good people to form mean and contemptible judgments. Let us suppose Moses and Aaron at the head of this great throng. Criticism would thus speak respecting the multitude : They must be better than they seem, or they would not follow the leadership of such men as Moses and Aaron; it is a very motley crowd, but it must be substantially good at heart, because look at the leadership which it has chosen. Or criticism might speak thus : Moses and Aaron cannot be much after all, or they would not allow this rag-tag-and-bob-tail following. Thus criticism, I repeat, is determined by quality. In the one case the multitudes get the benefit of the moral elevation of their leaders ; in the other case the leaders come in for depreciation because of the motley character of their followers. Blessed be heaven, the Judge is just who shall judge us all. We shall not be left at the disposal of imperfect and selfish criticism. A crowd, even in a church, is not to be judged indiscriminately or pronounced upon in some rough generalization. The crowd is "mixed." Men are not all in church for the same reason. Men are not all in church through the same motives. Some are in church who do not want to be there; they have a purpose to serve : some are there on account of mere curiosity. Others are in church to pray, to confess their life-sins, and seek the pity of God as expressed in pardon at the foot of the saving Cross. Outside criticism would thus judge us differently. Whilst we say this about the outward church, the great surging crowd that may be within the hallowed walls, we could say practically the same thing about the inner church. Even the inner church, gathered around the sacramental board, is a mixed multitude. For example, look at the difference of spiritual attainment. There is the veteran who knows his Bible almost by heart, and here is the little learner spelling out its earliest words. Have they a right to be in the same church? Their right is not in their attainments, but in their desire. But this makes church life very difficult to conduct: very difficult for the pastor and teacher, very difficult for the constituent members themselves. One can go at a great pace; another can only crawl. What is to be done when there is such a diversity of power? Then look at what a mixture of disposition there is even in the inner church. We are not all of one quality. Some men are born generous ; other men are born misers. It is easy for some men to pray; other men have to scourge themselves to their knees. Look at the difference of faculty for work you find in the church. One man will do anything for you in the way of music. He likes it ; it would be a burden to him not to do it. Thank God for such service! Another man will work in the Sunday school. He loves children ; their presence makes him young; he can never be old so long as he sees the light of little faces. Every man is himself a mixed multitude. That is the philosophy. Have you ever gone far enough in the task of self-analysis to find out how many men you, the individual man, really are? You are self-inconsistent ; you are not the same man at night you were in the morning; whatever you do, you do in a mixed way. It is human nature that is the mixed multitude. We know that we have motives; we have never seen them, but we have felt them; we know of a verity that we never do anything with a pure, simple, direct, frank motive. Sometimes the motive is as a whole good, with just one little taint in the middle of it. Sometimes the motive is predominantly bad, with just one little speck of white on the outside or on the left hand. So are we. It is the same way with our thoughts. We are not always impious. Sometimes even the unbeliever feels as though he could believe if one beam could be added to the light which already showers its glory upon his life. Sometimes the believer feels as if he had been misled, as if he were following some aerial sprite, some shadowy spectral nothing. At what point is he to be judged? God will judge him at his best. God accepts our prayers in their bloom. Do not, therefore, condemn yourselves because sometimes you are in moods that really distress the very soul; on the other hand, do not flatter yourselves and commit yourselves to the seduction that ends in utterest failure of life. What is the great work which the gospel has to do in the soul in relation to all this mixture of motive and thought? It has to take out all the bad and throw it away. Come, thou Holy Ghost, and take out of our hearts the selfish motive, the miser's greed, the debasing thought, the little, mean, contemptible purpose; tear it up, burn it in unquenchable fire. When a man can so pray he has a good hope that one day he shall be self-unanimous. Blessed will be the realization of self-unanimity. (*J. Parker, D.D.*)   *Hangers-on*:—The remora, instead of swimming far by its own exertions, greatly prefers being transported from place to place on ships' bottoms, or even the bodies of sharks. When one of the sharks to which a remora is clinging is caught by a hook, and is pulled out of the water, the little parasite is shrewd in its own interest, for it drops off and makes for the bottom of the ship. As long as a ship remains within the tropics, numbers of remoræ cling to its bottom, whether that be coppered or not, whence they dart off occasionally to pick up any morsels of greasy or farinaceous matter that may be thrown overboard, retiring again rapidly to their anchorage. These hangers-on resemble our social ones in the following particulars : they like travelling about ; they do not care what they attach themselves to so long as it suits their purpose for the time ; they will not get along by their own exertions if they can find others to carry them ; they are sharp in their own interests, and know quite well when to desert a supporter ; and they are ready to avail themselves of discarded or accidental ailment. (*Scientific Illustrations.*)

Vers. 40–41. **All the hosts of the Lord went out.**—*The Exodus :*—I. WE CANNOT TREAT THE EXODUS AS AN ISOLATED FACT IN HISTORY. Egypt is the type of the cunning, careless, wanton world, out of which in all ages God is calling His sons. The Exodus remained a living fact in history. The infant Jesus went down into Egypt, as the infant Israel went down, not to repeat the Exodus, but to illume afresh its fading lines. 1. The Children of Israel were an elect race, because they were of the seed of Abraham : that constituted their distinctity. You are of the race of the second Adam, of the same flesh and blood as Jesus ; and all who wear a human form and understand a human voice, God calls forth from Egypt ; His voice calls to His sons, "Come forth to freedom, life, and heaven." 2. You, like the Israelites, are called forth to the desert, the fiery pillar, the manna, the spiritual rock ; and while you aim at Canaan, His will, His heart, are on your side. II. NOTE THE MORAL FEATURES OF THE EXODUS. 1. There was a life in Egypt which had become insupportable to a man. That bondage is the picture of a soul round which the devil's toils are closing. 2. The Israelites saw the stroke of heaven fall on all that adorns, enriches, and nourishes a worldly life. 3. They had a Divine leader, a man commissioned and inspired by God. We have the Apostle and High Priest of our profession, Christ Jesus, who, in the house and the work in which Moses wrought as a servant, represents God as the Son. 4. We discern a condition of utter dependence on the strength and faithfulness of God. They and we were delivered by a Divine work. 5. Notice, lastly, the freedom of the delivered Israelites ; a broad, deep sea flowing between them and the land of bondage, and the tyrants dead upon the shore. Such is the glorious sense of liberty, of wealth, of life, when the deep sea of Divine forgiving love sweeps over the past and obliterates its shame. (*J. B. Brown, B.A.*)   *The Exodus :*—I. First, consider THE MODE OF THEIR GOING OUT. 1. When the Children of Israel went out of Egypt it is a remarkable thing that they were forced out by the Egyptians. The dove fleeth not to his cote unless the eagle doth pursue it ; so sins, like eagles, pursue the timid soul, making it fly into the clefts of the Rock Christ Jesus to hide itself. Once, our sins kept us from Christ ; but now every sin drives us to Him for pardon. I had not known Christ if I had not known sin ; I had not known a deliverer, if I had not smarted under the Egyptians. The Holy Spirit drives us to Christ, just as the Egyptians drove the people out of Egypt. 2. Again : the Children of Israel went out of Egypt covered with jewels and arranged in their best garments. Ah ! that is just how a child of God comes out of Egypt. He does not come out of his bondage with his old garments of self-righteousness on : oh ! no ; as long as he wears those he will always keep in Egypt ; but he marches out with the blood and righteousness of Jesus Christ upon him, and adorned with the goodly graces of the Holy Spirit. 3. Note, moreover, that these people obtained their jewels from the Egyptians. God's people never lose anything by going to the house of bondage. They win their choicest jewels from the Egyptians. "Strangely true it is, sins do me good," said an old writer once, "because they drive me to the Saviour ; and so I get good by them." Ask the humble Christian where he got his humility, and ten to one he will say that he got it in the furnace of deep sorrow on account of sin. See another who is tender in conscience : where did he get that jewel from ? It came from Egypt, I'll be bound. We get more by being in bondage, under conviction of sin, than we often do by liberty. 4. They came out in haste. I never met with a poor sinner under a sense of sin who was not in haste to get his burden off his back. No man has a broken heart, unless he wants to have it bound up directly. " To-day if ye will hear His voice, harden not your heart," says the Holy Ghost; He never says to-morrow; to-day is His continual cry, and every true-born Israelite will pant to get out of Egypt, whenever he has the opportunity. II. THE MAGNITUDE OF THIS DELIVERANCE. I would have you particularly remember one thing; and that is, that great as this emigration was, and enormous as were the multitudes that quitted Egypt, it was only one Passover that set them all free. One agonizing sacrifice, one death on Calvary, one bloody sweat on Gethsemane, one shriek of "It is finished" consummated all the work of redemption. III. THE COMPLETENESS OF THEIR DELIVERANCE. As Moses said, "Not an hoof shall be left behind." They were to have all their goods, as well as their persons. What does this teach us? Why, not only that all God's people shall be saved, but that all that God's people ever had shall be restored. All that Jacob ever took down to Egypt shall be brought out again. Have I lost a perfect righteousness in Adam? I shall have a perfect righteousness in Christ. Have I lost happiness on earth in Adam? God will give me much happiness here below in Christ. Have I lost heaven in Adam? I shall have heaven in Christ; for Christ came not only to seek and to save the people that were lost, but that which was lost: that is, all the inheritance, as well as the people; all their property. IV. THE TIME WHEN THE ISRAELITES CAME OUT OF EGYPT. God had promised to Abraham that His people should be in bondage four hundred and thirty years, and they were not in bondage one day more. As soon as God's bond became due, though it had been drawn four hundred and thirty years before, He paid the bill; He required no more time to do it in, but He did it at once. Christopher Ness says, they had to tarry for the fulfilment of the promise till the night came; for though He fulfilled it the selfsame day, He made them stay to the end of it, to prove their faith. He was wrong there, because Scripture days begin at night. " The evening and the morning were the second day." So that God did not make them wait, but paid them at once. As soon as the day came, beginning with our night, as the Jewish day does now, and the Scriptural day always did—as soon as the clock struck—God paid His bond. (*C. H. Spurgeon.*)

Ver. 42. **A night to be much observed unto the Lord.**—*The Passover:*—I. THE PASSOVER THE APPOINTED MEANS OF A GREAT DELIVERANCE. The destruction of the firstborn secured Israel's freedom; the rite itself saved Israel's firstborn. 1. Wrath was averted. 2. Individual faith and action were required. 3. Perfect safety was thus obtained. II. THE PASSOVER AN ORDAINED FEAST OF REMEMBRANCE. 1. Not a formal service, but gratefully rendered, and intelligently observed; the father instructing the child as to its meaning (vers. 26, 27). 2. To be kept by all the people (ver. 4). The redemption to be celebrated by all the redeemed. 3. In each successive generation. A perpetual witness of Jehovah's delivering mercy; an unfailing type; a constant test and measure of religious life. Kept by Moses (Num. ix.); by Joshua (chap. v.); revived by Josiah; in Nehemiah's time (Ezra. vi.); in our Lord's time widely observed. 4. Every detail was divinely ordered. 5. The lamb was eaten with special accompaniments   Bitter herbs denoted penitence; unleavened bread, sincerity. Godly sorrow chastens Christian joy. True consecration marks the believer's praise. 6. In a pilgrim spirit. Loins girded, shoes on feet, staff in hand. Christ's service here is not the Christian's rest. His eye is fixed on heaven; and, while he works and praises, his true cry ever is, "Come, Lord Jesus." (*W. S. Bruce, M.A.*)   *Freedom and discipline:*—I. Scholars have said that the old Greeks were the fathers of freedom; and there have been other people in the world's history who have made glorious and successful struggles to throw off their tyrants and be free. But liberty is of a far older and nobler house. It was born on the first Easter night, when God Himself stooped from heaven to set the oppressed free. II. The history of the Jews is the history of the whole Church and of every nation in Christendom. The Jews had to wander forty years in the wilderness, and Christendom has had to wander too, in strange and blood-stained paths, for eighteen hundred years and more. For as the Israelites were not worthy to enter at once into rest, no more have the nation of Christ's Church been worthy. As the new generation sprang up in the wilderness, trained under Moses' stern law, to the fear of God, so for eighteen hundred years have the generations of Christendom, by the training of the Church and the light of the gospel, been growing in wisdom and knowledge, growing in morality and humanity, in that true discipline and loyalty which are the yokefellows of freedom and independence. (*C. Kingsley, M.A.*)   *A holy celebration :*—It is the night of our regeneration; it is the night of our conversion (night or day, it matters not which); the time in which we actually received salvation, and were made partakers of this Passover, that we would just now admonish you to remember. At that particular time important events transpired for us. The most important events, to us, that ever occurred in our history, happened on that occasion. There was a point in our life up to which we were dead : then we were made alive. There was a point up to which we were condemned : then, in an instant, we were acquitted. Now, what events transpired on that occasion? 1. Well, the first was, it pleased God then to show us the blood of Jesus, and to apply it to our souls. That night, too, or that day, whichever it may have been, we do remember that we enjoyed a feast upon our Saviour. The blood was sprinkled, and so we were saved; and then we sat down at the table, and began at once to feast upon the precious things stored up in the person of Christ. 2. And then it was that for the first time in your life you felt that you were free. You were free; but finding yourself free, you also discovered, for the first time, that you were a pilgrim; for the Israelites, as they ate that paschal supper, had to do so with their loins girt and staves in their hands, like men that were to leave that country. You found that now you were a stranger. If you had an unconverted parent, you could not talk to him or her about your soul. If you had old companions, you felt you must bid them farewell, for they would not understand you; if you did not know you were a pilgrim before, you found it out the very next day, when you began to talk with them. O! it was a time to be remembered, and I want you to remember it now—those blessed days when we began to live! 3. Important results will flow to you from the preservation of this memorial. It will humble you and foster the grace of humility. Have you become an old experienced Christian, my brother? Go back to the hole of the pit whence you were digged. (*C. H. Spurgeon.*)

Vers. 43–48. **The ordinance of the Passover.**—*Minute instructions in reference to the observance of the Passover :*—I. THAT GOD NOT ONLY INSTITUTES ORDINANCES FOR MEN, BUT ALSO SHOWS IN WHAT WAY THEY ARE TO BE OBSERVED. II. THAT GOD WILL NOT ALLOW ANY STRANGER TO THE DEATH OF CHRIST TO PARTAKE OF HIS HOLY SACRAMENT. "There shall no stranger eat thereof." III. THAT A MERE HIRED AND NOMINAL RELATION TO THE CHURCH DOES NOT GIVE A TRUE RIGHT TO THE HOLY SACRAMENT. "An hired servant shall not eat thereof." IV. THAT CIRCUMCISION OF HEART IS NECESSARY (ver. 48). (*J. S. Exell, M.A.*)

CHAPTER XIII.

VERS. 1, 2. **Sanctify unto Me all the firstborn.**—*The sanctification of the firstborn to the Lord :*—I. THAT THE GOOD ARE REQUIRED TO SANCTIFY THEIR FIRSTBORN UNTO THE LORD. "All the firstborn"—that is to say, the most excellent of their possessions, the most valuable, and that which is viewed with the greatest regard. 1. This sanctification of the firstborn was required by the Divine commandment. 2. This sanctification of the firstborn was a grateful acknowledgment of the Divine mercy in sparing the firstborn from the midnight destruction. Heaven never asks more than it gives, or more than is consistent with the gratitude of a devout heart to bestow. 3. This sanctification of the firstborn was to be associated with the deliverance of the Israelites from the bondage of Egypt. II. THAT THE GOOD, IN SANCTIFYING THEIR FIRSTBORN UNTO THE LORD, ARE NOT CALLED UPON TO GIVE UP THE SOLE USE OF THEIR PROPERTY, BUT TO REDEEM AND TO PUT IT TO A LAWFUL USE. Who would not desire his firstborn to be the Lord's? III. THAT THE GOOD ARE REQUIRED TO CONNECT THE SANCTIFICATION OF THEIR FIRSTBORN WITH SACRIFICE. "And all the firstborn of man among thy children shalt thou redeem" (ver. 14). This redemption was to be by sacrifice. Parents need reminding of this duty. 1. Because they are liable to forget the service which past mercy requires of them. 2. Because they are apt to be selfish in the use of their property. 3. Because they are not sufficiently spiritually minded to see God in their property, and therefore forget His claims. 4. Because they do not like to pay the redemption price. IV. THAT THE GOOD ARE TO TEACH THE RIGHT OF GOD TO THE FIRSTBORN, TO THEIR POSTERITY (vers. 14, 15). Children are very inquisitive. They will ask questions, even about religious matters. At such times they should be carefully and solemnly instructed in Divine truth. The family is the best school for the young. They should early be taught the meaning of self-sacrifice, and the moral grandeur of giving to the Lord. Even the young have their firstborn, which they can be taught to give to the Lord; and if they grow up in the spirit of this obligation they will, in after days, impart to it a truer meaning, and give to it a more solemn influence than before they were capable of. Lessons: 1. That the good must sanctify their best things to the Lord. 2. That this can only be done by the redemption of the Cross. 3. That the young must be early taught their obligation to the Lord. (*J. S. Exell, M.A.*) *Sanctify unto Me all the firstborn:*—1. A command. 2. A duty. 3. A privilege. 4. A benediction. 5. A prophecy. (*Ibid.*) *The man-tithe:*— I. OBSERVE THE FIRST RULE: "Sanctify unto Me all the firstborn of man." As the redemption of the firstborn of the more valuable animals was graciously commuted by the sacrifice of less valuable ones, so there was a commutation for the firstborn of man; not indeed by inferior substitutes as in the former case, but by his fellow-man—by the institution of a priesthood, "sanctifying," or setting apart, the whole tribe of Levi in place of the firstborn of all Israel. But as this arrangement had not yet transpired at the period of the text, the explanation was deferred till then, that in the meanwhile the whole nation might fully realize the amount and weight of their liability to God; and further, that when Levi was sanctified, the whole Levitical priesthood—a priesthood of their brethren, " bone of their bone, and flesh of their flesh "—might symbolize the High Priesthood of the Mediator who " was in all things made like unto His brethren," that He too " might also make intercession for the sins of the people." This lies at the root of the Levitical principle, the lay-agency in the church of God. Admirable is the advice of Jethro to his son-in-law, and incidentally it bears upon this subject. " This thing," that is, the whole burthen of the work, " is too heavy for thee; thou art not able to perform it thyself alone. . . . Thou shalt provide out of all the people able men, such as fear God, men of truth, hating covetousness; and place such over them, to be rulers of thousands, and rulers of hundreds, rulers of fifties, and rulers of tens." Thus the work of religion, benevolence, and rule was divided, subdivided, and redivided still, from considerable districts down to classes of tens, as we should desire to see the work of God among ourselves distributed among our lay deacons and elders, district visitors, collectors and Sabbath-school teachers, who in their respective ministries should act on the suggestion of Jethro, " The hard causes they brought unto Moses, but every small matter they judged themselves." II. Secondly, the text presents the rule of consecrated WEALTH—" Sanctify unto Me all the firstborn of beasts." On this point there is some difficulty. " All the firstborn of cattle " were given to the Lord by sacrifice; and yet in the forty-fifth verse of the third chapter of Numbers the whole of the cattle of the Levites were considered as a substitute for the firstlings of the general cattle, just as all the men of the Levites were accepted as the substitute for all the firstborn of men from the rest of the tribes. Possibly the cattle firstlings were redeemed, as the excess of human firstborn over the number of the firstborn of the Levites were, by the half-shekel atonement for each, which was payable at the census or periodical numbering of the people. It is probable that David's omission of this payment was the sin which incurred God's heavy displeasure in that unseasonable numbering of the people, which, in omitting the soul-tax for atonement, seemed numbered for David himself, and not for God. Be this as it may, the Lord claimed all the firstborn of their beasts, which were the staple property in the ruder forms of society. III. The text presents its demand for consecrated TIME. We need not dwell upon the Sabbath, or the Divine claim upon the sevenths of our time. Assuming we are all agreed that this, the minimum of God's requirement, is due from every man, we may deplore the manner in which, for the most part, even this holy debt is discharged. The abuse of the Sabbath and insubordination to its constantly recurring, bounden, and emphatic law, lies at the root of the national irreligion. There is a significancy in the proportion of the Divine demand of only a tenth of all other things, but a seventh of our time. (*J. B. Owen, M.A.*) *The Divine right to the best things of man:*—" It is Mine." This is the language of God in reference to each one of us. It is Mine. I. BECAUSE I CREATED IT. II. BECAUSE I PRESERVED IT. III. BECAUSE I ENDOWED

IT WITH EVERYTHING THAT MAKES IT VALUABLE. (*J. S. Exell, M.A.*) *The first-born, types of Christ:*—I. AS THEY WERE GOD'S PECULIAR. 1. By common nature, 2. By common grace. 3. By a special right. (1) In His nature, Christ is Firstborn, as Son of God. (2) In His office, by special prerogative. (*a*) For the kind, in that He was Mediator, God and Man in unity of person, and the only Redeemer of His Church. (*b*) For undertaking of His office. (*c*) For the accomplishing His office, in His resurrection. He is called the First-begotten, or Firstborn of the dead, two ways: (i) In respect of His Father, who first begot Him from the dead; (ii) In regard of Himself, whose privilege it was to raise up Himself from the dead by His own power. II. The firstborn of Israel was the second, and NEXT TO THE FATHER OF THE FAMILY, yea, after the father instead of the father. So is Christ to His family, the Church; He performs all offices of a careful and tender father, and takes on Him, not the affection only of a father, but even—1. The name of a father (Isa. ix. 6). 2. The office of a father. (1) He supplies the means of spiritual life, as they of natural. (2) He nurtures and teacheth His Church. (3) He provides for the present, and bestows the inheritance of eternal life. III. The firstborn HAD THE PRE-EMINENCE AMONG THE BRETHREN, and were chief in office and authority, rulers in the house after their fathers, and priests in the family, before the Levitical order was established. Herein they were special types of Jesus Christ; who in all things must have the pre-eminence, as first in time, in order, in precedency, and in the excellency and dignity of His person. IV. The firstborn HAD A DOUBLE PORTION IN GOODS (Deut. xxi. 17). Signifying—1. The plenitude of the spirit and grace in Christ, who was anointed with oil of gladness above His fellows. 2. The pre-eminency of Christ in His glorious inheritance, advanced in glory and majesty incomprehensible by all creatures. Use—(1) Out of the occasion of the law of the firstborn, learn that the more God doth for any man, the more he ought to conceive himself to be the Lord's, and the more right and interest the Lord challengeth in him. (2) If Christ be the true firstborn, of whom all they are but types, we must give Him the honour of His birthright. (3) Here is a ground of much consolation. (*a*) In that Christ being the truth of the firstborn, from Him the birthright is derived unto us believers, as it was from Reuben unto Judah, and we partake of the same birthright with our head. For here is a difference between the type and truth of the firstborn. They had all their privileges for themselves: but Christ not for Himself but for us. (*b*) Being God's firstborn throughout, we are dear unto God. (*c*) God takes notice, and avenges all wrongs done to the saints, because they are His firstborn. (4) Seeing in Christ the firstborn we attain the birthright; let every Christian beware of profaneness, and passing away his birthright as Esau, who sold his birthright for pottage (Heb. xii. 16). (5) Learn to grow in conformity with our Elder Brother Christ, with whom we cannot be equal, but like as brothers. We must be like Him in affection, like Him in affliction, like Him in the combat, and like Him in the crown. (*T. Taylor, D.D.*) *Consecrated to the Lord:*—When Bishop Selwyn spoke to Sir John Patteson, then a widower, of the desire of his splendidly gifted son, Coleridge, to join him in the New Zealand Mission, the father's first exclamation was: "I cannot let him go!" but he immediately added, "God forbid I should stop him!" And he closed the conversation by saying: "Mind, I give him wholly, not with any thought of seeing him again. I will not have him thinking he must come home to see me." *A consecrated child:*—A young man was about to enter the foreign missionary work. A gentleman said to the young man's father, "It's hard to give up the boy." "Yes," replied the father, "but it's just what we've been expecting." "How so?" inquired the friend. "When he was a little baby," answered the father, "his mother and I went to a missionary meeting. An appeal, most earnest and touching, was made for men to become missionaries. We ourselves could not go. When we returned home the baby lay asleep in his crib. We went to the crib. His mother stood on one side, I on the other. We together laid our hands on his forehead, and prayed that it might be God's will for him to become a foreign missionary. We never spoke to him of what we did. But all through these twenty-five years we have believed that our prayer about him would be answered, and answered it now is. Yes, it is hard to give up the boy, but it's what we've been expecting."

Vers. 3, 4. **Remember this day.**—*A day to be remembered:*—1. God's commands and His servants' obedience are sweetly united together. 2. Deliverance of the Church from Egyptian bondage is justly chargeable on their memory. 3. Jehovah the Author of deliverance is to be minded with His work, and power of doing it.

4. Remembrance of Jehovah carrieth with it mindfulness of duty and service to Him (ver. 3). 5. Days and months of mercy are ordered by God to be remembered (ver. 4). (*G. Hughes, B.D.*) *Days to be remembered :*—I. THERE ARE DAYS IN THE HISTORY OF INDIVIDUALS WHICH OUGHT TO BE CELEBRATED. II. THERE ARE DAYS IN THE HISTORY OF CHURCHES WHICH OUGHT TO BE CELEBRATED. III. THERE ARE DAYS IN THE HISTORY OF NATIONS WHICH OUGHT TO BE CELEBRATED. (*J. S. Exell, M.A.*)

Vers. 5–7. **Keep this service.**—*The ordinances of the Lord :*—I. THAT THE ORDI-NANCES OF THE LORD MUST BE OBSERVED IN THE TIMES OF PROSPERITY (ver. 5). II. THAT THE ORDINANCES OF THE LORD MUST BE OBSERVED WITH TRUE INTELLI-GENCE (vers. 8, 9). III. THAT THE ORDINANCES OF THE LORD MUST BE OBSERVED WITH PARENTAL SOLICITUDE. God has appointed the family the moral nursery of the young. Lessons : 1. To attend to all the ordinances of the Lord. 2. To attend to them at the most appropriate time. 3. To attend to them in right spirit and temper. (*Ibid.*)

Vers. 8–10. **Show thy son in that day.**—*Lessons :*—1. The instruction of children is a duty upon parents. 2. God commands continuance of ordinances for instruc-tion of posterity. 3. The reason of God's ordinances must be understood by parents and children (ver. 8). 4. Sacramental signs, and memorials of God, He is pleased to give His Church. 5. God would have these signal memorials at hand and before the eyes of His. 6. The Passover was a true sacramental sign and seal of God's covenant. 7. By sacraments rightly used God's covenant is confirmed on hearts and in profession. 8. God's mighty gracious redemption is a just cause of such memorials (ver. 9). 9. God's sacraments are His statutes and positive laws. 10. It is God's prerogative, to make anniversary memorials of His mercies (ver. 10). (*G. Hughes, B.D.*) *Truth embodied :*—As the soul is clothed in flesh, and only thus is able to perform its functions in this earth, where it is sent to live ; as the thought must find a word before it can pass from mind to mind ; so every great truth seeks some body, some outward form, in which to exhibit its powers. It appears in the world, and men lay hold of it, and represent it to themselves, in histories, in forms of words, in sacramental symbols ; and these things, which in their proper nature are but illustrations, stiffen into essential fact, and become part of the reality. (*J. A. Froude.*) *Importance of commemorative days and ordinances :*— The following sentence is attributed to Voltaire :—" I despair of destroying Chris-tianity in any country, so long as millions of human beings meet on Sunday to worship God." Many things have been fathered on Voltaire of which he never heard, but if he really said or wrote this he uttered an unusually sensible thing. It is curious that sceptical writers have regarded so little the testimony of Christian rites to the facts with which they are indissolubly connected. How did the Lord's Supper and the Lord's Day come to be established institutions ? Rites and observ-ances do not establish and perpetuate themselves. The origin of these two Chris-tian institutions can only be explained by their connection with the events they commemorate. If the written records of the apostolic age could be blotted from the memory of man, the Lord's Supper would still bear testimony to Christ's death for man's salvation, as the Lord's Day would eloquently witness to His resurrection from the dead.

Vers. 11–13. **All the firstborn.**—*Firstborn to be dedicated to God :*—1. Jehovah is the beginning and end of His own ordinances. He sets them for Himself. 2. The Church must act these duties from God unto God Himself. 3. All that God requires must His people make to pass from them to Him. 4. Firstborn males of beasts God required in the law for special use to Himself (ver. 12). 5. Clean and unclean among creatures is a distinction made by God for men, not for Himself. 6. God hath a proprietary in all creatures be they never so unclean. 7. God hath ordered redemption for unclean by putting the clean in their stead. 8. Unclean unredeemed must be destroyed. 9. A price hath God set for man's redemption to gain a Church of the firstborn. 10. The law of the firstborn hath its truth and accomplishment in Christ Jesus, " the Firstborn of every creature " (Col. i. 15 ; ver. 13). (*G. Hughes, B.D.*)

Vers. 14–16. **When thy son asketh thee.**—The Book of Exodus introduces that new epoch in the scriptural history of sacrifices when they began to be regulated by fixed laws, to be part of a national economy. ʻI. The offering of the firstborn was THE DEDICATION AND CONSECRATION OF THE WHOLE JEWISH NATION. The firstborn represented its strength, its vitality, its endurance. This act signified that its strength lay only in its dependence on God's strength, that its vitality came from the life which is in Him, that it would endure from generation to generation, because He is the same and His years fail not. The calling of the Israelites was the calling to confess a Redeemer of Israel, a righteous Being who had brought out their fathers from the house of bondage. II. Moses taught the people that by looking upon themselves as beings surrendered and sacrificed to the God of truth, the Deliverer of men, by feeling that they held all the powers of their minds and bodies as instruments for the great work in which He is engaged, thus THEY MIGHT BE A NATION INDEED, one which would be a pattern to the nations, one which, in due time, would break the chains which bound them to visible and invisible oppressors. III. When once we understand that we are witnesses for God, and do His work, SELF-SACRIFICE CAN NEVER BE AN AMBITIOUS THING—a fine way to get the reputation of saints or the rewards of another world. It will be regarded as the true ground of all action ; that on which all the blessed relations of life stand ; that which is at the same time the only impulse to and security for the hard and rough work of the world. (*F. D. Maurice, M.A.*) *Meaning of ordinances to be explained :*—1. Ancient ordinances may be justly questioned in succeeding ages to know the meaning of them. 2. Reason is to be given of our religion to such as reasonably demand it. 3. Children may ask of parents and they must inform them of the ordinances of God. 4. Redemption mercies are to be recorded and reported as just ground of God's ordinance (ver. 14). 5. Opposition against redemptions are justly declared to make the work glorious, and God's people obedient. 6. Vengeance upon the enemies of the Church's redemption is fit to be known to quicken them to duty. 7. The Church's reason for its religion to God is rightly taken from its redemption (ver. 15). 8. God's redeeming mercies ought to work in the Church eternal memorials of Him (ver. 16). (*G. Hughes, B.D.*) *Lessons :*—1. After redemption of His Church God provideth for guiding them in the way to rest. 2. Nearest ways to rest with men are not always approved by God for His people. 3. God's foreknowledge of dangerous ways to His Church doth prevent them. 4. God will not put His people upon war or hard trials until He have fitted them for it. 5. God's special care of His Church is to keep them from a retreat to bondage after redemption (ver. 17). (*Ibid.*) *Imparting knowledge :*—Knowledge cannot be stolen by or from you. It cannot be sold or bought. You may be poor, and be troubled by the sheriff on the journey of life. He may break into your house and sell your furniture at auction ; drive away your cow ; take away your ewe lamb, and leave you homeless and penniless ; but he cannot lay the law's hand upon the jewellery of your mind. This cannot be taken for debt ; neither can you give it away, though you give enough of it to fill a million minds. In getting rich in the things which perish with the using, men have often obeyed to the letter that first commandment of selfishness : " Keep what you can get, and get what you can." In filling your minds with the wealth of knowledge, you must reverse this rule, and obey this law : " Keep what you give, and give what you can." The fountain of knowledge is filled by its outlets, not by its inlets. You can learn nothing which you do not teach ; you can acquire nothing of intellectual wealth except by giving. (*Elihu Burritt.*)

Vers. 17–18. Through the way of the wilderness.—*The way of the wilderness :*— I. THE WAY BY WHICH GOD OFTEN LEADS HIS PEOPLE MAY BE DESCRIBED AS THE "WAY OF THE WILDERNESS." There are several points of analogy or similarity between the journey of Israel from Egypt to Canaan, and the path of God's people through this world. For one thing, the journey of the sons of Jacob was circuitous. There can be little doubt that, after their release from bondage, they looked forward to a speedy occupation of the Promised Land ; but in this they were disappointed. They were not permitted to go direct and at once to their inheritance. Then, again, it was not a way of their own choosing. There were two routes, either of which they might have followed ; one, the ordinary caravan route through the country of the Philistines, entering Canaan from the south ; the other, by the Red Sea and the wilderness of Sinai, entering Canaan from the west. There was no geographical necessity for taking the more circuitous route through Sinai. Indeed, without an explicit command from God, it would have been the height of folly for any leader, even Moses, to have attempted to conduct such a vast host all unprovided for into the desert. Now, the discerning reader cannot fail to be struck with the similarity of all this to the Providential ordering of human life. The current of our earthly being seldom runs straight. There are often many windings before it reaches its goal; and it may be that few of those windings would have been in accordance with our wishes. How true is this of Moses, who, in his impatience for the release of his countrymen, struck the blow for freedom too soon. And instead of being permitted to go direct to the work, he had to undergo forty years of preparatory service among the solitudes of Midian. Take Joseph, and you see the working of the same principle. How strikingly is the hand of Providence seen in his life! His experiences in Egypt before his promotion may seem a strange preparation for his after eminence, and certainly not of his own choosing. God was " leading him about." The pit in Dothan, servitude under Potiphar, confinement in prison, were so many steps or turnings in a life that rose to such distinction. Then again take the apostle Paul. The great ambition of his life was to preach the gospel at Rome. The noble apostle got his wish. He was permitted to go to Rome, but he went as a prisoner. The chains might seem to confine his influence, but, for aught we know, they may have added to the impressiveness of his message and testimony for his Master. God was leading him about, an ambassador in bonds. So in our life. The course of Providence sometimes takes strange turns. Our life-path is seldom what at one time we expected it to be, any more than the journey from Egypt to Canaan was what the Israelites expected. We come to our Etham on the edge of the wilderness, and at that point the current of our life is altered and its winding course begins. The altered current may lead us into the desert of adversity, or into the wilderness of affliction, where for years we may have to endure. Many a Christian has been led home through the winding path of pain. It is God " leading us about." II. We now proceed to inquire into THE PURPOSE OF THIS ROUNDABOUT JOURNEY THROUGH THE WILDERNESS. When the sons of Jacob left Egypt, they were little better than a band of undisciplined slaves, and they had to be trained. The growth of every noble quality had been cramped and hampered by degrading bondage, and the wilderness was to be their training-school. There was, therefore, a moral purpose in the forty years' wandering. It was intended to train them to be and to do, to develop in them noble qualities, and train them for noble deeds. They could have marched to Canaan in eight or ten days; but eight or ten days would have been too short a period for the growth of character. No one can read their history without observing the change which forty years had produced on them. They gained new experiences, and developed those manly qualities needed to fight their way to the possession of Canaan. Now, is it not in this way still that God prepares His people for their mission? As a general rule the men who have made the deepest impression for good on the world's history have been led up to their throne of influence by a long path of preparation. Few leap into their position at a bound. The shortest way is not always the best. There is, perhaps, no station in life in which difficulties have not to be encountered and overcome before any decided measure of success can be achieved. Those difficulties are, however, our best instructors, as our mistakes often form our best experience. Horne Tooke used to say of his studies in intellectual philosophy, that he had become all the better acquainted with the country through having had the good luck sometimes to lose his way. And a distinguished investigator of physical science has left it on record that whenever, in the course of his researches, he encountered an apparently insuperable obstacle, he generally found himself on the brink of some novel discovery. The severe preparatory discipline which God's men have to undergo is for most part unknown to the world. We cannot tell how the Israelites spent thirty-eight years of their desert life, we only know the effect it had on them. We might further extend this thought to the discipline which God applies for the soul's sanctification. The ultimate end of all the Divine dealings with man in this life must be sought in the life to come. The soul has often to pass through the path of affliction or adversity ere it is fit for the fellowship of the pure in heart in the Promised Land. The reward will be more prized and the rest the sweeter on account of the experience gained when God led you about through the way of the wilderness. III. IN ORDER TO DERIVE FULL BENEFIT FROM THE EXPERIENCES OF LIFE, SEVERAL THINGS HAVE TO BE ATTENDED TO. Discipline, however suitable it may seem, will not of itself further the work of grace in the heart, unless it is accepted as from God. Confining ourselves to this narrative, we find two or three conditions without which Divine discipline will yield no moral profit. 1. In the first place, we must not harbour a spirit of discontent with our lot. To this spirit are traceable many of the calamities of the wilderness, and it barred the gates of Canaan against the generation that left Egypt. That generation did not benefit by God's dealings. Now all this is true in our life. We often miss the good that is meant for us by dissatisfaction with the channel through which it comes. The apprentice lad must not chafe if he is put to distasteful work and at a low wage : let him learn that this is the price to be paid for future advancement, and let him cheerfully accept his post. Murmuring at cross-bearing will do us no good, but rather harm, as it will prevent us from attaining to acquiescence in the Divine will. 2. Secondly, in order to secure the greatest good from our lot, we must banish from our company whatever tends to lead us astray. When the Israelites left Egypt they were joined by a group called the " mixed multitude." The Church's greatest danger lies not so much in attacks from without, as in temporizing with worldly-minded men, and harbouring in her midst those who are not of her in spirit. But this "mixed multitude," while it is typical of nominal Christians in the Church, may be regarded as a type of those unholy desires and passions that are more or less to be found in the heart of every one of us. We all carry about with us a " mixed multitude " of unsubdued appetites which crave for gratification ; and not more surely did the Israelites suffer from the presence of this base throng, than we shall have the peace of our life marred, and its usefulness impaired, by giving reins to those unholy forces. They need to be constantly kept in check, else they are sure to lead us astray. Let us lay aside every weight and the sin that doth so easily beset us ; and let us run with patience the race that is set before us, looking unto Jesus, the author and the finisher of our faith. 3. There is one more condition that we must comply with, if we would finish our course with joy, and that is, we must loyally follow the guidance of our Heavenly Leader. (*D. Merson, M.A.*) *Why the Israelites were guided by the way of the wilderness :*—I. They had been sated with the magnificence of man's works ; God led them forth into the wilderness TO SHOW THEM HIS WORKS IN THEIR NATIVE GRANDEUR, and to refresh their exhausted hearts and spirits by the vision of the splendour of His world. II. God led them forth by the way of the wilderness, that He might reveal not nature only, BUT HIMSELF. He led them into the wilderness, as He leads us, that He might meet with them, speak with them, reveal Himself to them, and teach them to know themselves in knowing Him. III. God led them into the wilderness, THAT HE MIGHT THERE CULTIVATE THEIR MANLY QUALITIES, and fit them to hold the possessions they might win. (*J. B. Brown, B.A.*) *God's path :*—1. God does not order salvation to His as it pleaseth man, but as it pleaseth Himself. 2. God in wisdom sometimes translates His Church from the house of bondage to a wilderness. 3. Wilderness and Red Sea paths, are the way of God's people here below. 4. God makes the way to rest not always straight, but to be about. 5. Israel, or God's people, go the round that God doth lead them. 6. Orderly and well instructed are the Church's motions under God in wilderness-ways. (*G. Hughes, B.D.*) *God's people in the wilderness :*—I. THAT BY ISRAEL IN EGYPT WE MAY UNDERSTAND THE SPIRITUAL BONDAGE OF GOD'S CHOSEN PEOPLE AT LARGE. 1. Israel was in an enemy's country. So are the elect by nature. 2. Their bondage was rigorous. So was the Christian's. 3. Their departure, like the believer's, was opposed. 4. And when liberated, their enemies pursued them. II. SOME REASONS WHY GOD DID NOT ADMIT THE CHILDREN OF ISRAEL INTO THE PROMISED LAND, IMMEDIATELY ON THEIR COMING OUT OF EGYPT, AND WHY HE DOES NOT ADMIT HIS ELECT INTO GLORY IMMEDIATELY ON THEIR CONVERSION. 1. The Egyptians must be drowned —enemies subdued. 2. The Israelites must be humbled (Psa. lxvi. 10–12). 3. He led them some hundreds of miles about ; yet it was the right way (Psa. cvii. 7). 4. God's way is right, although it may appear round about (Psa. xviii. 30). III. SOME REASONS FOR GOD'S CONDUCT IN KEEPING THEM IN THE WILDERNESS. 1. They were not fit as yet for severe warfare. 2. Their enemies were great, and themselves weak. 3. He had much to teach them. IV. THE MANNER IN WHICH THEY WENT UP. " Harnessed "—or by fives, or five in a rank, or rather by five bodies or squadrons, and so marched out, not in a disorderly or confused way, but in great order and regularity. 1. Their loins were girt (Eph. vi. 14). 2. Their heart was secured (Eph. vi. 14). 3. Their feet were shod (Eph. vi. 15). 4. Having a shield, helmet, and sword (Eph. vi. 16, 17). (*T. B. Baker.*) *The way of God in conducting the life of the good :*—I. THAT IT IS THE WAY OF GOD TO BRING THE GOOD TO A PLACE OF REST. This is the object of all life's discipline. II. THAT IT IS THE WAY OF GOD TO BRING THE GOOD AWAY FROM THE THINGS THAT WOULD BE UNFRIENDLY TO THEIR WELFARE. He selects the life path of the good—1. Wisely. 2. Kindly. III. THAT IT IS OFTEN THE WAY OF GOD TO BRING THE GOOD A CIRCUITOUS ROUTE TO THEIR DESTINATION. The nearest way is not always the best. IV. THAT IT IS THE WAY OF GOD TO BRING THE GOOD

ALONG UNWELCOME PATHS. Impossible to get to Canaan without perplexities. God is always with the good in their wilderness wanderings. V. THAT IT IS THE WAY OF GOD TO BRING THE GOOD INTO A BETTER AND MORE THOROUGH KNOWLEDGE OF THEMSELVES. Men get to know more in the desert. Some Christians are taken to heaven through a long route of pain. They long for home, but the journey is prolonged. It is hard to see the reason of their protracted existence. The Divine purpose is not yet accomplished in them. VI. THAT IT IS THE WAY OF GOD TO BRING THE GOOD INTO A WISE EXERCISE OF THEIR OWN STRENGTH. "And the children of Israel went up harnessed out of the land of Egypt." They walked in battle array. And so, while it is the way of God to conduct human life to its destination, it is also the duty of man to exercise his own wisdom and strength, so that he may do all to aid the plans of God concerning him. Lessons : 1. That God leads men from Egypt to Canaan. 2. That men must give themselves up to the guidance of God. 3. That life is often through a long wilderness. 4. However long the journey, men must trust in God. (*J. S. Exell, M.A.*)   *The roundabout way :*—I. GOD LED THEM. " Man's extremity is God's opportunity." When He calls you up the slopes of the mount of sacrifice, it is to bring you within the sound of Divine voices at the summit ; when He calls you to the "edge of the wilderness," or to a " desert place apart," it is to " speak comfortably " unto you " out of the cloud." II. GOD LED THEM NOT THROUGH THE LAND OF THE PHILISTINES, ALTHOUGH THAT WAS NEAR . . . BUT HE LED THEM ABOUT BY THE WAY OF THE WILDERNESS OF THE RED SEA. He had not taken them into His confidence, they could not understand Him, they had no sympathy with His vast and gracious designs, therefore He did not " give an account of any of His matters." " What I do thou knowest not now, but thou shalt know hereafter." Let no one hesitate to " go up and possess the land," for fear he be overpowered with temptations that beset the path of Peter or Paul or Luther, or of some venerable man of God who but too faithfully has given an account of his conflict with the world and the flesh and the devil. God will take you to heaven, but He has not promised to take you by the near way. It may be by a very long way. One thing I know, it will not be through the way of the land of the Philistines, or of any foes who would effect your ruin and drive you back in despair to the country from whence you came out. Only one enemy will encounter you at a time, and you will be prepared for each as he comes, and the " last enemy " will be kept to the last, and you will be made "more than conquerors." " God is faithful who will not suffer you to be tempted above that ye are able." III. " AND THE CHILDREN OF ISRAEL WENT UP IN BATTLE ARRAY OUT OF THE LAND OF EGYPT." The great work given the Church to do is the conquest of the world. These are the marching orders of the Captain of Salvation. IV. IF THE CHILDREN OF ISRAEL HAD ENTERED PALESTINE BY THE NEAR WAY, HOW MUCH WOULD THEY HAVE MISSED ! The sojourn in the wilderness was not a scene of unrelieved gloom. They bought and sold, they increased in cattle and in riches. " Their garments waxed not old, nor their shoes upon their feet." They were left generally unmolested by any of the tribes, and when attacked, they were as a rule able to hold their own. Had they not come by the roundabout way, the song of Moses had been unsung, Miriam's harp had been untuned, Elim, with its wells and palms had been undiscovered, Sinai, with its words of love and law had been unknown, the cloud had never been seen, the manna had not been tasted, the water from the rock had not followed them. They would have had no opportunity of partaking in a sacramental feast with the princely Jethro, and of exerting such a favourable impression upon his tribe that many who were "without" were induced to come within and to respond to the invitation, " Come with us and we will do you good, for the Lord hath spoken good concerning Israel." Theirs would not have been the joy which they did experience when, Jordan crossed, they did eat at last the old corn in the land in a city of habitation ; they would not have left behind them "footprints on the sands of time," which will cheer the hearts of countless generations of pilgrims until the world shall have an end ; they could never have conceived how good and how patient God was, they could never have believed how corrupt their own hearts were, had not Moses at the end of all the wanderings recalled one scene after another, one act of rebellion after another committed in the light of the unwearied love which "blackened every blot." This last point deserves more than passing notice. " Thou shalt remember all the way which the Lord thy God led thee these forty years in the wilderness to humble thee, to prove thee, to know what was in thine heart, to know whether thou wouldst keep His commandments or no." God knew what was in their hearts. The people did not know their own hearts. Some one will say, "I would that I had died in the days of childhood, I should have been saved many a weary march." But you would have missed many a providence, the memory of which will cast a shadow of seraphic loveliness on the background of your eternal home, and which will enable you to strike a higher note than otherwise you could ever have reached. Had you not passed through that night of bitter anguish, you could not have fathomed the depths of the words as you did, "Thy way is in the sea, Thy path is in the great waters, and Thy footsteps are not known." Had you not been forced to take thought for the morrow, you could never have said as sincerely as you did say, "My heavenly Father knoweth that I have need of all these things." Had it not been for that sore sickness, there would not have been lying upon your life, consecrating it, a "light that never was on land or sea." The scars of your suffering are "marks of the Lord Jesus." Your little bits of experience are so many types which to-day you can set up, and from which you can spell out the might, and majesty, and mercy of the blessed God. (*J. Macmillan, M.A.*) *The nearest way home:*—You and I often mark a path out for ourselves; and to us it seems so easy, so likely, so promising of success. Then all at once something happens that disappoints us, and directs us another road that we find further round, and apparently much harder; and we call it a "mysterious providence." Of course, all is mysterious that is the result of wider knowledge than our own. Do you remember old Quarles' lines:—

> " I say this way ; God says that.
> His way is best, for He knows what
> Of lions may beset my road.
> I'll follow Thee! Lead on, my God!"

He knew what was best and safest, and, in the long run, surest; and by the good hand of God they were kept out of mischief and away from danger. The old proverb is still very true: "The longest way about is often the nearest way home." "He that goes straight across, may have to carry a cross. He that goes round about, may have the chance to go without." His thoughts are not our thoughts, and it is a grand thing to be under His guidance; for "the way of man," as the good Book says, "is not in himself; it is not in man that walketh to direct his steps." We know not what is good for us, and, like children, if we were to run alone, we should soon run into mischief. You and I have often been imposed on, both by what we hope and what we fear. Many a time we have tried to run away from what afterwards turned out to be a blessing, and many a time we have been disappointed to save us from being destroyed. I remember on one occasion, when I was young, I got it into my head that I was able to drive. Having narrowly escaped an upset, and frightened myself almost out of my wits, I resigned the reins into more skilful hands than mine, and travelled safely. Let us be as wise as the psalmist, and say, "The Lord shall choose mine inheritance for me!" Let us learn a lesson of patience, too. We may be very anxious to pluck the fruit; but we had better wait till it's mellow, for fear the pain kills all the pleasure. God's time is a good time, and God's way is a safe way, both to-day and to-morrow, too! (*J. J. Wray.*) *The tender consideration manifested by God towards the Israelites:*— The Christian life is a growth, and if assailed by some temptations in its infancy, the consequences might be fatal. He, therefore, who commences and maintains the process of our salvation, gradually accustoms His soldiers and servants to the difficulties of their warfare. Their faith, love, zeal, and self-denial are thus exercised rather than oppressed. The text confirms this consolatory view of the Divine procedure. I. THE CIRCUMSTANCES OF THE ISRAELITES. The deliverance of the chosen tribes was at this moment like the first rays of the morning spread upon the mountains. They had been redeemed from bondage. They were commencing their journey to the promised land, every spirit filled with pleasure. They were confident of their power to endure the trials of the way. The heart-searching God knew their deficiencies; and a variety of circumstances connected with their feeble faith determined Him in wisdom to divert their feet towards Canaan by a devious path. 1. The Philistines, who lay between them and the promised inheritance, were a brave and warlike people, against whom the sons of Jacob, numerous as they were, could not hope to succeed in battle. Wisely, therefore, did the Lord judge that they would shrink from such enemies. Such are the Christian's foes. They are well practised. Satan has triumphed over man in every age, over the philosophy of Greece, the wisdom of Rome, and the refinement of Britain. And thinkest thou, Christian, that the enemies of thy soul are enfeebled? No! What, then, would be the consequences if God led thee past them to Canaan? Wisely and graciously are you led by the wilderness. 2. The Israelites were disarmed, and therefore utterly unable to cope with the Philistines, who were prepared with every means of defence which a people whose delight was in war could invent. The young believer just escaped from the house of bondage is defenceless. His enemies are armed. He cannot expect to wield the sword of the Spirit with the full energy of one who has been accustomed to fight with it. 3. In thus estimating the goodness of God towards the children in their need, we must add that their spirits were bowed down by long captivity. The hard bondage in mortar and brick was not the school in which to learn courage. Hence Israel was not fitted to match against the free soldiers of Philistia. The slavery of Satan unfits for conflict with the foes of the soul. II. THE DEALING OF GOD TOWARDS THEM. God might have made Israel at peace with the Philistines; or have given them courage to defeat their foes. But this procedure would have comprehended less of moral discipline. 1. He avoided the nearest way to the promised land, and led them by the way of the wilderness. The Israelites would be astonished at the line of march; they would be disposed to murmur. Has not God often contradicted your desires? You ought not to impugn His wisdom. The passenger ignorant of navigation cannot direct the course of the ship. The shipmaster knows the rocks: God knows our path best. 2. The Most High saw fit, not only that His chosen tribes should avoid the shortest way, but that they should pass through the dangers of the Red Sea, and sojourn in the wilderness of Zin. Could this be the result of wisdom? Clouds and darkness are round about Him. It is the exclusive province of unerring wisdom to draw a line between the discipline necessary for our moral good, and that severity of affliction, which might overwhelm us with despondency. We must confide in our heavenly Father. 3. Never, then, should it be forgotten, that although the journey of the Israelites was contrary to their expectations, their wishes, and their clouded judgment, it was the safest and the best path to Canaan. (*R. P. Buddicom.*) *Walking through the wilderness:*—Let us try to apply this, so far as the circumstances of the case permit, to the Christian's experience in his religious life. That life must have had somewhere a conscious beginning. I say a conscious one, because its actual beginning precedes our knowledge of the fact. Our Christian life really began, through God's grace, in our baptism, wherein we were made, though unconscious of the blessed truth, the children of God. But to know what then was done for us; to know that we have been made and are alive unto God, to perceive what we are and whose we are—this is like a second beginning. This new beginning is made, ordinarily, at the time of confirmation and first communion; then the Christian's conscious life begins. If at that time you were really in earnest, and knew what you were about, and did what you did in love and sincerity, then first you felt yourself to be a Christian, and for the first time saw yourself to be on the march towards the Celestial City. Now how, by what route, or what line, was your journey to be made? I say at once and emphatically that its best typical picture must still be found in the forty years of wandering, with what they brought by way of trial, and proof, and weaning from the love of this present world; and that without such steady, quiet discipline, the work runs the risk of being brought to naught. For persons recently awakened to sober reflection on their state, and newly brought to Christ, should not be thought of as able, competent, and strong. They are not yet veterans; they are not yet fairly drilled reserves; they are but raw and awkward recruits. It must be so, unless in rare instances, as when in some sweet, holy child one sees the certain making of a saint. If they make their profession of Christ at a very early age, and ere yet they have left the secure protection of a holy family and a religious household, then their weakness is that of a fallen nature which has not been tried by severe temptations from outside. If, on the other hand, they make their open profession of the faith at a later date of life, then, in addition to that congenital weakness, they have what comes of loss of time, delay without sufficient cause, and commerce with the world, and some past relish for the paths of sin. Either way, this new recruit is weak, and liable to fall. Now suppose such an one brought face to face with the Philistines, with a race that know not God, with Goliath and the other giants, with the vast and splendid array of the notable enemies of the Church, with the temptations and trials of this world. Such an encounter can hardly, by any possibility, be avoided. The world is become one great Philistine camp. Strong races, hardened against religion, hold its chief places. What is likely to result when our young Christian falls on such terrible appearances and is called on to surrender? Here surely is work for veterans and champions; but he is no champion, and as yet has hardly proved his arms. There is danger of discouragement, of terror, of flight. And Egypt calls to him to come back, fair to the eye, sweet to the taste, with many allurements, and a bondage which many find agreeable, as if one were bound in fetters of silk or chains of gold. Yes, the danger, if one were to go right on by the way that is near, would be that of losing heart under the first fire, and wishing one's self out of the battle; and taking back, or at least forgetting, the promise he had made, and sinking down, a backslider from Christ. What he wants is hardening, proving, tempering. But that comes in the roundabout way. It is effected by means of the discipline of long and slow-moving years; it is the result of innumerable trials and temptations, the fruit of many painful incidents. St. James bids us count it all joy when we fall into divers temptations. Why? Because they constitute the precious discipline of life. If we fail not, we shall be purified thereby, and made ready for the great and final conflict in our own valley of decision. (*Morgan Dix, D.D.*) *The way of the wilderness :*—To spare a child the toils and pains of education, is the most grievous wrong that a father can inflict on him. Thus did not God spare His sons! From the day when they sang their triumphal hymn upon the desert shore, to the day when they "passed over Jordan," their life was one continued discipline: each station, each experience, had a distinct office in relation to the formation of their character; was sent to add to them a virtue which would be an instrument of conquest or government, and a spring of strength, not in time only, but eternity. Not simply to keep them out of the way of the Philistines, but to drill them till they could master their enemies; to nurse them till they could bring forth a Samson, a David, who could compel the Philistines to own their supremacy, He led them by Sinai, and trained them, by self-conquest, to conquer the strongest foes. They came at last on Canaan, not as a scattered band of marauders, but with the shock of a thunderbolt; you feel that the battle is won the first moment that they set their feet on the land. And those men in the desert, hard as was their way and fare, were making history. Bunsen says, "History was born that night, when Moses led forth his people from Goshen." The narrative of their toils and struggles is the oldest and most precious of historic records, and their waybook has become the heirloom of the pilgrim world. "Behold, we count them happy which endure." And you who are out in the wilderness, faithless and heartless, like a sailor on a dark sea unlit by stars, learn from Israel the grand reason of your pilgrim vocation, and the end to which it will be guided if you follow the highway of God. God finds you a slave; He would make you a son. You are not the lawful slave of wanton Egypt; you have the King's mark upon you—the King of kings is waiting to redeem His own. Come forth, then, come forth to freedom! breathe the free air, scan the broad horizon—it is your land of wandering; see the soft blue hills swelling in the distance, the gleaming of rivers, the shadow of woodlands—it is your land of rest. (*J. B. Brown, B.A.*) *God's guidance :*—When the English soldiers were marching up the heights of Alma, meeting the Russians who were marching down towards the English lines, there came a command for the English company to divide, part turning to the left and marching along the side of the hill. It seemed a foolish order when first received by the soldiers. There were Russians marching right in their teeth, and yet half of them were to turn away when the foe was close upon them! But the order was not long considered foolish. Those that turned to the left soon found that a company of Russians had been secretly coming up the side of the hill to fall upon the English unawares. The commander-in-chief from the hill on which he stood could see all the movements of the foe, while those that were perplexed at his orders could see only a small portion of the field. So He who orders our life and lot sees all the movements of the powers of darkness, and to deliver us from their plots and designs, He often leads us by a way we know not. (*H. Starmer.*) *God's wondrous providence :*—What do you do when, in reading the massive folios of ancient English authors, you meet passages written in an unknown tongue? Paragraph after paragraph you read with all possible fluency, instantly apprehending the author's purpose; but suddenly the writer throws before you a handful of Latin, or a handful of Greek; what then? If you are absorbed by the interest of the book, you eagerly look out for the next paragraph in English, and continue your pursuit of the leading thought. Do likewise with God's wondrous Providence-book. Much of it is written in your own tongue—in large-lettered English, so to speak; read that, master its deep significance, and leave the passages of unknown language until you are further advanced in the rugged literature of life; until you are older, and better scholars in God's probationary school. The day of interpretation will assuredly come. (*J. Parker, D.D.*)

Ver. 19.—**Moses took the bones of Joseph.**—*An interesting incident in Israel's departure from Egypt :*—I. THE DISCHARGE OF A SACRED TRUST (Gen. l. 24, 25). Pay attention to the requests of the dead. II. THE FULFILMENT OF AN ANCIENT PROPHECY (Gen. l. 25). God can kindle the fire of prophecy in the soul of a dying saint, that the sorrowful may be encouraged. III. THE GIVING OF A TIMELY ENCOURAGEMENT. IV. THE BESTOWAL OF AN APPROPRIATE HONOUR ON AN ILLUS-TRIOUS ANCESTOR. (*J. S. Exell, M.A.*) *A memento and a pledge :*—And Moses took the bones of Joseph with him. This rendered the march a kind of funeral procession, and such as no other history relates. Never was body so long in its conveyance to the grave, for forty years were taken up in bearing Joseph to his burial. We read at the death of Joseph that "they embalmed him, and he was put in a coffin in Egypt." The precious deposit, likely to be cared for by some of the descendants of his own family, was dear to all. It was a memento of the vanity of human greatness. It was also a moral as well as a mortal memento. Joseph was a very pious character ; he had been highly exemplary in every relation and condition of life, and much of God, of providence, and of grace was to be read in his history. What an advantage to be always reminded of such a man in having his remains always in the midst of them ! But the body would be above all valuable as a pledge of their future destination. It was a present palpable sign of God's covenant with their fathers in their behalf. (*A. Nevin, D.D.*) *Rest in native land :*—Sir Bartle Frere was often asked at the Cape, "What do you expect when you reach England ?" His reply, which was found written on a slip in his Bible after his death, was thus expressed :

> " Where in the summer sun the early grasses grow,
> Six feet of English ground, a Briton's grave,
> Rest in my native land is all I crave."

Burial places :—It is the almost universal custom in America, and seems to be growing in favour here, for great men to be buried in the place where they have mostly lived, and among their own kith and kin. Washington lies at Mount Vernon ; Lincoln at Springfield ; Emerson and Hawthorne under the pines of New England ; Irving on the banks of the Hudson ; Clay in Kentucky. They are laid to rest not in some central city or great structure, but where they have lived, and where their families and neighbours may accompany them in their long sleep. (*H. O. Mackey.*)

Ver. 21.—**By day in a pillar of a cloud.**—*The prophetic element in life :*— " The Lord went before them in a cloud." So God ever goes before His people, and standing as we do now on the threshold of a new year, we may recall this truth to our great comfort. The future, unknown to us, is not unknown to Him ; He has gone before us, and is evermore delicately adjusting things to our discipline, our perfecting, our utmost salvation and bliss, I. We find an illustration of the text IN THE PREPARATION OF THE WORLD AS A DWELLING-PLACE FOR MAN. Ages before man appeared on this planet, God was preparing it as a habitation for us to dwell in. You talk of " getting the house ready" for some newly married pair ; but consider the getting ready of this globe as the scene for humanity to dwell in, and in which to work out its fortunes. What vast ages ! What complex and far-seeing adjustments ! And so we find to-day that the world has been provisioned for ages, the storehouses of nature are full, we do not lack any good thing. And God also anticipated the moral exigencies of the race. II. We find another illustration of the text IN GOD'S GOVERNMENT OF THE RACE. We are not moving at random, the world is full of design, the law is progress, we are always entering into our inheritance. The races of man form a vast motley multitude, and the Lord goes before us preparing for us paths, resting places, wells, palm-trees. " He sent a man before them, even Joseph, who was sold for a servant" (Psa. cv. 17). " He sent a man before them." And this was not some exceptional thing ; God is always sending out pioneers, outriders, heralds to prepare the way for the general host in its march through the ages. They come in science, they come in politics, they come in philosophy, they come in religion : men full of the prophetic instinct, men who anticipate a new world, and who prepare us for it. So these Josephs, these dreamers, go before us, making possible to us new creations, new redemptions, We ought all of us, as God's people, to have a bit of this prophetic instinct in us, helping to usher in a new and better state of things—God's messengers preparing the way. God has gone before us; He is preparing happier things for our race ; and although He works mysteriously, He works certainly to His glorious purpose. And all this is true in relation to our universal life. In our worldly life God is ever providing for us new blessings, glad surprises. Some do not see God because of the cloud, but He is in it nevertheless, working out His gracious purpose. And as to our spiritual life and need, God goes before us. We believe in "prevenient" grace—the grace that goes before. Grace that comes before our trials, preparing us for them, so that they do not overwhelm us. Grace that comes before our temptations, warning us of them, strengthening us against them. Grace that comes before our duties, so that we no sooner hear the call than we feel the strength to obey. We may enter a new year with tranquil confidence. Sydney Smith recommended people to take "short views," and we can afford to do that, because God on our behalf takes long views. III. We find our last illustration of the text in the fact THAT CHRIST HAS GONE BEFORE US INTO THE HEAVENLY PLACES. "A cloud received Him out of their sight." In that cloud He has gone before us to make ready for us once more. (*W. L. Watkinson.*)　　*The pillar of cloud; a symbol of the Bible:*—I. THE MYSTIC PILLAR RESEMBLED THE BIBLE IN THE ENDS IT ANSWERED. 1. The mystic pillar promoted their emancipation. So the Bible opens the soul's prison doors, snaps its chains, delivers it from the despotism of sin, and makes its way clear into the kingdom of God. 2. The mystic pillar guided them through the wilderness. So does the Bible show us the path of life. It is ever in advance of humanity, &c. 3. The mystic pillar protected them from all that would injure. The Bible is the sword of the Spirit ; the armour of the soul. II. THE MYSTIC PILLAR RESEMBLED THE BIBLE IN THE ATTRIBUTES IT DISPLAYED. 1. Supernatural- ness. 2. Adaptation. 3. Many-sidedness. III. THE MYSTIC PILLAR RESEMBLED THE BIBLE IN THE CONDITIONS IT REQUIRED. 1. It required a constant observance of its movements. Bible of no service unless studied. 2. It required a constant following of its movements. You must go as the Bible goes in relation to sin. Satan, holiness, and God ; life and death, time and eternity. (*Homilist.*)　　*The Divine leadership of the good:*—I. THAT THE GOOD ARE DIVINELY LED IN THE WANDERINGS OF LIFE. "The Lord went before them." 1. A visible Guide.　2. A competent Guide.　3. A faithful Guide, II. THAT THE GOOD ARE OFTEN DIVINELY LED DURING THE WANDERINGS OF LIFE INTO VARIED AND UNSUSPECTED PATHS. "The edge of the wilderness." 1. God sometimes leads His people contrary to their expectations. 2. God sometimes leads His people contrary to the dictates of their reason. 3. God always leads His people into those paths which shall yield the most sacred and safe discipline to them. III. THAT THE METHOD OF THE DIVINE LEADERSHIP IS ADAPTED TO THE CHANGING CIRCUMSTANCES OF THE GOOD. "By day in a pillar of cloud," &c. IV. THAT THE DIVINE LEADERSHIP SHOULD NOT BE MISTAKEN IN ASSOCIATION WITH THE ORDINARY AGENCIES OF LIFE. V. THAT THE DIVINE LEADERSHIP IS SOLICITOUS TO LEAD THE GOOD TO THEIR PROMISED AND PEACEFUL DESTINY. (*J. S. Exell, M.A.*)　　*The cloudy and fiery pillar a symbol of the Bible.* I. AS THE PILLAR OF CLOUD WAS GIVEN TO GUIDE AND COMFORT, SO THE BIBLE IS DESIGNED TO LEAD THE THOUGHT AND CONSOLE THE SORROW OF MAN. Without the Bible man would be lost in the wide waste of error. It is also intended to console the human heart in all the troubled moods of life, when its joys grow dim, when it is rendered lonely by bereavement, and when it comes to death. At such times the Bible is our chief consolation, it enables us to sorrow in hope, it shows us One who is the Resurrection and the Life. II. AS THE PILLAR COMBINED BOTH CLOUD AND FIRE, SO THE BIBLE UNITES ILLUMINATION AND MYSTERY. There is mystery in it which the finest genius cannot attain, which angelic intel- ligence cannot interpret, and which eternity may not simplify. Deity dwells in the volume, and we expect that clouds and darkness will be round about Him. But there is fire in the Book which illumines the doctrines and morality of the Christian life. III. AS THE PILLAR OF CLOUD AIDED THE OUTGOING OF ISRAEL FROM BONDAGE TO REST, SO THE BIBLE IS THE BEST HELP MAN CAN HAVE IN WALKING THROUGH THIS LIFE TO THE NEXT. They walk the best in the wilderness of life who pay the most heed to the Word of God (Psa. cxix. 105). Lessons : 1. Be thankful for the Bible. 2. Follow the directions of the Bible. 3. Seek the consolation of the Bible.

(*Ibid.*) *Divine guidance:*—I. EXPLAIN THE TEXT. 1. We may observe that God's people in every age stand in need of a guide, and without it they would miss the path of duty and of happiness. 2. The Lord Himself graciously condescends to become the guide of His people, and He alone is fit to be so. He only has a perfect knowledge of the way, and of all the difficulties that may befall them in it; and He only is able to support and defend them against the designs of all their enemies. 3. The Lord guides His people in different ages of the world, by various means adapted to their circumstances, and to the peculiar dispensations under which they live. (1) By His Providence. (2) By His Word. (3) By His Spirit. II. SYMBOLIC MEANING. 1. It was altogether miraculous, and a symbol of the Divine presence. It was called the cloud of the Lord; there it was He dwelt in the midst of His people, and spake with them face to face (Num. xix. 14). 2. This mysterious cloud was intended to direct the Israelites in their journey, and by it the Lord communicated to them His will. 3. The cloudy pillar in the wilderness afforded refreshment by its shade, as well as guidance by its light. And is not Jesus both our sun and shield, our light and shade, as our different necessities require? In a season of darkness, He sends forth His cheering beams; and when our soul is ready to faint within us, He ministers to our refreshment and relief. 4. The cloudy pillar was designed for safety and defence, as well as for a guide through the wilderness. (*B. Beddome, M.A.*) *Need of guidance:*—General Hill says: "In many of the battles the great want with the Confederates, strange as it may seem, was accurate knowledge of the country in their front. The map furnished me (and I suppose the six other major-generals had no better) was very full in regard to everything within our own lines, but a red line without any points marked on it was our only guide to the route on which our march was to be made." (*H. O. Mackey.*) *God's guidance:*—The other day I was walking across the Northumbrian fells to call at a shepherd's house that lay distinctly enough before me on the Fell side. The directions I received from a Fellsider whom I had just left, after the manner of those who live every day in the midst of ample space, were vague indeed. The rutty, half-formed road on which I was walking was distinct enough immediately before me, but when I strove to trace the course of the road a greater distance ahead it became blended with the frowsy bracken and bronzed heather, and was utterly lost to view. To have struck boldly out across country to reach my destination by what seemed the shortest route would have entangled me among the spongy bogs and numerous streams with which the hillside was intersected. However, by carefully following the road that was visible before me I managed to pick my way and reached my calling-place in safety. So is it in our daily search after the knowledge of the Divine will. When in our impatient eagerness we wish to look too far into the future, all is indistinct and hazy; but, if we carefully note what is near and sufficiently revealed, we shall be led up infallibly to safety and to rest. (*Christian Journal.*) *God's guidance of the Israelites:*—There was an old fisherman who got converted in his old age. He was not able to read, and therefore had to do his own thinking, not being able to catch up all ideas aired in our newspapers. A friend of mine visited him, and knowing how he loved the Word of God, said to him, "Now, John, shall I read you a chapter?" "Yes, if you please, I should so much like to hear a chapter. I do dearly love to hear the Word read." "And what part shall I read to you?" "About the Lizard Lights, please. Do read about them, for when I see them I always think I am near my heavenly home. I have often been out on the Atlantic on dark stormy nights, and when I caught sight of the Lizard Lights I knew I was near Falmouth harbour, and would soon be safely moored." "I am afraid," ventured my friend, "that I do not know about the Lizard Lights!" "Not know about them! Well, I thought you a gentleman, and had Scripture knowledge, but if you don't know about the Lizard Lights, you must just wait until Mary comes in." In a short time Mary, who was his daughter, came in, and the old man said, "Mary, where is that in the Book about the Lizard Lights? You know you were reading about them last Sunday night." "Oh, father," she said, "that was not the Lizard Lights. It was the Israelites." That old man had made a mistake in the apprehension but not in the application. The story of the Israelites told of the guidance of God, in their wanderings, and the Lizard Lights had frequently been the beacon that had guided the fisherman to his desired haven. (*Mark G. Pearse.*) *The pillar of cloud; historical parallels:*—Xenophon mentions, in his Spartan republic, in describing the military expedition of a Spartan king, that a servant, or officer, who was called "firebearer," preceded the king with the fire, which had been taken from the altar, on which he had just before sacrificed at the frontier of the Spartan territory. After they had sacrificed once more, and the march had commenced, a fire which was lighted at the second sacrifice preceded the lines, without ever extinguishing. In Curtius we read, "He (Alexander the Great) ordered a lofty pole, visible from all sides, to be raised over the general's tent, and from the top of this pole streamed a signal conspicuous everywhere to every one, *smoke by day and fire by n ght.*" Alexander had in this, as in many other points, imitated the custom of the Persians, who, in common with most of the eastern nations, on their marches through deserted regions, bear before the army high poles, on which iron pots are affixed, filled with lighted combustibles; so that, the smoke by day, and the flame by night, signalized the way to the troops. Thus we cannot but acknowledge a certain curious similarity between the Biblical miracle and a general military custom prevailing in the East. Under these circumstances we entirely approve of Faber's remarks: "Both the miracle and the custom, collated and compared, give light to each other. The custom effects, that we find the miracle dignified and worthy of God; and the miracle shows, that that very custom cannot have been quite unknown to the Israelites." (*M. M. Kalisch, Ph.D.*)　*The pillar of the cloud and of fire:*—The pillar of cloud and of fire was certainly (1) sacramental (1 Cor. x. 1, 2); (2) of a typical character (Isa. iv. 5; Num. xiv. 42). He whom the cloudy and fiery pillar typified was the same Almighty Being who hath said to the faithful members of his militant Church, in every age of its warfare, "Lo, I am with you always, even unto the end of the world." The cloud was manifestly intended—I. To GUIDE THE ISRAELITES THROUGH THE WILDERNESS. 1. The pillar of cloud guided the children of Israel with infallible certainty. God Himself was in it; and unless He could err, their way could not be mistaken. Mark here, the glorious character of the Bible,—that light to our feet with which the unsearchable compassion of our Saviour's love has provided us. It testifies of Christ. It embodies His teaching and salvation, as the pillar contained them in the wilderness. 2. This wondrous appearance in the heavens was a constant director to Israel. In every emergency the page of divine truth may be consulted. II. The cloudy and fiery pillar afforded not merely guidance, but PROTECTION to the Israelites in their eventful march. Sin invades, temptation threatens, and every spiritual enemy seems permitted to assail with a fierceness which might well gather gloom and despondency around the heart; but the fainting Christian is encouraged by that voice which speaks as from the cloud between him and his enemies. "Fear thou not, for I am with thee: be not dismayed, for I am thy God." His life is hid with Christ in God; and amidst every trial and seduction by which his salvation is endangered, he may lay hold upon One who walks with him, and has promised to uphold him with the sufficiency of an Almighty arm. III. The pillar of cloud and of fire had yet another office to perform for the children of Israel. IT GAVE THEM REFRESHMENT AND COMFORT IN THE WILDERNESS. Now say, O Christian, is it not thus with thee in the hour of thy most oppressive trial? (*R. P. Buddicom.*)　*The pillar of cloud and fire:*—I. THE WAY ALONG WHICH GOD LED HIS PEOPLE. II. THE MANNER IN WHICH GOD GUIDED AND PROTECTED THEM. 1. Pillar of cloud and fire only *means:* Jehovah Himself their true guide. God is with His people. What decision, blended with humility, will the realization of this great truth give us! What calmness in the midst of excitement; submission under trial; perseverance under difficulties. 2. Mark the adaptation of God's method of guidance to the condition and necessities of the Israelites. Gradual progress. (*G. Wagner.*)　*The fiery cloudy pillar:*—The fiery cloudy pillar performed many friendly offices to the Israelites, It was—1. A guide. To lead was its main mission. It was a striking illustration of the longsuffering kindness of God. Neither murmurings, nor rebellion, nor idolatry, ever drove away the angel of His presence. The guidance vouchsafed, too, was of the most gracious kind—that of a shepherd (Psa. lxxviii. 52), and that of a loving and affectionate parent (Deut. i. 31). 2. A light (see Neh ix. 19). 3. A shade (see Psa. cv. 39). 4. A shield (see Deut. i. 30; Exod. xiv. 19). 5. An oracle (see Psa. cxix. 7). He who opened His mouth in the burning bush at Horeb, opened His mouth in the cloudy pillar, and frequently spake to Israel's leader for Israel's benefit. 6. An avenger. When God wished to mark His displeasure, the cloud assumed a very wrathful appearance. The Lord looked unto the host of the Egyptians through the pillar of fire, and troubled the host of the Egyptians. What a dreadful visage it must have worn when flashes went forth from it and devoured Nadab and Abihu (Lev. x. 2), and also when fire came out from it and consumed two hundred and fifty men! (Num. xxi. 35). If the aspect of the cloud was thus at times such as to trouble those with whom God was angry, it would, no doubt, have a very pleasing one when He desired to manifest His favour to the congregation. As they looked up, they would behold the smiling face of their Divine leader cheering and encouraging them to go on in the path of duty. (*W. Brown.*) *The presence of God adapted to human need* :—The consciousness of the Divine presence is in proportion to the circumstances in which we are placed. In other words, our circumstances determine our consciousness of the Divine nearness. Sometimes life is all day—almost a summer day with great spans of blue sky over-head, and where the clouds gather they gather in beautiful whiteness, as of purity akin to the holiness of the inner and upper cities of the universe. Then what do we want with fiery displays of God ?—they would be out of keeping, out of reason and out of proportion. There are days that are themselves so bright, so hospitable, so long ending, and so poetic in all their breezes, and suggestions, and ministries, that we seem not to want any dogmatic teaching about the personality and near-ness of God. All beauty represents Him. Any more emphatic demonstration would be out of harmony with the splendid serenity of the occasion. Then there are periods in life all night, all darkness, all storm or weariness. We cannot say where the door of liberty is, nor dare we step out lest we fall over a precipice ; all is dark, all is trouble ; friends are as absent as if they were dead, and all the sanctuaries to which we have hitherto resorted are concealed by the infinite darkness. What do we want then ? A bird to sing to us ? That would be helpful. A little tiny voice to break the troubled silence ? That would not be amiss. But what do we really want ? A column of fire, a pillar of glory, an emphatic incarnation and vision of Providence ; and the soul gets both these manifestations of God according to the circumstances under which the soul is living. Take it, therefore, simply as an analogy, and then it is a rational analogy ; it is true to every man's experience. And if the pillar of cloud and fire should drop off, there will remain the eternal truth, that according to the soul's circumstances is the Divine revelation of itself. Where the visible is enough, why add more ? A man should not want much theology of a formal sort on a bright summer day. Some little tuft of cloud will represent the Infinite. Some almost invisible wing in the air—more a thought than a thing—hardly to be identified by the bodily eye, will symbolize the all-embracing power and the all-brooding love. Then at night we want what is called dogmatic teaching, broad emphasis, piercing declaration, vividness that cannot be mistaken, God almost within the clasping of the poor arms, God almost in sight of the eyes of the body. Thus God deals with us. This is true to our history. The mere cloud may go, the pillar of fire may be accepted as figurative ; but the eternal truth that God comes to us in different ways under different circumstances—now as a cloud, now as a fire, now as a judgment, now as without mercy, now a roaring tempest, now a still small voice,—is a truth that remains, whatever havoc may be wrought amid the mere figurativeness by which that truth is symbolized. (*J. Parker, D.D.*) *Divine guidance:*—How does this remarkable narrative exhibit to us in every variety the picture of God's daily guidance of His people ! 1. The guidance is as indispensable, and at the same time as obvious now as it was then. God still leads His people, through the voice of the purified conscience, through the evident suggestions of His exalted Providence, through the utterances especially of His infallible Word ; and all these indications differ sufficiently from what flesh and blood make known to us in order to preserve us from wandering. 2. The guidance now is indeed as mysterious, but yet as well adapted to its purpose, as that of which the history of Israel tells us. Our countless whys and wherefores are still as little answered as the questions concerning the peculiar nature and essence of the pillar of fire and of cloud which probably disturbed the minds of the ancient Israelites. But as regards the question whither, the answer, God be praised, has not remained unknown to us ; all God's guidance of His people, we know, has one good—to bring us out of disquietude into rest, out of bondage to liberty, along the path of faith to the land of sight. 3. Also in our case God's guidance is as varied, but still as faithful, as was the promise to the ancient people. In the day of prosperity He goes before us as in the cloudy pillar, in order to temper the glow of our joy through the remembrance of His close neighbourhood ; in the night of adversity the word of His promise beams on us in as friendly and consoling a manner as did the fiery pillar on Israel in midst of the darkness. But as Moses beheld in the fortieth year of his pilgrimage the same sign in the heavens which had guided and encouraged him in the first, so God's presence is never lost to His redeemed ones in Christ, whatever else around may faint or fail. Neither by day nor by night does He take from us the tokens of His nearness ; and even when He seems to hide His face from us, new thoughts of mercy and of peace are in His heart. 4. Who does not perceive how such a guidance promises as much, but also claims as much return as that of Israel ? It guarantees us the entrance into Canaan, but only along the path of believing perseverance and obedience. When the way indicated through the wilderness was despised, the pillar of cloud and fire rose above many a grave, and yet there is no single promise of God to him who chooses his own path.   (*J. J. Van Oosterzee, D.D.*)   *The mystic pillar :*—I have called it a mystic pillar—that cloud in the desert ; and so to them who saw it, and to us who read of it, it was. Of what it was composed ; by what means it was kept pillar-like and intact while all other clouds were carried and scattered by the winds of heaven ; by what strange secret force the cloud-pillar was nightly transformed to a column of bright flame?—these are questions that no doubt often exercised the minds of the spectators, only to be dismissed again as a baffling mystery that could not be explored. And not only its nature and changes, but its direction, its movements as to time and place—they had no knowledge, could make no sure prediction. Whether it would bend to the right, turn to the left, or move straight onward ; whether it would remain stationary, or begin to move night or morning, or at noon—all this, and all concerning it, was above and beyond their knowledge ; the laws that governed it and the will that led it was as entirely outside their information as it was beyond their control. What they did know was that Jehovah was the God of the cloud ; what they could do was to trust it implicitly, follow it constantly, seeing in it all the while the good hand of their God over them for good.   In all this, for my learning and for yours, I see a picture—a true and instructive picture—of the providence of God. From the beginning until now, the ways of God to man have been shrouded in mystery, have exercised inquiring but baffled minds, have furnished material for the sneer of the infidel, the sophistry of the sceptic, and the logic of the merely scientific mind ; ay, and have strained and tested the faith of the pious, and placed stumblingblocks before his faith, on which his foot hath well-nigh slipped. All this arises from the fact that men *will* strive to be equal with God ; that their mind will cope with that of Deity, and by their finite feebleness gauge the plans and purposes of the Infinite and Eternal Lord of all. (*J. J. Wray.*)   *Providential mercies :*—A clergyman who, with some others, had escaped in a boat from a burning ship, was discoursing in a large company of the marvellous favour of Divine Providence, that had so specially watched over and preserved him. A wonderful providence ! A special intervention of God's goodness ! "That was a very great mercy, sir," said Archbishop Whately, seriously, "but I can record a greater in my own experience. I once sailed across the sea in just such a ship, and bound for just the same port, and—would you believe it ?—the vessel never caught fire at all ! "   My friends, that is the way I would have you think of, and trust in Providence, as being ever present, ever wise and watchful, and, like the cloud-pillar of Israel, ever for your real good—pursuing its Divine and gracious path. Good and bad, light and shade, joy and sorrow, prosperity and adversity, things present and things to come, all are proceeding on precisely the same plan,—namely, the working of the soul and mind of God for His glory in the true well-being of His creatures, and for the ultimate advancement and elevation of mankind. Wherever the pillar went, with whatever seemingly reasonless vagaries the pillar moved, and however widely experiences and opinions differed about its moving, we know now that it led them safe enough and sure enough to the Canaan which was the longing desire of every heart. The mind of a pious and thoughtful artisan named Albert Thierney was much occupied with the ways of God, which seemed to him to be full of inscrutable mysteries. The two questions, " How ? " and " Why ? " were constantly in his thoughts, both as to the events of his own life and the government of the world. One day, in visiting a large ribbon manufactory, his attention was attracted by a large and extraordinary piece of machinery. His eye was that of a cultivated artisan, and he was immensely interested. Countless wheels were revolving in intricate motions, and thousands of threads were twirling and twisting in all directions. He could not understand its movements, and closer study only deepened his interest and increased the mystery. He was informed that all this work and motion was connected with a common centre where there was a large chest which was kept shut. Anxious to understand the principle of the machine, he asked permission to look inside the chest. " The master holds the key," was the reply. The words came to him like a flash of light. Here was the answer to all his perplexing thoughts—his anxious questionings about Providence. " Yes," thought he, "the Master holds the key ; He knows, He governs, He directs all—God ! That is enough ! what need I more ? " (*Ibid.*)

CHAPTER XIV.

VERS. 1–4. Encamp before Pi-hahiroth.—*The good in the trying situations of life* :—I. THAT THE GOOD ARE OFTEN BROUGHT, BY THE PROVIDENCE OF GOD, INTO THE MOST TRYING SITUATIONS IN LIFE (ver. 1). It is in the trying situations of life that we get the best revelations of the love and power of God. When men feel that they cannot help themselves, then God helps them. Thus they are humbled. They are brought to despair of creature aids. Then the promises become precious. The circumstances of life are all divinely ordered with immediate reference to the moral culture of the good ; the Israelites were taught a great lesson before Pi-hahiroth. When God fixes our position, it is sure to be a salutary one, even though it be perplexing. II. THAT THE TRYING CIRCUMSTANCES INTO WHICH THE GOOD ARE PROVIDENTIALLY BROUGHT ARE VIGILANTLY OBSERVED BY THE WICKED (ver. 3). Satan watches the best opportunity of frustrating the march of the soul into freedom. But the wicked often misinterpret the providence of God in reference to the good, and hence pursue their plans to their own ruin. III. THAT THE TRYING SITUATIONS INTO WHICH THE GOOD ARE BROUGHT ARE DESIGNED ULTIMATELY TO ENHANCE THE GLORY OF GOD AND THE RETRIBUTION OF WICKED MEN. " I will be honoured upon Pharaoh," " That the Egyptians may know that I am the Lord." Lessons : 1. Rest patiently in the circumstances in which God has placed you. 2. God is greater than all the hindrances to your true freedom. 3. Follow God, even though it be through the great waters. (*J. S. Exell, M.A.*)　　*In a fix* :—I was led to take this subject from seeing a sheet almanac upon which was painted a boy who had got his satchel full of apples, which, I presume, he had been stealing. He was hanging by the tips of his fingers from the top of a wall, and just above the wall on the other side was the owner, while at the bottom was a big bulldog, chained to a kennel—he could not go up for fear of the owner, he dare not drop down for fear of the dog ; and it said at the bottom, " In a fix." It would be very well for us if that represented the only fix in which we had ever been. I might talk for a considerable time in a general way about men who have been in a fix, but now I want you to give me your attention while I try to point out to you a nation that was once in a fix, and, if I can, teach some lessons that may be of use to you and me. There they are—the river before them, rocks on either hand, and the Egyptians behind them. They could not make boats to cross the sea ; they could not fly ; and were unable to fight—they had not the skill, neither the weapons. The most remarkable thing is this, that God, who had sent Moses to deliver them, had brought them into this very position ! Observe, they were in the path of duty—doing just as He had commanded them ; suggesting to us the thought that if we would serve our God faithfully, sometimes we may find ourselves " in a fix." There will be times when dark clouds will gather, and we cannot see our way, and we shall feel inclined to give up in despair. But wait a bit. If God has brought them into this fix, He will bring them out of it. There they are ; and, see ! Pharaoh is following. He did not let the people go until he had been compelled ; and, like a man shamed out of half-a-crown for some charitable purpose, he repented afterwards. He went after them designing their ruin, but God designed to ruin him. He designed to put the Lord's people into a fix, and the Lord—who always protects His own—designed to fix him. And then comes this thought : That what seems to tend to our ruin is often over-ruled to our good. A great many years ago there used to be the old stage coach, and in those days they were the chief means of travelling. I have heard some old men say what a terrible thing it was to take a long journey. One day the locomotive was invented ; they were going to take goods and people in such quantities and at such a speed as the stage coach never could. The owners of the coaches might declare they were all to be ruined ! What would become of them ? The stage coach was ruined, but what of its owners ? They shared the common advantages of the " puffing billy." This same principle will apply to things of the present day. Years ago, tailoring was said to be a good business. Their sewing was then done by hand. By and by the sewing-machine was invented; and when it was brought to something like perfection, clothing was sewn with it. The tailors were in such a state—it would destroy their prospects! it would ruin their trade! And the dressmakers were in the same excited condition. When were tailoring and dressmaking better than now? They are, I am told, more profitable than they ever were. I give you these illustrations to prove my statement—that very often that which seems to tend to our injury is over-ruled by a merciful Providence to our good. These Egyptians were following the Israelites, and were about to destroy them; they appeared now in the jaws of death, but it was over-ruled. "The wicked," says Solomon, "diggeth a pit, and falleth into it." "He layeth a snare, and his own feet are taken therein." Ah! there are many things you and I cannot understand now. Many a cloud sweeps over our path; many dark things we cannot quite see through. If we could rise above all these things, and see God's doings, perhaps we should rejoice that He sometimes puts us in a fix. We do not see through it all now; we shall by and by. "Sometimes God brings us into straits that He may bring us to our knees." You know that to be true. Often in your sorrow you have looked unto your Father for the help you could not get elsewhere. Observe, if they were in a fix, Moses was not. What did he do? He cried, "Fear not, God will fight for you"; though God has led you here, He will lead you elsewhere. He knew they could do nothing, so he commanded them to stand still. Man's extremity is God's opportunity. Have you never been in a fix like this? Your business has failed, your prospects blighted, your heart smarting through some bereavement. A darling child or wife has been snatched from you. In utter helplessness you have cried, "What can I do?" You can do nothing. You have been doing too long. God has brought all this to teach you to stand still, and let Him do. "Stand still." Oh! there is reason in that. If your God brings you to see your helplessness and poverty, and He reveals His true riches to you, it is worth your while to "stand still." Have salvation; you may. Get His love into your hearts; stand till He makes you free; and when once He does, then comes the cry as Moses gave it, "Forward!" and though there be before you a dark night and a troubled sea, you may go forward with safety. There is this further thought: that though sometimes God allows the enemies of His people to bring them into a fix, be assured the Lord will turn the scales, and bring the enemies into a fix. What He did for these Egyptians—the haters of the friends of God—He may do for you. Many a faithful man of God has been annoyed, perhaps by you; but be assured, God will annoy you. See what He did for these Egyptians. There was, first, darkness. That which gave light to His people became dark to His enemies. It is dark where the enemies of God are—so dark! Secondly, God troubled them. The children of God crossed the sea, and you know how in following them the Egyptians all perished in the waters, through which the Israelites had passed in safety. One word more. If you are on the side of God and truth, He will be with you, and bring you out of every fix into which you may get whilst serving Him. On the other hand, if you refuse to acknowledge Him, you may get into a fix which you will never be able to get out of. (*Charles Leach.*) *Right beginnings; or, no "progress"*:—Every true and strong life has its sharp transitions, its critical choice, its decisive moment between Migdol and the sea. It is true enough, most of our time we move on in a path no way remarkable, or in a routine with nothing signal or memorable about it. Day takes after day, and the scene, the occupation, the company, helps and hindrances, are much the same from month to month. But look longer, and you find that, however the wheels of habit may run on in a kind of groove, with few startling outside changes, yet somewhere there was a spot where this regular drift got its start and its new direction. You stood alone somewhere, at a parting of two ways, and you chose; and then, as the consequence of that choice, your life went thenceforth in a particular channel, pure or filthy, straight or crooked, heavenward or hellward, long after. And there is nothing exceptional about this. The same law governs national concerns, processes in nature, and mechanics. War, for instance, is well-nigh the staple of history; and yet historians count but fifteen decisive battles of the world, all other vast movements of ages and empires winding like a whirlpool around these bloody centres. So in mechanics. Only now and then, on its turn-table, the engine is set in its new direction; but all it does, or draws, afterwards, proceeds from that momentary pivotal determination. The grain grows day and night all summer till harvest;

but there is a single time of planting. The patriarch lodged only one night at Bethel; but then, afterward, all his journeyings over the Eastern lands were at the bidding of his God. How did you come to be the man you are to-day? There was most likely some hour of choice. Two forms of apparent good lay before you. Two voices spoke. Among all the common questions that rise, this one question rose. It was the question of your soul's eternity. Very likely it had relation, too, to some other soul besides your own—your affection, your duty, to him or her. Perhaps it was in the line of your common doing, only an emergency of larger and uncommon concern. How did you act? Did you say Yes, or No? Did you go or stay? Did you accept the partnership, the companionship, the offer—or refuse? The question is not one of expediency, or taste, or convenience, or profit. It has to do with your soul's life, honour, uprightness, salvation. Such periods can be recalled in memory, I think, by most persons; but never recalled in fact. The rest of life depends on them, and on the way we meet them. We are between Migdol and the sea. Egypt and Pharaoh—an old, bad life, and its despotism of darkness —are behind; the other way the road runs where God will. With Israel it was well that it ran to the baptism in the cloud and in the sea. We have only to enlarge the reach of such a decision, carrying it through the roots and springs of character, to find in it that one all-including, all-controlling choice which turns a bad man into a good one, or creates a living Christian. Indeed, it is of that one radical renewing that the exodus of Israel has always been regarded as the type. (*Bp. F. D. Huntington.*)

Vers. 5-10. **The Egyptians marched after them.**—*Israel pursued:*—Notice some analogies between the flight of Israel from Egypt and the progress of the sinner from the captivity of the devil. In both cases we have a debased condition of mankind, a powerful enemy, a pursuing foe, a perilous road, a human ministry, and an omnipotent and gracious Redeemer. I. THE STATE OF ISRAEL IN EGYPT WAS A STATE OF THE UTMOST ABASEMENT. Every sinner is a slave. The wicked man serves a cruel master. He is watched on every hand; all his movements are understood: every desire or aspiration after liberty is turned into an occasion of augmented suffering. Wickedness reduces the volume and quality of manhood. Every bad thought and every wicked deed is so much taken from the completeness and dignity of human nature. II. THE ENEMY OF ISRAEL WAS POWERFUL. So with the great enemy of man. His resources are all but inexhaustible. He is not confined to one series of temptations. The diabolic genius in luring and seducing men to evil dispositions and courses is fertile beyond all parallel. He assaults us through the flesh; he insinuates ruinous ideas into the mind; he secretly touches the very fountains of life. He can touch our nature with a light hand, or he can smite us with tremendous force. III. ISRAEL WAS PURSUED—SO IS THE REDEEMED MAN. It is too frequently expected that when a man forsakes his evil ways, he will at once become an exemplary saint. It is forgotten that the devil relinquishes his hold reluctantly. Years upon years after our conversion to God we are conscious of the presence of the old nature; there are sudden uprisings of forces which we supposed to be extinct. IV. THERE IS AN OMNIPOTENT AND GRACIOUS REDEEMER. In the course of our Christian experience we are often called upon simply to stand still. Herein is shown the tender grace of the living Redeemer. We are weak, we are weary, and there is no more strength left in us; at that point He says, "Waiting shall be accounted as serving, and standing still as the progress of triumphant strength." Israel was not self-redeemed, nor are we; Jesus Christ is the angel of our redemption; trusting to His leadership, neither mountain nor sea shall keep us back from the Canaan of God. (*J. Parker, D.D.*)   *Difficulty in duty :*—I. DIFFICULTY IN DUTY DEEPLY FELT. 1. Our temporary well-being here greatly depends upon the conduct of our contemporaries toward us. 2. The majority of our contemporaries are governed by corrupt principle. 3. The man, therefore, who carries out in his daily life the principles of duty, must more or less excite the anger and create the antagonism of his contemporaries. II. DIFFICULTIES IN DUTY TESTING CHARACTER. 1. Look at the influence of this difficulty upon the Israelites. (1) Their cowardice. (2) Their ingratitude. (3) Their apostacy. 2. Look at the influences of difficulty upon Moses. He now rises into the majesty of the hero. III. DIFFICULTY IN DUTY DIVINELY OVERCOME. Thus it is ever. 1. The nature of moral progress shows this. 2. The promises of God's Word ensure this. (*Homilist.*)   *The good pursued by old enemies :*—I. THAT THE GOOD, IN SEEKING TO COME OUT OF THE BONDAGE OF SIN, ARE FREQUENTLY PURSUED BY OLD ENEMIES.

1. Satan. He is powerful. He has great resources. He will arouse indwelling corruption. To sense all seems dark. To faith all is bright. We cannot get to the Promised Land without much resistance from the devil. 2. Wicked habits. The habits of youth are not easily conquered, hence they should be carefully formed, or they may impair the Christian career of the future. 3. Wicked companions pursuing with taunts and slanders even to the banks of the Red Sea. These are a terror to many a godly soul. Thus we see that Satan pursues the good with a great army, with many allies, in splendid array, and often strikes fear into their hearts. II. THAT SOMETIMES THE CIRCUMSTANCES OF LIFE APPEAR TO FAVOUR THE PURSUIT OF THE OLD ENEMIES OF THE SOUL. "And overtook them encamping by the sea," &c. The world in which we live is a Pi-hahiroth, and the devil knows it : but the God who has brought us from Egypt can bring us from before Pi-hahiroth, if we trust in Him—He is greater than the pursuing enemies. III. THAT THE PURSUIT OF THE OLD ENEMIES OF THE SOUL OFTEN AWAKENS THE SORROWFUL APPREHENSION OF THE GOOD. "And when Pharaoh drew near . . . sore afraid." How often does it happen that when the good are followed by their old enemies, they forget the mercies of the past, the power of God, and look only to the on-coming foe. They think they will have to yield to the prowess of Satan, and go back to the old bondage of the soul. But we see in this narrative the folly of allowing the advance of old enemies to awaken terror in the heart of the good ; for they are only advancing that the power of God may be seen in their defeat. Good people of melancholy temperament sometimes think that they made a mistake in coming out of Egypt, and that they will never reach Canaan. Such fears are dishonouring to the grace of God. IV. THAT THE PURSUIT OF THE OLD ENEMIES OF THE SOUL MUST BE MET UNDER THE GUIDANCE OF HEAVEN. "Fear ye not, stand still, and see the salvation of the Lord." It is a blessed fact that God adapts the method of His redemption to the weak condition of His people. 1. The enemies of the soul are overcome by God. He alone can give salvation from the enmity of Satan, from the weakness of self, and from the perilous circumstances of the wilderness life. 2. The soul must wait patiently the outcome of this aid. The good know not by what method of discipline the Lord will deliver them from their old habits of evil. We see here the advantage of having God as our Helper, in that He can make a way for our feet through the sea. Lessons : 1. That the good, being pursued by the enemies of their old life, are in constant need of Divine grace. 2. That progress in the freedom of the soul is in spite of the enmity of Satan. 3. That all moral progress is the outcome of the help of God to the soul. (*J. S. Exell, M.A.*) *Pursuit of the entangled :*—The things of the world are so many purveyors for Satan. When Pharaoh had let the people go, he heard after a while that they were entangled in the wilderness, and supposes that he shall, therefore, now overtake them and destroy them. This stirs him up to pursue them. Satan, finding those whom he has been cast out from entangled in the things of the world, by which he is sure to find an easy access unto them, is encouraged to attempt upon them afresh, as the spider to come down upon the strongest fly that is entangled in his web : for he comes by his temptations only to impel them unto that whereunto by their own lusts they are inclined, by adding poison to their lusts, and painting to the objects of them. And oftentimes by this advantage he gets so in upon the souls of men, that they are never well free of him more whilst they live. And as men's diversions increase from the world, so do their entanglements from Satan. When they have more to do in the world than they can well manage, they shall have more to do from Satan than they can well withstand. When men are made spiritually faint, Satan sets on them as Amalek did on the faint and weak of the people that came out of Egypt. (*J. Owen, D.D.*)

Vers. 11, 12. **Hast thou taken us away to die in the wilderness ?**—*The foolish way in which many people anticipate difficulties :*—1. THAT MANY PEOPLE MEET ANTICIPATED DIFFICULTIES IN A SPIRIT OF GREAT FEAR. II. THAT MANY PEOPLE MEET ANTICIPATED DIFFICULTY IN A SPIRIT OF COMPLAINT AGAINST THOSE WHO HAVE GENEROUSLY AIDED THEM IN THEIR ENTERPRISE. It is base to turn upon men who have spent their best energy and wisdom in our service when trouble seems to threaten. But this is the way of the world, a momentary cloud will eclipse a lifetime of heroic work. III. THAT MANY PEOPLE MEET ANTICIPATED DIFFICULTIES IN A SPIRIT WHICH DEGRADES PREVIOUS EVENTS OF A GLORIOUS CHARACTER. Lessons : 1. That when trials threaten we should trust in God. 2. That fear weakens men in the hour of trial. 3. That it is ungenerous to murmur against those who earnestly seek our good. (*J. S. Exell, M.A.*)- *An unreasonable complaint :*—During one of the campaigns in the American Civil War, when the winter weather was very severe, some of Stonewall Jackson's men, having crawled out in the morning from their snow-laden blankets half frozen, began to curse him as the cause of their sufferings. He lay close by under a tree, also snowed up, and heard all this; but, without noticing it, presently crawled out too, and, shaking off the snow, made some jocular remark to the nearest men, who had no idea he had ridden up in the night and lain down amongst them ! The incident ran through the army in a few hours, and reconciled his followers to all the hardships of the expedition, and fully re-established his popularity.

Ver. 13. **Fear ye not, stand still, and see the salvation of the Lord.**—*The temper for the crises of life :*—I. The question was once asked by an eminent thinker, WHETHER NATIONS, LIKE INDIVIDUALS, COULD GO MAD. There certainly have been movements, like the Reformation or the French Revolution, of which no one could foretell the existence or power. But such movements, like the cataclysms of geology, have been rare, and they seem likely to be rarer as the world goes on. Yet this is not the aspect of the world which our imagination presents to us. There are the two opposite poles of feeling, the one exaggerating, the other minimizing, actions and events ; the one all enthusiasm and alarm, the other cynical and hopeless. The true temper in politics is the temper of confidence and hope. " Stand still, and see the salvation of the Lord." Be patient, and instead of changing every day with the gusts of public opinion, observe how curiously, not without a Divine providence, many things work themselves out into results which we never foresaw. II. A TEMPER OF CONFIDENCE AND REPOSE IS NEEDED IN MATTERS OF RELIGION. The great changes in religious opinion during the last forty years have taken two directions—Rome and Germany. These changes are far from unimportant, but the temper of alarm and exaggeration is not the right way of dealing with them. Amid the changes of religious opinions and the theological discord which distracts the world, we may possess our souls in peace. If sometimes our ears are thrilled and our minds confused by the Babel of voices which dins around us, we may turn from without, and listen calmly to that voice which speaks to us from within, of love, and righteousness, and peace. III. LET US APPLY THE SAME PRINCIPLE TO OUR OWN LIVES. We need to see ourselves as we truly are, in all our relations to God and to our fellow-men. We need to carry into the whole of life that presence of mind which is required of the warrior who in the hour of conflict is calm, and sees what he foresaw. (*R. Jowett, M.A.*) *A duty and a blessing :*—I. These words which to fleshly Israel must have seemed so strange, and which to weak faith echo so strangely still, contain two parts, A DUTY AND A BLESSING. They were to " stand still," and so should they see the salvation of God. And this condition of blessing runs continually through the whole history of the Jewish and Christian Church. When God has tried His chosen servants or His chosen people, the most frequent trial perhaps has been this, whether they would tarry the Lord's leisure, be content to receive God's gift in God's way, hasten not, turn not to the right hand or the left, but " stand still " and see the salvation of God. By patient (the word implies suffering) waiting for God, an unresisting resistance unto blood, did the Church take root in the whole world. II. It is for instruction only that we may ask WHY GOD SHOULD SO HAVE ANNEXED THE BLESSING OF CONQUEST TO ENDURING SUFFERING, AND MADE PATIENCE MIGHTIER THAN WHAT MEN CALL ACTIVE VIRTUES. 1. It may be that it has some mysterious connection with the sufferings of Christ. Vicarious suffering may be so far well-pleasing to God as having a communion with the sufferings of His beloved Son, and doubtless it may make those who are partakers of it more capable of the communication of the merits and influence of His passion. 2. Then, also, it may be needful, in the wisdom of God, for the perfecting of His saints. As all trial implies pain, so the trial of the most precious vessels, it may be, is to be accompanied by pains proportionate. 3. It is evident, that so God's power and glory are most shown in averting suffering, or in crowning the enduring faith by His blessing. 4. Since man's self-will was the cause of his fall, God would thus teach him to renounce dependence upon himself, to quit his own wisdom and his own schemes, and do God's will. (*E. B. Pusey, D.D.*) *Lessons :*—1. It concerns God's instruments of salvation to reason quietly with a froward people who despise it. 2. God much contends by His ministers to remove the unbelieving fears of His people. 3. Stability in faith is God's command to cure fears in unbelief. 4. Jehovah's salvation is worth the looking unto by His poor creatures in faith. 5. Present salvation

God can and will give to His people to quiet them·in believing. 6. God's command for faith carries proportionable reason for it in all cases. 7. Causes of fear which hinder faith God removeth at His pleasure. 8. In God's great redemption, typical and real, the Church is passive, not a word to it. 9. In such appearances of God it is but just with men to be silent from murmuring (ver. 14). (*G. Hughes, B.D.*) *Faith and fear :*—As man is capable of different forms of actions, so is he susceptible of various kinds of emotions. There are two kinds of emotions which govern mankind more than any others—faith and fear. These comprehend almost all the interests, and sway almost all the actions of life. They are often opposed to each other, and frequently fear conquers faith. Fear is a power governed more by sense than faith ; it is more selfish and timid than it. Faith is a more spiritual and religious power than fear, and must conquer all fear and all opposing powers before men can be powerful and triumphant. I. Let us observe, first, THE TRIUMPH OF FEAR OR FEELING OVER FAITH. 1. Faith is often opposed and conquered when immediate danger appears, and when it cannot point to immediate deliverance. 2. When the superficial inclination of man is opposed and self-denial demanded, faith often is vanquished, and feeling triumphs. 3. Faith is often conquered by sense or feeling when reason cannot comprehend and explain things in God's dealings towards His creatures. 4. Feeling often overcomes faith when religion appears to militate against what men consider their present interest. 5. Feeling sometimes gets the advantage over faith on the ground of ease and indulgence. 6. Faith also is often conquered for want of free and open heart and mind to receive truth and conviction. Prejudice and narrowness of mind are deadly enemies to faith, as they are to the advancement of truth and right life everywhere. 7. I mention another ground on which faith is too often conquered by feeling—namely, because it looks to the future for its full reward. Feeling has no patience to wait; it must be satisfied with its objects now ; whilst faith rises above the visible and the present to the unseen and the future. II. We shall now notice THE TRIUMPH OF FAITH OVER SENSE AND FEELING. Though faith is above feeling, it is not necessarily opposed to it; it works through it, and makes it subordinate to its influence and end. The unity of the two is essential to make men strong and happy ; when they are divided the happiness of men is marred, and their strength of heart and character is shorn. 1. When the mind is profoundly convinced of truth it conquers. In the degree the mind is capable of deep conviction, it is strong, and this also is one of the strongholds of faith. When the mind becomes thoroughly imbued with the importance and truth of anything, it possesses the first qualification of conquest over all opposition and difficulty ; and never till then can great things be accomplished. 2. Another condition under which faith proves itself triumphant is a deep conviction of need. Conviction of need, either personally or relatively, is both the reason and power of any and every effort, and no great sacrifice and conquest will be accomplished without. 3. For the development and triumph of faith, it is requisite as a condition that the soul should be convinced of the failure and insufficiency of all sensuous and finite things to satisfy its requirements. 4. It is requisite that the moral perception and feeling of the soul should be opened and awakened to see and feel things as they are before faith can conquer. Though faith is a power of confidence in the dark, it is nevertheless a power that thrives in light, and demands all the evidence the case in hand permits. 5. Faith conquers whilst the soul lives in close union with God, and carries with it a consciousness of His presence ; for conscious communion with God is the power as well as the life of the soul, and so long as this is enjoyed faith is triumphant. III. We come now to THE TRIUMPH OF GOD OVER NATURE—" See the salvation of the Lord, which He will show to you to-day." Such a salvation was not wrought in the ordinary course of nature. Apparently the forces and laws of nature were against the possibility of it; it was a Divine display of Divine triumph of God over nature. 1. The event is represented as authentic and real. It is not an allegory, or any ideal manifestation representing a potential possibility, or a thing to excite human fancy. 2. The event was a manifestation, and produced in subordination to the purpose of mercy. 3. The event was produced for a moral and religious end. God had repeatedly promised to deliver them, and the act was a fulfilment of an old and repeated engagement. The promise was made and performed on the ground of religion. 4. The event is in harmony with its conditions. The event is not professed to be the production of ordinary power, which would be inconsistent; for it is an extraordinary one, and there must be some equality between the power of production and the production itself. The event is professed to be an extraordinary manifestation of an infinite power; and unless this power itself is denied in the fact of its existence, it is hard to guess how the event can be considered impossible. The event is professed to have been produced for a wise and sufficient reason. Lessons: 1. The dealings of God are suitable always to the occasion. He works in the right time and place, when and where the thing is needed. 2. It is possible to be in a condition which is beyond all human and natural deliverance. 3. God sometimes delays His deliverance to an extreme hour. 4. Where duty is clear, difficulties should not prevent an effort to perform it. 5. The difference between the real and the unreal is seen most clearly in extreme conditions. 6. There are things in life which we meet once, and we pass on and never meet again. 7. Genuine and deep-rooted faith shows its superiority in circumstances that baffle sensuous reasoning. (*T. Hughes.*) *Direction in dilemma:*—Our text exhibits the posture in which a man should be found while exercised with trial. Methinks, also, it shows the position in which a sinner should be found when he is under trouble on account of sin. We will employ it in both ways. I. Take our text first as A PICTURE OF THE BELIEVER WHEN HE IS REDUCED TO GREAT STRAITS. Then God's command to him is, "Stand still, and see the salvation of the Lord." In this brief sentence there are two things very conspicuous: first, what is to be done, "Stand still"; and secondly, what is to be seen, "See the salvation of the Lord." 1. What is to be done? Faith hears the bidding of her faithful God, and is not willing to be shut up in the iron cage of despair; nay, she defies the old giant to put so much as a finger upon her. Lie down and die? that she never will while her God bids her stand. See the word "stand." What does it mean? Keep the posture of an upright man, ready for action, expecting further orders, cheerfully and patiently awaiting the directing voice. But in what way are we to "stand still"? Surely it means, among other things, that we are to wait awhile. Time is precious, but there are occasions when the best use we can make of it is to let it run on. A man who would ride post-haste had better wait till he is perfectly mounted, or he may slip from the saddle. He who glorifies God by standing still is better employed than he who diligently serves his own self-will. (1) Wait in prayer, however. Call upon God and spread the case before Him; tell Him your difficulty, and plead His promise of aid. (2) Wait in faith, for unfaithful, untrusting waiting is but an insult to the Lord. Believe that if He shall keep you tarrying even till midnight, yet He will come at the right time; the vision shall come and shall not tarry. (3) Wait in quiet patience, not murmuring because you are under the affliction, but blessing God for it. 2. But now, secondly, what is to be seen? You are to see the salvation of God. In your present temporal trials you are to see God's power and love manifested. Now, I think I hear you say, "Well, one thing I know, I cannot deliver myself out of the dilemma in which I am now placed. I had some dependence once upon my own judgment and upon my own ability, but that dependence is entirely gone." It is a good thing for you sometimes, Christian, to be wholly weaned from yourself. But you are saying, "What shall I see?" Well, I know not precisely what you shall see, except I am sure of this, you shall see the salvation of God, and in that salvation you shall see two or three things, just as the children of Israel saw them. (1) You shall see, if needs be, all nature and all providence subservient to God's love. (2) You will see again, if you will but stand still and see it, that the Lord reigneth. You shall have such a picture of Jehovah sitting upon His throne, controlling and overruling all things, that you shall extol Him with your whole heart as your God and King for ever. You shall see most distinctly, if you will but wait and look for it, how He can make you a wonder. (3) You shall be a wonder to yourself, and marvel how it is that God supports you. You shall be a wonder to your enemies. You shall do what they cannot do; you shall walk through the depths of the sea, which the Egyptians, assaying to do, were drowned. (4) You shall see your enemies utterly destroyed, if you will but wait. II. I intend to take the text in reference to THE SINNER BROUGHT INTO THE SAME CON-DITION IN A MORAL SENSE. 1. "Stand still" in the renunciation of all thine own righteousness, and of all attempts to seek a righteousness by thine own doings. 2. But now the sinner says, "Suppose, then, I give up all hope, and do no more by way of trusting to myself, what shall I see?" Do remark that all the sinner can do is to see the salvation. He is not to work it out, he is not to help it on, but he is to see it; yet, mark you, that sinner cannot even find out that salvation of itself, for if you notice, the next sentence to our text is, "which He will show you to-day." God must show it to us, or else we cannot see it. I will tell thee of it. (1) First, it was ordained of old, like the deliverance of the Red Sea. If God's election comes to those who are without merit, without hope, without strength, here is hope for thee. (2) In the next place, the salvation which God shows is one wrought by a mediator. (*C. H. Spurgeon.*) *Salvation of the Lord :*—John Lyons, a well-known citizen in Arizona, while at work in the shaft of his mine near Tres Alamos, had just put in a blast and lighted the fuse, when, on reaching the top of the shaft, he beheld four mounted Apaches rapidly approaching. Their horrible yells and hostile gestures revealed their murderous intent, and Mr. Lyons was for an instant paralyzed with terror. His first impulse was to hurl himself into the shaft and be blown to atoms by the explosion of the blast rather than perish miserably at the hands of the remorseless foe. Suddenly the blast at the bottom of the shaft exploded with terrific effect, throwing a shower of rock and *débris* high in the air, which was followed by a dense volume of smoke rolling up from the shaft. The Indians checked their horses, appalled by the unexpected and to them mysterious eruption, then, with a yell of terror, wheeled round and galloped off in the direction whence they came. But for the coincidence of the blast igniting at that particular moment, the man would, doubtless, have been tortured to death in the true Apache style. In the Christian life there come times when destruction seems inevitable, as it seemed to the miner, but those who trust in God experience deliverance as unexpected as his. *Fitness before action:*—The first thing this proud and sinful soul of mine needs is to be emptied of self and become like a little child. Action by and by. Work when you are ready and fit for work. March when you have been told where to go, and can see your way—not before. First of all, if we would do anything good or great we must get into a right attitude with God, from whom all goodness and greatness come. First of all get you to the Fountain Head, and see that the channels are open for real streams of light and life to flow down from the unseen and supernatural Heart into your own. Make sure that there is a God, and that He is your God; and that, being yours, His course is your course and His fight is your fight. It is not the atheist that is told to go forward; for his very going will be godless and he will blunder into Egypt again. The farther he goes the worse. It is not the pantheist that is bidden to go forward; for no fatherly hand will lead him but a blind force, the blind leading the blind. It is not the arrogant and unreligious moralist; for he will have to build his system out of the same materials that have failed him so often, or else trust the poor instinct which has already cast him helpless between the wilderness and the sea. When Christ and the apostles were asked, "What shall I do to be a Christian"? the answer was always in the same order—it was a pointing upward, first, not forward: Believe; lay hold on Heaven; take the hand of Christ; see that spiritual things are real; make your first act one of devotion; repent; be baptized; be confirmed; pray. Fill your mind and will with power from on high. (*Bp. F. D. Huntington.*) *The Christian must both* "*stand still*" *and* "*go forward*" :—Twice the Divine voice speaks. It says, first, "Stand still." Stand still, O impatient, eager, unthinking, unbelieving men! Stand still, men of unregulated activity, of unconsecrated knowledge, of swift and sweeping passion, of intemperate desire! Stand still, reckless competitions, grasping enterprises, immoderate labours and furious amusements, of these hurrying days and heated nights! Stand still, boundless ambition, over-wrought and over-confident brain, from your wild chase for bubbles in the air! Stand still, selfish traffic, corrupted legislation, Mammon and Passion and Vanity Fair, an unprincipled press, a frivolous society, a worldly-minded and mercenary Church! Stand still and see the salvation of God! Stand still, O lustful appetite and unfeeling avarice and cruel pride and headstrong self-will in the unchildlike and unchristian heart! But go forward, men of duty, men of honour, men of faith, men of God! Speak to the children of the Christian Israel soberly; speak encouragingly to one another, you who have long borne a burden that presses hard and borne it for your covenant's and your sanctuary's sake. "The Lord shall fight for you." Go forward, mercy and charity, works of faith and love, missions, healings, sacrifices, praises, reconciliations—go forward, O kingdom, in every soul and every land till they all are the kingdom of our God! (*Ibid.*) *Sit still and trust :*—One day when Stonewall Jackson, with his sister-in-law, was crossing the boiling torrent, just below the American falls at Niagara, in a slight boat manned by two oarsmen, the current so swirled the boat that the lady became terrified, believing they were going to the bottom. Jackson seized her by the arms, and turned to one of the men and said, "How often have you crossed here?" "I have been rowing people across, sir, for twelve years." "Did you ever meet with an accident?" "Never, sir."

"Never were capsized? never lost a life?" "Nothing of the kind, sir!" Then turning, in a somewhat peremptory tone, he said to the lady, "You hear what the boatman says, and unless you think you can take the oars and row better than he does, sit still and trust him as I do." *Stand still :*—These words contain God's command to the believer when he is reduced to great straits and brought into extraordinary difficulties. "Stand still." Despair whispers, "Lie down and die; give it all up." But God would have us put on a cheerful courage, and even in our worst times rejoice in His love and faithfulness. Cowardice says, "Retreat, go back to the worldling's way of action; you cannot play the Christian's part, it is too difficult. Relinquish your principles." But, however much Satan may urge this course upon you, you cannot follow it, if you are a child of God. The Divine fiat has bid thee go from strength to strength, and so thou shalt; and neither death nor hell shall turn thee from thy course. Precipitancy says, "Do something; stir yourself—to stand still and wait is sheer idleness." We must be doing something at once. Presumption boasts, "If the sea be before you, march into it and expect a miracle." But Faith listens neither to Presumption, nor to Despair, nor to Cowardice, nor to Precipitancy, but it hears God say, "STAND STILL," and immovable as a rock it stands. (*C. H. Spurgeon.*) **Ye shall see them again no more for ever.**—*Social separations :*—Although the Israelites beheld the next morning the Egyptian host dead upon the beach, they saw them no more in their pomp and power, fierceness and anger; they saw them no more in this world for ever. Let us look at the fact in three aspects. I. As AFFORDING A GLIMPSE OF THE MORAL GOVERNMENT OF GOD. A signal interposition displaying justice towards the oppressor, and mercy towards the oppressed. 1. Moral government takes cognizance of man's conduct. 2. Moral government righteously visits man's conduct. II. As ILLUSTRATING SEPARATIONS THAT ARE GOING ON BETWEEN MEN EVERY DAY. 1. Every day we see men that we shall see no more in this world for ever. 2. Every day we see men that we shall see no more in their present circumstances for ever. 3. Every day we see men that we shall see no more in their present character for ever. III. As FORESHADOWING THAT FINAL SEPARATION WHICH MUST TAKE PLACE BETWEEN THE WICKED AND THE RIGHTEOUS. 1. This takes place really at death. No more sensualists with their seductions, sceptics with their insinuations, devil with his temptations. 2. This takes place publicly in the day of judgment. (*Homilist.*)   *Lessons :*—I. THEN WICKED MEN SHALL PERISH IN THE VERY HOUR OF THEIR SPLENDOUR AND PRIDE. II. THEN WICKED MEN ARE OFTEN POWERLESS TO INFLICT THE INJURY THEY DESIRE UPON THE GOOD. If we are injured by these enemies of the soul, it is because of our unbelief. III. THEN THE WICKED AND THE GOOD WILL BE ETERNALLY SEPARATED IN THE LIFE TO COME. (*J. S. Exell, M.A.*) *Never again :*—I have seen one person at least, to-day, whom I have seen for the last time in this life. He may live many days or many years—I may live many days or many years; but in a crowded city like this it must needs be that there is one among that throng whom I have passed whom I never again will see. He stands, therefore, as a messenger direct from me to the judgment seat of God. Little did I think, when I spoke to him, with what a message I was freighting him! It is the last look that strikes, the last touch that tells, and if it was an unkind or a false word I then spoke, that unkind or false word has sunk like a die on the molten memory of him from whom I have just parted, as well as of myself. What testimony will he bear against me in the judgment of the future? 1. Perhaps it was one whom I was bound to love on whom my words fell. If it were, may God forgive me! for if they burned and seared that heart, far more deeply will they burn and sear mine, when I find that the ear that listened so eagerly for love, and shrank so agonizingly from unkindness, is now closed in death. 2. Perhaps it was one whom I was bound to protect, and whom with words of cunning I have overreached. If so, may God forgive me, for I have thus sent direct to His throne of justice this accusation against myself! Never again! And yet again when I go forth to-morrow there is at least one other whom I will meet whom I may meet never again! Guard my tongue and my heart, O God, that my account as to him may be just before Thee! (*Episcopal Recorder.*)   *The resource of God against the enemies of the good :*—During the American Civil War an English ship was boarded by the crew of a confederate cruiser. They drew their swords. But the gallant English Captain Williams marched forward and said, "Gentlemen, I am a simple sailor, but do not forget that behind this flag which I hold in my hand lies all the power of the army and navy of England. If you strike me you strike the might of England." So we may be simple men and women, but when we are engaged in the Lord's work we do not stand alone. (*G. Howard James.*)

Ver. 15. **Wherefore criest thou unto Me?** . . . **Go forward.**—*Go forward :*—Men are more ready to cry out for help than to help themselves. They are more ready to call for more light, means, privileges, than to use faithfully what they possess. They are more ready to complain than to exert themselves; to wonder at what the Divine Providence has done, or to speculate on what it intends to do, than to observe its will, and stand in the line of their duty, and "go forward." 1. And first, when we are confused with uncertain speculations as to points of religious doctrine and the designs of Providence, let us rest from the questions that are beyond mortal solving, from the debate and from those who would pretend to settle it for us, and obey the practical exhortation of the text. What we can discover and know may not be much; but what we have to do is plain enough, and deserves the chief place in our attention. Theories are many, and the counsel of the Lord is hid; but what He requires of us there needs but singleness of heart to discern and follow. The absolute truth may often be beyond us; but the right, as distinct from the wrong, is in the sentiment of every one's conscience and in the power of his hand. The present age is remarkably bent upon a prying kind of research into the deep things of religious faith. Let me not find fault with this tendency, so long as it is reverent, and not presumptuous; so long as it is humble, and not disputatious; so long as it is neither carping, nor over-anxious, nor neglectful of nearer claims. But it has its dangers. Sometimes it distracts the thoughts with fears and unprofitable conjectures; and sometimes it absorbs them in cares that are intense, but stationary, holding back the mind from a manly progress and impeding the cheerful diligence of life. Do not gaze backward, nor pause to contemplate anxiously what is in front, but move. If you are faithful, God will carry you through. Work and you shall believe. Do and you shall know. You shall learn more that is worth the learning through your conscience than through your researches. You will be guided to the best convictions, by being heartily engaged in an obedient service. 2. Thus, duty is better than speculation; and this is the first lesson that our subject teaches. But the mind is troubled with other things than the doubtful aspects of truth. There are afflicted and dejected hours, when we hardly care to inquire about anything. A feeling of discouragement hangs about the heart. Now, sorrow is naturally sluggish, selfish—as indisposed to strive for anything as to be thankful for anything. It chooses to sit. It looks upon the ground. It nurses its gloomy meditations. When it is caused by losses and disappointments, it is apt to make men think that there is nothing that deserves their winning, or at least that it is not worth while for them any longer to try. No doubt it makes many a man better. It brings the thoughtless to reflection. Sorrow is a holy thing when it is rightly accepted. It gives a consecrated turn to the experiences and affections of our humanity. And yet it has a power of an opposite kind; and they who come under that power are rendered worse instead of better by it. They lose their usefulness, as well as give up their own good. Others add the sin of murmuring to that of supineness. Why have they been thus distressed? What have they done to be so hemmed in? They complain of the very prophets and guiding messengers of God, because they show them no more mercy, and will encourage them in no other way than one that they refuse to follow. They want to be relieved just where they stand. They want to be delivered without any thought or effort of their own. But it is not so that God will have it. "Speak unto them," is His word still, "that they go forward." The best consolation is in your tasks, with their straining toil or their steady and quiet occupation. 3. But it is perhaps the labour imposed upon your unwilling strength that most disconcerts you. The apprehension of coming calamities has fastened its terrors upon you. The fears of a faint heart form the chief trial of your lot. Not an arrow has reached you yet from the pursuing host of your enemies, but you hear their trumpets, and you are dismayed at the trampling of their approach. You have not yet wet your shoes in the waves of the intercepting sea; but you look at its broad flow, and are dismayed at what seems to you its unfathomable and impassable depth. You are afraid of what you may be compelled to do; or you are afraid of what you may be appointed to suffer. What is so depressing as this dread, when once it settles down upon a man? How it paralyzes his resolution! But no power can assist him, at least not in the manner he would choose—by interfering to change his whole situation, and that without any step of his own taking. He must stand in his lot. He must march at command. There will be always something like a chase in the rear. There will be some gulf crossing his advanced post. He will not be listened to, if he sits and prays that all this may be otherwise. At the same time the help that was refused to his complaint

and his supplication awaits his diligence. Let him "go forward." The cowardice
that was his worst enemy shall then be vanquished. Beware how you waste in
sighs the time that should be spent in exertion. Beware how you look abroad for
the succour that you will contribute nothing to bring. Beware how you abandon
your own cause. Bear your part, according to the imperfect ability that you have
received, in the work of your deliverance. Commit the issues of events to the
Sovereign Disposer. They may venture, as long as their trust is in Him. "Speak
unto all My people," saith God, " that they go forward." Their prayer is good ;
but their obedience is better. His grace shall be sufficient for them while they
move towards it. (N. L. Frothingham.)   The journey through life :—It points
out, with sufficient clearness, the best mode of journeying through life. " Go forward "—(1) from that point to which God has conducted us ; (2) along the path
God bids us take ; (3) by the light which God affords ; (4) with the staff which God
provides ; and (5) to the land which God prepares. I. You are, then, willing to go
forward ? But whether you will or not, you must. What better starting-point can
you discover than that from which Israel began—THE POINT TO WHICH GOD HAS
BROUGHT YOU NOW ? Stop for a moment, my impatient fellow-traveller ; we are not
speaking of the point to which you have now brought yourself, but of that to which
God has conducted you ; and you must very soon, I think, feel that there may be
an important difference between these two. God may, indeed, command us to go
forward from the point to which He has Himself conducted us, but not by any
means to make advance on that wrong path which we have chosen through our own
folly and our sin. In such a case, God must have rather asked, " Why do you cry
to Me ? You are yourselves the cause of your distress and misery ; there is no
safety on this road, but only death and horror ; speak unto the Israelites that they
return immediately ! " But now, because the Lord Himself has pointed out the
place where they were to encamp, between Pi-hahiroth and Baal-Zephon, they are
in the position which He bade them occupy ; they now are standing in the place
where He would have them be : now we may speak of going on. " Advance ! "—
it is a glorious word ; and that which it denotes deserves the application of our
noblest powers. But, in advancing, the main question is—not whether we are
rising rapidly enough, but simply whether we are really on the right track, and
keeping the great end in view. Yes ; " Forward " is still a glorious word, but not
the first, scarcely the second that we should employ ; and you will be in a position
to apply it with advantage to yourselves only when, like these ransomed ones, you
have an Egypt at your back, and a Canaan before. But what think you ? O man
of sin, the path you now pursue leads down to death ; repentance is the only way
to life—regeneration of the soul the first, although perhaps the least felt requisite
for entering on the new period. Nay, no advance ere you have first stood still, made
full confession of your guilt, sought for deliverance from worse than Egypt's bondage, and cried for blood more precious than the blood of even the spotless Paschal
Lamb, to hide your sins ! II. " Advance ! " The order may be given easily, but
is it quite as speedily performed ? Then listen, in the second place, to what is
further given in the summons—ADVANCE ALONG THE WAY WHICH GOD COMMANDS.
" Which God commands." This, in a certain aspect, makes the thing much easier,
but in another much more difficult. You will at once perceive this when you place
yourself again in the position of the Israelites. Moses need not, in deep anxiety,
inquire, " Whither ? " for there is but one path, and not another given him to
choose. There is the most peremptory command not to go back ; nor would good
come of turning to the right or left ; moreover, there are mountains rising up to
heaven, and rocks, which shut the people in, as if within a fortress. Forward,
then ! But well may we, also, in spite of not a little difference, find a resemblance
to the path on which the Lord once more calls you and me to make advance. That
way itself is, in its leading features, quite as plain, as difficult, and yet withal as
safe, as that for which the Israelites now looked. If we are Christians, there is only
one way possible for our understanding, our faith, our conscience ; and that is the
way God bids us go. See that the path before you is indeed the way appointed by
the Lord ; and do not venture on a single step before you bow the knee to Him in
deep humility. But if it be quite evident that just this, and no other, is the road
which God deems best for you, then act as if you heard His voice from heaven saying, " Why do you cry to Me ? Surely you know that I am not a God who says,
' Go forward,' without giving strength wherewith to go." Nay, verily, God has not
changed, so that He now should call His people to advance into the sea, and leave
them there to perish in the flood. Suppose the Israelites, alarmed at the idea of

advancing through the waves, had taken time to think, and then attempted to retreat; or sought, amidst the mountains on each side, an opening by which they might escape approaching death: according to the judgment of the natural man, they would have acted with the utmost prudence, yet they would have but been hastening into the yawning grave. The passage through the sea turns out to be much safer than the path along the quiet shore, as soon as it appears that God is with us. It is precisely when the prophet Jonah seeks to flee from Nineveh, and find a safe retreat in Tarshish, that such mortal danger comes so close on him; and, on the other hand, when Paul, led by the Lord to Rome, courageously defies Euroclydon and every storm, his life is saved, although the ship is lost. Our life is ever free from danger when we risk it in the service of the Lord; because, as has been truly said, we are immortal while God needs us here. III. "But what avails it me, even though I know the way, so long as, in short-sightedness, I still must grope about under dark clouds?" You are quite right; but you too, just like Israel, are this day summoned to advance UNDER THE LIGHT THAT GOD AFFORDS. You can imagine that you now behold the mysterious fiery pillar, scattering its golden rays upon the silvery waters in the darkness of the night, and straightway turning its fierce lightnings on the host of the Egyptians. But say, has not God, in His written word, sent light from heaven sufficient in amount and clear enough to brighten, with its friendly rays, many a gloomy night and many a cloudy day? And have you ever been kept waiting long without an answer, when, with the earnest question, "What will the Lord have me to do?" you took your precious Bible up, in silent solitude, not to consult it, like so many, just as if it were a kind of heathen oracle—examining the first page that might open up to you—but earnestly endeavouring to find out what the Lord desires? But is it not the case that we are just like that rebellious Israel—constantly inclined to choose their own way rather than simply pursue the path to which the cloudy pillar guided them? And even after we have been already taught, on numberless occasions, through the shame and injury that have befallen us, we still direct our eyes continually to the *ignis fatuus* of human wisdom, when we rather should fear God, and give attention to His word. And what should hinder you from choosing that same word of God to be a lamp unto your feet, a light unto your path? Should the obscurities and enigmas that here present themselves to you prove such a barrier? Even the fiery pillar had for Israel its impenetrable and mysterious side; but this much they perceived quite well, that it afforded them more light than a thousand other lights. And there is something wondrous in the fact that this great light illumines everything, although you know not where it has its seat; nor can you find in anything besides a proper substitute when it has been removed. Or—just acknowledge it—are you offended at the vehemence with which the Word of God denounces sin? Yes, verily, the cloudy pillar sent forth dreadful thunderbolts, but they were only aimed at hardened ones like Pharaoh; and that same light of God's unspotted holiness, which is so terrible to sinners, is the consolation of all those who make His mercy the foundation of their hopes. Or has that light no longer an attraction for you, inasmuch as it has lost the splendour of most novelties? Surely the fiery pillar was quite as invaluable in the fortieth year that followed Israel's Exodus, as in the first night when they were redeemed? And should you not be rather cheered by the consideration that, when everthing to-day announces instability and change, the word of God endures for aye? IV. But do you make complaint—not against God, but rather against yourself? And do you fear your strength will fail? We could not urge you to advance, did we not also, in the fourth place, indicate THE STAFF WHICH GOD BESTOWS ON US. Let it suffice to state that, without living faith working within the heart, it is as hopeless to set out upon life's journey as it would have been impossible to march through the Red Sea without the all-prevailing, wonder-working rod. Poor man, you rise up, but you know not whence; you wander here and there, but do not know how long; you ask for strength, yet know not whence it may be gained! The Lord's words are most true: "Cursed is the man that maketh flesh his arm. . . Blessed is the man that trusteth in the Lord." But have you never found that all things are possible to him that believeth, and that even mountains of difficulties seemed to dwindle away into molehills when touched by this wonder-working staff? The time will often come when you shall stand before a task for which your own unaided wisdom will be quite unequal; but the prayer of faith works wonders, and strength comes down from above into the heart which owns, in deep humility, that it is naught but weakness when apart from God. V. The Lord arouses us to march on TO THE LAND WHICH HE PREPARES FOR US. You are aware that Israel was called not merely to forsake the land of Egypt, nor even to spend a desert life in peace and liberty, but to march on into a land which God, ages before, had promised to bestow on the posterity of those who were His friends. Not one of all those multitudes who passed through the Red Sea had ever seen that promised land. Upon the ground of credible authority, they were constrained to the belief that it was a reality awaiting them beyond the flood. Not even the wisest of them all was free to choose the mode of access to that land which flowed with milk and honey. But their great Leader ever held Himself responsible for the result, although the moment when the earthly paradise was to unfold its gates was still kept in deep secrecy. Nor are we called to wander aimlessly, and to march on without exactly knowing where we are to go. The Lord from heaven has appeared on this vile earth that we, exiles from Eden, might have an eternal dwelling-place; and though no messenger has come back from the habitations where He has prepared us room, we know, as surely as we live, that what no eye hath seen, what ear hath never heard, what hath not entered into any human heart, is hid with Christ in God for all who know and love Him. Whoever will draw back unto perdition may perceive, in Israel's case, that while God presses upon sinful men His heavenly gift, He will by no means let Himself be mocked. The way that leads to it may not, perhaps, be quite the shortest (and those who, like Israel, are slow to learn require a longer training-time), still less is it the most agreeable, but most assuredly it is the best. And the inheritance itself will only seem more beautiful if we, like Moses, are obliged to wait a long time on God that we may get possession of the whole. Do you know any prospect more inspiriting than that of one day having done entirely with that daily dying which we now call "life"; of our at last, some time or other, breathing with a pleasure and a freedom we have never yet felt here, where every day brought us more than enough of its own ills; of once more hearing there, too, the command, "Forward!" and then advancing through the spacious fields of heaven, but finding nowhere near us any foe, nor seeing any wilderness before? Surely, even though it cost us other forty anxious years, as it cost Israel the Promised Land, what one of us would think the price of such a calling far too dear? (*J. J. Van Oosterzee, D.D.*) *Unseasonable prayer :*—I. SOMETIMES THE ANSWER WILL BE VERY UNSATISFACTORY. 1. Because I was brought up to do so. 2. It is a part of my religion. These pray as a Dervish dances or a Fakir holds his arm aloft; but they know nothing of the spiritual reality of prayer (Matt. vi. 7). 3. It is a right thing to do. So indeed it is if we pray aright, but the mere repetition of pious words is vanity (Isa. xxix. 13). 4. I feel easier in my mind after it. Ought you to feel easier? May not your formal prayers be a mockery of God, and so an increase of sin (Isa. i. 12–15 ; Ezek. xx. 31)? 5. I think it meritorious and saving. This is sheer falsehood, and a high offence against the merit and sacrifice of the Lord Jesus. II. SOMETIMES THE ANSWER WILL BETRAY IGNORANCE. 1. When it hinders immediate repentance. Instead of quitting sin and mourning over it, some men talk of praying. "To obey is better than sacrifice," and better than supplication. 2. When it keeps from faith in Jesus. The gospel is not "pray and be saved"; but "believe on the Lord Jesus Christ and thou shalt be saved" (Matt. vii. 21 ; John vi. 47). 3. When we suppose that it fits us for Jesus. We must come to Him as sinners, and not set up our prayers as a sort of righteousness (Luke xviii. 11, 12). 4. When we think that prayer alone will bring a blessing. III. SOMETIMES THE ANSWER WILL BE QUITE CORRECT. 1. Because I must. I am in trouble, and must pray or perish. Sighs and cries are not made to order, they are the irresistible outbursts of the heart (Psa. xlii. 1 ; Rom viii. 26). 2. Because I know I shall be heard, and therefore I feel a strong desire to deal with God in supplication. "Because He hath inclined His ear unto me, therefore will I call upon Him" (Psa. cxvi. 2). 3. Because I delight in it: it brings rest to my mind, and hope to my heart. It is a sweet means of communion with my God. "It is good for me to draw near to God" (Psa. lxxiii. 28). 4. Because I feel that I can best express the little faith and repentance I have by crying to the Lord for more. 5. Because these grow as I pray. No doubt we may pray ourselves into a good frame if God the Holy Ghost blesses us. 6. Because I look for all from God, and therefore I cry to Him (Psa. lxxii. 5). (*C. H. Spurgeon.*) *Self-help :*—Self-help is one of the popular topics of the day, and seems to be commended in the passage which contains the text. Help thyself, and Heaven will help thee, is a proverb which, both in its French and its English form, is widely current ; and wisely current, if we understand the Divine principle on which it rests. Read in the light of Scripture, it does not run, Venture, and the Almighty hand will meet thee, the help will come; but rather, Venture, for the

Everlasting Arms are around thee, the help is here. Thus read, it is an all-mastering truth. But what is the principle here, the essential principle of the progress? Is it, March, and I will meet you; or March, for I have led you; I, not you, am responsible for these straits; you are here because through them lies the path to victory and glory. Therefore "cry not unto Me"; your being here is My answer to your cry. "Speak unto the children of Israel that they go forward." I. THEIR STANDING THERE AT ALL WAS A MIRACLE OF ALMIGHTY POWER AND LOVE. By a series of the most tremendous miracles recorded in history, God's hand had led them out to that mountain gorge, and shut them in between the moaning sea and their raging foes. Pharaoh drew near, but God was even visibly more near. A great army was gathering behind them; but the angel of God's presence was visibly in the midst of them. They distrusted and despised Emmanuel—God with them, a visible glory over their host. II. They ought to have accepted God's guidance thither as THE ABSOLUTE ASSURANCE THAT THEIR WAY ON LAY CLEAR BEFORE HIS EYES, and that all the difficulties which beset it were under the firm control of His hand. (*J. B. Brown, B.A.*)   *Effort needed as well as prayer:*—A scholar was remarkable for repeating her lessons well. Her schoolfellow, rather idly inclined, said to her one day, "How is it that you always say your lessons so perfectly?" She replied, "I always pray that I may say my lessons well." "Do you?" said the other; "well then, I will pray, too": but alas! the next morning she could not even repeat a word of her usual task. Very much confounded, she ran to her friend, and reproached her as deceitful: "I prayed," said she, "but I could not say a single word of my lesson." "Perhaps," rejoined the other, "you took no pains to learn it." "Learn it! Learn it! I did not learn it at all," answered the first, "I thought I had no occasion to learn it, when I prayed that I might say it." The mistake is a very common one. (*C. H. Spurgeon.*)   *The flight from Egypt:*— I. THEIR DANGER. Foe behind, sea in front, mountains on each side. II. THEIR DILEMMA. Knew not which way to turn. III. THEIR DELIVERER. Man's extremity God's opportunity. IV. THEIR DUTY. "Go forward." This demanded faith. V. THEIR DETERMINATION. They obeyed. VI. THEIR DELIGHT. Song of Moses. (*G. Weller.*)   *Go forward:*—I. The story from which these words are taken is A STORY OF NATIONAL PROGRESS. It is also one of supernatural progress. For us the supernatural is, in the highest and truest sense of the word, natural, for it is the revelation of the nature of God. We accept the possibility of the supernatural and miraculous, but all the more for that do we hold that if God interferes in the affairs of men miraculously, He will not do it capriciously, unnecessarily, wantonly. Upon the whole story of these Jewish miracles there is stamped a character which marks distinctly the reason for which they were wrought; that reason was the religious education of the world. By these miracles the Jew was taught that for nations and men there is a God, an eternal and a personal will above us and around us, that works for righteousness. This great fact was taught him by illustrated lessons, by pictures illuminated with the Divine light and so filled with the Divine colour that they stand and last for all time. II. The lesson that seems definitely stamped on the story of the miraculous passage of the Red Sea is THE LESSON OF FEARLESSNESS IN THE DISCHARGE OF DUTY, of resolute walking in the way that we know to be God's way for us. We find this true—1. In the case of individuals. 2. In the case of nations. For individuals and for nations God has appointed a law of progress. All who have ever striven to raise the tone of a nation's life, to bring the nation onward on the path that leads to peace and righteousness, have been preaching to mankind this great word of God's, "Go forward where God would have you go." (*Bp. Magee.*)   *Christian progress:*— Progress is the great test of a Christian. It is not what we are absolutely, but what we are relatively, relatively to what we were. Religion must always be "a walk," and the child of God a traveller. Old things get further and further behind, and as they recede look smaller and smaller; new things constantly come into view, and there is no stagnation. The man, though slowly, and with much struggle, and with many humiliations, is stretching on to the ever-rising level of his own spiritual and heaven-drawn conscience. I. We may be discouraged because of PAST FAILURES. Still we have no choice but to go on. Life is made up of rash beginnings and premature endings. We have nothing for it but to begin again. II. We may feel ourselves utterly GRACELESS AND GODLESS. The remedy is, at once to determine to be a great Christian. We must aim at things far in advance. We must go forward. III. Perhaps SOME GREAT TEMPTATION OR SIN BARS THE WAY. Then we must not stand calculating. We must not look at consequences, but simply "go forward" to the new life of self-denial and holiness. (*J. Vaughan, M.A.*) *Going forward:*—Both the Israelites and Egyptians went forward; but how? and to what?—I. THE ISRAELITES WENT FORWARD IN OBEDIENCE TO DIVINE COMMANDS; THE EGYPTIANS, IN OPPOSITION TO THE DIVINE WILL. 1. As regards the Israelites—In this particular crisis He commanded them to proceed (ver. 15). The means and mode of their advance were prescribed by Him (ver. 16). 2. The Egyptians went forward in defiance of the will of God. II. THE ISRAELITES WENT FORWARD HAVING THE PRESENCE OF GOD WITH THEM AS A HELP; THE EGYPTIANS HAVING THAT PRESENCE AS A HINDRANCE (ver. 19, 20). III. THE ISRAELITES WENT FORWARD IN WISE RELIANCE UPON GOD; THE EGYPTIANS IN INFATUATED DARING OF HIM. IV. THE ISRAELITES WENT FORWARD HAVING THE FORCES OF NATURE CONTROLLED IN THEIR FAVOUR; THE EGYPTIANS WITH THOSE FORCES USED TO THEIR CONFUSION AND OVERTHROW (vers. 21–27). Nature renders loyal obedience to its Lord. The Most High employs nature's elements and forces for the defence and deliverance of His people, and for the defeat and destruction of His foes. V. THE ISRAELITES WENT FORWARD TO SPLENDID VICTORY AND SPIRITUAL PROFIT; THE EGYPTIANS TO UTTER DEFEAT AND DEATH. 1. As to the Israelites—(1) Their triumph was complete and glorious (vers. 29, 30). (2) They also derived moral benefit from the event (ver. 31). Reverential fear of God was inspired within them, and their faith in Him and in His servant Moses was quickened and confirmed. 2. But the Egyptians were utterly overthrown and slain (ver. 28). Lessons: 1. Going forward is not always making progress. 2. Going forward is true progress only when it accords with the will of God. 3. The path of duty is often beset with difficulties. 4. Difficulties in the path of duty disappear before believing obedience. 5. Rebellion against God leads to trouble and distress, and if persisted in must end in irretrievable ruin. 6. Faith in God and obedience to Him lead onward and upward to glorious triumph. 7. The deliverances wrought for us by the hand of God should encourage us to reverence and trust Him. (*William Jones.*) *Christian progress in the face of difficulties:*—I. In the Christian life ADVANCEMENT IS DEMANDED. Forward, upward, heavenward, Godward. II. In the Christian life advancement is demanded, WITH A FULL RECOGNITION OF THE OBSTACLES IN THE WAY OF IT. We pass from conquest to renew the conflict. III. In the Christian life, OBSTACLES TO PROGRESS, MANFULLY ENCOUNTERED, MAY BE SURMOUNTED. Difficulties vanish, in the presence of believing obedience. IV. In the Christian life, obstacles to progress, manfully encountered, CONTRIBUTE TO OUR ADVANCEMENT. V. In the Christian life we are INCITED TO PROGRESS, NOTWITHSTANDING OBSTACLES, BY A GREAT HOST OF ENCOURAGEMENTS. 1. Believing prayer is mighty with God. 2. Glorious examples encourage us onward. 3. The character of our Leader encourages us onward. (*Ibid.*) *Forward:*—Into whatever province of Divine government we look, we find that "Forward" is one of God's great watchwords, onward to that state which is higher, more perfect. On Christian believers is laid the obligation to "go on unto perfection," to "press toward the mark," &c. I. As the children of Israel, in obedience to the command of God, were on their way from A LOWER TO A HIGHER AND MORE BLESSED LIFE, so are Christians. II. As the children of Israel were required to go forward FOR THE DISCIPLINE OF THEIR FAITH, so are Christian believers. III. As the Israelites were required to go forward IN THE INTERESTS OF THE KINGDOM OF GOD IN THE WORLD, so are Christian disciples. (*R. Ann.*) *The Christian's watchword:*—I. IN WHAT THE CHRISTIAN IS TO GO FORWARD. Now this is evident; he must go forward in the path to eternal life. More particularly, he must go forward—1. In the increase of Christian graces. 2. In the exhibition of Christian virtues. Such as justice, temperance, brotherly kindness, and charity. 3. In the performance of Christian duties. In reading the holy oracles, and in holy meditation, forward. In secret and public prayer, forward. In family worship and discipline, forward. In the services of the sanctuary, forward. In enterprises of usefulness and plans of benevolence, forward. In all the personal and relative obligations of life, forward. 4. In the attainment of Christian privileges and blessings. "Peace flowing as a river, and righteousness abounding as the waves of the sea." II. WHY THE CHRISTIAN SHOULD GO FORWARD. 1. God commands it, and His authority is imperative. 2. Christ enforces it, and His claims are irresistible. 3. The Holy Spirit moves us to it, and His influences must not be quenched. 4. By the examples of saints with whom we are for ever to be associated. 5. By the sufficiency of the means provided for our progress and safety. 6. By the dreadful and calamitous effects produced by apostasy. 7. By the glorious rewards which God shall bestow upon His persevering people. Application: 1. Let the subject be addressed to all classes and ages of Christian professors. To the young believer, and the aged disciple, the motto is the same—forward. To the illiterate, and the learned Christian. Forward, in prosperity and adversity; in sickness and health; in life and until death. 2. The subject must be reversed to the sinner. He is in the wrong path; far enough already from God and happiness and heaven. Turn from thy evil ways and live. (*J. Burns, D.D.*)   *Progress :*—I. THE NECESSITY FOR PROGRESS AS A CONDITION FOR HEALTHY LIFE. The advancing tide has no sooner touched its highest point than it begins to recede. In the spiritual life, progress is needful to secure past attainments, as well as to gain fresh victories. II. THE DIRECTIONS IN WHICH PROGRESS SHOULD BE SOUGHT. 1. Go forward to clearer and higher conceptions of spiritual truth. 2. Go forward in further development of the Church's social life. 3. Go forward in all works of Christian beneficence. 4. Go forward individually in the cultivation of the spiritual life. (*J. Legge, M.A.*) *Go forward—a New Year's sermon for the young :*—We have been spared to see the beginning of another year, we may therefore think of ourselves as having reached a certain halting-place in our journey. I. WE SHOULD BELIEVE IN CHRIST, AND ALSO OBEY HIM. Without believing in Christ, we have no true love to God in our hearts; and without love, we cannot give Him the obedience of children. II. WE ARE TAUGHT HERE ALSO THAT WE SHOULD BOTH WORSHIP GOD AND WORK FOR HIM. I have heard of a heathen king who was wounded in battle, and who, in his dying hours, sending for his trusted servant, said to him, " Go, tell the dead I am come." That soldier-servant, without hesitating for a moment, drew his sword and stabbed himself to the heart, that he might go to the dead before his master, and prepare them for his coming. Oh ! that we had this spirit of service and of sacrifice for the King of kings ! In His dying hour, He also said to us, "Go, tell the dead, I come." He asks us to go to a world dead in trespasses and sins, to tell them of His coming, and to preach to them glad tidings of great joy. Alas ! how many of us are content to worship Him, and say, " O King, rule for ever ! " without spending and being spent, that His kingdom may come. III. THIS PASSAGE FURTHER TEACHES US, THAT, WHILE WE ENJOY RELIGIOUS PRIVILEGES, WE SHOULD SEEK TO MAKE YEARLY AND DAILY PROGRESS BY MEANS OF THEM. We should become liker to Christ, and seek to learn more perfectly the language of heaven. Christ's work for us is complete. Christ's work in us is only begun, and God loves to see His believing children growing in likeness to that Elder Brother who is the very image of Himself. If you ask me why you should thus go on towards perfection, I answer—1. It is the will of God. We are to be perfect as our Father who is in heaven is perfect ; and we see, from all that goes on around us and within us, that this perfection is not to be reached by a single effort, or in a single day. 2. But not only should we go forward in obedience to the will of God ; we should also feel that it is needful for our own sakes to obey our heavenly Father. For—(1) If we refuse to go forward, it is ruin to our highest interests. On the lake of Geneva, some years ago, I saw a gloomy castle where prisoners used to be confined ; and in it there was a dark dungeon, with a dreadful staircase, called the *oubliettes*. I was told that sometimes the keeper went to a poor prisoner confined in that dungeon-castle, and told him that now he was to obtain his life and liberty, and requested him to follow him. The prisoner was delighted, and left his cell, and went along very thankful and very glad, with hopes and visions of home and happiness. He reached the staircase I have spoken of, and was told to go down, step by step, in the darkness, that he might reach the castle gate, and so be free. Alas ! it was a broken stair ! A few steps down into the darkness, and the next step he took he found no footing, but fell down fifty or sixty feet, to be dashed to pieces among rocks, and then to have his mangled body buried in the lake. So the sinner thinks that the way of self-indulgence and self-pleasing he takes will give him all he wishes, but it leads to death. And if we willingly and knowingly go back to our sins, as the Israelites might have gone back with Pharaoh's hosts, our last condition will be worst than our first. But, as it is death to disobey, so—(2) It is life to go forward in the way of obedience and persistent service. The pleasures of sin, indeed, we cannot have. But the Christian's is, after all, the better part. " Godliness is profitable unto all things, having promise of the life that now is, and of that which is to come." We have the light of Christian knowledge, the blessings of religious faith, the hope of a happy immortality, and the blessedness of holy love. Before I conclude, let me give you this one counsel : Do not, as pilgrims of immortality, think lightly of little steps. These Israelites had to go all their long journey to Canaan one step at a time, and so it is with you. And, alas ! you may go a far way from the path of duty, and the path of safety, though you only take one step at a time. And, as bad persons become wicked step by step, so it needs many little steps to go forward to the love and likeness of Christ. It was told of a painter, that he had "no day without its line." Every day he added some touches to his picture. So let it be with ours. Thus we shall make it liker and liker to Christ, the perfect image of the invisible God. (*W. H. Grey, D.D.*) *The memorial charge to the Israelites :*—I. Let us consider THIS COMMAND IN REFERENCE TO THE JOURNEY OF THE ISRAELITES. It became them, and it becomes us, to obey whenever God commands ; and to do whatever He enjoins us, and that for four reasons. 1. Because He has a right to command. He is the Sovereign, we are the subjects. He is the Master, we are the servants. 2. Because none of His commands are arbitrary. We may not be able to perceive the reasons upon which they are founded ; but there are reasons. 3. Because all His commands are beneficial. They all regard our welfare, as well as His own glory. 4. Because they are all practicable. They all imply a power to obey. If not possessed, yet attainable—if not in nature, yet in grace. Now, men may enjoin what is really impossible ; but God never does. II. THE ADVANCEMENT OF CHRISTIANS IN THE DIVINE LIFE. For Christians are now on their way from Egypt to Canaan. An old writer says, "A Christian should never pitch his tent twice in the same place," but with every fresh rising sun there should be some fresh advancement. 1. In order to see the possibility, the propriety, the importance, of thus advancing in the Divine life, turn to the commands of the Scriptures, "Grow in grace, and in the knowledge of our Lord and Saviour Jesus Christ." "Add to your faith virtue," &c. 2. Then turn to the advantages of progression in your Christian course ; for, as you advance, you will improve, and will rise higher in Divine attainments. As you advance, you are "changing from glory to glory." Every step you take adds to your dignity ; every step adds to your usefulness, and enables you more to adorn the " doctrine of God your Saviour in all things," and to recommend His service to those around you. Every step you take adds to your comfort ; it adds to the evidences of your state, and to your character ; and so far exemplifies the words of the Saviour, " Herein is My Father glorified, that ye bear much fruit, so shall ye be My disciples " ; appear as such, and exemplify yourselves as such. III. Let us consider this command in reference to THE PROGRESS OF TIME. Time is always advancing ; the hour-glass, the day, the week, the year—all go forward. And do they leave you behind ? No ; you advance with as much speed as the vessel which bears you along. You are not, therefore, to consider us here as exhorting you to go forward with time, but how to go forward, and in what way you ought to advance. 1. " Go forward " with humbleness of mind, not strutting into the new year, as if you had been acting wisely, worthily and meritoriously, throughout the year that is past ; but "clothed with humility," and "walking humbly with your God." 2. " Go forward with gratitude in the remembrance of His mercies." Have they not been "new every morning"? 3. " Go forward " under a sense of present aid, in opposition to complainings and murmurings. 4. " Go forward " also with a firm confidence as to what may befall you in the future. 5. " Go forward " with earnest and constant prayer. 6. " Go forward " with frequent thoughts of your journey's end : for it will have an end, and you are brought one year nearer to it. (*W. Jay.*) *The pilgrimage of the saints :*—I. THE CHARACTER AND COURSE OF THE PEOPLE OF GOD. 1. These circumstances of Israel, illustrating the spiritual character and course of those who form the new-covenant Church, may apply to them as they are redeemed and called out of the world. 2. The circumstances of Israel apply to those who form the spiritual Church of God, as their redemption and calling out of the world are connected with a career of pilgrimage to a state of future happiness. II. THE IMPEDIMENTS EXISTING TO THE CONTINUANCE OF THEIR PROGRESS. 1. An impediment is found, in the actual presence of adversaries, and the view of the danger which thence appears to exist. 2. An impediment is found also, in the fears excited by the prospect of future perils and opposition. 3. An impediment is found also, in the guilty remembrances of past ease and enjoyments. III. THE COMMAND UNDER WHICH THEY ARE PLACED, AND WHICH IS CONNECTED WITH POWERFUL EXCITEMENTS TO OBEDIENCE. "Forward," is a word comprehending what must be the exclusive spirit of the Christian calling. Perils, foes, and fears, are not to be regarded ; above them all, the mandate sounds its imperious note—"Go forward." 1. Let us reflect on the danger of return. 2. Let us reflect on the sufficiency of the Divine protection. 3. Let us reflect on the value of the possessions, by the enjoyment of which our progress is to be closed. (*J. Parsons.*) *Encouragement in difficulties :*—I. THE

SITUATION OF THE ISRAELITES. It is no uncommon thing for many past mercies to be lost in one present perplexity. II. THE CONDUCT OF MOSES. We see here—1. Piety. 2. Meekness. 3. Faith. III. THE INTERPOSITION OF JEHOVAH. It was most seasonable and beneficial. Conclusion : It is plain that such an admonition as this in the text, must not be indiscriminately urged. It belongs to Christians. To as many as are of this character, we affectionately say, Go forward. More particularly. 1. You are engaged in a high spiritual pursuit. Your object now is, the acquisition of scriptural knowledge ; not the knowledge of froth and folly ; the cherishing and improving of religious impressions ; not to stifle and strive against them. Your object is to vanquish sin in all its various forms, to make progress in the way of holiness ; not to sit down at the entrance of the way. Your object is to increase in spiritual consolation. Much of this is yet to be enjoyed. 2. In this pursuit you must expect difficulties. And be not surprised if you meet with them at the very entrance of your religious course. 3. Notwithstanding difficulties, you must "go forward." Backward you cannot go, but at the hazard of life, at the cost of utter destruction. " If any man draw back, My soul," saith the Lord, " shall have no pleasure in him " ; and to lie under the displeasure of the Almighty is to be wretched and undone for ever. 4. In your progress there is much to encourage you. What is there? (1) The command of God is evident. (2) The example of others is encouraging. (3) The guidance which God gives is greatly encouraging. (4) The refreshments of the way must encourage you. The gospel is food, affording the best support ; the promises are a cordial, administering the richest consolation. Divine ordinances are wisely adapted to the same end. The Lord's Supper is a feast, a feast for refreshment. And what shall we say of heaven at the end of your course ? The Israelites had the prospect of Canaan, and it encouraged them : the hope of the promised land helped them through many trials. But yours is a much better hope, a much more animating prospect! (*T. Kidd.*) *On going forward :*—The Hebrew life was a camp-life, and as such is the picture of ours. For a while we rest beneath the shadow of Elim's palm-trees, or lie down beside the green pastures ; but ere long the bugle-note of our great Leader's voice is heard, calling us to the onward march. I. THE CALL TO GO FORWARD SHOWS THAT THERE ARE SEASONS FOR SWIFT OBEDIENCE, AS WELL AS EARNEST PRAYER. " Wherefore criest thou unto Me? " says God. Strange language from the lips of Him who has taught us to be instant in prayer. Even prayer must not be a medium for distrust to unveil itself. Prayer must bespeak faith, not doubt. We want brave hearts, as well as suppliant knees. We must fight against distrust. Doubt is defeat. II. THE CALL TO GO FORWARD WAS ACCOMPANIED BY EXAMPLE. Men crave leaders—in the State, in the senate, in the field, and in the Church. Fix your eye on the unfaltering Moses. "Forward! " says a voice from the better land. III. THE CALL TO GO FORWARD TEACHES US THAT GOD HIDES DIFFICULTIES TILL THEY COME. They had no forewarning of this event. But God keeps the veil down before each life's future hour. We never know what shall be on the morrow : save that grace will be there if we live, and glory if we die. To-morrow, the fairest lamb in the fold may wander, the most loved friend be gone; the thorn may spring from the pillow, and the garden contain a grave. IV. THE CALL TO GO FORWARD TELLS US THAT WE ARE NOT TO LIVE IN THE PAST. Neither in its successes nor in its sorrows. " Let the dead past bury its dead." Piety should be no fossil relic of past experience. Yesterday's religion will not save us ! V. THE CALL TO GO FORWARD ANSWERS TO THE SPIRITUAL INSTINCTS OF THE SOUL. Forward ! Not to the grave, but through the grave. The Christian revelation gives us the principles of progress, and opens up the sphere for their exercise, by its unveiling of the immortal state. VI. THE CALL TO GO FORWARD TELLS US THAT WE HAVE SUPERNATURAL ASSISTANCE TO GO FORWARD. When in our earthly life, God calls us to human progress, what aids He gives us in fellowship, friendship, and love! And when in a spiritual sense God says, Go forward, He does not leave us to ourselves. Go back to your first Communion—to brotherly sympathy and prayer—to tender help from hearts that now rest. What a way it has been ! (*W. M. Statham, M.A.*)   *Excelsior :*—1. Going forward supposes difficulty. You will find sometimes the path to be steep and uneven, rugged and rough. None but the brave go forward. The way, though right, is not always smooth and pleasant, charmed with music and song and perfumed with the fragrance of flowers, but much of a contrary kind. This is true of every enterprise in which men are engaged where either fame or opulence are sought. Thus, a man will be a successful painter, sculptor, mechanic, or merchant. Napoleon said of Massena that he was not himself till the battle began to go against him ; then, when the dead began to fall in ranks around him, awoke his powers of combination, and he put on terrors and victory as a robe. So it is in rugged crises, in unweariable endurance, and in aims which put human sympathy out of question that the angel is shown. Nothing is gained that is worth the having without difficulty. Things easily got readily go. 2. To go forward implies decision and energy. Indecision is relaxing to the moral nature, it weakens, and has often proved fatal to the deepest interests in some of life's most solemn crises. To swing this way and that, like the pendulum of the clock in the plane of its oscillation, without making any advance forward, is most pitiable in a man. A French orator says, "Indecision of movement shows lack, both in mind and heart ; to wish and not to wish, is most wretched ; he who hesitates, totters, falls back, and is lost." Then, what is needed to secure true advancement is energy, decision of character, force, concentration, the power to will and to execute. And this implies having an aim, a definite object before us, and fixing the mind on that, moving steadily, unfalteringly towards its attainment ; to know where we are going, looking to the grand final results, and measuring our steps accordingly. 3. To go forward implies patient endurance. The march sometimes will be slow and weary—you will not always be able to go with " alacrity and delight," nor shall you find it "all glory going to glory." Times will be when the apostle's saying will have a deep significance—" Ye have need of patience " ; and when obedience to the injunction—"In patience possess your souls," will be the highest point of heroism. Times when the way is dark and slippery, and adverse forces combine to stop your progress, and when, if you can move at all, it will be but a step at a time. 4. This going forward implies an object. Something before and above us as yet, and that may be attained to and won by diligent toil, application, study, and earnest pressing after. This, then, is the grand end of all going forward—the attainment of glory. It is not now, nor here, but beyond and above. (*J. Higgins.*) *Forward :*—I. First, we will contemplate THE CHILDREN OF ISRAEL AS A FLOCK OF FUGITIVES ; and in this light they give encouragement to trembling sinners, flying from the curse of the law and from the power of their sins. You are trying to escape from your sins ; you are not, as you used to be, a contented bondsman. You have been flying as best you could from sin ; but the whole of your sins are after you, and your conscience with its quick ear can hear the sound of threatening judgment. "Alas ! " your heart is saying, "unless God help me, I shall be in hell." "Alas ! " says your judgment, " unless God be merciful, I shall soon perish." Every power of your manhood is now upon the alarm. Now, what shall I do for you? Shall I pray for you? Ay, that I will. But, methinks, while I am praying for you, I hear my Master saying, "Wherefore criest thou unto Me ? " Tell them to go forward ; preach Christ to them, instead of praying any longer, or bidding *them* pray. Deliver to them the message of the gospel—" Forward, sinner, forward to the Cross ! " II. Secondly, we may view the great company who came out of Egypt as AN ARMY UNDER COMMAND; therefore, they must obey. The command given to them is, "Forward ! " "Sir, I have begun to be a Christian, but, if I continue in it, I shall lose my business. My calling is such that I cannot be honest in it, and serve my God faithfully. What ought I to do? Ought I not to give up my religion ? " Forward ! no matter what is before you. Forward ! you are not fit to be a soldier of Christ unless you can count all costs, and still hold fast to the Cross of Christ. "Ah ! " says one, " but what is to become of my children, my household? " Friend, *I* cannot tell thee, but *God* can. It is thine to trust them with Him, for the only command I have for you is, Forward ! forward ! "But my husband says, I shall never come into the house again ; my father tells me he will turn me out of doors." Be it so, no one pities you more than I do ; but I dare not alter my message to your soul. "Go forward ! " "Well," says one, "these are hard commands." Yes, but the martyrs had harder still. III. Let us view these people as ON THE MARCH TOWARDS CANAAN. Many of you are on your way towards heaven, and the Lord's command to you is "Forward ! forward ! " There are some persons who cannot be persuaded to make an advance in the Divine life. We ought to go forward in—1. Knowledge; 2. Faith; 3. Fellowship with Christ; 4. Work for our Master. IV. To CHRISTIANS IN TROUBLE our text is applicable. The children of Israel were in a trial into which God had brought them ; and it is an absolute certainty, that if God brings you in, He will bring you out. He never did take a saint where he must of necessity perish. What is to be done now? God's word is—"Forward ! " God shall fight for you, and you shall hold your peace. V. THE ISRAELITES WERE UPON A DIVINE MISSION. They were going up to slay the

Canaanites. Preaching is the great weapon of God for pulling down strongholds; it will pull down the hugest blocks of stone the enemy can pile together. I would I could make every member of this Church feel in earnest about doing good. VI. Soon you and I will stand on the brink of Jordan's river; the deep sea of death will roll before us; trusting in Jesus, we shall not fear the last solemn hour. We shall hear the angel say, "Forward!" we shall touch the chilly stream with our feet, the flood shall fly, and we shall go through the stream dry-shod. (*C. H. Spurgeon.*) *Don't halt; "go forward"*:—It is the first step that costs. When the Israelites came up to the Red Sea, the command of God was: "Speak to the Children of Israel that they go forward." The command is peremptory. It admits of no delay. "Go forward." Death is behind you. Hell followeth hard after you. There is no salvation in retreat. Heaven lies before you, not behind. No man ever saved his soul by relapsing into indifference. 1. Perhaps you say, "I have prayed many a time already, and no blessing has yet come." Will you cease to pray then? Will that bring an answer? How many a soul has quit praying when the door of mercy was just about opening! Go forward. 2. Another one is kept back by fear of ridicule. He cannot stand a laugh. There is a sneer waiting for him at his father's table, or a cutting sarcasm in his counting-room. He wavers before it. Go forward; the sea will open to you, and so will many a heart to cheer you on. You will inspire respect in the very quarters from which you now expect opposition. 3. A third person complains: "I am in the dark; I cannot see my way." Then go forward, and get out of the dark. The determination to do your duty will be attended by a luminous discernment of the path of duty. 4. Unbelief draws back a fourth. There is only one way to conquer doubt. It is, to believe. End the torturing uncertainty by going forward, "looking unto Jesus." The only way to do a thing is to do it. God gives strength to the obedient. He has no promises for cowards, or double-minded vacillating doubters. (*T. L. Cuyler, D.D.*) *Safety in progress:*—Flying birds are never taken in a fowler's snare. (*Archbp. Secker.*) *Go forward:*—And why were they to go forward? Not because there was less danger in the one path than in the other; there was much in both, and apparently more in the advancing than in the retreating path; but because to go forward was the path of duty and the command of God. Certainly advance is the great law of the Christian life, as well as of the universe. All things in nature and history go forward. The stream moves forward, not a wave of it turns back; its every eddy, even, is, in reality, advancing. The winds move forward, pausing, indeed, often on their journey, lingering amidst the locks of the pine, or in the cleft of the rock, but speedily resuming their onward sweep again. The stars—the earth included—move forward, "hasting not, resting not," seeking, it is said, some distant centre. Science, art, philosophy, literature, every species of knowledge, move forward; invention following invention, discovery, discovery; one man of genius eclipsing another, to be in his turn outshone. Time moves forward, oh, how rapidly! and how his vast wings seem to say, as they rush along, "I have an engagement at the judgment seat; I have an appointment in eternity, and I must fulfil it. My King's business requireth haste." Christ Himself never rested. He was never in a hurry, but He was always in haste. The difference between Him and many of His people is, His life was short, and He knew it, and did the most in it; theirs, too, is short, but they know it not, and do not with their might what their hand findeth to do. God Himself even, with all the leisure of eternity, is not losing an hour, but is carrying on His broad plans, with undeviating regularity and increasing swiftness, and surely men should aspire in this respect to be imitators of, and fellow-workers with, God. Christ's religion, too, has been active and progressive; sometimes frozen up for a time like a river, but, like a river, working under the ice, and when spring arrived making up for the time lost by the increased rapidity of its course. And so with the path of the individual; like the river, the winds, the stars, the Eternal Himself, it must advance. Our motto should be "Excelsior." The progress of the Christian, indeed, is often from one difficulty to another; and very idle for him, in this earth, to expect an unvaried course of even moderate peace and happiness. No, no! he only exchanges one difficulty for another. True, there is a difference between the character of the difficulties. In becoming a Christian, a man quits the path of destruction for the Hill Difficulty, midnight for morning twilight, the wrath of a judge for the discipline of a father, the brink of hell for the thorny road to heaven; Pharaoh, the devil's agent, for the Red Sea, which is God's ocean, and through which He can provide a passage. We are urged forward alike by the command of God, the expectation of rest, and the hope of heaven. Ay! and even there the word of command is to be "Forward!" No more Red Seas, indeed, no wilderness, no battles to be fought, no enemies to be overcome; but still it is an onward course which shall be pursued for ever by the people of God. Heaven would cease to be heaven were this progress to stop. For what is heaven but the fire of the Infinite Mind for ever unfolding itself to the view and reception of God's creatures? We hear of people on earth whose "education is finished." Ah, Christian, thy education shall never be finished! There is only one Being whose education was ever finished, or, rather, whose education never began— God. All others, having entered on their future abode, are to go onwards, pressing toward the mark, panting, running, hoping, believing, loving more and more, throughout the ages of eternity. All difficulties, we should remember, will yield to faith, prayer, and perseverance. (*G. Gilfillan.*) *Forward, the true direction:*—Livingstone, having broken fresh ground among the Bakh-atlas, wrote to the Directors of the London Missionary Society, explaining what he had done, and expressing the hope that it would meet with their approval. At the same time he said he was at their disposal "to go anywhere—*provided it be* FORWARD." *Pushing through obstacles:*—What won't, must be made to. On these wintry days, when I cross the ferry to New York, I sometimes see large thick cakes of ice lying across the path of the boat. They will not take themselves out of the way; so the pilot drives the copper-cased bow of his boat squarely against the ice-floes, cleaving them asunder. If they will not get out of the way, they must be made to, and the propelling power within is more than a match for the obstacles without. That is a fine passage in the "Pilgrim's Progress" where Christian approaches the Valley of the Shadow of Death, and hears the howlings of the dragons, and sees the "discouraging clouds of confusion" hanging heavy and black over the horrible place. He does not flinch an instant. Crying out "I perceive not but that this is my way to the desired haven," he pushes his way through the frightful fiends and past the mouth of the burning pit. The road to heaven is full of obstacles. They lie right across every sinner's path, and like the ice-floes around the boat, they will not remove themselves. An energetic young man who starts life with a pile of hindrances at his bow, understands that the battle of life is to smash through them. David Livingstone, when a factory boy, and fastening his school books on his loom to study Latin, was practising this process. You have to contend with a depraved heart. It is just in the condition of a clock whose inner works are a heap of disordered wheels and springs. They can be repaired, and the clock will go. Your soul is dislocated and disordered by sin. The Divine hand that made it can mend it. Sinful habits, long indulged, are obstacles in your way. They are tendencies of the mind strengthened by frequent repetition. If you have not any such horrible habits as swearing, or cheating, or hard drinking, you have formed the habit of refusing all Christ's rich offers of salvation. This has been a hardening process—as the cart-wheels made a hard beaten road across certain fields of my grandfather's farm. Persistent push is indispensable to your salvation. To enter into the strait gate requires striving. To overcome obstacles requires might in the inner man, and that comes from the Holy Spirit. Dr. Spencer tells us of a man who once came bursting into his inquiry-meeting in almost breathless excitement. The poor man had been walking back and forth between his own door and the meeting, until at last he said, "I am determined to go into that inquiry-room or die in the attempt." In that fierce fight with a wicked heart, he not only had to call on God's help, but he said afterwards—"If you expect God to help you, you must be perfectly decided." (*T. L. Cuyler, D.D.*)

Ver. 16. **Through the midst of the sea.**—*The Red Sea :*—I. GOD'S DELIVERANCE OF ISRAEL. II. JUDGMENT ON GOD'S ENEMIES, as well as a deliverance of His friends. III. GOD'S SEPARATION OF ISRAEL FOR HIS SERVICE. IV. THE UNITY OF GOD'S REDEEMED ONES. (*E. N. Packard.*) *The Red Sea :*—I. PROTECTION AT THE RED SEA. 1. The nature of the protection. 2. The all-sufficiency of the protection. II. DELIVERANCE THROUGH THE RED SEA. 1. Its means. A blending of the human and the Divine. 2. Its method. (1) Obedience a condition of deliverance. (2) Nothing can harm the obedient soul (ver. 29). III. THE ENEMY DESTROYED IN THE RED SEA. 1. The superinducing cause. The daring persistency of Pharaoh brought him and his hosts into danger. So even with sinners. "Thou hast destroyed thyself." 2. God left Pharaoh and his hosts to themselves in the peril. 3. God caused the waters to return to their normal state. (1) If we stand in the way of danger, we have no one to blame but ourselves for the consequences. (2) Every sinner places himself in the way of peril. Lessons : 1. Pharaoh undertook what no one has ever succeeded in—to fight against God. 2. Moses placed himself and Israel in a relation to God, in which no one has ever failed. (*D. C. Hughes, M.A.*) *The passage of the Red Sea :*—1. Israel leaves Egypt for the purpose of proceeding to Canaan, the promised land. A figure of an awakened soul, drawn to God, which takes the firm and noble resolution to renounce all sin, and serve God, seeking first the kingdom of God and His righteousness. 2. The fiery and cloudy pillar is the secret but powerful attraction of the Father to the Son, which the soul follows, and by which it is faithfully and correctly guided. Here the individual is brought to the salutary means of grace, or they to him, in such a manner that he is afterwards obliged to confess, that if a single, and often inconsiderable, circumstance of his life had been otherwise, his whole course would have assumed another form. 3. The pursuing Pharaoh is a figure of the law in its strict and insatiate requirements, as well as of Satan and the powers of darkness. The latter soon perceives when any one is desirous of escaping from him, and consequently opposes him in every way. Some he torments with blasphemous, others with unbelieving thoughts, &c. 4. The utterly helpless condition of the children of Israel represents the oppressive weakness felt by the awakened soul. 5. But the Red Sea, which threatened destruction to the Israelites, proved of the greatest benefit to them. And this very feeling of sin, misery, and inability, which causes an awakened person so much uneasiness, turns to his greatest advantage. For it serves, like the blindness of the man born blind, and the death of Lazarus, to promote the Divine glory that Christ may be honoured by it. 6. The way by which Israel was delivered was one which was most miraculously opened ; a way apparently dangerous and terrific, and hidden from the Egyptians. This may be also said of the way by which the Lord leads His people to life. For how wonderful is the way of salvation through the birth, sufferings, death, and resurrection of Christ! 7. A strong east wind arose, and dried the sea ; and a rushing, like the sound of a mighty wind, was the signal to the holy apostles of the approach of the Holy Spirit. When He blows upon man, "all flesh is as grass, and all the goodliness thereof as the flower of the field." He it is that quickens. 8. The cloud, which overshadowed the people of Israel, protecting them from the pursuing foe, descending upon them as a refreshing dew, and serving by its radiance instead of a lamp, may be regarded as an emblem of the Redeemer's blissful mediation between God and man. From it drops a refreshing dew upon the troubled heart, and a healing balm for the wounded conscience, yea, a peace of God which passeth understanding. 9. Lastly, the divided sea is a type of baptism, and consequently of all that which is requisite to purify the soul from sin. The Red Sea of the Redeemer's blood is the abyss into which the sins of believers are so deeply plunged, that, if sought for, they can never be found ; the sea which swallows up, overwhelms, and drowns Satan, with all his host, and the old man, and quickens in us a new man, who after God is created in righteousness and true holiness. This precious blood of Christ, who offered Himself to God by the Holy Spirit, is that which alone perfectly cleanses our consciences from dead works, to serve the living God. (*G. D. Krummacher.*) *The Red Sea :*—Regarding this passage of the Red Sea as typical of some events in the pilgrim-life of every Christian, let us say—I. WE ARE NOT DELIVERED AT THE BEGINNING OF THE LIFE OF FAITH FROM ALL THE OLD ENEMIES OF THE HOUSE OF BONDAGE. II. The hour when old enemies return may reveal the fact that NO ACCUMULATION OF CONFIDENCE IN GOD HAS BEEN GAINED BY THE EXPERIENCE OF PAST DELIVERANCES. To most men the great events of life seem to be disconnected. They bear no relation one to another. If Fremont's Peak and Pike's Peak and the Spanish Peaks stood apart, connected by no mountain-ridge, no great results would come from them upon soil or climate. They would not determine the rain-fall or fix the trend of the rivers. But, linked together by lofty mountain-chains, they become part of the vast water-shed of a continent, fixed the length and course of the rivers and causing the humid atmosphere and fertile soil on one side, the dry air and arid wastes upon the other. So the great facts of Divine Providence, isolated and separate one from another, have no determinative influence over life. But linked together they make its moral atmosphere. III. SOME OLD ENEMIES OF THE SOUL MAY BE UTTERLY DESTROYED. Evil companionships abandoned, &c. IV. THE PROVIDENTIAL WAY OF DELIVERANCE IS OFTEN MYSTERIOUS. V. DELIVERANCE CAME TO ISRAEL NOT BY HUMAN ACHIEVEMENT,

BUT BY THE POWER OF GOD. The most solemn hours of life are not times of great endeavour and of high achievement. They are times when we are called to "Stand still, and see the salvation of the Lord." Such an hour is that when we begin the life of faith, not a time of achievement when, by mental struggle and spiritual travail, we win the favour of God. It is rather the time of self-surrender, when unreservedly we commit our ways to the Lord, that He may work for us, and in us, His redeeming work. (*W. G. Sperry.*)

Vers. 19, 20. **Between the camp of the Egyptians and the camp of Israel.**— *Lessons :*—1. God in Christ moveth Himself in His hand or work where the Church doth most need help. Before and behind Israel is He. 2. God by Christ the Angel of His Covenant hath given and doth give all help to His Church (ver. 19). 3. God sets His posture for help between cruel persecutors and His Church. 4. The very same means God makes to darken His enemies which enlighten His people. So the gospel. 5. This interposition of God keeps the wicked world from destroying His Church (ver. 20). (*G. Hughes, B.D.*) *The removal of Israel's cloud to the rear :*—This passage leads me to speak of God our Rearward. It is God alone who can make the past a source of peace and comfort. We think much of the future ; we desire greatly to have an assurance that all will be well with us in time to come. We accept with gratitude the promise, "The Lord shall go before thee " ; but do we fully consider how important the concluding part of that passage is—"and be thy rearward " ? I. WE OFTEN NEED TO BE DEEPLY IMPRESSED WITH THE MEMORY OF PAST BLESSINGS. II. WE NEED THE PILLAR OF CLOUD BEHIND US FOR OUR PROTECTION FROM THE EVIL CONSEQUENCES OF THE PAST. Wonderful sight ! the angel of the Lord breaking camp and going to their rear ! that beautiful meteor, the guiding cloud, sailing back over their six hundred thousand fighting men, powerless as their infants, while Egypt was pouring out its swarming myriads to swallow them up. So, my soul ! thy sins and the hosts of hell are ready this day to destroy thee ; but the angel of the covenant has not forsaken thee ; faith can see Him, as plainly as Israel beheld Him going to their rear to stand between them and danger ; are not His promises a pillar of cloud to you, and do they not stand between you and the past, saying, "I, even I, am He that blotteth out thy transgressions for Mine own sake, and will not remember thy sins " ? III. THIS REARWARD ANGEL AND THIS PILLAR OF CLOUD SEEM TO BID ME TO SAY TO BELIEVERS, IT SHALL BE WELL WITH YOU. For these two things are true concerning all who believe in Jesus. First, you have not seen your best days ; and, secondly, you never will. Never through eternity, will you arrive at that summit of bliss from which you will anticipate declension. Onward and upward is to be your way. (*N. Adams, D.D.*) *Different effects of the same events and dealings :*— 1. A family is visited by dreadful calamity ; is reduced from a state of ease and affluence to comparative want. The members of this family are of very different characters ; some of them sincere believers, devout worshippers, faithful servants of God ; ever considering their talents, as lent for God's use. Other members of the family are the reverse of all this ; sensual, worldly, regardless of spiritual things ; caring for nothing, but that "to-morrow may be as this day, and much more abundant." Observe, now, how differently these members of the same family will be affected by what has befallen them : how the calamity will wear a bright side to some, and a dark side to others. Trouble of another kind overtakes the same family ; a friend, a relation, upon whom the comfort of their life depended, is suddenly removed by the stroke of death. Some acknowledge the providential hand of God, inflicting a wound, but supplying a gracious remedy ; they are drawn the more closely to their sure, unchangeable Friend. But who are they, that are sitting down gloomy and disconsolate and "refusing to be comforted"? They are the godless members of this family, whose all is in the world, in the creature. And thus, while some are utterly discomfited by this loss, others can find it to be their gain. 2. This leads me to speak upon the different impressions made upon different persons by the means of grace, by the doctrines, and promises, and precepts of the gospel. The humble, faithful servant of God, derives light and life from every portion of Divine revelation. Very contrary to this are the views and feelings of the blinded sinner ; nay, of the careless, lukewarm, outward believer. The same doctrines, which afford so much satisfaction and peace to the godly wear to him a different aspect ; "there is no beauty in them that he should desire them " ; no power derived from them even to affect, much less to change, the heart. The same promises also appeal to him without any encouraging, life-giving effect. And the same holy precepts, instead of being loved and honoured, are a trouble to his soul : conscience whispers, that he ought to obey them; and the law of God, instead of being his guide, stands in opposition to him, and fills him with fear. " The light that is in him is darkness"; that which is a light to others, and should be a light to him, is perverted into darkness; and then, " how great is that darkness!" (*J. Slade, M.A.*)   *The glory in the rear :*—God is always with those who are with Him.   If we trust Him, He hath said, " I will never leave thee, nor forsake thee."   There is a special and familiar presence of God with those who walk uprightly, both in the night of their sorrow, and in the day of their joy.   Yet we do not always in the same way perceive that presence so as to enjoy it.   God never leaves us, but we sometimes think He has done so.   The sun shines on, but we do not always bask in his beams; we some-times mourn an absent God.   I.   In considering the subject of the Lord's abiding with His people, I shall first call attention to THE DIVINE PRESENCE MYSTERIOUSLY REMOVED.   " The angel of God, which went before the camp of Israel, removed." 1. The symbol of God's presence removed from where it had usually been.   So has it been with us at times: we have walked day after day in the light of God's countenance, we have enjoyed sweet fellowship with Jesus Christ our Lord, and on a sudden we have missed His glorious manifestation.   2. Moreover, they missed the light from where they hoped it would always be.   Sometimes you also may imagine that God's promise is failing you; even the word of God which you had laid hold upon may appear to you to be contradicted by your circumstances.   Then your heart sinks to the depths, for " if the foundations be destroyed, what can the righteous do?"   3. The pillar of fire also removed from where it seemed more than ever to be needed.   Even thus is it with you, who once walked in the light of God's countenance ; you perhaps have fallen into temporal trouble, and at the same moment the heavenly light has departed from your soul.   Now, it is bad to be in the dark on the king's highway ; but it is worse to be in the dark when you are out on the open common, and do not know your road.   It is well to have a guide when the road is easy ; but you must have one when you are coming upon precipitous and dangerous places.   Then let him trust ; but he will need all the faith of which he can be master.   Oh, my Lord, if ever Thou dost leave me, forsake me not in the day of trouble.   Yet what have I said?   It is a day of trouble when Thou art gone, whatever my condition may be.   4. Thus it did seem a mysterious thing that the Covenant Angel should no longer direct the marchings of the host of God, and I dare say that some of them began to account for it by a reason which their fears would suggest.   I should not wonder that, if they had been asked why the blazing pillar was no longer in the van, they would have replied, " Because of our murmurings against the Lord and His servant Moses.   God will not go before us because of our sins."   This, however, would have been a mistake.   There was not a touch of the rod about this withdrawing of His presence from the van, not even a trace of [anger ; it was all done in lovingkindness.   So you must not always conclude that the loss of conscious joy is necessarily a punishment for sin.   Dark-ness of soul is not always the fruit of Divine anger, though it is often so.   Some-times it is sent for a test of faith, for the excitement of desire, and for the increase of our sympathy with others who walk in darkness.   There are a thousand precious uses in this adversity.   Yet it is a mysterious thing when the light of the future fades, and we seem to be without a guide.   II. Now all this while THE DIVINE PRESENCE WAS GRACIOUSLY NEAR.   1. The Angel of the Lord had removed, but it is added, He " removed and went behind them," and He was just as close to them when He was in the rear, as when He led the van.   He might not seem to be their guide, but He had all the more evidently become their guard.   He might not for the moment be their Sun before, but then He had become their Shield behind.   " The glory of the Lord was their rereward."   Oh, soul, the Lord may be very near thee, and yet He may be behind thee, so that thine outlook for the future may not be filled with the vision of His glory.   2. Note in the text that it is said the pillar went, and " stood behind them."   I like that, for it is a settled, permanent matter. The Lord had removed, but He was not removing still.   Even thus the Lord remaineth with the dear child of God.   Thou canst not see anything before thee to make thee glad, but the living God stands behind thee to ward off the adversary. He cannot forsake thee.   3. What is more, these people had God so near that they could see Him if they did but look back.   See how the Lord has helped you hitherto.   4. A thoughtful person would conclude the Lord to be all the more evidently near because of the change of His position.   When a symbol of mercy comes to be usual and fixed, we may be tempted to think that it remains as a matter of routine. If the rainbow were always visible it might not be so assuring a token of the covenant. Hence the Lord often changes His hand, and blesses His people in another way, to let them see that He is thinking of them. III. THE DIVINE PRESENCE WISELY REVEALED. That the symbol of God's presence should be withdrawn from the front and become visible behind, was a wise thing. 1. Observe, there was no fiery pillar of cloud before them, and that was wise ; for the going down into the Red Sea was intended to be an act of lofty faith. The more of the visible the less is faith visible. 2. Moreover, let us mark that the cloudy pillar was taken away from the front because the Lord meant them simply to accept His word as their best guidance. 3. Moreover, God was teaching them another lesson, namely, that He may be near His people when He does not give them the usual tokens of His presence. 4. The host of Israel did not require any guide in front when they came to the sea. "How is that ? " say you. There were no two ways to choose from : they could not miss the way, for they must needs march through the sea. So when men come into deep trouble, and cannot get out of it, they scarcely need a guide ; for their own plain path is submission and patience. 5. What they did want was the pillar of cloud behind them, and that is where they had it. What was that cloud behind them for? Well, it was there for several reasons : the first was to shut out the sight of their enemies from them. The cloudy pillar went behind for another reason, namely, that the Egyptians might not see them. Their enemies were made to stumble, and were compelled to come to a dead stand. Be calm, O child of God ; for the Covenant Angel is dealing with your adversaries, and His time is generally the night. IV. That THE DIVINE PRESENCE WILL ONE DAY BE MORE GLORIOUSLY REVEALED. " The Lord will go before you ; and the God of Israel will be your rereward." This is the condition into which the Lord brings His people when they depart from Babylon, and are no more conformed to this present evil world. V. THIS DIVINE PRESENCE HAS A TWOFOLD ASPECT : that same glory which lit up the canvas city, and made it bright as the day, darkened all the camps of Egypt. They could see nothing, for the dark side of God was turned to them. Oh, is it not a dreadful thing that to some men the most terrible thing in the world would be God? If you could get away from God, how happy you would be ! One of these days Jesus will tell you to depart. " Keep on as you were," says He, " you were always departing from God ; keep on departing. Depart from Me ye cursed ! " That will be the consummation of your life. (*C. H. Spurgeon.*) *Lessons :*—I. THE SURENESS OF GOD'S INTERPOSITION WHEN HE IS NEEDED, IN THE WAY HIS WISDOM CHOOSES (ver. 19). When we are called to difficult duty, God will keep His promise to be with us, and always His help will be found stationed at the exposed point. II. THE REVELATION OF A TWOFOLD CHARACTER IN GOD'S DEALINGS WITH MEN (ver. 20 ; see Luke ii. 34 ; 2 Cor. ii. 16 ; Rev. xi. 5 ; Matt. xxi. 42–44 ; John ix. 39). III. THE PRACTICAL BEARING OF A COURAGEOUS FAITH (ver. 21). We may never be put before an actual ocean tossing with billows under difficult stress of demand like this ; but we shall often be placed where mere obedience is commanded, and where God's covenant is all that ensures success. "Doing duty belongs to us ; achieving deliverance belongs to God." Then it is that an unbroken faith "laughs at impossibility," and says, "It shall be done ! " IV. THE PERFECT SAFETY OF A BELIEVER'S EXPOSURE, UPON A PROMISE OF THE LIVING GOD (ver. 22). One of Aristotle's sayings may well be quoted here. He says : "Every how rests upon a that." That is, if God has declared that a difficult duty is to be done, He may be trusted to show how it is to be done. He will never ask us into straits of obedience without providing for our preservation. And when once a path of service is lying out before us, it does not matter at all how dangerous it appears ; we shall go through it without harm. So our safety is in the exposure when God is our companion. His love will hold the sea-walls steady, and the sea-walls will keep back Pharaoh. Some solicitous friends once warned Whitefield to spare himself in such extraordinary efforts ; he only answered with words that long ago went into history "I am immortal till my work is done ! " V. THE FORGETFULNESS AND INCORRIGIBLENESS OF A DARING UNBELIEF (ver. 23). VI. THE MERCY OF GOD, EXHIBITED IN THE FACT THAT THE WAY OF THE TRANSGRESSOR IS HARD (ver. 24). Up to the last moment there was a chance for that pursuing army to retreat by the way they came. So it was a manifest benevolence to them on the part of God to hinder them as much as possible. Chrysostom calls attention to the familiar fact that God always warns before He waits, and waits before He strikes, and strikes before He crushes, so as to give space for repentance. He threatens plagues so that we may avoid plagues; and indeed, remarks the golden-tongued orator, it is doubtful whether the prospect of hell has not availed as much as the promise of heaven in hindering the blasphemies of open sin. We may safely assert now that many a man has had occasion to thank God that his chariot-wheels drave heavily, so that he recognized the hindering hand of his Maker (ver. 25). VII. Our last lesson is concerning THE SURE JUDGMENTS OF ALMIGHTY WRATH WHEN ONCE THE CUP OF INIQUITY IS FULL (ver. 26). (*C. S. Robinson, D.D.*) *A double aspect :*—It makes a good deal of difference which side of a barrier you are on, in your estimate of the actual worth of that barrier. To the burglar, a strongly barred door is a great annoyance. It is a real comfort to those who can lie down to sleep behind it at night. A garden wall is a pleasant protection to those who can walk freely within its enclosure. It frowns gloomily on those whom it shuts out from a share of the joys within. Another's wrong-doing which separates him from us, may be a source of light to us and of only despair to him. Even a cause of misunderstanding with others may be a source of advantage to us and of worry to them. The cloud of trouble which they and we faced together for a while, now that it has been put behind us, and before them, may shed light on our path by the lessons it teaches us, while it confuses them just as much as ever. The knowledge of the Scriptures, and the commandments of the moral law, only make plainer the course of the child of God; but they are a cause of continued trial and discomfort to him who is unwilling to walk in the way God has pointed out. (*H. C. Trumbull.*) *The dividing pillar :*—A tradition current in the west of Scotland tells that when one of the Covenanting preachers and his little band of hearers had been surprised on a hill-side by the military, the minister cried out, "Lord, throw Thy mantle over us, and protect us." And immediately out of the clear sky there fell a mist, which sundered and protected the pursued frem the pursuers. And a Netherland tradition tells how a little army of Protestants was once saved from the king of Spain's troops by the flashing lights and noise as of an army sent by the Lord to throw confusion into the camp of the enemy. The teacher will recollect the story of the Christian woman, who calmly awaiting in her home the approach of the enemy, was, in answer to her prayer, saved from them by a circling wall of snow. The dividing pillar is a reality yet. (*S. S. Times.*) *Different aspects of the same thing :*—There are many scenes in life which are either sad or beautiful, cheerless or refreshing, according to the direction from which we approach them. If, on a morning in spring, we behold the ridges of a fresh-turned ploughed field from their northern side, our eyes, catching cnly the shadowed slopes of the successive furrows, see an expanse of white, the unmelted remains of the night's hailstorm, or the hoar-frost of the dawn. We make a circuit, or we cross over, and look behind us, and on the very same ground there is nothing to be seen but the rich brown soil, swelling in the sunshine, warm with promise, and chequered perhaps here and there with a green blade bursting through the surface. (*J. A. Froude.*)

Vers. 21–25 **Made the sea dry land.**—*The sea-path :*—I. THE DEED OF VALOUR. Moses walking down the gravelly beach into the sea; Israel following. A lesson to us to come with boldness. II. The MIRACULOUS way. We walk in new and unseen ways. III. THE OVERTHROW OF THE ENEMY. 1. His wrath. 2. His foolhardiness; forgettin; the plagues. All sin is irrational. 3. His sudden destruction. Death surprises the impenitent. IV. THE SAME INSTRUMENTS BOTH DEFENDING AND DESTROYING. 1. The cloud. 2. The water. 3. The gospel. V. WHAT ISRAEL FOUND IN THE SEA-PATH. 1. Rebuke for the murmuring. 2. Filial fear. 3. Trust in God. 4. Trust in Moses. 5. Nationality; before, they were all slaves, then free men, now a nation. Learn: 1. All people must struggle and dare. 2. Our characters come from soul-struggles where self is abandoned, and trust is put in God. 3. Man's extremity is God's opportunity. 4. God will, out of every temptation, make a way of escape. (*Dr. Fowler.*) *A treacherous element :*—"An easy conquest!" said the eagle, attracted by the glittering scales of a large fish, which shone through the clear, deep waters of the lake. "An easy conquest!" As he dashed into the water, it was as if lightning had smitten the cliff and a fragment of it had fallen into the lake. There was a struggle; the fish dived, and drew the eagle with it. "Ah!" exclaimed the drowning king of birds, "had I been in the air, who would have dared to measure strength with me? But in this strange and treacherous element, I am overcome by one whom elsewhere I should have despised." (*Great Thoughts.*)   *Safe in the danger of duty :*—"The waters were a wall unto them on their right hand, and on their left." It is amazing what a blessing the things that we dreaded most become to us, when we go straight toward them at the call of God! The sea of business troubles, which looked as if it never could be crossed, but which we had no choice but to enter, how it opened right and left as we came to it, and then became to us a wall against competitors on either side, because we had ventured into its very depths when it was our clear duty to do that and nothing else ! That desert life of danger which we entered with fear and trembling, at the call of our country, or of some loved one of our family, or of some dear friend, how its very exposures and trying experiences toughened us and trained us, and made us stronger and manlier and happier, so that its results to-day—its physical and mental and moral results— are as a wall of protection to us on our right hand and on our left! There is no place in all the world so safe for us as the place of danger, when danger is a duty. The best way of caring for ourselves is not to care for ourselves. If we want to walk dry shod, with a wall shielding us on either hand, the better way is to plunge right overboard into a sea of work or of trial or of peril, when God says Go forward. (*H. C. Trumbull.*)   **Overthrew the Egyptians.**—*The destruction of the Egyptians :*— Consider this destruction of Pharaoh and his host as—I. A JUDGMENT. It was—1. Sudden in its execution. No warning given. 2. Terrible in its nature. Involving the destruction of a whole army, the picked men of the most powerful nation in the world. 3. Well merited by the subjects of it. Repeated warnings were conveyed in the plagues, yet all were now disregarded. II. A DELIVERANCE. Israel delivered from Pharaoh—1. Out of a perilous situation. 2. Notwithstanding their want of faith. 3. By a glorious miracle. III. A LESSON to—1. The sinner. Beware lest your end be like Pharaoh's; heed the warnings given to you. 2. The Christian. Learn to know the greatness of your deliverance from the host of Satan. (*H. Barnard, B.A.*)   *It is not always safe to follow those who are in the path of duty :*—A place that is the safest in the world for one man may be the most dangerous in the world for the next man. The portcullis which comes down to shut in the endangered refugee, may crush to death his close pursuer. Because another man actually saves his life and acquires new strength by exposing himself in some sea of battle, or pestilence, or perils of search for a lost one, it is no reason why you should venture in that same line. If God told him to go there, the very waves of danger were a shield to him; but if you have no call there, those waves may overwhelm you. His risks in business prove his safety, because he made them in faith, when God commanded them. They would be your ruin if you presumed on them without a command from God, The question for you is not, Is that other man safe in that sea? but, Do I belong there ? The call of God settles the question of your place of duty and your place of safety. God gives the walls of protection to His children when they are where He tells them to be. God throws down those very walls on those who have no business to be there. (*H. C. Trumbull.*)

Vers. 30, 31. **Thus the Lord saved Israel.**—*The great deliverance:*—Had it not been for this great deliverance, the children of Israel would only have been re- membered in the after-history of the world as the slaves who helped to build the Pyramids. Their religion was fast perishing among them, their religious rites forgotten; and they would soon have been found among the worshippers of the monster gods of Egypt. But God had better things in store for them, when He led them through the Red Sea, making a path for them amid the waters. I. IT WAS ONE OF THE GREATEST BLESSINGS FOR THE HUMAN RACE, that during the preservation of the Jewish people, the great truth of the personality of God, and His nearness to His people, was set before them in language which could not be mistaken. And it is one of the greatest blessings which we enjoy, that we have the same Lord personally presented to us, revealed in the risen and glorified Lord Jesus Christ. II. God is set before us here not only as a Person, but as A PERSON WHO CARES WITH ALL A FATHER'S LOVE AND WATCHFULNESS FOR HIS OWN PEOPLE. Our hopes in days of doubt and difficulty are directed to the same personal fatherly care of the great God who loves all His creatures, and who loves Christians above all in the Lord Jesus Christ. III. WHEN A GREAT NATIONAL VICTORY IS ACHIEVED, WHAT BOOTS IT TO HIM WHO LOSES HIS LIFE IN THE HOUR OF VICTORY? The question for us is, not whether God has wrought a great deliverance, but whether we as individuals are partakers of that deliverance, partakers of the victory of the Lord Jesus Christ. (*Archbishop Tait.*)   *Israel's deliverance :*—I. THE STATE OF THE ISRAELITES WHEN MOSES CAME TO THEM. 1.

They were in bondage. 2. They were so far conscious of the misery of their position that they had a strong desire for liberty. 3. They were by no means ready at first to accept the message of God's deliverance. 4. They had their comforts even in slavery. In all these things we have a picture of ourselves. II. The deliverance. 1. The moment the Passover is observed, that moment Pharoah's power is broken. The moment that all is right between us and God, that moment Satan's power is broken, and he can no longer hold us in bondage. 2. The waters of judgment which saved the Israelites were the means of destroying the vast hosts of Egypt. The power of Satan is broken by the very means by which he intended to destroy. 3. It is our privilege to take our stand on the other side of the Red Sea, and see ourselves "raised up with Christ" into a new life. (*W. Hay Aitken, M.A.*) *The Divine deliverer recognized:*—And this mighty God, who so delivered Israel in ancient time, is our God for ever and ever. The walls and covering of our habitations are as truly upheld and kept from falling and crushing us to death, by the Divine hand, as were the walls of waters kept upright, like solid stone, by Almighty power, while the Hebrews passed safely between. We say that it was miracle which protected them, and the laws of nature which protect us. But in both cases it is God. The deepest and truest philosophy of life and faith for us is to bring ourselves into the most intimate relations with the infinite God. The most profound and accurate student of nature is he whose eye is quickest to see the plan and purpose of an intelligent, governing Mind in everything that exists. What should we think of an Israelite walking through the depths of the sea on dry ground, between walls of water standing up like marble on either hand, and yet not recognizing the intended and merciful display of the Divine power for his protection? What should we think of a ransomed Hebrew standing on the safe shore of the Red Sea on that memorable morning, and yet refusing to join in the song of thanksgiving for the great deliverance of the night? The same that we ought to think of one who lies down to sleep at night in his own house, and goes to his daily occupation in the morning, and never prays, never offers thanksgiving to God, for the mercy which redeems his life from destruction every moment. In God we live, and move, and have our being. Every use of our faculties, every sensation of pleasure, every emotion of happiness, every possession, experience, and hope that makes existence a blessing, is a witness to us of God's special, minute, and ceaseless attention to our welfare. (*D. March, D.D.*)

CHAPTER XV.

Ver. 1. Then sang Moses and the Children of Israel.—*The Song of Moses at the Red Sea :*—Unwonted interest attaches to this song—the earliest on record of all the sacred odes, and the very foremost in the annals of Hebrew anthology. To the Jewish people themselves, it is what they have long called it, " The Song "; a designation to which it is entitled, alike from its inherent pre-eminence and its unrivalled associations. 1. It is Israel's natal song. For, in crossing the Red Sea, they passed through the birth-throes of their national existence, and from this epoch dates a new chronology in Israel's calendar. The oppressed tribes have become a commonwealth; and a commonwealth of the free. 2. It is Israel's emancipation song, or song of liberty. It signalises a triple deliverance ; marking the supreme moment of rescue from the threefold evils of domestic slavery, political bondage, and religious thraldom. 3. It is Israel's first National Anthem and Te Deum in one. The Exodus was not a mere effort on the part of the Hebrew race to achieve their independence and realize their aspirations after a separate nationality. The spirit of even this idea had yet to be created within them ; but everything depended on their being first delivered from the corrupting influences of Egyptian fetichism and idolatry, no less than from the yoke of Egyptian bondage. Not that the mass of them could at all appreciate the full meaning of the grand event as a mighty religious movement, repeating on a larger scale the migration of Abraham from Ur of the Chaldees, and breaking away from idolatrous and debasing superstitions, to find a home for the free development of a higher creed and worship. But the eye of their great leader descried this Divine purpose ; and he had gone with this first tentative proposal to Pharaoh from God

"Let My people go, that they may serve Me in the wilderness." It is Israel's Te Deum, or song of thanks and praise to God. An overwhelming sense of the Divine interposition is the predominant sentiment in the song from first to last. It is no mere secular ode ; no mere war-song or outburst of patriotic triumph ; no exultant shriek of insult over a fallen foe ; but an anthem of blessing and gratitude for a great deliverance, a devout and solemn psalm before God, to whom, of whom, and for whom it is sung. This high and sacred intent keeps it from degenerating into a wild strain of vindictiveness or vainglory. 4. It is Israel's Church-song ; the type of all songs of redemption and salvation. The very words "redemption" and " salvation " are first introduced in connection with this great deliverance. " I will redeem you with an outstretched arm " ; and again, " Fear ye not ; stand still, and see the salvation of the Lord." The people had become unified into a worshipping assembly. It is Israel's triumph-song of deliverance. The note is that of joy and victory ; and is prophetic of the success of every battle and struggle for the Lord's cause and kingdom, fought in the Lord's name and in His strength. This triumph is the precursor especially of that final and glorious one at the end of the ages, when the spiritual Israel, which no man can number, from every people, and tribe and language, " having gotten the victory over the beast, and over his image, and over his mark, and over the number of his name," shall take up a position like their prototypes of old—not, however, by the shore of the Red Sea, with the mere emblem of God's presence before them—but as John saw them in apocalyptic vision, standing by the sea of glass mingled with fire ; no longer led merely by Miriam and her chorus, but all of them having the harp of God in their hand, singing, not only " the Song of Moses, the servant of God," but "the Song of the Lamb." I. INTRODUCTION : OR THE TRIPLE AIM OF THE SONG (vers. 1, 2). Thus the song is, first of all, inscribed and offered to the Lord. He also is its great theme or subject ; and it is His exaltation that constitutes its one and expressly avowed aim. To God, of God, for God—these are the three pivot-thoughts regulating and determining the movement of the opening strophe, and, indeed, of the entire hymn. Here, as not infrequently with later psalms, we have the whole song concentrated in the first verse. The occasion of the song, its subject, its design, are all indicated. First, there is here a singing to the Lord. The simplest idea we can attach to the opening words, " I will sing to the Lord," is this—I will bring myself into the immediate and felt presence of Jehovah, and will address and offer my song to Him ! How near has He been to us during the eventful and stupendous transactions of the night ! Under a realizing sense of that nearness I will direct my song to Him. To what a pitch of solemnity this conception raises the singer ! But, while this idea of singing to the Lord is expressive of the singer's attitude as immediately before the very face of the Supreme, it no less indicates that the song is an acceptable offering and oblation to the Lord. It is no self-pleasing exercise of gift and faculty, but " a sacrifice to the Lord, the fruit of the lips." " Singing," says one, " is as much the language of holy joy as prayer is the language of holy desire." How sublime a sight ! The whole of a people singing before the one invisible God, and consciously realizing more or less their direct relation to the Eternal, under no outward form or image or material symbol ! Secondly, the Lord is the subject or theme of the song. Underlying all is the sense of the Divine personality. Nothing but this could have kindled the soul to song. If God is to be the subject of hymning praise, it must needs be the thought of a living, personal One, to evoke the spirit of glorying in and praising His name. Thirdly, there is here a singing, not only to the Lord and of the Lord, but for the Lord. To extol and exalt the Lord is declared to be the ultimate end and aim of this song. And indeed this is the highest reach and the final purpose of all praise —to manifest and express the Divine character, the Divine working and ways, the Divine glory and honour. We are taught to pray for God as well as to Him ; and to put this ever in the foreground of our prayers, as of all things the first, the best, the supremely desirable. "Hallowed be Thy name : Thy kingdom come : Thy will be done "—these petitions have the precedence over any for either ourselves or others. But not only to do this, but also to express it and set forth our purpose to do it—this is the special aim and function of praise, of which "Doxology," or the ascription of power, blessing, dominion, and every excellency, is the highest climax. It is the very anticipation of heaven itself and of all its worship. II. THE BODY, OR SUBJECT-MATTER OF THE SONG (vers. 3–13). The third verse seems to be designed for a great chorus—probably meant to be re-echoed by a body of deep-voiced warriors. It marks a transition from the declarative style of the introduction, to the alternation of recitative and ascriptive portions in the main body of the song. It forms also a suitable link between the two, being a fit climax to what precedes, because it sets forth why and in what character the Lord is to be exalted—" the Lord is a Man of War "—and a fit index to what follows, because it suggests, so strikingly, the nature of His triumph which is now about to be celebrated; a triumph involving struggle and conflict. He is "a Man of War" in accordance always with His sublime and sacred name Jehovah. The song proceeds to develop the three great qualities of the Jehovah-warrior, the Warrior who is Divine. 1. He is in power resistless. This power is seen first in the magnitude of the scale on which it operates—the sense of this being enhanced by the detail of particulars in verse 4. Pharaoh's chariots, and his host, and his chosen captains. Then, again, in the ease with which it effects its object as He " casts " them into the sea—it is as if He had caught up the whole host in His hand, and slung it like a stone into the deep; and finally, in the completeness of the overthrow and the irreversible and irretrievable nature of the result. Having thus signalized the catastrophe, the poet's inspiration seems to catch a new afflatus. The style suddenly changes in verses 6, 7, and 8; it ceases to be merely descriptive, and becomes directly ascriptive. The tone is now lofty and devout, God being addressed immediately in the second person, and the whole event being attributed to the interposition and miraculous operation of His power alone. 2. He is in equity and righteousness unchallengeable. The " equity and righteousness " is as manifest as the power. We are taught in verse 7 to regard the whole situation as intended for a display of " the Divine excellency " : so true, so timely, and so exemplary it is in its manifestation. With consummate ease, but with no less consummate justice, the dread penalty is enacted; to show how " He is glorious in holiness and fearful in praises " while " doing wonders." For it is intimated that Egypt, in what it was doing, was not only " the enemy " of Israel, but it was " of them that rose up against Thee "; fighting against the Almighty and violating the first principles of Divine justice, truth, and mercy. The victims of the catastrophe were the fit subjects of a retributive and self-vindicating economy. Moreover, it was so well-timed. They were taken, as it were, red-handed, in the very act; at the very moment they were anticipating their revenge and gloating in its gratification. While they were intoxicated with insolence and pride : while they were breathing out threatening and cruelty, the Lord speaks to them in wrath; the Lord holds them in derision. 3. Yet, finally, He is in mercy plenteous. We have to note the goodness, no less than the severity, of God here. The reiteration in verse 12 of what has been said before, seems designedly made to enhance the sublime and suggestive contrast. III. THE THREEFOLD ISSUES (vers. 14–18). In this third and last wave of the anthem, the Divine mercy in the redemption of Israel is illustrated. The song becomes prophetic; and three grand issues are described and anticipated, an immediate, an intermediate, and a final one. 1. The immediate influence of the Exodus and passage of the Red Sea, on the tribes and peoples around, verses 14–16. A striking gradation is observed in describing the various effects : there is first a widespread panic and commotion in general, then the chiefs or "phylarchs" of Edom are paralyzed with terror; the mighty men of Moab tremble with uncontrollable fear; and finally the Canaanites melt away in despair. 2. There is an intermediate or remoter influence on the ultimate settlement and final destiny of Israel. So great an initial triumph was a happy augury and a sure prognostication of coming success. It was to be accepted as a Divine pledge of all needful aid and succour, until at length they should be firmly established in the promised land, as a nation, a race or family, and a Church. For in verse 17 we have a climax with three particulars, in which Israel is presented in three aspects, and their land is set forth in the triple character of an inheritance, a home, and a sanctuary, awakening the chords of patriotism, ancestry, and worship. 3. There is the last great issue of all, " The Lord shall reign for ever and ever." The prophecy of this song reaches thus onward to the end of all things; for the deliverance of Israel was not merely typical of, but actually a part and instalment of, the final redemption. And therefore, this song of Moses is not only the key-note and inspiration of the songs of the Old Testament Church, but a song of the Church in every age, celebrating as it does an event and deliverance not only pledging but vitally contributing to the last great acts in the onward triumph of Christ's complete redemption. (*A. H. Drysdale, M.A.*) *The Song of Moses :*—I. THE HISTORY WHICH THE SONG CELEBRATES. II. THE REFLECTIONS WHICH THE HISTORY THUS CELEBRATED SUGGESTS. 1. The history affords an awful instance of persevering rebellion against God, notwithstanding the infliction of repeated and awakening chastisements. 2. The tendency of the human mind to forget past mercies, when we are involved in present afflictions. 3. The duty of yielding obedience to God, even when His commands seem to be opposed to our interests and our happiness. 4. The certainty that God will appear on behalf of His people, however long His interposition may be delayed. 5. The history reminds us of a nobler deliverance which God has effected for His people by Jesus Christ. 6. We may learn from the history with what grateful joy the disciples of Christ will celebrate His power and grace, when they have crossed the river of death. (*J. Alexander.*)   *Jubilate :—* I. It will be instructive to notice THE TIME OF THE SINGING OF THIS SONG. To everything there is a season: there is a time of the singing of birds, and there is a time for the singing of saints. "Then sang Moses." 1. It was first of all at the moment of realized salvation. When we doubt our salvation we suspend our singing; but when we realize it, when we see clearly the great work that God has done for us, then we sing unto the Lord who hath for us also triumphed gloriously. How can our joy of heart any longer be pent up? 2. So is it also in times of distinct consecration. I would remind you that the apostle assures us that all Israel were "baptized unto Moses in the cloud and in the sea." That passage through the Red Sea was the type of their death, their burial, and their resurrection to a new life; it was their national baptism unto God: and therefore they sang as it were a new song. It is the happiest thing that can ever happen to a mortal man, to be dedicated to God. 3. It was also a day of the manifest display of God's power. 4. But this song may be sung at all times throughout the life of faith. Let your hearts begin to ring all their bells, and let not their sweet chimes cease for evermore. II. THE TONE OF THIS SONG. 1. Note, first, that the tone is enthusiastic. 2. The tone is also congregational, being intended for every Israelite to join in it. Though Moses began by saying, "I will sing unto the Lord," yet Miriam concluded with, "Sing ye to the Lord, for He hath triumphed gloriously." This is a hymn for every child of God, for all that have come out of Egypt. Let the song be enthusiastic and unanimous. 3. Yet please to notice how very distinctly personal it is. "I will sing unto the Lord, for He hath triumphed gloriously. The Lord is *my* strength and song, and He is become *my* salvation; He is *my* God, and I will prepare Him an habitation; *my* father's God, and I will exalt Him." Do not lose yourself in the throng. 4. Note, again, the tone of this song is exceeding confident. There is not a shadow of doubt in it: it is all the way through most positive in its ascriptions of praise. 5. And this song is exceeding comprehensive. It sings of what God has done, and then of what God will do in bringing His people into the Promised Land; nor does it finish till it rises to that loftiest strain of all: "The Lord shall reign for ever and ever." 6. Note, too, all through, that this song is immeasurably joyous. The Israelites were slaves enjoying new liberty; children let out to play. They did not know how to be glad enough. Let us give to God our unlimited joy. 7. Yet I must say, however enthusiastic that song was, and however full of joy it was, it was only such a song as was due unto the Lord. III. THE FIRST CLAUSES OF THIS SONG. "The Lord is my strength and my song," &c. 1. Notice, the song is all of God: there is not a word about Moses. Let us forget men, forget earth, forget time, forget self, forget this mortal life, and only think of our God. 2. Observe, the song dwells upon what God has done: "The horse and his rider hath He thrown into the sea." Let us trace all the mercies we get to our God, for He hath wrought all our works in us; He hath chosen us, He hath redeemed us, He hath called us, He hath quickened us, He hath preserved us, He hath sanctified us, and He will perfect us in Christ Jesus. The glory is all His. 3. The song also declares what the Lord will yet do. We shall conquer yet in the great name of Jehovah. Take up the first note: "The Lord is my strength." What a noble utterance! Poor Israel had no strength! She had cried out by reason of her sore bondage, making bricks without straw: The Lord is my strength when I have no strength of my own. It is well to say, "The Lord is my strength" when we are weak and the enemy is strong; but we must mind that we say the same when we are strong and our enemies are routed. The next is, "The Lord is my song," that is to say, the Lord is the giver of our songs; He breathes the music into the hearts of His people; He is the Creator of their joy. The Lord is also the subject of their songs: they sing of Him and of all that He does on their behalf. The Lord is, moreover, the object of their song: they sing unto the Lord. Their praise is meant for Him alone. (*C. H. Spurgeon.*)   *The Song of triumph :—*The Song of Moses has never been surpassed for the poetical beauty of its imagery and its expressions. It is, besides, so full of holiness and adoration, as to render it incomparable. I. Let us recount ALL THE CAUSES FOR GRATITUDE WHICH ARE ENUMERATED IN IT. 1. The Israelites had been delivered from a terrible danger. The enemy had said, "I will pursue, I will overtake, I will divide the spoil; I will draw my sword, my hand shall destroy them." 2. They had been delivered from inevitable danger. None could save them but God only. Before them was the sea; behind them were Pharaoh and his host. 3. They had been delivered from universal danger. Not the lives of a thousand only, or even of ten thousand, among them had been threatened; all, old and young together, were to have been slain. 4. They had been delivered by most glorious miracles; the strong east wind, the pillar of light, the sea changed, as it were, into walls of ice. 5. They had been delivered notwithstanding their sins. Oh, what an example of the free grace of God! They had scorned His words, had murmured; it was, so to speak, in spite of themselves that God had saved them. 6. They had been delivered altogether, not one was missing, not one had perished, not even the youngest child. No mourning marred their triumph, as often happens to the nations of the earth when they are celebrating a great victory. 7. They had been saved by the power of God alone. It was not their work, it was that of the Lord, who had said to them, "Stand still, and ye shall see the salvation of the Lord; the Lord shall fight for you." 8. Lastly, their deliverance was accompanied by promises for the future. God had brought them out of Egypt, but it was to lead them to Canaan. II. If we are true believers, and if Jesus is our Saviour, WE HAVE THE SAME REASONS THAT THE ISRAELITES HAD FOR SINGING THE SONG OF PRAISE. 1. Like them, we have been delivered from a terrible danger. It was the danger of death,—not of the body, for that is comparatively nothing, as our Lord has said,—but of the soul; that is to say, condemnation, alienation from God, a whole eternity passed "in outer darkness, where there is weeping and gnashing of teeth." 2. Like the Israelites, we have been delivered from inevitable danger. There is no way of escape—no salvation in any other than in the Lord Jesus Christ. 3. We have been delivered from a universal danger. Indeed, we are all by nature under condemnation. "There is no difference: for all have sinned, and come short of the glory of God." 4. We have been delivered by most glorious marvels. "Behold what manner of love the Father hath bestowed upon us, that we should be called the sons of God," exclaims the apostle John. These things are so sublime, that the angels desire to look into them. 5. We have been delivered notwithstanding our sins; for "God commendeth His love towards us, in that, while we were yet sinners, Christ died for us." 6. Like Israel, we have been delivered altogether. Not one of the chosen people of God will be missing; the youngest child, the most despised, the most forgotten of men, if he has put his trust in the Lord, will not perish. 7. God has saved us without any strength of our own, for we were incapable of doing anything. "I have trodden the winepress alone," saith the Saviour by the mouth of Isaiah. He obeyed for us, He has borne our sins, He has accomplished all the work of our salvation. 8. Lastly, our deliverance has been accompanied, like that of the Israelites, with glorious promises. The Lord will guide us with His counsel, and afterwards He will receive us to glory. He will be our strength, because He has been our Saviour. (*Prof. Gaussen.*) *Manly gratitude* :—Among the mass of men how little there is of that frank, manly gratitude, that openly, and in the sight of a scoffing world, acknowledges the delivering, saving hand of God. Amid such wide-spread forgetfulness of the hand of an overruling Providence, it is a satisfaction to record the case of a thankful British seaman, a fine young man in the naval service on board Her Majesty's ship, *Queen.* They were cruising off Cape Finisterre. The hands had been turned up to reef top sails for the night; the work was just finished, when the young captain of the mizzen top overbalanced himself and fell. He came down a distance of a hundred feet or more, and would have fallen on the deck, where no doubt he would have been instantly killed or seriously injured; but as he fell he clutched the footbrail of the mizzen—this threw him against the sail, which broke his fall, and he was saved! And as he touched the deck he knelt down in the sight of the throng of officers and men who composed the crew, and offered up his thanks to Almighty God for his safe deliverance, during which time the silence and discipline was such one might have heard a pin drop on the deck. *After deliverance there should come a song* :—Gratitude is an imperative duty; and one of its first and finest forms is a hymn of thanksgiving and praise. It is true that it will not be worth much if it expends itself only in song; but wherever the psalm is sincere, it will communicate its melody also to the life. Too often, however, it does not even give a song. You remember how only one of the ten lepers returned to thank the Lord for His cleansing; and, perhaps, we should not be far wrong if we were to affirm that a similar proportion prevails to-day between the thankful and the ungrateful. Yet it would be wrong if we were to leave the impression that such gratitude as this of Moses is almost unknown. On the contrary, the pages of our hymn-books are covered with songs which have been born, like this one, out of deliverance. Many of the finest of David's psalms are the utterances of his heart in thanksgiving for mercies similar to those which Moses celebrated; and some of the noblest lyrics of Watts and Wesley, of Mont-gomery and Lyte, have had a similar origin. Nor is this all; we can see that in all times of great national revival there has been an outburst of song. At the Refor-mation, no result of Luther's work was more remarkable than the stimulus it gave to the hymnology of the Fatherland. In fact, that may be said to have been as good as created by the Reformation; and in our own country each successive revival of religion has had its own special hymn. But we have not all the genius of Wesley, or the inspiration of Moses, or of David; and what shall we do then? We can at least appropriate the lyrics of those who have gone before us, and use them in so far as they meet our case; and I can conceive no more pleasant or profitable occupation for the household than the singing of those hymns which have become dear to us because of the personal experiences which we can read between the lines. But we can do better still than that; for we can set our daily deeds to the music of a grateful heart, and seek to round our lives into a hymn—the melody of which will be recognized by all who come into contact with us, and the power of which shall not be evanescent, like the voice of the singer, but perennial, like the music of the spheres. To this hymnology of life let me incite you; for only they who carry this music in their hearts shall sing at last on the shore of the heavenly land, that song of "pure concert" for which John could find no better description than that it was "the song of Moses, the servant of God, and the song of the Lamb." But to sing of deliverance, you must accept deliverance. Open your hearts, therefore, for the reception of salvation. (*W. M. Taylor, D.D.*) **The Lord is my strength and my song.**—*The citadel and the temple :*—I. WHAT THE LORD IS TO HIS PEOPLE. 1. "The Lord is my strength," sang the enraptured host, when they saw how He had "triumphed gloriously" for them—and this has ever been the song of God's people as they have passed through dangers and tribulations in their way to the heavenly Canaan (Isa. xxvi. 4). 2. But if the Lord be the strength of His people, it must imply that they themselves are weak. 3. But the Lord is our strength; and if the Church be likened unto things which are weak, the figurative language of the Bible is equally strong in setting forth the Lord as her strength (Prov. xxviii. 10; Psa. xviii. 2). The Lord Jesus is called the Captain of her salvation, her Deliverer, Governor, Guide. 4. But the Lord is not only the strength of His people, but also their song. He is a very present help in trouble, and He sometimes raises the head, and cheers the heart, even in the midst of sorrows and trials (Hab. iii. 17–19). 5. The Lord is also the salvation of His people. He sometimes saves them, in a miraculous manner, from temporal evils. 6. He is their God: and this is every-thing. Infinite power, wisdom, mercy, goodness, love, pity, truth, justice, are all exerted in their behalf; for, in one delightful word, He is their God—yea, and He will be their God for ever and ever, and their Guide even unto death. II. THE RESOLUTIONS WHICH A SENSE OF HIS GOODNESS LEADS THEM TO MAKE. 1. "I will pre-pare Him an habitation," alluding, probably, to the Temple which the Jews after-wards built. But it is in the humble, contrite heart that the Lord delights to dwell; and we prepare Him a habitation when we open our hearts to receive Him, when we devote them entirely to Him, and when we make Him the principal object of our desires. 2. "My father's God"—the God of Abraham, Isaac, and Jacob, and of all our pious ancestors—"and I will exalt Him." With my tongue will I praise His name, and my soul shall exalt in Him. (*B. Bailey.*) **My father's God.**—*The pathos of theology :*—A song is the proper conclusion of a victory. Fasting is the worship of sorrow; singing is the worship of joy. The words specially chosen for meditation show that the victory did not end in itself; it touched the holy past; it consummated the promises and hopes of ages. I. "My father's God." THEN RELIGION WAS NO NEW THING TO THEM. They were not sur-prised when they heard the name of God associated with their victory. Religion should not be an originality to us; it should not be a novel sensation; it should be the common breath of our daily life, and the mention of the name of God in the relation of our experience sought to excite no mere amazement. II. " My father's God." THEN THEIR FATHER'S RELIGION WAS NOT CONCEALED FROM THEM. They knew that their father had a God. It is possible not to suspect that a man has any regard for God until we see his name announced in connection with some religious event. We cannot read this holy book without being impressed with the fact that the men who made the history of the world were men who lived in continual communion with the spiritual and unseen. III. " My father's God." YET IT DOES NOT FOLLOW THAT THE FATHER AND THE CHILD MUST HAVE THE SAME GOD. You have power deliberately to serve the connection between yourself and the God of your fathers. It is a terrible power! IV. " My father's God." THEN WE ARE DEBTORS TO THE RELIGIOUS PAST. There are some results of goodness we inherit independently of our own will. This age inherits the civilization of the past. The child is the better for his father's temperance. Mephibosheth received honours for Jonathan's sake. The processes of God are not always consummated in the age with which they begin. Generations may pass away, and then the full blessing may come. Practical questions: 1. Your father was a Christian,—are you so much wiser than your father that you can afford to set aside his example? There are some things in which you are bound to improve upon the actions of your father; but are you quite sure that the worship of the God of heaven is one of them? 2. Your father was a holy man—will you under-take to break the line of a holy succession? Ought not the fame of his holiness to awaken your own religious concern? 3. Your father was deeply religious,—will you inherit all he has given you in name, in reputation, in social position, and throw away all the religious elements which made him what he was? 4. Your father could not live without God,—can you? *(J. Parker, D.D.)* *A noble ancestry and a glorious resolution:*—I. A NOBLE ANCESTRY. " My father's God." Who are the men who have the most illustrious ancestry? The men who honoured, served, and trusted the one true and living God. The same God does for all ages; His character commends itself to the adoration of all souls. It is natural to value anything our loving fathers love. We value their favourite books, but how much more their God, the totality of goodness, the fountain of all blessedness? II. A GLORIOUS RESOLU-TION. " I will exalt Him." How can we " exalt Him? " Enthrone Him in our affections as Lord of lords, and King of kings, ruling all thoughts, animating and directing all activities. *(Homilist.)* *The living God:*—I. WHO WAS THE GOD OF OUR FATHERS? 1. A pure Being, not the " chance " of the atheist. 2. A conscious Being, not the "mere law " of the deist. 3. A personal Being, not "the all " of the pantheist. 4. A perfect Being, as revealed in the Bible. 5. An emotional Being, as manifested in Christ. 6. A communicative Being, as imparted by the Holy Spirit. II. WHAT IS IT TO EXALT HIM? 1. Not by tall spires. 2. Not by gorgeous ritual. 3. To adore Him as the object of our worship. 4. To give Him the chief place in our affections. *(W. W. Wythe.)* *My mother's God:*—At a fashionable party a young physician present spoke of one of his patients, whose case he con-sidered a very critical one. He said he was " very sorry to lose him, for he was a noble young man, but very unnecessarily concerned about his soul, and Christians increased his agitation by talking with him and praying for him. He wished Chris-tians would let his patients alone. Death was but an endless sleep, the religion of Christ a delusion, and its followers were not persons of the highest culture or intelli-gence." A young lady sitting near, and one of the gayest of that company, said, " Pardon me, doctor, but I cannot hear you talk thus and remain silent. I am not a professor of religion; I never knew anything about it experimentally, but my mother was a Christian. Times without number she has taken me with her to her room, and with her hand upon my head, she has prayed that God would give her grace to train me for the skies. Two years ago my precious mother died, and the religion she loved through life sustained her in her dying hour. She called us to her bed-side, and with her face shining with glory, asked us to meet her in heaven, and I promised to do so. And now," said the young lady, displaying deep emotion, " can I believe that this is all a delusion? that my mother sleeps an eternal sleep? that she will never waken again in the morning of the resurrection, and that I shall see her no more? No, I cannot, I will not believe it." Her brother tried to quiet her, for by this time she had the attention of all present. " No! " said she. "Brother, let me alone; I must defend my mother's God, my religion." The physician made no reply, and soon left the room. He was found shortly afterwards pacing the floor of an adjoining room, in great agitation and distress of spirit. " What is the matter? " a friend inquired. " Oh," said he, " that young lady is right. Her words have pierced my soul like an arrow. I too must have the religion I have despised, or I am lost for ever." And the result of the convictions thus awakened was that both the young lady and the physician were converted to Christ, and are useful and influential members of the Church of God.

Ver. 3. **The Lord is a man of war.**—*The triumphs of Jehovah :*—I. THE THOUGHT OF GOD'S TRIUMPHS AS A MAN OF WAR SEEMS TO BE VALUABLE AS GIVING IN ITS DEGREE A PROOF OF THE TRUTH OF HOLY WRIT. The moral expectations raised by our Lord's first sermon on the Mount are being actually realized in many separate souls now. The prayer for strength to triumph against the devil, the world, and the flesh is becoming daily more visibly proved in the triumph of the Spirit, in the individual lives of the redeemed. II. THE TRIUMPHS OF THE LORD IN THE INDIVIDUAL HEARTS AMONG US GIVE AN INCREASING HOPE FOR UNITY THROUGHOUT CHRISTENDOM. We cannot deny the debt we owe to the labours of Nonconformists in the days of the Church's lethargy and neglect. We cannot join them now, but we are preparing for a more close and lasting union, in God's own time, by the individual progress in spiritual things. III. WE MUST DO OUR PART TO SET OUR SEAL TO THE TRIUMPHANT POWER OF DIVINE GRACE. It is the half-lives of Christians which are such a poor proof of the truth of our Lord's words. They do not begin early enough; they do not work thoroughly enough. We have the promise that this song shall be at last on the lips of all who prevail, for St. John tells us in the Revelation that he saw those who had overcome standing on the sea of glass, having the harps of God, singing the song of Moses and the Lamb. (*Bp. King.*)

Ver. 9, 10. **The enemy said.**—*The enemy's spirit :*—Observe the spirit of the enemy of Israel. It was characterized—1. By great ambition. It was the love of power and dominion. To hold human beings as property is the vilest display of ambition. 2. Great arrogance and pride. I will pursue (rather " repossess "), overtake, divide, &c. What self-confidence ! What boasting ! What assumption ! Pride goeth before destruction. 3. Insatiable avarice. Divide the spoil. Had not Pharaoh enough? An avaricious spirit unceasingly cries, Give! give! What a cursed spirit it is! Well has it been said that nature is content with little, grace with less, but the lust of avarice not even with all things. 4. Reckless malevolence and cruelty. " My lust shall be satisfied, I will draw my sword," &c. What thirsting for blood ! Ambition and avarice render the mind cold and the heart callous. Tears, wailings, groans, mangled bodies and the flowing blood of mankind allay not the fires of human malevolence and lust. 5. Presumptuous confidence and security. I will do, not endeavour, no peradventure. Contingency and doubt have no place. How foolish for the man who puts on the armour to boast. (*A. Nevin, D.D.*)   *God's Church and her enemies :*—Israel was a type of the Church, Pharaoh a type of the Church's enemies in all ages of the world, both of the spiritual enemy Satan, and of the temporal, his instruments. The deliverance was a type of the deliverance that Christ wrought upon the cross by His blood; also of that Christ works upon His throne, the one from the reign of sin, the other from the empire of antichrist. The text is a part of Moses' song; a song after victory, a panegyric; the praise of God, attended with dancing, at the sight of the Egyptian wrecks (ver. 20). 1. It was then real; the Israelites then sang it. 2. It is typical; the conquerors of antichrist shall again triumph in the same manner (Rev. xv. 3). 3. It was an earnest of future deliverance to the Israelites. General observations. 1. The greatest idolaters are the fiercest enemies against the Church of God. It is the Egyptian is the enemy. No nation had more and more sordid idols. 2. The Church's enemies are not for her correction, but her destruction: "I will pursue; my hand shall destroy them." 3. How desperate are sometimes the straits of God's Israel in the eye of man! How low their spirits before deliverance. 4. God orders the lusts of men for His own praise. 5. The nearer the deliverance of the Church is, the fiercer are God's judgments on the enemies of it, and the higher the enemies' rage. 6. All creatures are absolutely under the sovereignty of God, and are acted by His power in all their services. 7. By the same means God saves His people, whereby He destroys His enemies: the one sank, the other passed through. That which makes one balance sink makes the other rise the higher. 8. The strength and glory of a people is more wasted by opposing the interests of the Church than in conflicts with any other enemy. 9. We may take notice of the folly of the Church's enemies. Former plagues might have warned them of the power of God, they had but burned their own fingers by pinching her, yet they would set their force against almighty power, that so often had worsted them; it is as if men would pull down a steeple with a string. But the observations I shall treat of are—1. When the enemies of the Church are in the highest fury and resolution, and the Church in the greatest extremity and dejection, then is the fittest time for God to work her deliverance fully and perfectly. When the enemy said, "I will pursue, I will overtake, I will divide the spoil," &c., then "God blowed with His wind," then "they sank." 2. God is the author of all the deliverances of the Church, whosoever are the instruments. "Thou didst blow with Thy wind; who is like unto the Lord among the gods." Uses: How dear is the Church to God! 2. Remember former deliverances in time of straits. 3. Thankfully remember former deliverances. (*S. Charnock, B.D.*) *Vanity of boasting:*—When Bonaparte was about to invade Russia, a person who had endeavoured to dissuade him from his purpose, finding he could not prevail, quoted to him the proverb, "Man proposes, but God disposes"; to which he indignantly replied, "I dispose as well as propose." A Christian lady, on hearing the impious boast, remarked, "I set that down as the turning-point of Bonaparte's fortunes. God will not suffer a creature with impunity thus to usurp His prerogative." It happened to Bonaparte just as the lady predicted. His invasion of Russia was the commencement of his fall. *Triumphing before the battle :*— Nothing can be got, but much may be lost, by triumphing before a battle. When Charles V. invaded France, he lost his generals and a great part of his army by famine and disease; and returned baffled and thoroughly mortified from an enterprize which he began with such confidence of its happy issue, that he desired Paul Jovius, the historian, to make a large provision of paper sufficient to record the victories which he was going to acquire! *Providentially destroyed :*—During the last summer, at Coblentz, we saw a monument erected to commemorate the French campaign against the Russians in 1812. It was a gigantic failure; 400,000 men set forth for Moscow; 25,000, battered and worn and weary, tattered and half famished, returned. Do you ask how it was done? Not by the timid Alexander's guns and swords. We read in one place that "the stars in their courses fought against Sisera"; in another, how God has sent an army of locusts to overthrow an army of men; but here the very elements combine to drive the invader back in disgrace. Yes. "He gave snow like wool, He scattered His hoar-frost like ashes, He cast forth His ice like morsels—who can stand before His cold?" Who? Not Napoleon, who, with self-sufficient heart, boasted in his own right hand, and sacrificed to his insatiable ambition the blood of myriads of murdered men. No! God blows upon him with His wind out of the north, and, shivering and half-starved, he slinks back in defeat. What a picture! But Alexander had not forgotten to prepare his ways before the Lord and seek the God of Jacob's aid. And in recognition of the Divine interposition and help, he struck a medal with a legend : "Not to me, not to us, but unto Thy Name." Thus the lesson taught by ancient and modern history is, that the race is not to the swift, nor the battle to the strong, but to the man who prepares his ways before the Lord his God. (*Enoch Hall.*)

VER. 11. **Who is like unto Thee, O Lord, among the gods ?**—*The incomparable God :*—I. WHO IS LIKE UNTO THEE, O LORD, AMONG THE GODS ? 1. King of kings and Lord of lords! Who among the gods is like unto Thee in majesty and power? Well might Israel exultingly make this inquiry. 2. Who is like unto Thee in the ineffable purity of Thy nature? "Glorious in holiness !" 3. Who is like unto Thee in the solemnity and sanctity of Thy worship ?—"fearful in praises!" The gloriously holy God is alone worthy to be praised, but that praise ought to be offered with "reverence and godly fear." II. WHO DOES LIKE THEE ?—"doing wonders." 1. The wonders alluded in the text were undoubtedly the miracles recently wrought by Jehovah for the salvation of His people. "Thou art the God that doest wonders," &c. (Psa. lxxvii. 14-20). 2. But not only miracles, which imply an inversion or suspension of the laws of nature, but nature and her laws— every part of the work of God in the heavens and in the earth is wonderful, and amply shows forth the power and wisdom of the Creator (Job xxxvii. 14-23; Psa. viii. 3, 4, xix. 1-7). If we only study our own frame, we shall be led to exclaim with the Psalmist, "I am fearfully and wonderfully made !" 3. The Lord sometimes does wonders in judgment, flood, &c. 4. The Lord does wonders in mercy. Redemption. (*B. Bailey.*)　　**Glorious in holiness.**—*The holiness of God :*— Plutarch said not amiss, that he should count himself less injured by that man that should deny that there was such a man as Plutarch, than by him that should affirm that there was such a one indeed, but he was a debauched fellow, a loose and vicious person. He that saith, God is not holy, speaks much worse than he that saith, There is no God at all. Let these two things be considered : 1. If any, this attribute hath an excellency above His other perfections. (1) None is sounded out with such solemnity, and so frequently by angels that stand before His throne, as this. (2) He singles it out to swear by (Psa. lxxxix. 35 ; Amos iv. 2). (3) It is His glory and beauty. Holiness is the honour of the creature—sanctification and honour are linked together (1 Thess. iv. 4)— much more is it the honour of God ; it is the image of God in the creature (Eph. iv. 24). (4) It is His very life ; so it is called (Eph. iv. 18). 2. As it seems to challenge an excellency above all His other perfections, so it is the glory of all the rest ; as it is the glory of the Godhead, so it is the glory of every perfection in the Godhead ; as His power is the strength of them, so His holiness is the beauty of them ; as all would be weak without almightiness to back them, so all would be uncomely without holiness to adorn them. Should this be sullied, all the rest would lose their honour and their comfortable efficacy ; as at the same instant that the sun should lose its light, it would lose its heat, its strength, its generative and quickening virtue. I. THE NATURE OF DIVINE HOLINESS. The holiness of God negatively is a perfect freedom from all evil. As we call gold pure that is not imbased by any dross, and that garment clean that is free from any spot, so the nature of God is estranged from all shadow of evil, all imaginable contagion. Positively, it is the rectitude of the Divine nature, or that conformity of it in affection and action to the Divine will as to His eternal law, whereby He works with a becomingness to His own excellency, and whereby He hath a complacency in everything agreeable to His will, and an abhorrency of everything contrary thereunto. In particular. This property of the Divine nature is—1. An essential and necessary perfection. He is essentially and necessarily holy. His holiness is as necessary as His being, as necessary as His omniscience. 2. God is absolutely holy (1 Sam. ii. 2). 3. God is so holy, that He cannot possibly approve of any evil done by another, but doth perfectly abhor it ; it would not else be a glorious holiness (Psa. v. 3), "He hath no pleasure in wickedness." He doth not only love that which is just, but abhor with a perfect hatred all things contrary to the rule of righteousness. Holiness can no more approve of sin than it can commit it. 4. God is so holy, that He cannot but love holiness in others. Not that He owes anything to His creature, but from the unspeakable holiness of His nature, whence affections to all things that bear a resemblance of Him do flow ; as light shoots out from the sun, or any glittering body. It is essential to the infinite righteousness of His nature, to love righteousness wherever He beholds it (Psa. xi. 7). 5. God is so holy, that He cannot positively will or encourage sin in any. 6. God cannot act any evil in or by Himself. II. THE PROOF THAT GOD IS HOLY. 1. His holiness appears as He is Creator, in framing man in a perfect uprightness. 2. His holiness appears in His laws, as He is a Lawgiver and a Judge. This purity is evident—(1) In the moral law, or law of nature ; (2) In the ceremonial law ; (3) In the allurements annexed to it for keeping it, and the affrightments to restrain from the breaking of it ; (4) In the judgments inflicted for the violation of it. 3. The holiness of God appears in our restoration. It is in the glass of the gospel we "behold the glory of the Lord" (2 Cor. iii. 18) ; that is, the glory of the Lord, into whose image we are changed ; but we are changed into nothing as the image of God but into holiness. We bore not upon us by creation, nor by regeneration, the image of any other perfection. We cannot be changed into His omnipotence, omniscience, &c., but into the image of His righteousness. This is the pleasing and glorious sight the gospel mirror darts in our eyes. The whole scene of redemption is nothing else but a discovery of judgment and righteousness. " Zion shall be redeemed with judgment, and her converts with righteousness " (Isa. i. 27). (1) This holiness of God appears in the manner of our restoration, viz., by the death of Christ. (2) The holiness of God in His hatred of sin appears in our justification, and the conditions He requires of all that would enjoy the benefit of redemption. (3) It appears in the actual regeneration of the redeemed soul, and a carrying it on to a full perfection. As election is the effect of God's sovereignty, our pardon the fruit of His mercy, our knowledge a stream from His wisdom, our strength an impression of His power, so our purity is a beam from His holiness. The whole work of sanctification, and the preservation of it, our Saviour begs for His disciples of His Father under this title (John xvii. 11, 17). III. The third thing I am to do, is to lay down SOME PROPOSITIONS IN THE DEFENCE OF GOD'S HOLINESS IN ALL HIS ACTS ABOUT OR CONCERNING SIN. 1. God's holiness is not chargeable with any blemish, for His creating man in a mutable state. It was suitable to the wisdom of God to give the rational creature, whom He had furnished with a power of acting righteously, the liberty of choice, and not fix him in an unchangeable state, without a trial of him in his natural. And if he did obey, his obedience might be the more valuable ; and if he did freely offend, his offence might be more inexcusable. (1) No creature can be capable of immutability by nature. Mutability is so essential to a creature, that a creature cannot be supposed without it. (2) Though God made the creature mutable, yet He made Him not evil. There could be nothing of evil in him that God created after His own image, and pronounced good (Gen. i. 27, 31). (3) There-fore it follows, that though God created man changeable, yet He was not the cause of his change by his fall. 2. God's holiness is not blemished by enjoining man a law which He knew he would not observe. (1) The law was not above his strength. (2) Though the law now be above the strength of man, yet is not the holiness of God blemished by keeping it up. It is true, God hath been graciously pleased to mitigate the severity of the law by the entrance of the gospel ; yet, where men refuse the terms of the gospel they continue themselves under the condemnation of the law, and are justly guilty of the breach of it, though they have no strength to observe it. (3) God's foreknowledge that His law would not be observed lays no blame upon Him. Though the foreknowledge of God be infallible, yet it doth not necessitate the creature in acting. 3. The holiness of God is not blemished by decreeing the eternal rejection of some men. 4. The holiness of God is not blemished by His secret will to suffer sin to enter into the world. God never willed sin by His preceptive will. It was never founded upon, or produced by any word of His, as the creation was. Nor doth He will it by His approving will ; it is detest-able to Him, nor ever can be otherwise. He cannot approve it either before com-mission or after. IV. The point was, THAT HOLINESS IS A GLORIOUS PERFECTION OF THE NATURE OF GOD. We have showed the nature of this holiness in God, what it is, and we have demonstrated it, and proved that God is holy, and must needs be so, and also the purity of His nature in all His acts about sin. Let us now improve it by way of use. 1. Is holiness a transcendent perfection belonging to the nature of God ? The first use shall be of instruction and information. (1) How great and how frequent is the contempt of this eminent perfection in the Deity ! (2) It may inform us how great is our fall from God, and how distant we are from Him. (3) All unholiness is vile and opposite to the nature of God. (4) Sin cannot escape a due punishment. A hatred of unrighteousness, and consequently a will to punish it, is as essential to God as a love of righteousness. (5) There is therefore a neces-sity of the satisfaction of the holiness of God by some sufficient mediator. The Divine purity could not meet with any acquiescence in all mankind after the Fall. (6) Hence it will follow, there is no justification of a sinner by anything in himself. 2. The second use is for comfort. This attribute frowns upon lapsed nature, but smiles in the restorations made by the gospel. 3. Is holiness an eminent perfection of the Divine nature? Then—(1) Let us get and preserve right and strong apprehensions of this Divine perfection. (2) Is holiness a perfection of the Divine nature ? Is it the glory of the Deity? Then let us glorify this holiness of God. (3) Since holiness is an eminent perfection of the Divine nature, let us labour after a conformity to God in this perfection. (4) If holiness be a perfection belonging to the nature of God, then, where there is some weak conformity to the holiness of God, let us labour to grow up in it, and breathe after fuller measures of it. (5) Let us carry ourselves holily in a spiritual manner in all our religious approaches to God (Psa. xciii. 5). (6) Let us address for holiness to God the fountain of it. As He is the author of bodily life in the creature, so He is the author of His own life, the life of God in the soul. (*S. Charnock, B.D.*)   *God the pattern of holiness :*—No creature can be essentially holy but by participation from the chief fountain of holiness, but we must have the same kind of holiness, the same truth of holiness; as a short line may be as straight as another, though it parallel it not in the immense length of it ; a copy may have the likeness of the original, though not the same perfection. We cannot be good without eyeing some exemplar of goodness as the pattern. No pattern is so suitable as that which is the highest goodness and purity. That limner that would draw the most excellent piece fixes his eye upon the most excellent pattern. He that would be a good orator, or poet, or artificer, considers some person most excellent in each kind as the object of his imitation. Who so fit as God to be viewed as the pattern of holiness in our intendment of, and endeavours after, holiness? The Stoics, one of the best sects of philosophers, advised their disciples to pitch upon some eminent example of virtue, according to which to form their lives, as Socrates, &c. But true holiness doth not only endeavour to live the life of a good man, but chooses to live a Divine life. As before the man was "alienated from the life of God," so upon his return he aspires after the life of God. To endeavour to be like a good man is to make one image like another, to set our clocks by other clocks without regarding the sun; but true holiness consists in a likeness to the most exact sampler. God being the first purity, is the rule as well as the spring of all purity in the creature, the chief and first object of imitation. (*Ibid.*) *The holiness of God and that of His best saints:*—There is as little proportion between the holiness of the Divine majesty and that of the most righteous creature, as there is between the nearness of a person that stands upon a mountain to the sun, and of him that beholds him in a vale; one is nearer than the other, but it is an advantage not to be boasted, in regard of the vast distance that is between the sun and the elevated spectator. (*Ibid.*) *God loves holiness:*—God is essentially, originally, and efficiently holy: all the holiness in men and angels is but a crystal stream that runs from this glorious ocean. God loves holiness, because it is His own image. A king cannot but love to see his own effigies stamped on coin. God counts holiness His own glory, and the most sparkling jewel of His crown. "Glorious in holiness." (*T. Watson.*)

Ver. 13. **Hast led forth the people which Thou hast redeemed.**—*Lessons:*—1. God's future providence as well as past deliverance is the matter of faith's praise. 2. God, as a shepherd, leadeth His people through their course to rest, and will lead, as if it were done. 3. Mercy is the rule of all God's conduct to His Church here below. 4. God hath saved, and will redeem His Israel out of all their troubles. It is His promise (Psa. cxxx. 8). 5. God's holy habitation, Sion in type and heaven in truth, is the end of all His providential guidance unto His. 6. God's strength secureth the Church's conduct to His holy habitation. 7. Tender, sweet, and gentle is God's guidance of His Church through their way to rest (Isa. xl. 11). 8. All this promised guidance faith must return to the praise of God. (*G. Hughes, B.D.*) *The song of Moses:*—I. Past mercies acknowledged. The fact celebrated is redemption from Egypt—"Thou in Thy mercy hast led forth Thy people which Thou hast redeemed." The whole glory of deliverance is ascribed to the Lord, without any reference to second causes. The believer will often look back and contemplate his mercies, and celebrate his deliverances; like Samuel, he will raise his Ebenezer (1 Sam. vii. 12). II. Future mercies anticipated. "Thou hast guided them, in Thy strength, unto Thy holy habitation." Here is the language of strong faith, as if they were already in Canaan. Moses knew that God had promised to bring them to His holy hill, and to His dwelling; he knew that God's promises were as good as His performances; and we may say so too, for they are all yea and amen in Christ Jesus. The Lord had done so much for Israel, that Moses felt no doubt as to the future—"Thou shalt bring them in, and plant them in the mountain of Thine inheritance." III. Israel's enemies confounded. "The people shall hear and be afraid, sorrow shall take hold of the inhabitants of Palestine," &c. The world has now much to say against the people and cause of God. Religion is denounced by them as a delusion—a gloomy thing—as madness; but then every objection will be silenced. Satan, too, is now very busy with his temptations and accusations; but this state of things shall not always last. Trembling shall take hold of the believer's enemies, when the people of God are safely brought to the heavenly Canaan. Then where will be the venom of the world? where the accusations of Satan? Not one mouth will then be opened against the meanest and most neglected of God's people on earth. He shall then have nothing to fear; admitted within the pearly gates of the heavenly Jerusalem, he shall be for ever with the Lord. All enemies will be for ever excluded. The Church shall be saved and God glorified. IV. The kingdom of God permanently triumphant. "The Lord shall reign for ever and ever." 1. To the enemies of Christ. You see that the Lord must reign; then what must become of you? 2. To the friends of Christ, yea, to those who wish to love the Saviour. (1) Look back and review your mercies; how numerous, how seasonable, how undeserved! See the Lord's hand in them, and this will add to their sweetness. (2) Look forward.

Consider what God has promised to do for you. You have your trials, and you will have them ; but you have not one too many. (3) Look upward to that promised rest—that " inheritance which is incorruptible, undefiled, and fadeth not away," &c. (*George Breay, B.A.*)

Vers. 14–16. **The people shall hear, and be afraid.**—*The world afraid of God's people :*—What shall make these mighty men melt away ? Seeing two or three millions of unwarlike folks marching towards them—an unarmed rabble, without military discipline, and without the appliances of war ? Is it before such that the mighty men of Moab are to fall back, that the chivalrous sons of Edom are to be put to flight; that all the inhabitants of Palestine are to melt away ? Nothing of the kind. Those Israelites were not going to terrify all these nations with any display of their own power or prowess. It was the story of the Exodus, the story of a divided sea, the story of a certain mysterious pillar of fire, the story of the wonderful overthrow of Pharaoh and his hosts in the Red Sea ; it was this that was to fill them with despair. Many of us are at the outset terribly afraid of these hostile forces ; is it not a comfort to know that on account of redemption they are actually afraid of us ? In a very memorable period in " our island story," when Admiral Howard and Drake had defeated the Spanish Armada after the first great battle, they continued to pursue them for a fortnight without having a single shot or a single charge of powder left in their ships. They had nothing left but air to fill their guns with. Yet thus without any ammunition our fleet went sailing on and sailing on, while the terrified strangers fled before them, until they were driven right into the Northern Sea. Then the Admiral thought they could not do much harm there, and so he left them and came back to get powder and shot for his own ships. Our fleet, with empty guns, chased their enemies because that enemy was afraid of them. They had had one terrible defeat, and that was enough. And even so may we deal with the forces of this world. Count upon your enemies being afraid of you. If instead of being afraid of them you will only carry the war into the enemy's camp, and seek to win them for Christ, instead of allowing them to draw you away from Him, you will find that redemption has already stripped them of their courage and paralyzed their power to do you any injury. (*W. Hay Aitken, M.A.*)

Vers. 17, 18. **Thou shalt bring them in.**—*Anticipations of faith :*—We are, perhaps, hardly surprised at the tone of jubilant confidence which pervades this glorious psalm of thanksgiving. Very strong indeed is the language used; but perhaps not stronger than might naturally have been expected to spring from such circumstances ; for what a wonderful event had just transpired ! Here they were then, on the other side of the Red Sea, the vast wilderness stretching before them, their long weary march not yet commenced, and wholly destitute of any adequate supplies, and without either arms, or discipline, or any capacity for warfare. Surely the prospect might have seemed most discouraging. They must have known perfectly well—what they soon found out to be a fact—that the wilderness swarmed with wandering nomad hordes, Bedouins of the desert, men of war, who might at any moment come down upon them, cut off their stragglers, or even put the whole undisciplined rabble to rout and make a prey of them. And even supposing they should overcome these difficulties of the journey, what then ? There lay Canaan before them, but how were they, who could hardly hold their own against the tribes of the desert, to undertake aggressive warfare against nations dwelling in cities with walls great and high, and equipped with all the appliances of ancient warfare ? How chimerical their enterprise would seem on reflection ! how improbable that they would ever succeed in taking possession of the land which God had promised to them ! But faith looked on beyond all difficulties. Faith never stops for commissariat supplies ! Faith does not ask, Where is my daily bread to come from ? Faith does not wait to be clothed with armour, save such armour as the power of God supplies. Faith does not stop to weigh the adequacy of the means within our reach to induce the end. Children of God, it is time we endeavoured to apply the lessons suggested by all this to ourselves. We too have been the subjects of a great deliverance, a deliverance as supernatural in its character and as astonishing in its conditions as ever was the deliverance of Israel from Egypt. This deliverance is also the product of redemption. We are saved in order that we may rise to the prize of our high calling, and become inheritors of our true Land of Promise ; and the first great deliverance is with us also surely an earnest and a pledge of all that is to follow. I suppose it is because we so imperfectly apprehend the miracle of our deliverance and its completeness, and the new relations which it establishes between ourselves and God, and between ourselves and sin, that our feelings at the outset of our new life are so often just the opposite of those depicted in this triumphant song. Instead of joyous anticipation, how common a thing it is to meet with gloomy forebodings on the part of the newborn children of God, fresh from the Cross of Christ, just rising, as we may say, spiritually out of the waters of the Red Sea. And many of us have scarcely been saved from our condition of condemnation and spiritual bondage before we begin to consider the difficulties that lie before us, the enemies that we shall have to encounter, the sacrifices that we may have to make, the trials that we may have to undergo. The wilderness seems so vast, the enemies so mighty, the supplies so inadequate or precarious; and while our eyes of unbelief are resting upon all these adverse considerations, our heart seems to sink within us until we are ready to turn back again into Egypt. How common a thing it is to meet with young Christians who seem indeed to be on the right side of the Red Sea, but who appear to be more inclined to wring their hands in terror than to " sound the loud timbrel " in exultation ! (*W. Hay Aitken, M.A.*)   *An encouraging deliverance :*—Two ways this great deliverance was encouraging. 1. It was such an instance of God's power as would terrify their enemies and quite dishearten them (vers. 14–16). It had this effect (see Deut. ii. 4; Num. xxii. 3; Josh. ii. 9, 10). 2. It was such a beginning of God's favour to them as gave them an earnest of the perfection of His kindness. This was but in order to something further (ver. 17). (*M. Henry, D.D.*)   *Christ for ever :*— When Luther went to his trial at Augsburg from Wittemberg he walked all the distance. Clad in his monk's brown frock, with all his wardrobe on his back, the citizens, high and low, attended him in enthusiastic admiration. As they went they cried, " Luther for ever ! "   " Nay ! nay ! " he answered, " Christ for ever ! "

Vers. 19–21. With timbrels and with dances.—*Song, timbrel, and dance :*—The monuments reproduce this scene in all its parts. Separate choirs of men and women are represented on them, singing in alternate responses; the timbrel, or tambourine, is represented as the instrument of the women, as the flute is that of the men; and the playing of the tambourine, unaccompanied, as here, by other instruments, is represented in connection with singing and the dance. Further, it appears from the monuments that music had eminently a religious destination in Egypt, that the timbrel was specially devoted to sacred uses, and that religious dances were performed in the worship of Osiris. (*E. C. Wines, D.D.*)   In the tombs at Thebes timbrels, like Miriam's, round and square, are seen in the hands of the women; while pipes, trumpets, sistrums, drums, and guitars are there in great abundance and variety; and harps, not much unlike the modern instrument, with varying numbers of strings up to twenty-two. (*S. C. Bartlett, D.D.*) *Cheering effect of music :*—Whilst the Federal army lay before the city of Richmond, the regimental bands were silent. When they began to retreat to Malvern, the troops marched through the acres of ripe grain, cutting off the tops and gathering them into their haversacks, being out of rations, as well as lame and stiff from marching. Orders were here given for the bands to strike up playing, and the effect on the dispirited men was almost magical as the patriotic airs were played. They seemed to catch new hope and enthusiasm, and a cheer went up from each regiment.   *Serving God with a cheerful spirit :*—When the poet Carpani inquired of his friend Haydn how it happened that his church music was always so cheerful, the great composer made a most beautiful reply. " I cannot," said he, " make it otherwise; I write according to the thoughts I feel. When I think upon God, my heart is so full of joy that the notes dance and leap, as it were, from my pen ; and since God has given me a cheerful heart, it will be pardoned me that I serve Him with a cheerful spirit."

Vers. 22–27. They came to Marah.—*Marah :*—I. The water was DELETERIOUS, not distasteful only. Had the people drunk it, it would have wrought disease; but it was healed by the obedience of Moses to God's directions. So if we are attentive and obedient to His voice He will find us remedies from all things that might hurt us. II. It was not possible, perhaps, that the children of Israel should, by persevering in the unwholesome draught which is there typical of sin, HAVE VITIATED THEIR TASTE TILL THEY DELIGHTED IN IT. But it is too possible in the antitype. III. Though we are compelled by God's providence to pass through difficulty and temptation, WE ARE NOT DOOMED TO DWELL THERE. If we are faithful, it is but in passing that we shall be endangered. If we use the remedy of obedience to God's Word to-day, to-morrow we shall be beside the twelve ever-springing fountains, and under the shade of the palm-trees of Elim. (*Archbishop Benson.*) *The waters of Marah* :—We have here a parable of the deep things of Christ. I. Israel was in those days FRESH FROM THE GLORIOUS DELIVERANCE OUT OF EGYPT; they had sung their first national song of victory; they had breathed the air of liberty. This was their first disappointment, and it was a very sharp one; from the height of exultation they fell almost at once to the depths of despair. Such disappointments we have all experienced, especially in the outset of our actual march, after the first conscious sense of spiritual triumph and freedom. II. Of us also it is true that GOD HATH SHOWED US A CERTAIN TREE, and that tree is the once accursed tree on which Christ died. This is the tree of life to us, though of death to Him. III. IT WAS GOD WHO SHOWED THIS TREE UNTO MOSES. And it was God who showed it to us in the gospel. Applied by our faith to the bitter waters of disappointment and distress, it will surely heal them and make them sweet. Two things there are about the tree of scorn which will never lose their healing power—the lesson of the Cross and the consolation of the Cross; the example and the companionship of Christ crucified. IV. THE LIFE WHICH FOUND ITS FITTING CLOSE UPON THE CROSS WAS not a life of suffering only, but EMPHATICALLY A LIFE OF DISAPPOINTMENT. Here there is comfort for us. Our dying Lord must certainly have reflected that He, the Son of God, was leaving the world rather worse than He found it in all human appearance. V. WHATEVER OUR TRIALS AND DISAPPOINTMENTS, LET US USE THIS REMEDY; it will not fail us even at the worst. (*R. Winterbotham, M.A.*) *Bitter-sweet* :— I. THAT GREAT JOY IS OFTEN CLOSELY FOLLOWED BY A GREAT TRIAL. "Thou hast made my mountain to stand strong" is the grateful word of many a rejoicing Christian; and lo! suddenly touched by the finger of Providence, it reels and rocks as though heaved by an earthquake, and falls into the depths of the sea. In the day of prosperity be wise! Rejoice with trembling! Do not presume on the possession of present good. In the hour of peace forget not the preparation for a possible storm. Trust in God with a firm hand, both in sunshine and in shade. II. HERE IS A GREAT TRIAL TRANSFORMED INTO A GREAT BLESSING. The bitter was not removed, but converted into sweet. So God can make the grief a grace and change the burden into a blessing. The rod itself shall bud and blossom and bring forth almonds, so that the very thing that chastens the trustful soul shall present beauty to the eye and fruit to the taste. It was a Divine work. The Israelites, even with Moses at their head, had no skill to meet the given necessities of the hour. "The Lord showed them a tree," and so miraculously healed the forbidding spring. Brothers! human wisdom, earth's philosophies, the world's limited resources are all useless in the midst of our desperate needs. III. HERE IS A GREAT TRIAL, SO TRANSFORMED, PREPARING FOR AND LEADING TO A STILL GREATER BLESSING (see ver. 27). Christian, be of good courage. Egypt's chains were heavy; but the Red Sea victory made thee glad. Marah's waters were bitter; but the Lord distilled sweet streams therefrom to strengthen and refresh thy soul. Then He led thee to beautiful Elim, with its springs and palm-trees, and its grateful rest, and in all and through all thou art "nearer" Canaan than when first thou didst believe. Amid all thine alternations of joy and sorrow there shall be, if thou art faithful to thy God, a clear current, progressive gain, and it shall still be better further on. IV. THIS GRACIOUS ALTERNATION AND ABUNDANT DELIVERANCE WAS ALL EXPERIENCED ON THE LINE OF MARCH. Let the Christian never forget that these are the conditions necessary to secure his gracious progression of conquest, transformation, and exceeding joy. (*J. J. Wray.*) *The sweetening tree in life's bitter streams* :— Heaven has prepared a sweetening tree for the bitter waters. I. OF OUR SECULAR LIFE. Wrecked plans, blasted hopes, &c. The "tree" to sweeten this is Christ's doctrine of a Fatherly providence. II. OF OUR MORAL LIFE. The bitter waters of an accusing conscience. "Whom God hath set forth," &c. III. OF AN INTELLECTUAL LIFE. God's revealed character in Christ—all-wise, all-loving, all-powerful. IV. OF OUR SOCIAL LIFE. "I am the Resurrection," &c. "Them that sleep in Jesus will God bring with Him." V. OF OUR DYING LIFE. (*Homilist.*) *The mysterious tree* :—I. THAT PRAYER WILL MEET EVERY PAINFUL CRISIS IN HUMAN EXPERIENCE. II. THAT ALL MEN, EVERYWHERE, ARE ATHIRST. III. THAT EVERY MAN WILL AT LENGTH COME TO HIS WELL; BUT THE WATER THEREOF WILL BE BITTER TO HIS TASTE. Sensual indulgence. Fashionable amusement; inebriety; riches; worldly renown; infidelity. All mere earthly pools are acrid and unsatisfying. IV. THAT THERE IS A TREE WHICH

CAN SWEETEN ALL EARTH'S WATERS. "The tree of life"—the Cross of Christ. "Ho, every one that thirsteth, come." (*S. D. Burchard, D.D.*) *Life's bitterness :—* The wilderness brings out what is within. It also discovers God's goodness and our unworthiness. I. EARTH'S BITTERNESS. 1. We must expect bitter pools in a bitter world. 2. Many of us make our own Marahs. II. HEAVEN'S REMEDY. 1. To the praying man the Lord reveals the remedy. 2. God uses instrumentality. 3. God does not always take away the Marah, but drops an ingredient into it to sweeten its bitterness. (*Homilist.*)   *The waters of Marah:—*Had they been allowed to select their path, they would have taken the short cut by the seaboard to their own promised land. But the cloud steered their pathway through difficulty and into difficulty. Behind them was the blood of the lamb. They were ransomed. Behind them the wonders of Egypt wrought on their behalf. Behind them the passage of the Red Sea. And they might have expected that, the moment they had left their foes behind, they had left all trouble and sorrow too. But instead of that, their redemption from Egypt was their redemption from comparatively easy circumstances into arduous and difficult straits. God led His redeemed in the very heart and teeth of difficulty. I am often met by men who have been redeemed by the blood of Christ, who are truly His servants, behind whom there lies a wondrous story of deliverance, and they have come to me with complaints, and they have said, "I thought when I had given up my old sins that my life would be calm and placid, and that difficulty would be at an end; but instead, I never did in all my life go through such a sea of difficulty as I have known since I became a Christian." Friend, that is always God's way with His redeemed ones. You must not think that difficulty is a proof that you are wrong. Difficulty is most likely an evidence that you are right. Never be daunted by it. Why? Those verses we read from Deuteronomy answer the question. It is in order to humble us, to prove us, and to know what is in our heart. Difficulty is sent to humble you. If I offer my hand to a little maiden on a cold and frosty day, and she thinks she can keep her feet by herself, she is not likely to take my strong hand until she has been humbled by a tumble or two. God has been compelled to break down your self-confidence. When you started the Christian life you thought your arm was so strong it could beat down every barrier, or that you were so elastic that you could leap over any wall, or that your brain was so keen that you could see through any difficulty. God began by little difficulties, and you leapt over them; and then He put greater ones, and you successfully overcame them; and God has been compelled to pile difficulty upon difficulty until you are now face to face with a very desert on the one hand, and an Alpine range upon the other; and now broken, cowed, defeated, you are just at the very position in which to learn to appreciate, and to appropriate, the infinite resources of God. And there is another thing that difficulty does for a man. It proves him. "He made a statute and an ordinance, and proved them." There are so many counterfeits, you do not know that you have got the real thing till you have tested it. You do not know the stability of a house till it has been tested by the storm. And it is only when difficulty comes that we really know what we are. You say that you have faith. How do you know? All your life has been sunny. Wait till God hides Himself in a pavilion of cloud. You think that you obey God, but up till now the path that God has led you hath been such an easy path, through a meadow where the flowers have been bestrewn. You do not know how much you will obey until you are proved. You say you have got patience; and there is nothing sweeter than patience—the patience and gentleness of Christ. Yet you wait until you are put into the midst of trying and difficult circumstances, and then you may talk about possessing patience. And then, once more, God not only humbles and proves us, but He tries what is in our hearts; not that He needs to know, but that He may give us the opportunity of equipping ourselves for larger work. For God thus deals with us: He puts us into difficulty and watches us lovingly to see how we act, for every day He stands before His judgment bar, and every hour is the crisis of our life. If we stand the test, He says, "Come up higher," and we step up to the wider platform and plateau of usefulness. But if, on the other hand, we cannot stand the test, we step down. Will you take heart from this? Will you mind the difficulties? Oh, meet difficulty in God, and see if it be not a training-ground for great and noble work in the hereafter. But there is disappointment too. It was hard enough to have difficulty, but it was harder to be tantalized. They marched on three days; they exhausted the water they had brought, or what was left was stinking, and they could not drink it. Ah, how weary they were! Ah, you men and women, so disappointment comes to all of us. The youth has disappointments. The lad at school thinks that he is a slave, that the drudgery of Egypt was nothing compared to this. How he longs for the time when he will be his own master! And off he starts. He buries his school books, and goes forth into the world. Alas, poor lad! he finds there is no way to Canaan except by the hard plodding sultry desert march. So it is with age—mature life I mean. So it is with the young convert. They think Christian living is a great holiday, a march-past with banners and bands. But they soon find that there is a stern warfare. They are disappointed in the Church they join, they find all Christian people do not act as they thought; they are disappointed because they do not at once find sin die within them, or the devil yield, or Christianity become what they hoped, just wandering through a pleasant garden plucking flowers. (*F. B. Meyer, B.A.*) *Moses at Marah :*—I. "They could not drink of the waters of Marah, for they were bitter"—SO THE GREATEST TRIUMPHS OF LIFE MAY BE SUCCEEDED BY THE MOST VEXATIOUS INCONVENIENCES. You may be right, even when the heaviest trial is oppressing you. You may be losing your property, your health may be sinking, your prospects may be clouded, and your friends may be leaving you one by one, yet in the midst of such disasters your heart may be stedfast in faithfulness to God. II. "The people murmured against Moses"—SO THE GREATEST SERVICES OF LIFE ARE SOON FORGOTTEN. III. "And Moses cried unto the Lord"! —SO MAGNANIMOUS PRAYER IS BETTER THAN OFFICIAL RESIGNATION. All great leaderships should be intensely religious, or they will assuredly fail in the patience without which no strength can be complete. Parents, instead of resigning the oversight of your children, pray for them! Pastors, instead of resigning your official positions, pray for those who despitefully use you! All who in anywise seek to defend the weak, or lead the blind or teach the ignorant, instead of being driven off by every unreasonable murmuring, renew your patience by waiting upon God! IV. "And the Lord showed him a tree"—SO WHERE THERE IS A BANE IN LIFE THERE IS ALWAYS AN ANTIDOTE. (*J. Parker, D.D.*) *The waters of Marah :*—I. A GRIEVOUS NEED. Do we not see in mankind a weary marching host of pilgrims, looking eagerly for the next well, and hoping there to find satisfaction? It is trite but true of the greater part of them, "Man never is; but always to be blest." There are deep yearnings after unattained good; a burning desire for rest. Moreover, even to them who have found "the living waters" there may be many a weary march. II. A SORE DISAPPOINTMENT. Intense as are human desires for final good, they are doomed, so long as fixed upon created objects, to perpetual and agonizing disappointment. The apples that seemed ripe for the gathering and fit for "baskets of silver" are found to contain only rottenness and dust. It is wisely ordered that no creature should give satisfaction to the heart. Even those who have chosen "the Lord" as their "portion" need to be perpetually quickened, lest they should cleave to the dust. III. A REBELLIOUS and UNREASONABLE treatment of afflictions. "The people murmured against Moses." So men complain still. They "charge God foolishly"; and governmental measures, blights, panics, failure of success, &c., are suffered to engender their thoughts and hard speeches. IV. THE TRUE AND SURE REFUGE IN TIME OF AFFLICTION. There is no might of influence like that which is wielded by those who are "hid in the pavilion" of "the blessed and only Potentate, the King of kings and Lord of lords." V. THE DIVINE SOVEREIGNTY. When men are "willing" to see what God shows, how quickly is the bitterness of life changed into "peace and joy through believing" "Looking away unto Jesus," they hear Him saying, "I am the Lord that healeth thee!" The mystic tree is "set forth" before the eye of faith, and its goodly boughs bend to the touch even of the chief of sinners. VI. Another and most significant passage occurs in connection with Israel's sojourn by the bitter well, and which shows THE CONTINUAL OBLIGATION OF DIVINE ORDINANCES EVEN IN GREAT EXIGENCIES. "There He made for them a statute and an ordinance, and there He proved them." They were now tested as to their disposition to obey alike the stated and occasional commandments of God; and it is possible that some further instructions were conveyed on Divine authority. But "the statute and ordinance" plainly refer to the "solemn assembly" which was now to be observed. VII. Once again, we learn beside the waters of Marah the COMPENSATORY LAW OF DIVINE PROCEEDINGS. We are "pilgrims as all our fathers were," and often reach a bitter well in our march through the wilderness; but beside each there is a tree whose virtue makes the nauseous waters sweeter than all the streams of Goshen. (*J. D. Brocklehurst, D.D.*) *Bitter things made sweet :*—But we have here also the means of sweetening all bitterness. The bitterness of repentance is sweetened by this consideration, that, being a godly sorrow, it worketh a repentance unto life, which no one repenteth of. The bitterness of denying the world and self is sweetened by this, that he who renounces everything for His sake receives it again a hundredfold. The bitterness of the spiritual combat is alleviated by this, that it is the good fight of faith to which the victory and the crown of glory is held out. The bitterness of the various sufferings we have to endure is sweetened by the consideration that they are not worthy of the glory that shall be revealed; and also of the various temptations by which we are assailed, of which it is said, "Blessed is the man that endureth temptation; for after he is tried, he shall receive the crown of life, which God has promised to them that love Him." In short, this wondrous tree can sweeten all the suffering that would be otherwise intolerable. But still it is necessary that the remedy be shown and pointed out to us by the Holy Spirit. (*G.* (*D. Krummacher.*) *Marah; or, the bitter waters sweetened:*—I. THE EVILS OF THE WILDERNESS. 1. The perils and trials of the wilderness occur very early in the pilgrim life. 2. These evils assume varied shapes. 3. They touch very vital matters. God may touch you in the most beloved object of your heart. 4. There is a reason why the earthly mercies which supply our necessities must be more or less bitter. What can you hope for in a wilderness but productions congruous to it? Canaan! Who looks for bitterness there? II. THE TENDENCY OF HUMAN NATURE. 1. They murmured, complained, found fault. A very easy thing. No sense in it, no wit in it, no thought in it: it is the cry rather of a brute than of a man—murmur—just a double groan. Easy is it for us to kick against the dispensations of God, to give utterance to our griefs, and what is worse, to the inference we drew from them that God has forgotten to be gracious. To murmur is our tendency; but do we mean to let the tendencies of the old nature rule us? 2. Observe that the murmuring was not ostensibly against God. They murmured against Moses. And have you ever noticed how the most of us, when we are in a murmuring vein, are not honest enough to murmur distinctly against God. No; the child is dead, and we form a conjecture that there was some wrong treatment on the part of nurse, or surgeon, or ourselves. Or we have lost money, and have been brought down from opulence to almost poverty; then some one person was dishonest, a certain party betrayed us in a transaction by failing to fulfil his part; all the murmuring is heaped on that person. We deny, perhaps indignantly, that we murmur against God; and to prove it we double the zeal with which we murmur against Moses. To complain of the second cause is about as sensible as the conduct of the dog, which bites the sticks with which it is beaten. 3. Once more, while we speak of this tendency in human nature, I want you to observe how they betrayed an utter unbelief in God. They said unto Moses, "What shall we drink?" They meant by it, "By what means can God supply our want of water?" They were at the Red Sea, and God cleft the intervening gulf in twain, through the depths thereof they marched dryshod; there is Marah's water—shall it be more difficult for God to purify than to divide? To sweeten a fountain—is that more difficult than to cleanse a sea? Is anything too hard for the Lord? III. THE REMEDY OF GRACE. 1. Take the case of prayer to God. 2. As soon as we have a prayer, God has a remedy. "The Lord showed him a tree." I am persuaded that for every lock in Doubting Castle there is a key, but the promises are often in great confusion to our minds, so that we are perplexed. If a blacksmith should bring you his great bundle of picklocks, you would have to turn them over, and over, and over; and try half of them, perhaps two-thirds, before you would find the right one; ay, and perhaps the right one would be left to the last. It is always a blessing to remember that for every affliction there is a promise in the Word of God; a promise which meets the case, and was made on purpose for it. But you may not be always able to find it—no, you may go fumbling over the Scriptures long before you get the true word; but when the Lord shows it to you, when it comes with power to the soul, oh, what a bliss it is! 3. Now that remedy for the healing of Marah's water was a very strange one. Why should a tree sweeten the waters? This was no doubt a miraculous incident, and it was also meant to teach us something. The fruit of the tree of knowledge of good and evil was eaten by our first parents and embittered all; there is a tree of life, the leaves of which are for the healing of the nations. 4. That remedy was most effective. When they cut down the tree, and put it into the water, it turned the water sweet—they could drink of it; and let me assure you, that in the case of our trouble, the Cross is a most effective sweetener. 5. It is transcendent. The water was bitter, but it became absolutely sweet. The same water that was bitter became sweet, and the grace of God, by leading us into contemplations that spring out of the Cross of Christ, can make our trials themselves to become pleasant to us. It is a triumph of grace in the heart when we not only acquiesce in trouble, but even rejoice in it. (*C. H. Spurgeon.*) *The well of bitterness :*—I. THAT THE FIRST DAY'S JOURNEY, in spite of the splendid scenery of the coasts of the gulf, IS PROBABLY THE MOST WEARISOME AND MONOTONOUS OF THE WHOLE WAY. Sand-storms, white limestone plains, the dust caked into a hard surface intensely hot and dazzling, no water, no trees—it is as if the desert put on its dreariest dress to greet its pilgrims, and gave to them at once a full taste of the toils and wants which they must endure in traversing its wastes. And is it otherwise in life? Is not the same character impressed for us on earth and life, when we enter on its sterner era, when we leave the home of our childhood, the Egypt of our careless, half-developed youth, and go out into the wilderness, to wander freely there under the law of duty, and before the face of God. Does it not seem to all of us strange and dreary? Who ever found the first aspects of duty pleasant? Is it holiday pastime, the first grappling with the realities of life? Who has not been choked and parched by the hot dust of the great desert! though it be full of looms, and mill-wheels, and manifold activity, it is a desert at first to us before we get accustomed to its atmosphere and at home in its life. Well does the schoolboy know it, as he plods into the wilderness of study, and faints under the first experience of its dryness and dust. Let him but hold on awhile, and he will find springs and palm-trees, where he may rest and play; but it wants large faith and a goad of sharp necessity to get him through the weariness of those first days. God does not conceal from any one of us the stern conditions of our discipline. II. It is a trite saying, THAT DISAPPOINTMENT IS THE HARDEST OF ALL THINGS TO BEAR. Hardest, because it finds the soul unbraced to meet it—relaxed, at ease, and tuned to indulgence and joy. Who has not muttered "Marah" over some well in the desert, which he strained himself to reach and found to be bitterness? It strikes me that we have, in this miracle, most important suggestions as to the philosophy of all miracles. I believe that the object of all miracles is to maintain, and not to violate—to reveal, and not to confound—the order of God's world. (*J. B. Brown, B.A.*) *Marah and Elim :*—I. THE THOUGHTS SUGGESTED BY THE CHANGES HERE DESCRIBED. 1. That the life of a God-led man is full of changes in outward circumstances. 2. That these changes are divinely ordained. 3. That each change brings its own temptations. 4. That these varied changes are intended to develop all our graces. II. THOUGHTS SUGGESTED BY THE HALTING-PLACES HERE MENTIONED. 1. Marah was a place of temptation. 2. Marah was a place of disappointment. 3. Marah was a place of trustfulness and prayer. 4. Elim has its suggestiveness. God's bountiful goodness. (*A. Rowland, LL.B.*)   *The moral lessons of Marah :*— I. WE HAVE AN EXPRESSIVE TYPE OF HUMAN TRIAL IN THE BITTERNESS OF THE WATERS. 1. The bitterness of the waters disappointed their most eager expectations. 2. The bitterness of the waters left them apparently without a grand necessity of life. 3. The bitterness of the waters immediately succeeded a remarkable deliverance. II. WE HAVE UNREASONING MISTRUST OF THE DIVINE PROVIDENCE IN THE MURMURING OF THE PEOPLE. 1. Their mistrust was unreasoning, considering the person against whom they murmured. Not Moses, but God, was their Guide, as they well knew. 2. Their mistrust was unreasoning, considering the Divine promises they had received. 3. Their mistrust was unreasoning, considering the displays of Divine power which they had witnessed. III. WE HAVE AN INSTRUCTIVE APPEAL FOR DIVINE HELP IN THE PRAYER OF MOSES. 1. It indicates the importance of earnest supplication to God in all our trials. 2. It suggests the importance of a submissive spirit in supplicating deliverance from our trials. IV. WE HAVE A GRACIOUS DISPLAY OF DIVINE POWER IN THE SWEETENING OF THE WATERS. God answers prayer in the hour of trouble. 1. By influencing the mind in the direction whence relief may be obtained. 2. By transmuting the temporal affliction into a rich spiritual blessing. V. WE HAVE AN INTIMATION OF THE DESIGN OF ALL AFFLICTION IN THE DECLARED PURPOSE OF THIS PARTICULAR TRIAL. "There He proved them"— tested their faith and obedience. Afflictions prove us. 1. By discovering to us the unsatisfying nature of earthly things. 2. By disclosing the true measure of our piety. (*W. Kirkman.*) *Poisoned waters :*—What is all this, but a striking picture of human life, and of that which the grace of God can and does effect? All the waters of human life have been poisoned by sin. There is not one drop that has been left quite pure,—all has been made bitter. Much there is still which at a distance looks beautiful and refreshing; and those who walk by sense and not by faith, are often, nay, always, deceived by appearances just as Israel was. It is not until they taste for themselves that they find out the truth of Solomon's words, that all is "vanity and vexation of spirit." Look at the attractions of the world, which cause so many souls to wander. What are they all but a vain show, which can intoxicate or lull the soul for a time, but which leave it, oh, how weary and restless afterwards! The waters of the world are truly bitter waters. Or, look at the occupations of life. To some energetic spirits the very difficulty and toil of labour are attractive; but, after a while, will not the question thrust itself upon the busy mind—oh, what is the profit? what the end of all this? Suppose that everything prospers. Suppose that I have enough to satisfy every earthly want, to secure me every gratification, to encompass myself and children with every luxury. What then? There is a voice, a penetrating voice, that says, "Prepare to meet thy God!" that proclaims, "It is appointed unto men once to die, but after that the judgment." And then, what will become of me? Or, look again at the relationships of life. Instituted though they are by God, yet sin has embittered them also. Whence is it, that some of the deepest and most certain trials of life come to us? It is through our relationships and our friendships. Deep affection, sacred as it is, has always many anxieties associated with it. How many a mother's heart is gradually worn out by cares about her children! How many a father, when surveying the disturbances of his family, is impelled to adopt the words of the aged Jacob, "All these things are against me!" And then, how many a heart is left widowed even early in life, with a void which nothing earthly can ever fill! Is it too much to say that this world, viewed as it is in itself, is "Marah"? Its waters are bitter. Have not numbers who have embraced it as their all, gone down to the grave, restless, discontented and murmuring? It may seem to some as if we had invested the world with its pleasures, its occupations, and its relationships, in too thick a gloom. If so, we would remind you that we have been speaking of the world, as such, as it is in itself—of pleasures which are far from God—of business and occupation from which God is excluded—and of relationships which are put in the place of God. (*G. Wagner.*)   *Bitter waters:*—Such are often the consolations of this world. We ardently long for them, and when we obtain them they are bitter. The things we have most wished for become new sorrows. And this is to teach us to seek our true joys in God alone, to make the wilderness of this world distasteful to us, and to cause us to long for eternal life. Suppose a man to be so poor as to earn his bread with difficulty; he can scarcely provide for his family. "Ah!" he may perhaps say to himself, "if I were only like so many people around me, who are not obliged to work, and are so happy in this world!" Suppose this man to become rich; but still a prey to care, surrounded by enemies, and unhappy in his children. How many bitter sorrows are still his lot: he was once in the desert of Shur, now he is at the waters of Marah! A woman finds herself solitary and lonely; she wishes for a friend and protector; she marries. But she finds out too late that her husband is a man of bad character or of bad habits. She was in the desert, she is now at Marah. (*Professor Gaussen.*) *Sweetening the waters:*—I. MARAHS OF DISAPPOINTMENT. I. The young convert imagines that when he has got to the Cross he has got, so to speak, next door to heaven; he imagines that, once he has got pardon, he will never have another sigh; but oh! it is only a three days' march from the City of Destruction to the Slough of Despond, only a little way out to the darkness and the trouble; and then, when it comes, the young convert is sometimes tempted to look back to the delights of the old days, when he had not any fear of God before his eyes; for he has thus to learn in bitterness and disappointment that it is through much tribulation he is to be perfected for the kingdom. 2. So, too, with the mature believer; life is full of disappointments. It takes very little to turn the waters of our best comforts into bitterness; and disappointment in any case is hard to bear; but sometimes it is doubly hard when it comes upon the back of other trials. II. MARAHS OF MERCY. 1. God sends no needless trials. He does not afflict for His own pleasure, but for our good. 2. For every need God has provided the supply, for every bane the antidote. But you will not discover it yourself. He must point it out. 3. Notice the method of the Divine mercy. God does not take away the burden; He will give you more strength; and then you will have the strength, even after the burden is removed. You will be permanently the better for it. (*G. Davidson, B.Sc.*)   *The tree of healing:*—God's plans of mercy to mankind are remedial. He allows sin and suffering to exist, but He provides means for the cure of these evils. The religion of Jesus Christ is the great healing and curative influence in the world. 1. Take, for example, the bitterness of temptation. A man has made noble resolutions, formed high plans of life, and lo, he finds, to his utter mortification, that his sinful nature still yields to any blast of temptation. He is like one who has built a noble palace and finds that some foul infection renders it hateful. Before the solemn aspect of the Crucified, the powers of evil lose their fascinating glow. 2. And then there is the bitterness of remorse, the sting of remembered guilt. A German writer describes a youth who returned, after a long absence, to his home. All welcomed him with joy. Everything was done to make him happy; but he still was oppressed with a silent gloom. Some friend urged him to say what ailed him and kept him so depressed amidst their happiness, and at length, with a groan, he explained, "A sin lies heavy on my soul." But the Cross of Christ removes this bitter sorrow, for He who is our peace has nailed "the writing which was against us" to His Cross. 3. What shall we say about the bitter cup of suffering which God, in His inscrutable dealings, places in the hands of so many to drink? Yet the sufferer finds succour in remembering that his Saviour has also suffered, and for his salvation. A poor woman in a ward of one of the great London hospitals had to undergo a fearful operation, and, as a special favour, besought that it might be performed on Good Friday, which was close at hand, that the reflection on her Redeemer's agony might the better enable her to endure her own sufferings. Is the bitterness of poverty, or of contempt, our lot? So was it that of Jesus, our Lord; and turning to Him, with all confidence we appeal to His sympathy. Are we called on to feel the terrible bitterness of bereavement, to gaze on the empty cradle, or the unoccupied chair? Then think how the Cross points upward! (*W. Hardman, LL.D.*) *Anticipated pleasure alloyed :*—We look with great expectancy for the arrival of some pleasure which we imagine will afford us the most complete satisfaction, and no sooner does it arrive than we find in its train a whole host of petty annoyances and unwelcome accompaniments. It is not only so in social life, but also in the material world. Mr. Matthew Lewis, M.P., in his interesting "Journal" of a residence among the negroes in the West Indies, relates how eagerly in Jamaica, after three months of drought, the inhabitants long for rain; and when the blessing at last descends, it is accompanied by terrific thunder and lightning, and has the effect of bringing out all sorts of insects and reptiles in crowds, the ground being covered with lizards, the air filled with mosquitoes, the rooms of the houses with centipedes and legions of mosquitoes. And it will, on inquiry, be found that the enjoyment of nearly every anticipated pleasure is in like manner more or less alloyed by reason of the unpleasant things which seem inevitably to attend it. (*Scientific Illustrations.*) *We have not done with hardship when we have left Egypt :*—This may be regarded as a universal law so long as we are in the present life, and may be illustrated as really in common and secular matters as in spiritual things. The schoolboy is apt to imagine that he is a slave. He is under tutors and governors; and as he grinds away at his studies, not seeing any relation between them and what he is to do in the future, he is tempted to think that the drudgery of the Hebrews in the brickyard was nothing to that which he has to undergo, and he longs for the day when he shall be a free man and enter upon the active duties of life. His emancipation from the dry and uninteresting labours at which he has so long been held marks an epoch in his history, and he sings over it a song as sincere, if not as exalted, as that of Moses at the sea. The burial of the books by our graduating classes may be in the main a foolish freak; but yet it is the expression, in its own way, of relief from that which has hitherto been felt to be a restraint, and each of those who take part in it is intensely jubilant. But after he has entered on the active duties of the work to which he devotes himself, the youth has not gone far before he comes to Marah, and his first experience is one of disappointment. Ah! well for him then if he cries to God, and finds the healing tree which alone can sweeten its waters of bitterness! So it is, also, with every new enterprise in which a man engages. After his first victory comes something which empties it of half its glory. Pure and unmingled success is unknown in the world, and would be, let me add, a great calamity if it were to be enjoyed; for then the man would become proud and forget God, and lose all remembrance of that precious influence by which the disappointments in our experience are transmuted into means of grace. (*W. M. Taylor, D.D.*) *A valuable tree :*—The eucalyptus tree is efficacious in preventing malaria. The cause is supposed to be that its thirsty roots drain the soil for many yards around, and that its large leaves exhale an aromatic oil and intercept the malarious germs. An incident shows its efficacy: An officer in India whose troops were often attacked by sickness removed their huts to a place where several large trees grew between them and the swamp, and from that time until the trees were cut down the troops enjoyed excellent health ; afterwards sickness reappeared. It appears to be only in the case of zymotic diseases that the trees operate as a preventative, but that is of no slight value in many districts. (*Youth's Companion.*) *A heaven-sent plant :*—It is impossible for us to win any victory over this terrible evil in our own strength. Even heathen teachers acknowledge this. Many of you will remember the classic fable when Ulysses was on his way from the ship to deliver from Circe those companions of his who had been changed into swine by the power of the enchantress of sensuality, he was met by the legendary god Mercury, who told him that he would never be able to overcome the enchantress by his own sword. Mercury gave him a plant, the root of which was black and the flower of which was white, and it was by the power of this plant that he was to win his victory over the enchantress. There is a deep moral truth in that myth of the old Greek poet. We have an enchantress to contend against ; we have to contend against a mighty power that is changing our fellow-men into swine every day, and we cannot attain the victory over that power except by means of a heaven-sent plant, the Tree of Life, the blessed Cross of Christ. (*Dean Edwards.*) *Difficulties of leaders through opposition among followers :*—What a hard place was this of Moses here ! Every great reformer has had to go through a wilderness to the promised land of his success ; and always some of those who left Egypt with him have turned against him before he had gone far. I think of the almost mutiny of his men against Columbus, as, day after day, he steered westward and saw no land ; I think of the trouble which Luther and Calvin had so often with their own followers, and of the banishment at one time of the latter from that Geneva, which, even to this day, is the creation of his greatness ; I think of the curs that yelped at the heels of the Father of his country, when he was following that course which now the universal voice of posterity has applauded ; I think of the difficulties which have embarrassed many meaner men in lower works of reformation, which have at length benefited and blessed the world ; and I blush for the selfishness of those who prefer their own interest to the welfare of the community, while, at the same time, I honour the conscientious courage which determines to go on, in spite of opposition in the front and dissatisfaction in the rear. Oh ! ye who are bravely battling for the right, the pure, the benevolent, whether it be in the sweeping out of corruption from political offices, or in the closing of these pestilential houses which are feeding the intemperance of our streets, or in the maintenance in the churches of the faith once delivered to the saints—take heart of grace from Moses here. Go with your causes to the Lord, and be sure that they who are on His side are always in the end victorious. (*W. M. Taylor, D.D.*) *The sin of murmuring :* —Consider that murmuring is a mercy-embittering sin, a mercy-souring sin. As the sweetest things put into a sour vessel are soured, or put into a bitter vessel are embittered ; so murmuring puts gall and wormwood into every cup of mercy that God gives into our hands. The murmurer writes " Marah," that is, bitterness, upon all his mercies, and he reads and tastes bitterness in them all. As " to the hungry soul every bitter thing is sweet," so to the murmuring soul every sweet thing is bitter. (*T. Brooks.*) *The evil of murmuring :*—I have read of Cæsar, that, having prepared a great feast for his nobles and friends, it so fell out that the day appointed was so extremely foul, that nothing could be done to the honour of the meeting ; whereupon he was so displeased and enraged that he commanded all them that had bows to shoot up their arrows at Jupiter, their chief god, as in defiance of him for that rainy weather ; which, when they did, their arrows fell short of heaven and fell upon their own heads, so that many of them were very sorely wounded. So all our murmurings, which are as so many arrows shot at God Himself, they will return upon our own pates' hearts ; they reach not Him, but they will hit us ; they hurt not Him, but they will wound us ; therefore it is better to be mute than to murmur ; it is dangerous to provoke a " consuming fire " (Heb. xii,). (*Ibid.*) *Murmuring, the mother sin, to be fought against :*—As the king of Syria said to his captains, " Fight neither with small nor great, but with the king of Israel," so say I, Fight not so much against this sin or that, but fight against your murmuring, which is a mother-sin ; make use of all your Christian armour, make use of all the ammunition of heaven, to destroy the mother, and in destroying of her, you will destroy the daughters. When Goliath was slain, the Philistines fled ; when a general in an army is cut off, the common soldiers are easily and quickly routed and destroyed : so destroy but murmuring, and you will quickly destroy disobedience, ingratitude, impatience, distrust, &c. (*Ibid.*) *Misery of murmurers :*— Every murmurer is his own tormentor ; murmuring is a fire within that will burn up all; it is an earthquake within that will overturn all; it is a disease within that will infect all; it is poison within that will prey upon all. (*Ibid.*) *Murmuring, the parent of other sins:*—As the river Nile bringeth forth many crocodiles, and the scorpion many serpents at one birth, so murmuring is a sin that breeds and brings forth many sins at once. It is like the monster Hydra—cut off one head, and many will rise up in its room. It is the mother of harlots—the mother of all abominations—a sin that breeds many other sins (Numb. xvi. 41; xvii. 10); viz., disobedience, contempt, ingratitude, impatience, distrust, rebellion, cursing, carnality; yea, it charges God with folly, yea, with blasphemy. The language of a murmuring soul is this: Surely God might have done this sooner, and that wiser, and the other thing better. (*Ibid.*) *Murmuring, a time-destroying sin:*—The murmurer spends much precious time in musing—in musing how to get out of such a trouble, how to get off such a yoke, how to be rid of such a burden, how to revenge himself for such a wrong; how to supplant such a person, how to reproach those that are above him, and how to affront those that are below him; and a thousand other ways murmurers have to expend that precious time that some would redeem with a world. Cæsar, observing some ladies at Rome to spend much of their time in making much of little dogs and monkeys, asked them whether the women in that country had no children to make much of. Ah, murmurers, murmurers! you who by your murmuring trifle away so many golden hours and seasons of mercy, have you no God to honour? Have you no Christ to believe in? Have you no hearts to change, no sin to be pardoned, no souls to save, no hell to escape, no heaven to seek after? Oh! if you have, why do you spend so much of your precious time in murmuring against God, against men, against this or that thing? (*Ibid.*) *Murmuring at joys:*—I was tired of washing dishes; I was tired of drudgery. It had always been so, and I was dissatisfied. I never sat down a moment to read that Jamie didn't want a cake, or a piece of paper to scribble on, or a bit of soap to make bubbles. "I'd rather be in prison," I said one day, "than to have my life teased out," as Jamie knocked my elbow, when I was writing to a friend. But a morning came when I had one plate less to wash, one chair less to set away by the wall in the dining-room; when Jamie's little crib was put away in the garret, and it has never come down since. I had been unusually fretful and discontented with him that damp May morning that he took the croup. Gloomy weather gave me the headache, and I had less patience than at any other time. By and by he was singing in another room, "I want to be an angel," and presently rang out that metallic cough. I never hear that hymn since that it don't cut me to the heart; for the croup-cough rings out with it. He grew worse towards night, and when my husband came home he went for the doctor. At first he seemed to help him, but it merged into inflammatory croup, and all was soon over. "I ought to have been called in sooner," said the doctor. I have a servant to wash the dishes now; and when a visitor comes, I can sit down and entertain her without having to work all the time. There is no little boy worrying me to open his jack-knife, and there are no shavings over the floor. The magazines are not soiled at looking over the pictures, but stand prim and neat on the reading-table just as I leave them. "Your carpet never looks dirty," said a weary-worn mother to me. "Oh! no," I mutter to myself, "there are no little boots to dirty it now." But my fate is as weary as theirs—weary with sitting in my lonesome parlour at twilight, weary with watching for the arms that used to twine around my neck, for the curls that brushed against my cheek, for the young laugh that rang out with mine, as we watched the blazing fire, or made rabbits with the shadow on the wall, waiting merrily together for papa coming home. I have the wealth and ease I longed for, but at what a price! And when I see other mothers with grown-up sons, driving to town or church, and my hair silvered over with grey, I wish I had murmured less. *Murmuring foolish:*—Seneca hath his similitude to set out the great evil of murmuring under small afflictions. Suppose, saith he, a man to have a very fair house to dwell in, with very fair orchards and gardens, set about with brave tall trees for ornament; what a most unreasonable thing were it in this man to murmur because the wind blows a few leaves off the trees, though they hang full of fruit. If God take a little and give us much, shall we be discontent? If He take our son and give us His own; if He cause the trees to bring forth the fruit, shall we be angry if the wind blow away the leaves? (*J. Venning.*) *Murmuring injurious:*—It is not wise to fret under our trials: the high-mettled horse that is restive in the yoke only galls his shoulder—the poor bird that dashes itself against the bars of the cage only ruffles her feathers and aggravates the sufferings of captivity.   **The Lord that**

healeth thee.—*Jehovah-Ropheka :*—No human experience is uniformly joyful or sorrowful. A great triumph is succeeded by a great obstacle and sometimes by a great defeat. But there is another equally constant fact to offset this. As we look at this alternation of Elims and Marahs in our life, and recognize it as a law of our human experience, we find it supplemented by something else which is equally a law; and that is the economy of God by which this alternation is happily adjusted. In other words, I mean this: that if it is a law of our life that joy and sorrow succeed each other, it is equally a law of our life that God interposes and keeps the joy from corrupting and the sorrow from crushing us. If sorrow is a part of God's economy, healing is equally a part. You hear abundance of popular proverbs to the effect that clouds have often silver linings; that calamity usually stops short of the very worst; that time dulls grief; that nature reacts from its depression, and much more of the same sort, all which may be more or less true, but which do not cover the same ground as this blessed name, " Jehovah that healeth thee " : which throw man for his compensation for sorrow merely upon nature and circumstances. Both are lawless and accidental, the alleviations no less than the sorrow itself. But there is a radical difference between a grief which is accidental, and a grief which falls in with happier things into an order arranged to make the man purer and more blessed. There is a radical difference between accidental mitigations, and the firm, wise, tender touch of an omnipotent Healer upon a sorrow : and there is a radical difference between that conception of sorrow which makes it an intrusion and an interruption, and a conception which sees both sorrow and healing as parts of one Divine plan, adjusted by that same Divine hand all along the line of man's life. With the alleviations of sorrow which come in what we call the natural order of things, I have therefore nothing to do here. That nature has certain recuperative powers is a familiar fact : that God often uses these or other natural means in His own processes of healing, as a physician uses for medicine the herbs and flowers which he gathers by the roadside, is an equally familiar fact. But we are not concerned with the question of means. Our text leads us back of the means. That to which alone sorrow can grapple securely is not means but God. God, on this occasion, though He uses a branch to sweeten the water, also uses it to direct the attention of the people to Himself. When He gives Himself a name by which they are to know and remember Him all through this desert journey, it is not, " the God of the branch," nor " the God of the rod," nor " the God of the strong east wind," but simply, " I am Jehovah that healeth thee." No matter what means I use. If He had called Himself the God of the rod, the people would have despaired of healing in any case where there was not a branch or a rod present. He would have them know that healing was in Him, by any means or by no means as He might choose. And thus it is well for us to bring every bitter experience of life at once to God— directly. The fountain of healing is there, and there is no need of our taking the smallest trouble in seeking any lower source of comfort. God is not like certain great medical authorities who leave all minor maladies to subordinates and hold themselves in reserve merely for consultation on cases of life and death. He wrought the great miracle at Marah, not only to relieve the people's thirst on that occasion, but to encourage them to seek His help in smaller matters. God sometimes reduces a man to terrible straits so that he may learn that lesson. The branch which he throws in is this : " Rest in the Lord and wait patiently for Him." When one is in such confusion and bewilderment, a great deal of the distress is thrown off in the throwing off of all responsibility for the way out. Many years ago, while in Rome, I went down into the Catacombs. I had not gone five feet from the entrance when I saw that if I should try to find my way back, I should be hopelessly lost. Passages opened out on every side, and crossed and interlaced, and my life was literally in the hands of the cowled monk who led the way with his lighted taper. But that was a relief. Having no responsibility for finding the way, and having faith in my guide, I could give myself up to the impression of the place. There is a beautiful passage in the one hundred and forty-second Psalm which brings out this truth. The Psalm is ascribed to David when he was fleeing from Saul's persecution and wandering in a labyrinth of caves and secret paths. "When my spirit is overwhelmed within me, Thou knowest my path." Few things are more painful or humiliating than the sense of having lost the way. The sweetening branch then is just this blessed consciousness that Divine omniscience knows the path ; that the knowledge is with one who knows just how to use it, who knows the path through, the path out, knows what the trend of the trouble is and what its meaning is. But let us not forget the other great truth of this story, a truth quite as important as the first, and perhaps quite as hard to learn ; and that is, that God's healing is a lesson no less than a comfort. The aim of a physician's treatment is not merely to relieve his patient from pain. It is, further, to get him on his feet for active duty. God did not sweeten the waters of Marah in order that the people might stay there. Marah was only a stage on the way to Canaan ; and the draught at the sweetened spring was but to give strength for a long march. And God never heals His people simply to make them easy. If He takes off a load it is that they may walk the better in the way of His commandments. Whatever God may say to us by sickness, when He comes to us as the Lord of healing He says, " I will raise thee up that thou mayst do that which is right in My sight ; that thou mayst give ear to My commandments and keep My statutes." Healing means more toil and more burdens and more conflict, and these will continue to the end. But let us remember that God never forgets to give rest along the road, and refreshment at the right places to His faithful ones. Even on earth there will be intervals of sweet rest, though the desert lie on beyond. (*M. R. Vincent, D.D.*) *The Lord that healeth :*—It is with healing power in the lowest form of its development, viz., the supplying of bodily wants—the healing of physical diseases—that this precious name is first brought to our notice. And even this is a blessing not to be lightly esteemed. But, if our powers of perception were so adjusted that we could estimate spiritual diseases, as God estimates them ; then, we should see, in the walks of daily life, even in the case of those who are said to possess sound minds in sound bodies, sights sadder far than any to be met with in our hospitals and asylums for physical and mental diseases. And the power to heal which the Lord claims when He is pleased to reveal Himself as Jehovah-Ropheka, is this power in its higher form—the power to heal the diseases of the soul. I. HE IS AN EFFICIENT HEALER. He puts His own Omnipotence into the grace by which He heals ; and what can resist that grace ? He has fathomed the lowest depths of human depravity, and the chain of His grace has reached even unto that. II. HE IS A PRACTICAL HEALER. It sometimes happens with earthly physicians that the medicine is mingled with our daily food, and that the food itself of which the patient partakes is made the means of healing. But this is what our heavenly Healer does continually. He connects the process of His healing with the food on which the souls of His people live, and the daily experience of life through which they are passing. III. HE IS A UNIVERSAL HEALER. In many of our hospitals there is a ward for incurables. There are cases which every physician will decline to undertake because he knows that nothing can be done with them. But Jehovah-Ropheka knows no such cases. In the hospital of His grace there is no ward for incurables. There are no limits to the range and operation of His wisdom and power. He has not made a specialty of any particular case. There is no form of spiritual disease that can be incurable to Him. IV. HE IS A PERMANENT HEALER. No earthly physician will undertake both to restore his patient to health, and at the same time to give him the assurance that the disease from which he has suffered shall never return to him. This is a matter quite beyond the reach of ordinary medical ability. But it is not so with our heavenly Healer. He undertakes to make His healing work not only perfect but permanent. Two things show us this. 1. One of these is the state into which Christ introduces the saved soul after death. It is a state in which there will be no sickness, sorrow, or sin. And what that state is, as the healed soul enters into it, it will be for ever. It is a " continuing city." 2. And then the state of the soul as it enters that blessed abode will show the same thing. " Presented perfect in Christ Jesus " (Col. i. 28). V. HE IS A GLORIOUS HEALER. Most physicians are satisfied if they can restore their patients to the condition in which they were before the disease seized upon them. If they can heal a man's wounds they are satisfied. They will not pledge that in securing this result there shall be no disfiguring scars remaining. But it is different with our heavenly Healer. He restores the sin-sick soul, not to its original state, but to one infinitely better than that. The creation state of the soul was pronounced good, the redeemed state of the soul is declared to be perfect. (*R. Newton, D.D.*) *The Lord that healeth :*—" Many a time have I been brought very low, and received the sentence of death in myself, when my poor, honest, praying neighbours have met, and, upon their fasting and earnest prayers, I have recovered. Once, when I had continued weak three weeks, and was unable to go abroad, the very day that they prayed for me, being Good Friday, I recovered, and was able to preach and administer the sacrament the next Lord's day ; and was better after it, it being the first time that ever I administered it. And ever after that, whatever weakness was upon me, when I had, after preaching, administered that sacrament to many hundred people, I was much revived and eased of my infirmities." "Oh how often," he writes in his "Dying Thoughts," "have I cried to Him when men and means were nothing, and when no help in second causes did appear, and how often, and suddenly, and mercifully hath He delivered me! What sudden ease, what removal of long affliction have I had! Such extraordinary changes, and beyond my own and others' expectations, when many plain-hearted, upright Christians have, by fasting and prayer, sought God on my behalf, as have over and over convinced me of special providence and that God is indeed a hearer of prayers. And wonders have I seen done for others also, upon such prayer, more than for myself; yea, and wonders for the Church, and for public societies." "Shall I therefore forget how often He hath heard prayers for me, and how wonderfully He often hath helped both me and others? My faith hath been helped by such experiences, and shall I forget them, or question them without cause at last?" (*Richard Baxter.*)   **Elim.**—*The pilgrim's pathway* :—I. THAT, IN LIFE'S PILGRIMAGE, GOD CROWNS HIS PEOPLE WITH CONSTANT BLESSINGS AND DIVERSIFIED TOKENS OF HIS GOODNESS. These blessings, as here implied, are of great practical utility; they are—1. Essential—"Water." 2. Refreshing—"Palm-trees." 3. Diversified—"Wells and palm-trees." 4. Proportionate,—"Twelve wells and threescore and ten palm-trees." II. THAT, IN LIFE'S PILGRIMAGE, GOD'S BLESSINGS SHOULD BE APPROPRIATED AND ENJOYED. "They encamped there." III. THAT, IN LIFE'S PILGRIMAGE, ELIM, WITH ITS REFRESHING SHADE, IS FREQUENTLY NOT FAR FROM MARAH, WITH ITS BITTER WATERS. Therefore, as pilgrims, we should not be too much elated or depressed with our camping-places. In the history of the Zion-bound traveller, it should not be forgotten, that it is always better further on. IV. THAT, IN LIFE'S PILGRIMAGE, WE SHOULD REMEMBER THAT WE ARE NOT YET HOME, ONLY PILGRIMS ON THE WAY. Our immortality would starve to death on the richest oasis this desert world could give us, if we should attempt to make it our abiding home. So, they did not buy the land, or build a city, they only "encamped there." (*T. Kelly.*)   *Marah and Elim :*—I. THE VARIED EXPERIENCE OF HUMAN LIFE. 1. There are the sorrowful scenes of life. You know well the sources from whence these sorrows arise. There is the sorrow that comes to us from our disappointments. We are constantly deceived and disappointed, partly because we indulge in unreasonable expectations, and partly because things differ so much in their reality from what they are in their outward appearance. Then there is the sorrow that proceeds from physical suffering. Another source of sorrow is our bereavements. A whole generation fell in the wilderness, and as the Israelites travelled onward, they had again and again to pause in their journey and bury their dead. Another source of sorrow is sin. This indeed is the great source of all sorrow, the fountain from whence these bitter waters flow. 2. There are the joys of life. Another day's march, and the scene was changed; verdure refreshed the eye, there was water in abundance to quench the thirst, and the weary pilgrim could repose under the palm-tree's welcome shade. True type again of human life—"Weeping endures for a night, joy cometh in the morning." "For a small moment have I forsaken thee, but with great mercies will I gather thee." The most weary pilgrimage has its quiet resting-places, and the saddest heart is not without its joys. God is kind even to the unthankful, for on them He bestows His providential bounties, but "the secret of the Lord is with them that fear Him." He gives to them a "peace which passeth understanding," a "hope which maketh not ashamed," and "a joy that is unspeakable and full of glory." Life, then, has a varied experience. II. BUT WHAT ARE THE REASONS FOR IT? There can be little doubt that if it were left to our choice, we should choose a less chequered course—we should avoid the bitter waters of Marah, and seek the palm-trees of Elim. Why is it that joy and sorrow, hope and fear, health and sickness, blessings bestowed and blessing removed, follow each other in such rapid succession. 1. It is to correct our self-will. Many whose hearts were stubborn enough when they began life, have found life so different to what they expected, that they have at length confessed—It is vain to fight against God; henceforth I place myself under His government—His will, not mine, be done. 2. To develop our character. If the events of life were exclusively sorrowful, then the test of our character would be but partial; so would it be if these events were exclusively joyful; and therefore it is sorrow to-day and joy to-morrow. Thus our whole character is developed. 3. To open our hearts to those sacred influences which soften and purify them. (*H. J. Gamble.*)   *Elim : the springs and the palms :*

—I. Elim rises before us as the representative of the green oases, THE SPOTS OF SUNNY VERDURE, the scenes of heavenly beauty, WHEREWITH GOD HATH ENRICHED, though sparingly, OUR WILDERNESS WORLD. This world is not all bad; its marches are not all bare. " Cursed is the ground for thy sake "—and because for thy sake, it is not cursed utterly. It is not all black, bare, lifeless, as the crust of a cold lava flood; a prison-house for reprobates, instead of a training school for sons. II. THE NEARNESS OF ELIM TO MARAH OPENS UP TO US A DEEP TRUTH IN THE SPIRITUAL HISTORY OF MAN. 1. Had they pushed on instead of murmuring at Marah, they would have found all they sought, and more than they hoped for, at Elim. Ah! the time we waste in repining and rebelling—scheming to mend God's counsels! How many Elims would it find for us, if employed in courage and faith! 2. How near is the sweetness to the bitterness in every trial! it is but a short step to Elim, where we may encamp and rest. The brightest spots of earth are amidst its most savage wildernesses, and the richest joys of the Christian spring ever out of his sharpest pains. The humbling pains of disappointment tune the soul for the joys which the next station of the journey affords. It is when we have learnt the lessons of the wilderness, and are resolved to press on, cost what it may, in our heavenly path, that springs of unexpected sweetness gush up at our very feet, and we find shade and rest, which give foretaste of heaven. III. Let us endeavour to DIS-CERN THE PRINCIPLE OF THIS ALTERNATE SWEETNESS AND BITTERNESS OF LIFE. These lights and shadows of nature, this glow and gloom, are caught from a higher sphere. Nature is but the reverse of the medal whose obverse is man. The ultimate reason of the bitterness of Marah is the sin in the heart of Israel and all pilgrims; the ultimate reason of the sweetness and freshness of Elim is the mercy that is in the heart of God. There is a fearful power in the human spirit to make God's brightest blessings bitter curses. Who was it who wanted to die, because God had found a deliverance for a great city in which were half a million of doomed men? At the door of your own spirit lie all the pangs and wretchedness you have known. You have cursed fate and fortune, and protested that you were the most wronged and persecuted of men. But the mischief lies not in God's constitution of the world, nor in His government of it, but in your hearts. (*J. B. Brown, B.A.*) *Sweetness not far from bitterness :*—Sorrow is not all a wilderness, even to the most sorrowful. Amid all its bleakness and desolation it has oases of beauty and fertility. It has Elims as well as Marahs, and frequently these Elims are very near the Marahs—if we only knew it. But six short miles separated the twelve wells of water and the three-score and ten palm-trees from the bitter, nauseous well that filled the hearts of the thirsting multitudes with disappointment. And so near in human life is the sweetness to the bitterness in every trial. A few steps will take us through the valley of the shadow of death out into the green pastures and beside the still waters upon which it opens. Had the Israelites of old, instead of murmuring at Marah, pushed on a little further, they would, in two short hours, have found at Elim all they sought and more than they expected. And so the time we waste in repining and rebelling would be better employed in living faith and active duty, for thus would consolation be found. Instead of sitting down to murmur at Marah, let us march in faith under the guidance of our tender Shepherd, who will bring us to the next station, where we may lie down in green pastures and beside still waters. (*Christian Age.*) *The comparative duration of sorrow and joy :*—Is there ever a Marah without an Elim near it, if only we follow on in the way the Lord marks out for us through the wilderness? The notice of Elim occupies less than four lines, while there are as many verses in the record of Marah, and a whole chapter following about the wilderness of sin; and we are apt to draw the hasty inference that the bitter experiences were the rule, and the delightful ones the exception. And so it often seems in the checkered life of the tried disciple of the Lord. But look again. The bitter time at Marah was quite short, though it occupies a great deal of space in the history. These four verses tell the story probably of as many hours or less. But the four lines about Elim are the story of three weeks, during which they " encamped there by the waters." When troubles come, the time seems long; when troubles have gone, the time seems short; and so many are apt to think that they are hardly dealt with, whereas if they would look more carefully into the Lord's dealings with them, they might find that they have far more to be thankful for than to grieve over. Hours at Marah are followed by weeks at Elim. (*J. M. Gibson, D.D.*)

CHAPTER XVI.

VERS. 1–12. **The wilderness of Sin.**—*Moses in the wilderness of Sin:*—People may be strong and hopeful at the beginning of a project, and most effusively and devoutly thankful at its close, but the difficulty is to go manfully through the process. 1. PROCESSES TRY MEN'S TEMPER. See how the temper of Israel was tried in the wilderness! No bread, no water, no rest! How do processes try men's temper? 1. They are often tedious. 2. They are often uncontrollable. 3. They often seem to be made worse by the incompetency of others. II. THE TRIALS OF PROCESSES ARE TO BE MET, NOT ALL AT ONCE, BUT A DAY AT A TIME. Daily hunger was met by daily bread. This daily display of Divine care teaches—1. That physical as well as spiritual gifts are God's. 2. That one of God's gifts is the pledge of another. "Not as the world giveth, give I unto you." Why am I to be easy about to-morrow? Because God is good to-day! "He is the same yesterday, and to-day, and for ever." III. PROCESSES SHOW THE DIFFERENT DISPOSITIONS OF MEN. Though the people were told in the distinctest manner that there would be no manna on the seventh day, yet they went out to gather it just as if they had never been warned! Such men are the vexation of the world. They plague every community of which they are a portion. 1. We have the means of life at our disposal: the manna lies at our tent-door! 2. We are distinctly assured that such means are given under law: there is a set time for the duration of the opportunity: the night cometh! IV. ALL THE PROCESSES OF LIFE SHOULD BE HALLOWED BY RELIGIOUS EXERCISES. There was a Sabbath even in the wilderness. 1. The Sabbath is more than a mere law; it is an expression of mercy. 2. No man ever loses anything by keeping the Sabbath: "The Lord giveth you on the sixth day the bread of two days." 3. He is the loser who has no day of rest. V. PROCESSES SHOULD LEAVE SOME TENDER AND HOPE-INSPIRING MEMORIES BEHIND THEM. "Fill an omer of it to be kept," &c. VI. THE PROCESS WILL END. Are you ready? (*J. Parker, D.D.*) *The pilgrimage of life:*—In the anecdote books of our boyhood we used to be told the story of an Indian faquir who entered an Eastern palace and spread his bed in one of its ante-chambers, pretending that he had mistaken the building for a caravanserai or inn. The prince, amused by the oddity of the circumstance, ordered—so ran the tale—the man to be brought before him, and asked him how he came to make such a mistake. "What is an inn?" the faquir asked. "A place," was the reply, "where travellers rest a little while before proceeding on their journey." "Who dwelt here before you?" again asked the faquir. "My father," was the prince's reply. "And did he remain here?" "No," was the answer; "he died and went away." "And who dwelt here before him?" "His ancestors." "And did they remain here?" "No; they also died and went away." "Then," rejoined the faquir, "I have made no mistake, for your palace is but an inn after all." The faquir was right. Our houses are but inns, and the whole world a caravanserai. (*Clerical Library.*) *Bread, the supreme question:*—During the French Revolution hundreds of market-women, attended by an armed mob of men, went to Versailles to demand bread of the National Assembly, there being great destitution in Paris. They entered the hall. There was a discussion upon the criminal laws going on. A fishwoman cried out, "Stop that babbler! That is not the question; the question is about bread." (*Little's "Historical Lights."*) *Murmuring, the result of forgetfulness:*—What unbelief and sad forgetfulness of God betrayed itself in these words! They quite forgot the bitter bondage of Egypt under which they had sighed and groaned so long. They now thought only of its "flesh-pots" and "its bread." They altogether overlooked the mercy and the grace which had spared them when the firstborn of the Egyptians were slain. The miracles of love at the Red Sea and at Marah, so great and so recent, had passed away from their memories. They thought nothing of the promise of the land flowing with milk and honey. The argument, so evident and so comforting, "Can the faithful God who has brought us out of bondage mean to let us perish in the wilderness?" did not withhold them from the impatient conclusion, "Ye have brought us forth into the wilderness, to kill this whole assembly with hunger." And if you watch your own hearts, you will find that there is always this forgetfulness in a murmuring and discontented spirit. We forget, first, that we deserve nothing but punishment at God's hands; and, secondly, we forget all the mercy and love which He has shown us in His acts and promises. (*G. Wagner.*) *Grumbling, an added* *burden :*—If I grumble because life is so arranged that I tear my clothes, and get many a scratch in the upward journey, my grumble is only an added burden. The difference between a soul that is soured by unbelief and a soul that honestly struggles and strives as the gymnast does, who tries to lift the heavy weight, knowing that, whether he succeeds or fails, the muscular development, which is the end sought, is still attained, is incalculable.   To trudge along the moor after nightfall, the: now knee deep, with the feeling that you are going nowhere, is indeed discouraging ; but to do the same thing with the feeling that you are going home to the fireside of the loved and expectant, is to keep both feet and hands warm through our power of anticipating the heat and the welcome under the roof tree not far off.   Rude, discourteous experience has taught us that an evil which is all an evil is a double evil, and that an evil with a joy behind it or beyond it is the healthy and invigorating toil by means of which a man may acquire a lasting good.   *Ingratitude of the public :*—Daniel Webster, after his wonderful career, and in the close of his life, writes : "If I were to live my life over again, with my present experiences, I would under no considerations allow myself to enter public life.   The public are ungrateful.   The man who serves the public most faithfully receives no adequate reward.   In my own history those acts which have been, before God, most disinterested and the least stained by selfish considerations, have been precisely those for which I have been most freely abused.   No, no ; have nothing to do with politics.   Sell your iron, eat the bread of independ-ence, support your family with the rewards of honest toil, do your duty as a private citizen to your country, but let politics alone.   It is a hard life, a thank-less life.   I have had in the course of my political life, which is not a short one, my full share of ingratitude, but the 'unkindest cut of all,' the shaft that has sunk the deepest in my heart, has been the refusal of this administration to grant my request for an office of small pecuniary consideration for my only son."   (*T. De Witt Talmage*)   *Ingratitude of grumbling :*—I heard a good man say once, as we passed the home of a millionaire : "It doesn't seem right that such a man as he is should be rolling in wealth, while I have to work hard for my daily bread."   I made no reply.   But when we reached the home of the grumbler, and a troop of rosy children ran out to meet us, I caught one in my arms, and, holding him up, said : "John, how much will you take for this boy ?"   And he answered, while the moisture gathered in his eyes : "That boy, my namesake! I wouldn't sell him for his weight in gold."   "Why, John, he weighs forty pounds at least, and forty pounds of gold would make you many times a millionaire.   And you would probably ask as much for each of the others.   So, according to your own admission, you are immensely rich.   Yes, a great deal richer than that cold, selfish, childless millionaire whom you were envying as we came along.   Nothing would tempt you to change places with him.   Then you ought to be grateful instead of grumbling.   You are the favourite of fortune, or, rather, of Providence, and not he."   (*H. W. Beecher.*)

Ver. 4. **That I may prove them.**—*Life a probation :*—There can be nothing more sobering than the truth that this life is a state of trial and preparation for another. There is at the same time something wonderfully satisfying in the idea.   It puts life before us in a point of view which satisfactorily explains it.   I. THIS ACCOUNT OF THE END OF LIFE SIMPLIFIES MATTERS IN OUR JOURNEY THROUGH LIFE.   The principle of trial as the end of life shoves aside a multiplicity of irrevelent ends to make way for the true one ; it reduces the purpose of life to the greatest possible simplicity, reduces it, as we may say, to a unit—to the effect upon the individual himself, what he does and how he turns out under these circumstances.   The idea of probation thus gives a singular unity to the whole design and plan of life.   It throws the individual upon himself as the rational of the whole.   II. The principle of the end of life being probative applies mainly to all the ordinary external advantages of life and our pursuit of them ; but it also affects another and less ordinary class of human objects—THE OBJECTS CONNECTED WITH THE GOOD OF OTHERS, THOSE USEFUL AND BENEVOLENT WORKS AND THOSE PUBLIC AND RELIGIOUS WORKS WHICH GOOD MEN PROPOSE TO THEMSELVES.   There is one defect to which good men are liable : they become to much absorbed in the success of their own plans.   The important truth for such men to realize is this very principle, viz., that of the end of life being trial.   If they brought this truth home to themselves, they would see that the only important thing to them was, not that a useful undertaking should answer, but that they should have done faithfully their best for that purpose.   III.

God makes use of us as His instruments, but THE WORK THAT WE DO AS INSTRUMENTS IS A FAR INFERIOR WORK TO THAT WHICH WE DO TO FULFIL OUR OWN PERSONAL TRIAL. The general end of life, as trial, is superior to all special ends; it is the end which concerns the individual being, his spiritual condition, his ultimate prospects. (*Prof. J. B. Mozley.*) *The Divine bestowal of physical good :*—I. PHYSICAL BLESSINGS ARE GIVEN TO SUPPLY OUR WANTS. 1. This provision was providential. God's hand directs the movements of the tiniest creatures in the universe. He clothes the grass, and paints the flower. 2. This provision was abundant. There was enough for each man, woman, and child. (1) The supply was varied—bread and meat. (2) The supply was regular—morning and evening. (3) The supply was constant— "They did eat manna for forty years." God's least thought is more prolific than man's greatest abundance. Nature is the expression of God's fulness. II. PHYSICAL BLESSINGS ARE GIVEN TO DEVELOP OUR ENERGIES. 1. The blessings of life must be secured by diligent application. "Go out and gather." No prize is beyond the reach of the earnest worker. 2. The blessings of life must be sought in a patient spirit. "A certain portion every day." We want to accumulate the treasures of life quickly, to provide in youth for age, and retire upon our gains. God does not forbid prudence, foresight; but He sometimes overturns our plans, and sends day by day our daily bread. To the anxious, fearful soul, He says, "Gather," "Trust." III. PHYSICAL BLESSINGS ARE GIVEN TO TEST OUR OBEDIENCE. "That I may prove them, whether they will walk in My law, or no." God has many ways of testing the sincerity of His people. He proves them by poverty, affliction, persecution, and prosperity. He spreads our tables with dainties, and says, I will test their love, and liberality, and devotion. 1. The recipients of material possessions often hoard their wealth. Hoarded wealth never satisfies the possessor. It begets selfishness, fear, unrest, and disappointment. 2. The recipients of material possessions often squander their wealth. (*J. T. Woodhouse.*) *The manna a test of faith :*—"That I may prove them, whether they will walk in My law, or no." How did the manna become a test of this? By means of the law prescribed for gathering it. There was to be a given quantity daily, and twice as much on the sixth day. If a man trusted God for to-morrow, he would be content to stop collecting when he had filled his omer, tempting as the easily gathered abundance would be. Greed and unbelief would masquerade then, as now, under the guise of prudent foresight. The old Egyptian parallels to "make hay while the sun shines," and such like wise sayings of the philosophy of distrust, would be solemnly spoken, and listened to as pearls of wisdom. When experience had taught that, however much a man gathered, he had no more than his omer full, after all—and is not that true yet?—then the next temptation would be to practise economy, and have something over for to-morrow. Only he who absolutely trusted God to provide for him, would eat up his portion, and lie down at night with a quiet heart, knowing that He who had fed him would feed. When experience taught that what was saved rotted, then laziness would come in, and say, "What is the use of gathering twice as much on the sixth day? Don't we know that it will not keep?" So the whole of the gift was a continual training, and therefore a continual test, for faith. God willed to let His gifts come in this hand-to-mouth fashion, though He could have provided at once what would have obviously lasted them all their wilderness life, in order that they might be habituated to cling to Him, and that their daily bread might be doubly for their nourishment, feeding their bodies, and strengthening that faith which, to them as to us, is the condition of all blessedness. God lets our blessings, too, trickle to us drop by drop, instead of pouring them in a flood all at once upon us, for the same reason. He does so, not because of any good to Him, from our faith, except that the Infinite love loves infinitely to be loved. But for our sakes, that we may taste the peace and strength of continual dependence, and the joy of continual receiving. He could give us the principal down; but He prefers to pay us the interest as we need it. Christianity does not absolutely forbid laying up money or other resources for future wants. But the love of accumulating, which is so strong in many professing Christians, and the habit of amassing beyond all reasonable future wants, is surely scarcely permitted to those who profess to believe that incarnate wisdom forbade taking anxious care for the morrow, and sent its disciples to lilies and birds to learn the happy immunities of faith. We, too, get our daily mercies to prove us. The letter of the law for the manna is not applicable to us who gain our bread by God's blessing on our labour. But the spirit is, and the members of great commercial nations have surely little need to be reminded that still the portion put away is apt to breed worms. How often it vanishes! Or, if it lasts, tortures its owner, who has more trouble keeping it than he had in getting it; or fatally corrupts his own character, or ruins his children. All God's gifts are tests, which—thanks be to Him—is the same as to say that they are means of increasing faith, and so adding joy. (*A. Maclaren, D.D.*)

Vers. 13-15. **Manna.**—*The manna :*—I. ITS MYSTIC CHARACTER. "What is this?" Christ was a mystery to His contemporaries. So is the Christian to his. "The world knoweth you not." II. ITS USES. To save from starvation, famine, and death. Christ is "the Bread that cometh down from heaven." 1. The manna was for all. 2. The manna was for all, according to their wants—appetites. The Saviour is to us just what we make Him to be. All fulness dwells in Him, infinite satisfaction; but we are straitened in ourselves, by our limited cravings, &c. III. THE PRESCRIPTIONS ATTENDING IT. 1. To be gathered early. 2. To be gathered every morning. "They that wait upon the Lord shall renew their strength." 3. To be used. 4. To be gathered within six days. Life has its appointed time for salvation. If we allow the end of life's week to come without a store of God's manna, we shall find none in the future. 5. To be gathered for others—for those who could not go out themselves. (*F. R. Young.*) *The manna :*—An army must have a commissary department well administered. The ordnance, or recruiting, or medical, divisions are not more essential to its existence, whether in peace or war. A soldier's pay is but a trifle compared with the expense of maintaining him in vigour. Yet a more strange venture and gross neglect would seem to be recorded in the early history of Israel than has ever since been seen. Here were some two million souls led out of bondage, of whom it is said : "They had not prepared for themselves any victual." Every hour increased the peril and the need. Desperation was in their threats. Bread-riots have always been the fiercest outbreaks. The great camp was on the verge of mutiny. I. THE LORD DID DAILY AND AMPLY PROVIDE FOR HIS PEOPLE. The fact of abundant food is clear and indisputable. There is no hint, however, as to its immediate source or methods of distribution. A similar mystery veils the agencies through which we find our present necessities met. Here the natural and the supernatural seem to work together. The political economist makes them his study, and extremists undertake to tell exactly how the nations of the earth are kept alive. The farmer, manufacturer, artisan, carrier, trader, accountant, teacher, labouring with hand or head, or both—each furnishing just that without which the rest must languish—constitute a most complex problem. Laplace set himself at no such intricate task when attempting the solution of the solar system. We fall back on the conviction that while none can see the vast organism, or all the forces which are operative in it, yet it does move by an instinctive impulse under a beneficent direction whose secrets none can wrest, whose failure no one can imagine. The suspension of one class of labourers affects, more or less, every other. But to trace, or tell, the infinite processes through which every person in the land finds daily that which will maintain the body and restore its energies, as they are constantly spent, is beyond the ability of any mortal. Over all is He upon whom all eyes, though so blind, wait. Men call Him God, or Nature, or Chance, or Law, each term being somewhat of a cloak for their ignorance. II. THE LORD REQUIRED EACH MAN TO PROVIDE FOR HIMSELF. The combined wisdom and efforts of men could not create a grain of corn. Yet each and all must gather for themselves. The increase will vary as occasions and necessities do. But how often has the world seen that they who would for their own selfish ends heap up their stores find to their surprise and horror that it breeds only loathsome and hateful forms of death! Capital, unscrupulously held and wielded, is becoming the terror even of its possessors. Vast fortunes have generally proved vast vexations, while Agur's prayer, "Give me neither poverty nor riches," &c., seems to have its happiest answer in the state of those who are most observant of these very precepts given to Israel. To idle, or hoard, or squander, or fret, is sin now as then. III. THE LORD PUT SPECIAL HONOUR ON THE SEVENTH. Good doctrine still, neither abrogated nor superseded, ye buoy men in these days of railroads, and steamships, and telegraphs, and fast mails, and Sunday papers, and apoplectic fits! Feel you not the Almighty hand on these flying wheels, bringing them to pause? Will you say, we *must* work a few of these forbidden hours to gain reprieve for the rest? Will you make hay, or post accounts, or write your commercial letters, or draw out your plans for greater barns, or repair your machine, or set foot on the train, to be first at the market on the morrow? Thus you do but repeat their folly, who hoped to gather the needful food, but failed.

Emptiness will fill all your omers when the results of such disobedience are weighed. (*De W. S. Clarke.*)　　*The bread of the wilderness :*—I. THEY BROKE UP FROM THEIR ENCAMPMENT IN ELIM IN AN ENERVATED AND MURMURING MOOD. They had eaten of the fat of the wilderness and become wanton, and they began to lust even for the fat of Egypt, the slave's portion ; the lot of the freeman already seemed too spare and hard. Wisely, indeed, was the wilderness appointed for our wanderings. Wisely was Adam sent forth into the land in which " in the sweat of his brow he must eat bread." Bread won more cheaply may fatten the body, but it sends " leanness into the soul." I never heard that money won by gambling or thieving brought a blessing with it to its possessor. Did you ever hear of speculation enriching either mind or heart ? Money which comes cheaply goes cheaply, and leaves no benediction. God's inscription on His coin is " Labour." It is of another mintage when that impression cannot be traced. II. THE FIRST STAGE OF THEIR JOURNEY BROUGHT THEM OUT INTO A VAST SANDY PLAIN, WHERE THERE WAS REAL DANGER, TO THE EYE OF SENSE, OF THEIR DYING OF HUNGER. Elim had re-heartened them after Marah. But the wilderness of Sin renewed their pains and terrors, and " the whole congregation of the Children of Israel murmured against Moses and Aaron." Their cry after the flesh-pots was the fruit of Elim. They had renewed there the blunt edge of their lust. The old appetites resumed their sway, as they sat by the waters and ate of their flocks ; when they went forth their murmurs broke out with new fierceness, as of lust rekindled, and in spirit, at any rate, they gave themselves again to be slaves. Beware of rekindling the flame of a dying lust or appetite. Starve it—it is the only policy. Let it taste again, let it look again, it flushes up into full fever glow, and you are once more enslaved. III. REPHIDIM WAS THE SCENE OF THEIR FIRST BATTLE AND THEIR FIRST VICTORY. In the first great act of the drama of deliverance, their duty had been simply to " Stand still and see the salvation of God." The hour was now come when they must " quit them like men and fight." Not otherwise is it in the Christian life. To rest on Christ, to " stand still and see His salvation," is the true deliverance of a spirit : this is redemption. But we must fight hard, as if the victory depended on ourselves—not for redemption, but as redeemed, if we would reap all its glorious fruits. The first foes of Israel were their kinsmen. " And a man's foes shall be those of his own house." But come whence they may, foes soon beset the young pilgrim : before he has gone far, a long day's battle will test his courage and strain his strength. Lusts and passions, which he thought he had slain for ever, stand forth alive, and renew the conflict. The Egyptians slain, new enemies throng around us. Our pilgrimage must be a war-march, with battle-music and banners : " Jehovah nissi," (" the Lord my banner ") we cry, and renew the fight. (*J. B. Brown, B.A.*)　　*Physical providence :*—I. THAT GOD'S PHYSICAL PROVIDENCE RECOGNIZES THE PERSONAL WANTS OF EACH INDIVIDUAL. Manna fell for each, babe and man ; not one overlooked. Poverty is not the institution of heaven. The causes of poverty being with us, let us seek to remove them. II. THAT THE ENJOYMENT OF GOD'S PHYSICAL PROVIDENCE DEPENDS ON TRUSTFUL LABOUR. Each was to gather for himself, and to gather no more than his portion for the day. Labour is necessary to give a relish and felt value to our blessings; and trust in God is necessary to exclude all anxious thought about the future. III. THAT AN AVARICIOUS ACCUMULATION OF THE BLESSINGS OF PHYSICAL PROVIDENCE WILL DIS-APPOINT THE POSSESSOR. Hoarded wealth never satisfies. It is noisome ; it gene-rates reptiles. IV. THAT THE SEEKING OF THE BLESSINGS OF PHYSICAL PROVIDENCE SHOULD NEVER INTERFERE WITH RELIGIOUS INSTITUTIONS. 1. Religion does not require us to neglect the body. 2. Religion has special claims. It has to do with man's spiritual nature, relations, and interests. (*Homilist.*)　　*Spiritual provi-dence :*—I. THE MANNA WAS A PROVISION FOR A GREAT EMERGENCY. " When we were yet without strength "—to do the true work of life, to prepare for death, to gain acceptance with God—" in due time Christ died for the ungodly." II. THE MANNA COMES AS A MIRACULOUS INTERPOSITION. 1. Undeserved. 2. Unsought. III. THE MANNA CAME AS A UNIVERSAL SUPPLY. 1. In quantities commensurate with the wants of all. 2. Within reach of all. IV. THE MANNA CAME WITH DIVINE DIRECTIONS. Gather for yourselves, and distribute to those who need help. 1. Proportionately. 2. Betimes. 3. Regularly. Constancy is the condition of religious life and growth. V. THE MANNA DEMANDED THE REMEMBRANCE OF POSTERITY (ver. 32). All God's interpositions on behalf of the fallen world are facts that shall be had in everlasting remembrance. For this purpose they are recorded in His Word. His interposition in Christ specially calls for our commemoration in the ordinance instituted for that purpose. (*Ibid.*)　　*The manna :*—I. THE OCCASION FOR THE MANNA. The supplies brought from Egypt exhausted. II. THE MORAL PURPOSES OF THE MANNA. 1. To test the people. 2. To give an indisputable proof of the reality of their deliverance from Egypt by God's own hand. 3. To show the unreasonableness of their murmurings. III. THE TYPICAL SIGNIFICANCE OF THE MANNA. Lessons : 1. This standing miracle of forty years' duration is an irrefragable proof of all the Bible assumes concerning the personality, love, and power of God. 2. It teaches the faithfulness and deep interest of our heavenly Father, in all His children. 3. The murmurings and loss of appetite for the manna on the part of the Israelites are fraught with lessons of deepest practical moment to us. 4. The constant dependence on Christ as the true Manna is clear and emphatic. 5. The memorial pot of manna in the ark is a type of the "hidden manna" laid up in heaven for the believer (Rev. ii. 17). (*D. C. Hughes, M.A.*) *Threefold aspects of Providence :—* I. THE TEMPORAL ASPECT OF PROVIDENCE. 1. Providence is always timely in its assistance. Never too soon, never too late ; never before the time, never after the time. Forgetting this, we bring upon ourselves no end of trouble by being over-anxious for the morrow. 2. Providence is always ample in its resources. There were many mouths to be filled and voracious appetites to be satisfied, and yet we have not heard that the supply failed for a single morning. You remember reading in the account of the Franco-Prussian war, that the army of Napoleon III. loitered for days on the banks of the Rhine, when they ought to have advanced into the heart of Germany. What was the cause of this fatal delay ? Want of provision ; the commissariat was inadequate to supply the demands of three hundred thousand soldiers, and at Sedan the campaign proved disastrous to the empire. "He that walketh righteously, and speaketh uprightly . . . bread shall be given him; his waters shall be sure." Providence is conditional in its method of support. God rained down manna from heaven in small grain, like coriander seed, not in ready-made loaves. "Society," says Emerson, "expects every man to find his own loaf." God expects it too. II. THE SPIRITUAL ASPECTS OF PROVIDENCE. "See that the Lord hath given you the Sabbath, therefore He giveth you on the sixth day the bread of two days." 1. Its value as a day of rest for the body is very great. 2. Its importance as a day for spiritual contemplation and holy delight is incalculable. III. THE HISTORICAL ASPECT OF PROVIDENCE. "This is the thing which the Lord commandeth, fill an omer of it to be kept for your generations, that they may see the bread wherewith I have fed you in the wilderness." 1. The omer full of manna was meant to teach coming generations the greatness of God's power and the faithfulness of His promise. "Power belongeth unto God" as it belongeth to no other being, because it is absolute and independent. This is what makes His promises "exceeding great and precious," that He has abundance of resources to make good His word to man. 2. The omer full of manna was meant to teach coming generations the evil of hoarding up covetously the bounties of Providence. (*W. A. Griffiths.*) *Manna :—* The manna was a type of Christ. I. AS THE MANNA WAS A SPECIAL MERCY TO THE ISRAELITES IN THEIR EXTREMITY, SO THE SAVIOUR IS GOD'S SPECIAL GIFT TO SINFUL MEN. II. AS THE DIVINE GIFT OF THE MANNA APPEARED IN THE GARB OF EXTREME SIMPLICITY, SO THE LIFE OF THE SAVIOUR IS EMBODIED IN THE CIRCUMSTANCES OF LIFE, THROUGH WHICH HE BECOMES OUR LIFE. III. AS THE MANNA WAS PROPORTIONED IN DAILY RATIONS, SO WE MUST HAVE COMMUNION WITH CHRIST EVERY DAY. Religious exercises are framed to recur. Thoughts of Jesus and communion with God cannot be stored ; they must be repeated. IV. THE MANNA WAS IN PERPETUAL REMEMBRANCE AFTER THEY ENTERED CANAAN, SO JESUS AND HIS CROSS WILL BE THE THEME OF ETERNITY. The manna was placed in the golden pot, and put, with the ark, in the most holy place, when they began to live on the old corn of the land. The daily gathering was over, and the journey, but the remembrance remained. Faith must make way to sight. Grand sight ! We shall not forget Calvary. The scenes with Jesus must remain. (*British Weekly.*) *Angel's food :—* I. DIVINE CARE. 1. Anticipating human need. He was before them in the way ; to turn "the barren wilderness" into "a fruitful field." 2. Providing a suitable supply. (1) Suitable to their bodily need. Pleasant to the taste. Nourishing. (2) Suited to a wandering life. No time to sow and reap, even had the soil permitted. 3. Furnishing a sufficient supply. Day by day ; for forty years. 4. Watching over spiritual interests in meeting physical need. The Sabbath guarded. Both body and soul cared for ; and at the same time. II. HUMAN DUTY. 1. To expect. Eyes of all wait on Him. The manna to be looked for. We are to expect that God will supply our wants. He has promised to do so. 2. To collect. This work might have been saved them. It had its use. Some collect for others. Young for aged, &c. All secular labour in fields or factories, but a collecting of the good gifts of God. So is prayer, study of the Bible, &c. 3. To economize. None to be wasted. Those who had gathered less were to be supplied out of another's abundance. A wise distribution of our good things is true economy. Sowing for eternity. III. SPIRITUAL INSTRUCTION. The manna a type of Christ. So Jesus Himself regarded it (John vi.). It was so—1. Because unexpected in its coming. 2. Came in time of great need. 3. Unostentatious in its form. 4. Pleasant to the taste. 5. Spread silently over the ground. 6. Lasted all the journey through. 7. The remembrance of it treasured for ever. 8. Mysterious in nature. "What is it ? " Compare with " Who is He?" "Great is the mystery of godliness," &c. While curious minds are trying to understand a mystery into which angels desire to look, let our exhortation be, "O taste and see that the Lord is good," &c. Learn—I. To trust in the care of Providence. II. To act in harmony with Providence. III. To seek the true Bread of Life. (*J. C. Gray.*) *Lessons from the manna :*—1. It was given in consideration of a great and urgent necessity. A like necessity lies at the foundation of God's gift of His Son to the world; it was not possible in the nature of things for any other resource to be found. 2. The manna was peculiarly the gift of God, coming freely and directly from His hand. How striking a representation in this respect of Christ all Scripture may be said to testify, as both in His person and in the purchased blessings of His redemption He is always presented to sinful men as the free gift of the Father's love. 3. The whole fulness of the Godhead is in Jesus, so that all may receive as their necessities require. So was it also with the manna ; there was enough for all. 4. Then, falling as it did round about the camp, it was near enough to be within the reach of all ; if any should perish for want, it could be from no outward necessity or hardship, for the means of supply were brought almost to their very hand. Nor is it otherwise in regard to Christ, who in the gospel of His grace is laid, in a manner, at the very door of every sinner; the word is nigh him ; and if he should still perish, he must be without excuse—it is in sight of the Bread of Life. 5. The supply of manna came daily, and faith had to be exercised on the providence of God, that each day would bring its appointed provision ; if they attempted to hoard for the morrow, their store became a mass of corruption. In like manner must the child of God pray for his soul every morning as it dawns, " Give me this day my daily bread." He can lay up no stock of grace which is to last him for a continuance without needing to repair to the treasury of Christ. 6. Finally, as the manna had to be gathered in the morning of each day, and a double portion provided on the sixth day, that the seventh might be hallowed as a day of sacred rest, so Christ and the things of His salvation must be sought with diligence and regularity, but only in the appointed way and through the divinely-provided channels. (*A. Nevin, D.D.*) *The rain of bread :*—I. THE BACKWARD LOOK OF THIS BIT OF HISTORY. Culminating point of a fit of murmuring. Shows sin and folly of persistent distrust. 1. Murmuring is a most unprofitable state of mind. Never did anybody any good. Source of all Israelites' troubles. Once a child was reading, apparently absorbed in the act : her parent asked what was the book ; and looking up, she answered, with a sudden overflow of tears, "Oh father, the people have begun to murmur again, and now God will have to punish them some more !" 2. Murmuring is a most delusive disposition. It leads to dangerous self-deception in almost all instances. Christians reply to those who attempt to rebuke them, "It is my temperament." Often mere habit. Should be checked. 3. Murmuring is a most unwelcome indulgence. It prejudices piety. Makes a Christian disagreeable. 4. Murmuring is a growing sin in the heart. Israelites—sullen at first—now suspicious. They openly find fault. 5. Murmuring is contagious, and propagates itself far and wide. II. THE PRESENT APPEARANCE OF THIS BIT OF HISTORY. 1. Man's perversity. Little vexations make us petulant and revengeful. 2. God's patience. Lord Bacon quotes an old Spanish writer as saying: "To return evil for good is devilish ; to return good for good is human ; but to return good for evil is even godlike." Certainly this is what our God often does ; but it would not do for any of us to presume upon such wonderful long-suffering. In ancient history we are told that there was once a statue of Jupiter erected at Crete ; but the Cretans were liars, and the maker of the stone image had fashioned it without ears. The exultant people may have been pleased to think they had a god who could not hear their falsehoods ; but they soon found that a deity who had no ears to hear prevarications had no ears to hear prayers either. We must remember that our God knows all our wickedness, and bears with us for a while; but it is to test our obedience to His law. 3. Heaven's sufficiency is also illustrated here. For in the story the promise takes a very significant and beautiful form; God says He will "rain bread from heaven" for their need (see Psa. lxxviii. 22–25; Phil. iv. 19). III. THE FORWARD REACH OF THIS BIT OF HISTORY. 1. It was designed to be a type of Christ. (1) It came down to earth from heaven, as He did. (2) Every man must take of it for himself as he would need to take his own food. (3) It would work an individual experience of the new life; the book of Wisdom says that in the day of it the manna tasted to every one as he pleased. (4) It was free and sufficient for all: the rich and the poor, the sick and the well, the young and the old. (5) It must be sought not once for all, but daily. (6) It must be eaten; it must become part of one's self. (7) It was exclusive: there was no other food so safe in the desert. (8) It would cease only when no longer needed. 2. It was accepted as a type by our Lord Jesus Christ (see John vi.). (*C. S. Robinson, D.D.*) *The food from heaven:*—Manna was prepared for food by grinding and baking. It tasted like cakes made of meal and honey in its natural state, and like fresh olive oil when cooked; its shape resembled coriander seed, and its colour was white; its supply continued for forty years, and failed with their use of the first new corn in the land of Canaan. That it was altogether a miraculous gift and not a product of nature is clear from the following considerations. It fell in enormous quantity, with unfailing regularity, even in the exceptional failure of the Sabbath-day; its composition was exactly suited to the tastes of the people; heat both melted and hardened it; gathered in distrust, it bred worms and putrefied; in faith, it was preserved for generations. The natural products of the Arabian desert and other Eastern lands, called manna, fail almost in every particular noticed in the miraculous food from heaven. All serve rather medicinal than nutritious purposes. They can be gathered only three months in the year, and not all the year round, and then only in small quantities, out of all proportion to the actual consumption of the Israelites, which, calculating the omer at three English quarts (each man had an omer a day, ver. 16), could not have been less than 15,000,000 of pounds a week; they may be preserved for a long time, may be gathered on all days, indiscriminately, without a perceptible increase or diminution in their supply. The manna now found in the Arabian desert is the product of the tamarisk (*Tamarix gallica*), gathered in June. According to Burckhardt, "it drops from the thorns on the sticks and leaves with which the ground is covered, and must be gathered early in the day or it will be melted by the sun. The Arabs cleanse and boil it, strain it through a cloth, and put it in leather bottles; and in this way it can be kept uninjured for several years. They use it like honey or butter with their unleavened bread, but never make it into cakes or eat it by itself. It abounds only in very wet years, and in dry seasons it sometimes disappears entirely." The same traveller found in the valley of Jordan "manna like gum on the leaves and branches of the tree *gharrob*, which is as large as the olive-tree, having a leaf like the poplar, though somewhat broader. It appears like dew upon the leaves, is of a brown or grey colour, and drops on the ground. When first gathered it is sweet, but in a day or two becomes acid. The Arabs use it like honey or butter, and eat it in their oatmeal gruel. They also use it in cleaning their leather bottles and making them air-tight. The season for gathering this is in May or June. Two other shrubs which have been supposed to yield the manna of Scripture are the *Alhagi maurorum*, or Persian manna, and the *Alhagi desertorum*, thorny plants common in Syria." In addition to what has been said of the miraculous nature of the manna supply and the character of the natural products just specified, a brief reference to three explanations of the manna may be in place. 1. It is said to be miraculous food, that is, dew changed into bread. "The dew of heaven" promotes the fertility of the earth. During the wanderings of Israel through the wilderness, which is "no place of seed," the dew, without sowing, brought bread from heaven (ver. 4; Psa. lxxviii. 24; cv. 40). So that the manna answers to the wine at the marriage of Cana. 2. The manna is the same food of the desert still found in the peninsula of Sinai. This, of course, lands us in the region of mythical embellishment, and requires a degree of credulity which the writer does not possess. 3. The manna is a miracle of accretion, answering to the miraculous feeding of the multitude in the New Testament, and to the increase of meal and oil by Elijah in the Old. (*J. I. Mombert, D.D.*) *Manna:*—Bonar gives the following twelve reasons why manna cannot be identified with the exudation of the tarfa-tree. 1. The tarfa exudes only small quantities. The Arabs could not live on it for a week. 2. The tarfa only exudes at certain seasons—March and

April. 3. The tarfa does not yield its exudation regularly, even once a year. 4. The exudations of the tarfa come out from the branches of the tree, they do not come down from the air or sky. 5. The tarfa exudations are in composition and consistency somewhat like honey. They are quite unfit for grinding, or pounding, or baking, or boiling. 6. The taste of manna is said to have been as fresh oil (Numb. xi. 8). No one who has tasted the tarfa-manna would compare it to oil. 7. The tarfa-manna does not stink, or breed worms, in a single night. 8. The tarfa-produce does not evaporate as soon as the sun arises (ver. 21). 9. Tarfa-manna does not give particular quantities on particular days. 10. The tarfa-manna is purgative medicine, not food. 11. The Israelites knew well the tarfa-tree, but they did not recognize the manna. 12. Israel could not have subsisted so long on this one food. *Dew and manna:*—Dew corresponds to that inward truth which descends into the soul from the Lord when all is peaceful and happy within. When, in a spiritual morning, this dew has descended upon him, fear is unfelt, solicitude no longer disturbs him; he relies with a child's confiding trust on the Giver of all good, and feels a freshness and vigour like those of heaven's own morning over the soul. This cheering, inward, blessed sensation is often in the Word described by dew (Mic. v. 7; Isa. xviii. 4; Hos. xiv. 5). When, on a summer's morning, we walk forth in a beautiful country, the red light of the early dawn tinging the whole eastern horizon with golden splendour, a holy quiet reigning round, not broken, but charmed and enriched with the thrilling songs of the birds, while every leaf, blade, hedgerow, and flower are gemmed with pearly dew glittering like diamonds in the sun's new beams, there is an image of the soul—calmed, illuminated, and blessed with the truth of peace. But after the dew we come to the manna—the substantial food which gave so much pleasure and so much support. When it is seen that solid food in Divine language corresponds to goodness, which supplies the will of every one who is living for heaven with energy and delight, and remember that this manna was given to supply food to the Israelites while they were in the transition period between living in Egypt and living in Canaan, we shall easily perceive that it is the symbol of that heavenly goodness which the Lord can impart to the soul of man while it is in the transition state, labouring to become regenerate, following the truth, fighting against its evils as they from time to time present themselves, but not yet entered into that phase of the spiritual life in which he feels at home in heavenly things. Hence the manna describes the goodness and the delight which the Divine mercy imparts to man while labouring to become regenerate. It is small, because, as compared with true angelic joy, it is of little account. It is round, because roundness expresses the smoothness, and also the completeness, of goodness, as compared with truth—truth is ever sharp and piercing. It is white, to denote its purity, and sweet, to express its deliciousness. It is like a thin cake, or wafer, to mark its inferiority, its shallowness, so to speak, when compared with true celestial joy. Yet feeble as it is, so far does it transcend all merely human and external joy, that when it is first truly awakened in the soul, all other delights in the estimation of the possessor become as nothing, and he cries out in the spirit, "What is this?"—for he knows not what it is. It is a state of peace, of richness, of sweetness that passeth all understanding. It may be felt, but cannot be described. It is as if every fibre of the soul thrilled with joy. It is blessedness unspeakable. All other delights seem now unutterably poor. They are as the lights of earth in the presence of the sun. By receiving each day the food for the day, and no more, the important lesson is conveyed that we should ever be guided in our wish to receive heavenly blessings not by the desire of selfish gratification, but by the love of use. So much as we need for our work, so much should we desire to receive. Seek food for use and delight will be given in. Seek it also for the duties of to-day. The only way to make any advance in heavenly things is to do our duty now. The good not used now will vanish when the sun of selfishness becomes vigorous within us. If we attempt to save it for the future, and to deceive ourselves with the good we will some day do, it will breed the worms of vain conceits, flattering and false. It may become polluted hypocrisy, most abhorrent in the sight of God and angels, but can never be saving good. The lesson involved in the corruption of the manna in the hands of those who gathered to hoard and not to use is of inestimable value. To be a miser is bad in earthly things, but far worse in heavenly. And it is to be feared that spiritual hoarding is even more prevalent than natural. How many sermons do we hear with delight, but whose influence goes no farther than to stock our memories! How many good books do we read whose pages unfold to us exalted lessons and truths of sterling worth! We hear, we read, and we admire, but our hearts remain as cold, heedless, and unpractical as before. We are no better, we admit; but we do not suspect what is the real truth—that we are worse. The manna we are hoping to preserve for future use is becoming corrupted and defiled. We are gliding into states of self-dependency, self-complacency, self-flattery. We are supposing we are righteous, or, at least, in no danger, because we know righteous things, while with every effort we make we are strengthening our inherent evils, our hereditary tendencies. We are not searching out our frailties and opposing them, but indulging them and salving them over with our religious knowledge and pious observances. The richest substances become, when corrupted, the most loathsome; and nothing is so abhorrent in the Divine sight as a religion unused for good, pandering only to self-gratulation and deceit. Our whole progress depends on eating to-day what God gives to-day. The same lesson would teach us also the duty of doing as it comes the work of each successive stage of our business of life and the reception of its proper and present blessing. "Gather of it every man according to his eating, an omer for every man. Let no man leave it until the morning" (vers. 16, 19). One exception to this rule, however, there was (ver. 29). Days for the soul are states. The six days of labour represent the states of the soul in which it is striving to obey a truth, although as yet it is laborious to do so in consequence of oppositions within and without. The sixth day is the end of this struggle, when the soul has succeeded in realizing not only the truth of a duty or a principle but also the good, the blessedness of it. Two omers are then received, the bread of two days. One more incident we would notice. The manna was gathered by an omer full at once, and no otherwise; and we are informed at the conclusion of the narrative, "Now an omer is the tenth part of an ephah" (ver. 36). There were three chief measures for dry articles, each ten times larger than the other—the omer, the ephah, and the homer (Ezek. xlv. 11). These three measures, like the three kinds of bread of the tabernacle—the loaf, the cake, and the wafer—we may readily conceive, have relation to the reception of heavenly good by the three grand classes of Christians who form afterwards the three heavens of the Lord (2 Cor. xii. 2). The good which they receive who have entered fully into love to the Lord as the supreme source of all their operations is of the largest measure, the homer. The good of those who glory rather in the light than the love of heaven, though they are true to the light and sons of the light, is of the second measure, the ephah. The good of those who are not even intellectual Christians, but still steadily obey what they see to be enjoined in the Word, is the lowest measure, the omer, which is the tenth part of the ephah. And this is the measure by which we all receive heavenly good in our spiritual journey. Our law of duty is to obey the Ten Commandments. Each commandment obeyed brings its omer of blessing. (*J. Bailey, Ph.D.*) *Christ the true Manna* :—I am told there is a country where men in times of want eat clay in great lumps, and fill themselves with it so as to deaden their hunger. I know that many people in England do the same. There is a kind of yellow clay (gold) which is much cried up for staying spiritual hunger: heavy stuff it is, but many have a vast appetite for it. They prefer it to the choicest dainties. Many try to stave off hunger by indifference, like bears in winter, which are not hungry because they are asleep. They would not like to be aroused, because if they were they would wake up to an awful hunger. I wish they could be awakened, for that hunger which they dread would drive them to a soul-satisfying Saviour. Depend upon it, the only way to meet hunger is to get bread, and the only way to meet your soul's want is to get Christ, in whom there is enough and to spare, but nowhere else. (*C. H. Spurgeon.*) *Satisfied with God's provision* :—Another time Billy Bray tells us that his crop of potatoes turned out poorly; and as he was digging them in the autumn, Satan was at his elbow, and said, "There, Billy, isn't that poor pay for serving your Father the way you have all the year? Just see those small potatoes." He stopped his hoeing, and replied, "Ah, Satan, at it again, talking against my Father, bless His name. Why, when I served you, I didn't get any potatoes at all. What are you talking against Father for?" And on he went hoeing and praising the Lord for small potatoes. A valuable lesson for us all. *Bread from God* :—Some time ago a good Christian man was living among the hills of Scotland. He was very poor, but so good that every one who knew him loved and honoured him. One winter there was a violent snowstorm. The wind was high, and drifting snow blocked up the roads, and quite covered the humble dwelling of poor Caleb, as this good man was called. For three days he had been unable to go out and get food for himself and family. They were in great need, and had prayed earnestly for relief. A gentleman living in that neighbourhood, who knew Caleb well, awoke suddenly one night. It seemed as if a voice was calling to him which said, " Send provisions to Caleb." He thought little of it, but turned on his pillow and went to sleep again. Again the voice seemed to sound in his ears, " Send provisions to Caleb." Again he slept. A third time the call came. Then he arose hastily, dressed himself, called up his servant, and told him to harness the horse, while he filled a basket with provisions of all kinds. " Take this basket to Caleb," said he, " and if he asks who sent it, tell him it comes from God." The servant did as he was bidden. A path was made through the snow. The basket of food was left at Caleb's cottage : and he and his family received it with hearty rejoicings. They felt sure that it was food from heaven, just as truly as the manna was in the wilderness on which the Israelites lived. Moses secured the blessing of bread for the Israelites in the wilderness, and Jesus is " the Prophet like Moses," because He secures this blessing both for the bodies and the souls of His people. (*R. Newton.*) *Food providentially supplied :*—At the Turners' banquet given in his honour a short time since, Mr. Stanley alluded to the strange sufferings in which he shared fifteen or sixteen months ago. For six weeks they had not seen a bit of meat ; for ten days they had not seen a banana or a grain, and the faces of the people were getting leaner, and their bodies were getting thinner, and their strength was fading day by day. One day the officers asked him if he had seen anything like it in any African expedition before. He replied " No," though he remembered on a former occasion when they were nine days without food, and ended their famine with a fight. Then, however, they knew where there was grain, and all they had to do was to hurry on ; but in the late expedition they had been ten days without, and they did not know when their hunger was to terminate. They were all sitting down at the time, and he expressed his belief that the age of miracles was not altogether past. Moses struck water out of the Horeb rock, the Israelites were fed with manna in the wilderness, and he told them that he did not think they should be surprised to see some miracle for themselves—perhaps on the morrow or the following day. He had scarcely finished when some guinea fowl flocked round them and were at once seized. *Soul food necessary :*—A man was leaving a church at St. Louis where Mr. Moody had been holding a service. The eminent preacher noticed him, and gives the following account of their conversation—" I said to him, ' My friend, why is it that you don't accept Christ ? ' He shook his head, and said he didn't know. ' Well, what is your soul feeding on ? ' He said it was feeding on nothing. ' Well,' I said, ' that is pretty hard for the soul, isn't it—giving it nothing to feed on ? ' He was a man about my age, forty years old, and he had given his soul nothing for forty years ; he had been starving that soul. And that man is but a type of thousands and tens of thousands in this city to-day ; their poor souls are starving. This body that we inhabit for a day and then leave, we take good care of that ; we feed it three times a day, and we clothe it and take care of it and deck it, and by and by it is going into the grave to be eaten up by the worms ; but the inner man, that is to live on and on for ever, is lean and starved." *Symbolic meaning of the manna :*—In the sixth chapter of St. John, where our Lord so emphatically applies to Himself the miracle of the manna, it will be seen He discovers no wish to take from the high estimate which the Jews entertained of this ancient miracle, so only that it was considered as a type, not a mere interposition of Providence to provide by miracles means for their daily support. And casting aside many minor analogies which have been contended for, but which are too much of the nature of fanciful refinements, it is not difficult to trace between the manna and Christ, the True Bread, several broad and instructive resemblances. 1. Thus both were the free, unsolicited gift of heaven, prompted by the sight of man's helplessness and man's misery. " Moses gave you not that bread from heaven," saith our Lord ; " but My Father giveth you the true bread from heaven." But observe, the gift in either case was the unmerited bestowment of the Eternal Father ; whether to nourish the physical life of those wilderness wanderers or to support the spiritual life of believers to the end of time. Jesus Christ is a gift, the eternal life is a gift, enlightening, converting grace is a gift. Human efforts could no more avail to procure these things than the sowing of coriander seed could produce a harvest of manna. 2. Again, this gift was to preserve life. '' Ye have brought us forth into the wilderness," said the Israelites to Moses, "to kill this whole assembly with hunger." They saw nothing before them but certain death. The place was desert; a curse of barrenness and drought laid upon it. The whole is a picture of man in this wilderness-world. His soul perishes with hunger; he has the sentence of death within him, a prospect of death before him. But God has rained bread from heaven. Christ, the Wellspring of all spiritual life; Christ, the Source of every active and passive grace; Christ, the energizing Principle of all acceptable obedience. "Your fathers did eat manna in the wilderness, and are dead." It saved them not from the common lot of all men, this bread ye boast of, but "I am the living Bread which came down from heaven. If any man eat of this Bread he shall live for ever." 3. Trace this parallel further, in the universality of the gift. There were in that wilderness all diversities of character—masters and disciples, owners of flocks and keepers of flocks; rulers of thousands, and rulers of hundreds, and rulers of fifties, and rulers of tens: yet to all was to be given the same portion, "an omer to every man, according to the number in their tents." And in like manner, as far as concerns the offer of the blessing, Christ is a universal portion. (*D. Moore, M.A.*) *Manna and dew :*—Does not the manner in which this bread descended from above, along with the gentle, silent dew, apply very beautifully to the True Bread from heaven? It is not in the bustle of the world or in the excitement of religion, but in secret and in silence that Jesus descends upon the soul, when the spirit communes with God—when the eye is turned within in earnest searching self-examination—when the heart calmly meditates on the Divine Word. And what is the "dew" on and with which He descends? What but the Spirit of God, of which the dew is the constant symbol in Scripture? When the Spirit falls gently upon our hearts, then Jesus descends there. Where the one is, the other is—yet they are distinct. It is not the Spirit, but Christ in His living Person who is the Bread of Life. The Spirit is as the dew; Jesus as the manna, the Bread from heaven. We must, then, cherish every gentle influence of the Spirit of God if we would have our souls nourished. (*G. Wagner.*) *Sufficiency of Providence :*—The following anecdote of Mr. Spurgeon is well authenticated:—On a certain occasion, when dining at a lady's house in Regent's Park, with the late Dr. Brock, he (Mr. S.) remarked that £2,000 had to be forthcoming for his builder to-morrow, and though nothing was in hand, the money would be paid at ten o'clock. "I wish you would not say that," Dr. Brock replied; but immediately after, while they were still at the table, a telegram came to say that A. B. had just left £2,000 for the Orphanage; and then, confessing that he had never seen anything like that, the doctor called upon all to put down their knives and forks and return thanks to God. They never knew who A. B. was, nor whence he came. (*Gleanings in Harvest Fields.*) *Supply of Providence :*—Harms of Hermannsburg, the pastor of a poor village on the Luneberg Heath in Hanover, said in his annual missionary sermon in 1857 : "I have expended much in the past year in sending out the ship with her fifteen passengers, for the printing house, the press, and the paper, altogether 14,781 dollars, and I have received altogether 14,796 dollars, so I have fifteen dollars over. Is not that a wonder? So much spent, and yet something over! And I thank God that He has given us the fifteen dollars overplus. Riches only make cares. God has heard all my prayers. He has given me no riches, and I have also no debts. We have neither collected nor begged, but waited patiently on God in prayer." *Constancy of Providence :*—"Never did man die of hunger who served God faithfully," was a saying of Cuthbert, the apostle of Northumbria, when he and his companions were overtaken by night without food or shelter. "Look at the eagle overhead," he would add; "God can feed us through him if He will." And this faith was on one occasion signally justified by the bird in question letting fall a fish, which furnished the needed meal. (*J. R. Green's Short History.*)

Vers. 16–18. **Gather of it every man according to his eating.**—*Spiritual assimilation :*—Why did each receive but three quarts a day? Might not a nutritious and delicious food like this be stored, and become an article of merchandise and a source of wealth? No, the Edenic law was not merely a penalty, but a method of mercy, of life, and health. It required labour. But there is a profounder reason for the prayer, "Give us *this day* our daily bread." We are to get out of to-day all we can, and trust God for to-morrow. We possess only what we can assimilate, so the miracle does no more than provide for one day. You say that you possess property. No; another may more truly possess it. I who tarry by your garden, or the beggar who feasts upon its beauty with appreciating and admiring eyes, gets more out of

it than you. You hurry away to business early in the morning, and are gone till
dark, too burdened, it may be, to give it a glance. So with your library or pictures.
He possesses who assimilates. If your wealth makes you anxious, or leads you to
dissipation, then you possess not wealth, but anxiety and disease. You may give
your child wealth, but it is better to put moral wealth into mind and heart than to
burden down with money, which may sink his soul in ruin. So with books and
associates. We grow by what we eat. What does that child read? Who are his
friends? We really eat both. Christ used this figure, and said we were to eat His
flesh and drink His blood. This means the assimilation of spiritual forces, the
incorporation of His life and character as we grow to be like those we make our
bosom friends. Our character is warped, shrivelled, and weakened, or it is enriched
and ennobled by those with whom we habitually and intimately live, as they are
mean and wicked, or pure and princely. (*E. Braislin, D.D.*)   *Lessons:*—We are
hereby taught—1. Prudence and diligence in providing food convenient for ourselves and our households; what God graciously gives we must industriously
gather, with quietness working, and eating our own bread, not the bread either of
idleness or deceit. God's bounty leaves room for man's duty. 2. Contentment
and satisfaction with a sufficiency; they must gather, "every man according to his
eating"; enough is as good as a feast, and more than enough is as bad as a surfeit.
They that have most have for themselves but food and raiment and mirth; and
they that have least generally have these; so that "he who gathers much," &c.
There is not so great a disproportion between one and another, in the comforts and
enjoyments of the things of this life, as there is in the property and possession of
the things themselves. 3. Dependence upon Providence. "Let no man leave till
morning" (ver. 19), but let them learn to go to bed and sleep quietly, though they
have not a bit of bread in their tent, nor in all their camp, trusting that God, with the
following day, will bring them their daily bread. It was surer and safer in God's
storehouse than in their own, and would thence come to them sweeter and fresher.
(*M. Henry, D.D.*)   *Nothing over:*—It is said that when J. C. Astor was once
congratulated by a certain person for his wealth, he replied by pointing to his pile
of bonds and maps of property, at the same time inquiring, "Would you like to
manage these matters for your board and clothes?" The man demurred. "Sir,"
continued the rich man, "it is all that I get." (*J. Denton.*)   *Self-help enforced:*—
A young man stood listlessly watching some anglers on a bridge. He was poor and
dejected. At last, approaching a basket filled with fish he sighed, "If now I had
these I would be happy. I could sell them and buy food and lodgings." "I will give
you just as many, and just as good," said the owner, who chanced to overhear his
words, "if you will do me a trifling favour." "And what is that?" asked the other.
"Only to tend this line till I come back; I wish to go on a short errand." The
proposal was gladly accepted. The old man was gone so long that the young man
began to get impatient. Meanwhile the fish snapped greedily at the hook, and the
young man lost all his depression in the excitement of pulling them in; and when
the owner returned he had caught a large number. Counting out from them as
many as were in the basket, and presenting them to the young man, the old fisherman said, "I fulfil my promise from the fish you have caught, to teach you, whenever you see others earning what you need, to waste no time in foolish wishing, but
cast a line for yourself." (*W. Baxendale.*)   *No position has a surplus of happiness:*—When Napoleon returned to his palace, immediately after his defeat at
Waterloo, he continued many hours without taking any refreshment. One of the
grooms of the chamber ventured to serve up some coffee, in his cabinet, by the
hands of a child whom Napoleon had occasionally distinguished by his notice. The
Emperor sat motionless, with his hands spread over his eyes. The page stood
patiently before him, gazing with infantine curiosity on an image which presented
so strong a contrast to his own figure of simplicity and peace; at last the little
attendant presented his tray, exclaiming, in the familiarity of an age which knows
so little distinctions: "Eat, sire; it will do you good." The emperor looked at
him, and asked: "Do you not belong to Gonesse?" (a village near Paris). "No,
sire; I come from Pierrefite." "Where your parents have a cottage and some
acres of land?" "Yes, sire." "There is happiness," replied the man who was
still the Emperor of France and King of Italy. (*J. Arvine.*)   *No satisfaction in
mere accumulation:*—"I once had occasion to speak of a certain charity to a
prosperous mechanic. He seemed not much inclined to help it, but after listening
to my representations awhile, he suddenly gave way and promised a handsome
subscription. In due time he paid it cheerfully, and said, "Do you know what

carried the point with me that day when you made the application?" "No," I replied. "Well, I'll tell you. I was not so much moved by anything you said till you came to mention the fact about the Israelites, 'He that gathered much had nothing over, and he that gathered little had no lack.' Thinks I, that is just my own history. Once I was a poor, hard-working young man; now I've got a good deal of property, but as for real comfort and use, I get no more out of it now than I did then. Now, when I gather much, I've nothing over, and then, when I gathered little, I had no lack." (*Family Treasury.*)

Vers. 23–26. **To-day ye shall not find it in the field.** — *The Sabbath in relation to secular toil* :—I. THAT MAN MUST NOT ENGAGE IN SECULAR TOIL ON THE SABBATH. Men must not even earn their daily bread on the Lord's day,—they must provide it before. II. THAT MEN ENGAGED IN SECULAR TOIL ON THE SABBATH WILL, AS A RULE, FIND THEIR LABOUR VAIN AND PROFITLESS. III. THAT MEN ENGAGED IN SECULAR TOIL ON THE SABBATH SHOW PLAINLY THAT THEY HAVE NO REGARD FOR THE COMMANDS OF GOD. They are selling their souls for gain. IV. THAT MEN ENGAGED IN SECULAR TOIL ON THE SABBATH HAVE NO DELIGHT IN THE CULTURE OF THEIR MORAL NATURE. It is especially on the day of rest that men of secular toil have the leisure and opportunity for soul-culture, by inward meditation, by earnest devotion, by wise reading, and by the ministry of the sanctuary. (*J. S. Exell, M.A.*) *The day of rest* :— In one of the most densely populated parts of the city a gentleman lately visited the house of a poor, hard-working, infidel cobbler. The man was busy at his last, and had scarce time to look up at his unwelcome visitor. "That is hard work." "It is, sir. "For how many hours a day have you to labour here—twelve?" "Yes, and more, sir. I am never off this seat under a fourteen or fifteen hours' spell of it." "That is sore toil for a bit of bread." "Indeed it is, sir; and very thankful am I when the week's end comes. What would become of me, and the likes of me, without that rest?" "And who, friend, think you, gave you that rest? Came it by accident, or arrangement, or how?" There came no answer to that; the cobbler hung his head; the man was honest; the sceptic was ashamed. *Queen Victoria and the Sabbath* :—One Saturday night, in this first year of Queen Victoria's reign, a certain noble visitor came at a late hour to Windsor. He informed the Queen that he had brought down some documents of great importance for her inspection, but that, as they would require to be examined in detail, he would not encroach on Her Majesty's time that night, but would request her attention the next morning. "To-morrow is Sunday, my lord," said the Queen. "True, your Majesty, but business of the State will not admit of delay." The Queen then consented to attend to the papers after Church the next morning. The nobleman was somewhat surprised that the subject of the sermon next day turned out to be the duties and obligations of the Christian Sabbath. "How did your lordship like the sermon?" asked the Queen on their return from Church. "Very much indeed, your Majesty," was the reply. "Well then," said the Queen, "I will not conceal from you that last night I sent the clergyman the text from which he preached. I hope we shall all be improved by the sermon." Sunday passed over without another word being said about the State papers, until at night, when the party was breaking up, the Queen said to the nobleman, "To-morrow morning, my lord, at any hour you please—as early as seven, my lord, if you like—we will look into the papers." His lordship said he would not think of intruding upon Her Majesty so early as that, and he thought nine o'clock would be quite early enough. "No, no, my lord," said the Queen, " as the papers are of importance I should like them to be attended to very early; however, if you wish it to be nine, be it so." Accordingly, at nine o'clock next morning the Queen was in readiness to confer with the nobleman about his papers. (*T. E. Ball.*) *Training for Sabbath observance* :—No doubt, in the oppression and darkness of Egypt, the seventh-day (Sabbath) observance had fallen into partial disuse; though even in Egypt in that era, as among the more eastern peoples, the traditional seventh-day rest seems to have lingered, and therefore the usages of Egypt may not have militated against the rest on the seventh day. However that may be, still there was need of this training to the Sabbath observance; and this ordinance of the manna was just the preparation needful for their receiving heartily the statute, "Remember the Sabbath day," when it came to them through Moses from the mount. (*S. Robinson, D.D.*) *A lesson on Sabbath keeping* :—In all the Jewish history there never again occurred as favourable a time for imposing the Sabbath observance upon the people as at the giving of the manna. For forty years, comprising more than two thousand weeks, they were to subsist upon manna as their daily food. God was to furnish it every day; they were to gather it every day. Thus was presented the opportunity both for God to mark the day and for man to keep it. During all these two thousand weeks God gave them a double supply on the sixth day, and preserved that given on that day fresh for two days instead of one. Two thousand Sabbaths came, but on them no manna. It was vain for them to look for it. Soon they ceased to do so altogether. What a lesson for beginners! The most stupid and the most obdurate alike learned it. Time and the world may be searched for another series of events by which it would be possible to impress the idea of a Sabbath upon the minds of the people as effectually as by this. (*A. M. Weston, D.D.*) *Sabbath gains a curse :—*Whatever is earned on the Sabbath is a curse in a man's property. (*A. Clarke, D.D.*) *Faithful to God's command :—*A delicate man, once a ringleader in all sorts of mischief, was recently found by some of the Mildmay Deaconesses in a common London lodging-house, and as it was discovered that the poor fellow could not work continuously at his trade, he was started in business in a small shop. Late one Saturday night, as many, through curiosity, or seeing the contents of the shop looking fresh and new, filled it up, and were asking one question and another, one woman said : "Here is 4d. ; I'll come in to-morrow with the other few pence, and you will give me the parcel then." "This shop will never be open for traffic on the Lord's Day," was the answer, at which announcement the people all turned to gaze at the speaker. A quiet look of firm resolve was on his delicate face, which seemed to make the crowd silent for a minute or two; then one laughed, and said : "Are you religious?" "Yes," said the proprietor; "I may as well declare it from the very first night of opening. You will never, with God's help, see either buying or selling here on Sundays." "Oh!" said a scoffer; "then you will soon shut shop." The owner of the shop replied : "Do you see that little card with the blue ribbon tying it up?" The eyes of all were turned towards the card, on which were the words, "Kept by the power of God." "This," continued the speaker, "is my motto ; He is able to keep me, and maybe some of you will find out 'tis better to have Him as a friend than any one in the world." (*Christian Herald.*)

Vers. 32–36. **Put an omer full of manna therein.**—*An instructive memorial :—*
I. BY WHOM THE MEMORIAL WAS ENJOINED. "The Lord." We have need to set up memorials in our lives which shall call upon our souls to remember the benefits of the Lord. It is the will of heaven that its gifts should be held in constant remembrance. II. IN WHAT THE MEMORIAL CONSISTED. "Fill an omer of it to be kept for your generations." 1. This memorial was reasonable. 2. Expressive. 3. Instructive. 4. Valuable. Golden pot (Heb. ix. 2). And the memorials of the soul should not find expression in valueless things, but in the richest treasures of man. God is worthy our best offerings. III. WHERE THE MEMORIAL WAS DEPOSITED. "And lay it up before the Lord." "So Aaron laid it up before the Testimony, to be kept." And so this memorial was laid up before the Lord, in the ark of the covenant. Thus we must keep the memorials of the soul in devout spirit, and with a constant trust in the mediatorial work of Christ. IV. THE DESIGN THE MEMORIAL CONTEMPLATED. "That ye may see the bread wherewith I have fed you in the wilderness." "To be kept for your generations." Each generation leaves a moral deposit behind it, for good or evil. Lessons : 1. The soul must have a memorial of the Divine mercy. 2. The memorial of the soul must consist of the best thing it possesses. 3. The memorial of the soul will have respect to the redemp ive work of Christ. (*J. S. Exell, M.A.*) *An instructive memorial :—*One day when George Moore—now a man of wealth—was accompanying his friend, Colonel Henderson, through the Waver wood on a partridge-shooting expedition, a curious ramshackle object appeared before them. It seemed to be a sort of big dhrosky with a long, broad trunk at the back end. "What is that?" asked the colonel. "Why," said George Moore, "that is the trap which I have driven into every market town in Great Britain and Ireland!" It was the carriage he had used whilst achieving such great success as a commercial traveller. (*H. O. Mackey.*) *Former mercies remembered :—*Mr. Kidd, minister of Queensferry, near Edinburgh, was one day very much depressed and discouraged. He sent a note to Mr. L—— minister of Culross, a few miles off, informing him of his distress of mind, and desiring a visit as soon as possible. Mr. L—— told the servant he was so busy that he could not wait upon his master, but desired him to tell Mr. Kidd to remember Torwood. When the servant returned, he said to his master, "Mr. L—— could

not come, but he desired me to tell you to remember Torwood." This answer immediately struck Mr. Kidd, and he cried out, "Yes, Lord! I will remember Thee, from the hill Mizar, and from the Hermonites!" All his troubles and darkness vanished upon the recollection of a day which he had formerly spent in prayer along with Mr. L—— in Torwood, where he had enjoyed eminent communion with God. (*W. Baxendale.*)   *An expressive memorial:*—It was during the wars that raged from 1652 to 1660, between Frederick III. of Denmark, and Charles Gustavus, of Sweden, that after a battle in which the victory had remained with the Danes, a stout burgher of Flensburg was about to refresh himself, ere retiring to have his wounds dressed, with a draught of beer from a wooden bottle, when an imploring cry from a wounded Swede lying on the field made him turn, and, with the very words of Sidney—"Thy need is greater than mine," he knelt down by the fallen enemy to pour the liquor into his mouth. His requital was a pistol-shot in the shoulder from the treacherous Swede. "Rascal!" he cried, "I would have befriended you, and you would murder me in return! Now will I punish you. I would have given you the whole bottle, but now you shall only have half." And drinking off half himself, he gave the rest to the Swede. The king, hearing the story, sent for the burgher, and asked him how he came to spare the life of such a rascal. "Sire," said the honest burgher, "I could never kill a wounded enemy." "Thou meritest to be a noble," the king said, and created him one immediately, giving him as armorial bearings a wooden bottle pierced with an arrow. The family only lately became extinct in the person of an old maiden lady.

CHAPTER XVII.

VERS. 1-3. **Give us water, that we may drink.**—*Rephidim: ancient and modern:*—How far have we travelled from Rephidim? This is more than a question in geography: it is a profound inquiry in morals. How far have we advanced morally, spiritually, and in all the higher ranges and Diviner outlooks of our being? Here we seem to be still at Rephidim. Geographers say they cannot find out the exact locality. Verily, there need be no difficulty about the exact locality—it is just where we are. Why be so emphatic about our being at Rephidim? I. BECAUSE THE PEOPLE AT REPHIDIM WERE TORMENTED BY A CONTINUAL CONSCIOUSNESS OF NECESSITY. How far have we got from necessity? Not one inch. Necessity has followed us all the time. We must advance from the lower to the higher. We have it before us as a certain and indisputable fact that for the support of the body we need external help: we need the whole ministry of kind and gracious nature. What wonder if in the education, and culture, and strengthening of the soul we need all heaven, with its infinite Trinity of Father, Son, and Holy Ghost? Were we pressed to affirm that necessity it would be in strict consonance with all the other wants that follow and devour our wasting life. II. BECAUSE AT REPHIDIM HELP WAS FOUND IN UNEXPECTED PLACES AND GIVEN IN UNEXPECTED WAYS: "Thou shalt smite the rock, and there shall come water out of it, that the people may drink." We are always helped by unexpected people, in unexpected ways, and at unexpected places. God would appear to delight in baffling the ingenuity that would forecast the future with too exclusive a minuteness. God will not allow us to trifle with His prerogatives. He will find water where we should find none. Why be so emphatic about still being at Rephidim? III. BECAUSE PEEVISH TEMPERS WERE CORRECTED BY GREAT DUTIES IN THAT ANCIENT LOCALITY. Israel fell into fretfulness, and whining, and dissatisfaction, and rebellion. What did God do? He sent Amalek upon Israel. That is the function of war among the nations. It is no use reasoning with peevishness. It is time wasted to try to expostulate with any man who is in a whining mood of soul, displeased because of his bread, discontented because of the scarcity of water, making no allowance for the undulations of life— reasoning, remonstrance, expostulation would be lost. What must be done? An enemy must be raised up to smite him with the sword. Then he will come into a new mood of mind, forget his littleness, and, springing forward to a realization of his true power, he will lose in service the discontent which he contracted in unbelief. What we want to-day is persecution. We do not want eloquence, criticism—new learning, some new invention in theological confectionery that shall tempt appetites that have been sated ; we want war—persecution—the enemy at the gate. Then we should begin to forgive one another, to pray for one another, to come more closely together at the altar and more near in that consent of soul which is blessed with insight into spiritual mysteries. We have lost in losing the enemy. The sting of Smithfield fire would correct our theology a good deal ; the old gibbet would take the fretfulness out of our tone ; the great earthquake rocking our cities would make us forget our animosities and unite us in bolder intercession. (*J. Parker, D.D.*) *Refreshing thoughts for the hot season :*—I was told by a gentleman who walked over one of the battle-fields on a hot summer night, after a day[of carnage, that the cry of the wounded was absolutely unbearable, ard after giving all supply that he could, he put his fingers to his ears, for the cry all over the plain was from hundreds of dying men, " Water ! Water ! For God's sake, give us water." Coming home from the store on a hot summer day, in the eventide, every muscle of your body exhausted with fatigue, what do you first ask for ? A cup of water—fresh, clear, sparkling water. This Bible is all agleam with fountains, and rivers, and seas. The prophet sees the millennium, and cries, " Streams in the desert." David thinks of the deep joy of the righteous, and calls it " A river, the streams whereof shall make glad the city of God." While the New Testament holds forth ten thousand chalices filled with living water for a thirsty world. I. Water is typical of the Gospel, because of its BRIGHTNESS. The fountain breaks forth from the side of the hill, flashing with gold, and silver, and beryl, and chrysolite ; and as you see it, you almost clap your hands with gladness. But there is no brightness in it compared with this living fountain of the Gospel ; for in each falling drop I see the glory of heaven. II. Water typifies the Gospel by its REFRESHMENT. How different you feel after you get a glass of cool water, or after you have plunged into a bath ! On a hot summer day there is nothing that so soon brings you back from a bad temper or a disturbed spirit, and puts you into a happy frame of mind and body, as cold water. Blessed be God for water. I love to hear it fall in the shower and dash in the cascade, and to see it rush from the ice pitcher into the clear glass. Hand round this nectar of the hills and drink, all of you, to the praise of Him who brewed it among the mountains. Thank God for water. But there is a better refreshment even than that. There was a time when you were hounded by convictions. Sinai thundered. The wrath of God cried, " Fly." Justice cried, " Fly." Your own fears cried, " Fly." Mercy said, " Come, come ! " and you plunged like a hart into the water brooks, and out of that flood your soul came up cool, and clean, and radiant ; and you looked round and said, " Come, and hear ye all that fear God, and I will tell you what He hath done for my soul." III. Water typifies the Gospel because of its ABUNDANCE. When we pour the water from the pitcher into the glass we have to be careful, or the glass will overflow, and we stop when the water has come to the rim. But when God, in summer, pours out His showers, He keeps pouring on and pouring on until the grass blades cry, " Enough ! " and the flowers, " Enough ! " and the trees, " Enough ! " but God keeps pouring on and pouring on, until the fields are soaked, and the rivers overflow, and the cisterns are all filled and the great reservoirs are supplied, and there is water to turn the wheel, water to slake the thirst of the city, water to cleanse the air, water to wash the hemisphere. Abundance ! And so with this glorious gospel. Enough for one, enough for all. Just after the battle of Antietam, with some of the other members of the Christian Commission, I went down to help look after the wounded, and on the afternoon of a very hot day I came to a pump of water. I saw a soldier, with musket, guarding the pump. I said, " Why do you not fill my cup ? " He replied, " Water is scarce ! Here is a great army, and we do not know where to get water after this is gone ; and I have orders to give no more than that." What a poor supply for a thirsty man on a hot day ! But, glory be to God ! that in this gospel fountain there is water enough for all the armies of the earth, and for all the armies of heaven. You cannot drink it dry. IV. Water typifies the Gospel in the fact that it is PERENNIAL. In this hot summer weather some of the fountains have dried up ; but stand you on the bank of the Amazon, or of the St. Lawrence, or of the Mississippi, or of the Ohio, and see if it runs dry. No ; they have been flowing on for thousands of years, and they will probably flow on for thousands of years more. The trees of the forest have cast their leaves for ages into the bosom of these waters, and the birds of heaven have dipped their wings in the wave. And so it is with this gospel. It is a perennial gospel. On earth we only see a portion of that great River of Life ; but after a while the river will rise, and it will join the tides of the celestial river that flows hard by the throne of God. (*T. De Witt Talmage, D.D.*) *Want of water a terrible experience :*—About 1858, while a number of routes from the proposed, now completed, Pacific railway were being surveyed, E. T. Scovill, of Cleveland, was in charge of a corps of engineers in Nevada. On one occasion they were obliged to leave their base of supplies for a trip of six days. On the fourth day's journey their water gave out, and the sufferings of men and beasts were terrible. The heat appeared to rise from the sand like vapour and dance a death dance before the sufferers' eyes. Not a breath of air stirred. The sun was like a great round furnace. The horses struggled on, their noses hung nearly to the ground, and their eyes bulged out of their heads like knots on a tree. Two of the men became delirious and were bound in the waggons. Near night a gulch was reached and all plunged into it expecting to find water. It was dry! The situation was desperate, when Mr. Scovill, taking in the situation at a glance, directed some to go up the gulch and some down and the one who found water to shout. Some found wet gravel and sand and with their hands dug a hole into which trickled water. It was brackish and warm, but it was water. Nothing ever tasted sweeter. They were saved. Next morning by digging a deep hole in the creek bed a good supply of water was obtained. As they were about to move away the next morning the thought struck Mr. Scovill that some other poor creature might come along the trail, strike the gulch, find a dry instead of a wet camp, and despair. So he took an empty flour-barrel and scrawled upon it : "Water 1,000 feet up the gulch, E. T. Scovill, chief of engineers." This he stuck in the sand by the side of the trail. Now the scene of the story shifts to South America. Mr. Scovill sat in the Llama Club, Lima. He had gone to Peru to help Henry Meigs build those wonderful railways in the mountains. Here, to a company of Americans and English, he told the story of his journey across the plains. There was one man in the party who was evidently excited. As Mr. Scovill reached the end of the story, and told how he had put up the sign that water could be found a thousand feet up the gulch, the nervous stranger, a man of giant frame, leaped from his seat and took Scovill in his arms as if the latter had been a child. "Then you are the man, are you"? he exclaimed ; " you are the man who saved my life. I went across the desert a few days after you. I—my companions and I—suffered as you suffered. On the way we killed our horses and drank their blood. When we finally reached the gulch we had just strength enough left to enable us to crawl down into the dry creek bed. There we lay down to die, when one of us happened to see your blessed guide board. A thousand feet up the gulch we found water. If we hadn't I should not be here to-night to take the hand of the man who saved our lives."

Ver. 4–7. **Thou shalt smite the rock.**—*Horeb ; or, great mercies from unlikely sources :*—I. THE SECULAR DEPARTMENT OF HUMAN HISTORY WILL FURNISH ABUNDANT ILLUSTRATIONS OF THIS PRINCIPLE. 1. Does intelligence conduce to this end? Undoubtedly knowledge tends to make men secularly happy. How often, then, do you find streams of intelligence gushing from the most unlikely sources. Demosthenes was a stammerer ; Homer and Milton were blind ; Shakespeare was the son of a butcher. 2. Do philanthropic institutions conduce to the secular well-being of man? Unquestionably. If you look to the origin of temperance societies, asylums, provident associations, &c., you will find they have generally sprung from the most unlikely sources. 3. Does political liberty conduce to the secular well-being of man? Undoubtedly. It, too, has come mostly from unlikely sources— Moses, Luther, &c. II. THE SPIRITUAL DEPARTMENT OF HUMAN HISTORY WILL FURNISH STILL GREATER ILLUSTRATIONS OF THIS PRINCIPLE. 1. See it exemplified in the spiritual Deliverer of the race. Babe in manger ; Son of carpenter ; Man of sorrows, &c. ; malefactor on cross. "This rock," says St. Paul, "is Christ"—is like Christ. How? (1) In the value of the blessings which emanate therefrom. (*a*) Most needed. (*b*) Most adequate. (2) In the method employed to secure the blessing. Rock smitten. (3) In the fact under notice, the unlikelihood of the source. 2. See it exemplified in the first preachers of the gospel. Poor fishermen, &c. 3. See it exemplified in the missionary enterprise. Carey, the shoemaker ; Williams, the blacksmith ; Moffat, the gardener, &c. Conclusion : This subject suggests—1. Good ground for trusting God in the greatest difficulty. 2. To remove all ground for glorying in your usefulness. God could make the meanest creatures do all and more than you can accomplish. (*Homilist.*) *Crying unto the Lord for help :*—Hiacoomes, an early Indian convert, was a remarkable man. Two years after his conversion (1743), having in the meantime been prepared by Mr. Mayhew, he commenced teaching to the Indians the things of Christianity. He was not suffered to proceed without opposition from the Paw-Waws, Sachems, and other Indians; but he made this improvement of the injustice done him. "I had," he remarked, "one hand for injuries and another hand for God; while I received wrong with the one, I laid the faster hold on God with the other." These words should be written in gold. (*New York Independent.*) *The needful things of life providentially supplied:*—I. THAT MEN ARE SOMETIMES BROUGHT INTO GREAT STRAITS THROUGH LACK OF THE ORDINARY THINGS OF LIFE. "And there was no water for the people to drink." Thus the Israelites lacked water. They had lacked bread only a few days previously. 1. It is not the lot of man to be long free from trial of some kind. Trials come successively. Job, Joseph, David. They are diversified according to the station in which our tent is fixed. Every sphere of life has something of perplexity connected with it, which tests our moral nature and brings the mercy of God near to us. We must learn both how to want and how to abound, to be sorrowful and yet always rejoicing. 2. Thus by the varied trials of life man is made to feel that earth cannot give him abiding satisfaction, and he is led to anticipate the rest of heaven. There the wilderness is unknown, and hunger and thirst are not experienced. The Lamb feeds them. They drink of the River of the Water of Life. 3. But we see from this narrative that each occasion of want on the part of Israel was signalized by a rich manifestation of the mercy of God. Their hunger was met by the manna. Their thirst was met by the streams of Horeb. The hour of man's need is often the hour of God's richest gift and blessing. II. THAT WHEN MEN ARE BROUGHT INTO GREAT STRAITS THROUGH LACK OF THE ORDINARY THINGS OF LIFE, THEY OFTEN APPEAL TO HUMAN AGENCIES RATHER THAN TO DIVINE. "Wherefore the people did chide with Moses, and said, Give us water that we may drink." How foolish, for did not he suffer from the same calamity? nor was it in his power to create fountains. How cruel, for was not he seeking their freedom? How fickle the approbation of men, it varies with the circumstances of life. People often go to the human in trouble when they ought to go to the Divine. III. THAT WHEN MEN ARE BROUGHT INTO STRAITS THROUGH THE LACK OF THINGS THEY VERY MUCH NEED, THEY OFTEN GET THEIR HELP IN THE PROVIDENCE OF GOD FROM THE MOST UNLIKELY SOURCES. "Behold, I will stand before thee there upon the rock in Horeb; and thou shalt smite the rock, and there shall come water out of it, that the people may drink." Thus we see that God did not flash immediate judgment upon these rebellious people. He is long-suffering toward the race. We must learn to be patient with those who injure us. God has regard to human need, and evil in men will not turn Him away from His promise. None need despair of His mercy. When the people chide, the minister should pray. Our heavenly Father is never absent from the good; goodness and mercy follow them all their days. IV. THAT WHEN MEN ARE BROUGHT INTO STRAITS, THE WAY IN WHICH THEY ACT THEREIN WILL LEAVE IRREPARABLE MEMORIALS OF SIN OR VICTORY. "And he called the name of the place Massah, and Meribah, because of the chiding of the children of Israel," &c. Let us not leave behind in our life memorials of strife and unbelief, but of faith and good works. Such memorials are abiding; once erected, they cannot be removed; hence the need that they should be worthy. Lessons: 1. That man is frequently called upon in this life to endure great physical need. 2. That the physical needs of life often reveal our real and inner character. 3. That the physical needs of life are no indication that God has failed us. 4. That the physical needs of life give us a great insight into the wealth and method of the Divine mercy. (*J. S. Exell, M.A.*) *The smitten rock:*—I. THE ROCK A TYPE OF CHRIST. 1. Its situation. In midst of wilderness. 2. Its stability (Isa. xxviii. 16). 3. Its durability. Jesus Christ is the same yesterday, to-day, and for ever. II. MOSES STRIKING THE ROCK. An act of violence required. When man is to be saved, the rod of Divine wrath strikes the Saviour, and "the rock" pours forth streams of everlasting salvation. III. THE PURPOSE OF THE MIRACLE. (*I. Saunders.*) *Water out of the rock, a type of Christ:*— I. AS A ROCK IT ELEGANTLY TYPED OUT JESUS CHRIST, FITLY COMPARED TO A ROCK IN FIVE RESEMBLANCES. 1. For the despicable appearance. The rock is in appearance dry and barren, the most unlikely thing in all the world to afford water, so as it was incredible to Moses and Aaron themselves to fetch water out of a rock. Even so Jesus Christ was (for outward form and appearance in the world) most unlikely of all men to afford any such waters of grace and salvation (Isa. liii. 2). 2. A Rock for exaltation and advancement. A rock is a promontory lifted up above the earth. Such a Rock was Christ advanced above the earth, yea, and the heavens; advanced above all men and creatures—(1) In holiness and purity. (2) In power and authority. (3) In place and dignity (John iii. 31). 3. A Rock for firmness and stability. He is the strength of Israel (Matt. xvi. 18). Hence He is a rock of defence and safety to His chosen ; and every wise man builds his house on this Rock. 4. A Rock of scandal and offence to wicked men (Rom. ix. 32). 5. A Rock for weight and danger and unavoidable judgment upon His adversaries, which, " on whomsoever it shall fall, it will grind him to powder" (Matt. xxi. 44). II. It was a type of Christ, AS IT SENT OUT WATER IN ABUNDANCE TO THE PEOPLE OF ISRAEL READY TO PERISH FOR THIRST. For so Jesus Christ is the only Rock that sends from Himself all the sweet waters of life for the salvation of His elect, otherwise ready to perish eternally. For explanation whereof, mark—1. As from that rock issued waters to wash and cleanse themselves and their garments, so from this Rock stream waters of ablution or washing, which serve to wash away both the guilt of sin and stain of sin. 2. As from that rock issued waters to cool and comfort Israel in their weariness and wanderings, so from Jesus Christ do issue the waters of refrigeration and comfort, to cool and refresh the dry and thirsty soul ; to allay the heat of a raging and accusing conscience, and to revive with new strength the fainting soul in temptation or persecution. 3. As from that rock streamed abundance of waters to make fruitful that barren wilderness wheresoever they ran, so only from the true Rock issue plentiful waters of grace to make our dry and barren hearts fruitful in all works of righteousness (Isa. xliv. 3, 4). III. IN THE MANNER OF ATTAINING THIS WATER ARE MANY SWEET RESEMBLANCES. 1. The people might ask Moses for water, but Moses cannot give it. It is God must give it, and miraculously fetch it out of a rock. 2. The rock gives water, but not till it be smitten (ver. 6). 3. It was the rod in Moses' hand that smites and breaks the rock. Even so it was the Law given by Moses' hand and our transgression against it that breaks the true Rock (Isa. liii. 5 ; Gal. iii. 13). 4. The rock was smitten, but it was not so much the striking on the rock, but the Lord's standing upon it that gets water for Israel (ver. 6). There was no virtue in the stroke, but all depended on God's commandment and presence ; even so it is not the death of Christ, nor an abundance of price and merit of His blood, nor the striking on this rock before men's eyes in the ministry of the Word and sacraments that can bring one drop of true water of comfort, but by the presence and word of God's blessing. The efficacy of grace depends not on any means or work wrought, but it is God's word and presence that doth all in them. (*T. Taylor, D.D.*) *Help from an unlikely source :*—The manna was simply sent from heaven, but the water, on the contrary, was brought out of the smitten rock—the most unlikely place that could be imagined. Some men went about collecting funds for an important charity. They arrived in course of time at a very rich man's door who was known to be churlish in his manner and niggardly in his gifts ; whereupon they said that there was no need to call on him, " he is not likely to give." However, they entered, and laid their case before him, and to their surprise he at once responded by giving them the largest donation they had yet received. Rephidim-Rock was a most unlikely place from which to receive supplies of water.

Ver. 7. **Is the Lord among us, or not ?**—*Evidences of the Divine presence :*—I. WE OBSERVE AN INCREASE OF SPIRITUAL ENLIGHTENMENT IS AN EVIDENCE OF THE DIVINE PRESENCE AMONG A PEOPLE. II. WE OBSERVE SPIRITUAL-MINDEDNESS IS AN EVIDENCE OF THE DIVINE PRESENCE AMONG A PEOPLE. III. WE OBSERVE CHRISTIAN LOVE IS AN EVIDENCE OF THE DIVINE PRESENCE AMONG A PEOPLE. IV. ACTIVITY AND DEVOTEDNESS IN THE CAUSE OF CHRIST IS AN EVIDENCE OF THE DIVINE PRESENCE AMONG A PEOPLE. We have three remarks in conclusion—1. The unrenewed may learn from this subject that there is no hope for him of any radical improvement save in the grace of God. The Holy Spirit is the sole agent for this work. 2. The Church of God should learn from this subject that the grace and presence of the Lord in the midst of them is the one thing needful. 3. Let all know that the Lord is to be found in the power and sufficiency of His grace by all who seek Him through the Saviour. (*H. F. Holmes.*) *" Is the Lord among us, or not ? "—a false inference :*—Notwithstanding all the other tokens of God's presence they thought that their renewed difficulties were a proof that God was no longer amongst them. And are not our hearts far too apt to come to the same conclusion on the same grounds ? We enter on some new path, on some fresh work, because we think that the hand of God is leading us to it, and, almost unconsciously to ourselves, we suppose that His presence will secure us from any great and discouraging difficulties. Our expectations are disappointed—one difficulty after another presents itself—one door after another is closed. What follows? Too often doubts begin to arise in our minds whether God is really with us. But these doubts should not be encouraged. It is altogether a false inference, that because our path is one of difficulty or trial, therefore the Lord is not among us. The very reverse will usually be found to be the true conclusion. (*G. Wagner.*)

Ver. 8. **Then came Amalek, and fought.**—*Fighting and praying :*—" Then came Amalek " ; that is, after the manna had fallen, after the rock had been smitten. First food, then conflict. God spared His people all battles in their early days. In our march to heaven, it may happen that one part of the way is free from conflict; but let no man wonder if things change. One of these days we shall read this despatch from the seat of war, " Then came Amalek, and fought with Israel." Do not court attack, nor even desire it. When you hear the older folk talk about their inward conflicts, do not lament if your chronicle of wars is a short one. It has often been the Lord's way to give His people space for refreshment before trying them. We cannot work for God too soon ; yet it is possible to go to work before you have sharpened your tools. There is a time for every purpose ; and each thing is good in its season. Learn, and then teach. I would have you serve the Lord successfully : wherefore, as God gave to Israel manna and water before He sent them to fight with Amalek, so should every believer feed on the truth himself, and then go forth to teach others also. Feed, that you may work, and work because you have been fed. After the manna and after the smitten rock, came the fight: " Then came Amalek." He was a descendant of Esau, full of his father's hate. Note well, that in this battle of the Lord, there were two kinds of fighting. The first was the Joshua-service ; and that was done in the plain by the fighting men. The second was the Moses-service ; and this was done upon the side of the hill, by the men of God, who communed with heaven. We need both modes of warfare. I. To begin with, we want much of THE JOSHUA-SERVICE. 1. This is the service of many. Moses said to Joshua, " Choose us out men, and go out, fight with Amalek." We have a battle against sin, error, pride, self, and everything that is contrary to God and to His Christ ; and in the Joshua-service many can be employed. Every believer should be a soldier in Christ's own army of salvation. 2. In this Joshua-service all the combatants were under due command. " Joshua did as Moses had said to him," and the people did as Joshua commanded them. In all holy service, willingness to be led is a great point. Certain workers may be very good personally ; but they will never combine with others to make a conquering band. They work very well alone, or as fore-horses in the team ; but they cannot trot in double harness. Soldiers without discipline become a mob, and not an army. Friend, will you be one of the steady workers ? 3. In Joshua-work courage was required. " Go out, fight with Amalek." The Amalekites were fierce, cruel, strong. They are said to have been the chief among the nations ; by which I understand first among the plunderers of the desert. The soldiers under Joshua had courage, and faced their wolfish foes. Saints need courage for Jesus in these days. May God, in His mercy, make His people bold against scepticism, superstition, and open wickedness ! We are called, not to flirt with error and evil, but to fight with it ; therefore, let us be brave, and push on the conflict. 4. Those fighting under Joshua did not grow weary. Moses had the more spiritual work, and his hands grew heavy : we sooner tire in private devotion than in public service. Joshua and his men were not weary : never let us be weary in well-doing. Do you ever grow weary in one peculiar way of serving God ? It may be useful to try something else. I mean, do something extra. Variety of labour serves for recreation. 5. In the Joshua-service they were successful, for " they discomfited Amalek and his people with the edge of the sword." Beloved workers for the Lord : may He grant you like success against evil ! The devil goes to be beaten, and he shall be beaten. II. THE MOSES-SERVICE—the service of Moses and his comrades. These did not go down to the battle-field themselves, but they climbed the mountain-side, where they could see the warriors in the conflict ; and there Moses lifted up the rod of God. 1. Note, that the Moses-service was essential to the battle ; for when Moses held up his hand, Israel prevailed ; and when he let down his hand, Amalek prevailed. The scales of the conflict were in the hand of Moses, and they turned as his prayer and testimony failed or continued. 2. This holy work was of a very special character. Only three were able to enter into it. I believe that, in every Church, the deeply spiritual, who prevalently commune with God, and bring down the blessing upon the work of the rest, are comparatively few.

3. This Moses-service lay in very close communion with God. Moses, and Aaron, and Hur were called to rise above the people, and to get alone, apart from the company. They climbed the hill as a symbol, and in retirement they silently communed with God. 4. In this sacred engagement there was a terrible strain upon the one man who led the others in it. In the process of bringing down the Divine power upon the people, the vehicle of communication was sorely tried. "Moses' hands were heavy." If God gives you spiritual power to lead in Christian work, you you will soon find out that the condition of such leadership is a costly one. 5. In this hallowed service help is very precious. When Moses' hands began to drop down, and he himself was faint, Aaron and Hur gave him substantial aid. Are you a worker? Have you a leader fit to lead you? Bring a stone and put under him: cheer his heart with some gracious promise from the Lord's Word, or with some happy sign from the work itself. Cheer the good man as much as possible. (*C. H. Spurgeon.*)   *The battle between good and evil :*—I.. THAT THE GOOD ARE REQUIRED TO DO BATTLE WITH INVETERATE ENEMIES (ver. 8). 1. Every soul has to contend with the Amalek of (1) an evil heart; (2) a wicked world ; (3) fallen angels. 2. The soul is led gradually into the moral battle of life. We cannot get to heaven without being interrupted by many enemies—by Satan, by poverty, by sickness, by prosperity; all these will seek to stop or slay us. II. THAT THE GOOD IN THIS CONFLICT MUST COMBINE PRAYER WITH THE UTMOST EXERTION TO OVERCOME THEIR ENEMIES (vers. 9-11). Truth has lost many a battle through bad generalship. Truth needs a man like Luther to lead the attack. If we would overcome evil within us and without us, we must summon the best energies of our mental and moral nature, and put them under the command of Christ ; then shall we be led to victory. Joshua fought. Moses went up the hill to pray. Prayer is often uphill work. And the conflict between Good and Evil necessitates the use of prayer and activity. Man must pray over his evil heart, and he must also fight against its sinful tendencies. Sin is persistent in its opposition to the soul. III. THAT THE GOOD IN THIS CONFLICT ARE OFTEN IMPEDED BY THE WEAKNESS CONSEQUENT UPON THE PHYSICAL CONDITION OF LIFE (ver. 12). Nature at the strongest is weak. But the hands of Moses were supported by Aaron and Hur. Holy companionship is helpful in the hour of severe moral conflict. Two are better far than one. Christians should seek to hold up the hands of ministers. They must bear one another's burdens. The insignificant members of the Church may render service to the most important ; Hur may strengthen Moses. The hands of our heavenly Intercessor never grow weary with pleading ; and the infirm Christian will soon be as the angels. It is consoling that God knows our frame, and remembers that we are dust. IV. THAT THE GOOD IN THEIR CONFLICT SHOULD KEEP FAITHFUL RECORD OF THEIR VICTORIES (vers. 13, 14). 1. To aid memory. 2. To inspire hope. 3. To awaken gratitude to God. V. THAT THE GOOD IN THIS CONFLICT SHOULD ASCRIBE ALL THE GLORY OF VICTORY TO GOD (vers. 15, 16). Lessons : 1. That there are inveterate enemies to moral goodness. 2. That these enemies are doomed to ultimate defeat and destruction. 3. That the good must pray and fight to this end. 4. There will be a final celebration of victory. (*J. S. Exell, M.A.*)   *War with Amalek :*—I. First, then, we have here THE EXPERIENCE OF EVERY INDIVIDUAL CHRISTIAN. 1. Observe, the Children of Israel were emancipated from bondage, and had left Egypt behind, even as you and I have been rescued from our natural state and are no longer the servants of sin. 2. The Children of Israel were probably anticipating ease, forgetting that the Promised Land was yet many days' journey beyond them. Inexperience made them expect a continuance of uninterrupted song and feasting, and there was a time when we indulged in the same foolish hopes. 3. Like Israel, we soon experienced tribulations. You must fight if you would win the crown, and your pathway to the other side of Jordan must be the pathway of an armed crusader, who has to contend for every inch of the way if he is to win it. 4. In proceeding with the narrative we notice that they found opposition from an unexpected quarter. It is just where we feel most safe that we should be most cautious. I do not think the Christian has so much to fear from open and avowed enemies as from those deceitful foes who feign to be his friends. Sin is never so much a Jezebel as when it paints its face with daubs of respectability and patches of innocence. Things dubious are more dangerous than things distinctly evil. 5. When the assault was made, the people were commanded to exert themselves. The message was given, "Go, choose out men, and fight with Amalek." Israel never fought with Egypt. God fought for them, and they held their peace. The yoke of sin has been broken by God's grace from off our necks, and now we have to fight

not as slaves against a master, but as freemen against a foe. 6. Spiritual fighting must be conducted on most earnest and prudent principles. They were to choose out men. So we must choose out our ways of contending with sin. The best part of a man should be engaged in warfare with his sins. 7. This makes me notice that though the men of Israel were to fight, and the chosen men were to be selected, yet they were to fight under the command of Joshua, that is, Jesus, the Saviour. 8. That where holy activity is joined with earnest supplication, the result as to our sins is absolutely sure—the enemy must be defeated; we shall put our feet upon the necks of all our sins. There is no fear of their overcoming us if we do but lay hold on Divine strength. 9. And, if ever we overcome sin once, it should be the signal for proclaiming a general war against all sin. The fight and victory over Amalek brought from God's mouth the solemn declaration that there should be war with Amalek for ever and ever. Have you mastered one sin? Slay the next, and the next, and the next. II. The whole narrative may be interpreted AS THE HISTORY OF ANY ONE CHRISTIAN CHURCH. In any one Church there will be, there must be, if it be a Church of God, earnest contention for the truth and against error. If we do indeed hold the very truth as it is in Jesus, we must fight for it valiantly, for if we do not fight Amalek, Amalek will certainly fight us, and the hindmost will always be suffering and the weakest go to the wall. It is on behalf of the weaker brethren, who are easily perverted, that we must watch and fight perpetually. To all Christian effort in every Church must be added unceasing intercession. III. But lastly, THE HISTORY OF THE WHOLE CHRISTIAN CHURCH IS HERE BEFORE US AS IN A PICTURE. The sacramental host of God's elect is warring still on earth, Jesus Christ being the Captain of their salvation. He has said, " Lo ! I am with you always, even to the end of the world." (*C. H. Spurgeon.*) *The war of truth :*—I. THE GREAT WARFARE. 1. Not with men, but with Satan and error. 2. A most righteous warfare. 3. A war of the greatest importance. 4. Insidious and very powerful foes. 5. A war of perpetual duration. II. THE APPOINTED MEANS OF WARFARE. 1. Hard blows. 2. Hard prayers. (*Ibid.*) *Both sides of the shield :*—I. First, let us look at PERSECUTION IN ITS DOUBLE ASPECT. On the one hand, notice that this attack upon Israel was Amalek's great sin, on account of which the nation was doomed to be extirpated. Because of this, God said, " I will utterly put out the remembrance of Amalek from under heaven." But, on the other hand, this assault was the result of Israel's sin; for it is significantly put after the strife of Massah and Meribah, " *Then* came Amalek, and fought with Israel in Rephidim." The point is this : persecution may come to you from evil men, distinctly from them, and it may be their wicked free will which makes them assail you ; and yet, at the same time, it may be your sin which lies at the bottom of it, and because you have erred they have been permitted, and even appointed, to bring trouble upon you. Let us think of these two things. 1. Notice well that assaults upon us may arise from the sins of others. It is right that we should recognize this, lest in the dark day we should become unduly discouraged. These Amalekites attacked Israel, and greatly sinned in so doing, for they were the first that made war against God's people. But the impiety was still worse ; for Amalek went out of his way to attack Israel. The people had not come into his territory ; they were a good way off it, and were passing quietly by ; but we read, " Then came Amalek." His envy was stirred up so much that he came away from his own region to fight with Israel without any provocation. Moreover, Amalek in this act went forth to fight against God Himself. It was not with Israel alone that he warred ; he battled also with Jehovah, the God of Israel. When you are persecuted for righteousness' sake, the Lord takes notice of it. " Saul, Saul, why persecutest thou Me ? " Let us now turn our thoughts to the other aspect of this subject. 2. The guilt of ungodly men in persecuting God's people is not inconsistent with my next statement, that assaults upon us may also arise from our own sins. We may have brought the evil upon ourselves. When they had chided with Moses, and murmured against God, " *Then* came Amalek." Israel had been quarrelling with God. Do you wonder, then, that other people quarrelled with them ? You may often read your sin in its punishment. They put a question about God, " Is the Lord among us, or not ? " But, because they questioned God, God makes it a serious question between them and Amalek. If we make God a question, God will make our safety a question, and we shall have a stern fight for it. Moreover, we find that Israel had uttered threats against Moses, so that he said, " They be almost ready to stone me." Now, if they would stone the man of God, is it at all wonderful that the men of the world were ready to kill them ? If you go against

Moses, God will sent Amalek against you, for remember that God does chasten His people. So, there is our first point. We may sometimes justly charge our afflictions upon the ill intent of ungodly men; and yet, at the same time, we may have to charge them also upon ourselves. II. In the second place, let us think of INSTRUMENTALITY IN ITS DOUBLE RELATION. Here, again, another contrast is to be found in the text and its connection. If you will notice, in the fifth verse, God says to Moses, "Take with thee of the elders of Israel; and thy rod, wherewith thou smotest the river"; but when Moses talks about the rod, in the ninth verse, which forms our text, he says, "To-morrow I will stand on the top of the hill with the rod of God in mine hand." In both verses it is the same rod which is spoken of. 1. One side is that God calls it the rod of Moses, and so honours him. Wherever there is an opportunity of doing honour to the faith of His own servants, God is never slow to use it. He is a King who delights to give glory to His warriors when they behave themselves bravely in the heat of battle. Moreover, it really was the rod of Moses, and would not so well have fitted any other hand. God does not put into a position of influence a man unfit for the post. Even Moses did not work wonders with the rod until he had renounced the riches of Egypt, and borne the burden of life in the wilderness. There was a fitness in the fact of the rod being in the hand of such a man. Thus, in a very real sense, it was the rod of Moses. In addition to this, it was the faith of Moses which gave power to his rod; he himself was the conductor of the Divine energy. Had the rod been wielded by another man, self-appointed, and lacking the confidence which Moses had come to possess in God, it would have been simply a powerless stick. 2. On the other hand, Moses calls it the rod of God, and so honours God. He whom God uses gives God the praise, for God is ever the source of our strength; and if any work is done that is worth the doing, unto Him must be ascribed all the glory. "Not unto us, O Lord; not unto us, but unto Thy name, give glory." Let us learn, from these words of Moses, that instrumentality is not to be decried, for God uses it; but the instrument must never be allowed to usurp the place of God, for it must be always remembered that it is God who uses it. The axe must not exalt itself against him that heweth therewith; but, when there are trees to be felled, it would be folly to throw the axe away. III. Behold, in this incident, PRUDENCE IN ITS DOUBLE ACTIVITY. You have that in the text. Moses said unto Joshua, "Choose us out men, and go out, fight with Amalek." To which Joshua might have replied, "Yes, I will gladly do that, and you will go too, Moses, and fight, will you not?" No, no, he will not. "To-morrow I will stand on the top of the hill with the rod of God in mine hand." Prudence prays with Moses, while it fights with Joshua. In like manner, in the activities of our holy faith, we must learn to balance work and worship, prayer for victory and conflict with the enemy. 1. In the case before us, we see that the means are not neglected. Moses did not call all the people to pray when it was time for fighting. He prayed, but at the same time he set the battle in array. This is true wisdom, for "faith without works is dead." The means must not be neglected. Observe how Moses prepared to fight the Amalekites. He said to Joshua, "Choose us out men." He did not lose sight of the necessity of having the fittest warriors, because his trust was in God. Let the Church always see to it that she tries to get the best men she can to fight the battles of the Lord. It is a mistake to suppose that anybody will do for Christian work. The leader was also chosen—"Moses said unto *Joshua*." He did not pick up the first youth that he met, and say to him, "Go and fight these Amalekites." The time for the battle was also chosen. "*To-morrow* I will stand on the top of the hill. Why not fight them at once? Well, because the people were not ready; it would take a little time to get the fighting men in order. Choose the best time. Serve God wisely. Go about the work as if all depended upon you, and then trust in God, knowing that all depends upon Him. Note, again, that the battle was most real. Moses did not say, "Choose you out men, and go and drive Amalek away like a flock of sheep." No; but "Go out, fight with Amalek." Believe me, we make a great mistake if we think that this world is to be conquered for Christ without mighty efforts. Some talk as if the expenditure of a few pounds, and the going forth of a few men, will end the whole war. 2. But, on the other hand, in this battle, reliance upon God is not neglected. Moses ascends the hill holding up his banner, and that banner is the rod of God. Unfortunately, in our work for God, we generally fall into one of two blunders. Either we get a lot of machinery, and think that we shall accomplish everything by that; or else we are like some whom I have known, who have confided so much in prayer that they have done nothing but pray. It is a very heinous fault to trust the means without God; but, though it is a much smaller fault to trust in God, and not use the means, yet still it is a fault. Practical prudence will lead you to do both. IV. Behold here, in a wondrous type, CHRIST IN HIS TWOFOLD CAPACITY. Christ is represented to us here as Moses on the hill pleading, and as Joshua in the valley fighting. 1. Learn, first, that Christ is pleading for us. He is not here: He is risen. It is because He intercedes for us that we win the victory. In His mediation is our confidence. 2. But, then, do not forget that He is also warring for us. On the very eve of His departure, He said, "Lo, I am with you alway, even unto the end of the world." This is the dispensation of the Holy Ghost, and in Him Christ is always with us, our greater Joshua, fighting for the people whom He will one day lead into the promised land, the heavenly Canaan. I think that I see our Joshua now, sword in hand, chasing our adversaries; and I turn my eye upwards, and see our Moses, rod in hand, pleading for His people. Let us see Him in both capacities. Believe in Christ in heaven, and trust Him with your prayers. Believe in Christ on earth, range yourself on His side, and rest assured that no foe will be able to stand against Him. So, you see that, though two things may look contradictory, they are often both really true, and are both different sides of one shield. Try, then, always to see both sides of every truth revealed in the Scriptures. (*Ibid.*) *The assistance of prayer:*—An unaccountable revival broke out in a congregation in a village, and about one hundred were converted in a few weeks. At last the minister discovers the secret of the revival, and relates it thus: "There is a sister in my Church who has for years been an invalid, and confined to her bed. She lives several miles from the village, and the other day I rode out to see her. As I sat by her bedside she said, ' You have had a very precious revival?' 'We have,' I answered. ' I knew it was coming,' she said." And then she proceeded to give her pastor an account of the burden that had been upon her for weeks, and the manner in which her soul had gone out in prayer for the unconverted, in midnight hours and at other times; and before the interview closed the pastor felt that the unaccountable revival was accounted for. Like Hur and Aaron, who held up the hands of Moses, this bedridden sister had by her prayers obtained victory for the soldiers of Christ. *Encouragement:*—There were four boys, all brothers, walking along the banks of a stream, and playing as they went. Like most boys, their idea of fun was to go as far into danger as they could, and at length one of them fell into a deep place. He could not swim, but immediately his brother who could, plunged in to rescue him. He got hold of him but could not bring him to the bank, then another brother, catching hold of a branch, stretched his body out its whole length so that the swimmer could catch hold, and thus all three were brought safe to land. When they got home they all began to tell their father about the affair. "Now give me time," he said, "and I'll hear you all." Turning to the oldest, he asked, "When your brother fell into the river what did you do towards his rescue?" "Well, father, at first I was paralyzed with fear, and I stood on the bank for some seconds trembling for his safety, then I recovered myself and plunging in, caught hold of him, and strove to bring him to shore." Then facing the second boy he said, "And what did you do to rescue your brother?" "I could not swim, father, but when I saw they could not reach the shore, I bridged the water between them and the bank so that they might pull themselves in." Now there only remained the youngest, a little fellow of four years, and turning to him the father asked, "And what did you do?" "Oh, father, I could do nothing. I just stood on the bank and clapped my hands and shouted, "Well done, well done!" "Yes, well done, my boys, all of you, I am proud to have such sons," exclaimed the happy father. Christians, standing safe on the bank, What have you done for the rescue of your brother? At least you can by your words and prayers encourage others who are stronger to go to the rescue of the lost. *The working layman:*—We shall find that the Church, like warring nations, expects every man to do his duty. If, as we suppose, Hur was not of the priestly office, we think the laymen of our day may find that this Scripture was written for their learning. They are, we fear, very far from walking in the steps of Hur, and from following his example. It will be noticed that it was a personal service in which he was engaged, one that required not only labour but the sacrifice of his time. Until the going down of the sun he stood by Moses and stayed up his hands. When Israel was at war with Amalek, he did not content himself with wishes for success, nor did he rejoice over a victory which he had not laboured to win. He did not serve God by proxy, nor send a substitute to perform his personal duties. When he was needed upon the mount, he did not beg to be excused; he pleaded no want of leisure and no press of worldly engagements. It is the great want of the Church in our day—working men and working women, especially working men; men with the true missionary spirit and zeal; men who, like Hur, will not grudge to spend a day on the mount, to stay up Moses' hands. While Aaron and Hur stood on the one side or on the other, the strength of Moses failed not. It is in vain to have officers if men will not fight, or men willing to fight if there are no officers to direct and guide them. There must be the co-operation of all, if we expect prosperity. Our strength is not to sit still. Here is a field which we all may equally occupy; where wealth has no advantage, and where poverty is no loss,—the field of religious influence and personal exertion. We all can do something, many of us can do much, to promote the prosperity of the Church. To destroy Amalek, to bless Israel, we must labour as well as give; we must stay up Moses' hands, as well as worship in the tabernacle. If the priest must pray and preach and toil, no less do we look for them to work. Hur, on the mount with Moses and Aaron, was a type of a working layman. (*G. F. Cushman, D.D.*)

Ver. 9. **The rod of God.**—*Moses' rod, the emblem of power and faith:*—I. THE ROD SERVED TO JOIN MAN AND GOD IN THE WORK OF THE LORD. At the one end, Faith; at the other, Almighty Power. II. THE ROD SERVED TO INCREASE THE CONFIDENCE OF THE PEOPLE IN THEIR GOD. Success everywhere attended the rod. III. THE ROD SERVED TO TEACH THE PEOPLE DEPENDENCE UPON GOD FOR THEIR SUCCESS IN BATTLE. IV. THE ROD SERVED TO TEACH THE PEOPLE THE NEED OF HOLY AND DEVOUT MEN. (*Homilist.*) *Man as a servant of God:*—The words (chap. iv. 17) lead us to contemplate man as a servant of God—a servant to promote the true progress of the race. They suggest four things which God requires man to do in this grand service. I. TO USE THE INSTRUMENT MOST AT HIS COMMAND. II. TO TURN OLD THINGS TO NEW USES. III. TO AIM AT MIGHTY ENDS BY APPARENTLY INSIGNIFICANT MEANS. IV. TO FOLLOW GOD'S WILL, RATHER THAN THE DICTATES OF OUR OWN WISDOM. (*Ibid.*) *The old rod, or the inspiration of common ministries:*—Wondrous is one little line in the history:—"And thy rod, wherewith thou smotest the river, take in thine hand, and go," and afterward Moses, having spoken to Joshua, said, "I will stand on the top of the hill with the rod of God in mine hand." Never forget the old rod, the old book, the old truth;—the sword that cut off the head of Goliath—"Give me that," said David, "there is none like it." Thus God hides inspiration in things of apparently little value, and touches the imagination and the faith by books, ministries, churches, altars, which we thought had passed away into desuetude, perhaps oblivion. Your first prayer may help you to-day. The faith of your youth may be the only thing to win the battle which now challenges your strength. One little hour with the old, old book may be all you need to obtain the sufficiency of light which will drive away the cloud of mystery and bring in the heaven of explanation. (*J. Parker, D.D.*)

Ver. 13. **Joshua discomfited Amalek.**—*Winning God's battles:*—I. Amalek, as we learn from Deut. xxv. 18, had "SMITTEN THE HINDMOST, EVEN ALL THAT WERE FEEBLE." The stragglers are always a temptation to the foe. The hindmost and the feeble are sure to be the first attacked, and therefore should have special care. II. Joshua discomfited AMALEK, not Moses or some other friend. Let us keep our bitterness for sin, and our swords for the King's enemies. III. AMALEK IS NOT TO BE BEATEN WITHOUT A FIGHT. The struggle against sin is real, as we shall find to our cost if we are not wary. IV. MOSES WAS FOR EACH MINDING HIS OWN WORK, Joshua to fight, and himself to take the top of the hill. V. Moses on the hill is AN EMBLEM OF PUBLIC PRAYER. There is a mystery about prayer that we cannot unravel. One of the bravest of Christian soldiers, scarred with many a fight, said, "I will therefore that men pray everywhere, lifting up holy hands." VI. HOW MUCH EVEN THE MIGHTIEST OF MEN ARE DEPENDENT UPON OTHERS MUCH WEAKER THAN THEMSELVES. It was well for the fortunes of the day that Moses was not alone. VII. AN ALTAR MARKED THE PLACE OF BATTLE, AND GLORY WAS GIVEN TO THE LORD OF HOSTS. The soldiers of the Cross should call the battle-fields where they have won their bravest fights by the name of Him to whom they ascribe all might and majesty. (*T. Champness.*) *The battle of Amalek, an instructive war:*—I. AS THE RECORD OF A WAR DISTINGUISHED FROM MOST MODERN WARS. 1. It was purely defensive on the Hebrew side. 2. It was Divinely sanctioned on the Hebrew side. 3. It was evidently judicial on the Hebrew side. II. AS THE RECORD OF A WAR SUGGESTING

PRINCIPLES OF GENERAL APPLICATION. 1. The propagating influence of evil. I find the primal cause of this war in the injury which Jacob perpetrated upon his brother Esau (Gen. xxvii. 18, 19). God only knows the influence of one evil act. 2. The Divine liberty allowed to wicked men. Full freedom to work out revengeful passions. 3. The variety of instrumentality by which God works out His designs. The Eternal ever works by means. 4. The dependence of man's progress on his relation to heaven. 5. The importance of transmitting to posterity the agency of God in history (see ver. 14). III. AS THE RECORD OF A WAR SYMBOLIZING THE MORAL STRUGGLE IN WHICH THE GOOD ARE ENGAGED. 1. That the good have spiritual enemies to contend with. 2. That the victory which the good are to obtain over their enemies depends on the help of others. 3. That whatever may be the amount of help obtained in the struggle, the victory must ever be ascribed to God. (*Homilist.*) *Israel and Amalek :*—I. THE CHRISTIAN'S EXAMPLE. 1. To fight. (1) An aggressive fight. "Go." (2) To be done wisely. "Choose you out men." (3) Earnestly "Fight." No parley. (4) Continually. 2. To pray. (1) For those who fight. (2) Earnestly. Not growing weary. (3) Confidently. "The rod"—symbol of past mercies. (4) Unitedly. II. THE CHRISTIAN'S ENCOURAGEMENT. 1. Christ, our Captain—(1) With us, to cheer. (2) With us, to direct. (3) With us, to defend. 2. Christ, our intercessor. (1) Prays, while we work. (2) Prays continually. (3) Prays successfully. III. THE CHRISTIAN'S PROSPECT. I. Of certain victory. 2. Of certain glory. (*B. D. Macmillan.*)　　*Amalek and Israel :*—I. THE BATTLE WAS FORCED UPON THE VICTORS. II. THE BATTLE WAS HOTLY CONTESTED. III. THE VANQUISHED OWED DEFEAT, AND THE VICTORS VICTORY, TO DIVINE POWER THROUGH HUMAN INTERCESSION. Lessons : 1. As soon as we become followers of Christ, war is forced upon us. 2. Every Christian possesses a Divine rod which, wielded, will bring him Divine help (Heb. iv. 16). 3. Christians in their conflict have an Intercessor on the hill, and a Leader in the valley. Christ makes intercession (Heb. vii. 25) ; and the Holy Spirit helps our infirmities (Rom. viii. 26), and guides into all truth (John xvi. 13). (*W. Harris.*)　　*Lessons :*—1. Hands of creature-instruments may be helpful under God, to give His Church success against its enemies. 2. Such hands lifted up to heaven in prayer, and for encouragement, God doth assist unto prevalency. 3. Hands hanging down and feeble in prayer, may give opportunity unto enemies to prevail. 4. Such languishings after strong strugglings, God sometimes orders upon His choicest servants. 5. Doubtful may be the fight of Israel as to success against its enemies for a time (ver. 11). 6. Heaviness of flesh and spirit in contending with God for Israel may sometimes befall Moses (Matt. xxvi. 41, 43). 7. Suitable support under such delinquencies are very requisite for God's servants. Christ the stone to us. 8. Good helpers to strengthen hearts and hands in faintings are specially useful. 9. By such helps souls may be stedfast and faithful unto God unto time of victory (ver. 12). 10. Moses praying and Joshua fighting, Amalek must fall, when prayer puts the edge on the sword it is furbished to the slaughter. 11. It is God's just ordering that they who first oppress with the sword, shall perish by the sword (ver. 13). (*G. Hughes, B.D.*)

Ver. 14. **I will utterly put out the remembrance of Amalek.**—*Lessons :*—1. Jehovah's victories over His Church's enemies He giveth in charge to be recorded. 2. Writing and tradition are both God's ways of recording His works for future ages. 3. God's book is the best record of His mighty works done for His Church. 4. A memorial would God have kept by the records of God's works to men. 5. God hath irreconcilable displeasure against some enemies above the rest. 6. Blotting out of the names of such enemies will God make, who would blot out the name of His Church. (*G. Hughes, B.D.*)　　*Destruction of Amalek :*—I. It is probable that from this time MOSES BEGAN TO KEEP A JOURNAL OF STRIKING AND USEFUL OCCURRENCES. Great men have frequently done the same for intellectual, and good men for religious, purposes. II. Whatever may be said of the particular mode, THE THING ITSELF IS OF IMPORTANCE. If we are to be affected with transactions and feelings, they must be in some way secured and retained. III. A reason is assigned for the recording and rehearsing of this transaction IN A DREADFUL MENACE. The threatening was executed partially by Saul ; but fully by David. IV. THE SCRIPTURES CANNOT BE BROKEN. Whatever improbabilities appear—whatever difficulties stand in the way— whatever delays intervene—God's counsels of old are faithfulness and truth ; not a jot of His Word shall fail. (*W. Jay.*)　　*Use of history :*—Lucius Lucullus, being appointed captain-general over the Roman forces against Mithridates, had not great experience or knowledge in war, but only what he had gotten by reading history,.

yet proved a discreet and valiant commander, and vanquished at that time two of the greatest princes in the East. Thus it is that history is, and may be, the director of meanest men in any of their actions, how others have behaved themselves upon several occasions, and what hath followed thereupon ; it is a trusty counsellor of state, by whose advice and direction a commonwealth may be framed, governed, reformed, and preserved, an army may be ordered, enemies vanquished, and victory obtained. In it, as in a glass, we see and behold God's providence guiding and ruling the world, and men's actions which arrive often at unexpected events, and even sometimes reach unto such ends as are quite contrary to the actor's intentions ; it is a punisher of vice, presenting aged folly green and fresh to posterity ; not suffering sin to die, much less to be buried in oblivion ; it is also a rewarder of virtue, reserving worthy deeds for imitation ; a good work, though it die in doing, is a reward to itself, yet that some dull natures might be stirred up the more, and all benefited by seeing gracious steps before them, this only is exempted by a firm decree from the stroke of death, to live in history. (*J. Crompton.*)

Ver. 15. **Jehovah-nissi, the Lord my banner.**—I. The fight with Amalek was Israel's first battle, and God made it to them THE REVELATION OF THE MYSTERY OF ALL BATTLES—the unseen spiritual things on which depend the final issues of all struggles and the progress of the world. 1. The main purpose of Israel's history is the revelation of the unseen influences which mould the character and guide the progress of all people or minister to their decay and death. (1) The first apparent condition of success was the courage and skill of the commander and of the troops. The successes of life are to the capable, the brave, the enduring ; but—and here is the great lesson of Rephidim—they are to capacity, courage, and energy married to, and not divorced from, the fear and the love of God. (2) There was a second and higher condition. Joshua fought while Moses was praying, and while he knew that Moses was praying. The people had a conscious hold on the strength of the arm of God. 2. It may be fairly asked if in all battles the victory is with those who can not only fight, but pray. The answer is that it is only on a very large scale that we can trace the ways of God. Yet we may say that in any conflict the best reinforcement, that which stands a man in best stead and raises our surest hope of victory, is the assurance that God is on his side. II. The text is THE REVELATION TO US OF THE MYSTERY OF THE GREAT BATTLE in which we are all combatants, the battle OF LIFE. "Jehovah-nissi" must be our watchword, if we would not doom ourselves to go down before the foe. 1. The Lord is our banner against self, that baser part of us which is ever ensnaring, enslaving, and dragging us down into the pit. 2. The Lord is our banner against the world. 3. The Lord is our banner against the devil. (*J. B. Brown, B.A.*) *Jehovah-nissi :*—I. THE ALTAR A MEMORIAL OF AN HISTORIC FACT. Great battle of Rephidim. One of the most remarkable. The enemy—crafty, cruel, cowardly—attacked the rear where the young, aged, women, &c. (Deut. xxv. 17, 18). Israelites unarmed, unused to warfare. Taken by surprise in the rear. They could succeed only by the help of God. II. THIS ALTAR A RECORD OF RELIGIOUS DUTY. 1. The duty of diligently using the means at hand in doing our proper and appointed work. Moses chose the general. Joshua chose the fittest men. The men chose their weapons. 2. The duty of encouraging those who may be in peculiar danger. Moses to Joshua (ver. 9). 3. The duty of rendering willing sympathy and aid. Israel hastening to the rescue of the feeble, &c., who were attacked. III. THIS ALTAR AN EXPRESSION OF PIOUS SENTIMENTS. 1. Of faith. Flushed with success, remembering much individual prowess, they acknowledge that their victory was from another source. 2. Of gratitude. The altar left behind would teach all desert travellers to trust in the Lord. 3. Resolution for the future. They would only fight for the right, and under this banner. We too have a banner (Isa. xi. 10). Must be united (Isa. xi. 12, 13), and rally round it (Psa. lx. 4 ; Song ii. 4). (*J. C. Gray.*) *Jehovah my banner :*—There are two names in Scripture conspicuous above all others, the names Jehovah and Jesus ; the one stamped upon the Old Testament, the other upon the New. Jesus is "the name which is above every name" ; it is the crowning word of Revelation. And the title Jehovah is that which lies beneath and sustains every other name, that on which all teaching about God contained in the Bible, and all true knowledge of Him, virtually rest. It is the foundation name of Scripture. With the name of Jesus we are very familiar. But the other word, the proper name of the God of Israel and of our Lord Jesus Christ, is too much overlooked and forgotten by the Church. And this greatly to our loss ; for in declaring it to Moses God said, "This is My name for ever, and My memorial

unto all generations." And this oblivion betokens the neglect of not a little belonging to the fundamental teaching about God contained in Scripture; to which in
turn we may attribute certain grave defects, painfully manifest in the religious life
and experience of our times. I mean the lack of reverence, the decay of that sober,
serious piety, that "fear of Jehovah" in which true wisdom begins. It is in rude
and violent surroundings that great spiritual principles are often first asserted, and
out of the throes of fierce conflict they come to birth. Upon this battle-field, with
routed Amalek disappearing over the edge of the desert, "Moses built 'his' altar,
and called the name of it Jehovah my banner." So he lifted up this mighty name
and flung it forth as the ensign under which God's Israel should march through all
its pilgrimage and warfare in the time to come. This great name of our God was,
however, in later times overlaid and almost destroyed by superstition. After the
age of prophecy had closed, when spiritual faith died down in Judaism, it ceased to
be a living word in the mouth of Israel. Through fear of "taking the name of
Jehovah in vain," the people no longer dared to pronounce it; and it is a saying of
the rabbis that "he who utters the name as it is written, has no place in the world
to come." But what does this mysterious word mean? I cannot give an answer
beyond all dispute. Its origin goes back to the very beginnings of Hebrew speech
and religion. The differences of interpretation, after all, lie within a narrow
compass. Most interpreters have taken it to signify "He is." Others render it
"He is becoming," "He goes on to be," or "will be." Others again, "He creates,"
"He makes to be." I have little doubt that the first is the proper, or, at least, the
principal sense of the word, although no very clear or sharp line can be drawn in
Hebrew between this and the second interpretation. But the third application, if
it were certainly established, is at any rate subordinate to the first. "He is,"
therefore "He makes to be." Creation rests upon the being of God. I. By the
name Jehovah, therefore, GOD IS DECLARED AS THE SUPREME REALITY. So the Greeks
render it, "He who is"; and John, in the Apocalypse, "Grace and peace to you
from Him which is, and which was, and which cometh." No grace or peace, verily,
from things that are not! "Say unto the children of Israel"—so He authenticated
Moses—"I AM hath sent me unto you." The finite demands the Infinite; the
chain of causes and effects hangs upon the Uncaused; all creatures unite to point
to their Creator, and by their very being proclaim His, "in whom they live, and
move, and are." But I hear some one saying, "This is metaphysics; this is very
obscure and transcendental doctrine, this talk about the Absolute and Uncaused.
How could ideas of this sort ever have existed or been entertained in these
early and barbarous times? But everything depends on the way in which you take
notions of this kind. To ancient Israel—the true Israel of spiritual faith—this
was no philosophical abstraction, arrived at by a process of difficult reasoning: it
was the revelation of an immediate and self-evidencing fact. Behind all sensible
objects, the forms of nature, the movements of human affairs—there He is! They
discerned, they felt the presence of Another—the real, the abiding, the living God,
breathing on their spirits by His breath, searching their hearts with holy eyes, as
of flame; He who said to their souls, "I AM," and concerning whom they could
say, as neither of their mortal selves nor of the fleeting world, "Yea, and of a truth,
He is." Hence their name was a standing protest and denouncement against all
idolatry. "The name of Jehovah," so their proverb ran, "is a strong tower; the
righteous runneth into it and is safe." "I am Jehovah," says the Lord in Isaiah,
"that is My name; and My glory will I not give to another, neither My praise to
graven images." You see the argument. If He is, then they are not. His very
name annihilates them. It was this sublime and solid faith in the unity and
sovereignty and spiritual reality of God, that lifted the Jewish people above superstition and the fear of worldly power. See the whole history of Israel gathered into
a single incident. "Thou comest unto me," said David to Goliath, "with a sword,
and with a spear, and with a shield; but I come to thee in the name of Jehovah of
Hosts, the God of the armies of Israel, whom thou hast defied!" Here is the one
immortal certainty, the Rock of Ages. II. THIS GLORIOUS NAME PROCLAIMS THE
ETERNITY OF GOD. His reality is our strength; His eternity our consolation. If
you turn to the French Bible you will find Jehovah translated, in place of our
English "Lord," by l'Eternel, "The Eternal." This rendering is often singularly
apt and true, as for instance in Psalm cii., where the Psalmist in melancholy mood
is sighing, "My days are as a shadow that declineth, and I am withered like grass."
But he remembers the name of his God, and he continues: "But Thou, O Eternal,
sittest King for ever; and Thy memorial is unto all generations." And from that

point in his song he mounts up as on the wings of eagles. God's name is the He Is—a timeless present, a perpetual now. John expands it backwards and forwards into the everlasting past and future : " Grace and peace to you from Him which is, and which was, and which cometh." Men live and die ; empires rise and fall ; worlds and systems of worlds run through their courses, and dissolve and vanish like a puff of smoke ; still He Is ; always He Is ; the unchanged, the abiding God, whose being fills and constitutes eternity. There is no thought so sublime and overwhelming to the human mind as that of the eternity of God. But there is none more restful, more soothing and satisfying. "We which have believed," it is written, "do enter into rest." Here we touch the calm of eternity, the "Sabbath of God." We have found a haven which no storm can ruffle, a rock to build upon which no earthquake will ever move. You find great religious minds, like that of St. Augustine in his Confessions, constantly returning to this thought as their solace and shelter, hovering round it as birds about their nest ; here they find an ever-renewed spring of mental strength, of spiritual joy and courage. The Jews have been not unfitly called "the people of eternity." Their monumental endurance, the toughness and indestructible vitality of their national fibre, are due, to no small extent, to the force with which the doctrine of Jehovah has possessed them. It would seem that the revelation of personal immortality was not made in the early ages to the men of Israel, that their souls might be the more completely filled and absorbed with the thought of God Himself—His being, His character ; that they might find in "Jehovah the portion of their inheritance and their cup." III. JEHOVAH IS THE SPECIFIC NAME, THE PROPER AND PERSONAL NAME OF THE GOD OF REVELATION AND REDEMPTION. It is, so to speak, the Divine autograph written across the face of Scripture ; it is nothing less than the signature of the Eternal attached to His covenant of grace ; its very presence on the page, the sublimity of its import, and the transcendent dignity and force with which it is employed, fill the mind with awe, and compel one to say as he reads and listens, "Surely God is in this place." To the believing Israelite this name was a summary of revelation past. The call of Moses, the judgment upon Pharaoh, the passage of the Red Sea, the lawgiving on Sinai, the conquest of Canaan—all these and a thousand glorious recollections clustered round this immortal name, and served for its verifying or illustration. And it was at the same time the basis and starting-point of future revelations. Having learnt to say He Is, they could go on to say: "He is just, He is wise, He is faithful, He is merciful and gracious—Jehovah of Hosts, Jehovah our Righteousness, Jehovah our Peace, Jehovah our Banner." In Himself unchange-able, in His manifestations to mankind God is perpetually new. He is ever ad-vancing and unfolding Himself to His creation. The "He Is" of the Bible is no frozen, silent Impersonality, like the Pure Being of Greek philosophy, or like Spinoza's Infinite Substance. This is the name of the living, self-declaring God, whose revelation is the single stream that runs through all cosmical and human history, the working of whose counsel forms the process of the ages. His name, like "His mercies," is "new every morning." IV. Finally, this glorious name of God IS A CREED, A CONFESSION OF FAITH. God says to Moses, through Moses to Israel, through Israel to the world, "I AM" : faith answers back, "He Is" ; and "this is His name for ever, and His memorial unto all generations." Pronouncing it in spirit and in truth, we "set to our seal that God is true." It is the com-munion of heaven and earth, the dialogue between man and his Creator ; it is the Church's Amen answering back to God's self-affirming Yea. And "Ye are My witnesses," saith Jehovah, "even Israel whom I have chosen." Despite its apos-tasies and its chastisements, nay, even by virtue of them, the Jewish nation has proved itself the people of Jehovah, the witness of the true God. Israel has made the nations hear the voice of her God ; and now they are sitting at the feet of her prophets, learning of His ways. It is the flag of conflict, the symbol of a faith which has the world to overcome. So our text continues, with a prophetic symbol-ism that has proved itself all too true : "And Moses said, Jehovah hath sworn that He will have war with Amalek from generation to generation." "All nations compassed me about," said Israel, in worldly power the smallest and least consider-able of the peoples—"Yea, they compassed me about ; but in the name of Jehovah I will destroy them !" And what is more, she has done it ; her faith, her Christ have done it ! Those gigantic and cruel empires of the East, with their vile and sensual idolatries, have passed away for ever. Isaiah sang their doom ages before : "They are dead, they shall not live ; they are deceased, they shall not rise. There-fore hast Thou visited and destroyed them, and made all their memory to perish."

Fact is stranger than fiction. The true God has lived down the false ones. The "He Is" must displace the "are nots." As it has been, so it will be. Moloch and Belial and Mammon—the gods of hate and lust and greed, the gods of this world that still rule in the nations and blind the souls of men—oldest of all false gods, which men formed out of their own evil passions, before they set them up in wood and stone—as the Lord liveth, they shall surely perish ! If the Church is worthy of her faith, she will say like David, "In the name of Jehovah I will destroy them." And these latest idols, which our fathers knew not, of modern nature-worship and scientific materialism, will they fare any better, do you suppose? The name Jehovah, we have said, is a confession of faith. It is a personal confession, which only personal experience qualifies us properly to make. It is not enough to read it in the Bible, to understand and assent to its theological and historical import; God Himself must pronounce His own "I AM," must "speak into our soul His name." Jesus is to us the revealer of Jehovah. "I have declared unto them Thy name," He said to the Father in leaving this world, "and will declare it." The name Jehovah—the Absolute, the Eternal, the Creator, the living God—Christ has rendered into the tender yet no less awful name of Father. (*G. G. Findlay, B.A.*) *Jehovah-nissi :*—A flag is in itself a simple thing enough. A piece of bunting, or of silk, having on it an emblematic device—that is all ! and, when so regarded, it is "nothing in the world." But when we view it as a symbol, it forthwith acquires transcendent importance. It becomes then the mark of nationality, and all the sentiments of patriotism are stirred in us by the sight of it. We think of the struggles of our fathers, when for the first time it fluttered over them in the breeze, as they resisted injustice and oppression. We recall the many bloody fields over which, amidst the smoke of battle, its streaming colours waved their proud defiance. The memories of centuries have woven themselves into its texture ; and as it floats serenely over us, we see in it at once the aggregated result of our history in the past, and the bright prophecy of our greatness in the future. Now, it is quite similar with the banner which God has given us, that it may be displayed because of the truth, and which, as this inscription declares, He is Himself. I. JEHOVAH IS OUR TOKEN OF DECISION. In the opening days of the first French Revolution, it is said that a timid trimmer fixed a cockade beneath the lappel of his coat on one breast, and a tricolour in the corresponding portion on the other ; and that when he met a royalist he exposed the cockade, and shouted, "Long live the king !" but when he met a republican he showed the tricolour, and cried, "Long live the Republic !" That, however, sufficed only for a short time : for as the strife increased, every man was forced to make a decision between the two. So sometimes, in times of indifference, it has been possible for men to seem to combine the services of God and mammon ; but happily, as I think, for us, we have fallen on an earnest age, in which it is becoming impossible even to seem to be neutral. Everywhere the cry is raised, "Who is on the Lord's side?" and it becomes us all to hoist our flag, and display to the world in its expanding folds this old inscription, "Jehovah-nissi—the Lord is my banner." When Hedley Vicars, the Christian soldier, was converted, he knew that he should be made the butt of much ridicule, and the victim of much petty persecution by his comrades ; so he resolved to be beforehand with them, and in the morning on which he made his decision he took his Bible and laid it down open on his table. Very soon a fellow-officer came in, and, looking at the book, exclaimed, "Hallo, Vicars ! turned Methodist?" To which he made reply, "That is my flag ; and, by the grace of God, I hope to be true to it as long as I live." That was his Rephidim, and there he, too, conquered Amalek by raising the banner of the Lord. So let it be with you. II. JEHOVAH IS OUR MARK OF DISTINCTION. When, in travelling through England, one comes on the stately residence of some duke or earl, and sees the flag floating in quiet dignity from its turret, he knows from that indication that the proprietor is himself within the walls. Now, the distinguishing peculiarity of the Christian is that God, to whom he belongs, is, by His Spirit, dwelling within him, and that shows itself in many ways. It is apparent in the love by which he is animated for all who are in suffering, sorrow, or want. It is seen in the purity of speech and conduct which he maintains ; in the earnestness of his devotion to the will of Christ ; and in the eager efforts which he makes to attain to that perfection of character which he sees in his Lord. III. JEHOVAH IS OUR JOY. When we make demonstration of our enthusiasm, we raise a whole forest of flagstaffs, and fix on each an appropriate banner. Let it be the commemoration of some victory, or the welcome to some foreign prince visiting our shores, and the whole city is gay with flags, while the emblems of many nationalities are seen fluttering in friendly fellowship from the mastheads of the ships in harbour. So we are reminded, by the inscription on this altar, that "the joy of the Lord" is "the strength" of the Christian. His life is one of constant gladness; his characteristic is what I may call a calm enthusiasm, or, to use the phrase of Jonathan Edwards, a "quiet rapture." IV. GOD IS THE PROTECTOR OF HIS PEOPLE. There is nothing of which a nation is so jealous as the honour of its flag, and he who is in reality a citizen has a right to the protection of the government. Great Britain has few prouder chapters in her recent history than that which tells of the expedition to Abyssinia some years ago. A great force was landed on the Red Sea shore; a large, troublesome, and dangerous march of many days was made into an enemy's country; a fierce assult was successfully attempted on a hitherto impregnable fortress; many lives were lost, and fifty millions of dollars were spent—and all for what? Because a brutal tyrant was keeping in horrid imprisonment two or three men who had a right to the protection of the British flag; and you can hardly conceive what an outburst of joy broke forth from the nation when the news came that they had been set free, and that the insulting monarch had been made to bite the dust. But what is the power of the British Empire, in comparison with Omnipotence? Yet he who sincerely raises this banner has God's pledge that He will protect him (see John x. 28, 29; xvi. 33; Isa. xli. 10; liv. 17). (*W. M. Taylor, D.D.*) *The Lord my banner:*—I. In the first place, this covenant banner is a wonderful banner when looked at with reference to its ANTIQUITY. It is very easy indeed to tell, for ourselves individually, when we were first made acquainted with this banner. With some it was in the lessons of earliest childhood. With others, it was later on in life, when our knowledge of it began. When this banner was first unfurled, for any of our race to gaze upon, it is easy enough to tell. We go back to the garden of Eden. But this is only the date of its first unfolding. The design of it was not first formed then. To get at this, we must go back far, far beyond that distant date. That takes us indeed to the farthest shores of time. Standing there we gaze upon the ocean that lies before us. It is the shoreless ocean of an unmeasured eternity. Far back in its hidden depths the design of this banner was formed. II. But now, let us take another look at this banner, and we shall see that it is not less wonderful in its MATERIAL than in its antiquity. The material of which our flags or banners are ordinarily composed is a coarse woollen substance known as bunting. True, we sometimes see banners made of more costly materials, as silk or satin. And gold and silver, and jems and jewels, are not unfrequently employed to enrich and adorn the material employed in making the banner. These things, of course, very greatly enhance the value of the banners on which they are employed. But when we speak of the Lord as our banner, and think of His revealed truth as the material of which this banner is composed, and then contrast it with the material of which our ordinary banners are made, how unspeakable the difference! Jehovah-nissi—the Lord my banner. All the names, or titles, or symbols applied to God in Scripture, are the elements of truth that make Him known. And so it is when He is spoken of as the covenant banner, unfurled over His people. The folds of this banner are woven out of the truth of His blessed word—"the truth as it is in Jesus." This constitutes the material of which this banner is composed. III. But in the third place, it is a wonderful banner when we consider THE MOTTOES inscribed upon it. The banner of England has in French the words—"God and my duty." The idea thus embodied is, "My duty to God—and my duty to my country." This simply expresses what should be the foremost thought and desire with every Christian patriot. And the mottoes on the banners of other nations are of a similar character. They are expressive, for the most part, of some sentiment of honour, or some principle of duty to the country over which they float. But the contrast is very striking, when we compare this banner of the covenant with other banners in regard to the mottoes which they bear. Each other banner bears but a single motto—while this bears many: those mainly refer to some matter of personal obligation and duty—while these refer to matters of high and glorious privilege. Every page of the volume of revealed truth may be regarded as a distinct fold of this covenant banner; and emblazoned on each fold is one or more of these inspiring mottoes. IV. It is a wonderful banner, in the fourth place, when considered with reference to its INFLUENCE on the hearts and lives of men. Doubtless the flag of every nation has a history, in this respect, that would be deeply interesting if the incidents connected with it could be collected and written out. But who can tell how many hearts have been stirred, and how many enterprises of great pith and moment have been started, and led on to successful issues, by the influence of this blessed banner ? Every motto emblazoned on its waving folds, or, in other words, every passage of saving truth within the leaves of the Bible, has a history of its own. How wanderers have been reclaimed !—how slumbering consciences have been aroused !—how anxious inquiries have been directed !—how depraved hearts have been renewed !—how sorrowing spirits have been comforted !—how listless energies have been quickened and consecrated !—how useless lives have been ennobled !— and lost souls have been saved, through the influence of the mottoes on this banner —or of particular passages of God's Word—who can tell ! V. And then, lastly, this is a wonderful banner in view of its DURABILITY. This is a quality which cannot be imparted to our national banners. The materials of which they are made is frail—and subject to decay. But how different it is with the banner of the covenant of our salvation ! This is something which the hand of violence cannot rend. Time, with his effacing finger, can make no impression upon it. (*R. Newton, D.D.*) *Jehovah-nissi :*—Jehovah my-banner. We acknowledge and honour Him as such four ways. 1. By voluntarily and inflexibly adhering to Him as our Leader and Commander. 2. By confessing Him the author of every success with which we have been crowned. 3. By our courageously trusting in Him to enable us to overcome in every future conflict. 4. By looking to Him for the remuneration of victory at last. As Jehovah's banner floated over the triumphant host, bearing the sweet and heart-sustaining inscription just explained, so should the assurance of victory be as complete as the sense of forgiveness, seeing both alike are founded upon the great fact that Jesus died and rose again. (*A. Nevin, D.D.*)

CHAPTER XVIII.

VERS. 1–6.—**I, thy father-in-law, Jethro, am come unto thee.**—*Family gatherings:* —I. THAT THIS FAMILY GATHERING WAS PERMITTED AFTER LONG ABSENCE, AND AFTER THE OCCURRENCE OF GREAT EVENTS. II. THAT THIS FAMILY GATHERING WAS CHARACTER-IZED BY COURTESY, BY A RELIGIOUS SPIRIT, AND BY DEVOUT CONVERSATION. III. THAT THIS FAMILY GATHERING DERIVED ITS HIGHEST JOY FROM THE MORAL EXPERIENCES WITH WHICH IT WAS FAVOURED. IV. THAT THIS FAMILY GATHERING WAS MADE THE OCCASION OF A SACRAMENTAL OFFERING TO GOD. Lessons : 1. That God can watch over the interests of a separate family. 2. That God unites families in a providential manner. 3. That united families should rejoice in God. 4. That the families of the good will meet in heaven, never more to part. 5. Pray for the completion of the Divine family in the Father's house. (*J. S. Exell, M.A.*) *Character not deteriorated by honour :*—Nothing tests a man more than his bearing toward his former friends after he has passed through some experiences which have brought him great honour and prosperity ; and when, as in the present instance, he comes back with his old frankness and cordiality, and is not ashamed of his old piety, he is a great man indeed. Too often, however, prosperity deteriorates character, and honour freezes the heart. The head swims on the giddy height, and the son returns a comparative stranger even to his father's house ; while the family worship, which used to be so enjoyed, is smiled at as a weakness of the old people's, and avoided as a weariness to himself. Old companions, too, are passed without recognition ; or, if recognized at all, it is with an air of condescension, and with an effort like that which one makes to stoop for something that is far beneath him. The development of character also estranges us from those whom we once knew intimately, and who were once, it may be, the better for our fellowship. But the consolation in all such cases is, that there can be no value in the further friendship of those who can thus forget the past. He is the really good friend—as well as the truly great man—who, in spite of his deserved eminence, resumes with us at the point at which we separated, and carries us at length with him to the throne of grace, to acknowledge there our obligations to the Lord. There are men whom one meets from time to time with whom he has always to begin anew. They are like a book in which you never get fully interested, and which, whenever you take it up, you must commence to read again at the very preface ; until, in absolute disgust, you cast it away from you, and never lift it more. There are others who are like a well-beloved volume, with a bookmark in it, which you can open at any moment, and resume where you broke off ; and which, though you may be often interrupted, you contrive to read through to the end. Such a friend was Moses to Jethro, and Jethro to Moses; and though there came a final separation of the one from the other on earth, they would renew their conference in heaven. (*W. M. Taylor, D.D.*) *Ashamed of parents :*—A fellow student of mine had very poor parents, but they had a great desire to give their son the very best possible education; and if you had looked into that home, you would have seen much pinching and self-denying on the part of those parents to give their boy a university training. Once, when he was away at college, they went up with proud hearts to see him, for was it not with great efforts on their part that he was there? He was walking in the street with a fellow student when he met them, and he tried to avoid them. You ask me, why? Because he was ashamed of them in their simple dress, and he was not going to own them until his friend had gone. That man reached the Presbyterian ministry, but he did not long stay in it. He fell from his position, and the broken-hearted parents followed him step by step. He went down lower and lower until a fellow minister and myself have rescued him again and again from police cells. Oh, the foulness of heart of one who is ashamed to own his mother, however poor. And yet there is still a greater sin; to be ashamed of that self-sacrificing love that nailed to the Cross the Son of God. (*J. Carstairs.*)

Ver. 7. **They asked each other of their welfare.**—*Friends meeting after separation :*—I. This world is not a scene adapted or intended to afford the pleasure and benefit of friendship entire. Men cannot collect and keep around them an assemblage of congenial spirits, to constitute, as it were, a bright social fire, ever glowing, ever burning, amidst the winter of this world. They cannot surround themselves with the selectest portion of humanity, so as to keep out of sight and interference the general character of human nature. They are left to be pressed upon by an intimate perception of what a depraved and unhappy world it is. And so they feel themselves strangers and pilgrims upon earth. II. It is contrary to the design of God that the more excellent of this world's inhabitants should form together little close assemblages and bands, within exclusive circles, detached as much as possible from the general multitude. On the contrary, it is appointed that they should be scattered and diffused hither and thither, to be useful and exemplary in a great number of situations; that there should be no large space without some of them. Thus it is a world that dissociates friends. Nevertheless, friends do sometimes meet; and then it is quite natural to do as Moses and Jethro did—"ask each other of their welfare." III. In the meeting of genuine friends, after considerable absence, these feelings will be present. 1. Kind affection. 2. Inquiry. 3. Reflective comparison. 4. Gratitude to God for watching over them both. 5. Faithful admonition and serious anticipation. (*J. Foster.*) *Family reunions :*—I. As to the salutations at meeting. 1. Courteousness. This excludes—(1) Excessive familiarity; (2) Rudeness; (3) Pride. 2. A hearty welcome. II. As to the subjects of conversation. 1. On public affairs. 2. On social matters. 3. With recognition of God. 4. Fit for mutual response (vers. 10, 11). III. As to the mode of festivity. 1. That such festivity may not be confined to the family. 2. That it may be preceded by an act of worship. 3. That it should be with consciousness of the Divine presence. To eat as before God will make us—(1) Happy and helpful; (2) Temperate; (3) Regardful of the soul's progress. (*D. G. Watt, M.A.*) *Lessons :*—1. It is not unbeseeming the highest places or persons in kingdom or Church of Christ to give due respect to relations. 2. Grace doth not unteach men manners and civil carriage respectively unto men. 3. Natural affection and expressions of it to friends beseemeth God's servants. 4. It is a natural duty for relations to inquire of and wish each other's peace. 5. Conduct to a tent for rest is suitable for travellers that visit their relations (ver. 7). (*G. Hughes, B.D.*) *Religious intercourse between parents and children :*— One Sunday night I said, "Ah! you mothers will say that your children are all in bed; never mind, go upstairs and wake them, and talk to them about their souls." A mother (this I know to be true) went home, and her little girl was in bed and asleep. She woke her and said, "Jane, I have not spoken to you, dear child, about your soul. The pastor has been exhorting us to-night, and saying that even if you were asleep you should be wakened." Then said Jane, "Mother, I have often wondered that you did not speak to me about Christ, but I have known Him these two years." The mother stood convicted. She brought her daughter round on Monday and said, "Let this dear girl be baptized and join the church." I said to her, "Why did you not tell your mother?" "Well," said she, "you know, mother never seemed to come up to the subject; she never gave me a chance." Then the mother said, "Quite right; I have not been to my children what I ought to have been; but, please God, there shall never be another child of mine that shall steal a march on her mother, and find Christ without her mother knowing it." God graciously rebuked that mother. (*C. H. Spurgeon.*) *Religious conversation :*—Among the means to be used in times of religious interest we may mention conversation. Many neglect it, but none can deny its power for good. Says Dr. Archibald Alexander, in his book on "Religious Experience": "Religious conversation, in which Christians freely tell of the dealings of God with their souls, has been often a powerful means of quickening the sluggish soul and communicating comfort." It is, in many cases, a great consolation to the desponding believer to know that his case is not entirely singular; and if a traveller can meet with one who has been over the difficult parts of the road before him, he may surely derive from his experience some salutary counsel and warning. The Scriptures are favourable to such communications. "Come and hear," says David, "all ye that fear God, and I will declare what He hath done for my soul." Dr. Watts thought so much of the "talent for parlour teaching," that he declared that the man who had it could do more good than the minister by his public discourses. Said one who was under sentence of death: "When the minister spoke to me he seemed like one who was standing far above me; but when Alexander, that good man that everybody knows is the holiest man in the place, came in, he stood like one at my side, and when he classed himself with me, and said, 'Sinners like me and you,' I could stand it no longer." Saurin, the great French preacher, said, in his sermon on Christian conversation: "Are we returning from a sermon? Why not entertain one another with the subjects we have been hearing? Why not endeavour to imprint on one another's memories the truths that have been proved, and to impress upon one another's hearts such precepts as have been enforced? Have we been visiting a dying person? Why not make such reflections as naturally occur on such occasions the matter of our conversations? Why not embrace such a fair opportunity of speaking on the vanity of life, the uncertainty of worldly enjoyments, and the happiness of a pious departure to rest? Have you been reading a good book? Why not converse with our companions on the information we have derived from it?"

Vers. 9–12. **Jethro rejoiced for all the goodness.**—*Lessons :*—1. The Church's friends rejoice in all the good done for it, and deliverance of it. 2. As Jehovah is the cause of good and deliverance to His Church, so He is the object of their joy (ver. 9). 3. Joyful hearts for the Church's good are thankful hearts to God for the same. 4. Deliverance of special relations, but especially of the Church, from powers of enemies is just matter of thanksgiving (ver. 10). 5. Experience of the mighty works of God perfects the knowledge of Himself. 6. The great works of God set Him above all that are so called. 7. The pride of enemies exalts the power of God above them (ver. 11). 8. Knowledge of God is best expressed in sacrificing and worship of Him. 9. Holy feasting is consistent with God's holy worship. 10. God's glory must terminate all sacrificing and eating among His people. 11. Eminent members of the Church may not disdain communion with true proselytes (ver. 12). (*G. Hughes, B.D.*)

Vers. 13–16. **Moses sat to judge the people.**—*Lessons :*—1. God's providence joins work to sacrifice, and His servants do unite them. 2. The morrow brings its own work from God unto His servants, not every day the same. 3. God's substitutes are careful as to worship Him, so to do judgment to God's people. 4. Good rulers sit close to deal judgment to their people. 5. Providence puts hard work upon God's ministers sometimes, from morning to evening. 6. It is just to be unwearied in giving and receiving judgment when God calleth (ver. 13). (*G. Hughes, B.D.*) *Lessons :*—1. The greatest and best rulers disdain not to give an account of their judgment to reasonable inquisitors. 2. The access of souls unto rulers to inquire of God, is a just ground for them to attend the work. 3. The appeal of souls to man's bar in matters, is and should be inquiring after God (ver. 15). 4. Duties of people and rulers are correlate, they come with matters, and these must judge. 5. God's laws and statutes are the best rule to order judgment between men. 6. It is duty to rulers to make people know the statutes and laws of God. (*Ibid.*) *Consulting with God :*—My heavenly Father is my "other partner" in my business. I consult with Him. It is remarkable how I am relieved from the worry and anxiety so common to business men. Frequently, when I desire to "think over a matter," it is really to consult with Him, after which my way is clear. And unto Him I render one-tenth. I often think this order should be reversed, and I take the tenth. (*William A. Lay.*)

Vers. 17–22. **Thou wilt surely wear away.**—*Undue application to laborious duties:*—Various lessons may be gathered from the fact that Moses was wearing himself away by undue application to the duties of his office, and that by adopting Jethro's suggestion and dividing the labour he was able to spare himself and nevertheless equally secure the administration of justice. I. We see the goodness of God in His dealings with our race in the fact THAT LABOUR MAY BE SO DIVIDED THAT MAN'S STRENGTH SHALL NOT BE OVERPASSED, but cannot be so divided that man's strength shall be dispensed with. II. It is a principle sufficiently evident in the infirmity of man that he cannot give himself incessantly to labour, whether bodily or mental, BUT MUST HAVE SEASONS OF REPOSE. We shrink from the thought and the mention of suicide, but there are other modes of self-destruction than that of laying hands on one's own person. There is the suicide of intemperance ; there is also the suicide of overlabour. It is as much our duty to relax when we feel our strength overpassed, as to persevere while that strength is sufficient. III. God has, with tender consideration, PROVIDED INTERVALS OF REPOSE, and so made it man's own fault if he sink beneath excessive labour. What a beautiful ordinance is that of day and night! What a gracious appointment is that of Sunday! When the Sabbath is spent in the duties that belong to it, its influence gives fresh edge to the blunted human powers. IV. EACH ONE OF US IS APT TO BE ENGROSSED WITH WORLDLY THINGS. It is well that some Jethro, some rough man from the wilderness, perhaps some startling calamity, should approach us with the message, "The thing that thou doest is not good; thou wilt surely wear away." V. AT LAST WE MUST ALL WEAR AWAY, but our comfort is that, though the outer man perish, the inner man shall be renewed day by day. (*H. Melvill, B.D.*)   *Jethro's advice to Moses; or, a word to ministers of the gospel:*—I. THE POWER WHICH MINISTERS OF THE GOSPEL SHOULD HAVE. "Be thou for the people to God-ward." II. THE WORK WHICH MINISTERS OF THE GOSPEL SHOULD DO. 1. Conduct Divine worship and establish suitable rules for the government of their people. 2. Give the right impetus to the moral and religious life of their people. 3. Explain to their people the duties devolving upon them. III. THE HELPS WHICH MINISTERS OF THE GOSPEL HAVE (vers. 21, 22). IV. THE QUALIFICATIONS WHICH MINISTERS OF THE GOSPEL SHOULD POSSESS. 1. Devout piety. 2. Truthfulness. 3. Disinterestedness. 4. Freedom. (*W. Edwards.*) *Lessons:*—1. God may use men of mean, calling, and endowments to help for prudentials, for government in His Church. 2. The most morally good government may not be good in natural or civil respects (ver. 17). 3. Imprudential over-acting in doing judgment may consume rulers and people. 4. Good and righteous work may be too heavy for the best and strongest shoulders. 5. Solitariness in dealing judgment may carry great weakness in it. 6. It is good prudence to undertake burdens proportionable for strength and no more (ver. 18). (*G. Hughes, B.D.*) *Lessons:*—1. Supreme governors had need of subordinate to carry on the burden of government. 2. Men entrusted with government should be eminently qualified with wisdom, knowledge, courage, &c. Each endowment may give a special observation. 3. Variety of bounds for power are requisite to the various capacities of rulers (ver. 21). 4. Men so designed to rule ought all times reasonably to attend on judgment. 5. Matters of greatest moment have a just way of appeal from lesser to superior judges. 6. Smaller matters are reasonably to be concluded by lesser hands. 7. Such distribution of work in government maketh the burden more easy (ver. 22). 8. Supreme rulers managing their affairs by others according to God's command, walk safely. 9. Prosperity to prince and people may be well expected by keeping God's commands (ver. 23). (*Ibid.*)   *The folly of solitary rulership :—* I. IT CAUSES AN UNDUE STRAIN UPON THE SOLITARY INDIVIDUAL. Wicked men sometimes kill themselves by excess of pleasure. Good men should not kill themselves by excess of work even in the service of God. Many great lives are lost to the Church through excessive toils. The Divine Judge can never grow weary in His administration of the universe. II. IT INTERFERES WITH THE EXECUTION OF THE HIGHER PART OF THE JUDICIAL OFFICE. How often are ministers engaged with the technical and local when they might be engaged in the spiritual and universal. Justice needs more than administrative power ; it needs spiritual discernment and those qualities of moral character which are the outcome of moral nearness to God ; hence it requires men to be for the people God-ward. Jesus Christ is now for the people God-ward, the one Mediator between God and man. III. IT LEAVES UNUTILIZED A VAST NUMBER OF ABLE MEN QUITE EQUAL TO THE ORDINARY REQUIREMENTS OF JUSTICE. Ministers should not do all the work of the Church; they should call out latent talent for it. Society has many unrecognized judges. IV. THAT THIS FOLLY IS EVIDENT TO WISE OLD MEN WHO SEE SOLITARY JUDGESHIPS IN OPERATION. Others can form a more correct estimate of our work than we can. We are too near it to take the perspective of it. We are too much interested in it to form unprejudiced judgments concerning it. Let us be open to the voice of wise old men who often speak to young men as in the fear of God. Lessons :—1. That positions of trust should not be monopolized by the few. 2. That the common crowds of men have unsuspected abilities. 3. That good men should not be prodigal of their physical and mental energy to the shortening of their lives. (*J. S. Exell, M.A.*) *Lessons on ver.* 17 :—I. OTHERS VIEW OUR ACTS. II. OTHERS CAN OFTEN SEE FAULTS WHERE WE CANNOT. III. OTHERS REPROVING US MAY LEAD TO A BETTER COURSE OF ACTION. Or—I. MEN SHOULD INTEREST THEMSELVES IN THE ACTS OF THEIR RELATIVES. II. MEN SHOULD BE FAITHFUL IN GIVING REPROOF AND ADVICE. Or—I. THE WISEST HAVE SOME DEFECTS IN THEIR CONDUCT. II. THE WISEST MAY BE BENEFITED BY THE ADVICE OF OTHERS. (*Ibid.*) *Jethro's justice of peace :*—Here is the archetype or first draught of magistracy. Scripture is the best man of counsel for the greatest statesman in the world. 1. It first gives order for the care and circumspection in the choice. "Provide." 2. Secondly, it directs the choice by four essential characters of magistrates:—(1) Men of ability. (2) Fearing God. (3) Men of truth. (4) Hating covetousness. 3. Thirdly, it applies these four to magistrates of all degrees, in an exact distribution of them, by way of gradation, descending step by step, from the highest to the lowest. "And place such over them to be rulers" —(1) Of thousands; (2) of hundreds; (3) of fifties; (4) of tens. 4. Fourthly, it prescribes to the magistrates, thus qualified and chosen, their offices, viz., to judge the people in the smaller causes, &c., and their assiduity and industry therein. "And let them judge the people at all seasons, &c. And it shall be that they shall bring every great matter to thee, but every small matter they shall judge." 5. Lastly, it propounds the blessed fruit and emolument that will necessarily ensue thereupon. (1) To Moses himself, "So shall it be easier for thyself, and they shall bear the burden with thee, and thou shalt be able to endure." (2) To the people, "And all this people shall go to their place in peace." (*T. Brooks.*) *Need of a heroic spirit in judges :*—What heroical spirit had he need have, that must encounter the Hydra of sin, oppose the current of the times, and the torrent of vice, that must turn the wheel over the wicked; especially such roaring monsters, and rebellious Korahs, such lawless sons of Belial, wherewith our times swarm, who stick not to oppose with crest and breast, whosoever stand in the way of their humours and lusts! Surely if Jethro called for courage in those modest primitive times, and among a people newly tamed with Egyptian yokes, what do our audacious and foreheadless swaggerers require? Our lees and dregs of time, not unlike to those wherein God was fain to raise up extraordinary judges to smite hip and thigh, &c. What Atlas shall support the state of the ruinous and tottering world, in these perilous ends of time? For all these fore-named purposes, how unapt is a man of soft, timorous, and flexible nature! for whom it is as possible to steer a right course, without swerving to the left hand or right, for fear or favour, as it is for a cockboat to keep head against wind and tide, without help of oars or sails : experience ever making this good, that cowards are slaves to their superiors, fellow-fools to their equals, tyrants to their inferiors, and windmills to popular breath, not being able to any of these to say so much as No! (*Ibid.*) *Divine ordinances of labour :*—How valuable is a little common-sense—and how scarce! Here was Moses, a man trained in kings' palaces, deeply skilled in all the wisdom of Egypt, and yet he has to wait till Jethro comes—a mere man of the desert, before to a self-evident evil he can apply a self-evident remedy. Labour is good; but if we labour unwisely, so as to overtask and enervate our faculties, the labour which in itself is good becomes, through our perversity, an evil. I. LABOUR IS AN ORDINANCE OF GOD. There is work for all, and need for every man's work, of whatever sort it may be—from thinking the thoughts or pursuing the scientific discoveries which clear the road along which the world is to advance, down to working a loom or digging a field; from managing a large estate so as to develop all its manifold capabilities of service, down to trimming its hedges or hauling its coal. II. THE DIVISION OF LABOUR IS AN ORDINANCE OF GOD. It is the wise division and distribution of labour to which we owe all the services and comforts of civilized life; and the wiser the distribution, the higher the civilization. It is this division of labour which multiplies the products of labour, and not only sets men free to invent improved methods of labour, but also puts them in the way of inventing them. If, for instance, one man could make a tent in ten days, ten men, each of whom was trained to make his separate part, would turn out not ten, but fifty or a hundred tents in the same time ; and each of the ten, always handling the same tools and working on the same substance—canvas, or wood for poles and pegs, or palm fibre or hemp for ropes—would naturally improve his tools to save his pains, and discover qualities and capabilities in the substance which only long familiarity could detect. From such simple beginnings as these has risen that division of the whole civilized community into separate trades and professions, and these trades and professions again into many component elements and specialities, which multiplies its productive power to an almost infinite extent, and keeps the discovery of our means and appliances of labour up to the level of our growing numbers and wants. III. THE INTROMISSION OF LABOUR IS AN ORDINANCE OF GOD. Not only has He given us an inward monitor which warns us when mental or vital powers are overtasked, to seek out holiday mirth and recreative sports, to change the air we breathe and the scenes on which we look if perchance we may thus change the wearing current of our thoughts ; He has also fixed the bounds to our labour beyond which we cannot or ought not to pass. Seven times a week the day draws to to an end, and the night comes on in which most of us, at least, are compelled to rest. Once every week, too, there returns the Day of Rest, on which we cease from our toils, and withdraw our minds from the noisy labours and corroding anxieties of traffic. And when we are over eager in our labours for present good, or what we think good, God sends some rugged Jethro—some warning sickness or calamitous loss, some sorrow that, passing through all our defences, smites and cleaves our very heart. Not because He grudges our prosperity, or would abate our happiness, but because He would have us rise to that sacred rest and satisfying peace which even adversity cannot take away, He often sends a chastening whose message, if we will hear it, is, " The thing thou doest is not good. Thou wilt surely wear thyself away, and wastefully expend thy life on things which perish as you handle them. Turn ye at My reproof ; for why should ye die ? " (*S. Cox, D.D.*) *Jethro's advice :*—I. THE GIVER OF THIS ADVICE. Jethro. 1. An old man. The father-in-law of Moses, who was now fully eighty years of age. Age has had experience of life. Time for observation. Old men have seen and noted causes of success and failure. Less likely than the young to give bad advice. Are less moved by passion. Taught by memory. Are near to eternity. 2. Thoughtful. His advice shows his thoughtfulness. Thought founded on observation. He saw the labour of Moses and the extent of the camp. 3. Affectionate. He was a relative of Moses. Looked kindly also on this great host of fugitives. Near relatives, amongst those who are most anxious for our welfare. 4. Disinterested. He had nothing to gain personally by giving it, save the satisfaction of his own mind and conscience. 5. Pious. Priest of Midian. Had a respect for the God of Israel. "Rejoiced for all the goodness which the Lord had done to Israel " (Acts xi. 22–24). The advice of men that fear God, who are men of prayer, and love the Bible, not to be slighted ; it will be agreeable to the mind of God. II. THE RECEIVER OF THIS ADVICE. Moses. He did not slight Jethro's advice, although—1. He was in direct communication with God. And we should respect the words of good men, although we have also the Word of God. We have need to be reminded of words, precepts, and promises, that we may overlook ; or of laws, &c., that we may not understand. 2. He had been eminently successful. Such a man, if not humble, might have been very self-reliant ; and have spurned the advice of another. Success makes some unmanageable and proud. 3. He was himself an aged man. Might have thought himself too old to be taught. As competent to give advice as Jethro. Inexperienced youth often puffed up by a little knowledge. The more one really knows the more one feels his ignorance. 4. He doubtless laid the advice he received before the Lord. Jethro made this a condition (ver. 23). Are we willing that the advice we give should be tested by the Word of God ? Do we so test the advice we receive ? 5. He acted upon it, and benefited by doing so. Much good advice is lost in this world. Evaded, though good, because of trouble, or indifference, or pride. The character of the adviser, or his opinion on other matters, made an excuse for neglecting his words. Will God excuse the neglecter ? Learn—1. To do good by word and deed, as we have opportunity, unto all men. 2. To get good, from all men, as opportunity offers. (*J. C.*

Gray.)   *Exhausting labour :*—Dr. Holland, after Mr. Bowles's death, wrote as follows : " As I think of my old associate and the earnest, exhausting work he was doing when I was with him, he seems to me like a great golden vessel, rich in colour and roughly embossed, filled with the elixir of life, which he poured out without the slightest stint for the consumption of this people. We did not know when we tasted it, and found it so charged with zest, that we were tasting heart's blood, but that was the priceless element that commended it to our appetites. A pale man, weary and nervous, crept home at midnight, or at one, two, or three o'clock in the morning, and while all nature was fresh and the birds were singing, and the eyes of thousands were bending eagerly over the results of his night's labour, he was tossing and trying to sleep. Yet this work, so terrible in its exactions and its consequences, was the joy of this man's life—it *was* his life." (*H. O. Mackey.*)   *A proposal for the public good :*—After Marcus Valerius had gained two great victories over the Sabines, in one of which he did not lose a single soldier, he was rewarded with a triumph, and a house was built for him upon Mount Palatine. The doors of the Roman houses generally opened inwards, but this was built to open outwards, to show that he who dwelt there was ready to listen to any proposal made to him for the public good. *God-fearing men for responsible positions :*—One of Stonewall Jackson's peculiarities was to select for his chief of staff, not a military man, but a Presbyterian clergyman, a professor in a theological seminary, and to clothe him with the power of carrying out his mysterious orders when he was temporarily absent. In this he acted as did the greatest of all English commanders—Oliver Cromwell ; who always surrounded himself with men of prayer. (*H. O. Mackey.*)   *Setting others to work :*—One of the best qualifications of a minister is the ability to set the membership at work. It is said that Mr. Spurgeon asks every person seeking admission to membership in his church. " Well, if you are received, what individual work are you going to take up and carry on for the Lord ? " As a result, he has now enrolled in his church register, 5,756 communicants, who represent just so many willing workers under his leadership. He saves his own strength by doing nothing that his hearers can do equally well. And every minister who tries can carry the same rule into practice with a membership of one hundred as well as five thousand. Many ministers fritter away valuable time in doing what the laity might do as well, and sometimes better, for them. (*Christian Age.*)   *Justice to be done in small matters :*—In one of the police courts up town in New York, one morning not long since, a very small boy in knickerbockers appeared. He had a dilapidated cap in one hand, and a green cotton bag in the other. Behind him came a big policeman, with a grin on his face. " Please, sir, are you the judge? " he asked in a voice that had a queer little quiver in it. " I am, my boy. What can I do for you? " asked the justice, as he looked wonderingly down at the mite before him. " If you please, sir, I'm Johnny Moore. I'm seven years old, and I live in One Hundred and Twenty-third street, near the avenue ; and the only good place to play miggles on is in the front of a lot near our house, where the ground is smooth. But a butcher on the corner, that hasn't any more right to the place than we have, keeps his waggon standing there ; and this morning we were playing at miggles there, and he drove us away, and took six of mine, and threw them away off over the fence into the lot. And I went to the police-station ; and they laughed at me and told me to come here and tell you about it." The big policeman and the spectators began to laugh, and the complainant at the bar trembled so violently with mingled indignation and fright that the marbles in his little green bag rattled together. The justice, however, rapped sharply on the desk, and quickly brought everybody to dead silence. " You did perfectly right, my boy," said he, gravely, " to come here and tell me about it. You have as much right to your six marbles as the richest man in this city has to his bank account. If every American citizen had as much regard for his rights as you show, there would be far less crime. And you, sir," he added, turning to the big policeman, " you go with this little man to that butcher and make him pay for those marbles, or else arrest him and bring him here." You see this boy knew that his rights had been interfered with, and he went to the one having authority to redress his wrongs. He did not throw stones or say naughty words, but in a manly, dignified way demanded his rights. (*S. S. Chronicle.*)   *Freedom of resort :*—It is an honourable memorial that James the Fifth, King of Scots, hath left behind him, that he was called the poor man's king ; and it is said of Radolphus Hapsburgius, that seeing some of his guard repulsing divers poor persons that made towards him for relief, was very much displeased, and charged them to suffer the poorest to have access unto him, saying, that he was called to the empire not to be shut up in a chest, as reserved for some few, but to be where all might have freedom of resort unto him. (*J. Spencer.*)   *Spiritual vocation the highest :*—Jethro counselled Moses to be "for the people God-ward, that he might bring the causes unto God." The highest of all vocations is the spiritual.   It is greater to pray than to rule. Moses was to set himself at the highest end of the individual, political, and religious life of Israel, and to occupy the position of intercessor.   He was to be the living link between the people and their God.   Is not this the proper calling of the preacher ? He is not to be a mere politician in the Church, he is not to enter into the detail of organization with the scrupulous care of a conscientious hireling : he is deeply and lovingly to study the truth as it is in Jesus, that he may be prepared to enrich the minds and stimulate the graces of those who hear him.   He is to live so closely with God, that his voice shall be to them as the voice of no other man, a voice from the better world, calling the heart to worship, to trust, and to hope, and through the medium of devotion to prepare men for all the engagements of common life.   The preacher is to live apart from the people, in order that he may in spiritual sympathy live the more truly with them.   He is not to stand afar off as an unsympathetic priest, but to live in the secret places of the Most High, that he may from time to time most correctly repronounce the will of God to all who wait upon his ministry.   When preachers live thus, the pulpit will reclaim its ancient power, and fill all rivalry with confusion and shame. Let the people themselves manage all subordinate affairs ; call up all the business talent that is in the Church, and honour all its successful and well-meant experiments ; give every man to feel that he has an obligation to answer. When you have done this, go yourself, O man of God, to the temple of the Living One, and acquaint yourself deeply with the wisdom and grace of God, that you may be as an angel from heaven when you come to speak the word of life to men who are worn by the anxieties and weakened by the temptations of a cruel world.   Many a man inquires, half in petulance and half in self-justification, "What more can I possibly do than I am already doing ? " Let the case of Moses be the answer. The question in his case was not whether he was doing enough, but whether he was not doing too much in one special direction. Some of the talent that is given to business might be more profitably given to devotion. Rule less, and pray more. Spare time from the business meeting that you may have leisure for communion with God. (*J. Parker, D.D.*)   *How to receive counsel :*—He might have thought : " what presumption in this Midianite to dictate to the ambassador of Jehovah ! " But Moses was a man of a very different spirit. In Montreal, some years ago, a certain English nobleman who had been recently converted, and was preaching the gospel to large multitudes who gathered to hear him, unfortunately had his heart lifted up within him, and began to speak bitterly and scornfully of the Churches of Christ in the city. An excellent and revered Presbyterian elder approached the young nobleman in the kindest way, spoke with great appreciation of the value of his work in preaching the gospel, but suggested that it would be better for the cause if he would cease abusing Christians and Christian Churches, and confine himself to the preaching of Christ. In reply he curled his lip in scorn, and said, "I take my counsel from the Lord ! " What a contrast between the grand nobleman of the olden time, and the small one of yesterday. Moses might with some reason have claimed a monopoly of Divine counsel. God had chosen him out from all other men to make known His will to him ; but when Jethro, though an outsider, and one who had only good common sense on his side, makes his suggestion, Moses does not scorn to listen to his advice, and take it too. And the event showed that the Lord fully approved His servant's course. (*J. M. Gibson, D.D.*)   *Division of labour :*—We recognize the value of the principle of division of labour in manufactures, because there it cheapens the manufactured article, but we fail to see its importance in our own work, because there, in the first instance, it involves additional outlay. We cannot get a man competent to be the head of a department without paying him a handsome salary ; for responsibility means character, and character always commands its price. So, to divide our work into so many departments, and to put over each a thoroughly capable man whom we will hold to a rigid account, requires the immediate expenditure of a large amount of money, and we say we cannot afford it. But all this is a shortsighted policy, for, in the long run, the greater amount of business done will more than reimburse the original outlay ; and, in addition, you can go home, not to fret and worry over trifles, but to be the companion of your wife and the guide and director of your children. Moreover, instead of breaking down hopelessly under the strain of carrying everything on your own shoulders, and requiring to go abroad for years, or, it may be, to leave business altogether, your strength remains unimpaired—nay, perhaps it even increases; and you have the satisfaction of seeing your home happy, and your children growing up to follow in your footsteps, and to declare that their God is dearer to them because He is the God of their father. . . . One said to me, when I began my ministry, "Never do yourself what you can get another to do for you as well as you can do it yourself"; and though I confess that I have not acted on the maxim as much as I ought to have done, I see the wisdom of it more clearly, the longer I live. "Divide et impera," was the maxim of the old Roman general—divide and conquer; and by dividing our labour into many sections, and holding some one responsible for each, we shall do more, we shall do it better, and we shall work longer than would be otherwise possible. (*W. M. Taylor, D.D.*)

CHAPTER XIX.

Vers. 1, 2. **Wilderness of Sinai.**—*Lessons:*—1. Months and days from Egyptian bondage are fit to be recorded. 2. Days are set by God for the Church's gradual progress to their rest; it fails not (ver. 1). 3. From Rephidim to Sinai, or from straits and trials to some rest and doctrine God removes His Church. 4. The Church's camp and God's mount are sweetly joined together (ver. 2). (*G. Hughes, B.D.*) *The wilderness of Sinai:*—After their long halt, exulting in their first victory, they advanced deeper into the mountain ranges, they knew not whither. They knew only that it was for some great end, for some solemn disclosure, such as they had never before witnessed. Onward they went, through winding valley, and under high cliff, and over rugged pass, and through gigantic forms, on which the marks of creation even now seem fresh and powerful; and at last, through all the different valleys, the whole body of the people were assembled. On their right hand and on their left rose long sucessions of lofty rocks, forming a vast avenue, like the approaches which they had seen leading to the Egyptian temples between colossal figures of men and of gods. At the end of this broad avenue, rising immediately out of the level plain on which they were encamped, towered the massive cliffs of Sinai, like the huge altar of some natural temple; encircled by peaks of every shape and height, the natural pyramids of the desert. In this sanctuary, secluded from all earthly things, they waited for the revelation of God. (*Dean Stanley.*)

Vers. 3, 4. **I bare you on eagles' wings.**—*Borne on eagles' wings:*—God here employs a similitude denoting the speed, the security and the tender care with which they were, as it were, transported from the house of bondage, and which is expanded in fuller significancy (Deut. xxxii. 11, 12). Here is a figurative illustration of an important work. We may apply it to three things in the history of the Christian. 1. To the period of conversion. Then God bears sinners on eagles' wings and brings them to Himself. He stirs up the nest of self-righteousness and carnal security; flutters over them, excites and teaches them to fly towards heaven in their desires and affections. 2. It will also apply to the season of deliverance, and is descriptive of the speed with which God comes to the help of His people, and the security He effects; for the eagle is not only a swift, but a powerful bird. 3. It will apply to their final happiness. He will bear His people on eagles' wings to heaven. It may be He may bear them through many a dark and trying scene, but they shall be brought to glory at last. (*A. Nevin, D.D.*) *God's deliverances:*— There is great beauty and truth in this expression, and it well displays all that God had done for this enslaved people. The eagle is the most powerful of the birds of prey of the ancient world; it is the most rapid in its flight, the highest and most majestic in its aerial courses, and, at the same time, one of the most tender towards its young. These four qualities of the eagle admirably depict—1. The power with which God had delivered Israel, destroying for them the most formidable nations, raising tempests in the heavens, and the waves of the sea, opening its abyss, and, as it is elsewhere expressed, saving them "through a mighty hand, and by a stretched-out arm." 2. The astonishing quickness of this deliverance: fifty days had scarcely elapsed since this multitude were slaves on the borders of the Nile employed in making bricks, under the lash of the task-masters; and lo! they were all gathered together at the foot of the mountains of Arabia, having passed, like an eagle, over deserts and seas. 3. The majesty which God had displayed in His intervention. As the eagle which, bearing its young upon its back, flies not near the earth, nor from tree to tree like other birds, but soars majestically at the height of the clouds, see with what brilliant grandeur God had delivered Israel: the Nile is turned into blood, the sun darkened, darkness covers the land for three days, thunder and hailstones rend the heavens, the Destroying Angel passes over Egypt in the terrible night of the death of its firstborn, the pillar of the cloud by day, and the pillar of fire by night goes before the camp of Israel, the voice of God is heard with power from the heights of heaven. 4. The tender care of the eagle for its cherished young presents to us a touching figure of the conduct of God towards Israel. The eagle broods over its young in its nest in the crevice of some rock, it cherishes them, it nourishes them, it carries them upon its wings, it deposits them tenderly, in such places as it deems good for them, and soon teaches them to fly alone in the sky. Well, such had been the conduct of God towards His people. Read what God Himself says about it in Deut. xxxii. 7–14. (*Prof. Gaussen.*) *And brought you unto Myself:*—The Israelites had, on the one side, by the Egyptian servitude; on the other, by the Egyptian idolatry, with which they had contaminated themselves, swerved far from God, His purity and sanctity—in a word, from truth and genuine faith; now God, in graciously granting them His revelation and His pure doctrines, brings them again back to Himself; He intends to make them "a kingdom of priests and a holy nation." (*M. M. Kalisch, Ph.D.*)

Vers. 5, 6. **A peculiar treasure unto Me.**—*God's people His treasure:*—1. A treasure is something searched for. The Holy Spirit is ever diligently seeking after Christians. 2. A treasure when found is carefully guarded. As the apple of His eye God protects those who trust Him. 3. The finding of a treasure is the occasion of rejoicing. "There is joy in heaven," &c. 4. To obtain a treasure we will make great sacrifices. "God gave His only begotten Son," &c. (*Homiletic Review.*) *National ideals:*—The problem was: How to convert a horde of demoralized slaves into a nation of virtuous freemen, paying a free obedience to law, as they had before paid a forced obedience to the lash of the taskmaster? The practical solution of the problem involved the application of three spiritual forces or living principles. We may describe them thus:—1. The revelation of the new name of God, "Jehovah," the Eternal, the unchangeable, the self-same. 2. The revelation of the ideal or standard, which the nation is to keep steadily before mind and conscience, as the thing to be aimed at and striven after. This revelation is given most explicitly and clearly in the words of our text: "A kingdom of priests, and an holy nation." 3. The actual legislation which is founded upon these two revelations:—of which legislation the law of the Ten Commandments is the eternal and indestructible substructure—as strong and durable now as when it was first uttered by the voice of God to Israel—as much the foundation of all legislation now as of the distinctively Mosaic legislation then. It was under the operation of these three forces that Israel became and continued to be a nation. It is under the operation of the same or analogous forces that any nation becomes and continues to be a nation. When such forces cease to operate upon a nation, it dies. To prove and illustrate this point must form the remainder of our subject. 1. It is impossible for any of us to overlook the importance of the words which introduce the Ten Commandments. "I am the Lord"—that is, the Eternal—"thy God." They are not an ornamental flourish or accidental prefix. They are the living root of all that follows. Again and again, in the course of the subsequent legislation, the words recur; even in those parts of the legislation which are most minute and temporary, sanitary or ceremonial. The new name, upon which the nation is to be built, is the name "Jehovah," the Eternal; to which is added the old name, "thy God," as a name to be cherished and dear as ever. Now, in this name Jehovah is involved the notion of permanence, unchangeableness; and this notion lies at the root of law, whether laws of man, or laws of nature, or laws of God. But to this tremendous, this oppressive, notion of unchangeableness, there is added the tender grace of the old name, "Thy God"—One with whom every Israelite and every human being may plead, as the Psalmist does, "O God, Thou art my God." It is the blending of the two together; it is the intertwining of the two subtle and mighty spiritual forces, implied in the two names, that made the revelation so potent for its great purpose—the creation of a nation, that should be a kingdom of priests, a holy nation. And just in proportion as the hold of those names upon heart and conscience relaxed, the nation decayed and died. For, indeed, it is everlastingly true, as one of our own poets has said, that "by the soul only the nations can be great and free." Any one can see, that a really free people must be a loyal or law-abiding people; and that laws, which are to receive the willing obedience of such a people, must be founded on the immutable principles of truth and justice and morality. Nor can any one doubt that the Mosaic legislation is founded on such principles. 2. But now I wish to speak to you about the second of those three spiritual forces, in the strength of which Israel was to be moulded into a nation. I have already described it as the revelation of the ideal which the nation was to keep steadily before mind and conscience, as the thing to be aimed at and striven after. Our text words it thus: "Now, therefore, if ye will obey My voice indeed, and keep My covenant." The destiny—the calling and election—of the nation of Israel was higher and holier than the destiny of any other nation. It was chosen to bear witness to the kingdom of God and His righteousness, before all the nations of the earth; a kingdom of priests, a royal and priestly race, each member of it uniting in his own person the attributes of a king and a priest: a king, to rule right loyally over his own lower and baser nature; a priest, to offer himself up in willing sacrifice to God. This pattern of righteousness the most choice and elect members of the nation did exhibit. You have only to think over the long list of truly kingly and priestly characters—from Moses to John the Baptist —to be satisfied of this. The fact that the election of Israel was what it was, does not deprive all other nations of an election of their own. On the contrary, the very words of our text, which affirm most strongly the election of Israel, do at least suggest the thought of a corresponding, though inferior, election of all other nations. At this distance of time we have not the data for determining the special calling of Egypt, for example, or of Assyria. But we can discern with very tolerable clearness the election, the manifest destiny, of Greece and of Rome; the call of Greece to catch the inspiration of beauty, and to be the nurse of freedom; the call of Rome to be the schoolmaster of the nations, with its iron rod of law and order. We can discern, also, with perfect clearness, the vast inferiority, even of such a calling and election as this, to the calling of Israel; and can therefore fully justify the language of our text: "Ye shall be a peculiar treasure unto Me above all people." But if this principle of a calling and election of nations holds true of the whole ancient world, why should it not hold true of the whole modern world also? So long as national distinctions and national characteristics exist at all, there must exist along with them corresponding national duties and national responsibilities. What is it, then, for England and for us? It may be said, that it is the manifest destiny of England to colonize and subdue the earth—to girdle it with rails of iron and steel, and lines of telegraph wire. It is in words like these, Duty and Justice— in the response which they awaken in our hearts—that we English people find the revelation of our national calling and election of God. As a nation, we are called, in a special sense, to be just and dutiful. And if our children are to go out into distant lands, and among subject peoples, to be models of duty and justice there, they must be nursed and trained in those principles first at home. A "kingdom of priests":—yes—and that title belongs also to us, as well as to Israel; though to us, not as Englishmen, but as Christians. For is it not written: "Unto Him who loveth us, and washed us from our sins in His own blood, and hath made us kings and priests unto God and His Father: to Him be glory and dominion for ever and ever. Amen." I need not say that there is no discrepancy whatever between our special calling as Englishmen, and our more general calling as disciples of Christ. On the contrary, the latter must and does sustain and verify the former. Just in proportion as we learn to rule, as kings, over our lower, baser, selfish nature; and to offer ourselves up as priests, living, reasonable, and spiritual sacrifices, in the power and virtue of the one perfect Sacrifice, to God; just in this proportion shall we be enabled to do justice and judgment, and to walk dutifully and uprightly, and so to uphold the true glory of the English name, in whatever circumstances we may be placed—whether at home, or amongst strangers and foreigners in some far distant land. It was so with the heroes of England in the past. (*D. J. Vaughan, M.A.*) *Lessons:*—1. In covenant-making or lawgiving from God there is need of some mediator to be with God. 2. God's call alone can qualify or authorize a mediator between Him and sinners. 3. It is incumbent on the mediator to declare fully God's mind unto His people. 4. A due recognition of God's gracious acts for souls against enemies is a good preparation to receive His law. 5. God's securing providence as well as selecting a people to Himself prepare them to hear His covenant (ver. 4). 6. God's covenanted people are His peculiar treasure in the world. 7. It is God's free grace who owneth all nations on earth to make one His peculiar above another (ver. 5). 8. Royalty, near communion with God, and sanctity are the privileges of God's peculiar ones. Kings, priests, and saints. 9. The words of duty and privilege must be spoken and made known unto the Church (ver. 6). (*G. Hughes, B.D.*) *God's promise to the Jews:*—I. THE RECITAL OF HIS WORKS. II. THE PROPOSALS OF HIS LOVE. III. THE PROMISES OF HIS GRACE. (*T. Mortimer.*) *"All the earth is Mine":*—I. GOD'S ASSERTION OF UNIVERSAL POSSESSION IN THE EARTH. 1. Nations. 2. Lands. 3. The animal and vegetable kingdoms. II. GOD'S ASSERTION EXCLUDES EVERY OTHER BEING FROM UNIVERSAL POSSESSION. 1. It is not man's earth. 2. It is not the devil's. 3. It does not belong to any created intelligence. III. GOD'S ASSERTION SHOULD AWAKEN CONFIDENCE IN HIS SAINTS AND TERROR IN SINNERS. 1. All forces are under His control. 2. Everything that is not of Him must fail. 3. His possession of the earth will be fully manifest in the end. (*J. S. Exell, M.A.*) *Explanation of the Divine preferences:*—Here is the explanation of the Divine preferences which have distressed so many hearts under the cruel name of sovereignty and election. There need be no torture in using those words. If we feel distressed by them, it is because we have come upon them along the wrong path. They are beautiful and noble words when set in their places according to the Divine intent. "Then ye shall be a peculiar treasure unto Me above all people." Is that partiality in any exclusive sense? Not at all; it is really meant to be inclusive. God elects humanity. "And ye shall be unto Me a kingdom." In what sense? In the ordinary sense—namely, a great aggregate of subjects ruled by one arbitrary and despotic king? In no such sense. The literal meaning is, ye shall all be kings. Now ye see the meaning of that great name, "King of kings"—not king of an individual monarch here and there, as in Britain, or Russia, or China, but of all believers. All obedient souls are lifted up unto kinghood. We are royal equals if we obey Heaven's will, and God is King of kings—King of all. We are a royal generation. All this language is typical. Beautiful is the historical line when seized and wisely applied. Let us attempt such seizure and application. The firstborn were chosen, and the firstborn were to be priests. In what sense are the firstborn chosen? Not as relegating the afterborn to positions subordinate and inferior; but in the sense of being their pledge and seal. God has the eldest Son, and therefore—that is the sacred logic—He has all the other children. Then the laws regarding the priesthood underwent a change, and the family of Aaron was called. We proceed from an individual, namely, the firstborn, to a family, namely, the Aaronic stock. But why were they chosen? That all the children of Aaron might also be priests, in the truly spiritual and eternal sense, though not in official and formal name and status. Then the family was deposed and a tribe is chosen— the tribe of Levi. Mark how the history accumulates and grows up into a prophecy and an argument! First the individual, then the family, then the tribe, then the Son of Man—absorbing all the past, gathering up into its true and official meaning all priesthood, all intercession. There is one Advocate with the Father, the Man Christ Jesus. A new light thus begins to dawn upon the cloud. There is nothing arbitrary in the movement of God when we can penetrate its infinite philosophy. Will God have the first-fruits of the harvest field? He claims all such. Why will He claim the first-fruits? That in having the first-fruits He might have all the field. He will not take the whole wheat acreage of the world into His heavens and devour our poor loaf of bread; but He will take the first ear of corn that we can find in all the fields, and, having taken that, He says: "In giving Me this you have given Me all." (*J. Parker, D.D.*) *God's peculiar treasure:*—Exotic flowers or foreign plants, if seeded on the mountain side, or inserted in the meadow amongst the promiscuous herbage growing there, soon become choked and disappear. Those who wish to preserve the flaming glories of the Cape, or the rich fruits of the tropic, must provide a garden enclosed—must keep out the weeds and rough weather. And so God, anxious to preserve "His Holy Law," fenced in the Hebrew nationality. He secluded them, and walled them in, and made them, as it were, His own conservatory—a conservatory where Divine truth should survive uninjured until Messiah should come. *God's covenant uniform:*—What covenant could this be, containing such promises, and by which a people should be a peculiar treasure to God, and above all others upon the earth; yea, a royal priesthood, a holy nation? This could be no other than the covenant of redemption by Christ, to the blessings of which man has no claim but in grace. The covenant of God, as the Church of God itself, under every diversity of dispensation has been the same. Whatever of a national character was peculiar to Israel, and that ceased under a better economy, was extraneous to this, and not an essential constituent or feature thereof. Uniformity of design is discoverable through the whole progress of Divine revelation, and under every form of religious ceremony. God has not at any period contradicted Himself, or set before man a covenant of grace at one time, and a covenant of works at another, for the hope of life. It would have been contrary to all that God had done, and to all that He yet promised to do, as also a break of an awful character, and the introduction of confusion into the whole system of redemption, to have here brought the nation under a covenant of works, by which they had virtually perished. True it is, that Sinai and Zion are, by the apostle, placed in contradistinction: the one as gendering to bondage; the other as free: the one as characterized by the law of condemnation; the other by the law of righteousness: but it is in certain respects only that that contrast holds good, not in the essential intention of things. The whole fabric of their ecclesiastical polity, conjoined in all its parts with exquisite wisdom, was the workmanship of mercy. By redemption it was that God claimed Israel as His own, a treasure, His best and greatest treasure, a treasure containing a treasure, His grace, His glory, the promised seed His Son. All the earth was His; yet in all the earth was nothing He so valued, nothing He held so dear. Still this treasure so great had been lost but for the security and grace of the covenant. The intrinsic value of His people was enhanced beyond all price by what this covenant embraced and required. It cost much to make them His people, and to secure them to Himself—a treasure for ever. (*W. Seaton.*) *The spirituality of the old covenant:*—The characteristic feature of the Sinai revelation is the law; but it is important to observe that it is not law as a means of salvation, but law as a sequel of salvation. If this simple and evident fact were only borne in mind in the reading of the Old Testament, endless perplexities and confusions of thought would be avoided. Observe, also, the kind of blessings which are promised. How many are there who will persist in maintaining that the old covenant offered mere temporal blessings, while it is the distinctive feature of the new to promise spiritual blessing. It is true that temporal blessings were included under the old covenant, just as they are under the new; and though they do hold a more prominent place in the old, as was indeed to be expected, yet it is a slander upon that covenant to say that these were the blessings it offered. The great blessings of the old covenant were undoubtedly spiritual, as is manifest here: " If ye will obey My voice and keep My covenant, then ye shall be to Me a peculiar treasure above all people"; "and ye shall be unto Me a kingdom of priests, and an holy nation." Nearness to God, dearness to God, holiness—these were the characteristic blessings of the old covenant. These promises are among the richest and most deeply spiritual in the whole Bible; and it is with great reluctance that, yielding to the exigency of our plan, we refrain from entering into the wealth of meaning which each separate word conveys. Let me only notice in leaving it, that when the apostle Peter wishes to express in the very strongest terms the highest privileges of the children of God under the new dispensation, he can do nothing better than quote these old but "exceeding great and precious promises" (1 Pet. ii. 9). (*J. M. Gibson, D.D.*) *Holiness ensured:*—A writer tells of going down with a party into a coal mine. On the side of the gangway grew a plant which was perfectly white. The visitors were astonished that there, where the coal-dust was continually flying, this little plant should be so clean. A miner who was with them took a handful of black dust and threw it on the plant, but not a particle of it adhered. There was a wonderful enamel on the plant to which no finest speck could cling. Living there, amid clouds of dust, nothing could stain its snowy whiteness. This is a picture of what every Christian life should be. Unholy influences breathe incessantly about us and upon us. But it is our mission to be pure amid all this vileness, undefiled, unspotted from the world. If God can make a little plant so wondrously that no dust can stain its whiteness, surely He can, by His grace, so transform our heart and life that sin shall not cling to us. He who can keep the plant stainless and white as snow amid clouds of dust, can guard us in purity in this world of sin. **A kingdom of priests.**—*Priests to the world:*—They were to be the trustees, for humanity at large, of the revelations, promises, and ordinances which God communicated, and they were to keep them for the benefit of all mankind. For a time, indeed, these heavenly communications were to be reserved to themselves; only, however, that they might be the more securely preserved; but at length all restrictions would be broken down, and that which, in its ritual exclusivism, had been confined to them would, in its spiritual persuasiveness, become the heritage of every true believer who should, like them, enter into covenant with the Lord, not over a merely typical sacrifice, but over the true and real atonement which Christ would make for the sins of men. Thus, in this peculiar promise, which looks at first as if it conferred a patent of protected privilege, we see that the present protection is in order to the future diffusion; and we have an echo of the Abrahamic blessing, "In thee and in thy seed shall all the nations of the earth be blessed." What the Levitical tribe ultimately was among the Israelites themselves, that the Israelites were to be among the nations; and the more faithfully they performed their duties, the richer would be the ultimate blessing to the Gentiles. Reading these words in the light of the history to which they form the introduction, it needs no keenness of insight to perceive the bearing of these principles upon ourselves; for we Christians are now the world's priests, custodians of those spiritual blessings by which our fellow-men are to be benefited; and only in proportion as we maintain holiness of character shall we discharge our duties to mankind at large. (*W. M. Taylor, D.D.*)

Vers. 7, 8. **All that the Lord hath spoken we will do.**—*Lessons :*—1. Command received from God by His ministers—they must go and call them whom they must bespeak. 2. Orderly proceeding to acquaint the people of God's will by their heads is rational. 3. Proposition and exposition of God's words must be made to souls that they may know them. 4. All God's words, and no more but His, Jehovah commands His ministers to speak to His people (ver. 7). (*G. Hughes, B.D.*) *God's revelation of Himself, &c. :*—The subject of this paragraph (vers. 7–24) is God's revelation of Himself,—the call to receive it, the manner in which it was made. I. When God reveals Himself man is summoned to attend. This is uniformly God's method. First the call, then the revelation. "Hear, O Israel," then, "the Lord thy God is one Lord." "This is My beloved Son, hear ye Him," then the New Testament dispensation. Moses was a type of the ministry of the Son of Man, and an example to Christian ministers in the manner in which he summoned men to God. He spoke—1. Authoritatively. 2. Clearly. 3. Completely. 4. Successfully. 5. Moses spoke for the people to God. So does Christ combine our poor prayers with the mighty eloquence of His intercession. II. When God reveals Himself, man must be prepared for the revelation (vers. 10–15). 1. Man must attend to the herald who proclaims God's coming. 2. Man must be prepared by personal sanctification. 3. Man must be prepared by a ready acquiescence in all that God commands. 4. Man must be prepared at the appointed time. "Be ready against the third day." (1) God has now appointed times in which He promises to reveal Himself to men. The Lord's day. All times of duty and religious privilege. Let no man be unprepared, or plead excuses, or make other engagements. (2) God has now appointed times which He has not chosen to reveal. Death, judgment. We "know not the day nor the hour when the Son of Man cometh." Hence the wisdom of immediate and constant preparation. "Watch and pray." III. When God reveals Himself it is in a manner suited to the occasion. It was necessary that He should speak to men who for years had been surrounded by idolatrous associations, and who had become debased by years of servitude, in a most solemn, startling, and impressive form. God has other methods than those employed here. Abraham, Elijah. Bethlehem, Pentecost, Patmos, &c. So in each individual case. Learn then—1. To listen when God speaks. Faith has a faculty not only of sight, but of hearing. 2. When God calls obey that call, and be prepared for the public revelation which that call precedes. "God now commandeth every man to repent" (2 Cor. vii. 1). 3. Receive God's revelation of Himself in His own way. (*J. W. Burn.*) *A commendable engagement rashly made and repeatedly broken :*—I. A commendable engagement. 1. Because of its righteousness. 2. Because of its advantageousness. (1) The highest character. "A holy nation." (2) The highest service. "Unto Me a kingdom of priests." (3) The highest privilege. "A peculiar treasure unto Me." 3. Because of its unanimity. "All the people answered together." II. A commendable engagement rashly made. 1. Without due consideration. 2. Without earnest purpose. 3. Without hearty concurrence with the will which they promised to obey. 4. Without any realization of their need of Divine help in order that they may keep it. "How easily overween we our own abilities!" III. A commendable engagement repeatedly and terribly broken. Their sin in violating this solemn promise was the more heinous because of (1) God's great goodness to them. (2) His invariable faithfulness in His portion of the covenant. (3) The comparatively trivial circumstances and slight influences which proved sufficient to induce them to break their engagement. Notwithstanding the strongest obligations to fulfil their promise, they broke it upon the slightest provocation. Conclusion—1. Let us heed well our obligation to do all that the Lord commands. 2. Let us be careful in the utterance of religious vows. 3. Let us be humbled by the recollection of the many religious vows we have made but not kept, and seek forgiveness for our failures. 4. Let us endeavour to perform our vows, looking to God for strength to enable us to do so. (*William Jones.*) *The response of the people to God's call :*—I. THE CALL (ver. 7). 1. The elders represented the people. In dealing with so great a multitude some such arrangement was necessary. So it is in many things—in the nation, the family, the Church. 2. God's commands were faithfully communicated. "Laid before their faces all," &c. : nothing was added and nothing kept back. The will of God was made known so plainly that none could plead ignorance ; so particularly that none could plead excuse. The truth was communicated to every man's conscience in the sight of God. II. THE RESPONSE (ver. 8). "And all the people answered together," &c. 1. Prompt. There was no hesitancy. 2. Hearty. There was no reservation. 3. Unanimous. There was no dissentient voice (Acts ii. 1). How grand the spectacle! The mighty multitude as with one heart and voice proclaimed their submission to God. But, alas! the sequel showed, that mixed with their apparent sincerity and enthusiasm there was much of ignorance, presumption, and self-conceit. III. THE REPORT TO GOD. "And Moses returned the words of the people unto the Lord" (cf. ver. 9). Such report was necessary to secure the favour of God and the faith of the people. It tended to—1. Exoneration of conscience. 2. Relief of the heart. 3. Invigoration of hope. 4. Accrediting of character. 5. Success of ministry. Nothing works more to give a man power with men than the belief that he has power with God. (*William Forsyth.*) *The preparation for meeting with God :*—Moses acted throughout according to Divine command. I. THE PEOPLE WERE CALLED TO SANCTIFY THEMSELVES. There must be separation from what is *not* of God, in order to fellowship with what *is*. Self-consecration required (Psa. xxvi. 6; Isa. i. 16–18; Rom. xii. 1; 1 Cor. vi. 9–20). II. THE PEOPLE WERE CHARGED TO BE READY AT THE APPOINTED TIME (ver. 11). Come into God's presence with humility, prayer, hope. III. THE PEOPLE WERE COMMANDED TO OBSERVE THE PRESCRIBED LAWS AND ORDINANCES AS TO APPROACH TO GOD. Bounds fixed as to place, action, behaviour (vers. 12–14; see 1 Cor. xiv. 10). (*Ibid.*) *Pleasantness of obedience :*—The pleasantest thing in the world is to be obedient. 1. Because it is so pleasant to know what we have to do. The word "law" comes from the verb "to lay"; it means "something laid down." The "law" is something that God has laid down quite plain for us to do. 2. Because it is a proof that God loves us. Do you remember, when Peter was so unhappy, Christ said to him : "Peter, feed My sheep, feed My lambs"? Christ said that to show that He trusted Peter again. Therefore, if God tells you to do anything, be sure God loves you. 3. Because it is practising for heaven. To obey the "law" is to prepare for heaven. There all will be obedience. Sir Henry Lawrence said, just before he died, "I wish this to be on my tombstone : 'Here lies Henry Lawrence, who tried to do his duty.'" Duty is preparing for heaven. Somebody perhaps will say, "Oh, but it is so difficult to do one's duty—to love the 'law.'" Listen to what a little girl said to her brother : "I tried with all my might to be good, and I prayed and read my Bible, but I was no better. At last I found Christ, and when I found Christ it was all easy; and from that time I have been so happy." (*Prof. Drummond.*) *Disobedience unhappy :*—A boy, when he entered his first place of employment, made an engagement with his master that he was to be in his place at nine o'clock in the morning. For a while the boy was always to be found at his post at the appointed hour, but he began to notice that his master did not come in until a quarter to ten, and he thought it would not matter if he did not come in until ten minutes past nine, for his master would never know. He got on very well for a time, but at length he began to grow very miserable. He had a feeling that he was cheating his master, consequently he was unhappy; he felt he had lost his faithfulness, and made up his mind to go in at the hour appointed, and when he did so his peace and joy returned, because he was conscious that he was doing right. It is the same with Christians in their daily life. As long as they are obeying God's commandments they are happy, but whenever they break one of them they become miserable. Want of faithfulness in the most trivial things often breaks our peace, and stops communion with God. (*George Müller.*)   *An inconsiderate promise:*—A story is told of a gentleman who visited President Lincoln, and who was in the habit of making promises more freely than he kept them. In order to induce one of Mr. Lincoln's boys, to sit on his lap, the gentleman offered to give him a charm which he wore on his watch chain. The boy climbed into his lap. Finally the gentleman arose to go, when Mr. Lincoln said to him, "Are you going to keep your promise to my boy?" "What promise?" said the visitor. "You said you would give him that charm." "Oh, I could not," said the visitor. "It is·not only valuable, but I prize it as an heirloom." "Give it to him," said Mr. Lincoln, sternly. "I would not want him to know that I entertained one who had no regard for his word." The gentleman coloured, undid the charm, and handed it to the boy, and went away with a lesson which he was not likely soon to forget, and which others may profit by learning.

Vers. 10, 11. **The third day the Lord will come down.**—*Lessons:*—1. The Mediator willingly cometh from God to impart His will to His people. 2. The true Mediator is as ready to sanctify His people as God would have Him. 3. Souls must follow their Mediator's command forsanctification (ver. 14). 4. It is the Mediator's care to prepare a people for God at His time, to whom He is sent. 5. Lawful enjoyments in the flesh sometimes must be denied for better attendance on God. 6. Great is the fitness required in souls for receiving rightly the law from God (ver. 15). (*G. Hughes, B.D.*)   *Getting ready for worship:*—What was the signification of this Divine command? God gets at the mind through the senses; and He doubtless intended to instruct the people by this act that their minds should be purified, and their hearts prepared for His service. And to us it points out the necessity of our hearts being cleansed from sin, from the defilement and the love of it, before we can serve the Lord acceptably; it teaches us also that we must not rush heedlessly into the presence of God, even in private prayer. This becoming reverence for the presence of the Divine Majesty will likewise show itself in our demeanour in the house of God. "Let them wash their clothes, and be ready against the third day." This will bring a man in time to the house of God. He will feel with David, "I was glad when they said, Let us go to the house of the Lord"; and if by any unavoidable circumstance he is later than he ought to be, his very step will testify his concern that it should be so, and a solicitude lest he disturb the solemnity of the worship of others. In the man who fulfils the spirit of this command there will be no wandering eye, but that general decorum of manner which shows that he has put off his shoes from his feet, for the place whereon he stands is holy ground. (*George Breay, B.A.*) *Salutary bounds:*—A traveller relates that, when passing through an Austrian town, his attention was directed to a forest on a slope near the road, and he was told that death was the penalty of cutting down one of those trees. He was incredulous until he was further informed that they were the protection of the city, breaking the force of the descending avalanche which, without this natural barrier, would sweep over the homes of thousands. When a Russian army was there and began to cut away the fence for fuel, the inhabitants besought them to take their dwellings instead, which was done. Such, he well thought, are the sanctions of God's moral law. On the integrity and support of that law depends the safety of the universe. "The soul that sinneth, it shall die," is a merciful proclamation. "He that offends in one point is guilty of all," is equally just and benevolent. To transgress once is to lay the axe at the root of the tree which represents the security and peace of every loyal soul in the wide dominions of the Almighty. (*Family Treasury.*)   *Importance of holiness:*—God has no ultimate use for a man that is not holy. A rose-tree that does not blossom is of no use in a garden. A vine that bears no grapes is of no use in a vineyard. A criminal has no place in the State. In that everlasting kingdom in which the glory of God and the perfection of man will be at last revealed, there can be no place for those that have not an intense passion for holiness, and who do not themselves illustrate its dignity and beauty. (*R. W. Dale.*)   *Purity of soul essential:*—"My son," said Nushirvan, king of Persia, in the directions of his last will to his successor, "present yourself often at the gate of heaven to implore its succour in your need, but purify your soul beforehand."

Vers. 16–25. **To meet with God.**—*Lessons:*—1. Upon Churches preparation, and sanctification God is ready to appear to them. 2. God will keep His day, His third day of appearance to His people. 3. In God's appearance for covenant-making He giveth the discovery of Himself as He pleaseth. 4. Terrible signals God useth sometimes to declare His majesty to men (Psa. xviii. 9). 5. The law given by Moses differs from Christ's in darkness and deadliness (Heb. xii.). 6. Suitable affections unto terrible appearances of God may be from nature and grace (ver. 16). It might be a spirit of bondage in some, but of free grace in others. (*G. Hughes, B.D.*) *Lessons :—*1. God's terrors in the law are not to drive men from Him, but to bring them humbly to Him. 2. God hath appointed a Mediator to bring souls unto Him. They come not of themselves. 3. Upon the Mediator's conduct souls may be bold to approach the terrors of the Lord. 4. Sinners must keep their standing appointed by the Mediator to find grace in the sight of God (ver. 17). (*Ibid.*) *Lessons :—*1. Great is the condescension of Jehovah unto men in giving law and covenant to them. 2. In God's humbling Himself He keeps His distance and place above men. 3. In giving His law to men God calleth the Mediator to be by Him. 4. God withholds no discovery from His Church but that which would be deadly to them (ver. 21). 5. Among the congregation God hath appointed some to office for ministering to Him. 6. Such persons must be sanctified in their special place according to God's will. 7. The more holy the persons and office are, the more deadly is their transgression. 8. Threatenings of death are primarily in grace to give life to souls (ver. 22). (*Ibid.*) *Lessons :—*1. God seeth need for His ministers testifying and pressing on people His will when men do not. 2. The Mediator's descent to men hinders not His ascent to God again for their good. 3. None but mediators must come so near to God as He appoints them. 4. Such as do, though under pretence of holiness, must perish (ver. 24). 5. The Mediator, as He must, so is He willing to be with God's people at the law-giving. 6. It is Mediator's work to teach all to souls that may fit them to a due reception of God's covenant (ver. 25). (*Ibid.*) *God on Mount Sinai :—*I. THE GREATNESS OF GOD. All powers of nature under His control. II. THE NEARNESS OF GOD (see iv. 7–12). III. THE MYSTERIOUSNESS OF GOD (see Psa. xcvii. 2). IV. THE HOLINESS OF GOD (see chap. xv. 11 ; Isa. vi. 1, 2 ; Rev. iv. 8 ; 1 Pet. i. 16). V. THE SOVEREIGNTY AND MERCY OF GOD (see Deut. v. 24). (*W. Forsyth.*) *The highest ministry* (ver. 17) :—The essence of religion is to realize the presence of God. Therefore we should hail as our highest benefactor the man who does for us as Moses did for Israel. "And Moses brought forth the people out of the camp to meet with God." I. IN THE OPERATIONS OF NATURE. Poets have sung of the sublimities and beauties of nature, and philosophers explain her secrets ; but he does the noblest work who brings us face to face with nature's God. II. THE EVENTS OF PROVIDENCE. Many writers have done well in history and fiction, and have depicted with wondrous skill the varieties of character and incident, and the strange vicissitudes of human life ; but he does best who shows us that there is a providence in the affairs of men, and that the Lord our God ruleth over all in righteousness and love. III. THE ORDINANCES OF THE GOSPEL. Preachers may be learned and eloquent, but it is only as they manifest God's law to the conscience and God's love to the heart that they do us real good. Prayer and praise are proper duties, but unless in them we rise to God they are meaningless and vain. (*Ibid.*) *Vain curiosity* (ver. 21) :—I. IT PRIES INTO SECRETS. II. BREAKS THROUGH BOUND-ARIES. III. SACRIFICES REVERENCE AND SELF-RESPECT. IV. RECKLESSLY RUSHES INTO DANGER. V. MULTIPLIES CONFUSIONS AND PERILS. Remember Eve, Uzziah. (*J. S. Exell, M.A.*) **To meet with God.**—*Coming to church to meet God :—*" The people stood at the nether part of the mount " ; they listened with this very end in view : they came out of the camp to meet God, as God had commanded they should do. When you come up to the house of God keep this in view. There is, in the present day, as there was in the days of the apostle, such a thing as having "itching ears," looking to man, instead of an humble and reverent desire to meet God. Brethren, be much in prayer ; and when you leave your closets to attend public worship, say, " I am now going to meet with God." As you enter His house, reflect, " This is none other than the house of God, this is the gate of heaven " ; oh that I may meet my Saviour ; oh that His love may be shed abroad in my heart ; oh that I may understand more of God's plan for the salvation of sinners ; oh that I may get my heart warmed by close communion with my God, and have my soul lifted up above the cares and pleasures of this sinful world ! Were all our congregations to assemble thus, oh what a savour, and unction, and blessing we should experience ! (*George Breay, B.A.*) *Communion with God :—*The windows of Somerset House that face the Strand are all double-cased, so as to deaden the roar of the traffic outside. It would be impossible to do mental work unless some such system were adopted. There is but one way to be "in the world and not of it"; it is to be shut in with God, away from the din of its cares, temptations, and strifes. Outside, confusion, hurly-burly; inside, quiet, peace, under the shadow of the Almighty. *Communion with God :*—When we think of Moses coming so near to Jehovah in His majesty, wielding the terrific agencies of flood and storm and fire, of darkness and lightning and the voice of trumpet exceeding loud—Mount Sinai rocking beneath His feet, and Moses alone drawing near the Awful Presence and talking with God face to face there—what shall we say of the possibilities of communion between man and his Maker? Whatever speculations we may have as to the means and methods by which the thought of God was borne to the mind of Moses, and the thought of Moses to the mind of God, the great fact of communion of mind with mind—thought meeting thought—of command from the superior party, received and obeyed by the inferior—is on the outer face of the whole history and admits of no question. God can speak to man so that man shall know the voice to be His, and comprehend perfectly its significance. Relations of obedience, confidence, and love on the part of man toward his Maker, are established, and God meets them with appropriate manifestations of His favour. (*H. Cowles, D.D.*) *Moses and Aaron united in the mount :*—The association of Aaron with Moses in the mount intimates evangelical instruction. It was the design of God, not only to declare the condemnation of sin, but to point out the way of justification and life. Their ministry united, the people cannot perish. It was in the presence of both that the words of the covenant were pronounced, showing that the functions of each were concerned in that dispensation. Moses would declare the law to the people; Aaron make reconciliation for sin. Infinitely glorious the surety of the everlasting covenant, our Divine Redeemer, of whom Moses in his prophetical office, and Aaron in his priestly, were but imperfect types. In Him was every qualification to mediate, and every right, that none need despair of redemption who trust in Him. (*W. Seaton.*)

CHAPTER XX.

VERS. 1, 2. **God spake all these words.**—*The Ten Words of God :*—I. Those Ten Commandments were to the Jews THE VERY UTTERANCE OF THE ETERNAL, and they hold in their grand imagination that the souls of all Jews even yet unborn were summoned to Sinai in their numbers numberless to hear that code; so that, in the East, to this day, if a Jew would indignantly deny the imputation of a wrong, he exclaims, "My soul too has been on Sinai." And not to Jews only but to all mankind there is this proof that the Ten Words were indeed the oracles of God, that, if they be written upon the heart, they are an "It is written" sufficient for our moral guidance—they are a great *non licet* strong enough to quell the fiercest passions. For the laws of the natural universe may mislead us. One tells us that they are just and beneficent; another that they are deadly and remorseless: but of these moral Laws we know that they are the will of God. No man has seen His face at any time. He seems far away in His infinite heaven; clouds and darkness are round about Him. Yes; but righteousness and judgment are the habitation of His seat. And this was the very idea which the Jews wished to symbolize in the building of their Tabernacle. They hung it with purple curtains; they overlaid it with solid gold; they filled its outer court with sacrifices, its inner chambers with incense;—but when the High Priest passed from the Holy into the Holy of Holies—when on the great Day of Atonement he stood with the censer in his hands, and the ardent Urim on his breast, before what did he stand? Not before Visible Epiphany; not before sculptured image. There was total darkness in the shrine; no sunlight streamed, no lamp shed its silver radiance; through the awful silence no whisper thrilled; but, through the dim gleam of the glowing thurible and the smoke of the wreathing incense, he saw only a golden Ark over which bent the golden figures of adoring Cherubim—and within that Ark, as its only treasure, lay two rough hewn tables of venerable stone, on which were carved the Ten Commandments of the fiery Law. Those stony Tables, that Ark, that Mercy-seat, those adoring Cherubim seen dimly through the darkness, were to him a visible symbol of all creation, up to its most celestial hierarchies, contemplating, with awful reverence, and on the basis of man's spiritual existence, the moral Law of God. II. AND IS THAT LAW ABROGATED NOW, OR SHORN OF ITS SIGNIFICANCE? Nay, it remains for the Gentile no less than for the Jew—for the nineteenth century after Christ no less than for the fifteenth before Him—the immutable expression of God's will. God, as the Italian proverb says, does not pay on Saturdays. He is very patient, and men may long deny His existence or blaspheme His name, but more than in the mighty strong wind which rent the mountains, and more than in fire, and more than in earthquake, is God in that still small voice which is sounding yet. Oh, it is not in Exodus alone, or in Deuteronomy alone, but in all nature that we hear His voice. In scene after scene of history, in discovery after discovery of science, in experience after experience of life, have we heard these words rolling in thunder across the centuries the eternal distinction of right and wrong. Confidently I appeal to you, and ask, Have you not, at some time in your lives, heard the voice of God utter to you distinctly these Commandments of the moral Law? Is there one here who has ever disobeyed that voice and prospered? If there be one here who feels, at this moment, in the depths of his soul, a peace which the world can neither give nor take away, is it not solely because by the aid of God's Holy Spirit he has striven to obey it? Yes, its infinite importance is that it is as old not as Sinai, but as humanity, and represents the will of God to all His children in the great family of man; so that if in this life we be passing from mystery to mystery, it is our surest proof that we are passing also from God to God. What matters it that we know not either whence we came or what we are, if " He hath shown thee, oh, man! what is good, and what doth the Lord require of thee but to do justly, and to love mercy, and to walk humbly with thy God?" III. And thus it is, lastly, THAT IF WE BE FAITHFUL THE LAW MAY LEAD US TO THE GOSPEL. For his must indeed be a shallow soul who thinks it an easy thing to keep the Commandments. When we observe that the summary of the first Table is that life is worship, and of the second that life is service; when we notice that the first Table forbids sin against God, first in thought, then in word, then in deed; while the second, proceeding in a reverse order, forbids sins against our neighbour first in deed, then in word, and then in thought; so that, unlike every other code that the world has ever known, the Commandments begin and end with the utter prohibition of evil thoughts, which of us is not conscious that we have utterly broken God's Law in this, that out of the heart proceed evil thoughts? And when we go from Moses to Jesus, from Sinai to Galilee, will Christ abolish the Law? will He teach us that we may keep both our sin and our Saviour, and that there is no distinction between a state of sin and a state of grace? There are no dim presences, no thundering clouds, no scorching wilderness, no rolling darkness around the trembling hill, but the sweet human voice of one seated in the dawn on the lilied grass that slopes down to the silver lake—but does that voice abrogate the Law? Nay, more stringently than to them of old time come the ten commandments now. Murder is extended to a furious thought; adultery to a lascivious look; and at first it might seem as if our last hope were extinguished, as if now our alienation from God be permanent, since admitted into a holier sanctuary we are but guilty of a deadlier sin. And when this has been indeed brought home to us, and we see the unfathomable gulf which yawns before a God of infinite holiness and a heart of desperate corruption, then indeed—and above all in the meeting of calamity with crime—then cometh the midnight. But after that midnight to the faithful soul there shall be light. With the personal conviction that the Law worketh wrath, come also the personal experience that Christ hath delivered us from its curse. In Him comes the sole antidote to guilt, the sole solution to the enigma of despair. True, He deepened the obligation of the Law, but for our sake He also fulfilled it. And thus by love, and hope, and gratitude, and help, He gives us a new impulse, a new inspiration, and this is Christianity; and this Christianity has redeemed, has ennobled, has regenerated the world. The "thou must" of Sinai becomes the "I ought," "I will," "I can." "I can do all things through Him that strengtheneth me." And then for us the Law has done its work. It has revealed to us the will of God, it has revealed to us the apostacy of man, it has driven us to know and to embrace the deliverance of Christ. (*Archdeacon Farrar.*)   *The Ten Commandments:*—The Ten Commandments hold a conspicuous position in that prolonged revelation of Himself—His character, His will, and His revelations to mankind—which God made to the Jews. They can, therefore, never become obsolete. I. The Ten Commandments rest on the principle THAT GOD CLAIMS AUTHORITY OVER THE MORAL LIFE OF MAN. II. There can be no doubt that GOD INTENDED THAT THESE COMMANDMENTS SHOULD BE KEPT. They are not merely to bring us to a sense of our guilt, as some seem to imagine. III. These commandments DEAL CHIEFLY WITH ACTIONS, not with mere thought or emotion. IV. Before God gave these commandments to the Jewish people, HE WROUGHT A MAGNIFICENT SERIES OF MIRACLES TO EFFECT THEIR EMANCIPATION FROM MISERABLE SLAVERY and to punish their oppressors. He first made them free, and then gave them the law. (*R. W. Dale, D.D.*)   *Comprehensive summary of the Ten Commandments :*—1. Its uniqueness: Compare this law with other so-called legislations—*e.g.*, Lycurgus, Draco, Solon, the Twelve Tables. There is found no counterpart; there is a gulf betwixt them and it. 2. Its origin: What is it that makes this separation but its divinity? Said a lawyer of eminence, who was led to renounce his infidelity by the study of the Decalogue: "I have been looking into the nature of that law: I have been trying to see whether I can add anything to it, or take anything from it, so as to make it better. Sir, I cannot; it is perfect." And then, having shown this to be so, he concluded: "I have been thinking where did Moses get that law? I have read history. The Egyptians and the adjacent nations were idolaters: so were the Greeks and Romans: and the wisest and best Greeks and Romans never gave a code of morals like this. Where did he get it? He could not have soared so far above his age as to have devised it himself. It came down from heaven. I am convinced of the truth of the religion of the Bible." 3. Its scope: Were we to keep this law, we should need no other codes and edicts— no courts and prisons. It would fill the sky with sunshine and the earth with righteousness. 4. Its simplicity: It is so easily interpreted. 5. But the attempt to keep the law in its spirit will lead to the revelation of self, and disclose both a disinclination and an inability; and, when this is the case, the law becomes a schoolmaster to lead to Christ. (*L. O. Thompson.*)   *Negative Commandments :*— The emphatic and repeated "Thou shalt not" from God teaches—I. MAN'S CAPACITY FOR EVIL. II. MAN'S TENDENCY TO EVIL. III. GOD'S KNOWLEDGE OF THIS CAPACITY AND TENDENCY OF MAN. IV. GOD, KNOWING THIS, NEVERTHELESS PROHIBITS SIN. This indicates—1. The guilt of sin. 2. The care of God. (*U. R. Thomas.*) *The Commandments :*—I. THE ORIGIN OF THESE COMMANDMENTS. 1. The Bible thus commits itself unequivocally to the highest origin for these laws. (1) Their Divine origin bespeaks their holy and righteous nature, and their absolute authority. (2) Their Divine origin bespeaks the deep interest we should take in their study, as well as in obeying them. 2. Divine as they are in their origin, they were transmitted first by the ministry of angels to Moses, and by Moses to us. (Psa. lxxviii. 17; Acts vii. 53; Gal. iii. 19; Heb. ii. 2; Deut. v. 5, x. 1–4.) II. THE NATURE OF THESE COMMANDMENTS. Lessons: 1. The awe-inspiring circumstances of the giving of the law suggest the solemnity of our relations to God. 2. Positive institutions of religion are a necessity. 3. They must be of God, or they are worse than worthless. 4. Those which bear the evidence of their Divine origin are alone worthy of obedience. 5. The only worthy obedience is that which is hearty and complete. (*D. C. Hughes, M.A.*)   *The character of the Decalogue :*—I. THE DECALOGUE IS IN FORM PROHIBITIVE. A solemn witness to the Fall. A bell to awaken conscience. II. Although the Decalogue is in form prohibitive, yet IN SPIRIT IT IS AFFIRMATIVE. A negative pole implies a positive. The Ten Words are divinely covenantal, rather than divinely statutory. Law is never as imperial as love. III. The Ten Words or Commandments are in their character GERMINAL AND SUGGESTIVE, RATHER THAN UNFOLDED AND EXHAUSTIVE. They are the rudimental principles of morality, the germs of ethics, the seminary, or seedplot, of religion. IV. But although the Ten Commandments are rudimental in their form, they are also ELEMENTAL IN THEIR MEANING, AND THEREFORE UNIVERSAL AND IMMORTAL IN THEIR APPLICATION. Just because they are germs, they are capable of all growth, or unfolding along the lines suggested in the embryo. In brief, the Ten Commandments are the axioms of morals, the summary of ethics, the itinerary of mankind, the framework of society, the vertebral column of humanity. (*G. D. Boardman.*)   *Characteristics of the Decalogue :*—The Law of the Ten Words constitutes the very heart or kernel of the entire Mosaic system. It was the Law which lent to Mosaism its peculiar character as a temporary interlude in the history of revelation. I. In the first place, EVERY CIRCUMSTANCE ATTENDING ITS PROMULGATION WAS ADJUSTED SO AS TO LEND TO IT A SOLEMN AND AWFUL EMPHASIS. II. THE SANCTION OF THE DECALOGUE WAS FEAR. In the infancy of the individual, when as yet the immature conscience lacks the power to enforce its convictions of duty upon the untutored passions, the first step in moral training consists in impressing upon the child's mind a wholesome dread for the constituted authorities of the home. Love is a preferable impulse to law-keeping, no doubt ; but love cannot be wholly depended on till the habit of obedience has been formed and principle has come to the aid of affection. III. It belongs to the same juvenile or primary character of this code, as designed for an infant people, THAT ITS REQUIREMENTS ARE CONCRETE, AND EXPRESSED IN A NEGATIVE OR PROHIBITORY FORM. When you have to deal with children, you do not enunciate principles but precepts. You do not bid a child revere all that is venerable in the social order ; but you say : "Honour thy father and mother." You do not tell a rude populace that hatred drives God out of the soul, but you say simply : "Do not kill !" Everything must be, at such a stage of moral education, concrete, portable, and unmistakable. For the same reason, it will usually take the shape of a prohibition rather than of a command : a "Do *not*" rather than a "Do." IV. While these remarks must be borne in mind if we would understand the archaic mould in which this code is cast, there is at the same time AN ADMIRABLE BREADTH AND MASSIVENESS ABOUT ITS CONTENTS. In Ten Words it succeeds in sweeping the whole field of duty. V. I have assumed above —what is indeed apparent to every careful reader—THAT THE DECALOGUE WAS DESIGNED PRIMARILY TO BE THE CODE OF A COMMONWEALTH. In the ancient world, and perhaps in the infancy of all societies, the idea of the community takes precedence over the idea of the individual. The family, the clan, the tribe, the nation : these are the ruling conceptions to which the interests of the private individual are subordinated. Then, each man exists as one of a larger body—heir of its past and parent of its future. VI. It is when one views the Decalogue under this aspect, that one can best see how it came to include two parts, A SACRED AND A CIVIL. In a theocracy there can be no such sharp distinction as we make between Church and State. Indeed, such a distinction would have been unintelligible to any ancient people. So far from comprehending the modern ideal of " a free Church in a free State," every people of antiquity took for granted that the Church and the State were one. Every public function was discharged, every expedition undertaken, every victory gained, under the immediate counsel and patronage of the Deity. All this was just as strongly felt by the devotees of Bel or Nebo, of Osiris, Chemosh or Baal, of Athenè or Jove, as by the Hebrew worshippers of Jehovah. So that, again, when it pleased God to throw into the form of a theocracy His peculiar relationship to Israel as a vehicle for teaching to the world a world-wide revelation of grace, He was simply accommodating His gracious ways to the thoughts of men and the fashions of the age that then was. (*J. O. Dykes, D.D.*) *The Law given from Mount Sinai suited to the circumstances of man, and of universal adoption :*—I. SOME PRELIMINARY REMARKS. 1. Man is a being possessed of a religious capacity. 2. Man is a moral agent. 3. It is possible for the reason, the understanding, and the moral sense of man to be brought to such a state, that he can have a right to have an opinion both upon morals and religion. II. THE LAW ITSELF (vers. 3–17). There are two parts of this law—that relating to—1. Religion. Here are four things—(1) The object of worship. (2) A mode of worship. (3) The inculcation of habitual reverence with respect to sacred things. (4) An appointed season for the cultivation and perfection of the religious capacity. 2. Morals. Here is—(1) Filial " honour." (2) Respect for life. (3) Reverence for purity. (4) Respect for property. (5) Respect for reputation. (6) Respect and regard to the source of all virtue—thine own heart. III. A few observations tending to show THAT THIS LAW, AS WE HAVE IT HERE, IS SUITED TO THE CIRCUMSTANCES OF MAN, AND OF UNIVERSAL ADAPTATION. It is suited to humanity—1. In that it meets the essential capacities and elements of human nature. 2. In its accidents ; that is, not only in its principles, but also in the mode in which these principles are to be carried out. 3. In spite of some of the accidental and peculiar topics which are here and there introduced into it. 4. If we consider what the world would be were this law universally obeyed ; and what if it were universally disobeyed. IV. The preceding point being made out, then I think THE PRESUMPTIONS ARE IN FAVOUR OF THIS LAW HAVING BEEN GIVEN BY GOD. 1. The history of man and the tendencies of human nature show that, if the original state of man had been barbarism, he never would have risen out of it by his own efforts, and never would have discovered such principles as are here put forth. 2. In the most refined ages of ancient times, no moral system equal or even approaching in rationality, purity, and simplicity to this was ever taught either by philosopher, statesman, or priest. 3. Even in our own times our philosophers, they who have rejected revelation and have given us moral systems, have taught principles subversive of these—Bolingbroke, Blount, Hume. 4. This law unquestionably was given about the time it was said to be. We find that it must have been given by Moses. From whom did he obtain it? 5. We now have the fact—"God spake all these words." V. PRACTICAL REMARKS. 1. Reflect on the internal evidence of the superhuman character of the Bible. 2. Notice that infidelity is always associated with impurity and blasphemy. 3. Meditate deeply how you stand in relation to the Law. 4. Accept, in addition to the law of judgment, the gospel of mercy. (*T. Binney.*) *The composition of the Law of God :*—There is a bell in the cathedral of Cologne, made by the melting together of French cannon. It would have been a very difficult task, indeed, to analyze the bell and determine whence the cannon came. Something like this, however, is the task before those who adopt the extreme theories of the rationalistic critics of the Pentateuch. You must be supposed to show in the minute literary traits of this series of documents the dates of their origin, the dates of their combination, and the dates of subsequent editorial supervisions. Even if it were to be granted that documents drawn from many polytheistic nations and ages were the original constituents of the Pentateuch, we have not touched the doctrine of the inspiration of the combined mass at all. The mass is strangely purified from all false doctrine. A Divine fire has burned all adulterate elements wholly out of it, and fused the constituents in a combination wholly new. These cannon are one set of objects ; melted together into a bell, hung in a cathedral tower, they are another object altogether. Mere white dust is one thing ; compacted into marble, in a vase, it has a ring, and is quite another. These cannon, melted and hung aloft in the form of a bell, are no longer cannon. They are an inspired work. It is our business, indeed, to know all we can as to the composition of this bronze ; but our highest business is to ring the bell in the cathedral tower. The moral law, and the ethical monotheism of the Pentateuch, have proved their resonance as often as they have been put in practice, age after age. The Pentateuch hung in the cathedral tower of the world has uttered God's voice, and it is our business to ask how we can ring the bell in the heights of history, rather than how it originated by the melting together of many fragments. (*Joseph Cook.*) *The inexhaustibility of the Law of God :*—I have many times essayed thoroughly to investigate the Ten Commandments, but at the very outset, "I am the Lord thy God," I stuck fast ; that very one word, I, put me to a *non-plus*. He that has but one word of God before him, and out of that word cannot make a sermon, can never be a preacher. (*Luther's Table Talk.*) *Usefulness of God's Commandments :*—Reconciliation to God is like entering the gate of a beautiful avenue, which conducts to a splendid mansion. But that avenue is long, and in some places it skirts the edge of dangerous cliffs, and, therefore, to save the traveller from falling over where he would be dashed to pieces, it is fenced all the way by a quick-set edge. That edge is the Commandments. They are planted there that we may do ourselves no harm. But, like a fence of the fragrant briar, they regale the pilgrim who keeps the path, and they only hurt him when he tries to break through. Temperance, justice, truthfulness ; purity of speech and behaviour ; obedience to parents ; mutual affection ; sanctification of the Sabbath ; the reverent worship of God ; all these are righteous requirements, and in keeping them there is a great reward. Happy he who only knows the precept in the perfume which it sheds, and who, never having kicked against the pricks, has never proved the sharpness of its thorns. (*J. Hamilton, D.D.*) *The Lawgiver :*—1. Let us recognize that this Law has its source in God. It comes to us from His will whose authority is beyond question, and our obligation to obey is complete. Since "God spake all these words," we find in them the law of our being. The conscience hears His voice, acknowledges His rightful authority, and bows before Him. 2. There is great need of the "I ought" power being developed in our nature so that it controls our lives ; a need at least as great in this age and in this country as it was in that early age and in the wilderness of Sinai. To be swayed not by impulse, nor by intense desire, nor by aroused wilfulness, but by a sense of obligation to God, insures a manhood which is a success in itself. What better start in life can the young have than a firm determination to obey God ? Can there be a better guide in life, in the perplexities of society, of business or of politics, than this same principle of obedience to God ? 3. While this law coming from God binds the conscience, it at the same time secures true liberty of conscience. Nothing can bind the conscience beyond or contrary to this law. It is the comprehensive and only law of the conscience. 4. This law coming from God repels many of the assaults of infidelity upon the Bible. Infidelity finds it impossible to account for the existence of this law in the Bible. Besides, infidelity is forced to honour the moral law in making it its standard of criticism. Much of its fault-finding of lives and measures is an unintended tribute to the law of God.   5. The fact that this law comes from God, carries with it another lesson and one of the utmost importance to us.   His authority runs through all the divisions of the law.   (1) Both tables must be fully observed, or the whole law is broken.   We cannot be devoted to God, correct in matters of faith and zealous in His worship, while we neglect charity of feeling, word and act toward our brother.   Neither can we truly love our neighbour while we neglect God, for we cannot keep any part of the law without supreme reverence for Him who commands.   Neither can we truly love our neighbour with recognizing that we are both and equally creatures of God.   (2) There is a tendency also to separate the commandments, and to claim virtue for keeping some while we make light of breaking others.   Now, the violation of one precept is not an actual violation of another, but it is the breaking of the whole law in that it sets aside the authority of God.   If he keeps other commandments, it must be from other considerations.   By breaking one commandment he shows he has the spirit of breaking them all, for he does not submit to the authority of God.   (*F. S. Schenck.*)   *For whom is the Law intended ?*—In the preface to the Law, God describes Himself not only as the self-existing Creator, but as having entered into close personal relation with the Israelites through promises made to their fathers, some of which had just been faithfully fulfilled in conferring great blessings upon them.   So He appeals not only to their respect for His authority, but to the relation to Him which they had inherited and accepted, and to the gratitude they should have for such benefits received.   This preface does not limit the following law to the Israelites, but makes a special appeal to them.   The law is general, for all mankind, the original law of their being, since it appeals to and arouses the universal conscience ; but a special revelation of God and rich favours bestowed form a strong appeal for the most hearty obedience.   God describes Himself to the full extent in which He had at that time revealed Himself.   Whatever increase of revelation we have received strengthens the appeal.   This shows the kind of obedience we should give : not reluctant, but eager ; not forced, but spontaneous ; not irksome, but with delight ; not heartless, but with the enthusiasm of love.   Created things obey the laws of their being joyously.   Stars shine, flowers bloom, birds sing.   Surely intelligent beings, recognizing the law of their being, should joyously obey it, especially when God reveals Himself fully and confers richest blessings upon them.   (*Ibid.*)   *Of the Commandments :*—I. QUESTIONS. 1. What is the difference between the moral law and the gospel ?   (1) The law requires that we worship God as our Creator ;   the gospel requires that we worship God in and through Christ.   God in Christ is propitious ; out of Christ we may see God's power, justice, holiness, in Christ we see His mercy displayed. (2) The moral law requires obedience, but gives no strength, as Pharaoh required brick, but gave no straw, but the gospel gives strength.   2. Of what use, then, is the moral law to us ?   A glass to show us our sins, and drive us to Christ.   3. Is the moral law still in force to believers ?   In some sense it is abolished to believers.   (1) In respect of justification ; they are not justified by their obedience to the moral law.   Believers are to make great use of the moral law, but they must trust only to Christ's righteousness for justification ; as Noah's dove made use of her wings to fly, but trusted to the ark for safety.   (2) The moral law is abolished to believers, in respect of the malediction of it ; they are freed from the curse and damnatory power of it (Gal. iii. 13).   4. How was Christ made a curse for us ?   As our pledge and surety.   Though the moral law be not their saviour, yet it is their guide ; though it be not a covenant of life, yet it is a rule of living ; every Christian is bound to conform to the moral law, and write, as exactly as he can, after this copy : " Do we then make void the law through faith ? God forbid."   Though a Christian is not under the condemning power of the law, yet he is under the commanding power. II. RULES FOR THE RIGHT UNDERSTANDING OF THE DECALOGUE.   1. The commands and prohibitions of the moral law reach the heart.   2. In the commandments there is a synecdoche, more is intended than is spoken.   Where any duty is commanded, there the contrary sin is forbidden, &c.   3. Where any sin is forbidden in the commandment, there the occasion of it is also forbidden.   4. Where one relation is named in the commandment, there another relation is included.   5. Where greater sins are forbidden, there lesser sins are also forbidden.   6. The law of God is copulative.   The first and second tables are knit together,—piety to God, and equity to our neighbour ; these two tables which God hath joined together must not be put asunder.   7. God's law forbids not only the acting of sin in our own persons, but being accessory to, or having any hand in the sins of others.   8. The last rule about the commandments is this, that though we cannot, by our own strength, fulfil all these commandments, yet doing what we are able, the Lord hath provided encouragement for us. There is a threefold encouragement. (1) That though we have not ability to obey any one command, yet God hath, in the new covenant, promised to work that in us which He requires : " I will cause you to walk in My statutes." The iron hath no power to move, but when the loadstone draws it, it can move; " Thou also hast wrought all our works in us." (2) Though we cannot exactly fulfil all the moral law, yet God will, for Christ's sake, mitigate the rigour of the law, and accept of something less than He requires. (3) Wherein our personal obedience comes short, God will be pleased to accept us in our surety : " He hath made us accepted in the beloved." (*T. Watson.*)

I am the Lord thy God.—*The preface of the Law :*—In this style or authority are three parts, according to three titles. 1. The first title, of His name— " Jehovah." 2. Secondly, the title of His jurisdiction—" thy God." 3. Thirdly, the title of that notable act He did last—" which brought thee out of the land of Egypt," &c. (*Bishop Andrewes.*)   *The preface :*—I. The Speaker and Giver of these commandments. 1. It is the Lord, particularly Jesus Christ, who gave this Law in the name of the Trinity. This is plain from the Scripture (Acts vii. 38; Heb. xii. 24-26). 2. The speech itself, wherein we have a description of the true God, bearing three reasons for the keeping His commands. (1) From His sovereignty; He is the Lord. (2) From His covenant-relation to His people—thy God. (3) From the great benefit of redemption, and deliverance wrought for them.   *The preface :*—I. I begin with the first, the preface to the preface : " God spake all these words, saying," &c. This is like the sounding of a trumpet before a solemn proclamation, " God spake "; other parts of the Bible are said to be uttered by the mouth of the holy prophets, but here God spake in His own Person. 1. The Lawgiver : " God spake." There are two things requisite in a lawgiver. (1) Wisdom. Laws are founded upon reason; and he must be wise that makes laws. God, in this respect, is most fit to be a lawgiver : " He is wise in heart "; He hath a monopoly of wisdom : " the only wise God." (2) Authority. God hath the supreme power in His hand; and He who gives men their lives hath most right to give them their laws. 2. The Law itself : " all these words "; that is, all the words of the moral Law, which is usually styled the Decalogue, or Ten Commandments. It is called the moral Law, because it is the rule of life and manners. St. Chrysostom compares the Scripture to a garden, the moral Law is a chief flower in it; the Scripture is a banquet, the moral Law the chief dish in it. (1) The moral Law is perfect : " The Law of the Lord is perfect." It is an exact model and platform of religion; it is the standard of truth, the judge of controversies, the polestar to direct us to heaven. (2) The moral Law is unalterable; it remains still in force. (3) The moral Law is very illustrious and full of glory. See Exod. xix. 10, 12; xxxi. 18; Deut xxxii. Use 1. Here we may take notice of God's goodness who hath not left us without a Law : therefore the Lord doth often set it down as a demonstration of His love in giving His Commandments. See Psa. cxlvii. 20; Neh. ix. 13 ; Rom. vii. 14.   The Law of God is a hedge to keep us within the bounds of sobriety and piety. Use 2. If God spake all these words, viz., of the moral Law, then this presseth upon us several duties : (1) If God spake all these words, then we must hear all these words. The words which God speaks are too precious to be lost. (2) If God spake all these words, then we must attend to them with reverence. (3) If God spake all these words of the moral Law, then we must remember them. Those words are weighty which concern salvation. (4) If God spake all these words, then we must believe them. Shall we not give credit to the God of heaven? (5) If God spake all these words, then love the Commandments : " Oh, how love I Thy Law ! it is my meditation all the day." (6) If God spake all these words, then teach your children the Law of God : " These words which I command thee this day shall be in thy heart, and thou shalt teach them diligently to thy children." He who is godly, is both a diamond and a loadstone; a diamond for the sparkling of his grace, and a loadstone for his attractive virtue in drawing others to the love of God's precepts; a good man doth more good to his neighbours than to himself. (7) If God spake all these words, then the moral Law must be obeyed. II. The preface itself. 1. " I am the Lord thy God." Here we have a description of God—(1) By His essential greatness : " I am the Lord "—Jehovah. Let us fear Him (Deut. xxviii. 58). (2) By His relative goodness : " Thy God." How? Through Jesus Christ—Emmanuel. (3) How may we come to know this covenant union, that God is our God? (*a*) By having His grace planted in us. Kings' children are known by their costly jewels: it is not having common gifts which shows we belong to God, many have the gifts of God without God, but it is grace gives us a true genuine title to God. In particular, faith is the grace of union; by this we may spell out our interest in God. (*b*) We may know God is our God, by having the earnest of His Spirit in our hearts. God often gives the purse to the wicked, but the Spirit only to such as He intends to make His heirs. Have we had the consecration of the Spirit? (*c*) We may know God is our God, if He hath given us the hearts of children. Have we obediential hearts? do we subscribe to God's commands, when His commands cross our will? A true saint is like the flower of the sun: it opens and shuts with the sun, he opens to God and shuts to sin. If we have the hearts of children, then God is our Father. (*d*) We may know God is ours, and we have an interest in Him, by our standing up for His interest. (*e*) We may know God is ours, and we have an interest in Him, by His having an interest in us: "My beloved is Mine, and I am His." Use 1. Above all things, let us get this great charter confirmed, that God is our God. Deity is not comfortable without propriety. Use 2. To all such as can make out this covenant union, it exhorts to several things. (1) If God be our God, let us improve our interest in Him, cast all our burdens upon Him, the burden of our fears, wants, sins. (2) If God be our God, let us learn to be contented, though we have the less of other things. Contentment is a rare jewel; it is the cure of care. If we have God to be our God, well may we be contented. (*a*) God is a sufficient good. Not only full as a vessel, but as a spring. The heart is a triangle, which only the Trinity can fill. (*b*) God is a sanctifying good. He sanctifies all our comforts, and turns them into blessings. He sanctifies all our crosses; they shall polish and refine our grace. The more the diamond is cut it sparkles the more. God's stretching the strings of His viol, is to make the music the better. (*c*) God is a choice good. All things under the sun are but the blessings of the footstool; but to have God Himself to be ours is the blessing of the throne. (*d*) God is the chief good. In the chief good there must be, first, delectability. "At God's right hand are pleasures." Secondly, in the chief good there must be transcendency, it must have a surpassing excellency. Thus God is infinitely better than all other things; it is below the Deity to compare other things with It. Who would go to weigh a feather with a mountain of gold? Thirdly, in the chief good there must be not only fulness, but variety; where variety is wanting we are apt to nauseate; to feed only on honey would breed loathing; but in God is all variety of fulness. (3) If we can clear up this covenant union that God is our God, let this cheer and revive us in all conditions. To be content with God is not enough, but to be cheerful. What greater cordial can you have than union with Deity? (4) If God be our God, then let us break forth into doxology and praise (Psa. cxviii. 28). (5) Let us carry ourselves as those who have God to be their God. Live holily. 2. The second part of the preface: "which have brought," &c. God mentions this deliverance, because of— (1) Its strangeness. (2) Greatness. 3. The third part of the preface: "out of the house of bondage." (1) God's children may sometimes be under sore afflictions. (*a*) For probation, or trial. Affliction is the touchstone of sincerity. (*b*) For purgation; to purge our corruption. "God's fire is in Zion." This is not to consume, but to refine; what if we have more affliction, if by this means we have less sin. (*c*) For augmentation; to increase the graces of the Spirit. Grace thrives most in the iron furnace; sharp frosts nourish the corn, so do sharp afflictions grace: grace in the saints is often as fire hid in the embers, affliction is the bellows to blow it up into a flame. (*d*) For preparation: to fit and prepare us for glory. (2) God will in His due time bring His people out of their afflicted state. The tree which in the winter seems dead, in the spring revives: after darkness cometh sunshine. Affliction may leap on us as the viper did on Paul, but at last this viper shall be shaken off. (*T. Watson.*) *The revelation of the Divine Name* :— I. GOD IN COVENANT WITH MAN IS THE CONDITION OF THE EXISTENCE AND DEVELOPMENT OF MAN'S SPIRITUAL LIFE. The despair of the sinner, but for God's mercy, would crush him. And what know we of God's mercy? For ages our forefathers have been living consciously in a covenant, and all our ideas of God have been formed by it. But ask that agonized father, plunging the bare knife into the throat of his daughter, or flinging his tender infant into that seething cauldron of fire, what man, ignorant of the covenant, knows of the mercy and forgiveness of God. Man lives on the covenant; he builds his life on the promises; it is the condition of his living at all in the sense in which a man may live. II. GOD WAS

SEEKING THE COVENANT, NOT MAN.   It is God who acts, man who accepts; God who gives, man who receives; and thus the hope of man has its strong resting-place, not on the strivings of his own weak will, not on the searchings of his own too easily bewildered and blinded intellect, but on the eternal purpose and love of God.   God cannot dispense with man's heart, will, and intellect; He led that people there that He might engage them in His service.   Refuse Him that service, and the covenant is worthless to you, nay, is a witness against you to condemnation; yield them to Him, and rest in the assurance that your salvation depends not on your own weak work but on the strong arm of God.   III. You will find two grand features in that which was transacted there on the Mount of God: GOD REVEALING HIMSELF—GOD DECLARING HIS LAW.   This was God's covenant; the people had but to say in heart and with voice " Amen."   1. Nature, circumstance, the currents of life, master us, till we know the Divine Name.   We know ourselves in knowing Him, and find in ourselves the broken features of His likeness.   The first step towards the establishment of the covenant was the revelation of the Divine name.   2. It was a merciful name which the Lord made known: " I am the Lord thy God, which have brought thee out of the land of Egypt, out of the house of bondage.   I am the God of thy fathers."   How tender, how blessed the assurance!   3. The Lord's name is holy.   " The Lord thy God is a holy Lord." A sensual-hearted man will fashion gods like unto himself.   A wise and earnest-hearted man will " give thanks at the remembrance of God's holiness."   (*J. B. Brown, B.A.*)   *The Jewish knowledge of God :*—To the Jews, Jehovah was not a mere idea or a system of attributes.   They did not think of Him as the Necessary Cause of the universe, or as a Being inaccessible to human knowledge, but whom it was their duty to invest with whatever perfections could exalt and glorify Him— infinite wisdom, infinite power, awful righteousness, inflexible truth, and tenderest love.   It never occurred to them to suppose that they had to think out a God for themselves any more than it occurred to them that they had to think out a king of Egypt.   They knew Jehovah as the God who had held back the waves like a wall while they fled across the sea to escape the vengeance of their enemies; they knew Him as the God who had sent thunder, and lightning, and hail, plagues on cattle, and plagues on men, to punish the Egyptians and to compel them to let the children of Israel go; they knew Him as the God whose angel had slain the firstborn of their oppressors, and filled the land from end to end with death, and agony, and terror.   He was the same God, so Moses and Aaron told them, who by visions and voices, in promises and precepts, had revealed Himself long before to Abraham, Isaac, and Jacob.   We learn what men are from what they say and what they do.   A biography of Luther gives us a more vivid and trustworthy knowledge of the man than the most philosophical essay on his character and creed.   The story of his imprisonment and of his journey to Worms, his Letters, his Sermons, and his Table Talk, are worth more than the most elaborate speculations about him.   The Jews learnt what God is, not from theological dissertations on the Divine attributes, but from the facts of a Divine history. They knew Him for themselves in His own acts and in His own words.   (*R. W. Dale, D.D.*)   *Man's religious craving satisfied :*—Man's nature is religious.   He instinctively worships some being, whom he regards as God.   It is the nature of religious worship to assimilate the character of the worshipper to that of the being worshipped.   The objects of worship, everywhere throughout the ancient world, were corrupt and corrupting.   In order to man's moral improvement, he must have a holy object of worship.   It is obviously impossible for an imperfect and sinful man to originate the idea of a perfect and sinless God.   The gods whom men invented and set up were as imperfect and wicked as themselves; and from the nature of the case, they could not be otherwise.   Moses, on the contrary, revealed a holy and a perfect God.   How pure, how amiable, how sublime, how transcendently glorious the character with which this God is invested by the Hebrew law-giver!   How striking the contrast which his sublime delineation of Jehovah as the Maker, Proprietor, and Sovereign of the universe, invested with every conceivable excellence, presents to the grovelling mythology of the most enlightened portions of the ancient world, in which the objects of religious worship were pictured with the passions and vices of the fierce and licentious chieftains of the primitive ages!   The publication of such a theology in such an age, when polytheism had covered the earth with the temples and altars of its monster gods, cannot be satisfactorily accounted for without allowing, and is satisfactorily accounted for by allowing, the truth of the Mosaic history, and the establishment of the Mosaic constitution by Divine authority. (*E. C. Wines, D.D.*) "*I am the Lord thy God*"—*a word to rest on in death :*—When Ebenezer Erskine lay on his deathbed, one of his elders said to him, "Sir, you have given us many good advices; may I ask what you are now doing with your own soul?" "I am jus. doing with it," he replied, "what I did forty years ago : I am resting on that word —'I am the Lord thy God.'" **Out of the land of Egypt.**—*God's deliverance of His people :*—Bearing in mind the universality of the Decalogue, this "land of Egypt" and "house of bondage" must have a far deeper and wider signification than the valley of the Nile. Egypt is a synonym for an ungodly world, which captivates the heart of man, and from which the grace of God releases the renewed soul. The Law of God is, therefore, in its holiness, justice, and goodness, held up to those who have been delivered from the bondage of sin. It is not so held up to the ungodly—they cannot love it, they cannot see its beauty. By the Lord's telling us that He has already brought us out of Egypt and bondage, He does not say when He gives us the Law: "Do this and live," but "Since ye live, do this"; "Since My grace has redeemed you, and you rejoice in the liberty of the children of God, use My Law, the reflection of My perfections, as your beloved guide." There is one other expression in this preface which should be noted. It is the use of the second person singular, "which have brought *thee* out of the land of Egypt." There are two thoughts connected with this use. 1. The first is that God deals with all Israel as one man. He expects them to be one, of one mind and one heart, before Him. There must be no antagonisms among God's people. He has taken us out of the contentious world, not that we should be only another contentious world, but that we should show our distracted earth the harmony of heaven. He wishes to reconcile all things unto Himself. Sin divides men, grace unites them. 2. The other thought regarding the use of the second person singular here is this: God treats man individually. Man enters heaven or hell, not in companies or battalions, but in naked individuality. It was thyself personally that wert delivered from that dark Egypt of condemnation, was it not? And so you can say : "Who loved me and gave Himself for me." (*H. Crosby, D.D.*)

Ver. 3. **Thou shalt have no other gods before Me.**—*The First Commandment :*—I. This Commandment DOES NOT TELL THE JEWS THAT THE GODS WORSHIPPED BY OTHER NATIONS HAVE NO EXISTENCE ; it tells him that he must offer them no homage, and that from him they must receive no recognition of their authority and power. The Jew must serve Jehovah, and Jehovah alone. This was the truest method of securing the ultimate triumph of monotheism. A religious dogma, true or false, perishes if it is not rooted in the religious affections and sustained by religious observances. But although the First Commandment does not declare that there is one God, the whole system of Judaism rests on that sublime truth, and what the Jews had witnessed in Egypt and since their escape from slavery must have done more to destroy their reverence for the gods of their old masters than could have been effected by any dogmatic declaration that the gods of the nations were idols. II. THE FIRST COMMANDMENT MAY APPEAR TO HAVE NO DIRECT PRACTICAL VALUE FOR OURSELVES. It would be a perversion of its obvious intention to denounce covetousness, social ambition, or excessive love of children. These are not the sins which this Commandment was meant to forbid. It must be admitted that there is no reason why God should say to any of us, "Thou shalt have no other gods before Me." If He were to speak to many of us, it would be necessary to condemn us for having no god at all. The appalling truth is, that many of us have sunk into atheism. We all shrink from contact with God. And yet He loves us. But even His love would be unavailing if He did not inspire those who are filled with shame and sorrow by the discovery of their estrangement from Him, with a new and supernatural life. (*R. W. Dale, D.D.*)　　*The First Commandment :*—I. ALL WANT OF A POSITIVE ALLEGIANCE TO JEHOVAH IS A POSITIVE ALLEGIANCE TO ANOTHER ELOHIM OR SUPREME GOD. A self-reliant man, in the strict sense of the word, never yet existed. Man's nature is such that he looks without him for support, as the ivy feels for the tree or the wall. If he has not the true and living God as his stay, then he is an idolater. II. ALL ALLEGIANCE TO GOD THAT DOES NOT RECOGNIZE HIM AS HE HAS REVEALED HIMSELF IS ALLEGIANCE TO A FALSE GOD. So a view of God as careless of personal holiness in His creatures, or as too exalted to notice all their minute acts and thoughts, or as tyrannical and arbitrary in His dealings with them, or as appeasable by self-denials and penances, is a view of a false god, and not a view of Jehovah, the only living and true God. And the man who, despising or neglecting the Holy Scriptures, and trusting to his reason or his dreams, or to nature, or to nothing, holds such a god before his mind, is an idolater ; he has put another Elohim before Jehovah Elohim. Because the thought of the Divine Being which he thus introduces into his heart becomes the substitute for the true motion that should guide his life, he puts the helm into as false hands as if he had delivered it to Mammon. Several subordinate thoughts naturally follow. 1. The help of the true God, Jehovah-Jesus, should be sought by us to overthrow our false gods. By that very act we should offer rightful allegiance, and, in so doing, consecrate our life to the rightful service of Him who is our rightful King. 2. How watchful we should be in this earth, where the false gods are not only plenty, but exactly after the fashion of our own depraved hearts ! It was said of Athens that at each corner there was a new god, and some have even said that in population Athens had more gods than men. It is so with our unseen gods of the unregenerate heart. They abound with different names and different characters, according to the tastes and characters of different men. 3. The Word of God ought to be in our hands all the while. This is the only offensive weapon against our false gods. (*H. Crosby, D.D.*) *The First Commandment :*—This Commandment, as all the rest, hath a positive part requiring something, and a negative part prohibiting something. I. We shall, in the first place, speak to WHAT IS REQUIRED here, and we take it up in these three things. 1. And first, it requireth the right knowledge of God ; for there can be no true worship given to Him, there can be no right thought or conception of Him, or faith in Him, till He be known. 2. It requireth from us a suitable acknowledging of God in all these His properties. As—(1) That He be highly esteemed above all. (2) Loved. (3) Feared. (4) Believed and trusted in. (5) Hoped in. (6) Adored. (7) Honoured. (8) Served and obeyed. And so—(9) He must be the supreme end in all our actions that should mainly be aimed at by us. 3. It requireth such duties as result from His excellency, and our acknowledging Him to be such a one. As—(1) Dependence upon Him. (2) Submission to Him, and patience under cross dispensations from Him. (3) Faith resting on Him. (4) Prayers put up to Him. (5) Repentance for wronging Him. (6) Communion, and a constant walking with Him. (7) Delighting in Him. (8) Meditating on Him ; and such other as necessarily may be inferred as duties incumbent on creatures in such a relation to such a God, whose excellency and worth calleth and inviteth men to all suitable duties. 4. Next, it is necessary that we add some advertisements to these generals. (1) That the Commandment requireth all these, and in the highest and most perfect degree. (2) That it not only requireth them in ourselves, but obligeth us to further them in all others, according to our places and callings. (3) That it requireth the diligent use of all means that may help and further us in these ; as reading and meditation, study, &c. (4) That these things, which in some respect may be given to creatures, as love, fear, &c., yet, when they are required as duties to God, they are required in a far more imminent way. II. In the next place, we should consider THE NEGATIVE PART of this Commandment, for the extent thereof will be best discerned by considering what is forbidden therein, and how it may be broken. This idolatry is either— 1. Doctrinal, or idolatry in the judgment, when one professedly believeth such a thing besides God to have some divinity in it; as heathens do of their Mars and Jupiter ; or—2. Practical, when men believe no such thing, and will not own any such opinion, yet are guilty of the same thing, as covetous men, &c. 3. It may be distinguished into idolatry that hath something for its object, as the Egyptians worshipped beasts, and the Persians the sun or fire, and that which has nothing but men's imaginations for its object, as these who worship feigned gods; in which respect the apostle saith, "an idol is nothing" (1 Cor. viii. 4). 4. We would distinguish betwixt the objects of idolatry ; and they are either such as are in themselves simply sinful, as devils, profane men ; or they are such as are good in themselves, but abused and wronged, when they are made objects of idolatry, as angels, saints, sun, moon, &c. 5. Distinguish betwixt idolatry that is more gross and professed, and that which is more latent, subtle, and denied. This distinction is like that before mentioned, in opinion and practice, and much coincideth with it. 6. Distinguish betwixt heart-idolatry (Ezek. xiv. 1 ; chap. xiv. 11, 12, and xvi. 2, 3), and external idolatry. The former consisteth in an inward heart-respect to some idol, as this tumultuous people were enslaved to their ease and bellies in the last two fore-cited places ; the other in some external idolatrous gesture or action. (*James Durham.*) *The First Commandment :*—First, there is the positive declara tion of a personal God ; and secondly, His claim to be worshipped as the one true and living God. The most obvious errors requiring our attention are four in number—Atheism, Polytheism, Pantheism, and Deism. 1. Except as a cloke for immorality and sinful indulgence, I am inclined to doubt the existence of Atheism, and the study of history confirms me in the doubt. 2. But what of the Polytheist, the worshipper, that is, of many gods ; in this respect, at least, the very opposite to the last? It is not difficult to trace his origin. When time was young, men lived together in families, tribes, or small communities ; beyond the circle of these they very rarely travelled. Before they were able to realize the idea of the oneness of the human race, each family would not unnaturally aim at being complete in itself ; and as tending, especially to this, they would place themselves under the protection of some one particular god, and then gods multiplied, as a necessary consequence, upon the increase of people and subdivision of tribes. This was one cause. We might discover, without difficulty, others of a different nature. To take one instance, in times of ignorance, when the mind was unable to grasp the Infinite, men seized upon what was best in themselves, or what was noblest in nature, and deified this ; and so at one time we find Earth, Air, Fire, and Water, receiving the homage of men ; and at another we see temples arising to Faith, or Modesty, or Constancy, or Hope. But all this, whatever its origin, was openly denounced by the simple declaration standing at the head of the first table : " I am," &c. 3. Of the Pantheist I shall only speak briefly. The meaning of the term is : " one who believes that everything is God, and God is everything." He deifies all that is best in nature, especially the intellect or mind, and His Supreme Being is a combination of the united intelligences of the world. But if all that is intelligent, all that is best in created things, is God, then that which is best in myself is God, and demands my worship and adoration. And what is this but to give to the creature what belongs and is due to the Creator alone ? 4. The Deist believes in a God, as his name implies, but does not believe that that God has ever revealed Himself to man ; and this is to deny the Bible, to deny Christianity, to deny Christ. He holds that when the Supreme Being finished the creation of the world, He assigned to nature " Laws that should never be broken," and then withdrew Himself from the government of the universe. Again, besides the fact that the Deist will not allow to God any superintendence or control over the works of His hands, thereby cutting off from man his most consoling faith in an all-wise and merciful Providence, He casts him adrift on the wide ocean of life, with no compass to steer by, and no chart to preserve his vessel from shoals and rocks, and all the countless perils of the deep. If God has not revealed Himself to man, then what can he know of a future life, what of the immortality of his soul? And with this unknown, it matters not what be his life and conduct on earth, for death is the close of all things, and there is nothing but darkness beyond the grave ! (*H. M. Luckock, D.D.*)   *On going after other gods :*—Going after other gods is a snare of the spiritual life into which we are liable to drift before suspecting any danger, for it does not necessarily mean the pursuit of things evil in their nature, but of things, innocent enough perhaps in themselves, which, by impressing us with an exaggerated idea of their importance or blessing, absorb that devotion which we owe to God, and demand from us a service which is due to Him alone. I. There is the God of PUBLIC OPINION. There is such a thing as healthy public opinion ; but there are times when its tone becomes lowered, and a very imperfect standard of conduct is all that is needed to satisfy its requirements. It involves a moral effort to which many are unequal to retain, in its integrity, the sense of sinfulness attached to any course of conduct which God forbids when public opinion gives its sanction. II. There is the god of PLEASURE. This is a deity which, when once installed in the heart of a man, is insatiable in its demands. Instead of remaining the handmaid of duty, it becomes its sworn foe ; instead of being the solace and refreshment of toil, it harasses and interferes with our work. The man who is a slave to pleasure looks upon all work as a grievance more or less ; to be shirked altogether, if possible, or to be got through as quickly as may be. His main interest in life is not centred in duty, but in amusement. But this exacting deity not only grudges every moment of our time which is not given up to its service, it grudges, too, every penny of our money which is not spent for its gratification. III. There is the god of SUCCESS. The dangers of the spiritual life attached to the worship of this god are very real. The man who worships success, who in his innermost heart values it more than anything else, and looks upon it as the one object to set before himself, by a natural law of his being, is prepared, if the need arises, to make any sacrifice for it, including even the incurring of God's displeasure. There is no more dangerous rival deity which we can admit into our hearts than success. It blinds us to all that is by the way. It makes us inconsiderate and unscrupulous in the struggle of life ; and as the competition of life increases, and the chances of getting on become fewer, we are tempted to subordinate all higher considerations to the one idea of personal advancement. Another and by no means the least mischievous effect of putting too great store by success in any shape, is that it leads us to look to it for our sole encouragement and reward in the efforts both of spiritual and secular life. As " it is not in man to command success," it follows that those who make success their god can have nothing to fall back upon in the hour of failure. (*M. Tweddell, M.A.*) *The First Commandment :*—How shall we conceive of God ? Who is He ? What is His name ? The First Commandment answers these questions. The language is local, but the meaning is universal. I. THE MEANING OF THE FIRST COMMANDMENT FOR THE ANCIENT JEW. II. THE MEANING OF THE FIRST COMMANDMENT FOR OURSELVES. 1. The Divine declaration. (1) The name " Jehovah." Jesus of Nazareth is Deity in exposition—the Word of God. See how the " I AM " of the burning bush reappears in the " *I am* " of the Nazarene (Matt. xviii. 20 ; xxviii. 20 ; John viii. 58; xiv. 3; xvii. 24; Rev. i. 8). (2) The Divine relation. Who is Jehovah's Israel in our day and land? It is the Church of the Living God (see Rom. ii. 28, 29 ; 1 Cor. xii. 27). If we really belong to Christ, truly loving Him and obeying Him and sharing His character, we are, in spite of all our diversities, one Christian personality ; for in Christ Jesus there can be neither Jew nor Gentile, neither Greek nor Scythian, neither male nor female ; for all in Christ are one, and Christ is all and in all. (3) The Divine deliverance. As it is the Church that is the true Israel, so it is Diabolus who is the true Pharaoh, and Sin which is the true Egypt, and Jesus who is the true Deliverer. 2. The Divine prohibition. We ourselves need this prohibition.no less than did ancient Israel. For, although Christendom, theoretically speaking, is monotheistic, yet Christendom, practically speaking, is largely polytheistic. Recall, for example, the practical tritheism of many Trinitarians, conceiving the three Persons in the Trinity as three distinct Gods ; or the practical dualism of many Christians, conceiving the Father as the God of wrath, and the Son as the God of love : or, again, conceiving the Creator as the God of nature, and the Redeemer as the God of Scripture. Behold in the Pantheon of our Christendom how many niches there are for various gods—the god of the deist, the god of the materialist, the god of the fatalist, the god of the sentimentalist, the god of the churchman, the god of the pantheist. CONCLUDING LESSONS : 1. Our indebtedness to the Jew for monotheism. 2. Jehovah is to be worshipped. 3. Jehovah alone is to be worshipped. (*G. D. Boardman.*) *The First Commandment :*—I. WHAT IS IT TO MAKE GOD TO BE A GOD TO US ? 1. To acknowledge Him for a God. Deity is a jewel that belongs only to His crown. 2. To choose Him. An act of mature deliberation and self-dedication. 3. To enter into a solemn covenant with Him. 4. To give Him adoration. (1) Reverence. (2) Worship. 5. To fear Him. This fearing of God is (1)— To have God always in our eye, " I have set the Lord always before me "; " mine eyes are ever towards the Lord." He who fears God, imagines that whatever he is doing God looks on, and, as a Judge, weighs all his actions. (2) To fear God, is when we have such a holy awe of God upon our hearts that we dare not sin; " Stand in awe and sin not." It is a saying of Anselm, " If hell were on one side and sin on the other, I would rather leap into hell than willingly sin against my God." 6. To love Him. In the godly, fear and love kiss each other. 7. To obey Him. II. THAT WE MUST HAVE NO OTHER GOD. 1. There is really no other God. (1) There is but one First Cause. (2) There is but one Omnipotent Power. 2. We must have no other God. This forbids—(1) Serving a false God. (2) Joining a false God with a true. III. WHAT IS IT TO HAVE OTHER GODS BESIDES THE TRUE GOD ? 1. To trust in anything more than God. (1) Riches. (2) Arm of flesh. (3) Wisdom. (4) Civility. (5) Grace. 2. To love anything more than God. (1) Our estate. (2) Our pleasures. (3) Our belly. (4) A child. If we love the jewel more than Him that gave it, God will take away the jewel, that our love may return to Him again. Use 1. It reproves such as have other gods, and so renounce the true God. (1) Such as set up idols ; " According to the number of thy cities are thy gods, O Judah " ; " Their altars are as heaps in the furrows of the field." (2) Such as seek to familiar spirits (see 2 Kings i. 6). Use 2. It sounds a retreat in our ears. Let it call us off from the idolizing any creature ; and renouncing other gods, let us cleave to the true God and His service. If we go away from God, we know not where to mend ourselves. (1) It is honourable serving of the true God ; it is more honour to serve God than to have kings serve us. (2) Serving the true God is delightful, "I will make them joyful in My house of prayer." (3) Serving the true God is beneficial ; they have great gain here—the hidden manna, inward peace, and a great reward to come. (4) You have covenanted to serve the true Jehovah, renouncing all others. You cannot go back from God without the highest perjury. (5) None had ever cause to repent of cleaving to God and His service. (*T. Watson.*) *The First Commandment :*—I. FOUR THINGS ARE HERE REQUIRED. 1. That we must have a God—against atheism. 2. That we must have the Lord Jehovah for our God—which forbids idolatry. 3. That we must have the only true God the Lord Jehovah alone for our God. 4. It requires that all these services and acts of worship, which we tender unto the true and only God, be performed with sincerity and true devotion. This is implied in that expression "before Me," or in My sight. And this forbids both profaneness on the one hand and hypocrisy on the other. II. IT FORBIDS US FOUR THINGS. 1. Atheism, or the belief and acknowledgment of no God. 2. Ignorance of the true God. 3. Profaneness, or the wretched neglect of the worship and service of God. 4. Idolatry, or the setting up and worshipping of false gods. (*Bp. E. Hopkins.*) *The First Commandment :*—The object of religious devotion has to be defined, and it has to be set into some ascertained relationship with ourselves. I. What we have first to look at, therefore, is THE SELF-DISCLOSURE OF GOD, upon which He grounds His claim to Israel's devotion. God is a Person ; a personal Spirit like our own ; a self-existent, eternal Spirit, apart from and above His world ; a Person capable of entering into converse with men, and acting towards them as Deliverer and Saviour from evil. What follows ? This follows—" This God shalt thou have for thy God; and thou shalt have no other ! " A tie on both its sides solitary and unique must bind the human person with the Divine ; saved with Saviour ; Jehovah's people with Jehovah's self. II. We are now, you perceive, in a position to examine our fundamental law, or First Commandment, DEFINING THE OBJECT OF WORSHIP. It has resolved itself into this—a mutual relationship exists betwixt God and His human people, absolutely unique and exclusive. Besides Jehovah, Israel has no other Saviour ; Israel, therefore, ought to know no other God. Jehovah is not simply first ; He is first without a second. He is not the highest of a class of beings, but in His class He stands alone. Other Helper have we nowhere ; beneath the covert of His everlasting wings must we run to hide. If we are not to people the heavens with shadowy powers, half Divine, or parcel earth among forces of nature, as the provinces of an empire are parcelled among satraps, or elevate human aid into the remotest competition with the Almighty's ; if to us there is but one seat of power, source of help, well-head of blessing, Author and Finisher of deliverance from every species and form of evil : then, what undivided dependence upon God results ! what absoluteness of trust ! what singleness of loyalty ! what unstinted gratitude ! what perfect love ! More is shut out than polytheistic rites. Superstition is shut out, which trusts in mechanical aids and not in the free, living, and righteous Will. Magic is shut out, which seeks to extort deliverance by spells from unholy spirits. Luck is shut out, and the vague hope in what will turn up. Spiritual tyranny is shut out, which makes one man the lord of another's faith and conscience. Policy is shut out, or godless state-craft, with its trust in human foresight, but none in the justice of Providence. Irreligion is shut out, which doubts if prayer avail or God can help, and puts its confidence only in the strongest battalions. Everything, in short, which divides the deep trust and hope of the heart between God and that which is not God, becomes a breach of loyalty to the unique, the solitary Deliverer. (*J. O. Dykes, D.D.*) *The First Commandment :*—1. It is quite evident that this Commandment prescribes a general "fitness of things," the proper relation of man to God ; aims to promote the highest happiness, directing man to seek his good in the highest source—God Himself ; and describes the nature of man, setting forth a great principle of his being, that he is capable of giving allegiance to God, has faculties and powers capable of knowing and loving God. Our power of knowing and loving Him in the distinguishing power of man, separating him from the brutes with whom he is in many other respects allied. Not to exercise this power is to cast away the crown of our manhood. Of course, we cannot know God fully. Our weak, limited minds cannot comprehend the Infinite One. If we could comprehend God, we would be greater than He. The unknowable in God leads us to worship the God we know. This command calls us to a constant advance in the knowledge of God, so securing the activity and development of our power of knowing, and making it our duty to carefully attend to the revelation He has made of Himself. This certainly commends the study of nature; not only the poetic listening to its subtle teaching, but the scientific research for its great truths. This certainly commends the study of the Scriptures. Every neglected Bible should thrill the conscience with the charge, "You have not yet taken the first step towards obeying this commandment." God's revelation of Himself in the Bible is progressive. It had reached a certain stage at the time the Law was given at Sinai, sufficiently clear and full to make man's duty plain. But it did not stop there. It unfolded through succeeding ages until it culminated in the Lord Jesus Christ. So this first commandment makes it our duty to believe in the Lord Jesus Christ. To reject Him is not merely to reject an offer of mercy; it is to refuse to receive the complete revelation of God made in His Son. 2. The prohibitory form of the Commandment shows that there are tendencies in our nature to break this law of our being. We are prone to give supreme allegiance to and find our highest good in some person or thing other than God. 3. But even if we had full and accurate knowledge of the one true God, and were free from all debasing superstitions, we would still have tendencies drawing us away from entire consecration to Him. Whatever we value more than God, is our god. Wherever a man makes the gratification of himself his chief aim, he takes the crown belonging to God and crowns himself. (1) There is a strong tendency to make the gratification of even the lowest portion of our nature our chief aim and greatest delight. He only can have the highest animal enjoyment who remembers that he is more than an animal, and honouring God, seeks to discover and obey His laws of healthful living. (2) One would think that the exercise of our reasoning powers would lead the soul to God, yet there is a very strong tendency to make this exercise end in itself. Many of the great thinkers of the world have been worshippers of their own powers of thinking, and we who can with difficulty follow their great thoughts are prone to worship our own intellectual culture and acquirements, and to claim a considerable amount of incense from our fellow-men. (3) How prone we are to make our loved ones idols! Now the idolatry of loved ones does not consist in loving them too much, but in not loving them enough. The father who allows his child to so absorb his love that he has no thought of or love for God, does not love his child as an immortal spiritual being, nor does he regard himself as such. (4) Above the animal, the intellectual, and the social nature in man, is the spiritual. To ignore this nature, or dwarf it, is to degrade man. To have this nature in healthful control, and giving supreme allegiance to God, is to bring the whole man into obedience to this Commandment; it is to ennoble his social, inspire his intellectual, and elevate his animal natures; it is to reach the noble manhood God designs for us. (*F. S. Schenck.*) *The First Commandment* :—I. The question we are now to try and answer is, WHAT IS IT TO HAVE A GOD? I mean by this a true God, such as the Lord Jesus Christ is to us. 1. To have a God is to have one who can do three things for us. (1) The first thing we want our God to be able to do is, always to help. The little child always needs the help of its mother. The blind man always needs the help of some one to guide him. The sick man always needs the help of a physician. We need some one who can always help us. Then it must be some one who is present in every place, whose eye never slumbers, and whose arm never grows weary. Is there such a one to be found? Yes, God our Saviour is just such a one. (2) The second thing we want our God to be able to do is, always to save us. Our bodies are often in danger as well as our souls, and we want a God who can save them both. We can't preserve ourselves; and our best friends can't preserve us. Jesus says, "Look unto Me, all ye ends of the earth; for I am God, and there is none else. Besides Me there is no Saviour." We need a God who can always save. (3) But, then, there is a third thing that we expect God to be able to do for us, and that is, always to make us happy. When we are in health, and have affectionate parents and kind friends, and many comforts and enjoyments around us, we do not feel so much our need of God. 2. But, then, there are three things that He who is our God has a right to expect from us. (1) He has a right to expect our highest love. He is good; He is holy. "God is love." He expects, and He deserves, our highest love. It is right to love Him better than any one else; but it is neither right nor possible to love any one else in this way. (2) The second thing He has a right to expect from us is, our unquestioning obedience. It may not be always right to obey, without questioning, all that others command us; but it is always right to obey, without questioning, everything that God commands. He never does wrong Himself, and never commands others to do wrong. (3) Then there is a third thing God expects from us, and that is, sincere worship. Sincere means that which is true or pure. Worship. Let us see what this means. Worship is a word made up of two other words, viz., "worth," and "ship" or "shape." It means, then, that we should put ourselves in the position or shape that is worthy of God. Or, it means that we should render to Him the service that is worthy of Him. And what is the proper shape or position for sinners such as we are to put ourselves in before God? David tells us, when he says, "O come, let us worship and fall down; and kneel before the Lord our Maker." Yes, a position of humble reverence is what we should put ourselves in when we would worship God. This is the shape or condition worthy of God for sinful creatures to appear in. But the shape of a thing denotes its use or service. If you see iron put in the shape of a bright, sharp blade, you know it is designed to cut. If you see it put into a round shape, like a ball, you know it is designed to roll. If you see a pile of wood broken up into the shape of kindling, you know it is designed to burn. And if you see a man in the form of a servant, with an apron on, and his sleeves rolled up, you know he is designed for work. And so when we appear before God as His worshippers—in the form or shape worthy of Him—we mean to say that we are ready to offer Him our prayers and praises, and that we desire to serve Him. And when we do this honestly and earnestly, with all our hearts, that is sincere worship. This is the service God deserves. He is worthy of it. II. THE REASON WHY WE SHOULD HAVE NO OTHER GODS THAN THE LORD. I wish to speak of three reasons. 1. The first reason is, because it is very foolish to do so. (1) God is too rich for any one to take His place. All the gold and silver, all the gems and jewels and precious things in the world, and in all other worlds, belong to Him. He has need of them to supply the wants of His creatures. It is very foolish to have any one else than the Lord for our God, because no one else is rich enough to be our God. (2) God is too great for any one to take His place. He is the greatest of all beings. How foolish it would be to blot out the sun from the sky, and then try to light up the world with candles! Yet it would be easier to do this than to put anything in the place of God. (3) And then God is too wise for any one to take His place. How strange it is that anybody should ever think of putting stupid idols of wood or stone in the place of God! 2. The second reason why we ought to have no other gods than the Lord is, because it is very injurious. (1) To have any other God than the Lord is injurious in two ways: one way in which it is so is, that it leaves us without help. Wouldn't it be very injurious to a sick man to leave him in a place where he could get no physician, no medicine, and no nurse? Wouldn't it be very injurious to a hungry man to leave him in a position where he could get no food? (2) The other way is this: it exposes us to many troubles. We are told in the Bible, "Their sorrows shall be greatly multiplied who go after other gods." All who are not Christians have some other god but the Lord. And all who do this will be made to feel how very injurious it is. When trouble and sorrow come upon them, they will have none to comfort them. When their sins press upon them as a heavy burden, they will have none who can give them pardon, and so lift off that burden. When they come to die, they will have no one to lean on as they go through the dark valley. At the judgment seat they will have no one to be their friend. In eternity they will have nothing to make them happy. 3. The third and last reason is, that it is very wicked. There are two things about this which show how wicked it is. (1) There is robbery in it. And it is not robbing our friends, or our relations, or our fellow-creatures, or the angels of heaven. Any of these would be bad enough; but this is worse than all of them put together. It is robbing God! (2) There is treason in it. (*R. Newton, D.D.*) *God supplemented*:—"No other gods before Me." That is, "No other gods in My presence; in sight of Me." God will not share His sovereignty with any being. And this is the commonest way of breaking this Commandment in our day. There is no danger of breaking it through over-loving a fellow-creature, through loving a child, or a wife, or a parent, or a friend, too dearly. It is a frightful error to suppose that. But it is possible for us to think that God's power must be supplemented by man's power, by man's influence, by man's wealth, by man's work. A pastor may lean on God— and a rich member of his congregation; but not without breaking the First Commandment. A politician may think that, besides God's favour, he must have popular favour, to give him success. A business man may have it in his mind that public sentiment—even against strict right—must be yielded to in his business, although he believes in God as above all. A parent may feel that fashion and wealth have a power that cannot be dispensed with in giving his child a desirable place in life. A professed Christian may feel that Jesus Christ will save him, if only he does enough for his own salvation. All these are ways of breaking the First Commandment; not very uncommon ways, either! (*H. C. Trumbull.*)

Vers. 4–6. **Thou shalt not bow down thyself to them, nor serve them.**—*The law of worship :*—I. A REVELATION OF THE WILL OF GOD. 1. What is forbidden is not the culture of the plastic arts, but their abuse in furnishing symbols for purposes of devotion. Statuary is lawful, and painting is lawful; but sculptor and artist are alike restricted from attempting to represent the Deity; and all men are prohibited from taking such representations as objects of worship. 2. There was a special reason for this prohibition as it affected the Hebrews. They had come away from Egypt—a country where the employment of beasts and images in religious symbolism had descended to the very nadir of human degradation. They were on their way to Canaan, a land given to them because its inhabitants had outraged all forbearance by the filthy and bloody rites of Baal and Astarte. Above all, the chief reason of their own election as the chosen nation was that they might become faithful witnesses of Jehovah. 3. The bearing of this law upon Christian duty is manifest. Material images are forbidden, but mental images may be framed, provided always that they be fashioned out of the Divine manifestations. Every historic act, in which God is seen by the individual or the community, is a revelation of God; and the sum of such revelations gives a mental image of the Divine Being which we can and may adore. Furthermore, the focus of all God's self-revelation is the Lord Jesus Christ. II. A REVELATION OF THE CHARACTER OF GOD. 1. God is jealous for the truth of His own nature. How could any graven image ever be an accurate or an adequate similitude of the infinite invisible Spirit? 2. God is jealous for the character of His people. By the act of homage men acknowledge themselves inferior to that which they adore; so that every degradation of the Object of worship involves a simultaneous abasement of the worshipper. 3. God is jealous for the influence of His people upon the world. Israel was appointed to be a guardian of truth, an apostle of the one God, a harbour-light for benighted nations upon the sea of time. It was peculiarly wounding to the King of Heaven that *they* should insult Him by representing Him as a calf of gold, and should degrade themselves by their debasing homage. III. A REVELATION OF THE PROVIDENCE OF GOD. 1. Hereditary penalties follow the breach of this law of spiritual worship. Sensuous worship leads to sensuous living; and the fruits of sensuous living may linger on in miseries untold which our children shall suffer when we who did the wrong lie forgotten in the grave. 2. On the other hand, hereditary blessings follow the keeping of this law. True spiritual life begets true spiritual life, and hands on a heritage of reward to succeeding generations. 3. And it is the fittest which survives the longest! Evil is for a time; good is for eternity. (*W. J. Woods, B.A.*) *The Second Commandment :*—I. THE DIVINE PROHIBITION. 1. Observe precisely what this second commandment forbids. (1) And, first, negatively: It does not forbid all use of art in worship. For Jehovah Himself commanded Moses to adorn the tabernacle with figures of cherubim, and trees, and flowers, and pomegranates, and bells, and all manner of cunning workmanship. The imaging faculty, or faculty of making images—imagination in the primary sense of the term—is itself a Divine endowment, and must therefore be cultivated. (2) What, then, does the second commandment forbid? It forbids all idolatrous representations of Deity (see John iv. 24). We must worship God according to His nature; His nature is spiritual, and, therefore, we must worship Him spiritually—spirit-wise, not image-wise; for only what is spiritual in us can worship what is spiritual above us. 2. The prohibition, then, of the second commandment is a universal need. (1) The Jew at the foot of Mount Sinai needed it. He had just emerged from idolatrous Egypt—that Egypt which was wholly given over to image-worship. (2) Modern Christianity needs it. We need not go to the Roman Catholic Church for examples of image-worship. Behold our own Protestant Ecclesiolatry, or worship of the Church as an institution, bowing down before her ordinances as though they were ends instead of using them as means, worshipping her sacraments and creeds and traditions and ceremonies. Behold our Protestant Bibliolatry, or rabbinic worship of the Bible as a letter and even sacrament. These, and such as these, are, practically speaking, more or less revered as symbols of Deity. II. THE DIVINE REASON FOR THE PROHIBITION. 1. Jehovah our God is a jealous God. 2. Law of heredity (see Gal. vi. 7). (1) The merciless aspect of heredity. Everybody knows that there are hereditary diseases; for instance, leprosy, scrofula, consumption, insanity, and a nameless disease far more dreadful. And as there are hereditary diseases, so there are hereditary vices; for example, indolence, mendacity, avarice, intemperance, crime. Moral habit is as hereditable as bodily gait. As Dr. Oliver Wendell Holmes has somewhere stated: "A man is an omnibus, in which all his ancestors are seated." Yes; the soul, not less than the body, has its physiology. This law it is which accounts for the sad fact of the universal sinfulness. But you interrupt me with an objection. "This law of heredity," you tell me, "tends to quench personal responsibility." Learn, then, I answer, a lesson from the analogy of the human body: although confessedly propagated, it is also confessedly a separate, independent individuality. Again: it is of the utmost importance in this discussion to keep clearly and steadily in mind the distinction between personal guilt and inherited disaster, or, as the philosophers phrase it, unfortunate "environment." But I hear another objection: "This law of heredity," you tell me, "is unjust and cruel; it makes the innocent suffer for the guilty. How, then, will you reconcile the awful working of this law of heredity with the character of a holy and loving God?" Answer: Man is mortal. How, then, shall the continuance of the race on earth be secured? I can conceive of but two ways. First, by the continuous creation of men, or a perpetual repetition of the miracle of Eden, the ceaseless bringing into the world, fresh from the Maker's hand, of a succession of created Adams, or parentless Melchizedeks. But under such a condition of things there would be, in all probability, a repetition of Adam's painful story. Secondly, the continuance of the race on earth can be secured in the way in which the Creator does actually secure it—namely, by the law of propagation. Heredity it is which renders this profound fact—Society—possible. There is such a thing as man-kind, because there is such a thing as men-kinned. It is almost impossible to overestimate the value of consanguinity as a curbing, uplifting, unifying force. Heredity! Why it is my real hope under God for humanity. (2) Merciful aspect of heredity. This law is a real inspiration for foreign missions. Special pains must be taken to save the heathen children; for converted children are, according to God's own law, the mighty hope of our world's future. Lessons: 1. Heredity the key to social regeneration. Men, not less than animals, can be improved by stirpiculture, or selective breeding. 2. A summons to personal heroism. God judges us, not by our capacities, but by our efforts. 3. Worship the Divine Man Himself. He is the Image of the Invisible God, and we need no other. (*G. D. Boardman.*) *Idolatry :*—I. THE NATURE OF IDOLATRY. A giving to something below God of that worship which is due to God alone. It may be outward, or inward; an act of the body, or an act of the mind. II. THE EVIL OF IDOLATRY. 1. It has a strange power to perpetuate and increase itself. 2. It ever engenders falsehood and deceit. 3. It is almost always accompanied with cruelty. "The dark places of the earth," says Scripture, "are full of the habitations of cruelty," and all experience confirms the saying. Think of Mexico, as she was when first discovered, and of her fearful hecatombs of slaughtered men. Think of our country, and of other countries around it, in Druidical times. Follow Captain Cook in his voyages from island to island in the great Pacific. Wherever we find idols we find bloodshed, bloodshed for those idols. As for idolatrous Rome, I will not speak of her wholesale slaughters in years gone by. 4. There is one point more which I wished to notice, it is the licentiousness that accompanies idolatry, arising, beyond doubt, in part out of it. English minds cannot conceive the extent of this, nor the nature of it. III. There is another thing, far more fearful than the idolatry of Rome, and far more difficult to keep ourselves from—THE IDOLATRY OF THE MIND AND HEART. We may have idols within us, and, as for worshipping them, it may be the main business of our lives. (*C. Bradley. M.A.*)   *Image-worship :*—To set up an image to represent God is a debasing of the Deity, it is below God. If one should make images of snakes or spiders, saying he did it to represent his prince, would not the prince take this in high disdain? What greater disparagement to God, than to represent the infinite God by that which is finite,—the living God, by that which is without life, and the Maker of all, by a thing which is made? 1. To make a true image of God is impossible. What is invisible cannot be portrayed. 2. To worship God by an image is both absurd and unlawful. (1) It is absurd and irrational; for, the workman is better than the work: "he who hath builded the house hath more honour than the house." If the workman be better than the work, and none bow to the workman, how absurd then is it to bow to the work of his hands! Is it not an absurd thing to bow down to the king's picture, when the king himself is present? more so to bow down to an image of God, when God Himself is everywhere present.

(2) It is unlawful to worship God by an image; for it is against the homily of the Church; "the images of God, our Saviour, the Virgin Mary, are of all others the most dangerous; therefore the greatest care ought to be had that they stand not in temples and churches." Use: Take heed of idolatry, namely, image-worship. (1) Get good principles, that you may be able to oppose the gainsayer. (2) Get love to God. (3) Pray God to keep you. (*T. Watson.*) *The Second Commandment, and its influence upon the Jews:*—Some go so far as to say that it forbad the Jew to make any carved work at all. Certainly, judging by national results, it would almost seem as if Israel had so understood it. The Jews are a people famous for many things, for intellectual and administrative ability, and for a marvellous power of sustaining themselves in the midst of the most difficult circumstances. But whilst there have been Jewish warriors and poets, statesmen and financiers, musicians and singers of world-wide reputation, where are their artists and architects? The very temple of Solomon was a Phœnician structure. You may count easily a half-dozen distinguished musical Jewish composers—Mozart, Beethoven, Meyerbeer, Mendelssohn, and Rossini—but where is the distinguished Jewish sculptor or painter? Still, whilst all this is very suggestive as to the formative influence of the commandment, it seems most reasonable to decide that the sentence, "Thou shalt not make," is qualified by the sentence, "Thou shalt not bow down nor worship." The Jews were really only forbidden to make carved images as symbols of Deity, as objects of adoration. (*W. Senior, B.A.*) *The offence of symbolism:*—It becomes obvious that an imaged representation of the Invisible One must involve dishonour. Before the Infinite One can be bodied forth He must first of necessity be sensualized. Here is the deep insult. And the guilt of irreverance clings to the human mind in the very fact that it thinks itself capable of such an impossibility, and fails to perceive how it befouls what it touches. What difference then is there between the image of the artist and an intellectual conception of God? None in reality. What is the image? It is more than the carving of the sculptor; it is first his thought. The image is really thought embodied. Words may be used instead of marble, or wood, or colours, but essentially they are the same if they present to the imagination a shape, a form, or an intellectual conception. In this sense words are as finite as images or symbols, and therefore may be as guilty of degradation. Thus it follows that the reason of man has no more right to touch the Invisible Creator than the hands. God refuses also to be the subject of the human intellect. That the human mind should think itself capable of compassing the Infinite is to insult Him with deepest irreverence. "Who by searching can find out God?" God Himself must instruct us how to conceive of Him, and by what faculties of our nature we must draw near to Him. And this He has done. Through Abraham and through Moses, through David and the prophets, and, including all and perfecting all, through Jesus Christ the Divine Son, He has made Himself known to man. (*Ibid.*) **A jealous God.**—I. Reverently, let us remember that the LORD IS EXCEEDINGLY JEALOUS OF HIS DEITY. The whole history of the human race is a record of the wars of the Lord against idolatry. The right hand of the Lord hath dashed in pieces the enemy and cast the ancient idols to the ground. Behold the heaps of Nineveh! Search for the desolations of Babylon! Look upon the broken temples of Greece! See the ruins of Pagan Rome! Journey where you will, you behold the dilapidated temples of the gods and the ruined empires of their foolish votaries. The Lord hath made bare His arm and eased Him of His adversaries, for Jehovah, whose name is Jealous, is a jealous God. With what jealousy must the Lord regard the great mass of the people of this country, who have another god beside Himself! Even believers may be reproved on this subject. God is very jealous of His Deity in the hearts of His own people. II. THE LORD IS JEALOUS OF HIS SOVEREIGNTY. He that made heaven and earth has a right to rule His creatures as He wills. 1. This reminds us of the Lord's hatred of sin. Every time we sin, we do as much as say, "I do not acknowledge God to be my Sovereign; I will do as I please." 2. Surely if sin attacks the sovereignty of God, self-righteousness is equally guilty of treason: for as sin boasts, "I will not keep God's law," self-righteousness exclaims, "I will not be saved in God's way; I will make a new road to heaven." III. THE LORD IS JEALOUS OF HIS GLORY. God's glory is the result of His nature and acts. 1. How, careful, then, should we be when we do anything for God, and God is pleased to accept of our doings, that we never congratulate ourselves. The worms which ate Herod when he gave not God the glory are ready for another meal; beware of vain glory! 2. How careful ought we to be to walk humbly before the Lord. The moment we glorify

ourselves, since there is room for one glory only in the universe, we set ourselves up as rivals to the Most High. 3. Let us see to it that we never misrepresent God, so as to rob Him of His honour. If any minister shall preach of God so as to dishonour Him, God will be jealous against that man. IV. In the highest sense, THE LORD IS JEALOUS OVER HIS OWN PEOPLE. 1. The Lord Jesus Christ, of whom I now speak, is very jealous of your love, O believer. 2. He is very jealous of your trust. He will not permit you to trust in an arm of flesh. 3. He is also very jealous of our company. It were well if a Christian could see nothing but Christ. (*C. H. Spurgeon.*) *The jealousy of God :*—Jealousy is but the anger and pain of injured and insulted love. When God resents the illegitimate transfer to material symbols of the devotion inspired by His own acts, it is not because His greatness suffers any diminution or because His authority is impaired. It is His love which is wounded. He cannot endure to lose any of the affection, trust, or reverence by which He has stirred our souls. One of the fairest-looking falsehoods by which men excuse themselves for living a life in which God has no place, is the plea that the infinite God cannot care for the love and reverence of such creatures as we are. When will men understand that no father can ever be great enough to be indifferent to the affection, the obedience, and the confidence of his children? (*R. W. Dale, D.D.*) **Visiting the iniquity of the fathers upon the children.**—*Visiting the sins of the fathers on the children:*—I. THAT THE DENUNCIATION AND SENTENCE RELATE TO THE SIN OF IDOLATRY IN PARTICULAR, IF NOT TO THAT ALONE. II. THAT IT RELATES TO TEMPORAL, OR, MORE PROPERLY SPEAKING, TO FAMILY PROSPERITY AND ADVERSITY. III. THAT IT RELATES TO THE JEWISH ECONOMY, IN THAT PARTICULAR ADMINISTRATION OF A VISIBLE PROVIDENCE UNDER WHICH THEY LIVED. IV. THAT AT NO RATE DOES IT AFFECT (OR WAS EVER MEANT TO AFFECT) THE ACCEPTANCE OR SALVATION OF INDIVIDUALS IN A FUTURE LIFE. (*Archdeacon Paley.*) *The children bearing the fathers' iniquities :*— I. As to THE MATTER OF FACT—that God does visit on the children the iniquities of the fathers—the evidence is so broad and conclusive that, without a singular careless-ness it cannot be overlooked. The sin of one man brought death into the world, and caused that, throughout the vast spreadings of humanity, wretchedness, both physical and moral, shall hold a kind of undisputed supremacy. II. WHETHER SUCH A VISITATION CONSISTS WITH THE PRINCIPLES OF JUSTICE AND EQUITY. In most men's minds, when this question is proposed, there is a feeling that the visitation is not thus consistent : we think it a righteous procedure that every man should bear his own burden; but we see no equity in the appointment that the innocent should suffer for the fault of the guilty. It is, however, worthy of observation, that the proceeding after all cannot be repugnant to our notions of justice, since its exact parallel occurs in human legislation. If the statute-book of the country enact the visiting on children the sin of the father, it will be hard to show that the visitation is counter to common sense and equity. In cases of treason, we all know that it is not the traitor alone who is punished : his estates are confiscated, his honours destroyed ; so that, in place of transmitting rank and affluence to his son, he trans-mits him nothing but shame and beggary. We do not say that the thing must be just because enacted by human laws ; we only say that there can be no felt and acknowledged contradiction between the proceeding and the principles of equity, since human laws involve the children in the doom of the parent. If you can show the child to be innocent, and therefore to deserve nothing of what it receives, you will have made good your point that the visitation is unjust ; but to maintain the thorough innocence of the child would be to maintain the purity of human nature. Still, you will say, the child is confessedly worse off than it would have been had the parent not sinned ; and though we may deserve all we endure for ourselves, we still practically suffer for the misdoings of another. We admit this ; but at the same time we contend that you are shifting the argument. If the child endured no more than it has deserved you admit that the course of justice is unimpeached—and this is the main thing we are anxious to establish : but, if after conceding the strict justice of the measure, you profess to think it hard that the child should endure what, but for the parent's offence, it would not have deserved, we are ready to follow you into the new field of debate, and to show you, as we think, the errone-ousness of your opinion. The child, for example, is of a diseased constitution, of a dishonoured name, of a broken fortune ; these constitute the visitation of whose hardship you complain ; but who can prove to us that the child is really injured by the visitation? Nay, who can prove to us that the child is not really advantaged? If we were told that, because the parent died in unrighteousness, the child also must be shipwrecked for eternity, the wrought injury would be tremendous and overwhelming : but there is not the least ground for supposing that the threatened visitation extends to the next world ; on the contrary, the whole tenor of Scripture —inasmuch as salvation is offered to all—requires us to believe, that the consequences to the children of the father's transgressions lie confined within our present sphere of being.   Why then is it certain that the child is dealt with injuriously, if sentenced for the parent's iniquity to penury and affliction ?   Are penury and affliction never overruled for good ?   Is it necessarily an evil to have been born poor in place of rich—to be of weak health instead of strong—to struggle with adversity, in place of being lapped in prosperity ?   No man who feels himself immortal, who is conscious that this confined theatre of existence is but the school in which he is trained for a wider and nobler still, will contend for the necessary injuriousness of want and calamity : and yet unless this necessary injuriousness is supposed, it cannot be proved that the children who are visited for the father's iniquity are on the whole worse off than they would have been had there been no visitation.   Thus the argument against the goodness of the Almighty as much falls to the ground as that against His justice ; for proceeding on the principle that physical evil is never subservient to moral good, we overthrow our position by assuming what we know to be false.   (*H. Melvill, B.D.*)   *Inherited character :—* An old man died a few years ago in the Massachusetts State Prison.   He was seventy-six years old, and had spent the last eight years of his life in a cell in that gloomy gaol.   His wife for years had been a prisoner there too, and so had his daughter, and seven of his sons.   Were not " the iniquities of the father visited upon the children " ?   In that same State, seventy years ago, a good minister died, who for forty-one years had been a beloved pastor over the same church.   He was the fourteenth eldest son of that same name and family who had been a preacher of the gospel.   Since his death, one hundred of his descendants have been Christians, and eight of his sons and grandsons have also been ministers.   Through that blessed family, for many long years, the Great Father of love has been " showing mercy to thousands in them that love Him and keep His commandments."   **Showing mercy unto thousands.**—*The place of mercy in the government of God :—* Look carefully at a very important feature of the appeal which is not brought out clearly in our English translation.   He visits iniquity " unto the third and fourth," and shows mercy " unto the thousandth," the commandment reads.   Our translators have supplied the word " generation " in italics to the first numeral, and evidently they were right in doing so, but they should have supplied for the same reasons the same word to the second numeral : " He visits iniquity unto the third and fourth *generation,*" " He shows mercy unto the thousandth *generation.*"   The third and fourth show an indefinite number, the thousandth is also an indefinite number, but it is a much larger number.   The principle of the Divine government has a very decided leaning to the side of mercy.   Now, perhaps you will say : " I see that this feature of the Divine government works with absolute impartiality, with strict justice, but I can see no indication of its leaning to the side of mercy."   Then look again, and more closely, at the race and the individual.   1. Look at the individual first.   A child inherits an impaired constitution.   Two features of the Divine government respond at once.   First, the restorative forces within the child, the recuperative powers of man's nature ; and second, the restorative forces without, the whole realm of remedies and skill awakened in others in their application.   The child of ignorant parents is ignorant.   Two features here also are on the side of mercy.   The innate thirst of the mind for knowledge, present though weak in the child ; and the intelligence of the community in which the child lives, the atmosphere of enlightenment which he must breathe while he lives.   The child of irreligious parents is irreligious.   Here, too, there are two principles on the side of mercy.   However corrupt he may be, there is something in the soul of the child at unrest for God which may be touched into power ; and the surrounding Christianity —the Christ who has loved and died to save—lives in many believing hearts through whom He seeks to save the child.   2. Now, concerning the race, it may be said that the limit of degradation seems to be fixed, but the limit of progress cannot be even imagined.   How far man will advance in the control and use of the powers of nature, we who witness to-day the stupendous achievements of Christian civilization will not even dare to conjecture.   And how far man will be lifted up, in the knowledge and fellowship of God, the Bible tells us that we cannot even imagine.   In the whole race, also, the two principles we have seen working in individuals on the side of mercy exist.   However corrupted in idolatry men may become, however great the ascendancy of the flesh over the spirit in man, the spirit still exists, and in its very nature cannot be satisfied until it finds and lays hold upon the living God. There is something within men that cannot be satisfied with idolatry, or with sensual corruption, something that may be touched into strong and glorious life. And there is something to touch it. God makes the appeal of His infinite love in Jesus Christ, who has at infinite cost taken away sin and brought in new life to all who receive Him. And we who receive Him, as He lives in us, will touch all the dark souls we can reach with His light and life. We have received from our fathers the elevation and happiness of our Christian land. Let us cherish and transmit to our children the glorious inheritance, and let us send the light into the whole earth. Let us, receiving forgiveness and new life in our Saviour, bring our whole being into a shape worthy of God in moral likeness. (*F. S. Schenck.*) *God's mercies:*—I. WHAT ARE THE QUALIFICATIONS? 1. The spring of mercy which God shows is free and spontaneous. Say not then, I am unworthy; for mercy is free. If God should show mercy only to such as deserve it, He must show mercy to none at all. 2. The mercy God shows is powerful. How powerful is that mercy which softens a heart of stone! Of what sovereign power and efficacy is that mercy which subdues the pride and enmity of the heart, and beats off those chains of sin in which the soul is held! 3. The mercy which God shows is superabundant; "abundant in goodness, keeping mercy for thousands." The vial of God's wrath doth but drop; but the fountain of His mercy runs. 4. The mercy God shows is abiding (Psa. ciii. 17). II. HOW MANY WAYS IS GOD SAID TO SHOW MERCY? 1. We are all living monuments of God's mercy. He shows mercy to us in daily supplying us. 2. God shows mercy in lengthening out our gospel liberties. 3. God shows mercy in preventing many evils from invading us. 4. God shows mercy in delivering us. 5. God shows mercy in restraining us from sin; lusts within, are worse than lions without. 6. God shows mercy in guiding and directing us. 7. God shows mercy in correcting us. God is angry in love; He smites that He may save. Every cross to a child of God is like Paul's cross wind, which though it broke the ship, it brought Paul to shore upon the broken pieces. 8. God shows mercy in pardoning us; "who is a God like Thee, That pardonest iniquity?" It is mercy to feed us, rich mercy to pardon us. 9. God shows His mercy in sanctifying us (Lev. xx. 8). This prepares for happiness, as the seed prepares for harvest. 10. God shows mercy in hearing our prayers. God may sometimes delay an answer, when He will not deny. You do not presently throw a musician money, because you love to hear his music: God loves the music of prayer, therefore doth not presently let us hear from Him, but in due season He will give an answer of peace. 11. God shows mercy in saving us: "according to His mercy He saved us." This is the top-stone of mercy, and it is laid in heaven. Now mercy displays itself in all its orient colours; now mercy is mercy indeed, when God shall perfectly refine us from all the lees and dregs of corruption. As an argument against despair: see what a great encouragement here is to serve God,—He shows mercy to thousands. (1) Hope in God's mercies, "the Lord takes pleasure in them that fear Him, and hope in His mercy." (2) If God shows mercy to thousands, labour to know that His mercy is for you, "He is the God of my mercy." A man that was ready to drown saw a rainbow; said he, "What am I the better, though God will not drown the world, if I drown?" so, what are we the better God is merciful, if we perish? Let us labour to know God's special mercy is for us. (*T. Watson.*) "*Them that love Me*":— I. HOW MUST OUR LOVE TO GOD BE QUALIFIED? 1. Love to God must be pure and genuine; He must be loved chiefly for Himself. We must love God, not only for His benefits, but for those intrinsic excellencies wherewith He is crowned; we must love God not only for the good which flows from Him, but the good which is in Him. 2. Love to God must be with all the heart, "thou shalt love the Lord thy God with all thy heart." We must not love God a little,—give God a drop or two of our love,—but the main stream of our love must run after Him; the mind must think of God, the will choose Him, the affections pant after Him. 3. Love to God must be flaming; to love coldly is all one as not to love. II. HOW MAY WE KNOW WHETHER WE LOVE GOD? 1. He that loves God desires His sweet presence; lovers cannot be long asunder, they have their fainting fits, they want a sight of the object of their love. A soul deeply in love with God desires the enjoyment of Him in His ordinances, in word, prayer, sacraments. 2. He who loves God doth not love sin; "ye that love the Lord hate evil." The love of God and the love of sin can no more mix together than iron and clay; every sin loved strikes at the being of God, but he who loves God hath an antipathy against sin. 3. He who loves God is not much in love with anything else; his love is very cool to worldly things; his love to God moves as the sun in the firmament. swiftly; his love to the world moves as the sun on the dial, very slow. 4. He who loves God cannot live without Him. 5. He who loves God will be at any pains to get Him. Doth he love his friend that will not make a journey to see him? 6. He that loves God prefers Him before estate and life. Before estate: " For whom I have suffered the loss of all things." Who that loves a rich jewel would not part with a flower for it? Before life: " They loved not their lives to the death." Love to God carries the soul above the love of life and the fear of death. 7. He who loves God loves His favourites, namely, the saints (1 John v. 1). 8. If we love God, as we cannot but be fearful of dishonouring Him (the more a child loves his father, the more he is afraid to displease him), so we weep and mourn when we have offended Him. III. WHAT ARE THE INCENTIVES TO PROVOKE AND INFLAME OUR LOVE TO GOD? 1. God's benefits bestowed on us. Great is the love that is excited by love. Kindness works on a brute; the ox knows his owner. 2. Love to God would make duties of religion facile and pleasant. 3. It is advantageous (1 Cor. ii 9). 4. By our loving God we may know that He loves us (1 John iv. 19). If the ice melts, it is because the sun has shined upon it; if the frozen heart melts in love, it is because the Sun of Righteousness hath shined upon it. IV. WHAT MEANS MAY BE USED TO EXCITE OUR LOVE TO GOD? 1. Labour to know God aright. 2. Make the Scriptures familiar to you. 3. Meditate much of God, and this will be a means to love Him; " while I was musing, the fire burned." Meditation is the bellows of the affections. Who can meditate on God's love? who can tread on these hot coals, and his heart not burn in love to God? (*Ibid.*) " *And keep My commandments*" :—Love and obedience, like two sisters, must go hand in hand. A good Christian is like the sun, which doth not only send forth light, but goes its circuit round the world: so he hath not only the light of knowledge, but goes his circuit too, and moves in the sphere of obedience. In what manner must we keep God's commandments? 1. Our keeping the commandments must be fiducial. Our obedience to God's commandments must spring from faith; therefore it is called " the obedience of faith." 2. Our keeping the commandments must be uniform. We must make conscience of one commandment as well as another; " then shall I not be ashamed, when I have respect to all Thy commandments." Physicians have a rule, when the body sweats in one part, but is cold in another, it is a sign of a distemper: so when men seem zealous in some duties of religion, but are cold and frozen in others, it is a sign of hypocrisy. We must have respect to all God's commandments. 3. Our keeping God's commandments must be willing; " if ye be willing and obedient." A musician is not commended for playing long, but for playing well; it is obeying God willingly is accepted; the Lord hates that which is forced, it is rather paying a tax than an offering. If a willing mind be wanting, there wants that flower which should perfume our obedience, and make it a sweet smelling savour to God. That we may keep God's commandments willingly, let these things be well weighed. Our willingness is more esteemed than our service; therefore David counsels Solomon not only to serve God, but with a willing mind. The will makes sin to be worse, and makes duty to be better. To obey willingly shows we do it with love; and this crowns all our services. There is that in the Lawgiver, which may make us willing to obey the commandments, namely, God's indulgence to us. There is that in God's commandments which may make us willing; they are not burdensome. 1. For a Christian, so far as he is regenerate, consents to God's commands—" I consent to the law that it is good." 2. God's commandments are sweetened with joy and peace. Cicero questions whether that can properly be called a burden which one carries with delight and pleasure. If a man carries a bag of money given him, it is heavy, but the delight takes off the burden; when God gives inward joy, that makes the commandments delightful. 3. God's commandments are advantageous. (1) Preventive of evil. Had He not set them as a hedge or bar in our way, we might have run to hell, and never stopped. (2) Nothing in them but what is for our good. Not so much our duty as our privilege. 4. God's commandments are ornamental. It is an honour to be employed in a king's service. 5. The commands of God are infinitely better than the commands of sin, these are intolerable. Many have gone with more pains to hell than others have to heaven. This may make us obey the command- ments willingly. 6. Willingness in obedience makes us resemble the angels. Use: It reproves them who live in a wilful breach of God's commandments,—in malice, uncleanness, intemperance,—they walk antipodes to the commandment. To live in a wilful breach of the commandment is—1. Against reason. 2. Against equity. 3. Against nature. 4. Against kindness. (*Ibid.*) *Keeping the com-*

mandments :—I. ONE CONDITION, THEN, OF OBTAINING GOD'S MERCY IS OBEDIENCE. But what am I to obey? But I desire to ask whether, at heart, some of you do not know sufficiently the answer that should be given? Can you say that you know no difference between right and wrong? Is the liar and the man of truth the same to you? May we go together, then, thus far, that we admit the difference between right and wrong? A second step will, I think, be then admitted—to right and wrong we must add the words "ought" and "ought not." In other words, the distinction between right and wrong brings with it the words "ought," "ought not," "responsibility," "duty." Here it may be well further to remind you that in this word "duty" lies hid an inexplicable treasure of infinite value—I mean our freedom. In the "I ought" is practically included the "I can." But let me ask you, yet again, whence comes this power to distinguish right from wrong? Here we may differ in words, but in the existence of the power itself many will agree. We may call it moral feeling, moral sense, Divine reason, or use the word to which we have been accustomed—conscience. But, once more, why do we give to this mysterious power so much importance? Why, if this moral feeling, this conscience, is part of ourselves, why not deal with it as we please, and listen or not as it may serve our turn? The real answer, I believe (though all may not be able to give it), is because conscience does not speak as for herself, but as for another. She brings us to a bar of another, whom we fear and may resist, but One higher than ourselves, even God. Here is surely a point worthy of your most careful consideration. II. The text offers mercy for thousands, mercy for all, but on two conditions—obedience and love. Obedience of a kind we may practise to the moral law; but LOVE REQUIRES PERSONALITY. We must, by God's help, rise above the contemplation of the law to the Person of the Lawgiver, and love the law for His sake—"Lord, what love have I unto Thy law!"—and then love Him because He is what He is. 1. The first test I would suggest to you is this—what use do you make of your Bible? The step from obedience to love, we said, implied the step from an impersonal law to the personal Lawgiver, and this, the belief in one Personal God, we said, required for its fulness the aid of Divine revelation. Here, then, is one test—our Bible. Let me say it as plainly as I can: if you neglect the study, the habitual devotional study, of the one Book that above all others makes known to you the one Personal God, you will be in danger of living a mere moral life—fulfilling, in a sense, the condition of obedience, but falling short of the higher condition of love, and a narrow, selfish, unloving, uninfluential humanity will be the result. 2. Let me offer you another test which each can easily make for himself. What is your relation to prayer? Prayer is the test of belief in a Personal God. The man who never prays, never rises above himself, may be moral, may be obedient to the moral law, but he has lost one proof of his belief in a Personal Lawgiver, to whom the law was intended to lead him; has lost one proof that he has a Personal Guide through the perils of his life; has lost one proof that he is preserving the condition of love. If we can pray, we have faith in a Personal God; we may deplore our coldness from time to time, we may even pray from a sense of duty many times, but we have not lost the great condition of love, and we know by experience how our hearts may become again as the rivers in the south—dry water-beds for a season, but in due time flowing like a flood. 3. Let me give you but one more test, by which you may know whether you are fulfilling this condition of love, the great condition on which God's plentiful mercy may be obtained. It is the test of the love of our neighbour. (*Bp. E. King.*)

Ver. 7. **Thou shalt not take the name of the Lord thy God in vain.**—*The Third Commandment :*—The name of God stands for Himself and for that which He has revealed of Himself, not for our thoughts about Him. It is not surprising that this great name was invested with a superstitious sanctity. Even the Jews used it rarely. There is a tradition that it was heard but once a year, when it was uttered by the high-priest on the great day of atonement. In reading the Scriptures it became customary never to pronounce it, but to replace it with another Divine name, which was regarded as less awful and august. The Third Commandment requires something very different from this ceremonial homage to His name. His name stands for Himself, and it is to Him that our reverence is due. I. WE MAY TRANSGRESS THE COMMANDMENT IN MANY WAYS. 1. By perjury. 2. By swearing. 3. By the practice of finding material for jesting in Holy Scripture. 4. By the habit of scoffing at those who profess to live a religious life, and taking every opportunity of sneering at their imperfections. II. It is not enough to avoid the sin of profanity;

WE ARE BOUND TO CULTIVATE AND TO MANIFEST THAT REVERENCE FOR GOD'S MAJESTY AND HOLINESS WHICH LIES AT THE ROOT OF ALL RELIGION. We have to worship Him. It is the "pure in heart" who see God, and only when we see God face to face can we worship Him in spirit and in truth. (*R. W. Dale, D.D.*) *On taking God's name in vain :*—I. The first expression to which I refer is, "THE NAME OF THE LORD THY GOD," or strictly, "the name of Jehovah thy God." The name of the Lord is not, on the one hand, the mere articulate sound by which the mouth expresses the idea of Deity, nor is the phrase, on the other hand, a simple synonym for God. It holds up God in His special character of Jehovah, the covenant-making and covenant-keeping God of His own dear people. "The name of Jehovah" means God, known and served under His revealed aspect of mercy, God appreciated as the pardoner of sin and giver of the Spirit, the Jehovah or keeper of His precious promises to His people. For example, of the antediluvian piety it is said : "Then began men to call upon the name of the Lord"—*i.e.*, it was then that distinctive recognition was made of God's special provision of mercy for sinners. His name of Jehovah was received as indicating His relation to His believing people. A name is an expression of the personal substance—an exhibition of the essential character. God's name by which He delights to be known among men, is Love. His character of compassion is especially displayed in His Word, and hence the Psalmist says : "Thou hast magnified Thy Word above all Thy name"—that is, of all revelations of God's character, all expressions of His being, the written Word is most full and complete. Here is the way of pardon and acceptance clearly portrayed. Another conspicuous display of God's character, but only local and temporary in its personal contact, while universal in its possible application, is in the Lord Jesus Christ ; and so Jesus is in a high sense "the name of Jehovah." II. The second expression to which our attention should be directed is the phrase, "To TAKE IN VAIN." The literal rendering is, "Thou shalt not lift up the name of Jehovah thy God lightly." Taking God's name in vain is the flippant and thoughtless use of God's name. It is the taking up the name in the vacant, purposeless way in which we pluck off a leaf as we pass along the road—the use of the name, not only where the purpose is evil, but where there is no defined purpose at all. Again, there may be not only an absence of evil purpose, but, beyond an absence of all purpose, there may even be a purpose of good, but this purpose may be seized upon in so rash and ill-advised a way that the use of the Divine name in it is a taking the name in vain, just as Uzzah's touching the ark of God, even to stay it upon the cart and prevent its fall, was a sin of profanity, and called for the Divine punishment. 1. In respect to God's verbal name, we are not to be satisfied with our freedom from the coarse profanity which culture and good breeding forbid, but we are to remove the habit of using the holy name in ordinary conversation in which the use has no religious character. We are not to call a wretched and forlorn person or thing "God-forsaken," or to hail a gift as a "God-send," when, in using these epithets, we have no design to use their full meaning, and therefore have not the proper attitude of mind for their utterance. 2. In respect to God's written Word, we are to take it up with reverence both in our hearts and on our tongues. 3. But chiefly, in relation to Jesus and the great eternal truths which the Holy Spirit introduces to the soul. To each man comes through his conscience a summons from God to give heed to his future spiritual and eternal condition. If you slight that summons, given to you in the gospel, you are taking God's name in vain. (*H. Crosby, D.D.*) *The Third Commandment :*—I. THE DIVINE PROHIBITION—1. Forbids perjury. 2. Forbids hypocrisy—insincere worship. 3. Forbids profanity. II. THE DIVINE WARNING. Being in its very nature the most godless of sins, God from His very nature cannot allow it to go unpunished. Did you ever read that remarkable assertion of the famous mathematician, Charles Babbage, in the "Ninth Bridgwater Treatise," to the effect that the slightest word, though it be but a whispered interjection, vibrating in the air, sets in operation a series of changes which undulate to the very outskirts of creation, rising and falling like an everlasting tide ? The whole material universe is a mighty whispering-gallery, in which the Infinite One is everlastingly hearing every word, every whisper, breathed by every human being, from the day Adam pronounced his first vocable in Eden to the day when human time shall be no more. If, then, the scarcely audible rustle of an unconscious aspen leaf sets in inexorable motion atom after atom—from leaf to tree, from tree to earth, from earth to star, till the whole material creation responds in undulation—think you that an oath, spoken by conscious, responsible man, will ever die away, or go unpunished ? Oh, no ! Jehovah will not hold him guiltless that taketh His name in vain. (*G. D. Boardman.*)   *The Third Commandment:*—There are other ways besides making an image of Him by which the conception of Deity can be lowered. Man by his words embodies his thoughts of God as really as when by his hands he carves an image of Him. It bears significantly upon certain usages which tend, though perhaps unconsciously, to dissociate the name of God from the deep reverence which should invest it. Among these is the habit, formed often unthinkingly, of using frequent and almost meaningless repetitions of the name of God in prayer. Akin to this evil, and one equally opposed to the spirit of the Third Command, is the familiar and endearing use of God's name in prayer. Some, while praying, employ epithets as if they were on terms of special intimacy, and almost of equality, with their Heavenly Father. Christ has, indeed, taught us to call God "Father"; but He has, in the same breath, bid us gather around the name these reverent words, "which art in heaven, hallowed be Thy name." And there is nothing in Scripture to indicate a less hallowed aspect toward Christ in prayer than toward the Father. With what unvarying reverence do Paul and John, in their Epistles, refer to the ascended and glorified Redeemer! A true acquaintance with God produces reverence for Him; a correct knowledge of Christ exalts Him far above all principality and power, and gives Him a name that is above every name. (*P. B. Davis.*)   *The Third Commandment :*—I. WHAT IS REQUIRED. The holy and reverent use of God's names, titles, attributes, ordinances, words, and works. II. WHAT IS FORBIDDEN. All profaning or abusing of anything whereby God makes Himself known. This command is broken two ways—1. By not using the name of God as is required (Mal. ii. 2). So as many duties as are required, so many sins there are in omitting these duties. Hence this command is broken by our not hallowing and glorifying God's name, by not taking up the name of God into our minds, lips, and lives. 2. By profaning or abusing of the name of God; that is, anything whereby God makes. Himself known. 1. When it is used ignorantly, as it was by the Athenians, whom the apostle Paul charges with worshipping God ignorantly (Acts xviii. 23). 2. When it is used vainly and irreverently, that is, lightly and rashly. 3. When the name of God is used superstitiously. 4. When it is used profanely and wickedly. (1) Profane swearing. (2) Sinful imprecations or cursings, whereby people pray for some evil against themselves or others, whether absolutely or conditionally. (3) Perjury is falsehood confirmed with an oath. (4) Blasphemy, which is a wronging of the majesty of God, by speeches tending to His reproach. Having spoken of the more gross and palpable breaches of this command, I shall now consider other ways how the Lord's name is abused and taken in vain. 1. With respect to His names and titles. They are taken in vain—(1) When they are not improved for those uses to which they natively attend (see Mal. i. 6). (2) When we make an ill use of them, either to encourage ourselves in sin by them, or to drive us away from Him by terror, or to any other use dishonourable to God, and contrary to the intent of the revelation of them to us. 2. With respect to His attributes, God's name is abused—(1) By the working of unbelief against them, doubting of, questioning, and denying them. (2) By the aversion of the heart unto them, and its rising against them (Rom. viii. 7). (3) By using them to wrong ends and purposes. Thus the mercy of God is abused to encouragement in sin; His patience to continuance in it; His justice to desperation, &c. (Eccles. viii. 11; Rom. ii. 4, 5). 3. With respect to His ordinances. The name of God is abused in ordinances when we do not go about them after the right manner, &c. 4. With respect to His Word, men are guilty of profaning the name of God—(1) By misimproving and misapplying the Word of God, as the Pharisees did (Matt. v. ; Ezek. xiii. 19). (2) Jesting upon it (Jer. xxiii. 33). (3) Using it to the maintenance of erroneous principles, unprofitable questions, and vain janglings (2 Tim. ii. 14, 15). 5. With respect to His works, men are guilty of profaning the name of God, when they use the works and creatures of God to sinful lusts and practices. 6. Men profane the name of God, in respect of religion, and the profession of it. (1) By maligning, scorning, and reviling religion, and the profession of it. (2) By a hypocritical profession. (3) By a scandalous walk. III. THE REASON ANNEXED. This is, that however the breakers of this commandment may escape punishment from men, yet the Lord our God will not suffer them to escape His righteous judgment. 1. Whence it is that men think so lightly of the profaning of the name of God, so that in effect they hold themselves guiltless. (1) It proceeds from that wicked and malicious spirit the devil (James iii. 6). (2) It springs from the low and mean thoughts they have of God and His dreadful name (Psa. xxxvi. 1, 2). (3) There are many profanations of the name of God, that untender men will not allow to be such. They are not and will not be convinced of a fault in them, as in obsecrations, appeals to God, adjurations, &c. But a due sense of the majesty of that name would clear people's minds in these things (Matt. v. 37). (4) There are many profanations of that name which men do not at all observe, as profaning that holy name in duties by formality, and want of faith and fervency. (5) It proceeds from the passion of anger or malice. (6) Custom in taking the name of God in vain takes away the sense of it. (7) Swearing proceeds from unwatchfulness. (8) In some it proceeds from vanity and hellish bravery. 2. Whence it is that profaners of the name of God escape punishment from men. (1) Little zeal for God's honour. (2) Those who ought to put in operation the laws against swearing are themselves often guilty of that sin. 3. I proceed to show how God will not let men escape with it; that He will by no means hold them guiltless. Consider that the profaning of the name of God is a sin—(1) That brings wrath upon a land (Hos. iv. 1, 2; Jer. v. 7, 9). (2) It brings wrath upon families (Zech. v. 3, 4). (3) It brings a curse upon particular persons. 4. What is the great evil of this sin, that it is so severely punished? (1) It is a sin that is directly against God, His glorious greatness and infinite majesty. (2) It is a direct violation of the law of God, " Swear not at all "; " Thou shalt not take the name of the Lord thy God in vain." Have you no respect to the authority of God? (3) It is not only a violation of the law of God, but a breach of men's laws. (4) It is a sin that has a peculiar contempt of God in it, striking most directly against His honour (Psa. cxxxix. 20). (5) It is most directly contrary to the great end of all Divine revelation. The first petition in the Lord's Prayer is, " Hallowed be Thy name." (6) It has a particular malignity in it, and in a most special manner proceeds from the devil, as it has less to carry us to it than ordinary sins have. What profit or pleasure can be derived from it? (7) Common swearers and cursers will be found to be men either of consciences already seared, or next door to it. I shall conclude all with a very short word of improvement. 1. How can these lands escape a stroke that have so much of this guilt to answer for? 2. I warn all gross profaners of the name of God to repent and flee to the blood of Christ for pardon; certifying, that if ye do not, ye shall lie under the wrath of God for ever. 3. Let us endeavour not only to reform ourselves, but contribute to the reformation of others in this point. (*T. Boston. D.D.*) *The Third Commandment:*—I. WHAT IS MEANT BY THE NAME OF GOD? II. HOW IS GOD'S NAME TAKEN IN VAIN? 1. We take God's name in vain when we use it lightly or without thinking. 2. It is taking this name in vain when we use it falsely, or speak what is not true in connection with it. 3. But we break this commandment also when we use God's name profanely. III. WHY SHOULD WE NOT TAKE THIS NAME IN VAIN? 1. Because it is useless. 2. Because it is cowardly. 3. Because it is vulgar. 4. Because it is wicked. 5. Because it is dangerous. (*R. Newton, D.D.*) *The guilt of profaneness:*—1. God has forbidden all profane language, in a manner the most solemn, and best adapted to make the deepest impression on the hearts and consciences of men. 2. Taking the name of God in vain is destructive of all religion. A profane person cannot love, nor fear, nor obey, nor trust in God. 3. The profanation of God's name tends to weaken and destroy the force and obligation of every civil government. The profanation of God's name directly tends to bring religion and oaths into contempt; and when these are brought into contempt, how can civil government be administered to preserve the property, liberty, or lives of the subjects? 4. Profane swearing is the most unnatural sin in this wicked world. It does not originate from any natural propensity, instinct, or appetite in the human mind, but is contrary to every dictate of reason and conscience. No one ever heard profane language for the first time without being shocked. No child ever uses it until he has learned it from others. 5. To use profane language is below the dignity of any man. It requires no superior knowledge, learning, or intellectual talents to take the name of God in vain, or to rise to the highest attainments in the art of swearing. 6. Profane swearing is a vice which never lives alone. Who ever knew a profane swearer that was free from every other vice? It is true, a profane swearer may not be a liar, a thief, or a drunkard; but it is the nature and tendency of his profaneness to lead him into these and all other vices. For it takes off the most powerful restraints that can be laid upon the human mind. 7. Profane swearing is a land-defiling iniquity. It is a moral infection, a spreading leprosy, and more infectious than any natural disease. It is a sin which can be more easily and oftener repeated than any other sin. The profane man can utter his oaths and imprecations every hour in the day, and every day in the week, wherever he is, and wherever he goes, as long as he lives. 8. Profane swearing is a sin, which exhibits infallible evidence, that those who are guilty of it are pursuing the broad road which leads to future and endless ruin. (*N. Emmons, D.D.*) *Taking God's name in vain :*—There is a three-fold swearing forbidden. 1. Vain swearing ; when men in their ordinary discourse let fly oaths. 2. Vile swearing ; horrid, prodigious oaths not to be named. 3. Forswearing ; this is a heaven-daring sin : "Ye shall not swear by My name falsely, neither shalt thou profane the name of thy God." Perjury is a calling God to witness to a lie. In righteousness, therefore, it must not be an unlawful oath. In judgment, therefore, it must not be a rash oath. In truth, therefore, it must not be a false oath. 4. We take God's name in vain by rash and unlawful vows. (*T. Watson.*) *The law of reverence :*—What God approves is not the parade of homage for the letter, but the inward homage of the soul for what the name represents. I. In relation to public duty. 1. Perjury. Worthily to take an oath being one of the loftiest of human actions, it follows that to take it unworthily is one of the most infamous of crimes. The perjurer professes to believe in God. His pretence is that he confides in the presence, truth, majesty, justice of God. Yet he dons this fair cloak of piety that he may get a lie believed ! It is a dastardly attempt to make the righteous God his partner in wronging the innocent, by leading a jury to an unjust verdict, and a judge to an unrighteous sentence. 2. Blasphemy : to impute evil to God ; to scoff at the holiness and power of God ; to assume the prerogatives of God. II. In relation to private speech. 1. Profane swearing. Leave expletives to those who have more words than ideas, and more tongue than brains. Be sure that reverence is the saving salt of society, and the very soul of virtue. 2. Flippant talk of sacred things. III. In relation to Divine worship. 1. They who are in the pulpit are there on purpose to lift up the name of God like a standard. Let them beware that they do not, through utterance of false doctrine, lift it for a lie ! Let them beware of turning their piety into a mercantile profession, or using it for unworthy ends ! Let them beware of preaching Christ out of strife, and of the opposite vice of perfunctory utterance ; or unawares they may lift up the name of God for a thing of nought ! 2. They who are in the pew need the warning also. We want reverence in the house of prayer—reverence in attitude, reverence in demeanour, reverence in worship. (*W. J. Woods, B.A.*) *On oaths :*—1. For the matter of an oath, assertory oaths must be of things that are—(1) True. (2) Weighty. (3) They must be such to our knowledge. Again, promissory oaths must be things just and lawful, possible, profitable, and in our power, and which to our knowledge are such. 2. The form must be, By the true God, it being a peculiar part of His worship. 3. Its rise must be edification, that is, God's glory, our own vindication, or our neighbour's good, or the call of a magistrate putting us to it. 4. As to the expressions in which it is conceived, or the thing sworn, it is required that it sought not only truth to, and in the man's meaning that sweareth, but that the expressions be plain and intelligible to his meaning and understanding to whom the oath is given ; otherwise it deludeth, but doth not clear. 5. As to the right manner of swearing, these things ought to be noticed—(1) That it be in judgment, that we understand the thing we swear, and the nature of our oath, and Him we swear by (Jer. iv. 2). (2) Fear and reverence in going about it, as being in an especial way in God's own sight. (3) Singleness in the end, that it be not to deceive any, but to express the truth only and faithfully, called righteousness (Jer. iv. 2). (*J. Durham.*) *The Third Commandment :*—"For the Lord," &c. 1. This implies that the sin under consideration may be lightly thought of, and rarely punished, among men. 2. It is an aggravation of this sin, that there seems to be very little temptation to the commission of it. 3. In the next place, it is a sin most pernicious to those who indulge it, and to those with whom they are connected. 4. In conclusion, I observe that God notices, records, and will certainly, in this world or the next, avenge the insults done to His majesty by a violation of this command. (*G. Clayton.*) *Rules to avoid profanity :*—1. Beware of the first rudiments and beginnings of oaths, if thou wouldst not learn them. 2. Subdue, as much as you can, all inordinate passion and anger. 3. Labour to possess thy heart and over-awe it with the most serious considerations and apprehensions of the greatness and majesty of God. (*Bp. E. Hopkins.*) *A proper use to be made of the gift of speech :*—The Third Commandment shows man at the head of the material creation with the crowning glory of intelligent speech, and, as a social being, possessing the power of speech as the highest instrument of his social nature. God reveals Himself to him by word, by name, as to a speaking being, making language a bond of union between Him and man. God commands him to use this great gift in His worship, in honouring Him. 1. The tongue is the glory of man, and the glory of the tongue is to voice the praises of God. All nature praises God as it obeys His laws. Man stands at the head of creation to take up its many notes of praise and give them intelligent utterance. He stands thus not as a single individual, a great High Priest, but as a race whose myriad voices are to join and mingle in a vast chorus of intelligent and harmonious praise. We are to speak of Him, and to Him, with adoration. He is our Creator, Preserver, Governor, and Judge. We are to speak of Him, and to Him, with love and praise. Our lips should quiver with emotion when we speak of Him who is our Father and our Saviour. We are to speak to Him in His worship, and of Him to each other, only in such a way as shall promote His worship in our own hearts and in the hearts of others. 2. The command is in the prohibitory form. Man has broken this law, and is prone to break it. His voice is silent often when it should be praising God. A man uses the name of God as an exclamation of surprise at some trivial thing or assertion of another, or to sustain some unimportant statement of his own. Sometimes a story is dull, and the story-teller seasons it with a few oaths ; or some joke is without point, and so a curse is used to awaken a laugh. Man calls God to make sport for him. A man has become accustomed to exaggerate or to speak falsely, and, conscious that others hesitate to believe him, he continually calls upon the truth-loving God to witness to his lies. Sometimes he becomes heated in argument, or angry under contradiction, or in a quarrel, and he calls upon God to curse him if he is not right, or in his anger he calls upon God to curse the one who irritates him. Sometimes he so loses control of himself that curses pour out of his lips as dense smoke out of a chimney. (*F. S. Schenck.*)   *No excuse for swearing :*—The swearer tries to excuse himself. "I did not mean it. I was only in fun." There are some things not the proper subjects of fun. Surely a man ought not to make fun of God, or of invoking the wrath of God upon himself or others. But the swearer says: "It is a relief for me to swear. It cools off my heated spirits." Often it is the reverse, adding fuel to the flame, not only to himself, but to others, especially those he curses. But if it is a relief, what is it a relief of ? It is a relief to the storm-cloud to throw out its lightnings, because it is over-charged with electricity. So it is a relief for you to throw out your cursing because you are over-charged with cursing. Your heart is so full of hatred that when stirred in anger it overflows in curses. You had far better bring such a heart to God with a strong cry for mercy. Again the swearer says : "I know it is wrong, but it is a habit I have fallen into to such an extent that I often swear without knowing it." Do you not see that habit does not excuse but rather aggravates the offence ? No one can become wicked at once. Your habit only shows how often you have sinned, how far you have gone down in this kind of wickedness. Again the swearer says : "I may as well say it as think it." You should not think an oath or curse. But it is worse to speak it. The letter of the law forbids the word, and so checks the evil in the heart, and at any rate prevents its injuring others. You gain inward control by outward control. Come toward the spirit of the law, checking the thought by obeying the letter. You keep yourself also from being a curse. The swearer is a moral blight in a community, his oath-speaking is a spreading infection, he is himself a curse to others. (*Ibid.*) *Speaking of God :*—The positive side, underlying the negative, is the requirement that our speech of God shall fit our thought of God, and our thought of Him shall fit His name ; that our words shall mirror our affection, and our affection be a true reflection of His beauty and sweetness ; that cleansed lips shall reverently utter the name above every name, which, after all speech, must remain unspoken ; and that we shall feel it to be not the least wonderful or merciful of His condescensions, that He is "extolled with our tongues." (*A. Maclaren, D.D.*)   *God not to be trifled with :*—It is enough to make the blood curdle, to think of the name of God bandied about as a bauble and plaything of fools. This offence cannot go unpunished. If there be a God, He must vindicate His own majesty and glory. It is the very spirit and essence of all evil, the very core of iniquity. If you could see it as it is, in the naked enormity of its guilt, you would flee from it as from the very pestilence of death. You may sport with the whirlwind and trifle with the storm, you may lay your hand upon the lion's mane and play with the leopard's spots, you may go to the very crater of a burning volcano, and laugh at the lava which it belches out in thunder ; you may trifle with any and everything ; but trifle not with God. Let there be one holy thing upon which you dare not lay a profane hand, and let that be the name of God. (*J. H. Thornwell, D.D.*)   *Reverence :*—To swear by his gods was the most common usage of the heathen ; and it grew out of a worship that of necessity debased the heart of moral reverence. Unbelief comes oftener from irreverent association than intellectual doubt. The sneer of a Voltaire has killed more than all his arguments; for, in Paley's keen words, "who can refute a sneer?" The youth who grows in the midst of profane minds imbibes a scorn of truth before he has searched a single doctrine, as the breath of an infected garment may engender disease. In this light you perceive how this old commandment covers the whole ground of our Christian conduct. So shall we build our piety, as Israel built the Temple; without, the costliest work that faith could rear; the walls overlaid with gold, each door carved with cherubim and palms and open flowers: each pillar with its chapiters and wreaths; its vessels, its lamps, its censers of the beaten gold of Ophir; a house of God, finished throughout all the parts thereof; but within, the Holy of Holies, where the unseen God dwells alone behind the veil of the heart! (*E. A. Washburn, D.D.*) *Frivolous use of Scripture :*—Nothing is more easy than to create a laugh by a grotesque association of some frivolity with the grave and solemn words of Holy Scripture. But surely this is profanity of the worst kind. By this Book the religious life of men is quickened and sustained. It contains the highest revelations of Himself which God has made to man. It directly addresses the conscience and the heart, and all the noblest faculties of our nature, exalting our idea of duty, consoling us in sorrow, redeeming us from sin and despair, and inspiring us with the hope of immortal blessedness and glory. Listening to its words, millions have heard the very voice of God. It is associated with the sanctity of many generations of saints. Such a book cannot be a fit material for the manufacture of jests. For my own part, though I do not accept Dr. Johnson's well-known saying, that " a man who would make a pun would pick a pocket," I should be disposed to say that a man who deliberately and consciously uses the words of Christ, of apostles, and of prophets, for mere purposes of merriment, might have chalked a caricature on the wall of the Holy of Holies, or scrawled a witticism on the sepulchre in Joseph's garden. (*R. W. Dale, D.D.*) *Irreverence in prayer :*—An aged minister told me, says a correspondent of the *Morning Star*, that when he was a young man, he had, on a certain occasion, been praying in a family, and in his prayer he had made a very frequent and energetic use of the terms " Good God," and " God Almighty." At the close of his prayer, a little child, about four years of age, came to his mother and said, " Mother, I don't like to hear that minister pray." " Why ? " inquired the mother. " Because," replied the child, " he swears so when he prays." This reproof from the child broke the minister of swearing when he prayed. Prayer is *petition*, and no one would use the name of a ruler to whom he was making a petition in as harsh a manner as many use the name of the great God. *Profanity known to God :*—A coachman, pointing to one of his horses, said to a traveller, " That horse, sir, knows when I swear at him." " Yes," replied the traveller; "and so does your Maker." *Swearer rebuked :*—Mr. Meikle, a gentleman of eminent piety, was a surgeon at Carnwath, in Scotland. He was once called to attend a gentleman who had been stung in the face by a wasp or bee, and found him very impatient, and swearing, on account of his pain, in great wrath. " Oh, doctor," said he, " I am in great torment; can you any way help ? " " Do not fear," replied Mr. M., " all will be over in a little while." Still, however, the gentleman continued to swear, and at length his attendant determined to reprove him. " I see nothing the matter," said he, " only it might have been in a better place." " Where might it have been ? " asked the sufferer. " Why, on the tip of your tongue." *Payment for swearing :*—" What does Satan pay you for swearing ? " asked one gentleman of another. " He don't pay me anything," was the reply. " Well you work cheap—to lay aside the character of a gentleman ; to inflict so much pain on your friends and civil people; to suffer; and, lastly, to risk your own precious soul, and for nothing—you certainly do work cheap, very cheap indeed." *Satanic swearing :*—A thoughtless, conceited young man was boasting of the number of languages he knew. In French he was a complete Parisian ; Spanish and Portuguese were as familiar to him as his old gloves. In Italy he had passed for a native. Now and then he popped out an oath, swearing that he thought he knew almost all languages. An elderly man, who had listened attentively to his address, suddenly stopped him by asking him if he were at all acquainted with " the language of Canaan." (*J. Cope.*) *Swearing reproved :*—A good old man was once in company with a gentleman, who occasionally introduced into conversation the words " devil, deuce," &c., and who at last took the name of God in vain. " Stop, sir," said the old man, " I said nothing while you only used freedoms with the name of your own master, but I insist upon it that you shall use no freedoms with the name of mine." *A wise prohibition :*—It is interesting to know that when St. Paul's Cathedral was in building, Sir Christopher Wren, the architect, caused a printed notice to be affixed to the scaffolding, threatening with instant dismissal any workman guilty of swearing within those sacred precincts. *Profanity subjects the soul to Satan:*—In ancient feudal times, when a man paid a small " peppercorn rent " to the landlord, it was in token of submission. It was no onerous burden. But when the " landholder " fell to fighting with some neighbouring chief or baron, or when he was summoned by the king to join the royal army into France, the " peppercorn submission " brought its corresponding penalty and danger. The payee was bound to follow in the baron's train, to make any sacrifices required by the landholder, and encounter any dangers, even death, in his service. Such are " profane expressions." They are tokens of submission to Satan, and the prince of darkness does not scruple to make the utterers testify their allegiance whenever it suits him. Oaths are light things. Blasphemies are rents too readily paid to the " prince of this world " ; but they bring in their train heavy responsibilities from which there is no escape, except by sincere repentance. *Profanity:*—The perniciousness of profanity is its vulgarizing names that should never be uttered save with reverence and awe. The old monks, in their cloistered work on sacred manuscripts, wiped the pen and breathed an invocation before writing the name of the Most High. A great deal of the religious apathy of our day is the natural recoil of the heart from language about Deity and sacred things which shocks the sensibilities and makes piety seem akin to blasphemy. *Reverence for God's name:*—That great and good man, the Hon. Robert Boyle, a nobleman, a statesman, and an author, during his lifetime, before he ever said the name of God, always made a hush, a pause! *A signal light:*—I once knew a sweet little girl called Mary. Her papa was the captain of a big ship, and sometimes she went with him to sea, and it was on one of these trips that the incident, of which I am going to tell you, happened. One day she sat on a coil of rope, watching old Jim clean the signal lamps. " What are you doing? " she asked. " I am trimming the signal lamps, miss," said old Jim. " What are they for ? " asked Mary. " To keep other ships from running into us, miss ; if we do not hang out our lights, we might be wrecked." Mary watched him for some time, and then she ran away and seemed to forget all about the signal lights; but she did not, as was afterwards shown. The next day she came to watch old Jim trim the lamps, and after he had seated her on the coil of rope, he turned to do his work. Just then the wind carried away one of his cloths, and old Jim began to swear awfully. Mary slipped from her place and ran into the cabin; but she soon came back, and put a folded paper into his hand. Old Jim opened it, and there, printed in large letters—for Mary was too young to write—were these words : " Thou shalt not take the name of the Lord thy God in vain, for the Lord will not hold him guiltless that taketh His name in vain." The old man looked into her face, and asked : " What is this, Miss Mary ? " " It is a signal light, please. I saw that a bad ship was running against you because you did not have your signal lights hung out, so I thought you had forgotten it," said Mary. Old Jim bowed his head and wept like a little child. At last he said : " You are right, missy. I had forgotten it. My mother taught me that very commandment when I was no bigger than you ; and for the future I will hang out my signal lights, for I might be quite wrecked by that bad ship, as you call these oaths." Old Jim has a large Bible now, which Mary gave him, and on the cover he has painted : " Signal lights for souls bound for heaven." (*Great Thoughts.*) *Clothed with cursing:*—I remember, some time since, hearing of a rich man who had a large plantation. He was the most terribly profane man that had ever been known in the neighbourhood. He could hardly speak a word on any subject without mingling it with oaths. It was perfectly shocking to hear him speak. At length he was seized with a stroke of something like paralysis. This left him in good health, only he had lost the use of his limbs. And the remarkable thing about it was, that the power of speech was taken away from him, except that he could still swear. Profane words were all that he could utter. He used to be carried about his plantation by his servants in a sort of hand-carriage, and the only words that ever fell from his lips were dreadful oaths and curses. How awful this must have been ! What a terrible illustration it affords of that passage of Scripture in which God says that because the wicked " love cursing it shall come into their bones like oil, and they shall clothe themselves with cursing like a garment ! " (Psa. cix. 17–19) Surely this man was so clothed. A dreadful garment it must have been to wear ! *A just reproof:*—As the Rev. Dr. Gifford was one day showing the British Museum to some strangers, he was much shocked by the profane language of a young gentleman belonging to the party. Taking down an ancient copy of the Septuagint, he showed it to the youth, who, on seeing it, exclaimed, "Oh! I can read this." "Then," said the doctor, "read that passage," pointing to the Third Commandment.

Vers. 8-11. **Remember the Sabbath Day.**—*The Fourth Commandment :*—I. The first word of the Fourth Commandment reminds us that THE SABBATH DAY WAS ALREADY ESTABLISHED among the Israelites when the law was delivered on Sinai. That law created nothing. It preserved and enforced what God had already taught His people to observe by another method than that of formal decrees. II. IN THIS COMMANDMENT WORK IS ENJOINED, JUST AS MUCH AS REST IS ENJOINED. Man's sin has turned work into a curse. God has redeemed and restored work into a blessing by uniting it again to the rest with which, in His Divine original order, it was associated. III. GOD RESTS; THEREFORE HE WOULD HAVE MAN REST. God works; therefore He would have man work. Man cannot rest truly unless he remembers his relation to God, who rests. IV. It is not wonderful that the Jews after the Captivity, as they had been schooled by a long DISCIPLINE INTO AN UNDERSTANDING OF THE MEANING OF THE SECOND COMMANDMENT, SO HAD LEARNT ALSO TO APPRECIATE IN SOME DEGREE THE WORTH OF THE FOURTH. Nehemiah speaks frequently and with great emphasis of the Sabbath as a gift of God which their fathers had lightly esteemed, and which the new generation was bound most fondly to cherish. His words and acts were abused by the Jews who lived between his age and that of our Lord's nativity, and when Christ came, the Sabbath itself, all its human graciousness, all its Divine reasonableness, were becoming each day more obscured. V. JESUS, AS THE MEDIATOR, DECLARED HIMSELF TO BE THE LORD OF THE SABBATH, AND PROVED HIMSELF TO BE SO BY TURNING WHAT THE JEWS MADE A CURSE INTO A BLESSING. He asserted the true glory of the Sabbath Day in asserting the mystery of His own relation to God and to His creatures. (*F. D. Maurice, M.A.*)   *The Jewish Sabbath :*—1. The Jewish Sabbath was founded on a definite Divine command. 2. The particular day which was to be kept as a Sabbath was authoritatively determined. 3. The purpose of the day was expressly defined. 4. The manner in which the Sabbath was to be kept was very distinctly stated. 5. The sanction which defended the law of the Sabbath was most severe. The only similarity between the Lord's Day and the Jewish Sabbath is that both recur once a week, and that both are religious festivals. To the idea of the Jewish Sabbath rest was essential, worship was an accident; to the idea of the Christian Sunday worship is essential, rest an accident. The observance of Sunday as a religious institution is a question of privilege, not of duty. (*R. W. Dale, D.D.*)   *The Sabbath Day :*—I. THE DESIGN OF THE SABBATH. 1. A day of rest from physical toil. 2. A day of holy employment. "Keep it holy." (See also Deut. v. 12, Isa. lviii. 13, 14). It is to be a day of rest, but not a day of idleness. II. WHAT IS THE PRACTICAL RELIGIOUS VALUE OF THE SABBATH? 1. It is a perpetual reminder of spiritual things. 2. It is a great conservative of good, and a powerful barrier against evil. III. THE DUTY AND PRIVILEGE OF KEEPING THIS DAY. 1. It is a duty we owe to God. He made the Sabbath. He commands us to keep it. 2. It is a duty we owe to ourselves. As a day of rest it is essential to the highest condition of physical health. As a day of holy meditation and worship, it is essential to our spiritual education and growth. 3. It is a duty we owe to our fellow-men. You cannot violate the Sabbath without influencing your brother to do the same. (*George Brooks.*)   *The Fourth Commandment :*—This Commandment holds a remarkable position in the Decalogue. It lies between those which touch our duty to God and those which touch our duty to man. It belongs to both branches of the Decalogue. Its position tells us that a breach of the Sabbath is a direct insult to God, and is also a direct injury to man, weakening the power of a day which is eminently a blessing to the human race. This remarkable position of the Sabbath Commandment is proof incontrovertible of its binding character for all men in all time. There are two expressions in the command itself which testify to this universality of application. 1. "Remember the Sabbath Day." It is no new institution which you are now to learn about for the first, but it is an old observance, not Israelitish, but human, Noachic, and Adamic, which you, God's Israel, are to remember, that you may sustain it in its purity, just as you are to sustain a true and spiritual worship as against idolatry. 2. The other expression which proves the universality of its application (in addition to its very position in the Decalogue) is the reason given for the Divine order— "because in six days Jehovah made heaven and earth, the sea and all that in them is, and rested the seventh day; wherefore Jehovah blessed the Sabbath Day and hallowed it." The reason began at the creation, and therefore the observance began at the creation. I. WHAT IS THE IDEA OF THE SABBATH? It had its origin in God's resting on that day. II. WHAT IS ITS PROPER OBSERVANCE? God has given it His own holy name—" The Sabbath of the Lord thy God," and the Holy Spirit calls it " the Lord's Day," in the New Testament. This fact shows us that its rightful observance must have regard to our right relation to God. The soul must be turned Godward. (H. Crosby, D.D.) The Sabbath cheerful and holy :—Let us alway make the Sabbath a cheerful day, as Phariseeism does not, and let us always make it a holy day, as worldliness does not. (Ibid.) Sunday and suicide :—There is no one thing that kills, exhausts, or sends to the lunatic asylum more of the active and strong men of this country (United States) than the breach of the Fourth Commandment. 1. " He kept no Sunday." You may safely write that epitaph over hundreds of graves that will be dug this year for ambitious, prosperous, influential men, cut off in the midst of the race of life. There are suicides in scores where no apparent cause exists for what the newspapers call " the rash act." The man was doing well; his business was prospering; his family relations were pleasant and affectionate. 2. No law of God is arbitrary. It is for man's good that God has established all His statutes. Clear as that truth is about them all, it is especially clear about the day of rest. 3. As a matter of fact, there is no rest, no relaxation, so utter as that offered by a well-kept Sunday. There is perfect rest and quiet for the body, and, to the worker with his hands, that may be the main point. But there is far more than this. The mind is called away from all its cares and all its common vulgar interests. The man is called to rise out of the changing into the unchanging, out of the temporary into the eternal, out of the low into the infinitely lofty, out of the strife into the deep calm of the eternal peace. 4. It is the neglect of this provision of God that is the root-cause of the deaths and suicides from over-work, which shock us almost daily in the current items of news. 5. We are not placing this thing on the highest motive, because the highest motive is powerless to touch the transgressors. We only say the transgression does not pay. And by working on Sunday we do not mean only the formal going to the office or counting-room. We mean the carrying a man's business about with him on that day; the taking it home and poisoning the fireside with it; the taking it to church and poisoning the church with it. (Bp. H. M. Thompson.) The manner of keeping the Sabbath :—I. LET US FIRST TAKE THE NEGATIVE VIEW. 1. We are forbidden to do any work upon the Sabbath. 2. We are forbidden to make the Sabbath a day of pleasure (Isa. lviii. 13, 14). 3. The Sabbath is not to be a day of sloth. II. NOTICE THE POSITIVE DUTIES IMPLIED IN KEEPING THE SABBATH HOLY. 1. Portions of the Sabbath should be devoted to public religious worship. 2. Portions of the Sabbath are due to special private devotion. 3. Portions of the Sabbath should be devoted to religious reading. 4. A portion of the Sabbath is very properly adjudged to Sunday-school work. 5. What remains of the Sabbath, deducting the time for necessary temporal cares, should be devoted to family religion. (H. Winslow.) The Fourth Commandment :—I. DUTIES ENJOINED. 1. The duty of work. This is man's normal condition. (1) For the soil's sake. Nature's capacities are latent as well as vast, and need the quickening, unfolding, marshalling power of a tireless, and skilful labour. (2) For man's own sake. He who does not use his faculties is as though he had none. Indolence and barbarism go hand in hand. (3) For God's sake. Stewardship. 2. The duty of rest. The seventh day is to be a day of rest for the body, jaded with the toils of the week : a day of rest for the mind, jaded with the cares of the week : a day of rest for the heart, jaded with the griefs of the week. 3. The duty of worship. " Keep it holy." The Sabbath, if I may so say, is God's weekly toll on mankind, the periodical tribute which He demands in token of human fealty. II. REASON ASSIGNED. 1. Cessation of creative process. 2. The Creator's resting. Holy, blessed, festal contemplation. 3. The Creator's sanctification of the seventh day. III. CHRIST'S DOCTRINE OF THE SABBATH (see Mark ii. 23–28.) 1. Man himself is the basis of the Sabbath. (1) He needs it—for his secular nature, alike bodily and mental; (2) for his religious nature. (3) What man needs, God has appointed. 2. Man is greater than the Sabbath. It is to be used as a means, not as an end. Man is more sacred than ordinances. IV. TRUE METHOD OF KEEPING THE SABBATH. It is to be kept in such a way as will unfold man heavenward the most thoroughly, totally, symmetrically. The Sabbath being made for man, he must use it religiously; for the faculty of worship is man's chief definition. But full unfolding of man's spiritual nature is possible only in the sphere of edification—that is, society building. The Sabbath summons man to conjugate life in a new mood and tense; but still in the active voice. And here the Son of Man is our teacher and blessed model. No one truly keeps the Sabbath unless he keeps it as the Divine Man kept it: and He went about doing good, and healing all that were oppressed of the devil. Indeed, I cannot conceive how a young man can unfold himself more thoroughly or symmetrically than by devoting himself vigorously to study during the week, and then setting apart Sunday as a day of restful worship, first praising God in His sanctuary, and then praising Him in works of mercy, visiting the sick, comforting the sorrowful, teaching the ignorant, reclaiming the outcast. V. CHANGE OF DAY. Saturday was the Sabbath of nature, Sunday is the Sabbath of grace; Saturday the Sabbath of a rejected, executed, entombed Jesus, Sunday the Sabbath of a risen, exalted, triumphant Christ; Saturday Creator's day, Sunday Redeemer's day. VI. Lastly: JESUS CHRIST HIMSELF IS OUR SABBATH, ALIKE ITS ORIGIN, ITS MEANING, AND ITS END. In fact, the final cause of the Sabbath is to sabbatize each day and make all life sacramental. And Jesus Christ being our true Sabbath, Jesus Christ is also our true rest, even the spirit's everlasting Eden. (*G. D. Boardman.*) *The Sabbath:*—I. ITS PERPETUAL OBLIGATION. 1. Its early Divine institution. 2. The uninterrupted observance of this day. 3. Though the day be changed under the Christian dispensation, the obligation of it remains unaltered. 4. God has eminently honoured and signally blessed this day in every age of time. " Therefore the Lord *blessed* the Sabbath day, and hallowed it." II. THE MANNER OF ITS OBSERVANCE. 1. This requires, first, that we should diligently prepare for its approach. 2. We must carefully watch against the profanation of it. 3. There is required by this command an entire cessation from secular and worldly occupations. 4. The observation of the Sabbath requires the religious appropriation and occupation of *all* its hours. 5. We should guard against the two extremes, of excessive rigour on the one hand, and of excessive relaxation on the other hand, in our regard to this sacred institution. (*G. Clayton.*) *The Sabbath under the law of Moses:*—I. The endeavour to displace the Fourth Commandment is AN OPEN INVASION OF THE FIRST PRINCIPLES BOTH OF FAITH AND OBEDIENCE. For everything conspires to cast an importance around the Ten Commandments peculiar to themselves. As the First command fixes the object of worship, and the Second the means, and the Third the reverential manner, so the Fourth determines the time. II. But we proceed to show, that even when the CEREMONIAL USAGES WERE IN THEIR GREATEST VIGOUR, THE SABBATH APPEARED HIGH AND DISTINCT ABOVE THEM. For first, after the record of the promulgation of the Decalogue, three chapters of judicial statutes follow ; but in the midst of these, the people are reminded of the essential importance of the Sabbath, in a manner quite distinct and peculiar. Again, after six chapters more concerning the tabernacle and its various services and sacrifices, the whole communication of the forty days' abode on the mount is concluded with a re-inculcation of the Sabbath-rest, in a manner the most solemn and affecting. III. But proceed we to show that, in the latter ages of the Jewish Church, the weekly Sabbath was insisted upon BY THE PROPHETS AS OF ESSENTIAL MORAL OBLIGATION, AND AS DESTINED TO FORM A PART OF THE GOSPEL DISPENSATION. IV. Let us then turn from these discussions to some PRACTICAL POINTS which may affect our hearts. 1. Let us learn to give to the holy day of rest that prominency in our esteem which Moses was instructed to give it in his dispensation. 2. And to this end, let us imbibe the spirit of love and delight in the worship of God, which the Psalms and Prophets display. 3. But add to these motives the awful indignation of Almighty God against the contempt of His name and His day. (*D. Wilson, M.A.*) *The pearl of days:*—The Sabbath was spoken of as the " Prince and Sovereign of Days " by a good man, long ago. It might be called the " King of days." I wish I could get you to love it, so that, instead of it being a dull, wearisome day, and as coming after Saturday, just like passing out of bright sunshine into a dark night—or out of a palace into a prison, it should be wearied for, all the week round, and received with songs of welcome when it comes. The Sabbath comes to us as a holy visitant—as a messenger of love. It bears its message in its very name—Rest. I. REASONS for observing the Sabbath. 1. We have God's command. This of itself should be enough for us. 2. We have God's example. He does Himself what He bids us do. 3. God claims it as His own day. Here is His own direction—" Not doing thine own ways, nor finding thine own pleasure, nor speaking thine own words, on My holy day." 4. God is pleased and honoured by the keeping of it. 5. It is a memorial of a completed creation work and of Christ's resurrection. In an ironmonger's shop in a country town in Scotland, the shopkeeper sat at his desk at the window. A young apprentice in the cellar below had stuck the candle which he carried in a barrel of gunpowder; the gunpowder exploded, the shop window was blown out, and the good man who sat in it was carried in the current of air to the top of the street, and there landed safely on his feet, while the apprentice was blown to pieces. It was such a wonderful deliverance that the ironmonger observed the day as a day of prayer and thanksgiving to the end of his life. Is it difficult to understand how he should have done so? And shall we not gladly commemorate our deliverance—our emancipation—the announcement that the sinner's salvation was complete, by the rising of Jesus from the dead? Shall we ever suffer ourselves to be deprived of a day that has such happy and hallowed associations? *Sabbath-breaking is a sin:*—This Commandment is more than the setting forth of a need of our nature, more than advice for our own good. It is a command of God. Breaking the Sabbath is therefore more than an error, more than a mistake. It is a sin. 1. It is a sin because it contemns the authority of God, and that is the essence of all sin. 2. It is a sin further against the love of God. As a father invites his children home to a family gathering because he loves to have them in his presence, so God would have us, His children, come to Him on the Sabbath day because He loves us. 3. It is a sin further against our higher nature. God calls us to remember our spiritual nature and to guard against degrading ourselves to mere sensual beings. (*F. S. Schenck.*) *Some blessings of the rest day :*—Here, as everywhere, in keeping God's commandments there is great reward. There is great blessedness that comes from keeping the rest day holy—to the one keeping it so, and to his fellow-men. I. CONSIDER THE BLESSINGS TO OUR FELLOW-MEN. 1. The holy or religious observance of the day bestows the rest day upon mankind. The unbelieving world may rail against God and His Church, but while it does so it is receiving from Him through the Church the rich gift of the only rest day it has from grinding labour. 2. The religious observance of the day also preaches a powerful though silent sermon to the non-church-goer, telling him he is a man, not a beast of burden; that there is a God whom he should worship; that there is an eternal life beyond this fleeting one for which he should prepare. 3. The religious observance of the day does much also to educate the conscience of a community. 4. The religious observance of the day further secures the continuance and progress of Christianity in the world. The procession of secular days bears rich material gifts to man. The Holy day spreads heaven's glories over the earth. II. The religious observance of the day brings also rich BLESSING TO THE ONE SO OBSERVING IT. 1. Communion with God, to refresh and strengthen the soul. 2. A clear view of our heavenly home, the eternal holy rest from all this world's toil and care. (*Ibid.*) *Reasons for observing the Sabbath :*—I. The first consideration which I shall suggest is, THAT IF THE SABBATH IS ABOLISHED, THE CHRISTIAN RELIGION WILL BE ABOLISHED WITH IT. The question whether this day is to be observed or desecrated, is just a question of life and death in regard to Christianity. In former generations, attempts were made to destroy the gospel by the sword and the fagot; but all such attempts were foiled. Imperial power attempted to crush it; but imperial power found its arm too weak to contend with God. Argument and sophistry were then employed; ridicule lent its aid, and contempt pointed the finger of scorn; but all was in vain. Christianity survived all these, and rose with augmented power and more resplendent beauty—and would do so to the end of time. But there is one weapon which the enemy has employed to destroy Christianity, and to drive it from the world, which has never been employed but with signal success. It is the attempt to corrupt the Christian Sabbath; to make it a day of festivity; to cause Christians to feel that its sacred and rigid obligation has ceased; to induce them on that day to mingle in the scenes of pleasure, or the exciting plans of ambition. The "Book of Sports," did more to destroy Christianity than all the ten persecutions of the Roman Emperors; and the views of the second Charles and his court about the Lord's-day, tended more to drive religion from the British nation than all the fires that were enkindled by Mary. II. The second reason why this subject demands now the special attention of Christians is, THAT IF THE SABBATH IS NOT REGARDED AS HOLY TIME, IT WILL BE REGARDED AS PASTIME ; IF NOT A DAY SACRED TO DEVOTION, IT WILL BE A DAY OF RECREATION, OF PLEASURE, OF LICENTIOUSNESS. The Sabbath is not essentially an arbitrary appointment, for it is required in the very nature of the animal economy that there should be periodical seasons of relaxation. We must have periodical rest in all the functions of our nature. Buonaparte once passed three entire days and nights without sleep, but he could no longer contend against a great law of nature, and sank to sleep on his horse. There is not a muscle in the animal economy that does not demand rest after effort, that will not have it. If it is not granted voluntarily, it will be taken. In demanding, therefore, that the animal and mental economy should be allowed a day of periodical repose, God has acted in accordance with a great law of nature. III. A third reason why this subject demands the attention of Christians in a special manner now is, THAT THERE IS A STATE OF THINGS IN THIS LAND THAT IS TENDING TO OBLITERATE THE SABBATH ALTOGETHER. The Sabbath has more enemies in this land than the Lord's Supper, than baptism, than the Bible, than all the other institutions of religion put together. At the same time it is more difficult to meet the enemy here than anywhere else—for we come in conflict not with argument, but with interest, and pleasure, and the love of indulgence, and of gain. (*A. Barnes, D.D.*) *The holy day :*—The old principles of Mosaism, I contend, are doing duty still under higher forces in the new life in Christ. They are not abolished, only transformed. The idea of circumcision has been elevated and spiritualized into membership of the body of Christ with baptism as the sign and seal; and the whole sacrificial system has been transfigured into the sacrifice of praise and thanksgiving in the Holy Communion, &c. It seems, therefore, natural to expect that so prominent and important a part of the law as the principle of devoting time to God would reappear also in a higher but yet definite form as these parts have done, that is, in fact, in the form of the Lord's Day. There are two considerations which strongly support this expectation. 1. There is in the Commandment more than a Jewish ordinance. It expresses a physical law—a law of nature—and it does so most precisely. How all this suggests the beneficence of Jehovah! 2. The second suggestive consideration is the real purpose of the Sabbath as given to the slave-nation. That purpose was beneficent, from every point of view. Do you not see that in a time when men as men had no rights, this law brought a right of rest to the most helpless and defenceless? Do you not see that it imposed a check upon the greed and rapacious selfishness which is natural to those who have their fellow-creatures under their power? Without this law where would the poor slaves have been? (*W. Senior, B.A.*) *Reason for change of day :*—Now there is a grand reason for changing of the Jewish Sabbath to the Lord's Day, because this puts us in mind of the "mystery of our redemption by Christ." Great was the work of creation, but greater was the work of redemption. As it was said, "the glory of the second temple was greater than the glory of the first temple"; so the glory of the redemption was greater than the glory of the creation. Great wisdom was seen in curiously making us, but more miraculous wisdom in saving us. Great power was seen in bringing us out of nothing, but greater power in helping us when we were worse than nothing. It cost more to redeem us than to create us. In the creation there was but "speaking a word"; in the redeeming us, there was shedding of blood. In the creation God gave us ourselves; in the redemption He gave us Himself. By creation, we have a life in Adam; by redemption, we have a life in Christ. By creation, we had a right to an earthly paradise; by redemption, we have a title to an heavenly kingdom. So that well Christ might change the seventh day of the week into the first, because this day puts us in mind of our redemption, which is a more glorious work than the creation. (*T. Watson.*) *Honouring the Sabbath :*—Dr. Edward W. Hitchcock says: "While he was minister of the American Chapel in Paris, General Grant was invited by the President of the Republic of France to occupy the grand stand at "Le Grand Prix,' the great day of the races, which comes on Sunday. Such an invitation from the chief magistrate of a great nation is an honour which is almost a command. But General Grant, replying in a note to the President, said in substance, ' It is not in accordance with the custom of my countrymen, or with the spirit of my religion, to spend Sunday in this way. I beg that you will permit me to decline the honour.' Instead of accepting the invitation, he attended public worship at the American Chapel." *Sabbath breakers reproved :*—The late Dr. Lockhart of the College Church, Glasgow, when travelling in England, was sojourning at an inn when the Sabbath came round. On entering the public-room, and about to set out for church, he found two gentlemen preparing for a game of chess. He addressed them in words to this affect, " Gentlemen, have you locked up your portmanteaus carefully?" "No! What! are there thieves in this house?" "I do not say that," replied the doctor, "only I was thinking that if the waiter comes in and finds you making free with the *Fourth* Commandment, he may think of making free with the *Eighth*." The gentlemen said there was something in that, and so laid aside their game. *Benefit of keeping the Sabbath :*—In the "Life of Frank Buckland," the eminent naturalist, who devoted himself so thoroughly to the scientific and practical study of the river and sea fisheries of Great Britain, there is the following testimony to the value of Sunday rest:—March, 1866. I am now working from 8 a.m. to 6 p.m., and then a bit in the evening—fourteen hours a day; but, thank God, it does not hurt me. I should, however, collapse if it were not for Sunday. The machinery has time to get cool, the mill-wheel ceases to patter the water, the mill-head is ponded up, and the superfluous water let off by an easy, quiet current, which leads to things above." *Result of a weekly rest :—* "Tell me," said a gentleman, addressing a clean, tidy cabman, "how is it that *some* of the men on the stand look so smart on a Monday morning—they have clean shirts, and are much happier-looking than the other men; and their horses are sprightlier, too. What is the cause of the contrast?" "Oh, they are six-day men, sir. They have green plates; their cabs don't run on Sundays; both men and horses have now a weekly rest. That's the reason why they are not jaded like the others, sir." *Sabbath kept under difficulties :—*The *Mayflower*, a name now immortal, had crossed the ocean. It had borne its hundred passengers over the vast deep, and after a perilous voyage had reached the bleak shores of New England, in the beginning of winter. The spot which was to furnish a home and a burial-place was now to be selected. The shallop was unshipped, but needed repairs, and sixteen weary days elapsed before it was ready for service. Amidst ice and snow it was then sent out, with some half-a-dozen pilgrims, to find a suitable place where to land. The spray of the sea, says the historian, froze on them, and made their clothes like coats of iron. Five days they wandered about, searching in vain for a suitable landing-place. A storm came on, the snow and the rain fell, the sea swelled, the rudder broke, the mast and the sail fell overboard. In this storm and cold, without a tent, a house, or the shelter of a rock, the Christian Sabbath approached, the day which they regarded as holy unto God, a day on which they were not to "do any work." What should be done? As the evening before the Sabbath drew on, they pushed over the surf, entered a fair sound, sheltered themselves under the lee of a rise of land, kindled a fire, and on that little island they spent the day in the solemn worship of their Maker. On the next day their feet touched the rock, now sacred as the place of the landing of the pilgrims. Nothing more strikingly marks the character of this people than this act, and I do not know that I could refer to a better illustration, even in their history, showing that theirs was the religion of principle, and that this religion made them what they were. (*A. Barnes.*) *Grief at profanation of the Sabbath :—*Truly it should be a matter of grief to us to see so much Sabbath profanation. When one of Darius' eunuchs saw Alexander setting his feet on a rich table of Darius', he fell a-weeping; Alexander asked him why he wept? He said it was to see the table which his master so highly esteemed to be now made a footstool. So we may weep to see the Sabbath, which God so highly esteems, and has so honoured and blessed, made a footstool, and trampled upon by the feet of sinners. (*T. Watson.*) *Heaven seen on the Sabbath :—*A gentleman was once directing the attention of his friend to the objects of interest visible from his observatory. "Just beyond the river," he said, "is a city which on the Sabbath Day can be distinctly seen." "Why," asked the friend, "can it be better seen on the Sabbath than on other days?" "Because," was the reply, "on other days the smoke from its chimneys settles about the city and hides it from sight; but on the Sabbath, when the factories are still and the smoke is gone, the city, with its glittering spires, is clearly seen." So on the Sabbath, when the smoke and dust of earth and its cares have settled away, through the clear transparent air can be distinctly seen the City of God and the pathway leading thither. (*P. B. Davis.*) *Bible law recognized :—*A motion was once made in the House of Commons for raising and embodying the militia, and, for the purpose of saving time, to exercise them on the Sabbath. When the resolution was about to pass, an old gentleman stood up, and said, "Mr. Speaker, I have one objection to make to this; I believe in an old book called the Bible." The members looked at one another, and the motion was dropped. *The Sabbath appointed by God :—*The Governor Turnusrupis once asked Rabbi Akiba, "What is this day you call the Sabbath, more than any other day?" The Rabbi responded, "What art thou, more than any other person?" "I am superior to others," he replied, "because the Emperor has appointed me governor over them." Then said Akiba, "The Lord our God, who is greater than your Emperor, has appointed the Sabbath day to be holier than the other days." (*Talmud.*) *Honouring the Sabbath :—* When King George III. was repairing his palace at Kew, one of the workmen, a pious man, was particularly noticed by His Majesty, and he often held conversations with him upon serious subjects. One Monday morning the king went as usual to watch the progress of the work, and not seeing this man in his customary place, inquired the reason of his absence. He was answered evasively, and for some time the other workmen avoided telling His Majesty the truth ; at last, however, upon being more strictly interrogated, they acknowledged that, not having been able to complete a particular job on the Saturday night, they had returned to finish it on the following morning. This man alone had refused to comply, because he considered it a violation of the Christian Sabbath ; and in consequence of what they called his obstinacy, he had been dismissed entirely from his employment. " Call him back immediately," exclaimed the good King; "the man who refused doing his ordinary work on the Lord's Day is the man for me. Let him be sent for." The man was accordingly replaced, and the King ever after showed him particular favour.

Ver. 12. **Honour thy father and thy mother.**—*The Fifth Commandment :*—I. THE RELATIONSHIP in which we stand to our parents, a relationship based upon the fact that we owe our existence to them, that we are made in their image, that for so long a time we depend on them for the actual maintenance of life, and that, as the necessary result of all this, we are completely under their authority during childhood. This relationship is naturally made the highest symbol of our relationship to God Himself. II. Honouring our parents INCLUDES RESPECT, LOVE, AND OBEDIENCE, as long as childhood and youth continue, and the gradual modification and transformation of these affections and duties into higher forms as manhood and womanhood draw on. III. The promise attached to the Commandment is A PROMISE OF PROLONGED NATIONAL STABILITY. St. Paul, slightly changing its form, makes it a promise of long life to individuals. Common experience justifies the change. IV. There is one consideration that may induce us to obey this Commandment which does not belong to the other nine: THE TIME WILL COME WHEN IT WILL BE NO LONGER POSSIBLE FOR US TO OBEY IT. (*R. W. Dale, D.D.*) *The duties of youth:*—I. CONSIDER VARIOUS WAYS IN WHICH A MAN MAY HONOUR HIS FATHER AND MOTHER. 1. By doing his best in the way of self-improvement. 2. By habits of care and frugality. 3. By keeping himself in soberness, temperance, and chastity. II. HONOUR TO PARENTS IS ONLY THE PRINCIPAL AND MOST IMPORTANT APPLICATION OF A GENERAL PRINCIPLE. The apostle bids us honour all men, and again, "In lowliness of mind let each esteem other better than themselves." III. FROM THE CONCEPTION OF LOVE DUE TO FATHER AND MOTHER WE RISE TO THE CONCEPTION OF THE LOVE DUE TO GOD. By what heavenly process shall we melt the cold, hard law which forbids idolatry, into the sweet, gentle principle of heart-worship and love? I believe that in this respect the First Commandment is much indebted to the Second, which is like unto it, "Honour thy father." And so, when God condescends to call Himself our Father, the clouds which conceal Him from our sight seem to break and vanish, and we feel that we can love and honour Him, not merely acknowledge Him, and refuse to accept others besides Him: not merely fear Him, as one too powerful to be safely set at naught; not merely philosophize about Him, and try to express His Infinite Being in some scientific formula of human words. No ; but love Him as a father ought to be loved—with all our hearts, and souls, and strength. (*Bp. Harvey Goodwin.*)   *A promise and a duty :*—I. THE PROMISE. Expanded in Deut. v. 16. The promise is of a long and prosperous life. It is so plain that it can admit of no other interpretation. The only question can be, " Is it an individual or a national life that is here meant?" But this is answered, first, by noticing that the command can only be kept by an individual person, and by a nation only as a number of individuals ; and hence, as the command is only addressed to the individual, the prolongation of the individual life must be intended. The "thy " of " thy days " must refer to the same person as the " thy " of " thy father and thy mother." It is answered, secondly, that a long national career of prosperity presupposes and implies a goodly degree of personal longevity and prosperity, and that the latter is a cause of the former, while the former could in no sense be considered a cause of the latter. II. THE NATURE OF THE DUTY ENJOINED. The word " cabbed " is very strong ; it strictly means " load with honour," and is often used in reference to the Deity. Obedience is only one of the more prominent practical forms of this honour. The honour strikes deeper than mere obedience— it touches the heart, it bespeaks the affections. It is a reverence inwoven in the very nature, connected with all the chords of being, and so coming to the surface in obedience and outward respect. We notice—1. That the command is not " Honour thy father and thy mother when they do right." Our parents, like ourselves, are frail, and may commit error. If their error absolved their children from respect, there could be no filial piety in the world. While the honour due to parents will not go to wicked or foolish lengths, it will go to all reasonable and allowable lengths. It will submit to inconvenience and loss; it will hold its private judgment of what is better in abeyance; it will even keep its own clearly superior wisdom subject to the parental prejudice. So long as conformity to the views and expressed wishes of parents does not harm any third party, a right respect for father and mother will gracefully yield and lay the self-denial on the altar of filial piety. 2. The command is not, "Honour thy father and thy mother while thou art a little child." Many act as if they had no parents after they had reached their full stature, and some use this theory even earlier. Now, if to anybody this command is not given, it is to the little child, for in his case nature and necessity teach some degree of obedience and respect to parents, and hence the command is comparatively unnecessary to these. III. Lastly I would ask if there is not NEED THAT GOD'S WILL IN THIS MATTER BE OFTEN REHEARSED IN OUR EARS. I would say not to little children, "Be obedient to your parents," but rather to parents, "Make your children obedient." It is all in your power. If you indulge your little ones in little irreverences and little disobediences because it looks "so cunning," and foolish friends urge you to the dangerous pastime, then you will have the little disobedient children grow to be big disobedient children, and they will bring down your grey hairs with sorrow to the grave. Or if, through sheer carelessness and selfish laziness, you avoid the active watchfulness and discipline that are necessary to ensure obedience, and to promote an obedient habit, you will obtain the same disastrous result. Beware, too, how, in your anxiety to have your boy a man before the time, you consent to his consequential swagger at sixteen, and furnish him with a night-key as a help to independence, in which you are destroying the bonds of dutiful humility and respectful submission with which God bound him to you to preserve. It is in this way I would apply the Fifth Commandment to young children through the parents, who are responsible before God and man. But I also make the special application of the text to children of maturer growth. Let our continued reverence for parent or parents still living, be of itself a glorious example, deeply written on the thoughts and future memories of your own children. Surround the old age which adorns and honours your household with the tribute of your assiduous care, jealous of its comfort and its dignity, and cover its defects with the mantle, not of your charity, but of your filial love and sympathy. (*H. Crosby, D.D.*) *The Fifth Commandment:*—I. THE DIVINE MANDATE. 1. It is not an arbitrary edict; but a natural principle, having its constitutional basis in the very essence of the relation which subsists between parents and children. The parent is to his child, in a certain sense, the representative and symbol of God. It is a significant fact that the Romans denoted dutifulness to the gods and dutifulness to parents by the same word, namely, *pietas.* Allegiance, or amenability to law, this is a constitutional, constituent part of manhood. And it is the parent (father and mother equally) who is the natural symbol of authority. Parentage, in simple virtue of its being parentage, is inherently imperative; it is of the very essence of parentage that it is constitutively and rightfully authoritative. Authorhood, genealogically as well as etymologically, is the sire of authority. 2. But you interrupt me with a question, " Must the child always obey his parents?" In the sphere of fundamental moral obligations, my father and I stand on an equality before God; in this sphere he has no more right to command me than I have to command him. But in the sphere of incidental, shifting duties, my father is over me, and has a right to command me. II. THE DIVINE PROMISE. Nothing is more certain, at least in a physiological way, than this: Respect for parental authority tends to longevity; filial reverence is itself an admirable hygiene. What was it that gave to Rome its long-continued tremendous power and majesty? It was the *patria potestas,* or paternal authority, before which every Roman youth unquestioningly bowed; for loyalty is the sire of royalty. Even China herself, although her civilization was long ago arrested and petrified, owes, I doubt not, her preservation through millenniums to the fealty of her children to their ancestral commandments and traditions. III. THE PARENT IS A SYMBOL OF THE STATE. What the parent is to the child, that the State in many particulars is to the citizen, only vastly augmented. In fact, no sooner is the infant born than he enters the jurisdiction of law. As soon as he is able to notice relations and reason about them, so soon does he perceive that he is under authority. One of the first lessons he learns is this: There are some things which he must do, and some things which he must not do; and these commands and prohibitions awaken the ideas of law and subordination. As he grows older, these ideas become more vivid and dominant.

And, finally, when he leaves home to take his position as a member of society, he finds that the authority which had hitherto resided in his parents has been transferred to the State. Accordingly, parental authority is the grand, divinely-appointed educator for citizenship. Loyalty to parental law prepares the way for loyalty to civic law. IV. OUR THEME IS ESPECIALLY PERTINENT TO OUR OWN TIMES. There are two tendencies in our land and age which make the discussion of the Fifth Commandment particularly appropriate. 1. And first, our age is an age of innovation. Rage and frenzy will pull down more in half an hour than prudence, deliberation, and foresight can build up in a hundred years. Therefore do I lift up my voice in behalf of reverend antiquity ; doubly reverend, first, because it is antiquity; and secondly, because, being antiquity, it is an oracle. 2. Secondly, our age is an age of anarchy or moral lawlessness. V. HUMAN PARENTAGE IS A SYMBOL OF THE DIVINE. The Creator ordained it, not so much for man's sake as for His own sake, meaning that it should serve as the ladder by which we may ascend to His own blessed fatherhood, and joyously feel His paternal sway. And this is majesty indeed. It is told of Daniel Webster that, when a party of distinguished gentlemen were dining with him at his Marshfield home, and one of his guests asked him what single thing had contributed most to his personal success, the famous statesman paused for a moment, and then, with great solemnity, replied, " I think that the most fruitful and elevating influence I have ever felt has been my impression of my obligation to God." Believe me, no man is ever so sublime as when he is consciously loyal to the King of kings ; no man is ever so supremely blessed as when he reverently sits at the feet of the Infinite Father. (*G. D. Boardman.*) *The parent and the nation* :—1. First, Jehovah is the source of all life. " In Him we have our being." But the parent is God's means by which He imparts life, the human channel through which Divine life creates. The parent is the shrine of Divine power working creatively. The parent, therefore, as the secondary author of life, is to the child a representative of God. A Divine sacredness, a reflection of the Creator, invests parents through whom life came and grew and was begotten into time. In the mysterious law of life, the link between the child and God is the parent. 2. Secondly, it is true that parental honour is here set down as a statute law of Israel, but have we yet to learn that these " Ten Words " express the profoundest principles of human life ? We may rest assured that the honour which God claims for father and mother forms the germ of man at his best and noblest state. Plato would fain have reconstructed the Athenian national life without the family life. Disraeli once said in the House of Commons, " The family is the unit of the nation." Plato came to the opposite conclusion, viz., the family life is the bane of the nation. He thought it bred selfishness, that it was detrimental to courage, that it narrowed men's interests and dulled the spirit of patriotism, which prefers country to everything. Blot out reverence for parents and life neither at the beginning nor the end is safe. What is the true wealth of a nation ? Is it not patriotic men and virtuous women ? But family life alone can produce these ; the family life which is overshadowed by a sense of God. Home obedience is the spirit which expands into the fine feeling of the sanctity of law. Parental honour develops into loyalty to the Queen and reverence for the constitution. The love of home and its dear ones grows big with the love of country and with the self-sacrificing energies of patriotism. But so it is also that the decline of home life, the loss of parental and filial feeling, is the sure precursor of national decline. Loyalty, reverence, faith—lose these, and the soul is lost out of the body politic. Its very heart and strength are gone when these are gone. But these are the fruit of home. There are three sources of danger—literary, political, and social. 1. As to the first, all atheistic theories which take away the glory from the head of the parent rob the parental tie of its highest sanctity. When life is only the result of material laws, reverence cannot rise higher than the nature of the fact. A mere flesh and blood relationship will not yield a spiritual feeling. Reverence cannot sustain itself on humanity alone, without God in the background ; no, neither reverence for man as man, nor for woman as woman. All lustre dies away, and only commonness remains, barren of the emotions which are the riches of human life. 2. Again, in the sphere of politics it has begun to look wise and liberal, and the only practical thing, to separate civil life from religion, and to draw a line of distinction between Christianity and the nation. The tendency is setting in to look to citizenship in the narrowest sense of commerce and material progress. As certain as moral feeling is the truth of manhood, so certain is it that education or legislation which forgets or ignores the heart is guilty of a fatal defect. When cleverness is divorced from the fear of God, rational selfishness takes the place of honour and faith. It is this radical bias of the heart which will confound all the hopes of mere secularists. Morals need to be sustained in the affections or they are barren precepts only; and they cannot be sustained there except by a power which is able to cope with our radical selfishness and overcome it. We have strong reasons, derived from history and human nature, for believing that Christianity alone is capable of this. The immoral or even the selfish will never think rightly. Stop wrong feeling in one direction, it will burst out in another. Out of the heart are the issues of life. The voice of prudence will never be the law of morals. It is an inference almost as certain as actual fact that the spirit of atheistic communism has had no true home, that is, no true moral training of the heart. It drifted loose from true feeling before it drifted loose from true reasoning, though the two processes were doubtless deeply and inextricably intermingled. 3. But let us turn to the enemies of home in the social sphere. I pass by the danger of conceited superficiality at home. But there is one danger to the English home which must be patent to all, vast, portentous, fearful—the public-house. It swallows up comforts, decencies, and every possibility of religiousness and good citizenship. Materially and morally it works an awful ruin. Homes being deteriorated and parents degraded, then young people abandon them as early as possible. Novelty and sensation are the order of the day. Like a fever it penetrates the very blood. To sit still, to meditate, to enjoy home is getting beyond us. The Church, too, has been compelled to enter into the competition. She must do it to fight against social temptations and moral decline. But let the Church of Christ ever keep her high purpose in view. Let her not degrade herself into a mere rival of sensational amusement. She is the mother of the nation, the ideal of the true home. Let her seek to restore it on the Divine pattern by setting up the family altar and the Word of God. So shall it be well with us, and so will our children live long on the earth. (*W. Senior, B.A.*) *Parent and child:*—The command is reflexive. It speaks to the child and says, "Honour"; but in that very word it springs back upon the parent and says, "Be honourable; because in your honourableness your child shall grow reverent." Of all things in this world the soul of a reverent child is the most beautiful and precious, and therefore of all things in this world honourable parents are the most important. One thing cannot be too strongly insisted on. Parental goodness must be genuine and unaffected, of the heart, flowing easily through the life, in order to evoke reverence. Unreality is sure to be detected by-and-by, and when children find out unreality in those who stand in the place of God—God help them! It never does to give precept instead of example. Children have strangely sensitive natures. They don't see through pretence, but after a while they do more, they feel it. Brethren, there is much talk of culture now-a-days. I venture to suggest, in the light of the requirements of this Commandment, that the finest culture of all lies within the sphere of home life, the life we seem to be in danger of losing. The finest culture would come from the endeavour to be worthy of a child's reverence, and trust, and love. What does it need in the parent to be the child's ideal? It needs the cultivation of truthfulness, and love, and unselfishness. To your own selves, to your own higher nature, you must first be true in order to be true to them. The true heaven of home can only be entered by the parents becoming as their own darling child in innocence, sweetness, and goodness. There is even something higher still. It is through true parentage that the heart of God is best understood, and best realized. He calls Himself "Father," and likens Himself to a "Mother." The names are revelations; they are profound instructions. God wants to shine down into His children's hearts through father and mother. Only two last words. 1. First, to the young unmarried. Some may be thinking of marriage. Well, marriage is of God, but mark the solemn importance with which this Commandment invests it. It is for God also. Marriage means parentage, and parentage involves all this home life, all these influences of which we have been speaking. Are you morally equal to marriage? Are you fit to be a parent when you think of all that is in this word "honour"? What sort of a mother shall you give your children? What sort of a father? 2. Secondly, a word to the married who have children. It is in the nature of things that parents love their children more than children love their parents. The world is all new, to the young, their interests fly abroad. The parents have more or less gone through that phase of life, and now concentrate their thoughts and hopes upon the children's welfare. The child turns from the parent after the illusions of life, the parent begins to live over again in the child. The child accepts all the thoughts, and love, and sacrifice as a matter of course, unable, in fact, to realize the hidden life below them. Yes, such times bring moments of almost anguish, but parents see. We are only feeling in our turn what our parents felt before over us. Love on, and knowledge of you and reverence shall surely come to your children. You shall have your reward, it may be, even here, in the protecting love which clings to your old age, and warms and beautifies it, and prolongs the joys of home to the very gates of death, and fills beyond them with visions of union and perfect bliss. But if not here, then when the green sod covers you your reward shall come in tears which melt the soul of your wilful boy back into your arms; in memories which make your wayward girl long passionately to be pressed to a mother's bosom. Then, I say, your love shall have its due reward. Only be true and faithful, and kind and upright, and father and mother shall be known at last. Be comforted, your love is never lost. (*Ibid.*) *The Fifth Commandment :*—I. Who is meant here by "father"? 1. The political father, the magistrate. These fathers are to be honoured; for, (1) Their place deserves honour. (2) God hath promoted kings, that they may promote justice. These political fathers are to be honoured: "honour the king." And this honour is to be shown by a civil respect to their persons, and a cheerful submission to their laws, so far as they agree and run parallel with God's law. 2. There is the grave ancient father who is venerable for old age, whose grey hairs are resembled to the white flowers of the almond-tree. There are fathers for seniority, on whose wrinkled brows, and in the furrows of whose cheeks is pictured the map of old age. These fathers are to be honoured: "thou shalt rise up before the hoary head, and honour the face of the old man." 3. There are spiritual fathers, as pastors and ministers. The spiritual fathers are to be honoured. (1) In respect of their office (Mal. ii. 7; 2 Cor. v. 20). (2) Ministers, these spiritual fathers, are to be "honoured for their work's sake." 4. There is the economical father, that is, the master; he is the father of the family, therefore Naaman's servants called their master, "father." And the centurion calls his servant, "son." (1) In obeying his master in things that are lawful and honest (1 Pet. ii. 18). (2) In being diligent in his service. (3) By being faithful. That servant who is not true to his master, will never be true to God or his own soul. (4) The servant is to honour his master by serving him, as with love, for willingness is more than the work, so with silence, that is, without repining, and without replying: "exhort servants to be obedient to their masters, not answering again"; Greek, "not giving cross answers." 5. The natural father, the father of the flesh. Honour thy natural father. Children are the vineyard of the parent's planting, and honour done to the parent is some of the fruit of the vineyard. II. Wherein are children to show their honour to their parents? 1. In a reverential esteem of their persons. (1) Inwardly, by fear mixed with love. (2) Outwardly, in word and gesture. 2. In a careful obedience. (1) In hearkening to their counsel. (2) In subscribing to their commands. (3) In relieving their wants. It is but paying the just debt. The young storks, by the instinct of nature, bring meat to the old storks, when by reason of age they are not able to fly. The memory of Eneas was honoured, for carrying his aged father out of Troy when it was on fire. (*T. Watson.*) *The law of subordination :*—The importance of this commandment is indicated by 1. Its positive form; 2. Its relative place; and, 3. Its accompanying promise. I. The scope of this precept embraces an universal law of subordination with corresponding relative duties. 1. A law of subordination is implied in the relation of a child to its parent. 2. This law of subordination is seen in similar relations to be the foundation of society. (1) Everywhere the older men are in authority, and the new comers must accept subjection. (2) Rank, wealth, station, genius, scholarship, and other phases of power exist around us, distinguishing certain individuals, and enriching them with definite advantages which in effect do subordinate other persons to them. (3) The king is the father of a larger household. Patriotism is the love of home upon a grander scale. 3. The law of subordination being thus the broad foundation of society, and the principle on which it is evidently constituted, this Divine order witnesses for the Divine origin of man. Society is now seen to be not a heap of unconnected sand, but a living tree, whose multitudinous branches, meeting in one stem, have their root in Him "from whom every fatherhood in heaven and on earth is named." II. Some of the more prominent applications of this law. All these include responsibility as well as authority in the superior, and therefore rights as well as duties in the subordinate. 1. There is first the typical case of parent and child. 2. Closely connected with the relation of parent and child, and even influencing it, is that mutual bond of husband and wife which affords the next great instance of the law of subordination. In her mother-hood woman is the equal, in her wifehood the subordinate of man. 3. There are manifold other relations which illustrate the law of subordination—teachers and pupils, seniors and juniors, masters and servants, monarchs and subjects, magis-trates and citizens, pastors and people. (*W. J. Woods, B.A.*) *Lessons from the position of the Fifth Commandment :*—The position of this Commandment among the others has important teachings. It is the centre, the heart of the whole law. Not only has God given us the power to love, but He has placed us in relationships which call this power into exercise and give it right direction, especially the rela-tionship of parents and children. God says here to parents: "As you love your children, so I love you. As you yearn for their responsive love, so I yearn for yours. I am your Father." God says here to children: "Love your parents, and therein learn to love Me, your Father." The position of this Commandment among the others has a further teaching of great importance. The place of division into the Two Tables of the Law is somewhat indistinct. It is in this Commandment, but whether it belongs to the First Table, or to the Second, is not quite clear. It cer-tainly treats of duties to man, and so must belong to the Second Table. But hold! May not the parents be regarded as the representatives of God? Then it belongs to the First Table. There is certainly a strong analogy in the relationships. The parents are the nearest cause to the child of its being, its continued existence and its welfare, and this through that wonderful thing God has given them, parental love, which allies them so closely to Himself. We need not try to determine what God seems purposely to have left indistinct. In the indistinctness is the lesson. We are apt to consider duties to man separately, but God joins them indissolubly with duties to Himself. The position of the Commandment in this indistinctness also shows its great importance. Considering it as the last of the First Table we see that in order that children shall become men and women worshipping God in spirit and in truth, they are to be taught and trained by honouring their parents. Considering it as the first of the Second Table, we see that in order that children shall become men and women fulfilling their duties in the various relations of life, they are to be taught and trained by honouring their parents. Both religion and morality have their foundations laid in the home life of children. (*F. S. Schenck.*) *Reasons for honouring parents :*—1. The first and greatest is because God com-mands. His command is written in our own natures and in this holy law. This reason is above all others and embraces all. 2. Such conduct gives the greatest pleasure to our parents, as the reverse conduct brings to their hearts the keenest suffering. We can never fully appreciate all the care and love father and mother have bestowed upon us in infancy and youth, in sickness and in health, and the yearning of their hearts for our love. Surely we should respond to their love—we should seek their happiness. 3. Such conduct is itself excellent. There is something within us that approves it, and condemns the reverse. 4. The Com-mandment itself contains a reason for obedience, in that it gives a promise, an assurance that in the providence of God obedience to this Commandment will result in long life and prosperity. This sets forth a general rule in the Divine government of the race, promoting stability in social welfare. The child honouring his parents learns self-control, and obedience to law, submission hearty and prompt to rightly constituted authority as a principle of action. Such a child will in all probability become a man of like character. He will obey the laws of health. Entering busi-ness he will obey the laws of success, industry, perseverance, economy, enterprise. His powers under full control, he will be also a law-abiding citizen in society. Such character tends to long life and the enjoyment of the gifts of God. A good citizen enjoys the protection of the state not only, but helps to form a condition of social well-being. The child, on the other hand, who is disobedient and disrespectful to his parents, who sets aside their authority and God's authority, is cultivating a law-breaking character. He will in all probability become a self-willed man, setting at defiance the laws of God and man. Such a life tends to the undermining of health by excesses, to the waste of property by abuse, to the running into dangers recklessly, and to the overthrow of social well-being. Such a character tends to shorten life and to forfeit the gifts of God. (*Ibid.*) *Forbearance towards erring parents :*—How is a religious son or daughter to act towards an irreligious parent? To answer that question in detail would require a long discourse. Circumstances sometimes make the duty of a child very perplexing. When a father comes home drunk three times a week, violently abuses his daughter who opens the door for him half dead with weariness and fright, curses her, sometimes strikes her, drinks half her wages and nearly all his own, what ought she to do? The principle which determines her duty is clear. The obligation to honour her father is not relaxed. You are not released from a debt because the man to whom you owe it is a drunkard or a profligate; and so irreligion, or even vice in a parent, cannot release a child from filial duty. The application of the principle to particular cases is, I acknowledge, sometimes extremely difficult. Parental cruelty occasionally becomes intolerable. For a child to remain in some houses is to suffer perpetual misery. But the noble and Christian course, as long as your strength is not utterly exhausted, is to manifest the charity which "endureth all things." If your religion makes you more sensitive to the vices which disgrace the character of your parents, it should also enable you to bear their ill-treatment with more meekness and patience. The consciousness of your own sins should make you more merciful to theirs. (*R. W. Dale, D.D.*) *Filial duty:*—Tenderness and sympathy were conspicuously displayed in the character of the late Dr. Alexander Waugh. A young man of unimpeachable character was desirous of entering upon missionary labour, and was recommended to the notice of the London Missionary Society. He had passed through the usual examination, but stated that he had one difficulty—he had an aged mother dependent upon an elder brother and himself for maintenance; in case of his brother's death, he wished to be at liberty to return home to support her. Scarcely had he made this natural request than he heard the voice of one of the directors exclaim, "If you love your mother more than the Lord Jesus, you won't do for us." The young man was abashed and confounded, and he was asked to retire while his case was considered. Upon his return, Dr. Waugh, who was in the chair, addressed him with patriarchal dignity, telling him that the committee did not feel themselves at liberty to accept his services on a condition involving uncertainty as to the term; but immediately added, "We think none the worse of you, my good lad, for your beautiful regard to your aged parent. You are following the example of Him whose gospel you wish to proclaim among the heathen, who, when He hung upon the cross in dying agonies, beholding His mother and His beloved disciple standing by, said to the one, "Behold thy son!" and to John, "Behold thy mother!" *Filial piety:*—David Livingstone is said to have learned Gaelic in order that he might be able to read the Bible to his mother in that language, which was the one she knew best. *Obligation to parents:*—The celebrated Jonathan Edwards, who had the advantage of being trained by singularly pious and judicious parents, wrote, when about twenty years of age, in his diary: "I now plainly perceive what great obligations I am under to love and honour my parents. I have great reason to believe that their counsel and education have been my making; notwithstanding in the time of it, it seemed to do me so little good." *A noble sentiment:*—A little boy hearing a party of gentlemen applauding the sentiment, "an honest man is the noblest work of God," boldly said, "No "; and being asked, "What do you think is the noblest work of God?" replied, "My mother." That boy made a good man. Who can doubt it? *Archbishop Tillotson's respect for his father:*—There are some children who are almost ashamed to own their parents, because they are poor, or in a low situation of life. We will, therefore, give an example of the contrary, as displayed by the Dean of Canterbury, afterwards Archbishop Tillotson. His father, who was a plain Yorkshireman, approached the house where his son resided, and inquired whether "John Tillotson was at home." The servant, indignant at what he thought his insolence, drove him from the door; but the Dean, who was within, hearing the voice of his father, came running out, exclaiming, in the presence of his astonished servants, "It is my beloved father!" and falling down on his knees, asked for his blessing. *Honouring a parent:*—Frederick the Great one day rang his bell several times, and nobody came. He opened the door, and found his page asleep in an arm-chair. Advancing to awake him, he perceived the corner of a note peeping out of his pocket. Curious to know what it was, he took it, and read it. It was a letter from the mother of the youth, thanking him for sending her part of his wages, to relieve her poverty. She concluded by telling him, that God would bless him for his good conduct. The king, after having read it, went softly into his room, took a purse of ducats, and slipped it, with the letter, into the pocket of the page. He returned, and rang his bell so loud, that the page awoke, and went in. "Thou hast slept well!" said the king. The page wished to excuse himself, and in his confusion put his hand by chance into his pocket, and felt the purse with astonishment. He drew it out, turned pale, and looking at the king, burst into tears, without being able to utter a word. "What is the matter?" said the king; "what hast thou?" "Ah!

Sire," replied the youth, falling on his knees, "they wish to ruin me; I do not know how this money came into my pocket." "My friend," said Frederick, "God often sends us blessings while we are asleep. Send that to thy mother, salute her from me, and say that I will take care of her and thee." *Honour thy parents :*— An amiable youth was lamenting the death of a most affectionate parent. His companions endeavoured to console him by the reflection that he had always behaved to the deceased with duty, tenderness, and respect. "So I thought," replied the youth, "whilst my parent was living; but now I recollect, with pain and sorrow, many instances of disobedience and neglect; for which, alas! it is too late to make atonement." *Pleasing parents :*—Epaminondas, the Theban, after winning a battle, said, "My chief pleasure is, that my parents will hear of my victory." *Begin right :*—If you begin to put up a house, and lay the foundation wrong, or to build a ship, and make a mistake in laying the keel, you'll have to take it all down and begin again. Oh, it is very important to begin right! It is so in everything. And it is so in trying to do our duty to our neighbour. The Fifth Commandment shows us how we must begin to do this. We must begin at home. You show me a boy or girl who is not a good son or daughter, who does not honour his own father and mother, and I will show you one who will not make a good man or woman. (*R. Newton, D.D.*) *Kindness to parents :*—There is a celebrated charity school in London, called the "Blue Coat School." It bears this name because the scholars there all wear blue coats with long skirts to them. I remember reading about one of the boys in this school, who was in the habit of saving part of his own meals, and all the bits and scraps he could gather from the table after their meals were over. He used to put them in a box near his bed, and keep them there. This led the other scholars to talk against him very much. At first they thought he was greedy, and kept them there to eat at night, when the rest were asleep. Some of them watched him, but he was never seen to eat them. Once or twice a week he used to make a bundle of the contents of the box, and go away with it. Then the boys thought that he meant to sell them and keep the money. They concluded that he was a mean, miserly fellow. They refused to let him play with them. They joked about him, and called him hard names, and persecuted him in many ways. But he bore it all patiently, and still went on, saving and carrying away all he could honestly get. At last they complained of him to their teacher. The boy was watched when he took away the next bundle. He was seen to go into an old, worn-out building, occupied by some of the poorest people in the city. There he made his way up to the fourth storey of the building, and left his bundle with a poor old couple. On inquiry it was found that these were his parents. They were honest, worthy people, whom age and poverty had reduced to such a condition of want that their chief dependence was the food thus furnished by their son. He was willing to deprive himself of food, and bear the reproach and persecution of his schoolmates, in order to do what he could for the support of his parents. When the managers of the school heard of it, they provided relief for the poor boy's parents, and gave him a silver medal for his praiseworthy conduct. *Dr. Johnson and his father :*—The great Dr. Johnson was a very learned man; he wrote a "dictionary." I know what I am going to say is true. He lived in Uttoxeter. His father was a bookseller, not in a very grand way, because he used to sell his books in the market-place. One day he asked his son Samuel (for that was the Christian name of Dr. Johnson) to come down and help him in the sale of his books in the market-place. Little Samuel was rather a sort of a dandy, a conceited fellow; and he thought it beneath his dignity to sell books in the market-place. "He demean himself to stand in the market-place to sell books, indeed, for his father! He was too great a gentleman for that!" Fifty years passed away, and Dr. Johnson had become now an old man. It haunted him; he could not forget, though more than fifty years had passed,—what he had done to his father, in refusing to sell books in the market-place. He was very sad and unhappy about it. So, one day, the doctor took off his hat, and went and stood in the same market-place, on the very spot where he said he would not stand to sell books for his father. And all the boys laughed at him; but there he stood with his bald head, not feeling the rain, or caring for the boys' laughter, that he might do a sort of act of penance, to ease his conscience! He did not "honour his father" when a boy, and he remembered it fifty years after, and it was a pain to him. A statue to Dr. Johnson now stands on the spot, and this noble act of his is depicted upon it. (*J. Vaughan.*) *Parents are God's representatives :*—In battle, men will give their lives to prevent the ragged and shot-torn colours of their country from falling into the hands of the enemy. These ragged colours represent their country. The dust-covered messenger who carries private despatches to an embassy in a foreign country is received with all respect, because he represents his king. Even the child who carries an important message is treated with the reverence due to the sender of the message. So parents are to be honoured, not alone as parents, but as the representatives of God Himself. (*S. S. Times.*) **That thy days may be long.**—*Long life :*—1. My design is to show you that practical religion is the friend of long life, and I prove it first from the fact that it makes the care of our physical health a positive Christian duty. The Christian man lifts this whole problem of health into the accountable and the Divine. He says : " God has given me this body, and He has called it the temple of the Holy Ghost, and to deface its altars, or mar its walls, or crumble its pillars, is a sacrilege." The Christian man says to himself : " If I hurt my nerves, if I hurt my brain, if I hurt any of my physical faculties, I insult God and call for dire retribution." An intelligent Christian man would consider it an absurdity to kneel down at night and pray, and ask God's protection, while at the same time he kept the windows of his bedroom tight shut against fresh air. The care of all your physical forces—nervous, muscular, bone, brain, cellular, tissue—for all you must be brought to judgment. 2. Again, I remark that practical religion is a friend of long life in the fact that it is a protest against all the dissipations which injure and destroy the health. Bad men and women live a very short life ; their sins kill them. Napoleon Bonaparte lived only just beyond mid-life, then died at St. Helena, and one of his doctors said that his disease was due to excessive snuffing. The hero of Austerlitz, the man who by one step of his foot in the centre of Europe shook the earth, killed by a snuff-box! Oh, how many people we have known who have not lived out half their days because of their dissipations and indulgences ! Now, practical religion is a protest against all dissipation of any kind. 3. Again, religion is a friend of long life in the fact that it takes the worry out of our temporalities. It is not work that kills men; it is worry. When a man becomes a genuine Christian he makes over to God not only his affections, but his family, his business, his reputation, his body, his mind, his soul—everything. Oh, nervous and feverish people of the world, try this mighty sedative ! You will live twenty-five years longer under its soothing power. It is not chloral that you want, or more time that you want ; it is the Gospel of Jesus Christ. 4. Again, practical religion is a friend of long life in the fact that it removes all corroding care about a future existence. You have been accustomed to open the door on this side the sepulchre ; this morning I open the door on the other side the sepulchre. Glory be to God for this robust, healthy religion. It will have a tendency to make you live long in this world, and in the world to come you will have eternal longevity. (*Dr. Talmage.*) *Vindication of God's faithfulness, in the performance of the promise of long life :*—We may boldly challenge long life, when all the circumstances of it will tend to our everlasting welfare. But God, who knows how frail and yielding the best of us are, and in the series of His Divine Providence seeth what prevailing temptations we shall be exposed unto, doth oftentimes, in mercy, abridge this promise; and takes us from the world, lest the world should take us from Him; and deals with us, as princes deal with duellists, they make them prisoners, that they might preserve them : so God, that He might preserve His people from their great enemy, commits them to safe custody of the grave. And, if this be to be unfaithful, certainly His faithfulness would be nothing else but an art to circumvent and undo us ; should He, only to keep that inviolate, perform those promises, which would be to our hurt and detriment. Nor, indeed, can any man, whom God hath blessed with a right judgment and due esteem of things, be willing to compound for the continuance of this present life, with the hazard or diminution of his future happiness. (*Bp. E. Hopkins.*)

Ver. 13. Thou shalt not kill.—*The Sixth Commandment :*—I. THAT THIS COMMANDMENT WAS INTENDED, AS SOME SUPPOSE, TO FORBID THE INFLICTION OF CAPITAL PUNISHMENT, IS INCONCEIVABLE. The Mosaic law itself inflicted death for murder, Sabbath-breaking, and the selling of a Jew into slavery. The root of the Commandment lies in the greatness of human nature ; man is invested with a supernatural and Divine glory ; to maintain the greatness of man it may be sometimes necessary that the murderer, who in his malice forgets the mystery and wonderfulness of his intended victim, should be put to death. II. DOES THE COMMANDMENT ABSOLUTELY FORBID WAR BETWEEN NATIONS ? Certainly not. The nation to which it was given had a strict military organization, organized by the very authority from which the Commandment came. Moses himself prayed to God that the hosts of Israel might be victorious over their enemies. Wars of ambition, wars of revenge —these are crimes. But the moral sense of the purest and noblest of mankind has sanctioned and honoured the courage and heroism which repel by force of arms an assault on a nation's integrity, and the great principle which underlies this Commandment sanctions and honours them too. (*R. W. Dale, D.D.*) *The Sixth and Seventh Commandments :*—There are very sad and fearful thoughts connected with these Commandments. But there are also very blessed thoughts connected with them. I. Is it nothing to remember that THE LORD GOD HIMSELF WATCHES OVER THE LIFE OF EVERY ONE OF US, POOR CREATURES AS WE ARE, that He has declared, and does declare, how precious it is in His eyes? Our life is subject to a thousand accidents. All things seem to conspire against it. Death seems to get the mastery over it at last. But no ; He has said, " Death, I will be thy plague." As every plant and tree seems to die in winter and revive in spring, so He says to this more wonderful life in our bodies, "It shall go on, and this is the pledge and witness that it shall : the Head of you all, the Son of man, the only-begotten Son of God, died Himself and rose again. God's conflict with death is accomplished. The grave shall not kill." II. And so, again, THE LORD IS THE GOD OVER THE HOUSEHOLD. He who says, " Thou shalt not kill," bids us understand that it is well to pour out blood as if it were water rather than to become base and foul creatures, beasts instead of His servants and children. That was the reason He sent the Israelites to drive out the Canaanites. They were corrupting and defiling the earth with their abominations. It was time that the earth should be cleared of them. The God who gave these Commandments is King now, and there is no respect of persons with Him. III. CHRIST DIED TO TAKE AWAY THE SINS OF MEN. He died to unite men to the righteous and sinless God. The Lord our God, who has redeemed us out of the house of bondage, will always deliver us from sin, will give us a new, right, and clean heart. (*F. D. Maurice, M.A.*) *The Sixth Commandment :*—I. THE SIN FORBIDDEN. In this, " thou shalt not kill," is meant the not injuring another. 1. We must not injure another in his name. We injure others in their name when we calumniate and slander them. No physician can heal the wounds of the tongue. 2. We must not injure another in his body. The life is the most precious thing ; and God hath set this Commandment as a fence about it, to preserve it. All these sins which lead to murder are here forbidden : As (1) Unadvised anger. Anger boils up the blood in the veins, and oft produceth murder ; "in their anger they slew a man." (2) Envy. Anger is sometimes "soon over," like fire kindled in straw, which is quickly out ; but envy is a radicated thing, and will not quench its thirst without blood ; "who is able to stand before envy ?" (3) Hatred. How many ways is murder committed ? We may be said to murder another : 1. With the hand : as Joab killed Abner and Amasa ; "he smote him in the fifth rib, and shed out his bowels." 2. Murder is committed with the mind. Malice is mental murder ; "whoso hateth his brother is a murderer." 3. Murder is committed with the tongue, by speaking to the prejudice of another, and causing him to be put to death. 4. Murder is committed with the pen. Uriah. 5. By consenting to another's death. Saul. 6. By not hindering the death of another when in our power. Pilate. 7. By unmercifulness. 8. By taking away that which is necessary for the sustentation of life. 9. By not helping him when he is ready to perish. We must not injure another's soul. Who do this ? (1) Such as corrupt others by bad example. (2) Such as entice others to sin. (3) Ministers are murderers, who starve, poison, or infect souls. (4) Such as destroy others, by getting them into bad company, and so making them proselytes to the devil. 2. The second thing forbidden in it is, the injuring one-self ; "thou shalt not kill" : thou shalt do no hurt to thyself. 1. Thou shalt not hurt thy own body. One may be guilty of self-murder, either (1) Indirectly and occasionally ; as, first, when a man thrusts himself into danger which he might prevent. Secondly, a person may be in some sense guilty of his own death, by neglecting the use of means. If sick, and use no physic, if he hath received a wound and will not apply balsam, he hastens his own death. Thirdly, by immoderate grief : "the sorrow of the world worketh death" ; when God takes away a dear relation, and one is swallowed up with sorrow. How many weep themselves into their graves ! Queen Mary grieved so excessively for the loss of Calais, that it brake her heart. Fourthly, by intemperance, excess in diet. Surfeiting shortens life ; "more die of it than by the sword" ; many dig their grave with their teeth ; too much oil chokes the lamp; the cup kills more than the cannon. (2) One may be guilty of self-murder, directly and absolutely. First, by envy. Envy corrodes the heart, dries up the blood, rots the bones; "envy is the rottenness of the bones." It is to the body, as the moth to the cloth, it eats it, and makes its beauty consume; envy drinks its own venom. Second, by laying violent hands on himself, and thus he is *felo de se ;* as Saul fell upon his own sword and killed himself. A man's self is most near to him, therefore this sin of self-murder breaks both the law of God, and the bonds of nature. Self-murderers are worse than the brute-creatures; they will tear and gore one another, but no beast will go to destroy itself. Self-murder is occasioned usually from discontent; discontent is joined with a sullen melancholy. The bird that beats herself in the cage, and is ready to kill herself, is the true emblem of a discontented spirit. 2. Here is forbidden hurting one's own soul. Who are they that go about desperately to murder their own souls? 1. Such wilfully go about to murder their souls, who have no sense of God, or the other world; they are "past feeling." 2. Such as are set wilfully to murder their own souls, are they who are resolved upon their lusts, let what will come of it. Men will, for a drop of pleasure, drink a sea of wrath. 3. They murder their souls, who avoid all means of saving their souls. 4. They do voluntarily murder their souls, who suck in false prejudices against religion; as if religion were so strict and severe, that they who espouse holiness, must live a melancholy life, like hermits and anchorites, and drown all their joy in tears. This is a slander which the devil hath cast upon religion: for there is no true joy but in believing. 5. They are wilfully set to murder their own souls, who will neither be good themselves, nor suffer others to be so. II. The duty implied. That we should do all the good we can to ourselves and others. 1. In reference to others. (1) To preserve the life of others. Comfort them in their sorrows, relieve them in their wants, be as the good Samaritan, pour wine and oil into their wounds. Grace makes the heart tender, it causeth sympathy and charity; as it melts the heart, in contrition towards God, so in compassion towards others. (2) Love. Love loves mercy : it is a noble bountiful grace. Love, like a full vessel, will have vent; it vents itself in acts of liberality. To communicate to the necessities of others, is not arbitrary, it is not left to our choice whether we will or no, but it is a duty incumbent; "charge them that are rich in this world that they do good, that they be rich in good works." God supplies our wants, and shall not we supply the wants of others? Shall we be only as a sponge to suck in mercy, and not as breasts to milk it out to others? (3) It is implied, that we should endeavour to preserve the souls of others; counsel them about their souls, set life and death before them, help them to heaven. 2. In reference to ourselves. The Commandment, "thou shalt not kill," requires that we should preserve our own life and soul. 1. It is engraven upon every creature, that we should preserve our own natural life. 2. This Commandment requires, that we should endeavour, as to preserve our own life, so especially, to preserve our own souls. (*T. Watson.*) *The Sixth Commandment :*— This command forbids the illegal and unrighteous taking of life. What a terrible commentary upon the condition of man that there needs to be such a command as this, "Thou shalt not kill"! Sin is its only explanation. Consider—I. The murderer. 1. This crime comes as the sequence to a life of terrible guilt. 2. It subjects him to the extreme penalty of the law, and holds him up as a monster unfit for human fellowship and life. 3. It does violence to the highest interests of his soul. II. The murdered man. 1. Murder cuts him off in the midst of his days. 2. It destroys all his earthly interests, and does him the greatest injustice. No time given to set business in order or provide for household. 3. It endangers his eternal welfare. III. Society. 1. Murder outrages the rights of life and property. (1) It brings disgrace to the relations of the murderer. (2) It injures the connections of the murdered one. (3) It disturbs the peace of society, and even threatens the stability of good government. 2. Hence to defend life becomes a duty (Psa. lxxxii. 3, 4 ; Job xxix. 13). (1) We are not at liberty to take our own life (Acts xvi. 28). (2) When a man is attacked he should defend himself; or, if others need help, he should assist them (Prov. xxiv. 11, 12). (3) The welfare of society demands that the life of the murderer should be exacted by the government, or that he should be kept in perpetual durance (Gen. ix. 6). IV. Applications. 1. We should keep the heart free from hatred and the like. 2. We should cultivate a sweet disposition and control over temper and passion. The passionate man may commit murder in the frenzy of his excitement. 3. We should avoid everything that tends toward this crime, such as quarrels, differences, strong drink, and all other things whose tendency is to evolve passion and destroy self-control. (*L. O. Thompson.*) *The Sixth Commandment:*—Man alone has the inspiration of Deity. This Divine inbreathing is the august peculiarity which separates man discretively and everlastingly from the animal creation. On his body side he sprang from dust ; on his soul side he sprang with the animals ; on his spirit side he sprang from God. Thus in his very beginning, in the original make-up of him, man was a religious being. Coming into existence as Jehovah's inbreathing, man was, in the very fact of being Divinely inbreathed, God's Son and Image. Hence it is that the human body is such a sacred thing. It is the shrine of God's Son, God's image, God's likeness, God's spirit, God's breath. As such it is the priceless casket of unknown sacred potentialities. Hence, murder is, in the intensest sense of the word, sacrilege : not only a crime against man, but a crime against God, in whose image man is made. But murder may be of varying degrees of atrocity. Accordingly, let us now glance at some of the various forms of murder. 1. And, first, there is the murder which is born of malice, or murder in the common acceptation of the term. Murder of this kind, whether perpetrated swiftly, as by the bullet, or slowly, as by arsenic, is the most fiendish of crimes. And nature, in an especial manner, ever waits to avenge it. Nor is this strange ; for, as we have seen, man, on his body side, is linked with the material creation. The same elements which compose our physical organism compose, although in different proportions, the water we drink, the food we eat, the air we breathe, the dust we await. Hence nature herself often becomes a principal factor in the detection of the murderer. She ever stands ready to be murder's avenger, supplying the prosecuting attorney with her re-agents, even with blood-corpuscles themselves. 2. Again, there is the murder which is born of sudden passion : the murder, for example, of lynch-law, when a mob usurps the functions of a court of justice ; the murder of sudden vengeance, as when an outraged husband encounters and slays the destroyer of his home ; the murder of manslaughter, whether voluntary or involuntary, whether provoked by insult, by menace, or by alcohol. 3. Again, there is the murder which is born of despair. Suicide, when committed by a sane person, is murder. Indeed, how often the two crimes are committed by the same person—the murderer first slaying his victim, then slaying himself. Justly does the law pronounce a suicide a *felo de se*—that is, one who makes a felon of himself, suicide being felonious self-murder. 4. Again, there is the murder which is born of shame : I mean infanticide. 5. Again, there is the murder which is born of harmful occupations. First in this list I would put the dram shop ; it matters not that the killing is slow ; the killing is moral murder ; and before every saloon I would post a placard bearing the Sinaitic legend: "Thou shalt not kill." Again, there is the sale, when not prescribed by the physician, of narcotic drugs, in their various forms, from opium joints to chloral drops. Again, there are the slow murders which are perpetrated in houses of nameless sin— murders which are particularly sacrilegious, because, as we have seen, the body is the temple of the Holy Spirit. 6. Again, there is the murder which is born of thoughtlessness (see Deut. xxii. 8). It is one of the cheering signs of the times that the public is awakening to the sense of its grave responsibility in this direction, for example, demanding that life shall not be imperiled by the failure to provide substantial structures, fire-escapes, life-preservers, railway precautions, sanitary arrangements of fresh air and wholesome food and pure water and clean streets, isolated refuges for sufferers from contagious and infectious diseases, competent physicians and druggists and nurses, sufficient hours for rest on the part of operatives, excursions for children, sanitariums for the poor, parks and recreation grounds—in brief, hygienic regulations in general. 7. And now let us ponder Christ's interpretation of the law against murder (Matt. v. 21, 22). According to Him, murder is not a matter of outward act, but of inward feeling : not a question of standing before the community, but of character before the All-seeing. No murder was ever committed which did not begin in the heart. Who of us has kept the Sixth Commandment as the Divine Man has interpreted it? Who of us has not been angry, passionate, revengeful, petulant? Remembering, then, these quarrels of ours, these grudges and piques and faults of temper, who of us is not in danger of the eternal Gehenna? But we are not yet through with the Sixth Commandment. Although it is prohibitive in form, saying, Thou shalt not kill, yet it is affirmative in spirit, saying, Thou shalt love. (*G. D. Boardman.*)   *The law of mercy :*—I. THE ESSENTIAL PRINCIPLE OF THIS COMMANDMENT. 1. In preferring the old Prayer Book reading, " Thou shalt do no murder," the revisers have done well. Killing may be no murder. The right of self-defence belongs both to the individual and the community. 2. Human life is sacred, but not so sacred as the end for which it is given, viz., that man created in the image of God should do His will. That is the paramount obligation. The will of God may make it right for us to lay down our lives, or right to defend them at the cost of death to others. II. THE MOSAIC ENUNCIATION OF THIS COMMANDMENT. 1. It is inconceivable that the great law-giver can have read it in the sense of an absolute " Thou shalt not kill." (1) If he had condemned killing in self-defence, he could not have formed the regulation in chap. xxii. 2. (2) If he had condemned killing by public justice, he would not have ordained capital punishment, as he did not only for murder, but also for kidnapping, insolence to parents, adultery, sorcery, blasphemy, and Sabbath-breaking. (3) If he had condemned killing in war, he would neither have engaged in it himself nor have left it as a solemn legacy to his successor. (4) Against actual murder the law of Moses was uncompromising (see Deut. xix. 11–13 ; Exod. xxi. 14.) 2. In this stern impartiality the Hebrew legislator rose head and shoulders, not only above his contemporaries, but above generations very far subsequent to him. Even in Christian England, and in our own day, we tolerate in connection with many offences, an alternative of " fine or imprisonment " ; a bad remainder of feudal times, which lets the rich man lightly off, but crushes his poorer neighbour—an inequality with which Moses could not be charged. But he went further than this. He laid down the principle that criminal carelessness and selfish indifference to human life ought to be regarded as tantamount to murder (see chap. xxi. 28, 29). If our own British laws were as clear as this in their denunciation of criminal care-lessness and wicked recklessness of human life, it would be vastly to the public advantage. What of the jerry-builders heaping rotting garbage into the foundations of houses, putting cheap arsenicated papers on the walls, and scamping drains that they may net exorbitant rents at the price of human lives ? What of smug railway-directors sweeping in golden dividends, but leaving poor signalmen to toil for such long hours that exhausted nature muddles the points, and horrible collisions follow? What of the chemist who adulterates his drugs, the inn-keeper who puts damp sheets on the traveller's bed, and the butcher who sends diseased meat into market ? The plain truth is, that these people are murderers. We are yet as to legislation a long way behind the brave old ruler who said out forcibly what such criminals should suffer ; but our moral sense sees clearly that they inflict death upon innocent people, a death as sure as if they had put knife to the throats or revolver to the hearts of their victims, a death often slower and more cruel in its torture. III. THE SAVIOUR'S COMMENT UPON THIS WORD (see Matt. v. 21, 22). Nothing condemned by Moses as a breach of the sixth word is excused by Jesus. Instead of loosing, He tightens the reins. He tracks the lurking murder in many an unsuspected heart. He marks three degrees of murderous guilt, all of which may be manifested without a blow being struck : secret anger ; spiteful jeer ; open, unrestrained outburst of violent, abusive speech. IV. THE POSITIVE INTERPRETATION OF THIS COMMANDMENT will lift us to the true platform of Christian morality by transfiguring it into a law of mercy. The same essential principle which forbids murder ordains brotherhood. (*W. J. Woods, B.A.*) *Injuring man prohibited :—* We now come to the commandments which refer exclusively to our duty to man. Of these there are five. The first four we group together. They each read: " Thou shalt not injure thy fellow-man." We cannot injure God—we can only act irreverently and carelessly toward God, and so injure, not Him, but ourselves. Sin has made us natural enemies to one another—Ishmaelites, whose hands are against every man, and every man's hand against us. Man's condition by nature is not seen in man's condition in England, France, or civilized America, but in man's condition in the savage island of the Pacific, where the heavenly rays of the gospel have least penetrated. The civilizations of Christianity exhibit, not humanity, but Christianity. The civilizations of ancient Persia, Greece, and Rome (although a little revelation filtered through upon them) exhibit humanity, in its best estate, as a refined selfishness, where every man seeks (adroitly, perhaps, and not openly) to injure his neighbour. The injury which man can do to his fellow-man can be divided into four kinds—injury to person, injury to society, injury to property, and injury to reputation. (*H. Crosby, D.D.*) *Personal application of the Commandment :—*The Commandment is addressed to each man, and applies to his own life and the life of his neighbour. 1. His own life he is forbidden to take. He is commanded to care for it. Man does not own himself, has no title in his own life as before God, has no right to destroy it, but should take good care of it, for it belongs to God. We are here forbidden to brood over our troubles.

It is wrong to cultivate a melancholy spirit, or a rebellious one. We should strive against these natural tendencies which threaten life and dishonour God. God requires us further to have that high regard for our lives which shall lead us to guard and maintain them in the best possible condition. We are to become familiar with the laws of health, and obedient to them. The Commandment tells us how we shall dress. Adornment should be subordinate to comfort. Thin shoes and bare arms venture out to a late party on a winter's night; a severe cold sometimes follows, and a speedy death. We say, What a mysterious providence to take one so young! Do we not know that the laws of providence are in favour of good health and long life, and that sickness and death often come directly from our disobedience of these laws. This Commandment directs us in the conduct of our business. In gaining our living we are not needlessly to risk our lives. We are to be masters of our business, not mastered by it. 2. God requires further that each one shall hold the life of others sacred as well as his own. He is forbidden to take it. He is commanded to care for it. The contentious spirit is to be checked in its small beginnings, for its natural tendency is to hard feelings and deadly hatred. Our pride is not to be cultivated, for an over-estimate of our own importance is sure to be cut to the quick by the slights of others, and arousing into anger will cherish the desire for revenge. High temper quickly flies into anger when provoked, and often acts and speaks in the heat of passion, adding fuel to its own flame and striking fire into other hearts. It is said that Julius Cæsar won many victories over his own spirit by the simple rule never to speak or act when provoked until he had repeated slowly the Roman alphabet. We are to beware of having any prejudice against our neighbour. We are to think of him kindly, and speak of him and to him kindly, no matter what he thinks of us, or how he speaks of us or to us, or even if he will not speak to us at all. All private grudges and neighbourhood feuds, if they stand at all, must stand under the frowning face of this Commandment. Neither can cool indifference to our neighbour's welfare find any place in our hearts under this law of God. In the social arrangements of the day lives are often placed in the charge of others. Those having this charge should pay special attention to this Commandment. The owner of a tenement house, if he regards this Commandment at all, will seek the health, comfort, and welfare of his tenants. Builders of roads, bridges, and houses, if they regard this Commandment at all, will seek not only good wages, but mainly to do good work, that men's lives may be safe. This Commandment directs us to be good citizens and to seek the health and welfare of all the members of the community where we dwell. The sanitary arrangements of city, town, and village, are commended to our attention. We may not neglect them without guilt. The sacredness of life enjoined in the Commandment covers not merely the bodily life, it lies specially in our spiritual life, in the image of God. Is life worth living? asks the worldly philosopher, as if there was some doubt about it. Worth living? Surely it is, since our spiritual life though fallen may be brought into a shape worthy of God our Father. Herein we see the highest realm of this Commandment, the true sacredness of life. We are carefully to avoid in ourselves and in our influence all those things which would have any tendency to destroy the soul. (*F. S. Schenck.*) *Anger leading to murder :*—I remember when I was a boy at school a case of this kind occurred. One of the scholars, whose name was James, had a terrible temper. The least thing that displeased him would throw him into a rage, and then he would act in the most violent manner. He never seemed to feel how dreadfully wicked it was, or to be afraid of the consequences that might follow from it. One day, during recess, he stretched himself on a bench to take a nap. One of the boys thought he would have a little fun with James. He took a feather, and leaned over the bench, and began to tickle him in the ear. James shook his head, and cried "Quit that." Presently he felt the feather again. "You quit that, I say!" he exclaimed, very angrily. The boy very thoughtlessly went on with his mischief. Then James sprang from the bench, seized a pair of compasses lying on the desk near him, and threw them at the boy with all his might. They struck him on the side of the head. They entered his brain. He fell down, never spoke again, and was carried home a corpse. How dreadful this was! Here was the young serpent that had been allowed to nestle in this boy's heart springing up suddenly to its full growth, and making a murderer of him. Oh, watch against these young serpents! (*R. Newton, D.D.*) *Refusing to fight a duel :*—Colonel Gardiner, having received a challenge to fight a duel, made the following truly noble and Christian reply: "I fear sinning, though you know, sir, I do not fear fighting"; thus showing his conviction of a fact too often forgotten, that the most impressive manifestation of courage is to "obey God rather than man."

Ver. 14. **Thou shalt not commit adultery.**—*The Seventh Commandment :*—I. WHAT IT FORBIDS. 1. Unchastity in thought and desire (Matt. v. 28 ; Prov. vi. 18). 2. Unchastity in conversation (Eph. v. 3, 4). 3. Sensuality in all its forms and actions. II. WHAT IT REQUIRES. 1. To avoid temptation, by carefully keeping the heart (Prov. iv. 23). 2. To cherish a regard for God and His will (Prov. v. 21). 3. To keep the body pure as a temple of the Holy Ghost (1 Cor. vi. 17, 18). 4. To seek lawful wedlock when chastity cannot otherwise be retained (1 Cor. vii. 2). 5. To honour the estate of matrimony (Heb. xiii. 4). III. ITS PENALTIES. 1. It consumes the body and destroys the soul (Prov. v. 11 ; vi. 32). 2. It destroys a man's name and family (Prov. vi. 33). 3. It involves others in guilt. 4. It breaks down moral principles, and does violence to all the virtues. 5. It incurs the displeasure of God. He has denounced this sin in almost every book of the Bible. 6. It excludes from heaven, unless the sin be repented of and, by the help of God, forsaken (Eph. v. 5). 7. It will be visited by condign punishment (Heb. xiii. 4 with x. 31). (*L. O. Thompson.*) *The Seventh Commandment :*—The faithful observance of the matrimonial contract is guarded by this Commandment. Marriage holds both socially and morally a quite exceptional rank among contracts. I. Glance for a moment at its SOCIAL consequences, which are those that bulk most largely in the view of a civil legislator. No community can be more orderly, healthy, rich, or happy, than the sum of the families which compose it. II. The MORAL aspects of marriage, however, are those which in this place deserve the most careful attention. 1. The law of marriage is a restraint upon the relations of the sexes which at first sight may appear arbitrary or conventional. It is less so than it looks. Monogamy is suggested by the proportion which exists between males and females in the population, and is found to be conducive both to individual well-being and to the growth of society. Manifestly, therefore, it has its roots in the nature of man himself, and is in harmony with the best conditions of his being. Still, it is a restraint ; and a restraint imposed just where the animal nature of man is most pronounced and his personal passions are most head-strong. The limitations of the marriage-bond constitute only a single department (though an important one) of that old-fashioned and manly virtue called "temperance," or the due control of oneself. It is a virtue which has to be learned in youth ; and in learning it we need to bear in remembrance what St. Peter says, that the lusts of the flesh are the peculiar foes of the spiritual life ; its incessant and its mortal foes : "Beloved, I beseech you as sojourners and pilgrims, to abstain from fleshly lusts, which war against the soul." 2. There is a second aspect of this law of marriage to which I must venture to invite your attention. I have said that it testifies to the need for restraint upon the physical appetites. It shows no less the extreme consequence of associating the strongest and most necessary of all appetites with a whole cluster of higher moral and social affections before it can be worthy of human beings. The union of true husband and wife in holy wedlock involves a crowd of complex elements, many of which touch the spiritual nature. It assumes a "marriage of true minds" ; for that is not an ideal marriage which is not first a union of souls before the "twain become one flesh." It reposes upon mutual esteem. It presupposes common tastes and establishes a most perfect system of common interests. It is, to begin with, a friendship, although the closest of all friendships. It leads to a noble dependence of weakness upon strength, and a chivalrous guardianship of strength over weakness. It asks for a self-renunciation on the part of each to the welfare of the other, which is the very perfection of disinterested love. It engages principle and honour to sustain mere inclination, and raises what would otherwise be the passion of an hour into a permanent devotion. By means of all this, the nobler social and moral emotions are enlisted in the service of "love," so that there emerges that lofty ideal of chaste wedded affection in which lies the chief poetry of common lives. (*J. O. Dykes, D.D.*) *The Seventh Commandment :*—Leighton, in explaining this precept, says, I purpose not to reckon up particularly the several sorts and degrees of sin here forbidden, for chastity is a delicate, tender grace, and can scarcely endure the much naming of itself, far less of those things that are so contrary to it. If you would be freed from the danger and importunity of this evil, make use of these usual and very useful rules : 1. Be sober and temperate in diet : withdraw fuel. 2. Be modest and circumspect in your carriage. Guard your ears and eyes, and watch over all your deportment. Beware of undue and dangerous familiarities with any, upon what pretence soever. 3. Be choice in your society, for there is much in that. 4. In general flee all occasions and incentives to uncleanness. But the solid cure must begin within, otherwise all outward remedies will fail. Then,

(1) Seek a total entire change of heart and to find the sanctifying Spirit of grace within you. (2) Labour to have the heart possessed with a deep apprehension of the holiness and purity of God, and then of His presence and eye upon all your actions and thoughts. (3) Acquaint yourselves with spiritual enjoyments. (4) Increase in the love of Christ. Alas! the misery which the sin here forbidden produces! *The Seventh Commandment :*—I. GOD FORBIDS UNFAITHFULNESS TOWARDS HUSBAND OR WIFE. Any previous step in course of infamy—any kind of incentive to impurity. Indecent conversation. Immodesty in dress. Evil thoughts. II. RULES FAVOURABLE TO MORAL CHASTITY. 1. Mortify any evil propensity. 2. Strengthen spirituality of mind. 3. Seek society and friendship of good and holy. 4. Fill up time with wholesome and right employment. 5. Observe temperance in all things —eating, sleeping, drinking. (*W. B. Noel, M.A.*) *The Seventh Commandment :*—I. THE ESSENTIAL UNITY OF MAN AND WOMAN. 1. Community. Woman is man's complement, his essential peer, his *alter ego,* his second self ; constituting with him the genus mankind, or *Homo.* 2. Diversity. Man and woman are the two poles of the sphere of mankind—the one implying the other. Like the stars, they differ in their glory. II. MARRIAGE A DIVINE INSTITUTION. A constituent elemental fact of humanity. III. THE MARRIAGE RELATION TAKES PRECEDENCE OF EVERY OTHER HUMAN RELATION (Gen. ii. 24). None but the Lord who joins, can disjoin. "Thou shalt not commit adultery." It is the Divine Lawgiver's ordinance, guarding the chastity of marriage, the sanctity of home, the blessedness of the household, the preservation of society, the upbuilding of mankind. Let earth's civic authorities, then, take exceeding care that they legislate and administer in this supreme matter of marriage according to the Divine oracle. Would God they all conceived it according to the standard and in the spirit of the Nazarine Teacher! And so we pass from the Seventh Commandment itself to the Divine Man's exposition of it (Matt. v. 27–32). Here at least is freshness of moral statement, radiant in beauties of holiness, born from the morning, sparkling with the dew of perpetual youth. Our topic, I must sorrowfully add, is pertinent to our age and land. Loose notions touching marriage, divorce, re-marriage, are painfully, alarmingly prevalent. We need not go so far as Utah to find Mormons, theoretical and practical. Let it be thundered from the pulpit, from the academy, from the forum, that divorce (absolute divorce, allowing re-marriage), saving for one solitary cause, is a threefold crime—a crime against home, a crime against society, a crime against God. And now let us ponder the Divine Man's prescription for the cure of unchastity : "If thy right eye causeth thee to stumble, pluck it out, and cast it from thee : and if thy right hand causeth thee to stumble, cut it off, and cast it from thee." No ; Christ's asceticism is not asceticism for its own sake, but asceticism for the sake of the moral discipline and rectification of character. Enough that I simply remind you that whatever fosters or suggests unchaste desire or thought—whether it be painting or statuary, opera or dance, romance or song, ambiguous allusion or the figment of one's own imagination, as in the prophet Ezekiel's vision of the chambers of imagery—it must be instantly, remorselessly, everlastingly renounced. (*G. D. Boardman.*) *The Seventh Commandment :*—I. THE DUTIES REQUIRED. 1. The preservation of our own chastity and purity. There is a twofold chastity. (1) In single life ; when it is led in purity, it is like the angelical ; when in impurity, it is devilish. (2) There is conjugal chastity, when married persons keep themselves within the bounds of the law of that state. This lies in two things. (*a*) With respect to all others, keeping themselves pure and uncorrupted. (*b*) With respect to one another, keeping themselves within the bounds of Christian sobriety and moderation. 2. This command requires us to preserve the chastity of others, and that so far as we can, in their hearts, lips, and lives. Our duty in this point may be reduced to these two heads. (1) That we may do nothing which may ensnare others. For whosoever lays the snare is partner in the sin that comes by it. (2) That we do everything incumbent on us to preserve the chastity of others, in heart, speech, and behaviour. Let married persons live together in due love and affection to one another. Let each one be an example of purity to others. Let those whom ye see in danger be rescued by all means, whether by force or persuasion, as the circumstances require. And let none bring others' guilt on their own heads, by being silent when they see the smoke, till the flame rise and discover itself. Let parents and masters do what they can to prevent the ruin of their children and servants, by rebuking any lightness about them, exhorting them, and praying for them ; keeping them out of ill company, not suffering them to be idle or vague, and seasonably disposing of

children in marriage. II. THE SINS FORBIDDEN. 1. Uncleanness in heart, all speculative filthiness, unclean imaginations, thoughts, purposes, and affections, though people do not intend to pursue them to the gross act (Matt. v. 28). 2. Uncleanness in words, all filthy communications and obscene language (Eph. iv. 29). 3. Uncleanness in actions. Besides the gross acts, there are others leading thereunto, which are there also forbidden. As, (1) Wanton looks : there are "eyes full of adultery" (2 Peter ii. 14) ; "wanton eyes" (Isa. iii. 16). (2) Impudent and light behaviour, and immodest gestures (Isa. iii. 16) ; indecent postures, contrary to religion and good manners. (3) Luxurious embraces and dalliances. These are as smoke going before the flame, and were practised by the adulterous whore (Prov. vii. 13). I shall next make some improvement of this subject. 1. Let those that have fallen into the sin of uncleanness, repent, and walk humbly all the days of their life under the sense of it. 2. Let those that stand take heed lest they fall. Labour to get your hearts possessed with a dread of this sin, and watch against it, especially ye that are young people, seeing it is a sin most incident to youth when the passions are most vigorous ; which yet may stick fast with the blue marks of God's displeasure upon you when you come to age. For motives, consider—(1) It is not only a sin, but ordinarily, if not always a plague and punishment for other sins. (2) It is a sin that very few ever get grace to repent of. It stupefies the conscience, and wastes all sense of sin from it (Hos. iv. 11). (3) It dishonours and debases the body (1 Cor vi. 18). (4) It leaves an indelible stain upon their reputation ; their honour is sunk, and there is no recovering of it (Prov. vi. 33). (5) Poverty and want oft-times follow it. It natively tends to poverty (Prov. v. 10), and there is a secret curse of that nature that often accompanies it (Prov. vi. 26). (6) It is ruining to the soul (Prov. vi. 32). "He that doth it"—commit adultery with a woman—"destroyeth his own soul." It ruins it here, in so far as it defiles the conscience, fetters the affections, blinds the mind, utterly unfits for communion with God, till the guilt be washed off by the application of Christ's blood, after a frightful awakening of the conscience. And if they do not repent of this sin, it will destroy the soul for ever. Let these Scriptures imprint a horror of it on the minds of all (Heb. xiii. 4 ; 1 Cor. vi. 9 ; Gal. v. 19 ; Rev. xxi. 8). (*T. Boston, D.D.*) *The Seventh Commandment :*—I. That which is here literally and expressly FORBIDDEN is—1. That detestable and loathsome sin of adultery. There are two things in this sin of adultery that make it so exceeding heinous. (1) The luxury and incontinency of it : in letting loose the reins to a brutish concupiscence ; and yielding up the body to pollution and the soul to damnation. (2) The injustice of it : being a deceit of the highest and most injurious nature that can be. 2. This Commandment forbids the uncleanness of fornication. Which, properly, is the sin committed betwixt two single persons. And, though it hath not some aggravations that belong to the other, yet it is an abominable sin in the sight of God (see 1 Cor. vi. 9, 10 ; Rev. xxii. 15 ; Gal. v. 19 ; Col. iii. 5). 3. Here, likewise, are forbidden all incestuous mixtures ; or uncleanness between those who are related to each other within the degrees of kindred specified (Lev. xviii. 6–18). 4. Here is likewise forbidden polygamy, or a taking a wife to her sister ; that is, to another (Lev. xviii. 18). 5. Here also are forbidden all those monsters of unnatural lust, and those prodigies of villany and filthiness, which are not fit to be named among men ; but thought fit to be punished upon beasts themselves : as ye may read (Lev. xx. 15, 16, xviii. 22, 23). 6. All those things that may be incentives to lust and add fuel to this fire are likewise forbidden in this Command. 7. Because this law is spiritual, therefore it not only forbids the gross outward acts of filthiness but the inward uncleanness of the heart ; all lustful contemplations, and ideas, and evil concupiscences. II. THE GREATNESS AND HEINOUS NATURE OF THIS SIN appears—1. In that it is a sin which murders two souls at once, and, therefore, the most uncharitable sin in the world. 2. This is the most degrading sin of all others. 3. This is a sin that doth, most of all others, obscure and extinguish the light of a man's natural reason and understanding. 4. This is a sin justly the most infamous and scandalous amongst men (Prov. vi. 32, 33). 5. Consider, that this sin of uncleanness is a kind of sacrilege ; a converting of that which is sacred and dedicated unto a profane use. 6. Consider, if all these things will not prevail, the dreadful punishment that God threatens to inflict upon all who are guilty of this sin. Yea, He speaks of it as a sin that He can hardly be persuaded to pardon ; a sin that puzzles infinite mercy to forgive (Jer. v. 7, 8, 9). And, indeed, God doth often, in this life, visit this sin : sometimes, by filling their loins with strange and loathsome diseases (Prov. vi. 26), sometimes, by reducing them to extreme beggary; for this sin, as Job speaks, is a fire that consumeth to destruction, and would root out all his increase. Yea, this very sin is so great a punishment for itself that the Wise Man tells us (Prov. xxii. 14) that those whom God hates shall fall into it. III. Let me now give you some CAUTIONARY RULES AND DIRECTIONS, by observing of which you may be preserved from it. 1. Be sure that you keep a narrow watch over your senses. For those are the sluices which, instead of letting in pleasant streams to refresh, do commonly let in nothing but mud to pollute the soul. 2. Addict thyself to sobriety and temperance; and, by these, beat down thy body and keep it in subjection to thy reason and religion. 3. Continually exercise thyself in some honest and lawful employment. Lust grows active when we grow idle. 4. Be earnest and frequent in prayer: and, if thou sometimes joinest fasting with thy prayers, they will be shot up to heaven with a cleaner strength. For this sin of uncleanness is one of those devils that goes not out but by fasting and prayer. God is a God of purity. Instantly beg of Him, that He would send down His pure and chaste Spirit into thy heart, to cleanse thy thoughts and thy affections from all unclean desires. (*Bp. E. Hopkins.*) *The Seventh Commandment* :—I. SOMETHING IMPLIED—that the ordinance of marriage should be observed; "let every man have his own wife, and let every woman have her own husband," "marriage is honourable in all, and the bed undefiled." Marriage is a type and resemblance of the mystical union between Christ and His Church. Special duties belonging to marriage are love and fidelity. 1. Love. Love is the marriage of the affections. 2. Fidelity. Among the Romans, on the day of marriage, the woman presented to her husband fire and water: fire refines metal, water cleanseth; hereby signifying, that she would live with her husband in chastity and sincerity. II. SOMETHING FORBIDDEN—the infecting ourselves with bodily pollution and uncleanness: "thou shalt not commit adultery." The fountain of this sin is lust. Since the fall, holy love is degenerated to lust. Lust is the fever of the soul. There is a twofold adultery: 1. Mental; "whosoever looketh on a woman to lust after her, hath committed adultery with her already in his heart." As a man may die of an inward bleeding, so he may be damned for the inward boilings of lust, if they be not mortified. 2. Corporal adultery, when sin hath conceived, and brought forth in the act. Wherein appears the heinousness of this sin of adultery? 1. In that adultery is the breach of the marriage oath. 2. The heinousness of adultery lies in this, that it is such a high dishonour done to God. 3. The heinousness of adultery lies in this, that it is committed with mature deliberation. First, there is the contriving the sin in the mind, then consent in the will, and then the sin is put forth in act. To sin against the light of nature, and to sin deliberately, is like the dye to the wool, it gives sin a tincture, and dyes it of a crimson colour. 4. That which makes adultery so heinous is, that it is a sin after remedy. God hath provided a remedy to prevent this sin; "to avoid fornication, let every man have his own wife." Therefore after this remedy prescribed, to be guilty of fornication or adultery, is inexcusable; it is like a rich thief, that steals when he hath no need. It is matter of lamentation to see this Commandment so slighted and violated among us. Now, that I may deter you from adultery, let me show you the great evil of it. First, it is a thievish sin. Adultery is the highest sort of theft; the adulterer steals from his neighbour that which is more than his goods and estate, he steals away his wife from him, "who is flesh of his flesh." Secondly, adultery debaseth a person; it makes him resemble the beasts; therefore the adulterer is described like a horse neighing: "every one neighed after his neighbour's wife." Nay, this is worse than brutish; for some creatures that are void of reason, yet, by the instinct of nature, observe a kind of decorum of chastity. The turtle-dove is a chaste creature, and keeps to its mate; the stork, wherever he flies, comes into no nest but his own. Naturalists write, if a stork, leaving his own mate, joineth with any other, all the rest of the storks fall upon him and pull his feathers from him. Adultery is worse than brutish, it degrades a person of his honour. Thirdly, adultery doth pollute and befilthy a person. The body of a harlot is a walking dunghill, and her soul a lesser hell. Fourthly, adultery is destructive to the body. Uncleanness turns the body into a hospital, it wastes the radical moisture, rots the skull, eats the beauty of the face. As the flame wastes the candle, so the fire of lust consumes the bones. Fifthly, adultery is a purgatory to the purse: as it wastes the body, so the estate, by means of a whorish woman a man is brought to a piece of bread. Sixthly, adultery blots and eclipseth the name; "whoso committeth adultery with a woman, a wound and dishonour shall he get, and his reproach shall not be wiped away." Some while they get wounds, get honour. The soldier's wounds are full of honour; the martyr's wounds for Christ are full of honour; these get honour while they get wounds: but the adulterer gets wounds in his name, but no honour: "his reproach shall not be wiped away." Seventhly, this sin doth much eclipse the light of reason, it steals away the understanding, it stupefies the heart; "whoredom takes away the heart." It eats out all heart for good. Solomon besotted himself with women, and they enticed him to idolatry. Eighthly, this sin of adultery ushers in temporal judgments. This sin, like a scorpion, carries a sting in the tail of it. The adultery of Paris and Helena, a beautiful strumpet, ended in the ruin of Troy, and was the death both of Paris and Helena. "Jealousy is the rage of a man"; and the adulterer is oft killed in the act of his sin. Ninthly, adultery, without repentance, damns the soul. How may we abstain from this sin of adultery? I shall lay down some directions, by way of antidote, to keep you from being infected with this sin. 1. Come not into the company of a whorish woman; avoid her house, as a seaman doth a rock; "come not near the door of her house." 2. Look to your eyes. 3. Look to your lips. 4. Look in a special manner to your heart. 5. Look to your attire. A wanton dress is a provocation to lust. 6. Take heed of evil company. 7. Beware of going to plays. A play-house is oft the preface to a whore-house. 8. Take heed of mixed dancing. Dances draw the heart to folly by wanton gestures, by unchaste touches, by lustful looks. 9. Take heed of lascivious books and pictures. 10. Take heed of excess in diet. The flesh pampered is apt to rebel. 11. Take heed of idleness. When a man is out of a calling, now he is fit to receive any temptation. 12. To avoid fornication and adultery let every man have a chaste, entire love to his own wife. It is not the having a wife, but the loving a wife makes a man live chastely. He who loves his wife, whom Solomon calls his fountain, will not go abroad to drink of muddy, poisoned waters. 13. Labour to get the fear of God into your hearts, "by the fear of the Lord men depart from evil." As the banks keep out the water, so the fear of the Lord keeps out uncleanness. Such as want the fear of God, want the bridle that should check them from sin. 14. Set a delight in the Word of God. "Let the Scriptures be my chaste delights." The reason why persons seek after unchaste, sinful pleasures is because they have no better. He that hath once tasted Christ in a promise, is ravished with delight; and how would he scorn a motion to sin! 15. If you would abstain from adultery, use serious consideration. Consider, (1) God sees thee in the act of sin. (2) Few that are entangled in the sin of adultery, recover out of the snare; "none that go to her return again." Soft pleasures harden the heart. (3) Consider what the Scripture saith, that it may lay a bar in the way to this sin, "I will be a swift witness against adulterers." (4) Consider the sad farewell this sin of adultery leaves: it leaves a hell in the conscience (Prov. v. 3, 4). 16. Pray against this sin. If the body must be kept pure from defilement, much more the soul of a Christian must be kept pure. (*T. Watson.*) *The law of chastity :*—I. THE LAW OF CHASTITY IS THAT WHICH REGULATES THE INTERCOURSE OF THE SEXES, whether in wedlock or other relations. 1. Marriage is the union of one man with one woman until death do them part. (1) A mutual compact. (2) A civil contract. (3) A vital and spiritual union. (4) A Divine institution. 2. The sacredness of the marriage contract as between one man and one woman was among the first things to be sullied by the fall, and through the lingering progress of many centuries has but slowly recovered. II. THE ESSENTIAL PRINCIPLE OF THIS LAW OF CHASTITY. 1. The man and the woman are the two halves of God's image. Not the masculine qualities alone, but also the feminine; not man's strength alone and vigour, but also woman's beauty and gentleness, are reflections of what, in the archetype, is found in God alone. 2. In this principle that the sexes are complemental to each other, together making one reflection of the image of God, we must learn that as a rule marriage is the appointed instrument for our highest moral development. When souls are wedded, when husband and wife alike are baptized into the Divine secret of utter self-abnegation, so that every drudgery is glorified, and every sacrifice made sweet, earth has no fairer picture of celestial joys. III. THE LEADING VIOLATIONS OF THE LAW OF CHASTITY. (*W. J. Woods, B.A.*) *The scope of the Seventh Commandment :*—The Jewish tradition in the time of our Lord taught that it forbad simply the act of adultery. More, says Christ (Matt. v. 27, 28), it forbids all impure thoughts and desires. Let us be as practical as possible about guarding against the beginnings of this sin. We who are parents should guard against its beginning in our children. We all agree that ignorance is not the mother of devotion, and yet act as if ignorance was the mother of purity. Knowledge is the basis of true religion, and the safeguard of virtue. Our children will learn concerning the new-born passions which fire their imagination, either from impure companions or from you, and it is a matter of tremendous importance whether they learn purely or impurely. These new-born passions have a wise purpose in the will of God, and governed by His law they become the source of the purest and richest blessings. They are as God's gift of fire to us. Controlled, it makes our firesides places of comfort and cheer; uncontrolled, it consumes our homes and leaves us miserable wanderers over a wintry waste. They are, like fire, excellent servants but terrible masters. It is well to know their nature and God's law for their control. We will all do well, and especially the young, to cultivate a taste for purity, so keen and sensitive that it will instinctively turn from the suggestion of impurity with loathing. We can do this in selecting our reading, and there is much need of it. There are many novels and poems of insinuating vice and suggestive impurity. It is wise to let our novel-reading be a very small proportion of the whole, simply for needed recreation, and then only the very best, of noble characters and heroic deeds; and our poetry, of fair ideals and beautiful scenes. We should cultivate the taste for purity in the choice of our companionship. Let our acquaintanceship even, as far as it is a matter of our choice, be of those whose delight is in pure thinking and feeling, in clean speaking and living; and let our friendship, which is altogether a matter of choice, be only with the pure. We strive to have in our gardens the most beautiful flowers, and the finest flavoured fruit, but we are careful to have no poison vine, however brilliant its colours, trail over the flowers, no poison berries, however tempting to the sight, hang side by side with the fruit. Let us take at least as good care of our minds and hearts as we do of our gardens. Now we may approach the subject of marriage. A high ideal of marriage is a great incentive to purity of heart. If young people anticipate a pure marriage, every step towards it must be in the way of virtue. If you wish to win a pure white soul for your lifelong companion, you will be unwilling to give less than you wish to receive. You will keep your own soul sweet and clean. (*F. S. Schenck.*) *Marriage* :— Marriage is a Divine institution founded in the nature of man as created by God. There is no higher mode of living for man and woman than to be husband and wife. It is the most intimate and sacred union that can exist on earth, to which all other relations are to give place. It is the union of one man and one woman for life, whose duties are not only to each other and to society, but to God. The legitimate power of the State is simply to enforce the law of God. If the State attempts to separate those whom God hath joined together, or to unite those whom God forbids to unite, her laws are nullities at the bar of conscience. God's institution of marriage is the foundation of the family, and the family is the foundation of society, the State, and the Church. Rome rose by the sanctity of her family life, and fell when it was undermined, as any fabric however stately will fall when the foundation is removed. Her rise was through the courage of her men and the virtue of her women. The perpetual fire on the altar of the Temple of Vesta, tended by a chosen band of white-robed virgins, was a true symbol of her strength. But the days of degeneration came, and the fire flickered and went out. There were no divorces in the early years of her history. There were many easily obtained divorces in the years of her luxury. Mutual consent was all that was needed to break the tie. Now the Roman laws in their later laxness are at the basis of much of our [American] legislation, and have displaced the law of God. We should be aroused from indifference by her experience. Like cause will produce like effect. Beyond love of our country Christian sentiment should arouse in its strength, and impress God's law of marriage upon the statute books of our States. It is enough to enshrine marriage in our regard, that it is ordained by God and governed by His law. Now all God's laws are for the highest good of man, and hence we find many inestimable blessings flowing from marriage. It confers happiness upon the married. True, there are unhappy marriages. Those who marry for property will be very apt to find the husband or wife an encumbrance. Those who marry heedlessly will find here as everywhere that heedlessness brings disaster. But the great majority of married people are happier for the marriage, as happy as their circumstances and character will allow. Poverty can never have the pleasures of wealth, but can have more pleasure in a loving marriage than in single loneliness. Love makes many a cottage happy. Covetousness can never have the pleasure of generosity, but in a loving marriage it finds dwarfing influences, and so becomes a smaller barrier to happiness. Selfishness in whatever form can never have real happiness, but true love in marriage tends to destroy selfishness. Marriage is God's grand institution for cultivating love in human hearts. What would this sin-stricken world be without the affections of the family circle, the love of husband and wife, parents and children, brothers and sisters? What refining influences come into this world with a little child! How selfish and narrow and hard our hearts and lives would become were it not for God's gift of children, awakening gratitude to Him, self-sacrificing love for them, and all the sweet sympathies and tender patient ministries of the home! What more helpless than a babe? God in marriage secures the might of love for its helplessness. What more ignorant? God secures teachers whose patience is well-nigh inexhaustible. Is there danger the child may become rough and selfish? In the required yielding to one another of brothers and sisters of different ages is found an antidote of selfishness, and the cultivation of gentle manners. Certainly the child will need government. The family is God's place for cultivating obedience to law from the earliest hours of childhood. Submission to right authority is the spirit of a good child, of a good citizen, of a good Christian. Is there any wonder, then, that God guards this blessed institution of marriage against all that would pollute and destroy it? If the frequency and earnestness of the warnings of the Holy Scripture against any sin measure the tendency of man to commit that sin, then impurity is one of the most fearfully prevalent and dreadful sins of the race; and so the history of the past and of to-day plainly teaches. Our laws are lax here too. They do not regard adultery and its hideous kindred as crimes. To steal ten dollars sends a man to prison. To steal happiness and honour only gives a right to sue for damages. And has society, the State, no interest in such things? Surely adultery is a crime. However silent our laws may be, let us never forget that God is not silent. The Bible does not whisper, it thunders peal on peal the hot denunciations of Divine wrath against the adulterer. Marriage is further ennobled in our thought since God has chosen this most intimate and sacred union to illustrate the union between Christ and His Church. On the plains of Northern Italy there stands an ancient and beautiful city. Near its centre rises a building of pure white marble, wonderful for its grandeur and beauty, seeming more like a dream from heaven than a creation of the earth. As one stands upon the roof of this cathedral of Milan, surrounded by the multitude of its dazzling pinnacles and spires, he may look far off to the north, over the plains and hills, until his eye rests upon the snowclad summits of the Alps, those other pinnacles and spires which God Himself created, and clothed with the ever pure white garments of the skies. So, from this purest of earth's relationships, we lift our thoughts to the mystical union of life and love, between the heaven and the earth, the marriage of the Church to her Divine Lord. Who shall speak of the love and faithfulness of this Divine Bridegroom, the love which knows no changing, which led Him to lay down His life for His Church? How steadily and warmly should her love go out to Him! (*Ibid.*) *Purity outward and inward:*—Sir Edward Coke was very neat in his dress, and it was one of his sentiments, " that the cleanness of a man's clothes ought to put him in mind of keeping all clean within." *Value of purity:*—A Greek maid, being asked what fortune she would bring her husband, answered: " I will bring him what is more valuable than any treasure—a heart unspotted, a virtue without a stain, which is all that descended to me from my parents." No woman could have a more valuable dowry! *The power of passion:*—One bright July morning I was driving to town. As I came to the top of the hill just above the bridge, on the outskirts of the place, a little boy, from a cottage on the north side of the road, fired off a small cannon. He was so near the road, the cannon made so great a noise, and the whole thing came so unexpectedly, that my little bay pony took fright, and shied, with a spring, to the other side of the road. He not only overturned the carriage in doing so, but was with great difficulty reined in and prevented from running away. " You should not fire your cannon so near the road," said I to the boy; "you frightened my horse badly, and nearly made him run away." " I didn't mean to do it," said he, " but it got agoing before I saw the horse, and then I couldn't stop it." I said no more, but drove on, thinking of the boy's answer, as I have often thought of it since, though all this happened years ago. " Couldn't stop it." How often, when we start " lust," there is no stopping. Do not begin, and the difficulty will not arise—it will not get " a-going."

Ver. 15. **Thou shalt not steal.**—*The Eighth Commandment :*—I. In this Commandment THE INSTITUTION OF PROPERTY IS RECOGNIZED AND SANCTIONED BY THE AUTHORITY OF GOD. The institution of property is necessary—1. For increasing the produce of the earth ; 2. For preserving the produce of the earth to maturity ; 3. For the cultivation and development of the nature of man ; 4. For the intellectual development of man.   II. The institution of property IMPOSES UPON ALL MEN THE DUTY OF INDUSTRY IN THEIR CALLINGS ; the duty of maintaining independence ; the duty of avoiding any, even the least, invasion of the rights of others ; the duty of self-restraint in expenditure, as well as of honesty in acquisition.   III. If property is a Divine institution, founded on a Divine idea, protected by Divine sanction, then IN THE USE OF IT GOD SHOULD BE REMEMBERED, and those whom God has entrusted to our pity and our care.   (*R. W. Dale, D.D.*)   *The Eighth Commandment :*—To steal, I am sorry to say, is a universal temptation, common to all sorts of people. It often springs from the sense of necessity : this it is which, as you remember, gives such tragic power to Victor Hugo's " Les Miserables," whose hero, Jean Valjean, stole a loaf of bread.   Again the temptation to steal springs from indolence, or, to use a good, or rather bad, old French-Latin word, laziness ; for there are not a few persons who, instead of getting an honest living by working, prefer to get it by what they call their wits, resorting to all sorts of shifts and tricks, which are really stealings.   Again, the temptation to steal springs from dissolute or what is called fast living ; how many of the embezzlements which so often startle the community spring from the fact that the embezzlers had entered on careers of personal debauchery !   Again, the temptation to steal springs from the love of display ; how many of the defalcations which land our citizens in prison or in Canada are owing to their passion for equipage, for furniture, for jewelry, for fashion !   Again, and chiefly, the temptation to steal springs from the haste to become rich ; how true it is that the love of money is a root of all kinds of evil ! Let us first glance at the case of private stealings.   For example : there is the taking advantage of the ignorant in a bargain.   Again, there is the taking advantage of the necessitous, when they lie prostrate and helpless, demanding from them, for instance, extortionate interest for the use of money, exorbitant rent for premises or tools, or extravagant prices for commodities.   Again, there is the refusing, I will not say lawful wages, but I do say fair wages—that is, just compensation to servants, whether in the family, the farm, the factory, the store, or the bank ; for every man born into this world is entitled, by the very fact of his existence upon this footstool of God, to a living.   Again, there is the delay in the payment of debts when due.   Again, there is the contracting of debts beyond any reasonable possibility of paying them, the indulgence in venturesome speculations, the living beyond income—these, and such as these, morally surveyed, are stealings.   Again, there is the practice of endorsing, or going security.   It is right for you to help your friend when he is in trouble ; but it is not right for you to help him, however much in trouble, if your endorsement of his note is going to cost some other friend of yours his comfortable home.   To aid one man by endorsing him may result in stealing from many men.   Again, there is the habit of begging for endorsements ; for example : tempting one to misrepresent, on the one hand, the amount of assets, and, on the other hand, the amount of liabilities ; contracting liabilities without the knowledge of the endorser ; keeping up appearances when insolvent ; in brief, offering a premium for the use of your name.   Again, there is the evading of government taxes and custom-house duties by making defective or ambiguous returns—a mode of stealing which, I regret to say, is not altogether unfashionable among people of position.   Once more, there is the lazy subsistence or dependence on charity (and there is a great deal more of this than we at first recognize) ; the dependence on friends to eke us out, when, if we had been a little less slothful in diligence as well as a little more fervent in spirit, we might not have needed their aid ; the sluggard, I take it, is quite a prince among thieves.   Let me now speak of the case of official stealings, no matter what the office is, whether public or private, whether in a bank, or in a store, or in an institution, or under the government.   Office is in its very nature a trust ; and as such it is a sacred thing.   And to betray a trust is the worst, because the meanest, kind of stealing.   And now let me pass from official stealings to what I may call associated or corporate stealings. There is something in the very nature of the organization of a company which somehow tends to the extinction of personal responsibility.   It is well understood that many a man will, as a member of a corporation—no matter what kind, whether a trust company, like a bank or a charitable institution, or an executive company, like a railroad or a telegraph organization—do things as a manager of that company which he would scorn himself for doing as a private individual on his own personal responsibility.   In fact, it has become an aphorism that corporations have no souls. And monopolies, or corporations granted the exclusive privilege of manufacturing or selling certain articles of commerce :—what are they but oftentimes organized robberies of society, thefts of your purse and my purse? But there are other kinds of property besides those which we call real and personal, which may also be stolen. For example : There is the stealing of time ; and time, you know, or will know, is money. When a man comes and takes up twice the time that is necessary in arranging with me for his own advantage, or even the advantage of a good institution, he steals my time, and in stealing my time, he steals my patience as well as my money. Again, there is the petty larceny of writing a letter of inquiry for your own advantage, and omitting to enclose a postage stamp ; for he that is faithful in a very little is faithful also in much ; and he that is unrighteous in a very little is unrighteous also in much. Again, there is the stealing of another's time and opportunity and serenity when you keep him waiting and fuming through your own failure to keep your engagement with him punctually. Again, there is the theft of plagiarism, the stealing of ideas, the withholding of credit or praise when credit or praise is due. Again, there is the stealing of reputation or character. Lastly, irreligion is the typical specimen of perfect theft. For while man in relation to his fellow-man has right to own property on his own account, yet man in his relation to his God is but a trustee. Steal not, then, O friend, from a greater than thy neighbour, even thy Divine Master! Language fails you when you undertake to denounce a defaulter against man. But where is your language when you think of a defaulter against Almighty God? (*G. D. Boardman.*)   *Property sacred :—*I. PROPERTY AS A SACRED RIGHT. A man's right in justly-acquired property is a reflection of God's rights in all His works. All property is the outgrowth of life, the results in houses, harvests, machinery, manufactures, commerce, and art of creative power. But that creative power is the gift of God, and therefore both its rights and responsibilities have their foundation and standard in God Himself. The property belongs to the man, but the man belongs to God. Thus the honest gains of toil, skill, judgment, self-denial, and good fortune are a man's own by a Divine right of which the civil right is the echo. II. PROPERTY AS A SACRED TRUST. The same fact which makes property sacred gives birth to sacred responsibilities. As in old feudal days lands were given by the king on certain conditions of service, so now God's gifts have always duties attached to them. Sacredly given, they are to be sacredly used. APPLICATION :—1. As to our use of our money. Is it not significant that God claimed tithes? Not to pay a tenth of His income into the temple treasury God considered a sacrilege in a Jew. Do we give a tenth to God? 2. Our use of ourselves. Wealth is more than money. It comprises all that God gives us, our talents, our influence, our whole self. He who might do good, who might heal and comfort and bless if he would, and yet does not, is guilty of unfaithfulness. (*W. Senior, B.A.*)   *The Eighth Commandment :—*I. WE MAY CAUSE INJURY TO OTHERS THROUGH LENDING AND BORROWING. II. WE SHALL DO WRONG TO OUR FELLOW-MEN BY INFLICTING INJURY ON PROPERTY THAT IS OPEN, THROUGH KINDNESS OF THE OWNERS, TO THE PUBLIC, as gardens, private picture-galleries, &c. It is mean, dishonourable, to do hurt to such property. III. THROUGH INCURRING OF DEBTS OR OBLIGATION TO OUR FELLOW-MEN. IV. THE WRONGS DONE IN MERCANTILE PURSUITS. This is done— 1. By selling to customers goods of inferior value. 2. By inferior weights. 3. By the adulteration of merchandise. 4. By false pretences. The placing the best strawberries or apples on top of the measure, &c. V. BREACHES OF TRUST. VI. GAMBLING. Property is a trust. You have no right to squander your own, or to lead another to squander what he has in trust. (*W. Ormiston, D.D.*)   *The law of property :—*I. Consider, first, what it means—THE RIGHTS OF PROPERTY. 1. In a country like this, long occupied and thickly peopled, almost everything belongs to somebody ; and most of us possess a few things that we call our own, either earned or inherited, or otherwise received. In a new country the first-comers enter upon unoccupied ground, and each, while making his own claim, recognizes the claims of others. The relations of property are expressed by the possessive pronouns, and it is remarked that these are found in all languages. On what, then, is this right of property grounded? Not on social compact, not on the law of the land, not on the principle of utility, but on the will of God revealed in the constitution of our nature, and in the teaching of His Word. All acquired property is the product of labour, or the fruits of labour ; and why do men labour ? Is it not for the means of living ? If, then, the constitution of our nature is such that we must labour for the means of living, it must be the will of Him who made us that we should receive and possess the fruits of our labour (see Prov. xvi. 26 ; Eph. iv. 28 ; 2 Thess. iii. 10). 2. The principle of possession excludes the principle of communism. If the fruit of my labour is mine, the fruit of another man's labour is his to do as he will with it. Communism has always ended in disaster; and always must. It is a tissue of mistakes. It is wrong in its original inference that the principle of property is the cause of destitution, whereas the real cause is selfishness and sin ; it is wrong in its ruling idea that all should share and share alike, a notion which would tax industrious people for the benefit of idlers, and rob the skilful for the advantage of the incompetent ; it is wrong in its proposed method, for force is no remedy, and the circumstances of men can only be mended by mending the men themselves ; and it is wrong in its cherished hopes, for if by some fatal success the communists should break down the present social system and suppress private wealth, the result would be to take all heart of enterprise out of the world's workers, to dry up the waters of progress at their source, and to crush the human race under a final incubus of intolerable woe. Not in the suppression of property, but in a wise understanding of its uses, and in a right direction of its powers, lies the redress of human wrongs, with the hope of a good time coming. II. What it ensures—THE USE OF PROPERTY. 1. Property has economical uses. It increases, protects, and stores, the produce of the earth. 2. Property has also its moral uses. (1) Its steady stimulation of labour is alone a mighty helper of our manhood. It is where men have to work that they acquire robustness of frame, alertness of mind, and firmness of moral fibre. (2) The way in which a man acquires property, and the way in which he uses it—resisting temptation to get it unlawfully, and making it a field for exercise of all the virtues ; or dealing oppositely, so as to win it by fraud, and use it for vice—these things make all the difference between a hero and a scoundrel, between a son of God and a child of the devil. III. What it forbids—THE VIOLATION OF PROPERTY. 1. There are robberies over and above those which policemen investigate. Private gambling. Betting. Extravagance and petty theft on the part of domestic servants. 2. Fraud, or the withholding of a man's due. "Trade practices." IV. What it involves—THE RESPONSIBILITIES OF PROPERTY. We are God's stewards. (*W. J. Woods, B.A.*) *The Eighth Commandment :*—I. WHAT IT FORBIDS. II. WHAT IT REQUIRES. 1. It requires restitution of whatever we have, at any time, unjustly taken or detained. For, that being in right not our own, but another's ; keeping it is continuing and carrying on the injustice. 2. This Commandment also requires industry ; without which, the generality of persons cannot maintain themselves honestly. 3. To observe it well, frugality must be joined with industry, else it will be all labour in vain. 4. This Commandment requires in the last place, that we neither deny ourselves, or those who belong to us, what is fit for our and their station, which is one kind of robbery ; nor omit to relieve the poor according to our ability, which is another kind. For whatever we enjoy of worldly plenty is given us in trust, that we should take our own share with moderation, and distribute out the remainder with liberality. (*Abp. Secker.*) *The Eighth Commandment :*—I. WHENCE DOTH THEFT ARISE ? 1. The internal causes are : (1) Unbelief. A man hath an high distrust of God's providence : "can God furnish a table in the wilderness ? " So saith the unbeliever, "can God spread a table for me ? no, He cannot." Therefore he is resolved he will spread a table for himself, but it shall be at other men's cost, and both first and second course shall be served in with stolen goods. (2) Covetousness. The Greek word for covetousness signifies " an immoderate desire of getting " ; this is the root of theft. A man covets more than his own, and this itch of covetousness makes him scratch what he can from another. 2. The external cause of theft is, Satan's solicitation : Judas was a thief ; how came he to be a thief ? "Satan entered into him." The devil is the great master-thief, he robbed us of our coat of innocency, and he persuades men to take up his trade ; he tells men how bravely they shall live by thieving, and how they may catch an estate. II. HOW MANY SORTS OF THEFTS ARE THERE ? 1. There is stealing from God ; and so they are thieves, who rob any part of God's day from Him. 2. There is a stealing from others. (1) A stealing away their souls ; and so heretics are thieves, by robbing men of the truth, they rob them of their souls. (2) A stealing away their money and goods from them ; and under this head of stealing away other's money, there may be several arraigned for thieves. The highway thief who takes a purse contrary to the letter of this Commandment. The house-thief, who purloins and filches out of his master's cash, or steals his wares and drugs. The house-thief is a hypocrite, as well as a thief ; he hath demure looks, and pretends he is helping his master, when he only helps to rob him. The thief that shrouds himself under law, as the unjust attorney or lawgiver, who prevaricates and deals falsely with his client. This is to steal from the client. The church-thief or pluralist, who holds several benefices, but seldom or never preacheth to the people ; he gets the golden fleece, but lets his flock starve. The shop-thief; he steals in selling, who useth false weights and measures, and so steals from others what is their due. The usurer who takes of others even to extortion ; he seems to help another by letting him have money in his necessity, but gets him into bonds, and sucks out his very blood and marrow. The feoffe in trust, who hath the orphan's estate committed to him ; he is deputed to be his guardian, and manage his estate for him, and he curtails the estate, and gets a fleece out of it for himself, and wrongs the orphan. This is a thief; this is worse than taking a purse, because he betrays his trust, which is the highest piece of treachery and injustice. The borrower, who borrows money from others, with an intention never to pay them again. The receiver of stolen goods. The root would die if it were not watered, and thievery would cease if it were not encouraged by the receiver. III. WHAT ARE THE AGGRAVATIONS OF THIS SIN OF STEALING? 1. To steal when one has no need. To be a rich thief. 2. To steal sacrilegiously. To devour things set apart to holy uses. 3. To commit the sin of theft against checks of conscience, and examples of God's justice : this is like the dye to the wool, it doth dye the sin of a crimson colour. 4. To rob the widow and orphan; "ye shall not afflict any widow or fatherless child " ; it is a crying sin; " if they cry unto Me, I will surely hear them." 5. To rob the poor. (*T. Watson.*) *The Eighth Commandment :*—I. Stealing by FORGETFULNESS. People with these bad memories borrow things from their neighbours and friends, and forget to return them. Now, to the persons who lend those things, it is just as bad as if a thief should come into their house and steal them. Umbrellas, and books, and things of that kind are most likely to suffer in this way. II. CUNNING, is another branch of it. Did you ever see a counterfeit bank-note? It passes for a good note, though it is not worth a straw. And gold and silver coin are counterfeited in the same manner. The people who make them think themselves very cunning. But they are not a bit better than thieves. But a great many other things may be counterfeited as well as money. When God shall come to reckon with them at last, they will find that the real name for what they called smartness was stealing. This is the name by which God calls it. III. Those who break the Eighth Commandment by DECEIT. For instance, a lady goes into a shop to buy a dress. She finds one of the colour she wants. If she could be sure that the colours would not fade she would take it. She says to the shopkeeper, " Will these colours stand ? " " Oh, yes, madam, they are the very best colours to wear. They will stand as long as the dress lasts." The lady buys the dress on this assurance, though all the while the shopkeeper knows the colours will not stand at all. In this way he steals the lady's money. IV. Those who break the Commandment by EXTORTION. V. Those who break the Commandment by VIOLENCE and FRAUD. We must resist little temptations. Everything must have a beginning. I remember reading once about a man who was going to be hung for robbery and murder. On the scaffold, he said he began to steal by taking a farthing from his mother's pocket while she was asleep. Many children begin to steal at the sugar-bowl or the cake-basket. To take the smallest thing that does not belong to us, without permission, is stealing. And, then, there is another thing to do: we must pray to God to keep us from temptation. (*R. Newton, D.D.*) *True honesty :*— There is an anecdote told of a brave general of the American Revolution, that he one day overheard the remark of a grandson, that "he hoped to be middling honest." The old gentleman stopped, turned short upon the speaker, and broke out: "What is that I hear? *Middling* honest! let me never hear again such a word from your lips. *Strictly* honest is the only thing you ought ever to think of being." *Praying better than stealing :*—Some poor families lived near a large wood-wharf. In one of the cabins was a man who, when he was sober, took pretty good care of his family ; but the public-house would get his earnings, and then they suffered. In consequence of a drunken frolic he fell sick. The cold crept into his cabin, and but one stick was left in his cellar. One night he called his eldest boy, John, to the bedside, and whispered something in his ear. " Can't do it, father," said John aloud. " Can't—why not? " asked his father, angrily. " Because I learned at Sabbath-school ' Thou shalt not steal,'" answered John. " And did you not learn ' Mind your parents,' too? " " Yes, father," answered the boy. " Well, then, mind and do what I tell you." The boy did not know how to argue with his father, for his father wanted him to go in the night and steal some sticks from the wood-wharf; so John said to his father: "I can pray to-night for some wood; it's better than stealing I know." And when he crept up into the loft where his straw bed was, he did go to God in prayer. He prayed the Lord's Prayer, which his Sabbath-school teacher taught him, only he put something in about the wood, for he knew God could give wood as well as " daily bread." The next noon, when he came home from school, what do you think he caught sight of, the first thing after turning the corner? A load of wood before the door, *his* door. Yes, there it was. His mother told him the overseers of the poor sent it; but he did not know who *they* were. He believed it was God; and so it was. *What is stealing ?*— Two old men were once arguing upon the question of venial sin. Their faces one could not forget. One said, " Well, after all you have to say, you will not tell me that the theft of a pin and a guinea are the same." The other said, " When you tell me the difference between a pin and a guinea to God, I will give you an answer." It at once settled the point; and there was no more said about venial sin. *The rights of property defended:*—It must be acknowledged that the sufferings and crimes which are incident to the institution of property are so grave as sometimes to provoke the inquiry whether, after all, the institution itself can be defended. Selfishness, covetousness, dishonesty, fierce and angry contention, are among the worst vices of which men can be guilty; and it may almost seem as though we might escape from them all by abolishing the rights of property. What are the grounds, then, on which the maintenance of these rights, in some form or another, can be defended? Archdeacon Paley, in one of the chapters of his " Moral Philosophy," has illustrated some of the advantages of the institution of property, with his usual clearness and felicity. He shows that it both increases the produce of the earth, and preserves it to maturity. Houses, ships, furniture, clothes, machinery, pictures, statues, books, require a great amount of labour to produce them; the stimulus to production would be altogether destroyed if after they were produced they belonged to nobody, and if people who had done no work were as free to use them as those by whose self-denial and labour they were produced. No mines would be worked, no fields would be cleared, no waste land would be brought into cultivation, no marshes would be drained, unless the men who did the work had the hope either of owning the property which they created, or of receiving in some other form compensation for their labour. The material wealth of the world would almost disappear, and the poorest and most wretched would have even less than they have now, if the rights of property were abolished. But there are other grounds on which the institution may be defended. The rights of property are essential not only to the creation and preservation of material wealth, but to the cultivation and development of the nature of man. It is only because corn belongs to the farmer, and coal to the mine proprietor, and bread to the baker, and meat to the butcher, it is only because clothes belong to the tailor, and houses to the builder, and because the law protects every one of them in the possession of his property until he is willing to part with it, that men work in order that they may get coal, and corn, and bread, and meat, and clothes, and house room. The Indian would sit idle in his cabin if the game he hunted did not become his own. Excessive physical labour is no doubt a great evil; but the evils of indolence are still greater. There are parts of the world where it is hardly necessary for men to work at all in order to get the bare necessaries of life, and the result is a miserable want of physical vigour and a portentous development of vice. We were made to work. It is by work that muscle is created and the whole body kept free from disease. Work as a rule is good for health, and good for morality and happiness too. Moreover, the institution of property supplies a most powerful motive to intellectual exertion. We want food, clothing, and a thousand other things; but they belong to people who will not part with them, except for the results of our own work. Inventive genius is stimulated to improve the processes of manufacture; administrative skill is exercised in lessening the cost of production; merchants watch the rise and fall of the markets in remote countries, estimate the effect of good and bad seasons and of political events on the probable price of commodities. There is not a counting house however small, there is not a workshop in a back court, where business can be carried on without thought. The institution of property secures an amount and variety of intellectual activity for which, perhaps, we have never given it credit. It has also very important relations to the moral life of man. The whole organization of the world is intended to discipline our moral nature; and the very variety of the sins to which the existence of property gives occasion, illustrates the variety of the virtues which it is intended to exercise. (*R. W. Dale, D.D.*) *Dishonesty in trade :*—If a manufacturer charges you twenty pounds for a hundred yards of cloth and sends you only half the quantity, he as really steals ten pounds as though he broke open your cash box and took out a ten pound note. If he engages to send you cloth of a certain quality and charges you for it, and then sends you cloth which is worth in the market only two-thirds the price, he is just as much a thief as though he stood behind you in a crowd and robbed you of your purse. No one disputes this. The same principle holds in every business transaction. To give short weight or short measure, is to steal. To supply an article of inferior quality to that which it is understood that the buyer expects, is to steal. To take a Government contract and send to Weedon or Portsmouth articles which you know will be worthless, or which you know are of a worse kind than it was understood that you would furnish, is to steal. To take advantage of your superior knowledge in order to pass off on any man articles for which he would never give the price that he pays for them but for his confidence in your integrity, is to steal. To start a company and to induce people to take shares in it by false representations of the amount of the subscribel capital and of its probable success, is to steal. If a workman who is paid to work ten hours, takes advantage of the absence of the master or foreman to smoke a pipe and read a newspaper for one hour out of the ten, he steals one-tenth of his day's wages. He does the very thing that a shopkeeper would do who gave him fourteen ounces of butter or sugar instead of a pound, or nine yards of calico when the bill charged ten. An assistant in a shop, who instead of caring for his master's interests as if they were his own, puts no heart into his work, exercises no ingenuity, treats customers carelessly instead of courteously, and so diminishes the chances of their coming again, gets his salary on false pretences, does not give the kind of service which he knows his employer expects, and which he would expect if he were an employer himself. (*Ibid.*) *An example of honesty :*—Speaking of the early American prairie settlements, a modern historian says : " Theft was almost unknown ; the pioneers brought with them the same rigid notions of honesty which they had previously maintained. A man in Mancoupin County left his waggon, loaded with corn, stuck in the prairie mud for two weeks near a frequented road. When he returned he found some of his corn gone, but there was money enough tied in the sacks to pay for what was taken. *Honesty :*—In Abraham Lincoln's youthful days he was storekeeper's clerk. Once after he had sold a woman a little bill of goods and received the money, he found, on looking over the account again, that she had given him six and a quarter cents too much. The money burned in his hands until he had locked the shop and started on a walk of several miles in the night to make restitution before he slept. On another occasion, after weighing and delivering a pound of tea, he found a small weight on the scales. He immediately weighed out the quantity of tea of which he had innocently defrauded the customer and went in search of her, his sensitive conscience not permitting any delay.

Ver. 16. **Thou shalt not bear false witness.**—*The Ninth Commandment :*—I. This Commandment is A RECOGNITION OF THOSE TRIBUNALS WHICH ARE NECESSARY TO THE PEACE AND TO THE VERY EXISTENCE OF THE STATE. II. In this Commandment there is A DIVINE RECOGNITION OF THE IMPORTANCE OF THE MORAL JUDGMENTS WHICH MEN PRONOUNCE ON EACH OTHER : the judgments which individual men form of other men as the result of the testimony to which they have listened, whether it was true or false ; the judgments which large classes of men or whole communities form of individuals, and which constitute what we call the opinion of society concerning them. III. MANY WAYS MIGHT BE MENTIONED IN WHICH WE MAY AVOID BEARING FALSE WITNESS AGAINST OUR NEIGHBOUR. 1. We should try to form a true and just judgment of other people before we say anything against them. 2. We have no right to give our mere inferences from what we know about the conduct and principles of others as though they were facts. 3. We have no right to spread an injurious report merely because somebody brought it to us. (*R. W. Dale, D.D.*) *The law of truth :*—1. There is no engine by which we help or harm one another more than by our speech. In one aspect words are mere counters, but he who supposes them to be only that is greatly mistaken ; more often they are very children of our inner selves, out-growing quickly the control of their parents, and entering upon an independent career which may be full as sunshine is of blessing, or more destructive than a prairie-fire. 2. What is truth ? It stands for the relation which God has established between things, the relation in which their harmony consists. It expresses conformity to fact—what really is seen as it is. It accords with, and is, the constitution of all things. It is of the essential substance of God; for if God were not true He would not be God. The more we think about this sublime theme, the more we see its ineffable dignity, and that the law which guards truth must be of supreme importance. I. Consider this law IN RELATION TO COURTS OF JUSTICE. 1. The literal form of the precept implies the existence of a court of justice. Here is a definite acknowledgment, at least by implication, of the principle of state tribunals; and if of tribunals, then also of governments, and of the necessary machinery of government. 2. Courts of justice exist, as their name implies, in order that justice may be done; and justice can only be done in proportion as truth prevails. The supreme business of every member of the court, from the judge to the humblest official, is with truth. II. Consider this law IN RELATION TO PUBLIC OPINION. 1. It is not by any means an ideal bar, this of public opinion: inconsistent in much, inconsequent in more; not patient in sifting evidence, nor impartial in hearing both sides, nor cautious in coming to conclusions; liable also to bursts of impulse, when, as in a wind-swept cornfield, all heads are bowed one way only to bend back again at the next breath: often its judgments are hasty, not seldom warped, sometimes cruelly unjust. Nevertheless, public opinion is a great natural assize, where every one of us passes judgment upon others, and where others pass judgment upon every one of us—a court with wider jurisdiction than any other in the world, a court always sitting, a court everywhere present. The special moment and consequence of its decisions lies in the fact that they affect our reputation. This being so, every man has a right to demand of every other man, and every man is bound to accord to every other man, a true and righteous witness. 2. In glancing at the more conspicuous forms of false witness in the court of public opinion, one dark and monstrous shape demands immediate notice. I mean slander, the deliberate invention of a lie to injure a neighbour. All forms of wilful misrepresentation, base insinuation, wanton detraction, damning with faint praise, and guilty silence that does the work of open defamation, belong to this category. Next to slander, I must mention tale-bearing, which signifies the spreading of evil reports. We ought not to carry stories to our neighbours' discredit, even if they are true (Lev. xix. 16). III. Consider this law IN RELATION TO THE PERSONAL CONSCIENCE. 1. When the Commandment says, "Thy neighbour must not be wronged by untruthful words," it manifestly says also, "Thou shalt not be a liar." Unless we are true, how can our witness be true? And if we are true, how can our witness be other than true? Three elements enter into a falsehood. It is a statement of what is not true; it is intended to deceive, and it violates a promise or obligation to speak the truth. 2. In this view of the obligation of every man to "put away lying and speak truth with his neighbour," the paramount importance of the law of truth stands forth conspicuous. Equivocation is seen to be nothing but a lie complicated with the meanness of evasion. Mental reservations are detected as lies blackened by breach of contract. Exaggerations and extenuations, fibs and white lies, are shown to be inexcusable. Pious frauds are branded as fraudulent piety. And the one only course open to a Christian man in his dealings with his neighbour is to speak truth. "Dare to be true; nothing can need a lie!" (*W. J. Woods, B.A.*) *The Ninth Commandment:*—This Commandment hath a prohibitory, and a mandatory part: the first is set down in plain words, the other is clearly implied. 1. The prohibitory part of the Commandment, or, what it forbids in general. It forbids anything which may tend to the disparagement or prejudice of our neighbour. More particularly, two things are forbidden in this Commandment. (1) Slandering our neighbour. The scorpion carries his poison in his tail; the slanderer carries his poison in his tongue. Slandering is to report things of others unjustly; "they laid things to my charge which I knew not." Eminency is commonly blasted by slander. Holiness itself is no shield from slander. The lamb's innocency will not preserve it from the wolf. We must not only not raise a false report, but not take it up. He that raiseth a slander, carries the devil in his tongue: and he that receives it, carries the devil in his ear. (2) The second thing forbidden in this Commandment is false witness. Here three sins are condemned: (*a*) Speaking that which is false; "lying lips are an abomination to the Lord." There is nothing more contrary to God than a lie. Imitate God who is the pattern of truth. Pythagoras being asked what made men like God answered, "When they speak truth." It is made the character of a man that shall go to heaven; "he speaketh the truth in his heart." (*b*) That which is condemned in the Commandment is witnessing that which is false; "thou shalt not bear false witness." There is a bearing of false witness for another, and a bearing false witness against another. (c) That which is condemned in the Commandment is swearing that which is false. When men take a false oath, and by that, take away the life of another. The Scythians made a law, when a man did bind two sins together, a lie with an oath, he was to lose his head, because this sin did take away all truth and faith from among men. The devil hath taken great possession of such who dare swear to a lie. 2. The mandatory part of this Commandment: that is, "that we stand up for others and vindicate them, when they are injured by lying lips." A man may wrong another as well by silence as by slander when he knows him to be wrongfully accused, yet doth not speak in his behalf. If others cast false aspersions on any, we should wipe them off. When the primitive Christians were falsely accused for incest, and killing their children, Tertullian made a famous apology in their vindication. This is to act the part both of a friend and of a Christian, to be an advocate for another, when he is wronged in his good name. (*T. Watson.*)　　*The scope of the Ninth Commandment :*—This Commandment checks all propensities to lying, and commands truthfulness of speech to and about our neighbour. It is very difficult to over-estimate the value of truth or the importance of being truthful in character and speech. There is a reality to the things and the laws which surround us and are within us which we call *truth*. When our thoughts exactly correspond with this reality we have apprehended truth. When we conform ourselves to this we are true. If our thought does not exactly correspond with this reality we are in error, and error is a mischief to us. We disobey the laws, we abuse the things about us, we are like blind men striking against obstacles, falling into pits. The nature of things remains unchanged, the laws are immutable, but we are false to them. Truth is not merely to be known, it is to be transmitted into life. Man is to be so hearty in his allegiance to the truth he knows, that he lives it and speaks it. The man who knows the truth and disobeys it, is false in his nature. He may not deceive his neighbours as to himself. Every one may know he is a false man, but his whole life is bearing false witness as to the truth, and as to it may deceive many. The greater part of the truth we possess we have derived from others. There is an exchange of truth. Men who search in one realm give the truth they find to their fellows who are searching in other realms, and receive truth from them in return, and each generation leaves its rich legacy of inherited and acquired truth to the following, and thus the race advances in the knowledge of truth. Wide is the realm of truth, in earth and sky, in matter and spirit, in time and eternity. Man should not shut his fellow out from any portion of it. If any one bears false witness to any part of the wide realm of truth, it is always against his neighbour, depriving him wrongfully of that which is of the greatest importance to his well-being. Great is the difference between truth and falsehood. Infinity and eternity cannot measure it. Of God it is said ; "He is light. He is the truth." Of the devil it is said : " There is no truth in him. He is a liar and the father of it." Hell is the home of universal falsehood and distrust. Each one there is alone in the midst of others, deceiving and being deceived, distrusting and being distrusted. Heaven is the home of universal truth and confidence. The more we follow truth, the nearer we advance to God. The truths in nature are His thoughts, written on the heavens in light, on the earth in beauty, on our souls in virtue. As we express truth we help others to advance to Him, by small steps or large, according to the importance of the truths we speak. The Commandment requires truth in ordinary conversation. Conjecture and partial information must be spoken of as such, not made to pass for complete knowledge. We must strive to know fully, that we may speak clearly. Vivid, sprightliness, and colour may be employed to interest in and set forth the truth, not to gain applause, and all exaggeration must be avoided. Our aim must not be selfish, to be considered as having had a wonderful experience, or as having fine descriptive powers, or as being well informed, but simply to convey truth to our neighbour. In all those cases in which we speak to our neighbour with intent to lead him to a desired line of conduct, our self-interest may be aroused against our loyalty to truth. Mental reservation, double meaning, significant silence, the end justifies the means, and all kindred evasions, may quiet a confused conscience, but will never do to plead before a truth-loving God. But, says the business man, must I reveal the defects in the property I am trying to sell? Must I reveal the fact I have skilfully acquired, that prices in the market will be much lower to-morrow? Certainly, you must, or you will both lie and steal in one act. We are to speak truth, again, not only *to* our neighbour, but *about* him. This Commandment guards a man's reputation—gives each man a right to have his reputation the exact expression of his character. We should guard against secret prejudice against our neighbour, or envy of him, and should cultivate such love for him that we will rejoice in his good qualities and in his good name, that we will sorrow over the faults in him we cannot help seeing, and throw over them the garment of Christian charity, rather than exulting to proclaim them to the world. This Commandment should govern not only our tongues, but our hearts and ears as well. It forbids an appetite for gossip, a desire to hear detraction, and a tendency to form unfavourable opinions of others. By holding our peace when we have it in our power to defend, by failing to mention the good when the evil is spoken of, by encouraging the telling of evil by eager listening, we assault the reputation of our neighbour by the assent of our silence. There is a modern statue of Truth, instinct with the fire of genius, which strongly incites an opposite spirit and action. A stately woman in pure white marble, with beautiful and firm face, wears on her head a helmet and carries a sword in her hand. At her feet lies a mask touched by the point of her sword. She has just smitten it from the face of Slander, and now she proudly draws her robe away from its polluting touch. (*F. S. Schenck.*) *The Ninth Commandment :*—I. This command prohibits LYING. 1. What a lie is. (1) A lie, according to St. Austin's definition of it, is a voluntary speaking of an untruth, with an intent to deceive. (2) Lies are usually distinguished into three kinds. (*a*) There is a jocular lie : a lie, framed to excite mirth and laughter ; not to deceive the hearer, only to please and divert him. (*b*) There is an officious lie : which is told for another's benefit and advantage ; and seems to make an abundant compensation for its falsehood, by its use and profit. (*c*) There is a malicious and pernicious lie : a lie, devised on purpose for the hurt and damage of my neighbour. 2. Now, for the aggravations of this sin, consider—(1) It is a sin, that makes you most like unto the devil. (2) Consider, that it is a sin most contrary to the nature of God, who is truth itself. (3) Consider, that it is a sin, that gives in a fearful evidence against us, that we belong to the devil, and are his children. (4) Consider, how dreadfully God hath threatened it with eternal death (Rev. xxii. 15). (5) A lie showeth a most degenerous and cowardly fear of men, and a most daring contempt of the great God. (6) Mankind generally account it the most infamous and reproachful sin of all others. (7) It is a sin that God will detect ; and exposeth those who are guilty of it to shame and contempt (Prov. xii. 19). II. There remain two other violations of this Commandment : the one is, by SLANDER AND DETRACTION ; the other, by base flattery and soothing. And both these may respect either ourselves or others. 1. Indeed slander and detraction seem somewhat to differ. For slander, properly, is a false imputation of vice ; but detraction is a causeless, diminishing report of virtue. (1) If thou wouldst keep thyself from being a slanderer of others, addict not thyself violently to any one party or persuasion of men. (2) If thou wouldst not be guilty of slander, be not busy in other men's affairs. (3) If thou wouldst not be guilty of slander, be frequent in reflecting upon thine own miscarriages ; or thy proneness to fall into the same, or greater faults. (4) If you would not be guilty of slander, listen not unto those who are slanderers and detractors. (5) If you would not be slanderers of others be not self-lovers. For self-love always causeth envy ; and envy detraction. (6) Be not too easy and facile to entertain suspicious and evil surmises against others. III. The third sin against this Commandment is BASE FLATTERY and SOOTHING ; which is a quite opposite extreme to the other, as both are opposite to truth. Now this is, either self-flattery, or the flattering of others. 1. There is a self-flattery. Learn, therefore, O Christian, to take the just measure of thyself. 2. There is a sinful flattering of others : and that, either by an immoderate extolling of their virtues ; or, what is worse, by a wicked commendation even of their very vices. This is a sin most odious unto God, who hath threatened to cut off all flattering lips (Psa. xii. 3). (*Bp. E. Hopkins.*) *Slander :*—A man of overweening curiosity who looked down his neighbour's chimney to see what he was cooking for supper, not only failed to find out what he desired to know, but was nearly blinded by the smoke. Somebody has conveyed a well-deserved rebuke to such unamiable people, who said, " If we would sit down by our neighbour's fire occasionally, instead of looking down his chimney, we would see many good points in his character that smoke will certainly obscure." There are so many ways of kindling a flame by the poisonous breath of slander, that only a few of them can now be referred to. I. PERVERTING ONE'S WORDS OR ACTIONS IS AN EVERY-DAY OCCURRENCE. II. Another way by which flames are often kindled to the damage of one's good name, is THE HABIT OF JUMPING TO CONCLUSIONS

WITHOUT SUFFICIENT EVIDENCE TO SUSTAIN THEM. While Wilberforce occupied his prominent place in the British parliament he was exceedingly annoyed by finding himself chronicled in opposition papers as "St. Wilberforce." "He was lately seen," said the slanderous print, "walking up and down in the pump-room at Bath, reading his prayers, like his predecessors of old, who prayed at the corners of the streets to be seen of men!" Mr. Wilberforce, who was not more distinguished for his brilliant mental gifts than for his unobtrusive goodness, remarked upon this wanton falsehood: " As there is generally some slight circumstance which perverseness turns into a charge or reproach, I began to reflect, and I soon found the occasion of the calumny. I was walking in the pump-room, in conversation with a friend; a passage from Horace was quoted, the accuracy of which was questioned, and as I had a copy of the Latin poet in my pocket, I took it out and read the words. This was the plain "bit of wire" which factious malignity sharpened into a pin to pierce my reputation." It is pitiful to think how many ugly pins have been fashioned out of smaller bits of wire than that! III. THE CRUEL PURPOSES OF SLANDER MAY ALSO BE ACCOMPLISHED BY SLY INSINUATIONS AND CRAFTY QUESTIONS CALCULATED TO AROUSE SERIOUS AND DAMAGING SUSPICIONS. When any one spoke evil of another in the presence of Peter the Great, he would promptly stop him and say, " Well, now; but has he not got a bright side? Come, tell me what good you know of him. It is easy to splash mud; but I would rather help a man to keep his coat clean!" IV. SLANDER IS ENCOURAGED BY THOSE WHO PATIENTLY LISTEN TO IT, and who prompt the cruel person to vent his venom on the innocent. (*J. H. Norton, D.D.*) *Violations of the law of truth :*—I. MISREPRESENTATION. It is an ingenious method to class an opponent with those whom the world has already condemned as heterodox. It is still another to make his truth responsible for all the folly that unwise minds have added to it. II. INSINUATION. A whisper dropped carelessly in some corner among the combustibles, a look, a shrug of the shoulders, a sneer, a laugh may serve the purpose. Rumour with most minds is presumptive evidence, and they will say with a knowing air, " There must be some fire in so much smoke." III. DETRACTION. If we be unable to find evil in the opinions or actions of another, we can attribute his good to doubtful motives. IV. TALEBEARING. Is there, I pray you, a creature more contemptible than this, who fattens on the griefs of others, and passes day and night in such petty larceny? How few dream of their responsibility in this! We know the power of strychnine or arsenic, but not of a word. What undesigned phrases we drop in conversation, and forget as soon as passed, yet they are never forgotten! What insignificant insects may have a fatal sting! (*E. A. Washburn, D.D.*) *The Ninth Commandment :*—This Commandment requires us, as the Catechism says, " to keep our tongues from evil-speaking, lying, and slandering." Slandering means saying anything that will injure the character of another person. There was a company of ladies once at the house of a clergyman. As he entered the room he heard them speaking in a low voice of an absent friend. " She's very odd," says one. " Yes, very singular indeed," says another. " Do you know, she often does so and so?" says a third, mentioning certain things to her discredit. The clergyman asked who it was. When told, he said, " Oh yes, she is odd ; she's very odd; she's remarkably singular. Why, would you believe it?" he added, in a slow, impressive manner; "she was never heard to speak ill of any absent friends!" A clergyman was once examining the children of an infant school upon the Commandments. He put his hand on the head of a little boy, and said, " My little man, can you tell me what the Ninth Commandment means by " bearing false witness against thy neighbour"? The boy hesitated a while, and then said, " It means telling lies, sir." The minister didn't exactly like this answer, so looking at a little girl who stood next to him, he asked, " What do you say?" Without waiting a moment, she replied, " It's when nobody does nothing, and somebody goes and tells of it." " Very good," said the minister. The little girl's answer was a very funny one; but the little boy's was true. Bearing false witness is telling lies, and telling lies is bearing false witness. We break the Ninth Commandment every time we tell a lie. I. The first reason why we should never bear false witness or tell a lie is, because it is a MEAN thing. Who was the first person of whom we know that ever told a lie? Satan. Where was this lie told? In the garden of Eden. Satan bore false witness against God. He contradicted God. This was mean of Satan. He did it out of spite. A gentleman once sent his servant to market with the direction to bring home the best thing he could find. He carried home a tongue. He was sent again with the direction to bring home the worst thing he could find. Again he brought home a tongue. This was right; for the tongue is the best thing in the world when properly used, or the worst when not so used. II. The second reason why we should not do it is, because it is an UNPROFITABLE thing. People generally expect to make something when they tell a lie. III. The third reason why we ought not to do this is, because it is DANGEROUS. Lying is like letting water through a bank. When it once begins to run, there is no telling where it will stop. Now, suppose it were possible all at once to draw every bolt and fastening out of that ship as she sails over the ocean, what would become of her? She would fall to pieces directly, and all her cargo would be lost. Well, every family, every village or town, is like such a ship. It is made up of a number of persons bound together. And what binds them together? Why, truth or confidence. Truth among people in society is like the bolt in the ship. If nobody told the truth, and people had no confidence in one another, they could no more live together in families or communities, and do business together, than a number of pieces of timber without bolts to fasten them together could make a ship. Would it not be very dangerous to have a person on board a ship who had a machine for drawing the bolts out, and who was trying to use it all the time? Certainly it would. Well, lying is such a machine. IV. Our fourth and last reason is, we ought not to do it because it is a WICKED thing. This is shown by—1. What God says of liars (see Prov. vi. 19; xii. 5). 2. What God does with liars (see Rev. xxi. 8). (*R. Newton, D.D.*) *On the sin of bearing false witness :*—I. First, WHAT ARE THE DIFFERENT SENSES IN WHICH A MAN MAY BE SAID TO BEAR FALSE WITNESS AGAINST HIS NEIGHBOUR. II. THE ENORMITY OF THE SIN OF BEARING FALSE WITNESS. The malignity of an offence arises either from the motives that prompted it or the consequences produced by it. The most usual incitement to defamation is envy, or impatience of the merit, or success of other; a malice raised not by any injury received, but merely by the sight of that happiness which we cannot attain. Calumnies are sometimes the offspring of resentment. When a man is opposed in a design which he cannot justify, and defeated in the prosecution of schemes of tyranny, extortion, or oppression, he seldom fails to revenge his overthrow by blackening that integrity which effected it. The consequences of this crime, whatever be the inducement to commit it, are equally pernicious. He that attacks the reputation of another, invades the most valuable part of his property, and perhaps the only part which he can call his own. (*Bp. J. Taylor, D.D.*) *Breaches of the Ninth Commandment :*—I. In HEART a man may fail—1. By suspecting others unjustly, this is called evil surmising (1 Tim. vi. 4), which is when men are suspected of some evil without ground, as Potiphar suspected Joseph. 2. By rash judging, and unjust concluding concerning a man's state, as Job's friends did; or his actions, as Eli did of Hannah, saying, that she was drunk, because of the moving of her lips. 3. By hasty judging, too often passing sentence in our mind from some seeming evidence of that which is only in the heart, and not in the outward practice; this is but to judge before the time, and hastily (Matt. vii. 1). 4. There is light judging, laying the weight of conclusions upon arguments that will not bear it, as Job's friends did, and as the barbarians suspected Paul, when they saw the viper on his hand, to be a murderer (Acts xxv. 4). 5. The breach of this command in the heart may be when suspicion of our neighbour's failing is kept up, and means not used to be satisfied about it, contrary to that (Matt. xviii. 15). If thy brother offend thee, &c., and when we seek not to be satisfied, but rest on presumptions, when they seem probable. II. In GESTURE this command may be broken, by nodding, winking, or such like (and even sometimes by silence), when these import in our accustomed way some tacit sinistrous insinuation, especially when either they are purposed for that end, or when others are known to mistake because of them, and we suffer them to continue under this mistake. III. By WRITING this command may be broken, as Ezra, v. 6.; Neh. vi. 5, where calumniating rebels are written, and sent by their enemies against the Jews and Nehemiah; in which respect many fail in these days. IV. But WORDS are most properly the seat wherein this sin is subjected, whether they be only or merely words, or also put in writing, because in these our conformity or disconformity to truth doth most appear. (*James Durham.*) *Slander :*—The false witness which was born against the Puritans by the profligate wits of the court of Charles II., produced in the mind of this country a strong antagonism to the great principles for which the Puritans contended. The calumnies which, during the first two centuries, were flung at the Christians, made many upright heathen believe that Christianity itself was an execrable superstition. Slander a clergyman and you help to make the principle of an Established Church odious, and you try to win the cause of ecclesiastical freedom before the tribunal of public opinion by " false witness " against your neighbour. Slander a Nonconformist and you help to make Non-conformity odious, and you try by " false witness " against your neighbour to induce the tribunal of public opinion to pronounce in favour of religious establishments. Pick up and circulate any scandal you may happen to hear—no matter how un-trustworthy the authority for it—to the dishonour of a religious man, and you do what lies in your power to create a conviction in the public mind that all religious men are hypocrites, and that religion itself is an imposture. It is by the opinion which society forms on individuals that its general opinions on all questions, moral, religious, and political, are to a very large extent created ; and to bear " false witness " either for or against any man is to attempt to deceive and to mislead that great Tribunal—whose decisions affect not merely the happiness and the reputation of particular men, but the formation of the conscience and the judgment of the whole nation. (*R. W. Dale, D.D.*)   *False witness :*—There was a boy of the name of John Busby. He said once, " What a wicked man Mr. Bradburry is." A gentleman said to him, " I do not think he is wicked ; I think he is very good ; he is always on the line of his duty." " I only know," said John, " that he went to church last Sunday, and he slept all through the sermon." The other was very much surprised, because he thought Mr. Bradburry was a very good man ; so he said to the boy, " Can you tell me what the text was ? " " No, I can't," said John ; " but I can tell you Mr. Bradburry was asleep all the time." " Then," said the gentleman to him, " I happen to know the text ; for Mr. Bradburry told me not only the text, but all about the sermon. You say he was fast asleep ; but I can tell you he has got very weak eyes, and there is a gas lamp between him and the pulpit ; and he is obliged to shut his eyes because he cannot stand the light." Do you see, that was " bearing false witness " on the part of John Busby ; that was slander, taking away his character. We must not bear " false witness." We used sometimes to play a game called " Scandal." It is a very good game. You all sit round in a circle, and somebody tells a person at one end a story he has heard about something or somebody—anything you like. He whispers it to the next one, and he again whispers it to the next, and he to the next, and to the next. When it comes to the last person, he is to say aloud what he has had whispered to him, and the first is to say what he had said. Often the act of repeating it all around makes it seem quite a different story. That is called " Scandal " or " Slander." You try that game some day, and it will teach you the importance of being very exact in repeating what you hear, if you would not " bear false witness." (*J. Vaughan.*)   *A cure for backbiting :*—A gentleman writes that he once saw the title " Slander Book," printed on the back of a small ledger in a friend's house. On examining it, he found that the various members of the household were charged so much for every piece of slander they were found uttering. The accounts were very neatly and correctly kept, credits entered, &c., as in a merchant's office. The plan originated with a good young girl, who had observed the wretched effects of evil-speaking in families and in the neighbourhood. *Scandal :*—The story is told of a woman who freely used her tongue to the scandal of others, and made con-fession to the priest of what she had done. He gave her a ripe thistle top, and told her to go out in various directions and scatter the seeds, one by one. Wonder-ing at the penance, she obeyed, and then returned and told her confessor. To her amazement, he bade her go back and gather the scattered seeds ; and when she objected that it would be impossible, he replied, that it would be still more difficult to gather up and destroy all evil reports which she had circulated about others. Any thoughtless, careless child can scatter a handful of thistle-seed before the wind in a moment, but the strongest and wisest man cannot gather them again.

Ver. 17. **Thou shalt not covet.**—*The Tenth Commandment :*—I. The history of the world is stained and darkened by the CRIMES TO WHICH NATIONS HAVE BEEN DRIVEN BY THE SPIRIT OF COVETOUSNESS. Covetousness is forbidden not merely to prevent the miseries, and horrors, and crimes of aggressive war, but to train the spirit of nations to the recognition of God's own idea of their relations to each other. Nations should see underlying this Commandment the Divine idea of the unity of the human race ; they should learn to seek greatness by ministering to each other's peace, security, prosperity, and happiness. II. INDIVIDUALS, AS WELL AS NATIONS, MAY VIOLATE THIS LAW. They may do it—1. By ambition. 2. By discontent and envy. 3. By the desire to win from another man the love which is the pride and joy of his life. The very end for which Christ came was to redeem us from selfishness. The last of the Ten Commandments touches the characteristic precept of the new law, "Thou shalt love thy neighbour as thyself." (*R. W. Dale, D.D.*)   *Coveting prohibited :*—I. WHAT IS COVETING? The Hebrew word is really but expressive of a strong controlling *desire.* This is not forbidden *per se* in the Commandment, but a special form of coveting, determined by the objects enumerated. Prussic acid in itself is not bad—it is just as good as bread or milk; but it would be evil in me to use or seek prussic acid as my food, because its relation to me in that case would be pernicious. II. WHAT ARE THE OBJECTS WHICH WE MUST NOT COVET? If anything belongs to our neighbour, either by the tie of property, as a house, or by the tie of domestic union, as a wife, it thereby partakes of the sacredness of his own person, and is so to be viewed by us. The coveting any such object for our-selves is directly at war with this view. It pollutes this sanctity, it destroys in our heart the harmony of things and introduces confusion. Anything appertaining to our neighbour is in such relation to us as to condemn all coveting. The elements of his wrath, his happiness, his fame, his success, are all included. His time, his talents, his opportunities, his advantages, so far as they are peculiarly his and are not common to all, are in the same category. III. WHAT IS THE HARM OF COVETING? 1. It degrades our neighbour in our heart. 2. We are nursing the brood of sin in our soul. It is spiritual corruption—gangrene. You are carefully cherishing the eggs of envy, jealousy, malice, anger, and revenge, when you indulge in your unhallowed desires; and these dire monsters will be hatched and become your irresistible masters before you are aware. IV. HOW SHALL WE AVOID THIS EVIL COVETING? "Set your affection on things above, not on things on the earth." The desires of the heart are not to be annihilated, man is not to be reduced to an inert lump, his passions are to burn as brightly as ever, his eager heart to beat as strongly as before, yet not for worldly jewels, but for heaven's crown. The current is to run as swiftly as before, but now in a new channel. We are to seek first—that is, as chief—the kingdom of God and His righteousness. (*H. Crosby, D.D.*) *Inordinate desire forbidden :*—Love is compatible with desire, but it is not consistent with inordinate desire. I. The violation of this command ARRAIGNS THE WISDOM OF PROVIDENCE. II. The violation of this command DISTURBS THE BALANCE OF SOCIETY. III. The violation of this command PRODUCES CRIMINAL DEEDS. IV. The violation of this command EMBITTERS EXISTENCE. V. This command can only be kept in THE SPIRIT OF THE GOSPEL. (*W. Burrows, B.A.*)   *The law of motive :*—1. Human laws cannot meddle with a man's desires; they may control his conduct, may even punish his utterances; but any attempt to fetter his wishes would be as futile as to chain the free winds, or restrain the ocean's tides. Therefore, when this Commandment says, "Thou shalt not covet," &c., it gives a plain warning that the Decalogue is something more than a criminal code. 2. Again, a man's desires can only be known to God and himself, and no other person has any right to rule them. Therefore, when this Commandment lays claim to such a right, it manifestly speaks in the name of God. I. What is THE ESSENTIAL PRINCIPLE of this Command-ment? 1. What is forbidden is unlawful desire. We are to cherish contentment; to avoid discontent and envy. (1) What is there in repining to induce success? Grumbling makes mischief, but it does no work. It sours men; renders them un-thankful to God, and unjust to their neighbours; destroys their peace and paralyzes their courage; blinds them to their blessings, so that they become "poor in abundance, and famished at a feast"; but far from helping them in the race of life it is the direst of hindrances. (2) And discontent is no whit wiser when it takes the name of ambition. He that would be wretched all his days, cold in the sun-shine, and parched beside the running stream, let him be ambitious! He that would sow scorpions to torment his latter days, let him be ambitious! "By that sin fell the angels." 2. But of all violations of this Commandment, the Scriptures single out for especial reprobation the greed of money. Even when there is no apparent disregard of the rights of others, the inordinate love of gain—"accursed hunger of pernicious gold"—is stigmatized with the name of covetousness. But, it may be asked, if it is lawful to make money, why is it unlawful to love money? The answer is, that money should be only a means to an end, the end being the glorifying of God with our substance; but a man cannot serve two masters. If we love the means, we cease to love the end; and the love of money is forbidden because it kills the love of God. II. THE SPECIAL FUNCTION of this Commandment. 1. To awaken a conviction of moral failure. The ordinary course of many a man's moral life might be compared to the glassy surface of a river, smooth because undisturbed. If in that swift torrent, at mid-channel, some firmly-bedded rock obtrudes itself, there is a sudden swirling and commotion, the opposition reveals the current. Like that rock is this law of motive. It does not cause, does not reverse the stream, but it discovers it. Oh, terrible illumination! 2. So in the providence of God the way is prepared for a gospel of grace and truth. III. THE SECRET OF THIS LAW'S FULFILMENT. We can perfectly keep no Commandment except as we have learned the law of motive; and we can keep the law of motive only as we do it with loving hearts. 1. Without love no law can be truly obeyed, whether to God or our neighbour; but he that loves as Christ loved, will love rightly; he that loves rightly will desire rightly; and he that desires rightly will keep both this Commandment and all the Decalogue. 2. This spirit of neighbourly love needs to be empowered by the grace of Christ. Our Saviour is not only the Pattern, but also the Source of it. (*W. J. Woods, B.A.*) *The Tenth Commandment :*—I. Let us inquire, WHAT IS COVETOUSNESS? 1. Covetousness is the unlawful desire of temporal good; when we wish for that which we have not, or when we wish for that which is another's. 2. Covetousness consists in an inordinate desire after natural good, although the desire itself be not unlawful. In the one case, the matter of the desire is to be condemned; in this case the measure and degree in which that desire is cherished and indulged. 3. An undue delight and satisfaction in created good, is another form of covetousness. 4. All discontentment of spirit, envious repining, and uncharitable judging towards our neighbour, his prosperity and possessions, partake of the nature of covetousness; discontent with the lot and station which God has appointed us; envious repinings at the prosperity and success of others. II. I am now to show you ITS HIGH CRIMINALITY; or, to use the language of Scripture, its "exceeding sinfulness." 1. That it stands directly opposed to the benevolence of Deity; God is infinitely good, and He is infinitely kind. 2. This is a sin which is peculiarly dishonouring to God, as well as expressly contrary to His revealed will. 3. This disposition of mind is a direct and too prevalent impediment to the introduction of Divine truth into the heart of man. It is the pre-occupancy which the world has insured in our thoughts, and affections, and desires, which keeps us at a distance from Christ, and the blessing of his redemption. 4. This sin is peculiarly destructive of the peace and happiness of human society. 5. This sin, above all others, deludes, hardens, and destroys. It deludes. Few persons, who are under the influence of covetousness, ever suspect it. It conceals itself under very plausible names, and specious disguises, such as prudence and foresight, frugality and good thrift. Terms much misapplied. And this sin not only deludes, but hardens. "Take heed, lest any of you be hardened through the deceitfulness of sin," and more particularly this sin. There is nothing which so indurates the soul, depriving it of its finest sensations, eradicating its tenderest sympathies, and drying up its noblest sensibilities, as covetousness. It tends to throw an armour of proof around the mind under its tyranny, which no arrow of conviction can pierce, and of which it is most difficult to strip the possessor. Whatever men may think or say, this sin, without intervening pardon and repentance, will assuredly destroy the soul. 6. This is a sin which, of all others, inflicts upon the subject of it the worst miseries here, while it prepares for eternal misery hereafter. (*G. Clayton.*) *The Tenth Commandment :*—I. THE DUTIES REQUIRED. 1. I shall consider the duty of this command as it respects ourselves. A thorough weanedness from and indifference to all those things that we have, in which our desire may be too eager. There are some things whereof our desire cannot be too much, as of God, Christ, grace, victory over sin; and therefore we read of a holy lusting (Gal. v. 17). There are other things to which our desires may be carried out too eagerly and inordinately. Thus we may sin, not only in the inordinate desire of sensual things, as meat, drink, &c., but in rational things, as honour, esteem, &c. (1) Hearty renunciation of our own will, saying, with the pattern of contentment, "Not my will, but Thine be done." We must no more be choosers for ourselves of our own lot; but as little children standing at the table, not to carve for themselves, but to take the bit that is given them. (2) Absolute resignation to the will of the Lord (Matt. xvi. 24; 1 Sam. iii. 18). 2. We are to consider the duty of this command, as it respects our neighbour. And that is a right and charitable or loving frame of spirit towards himself and all that is his. (1) Love to our neighbour's person, as to ourselves (Rom. xiii. 9). (2) An upright respect to what is his, for his sake. As we are to love himself for God's sake, so what is his for his sake (Deut. xxii. 1). (3) An hearty desire of his welfare and prosperity in all things, as of our own, his honour, life, chastity, wealth, good name, and whatever is his. (4)

A real complacency in his welfare and the welfare of what is his (Rom. xii. 15). (5) A cordial sympathy with him in any evil that befalls him (Rom. xii. 20). II. THE SINS FORBIDDEN. This command is a curb and bridle to the distempered heart of man, which of all parts of man is the hardest to be commanded and kept within bounds. Men may be of a courteous obliging behaviour, keep in their hands from killing, or what tendeth thereunto, their bodies from uncleanness, their hands from stealing, and their tongues from lying; while, in the meantime, the heart in all these respects may be going within the breast like a troubled sea, unto which this command by Divine authority saith, "Peace, be still." The heart distempered by original sins runs out in the irascible faculty in tormenting passions, bearing an aversion of the heart to what the Lord in His wisdom lays before men. I will show the evil of discontentment, and paint out this sin in its black colours. It is the hue of hell all over. 1. Discontent is, in the nature of it, a compound of the blackest ingredients, the scum of the corrupt heart boiling up, and mixed to make up the hellish composition. (1) Unsubjection to and rebellion against the will of God (Hos. iv. 16). (2) Sorrow of heart under the Divine dispensation towards them. (3) Anger and wrath against their lot (Jude 16). Thus the discontented do in their hearts bark at the mountains of brass (Zech. vi. 1); as dogs do at the moon, and with the same success. 2. If ye view discontentment in the rise of it, ye will see further into the evil of it. It takes its rise from—(1) A blinded judgment which puts darkness for light, and light for darkness, and cannot see into the wisdom of the conduct of Providence. (2) A proud heart. (3) An unmortified affection to the creature (1 Tim. vi. 9, 10). (4) A spirit of unbelief. 3. View it in the effect, and it will appear very black. The tree is known by its fruits. (1) It mars communion with and access to God. (2) It quite unfits a man for holy duties, so that he cannot perform them rightly or acceptably, for speaking to God in prayer, or His speaking to them by His Word. (3) Nay, it unfits people for the work of their ordinary calling. It is not only an enemy to grace, but to gifts too, and common prudence. (4) It mars the comfort of society, and makes people uneasy to those that are about them. (5) It is a torment to oneself, and makes a man his own tormentor (1 Kings xxi. 4). (6) It is not only tormenting to one's mind, but is ruinous to the body (Prov. xvii. 22). (7) It sucks the sap out of all one's enjoyments. As a few drops of gall will embitter a cup of wine, and a few drops of ink will blacken a cup of the clearest liquor; so discontent upon one ground will embitter and blacken all other enjoyments. (8) Hence it always makes one unthankful. Let Providence set the discontented man in a paradise, the fruit of that one tree which is forbidden him, and which he is so uneasy about, will so embitter him that he will not give God thanks for all the variety of other delights which the garden is furnished with. For all these avail him nothing while that is kept out of his reach. When once it entered into Adam's heart, it made him at one stroke break through all the Ten Commandments. 2. The branch that runs against our neighbour's condition is envying and grudging. The object of this sin is the good of our neighbour; and the better the object is, the worse is the sin. 1. View it in the ingredients thereof, whereof it is made up. (1) Sorrow and grief for the good of our neighbour (1 Cor. xiii. 4). (2) Fretting anger at their good (Psa. xxxvii. 1). 2. View it in the springs and rise thereof. (1) Covetousness of what is their neighbour's. (2) Discontent. (3) Pride and selfishness. 3. View it in the effects thereof. It has almost the same as those of discontent, which may be well applied thereto. I will only say that envy is a sword, and wounds three at once. (1) It strikes against God, being highly offensive and dishonourable to Him. It quarrels His government of the world, and accuses Him of folly, partiality, and injustice (Matt. xx. 15). (2) It strikes against our neighbour. It is a bitter disposition of spirit, wishing his ill-fare, and grudging his good; and not only binds up men's hands from doing him good, but natively tends to loose them to his hurt. It will be at him one way or other in word or deed, and there is no escaping the evil of it (Prov. xxvii. 4). (3) It strikes at oneself (Job v. 2). "Envy slayeth the silly man." Though it be so weak as to do no execution on others, yet be sure it never misses a man's self; and it wounds oneself the deeper, that it cannot do much hurt to the party envied. (*T. Boston, D.D.*)   *The Tenth Commandment:*—I. The sin here prohibited is CONCUPISCENCE, or an unlawful lusting after what is another man's. For since God had, in the other Commandments, forbidden the acts of sin against our neighbour, He well knew that the best means to keep men from committing sin in act would be to keep them from desiring it in heart; and therefore He, who is a Spirit, imposeth a law upon our spirits, and forbids us to covet what before He had forbidden us to perpetrate. There are four degrees of this sinful concupiscence. 1. There is the first film and shadow of an evil thought, the imperfect embryo of a sin before it is well shaped in us, or hath received any lineaments and features. And these the Scripture calls the imaginations of the thoughts of men's hearts (Gen. vi. 5). 2. A farther degree of this concupiscence is when these evil motions are entertained in the sensual mind with some measure of complacency and delight. 3. Hereupon follows assent and approbation of the sin in the practical judgment. 4. When any sinful motion hath thus gotten an allowance and pass from the judgment, then it betakes itself to the will for a decree. II. I shall close up all with some PRACTICAL USE AND IMPROVEMENT. 1. Learn here to adore the unlimited and boundless sovereignty of the great God. 2. Content not thyself with an outward conformity to the law, but labour to approve thy heart in sincerity and purity unto God ; otherwise thou art but a pharisaical hypocrite, and washest only the outside of the cup, when within thou art still full of unclean lusts. 3. See here the best and the surest methods, to keep us from the outward violation of God's laws; which is to mortify our corrupt concupiscence and desires. And therefore the wisdom of God hath set this Commandment in the last place, as a fence and guard to all the rest. (*Bp. E. Hopkins.*)　　*The Tenth Commandment :*—We have here at the close a startling enough reminder that the calling of Israel to be a state or commonwealth did not exhaust its calling. It is very easy to see that the idea thus introduced at the close of the covenant was sure to exert a profound influence on the Israelite's whole conception of duty. 1. For one thing, it served to lay emphasis upon the stainless purity required in each individual soul. To be a good citizen, it told him, might be enough in an earthly kingdom, but not in the kingdom of Jehovah. Jehovah looks upon every heart. He is each man's God as well as King over all the citizens ; Lord of the conscience and the interior life. The individual, therefore, must be holy as well as the state ; and if innocence from statutory transgression be much, purity in the soul is more. 2. In the next place, this sudden revelation of a deeper righteousness, which is so unexpectedly flashed out upon us at the close of the Commandments, flings its piercing light back upon all that had gone before. The truth is that illicit conduct always has its root in illicit desire. 3. In the next place, it was by thus appending, as it were, a rider to every other Commandment of the Ten that this last one awoke in earnest Hebrews the conviction not only of failure but of hopeless failure. A fatal commandment, truly, to one's self-righteous conceit ! Not content with disclosing ghastly depths of evil beneath the surface of a decorous and well-ordered life, it insists on probing the motives of our best conduct; it puts us upon an effort to "cleanse the very thoughts of our hearts," not "by the inspiration of the Holy Ghost," but by our own exertions; till the poor soul, stung to death by evil thoughts which it cannot expel, evil desires which it cannot prevent, and evil passions which it cannot master, is reduced to an extremity of despair : "Who shall deliver me out of this body of death ? " 4. It is in this way, finally, that the last of the Ten Words educated the Hebrew for the New Testament revelation of "grace and truth by Jesus Christ." (*J. O. Dykes, D.D.*) *On covetousness :*—I. We should not covet, in the first place, because it is UNSATIS-FYING. If we get the things we covet, instead of being satisfied, we shall only want more. Our covetous desires are like a tub without a bottom, and trying to get satisfied by indulging them is just like trying to fill a tub with water when there is no bottom to it. "How strange it is," said a young man one day to Dr. Franklin, "that when men get rich they are just as unsatisfied and anxious to make money as when they were poor." There was a little child playing in the room near them. "Johnny, come here," said Dr. F. The little fellow came up to him. "Here, my man, is an apple for you," said he, handing one from a fruit-basket on the table. It was so large that the child could hardly grasp it. He then gave it a second, which filled the other hand; and picking out a third, remarkable for its size and beauty, he said, "Here's another." The child tried hard to hold this last apple between the other two, but it dropped on the carpet, and rolled away over the floor. "See, ' said Dr. F., " there is a little man with more riches than he can enjoy, but not satisfied." II. Again, we should not covet, because it is DISGRACEFUL. A person who covets is very nearly related to a thief. Here is a chicken almost ready to be hatched, and there is a chicken that is already hatched. What is the difference between them ? Why, one is *in* the shell, while the other is *out* of it. That is all the difference. There is nothing in the world but the thickness of that thin shell which separates one of them from the other. A slight tapping, a very little pecking on the end of that shell, and it is broken through, and then out comes the chicken, as lively and active as its little brother that came out yesterday. Now, just such is the relation that exists between a covetous person and a thief. There is nothing but a thin shell that separates them from each other. The covetous person is a thief *in* the shell; the thief is a covetous person *out of* the shell. III. We should not covet, because it is INJURIOUS. Some years ago there was a large ship, called the *Kent,* going from England to the East Indies. On her voyage she caught fire. The flames could not be put out. While she was burning another vessel came in sight, and offered to take off her crew and passengers. The sea was very rough, and the only way to get the people off the burning ship was to let them down by ropes from the end of a boom into the little boats, that were tossed about like corks by the rough waves below. One of the sailors, who knew that the mate had a large quantity of gold in his possession, determined to get it and take it with him. So he broke into the mate's cabin, forced open his desk, and taking about four hundred pounds in gold pieces, put them in a belt, and fastened it round his waist. His turn came to leave the burning ship. He got out to the end of the boom, slipped down the rope, and let go, expecting to drop right into the boat that was beneath him. But a sudden movement of the waves carried the boat out of his reach, and he was plunged into the sea. He was an excellent swimmer, and if it had not been for the gold he had coveted, he would have risen like a cork to the surface, and soon been safe in the boat. But the weight of the money round his waist made him sink like lead in the mighty waters. He never rose again to the surface. Ah, as he felt the golden weight dragging him deeper and deeper down into the vast ocean, he must have understood plainly enough how injurious covetousness is! IV. The fourth and last reason why we should not covet is, because it is SINFUL. It breaks this Commandment. And the worst thing you can say of any sin is that it breaks God's law. But by coveting we break two Commandments at once. Besides breaking the Tenth, we at the same time break the First Commandment by committing this sin. You know the First Commandment forbids idolatry. It says, "Thou shalt have no other gods before Me." But the Bible tells us that "covetousness is idolatry" (Col. iii. 5). This means that when people become covetous they put their gold in the place of God. They love it more than they love God; they think of it more than they think of God; they trust to it more than they trust to God. But there is even more than this to be said about covetousness. The covetous man breaks the whole Ten Commandments at once. You know our Saviour said the Ten Commandments were all embraced in two, viz., to love God with all our hearts, and to love our neighbour as ourselves. But the covetous man loves his gold with all his heart: by this he breaks the first four Commandments. He loves his gold more than he loves his neighbour: by this he breaks the last six Commandments. What a dreadfully wicked thing covetousness is! (*R. Newton, D.D.*) *The sin of covetousness :*—Covetousness is—1. A subtle sin. It is called "a cloak" (1 Thess. ii. 5), because it cloaks itself under the name of frugality and prudence. 2. It is a dangerous sin. It hinders the efficacy of the preached Word (Matt. xiii. 7), and makes men have "a withered hand," which they cannot stretch out to the poor (see Luke xvi. 14). 3. It is a mother-sin, a radical vice (1 Tim. vi. 10). 4. It is a sin dishonourable to religion. How disgraceful for those who say their hopes are above to have their hearts below—for those who say they are born of God to be buried in the earth! 5. It exposes to God's abhorrence. 6. It shuts men out of heaven (Eph. v. 5). (*A. Nevin, D.D.*) *The Tenth Commandment :*—I. IT FORBIDS COVETOUSNESS IN GENERAL: "Thou shalt not covet." It is lawful to use the world; yea, and to desire so much of it as may—1. Keep us from the temptation of poverty: "Give me not poverty, lest I steal, and take the name of my God in vain." 2. As may enable us to honour God with works of mercy: "Honour the Lord with thy substance." But all the danger is when the world gets into the heart. The water is useful for the sailing of the ship; all the danger is when the water gets into the ship; so the fear is when the world gets into the heart. What is it to covet? There are two words in the Greek which set forth the nature of covetousness—1. *Pleonexia,* which signifies an "insatiable desire of getting the world." Covetousness is a dry dropsy. 2. *Philargyria,* which signifies an "inordinate love of the world." He may be said to be covetous, not only who gets the world unrighteously, but who loves the world inordinately. But, for a more full answer to the question, What is it to covet? I shall show you in six particulars when a man may be said to be given to covetousness. 1. When his thoughts are wholly taken up about the world. 2. A man may be said to be given to covetousness when he takes more pains for the getting of earth than for the getting of heaven. The Gauls, who were an ancient people of France, after they had tasted of the sweet wine of the Italian grape, inquired after the country, and never rested till they had arrived at it ; so a covetous man, having had a relish of the world, pursues after it, and never leaves it till he hath got it ; but he neglects the things of eternity. 3. A man may be said to be given to covetousness when all his discourse is about the world. 4. A man is given to covetousness when he doth so set his heart upon worldly things that for the love of them he will part with heavenly ; for the " wedge of gold " he will part with the " pearl of great price." 5. A man is given to covetousness when he overloads himself with worldly business. He takes so much business upon him that he cannot find time to serve God ; he hath scarce time to eat his meat, but no time to pray. 6. He is given to covetousness whose heart is so set upon the world that, to get it, he cares not what unlawful indirect means he useth ; he will have the world, " by right or wrong " ; he will wrong and defraud, and raise his estate upon the ruins of another. I shall prescribe some remedies and antidotes against this sin. 1. Faith : " This is the victory that overcometh the world, even our faith." The root of covetousness is the distrust of God's providence ; faith believes God will provide—God, who feeds the birds, will feed His children, He who clothes the lilies will clothe His lambs ; and so faith overcomes the world. 2. The second remedy is judicious consideration. (1) What poor things these things below are that we should covet them. (2) The frame and contexture of the body. " God hath made the face to look upward towards heaven." Can it be imagined that God gave us intellectual, immortal souls to covet only earthly things ? What wise man would fish for gudgeons with golden hooks ? Did God give us glorious souls only to fish for the world ? Sure our souls are made for a higher end—to aspire after the enjoyment of God in glory. (3) The examples of those who have been contemners and despisers of the world. The righteous are compared to a palm-tree. Philo observes that whereas all other trees have their sap in their root, the sap of the palm-tree is towards the top : the emblem of the saints, whose hearts are above in heaven, where their treasure is. Covet spiritual things more, and you will covet earthly things less. Covet grace ; grace is the best blessing—it is the seed of God, the angels' glory. Covet heaven ; heaven is the region of happiness, it is the most pleasant climate. Did we covet heaven more, we should covet earth less. II. I shall speak of it more particularly : " Thou shalt not covet thy neighbour's house, thou shalt not covet thy neighbour's wife," &c. Observe here THE HOLINESS AND PERFECTION OF GOD'S LAW ; it forbids the first motions and risings of sin in the heart : " Thou shalt not covet." The laws of men take hold of the actions, but the law of God goes further—it forbids not only the actions, but the affections. Though the tree bears no bad fruit, it may be faulty at the root ; though a man doth not commit any gross sin, yet who can say his heart is pure ? Let us be humbled for the sin of our nature, the risings of evil thoughts, coveting that which we ought not. Our nature is a seed-plot of iniquity ; it is like charcoal that is ever sparkling ; the sparkles of pride, envy, covetousness, arise in the mind. How should this humble us ! If there be not sinful actings, there are sinful covetings. Let us pray for mortifying grace which may be like the water of jealousy to make the thigh of sin to rot. Why is the house put before the wife? In Deuteronomy the wife is put first : " Neither shalt thou desire thy neighbour's wife, neither shalt thou covet thy neighbour's house." Here the house is put first. In Deuteronomy the wife is set down first, in respect of her value. She, if a good wife, is of far greater value and estimate than the house ; " her price is far above rubies." When Alexander had overcome King Darius in battle, Darius seemed not to be much dismayed ; but when he heard his wife was taken prisoner, now his eyes, like spouts, did gush forth water. The nest is built before the bird is in it ; the wife is first esteemed, but the house must be first provided. 1. Then, " Thou shalt not covet thy neighbour's house." How depraved is man since the Fall ! Man knows not how to keep within bounds, but is ever coveting more than his own. It is only the prisoner lives in such a tenement as he may be sure none will go about to take from him. 2. " Thou shalt not covet thy neighbour's wife." This Commandment is a bridle to check the inordinancy of brutish lusts. 3. " Thou shalt not covet thy neighbour's manservant, nor his maidservant." Servants, when faithful, are a treasure. But this sin of coveting servants is common ; if one hath a better servant, others will be inveigling and laying baits for him, and endeavour to draw him away from his master. 4. " Nor his ox, nor his ass, nor anything that is thy neighbour's." Were there not coveting of ox and ass, there would not be so much stealing. First men break the Tenth Commandment by coveting, and then they break the Eighth

Commandment by stealing. But what means may we use to keep us from coveting that which is our neighbour's? The best remedy is contentment. If we are content with our own, we shall not covet that which is another's. (*T. Watson.*) *Covetousness—its insidiousness :*—Beware of growing covetousness, for of all sins this is one of the most insidious. It is like the silting up of a river. As the stream comes down from the land, it brings with it sand and earth, and deposits all these at its mouth, so that by degrees, unless the conservators watch it carefully, it will block itself up, and leave no channel for ships of great burden. By daily deposit it imperceptibly creates a bar which is dangerous to navigation. Many a man when he begins to accumulate wealth commences at the same moment to ruin his soul, and the more he acquires, the more closely he blocks up his liberality, which is, so to speak, the very mouth of spiritual life. Instead of doing more for God, he does less; the more he saves the more he wants, and the more he wants of this world the less he cares for the world to come. *Coveting driven out by love :*—It may be said that this is a hard saying, and that it is one of the impossible precepts of which there are so many in the Old Testament and the New. But what is the moral idea on which it rests? It is only another form of the great Commandment : "Thou shalt love thy neighbour as thyself." If we can obey that law, we can obey this. It affords us more pleasure to see those who are dear to us prosperous than to be prosperous ourselves. I venture to say that if any man who had himself been senior wrangler had a son who achieved the same honour, he would have greater pride in his son's success than in his own; and that a prime minister would listen with greater delight to the cheers with which his son was received on entering the House of Commons, after being appointed to a high political office, than to the cheers which he himself received when he first took his seat as leader of the House. We never covet what belongs to those whom we love. This Commandment has its root in the Divine idea of the mutual relations which should exist among mankind. God means us to love our neighbours as we love ourselves. (*R. W. Dale, D.D.*) *God's great root-extractor :*—Suppose that we were farmers. We move out to the West and buy a farm. A large part of our farm is covered with forest trees. We want to clear a portion of it, and turn it into fields, where we can raise Indian corn or wheat. We cut down the trees and split up and haul away the timber. But after all this the stumps remain in the ground, and, if nothing is done to them, they will soon begin to sprout up again. It is very important for us as farmers to get those stumps removed. Somebody has invented a machine that is called a "root-extractor." It has great strong iron hooks. These are fastened to the roots, and then, by turning a wheel or crank connected with some very powerful machinery, the tough, crooked, gnarled roots are torn out by main force. It would be a grand thing for us on our western farm to have one of these root-extractors. Then how nicely we should get our field cleared ! We should go to work with one stump after another, and in a little while they would be all gone, and we should have no more trouble with them. My dear children, our hearts are like a field full of trees. This field has to be cleared. The trees here are our sins — the wicked feelings and tempers that belong to us. When we are converted, and our hearts are renewed by the grace of Jesus, then these trees are cut down. But the roots of them remain. Even when we become Christians we find the roots of our old sins springing up again. And covetousness is the worst of these roots. You remember that Paul says, " The love of money " (this means coveting or desiring money) " is the root of all evil " (1 Tim. vi. 10). It is very important for us to have these roots removed. Now the Tenth Commandment may well be called God's great " root-extractor." If we pray to Him for grace to understand and keep it, we shall find that it pulls up sin by the roots from our hearts, and prevents it from growing there. This is what the Commandment was intended to do ; and this is what it does, wherever it is properly kept. (*R. Newton, D.D.*) *Penalty of covetousness :*—In 1853 I knew a young girl whose great besetment was a love of dress. She looked pale and wretched whenever she saw any one among her companions better dressed than herself. She always lamented she was too poor to buy fine clothes. It happened that her aunt kept a lodging-house at a watering-place, and this girl lived with her as a servant. A lady from London went down to lodge in their house, and on the very night of her arrival she was seized with the worst form of cholera, and died in a few hours. The clothes the lady had on when she was attacked with the disease the doctor ordered should be burned, for fear of infection. There had not previously been a case of cholera in the town, and the authorities were anxious to take very vigorous measures, if possible, to stay the pestilence.

Now the lodger had worn a very handsome silk gown. Jane noticed it with covetous eyes when the poor lady came. She heard the order given that the clothes should be burnt, to which, of course, the lady's friends made no objection, and Jane's aunt threw out a large bundle from the window into an iron pot in the yard, in which there was some lighted tow. But Jane managed to get away the silk gown. She did not consider that she stole it, because it was condemned to the flames. She coveted it, and yielded to the temptation. Now, some people think that cholera is not infectious, and I cannot venture to say whether it is or not; but I know that no one shared the poor lady's fate but Jane. Ten days elapsed; she took an opportunity to wear that gown when she went to see her mother, and was taken ill with it on, and died after three days' illness, apparently from cholera. "Thou shalt not covet." (*Mrs. Balfour.*) *The folly of covetousness proved at death:*—It is told of Alexander the Great that he gave orders that when he should die his hands should be left outside his coffin, so that his friends might see that, though he had conquered the world, he could take nothing of his conquests into the hereafter. In like manner, the famous Saladin, it is said, ordered a long spear with a white flag attached to it to be carried through his camp bearing this inscription: "The mighty King Saladin, the conqueror of all Asia and Egypt, takes with him, when he dies, none of his possessions except this linen flag for a shroud." *Covetousness:*— The covetous man pines in plenty—like Tantalus, up to the chin in water, and yet thirsty. (*T. Adams.*)

Vers. 18–21. **They removed, and stood afar off.**—*Israel and Sinai:*—I. THAT ALL MEN AS SINNERS MUST BE BROUGHT INTO CONSCIOUS CONTACT WITH MORAL LAW. The guarantees of this conscious contact are found—1. In the law of our spiritual nature. 2. In the special Providence that is over us. 3. In the provisions of the gospel. 4. In the transactions of the final retribution. II. THAT THIS CONSCIOUS CONTACT IS EVER ASSOCIATED WITH FEELINGS OF THE MOST TERRIBLE ALARM. III. THAT UNDER THE INFLUENCE OF THIS MOST TERRIBLE ALARM THERE WILL ARISE A CONSCIOUS NECESSITY FOR A MEDIATOR. IV. THAT HEAVEN HAS GRACIOUSLY PROVIDED SUCH A MEDIATOR, WHO IS EQUAL TO THE EMERGENCY. (*Homilist.*) *The superficial and the profound:*—I. SUPERFICIAL VIEWS OF DIVINE PROCEEDINGS INDUCE FEAR. II. PROFOUND VIEWS OF DIVINE PROCEEDINGS ENCOURAGE CONFIDENCE. III. PROFOUND VIEWS OF DIVINE PROCEEDINGS LEAD TO A CORRECT UNDERSTANDING OF DIVINE PURPOSES. IV. THE UNENLIGHTENED AND THE FEARING STAND AFAR OFF. "And the people stood afar off." There is no reason to keep away from God. Why should we shut out the light of a Father's compassion? V. BUT THE HEAVEN-TAUGHT ARE TAKEN INTO THE THICK DARKNESS WHERE THE TRUE LIGHT APPEARS. Moses drew near, or more correctly, was made to draw near, unto the thick darkness where God was. (*W. Burrows, B.A.*) *God's revelation of Himself:*—I. THE MODE OF THIS REVELATION WAS STRIKING (ver. 18). 1. Such a mode was necessary— (1) To reveal God's majesty—to men familiar with the puerilities of heathen worship; (2) to show that God was not to be trifled with, and His laws broken with impunity; (3) to meet the case of those open only to impressions made on their fear. 2. Such a mode served some of the most important functions of the old dispensation. (1) Preparatory; (2) symbolic. 3. Such a mode was appropriate, as accompanying judicial proceedings. II. THE RECEPTION OF THIS REVELATION WAS WHAT GOD INTENDED IT SHOULD BE. 1. Intelligent. 2. Reverent. 3. Prayerful. III. THE COMFORT OF THIS REVELATION DISARMED IT OF ALL ITS TERRORS. 1. The God of their fathers had spoken. 2. God had spoken for their encouragement. 3. God had spoken but to prove their loyalty to Him. If they could stand the test, what could harm them? (Rom. viii. 39). 4. God had spoken for their moral elevation. (1) "That His fear may be before your faces." (2) "That ye sin not" (1 John ii. 1, 2). Learn—1. Not to dread God's revelation. 2. To approach God through the one new and living way which is ever open. 3. To keep all God's laws in the strength of the comfort which His presence brings. (*J. W. Burn.*) *The seriousness of life:*—The Hebrews had come up out of Egypt, and were standing in front of Sinai. They turn to Moses and beg him to stand between them and God. At first it seems as if their feeling were a strange one. This is their God who is speaking to them. Would it not seem as if they would be glad to have Him come to them directly, to have Him almost look on them with eyes that they could see? That is the first question, but very speedily we feel how natural that is which actually did take place. The Hebrews had delighted in God's mercy. They had come singing up out of the Red Sea. They had followed the pillar of fire and the pillar of cloud.　But now they were called on to face God Himself. In behind all the superficial aspects of their life they were called on to get at its centre and its heart.　There they recoiled.　We are willing to know that God is there.　We are willing, we are glad, that Moses should go into His presence and bring us His messages.　But we will not come in sight of Him ourselves.　Life would be awful.　"Let not God speak with us, lest we die!"　I want to bid you think how natural and how common such a temper is.　There are a few people among us who are always full of fear that life will become too trivial and petty. There are always a great many people who live in perpetual anxiety lest life should become too awful and serious and deep and solemn.　There is something in all of us which feels that fear.　We are always hiding behind effects to keep out of sight of their causes, behind events to keep out of sight of their meanings, behind facts to keep out of sight of principles, behind men to keep out of the sight of God.　We have all known men from whom it seemed as if it would be good to lift away some of the burden of life, to make the world seem easier and less serious.　Some such people perhaps we know to-day ; but as we look abroad generally do we not feel sure that such people are the exceptions?　The great mass of people are stunted and starved with superficialness.　They never touch the real reasons and meanings of living.　They turn and hide their faces, or else run away, when those profoundest things present themselves.　They will not let God speak with them.　So all their lives lack tone ; nothing brave, enterprising, or aspiring is in them.　For we may lay it down as a first principle that he who uses superficially any power or any person which he is capable of using profoundly gets harm out of that unaccepted opportunity which he lets slip.　You talk with some slight acquaintance, some man of small capacity and little depth, about ordinary things in very ordinary fashion ; and you do not suffer for it.　You get all that he has to give.　But you hold constant intercourse with some deep nature, some man of great thoughts and true spiritual standards, and you insist on dealing merely with the surface of him, touching him only at the most trivial points of living, and you do get harm.　The unused capacity of the man—all which he might be to you, but which you are refusing to let him be—is always there demoralizing you.　But—here is the point—for this man with his capacities to live in this world with its opportunities and yet to live on its surface and to refuse its depths, to turn away from its problems, to reject the voice of God that speaks out of it, is a demoralizing and degrading thing.　It mortifies the unused powers, and keeps the man always a traitor to his privileges and his duties.　Take one part of life and you can see it very plainly.　Take the part with which we are familiar here in church.　Take the religious life of man. True religion is, at its soul, spiritual sympathy with, spiritual obedience to, God. But religion has its superficial aspects—first of truth to be proved and accepted, and then, still more superficial, of forms to be practised and obeyed.　Now suppose that a man setting out to be religious confines himself to these superficial regions and refuses to go further down.　He learns his creed and says it.　He rehearses his ceremony and practises it.　The deeper voice of his religion cries to him from its unsounded depths, "Come, understand your soul !　Come, through repentance enter into holiness !　Come, hear the voice of God."　But he draws back ; he piles between himself and that importunate invitation the cushions of his dogma and his ceremony.　"Let God's voice come to me deadened and softened through these," he says.　"Let not God speak to me, lest I die.　Speak thou to me, and I will hear."　So he cries to his priest, to his sacrament, which is his Moses.　Is he not harmed by that ?　Is it only that he loses the deeper spiritual power which he might have had?　Is it not also that the fact of its being there and of his refusing to take it makes his life unreal, fills it with a suspicion of cowardice, and puts it on its guard lest at any time this ocean of spiritual life which has been shut out should burst through the barriers which exclude it and come pouring in?　Suppose the opposite.　Suppose the soul so summoned accepts the fulness of its life.　It opens its ears and cries, "Speak, Lord, for Thy servant heareth."　It invites the infinite and eternal aspects of life to show themselves.　Thankful to Moses for his faithful leadership, it is always pressing through him to the God for whom he speaks. Thankful to priest and church and dogma, it will always live in the truth of its direct, immediate relationship to God, and make them minister to that.　What a consciousness of thoroughness and safety ; what a certain, strong sense of resting on the foundation of all things is there then !　Oh ! do not let your religion satisfy itself with anything less than God.　Insist on having your soul get at Him and hear His voice.　Never, because of the mystery, the awe, perhaps the perplexity and doubt which come with the great experiences, let yourself take refuge in the superficial things of faith. It is better to be lost on the ocean than to be tied to the shore. Therefore seek great experiences of the soul, and never turn your back on them when God sends them, as He surely will! The whole world of thought is full of the same necessity and the same danger. A man sets himself to think of this world we live in. He discovers facts. He arranges facts into what he calls laws. Behind his laws he feels and owns the powers to which he gives the name of force. He will go no further. He dimly hears the depth below, of final causes, of personal purposes, roaring as the great ocean roars under the steamship which, with its clamorous machineries and its precious freight of life, goes sailing on the ocean's bosom. You say to him, "Take this into your account. Your laws are beautiful, your force is gracious and sublime. But neither is ultimate. You have not reached the end and source of things in these. Go further. Let God speak to you." Can you not hear the answer? "Nay, that perplexes all things. That throws confusion into what we have made plain and orderly and clear. Let not God speak to us, lest we die!" You think what the study of Nature might become if, keeping every accurate and careful method of investigation of the way in which the universe is governed and arranged, it yet was always hearing, always rejoicing to hear, behind all methods and governments and machineries, the sacred movement of the personal will and nature which is the soul of all. The same is true about all motive. How men shrink from the profoundest motives! I ask you why you toil at your business day in and day out, year after year. I beg you to tell me why you devote yourself to study, and you reply with certain statements about the attractiveness of study and the way in which every extension or increase of knowledge makes the world more rich. All that is true, but it is slight. This refusal to trace any act back more than an inch into that world of motive out of which all acts spring, this refusal especially to let acts root themselves in Him who is the one only really worthy cause why anything should be done at all—this is what makes life grow so thin to the feeling of men who live it; this is what makes men wonder sometimes that their brethren can find it worth while to keep on working and living, even while they themselves keep on at their life and work in the same way. · "Let us be quiet and natural," men say, "and all will be well." But the truth is that to be natural is to feel the seriousness and depth of life, and that no man does come to any worthy quietness who does not find God and rest on Him and talk with Him continually. The whole trouble comes from a wilful or a blind under-estimate of man. "Let not God speak to me, lest I die," the man exclaims. Is it not almost as if the fish cried, "Cast me not into the water, lest I drown"? or as if the eagle said, "Let not the sun shine on me, lest I be blind"? It is man fearing his native element. He was made to talk with God. It is not death, but his true life, to come into the Divine society and to take his thoughts, his standards, and his motives directly out of the hand of the eternal perfectness. We find a revelation of this in all the deepest and highest moments of our lives. Have you not often been surprised by seeing how men who seemed to have no capacity for such experiences passed into a sense of Divine companionship when anything disturbed their lives with supreme joy or sorrow? Once or twice, at least, in his own life, almost every one of us has found himself face to face with God, and felt how natural it was to be there. And often the question has come, "What possible reason is there why this should not be the habit and fixed condition of our life? Why should we ever go back from it?" And then, as we felt ourselves going back from it, we have been aware that we were growing unnatural again. And as this is the revelation of the highest moments of every life, so it is the revelation of the highest lives; especially it is the revelation of the highest of all lives, the life of Christ. Men had been saying, "Let not God speak to us, lest we die"; and here came Christ, the man—Jesus, the man; and God spoke with Him constantly, and yet He lived with the most complete vitality. And every now and then a great man or woman comes who is like Christ in this. There comes a man who naturally drinks of the fountain and eats of the essential bread of life. Where you deal with the mere borders of things, he gets at their hearts; where you ask counsel of expediencies, he talks with first principles; where you say, "This will be profitable," he says, "This is right." And in religion, may I not beg you to be vastly more radical and thorough? Do not avoid, but seek, the great, deep, simple things of faith. (*Bp. Phillips Brooks.*)

Vers. 22, 23. **Ye shall not make with Me gods of silver.**—*God's voice, but not* *a form :*—I. God's voice. Indicative of the Divine personality. II. God's abhorrence of idolatry. Our loftiest conceptions, embodied in the most costly and precious material forms, must fall short of Infinite perfectness. III. God's love of simplicity. Altars of earth, and altars of unhewn stone. The simplest is often the purest and the divinest. Man's superb altars lead to degrading conceptions of the Infinite. IV. God's respect to appearances. "Neither shalt thou go up by steps unto Mine altar, that thy nakedness be not discovered thereon." Let all things be done decently and in order, is the injunction of two economies. V. God's superiority to splendid structures. In all places where God's name is recorded there He will come, and there He will bless. (*W. Burrows, B.A.*) *Public worship :*—1. The end for which God reveals Himself is, that we should worship Him. 2. God's revelation of Himself should be kept in perpetual memory by acts of public worship. 3. God, having made a spiritual revelation of Himself, should not be worshipped under any symbolic form. I. Public worship involves cost. II. Public worship can dispense with elaborate ritual. III. Public worship carefully excludes all idea of merit on the part of the worshipper. IV. Public worship is not confined to set places. V. Public worship does not depend on the material or intellectual qualifications of the worshipper. VI. Public worship must be conducted with proper decency. VII. Public worship, when properly conducted, is uniformly attended with a blessing. 1. The Divine presence. 2. The Divine benediction. (*J. W. Burn.*)

Ver. 24. **In all places where I record My name, I will come unto thee.**— *The gospel in Exodus :*—I. That God demands from His creature man reverent and intelligent worship. II. That such worship, to be acceptable to God, must always be associated with Divinely-appointed sacrifice. III. That such worship and sacrifice obtain for man the best blessings of heaven. (*F. W. Brown.*) *God's promised presence essential to constitute a Church :*—I. The extent of the promise. What and where are the places where we are to receive this blessing ? Before God gave the promise, He gave instructions to the children of Israel about sacrifices—what kind of offerings to bring, what animals to offer, what kind of altars to build ; and having given these instructions, He follows them by the promise that "in all places where I record My name, I will come unto thee and bless thee." We must easily see that the places where God recorded His name were places where altars were built to Him—where lambs bled in sacrifice, and where the ordinances and commands of God were observed by the people. II. The blessing promised. 1. "I will come to thee." God's gracious presence. 2. "I will bless thee." Remind Him of His promise. 3. Make this a house of prayer. (*T. Guthrie, D.D.*) *Sanctuary blessings :*—I. What is meant by recording the name of the Lord in any place ? 1. By the name of the Lord is often understood God Himself, or the display of His infinite perfections in those works, whereby He makes His being and nature known.—Thus, Psa. xx. 1. But the name of the Lord, when used in a particular reference to the covenant of grace, always respects God considered as a Redeemer ; and expresses His Divine perfections, as they are gloriously displayed in the salvation of sinners. 2. Let us now see in what respects that name may be said to be recorded in any place. The words might be rendered, "In all places where I shall fix the memory of My name" ; or, "In all places where I shall make My name to be invoked." The Chaldaic paraphrase has it, "In every place where I shall make My majesty to dwell." The phrase, agreeably to either of these translations, evidently refers to the public worship of God, and has respect both to the place when, and the manner in which, it was to be celebrated. It is well known that the tabernacle was the place of public worship which God, exclusively of all others, determined for the Israelites while they were in the wilderness. After they had possession of the promised land, the ark of the covenant was lodged at Shiloh, and there, for a long while, the people celebrated Divine service. When the temple was finished, Jerusalem was fixed upon as the permanent seat. 3. If you now inquire how the name of the Lord was recorded in all these places, and by what means it might be said that He made Himself to be there remembered as the God of Salvation ; we refer you, for a general answer, to the genius and scope of the Mosaic institution. 4. But this great end was more especially attained by the sacrifices and burnt-offerings, which formed an essential part of the daily worship in Israel. Believers were then looking for the appearance of the promised Seed who was not yet come. What could be better calculated to assist their faith, to establish their hope, and instruct them in the method of salvation, than to be commanded of God to substitute a bloody offering in their own stead, and thus transfer the legal guilt and punishment upon a sacrifice? In this act of worship, the bleeding lamb and smoking altar directed them to the promised Surety, the precious Lamb of God, who, by His sufferings and death, was fully to atone for His people, and, by one perfect sacrifice, became the Author of salvation unto all that obey Him. II. THE IMPORT OF THESE WORDS, "I will come unto thee, and bless thee." The blessing of the Lord is always upon His people in every place. He hears their prayers in secret, and in their families. He has never said to the seed of Jacob, "Seek ye Me in vain." But to public worship peculiar mercies are annexed. 1. The Lord blesses His Church when He gives it a pure and faithful ministry. 2. The Lord blesses His Church when, in His good Providence, He preserves His people together in mutual peace, and prevents confusion, animosities, and schisms. 3. But especially He blesses His people in the place where He records His name, when He bestows that blessing of all blessings, the Holy Spirit. 4. The protection and defence of the Most High, whereby He preserves His Churches in the enjoyment of their privileges, and continues His blessing from the fathers to the children. Application: 1. We learn, "that the Son of God, from the beginning to the end of the world, gathers, defends, and preserves to Himself, by His Spirit and Word, out of the whole human race, a Church chosen to everlasting life and agreeing in true faith." 2. We learn, that there is forgiveness with our God, that He may be feared; and thus a foundation laid for true and spiritual worship. 3. We see, that the doctrines of the gospel, like their Divine Author, are the same yesterday, to-day, and for ever. (*J. H. Livingstone, D.D.*) *The promise of God at Sinai:*—I. THE PROMISE IS EVIDENTLY OF UNIVERSAL APPLICATION. Its language implies or rather asserts this. It speaks of "all places," and consequently it takes in or may take in the whole world, and every spot in the world. The Lord "records" His name in a place, when He declares His perfections and makes Himself known there; when He tells us what He is; unfolds to us His character. Now comes the question, Where has the Holy One of Israel thus revealed Himself? Where has He thus recorded His great name? It is engraven on the face of universal nature. The Cross of the Lord Jesus Christ is, in fact, the one great manifestation of a hidden God. II. Let us go on to consider HIS PROMISE. 1. It encourages us to expect in this house of prayer the presence of God with us. "I will come unto thee." And what more can we desire? It is rest to the soul; a something which not only quiets, and strengthens, and raises it, but leaves it nothing to wish for; it is the "fulness of joy"; no cistern of happiness, which a few moments or hours of enjoyment can empty; but a fountain of life, a spring that eternity cannot dry up nor a universe exhaust. "I will come unto thee, and I will bless thee"; "so bless thee, that My presence shall be known by the happiness I communicate, and the mercies I bestow." 2. We are warranted then to look for blessings from heaven in this place, and these real blessings, great blessings, mercies which God Himself esteems blessings. But here we must remember that anything, in order to be a blessing, must be adapted to the situation and condition of those to whom it is given. Hence when the Lord Jehovah says, "I will bless thee," before we can understand His words, we must have some acquaintance with the character and circumstances of those to whom they are addressed. If spoken to an angel or a redeemed saint in heaven, they may mean one thing; addressed to this sinner on the earth, another thing; and sent home to the heart of that poor child of the dust, yet something different. We must look to ourselves then. We must ask where we are standing and whither we are going; where we are and what we are. And to what a multitude of thoughts do such questions as these give rise! What wants, and burdens, and sins, and fears, do they bring before us! (*C. Bradley, M.A.*) *The presence of God in His Church:*—"I will come unto thee, and I will bless thee," said a faithful God on Sinai. And did the words, as they died on His lips, pass away from His remembrance? No; His Church in the wilderness beheld and owned His presence. He shone forth between the cherubim; He met His people in His tabernacle, and "made them joyful in His house of prayer." And when a temple was built at Jerusalem for His rest, He dwelt visibly in it. "The glory of the Lord filled the house of the Lord"; and this was His promise concerning it, "I have chosen this place to Myself for an house of sacrifice. Now Mine eyes shall be open, and Mine ears attend unto the prayer that is made in this place. Mine eyes and Mine heart shall be there perpetually." And when He left the heaven of His glory, and came down "a Man of sorrows" to the earth, was Sinai forgotten amidst His labours and griefs? A thousand years had not erased from His memory one word of the promise He had uttered there. He remembers it; He takes it up as His own; He confirms and extends it. "In all places," was His language on the mountain; "Wheresoever any are gathered together," is His language now. "I will come unto thee," said He to the hosts of Israel; He says to us, "Where only two or three are met together, I am." "I will come," was His promise in the wilderness; but this is His declaration in His Church, "I am come; there am I in the midst"; His presence is no longer a mercy to be hoped for, it is a blessing to be enjoyed. But all this, it may be said, was addressed to His disciples; and was intended only for the early ages of His Church. He foresaw the objection. Hear Him again; "Lo, I am with you alway, even unto the end of the world." What then is this house of prayer? It is a place where we are to meet our God. We see Him not, perhaps we think not of His presence; but if only two or three of us are seeking our happiness in Him, He is here, and here to bless us. His own faithful lips have told us so. May His Spirit grant that our own experience may often tell us the same! (*Ibid.*)

Ver. 25. **Thou shalt not build it of hewn stone.**—*The altar of "unhewn stone": simplicity of worship:*—I. RITUALISM IS NOT A NECESSITY OF WORSHIP. There can be worship at the rough "altar of unhewn stones," as well as in the temple where wealth has lavished its contributions and art exhausted its genius. Worship is not a form, but a spirit; not a service, but a life. And a life has many functions. II. MERITORIOUSNESS MUST BE EXCLUDED FROM WORSHIP. No "tool" to be used in constructing this altar. To culture the soul in true devotion, as God requires, is a harder task than to give money, &c. III. UNIVERSALITY IS A CHARACTERISTIC OF WORSHIP. 1. Not confined to places. 2. Not confined to persons. As mere earthen altars will do, where is the man who cannot build them? (*Homilist.*) *The Jewish altar as typical of Christ:*—One can hardly help connecting the words with Daniel's vision of "a stone cut out of the mountain without hands," which was a vision of Christ. The rough stone fashioned by no human instrumentality, this alone might be an altar of the Lord. It was forbidden that man should attempt by devices of his own to adorn the altar; if he made the endeavour, he utterly profaned and polluted the structure: and in all this, was it not, as though it had been said expressly to man, "Thou shalt have a Mediator, an Altar, on which thine offerings being laid, shall be consumed by the fires of Divine acceptance; but if thou shouldst attempt to add anything of thine own to the worthiness of this Mediator, if thou wouldst carve the altar, or ornament it with human merit or righteousness, the effect shall be that for yourself the altar shall be stripped of all virtue, and no flame break forth from the heavens to burn up the oblation"? Now, we believe, that so soon as man had fallen, God instituted a system of sacrifice, and taught those who had sullied their immortality that its lustre should be restored through a propitiation for sin. As we conclude that God first ordained sacrifice, we may also conclude that it was under His direction that the first altars were reared. Observe two things: an altar supported the gift, and an altar sanctified the gift. We believe that in both these respects Christ Jesus may be designated as an altar, whether you consider His Person or the work which He effects on our behalf. 1. If we look first at the Person of the Mediator, shall we not find the two properties of the altar, that it supported and sanctified the oblation which Christ made to the Almighty? The Person of Christ Jesus, as you know, was a Divine Person, whilst in it were gathered two natures, the human and the Divine. It was the human nature which was sacrificed, the Divine being inaccessible to suffering and incapable of pain. So that if you simply look at the Person of the Mediator, and consider that it was the design of the altar to support the gift that was presented in sacrifice, you must see that the Divine nature so bore up the human, that it so served as a platform on which the oblation might be laid when the fire of God's justice came down in its purity and its intenseness, that with as much reason as Christ Jesus is described as a sacrifice, may He also be described as an altar. 2. Not, however, that the altar only sustained the gift; it also sanctified the gift; and the fitness of considering the Divine nature in the Person of Christ as the altar on which the human was presented, will be still more apparent if you bring into account this sanctifying virtue. We have already stated that the Divine nature was of necessity incapable of suffering, and that t was, therefore, the human which made the Redeemer accessible to anguish; but it was the Divinity which gave worth to the sufferings of the humanity, and rendered them efficacious to the taking away sin. The Divine was to the human what the altar was to the sacrifice: it sanctified the gift and made it acceptable. Yes, blessed Saviour, we most thankfully own that through Thee, and Thee only, can we offer unto God any acceptable service. And here we would remind you of a very emphatic question put by our Lord to the Pharisees—"Whether is greater, the gift, or the altar that sanctifieth the gift?" We have to allude to the supposed efficacy in repentance, and the presumed virtue in the tears which the sinful may shed over their offences against God. The guilt of sin is removed by Christ's blood, not by man's tears. It is the altar that sanctifieth the gift. I depreciate not repentance, I strip it not of moral excellence, nor of moral prevalence, but we affirm that without the altar the gift would be unavailing, without Christ the most contrite would perish with the most hardy. (*H. Melvill, B.D.*)

CHAPTER XXI.

Ver. 1. **These are the judgments.**—*The judgments :*—These judgments stood related to the second table of the Law, just as the regulations concerning the worship of the altar stood related to the first. It is to be remembered also that these "judgments," and those of the same kind which afterward were added as occasion arose, are to be distinguished from the moral law, not only as applying to the state rather than the individual, but also as local and temporary in their nature, representing not what was ideally best, but only what was then practically possible in the direction of that which was best. Some very superficial people criticise them as if they were intended for the nineteenth century! The Decalogue was, and is, intrinsically perfect; the "judgments" were adapted to the circumstances and wants of Israel at the time. And it would be a good thing if reformers of modern times would always remember the same wise and necessary distinctions, between that which is ideally perfect and that which alone may be practically possible. Still further it is to be remembered, that these judgments were suitable to "the Theocracy" of Israel; and hence those are entirely wrong who attempt to use them as precedents for general legislation in the limited monarchies and republican governments, and otherwise entirely altered circumstances, of modern times. Yet if we could only compare these "judgments" with the laws and customs of the nations around, we should see by force of contrast how exceedingly pure, wise, just, and humane they are; and especially where private relations are dealt with, we have touches which would not shame the New Testament itself, however much they may in another sense shame us, as for instance Exod. xxiii. 4, 5. The third division of the book of the covenant has to do with matters which relate neither to worship exclusively, nor to civil relations exclusively, but to both. These are the Sabbath year, the Sabbath day, and the yearly festivals (xxiii. 10–19). As for the Sabbath year and the festivals, they will come up again in the fuller details given from the tabernacle and recorded in Leviticus. And as for the Sabbath day, we may simply remark the significance of its presence here in the book of the covenant, as well as in the Decalogue, indicating that while in its principle it belongs to universal and unchangeable law, in its letter it formed part of that national covenant which was merged in the new and better covenant of the later age. (*J. M. Gibson, D.D.*) *The Hebrew commonwealth founded on religion :*—There is a very common reflection upon the Hebrew lawgiver, which, though it does not call in question any particular law, is yet designed to vitiate and weaken the impression of the whole—that he was a stern and relentless ruler, who may indeed have understood the principles of justice, but whose justice was seldom tempered with mercy. This impression is derived partly at least from the summary way in which in several instances he dealt with rebellion. To this kind of argument there is one brief and sufficient answer: All bodies of men are acknowledged to have the right to resort to severe penalties when encompassed by extraordinary dangers. The children of Israel were in a position of great peril, and their safety depended on the wisdom and firmness of one man. Never had a ruler a more difficult task. Moses did not legislate for the ideal republic of Plato, a community of perfect beings, but for a people born in slavery, from which they had but just broken away, and that were in danger of becoming ungovernable. Here were two millions and a half who had not even a settled place of abode, mustered in one vast camp, through which rebellion might spread in a day. Moses had to govern them by his single will. . . . To preserve order, and to guard against hostile attacks, all the men capable of bearing arms were organized as a military body. . . . He suppressed rebellion as Cromwell would have suppressed it : he not only put it down, but stamped it out ; and such prompt severity was the truest humanity. But it is not acts of military discipline that provoke the criticism of modern humanitarians, so much as those religious laws which prescribed the God whom the Hebrews should worship, and punished idolatry and blasphemy as the greatest of crimes. This, it is said, transcends the proper sphere of human law ; it exalts ceremonies into duties, and denounces as crimes acts which have no moral wrong. Was not, then, the Hebrew law wanting in the first principle of justice —freedom to all religions ? Now it is quite absurd to suppose the Hebrews had conscientious scruples against this worship, or seriously doubted whether Jehovah or Baal were the true God. They had been rescued from slavery by a direct interposition of the Almighty, they had been led by an Almighty Deliverer ; and it was His voice which they heard from the cliffs of Sinai. But it was not merely because their religion was *true*, and the *only* true worship, that they were required to accept it ; but because also of the peculiar relation which its Divine Author had assumed towards the Hebrew state as its founder and protector. They had no king but God ; He was the only Lord. As such, no act of disobedience or disrespect to His authority could be light or small. Further : the unity of God was a centre of unity for the nation. The state was one because their God was one. The worship of Jehovah alone distinguished the Hebrews from all other people, and preserved their separate nationality. Admit other religions, and the bond which held together the twelve tribes was dissolved. How long could that union have lasted if the prophets of Baal had had the freedom of the camp and been permitted to go from tribe to tribe and from tent to tent, preaching the doctrine of human sacrifices ? Hence Moses did not suffer them for an hour. False prophets were to be stoned to death. . . . Such was the Hebrew commonwealth, a state founded in religion. Was it therefore founded in fanaticism and folly, or in profound wisdom and far-seeing sagacity ? " Religion, true or false," says Coleridge, " is, and ever has been, the centre of gravity in a realm, to which all other things must and will accommodate themselves." Would it not be well if some of our modern pretenders to statesmanship did not so completely ignore its existence and its power ? The religion which Moses gave to the Hebrews was not one merely of abstract ideas ; it was incarnated in an outward and visible worship by which it addressed the senses. Even in the desert the tabernacle and the altar were set up, and the daily sacrifice was offered ; the smoke and the incense below ascending towards the pillar of cloud above, and the fire on the altar answering to the pillar of fire in the midnight sky. This daily and nightly worship made religion a real because a visible thing ; it appealed to the senses and touched the imagination of the people, and held their spirits in awe. The feeling that God dwelt in the midst of them inspired them with courage for great efforts and great sacrifices. (*H. M. Field, D.D.*)

Vers. 2–6. **If thou buy an Hebrew servant.**—*Slavery and sovereignty :*—These judgments of God are the declarations of human rights. I. These judgments dealt WITH AN EXISTING INSTITUTION. The circumstances under which an Hebrew might be reduced to servitude were—1. Poverty. 2. The commission of theft. 3. The exercise of paternal authority. II. This admitted institution does NOT SANCTION MODERN SLAVERY. There is in the Divine revelation a spirit ever working to the enfranchisement of the race. More closely consider the conditions of Mosaic slavery—III. This system asserted the SLAVE'S PERSONAL SOVEREIGNTY. In modern systems, the man is a mere chattel, but in the Mosaic system the slave's manhood is declared. He is sovereign over himself, and is allowed the power of choice. The Southern slaveholder would not permit his slave to say, " I will not " ; but the Hebrew slave is permitted to say, " I love my master, my wife, and my children ; I will not go out free." IV. This system declared the slave's right TO BE A MAN OF FEELING. The man was not to be separated from the wife he had chosen prior to his days of servitude. This part of the Mosaic regulations would not harmonize with the painful scenes which took place at slave marts. V. This system proclaimed the SLAVE'S RIGHT TO FREEDOM, AND THAT IT IS THE HIGHEST CONDITION. The Hebrew slave worked on to the day of happy release. This term of service was

no longer than a modern apprenticeship. The bells of the seventh year rang out
the old order of slavery, and rang in the new glorious order of freedom. VI. This
system typically SETS FORTH THAT THE SERVICE OF LOVE IS THE HIGHEST, AND ALONE
ENDURING. He only was to serve "for ever" who chose continued servitude on
account of love to his master, and love to his wife and his children. The service of
love outstrips in dignity and surpasses in duration all other forms of service. (*W.
Burrows, B.A.*)   *Attachment to a master :*—The following anecdote is furnished
by an officer who went through the campaign in Egypt against the French in the
time of the first Napoleon. "I am glad," he says, "to recall to my memory the
remembrance of a deed done by a brave and faithful servant. While in Egypt, the
plague broke out in the 2nd Regiment of Guards. A large tent was immediately
set apart as a hospital for the stricken. It was, naturally, regarded with extreme
dread by the unfortunate sufferers, who despaired of ever leaving it alive. The
surgeon of the Guards, discovering that he had symptoms of the disorder about him,
bravely gave himself up as an inmate of the plague tent. His servant, who was
greatly attached to him, was in despair. 'At least,' he said, 'let me go with you,
and nurse you.' His master, however, made answer that such a step was impossible, since the tent was guarded by sentinels, who had orders to admit no one
without a pass. The breach of this rule was punishable with death. The man was
silenced for the moment, but at nightfall, regardless of the danger of disease or
detection, he crept on hands and knees past the sentinels, and slipping under the
cords of the doomed tent, he presented himself at his master's bedside. Here he went
through many days of patient and tender nursing of the sick man, till the plague
claimed another victim, and the good surgeon died. Then the servant walked
quietly out of the tent door, and went through the usual form of disinfection, after
that returning to his regiment, where he was received with open arms. To have
dared so much for a beloved master raised him to the rank of a hero, both among
officers and men. He had shown that love for a fellow-man was stronger even than
the love of life in his breast, and those who might not have been brave enough to
dare such fearful risks, were noble enough to own their admiration of one who had
done so.   Such faithful service is registered in heaven," the writer adds.   (*Great
Thoughts.*)   *Love for a master :*—In the latter days of Sir Walter Scott, when
poverty stared him in the face, he had to announce to his servants his inability to
retain them any longer. But they begged to be allowed to stay, saying they would
be content with the barest fare if only they might remain in his employ. This was
permitted, and they clung to him until the last. (*H. O. Mackey.*)   *The ear bored
with an aul :*—We are going to use this as a type, and get some moral out of it.
1. And the first use is this. Men are by nature the slaves of sin. Some are the
slaves of drunkenness, some of lasciviousness, some of covetousness, some of sloth ;
but there are generally times in men's lives when they have an opportunity of
breaking loose. There will happen providential changes which take them away
from old companions, and so give them a little hope of liberty, or there will come
times of sickness, which take them away from temptation, and give them opportunities for thought. Above all, seasons will occur when conscience is set to work
by the faithful preaching of the Word, and when the man pulls himself up, and
questions his spirit thus :—" Which shall it be ? I have been a servant of the devil,
but here is an opportunity of getting free. Shall I give up this sin ? Shall I pray
God to give me grace to break right away, and become a new man ; or shall I not ? "
2. Our text reads us a second lesson, namely, this. In the forty-first Psalm, in the
sixth verse, you will find the expression used by our Lord, or by David in prophecy
personifying our Lord, " Mine ear hast thou opened," or " Mine ear hast thou
digged." Jesus Christ is here, in all probability, speaking of Himself as being for
ever, for our sakes, the willing servant of God. Will you not say, " Let my ear be
bored to His service, even as His ear was digged for me "? I. First, let us speak
upon our CHOICE OF PERPETUAL SERVICE. 1. The first thing is, we have the power to
go free if we will. 2. We have not the remotest wish to do so. 3. We are willing
to take the consequences. The boring of our ear is a special pain, but both ears
are ready for the aul. The Lord's service involves peculiar trials, for He has told
us, " Every branch that beareth fruit He purgeth it." Are we willing to take the
purging ? II. Now, secondly, OUR REASONS FOR IT. A man ought to have a reason
for so weighty a decision as this. What reasons can we give for such decided
language ? 1. We can give some reasons connected with Himself. The servant in
our text who would not accept his liberty, said, " I love my master." Can we say
that ? The servant in our text, who would not go free, plainly declared that he

loved his wife, so that there are reasons connected not only with his Master, but with those in his Master's house, which detain each servant of Jesus in happy bondage. Some of us could not leave Jesus, not only because of what He is, but because of some that are very dear to us who are in His service. How could I leave my mother's God? Besides, let me add, there are some of us who must keep to Christ, because we have children in His family whom we could not leave—dear ones who first learned of Christ from us. 2. There are reasons also why we cannot forsake our Lord which arise out of ourselves; and the first is that reason which Peter felt to be so powerful. The Master said, "Will ye also go away?" Peter answered by another question. He said, "Lord, to whom shall we go?" 3. And why should we go? Can you find any reason why we should leave Jesus Christ? Can you imagine one? 4. And when should we leave Him if we must leave Him? Leave Him while we are young? It is then that we need Him to be the guide of our youth. Leave Him when we are in middle life? Why, then it is we want Him to help us to bear our cross, lest we sink under our daily load. Leave Him in old age? Ah, no! It is then we require Him to cheer our declining hours. Leave Him in life? How could we live without Him? Leave Him in death? How could we die without Him? No, we must cling to Him; we must follow Him whithersoever He goeth. III. In the last place, I WANT TO BORE YOUR EAR. Do you mean to be bound for life? Christians, do you really mean it? Come, sit ye down and count the cost. 1. And, first, let them be bored with the sharp awl of the Saviour's sufferings. No story wrings a Christian's heart with such anguish as the griefs and woes of Christ. The bleeding Lamb enthralls me. I am His, and His for ever. That is one way of marking the ear. 2. Next, let your ear be fastened by the truth, so that you are determined to hear only the gospel. The gospel ought to monopolize the believer's ear. 3. Furthermore, if you really give yourself to Christ, you must have your ear opened to hear and obey the whispers of the Spirit of God, so that you yield to His teaching, and to His teaching only. (*C. H. Spurgeon.*)

Vers. 7–11. **If a man sell his daughter to be a maidservant.**—*Degraded condition of girls in Africa :*—The condition of girls in Africa is thus described by a missionary : "A father looks upon his girl as being of the value only of so many goats, and he is ready to sell her as soon as any man offers him the required payment. Thus, while she is quite young—perhaps only four or five—her life and liberty may have been sold away by her own father, and sooner or later she must become the wife, the slave, the drudge of her owner. While at Mayumba, near the mouth of the Congo river, I one afternoon heard a child screaming frantically behind the house where I was staying, and going out I found a little Bavilla girl, not more than four years old, who had just been brought down the lagoon from her home away in the Mamba hills, where she had been bought by a Mayumba man. The crew of the canoe in which she had been brought down—six big, fierce-looking men —were standing around the little prisoner, pointing their guns and spears at her just for the sport of seeing her shake and scream with fright; and a band of women were dancing with wild delight at the heartless game. It was possible to save the poor child from the cruel treatment just then, but that was only the beginning of a lifetime of suffering for her in the midst of a strange people, with no friend at hand to help or protect her."

Vers. 12–14. **Shall be surely put to death.**—*Cases of homicide :*—I. HOMICIDE IN EFFECT. "He that hateth his brother is a murderer." Anger in the heart gives unconscious malicious power to the will. The man is responsible for the effects of his anger, even though these effects are more disastrous than he intended. II. HOMICIDE BY MISTAKE. Cities of refuge. And in the final adjustment of human affairs, merciful consideration will be dealt out to those who have done vast mischief by mistake ; upon sins of ignorance will fall the blessed light of Divine mercy. Embrace the glorious truth that through the sternest code the Divine love cannot help revealing its gracious tendencies. III. HOMICIDE BY DESIGN. Death is to be his portion. Life is God's most sacred gift. He bestows largely for its unfolding. He provides many safeguards for its preservation. (*W. Burrows, B.A.*) *Capital crimes in the Mosaic code :*—Complaint has been made against Moses on account of the number of crimes made capital in his code. But great injustice has been done him in this particular. The crimes punishable with death by his laws were either of a deep moral malignity or such as were aimed against the very being of the state. It will be found, too, on examination, that there were but four classes of capital offences known to his laws—treason, murder, deliberate and gross abuse of parents, and the more unnatural and horrid crimes arising out of the sexual relation. And all the specifications under these classes amounted to only seventeen; whereas it is not two hundred years since the criminal code of Great Britain numbered one hundred and forty-eight crimes punishable with death—many of them of a trivial nature, as petty thefts and trespasses upon property. But no injury simply affecting property could draw down upon an Israelite an ignominious death. The Mosaic law respected moral depravity more than gold. Moral turpitudes, and the most atrocious expressions of moral turpitude, these were the objects of its unsleeping severity. (*E. C. Wines, D.D.*)

Ver. 15. **He that smiteth his father.**—*God's indignation against the unfilial spirit:*—I. THE UNFILIAL SPIRIT IN TWO ASPECTS. 1. He that smiteth his father or his mother. (1) A child may smite his parent literally, as in the case of those brutes we read of in the newspapers every week. (2) A child may smite his parents' authority by rebellion in thought, word, or deed; *e.g.*, Absalom. (3) A child may smite his parents' wealth by extravagance or carelessness. (4) A child may smite his parents' character by an incautious revelation of domestic secrets. (5) A child may smite his parents' health, and, by misconduct, bring their grey hairs with sorrow to the grave; *e.g.*, Joseph's brethren. (6) A child may smite his parents' heart, and break it by disobedience and wilfulness; *e.g.*, sons of Eli. 2. "He that curseth (*lit.* revileth) his father or his mother." (1) A child may revile his parents by an assertion of personal independence. (2) A child may revile his parents by speaking of them in a careless and irreverent way. (3) A child may revile his parents by speaking to them in a familiar or impertinent way. (4) A child may revile his parents by treating their counsels with contempt; and (5) Alas! a child may revile his parents by cursing them to their face. II. THE UNIFORM PUNISHMENT OF THE UNFILIAL SPIRIT. "Shall surely be put to death." The letter of this condemnation is now repealed, but its spirit lives on through the ages. 1. An unfilial child dies to the respect of civilised society. 2. An unfilial child is morally dead. If the sign of the moral life is "love of the brethren," how dead must he be in whom filial respect and love is extinct! 3. An unfilial child, inasmuch as he breaks a moral law, and a law that partakes of the qualities of both tables and combines them, dies in a more terrible sense. "The soul that sinneth it shall die." (*J. W. Burn.*)   *Filial impiety :*—The books tell us of an old man whose son dragged him, by his hoary locks, to the threshold of his door, when the father said : "Now stop, my son, that is as far as I dragged my father by his hair." There is still a God that judgeth in the earth. He makes Himself known by the judgments which He executeth. Who has ever seen any one a loser by filial piety, or a gainer by the want of it? There still lives a man who, in a passion, cursed his own father, and then struck him several times with a horsewhip. Judgment against this evil work was not executed speedily. Time rolled on, but no ingenuous repentance followed. After some time the cruel son was blasting rock in a well. The fuse caught fire, and he was blown up with the loss of both his eyes, and his right hand, with which he had struck his father. Soon after this sad occurrence he was received in the year 1868 as a pauper at the county workhouse. He has habitually been restless and miserable. He is happy nowhere. He has gone to another county and to another workhouse. But he is well known as a very wretched man. By the law of Moses, cursing father or mother was punished with death. No reason for the law is given, but the atrocious nature of the act. What fearful force is in such words as these : "Whoso curseth his father or his mother, his lamp shall be put out in obscure darkness." "The eye that mocketh at his father, the ravens of the valley shall pick it out, and the young eagles shall eat it " (Prov. xx. 20; xxx. 17). (*W. S. Plumer.*)   *Cruelty to a mother :*—A young man, of whom I once heard, was often spoken to and often prayed for by his mother, until he said to her, "Mother, if you don't give up that praying for me, I will run away to sea." He ran away. Before he went, his mother packed his box. She put the writing paper at the top, and all she begged of him was, "My boy, when you are far away from me, write to me. I will write to you; but send me an answer." He went away; he stayed three years, and never sent a single syllable to that loving mother, who oftentimes was kneeling by her bedside praying for that runaway boy. At last he went back to the old village to see how she was. As he walked down the street his heart misgave him. He walked up the path to the house, he knocked at the door; it was opened by a person whom he did not know.

He asked for Mrs. So-and-so. "How is she?" The woman looked blank at him. He said, "Is not she here?" "Oh," said the woman, "you mean the old woman who used to live here. She died eight months ago of a broken heart. She had a bad son, who went away to sea and left her, and she wrote to him, and he never wrote back again." He turned away and went into the village churchyard. He looked at the graves, he found the one he sought, and threw himself down upon it, saying, "Oh, mother, I never meant it, I never meant it!" But he did it. (*Dr. Morgan.*)

Ver. 16. **He that stealeth a man.**—*About kidnapping :*—The same law is repeated in Deut. xxiv. 7; from which passage it is evident that it treats of kidnapping a *Hebrew.* And thus the severity of the punishment, death, without the possibility of redemption, cannot appear surprising. For all Israelites are considered as free citizens with inalienable and equal rights, of which they can never be entirely divested. Now it is natural that he who steals an Israelite will, in the rarest cases, keep him as his slave or sell him to an Israelite, as the injured person could, in the Holy Land, easily find means to inform the authorities of his fate, and thus cause the punishment of his criminal master. The latter, therefore, generally sold the kidnapped individual to foreign merchants into distant lands, either to Egyptians, who commanded the land commerce to the south, or to Phœnicians, who influenced the trade to the west; and opportunities of selling must have easily offered themselves, as Palestine was situated in the exact centre of the commerce of the East. But by such sale, free Israelites became *permanent* slaves; they forfeited with their liberty their chief characteristic as Hebrews, and were thus lost to the Hebrew community, the more so, as the exclusive intercourse with pagans must necessarily defile the purity of their faith, and gradually accustom their thoughts to idolatry. For this reason it was. in the Mosaic law, interdicted to sell even thieves into foreign countries, because thereby *souls* are, as it were, extirpated from Israel. Thus he who kidnapped Israelites and sold them to other countries justly deserved death, especially if we consider the most melancholy and bitter lot to which the slaves of heathen nations were generally doomed. (*M. M. Kalisch, Ph.D.*) *Unrighteousness of slave holding :*—At the time slaves were held in the State of New York, one of them, escaping into Vermont, was captured and taken before the court at Middlebury by his owner, who asked the court to give him possession of his slave property. Judge Harrington listened attentively to the proofs of ownership, but said that he was not convinced that the title was perfect. Then the counsel asked what more was required. "Until you bring me a bill of sale from God Almighty you cannot have this man." (*J. Swinton.*)

Vers. 18, 19. **If men strive together.**—*Lessons :*—1. Passions and contentions breed many sad events among neighbours. 2. Smitings, and wounds, and sickness, and death are usual effects of sudden passions. 3. In case it proceed not to death, God will not suffer injuries unpunished by men. 4. Not only the death, but the hurts of men, are in God's heart to prevent (ver. 18). 5. It is just with God that he who wounds must look to thorough healing of his neighbour. 6. Man's loss of time, as well as health, God will have recompensed by the injurious. 7. Security and prosperity of creatures is the end of God's judgments against violent men (vers. 18, 19). (*G. Hughes, B.D.*) *Human strife :*—Are our little personal strifes noted in heaven? Yes, every one of them. But *can* men strive together? Properly looked at that would seem to be the harder question of the two. Coming suddenly upon a line of this kind we should exclaim in surprise, "The assumption is impossible. We must begin our criticism of a statement of this kind by rejecting its probability, and, that being done, there is no case left. How can men strive together? Men are brothers, men are rational creatures, men recognize one another's rights, and interests, and welfare; society is not a competition, but a fraternal and sacred emulation; therefore, the assumption that men can strive together is a false one, and, the foundation being false, the whole edifice totters down." That would-be fine theory, that would be sweet poetry, it might almost be thrown into rhyme, but there are the facts staring us in the face. What are those facts? That all life is a strife, that every man in some way or degree, or at some time, begrudges the room which every other man takes up. The tragedy of Cain and Abel has never ceased, and can never cease until we become children of the Second Adam. Great degrees of modification may, of course, take effect. The vulgarity of smiting may be left to those who are in a low state of life—who are, in fact, in barbarous conditions; but they who smite with the fist are not the cruellest of men. There is a refined smiting—a daily, bitter, malignant opposition; there is a process of mutual undermining, or outreaching, or outrunning, in the very spirit of which is found the purpose of murder. But mark how beneficence enters into the arrangement here laid down. Not only is the man who smote his brother to pay for the loss of his brother's time; that would be a mere cash transaction. There are men ready enough to buy themselves out of any obligation; a handful of gold is nothing. Their language is, "Take it, and let us be free." That would be poor legislation in some cases, though heavy enough in others. To some men money has no meaning; they have outlived all its influences; they are so rich that they can bribe and pay, and secure silence or liberty by a mere outputting of the hand. But the beneficence is in the next clause, "and shall cause him to be thoroughly healed." The man must be made as good as he was before, therefore he must be inquired about; he must be taken an interest in; he must become a quantity in the life of the man who injured him, and, however impartial the man who inflicted the injury may become under such chafing, the impatience itself may be turned to good account. Some men can only be taught philanthropy by such rough and urgent schoolmasters. (*J. Parker, D.D.*)

Vers. 20, 21. **If a man smite his servant.**—*Masters and servants :*—1. It is supposed that masters in the Church of God may be cruel in correcting servants, but it is sin.   2. It is possible that death may follow upon such cruel smiting.   3. In such case the life of the vilest slaves is precious with God, and He requireth it with death (ver. 20).   4. Correction due unto servants which endangers not life, is supposed lawful.   5. No governor is guilty by God's law upon such due chastening.   6. Servants are the due purchase of their lords for their labours not for their lives.   7. The lives and comforts of poorest slaves are dear to God and secured by Him (ver. 21).   (*G. Hughes, B.D.*)

Vers. 22–25. **Life for life.**—*The criminal law : was it written in blood?*—The only sense in which retaliation was authorized was as a maxim of law, which helped to fix the measure of punishment for crime. It was the mode of punishment which was at once the simplest, the most natural, and the most easily administered. Indeed, in many cases it was the only mode possible. How would our modern reformers punish such offences? By putting the malefactor in prison? But where was the prison in the desert? In the desert the only possible penalty was one which could be inflicted on the person of the offender, and here the principle of strict retaliation for the crime committed, rigid as it may seem, was perfectly just. It was right that he who inflicted a wound upon his neighbour should feel himself how sharp and keen a wound may be; that he who ferociously tore his brother's eye from its socket should forfeit his own. The law against murder followed the same inexorable rule—"life for life"; a law in which there was no element of pardon or pity. But Moses did not create it; it had been the law of the desert long before he was born. When that old bearded sheik of all the Bedaween of Sinai, sitting under the shadow of a great rock in the desert, explained to us the operation of the *lex talionis* in his tribe, he set before us not only that which now is, but that which has been from the very beginning of time. It was somewhat startling, indeed, to find that laws and customs which we had supposed to belong only to an extreme antiquity still lingered among these mountains and deserts. The avenger of blood might follow with swift foot upon the murderer's track, and if he overtook him and put him to death the law held him free. But at the same time it gave the criminal a chance for his life. In the cities of refuge the manslayer was safe until he could have a fair trial. . . . Perhaps nothing shows more the spirit of a law than the modes of execution for those who are to suffer its extreme penalty. It is not two hundred years since torture was laid aside by European nations. James the Second himself witnessed the wrenching of "the boot" as a favourite diversion. The assassin who struck Henry the Fourth was torn limb from limb by horses, under the eye of ladies of the court. The Inquisition stretched its victims on the rack. Other modes of execution, such as burning alive, sawing asunder, and breaking on the wheel, were common in Europe until a late period. The Turks impaled men, or flayed them alive; and tied women in sacks with serpents, and threw them into the Bosphorus. Among the ancients, punishments were still more excruciating. The Roman people, so famous for the justice of their laws, inflicted the supreme agony of crucifixion, in which the victim lingered dying for hours, or even days. After the capture of Jerusalem, Titus ordered two thousand Jews to be crucified. How does this act of the imperial Romans compare with the criminal law of "a semi-savage race"? Under the Hebrew code all these atrocities were unknown. Moses prescribed but two modes of capital punishment—the sword and stoning. . . . And is this the law that was "written in blood"? No, not in blood, but in tears; for through the sternness of the lawgiver is continually breaking the heart of man. Behind the coat of mail that covers the breast of the warrior is sometimes found the heart of a woman. This union of gentleness with strength is one of the most infallible signs of a truly great nature. It is this mingling of the tender and the terrible that gives to the Hebrew law a character so unique—a majesty that awes with a gentleness that savours more of parental affection than of severity. Crime and its punishment is not in itself a pleasing subje t to dwell on; but when on this dark background is thrown the light of such provisions for the poor and the weak, the effect is like the glow of sunset on the red granite of the Sinai mountains. Even the peaks that were hard and cold, look warm in the flood of sunlight which is poured over them all. Thus uniting the character of the supporter of weakness and protector of innocence with that of the punisher of crime, Moses appears almost as the divinity of his nation—as not only the founder of the Hebrew state, but as its guardian genius through all the periods of its history. When he went up into Mount Nebo, and stretched out his arm toward the Promised Land, he gave to that land the inestimable blessings of laws founded in eternal justice; and not only in justice, but in which humanity was embodied almost as much as in the precepts of religion. Nor was that law given for the Israelites alone. It was an inheritance for all ages and generations. That mighty arm was to protect the oppressed so long as human governments endure. Moses was the king of legislators, and to the code which he left rulers of all times have turned for instruction. (*H. M. Field, D.D.*) *Lessons:—* 1. God supposeth the cruel smitings of masters, but alloweth them not. 2. God foreseeth the sufferings of poor slaves, and provides in His law against it. 3. The perishing of the least member of servants, even of a tooth, God will require of superiors (ver. 26). 4. God by His law depriveth those men of lordship, who abuse their power cruelly over servants. 5. Bond and free are equally considered by God in His law without respect of persons. He makes the oppressed free (vers. 26, 27). (*G. Hughes, B.D.*) *Stripe for stripe:—*A boy was one day sitting on the steps of a door. He had a broom in one hand, and in the other a large piece of bread-and-butter, which somebody had kindly given him. While he was eating it, and merrily humming a tune, he saw a poor little dog quietly sleeping not far from him. He called out to him: "Come here, poor fellow!" The dog, hearing himself kindly spoken to, rose, pricked up his ears, and wagged his tail. Seeing the boy eating, he came near him. The boy held out to him a piece of his bread-and-butter. As the dog stretched out his head to take it, the boy hastily drew back his hand, and hit him a hard rap on the nose. The poor dog ran away, howling most dreadfully, while the cruel boy sat laughing at the mischief he had done. A gentleman who was looking from a window on the other side of the street, saw what the wicked boy had done. Opening the street door, he called to him to cross over, at the same time holding up a sixpence between his finger and thumb. "Would you like this?" said the gentleman. "Yes, if you please, sir," said the boy, smiling; and he hastily ran over to seize the money. Just at the moment that he stretched out his hand, he got so severe a rap on the knuckles from a cane which the gentleman had behind him, that he roared out like a bull. "What did you do that for?" said he, making a very long face, and rubbing his hand. "I didn't hurt you, nor ask you for the sixpence." "What did you hurt that poor dog for just now?" said the gentleman. "He didn't hurt you, nor ask you for your bread-and-butter. As you served him, I have served you. Now, remember dogs can feel as well as boys, and learn to behave kindly towards dumb animals in future." (*Great Thoughts.*) *Life for life:—* Herbert was yet of tender age when his father, the huntsman of Farmstein, was, in the heart of the forest, shot down by an unknown poacher. His mother brought up her fatherless boy as well as she could, and at the age of twenty, when he had become a skilful forester, he obtained his father's situation. It happened that one day, when Herbert was hunting in the forest with many hunters, he shot at a large stag, and missed it. Presently a voice exclaimed piteously in the copse, "Oh, heaven! I am shot." Herbert moved forward, and found an old man, who was uttering loud groans, as he lay covered with blood. The whole company of hunters gathered around the dying man. Herbert, however, knelt down beside him, and begged his forgiveness, protesting that he had not seen him. The dying man, however, said, "I have nothing to forgive you, for that which has hitherto been concealed from all the world shall now come to light. I am the poacher who shot your father just here, under this old oak. The very ground where we now are was dyed with his blood; and it has evidently been destined that you, the son of the murdered man, should on this precise spot, without any thought or intention of such a thing, avenge the act on me. God is just!" he exclaimed, and presently expired.   *Equitable judgment :*—"A Teuton made a little fortune here not long ago in the milk business, and decided to return to Germany and enjoy it in his old home. In the ship that was bearing him homeward was a mischievous monkey. The monkey, prying around one day, found a heavy bag and ran up to the mast-head with it. The German clasped his hands in despair at seeing the bag; it was his money, all in gold. The monkey in a leisurely way pulled out a piece and flung it down to the deck, when the ex-milkman gathered it up. Then the beast tossed a second piece into the sea. Thus alternately the pieces went, one into the ocean and the next into the distracted man's pocket. 'Ah,' said the ex-milkman, as he pocketed just half of what he had started with, 'it is just. One-half of that milk I have sold was milk, and the money for it comes back; the other half was water, and half goes back to water.'"

Vers. 28–36. **If an ox gore.**—*God's regard for the safety of man and beast :*—I. GOD CARES FOR THE SAFETY OF MAN. 1. If an ox injured a man for the first time, the life of the ox only was forfeited (ver. 28). But—2. If the owner of the ox, acquainted with the proved vicious character of his beast, neglected to put him under restraint, and the ox killed his victim—as culpably negligent,—(1) the owner was put to death; or—(2) his life commuted for a fine. II. GOD CARES FOR THE SAFETY OF THE BEAST. Other Scriptures demonstrate this (Matt. vi. 26, &c.). III. PROVISION FOR THE SAFETY OF OTHERS SHOULD BE MADE. 1. This provision should be made promptly. 2. This provision should be permanent. Application: 1. Beware of injuring your neighbour's soul by an unguarded inconsistency. 2. Beware of injuring your neighbour's friendship by any unguarded passion. 3. Beware of injuring your neighbour's character by any unguarded word. 4. Beware of injuring your neighbour's peace by any unguarded look or action. 5. In all matters concerning your neighbour, remember that "Whatsoever ye would," &c. (*J. W. Burn.*)   *The penalties of carelessness :*—I. LIFE IS SUPERIOR TO PROPERTY. The ox that had gored a man to death was to be killed, and put out of the way. The ox is stoned to death; and, legally, it would involve physical uncleanness to eat of the flesh. II. THE CARELESS MAN IS CULPABLE. If the animal had been known to gore; if this fact had been testified to the owner, and proper precautions had not been taken, then the owner was in some measure participant in the evil doings of the vicious creature. Carelessness is culpable. He that knoweth to do good, and doeth it not, to him it is sin. To prevent evil by wise precaution is our bounden duty, and is an indirect method of doing good. All life is precious; but it seems to be indicated that some lives are more precious than others. Thirty shekels is a high price for some; but a hundred shekels would be a low price for others. After death has visited, then estimates nearer the truth of a man's worth will be formed. III. MAN IS RESPONSIBLE FOR PREVENTABLE EVIL. If into the uncovered pit an ox or an ass fall, the owner of the pit shall make good the damage. Will the Almighty hold us responsible for the moral pits we have left uncovered? We have not placed precautionary signals in sufficient number along those high-ways where moral pits and quagmires abound. (*W. Burrows, B.A.*)   *Punishment of criminal carelessness :*—If Moses had to regulate our legislation in reference to railway accidents, he would put it on altogether a new basis. If half-a-dozen people were killed and a score seriously injured through the mail running into a goods train, and Moses found that the engine driver who missed the signal had been on his engine twelve or fourteen hours, or that the pointsman who turned the mail into the goods siding had been kept at his post for, perhaps, a still longer period, I cannot help thinking that managers and directors would stand a chance of having a much sharper punishment than they commonly receive now. And if criminal carelessness which might be fatal to life was punished by Moses with death, I think that fraudulent acts which are certain to injure the health and perhaps the life of the community, would have been punished by him not less severely. He would certainly have approved the sentence under which a few months ago a large farmer, greatly to his own astonishment and the astonishment of his friends, was put in prison for sending diseased meat to market; only I think that the old Jewish legislator would have inflicted a still heavier punishment—a few years' penal servitude instead of a month or two's imprisonment. Chemists, who adulterate the drugs on which the rescue of life depends—the rescue of the life not only of ordinary members of the community like ourselves, whom also Moses would have protected, but of men of science, poets, and statesmen, whose death would be a calamity to the nation, and to the world—would I think, have been made responsible by him for the death of those who perished through their fault; and if they were not stoned or hung for murder, which I think would have been possible, a criminal penalty so heavy would have been inflicted on them, and they would have been branded with such imfamy, that other evil-disposed persons would have feared to repeat the crime. (*R. W. Dale, D.D.*)   *Responsibility respecting life :*—We have this principle certainly in our law, but with what beneficial effect a much wider application of it might be made! Look at a few instances of carelessness. There is a block of crowded, unventilated, and badly-drained houses, into which necessity drives the poor to herd, and where they sicken and die. Think you this principle would not lay hands on the owner of such property? Would it spare a corporation if it neglected to deal with a pestilence breeding quarter? Neither would trifling carelessness escape. What is trifling? A traveller goes to a strange hotel, and retires to damp sheets, and ever afterwards suffers from ill-health, sometimes speedily loses life. Think of the thousands who travel, and follow even one stricken one into a sorrowful and bereaved family! Carelessness, when seen in its consummation, speaks for itself. But worse than carelessness is selfishness which pursues its ends regardless of others. In the sloppy winter of the Franco-German war, an army contractor furnished boots with paper soles to the French. In the Crimean war we heard of manufacturers who supplied blankets which, so to speak, rotted on the backs of our soldiers. How much death and disaster was due to this selfishness! Because we cannot count the victims is there no guilt? Moses would say, if life be lost and can be traced to a man, let him atone for it; results must be dealt with. Life is the one sacred thing. Nor is it difficult to see that such a principle applies itself to the selfishness of those who by their trickery and roguery in business ruin the commerce of their country. Alas! for the advice because it is utopian, and more because it is needed, but it is true that no tribunal would better serve England at this juncture than one which held the terror of moral justice over manufacturers who send out worthless goods and taint our honest name, and impair our credit the wide world over. They rob others, and they destroy their country. There are traitors to-day as real as those who in olden days took a bribe and sold their armies or their castles to the enemy. (*W. Senior, B.A.*)   *A needful warning :*—On a cold Sabbath morning in February, a gentleman was walking along, somewhat hastily, through the snow. He noticed a bright-looking little lad standing upon the pavement, with his cap in his hand and his eyes fixed upon one spot on the sidewalk. As he approached him he looked up to him, and pointing to the place, said, "Please don't step there, sir. I slipped there and fell down." What a different world this would be if all Christians were as particular as this lad to warn others against dangers, whether temporal or spiritual. (*Christian Herald.*)   *A danger signal :*—At Saltcoats, not very far from the shore, stands a beacon in the winter. If you were to ask any one who belongs to that place, why it is there, you would be told this story :—"A merchant from Glasgow, with his family, was residing there for the summer months. One morning the merchant went out to bathe before breakfast, and he thought he was quite safe as long as he kept near the shore. But there was a pit there which he did not know anything of, and into this pit he fell, and nothing more was seen or heard of him. After this accident a beacon was put up as a warning to all others to keep from the spot." What were the feelings that prompted this beacon to be put up? It must have been feelings of love to keep all others from danger. (*Ibid.*)

CHAPTER XXII.

VERS. 1-5. **If a man steal.**—*The law of robbery :*—God made provision not only for the acquisition of property, but for its security. Hence this law, which respects

—1. Theft. 2. Housebreaking. I. THEFT (vers. 1–4). As the wealth of an Israelite consisted mainly in flocks and herds, the depredations of the thief were directed for the most part against them. II. HOUSEBREAKING (vers. 2, 3). Learn—1. That God's providence extends to property as well as persons. Both are His gift. 2. That those who endeavour to thwart that providence play a losing game. 3. That the recognition of that providence is not inconsistent with, but demands the use of, means. It is an abuse and perversion of it to tamely submit to wrong when the legitimate prevention of wrong is within our reach. 4. That providence protects even the life of the wrong-doer, and no man must wantonly interfere with that protection. (*J. W. Burn.*) *Actual and virtual criminality :*—I. MEN MUST SUFFER FOR CRIME. II. MEN MUST SUFFER, UNAVENGED, THE EXTREME CONSEQUENCES OF CRIMINAL CONDUCT. III. MEN MUST LEARN, BY DEGREES OF SUFFERING, THAT THERE ARE DEGREES OF CRIMINALITY. IV. MEN MUST LEARN THAT PROPERTY HAS RIGHTS. V. MEN MUST LEARN TO CONSIDER THE WELFARE OF THEIR NEIGHBOURS. (*W. Burrows, B.A.*) *How to get at a thief :*—This is the only way of getting at a thief. You cannot reason with him. He dismissed his reason before he committed his felony. He had first to strangle his reason ; he committed murder in the sanctuary of his soul before he committed theft in the fields of his neighbour. What, then, is to be done with him? He must be made to feel the folly of theft; he must be made to feel that theft is a bad investment ; he must be made to feel that he has played the fool even in the excess of his cleverness. The thief would be made to know what dishonesty is, when for the one ox he must pay five in its place. He could have evaded an argument; he could have doubled upon a covenant, and have quibbled about the ambiguity of its terms ; but he could not shuffle out of this four-square arithmetical arrangement. Five oxen for an ox, four sheep for a sheep ; and by the time the thief had played at that game two or three days, he would have put on the garb, at least, of an honest man! (*J. Parker, D.D.*) *Substitutionary resti-tution :*—A coal merchant in one of our American cities was approached by a minister in regard to the salvation of his soul. The merchant declared it an im-possibility for him ever to become a Christian. He gave as a reason his mode of business. For a long term of years, he had, according to a too general custom, given short weight. He had thus grown rich, and now felt the inconsistency of seeking religion without restitution. This was impossible: many of his customers were dead, others beyond his knowledge. The thought of the poor who had paid for coal they had never received rested heavily on him. He asked the minister if he thought the substitution of a gift to the poor would be acceptable to God. The minister advised him to try it. A large donation, more than equal in amount to his unjust gains, was made, and the merchant sought God in earnest. He was happily con-verted, and is to-day a prominent member of the church. *Tardy restitution :*—As a gentleman in London entered his house, he found a well-dressed female sitting on the stairs, who asked pardon for the liberty she had taken, saying that, hearing the alarm of a mad dog, she had taken refuge in his house. On hearing her story, he gave her some refreshment ; and she left, thanking him for his civility. In the evening his lady missed her gold watch ; and it was concluded the female was the thief. Fifteen years afterwards, the watch was returned, with a note from this woman, saying the gospel had changed her heart, and she desired to return the watch to its rightful owner. *Unrighteous restitution :*—What a shame then is this to Christians, who minding nothing less than restitution, make *ex rapina holo-caustum :* out of a world of ill-gotten goods, they cull out some small fragments to erect some poor hospital ; having cheated thousands, build alms-houses for some few, and then set a glorious inscription in front, whereas this one word, *Aceldama,* would be far more proper. (*J. Spencer.*) *Compensation for damage :*—A man in New Jersey told me the following circumstances respecting himself and one of his neighbours. "I once owned a large flock of hens. I generally kept them shut up. But one spring I concluded to let them run in my yard, after I had clipped their wings so that they could not fly. One day, when I came home to dinner, I learned that one of my neighbours had been there full of wrath, to let me know that my hens had been in his garden, and that he had killed several of them, and thrown them over into my yard. I determined at once to be revenged. I sat down and ate my dinner as calmly as I could. By the time I had finished I thought that perhaps it was not best to fight with my neighbour about hens, and thereby make him my bitter enemy. I concluded to try another way, being sure that it would be better. After dinner, I went to my neighbour's. He was in his garden. I went out and found him in pursuit of one of my hens with a club, trying to kill it. I accosted him. He turned upon me, his face inflamed with wrath, and broke out in a great fury, 'You have abused me. I will kill all your hens, if I can get them. I never was so abused. My garden is ruined.' 'I am sorry for it,' said I : 'I did not wish to injure you ; and now see that I have made a great mistake in letting out my hens. I ask your forgiveness, and am willing to pay you six times the damage.' The man seemed confounded. He did not know what to make of it. He looked up to the sky, then down at the earth, then at his neighbour, then at his club, then at the poor hen he had been pursuing, and said nothing. 'Tell me now,' said I, 'what is the damage and I will pay you six-fold ; and my hens shall trouble you no more. I will leave it entirely for you to say what I shall do. I cannot afford to lose the love and goodwill of my neighbours, and quarrel with them, for hens or anything else.' 'I am a great fool !' said my neighbour; 'the damage is not worth talking about ; and I have more need to compensate you than you me, and to ask your forgiveness than you mine.' " (*Mrs. Child's Letters from New York.*)

Ver. 6. **If fire break out.**—*Responsibility for actions :*—In the twenty-second chapter of Exodus the rights of property are defended, and the text before us may be considered as the law of fire insurance under the Mosaic dispensation. The law was a constant lesson to the people on their vast responsibility for the consequences of their conduct. God's law thus showed that Omnipotence identified itself with every just claim, and would insist on compensation for every wrong inflicted. I. This ancient law brings into view THE GENERAL DOCTRINE OF LIABILITY FOR THE CONSEQUENCES OF OUR ACTIONS AND NEGLECT. Nothing is more difficult than to raise in most men's minds a vivid sense of the widespreading results of their own character and conduct. They readily acknowledge the responsibility of others, but not their own. Men never take so modest a view of their own individuality, as when the object is to set forth the insignificance of their own contribution to " the evil that is in the world." But such calculations are founded on a gross delusion. The most commonplace sinner has a power of mischief in him which might sadden the blessed as they look at it. II. The dormant sense of liability for the consequences of our conduct OUGHT SURELY TO BE AWAKENED BY CONSIDERING HOW WE HOLD OTHER MEN RESPONSIBLE IN COMMON LIFE. III. THE RIGHT CONCEPTION OF JUDGMENT TO COME IS THE BRINGING TO THE CONSCIOUSNESS OF THE FINITE THE KNOWLEDGE OF THE INFINITE IN THIS REGARD. " This, hast thou done." He who subverts the faith or the conscience of one soul subverts in effect the faith and conscience of all souls, and " their blood will I require at the watchman's hand." IV. These considerations should impress the mind with A NEW SENSE OF THE INFINITE BEARINGS OF OUR THOUGHTS, WORDS, AND ACTIONS ; and should make us " swift to hear, slow to speak, slow to wrath." Let to-day be the day of salvation by becoming the day of judgment, for " if we would judge ourselves, we should not be condemned with the world." (*E. White.*) *The penalty of carelessness :*—Learn—1. To be careful of your neighbour's material, intellectual, and spiritual interests, and do not damage them by a careless word or action. 2. In order that these interests may not be invaded, put a strong check on those loose and vagrant so-called interests of your own. 3. In order to prevent any possibility of the transgression of these interests, see that those passions of avarice, envy, and revenge which cause so much mischief in the world, are quenched. 4. If these interests are invaded, render a frank, manly, and ample restitution. (1) Confess your fault. (2) In the case of loss make it up. (3) In the case of injury to character, let the acknowledgment be co-extensive with the slander. (4) Let those who have been injured forgive as they hope to be forgiven. (*J. W. Burn.*) *No trifling with bread :*—This is right. The Bible really builds upon granite bases ; there is nothing merely fanciful in this legislation. This is sound common-sense, and common-sense in the long run wins the esteem and confidence of the world. No man may trifle with bread. Bad enough to burn down any kind of property ; but to consume stacks of corn is to commit murder with both hands ; to light the standing corn when it waves in the fields is to thrust a knife, not into one heart, but into the very life of society. How can restitution be made ? It cannot be made. You cannot replace corn ; money bears no relation to corn ; corn is not an arithmetical quantity. Destroyed bread is destroyed life. Who destroys bread ? He who makes poison of it ; he who turns it into a drink that takes away the reason and deposes the conscience of men. He who holds back the bread-stuff until the time of famine that he may increase his own riches by an enhanced market value is not a political economist, unless, under such circumstances, a political economist is a heartless murderer. And if it is wicked to set fire to corn, is it a light or frivolous matter to set fire to convictions, faiths—the bread-stuff of the soul? Is he guiltless who takes away the bread of life, the bread sent down from heaven? Is he a pardonable incendiary who burns down the altar which was a stairway to the light, or reduces to ashes the Church which was a refuge in the day of storm? (*J. Parker, D.D.*)　　*Who kindled the fire?*—This statute had a peculiar necessity in such a hot, dry country as Palestine, where there was a peculiar danger from accidental conflagrations. If a man burned over his stubble field, it was necessary, before the dry grass was lighted, to see that the wind was in the right quarter, and every precaution taken that the flames should not kindle upon the property of a neighbour. The sound principle that underlies this law is that men must suffer for the evil they do through thoughtless recklessness, as well as for what they do with malicious intent. 1. If I invite a group of young men in my house to surround a card-table, I may simply design to furnish them an hour's amusement. But perhaps a lust for gambling may lie latent in some young man's breast, and I may quicken it into life by my offer of a temptation. There is fire in that pack of cards. And I deliberately place that fire amid the inflammable passions of that youthful breast. On me rest the consequences of that act, as well as upon him whom I lead into temptation. The motive does not alter the result by one iota. 2. Among social virtues none is more popular than that of hospitality. When bountifully practised toward the needy, it rises to the dignity of a Christian grace. And ordinary hospitalities may be set to the credit of a generous spirit. But here is the master or mistress of a house who spread their table with a lavish provision for the entertainment of their evening guests. Among the abundant viands of that table the lady of the house places the choicest brands of Madeira wine, and on a side-board she sets out a huge bowl of inviting punch. And among the invited guests of the evening comes a man who has promised the wife of his early love that he will never again yield to his awful appetite, and turn their sweet home into a hell. He sees the tempter in that accursed punch-bowl, and is pressed very courteously to "take a glass." The fire "catches in the dry thorns" in an instant. He drinks. He goes reeling into his own door that night, and his whole household is in a flame of excitement and terror, and agony and shame. Now, who kindled that fire? Let her who put the bottle to her neighbour's lips make answer. 3. The artillery of this Divine law against incendiarism has a wide range. It is pointed against that social nuisance, the slanderer. "Behold how great a matter his little fire kindleth." The utterance of evil reports may be well likened to playing with fire. 4. This law against incendiarism applies to every utterance of spiritual error and infidelity. He who utters a devilish suggestion to corrupt the innocence of chastity sets fire to passion, and becomes the incendiary of a soul. He who scatters a pernicious literature comes under the same condemnation. He who sows scepticism, by tongue or pen, sets fire to the "standing corn" of righteous opinion. Beware how you play with the sparks of falsehood. Beware how you play with the fire of wicked suggestion, that may kindle a blaze of sin in another's heart. (*T. L. Cuyler, D.D.*)

Vers. 7–13. **If a man shall deliver unto his neighbour money or stuff to keep.**— *The law of trusts:*—1. God's law provides strictly to keep men faithful to their trusts by men. 2. Theft may abuse and frustrate the trust of the most faithful men. 3. Such theft discovered is punished with double restitution by God. 4. In theft undiscovered and upon suspicion, trustees are bound to clear themselves by oath. 5. A right oath as it terminates upon God, so ought in some cases to be taken before magistrates (ver. 8). 6. In doubtful cases about trust, civil powers are enabled to try men, and judge by oath. 7. The falsifier of trust convicted must restore double (ver. 9). 8. Living stuff trusted to any and dying, none knowing how, the trustee's oath must clear him (vers. 10, 11). 9. Living goods trusted to keeping upon consideration if stolen, must be made good by the keeper (ver. 12). 10. No law binds men to restore what Providence takes away from men by wild beasts (ver. 13). (*G. Hughes, B.D.*)

Vers. 14, 15. **If a man borrow.**—*Borrowing:*—1. God in His law provideth against hurting our neighbour's goods by borrowing. 2. Hurt and death may come to things borrowed without the sin of the borrower. 3. In case of the borrower's faultlessness in hurt, no restitution doth God award. 4. In case of wilful hurt and spoil the borrower by God's law must make it good. 5. Things wilfully hurt which are borrowed by hire must be satisfied by God's law. 6. Perishing of such in a lawful use of them, God's law accounts satisfied by their hire (vers. 14, 15). (*G. Hughes, B.D.*) *Concerning borrowing :*—Learn : 1. On the one hand—(1) To be obliging. If you can do a needy neighbour a good turn by lending advice or material assistance, do so. (2) Don't make your needy but obliged neighbour answerable for any accident that may occur through your own misfortune or fault. 2. On the other hand —(1) Be careful not to abuse that which is in kindness lent you ; or—(2) Forget to return it, and thus render evil for good. Book-borrowers should note this. But— (3) Rather both in principle (2 Kings vi. 5) and in action suffer the loss than inflict it. (*J. W. Burn.*)

Vers. 16, 17. **If a man entice a maid.**—*Lessons :*—1. Providence may suffer men through strength of lust to entice and defile virgins. 2. Such enticing and polluting is grievous sin against God and man abhorred of the Lord. 3. In case of such sin God hath judged recompense to men, as He executeth vengeance for Himself. (*G. Hughes, B.D.*) *Want of wariness :*—Flamingoes are very shy and timid birds, and shun all attempts of man to approach them ; the vicinity of animals, however, they disregard. Any one who is acquainted with this fact can take advantage of it so as to effect the slaughter of these beautiful animals by dressing himself up in the skin of a horse or an ox. Thus disguised, the sportsman may get close to them and shoot them down at his ease. So long as their enemy is invisible they still remain immovable, the noise of the gun only stupefying them, so that they refuse to leave, although their companions are dropping down dead around them. They are taken in by appearances ; and so long as the man is disguised they accept him as the creature which he pretends to be, even though his actions clearly indicate that he is something else. Shy, beautiful, and harmless, the unfortunate bird meets destruction simply for want of wariness. Many a lovely human being with the like qualities has met her doom for want of that same trait. (*Scientific Illustrations.*)

Ver. 18. **Thou shalt not suffer a witch to live.**—*Spiritualism—modern witchcraft :*— The Bible regards witchcraft—1. As a stern and diabolical reality (Lev. xx. 27 ; Deut. xviii. 9). 2. As unlawful trafficking with the unseen world (Lev. xix. 31 ; Isa. viii. 19, "For the living to the dead," *i.e.*, on behalf the living to the dead). 3. As sometimes trickery and imposture (Isa. viii. 19), "that peep and mutter" (probably ventriloquise. See art. Pythoness, Smith's Dic. Bible). 4. As filthy defilement (Lev. xix. 31). 5. As deserving death (Lev. xx. 6. *cf.* text). 6. As one of the crimes for which the Canaanites were destroyed. 7. As inconsistent with a trust in God (Isa. viii. 19). 8. As frustrated by God (Isa. xliv. 25). 9. As a power from which the godly have nothing to fear, for there is no solitary prayer in the whole Bible to be protected from its enchantments, and no thanksgiving for deliverance from them. In this country we only meet with it now in the form of spiritualism, and as such—I. It is DANGEROUS. 1. Because it destroys all faith in the person and providence of God, and hence imperils the hopes, aspirations, and safety of the soul. 2. Because it tends to debase man's moral standards, and to obliterate the fact of sin. 3. Because its direct aim is to subvert Christianity, and to abolish the Word of God. 4. Because it comes before the imagination and the affections with plausible appeals. II. It SHUNS THE LIGHT. 1. Its performances, like the old witchcraft, take place in the dark, and under circumstances the force of which requires the exertions of the strongest will. On the contrary, the grand facts of both Old and New Testaments were "not done in a corner," but in the light of day. 2. It is chary of the open exhibition of its credentials to the critic and the unbeliever ; this privilege is reserved for those who first believe in the magician and in his powers. The miracles and other credentials of the Bible—court scrutiny— were mainly for the conviction of those who disbelieved. 3. And why does it shun the light ? For the old reason (John iii. 19–21). III. It is UNLAWFUL. 1. Because expressly forbidden in the Word of God. Christ and His apostles meet the spirits not in darkened cabinets but with open exorcism. 2. Because of its avowed mission to pry into and traffic with the unrevealed matters of the spirit-world. God has emphatically set His face against this (Deut. xxix. 29). 3. Because it is "another gospel" (Gal. i. 8). IV. It is partly gross IMPOSTURE. 1. Spiritual realities are solemn and imposing, and worthy in every way of the high source from which they emanate. When God communicated to the prophets and apostles we do not hear that it was on dancing tables, illegible inscriptions on slates, or through books made luminous by phosphoric oil. We do not hear of angels or spirits, whether in

Old Testament or New, pulling men's hair, scattering sweetmeats, rapping on walls, hurling bed pillows, appearing in regimentals, or handling hot coals. 2. Spiritual realities in the Bible were never discovered to be small tricks. 3. Spiritual realities in the Bible have never been explained by natural phenomena as have much of the legerdemain of modern magic. V. It is uniformly USELESS. 1. For harm (Isa. viii. 19), when there is a firm trust in God. 2. For good (Luke xvi. 27–31), when there is no such trust. (*J. W. Burn.*)

Ver. 21. **Neither vex a stranger.**—*The stranger :*—The spirit of the Hebrew law was broader than race, or country, or kindred. Among the ancients generally a foreigner had no rights in any country but his own. In some languages the very word " stranger " was synonymous with enemy. Against these race hatreds Moses set up this command. Not only were foreigners to be tolerated ; they were to receive the fullest protection (see Lev. xxiv. 22). (*H. M. Field, D.D.*)   *Sound policy :*—This was not only a humane law ; but it was a sound policy. Do not wrong a stranger ; remember ye were strangers. Do not oppress a stranger ; remember ye were oppressed. Therefore do unto all men as you would they should do to you. Let strangers be well treated among you, and many will come among you, and the strength of your country will be increased. If refugees of this kind be treated well, they will become proselytes to your religion, and thus their souls may be saved. (*A. Clarke, D.D.*)   *She was a stranger :*—A missionary was requested to go out to a new settlement to address a Sabbath-school. He had preached in the morning, and was wearied and felt quite unfitted for the task, but reluctantly consented to go. When he found himself at the spot, he looked round the assembly with great misgivings, not knowing what to say to them. He noticed a little girl, shabbily dressed and barefooted, shrinking in a corner, her little sunburnt face buried in her hands, the tears trickling between her small brown fingers, and sobbing as if her heart would break. Soon, however, another little girl, about eleven years old, got up and went to her, whispered kindly to her, and taking her by the hand, led her toward a brook, then seated her on a log, and kneeling beside her she took off her ragged sunbonnet, and dipping her hand in the water, bathed her hot eyes and tear-stained face, and smoothed her tangled hair, talking in a cheery manner all the while. The little one brightened up, the tears all went, and smiles came creeping around the rosy mouth. The missionary stepped forward and said : " Is that your little sister, my dear ? " " No, sir," answered the noble child, with tender, earnest eyes, " I have no sister, sir." " Oh, one of the neighbours' children," replied the missionary ; " a little school-mate, perhaps ? " " No, sir ; she is a stranger. I do not know where she came from ; I never saw her before." " Then how came you to take her out and have such a care for her if you do not know her ? " " Because she was a stranger, sir, and seemed all alone, and needed somebody to be kind to her." " Ah," said the missionary to himself, " here is a text for me to preach from— ' Because she was a stranger, and seemed all alone, and needed somebody to be kind to her.' " The words came to him, " Inasmuch as ye have done it unto one of the least of these My brethren, ye have done it unto Me." So, taking the little girls by the hand, he went back to the school-room and told the people the simple story ; then spoke of the great love that all should bear to one another, even as the dear Saviour sought out those who were humble and of low estate, making them His peculiar care. The missionary forgot his weariness, and felt that God had put a good word in his mouth.

Vers. 22–24. **Ye shall not afflict any widow, or fatherless child.**—*God's care for the widow and fatherless :*—I. THAT WIDOWS AND ORPHANS HAVE CLAIMS UPON OUR REGARD. 1. They have claims upon our sympathy. Their stay, comfort, defence is gone. What state can be more sorrowful and helpless ! 2. They have claims upon our protection and help. Our resources are only held in stewardship for God's purposes, and to what better purpose could they be applied, both as regards its intrinsic merits and the Divine will concerning it. II. THAT WIDOWS AND ORPHANS HAVE SPECIAL PRIVILEGES. 1. God has legislated for them. Not in the dry and hard manner in which penal and ceremonial codes are obliged to be enacted, but in a way which throws them on the broad and better principles of humanity and love. 2. God stands in a peculiar relation to them (Psa. lxviii. 5). In the absence of their natural guardians He takes them under His wing. 3. God is always ready to help them ; to hear their cry (ver. 23 ; Jer. xlix. 11). III. THAT ANY OPPRESSION OF THE WIDOW AND FATHERLESS WILL BE RIGOROUSLY PUNISHED (ver. 24). 1. The oppressor is left to the righteous judgment of God, who will surely avenge His own (Luke xviii. 7). 2. The oppressor is left to the terrible retribution of a hard and cruel heart, which inflicts as much punishment on the subject as on the object. 3. The oppressor is left to the certain contempt and execration of his fellow-men. Husbands and fathers, learn—1. To provide for the wants of those whom you may leave behind to mourn your loss. (1) Make diligent use of your time, and save all you can for them. (2) Your life is uncertain, insure it. (3) We don't know what a day or an hour may bring forth, have all your affairs in order so as not to add perplexity to trouble already too heavy to be borne. It is "afflicting them," not to do so (see 1 Tim. v. 8). 2. Then, having made a proper use of means, leave them with calm faith in the power and goodness of their "Father in heaven." 3. Help the widow and the orphan, as your wife may be left a widow and your children fatherless. (*J. W. Burn.*)

Ver. 25–27. **Any of My people that is poor.**—*Judgment on an usurer :*—There was once in this church a poor widow, and she wanted £20 to begin a small shop. Having no friends, she came to me, her minister ; and I happened to know a man —not of this church—who could advance the money to the poor widow. So we went to this man—the widow and I—and the man said he would be happy to help the widow. And he drew out a bill for £20, and the widow signed it, and I signed it too. Then he put the signed paper in his desk, and took out the money and gave it to the widow. But the widow, counting it, said, "Sir, there is only £15 here." "It is all right," said the man ; "that is the interest I charge." And as we had no redress, we came away. But the widow prospered. And she brought the £20 to me, and I took it myself to the office of the man who lent it, and I said to him, "Sir, there is the £20 from the widow." And he said, "Here is the paper you signed ; and if you know any other poor widow, I will be happy to help her in the same way." I said to him, "You help the widow ! Sir, you have robbed this widow, and you will be damned ! " And, my friends, I kept my eye on that man. Before six months were over God smote him, and he died. (*Wm. Anderson, D.D.*) *Regard for the poor and needy :*—While General Grant was President of the United States, he was at one time the guest of Marshall Jewell, at Hartford, Conn. At a reception tendered him by the Governor, where all the prominent men of the State were gathered, a roughly-pencilled note, in a common envelope, signed by a woman, was handed him. It was put into his hands by a young politician, who thought it a good joke that "an old woman in tatters" should presume to intrude upon the President at such a time. "You need not bother about her ; I sent her away—told her you were not here to be bored," the young man said to Grant. The President's answer much surprised the politician. "Where is this woman ; where can I find her ? " he inquired, hurrying from the room. The letter he held in his hand, written poorly in pencil, told a sorrowful story. It said in substance : "My son fought in your army, and he was killed by rebel bullets while fighting for you. Before he died he wrote me a letter which told how noble a man you were, and said you would look out for his mother. I am poor, and I haven't had money or influence to get anybody interested in me to get a pension. Dear General, will you please help me for my dead boy's sake ? " Sadly the woman had turned away from the mansion, her last hope dead. A servant pointed her out to President Grant, walking slowly up the street. The old soldier overtook her quickly. She was weeping, and turned towards him a puzzled face as he stopped her and stood bare-headed in the moonlight beside her. The few words the great, kind man spoke turned her tears into laughter, her sorrow into joy. The pension before refused her came to her speedily, and her last days were spent in comfort. (*Christian Age.*) *Take care of the poor :*—"Take care of the poor, and the Lord will take care of you," was the wise counsel of a bishop to a candidate for ordination. *The profit of helping the poor :*—The welfare of the lowest is bound up with that of the highest, so that the "injury done to the meanest subject is," as Solon said, "an insult upon the whole constitution," and a blow at the prosperity of all. Sir Robert Peel gave his daughter, on her birthday, a splendid riding-habit, and rode by her side for an airing in the park, his heart swelling with pride that he could call such a maiden daughter ! At once, however, she fell sick of the most malignant type of typhus fever, and despite all medical skill and parental care died. A careful inquiry as to the source of the germs of the fatal disease revealed the fact that the poor seam-stress, who had embroidered that robe in a wretched attic, had been compelled to use it to cover her husband when he shivered with the chills of the deadly fever.

And from that garret of poverty the infection of death passed into the mansion of the Premier. Society has her own ways of avenging our neglect of her poorest and neediest children. In one bundle are we all bound up, for weal or woe. We give, though we do not always know it, to save ourselves, not alone to save others. Ignorance and idleness are handmaids of vice, as intelligence and industry are handmaids of virtue. God sees that no one is so much profited as ourselves by those gifts to His poor, which are corrective of self-indulgence, expansive of our noblest sympathies, educative of our highest nature, and which, while they help to lift humanity to a higher level, as surely lift ourselves with the rest. (*Christian Age.*)   *Pious poverty :*—I have no legacy to leave my children but pious poverty, God's blessing, and a father's prayers. (*R. Prideaux.*)

Ver. 28. **The ruler of thy people.**—*The Divine right of magistrates to respect :*— I. THAT THE POWERS THAT BE ARE ORDAINED OF GOD (Rom. xiii. 1-5; 1 Peter ii. 13-15). II. THAT MAGISTRATES MUST BE TREATED WITH RESPECT, both their persons and their decisions (Josh i. 16-18). 1. Because they administer that which, when it is law at all, is based on the will and authority of God (Rom. xiii. 2). 2. Because they administer that which is the bulwark of national stability and personal safety (Rom. xiii. 3). III. That magistrates must receive respect, IRRESPECTIVE OF THE EFFECT OF THEIR DECISION (Prov. xvii. 26). 1. Because they are but the servants of the law. 2. Because if through human infirmities, justice should occasionally miscarry, it is better to suffer than to bring the law into disrepute (Prov. xxiv. 21, 22). 3. But if their decisions violate conscience, then Acts. iv. 19, 20 ; v. 29. IV. THAT MAGISTRATES MUST BE SECURE AGAINST ALL HOSTILE ACTION (Prov. xvii. 26 ; Job xxxiv. 17, 18). 1. Fear will warp the judgment. 2. Fear will divert the course of justice. V. That magistrates are not only entitled to respect, BUT TO OUR SYMPATHY AND PRAYERS (Psa. xxii. 1, 2; Ezra vi. 10; 1 Tim. ii. 2). VI. THAT DIS-RESPECT TO MAGISTRATES IS SEVERELY CONDEMNED (Jude 8). Let magistrates, all who are in authority and all who administer law whether civil or domestic, whether in law courts, homes, or houses of business, remember—1. That they are responsible to God (2 Sam. xxiii. 3). Let them see (1) that they accurately know the law, and (2) that their administration is conscientious and courageous (Psa. lxxii. ; iv. 12-14). 2. That they are responsible to man. Upon their decisions depend the well-being of the citizen, and the stability of the realm. 3. That their title to sympathy and veneration is recognized by the people at large. (*J. W. Burn.*)

Vers. 29, 30. **The firstborn.**—*First-fruits to God :*—God asks for nothing that we have not to give. He asks that we will give to Him of what He has given to us, that we will put to its true and highest use what He for that end has bestowed. We cannot give fruit that we do not bear, or that is green and unripe, but only that which is fresh and mature, waiting to be gathered in. I. God asks for the first ripe fruits of our EDUCATION. The wise man's education is never finished. To cease to learn is to cease to grow; to cease to grow is to decay in force and faculty. Yet there is a special sense in which education ceases. The youth leaves school, the scholar the university, the apprentice is "out of his time." Then we have to think and act for ourselves, and use the knowledge we have acquired. We have to face the great questions that concern man's life and destiny. Then God asks from us the first ripe fruits of our education in the use of our intelligence and feeling and con-science. He asks us to face these great questions; to think soberly and ponder the path of our feet. II. God asks from us the first ripe fruits of our TOIL. The Jews gave this in kind—from flock, vineyard, or field. We give an equivalent—money. The first money earned is the first-fruits of toil. From that lay by some-thing for God. III. God asks from us the first ripe fruits of our CONVERSION. I have often seen a child so overcome with an unexpected gift that he has forgotten to say "Thank you," but surely Christ does not expect such forgetfulness from those whom He has snatched from the burning. IV. Then there are some first-fruits of EXPERIENCE which God commands us to offer to Him. "I have learned by ex-perience" is the confession sometimes of self-convicted folly, sometimes of grateful wonder. How near have we been to spiritual death! How well hidden the pit-falls under our feet! How strong the arms that have held us up! How wonderful the consolations! How sweet the grace of the Divine! So experience enriches the soil in which we are planted to produce a lustier and richer growth. Now to offer to God the first ripe fruits of experience is surely to learn and profit by its lessons. It is to remember; to take warning; to know our own selves—our peculiar weaknesses and danger; it is to trust God more and self less; to look for larger answers to prayer, and more wonderful vindications of faith. V. Does not God want THOSE LOVELY AND PRECIOUS FRUITS WHICH GROW ON THE HOUSEHOLD VINE ? The only true dedication of children to God is that Christian nurture which leads to their dedicating themselves. (*R. B. Brindley.*)

CHAPTER XXIII.

VER. 1. **Thou shalt not raise a false report.**—*Slander characterized, prohibited, and punished :*—I. Slander is CHARACTERIZED. 1. Originating a false report. It may be from—(1) Envy. (2) Carelessness. (3) Hasty conclusions. 2. Listening to false reports. 3. Circulating a false report. II. Slander is PROHIBITED. 1. Affecting antecedents. 2. Affecting character. 3. Affecting family or social relations. 4. Affecting goods. III. Slander is PUNISHED. The slanderer is—1. Excluded from religious fellowship (Psa. xv. 3). 2. Exposed to contempt of mankind (Prov. x. 18). 3. Object of Divine vengeance (Psa. x. 5). 4. Excluded from kingdom of heaven (Rev. xxii. 15). (*J. W. Burn.*) *Description of slander :*— The tongue of the slanderer is a devouring fire, which tarnishes whatever it touches ; which exercises its fury on the good grain equally as on the chaff, on the profane as on the sacred : which, wherever it passes, leaves only desolation and ruin ; digs even into the bowels of the earth, and fixes itself on things the most hidden ; turns into vile ashes what only a moment before had appeared to us so precious and brilliant ; acts with more violence and danger than ever in the time when it was apparently smothered up and almost extinct ; which blackens what it cannot consume, and sometimes sparkles and delights before it destroys. (*Massillon.*) *Envious slander :*—The worthiest persons are frequently attacked by slanders, as we generally find that to be the best fruit which the birds have been pecking at. (*Bacon.*) *How to avoid slander :*—The celebrated Boerhaave, who had many enemies, used to say that he never thought it necessary to repeat their calumnies. "They are sparks," said he, "which, if you do not blow them, will go out of themselves. The surest method against scandal is to live it down by perseverance in well-doing, and by prayer to God, that He would cure the distempered minds of those who traduce and injure us." It was a good remark of another, that "the malice of ill tongues cast upon a good man is only like a mouthful of smoke blown upon a diamond, which, though it clouds its beauty for the present, yet it is easily rubbed off, and the gem restored, with little trouble to its owner." *Slander reproved :*—When any one was speaking ill of another in the presence of Peter the Great, he would shortly interrupt him, and say, "Well now ; but has he not a bright side? Come, tell me what have you noticed as excellent in him ! It is easy to splash mud ; but I would rather help a man to keep his coat clean." *Listening to slander :*—Calumny would soon starve and die of itself, if nobody took it in, and gave it lodging. (*Leighton.*) There would not be so many open mouths if there were not so many open ears. (*Bishop Hall.*) *The progress of slander :*—It is Ælian's observation, how that men being in danger to be stung by scorpions, use to place their beds in water, yet the politic serpents have a device to reach them : they get up to the top of the house, where one takes hold, the next hangs at the end of him, a third upon the second, a fourth upon the third, and so making a kind of serpentine rope, they at last wound the man. And thus it is, that amongst scandalizers and slanderers, one begins to whisper, another makes it a report, a third enlargeth it to a dangerous calumny, a fourth divulgeth it for a truth. So the innocent man's good name, which, like a merchant's wealth, got in many years, and lost in an hour, is maimed, and so secretly traduced, that it is somewhat hard to find out the villain that did it. (*J. Spencer.*) *False reports :*—The Rev. C. H. Spurgeon has given publicity to the following letter : "Dear Mr. Spurgeon,—As I see that you are still occasionally put to the trouble of answering inquiries as to the truth of various anecdotes, &c., concerning yourself, I thought the following brief statement might interest you, or some of your numerous readers, if you think it well to publish it. About seventeen years ago I was for some time at a well-known health resort on the south coast. At the *table d'hôte* I sat next to a young married lady, who was, alas ! consumptive, and of that temperament which is so common in such cases, *très spirituelle*, and very learned and accomplished. You may be sure she never lacked auditors for her lively conversation. At dessert one day she was 'telling stories' (in the literal and juvenile sense of the phrase) about yourself. I let her go on for some time, until I thought the fun was getting a little too fast; and then I said, 'I hope Mrs.——, you do not believe the stories you are detailing, because I assure you, I heard nearly all of them in my boyhood, before Mr. Spurgeon was born, and that most of them were then attributed to Rowland Hill—doubtless with equal lack of authenticity.' She looked me calmly in the face, with a comical expression, and replied, 'Oh, Mr.——, we never ask whether such stories are true; it is quite sufficient if we find them amusing.' 'Well,' I said, 'so long as that is understood all round, by all means keep on.' The poor, brilliant, thoughtless woman and her husband also have many years since passed away; but she has many, many successors, who are without her wit, and not quite so good-humouredly candid as to their practice. If only you can get it 'understood all round' that such folk really do not consider whether their 'anecdotes' are true or not, it might save you some trouble. Yours faithfully——." Mr. Spurgeon himself adds : "This is quite true, but it is a pity that people should lie in jest. The lady was let off very easily. Our friend has touched the root of the matter, It is not malice, but the passion for amusement, which creates the trade in falsehood, which never seems to decline." *Description of calumny* :—Apelles painted her thus : There sits a man with great and open ears, inviting Calumny, with his hand held out, to come to him ; and two women, Ignorance and Suspicion, stand near him. Calumny breaks out in a fury; her countenance is comely and beautiful, her eyes sparkle like fire, and her face is inflamed with anger; she holds a lighted torch in her left hand, and with her right twists a young man's neck, who holds up his hands in prayer to the gods. Before her goes Envy, pale and nasty; on her side are Fraud and Conspiracy; behind her follows Repentance, clad in mourning, and her clothes torn, with her head turned backwards, as if she looked for Truth, who comes slowly after. (*A. Tooke.*) *False insinuations* :—Often are the most painful wrongs inflicted through the medium of covert inuendoes and malignant insinuations. Half of a fact is a whole falsehood. He who gives the truth a false colouring by a false manner of telling it is the worst of liars. Such was Doeg in his testimony against the priests. He stated the facts in the case, but gave them such an artful interpretation as to impart to them the aspect and influence of the most flagrant falsehoods. It was through the same mode of precedure that our Lord was condemned. **An unrighteous witness.**—*The duties of witnesses* :—I. NOT TO CO-OPERATE IN AN UNRIGHTEOUS CAUSE (ver. 1). This "commandment is exceeding broad," and conveys a lesson—1. To judicial witnesses. (1) Personal friendships. (2) The guilt of the accused on some other point. (3) A show of justice must not influence us. 2. To all partisans, controversialists, politicians. 3. To trades unionists, &c. II. NOT TO CO-OPERATE IN ANY UNRIGHTEOUS CAUSE BECAUSE IT IS POPULAR (ver. 2). 1. Because majorities are no test of truth. Multitudes may be roused by passion, prejudice, or self-interest. 2. Because men should be weighed as well as counted. 3. Because righteousness, from the constitution of human nature, is often unpopular and in the minority. III. NOT TO CO-OPERATE IN AN UNRIGHTEOUS CAUSE BECAUSE IT IS APPARENTLY BENEVOLENT (ver. 3 ; Lev. xix. 15). 1. Because we may be putting a premium on vice which is the source of all misery. (1) By endeavouring to conceal the crime. (2) By extolling other virtues, so as to minimize the enormity of guilt. But to what purpose is it if we extol a man's honesty, if he is lazy, or a drunkard; or his sobriety, if a thief? 2. Because justice is above mere sentiment, and for the well-being of the whole community, and not for the exclusive benefit of a class. 3. Because of its influence on the object himself. Let a man feel that you do this or that for him simply because he is poor, and he will see no advantage in helping himself. Learn then—1. To entertain none but righteous considerations. 2. To pursue them at all cost. (*J. W. Burn.*)

Ver. 2. **Thou shalt not follow a multitude to do evil.**—*Following the multitude prohibited* :—I. EXPLAIN THE NATURE OF THIS PRECEPT. 1. It is here assumed that the multitude do evil. This may be inferred—(1) From the review of past ages. (2) From the cruel persecutions which have been raised against the righteous in various ages of the world. (3) From the common conduct of mankind. Is not vice more general than virtue? 2. Secondly, the precept in the text supposes that we are in danger of copying the example of the multitude. We may infer this— (1) From the innate tendencies we have to evil. (2) From the prevalence of bad

example. 3. From a variety of melancholy facts. The multitude who now do
evil were not always such adepts in depravity ; when they first entered into the
broad way their feet were not swift to do evil ; they proceeded with hesitating
steps, but by practice became hardened in crime. II. URGE REASONS TO INDUCE US
TO OBSERVE IT. The multitude doing evil should not be imitated, because they are
—1. Unlawful and unconstituted guides. 2. Bad guides. 3. Dishonourable guides.
4. Unprofitable guides. 5. Dangerous guides. III. IMPART ADVICE FOR THE DIREC-
TION OF THOSE WHO WISH TO ESCAPE THE ENSNARING WILES OF THE MULTITUDE. 1. Get
your minds deeply and thoroughly impressed with the awfulness of your situation.
Dangers unseen will be unavoided. 2. Seek the regenerating grace of God. 3. Be on
your guard against the seductive wiles and insinuating influence of the multitude.
Sinners will entice you ; but come out from among them ; have no communion
with the unfruitful works of darkness (Psa. i. 1). 4. Follow the happy few who
strive to do good. Show that you are with Christ by being with His people. Oh,
say, " This people shall be my people, and their God my God." Inferences—(1)
That the measures of right and wrong are not to be determined by the majority.
Good and evil are fixed immutable principles ; and their natures are unchangeable,
whether many or few follow them. (2) What gratitude is due to God for the revelation of His will, which marks the boundaries of right and wrong ; and for the gift
of His Son to redeem us from this present evil world : to whom be glory for ever
and ever. Amen. (*Sketches of Sermons.*)   *Individual responsibility :*—There is,
I suppose, no doctrine more clearly set forth in Scripture than the doctrine of personal responsibility. There is no doctrine more readily owned, no doctrine more
insisted upon by men. Yet I think I can show you that, in its application to a
great number of particular cases, you would not only act as though you disbelieved
it, but you would unconsciously maintain in words doctrines directly opposed to it.
The words which I have just read to you suggest one of the most universally employed modes of denying this universally received doctrine of individual responsibility. " Thou shalt not follow a multitude to do evil," was said long ago by the
Jewish law. I think you will find that the present condition of things, in whatever
place or class we are thinking of, grew up from something very small, and that by
degrees the sin acquired strength from the power and position, and then from the
mere number of its perpetrators, until in time it acquired positive dignity and became correct, or according to the absurd modern phraseology, became " good form,"
from the multitude of transgressors. I will begin with the sex which since the
creation of the world has almost uniformly carried its point against the opposite
sex, and which, nevertheless, is still facetiously called the weaker. They will, I believe, if you ask them, readily own themselves responsible for their use of time and
of money. Well, they certainly spend an excessive amount of the latter, money,
as I daresay their husbands know, in purchasing ; and of the former, time, as
everybody knows, in adjusting those ever-changing and most cumbrous absur-
dities which they pile upon themselves, and with which they surround themselves
to the general inconvenience of everybody and everywhere. They do this until I
should think they must feel uncomfortable, and I know that they look deformed.
Why do they do it ? Ask any one, and you will hear it all condemned at once,
solemnly, perhaps piously condemned at once, the responsibility being shifted immediately from the individual to fashion, and that is to everybody. What does
all that mean ? Their conscience is relieved by the multitude whom they follow.
Let us go a little further and take another view of the matter. Public bodies, I believe,
parliaments, ministries, corporations, town commissioners, Poor Law guardians,
boards of all kinds, and committees of all kinds, are known—every one of you
knows it as well as I do—to be guilty of neglect of duties and violations of honour of
which none of their members singly, in private transactions, would for one moment
be capable. Take another set of instances. Look at the recognized dishonesties of
different trades and businesses. The man who keeps light weights for selling, and
heavy weights for buying, as I once knew a most " pious " man do ; the man who
adulterates food ; the man who puts bad work or bad material where it is not to be
detected ; the servant who robs his master " in the usual way " ; " the workman who
to no greater extent than others of his craft plunders his employer " ; none of these
desire by any means, I fancy, to have their children taught at school that the
Eighth Commandment has no meaning. They like to hear it every Sunday. Why ?
Because they have an unwritten tradition in the craft or trade, by which it is dispensed with. But I am going into more dangerous ground now. In the present
day, the multitude has come to be considered something more than an excuser of

deviations from strict principles in the ordinary affairs of life. It is beginning to assume the functions of the highest authority on religious matters. To call in question its decision, or refuse submission to its commands, no matter how unin- structed it may be, is coming to be viewed in the light of standing up against an inspired prophet. It does not occur to the thoughtless throng, who will rush any- where to hear anybody, or to see anything, that when the multitude appears to have taken a " pious " turn it can be wrong to follow it whithersoever it leads. It does not seem to occur to them that when the multitude is longing to take Jesus by force and make Him a king, it may have just as little perception of His mission as when it clamorously demands His crucifixion. No, they are afraid to gainsay what the multitude asserts; they are afraid to do anything but echo its assertions, and thus each one among a multitude perpetuates the delusion of the others as to his real opinion, by being afraid to say it out, and act in conformity with it. This is the very spirit by which multitudes are created, by which they are enabled to assume formidable proportions, to become powerful for evil. The silence of cowardice is re- garded as satisfactory consent, and everybody's echo of what everybody else says is vaunted as the concurrence of numerous independent testimonies. Persons of this kind are the genuine followers of the multitude who are condemned in the text. (*J. C. Coghlan, D.D.*) *The sin of following the multitude to do evil:*—I. It im- plies that the majority or great mass of mankind are uniformly and constantly engaged in doing evil. II. The prohibition which we are considering implies that every person is naturally disposed to follow a multitude to do evil. III. The prohibition in the text implies that those are altogether criminal who follow the evil examples of evil-doers, though they are the great majority of mankind. For—1. They are free and voluntary in following the examples of those who do evil. 2. Every person acts contrary to his reason and conscience in follow- ing a multitude to do evil, which renders him altogether criminal and inexcusable. Conclusion: 1. If men are apt to follow bad examples, as has been said, then there is reason to think that bad examples are the great source of moral corruption in every part of the world. 2. If men are naturally disposed to follow the multitude to do evil, then the truly godly have much more concern in spreading moral corruption, and obstructing the cause of religion than they are apt to imagine. 3. Since men are naturally disposed to follow the bad examples of the multitude, it is easy to see why a people, declining in religion, are so apt to be insensible of their religious declensions. The minority are blended with the majority, and they are all im- perceptibly declining together. 4. If all men are naturally disposed to follow the multitude to do evil, then the rising generation are always in a peculiarly danger- ous situation. 5. If it be criminal to follow bad examples, it must be far more criminal to set bad examples. 6. If men are naturally disposed to follow the multi- tude to do evil, then every one in a state of nature has a great reason to fear that he shall live and die in his present unsanctified and impenitent state. Your belong- ing to the majority will not help you to turn about, but powerfully tend to hinder you. What will you say when He punishes you? (*N. Emmons, D.D.*) *Multi- tude no prevailing argument:*—The Lord that made us knoweth our mould and how easily we are persuaded to taste of the forbidden fruit, and how prone to be carried headlong to error, and therefore gives us a *caveat*, and sets a bar and a stop in our way, that we run not to evil because we see others run or lead the way before us. And we shall do well by the way to take notice of our own corruption, as the Lord doth, that in the same we may see the necessity of this precept; for first, nature corrupt is as attractive of evil as the adamant naturally draws iron; just as a spark to tinder or gunpowder. Secondly, evil is diffusive of itself, and such an acquaintance there is between it and us, as the plague cannot so easily infect our bodies as sin doth poison and suddenly infect our souls. Thirdly, our nature is social, and not as the brutes; we readily thrust into company, and therefore being naturally enemies to solitariness, we are ready to follow if any one lead us the way; but if many or a multitude (as here) then we run, and for haste never stay to reason the case, neither in what way nor upon what errand. And, therefore, the Lord would have His people to fence themselves with a rule of prudence, that they be not misled by the crooked steps of others and their own perverse inclinations. 1. One reason is in the text: because a multitude may err and run to evil, and may decline to overthrow truth. 2. Multitudes cannot make that to be good which is evil in itself, neither in doctrine nor manners; well they may make an evil worse, but none better. 3. Multitudes cannot keep off the revenge of evil; one evil mate may help his fellow into sin, but cannot help him out of punishment. 4.

Multitudes and most men are commonly the worst. The way to hell is broad and the gate wide that leads to destruction, and many go in thereat (Matt. vii. 13). "Hell enlargeth itself" (Isa. v. 14). "Tophet is large and wide" (chap xxx. 33). And therefore it cannot be the safest way which the most walk in. Contrarily, the fewest are commonly the best; pearls are rare; many hundred false prophets to one poor Micaiah; God's part in the world was ever but a gleaning and a small remnant; and the apostle (1 John v. 19) pronounceth in the name of believers, "We know we are of God, and the whole world lieth in unrighteousness." 5. It is better to walk the right way alone than to wander out of the way with company; better go to heaven alone, or with a few, than with multitudes to hell. Come we now to application of this point. 1. If it be so dangerous to follow a multitude to evil, what a fearful thing it is to lead a multitude to evil! as the magistrate that enacts and commands evil; like Jeroboam that made all Israel to sin. Or the minister that shall be weak as another man by whose example many are corrupted, through loose speeches, unseemly behaviours, libertine courses, fellowship with the abject, opposing the persons and strict courses of such as fear God. 2. See how desperately many men frame their courses while they live as if to do as the most do, were a good and warrantable plea. Because the most are irreligious, without the fear of God, and without conscience: so are they. The most scorn to attend God's ordinance: so do they. Commit a felony, riot, robbery, or rebellion with a multitude, and try if in thy trial before the judge it will be a good plea to say, "I was led, and followed the multitude." What then would you have us to do? In matters of faith build upon a surer foundation than upon numbers and multitudes, whom it was never safe to follow; nor was it ever a good argument either of the truth or true Church. In Christ's time the multitude followed the Scribes and Pharisees, but not Christ nor His apostles; and all the multitude cried, "Crucify Him." And how uncertain a rule this is the father tells us who observed, that in synods and councils the greater side doth oftentimes overcome the better; and another who saith, that in all Divine cases we must not number voices, but weigh them. What sure ground can be expected from the rude multitude, than which nothing is more fickle and uncertain? But we have a surer word, "Being built upon the foundation of the apostles and prophets, Jesus Christ Himself being the chief corner-stone" (Eph. ii. 20; 1 Cor. iii. 11). And we say as Hushai to Absolom (2 Sam. xvi. 18) "Nay, but whom the Lord and this people, and all the men of Israel chose, his will I be, and with him will I abide." (*T. Taylor, D.D.*) *Thou shalt not follow a multitude to do evil:*—I. IMITATION IS ONE OF THE GREAT CHARACTERISTICS OF THE HUMAN SPECIES. The same passion that impels us to society, impels us to take part with our companions in their interests and inclinations. Insensibly and without thought we fall into their customs and their manners; we adopt their sentiments, their passions, and even their foibles, and follow the same course as if we were actuated by the same spirit. II. BY WHAT MEANS WE ARE TO KEEP OURSELVES FROM FOLLOWING A MULTITUDE TO DO EVIL. 1. Let us be early and firmly established in the principles of an holy faith. It is education chiefly that forms the human character; and it is a virtuous and religious education that forms the character. 2. Let us beware with what company we associate. 3. Let us acquire firmness and fortitude of mind. (*James Logan.*) *The multitude an unsafe guide:*—It is said of the roes and hinds that they are most tender and fearful of all beasts, affrighted with any noise, checked with the least foil, turned out of course with the snapping of a stick, presently make head another way, and when they are once out of their wonted walk they run they know not whither, even to their own death. Such is the natural disposition of the multitude or common people, soon stirred up, quickly awry, sometimes running full head one way, on a sudden turned as much another, easily set agog, delighted with novelties. (*J. Spencer.*) *The multitude not to be followed:*—Said Horace Bushnell to his younger brother, who had been to a cheap show and came home crestfallen, "The next time that you see the whole world doing something, be sure not to go with them unless you have some better reason." That was the germ of manly independence out of which the sturdy manhood of that remarkable thinker grew. The sooner a young man learns that there are in this world more silly people than wise, more weak than strong, the better his chances of being a man. *Custom not the standard of right:*—"Know that the Lord has set apart him that is godly for Himself." Therefore it is no excuse for him to say, "I do but as others do." He is to reckon his hours by the sun, not the town clock; to take God's direction, not the vice of the multitudes, as one of their stamp and at liberty to comply with their fashions. (*T. Manton, D.D.*)

Vers. 4, 5. **Thine enemy's ox.**—*On duties to enemies :*—I. THAT DUTIES TO ENEMIES ARE ENJOINED (Prov. xxiv. 17; 1 Thess. v. 15). 1. It is our duty to protect the interests of our enemy. (1) If they are damaged, we should endeavour to retrieve them. (2) If they are in danger of damage, we should endeavour to prevent them (James v. 19, 20). 2. It is our duty to help the difficulties of our enemy. (1) His mind may be in difficulties. (2) His soul may be in difficulties. (3) His material interests may be in difficulties. II. THAT DUTIES TO ENEMIES ARE DIFFICULT : "and wouldest forbear to help him." 1. Such duties are against the grain of human nature. 2. Such duties are apparently against self-interest. 3. Such duties require self-denials and sacrifices. III. THAT DUTIES TO ENEMIES ARE REWARDED (Prov. xxv. 21, 22; Matt. v. 44, 45 ; Rom. xii. 20). IV. THAT NEGLECT OF DUTIES TO ENEMIES IS PUNISHED (Job xxxi. 29; Prov. xxiv. 18). In conclusion—1. Our text applies to all enmity, whether polemical, political, or national. 2. Its precepts should be obeyed, because we may be in the wrong and our enemy in the right. 3. Because God has Himself set us the sublime example. " When we were enemies, we were reconciled by the death of His Son." (*J. W. Burn.*)   *Neighbourly conduct :*—The horse of a pious man living in Massachusetts, North America, happening to stray into the road, a neighbour of the man who owned the horse put him into the pound. Meeting the owner soon after, he told him what he had done; "And if I catch him in the road again," said he, "I'll do it again." "Neighbour,' replied the other, "not long since I looked out of my window in the night and saw your cattle in my meadow, and I drove them out and shut them in your yard ; and I'll do it again." Struck with the reply, the man liberated the horse from the pound, and paid the charges himself. " A soft answer turneth away wrath."   *A humane disposition :*—In one of my temperance pilgrimages through Illinois I met a gentleman who was the companion of a dreary ride which Mr. Lincoln made in a light waggon, going the rounds of a circuit court where he had clients to look after. The weather was rainy, the road " heavy " with mud. Lincoln enlivened the way with anecdotes and recital, for few indeed were the incidents that relieved the tedium of the trip. At last, in wallowing through a slough, they came upon a poor hog, which was literally fast in the mud. The lawyers commented on the poor creature's pitiful condition and drove on. About half a mile was laboriously gone over, when Lincoln suddenly exclaimed, " I don't know how you feel about it, but I've got to go back and pull that pig out of the slough." His comrade laughed, thinking it merely a joke ; but what was his surprise when Lincoln dismounted, left him to his reflections, and striding slowly back, like a man on stilts picking his way as his long walking implements permitted, he grappled with the drowning swine, dragged him out of the ditch, left him on its edge to recover his strength, slowly measured off the distance back to his waggon, and the two men drove on as if nothing had happened. The grand and brotherly nature which could not consent to see the lowest of animals suffer without coming to its rescue at great personal discomfort was nurtured by years of self-abnegation for the great struggle, when he should be strong enough to " put a shoulder to the wheel," that should lift the chariot of State out of the mire and set a subject race upon its feet. (*Frances E. Willard.*)

Vers. 6–8. **Thou shalt not wrest the judgment.**—*Duties of judges :*—I. That judges should be IMPARTIAL. 1. In particular towards the poor (ver. 6). (1) Because the poor are most open to the oppression of the powerful. (2) Because the poor are often at a disadvantage for the want of technical knowledge or means to procure legal assistance. (3) Because the poor are easily overawed. 2. In general towards the right (ver 7, first clause). Not to aid or abet a wrong cause. II. That judges should be CAUTIOUS, particularly with regard to matters relating to capital punishment. " The innocent and righteous slay thou not." 1. The case must be clearly proved. 2. The accused to have the benefit of the doubt. 3. Because justice would be done. If the criminal escaped an earthly doom, God would " not justify the wicked" (Prov. xi. 21). III. That judges should be INCORRUPT (ver. 8), either in the shape of direct bribe or indirect present. 1. Because the bribe may blind him to the true merit of the case; and—2. Because the bribe may weigh down and pervert his judgment on the wrong side. IV. That judges should be CONSIDERATE (ver. 9), particularly in regard to foreigners. Because —1. They had been foreigners themselves, and had suffered for the want of consideration. 2. They therefore knew something of the sufferings of foreigners. (1) Foreigners may be ignorant of the law and unwittingly break it. (2) When broken, they may know nothing of legal technicalities, or be unable to pay legal expenses.

(*J. W. Burn.*)   *The administration of justice :*—There was a close connection between the civil and the military constitution of the Hebrews. The same men who were captains of thousands and captains of hundreds in war were magistrates in time of peace. In every Oriental state the point of greatest weakness is the administration of justice. Those who have lived long in the East testify that there is no such thing as justice ; that no cadi, sitting in the place of judgment, ever pretends to such exceptional virtue as to be above receiving bribes. The utmost that can be expected is the hypocrisy which is the homage of vice to virtue; and even this is seldom rendered, for where bribery is universal no one is constrained by shame to conceal it. Against this terrible demoralization no rock can stand but that of the Divine authority. In the administration of justice a theocracy is an ideal government, for it is Divinity enthroned on earth as in heaven ; and no other form of government enforces justice in a manner so absolute and peremptory. In the eyes of the Hebrew lawgiver, the civil tribunal was as sacred as the Holy of Holies. The office of the judge was as truly authorized and his duty as solemnly enjoined as that of the priest. " The judgment is God's," said Moses; and he who gave a false judgment disregarded the authority of Him whose nature is justice and truth. The judgment-seat was a holy place, which no private malice might profane. Evidence was received with religious care. Oaths were administered to give solemnity to the testimony (Lev. v. 1). Then the judge, standing in the place of God, was to pronounce equitably, whatever might be the rank of the contending parties (Deut. i. 17). He recognized no distinctions ; all were alike to him. The judge was to know no difference. He was not to be biased even by sympathy for the poor (chap. xxiii. 3 ; Lev. xix. 15). Magistrates were not allowed to accept a gift, for fear of bribery. (*H. M. Field, D.D.*)   *Bribery resisted :*—Persuaded that Marvell would be theirs (the Administration's) for properly asking, they sent his old schoolfellow, the Lord Treasurer Danby, to renew acquaintance with him in his garret. At parting, the Lord Treasurer, out of pure affection, slipped into his hand an order upon the Treasury for £1,000, and then went to his chariot. Marvell, looking at the paper, called after the Treasurer, " My lord, I request another moment." They went up again to the garret, and Jack, the servant-boy, was called. " Jack, child, what had I for dinner yesterday ? " " Don't you remember, sir ? You had the little shoulder of mutton that you ordered me to bring from the woman in the market." " Very right, child. What have I for dinner to-day ? " " Don't you know, sir, that you bade me lay by the blade-bone to broil ? " " 'Tis so ; very right, child ; go away. My lord, do you hear that ? Andrew Marvell's dinner is provided. There's your piece of paper—I want it not. I know the sort of kindness you intended. I live here to serve my constituents. The Ministry may seek men for their purpose. I am not one." (*Coleridge.*) *Bribes declined :*—" Why," asked one of the English Tories of the Tory Governor of Massachusetts—" why hath not Mr. Adams been taken off from his opposition by an office ? " To which the Governor replied, " Such is the obstinacy and inflexible disposition of the man, that he never would be conciliated by any office whatever." His daughter used to say that her father refused a pension from the British Government of £2,000 a year. Once, when a secret messenger from General Gage threatened him with a trial for treason if he persisted in his opposition to the Government and promised him honours and wealth if he would desist, Adams rose to his feet and replied, " Sir, I trust I have long since made my peace with the King of kings. No personal consideration shall induce me to abandon the righteous cause of my country."   *A judge to refuse bribes :*—I dare say many of you may have heard of the celebrated Sir Matthew Hale, that he was in the habit of receiving a present from a person annually ; and it happened once, that about the usual time when this friend made him the present, that he was accused of some offence, and was to appear as an accused person before Sir Matthew Hale. On this occasion Sir Matthew Hale returned him the present, lest it should afford even the shadow of a suspicion that the purity of judicial impartiality should be disturbed, or seem to be disturbed, by a gift from one who was to appear before the court accused of an offence, and demanding a fair trial. And I believe still it would be thought the most scandalous outrage upon our constitution, and every judge would repudiate it with scorn and disdain, were any one, expecting to have his cause tried by that judge, to attempt to propitiate his favour by gifts. Now, this beautiful rule—so just, so reasonable, so proper—was anticipated and was known, you observe, three thousand years ago, and was first revealed by Him who is the Fountain of all wisdom and justice. (*J. Cumming, D.D.*)   *Bribery resisted :*—A speculator heard that an amalgamation between two joint-stock companies was projected, which would afford an opportunity to make a large sum of money by prompt purchases of shares. He was acquainted with an official holding a subordinate and poorly paid position in one of the companies, and went to him to obtain reliable information. But the official was a Christian and a man of honour, and knowing the information would operate to the disadvantage of his employers, refused to say whether the amalgamation was contemplated or not. " I can make £60,000 by my speculation if you will tell me," said the tempter, " and I will give you half." " I cannot betray my trust," was the reply. " You need not speak," said the speculator ; " just wink your eye and I shall know, and you shall have £30,000." The temptation was fierce, but the Christian conquered it. A few days afterwards, when the amalgamation was completed, the speculator reproached his acquaintance for not giving the information, but he was told that an approving conscience was above price. It is satisfactory to learn that the faithful official prospered in his subsequent career, and is now receiving a salary of £5,000 a year.

Ver. 9. **Thou shalt not oppress a stranger, for ye know the heart of a stranger.** *The logic of law :*—The argument is that our conduct is to spring out of our experience ; we are to go back upon our own history and consciousness for the law that shall guide us in the treatment of our fellow-men. Why, could we do so, no more should we hear the rasping voice of rancour, hostile criticism, mean remark, or severe demand. 1. Thou shalt not oppress the struggling man, for thou thyself hast had thy struggle. Do not be hard upon those who are going up-hill. 2. Thou shall not oppress a doubting man, for thou thyself hast had thy doubts, if thou art more than half a man. 3. The text has a meaning in reference to ourselves, as well as to others. Thou shalt not renew old fears, for all thy fears have been round, black, blatant liars. Six fears have been with you, have lied to you, have made you play the fool in all the higher relations and issues of life, and yet I detect you this morning talking in the corner to a member of the same false family ! Why do you not throw it from you, or order it behind you, or mock it with the jibing of perfect rest in God ! 4. " Thou shalt not ——, because ——." That is the logic of the text. Now, what must *He* be who gave such laws ? In the character of the laws, find the character of the legislator. God must be tender ; He takes care of strangers. Not only so ; He must be aware of human history in all its changes and processes. He knows about the strangers who were in the land of Egypt ; He knows about their deliverance ; He knows that strangers are a tribe that must be on the earth from age to age ; He knows us altogether. He speaks a word for the stranger. Oh, man, friendless, lonely man, you should love God. Oh, woman, mother, sister, sinning woman, you should love Christ. Oh, little children, frail flowers that may wither in a moment, you should put out your little hands, if in but dumb prayer, and long to touch the Son of God. Oh, working man, led away by the demagogue, made to scoff where you ought to pray, the Bible has done more for you than any other book ever attempted to do ; this is a human book, a book for the nursery, the family, the market-place, the parliament, the universe ! (*J. Parker, D.D.*) *Kindly qualities developed by adversity :*—I suppose it is adversity that develops the kindly qualities of our nature. I believe the sense of common degradation has a tendency to make the degraded amiable—at least among themselves. I am told it is found so in the plantations in slave-gangs. (*Lord Beaconsfield.*)

Vers. 10, 11. **The seventh year thou shalt let it rest.**—*The Sabbatic year :*— This law was intended—1. To show the fertility of the land of promise. Every seventh year, without skill or toil, the land would produce of itself sufficient for the poor and the beasts of the field. 2. To encourage habits of thrift and forethought, so that they might provide for the year of rest. 3. To test (1) their faith in the providence, and (2) their obedience to the laws of God. The subject suggests—I. THAT PERIODS MAY ARRIVE BY THE ORDER OR PERMISSION OF GOD WHEN WORK MUST BE LAID ASIDE. Commercial depression, sickness, old age. II. THAT THE PROSPECT OF SUCH PERIODS SHOULD LEAD US TO PROVIDE FOR THEM. We are not like " fowls of the air," or "grass of the field," which have to be literally fed and clothed by the providence of God, and are utterly unable to forecast and provide for contingencies. III. THAT THE PROSPECT OF SUCH PERIODS SHOULD TEACH US RESIGNATION TO THE WILL OF GOD AND FAITH IN HIS GOODNESS (Matt. vi. 25-34). 1. There remaineth "a rest" for the people of God. 2. Prepare for that rest by faith and obedience. (*J. W. Burn.*)

Ver. 12. **On the seventh day thou shalt rest.**—*Labour and rest :*—I. That rest is NEEDFUL—"May be refreshed." 1. Rest is needful that the exhausted faculties may repose after past work. 2. Rest is needful that those faculties may be invigorated for future service. 3. Rest is needful that work may not become irksome; for if so (1) it will be done slovenly; and (2) done imperfectly. 4. Rest is needful that work may be free and joyous. II. That rest is MERCIFULLY PROVIDED. 1. This rest is provided by God, lest man should overlook its necessity. 2. This rest is provided by God lest the servant, the foreigner, or the beast should be defrauded of their right to it. III. That rest should be DILIGENTLY EARNED. "Six days shalt thou do thy work." 1. Not lounge over it; 2. Not neglect it; but 3. Do it earnestly, conscientiously, and well. Application : 1. A lesson to employers. God has provided this rest; beware how you steal what God has given to man. 2. A lesson to working-men. This rest is yours by right. Then (1) claim it; (2) don't abuse it; (3) don't curtail that of others; (4) work during your own time, rest during God's. 3. A lesson to the world at large. Sabbath-breaking is the direct cause of (1) intellectual evils; overtaxed brains, &c.; (2) moral evils; neglect of the rights of God and man ; (3) physical evils. Science has demonstrated the need of one day's rest in seven. (*J. W. Burn.*) *Need of rest :*—We know well enough that if trains are run at fifty miles an hour over roads built to endure only a speed of thirty miles an hour, everything in a short time begins to give way, and to wear out, and the whole road and all the rolling stock gets into a dangerous condition. Every rail, every tie, every joint, every nail, every wheel and bit of machinery feels the strain and wear. The human mechanism is not less sensitive than are railroads and locomotives. The tendency of the time is to increase the speed of individual movement and progress. The over-driven human being needs constant rest and repairs, as do railroads and locomotives, and a thousand-fold more, for his mechanism is infinitely more complicated and delicate. Instead of adding more fuel to a disordered engine to make it go, we would send it to the repair shop, and let it be restored by skilled workmen to soundness. So when the mind and body are worn and weary, send them to the repair shop for rest. Sleep, quiet, nutritious food, the absence of all stimulants and whips, and goads—these skilled positive and negative workmen of nature will restore (if anything can) the wasted vitality, and bring back health and strength and soundness. (*Christian Advocate.*)

Ver. 13. **Be circumspect.**—*Circumspection :*—I. IN GENERAL. "In all things." Moses is drawing to the close of these precepts, and looking back upon them, he says—"Be circumspect." The original suggests—1. That we should be fully awake to the importance of the Divine commands. (1) Give them intelligent and reverent examination. (2) Store them up in the memory. (3) Study them in their beneficent operation. 2. That we should be on our guard against temptations to break the Divine commands. Temptations are (1) sudden; (2) insidious; (3) deceiving. 3. That we should be careful "to remember His commandments to do them." (1) There is a danger lest an exaggerated estimate of human weakness should lead to despair on the one hand, and recklessness on the other. (2) God would not command the impossible. (3) There is "grace to help in time of need." II. IN PARTICULAR, "make no mention," &c. Because—1. That would be uncircumspect in the first and greatest commandment. 2. That would be to forfeit the help promised to the circumspect. 3. That would be to yield to a tendency to be uncircumspect in everything. Christians—1. "Watch and pray, lest ye enter into temptation." 2. Live so as "to adorn the doctrine of God your Saviour in all things." (*J. W. Burn.*) *Circumspection needed :*—The mysterious perturbation of a ship's compass is reported in a scientific journal. It appears that the compass of the ship *Penguin*, recently anchored off Australia, was deflected fifty-five degrees, and had a dip of eighty-three degrees. After the ship left the anchorage and proceeded on her voyage the disturbance ceased. At two miles from the point the variation was quite normal. The captain spent a day in investigating the phenomenon. He passed two or three times over the point where he had anchored, and found that whenever the ship crossed it, the compass was disturbed as before, and recovered when at a distance of two miles in any direction. This satisfied him that the centre of the submarine disturbance was limited to a circle of less than two miles magnetic minerals at the sea bottom. The journal reporting his observation says: "Great as is the gain to the navigator to be thus warned of a formidable danger in certain places, it lays upon him the imperative duty of being always on his guard against such sources of disaster elsewhere, and of promptly reporting any new magnetic disturbance, as he would a rock or shoal." Similar vigilance is necessary on the part of every voyager through life.

Ver. 16. **The feast of harvest.**—*The feast of harvest :*—I. THE INSTRUCTION IT COMMUNICATES. 1. It exhibits the wonderful power of God. 2. We have an establishment of the faithfulness and truth of God. 3. We have a manifestation of the goodness and bounty of God. 4. It displays the mercy and forbearance of God. 5. It shows us the connection between means and the end. II. WHAT FEELINGS IT SHOULD PRODUCE. It should produce feelings—1. Of deep humiliation. 2. Of heartfelt gratitude. 3. Our constant dependence upon God. 4. A constant desire to please Him. III. WHAT PRACTICAL INFLUENCE THE SUBJECT SHOULD EXERT UPON US. 1. To labour for the provision suited to our souls. 2. To do good in our respective spheres and stations in life. 3. Prepare for the final harvest. Application : 1. Let us gratefully enjoy the bounties of Providence. Many are abusing, many forgetting, &c. 2. Let us be especially anxious about the blessings of eternal life. 3. Let us always act in reference to the final harvest of the world. (*J. Burns, D.D.*) *Pilgrimage feasts :*—I. RELIGIOUS FEASTS ARE MEMORIALS. 1. Of God's past dealings. 2. Of our dependence on God's care. 3. Of our present condition. Pilgrims. This earth is not our rest. II. RELIGIOUS FEASTS ARE NOT TO INTERFERE WITH THE DUTIES OF LIFE. III. STATED RELIGIOUS FEASTS ARE HELPFUL TO A RELIGIOUS SPIRIT. IV. RELIGIOUS FEASTS MUST PROMOTE THE SOCIAL AND BENEVOLENT INSTINCTS OF OUR NATURE. V. THE OFFERINGS AT RELIGIOUS FEASTS must be—1. Pure. 2. Of the best. (*W. Burrows, B.A.*) *The feast of harvest :*—This was their Pentecost ; so called from a Greek word signifying "fifty"—because it occurred on the fiftieth day from the feast of unleavened bread. It was, properly, a harvest festival, in which the Jew offered thanksgiving unto God for the ripened fruits of the earth. To understand the peculiar interest the Jew took in this holiday, you must remember that the Israelites, after their establishment in Canaan, were almost entirely a nation of farmers. The peasant and the noble, in their respective spheres, were alike husbandmen. And the whole land of Israel was in the highest state of cultivation. Now, to such a people, inhabiting such a country, the feast of harvest was necessarily a grand festival. 1. We, too, want great national and religious holidays, to keep in mind great national providences. 2. We need them, moreover, as verily as the Jews, for their conservative political influence—to counteract the sectional and unsocial tendencies of our great tribal divisions. If we could come up nationally to such Pentecosts, then no living man would ever again dare breathe of discord and disunion—for chords, tender as our loves and stronger than our lives woven of religion and holy with old memories, as the memorial festivals uniting Judah and Ephraim, would bind us together and bind us to God ! 3. Meanwhile we need such pentecostal holidays for those personal advantages which they brought to the Hebrews. They furnish that harmless relaxation so constitutionally necessary to our highest well-being. Real pleasure, as well physical as moral, is always the true law of life. True virtue is genial and joyous, walking earth in bright raiment, and with bounding footsteps. And the nervous, restless, unreposing, devouring intensity of purpose wherewith our men follow their business, is as disastrous to the nobler moral bloom and aroma of the heart, as a roaring hurricane to a garden of roses. Above all, our religious nature needs them. The true joy of the Lord is the Christian's strength. Cheerfulness is a very element of godliness. 4. This is our Pentecost—our feast of harvest. And even in its lowest aspect, as a grateful acknowledgment of God's goodness, in preserving for our use the kindly fruits of the earth, it is a fitting occasion of thankfulness. It is scarcely possible to over-estimate the importance of agriculture. It surpasses commerce and manufacture, as a cause is superior to its effects—as an inner life is of more moment than its various outward functions. Meanwhile, the reflex influences of industrial agriculture on our physical and social well-being are as well incalculable. After all, the finest products of our farm-lands are found in our farm-houses. Things better than corn and cabbages are grown on plough-ground—bone, muscle, sinew, nerve, brain, heart ; these all thrive and strengthen by agriculture. The specimens of strong, hale, common-sense manhood seen at our annual fairs are a finer show than all the fat cattle and sheep, and noble horses, and the brave array of farm-fruits and implements. Agriculture purifies morals, chastens taste, deepens the religious element, develops the individual man. 5. Our thanksgiving is partly in view of the ripened fruits of the earth; but mainly in view of other and higher blessings. And in this regard as well, it is properly—a feast of harvest. In respect of all things—not merely the natural fruits of the earth, but all great human interests, political, intellectual, religious—we may be said to live in the world's great harvest time. We have reaped, and are reaping the ripened and ripening fruits of all earth's past generations. Consider this a little. (1) First: This is true—politically. Philosophically considered, the grand end and aim of all civil progress is human freedom—the highest development and culture of the individual and free manhood. Monarchy the one-man-power, oligarchy the few-men-power, are but the successive stages of the growing life, up to the ripened product of the true democracy—the all-men-power. To this end hath tendered all political progress; and beyond this there is no progress. This is the harvest of earth's long political husbandry, and we are reaping it. (2) Then passing from the political, the same thought is true in regard of the intellectual. It is a thought well worthy our pondering, on an occasion like this—that we live in the harvest-time of mind and thought! Carefully considered, the development of the "mental" follows the law of material development. "First, the blade, then the ear, after that the full corn in the ear." Genius is first poetical, then practical. First, the flaunting blossom; then the substantial fruit. From the beginning, man's law of intellectual progress has been from the abstract to the practical—from ideas to facts. The practical, being the fruit of the imaginative, as the ripened corn is the fruit of the plant's inner life. In past generations, intellect has been busy in a rudimental husbandry—felling the great forests; draining the low marshes; subduing the rugged soil; scattering the seed; and watching and waiting for the increase. The old philosophy; the old civilization; the old polities, civil and ecclesiastical; the old chivalry; the old poetry—these were the thought-germs, the thought-leaves, the thought-blossoms, which have ripened, and are ripening around us into God's glorious fruit! We live in earth's prodigal and luxuriant autumn—in times when marvellous things are the rule, and mean things the exception—in an economy of prodigies, each one a seeming miracle to men's earlier comprehension, and yet all, only the ripened development of their own thought-germs. And if the law of all husbandry be "to sow in tears and reap in joy," then our thanksgiving, that we live in these eventful times, should be unto God, this day, a great feast of harvest! (3) Passing this, we observe once more, and finally, That this same law of development we have been tracing through the political and intellectual, will be found to rule in the spiritual—and in this regard should we mainly rejoice that we live in life's harvest-time. 6. In respects, then, like these, political, intellectual, religious, we live in times of unexampled blessedness. We have come up to Zion from hills purple with vintage, and valleys golden with corn, in the rapturous harvest-home of the mortal! And it becomes us to keep festival before God as the old Jew kept his Pentecost. As men, as patriots, as philanthropists, as Christians, our cup of joy mantles brightly. What more could God have done for us that He hath not done? What people can be happy before God, if we are not happy? Living here, in this nineteenth century, free men—free Christians—we seem to stand on the very mount of God, flung up in the waste of ages, for the enthronement of His great man-child! We look backward, and lo! all the past has been working together for our national and individual beatitude. Patriarchs, prophets, bards, sages, mighty men, conquerors, have all been our servants. Generation after generation, that have lived and died—great empires, that have risen and flourished, and trod imperial paths, and passed away for ever—seem to rise from their old death-dust, and march in vision before us, laying down all their accumulated thoughts, and arts, and honours—all the trophies of their mighty triumphs, in homage, at our feet! We look forward, and the eye is dazzled with the vision of the glory about to be accorded to God's kingly creature, man! when standing upon this redeemed world, he shall assert his birthright—a child of God here! an heir of God for ever! Verily, we have cause for thanksgiving. "The Lord hath done great things for us, whereof we are glad." Let us give, then, free course to our grateful emotions! Thankful for the present, trustful for the future, let us rejoice before God "with the joy of harvest." (*C. Wadsworth.*)

Ver. 19. **Thou shalt not seethe a kid.**—*Cherish the finer instincts:*—The prohibition suggests the duty of cherishing the finer instincts of our nature. The act

here forbidden could hardly be called cruelty, the kid being dead, but it was
unnatural. It is beautiful to see the ancient Law inculcating this rare and delicate
fineness of feeling. The lesson is that everything is to be avoided which would tend
to blunt our moral sensibilities. (*J. Orr.*)

Ver. 20. **To bring thee into the place which I have prepared.**—*Life's pilgrimage :*—The angel, the way, the prepared place. It is the Divine key to the
mystery of life. Life is emphatically a way. Not by the way of the sea—a prompt
and easy path—but by the way of the wilderness, of old God led His pilgrims.
The vision of the angel in the way lights up the wilderness. Consider the suggestion of the text as to—I. The pilgrim's CONDITION. God's children must be pilgrims,
because this world is not good enough, not bright enough, not capable of being
blessed enough, for the pilgrim in his home. For—1. The instructed soul sees the
touch of essential imperfection and the bounds of close limitation in everything
here. 2. There is a constant aching of the heart through memory and hope. 3.
Life is a pilgrimage because it is far away from the Friend whom we supremely love.
II. The pilgrim's GUIDE. 1. God has sent His angel before us in the person of
His Son. 2. He sends His angel with us in the person of the Holy Ghost. III.
The pilgrim's WAY TO THE PILGRIM'S HOME. 1. It is a way of purposed toil and
difficulty, of wilderness, peril, and night. Suffer we must in the wilderness ; the
one question is, Shall it be with or without the angel of the Lord ? 2. It is a way
of stern, uncompromising duty. God asks us now simply to do and to bear, and to
wait to see the whole reason and reap the whole fruit on high. We must train
ourselves to the habit of righteous action, and leave the results to God and eternity.
3. It is a way of death. God promises to none of us an immunity from death.
The shadow hangs round life as a drear monitor to all of us. He only who can eye
it steadily and fix its form will see that it is angelic and lustrous with the glory
beyond. The grave is but the last step of the way by which the angel leads us to
the place which He has prepared. (*J. B. Brown, B.A.*) *Divine guidance :*—I.
THERE IS A DIVINE WAY. 1. Through the wilderness. 2. Beset with enemies. 3.
Many privations. 4. Contrary to mere human liking. God's way is not our way !
Ours may be pleasant at first but bitter at last, but God's way is the reverse ; and
yet not exactly, for sweets are graciously mingled with the bitters. There is
hunger, but there is manna. There is thirst, but there is clear water from the
smitten rock. There is perplexity, but there is an angel to guide and protect. II.
THIS WAY LEADS TO DIVINELY-PREPARED PLACES. Heaven is a specially prepared place.
" I go to prepare a place for you." A place in the best of all places. A home in
the best of homes. A dwelling-place where all the abodes are mansions. A seat
where all the seats are thrones. A city where all the citizens are kings. What
matters it though the way be long and sometimes dreary, so long as the place is so
attractive ; and we cannot fail to reach it if we obey Divine directions. III. THE
TRAVELLERS ON THIS WAY ARE FAVOURED WITH A DIVINE GUIDE. Jesus Christ, the
Angel of the new covenant, is fully competent to direct and protect. He has
trodden every inch of the way. IV. DIVINE PROMISES ARE CONTINGENT ON THE FAITH-
FUL PURSUIT OF DIVINE METHODS (ver. 21). The Divine methods are—Caution,
obedience, self-restraint, and the entire destruction of all that has the remotest
tendency to damage the moral nature. (*W. Burrows, B.A.*) *The angel of the
covenant :*—I. HIS NATURE WAS DIVINE. 1. Equal with God. (1) Bearing the
Divine name ; " My name is in Him." The incommunicable covenant name of
Jehovah. (2) Performing Divine actions ; " Mine angel shall go," &c., " I will
cut them off." So New Testament, " I and My father are one." 2. Distinct from
the personality of the speaker, " I send," so New Testament, " The Father which
sent Me." II. HIS OFFICE WAS TO CONDUCT THE COVENANT PEOPLE TO THE FULFILMENT
OF GOD'S COVENANT ENGAGEMENT. 1. Providence. " To keep thee in the way."
So Christ " upholds all things by the word of His power." " In Him all things
consist." Generally and particularly He preserves those who trust in Him (John x.
28). 2. Redemption. " To bring thee into the place which I have prepared."
Israel's redemption is only half accomplished as yet. So Christ's eternal redemption is not complete till the last enemy is destroyed (John xiv. 2, 3). III. THE
PROPER ATTITUDE TOWARDS HIM. 1. Fear. Carefulness not to displease Him.
Christ is the Saviour of those only who believe in Him. To others He is a " savour
of death unto death." 2. Obedience. " Obey His voice." So says the Father in
the New Testament (Matt. xvii. 5) ; and Himself (Matt. xxviii. 20). This implies—
(1) Trust in His person. (2) Subjection to His authority. (3) The prosecution of

His commands. IV. THE REWARD OF OBEDIENCE TO HIM (vers. 22, 23). 1. Identification and sympathy with us in our cause. " I will be an enemy," &c.   2. Victory
over our foes (1. Cor. xv. 57), world, flesh, devil, death, &c.   3. Inheritance in the
promised land.   Learn—1. (2 Tim. i. 9), That God's grace has been manifested in
Jesus Christ from the beginning of the world. 2. That God's grace has been,
through Jesus Christ, with His people up to the present moment. 3. And will be
till the end of the world. (*J. W. Burn.*)   *Christ at the head of the column :*—
It is said when the Duke of Wellington, on one occasion, rode up to his retreating
army, a soldier happened to see him first and cried out : " Yonder is the Duke of
Wellington ; God bless him ! " and the retreating army had courage to nerve itself
afresh and went forward and drove the enemy away.   One has said that the Duke
of Wellington was worth more at any time than five thousand men.   So it would
be if we had the Captain of our salvation in front, we would go forward.   How
gloriously would this Church contend if Christ were visibly in front of them ! But
the army was sometimes without the Duke of Wellington.   There was a place
where he could not be.   And if Christ were visibly present, He would be present at
the same time, only at one church in one locality ; it might be in Philadelphia, but
what of the thousand other cities?   But an unseen Saviour is at the head of the
column everywhere.   We know He is there.   The Captain of our salvation is where
two cr three are gathered in His Name to inspire us ; and to-day, in every city on
the face of this globe, where the columns meet to march, His voice sounds
"Onward ! " in their ears. (*M. Simpson, D.D.*)   *The angel in life :*—Laws without angels would turn life into weary drudgery.   Life has never been left without
some touch of the Divine presence and love.   From the very first this has been
characteristic of our history.   The solemn—the grand, fact is, that in our life there
is an angel, a spirit, a presence ; a ministry without definite name and altogether
without measurableness ! a gracious ministry, a most tender and comforting service,
always operating upon our life's necessity and our heart's pain.   Let us rest in
that conviction for a moment or two until we see how we can establish it by
references to facts, experiences, consciousness against which there can be no witness.   See how our life is redeemed from baseness by the assumption that an angel
is leading it.   Who can believe that an angel has been appointed to conduct a life
which must end in the grave?   The anticlimax is shocking ; the suggestion is
charged with the very spirit of profanity.   If an angel is leading us, is he leading
us to the grave ?   What is it within us that detests the grave, that turns away from
it with aversion, that will not be sent into so low and mean a prison ?   It is " the
Divinity that stirs within us."   Then again, who could ask an angel to be a guest
in a heart given up to evil thoughts and purposes ?   Given the consciousness that
an angel is leading us, and instantly a series of preparations must be set up corresponding with the quality and title of the leading angel of our pilgrimage.   We
prepare for some guests.   According to the quality of the guest is the range and
costliness of our preparation.   Whom our love expects our love provides for.
When we are longing for the coming one, saying, " The presence will make the
house the sweeter and the brighter, and the speech will fill our life with new poetry
and new hope.   Oh, why tarry the chariot wheels? " then we make adequate—
that is to say, proportionate—preparation.   The touch of love is dainty, the invention of love is fertile, the expenditure of love is without a grudge or a murmur,—
another touch must be given to the most delicate arrangement ; some addition must
be made to the most plentiful accommodation ; love must run over the programme
just once more to see that every line is worthily written.   Then the front door must
be opened widely, and the arms and the heart, and the whole being to receive the
guest of love.   And that is so in the higher regions.   If an angel is going to lead
me, the angel must have a chamber in my heart prepared worthy of myself.
Chamber !—nay, the whole heart must be the guest-room ; he must occupy every
corner of it, and I must array it with robes of purity and brightness that he may
feel himself at home, even though he may have come from heaven to do some
service for my poor life.   Any appeal that so works upon every kind of faculty,
upon imagination, conscience, will, force, must be an appeal that will do the life
good.   It calls us to perfectness, to preparedness, to a nobility corresponding in
some degree with the nobility of the guest whom we entertain.   The Divine presence
in life, by whatever name we may distinguish it, is pledged to two effects, supposing
our spirit and our conduct to be right.   God undertakes our cause as against our
enemies.   Would we could leave our enemies in His hands ! I do not now speak
altogether of merely human enemies—because where there is enmity between man

and man, though it never cen be justified, yet it admits of such modification in the system of words as to throw responsibility upon both sides—but I speak of other enemies,—the enmity expressed by evil desire, by the pressure of temptation, by all the array against the soul's health and weal of the principalities of the power of the air, the princes of darkness, the spirits of evil. Send the angel to fight the angel ; let the angel of light fight the angel of darkness. The second effect to which the Divine presence in our life is pledged is that we shall be blessed with the contentment which is riches. Thus we have mysteries amongst us which the common or carnal mind cannot understand. Men asking God's blessing upon what appears to be unblest poverty—men saying it is enough when we can discover next to nothing in the hand uplifted in recognition of Divine goodness. Thus we hear voices coming from the bed of affliction that have in them the subdued tones of absolute triumph ; thus the sick-chamber is turned into the church of the house, and if we would recover from dejection, and repining, and sorrow, we must go to the bedside of affliction and learn there how wondrous is the ministry of God's angel, how perfecting and ennobling the influence of God's grace. (*J. Parker, D.D.*)

Ver. 30. **By little and little I will drive them out before thee.**—*The gradual processes of God :*—It is important, not only to see, but to love, the gradual processes of God. There is more love in doing the little thing than in doing the great thing. A great mind is never so great as when it is throwing itself into something exceedingly minute. The special subject to which the text spiritually and allegorically refers is the conquest of sin. For such as the old inhabitants of the land of Canaan were to Israel, such the old inhabitants of our hearts are to us. But now here let me draw what appears to me to be a very important distinction before I proceed. If the processes of sanctification are exceedingly small, the work of justification is complete—perfectly complete—in its one defined isolated act. Never confound this —the advancement of your holiness with the perfection of your pardon. There are no degrees of pardon. Nevertheless, though, the Lord Jesus Christ being set up in his heart, sin has gone down, and grace is in the ascendancy—the sin is there—and there it is in tremendous rebellion and awful conflict. Make the distinction of the sin dominant, and the sin subservient, but rebellious against the grace dominant. Yet still, though the sin be thus so far subdued, it lives. Only " little by little," after it is put down from its throne, is it expelled. It goes on to that expulsion— till at last, as the condemnation of sin was exchanged for the rebellion of sin, the rebellion of sin is exchanged for the removal of the presence of sin, and sin is no longer there. Now I want to lead you to see the benefits of this " little by little." It is in infinite mercy. It is the discipline of life. And not only in the external event, but in the internal experiences, to a believer, it is all discipline. And that very gradual overcoming of sin is a great part of the discipline of life—to exercise many graces, patience, faith, waiting upon God, prayer, humiliation. And not only so, but remember in this discipline of life, God has His punishments. And do you know what God's heaviest punishment is? Sin. He makes sins scourge sins !— often a sin we hate to scourge a sin we love—often a sin of action to chasten a sin of feeling—often a sin of conscience to humble us in the dust and make us discover a sin of emotion. Sins punish sins. Therefore, as the old Canaanites were kept in the land of Canaan for this very end—that they might be thorns in the side of the Israelites, and whenever the Israelites fell into idolatry—for their grievous sin some were allowed to rise up and overcome them for awhile, till God raised up some judge to overcome that nation, so it is in your heart. And not only is it thus discipline and punishment—but remember it is for the manifestation of the glory of the Holy Ghost who exhibits His power and grace in the process of converting sinners into saints. Or look at it again thus. I do not believe that we could bear now to be perfectly holy. That inward light, if so unclouded, would be of such a brightness as would wither us and scorch us. The body would not be capable of it—the mind would not be capable of it. But when we have the disembodied spirit, or when we have the " spirit clothed upon with the new body," then, and then only, we shall be capable of perfect saintliness. And till that, it must be " little by little," —a gradual approaching to that state which we could not bear if introduced to at once. Now, just in conclusion, observe the expression " I will drive them out." It is one of God's high works ; it requires the power of Omnipotence to eradicate sin from the human soul. (*J. Vaughan M.A.*)   *The power of little things :*—I. IT IS THROUGH LITTLE THINGS THAT A MAN DESTROYS HIS SOUL ; he fails to take note of little things, and they accumulate into great ; he relaxes in little things, and thus in time loosens every bond. II. It is by little and little that men become great in piety. We become great in holiness through avoiding little faults, and being exact in little duties. III. There is great difficulty in little things. In daily dangers and duties, in the petty anxieties of common life, in the exercise of righteous principles, in trifles—in these we must seek and find the opportunity of ejecting "by little and little" the foes we have sworn to expel from our hearts. (*H. Melvill, B.D.*) *Little things :*—I. Great things are made up of little things. Highest mountain of grains of dust. Atlantic of drops of water. Year of 31,536,000 seconds. Deepest snow-fall came down one flake at a time. II. Great things depend on little ones. Falling of apple from tree insignificant enough ; yet led to discovery of law of gravitation. III. Great things spring from little ones. Oak once an acorn. Greatest hero once an infant. Explosion in coal-pit which destroyed life and property was caused by spark from match. Tract sent by child to India fell into hands of a chief, who was brought to Christ through reading it ; missionary was sent out and hundreds converted. IV. Great works are accomplished by little and little. Pyramids raised one stone at a time. Greatest paintings done stroke by stroke. Michael Angelo, when pointing out what progress he had made in a piece of sculpture on which he was engaged, was met with the remark, "But these are trifles." He replied, "Trifles make perfection ; but perfection is no trifle." V. Character is formed by little and little. Good characters are built up of little acts of kindness, industry, generosity, obedience, and integrity. One mean or dishonest act may destroy a reputation which it has taken years to acquire. (*W. H. Booth.*) *The power of moral forces :*—I. The strength of moral forces. II. The power of little, backed by moral force. III. Moral forces move to the production of distant results. IV. The movements of moral forces are not hurried. V. Moral forces will continue to move until the purpose is finally accomplished. VI. Moral forces are ever on the side of right doers. (*W. Burrows, B.A.*) *The conquering life :*—The upward road to success must always be over difficulties, and these are only overcome "little by little." The man who would conquer must not expect to do so at once, by one headlong charge. Yes, a man to succeed must be self-reliant, he must trust to God and his own right arm. When Stephen Colonna was taken prisoner by his enemies, and they sneeringly asked him, "Where is now your stronghold?" he laid his hand upon his heart, and answered, "Here." A man must dare to stand alone. If Clive had leaned upon others instead of himself, he would not have matched his few European and native troops against the overwhelming masses of Bengal, and have won the Battle of Plassey. If Columbus had been discouraged by delays, and obstacles and disappointments, he would never have found America. We have seen, then, that success means the overcoming of difficulties, by determination, by self-reliance, by patience, "little by little." This is equally true of the noblest of all pursuits, the pursuit of holiness, of the grandest and purest work, work for God ; of the hardest and most splendid of victories, victory over self. The victories which have been gained over ourselves will be remembered when the triumphs of Cæsar and Hannibal are uncared for. "He conquered himself" is a better epitaph than "He conquered the world." Well, then, in this daily life of ours we all have a Canaan to conquer ; and God promises that if we do our part, He will drive out our foes "little by little." No one becomes bad all at once, nor good all at once. Our life, if it be the true life, will be a gradual growth in grace, a daily dying to sin, and rising again unto righteousness, a daily mortifying of our evil and corrupt affections, and a daily proceeding in all virtue and godliness of living. (*H. J. Wilmot-Buxton, M.A.*) *Destructive power of "little" things :*—How does it commonly come to pass, that a man who had been thoroughly alive to his moral responsibility, and who had acted under a manifest consciousness of the account which must one day be rendered at the judgment seat of Christ, falls away from the striving for salvation, and mingles with the multitude that walks the broad road ? Is it ordinarily through one powerful and undisguised assault, that he is turned from the path—the enemies of his soul combining their strength in one united attack, and coming down on him with every weapon which their malice could suggest and their power obtain ? Nay, not so ; it is invariably through "little" things, that such a man destroys his soul. Like the heavenly bodies, the man of piety moves in a resisting medium, as he revolves about the Sun of righteousness, which is, and must be, the centre of our system. It may be only a very minute fraction of velocity, that this resisting medium is able at any one time to destroy ; but its operation is constant, and therefore if the destroyed fraction remain unobserved and unrepaired, the waste will go on, till the whole motion is lost, and the star recedes from its pathway of light. As Christians we profess ourselves strangers and pilgrims upon earth; we are not at home, and the atmosphere of the earth is one which tends to retard our movements, and diminish the speed with which we might otherwise run the race set before us; and although, beyond doubt, the world may occasionally put huge impediments in the way, which may tend to block up the path, and force us, on a sudden either to stand still or turn aside, yet our chief danger lies in the almost imperceptible influence exerted by the world, like that of the resisting medium on the planets—a hindrance which offers no violent opposition to our principles, but which, confining itself to trifles, is perhaps allowed to act undisturbed, as though either there could be trifles when the soul's good is in debate, or as though, if there were, trifles upon trifles would not make up large amounts. There is a sort of continued attraction, resulting from our necessary intercourse with the world, which of itself deadens the attainments of the soul. There is, moreover, a continued temptation to yield in little points under the impression of conciliating, to indulge in little things, to forego little strictnesses, to omit little duties, and all owing to the idea, that what looks so slight cannot be of real moment. (*H. Melvill, B.D.*)   *Gradual sancti-fication :*—We here have—I. A GRACIOUS PROMISE, ON GOD'S PART, TO THOSE WHO ARE NOW HIS TRUE ISRAEL, AND WHO LOOK FOR A BETTER POSSESSION THAN THE EARTHLY CANAAN. II. AN ADMIRABLE CRITERION BY WHICH TO DISCOVER THE SINCERITY OF OUR PROFESSION ; AND OUR PROGRESS IN IT. III. A WARNING THAT THE WORK OF SANCTIFI-CATION MUST BE GRADUAL. God does not give us a rapid victory over our sins. 1. In order to keep us humble ; 2. To incite us to prayer, watchfulness and exertion ; 3. To increase our desires after that land where peace and purity reign for ever. IV. A GUARANTEE OF FUTURE VICTORY, THOUGH IT MAY BE PROGRESSIVE. (*P. Maitland, B.A.*)   *The difficulty of little things :*—" By little and little." My brethren, think often of the mode in which God thus declares that He will drive out before Israel the Hivite, the Perizzite, and the Jebusite: it is the very mode by which His grace will enable you to drive out from your hearts those principles of evil which oppose the complete setting up of the kingdom of His Son. The difficulty in religion is the taking up the cross daily, rather than the taking it up on some set occasion, and under extraordinary circumstances. The serving God in little things, the carrying religious principle into all the minutiæ of life, the discipline of our tempers, the regulation of our speech, the domestic Christianity, the momentary sacrifices, the secret and unobserved self-denials—who that knows anything of the difficulties of piety does not know that there is greater danger of his falling in these, than in trials which apparently call for higher and sterner endurance ? If on no other account than from the very absence of what looks important, are trifles likely to throw him off his guard, make him careless or confident, and thereby almost ensure defeat. It is not comparatively hard to put the armour on, when the trumpet sounds, but it is to keep the armour on when there is no alarm of battle ; and our warfare with our spiritual enemies is not warfare in a series of pitched battles, with intervals for rest and recruiting—it is rather daily, hourly, momentary fighting. This is the " driving out by little and little," to which the Almighty promises " the reward of the inheritance." Understand, therefore, and remember, that there is great difficulty in little things. Be assured that daily dangers and duties, the little unevennesses which may ruffle the temper, the petty anxieties of common life, the exercise of righteous principle in trifles—in these must you seek, and in these will you find the opportunity of ejecting " by little and little " the foes which you have sworn to expel from the heart, but which still, like the Canaanites against Israel, dispute the territory with the Lord God of hosts. And if the warfare be tedious, forget not that you fight for an incorruptible crown. (*H. Melvill, B.D.*)   *Im-portance of little things :*—Giotto, a distinguished Roman painter, was desired by one of the Popes to paint a panel in the Vatican. Some doubt of his ability, however, being entertained, the Pope's messenger first asked him for an example of his art. Giotto's study was adorned with his paintings, but instead of offering any of these, he took a sheet of white paper, and with a single stroke of his pencil drew a perfect circle, and handed it to his visitor. The latter, in surprise, reminded him that he had asked for a design. " Go," said Giotto ; " I tell you, his Holiness asks nothing else of me." He was right, for the evidence of his command of the pencil was accepted as conclusive, and his eccentric though reasonable reply gave rise to the proverb, " Round as Giotto's O." To do a small thing well is the best proof of ability to do what is great. *Progressive sanctification :*—Those persons must have a very inadequate knowledge of the scheme of salvation, who suppose that the work of sanctification is sudden and rapid in its effects. And why? Because we find a consistency maintained between God's natural government of the world, and the plan of salvation as displayed in the gospel. And hence we are led to argue, that both must proceed from the same Divine hand. Now, when persons first resign this world as their portion, and give themselves up to the service of God, they frequently set out with highly raised expectations and, not fully conscious of the difficulties which lie in their path, suppose that the victory over sin will be easily accomplished, and a rapid progress made in the ways of godliness. It is with the inexperienced Christian, as it is with the young in the spring-tide of their existence. Then all is bright and glittering; and, exulting in the present, and buoyed up with joyous hopes for the future, they know not of the cloud gathering in the horizon. And this expectation is, in a measure, aided by the fact, that in the earlier stages of a Christian course, a much more rapid advance is frequently made than is found to be the case in after years. Moreover, the Christian, in the earlier stages of his course, is not fully aware of the extent of obedience which the law of God demands, and is not sufficiently conscious of the deep depravity of his own heart. Hence the terms of the gospel, which demand an irreconcileable war with every lust and passion, and call for a continued and persevering struggle with every known sin, cannot be fully appreciated, because these are not discovered. But it is the office of the Holy Spirit, gradually to make this discovery to the mind of the Christian. But has God ever undertaken that Satan and the world and the flesh shall at once be beaten down beneath your feet? No! What says my text? "By little and little." But, whilst it is only right, Christians, that I should thus set before you the difficulties which beset your path, at the same time that you take warning from the text not to expect a more rapid victory over sin than God has prescribed, take also to yourselves the encouragement which it affords. Here is the promise of Him who cannot lie, that He will eventually make us more than conquerors, though it will be by little and little, and not so rapidly as we could desire. "Being confident of this very thing, that He which hath begun a good work in you, will perform it unto the day of Jesus Christ." It will be gradual, but effectual—it will be progressive, but abiding; if left to yourselves, indeed, your strength must fail; and vain would be the attempt to contend successfully with your sins and infirmities. "The Lord is my strength and my song, and is become my salvation," says the Psalmist; and what he here speaks of—God's loving-kindness—is only that which is the portion of every true believer. "He giveth power to the faint," says the prophet, "and to them that have no might He increaseth strength." How cheering are such assurances to those who feel the burden of their sin, and how calculated to set at rest all doubts and misgivings with respect to our future perseverance! But, for this, let it ever be remembered that continued and fervent supplication must be made. "For all these things" are the words of God, "will I be inquired of by the house of Israel, to do it for them." And never let us complain that our enemies are mighty, and that we make so slow a progress against them, whilst we neglect to plead in prayer with the Almighty for the fulfilment of His own promises. And here let me turn to the well-tried Christian—to such as are firmly established and grounded in the faith; and I would ask, whether you cannot bear testimony to the faithfulness with which the promise of the text is verified? You, as well as others, need the encouragement which it affords, because, the more you grow in holiness, the more you will perceive how infinitely short you come of the standard at which you aim. But have you not reason from the past, to trust God for the future? With St. Paul, thank God, and take courage; and, whenever it shall happen (as it sometimes will with the holiest and best of men) that you entertain doubts and misgivings with respect to your ultimate safety, owing to your unworthiness, recall to your minds the promise of my text, and others of a similar character. Let these reassure and animate you: God is still the same unfailing Protector of those who trust in Him as He ever was, and will never forsake the true sheep of His pasture, but gradually drive out their enemies from before them, until they are established in their promised possession. (*P. Maitland, B.A.*)

Vers. 31–33. **They shall not dwell in thy land.**—*Lessons :*—1. God is the sovereign boundmaker to all nations on the earth. 2. Among all God hath promised to set the bounds of His Church on earth. 3. God's suppression of His adversaries is a token of His settling His Church's habitation (ver. 31). 4. No covenant with idolatrous adversaries must be made by the Church against God's will. 5. No covenant can be made with idolaters, but it will be with their idols, viz., devils (ver.

32). 6. Converse with idolaters is very dangerous to make men such sinners against God. 7. Such sinning with idolaters is a snare, which will keep souls to destruction. 8. All such sins must be avoided, that God's promise of good may be obtained (ver. 33). (*G. Hughes, B.D.*) *Associating with the ungodly :*—Those who willingly associate with the sinful are like the river Thames, which is a sweet and pretty river enough near its source; but in the great metropolis it has kept company with drains and sewers under the belief that its current was too powerful and too pure to be injured by them. It was meant that the river should purify the sewer; but, instead of that, the sewer has corrupted the river. (*Union Magazine.*) *The snare of worldliness :*—Serious people often complain of the snares they meet with from worldly people, and yet they must mix with them to get a livelihood. I advise them, if they can, to do their business with the world as they do it in the rain. If their business calls them abroad, they will not leave it undone for fear of being a little wet; but then, when it is done, they presently seek shelter, and will not stand in the rain for pleasure. So, providential and necessary calls of duty, that lead us into the world, will not hurt us, if we find the spirit of the world unpleasant, and are glad to retire from it, and keep out of it, as much as our relative duties will permit. That which is our cross is not so likely to be our snare; but if that spirit which we should always watch and pray against, infects and assimilates our minds to itself, then we are sure to suffer loss, and act below the dignity of our profession. (*Newton's Letters to a Nobleman.*)

CHAPTER XXIV.

VERS. 1–8. **Behold the blood of the covenant.**—*The sprinkling of blood :*—I. He sprinkled THE BOOK in his hand. It was the Bible of his day, and yet it needed sprinkling. And we hold our Bibles—do they need sprinkling? The Bible is the transmitted mind of God—it is perfect truth, it is essential holiness—must it be sprinkled? Human words are all unclean. The mind of God must pass to men through the organs of the human voice—and that humanity mingling even with the revelation of God, wants washing. The materials of which the book is made are human. And again and again with our defiled hands we have soiled it—and we never open the book but it is a sinner's hand that touches it. Our Bibles need the sprinkling of the blood of Jesus. II. And he sprinkled THE ALTAR—for he had reared it. The altar was a holy thing—dedicate, consecrated, yet for the manhood which was associated with it, it needed the sprinkling of the blood. And we have our altars. You rise in the morning, and you set up your altar on your bedside—and when you rise from your knees, how many wandering thoughts, what coldness and dulness of soul, what mixture of motive, calls out for mercy. The altar of the bedroom—it must be sprinkled. You come down, and you gather round the family altar. But is there no one there, in that little assembly, whose heart is wrong with God? Does the worship of the family all go up in purity? Is it not a dull thing —that family prayer each morning—a mere routine? And does not it want the sprinkling of the blood of Jesus? III. Moses sprinkled THE PEOPLE. There is no part of man that does not need that sprinkling. IV. The sprinkling of the blood was the token THAT WHATEVER IT TOUCHED BECAME COVENANT. We have our covenanted Bibles and our covenanted altars; we ourselves are in covenant with Christ. Do you know that the blood of the Lord Jesus Christ is on you? And all that you must recognize if you would obey God. You must not rely upon "All the words that the Lord hath spoken we will do." But you must go as a sprinkled and covenanted people, or you will not go at all. (*J. Vaughan, M.A.*) *The blood of the covenant :*—I. THE SACREDNESS OF BLOOD. This is taught both in Old and New Testament. II. THE CHRISTIAN covenant IS A COVENANT OF BLOOD. The blood of the eternal Son of God, shed on Calvary, sprinkled on the high altar of heaven and on all who approach with penitence and faith. III. THE COVENANT WHICH CHRIST HAS INSTITUTED WITH HIS PEOPLE IS THE MOST SACRED COVENANT WHICH GOD EVER MADE WITH MAN. IV. THE LORD'S SUPPER is a memorial and a solemn public ratification of this Divine blood covenant. It sprinkles us afresh with the blood of the great atonement. (*J. M. Sherwood, D.D.*) *The covenant :*—I. DIVINELY REVEALED. 1. Revealed faithfully. (1) "Words." for direction and encouragement. (2) Judgment, for warning. 2. Revealed intelligently. (1) Not an appeal to superstition and credulity. (2) In language which all could understand. (3) Under circumstances attesting Divine origin. (4) An appeal to reason, piety, interest. II. ACCEPTED BY MAN. 1. Unanimously. 2. Heartily. 3. Specifically. 4. Speedily. III. PERMANENTLY EMBODIED. A written revelation is—1. Necessary. 2. Advantageous. 3. Important. IV. ARRANGEMENTS CAREFULLY AND IMPRESSIVELY PREPARED. 1. Altar and pillars—representing God and people. 2. Young men—symbolizing strength and earnestness that should be exerted in keeping covenant engagement. 3. Sacrifices. (1) Burnt-offerings, to signify dedication of people to Jehovah. (2) Peace-offerings, as typifying Jehovah's reconciliation with people. V. RATIFIED WITH BLOOD. In conclusion—1. Christ is the Mediator of a better covenant. 2. That His blood is sprinkled on the altar of God (Heb. ix. 12), and in the heart of His people (Heb. ix. 13–15). 3. That He has instituted a " perpetual memorial of His precious death until His coming again " (1 Cor. ix. 25). (*J. W. Burn.*)   *God's covenant with Israel :*—I. THE PREPARATION AND SEPARATION. God and Israel were to bind themselves in sacred oath. God was ready. Was man ready? Reverence and humility were required, a deep sense of the full meaning of all that was to be said and done. Special preparation is always demanded for special exhibitions of the Divine glory and power, and for special seasons of covenanting with God. Man is never ready for pledges of love and loyalty until he has sanctified himself through penitence and prayer. II. THE PEOPLE INFORMED. Let the leaders of God's host plainly point out the path. The need of our age is not speculation but declaration of things revealed by those who have been on the mount with God, have beheld His glory, and have received a message for dying men. The people would know what God has said, not what men imagine or guess. How about our Father in heaven? What are His purposes of grace? What are the conditions of blessing? These are the burning questions of our age and of all ages. If any one has been on the mount and heard the voice, let him come down and tell us what he knows. The world is waiting. III. RATIFICATION OF THE COVENANT. Deliberation is always demanded before pledges of acceptance and obedience are made. No act of human life is more solemn than that of covenanting with God. Before men begin to build, they should count the cost. Many who run well for awhile afterwards halt and turn back because they started under the impulse of a sudden and ill-considered emotion. Christianity is righteous principle put in practice. IV. SEALING THE COVENANT. Remember the hour, the spot, all the circumstances attending your public avowal of faith in Jesus Christ, and your covenanting with God and with His people. How have these vows been kept? How have the conditions of blessing been fulfilled? God has never failed you. Have you failed Him? Oh, these covenants! How many have been broken! These vows! How many have been slighted! We should frequently go back to the altar " under the hill," and recall the sealing blood. V. NEW VISIONS OF GOD. This doubtless was a far more distinct vision than the former, when the law was given amid clouds and darkness and tempest. That was a display of majesty; this is of love. The language of the former was: Obey and thou shalt live. The language of the latter is: Love and confide. A little while before the vision was of a Law-giver. Now it is of a Saviour, inspiring confidence and peace. The mercy-seat appears. God's glory is seen in the face of Jesus Christ, typified by the sapphire stone and, as I suppose, by the dimly outlined form of the world's Redeemer. (*J. E. Twitchell.*)   *The strictness of God's law :*—" The Bible is so strict and old-fashioned," said a young man to a grey-haired friend who was advising him to study God's Word if he would learn how to live. " There are plenty of books written now-a-days that are moral enough in their teaching, and do not bind one down as the Bible." The old merchant turned to his desk, and took out two rulers, one of which was slightly bent. With each of these he ruled a line, and silently handed the ruled paper to his companion. " Well," said the lad, " what do you mean?" " One line is not straight and true, is it? When you mark out your path in life, do not take a crooked ruler!" (*S. S. Chronicle.*) *Belief and disobedience :*—Suppose, says the late Archbishop Whately, two men each received a letter from his father, giving directions for his children's conduct; and that one of these sons hastily, and without any good grounds, pronounced the letter a forgery, and refused to take any notice of it; while the other acknowledged it to be genuine, and laid it up with great reverence, and then acted without the least regard to the advice and commands contained in the letter : you would say that both of these men, indeed, were very wrong; but the latter was much the more undutiful son of the two. Now this is the case of a disobedient Christian, as compared with infidels. He does not like them pronounce his Father's letter a forgery; that is, deny the truth of the Christian revelation; but he acts in defiance in his life to that which he acknowledges to be the Divine command. *The sealing of the covenant :*—I. WHAT OCCURRED ? The Law had been given, amplified (chaps. xxi.-xxiii.), and endorsed by the people (xxiv. 3). Necessary now to uncover that atonement which is ever the ground of God's dealings with man. Hence the altar. No soul was to touch it, for the atonement is the creation of God. Still man had a part in these covenantal transactions, hence twelve pillars = twelve tribes. But sacrifice on the altar—the burnt offering = life surrendered—and the peace offering = communion with God and one another. The sacrifices were slain by young men = the flower of Israel. The Levitical priesthood not yet. Every age has its own special service for God. The blood was preserved. Now the blood stands for life. Half disappeared in fire on the altar. Gone! = forfeited life of the sinner. Half thrown back upon the people = life restored to man. How Israel ascended to a higher plane of life (ver. 9). In the only possible way—representatively. Then came the vision of God (ver. 10). Then the banquet (see Song of Sol. ii. 3, 4). II. WHAT DID IT MEAN ? 1. Salvation has its ground in God and God alone. Calvary potentially before the Christian era, actually since, the Divine ground of salvation. 2. Forfeited life is given back to man on the ground of Christ's atonement. Life, capacity, faculty, are all given back now to be man's very own. 3. Now again to be given back to God in consecration. Being now my very own (in the sense just hinted), I give my own to God. This self-surrender is vital. The surrender is to be complete in intent and purpose. And the obligation presses now. Delay is disloyalty. 4. There will then be peace. With God ; with ourselves ; with men. 5. Life will move on a higher level (vers. 9, 12, 13). (Emphasize the meaning in the words "And BE there": "And Moses went up into the Mount of God.") Valley men have no idea of the bracing atmosphere, the brilliant light, the wider view, the grander visions, to be found on the mountain-plateau. It is so in Switzerland ; so with the mountains celestial. 6. There shall be visions of God (ver. 10). Bushnell says : "So gloriously has my experience of God opened His greatness to me, I seem to have got beyond all physical images and measures, even those of astronomy, and simply to think God is to find and bring into my feeling more than even the imagination can reach. I bless God that it is so. I am cheered by it, encouraged, sent onward, and, in what He gives me, begin to have some very faint impression of the glory yet to be revealed." 7. And banquetings and satisfactions of soul (ver. 11). As the body has its nutriment, so the soul. No more "husks." High thought befitting immortal man. Manna: "Hidden manna." Here on earth. At the marriage supper of the Lamb. Thereafter to all eternity. (*H. T. Robjohns, B.A.*)

Vers. 9–11. **They saw God, and did eat and drink.**—*The vision of God, and the feast before Him :*—These are strangely bold words, both for the assertion with which they begin, and for the juxtaposition of the two things which they declare. They come at the close of the solemn ceremonial by which God and Israel entered into covenant. Lightly-uttered vows of obedience to all that God could speak had echoed among the rocks. On the basis of that promise a covenant was formed and ratified by sacrifice. They pass within the fence, they witness that access to God is possible on the footing of covenant and sacrifice. They behold, as I suppose, unclouded, the material and fiery symbol of His presence: witness that men through sacrifice and covenant can see God. But our eyes are stayed on the pavement beneath His feet. No form is described. Enough for us that there is spread beneath Him that which is blue and gleaming as the cloudless heaven above Sinai. "They eat and drink"—witness that men who draw nigh to God, on the footing of sacrifice and covenant, and thereby behold His face, have therein festal abundance for all their need. So this incident, in its form adapted to the infantile development of the people that first received it, carries in its symbols the deepest truths of the best communion of the Christian life, and may lend itself to the foreshadowing of the unspoken glories of the heavens. From that point of view I want to look at it. I. I ask you to consider THE VISION OF GOD POSSIBLE FOR US. Jesus Christ is the Revealer. This generation is very fond of saying, "No man hath seen God at any time, nor can see Him." It is a pity, but they would go on with the quotation and say, "the only-begotten Son, which is in the bosom of the Father, He hath declared Him." The eradiation of His brightness, "and the express image of His person," is that Divine man, God manifest in the flesh. The knowledge of God which we have in Jesus Christ is real, as sight is real. It is not complete, but it is genuine knowledge. We know the best of God, if I may use such a phrase, when we know what we know in Christ, that He is a loving and a righteous will; when we can say of Him "He is love," in no metaphor but in simple reality, and His will is a will towards all righteousness, and towards all blessing, anything that heaven has to teach us about God afterwards is less than that. We see Him in the reality of a genuine, central, though by no means complete, knowledge. Our knowledge of God in Christ is as sight, in reference to certitude. People say, "Seeing is believing." I should turn it the other way about, and say, "Believing is seeing." For we may be a great deal surer of God than ever we can be of this outer world. And the witness which is borne to us in Christ of the Divine nature is far more reliable than even the evidence that is borne to us by sense of an external universe. Then remember, too, that where we have learned to know, and absolutely to rely upon, and vividly to realize our Father's presence through Jesus Christ, there we shall see Him in all things and everywhere. Then, remember, further, that the degree of this vision depends upon ourselves, and is a matter of cultivation. "Blessed are the pure in heart, for they shall see God." There are three things wanted for sight—something to see; something to see by; something to see with. God has given us the two first, and He will help us to the last if we like. But we have to bring the eye, without which the sunbeam is vain, and that which it reveals also. Christ stands before us, at once the Master-Light of our seeing, and the Object that we are to behold. But for us there is needed that the eye shall be pure; that the heart shall turn towards Him. Faith is the eye of the soul. Meditation and habitual occupation of mind and heart with Jesus Christ, the Revealer of God, are needed if we are to "see God." II. Secondly, notice THE FEAST IN THE DIVINE PRESENCE. "They did eat and drink." That suggests in the singular juxtaposition of the two things, that the vision of God is consistent with, and consecrates, common enjoyment and everyday life. Even before that awful blaze these men sat down and fed, "eating their meal with gladness and singleness of heart," and finding no contradiction nor any profanity in the close juxtaposition of the meal and the vision. There is no false asceticism as the result of the Christian sight of God. It takes nothing out of life that ought to be in it. If we see God there is only one thing that we shall be ashamed to do in His presence, and that is to sin. For all the rest the vision of God blends sweetly and lovingly with common service and homely joys. It will interpret life. Nothing is small with such a background; nothing common-place when looked at in connection with Him. It will ennoble life; it will gladden life. But there is another thought here to which I must refer for a moment. That strange meal on the mountain was no doubt made on the sacrifices that had preceded, of which a part were peace-offerings. The ritual of that species of sacrifice partly consisted in a portion of the sacrifice being partaken of by the offerers. The same meaning lies in this meal on the mountain that lay in the sacrificial feast of the peace-offering, the same meaning that lies in the great feast of the new covenant, "This is My body; this is My blood." God spreads in His presence a table, and the food on that table is the "Bread which came down from heaven that it might give life to the world." The vision of God and the feast on the mountain are equally provided and made possible by Christ our Passover, who was sacrificed for us. III. And so, lastly, we may gather out of this incident A GLIMPSE OF A PROPHETIC CHARACTER, AND SEE IN IT THE PERFECTING OF THE VISION AND OF THE FEAST. We know the apostle's wonderful statement of the difference between the beatific knowledge of heaven and the indirect and partial knowledge of earth. Here we "see in a glass darkly; there face to face." It is not for us to try before the time to interpret the latter of these statements; only this, let us remember that whatever may be the change in manner of knowledge, and in measure of apprehension, and in proximity of presence, there is no change in heaven in the medium of revelation. For heaven as for earth God is the King invisible; for heaven as for earth no man can see Him, the only begotten Son declares Him. Christ is for ever the Manifester of God, and the glorified saints see God as we see Him in the face of Jesus Christ, though they see that Face as we do not. Yonder there are new capacities indeed. When there are more windows in the house there will be more sunshine in the rooms. When there is a new speculum in the telescope galaxies will be resolved that are now nebulous, and new brightnesses will be visible that are now veiled. But with all the new powers and the extension of present vision, there will be no corrections in the present vision. We shall see Him as He is, and learn that what we knew of Him in Christ here is true for ever. And on that perfect vision will follow the perfect meal, which will still be the feeding on the sacrifice. For there were no heaven except " He had offered one sacrifice for sins for ever," and there is no spiritual life above except a life derived from Him. The feast means perfect satisfaction, perfect repose, perfect gladness, perfect companionship. (*A. Maclaren, D.D.*)　　*The God of Sinai approached through sacrifice :*— Two distinct aspects of the Divine character had already been made known to the Israelites—His goodness and His severity, His tenderness and His righteousness. Now a third lesson is given them. The awful God of Sinai may be approached and communed with ; they need not be terrified away for ever from Him, or be afraid to approach Him. I. THE AWFUL GOD OF SINAI MAY BE APPROACHED BY SINFUL MEN THROUGH SACRIFICE. " Upon the nobles of Israel He laid not His hand." II. THE AWFUL GOD OF SINAI IS SEEN BY SINFUL MEN THROUGH SACRIFICE. " Also they saw God." III. THE AWFUL GOD OF SINAI IS COMMUNED WITH BY SINFUL MEN THROUGH SACRIFICE. " Also they did eat and drink." There is safety for the transgressor only under the shadow of the sacrifice—the atonement of Jesus Christ. Socrates once cried, " Plato, Plato, perhaps God can forgive wilful sin." You see the gospel of Socrates—" Perhaps." " But," he added, " I do not see how." In the gospel of Jesus Christ there is no " perhaps." " It is a faithful saying, and worthy of all acceptation, that Christ Jesus came into the world to save sinners." There is no " perhaps " about that. Socrates said, " I do not see how." We do see how. " Through this Man is preached forgiveness of sins." (*R. Roberts.*) *A glorious vision :*—I. GLORIOUS ASCENSION. Mountain climbing is always wholesome. The more we climb, the less will be our difficulty, on the summit of Divine mountains are gracious manifestations to reward the praying climbers. II. BLESSED VISION. " And they saw the God of Israel ; and there was under " &c. Calm repose. We may rest sweetly on the Divine fidelity. III. GLORIOUS PRESERVATION. God's hand will ever be laid on the spiritual nobility. They are under His protecting, preserving care. IV. WONDROUS FESTIVITY. The saints shall eat and drink in the Divine presence. Heavenly manna. New wine. (*W. Burrows, B.A.*) *Man's approach to God :*—I. That man's approach to God IS COMMANDED (ver. 1). This is both reasonable and necessary. Servant to master ; scholar to teacher ; child to parent ; sinner to Saviour. II. That man's approach to God MUST BE THROUGH A MEDIATOR ; " worship thou afar off, and Moses alone shall come near unto the Lord." So Jesus has entered into the holy place for us. He is the " one mediator," &c., " the new and living way " (John xiv. 6). We must remember that this was in answer to their own prayer (xx. 19). III. That man's approach to God must be REVERENT. " Worship ye afar off." IV. That man's approach to God is REWARDED BY A MANIFESTATION OF THE DIVINE GLORY (ver. 10). Not a literal or physical vision of " the king "—invisible (Deut. iv. 2 ; 1 Tim. vi. 16) ; but spiritual (Isa. vi. ; Acts ix. 3, 4, and refs. ; 1 Cor. xii. 2). V. That man's approach to God is NOT TO BE DREADED, BUT WELCOMED AND ENJOYED. " They find His presence no more a source of disturbance and dread, but radiant in all the bright loveliness of supernal glory : a beautiful sign that the higher religion and state of conformity to law, now established, shall work onward to eternal blessedness." (*J. W. Burn.*) *A glorious sight and a holy feast :*—I. THE SIGHT OF GOD, TO WHICH THE NOBLES OF ISRAEL WERE ADMITTED. II. THE SAFETY AND COMFORT WHICH THEY ENJOYED. III. THE FEAST WITH WHICH THEY WERE PROVIDED. They ate of the peace-offerings which had been recently sacrificed, and drank of the libations which had just been offered, on the ratification of the covenant. Even thus are the disciples of Christ invited to partake of Him by faith, and that in joy and gladness, as the great peace-offering of the Church. Thus are they seated at the table of their adorable Lord, in token of gracious communion with the family in heaven ; and thus is their fellowship manifested with the Father and with His Son Jesus Christ. In this fellowship His children truly see God in Christ. They behold, and they partake, the glory of His person, the glory of His covenant, the hidden glory of His Word, the glory of His redeeming and everlasting love. (*R. P. Buddicom, M.A.*)　　*The vision of God :*— We have here the conjunction of that which is the highest attainment of faith, namely, the vision of God, with that which is the commonest act of our lives, namely, eating and drinking. Again, eating and drinking is only one form, and that one of the lowest forms of human enjoyment. Therefore, if the vision of God be compatible with that, it may be, it must be, equally so with every proper mode of employment or enjoyment among men. I. In the first place, then, let it be noted, THAT THERE ARE SOME WHO EAT AND DRINK WITHOUT SEEING GOD. This is true in the very lowest sense in which the words can be employed ; for, unhappily, there are multitudes who partake of their ordinary food without any perception of the fact that they are indebted for it to a higher power. In the same way there are many successful men of business, who enjoy the blessings of prosperity without seeing that God has had any hand in the bestowment of them. They are, as the phrase is, " self-made." They have been the architects of their own fortunes. Similarly, there are those who have risen to places of power and influence, alike in the world and in the Church, who never think of God in their enjoyment of their eminence. It has come to them, so they say, all in the way of cause and effect. They have been able, diligent, and persevering, and, therefore, their prosperity or popularity is nothing more than the natural result of their use of appropriate means. And to mention only one other form of the same disposition : there are men among us whose delight it has been to unravel the secrets of the external world, and discover the operations of those forces which play so important a part in the physical universe. Their meat and their drink is to sit at the spectroscope, and by their wondrous analysis to bring out the composition of the sun, and of the various members of the planetary sphere. Their joy is to chain the lightning to their messages, and make it carry their words to the world's ends. They rise into ecstasies over the detection of some new fact which witnesses to the uniformity of law ; and they become enthusiastic at the prospect of being able to trace the mystery of the universe a step farther back than their predecessors have gone. But all this while they see nothing of God. No thrill of affection vibrates in their hearts to any personal agent ; and their emotions are similar to those which one feels as he looks upon a mighty machine moving on in rhythmic regularity at its unceasing work. I do not need to say that all our men of science are not such as I have now described, but every one acquainted with the recent utterances of some of them will admit that these confirm what I have said. Now I have grouped all these together because they are all alike practical atheists. They eat and drink, but they do not see God.

II. In the second place, let it be remarked THAT THERE ARE SOME WHO SEE GOD, BUT CANNOT EAT OR DRINK. They have a vivid sense of the personal existence of Jehovah, and they feel Him always near, but they take no comfort in His presence. Rather, it seems to haunt them as a spectre, and to threaten them as an executioner. Now how shall we account for this? The answer is not far to seek. It is caused by a sense of guilt. They have never entered, through Jesus, into covenant with God. But even among those who have done this, there are some who seem to have had their happiness poisoned by the thought of God. They see Him, they are always seeing Him : but the vision seems to have paralyzed them, and they go through life halting, solemn, and severe. If they would " see God, and eat and drink," they must rise out of service into sonship, and learn to think and speak of God as their Father in heaven. This will give sincerity and naturalness to their devotions, activity to their lives, happiness to their hearts, and cheerfulness to their deportment, so that men, as they behold them, will be won by the very radiance of their joy to Him from whom their gladness springs. But there are still others who, at certain times of their history, have had a vivid perception of the nearness of God, while yet they could neither eat nor drink. Affliction has come upon them. They have felt God very near them, but then they have felt as if He were having a controversy with them, as if, somehow, He were alienated from them, and that has made their sorrow all the deeper. But all this has sprung from a misinterpretation of His providence, and that again has its root in lack of faith in His fatherhood. III. Finally, let it be observed, THAT THERE ARE SOME WHO, LIKE THOSE HERE DESCRIBED, " SEE GOD AND DO EAT AND DRINK." They are reconciled to God through Jesus Christ, His Son ; they have learned to call Him Father, and the joy of their lives is that they have a constant sense of His presence. When they say, " Thou God seest me," it is not with a feeling of uneasiness, like that of a suspected person who feels himself watched by some detective ; but rather with an emotion of satisfaction, because they know that One is beside them who can make provision for every emerging necessity, and find for them also, as for Hagar, a fountain in the desert. When they think of Him, it is not so much as the Great Creator, Ruler, and Judge, as the Father ; and because they can say " Our Father," they have a sense of ownership in all His attributes and possessions. They have accepted His own assurance, " I am the Lord thy God," and His omnipresence is the very joy and rejoicing of their hearts. It is not a melancholy thing, which poisons every other experience. It is not, like the sword of Damocles, a threatening thing, that keeps us from sitting down to the feast. Rather it is itself that which gives the feast its real glory, and the festival to us is twice a feast because He is there. He makes the brightest element in our blessings; He gives to us the real joy of our prosperity. And when affliction comes He mitigates it with His sympathy and cheers us under it with His fellowship. He comes to us not as a spectre in the night, but as a father, to lap us in the mantle of His love. "Bane and blessing, pain and pleasure," alike are sanctified by His presence, and no darkness for us could be so dense as that which would envelop us if we were to be deprived of Him. (*W. M. Taylor, D.D.*) *The distinguishing privilege of God's faithful servants :—* That a sight of God in Christ, and a holy familiarity with Him, with all safety, is the privilege of God's covenant-people, especially in these solemn approaches to which He calls them. I. To show what is that sight of God in Christ, which is the privilege of His people in their solemn approaches to Him.—There is a two-fold solemn approach of God's people to Him. There is a right approach. 1. When God calls them up to the mount of myrrh, where our Lord abides till the day break (Song of Sol. iv. 6); when He calls them to come up to the hill of God in Emmanuel's land, where stands the King's palace, namely heaven. This call comes to the believing soul at death. 2. When God calls them to come up to the mount of ordinances to meet Him at the sacred feast, as the nobles of Israel in the text, and as we at this time are called to feast on the great sacrifice in the sacrament. This is a solemn approach. Now, what is the sight of God in Christ which is the privilege here? As to this we observe—(1) That it is a believing sight of God in their nature (John i. 14.). (2) That it is a sight of this God in the place of His special residence; on the mount to which they were invited, where He stood, as it were, on a pavement of sapphire. (3) It is a sight of the glory of the place of His feet (ver. 10). (4) It is a sight of God as reconciled in Christ. They saw God, and did eat and drink as in the house of their friend (2 Cor. v. 18-20). (5) It is a sight of God as their God. They saw the God of Israel. Here lay the surpassing sweetness of their sight. (6) It is a sight of transcendent glory in Him. Nothing is described but what was under His feet. For, search the universe, there is no person, no thing like Him. But the best things on earth are not sufficient to set forth the glory even of this, and therefore it is added, "as if it were the body of heaven in His clearness." They who see Him, see that of which they can never see the like. We are now—II. To show what is that holy familiarity which is the privilege of God's people in their solemn approaches to Him.—It is a believing, holy, humble freedom before their Lord (Eph. iii. 12)! "In whom we have boldness and access, with confidence, by the faith of Him." 1. They were allowed to come forward to God, when others must stand back (Isa. lvi. 6, 7); when others must abide at the foot of the hill, believers may come up to the mount and are welcome. 2. They were allowed to feast on the sacrifice set before them. Christ the sacrifice typically slain, and believers are allowed to feast on this sacrifice, to eat His flesh and drink His blood; to make a believing application of a whole Christ to their own souls for their spiritual nourishment : "Take, eat, this is My body broken for you." 3. They were allowed to converse with God freely, as one at the table of his friends. 4. They were allowed to be in His secrets, to see what others have no access ‡to. They saw God. Believers are allowed to see the glory of His person (John i. 14). The glory of His covenant (Psalm xxv. 14). The glory of His redeeming, His everlasting love to them (Jer. xxxi. 3). The hidden glory of His word (Luke xxiv. 32). 5. They were allowed to lay all their wants on Him. III. To make some practical improvement. 1. To show that it is a wonder of grace that sinful creatures are admitted to see God, and be familiar with Him. We think we need say little for proof of this. Only consider—(1) The infinite distance that there is between God and the creature in respect of perfection. (2) That it is the same God who is such a severe and dreadful avenger of sin (Psalm v. 5). 2. To show that it is a wonder of grace that sinful creatures, in their solemn approaches to God, and when they are thus favoured, come off safe. This will appear if we consider—(1) The infinite holiness and spotless purity of that God before whom the sinful creature appears. He is glorious in holiness, and fearful in praises (chap. xv. 11). (2) That the best carry a sinful nature even up into the mount with them. (3) That sinful creatures never miss to leave the marks of their foul feet, even when they are on holy ground (Rom. vii. 2). (4) The particular jealousy which God has manifested about His worship. 3. To explain how it comes to pass that the safety of God's people, when thus favoured, is secured. It is so—(1) Because they are God's covenant-people by marriage with His Son. (2) Because they come up under the covert of the Redeemer's blood (Heb. xii. 22–24). (3) Because God looks on them as in His own Son, and not as in themselves; and so after a sort He overlooks their infirmities (Numb. xxiii. 21). (4) Because, though they be unclean creatures, they come up into the mount, to bathe in the fountain opened there, for sin and for uncleanness (Zech. xiii. 1). (5) Because it is the end of the covenant, to bring them to God. 1. Let us, then, nevermore think lightly of solemn approaches to God, whether in private or in public ordinances. 2. Let this commend Christ and the covenant to us, especially to those who stand off from Him and His covenant. 3. Let us long for that day which will put an end to our sinfulness, weakness, and imperfection, when we shall see Him as He is, without any danger of sinning or suffering, which is far better (Phil. i. 23). It would be a token for good that we had seen the Lord, if we were now longing for that blessed day. (*T. Boston, D.D.*) *Seeing God:*—The soul has eyes. There are hours not related to the clock; there are birthdays for which the calendar provides no line of registry. How natural is this endeavour to make the conception plain by a visible picture, and how visible pictures are lifted up to new meanings and clothed with new solemnities by such sacred uses. There have been times, even in our cold experience, when nature has had to be called in to help the expression of the soul's delight. Every heart has its own image, or parable, or symbol, by which it sets forth to itself the best aspect of its supreme delight. When we want to represent God, and our view of Him, how naturally we turn to the heavens. No earthly object will suffice. There burns in us a sacred contempt for all things measurable. We want all the broad brilliance of noonday, all the tender glory of the midnight, all the pomp of the summer sky. There is verily a natural religion; it is a poor deity that can be set forth in clay, and iron, and carved stone. Find any race that has lifted up its religious conceptions so as to require for their imaging all heaven, and surely you have found a race that may at any moment alight upon the true God. What Ezekiel saw was as the appearance of the likeness of a throne. John said that the face he saw was like a jasper and a sardine stone, and the rainbow which gave tenderness to the throne was in sight like unto an emerald. When Jesus was transfigured, His face did shine as the sun, and His raiment was white as the light. Do not take these as equivalents, but as hints—some idea of the majesty which must have beamed upon the eyes of worship as they gazed with religious awe upon sights for which there is no language. It does us good to be wrought into passions which transcend all adequate speech— yes, it does the soul good to pray itself into silence. We may have clear vision of God to such an extent as to have every word taken away from our use and be left dumb in the eloquence of silence. (*J. Parker, D.D.*)

Vers. 12–18. **Come up to Me into the mount.**—*Divine preparations:*—I. Each one has his own position to occupy. II. Each man has his own Divine vision. To-day we may experience Divine chidings, and to-morrow we may be on the Mount of Beatitude. III. But there are specialities of work. IV. Therefore there must be speciality in the preparations. Learn to be much in the right, much in prayer, much in mountain solitude; but much also with the people. Let waiting and working go hand in hand. Above all things, obey the Divine voice. (*W. Burrows, B.A.*) *Communion with God:*—I. That communion with God is necessary. 1. For religious teachers. 2. For those engaged in business. 3. For parents, &c. II. That special places are appointed for communion with God. 1. House of God. 2. Privacy of own chamber. III. That preparation should be made for communion with God (ver. 14; see Matt. vi. 6). 1. Guard against interruptions from without. 2. Drive away worldly and anxious thoughts within. IV. That communion with God should be most frequently alone. 1. Presence of others may distract mind or embarrass thoughts. 2. Presence of others may divert attention from personal concerns of soul. 3. Private sins and wants to be laid bare. V. That in communion with God, the presence of others is sometimes helpful and even necessary. Family worship—prayer meetings—for those who have common wants, interests, &c. VI. That communion with God is the condition upon which man may witness the Divine glory (vers. 16, 17; see Isa. vi.) VII. That communion with God may be protracted, and man must not weary of it. VIII. That among the purposes of communion with God, are recognition of the Divine authority and preparation for future work. (*J. W. Burn.*) *The best recommendation:*—A young man once came to London bearing a letter of introduction to Baron Rothschild with the request that he would give him employment. The great banker received him warmly, but expressed his regret that he had no position for him. As the young man was going, the baron put on his hat and walked along with him, pointing out the various objects of interest. Passing a bank the rich man went in to transact some business. Afterwards the young man applied at that very bank for work, and they asked, " Are you not the young man who was walking with the baron this morning ? " " Yes." " Well, you were in good company : and since we need a young man we will consider this a sufficient recommendation." To walk with God is the best recommendation. When men of the world have need of an assistant or helper, they will be likely to consider such a fact as a commendation. (*A. J. Gordon.*)   *On the mount with God :*—Moses would never have been the lawgiver he was had he not remained there on the mount, in sight of the glory and in communion with his God. The disciples would never have wrought as they did, had they not tarried in Jerusalem. Eminent preachers and teachers would never have thrilled and won hearts to Christ as they have, had they not gained their power in long seasons of prayer and communion with God. 1. Spiritual endowment is always the measure of success in work for Christ. Preachers fail and teachers fail because they are so little on the mount with God. 2. The want of Christian workers everywhere is revelation of the Divine glory. From this, power springs. God can use us only as we become equipped by vision of, and communion with, Him. We can tell only as we know. We know only as we are taught of God. Have we been on the mount, under the cloud ? Have we seen the glory and heard the voice ? What is our message from God to men? (*J. E. Twitchell.*)

CHAPTER XXV

Vers. 1–9. **Make Me a sanctuary.**—*God dwelling with men :*—I. The dwelling of God among us in Christ Jesus, when it is a reality, and not merely an idea or a phrase, imports and of necessity secures the passing away from us of the things we have most reason to fear. When God comes to dwell among us, which can only be by dwelling in us individually, sin goes from us, in its guilt and its predominating power. II. God comes thus to dwell with men, for the development of character, and for the nourishment of all goodness. The putting away of sin is but the negative part of salvation. The presence in its place of truth and duty and love and obedience—this is what makes a saved man. III. For how long does God dwell with men ? Deep philosophy as well as high faith sanctions the conclusion that the God of grace, who makes covenant with man and dwells with him, is " our God for ever and ever," and that He " will never leave us or forsake us." (*A. Raleigh, D.D.*)   *The holy tent :*—I. We should mark that God makes himself dependent on the will of man. " Let them make Me." This is true, not only of material wealth, but of man's nature. 1. God wants human nature, He seems to covet to have the affection of our life, and yearns to be looked to by the creature He has made. Let us not cheat Him, for we shall rob ourselves most of all. 2. God may be thwarted by man. II. In this Divine conception of the Church, there is a place for the rich. It is not impossible for rich men to be good men. It is not easy, but still it can be done. God has given them a place. " This is the offering which ye shall take of them : *gold.*" God would not have accepted planks from those who had gold, and so God will not accept industry in His service in the place of wealth. III. Labour has its place. There was a great deal of timber required ; the wood of the acacia tree was used for the framework. Here was work which the poorest could do. Is it not so to-day ? In building the Church, what room for a holy industry ! IV. Woman has her rights here. We read in chap. xxxv. 24, 25, of women that were wise-hearted, who did spin with their hands, &c. Influence of Christian mothers. Sunday-school workers. Mothers' meetings. Let woman do her work well. We must have her work, or we cannot finish ours. V. There is room for genius. " Precious stones" are required. The onyx stones, and other jewels, took up but small room, but they added beauty and splendour to the rest. God does not create genius every day. Many rhymers, but few poets. VI. Still, we must not forget that the meanest is acceptable, if it is the best we can bring. There are times when cleverness is baffled, and wealth is powerless. But see to it God has your best. Acacia wood will not be accepted in the place of any-

thing else. But if the axe and saw are your talents, by all means use them. VII.
OUR BEST AND OUR ALL IS OF NO AVAIL WITHOUT THE ATONEMENT. Alms and deeds are
only safe as they rest upon Christ's merits. (*T. Champness.*) *The Tabernacle and
priesthood :*—I. THE TABERNACLE. 1. Its general character. 2. Its contents. II.
THE PRIESTHOOD FOR THE TABERNACLE. III. THE SYMBOLIC MEANING OF BOTH TABER-
NACLE AND PRIESTHOOD. 1. Scriptural evidence of the symbolic character of these.
(1) The Mosaic ritual, as a whole, is declared to be this (Heb. x. 1). (2) Parts of it
declared symbolic (Heb. ix. 6–9). 2. Some of its symbols explained. (1) The
propitiatory in the "Holy of Holies" (1 John ii. 2). (2) The veil dividing the
"holy place" from the "most holy" (Heb. x. 19, 20). (3) The sacrifices of the
Mosaic ritual (Heb. ix. 13, 14). 3. The priesthood a symbol. (1) In its appointment (Heb. v. 1–5, viii. 1–5, ix. 11, 12). (2) In its contrast (Heb. vii. 11–28, ix.
23–28, x. 1–13). Lessons: 1. The importance and duty of studying the Old
Testament in order to understand the New Testament. 2. The marked superiority
of the Christian over the Mosaic dispensation. 3. Our weightier responsibilities
over those of old. 4. The all-sufficiency of Christ as Redeemer, Priest, and Friend.
5. Our paramount duties—to accept, trust, and obey Him. (*D. C. Hughes, M.A.*)
The Tabernacle :—I. THE GRAND PURPOSE OF THE TABERNACLE WAS THAT THE ISRAELITES
MIGHT REALIZE GOD'S PRESENCE WITH THEM. 1. The unity of God had been lost in
the gradual transference of separate and independent sovereignty to every attempted
representation or localization of the Deity. This evil, God now corrects by the
strict confinement of His localization to one spot. 2. The conception of the Deity
had been demoralized through the forms in which men sought to represent God.
And so the God of Israel refuses to allow any image or outward representation of
Himself. II. THE MANIFESTATION OF GOD'S PRESENCE WAS SECURED BY THE CONSTRUC-
TION AND FURNITURE OF THE TABERNACLE. 1. The ark was constructed out of the
freewill offerings of the people. 2. The Tabernacle in its costliness was, in all the
circumstances of the case, wonderfully appreciative of the Divine Majesty. 3.
The Tabernacle was constructed in all respects according to Divine pattern.
(*W. Roberts, M.A.*) *Nature and design of the Tabernacle :*—I. ITS NATURE. 1.
It was a simple structure. The materials of which it was composed were costly
indeed. There was also much of artistic grace and beauty wrought up into its
composition, and yet, compared with the splendid cathedrals &c. which men have
erected, how simple and unpretending! 2. It was a structure of Divine origin.
Indebted for nothing to the force of man's creative faculty. God planned it. II.
ITS DESIGN. 1. In reference to the Jews. (1) The source of present blessing. The
bright spot in the midst of a dark and desert world ; for God was there, and walked
in the midst of His people, to bless and deliver them from their enemies. (2) A
pledge or promise to them of future good. A heaven-devised symbol, prefiguring God's salvation. 2. In reference to ourselves. (1) An illustration of the
blessings of the gospel. The relation which God sustained to Israel as a nation,
He now sustains to His people as individuals. He shades them by day, and
enlightens them by night ; strengthens and comforts ; guides and blesses them as
their own personal God. (2) The Tabernacle furnishes us with a figurative view of
our relation to the heavenly world (see Heb. ix. 23). We are often tempted to think
and feel as if that world must be at an immense distance, a vast remove from us.
A proper consideration of the Tabernacle would seem to correct this impression.
Here you see the Holy Place, or the Church on Earth, and the Most Holy Place, or
the Church in Heaven, in the closest possible contiguity to each other. There is
only that thin material veil to separate them. In CONCLUSION the subject we have
now considered suggests to us—How thankful we should be for the day in which
we live! It is "the day of salvation"; the dispensation of the substance which
succeeded to that of the shadow ; the time of direct and full revelation as opposed
to the time of type and figure. It is to the dispensation of the Tabernacle what the
hour of noon, with its radiant splendour, is to the hour of early dawn, with its dim
twilight and its gloom. In regard to light, and grace, and privilege, our position
under the gospel is exalted indeed. And if it be true that "to whom much is given,
of them much will be required," then it becomes us to see well to it, that we
improve diligently our privileges. (*R. Newton, D.D.*) *The Tabernacle a symbol
of holier things :*—1. The Tabernacle was the dwelling place of God. It tells us God
is great. It was a costly Tabernacle. The value of the structure was probably not
much less than £300,000. There was mystery. The Israelites were not to enter
the Tabernacle, but only the priests. Only the high priest could enter into the
Holy of Holies, and that but once a year. Thus God surrounded Himself with an

impenetrable veil of mystery. It has been said, " God is the greatest mystery in the universe." But, if there is mystery, there is mercy. There was also justice, holiness, and majesty. 2. The Israelites no doubt looked upon the Tabernacle as the palace of their King. The furniture was palace furniture, and the priests were ministers of state. 3. The Tabernacle was set up in the wilderness. In all our wanderings God is with us. 4. The Tabernacle was the first religious structure, in which Jehovah condescended to dwell. Symbol of Divine grace. Erected in midst of sinners. 5. God's presence is the cause of holiness and it alone removes the curse. God came down to dwell with His people, not because they were holy, but to make them so. No place is holy without God. That place—wherever it may be —is holy if God is there. 6. The Tabernacle was a place of worship. It was called " the tent of the congregation " (chap. xl. 22). They had a property in it. It was the palace of their King. It was the house of their God. There they came to confess their sin. There was no other place of the kind. It was the one Tabernacle for all the tribes, and for all the individual members of those tribes. 7. The Tabernacle was not a model for our imitation, but " a shadow of heavenly things " (Heb. viii. 5). The substance having come, we need not go back to the shadow. In the Tabernacle we have " the figures of the true " (Heb. ix. 24). In the gospel we have reality. Its blessings are everlasting. Jesus is the way, the truth, and the life. He is the truth of every figure, the way to a holy God, and the life of all who believe. (*R. E. Sears.*)　　*The Divine purpose in the erection of a Tabernacle :*—This introductory sentence of the symbolical dispensation involved much. It reiterated the great promise given at the fall, that man, although lapsed, should not be left unaided ; that there should be, in the fulness of time, an inter- ference on his behalf of the most remarkable character ; and that, to prepare men's minds for its reception, it should, first of all, be presented in a figure. I. GOD DWELT IN A TABERNACLE. In this a glorious reality was foreshadowed (John i. 14 ; Tim. iii.16 ; Gal. iv. 4 ; Heb. ii. 14). II. IN THAT TABERNACLE HE DWELT AMONGST HIS PEOPLE ISRAEL. Christ is the great centre round which all His people are grouped—those nearest to Him, the family within the veil ; the glorified ones, who, having finished their service here below, are at rest—while the outer circle is the Church militant, that portion of the family which is still in the midst of tribulation and conflict. But He is the great centre. To Him all eyes, all hearts are turned ; from Him all supplies are derived. The one see Him in actual fruition and enjoyment ; the other realize Him by faith. (*J. Ridgeway, M.A.*)　　*The Tabernacle of the testimony :*—So many things of a covenant form and character required to be placed under the security and covering of a covenant habitation, a habitation having relation to both God and His people. The Lord Himself had said, " I will dwell among them." Here was His habitation. Look at the model after which it was formed (ver. 40). God was His own architect, nor were there any deviations in after thought from His original plan : the design was perfect. But why such exact- ness in relation to this temporary residence, this wilderness habitation of the Lord of the whole earth ? A prefiguration of the body of Christ was intended, His assumption of our form and flesh, and which was an act of condescension, a veiling of the glories of His Godhead, a coming down to dwell in concealment. The personal assumption of our nature, therefore, made it of moment that what was to contain the inhabitation of Deity, like the body of Christ, curiously wrought, as it is said, in the lowest parts of the earth, should be of a form, and be put together exactly as God Himself had given the model to Moses in the mount. It was especially of God. In the spiritual worship of the gospel of Christ, and in the doctrines of grace, nothing is suffered to be misplaced, nothing left to be introduced. There is a show of wisdom in will-worship, an appearance of reverence and humility, but none in reality. If we worship God, we must worship Him, after His own instructions, and, under whatever dispensation, in spirit and in truth. The design was God's, but the execution of the work was man's. 1. Many hearts were in the work. As soon as required to be constructed, the people had a heart to it, and well they might, since it was bringing God nearer to them, and more visibly with them than He had been. How interesting the union of hearts in such a work, men and women, and, we might think, even children too, wise and willing in the work of the Lord ! Delightful was it to have their hearts in what had, from eternity, employed the heart of God, His whole will and under- standing, His counsels, grace, and love. How are our hearts affected towards the spiritual temple that is rising in this world of sin ? Sweet the frame of mind David was in when he said (1 Chron. xxix. 14, &c.). Their hearts were their offerings :

there were no niggardly restraints of covetousness. At what expense are many to support the pride of life, and to maintain the superfluities of naughtiness! The day is coming when they will bitterly lament the misapplication of wealth, and the want of a heart, in their fulness, for a ready yieldance to God. 2. Many hands, as well as many hearts, were in the work (chap. xxxv. 26). And how delightful is it to see the spiritual temple rising, and each employed as skill given him! Where there are hearts, hands will not be wanting. We see many employed about the great building God has in progress, and what has set them to work but love? It is this that is the great moving power in the machinery of those many institutions which are in truth the bulwark and glory of the land. (*W. Seaton.*) *The Tabernacle entire :*—We think the Tabernacle in its entireness was emblematical of—1. The incarnation. The glory of Jehovah filled it. 2. The Church. Unity in diversity, and diversity in unity. 3. The believer. As respects both his (1) present, and (2) future being. Weak and imperfect now ; to be glorified hereafter. 4. The millennial kingdom (Rev. xxi. 3, 4). (*W. Mudge.*) *Design and use of the ceremonial law :*—1. It served to cherish the religious sentiment. The Israelite was reminded by it in all his relations, even the most significant and external, of God ; the thought of God was introduced into the very midst of the popular life. 2. It required the recognition of sin, and thus called forth the first thing essential for the reception of redemption, a sense of the need of redemption. The law was, and was intended to be, a heavy yoke, and therefore would awaken a longing after the Redeemer. 3. It served to separate Israel from the heathen ; it erected between the two a wall of separation, by which communication was prevented. 4. Many things in the Ceremonial Law served, by impressions on the senses, to awaken reverence for holy things among a sensual people. 5. One principal object of the Ceremonial Law lay in its symbolic meaning. The people, enthralled in visible objects, were not yet capable of vitally appropriating supersensual truth in words, the form most suited to their nature. It was needful for the truth to condescend, to come down to their power of apprehension, to prepare itself a body from visible things, in order to free the people from the bondage of the visible. Would we rather not speak at all to the dumb than make use of signs? The Ceremonial Law was not the opposite to the worship of God in spirit and in truth, but only an imperfect form of the same, a necessary preparation for it. The accommodation was only formal, one which did not alter the essence, but only presented it in large capital letters to children who could not yet read a small running-hand. (*E. W. Hengstenberg, D.D.*) *The basis of symbolism :*—The altar was the basis of the sacred places, the priesthood was the basis of the sacred persons, the burnt-offerings were the basis of the sacred rites, and the Sabbath was the basis of the sacred times. Here we discover the links that connect the Ceremonial Laws given by Moses with the primeval ordinances of religion. In the altar set up in the family of Adam we have the genesis of the Tabernacle and Temple. At the beginning the minister of sacrifice was the patriarch of the existing family, and his sacred office passed over to the Mosaic priesthood. In the offering of the blood by Abel and the offering by fire of Noah, we discover the germs of the Jewish ritual. The Sabbath ordained in Paradise became the central institute in the sacred times appointed by Moses. (*E. P. Humphrey, D.D.*) *The Tabernacle a tent :*—The Tabernacle was a tent; it was a costly building, but still it was a tent ; it was God's tent in which He lived and walked with His people in the wilderness (chap. xxv. 8 ; Num. ix. 15 ; 2 Sam. vii. 6 ; Acts vii. 38–50). As His people were dwelling in tents, God would have a tent, and would live with them as their Guide and their Guard, their Father and their King ; but afterward, when they were settled in the land of Canaan and dwelt in ceiled houses, He permitted them to build Him a house at Jerusalem, which He then filled with His presence as He had before filled the Tabernacle. As God dwelt in the Tabernacle and afterwards in the Temple, and as men must then come to the Tabernacle or to the Temple to get to God, so God dwells in Christ (2 Cor. v. 19), and all who would come to God must come to Christ : in no other way can any one get to God (John xiv. 6 ; vi. 37). Moreover, as there was but one Tabernacle, so there is but one Christ, and none can be saved from the wrath to come but those who come to Him ; and as a man must come out of the camp to get to the Tabernacle, so a man must come out from the world, must be separated from it in spirit, before he can be really in Christ. (*G. Rodgers.*) *The edifice of the Tabernacle :*—Moses received on Sinai not only a command to make the Tabernacle, but plans and specifications according to which the work was to be executed. Its ground-plan was a parallelogram forty-five feet in length, and fifteen feet in width.

The material was of shittim, a species of acacia, the timber of which has a rich black colour like ebony, and is eminently light, solid, strong, and smooth. The frame of the Tabernacle consisted of forty-eight pieces of this acacia wood standing on end. Eight of them were at the rear, and twenty on each side; the front being left open to be covered with a curtain. They were each fifteen feet long, and, unless the two outside pieces on the rear end were exceptions, twenty-seven inches wide. The description of the corner planks is obscure, but favours the opinion that each consisted of two pieces fastened together at a right angle; so that it was a corner-plank not merely because it stood at the corner, but because it formed an angle. On the lower end of each of the planks, two tenons were wrought, to correspond with mortises in the sills on which it was to stand. Possibly there were also tenons and mortises on the edges where the planks came together; but of this we have no certain knowledge. Such a connection of one plank with another, by tenon and mortise, would give greater strength to the frame, but might not be necessary in addition to the horizontal bars which bound the planks together. There were five such bars on each side, and five on the rear, made of acacia wood, and overlaid with gold. These gilded planks when erected, stood on a base, or sill, of silver, which extended perhaps a little way both outward and inward, from the wall formed by the planks, and was divided into twice as many pieces as there were planks; so that each of the latter stood on two separate pieces of the base, one of its two tenons being inserted into a corresponding cavity in each division of the base. Besides the planks which formed the wall of the Tabernacle, there were four pillars, to support a curtain across the interior of the building, dividing it into two apartments, and five pillars to support another curtain over the entrance at the east end of the edifice. The four pillars for the partition-curtain stood on sills, or socket-pieces of silver, and the five for the entrance-curtain on sills of copper. The wooden frame of the Tabernacle having been prepared, it was necessary to cover it with suitable hangings, or curtains. Of these there were four layers; the innermost so far excelling the others in importance, that it was sometimes denominated "The Tabernacle," as if all else appertaining to the edifice were subsidiary to this. The frame, indeed, seems to have been chiefly designed to give support to the beautiful drapery with which it was covered. In the conception of a Hebrew travelling through the wilderness from Sinai to Canaan, the Tabernacle where Jehovah dwelt was of cloth, as was his own habitation. It was, indeed, of a more beautiful fabric than the other tents of the encampment, which were doubtless of goats' hair, like those of the nomadic inhabitants of the same region at the present day, while the Tabernacle of God was of fine linen variegated with brilliant colours. The several parts of the sanctuary having been constructed, it still remained to make an enclosure for the court in which it was to stand. The prescribed dimensions of this area were one hundred and fifty feet for the length, and seventy-five feet for the width. It was to be enclosed with hangings of cloth made of fine white linen, not interwoven, like the curtains of the Tabernacle, with figures and colours, but, so far as appears, woven plain. That portion of it, however, which covered the entrance-way at the east end of the court, was variegated with colours of blue, purple, and crimson. The height of these hangings was seven feet and a half; and they were suspended on pillars by means of silver hooks, the pillars standing on sills of copper. The distance between these pillars was equal to the height of the hangings, i.e., seven and a half feet. They were connected by a silver rod, or fillet, extending from one capital to another. The Tabernacle was to stand near the western end of this enclosure, and midway, doubtless, between its northern and southern curtains. A large area was therefore left in front of the edifice for the performance of those rites of worship which were appropriate to the place. (E. E. Atwater.) The oneness of the Tabernacle:—(see chap. xxvi. 6). It is to be one Tabernacle—not in the sense of singleness and uniqueness, as if God had forbidden more than one Tabernacle to be constructed for His service—but in the sense of a real and profound unity. By the golden taches or clasps binding together the curtains which covered it, the whole structure was made one tent or tabernacle, and all its parts and objects were united. Unity is the hall-mark which God stamps upon all His works. It is His autograph written in the stars of heaven and in the flowers of the field, attesting that they all proceed from the same Mind. The universe is a great kaleidoscope which He is perpetually turning round, in which a few simple elements are exhibited in endless diversity; in which the variety is not more wonderful than the unity. 1. In unfolding this sublime lesson, let us look, in the first place, at the illustration of it which the Tabernacle itself afforded. This remarkable structure was one in regard to its parts. Each vessel has its own distinct use, and each can be viewed apart from the others; and yet in every act of priestly service, all are joined together, and are in active operation at the same time. It needs the combination of the whole to make a complete and perfect act of worship, just as it needs the harmonious action of all the members of the body to constitute the act of living. And just as the golden taches link the curtains of the Tabernacle together, and make of them one covering for one structure, so the smaller golden vessels attached to the golden candlestick, the altar of incense, and the shewbread table—the tongs, snuff-dishes, spoons, and censer—linked together the different vessels of the sanctuary into one ministration, forming in this way one golden chain of service simultaneously carried on in the presence of God in behalf of Israel. 2. The words of the Lord to Moses have a wider reference than to the immediate object which called them forth. They may be applied to nature. It may be said that the Tabernacle pointed back to the creation. It was a symbol of the great world of nature, as at once manifesting and concealing God. It was, indeed, as a Rosetta stone, to explain to man the spiritual hieroglyphics in the typology of nature, which had become dark and insignificant to him when he sinned and fell, that God devised the clearer typology of the Tabernacle, and set the cherubim, which were the symbols of creation in connection with the redemption of man, above the mercy-seat in its holiest place, and embroidered them on the veil that divided the outer from the inner sanctuary. There was no typical object or service in the Tabernacle which might not have been seen in nature if man had not lost the key of interpretation. If the creation be thus a greater Tabernacle, in which all the objects are meant to show forth the praise of God, and to symbolize His work of grace, we should expect to find in it the same unity, the same oneness of design and harmony of all parts, that we see in the Jewish Tabernacle; and this is what we actually find. This is the great lesson which modern science has taught us so effectually. 3. But not only did the Tabernacle repeat in miniature the whole creation as God's dwelling-place, it also more especially typified the new creation— the Church of God. Under all the varying dispensations of His grace, God's Church has been one. The Jews were in the outer court because the way into the holiest was not yet made manifest. Gentiles, by the new and living way opened up through the rent veil of Christ's flesh, have entered into the inner shrine. But Jews and Gentiles alike are now united in one communion and fellowship in Christ. The Saviour the Jews looked forward to in rites and sacrifices, we look back to in the ordinances of the gospel. The religion that was veiled to them has been unveiled to us. They saw the types and shadows; we behold the living and glorious realities. Over all is the tabernacling of the same God; and the Church of Jews and Gentiles is "built upon the foundation," &c. 4. The Tabernacle was the Bible of the Israelites. God taught them by its object-lessons in their childhood and pupilage in the wilderness. But that age of shadows and symbols has disappeared; man has passed from the childhood's stage of education into the higher school. We have been trained for a clearer perception and a fuller possession of the truth. God has given to us His own written Word, in which His thoughts are woven with man's thoughts, making of the whole Book the speech to the world of Emmanuel, God with us. 5. Man's body is a tabernacle—the greatest of all temples. It is fearfully and wonderfully made, the very highest possible form of organization, the masterpiece of creation. (*H. Macmillan, D.D.*) *Means of interpretation:*—There are means of interpretation by the aid of which one may decipher the symbols of the Hebrews as correctly as Champollion deciphered the hieroglyphics of Egypt. I. First in the table may be placed THE PARALLELISM BETWEEN THE MOSAIC SYSTEM, AS OTHERWISE ASCERTAINED, AND ITS SYMBOLIC REPRESENTATION. The writings of Moses, like the Greek translation of the Rosetta stone give a clue to the meaning of what otherwise might be illegible. II. Another key of interpretation is found in the SCRIPTURAL EXPLANATION OF SYMBOLS. For instance, in the Apocalypse incense is explained as symbolizing the prayers of the holy; and fine linen is explained as meaning, when used for garments, that those thus arrayed were holy. III. THE DESIGN OF THE TABERNACLE AS DECLARED IN THE DIRECTIONS FOR ITS CONSTRUCTION, EQUIPMENT, AND SERVICES, IS A KEY TO ITS SIGNIFICANCE. If the edifice was a symbol it signified that Jehovah dwelt among the Israelites. It represented His true habitation, wherever and of whatever nature it may be, and the spiritual intercourse between Him and those who worship. Moreover, it was equipped in such a manner as to provide for

ministrations expressive of atonement, restoration to favour, assurance of reconciliation, and acceptable service ; and was thus both a sign and a seal of the
covenant relation and of the presence of Jehovah.   IV. THE SCRIPTURAL APPELLA
TIONS OF THE TABERNACLE ARE A MEANS OF INTERPRETATION.   V. THE SYMBOLISM
OF NATURE IS AN IMPORTANT MEANS OF INTERPRETATION.   VI. Another means of
interpretation is THE ARTIFICIAL SYMBOLISM OF THE ANCIENTS.   Kings wear crowns,
and sit on thrones; and so crowns and thrones indicate royalty.   Among
the ancients purple was worn by those in authority, and so became the badge of
power and distinction.   The temples of the Hindoos, the Chinese, the Chaldeans,
and the Egyptians, were built with an adherence to certain forms, proportions, and
repetitions, which leaves no room for doubt that their sacred architecture was
significant, and that with some difference in the ideas expressed, and some variety
in the mode of expressing the same ideas, they employed the relations of geometry
and arithmetic to represent the objects of their religious thought.   Colour was
employed for the same purpose.   The three kingdoms of nature—animal, vegetable,
mineral—were also made to subserve this artificial symbolism.   (E. E. Atwater.)
Gold, and silver, and brass.—Symbolism of minerals :—Gold, silver, and jewels have
in all ages and countries been regarded as significant of wealth, rank, power.   The
use of the precious metals for money has, however, rendered it impossible that they
should exert in modern times as much influence on the imagination as when used
only as insignia.   1. It is quite certain that in the time of Moses gold had not been
coined, and was not often used, even by weight, as a medium of exchange.   There
is a warrant in nature as well as in the universal custom of antiquity, for this
employment of the most splendid of the metals to illustrate the highest possible
dignity and glory ; for it never fails to excite in the mind of the beholder feelings
of admiration and awe.   Hence, as an emblem, it was among metals what
purple was among colours, and found its most appropriate place on the persons
and in the habitations of kings and gods.   The dedication of a large amount of
gold to the service of religion was, therefore, not peculiar to the Hebrews.   It was
the universal custom of the age thus to do homage to the objects of worship.
But, as Mosaism allowed no images of Jehovah, the symbolism of gold must be
confined to His habitation and its furniture.   It is worthy of observation, then,
that the God of the Hebrews dwelt in a golden house.   2. If the Tabernacle of
Jehovah was splendid by contrast between it and the ordinary tents of the surrounding encampment, it seems to have been designedly rendered still more splendid
by the ordained distinction between the Tabernacle and its court.   For while the
walls of the dwelling and all its utensils were of gold, so that (with the exception
of the sill) no other metal was visible within, the furniture of the court must,
according to the specifications furnished to Moses, be of copper.   The significance
of copper seems to depend chiefly on its rank among the metals, being more
esteemed than iron, and less so than silver and gold.   As a metal of honour and
beauty, it was an appropriate material for the utensils of Divine service, and by its
inferiority to gold furnished a background on which the latter seemed more splendid
by contrast.   Its resemblance to gold deepened the symbolic significance conveyed
by the exclusive use of one of the metals in the court, and of the other within the
habitation.   3. Between the copper outside and the gold inside, silver was the
mediating metal, being found both on the sill of the sanctuary and on the caps of
the pillars around the sacred enclosure, to indicate by another sign that the house
was higher in honour than the area in front, so much higher that its sill was of
the same material as the crowning ornament of the court.   Silver was at that time
in common use as money ; if not in the shape of coin, certainly of bullion, which,
when weighed, was current with the merchant (Gen. xxiii. 16).   Now, this silver
which had been wrought partly into the sill of the Tabernacle and partly into the
caps of the pillars around the court, had been used as money.   Indeed, it came
into the possession of Moses in half-shekels, which the people had paid as " atonement money," " every man a ransom for his soul " (chap. xxx. 12, 16).   The services
of the court culminated in redemption, and not till they were redeemed could
the people, even representatively, enter the sanctuary.   The shining silver on the
top of the pillars of the enclosure was " a memorial to the children of Israel before
Jehovah to make an atonement for their souls " (chap. xxx. 16), i.e., a permanent
reminder that their sins were expiated ; and the sill of the sanctuary, into which
the greater part of the ransom-money had been molten, was a token that in consequence of their redemption God dwelt among them, and received them to His
fellowship.   The silver, " as an expiation for souls, pointed to the unholiness of

Israel's nature, and reminded the people continually that by nature it was alienated from God, and could only remain in covenant with the Lord, and live in His kingdom, on the ground of His grace which covered its sin." May not the apostle have had this ransom-money in mind when he said to the people of the new covenant, " Ye were not redeemed with corruptible things, as silver and gold, but with the precious blood of Christ "? (*Ibid.*) *Gifts of materials for the construction of the Tabernacle :*—Many chapels are burdened with a load of debt occasioned by the bad habit of congregations building, either wholly or in part, with borrowed money. But the Hebrews acted more nobly than such builders, for they collected by voluntary contributions the entire materials with which the sanctuary was constructed ere they began to build (chap. xxv. 1–9, xxxv. 4–9, 20–30). Their free-will offering for the work of the Tabernacle is, in many respects, the most splendid one that was ever given for the purpose of raising a place of worship. (*W. Brown.*) *Gold :*—Foremost in the procession of willing-hearted offerers came men and women bringing " bracelets, and ear-rings, and seal-rings, and tablets," all of gold (chap. xxxv. 22), till the heap comprised many thousands of articles, and weighed no less than 29 talents and 730 shekels (chap. xxxviii. 24), equal to 43,865 ounces, the value of which at the present day is £180,000 sterling. (*Ibid.*) *Silver :*—Gold was contributed by men and women, but silver by men only. This, however, was not on account of the women, who cheerfully gave their gold ornaments, refusing to part with their silver ones, but because silver was to be taken from none but adult males, who were required to give half a shekel each as a ransom for the soul (person) (chap. xxx. 11–16). The sum of the silver brought was 100 talents and 1775 shekels, or 301,775 shekels (chap. xxxviii. 25–27), which proves that every one of the 603,550 men comprising the Hebrew encampment paid the price of his redemption. This was done, however, not by compulsion, but freely ; the silver as well as the gold was to be a free-will offering (chap. xxv. 2, 3). The whole was equal to 150,887½ ounces, and would now realize £40,000 sterling, Silver appears to have been the only metal used as money by the Hebrews, at least up to the period of the Exodus, and this circumstance no doubt accounts for the ransom price being paid in silver (Gen. xxiii. 15, xxxvii. 28). (*Ibid.*) *Brass :*— Gold and silver were the most precious metals, but brass (copper) was also needed for the work of the Tabernacle, and those who possessed it—and amongst them might be some who had no gold to bestow—brought 70 talents and 2,400 shekels (chap. xxxviii. 29), equal to 106,200 ounces. The original word rendered brass in the text is from a Hebrew root signifying to shine. (*Ibid.*) *Typical import of materials :*—1. Gold. Type of the Divine glory of the Lord Jesus as Son of God. 2. Silver. The preciousness of the Lord Jesus as the Ransom for the sinner. 3. Brass. The power of the Lord Jesus to endure the cross, because He is God. 4. Blue. The manifestation of God as love, in the ways and death of Christ. 5. Purple. The manifestation of the God-Man, God manifest in the flesh. 6. Scarlet. The manifestation of the true dignity and glory of man as seen in the Lord Jesus Christ, the Son of Man. 7. Fine linen. The righteous man exhibiting to the eye of faith " the glory as of the only begotten of the Father, full of grace and truth." 8. Goats' hair. The memorial of the death of the Lord Jesus as the offering for sin. 9. Rams' skins dyed red. The outward aspect of Christ as the Man of sorrows and acquainted with grief. Born in this world to die. 10. Badgers' skins. The outward aspect of Christ, as having no form nor comeliness to the heart of the natural man. 11. Shittim wood. The Lord Jesus, the incorruptible Man. " That holy thing," the Son of God. 12. Oil for the light. The Lord Jesus as the light ; filled with the Spirit. 13. Spices for anointing oil. The graces of the Spirit in all their fulness manifested by the Christ. 14. Spices for sweet incense. The fragrant graces of Christ made manifest on the cross, and perpetuated in His intercession. 15. Onyx stones, and stones to be set in the ephod and the breastplate. The glory and brilliancy of the Heavenly One reflected also in His saints. (*H. W. Soltau.*) *Offerings accompanied with devotion :*—Almost every hill in Mongolia is adorned with a cairn of stones on the very top. This cairn is a thing of the Mongolian religion. When it is determined to erect one, men, women, and children turn out and gather stones, repeating prayers over each stone ; and thus the raised heap represents much devotion on the part of the gatherers. Oh, that all contributions in Christian lands for Christian objects were raised in the same way. Gifts are good, but gifts accompanied by heart-felt devotion are better. (*S. S. Chronicle.*) *The pocket converted :*—John Wesley used to say that he never believed in a man's conversion until his pocket was converted. *A Divine plan for building :*—There is a beautiful story told of the plan by which Strasburg Cathedral was made. The architect, Erwin von Steinbach, who was given the commission to build it, was greatly troubled lest he should not get his plan sufficiently noble. He had a daughter named Sabine, who was skilful in drawing, and one night, after they had wept together over the plans, she said to her father, "Don't despair; God will help us." After she fell asleep she dreamed that a beautiful angel came, and when she had told her story, said; "You shall make the plan for the minster." The angel and Sabine then set to work, and soon the plan was done. When she awoke she uttered a loud scream, for there was a paper before her covered with wonderful drawing. Her father exclaimed, "Child, it was no dream. The angel really visited you, bringing the inspiration from heaven to help us." He built the cathedral after the plan, and it was so beautiful that the people really believed the story. (*Great Thoughts.*) **Blue, and purple, and scarlet, and fine linen.**—*Symbolism of colour :*—The symbolism of colour in the Tabernacle was confined to the curtains of the edifice and the garments of its priesthood, both of which were of fine-twined linen, blue, purple, and crimson. The four colours indicated all inhered in the same material subjected to different processes of manufacture; the fine thread of the byssus being in one process bleached to the greatest possible whiteness, and in the other three dyed with blue, purple, and crimson. 1. That white linen was employed as a symbol, appears from many passages of the New Testament, where its significance is declared and explained. It was a representative of light, resembling it somewhat in colour (Matt. xvii. 2), but more in brightness (Luke ix. 29, xxiv. 4; Mark ix. 3), and purity (Rev. xix. 8, 14, xv. 6). 2. The Hebrew word rendered "blue" is primarily the name of a shell-fish, and derivatively of the dye yielded by it. If Moses would represent that Jehovah, whose dwelling is in heaven, had come down to earth to dwell with His covenant people, how could he do it better than by employing in the habitation made with hands the azure hue of the visible heaven? If he wished to teach that the priests, and the sacrifices they offered were an "example and shadow of heavenly things," how pertinent would it be to weave into their official attire threads of that cerulean tint, which in his day communicated such thoughts to the eye as are now conveyed to the ear by the audible pronunciation of the word "heaven"! 3. Cloth of purple was much prized by the Greeks and Romans, who included under this appellation a wide range of colour, extending from red slightly tinged with blue to shades in which the blue was predominant; the dye being in all cases derived from shell-fish. In the earlier days of Rome, purple had been worn only by magistrates as a badge of office; but the progress of wealth and luxury was afterward so great, that the first of the emperors thought it necessary to put restriction on the use of it in order to preserve the significance of the ancient symbol; and eventually certain fabrics of this colour, including those held in highest estimation, were entirely interdicted to the Roman citizens, and reserved for the exclusive use of the imperial household. In the employment of purple as a mark of official distinction, the Romans followed the custom of some, if not all older nations (see Judges viii. 26; Dan. v. 7, margin). Not only kings, emperors, and their subordinates in civil authority, wore this colour, but sometimes priests, as a mark of honour to their office and the deities they served. Even the images of the gods were adorned with raiment of purple. The appearance of this colour, then, in the curtains of the Hebrew Tabernacle marked that central edifice as the habitation of the Ruler of the encampment. The purple in the garments of the priests indicated that they belonged to the royal household, and were officers of the King. 4. The two Hebrew words which taken together are rendered "scarlet," denote a colour derived from an insect called by naturalists *coccus ilicis*, found in large quantities on certain species of the oak. The Arabic name of the insect is *kermes*, the root of our word "crimson." The only natural object to which the tint is applied in the Old Testament is the lips (Song of Sol. iv. 3). It seems probable (see Gen. xxxviii. 28; Lev. xiv. 4–7; Num. xix. 6; Josh. ii. 18) that this colour was used as a symbol of life; deriving this significance from blood, which was itself the vehicle and representative of the vital force. (*E. E. Atwater.*) *The colours :*—1. Blue, being the colour of the heaven, as it appears to man looking up into it, may be regarded not unnaturally as speaking of God. The Israelites were bidden to have fringes on the borders of their garments, and upon the fringe of the borders a ribband of blue (Num. xv. 38), doubtless to be a perpetual reminder to them in their daily life that they were the people of God. 2. Scarlet, or red, is the colour which, after blue, occurs most frequently in connection with the Tabernacle. As blue speaks of God the Creator, so red, or scarlet, speaks of the world, or of man the creature. 3. Purple is formed from the intermingling of scarlet and blue, and thus corresponds to twelve among numbers, which is the result of three multiplied into four, and is, therefore, the colour of the Incarnation. In the Tabernacle, purple appears side by side with blue and scarlet in the interior hangings, in the veils, and in the vestments of the high-priest. When we remember that the Tabernacle, as a whole, was a type of the Word who "tabernacles in us" (John i. 14), we shall not, I think, find it difficult to acquiesce in the suggestion of a devout and learned writer, that "the purple appears to have foreshadowed the hypostatical union, *i.e.*, the union of the Divine and human natures in the person of our Lord." It would seem to have been selected to reveal the intimacy and perfection of this union; and the constituent colours of purple, red, and blue, to have been set in juxtaposition with it, to teach that, although the two natures are thus combined in Him, yet are they not absorbed in each other, as if the Divine had been lost in the human, or the human in the Divine, but ever remain to co-exist, notwithstanding their most perfect union. 4. The three colours already spoken of were conjoined with the whiteness of fine linen. White is symbolic of cleansing from sin (Isa. i. 18; *cf.* Rev. vii. 14; Psa. li. 7). White is also symbolical of perfect dazzling holiness (Dan. vii. 9; *cf.* Rev. vi. 2, xiv. 14, xix. 11, xx. 11). In the Tabernacle the fine white linen would tell of the purity and holiness which results from that union of the Divine with the human which was already indicated by the three colours with which it was conjoined. The great lesson, therefore, which everywhere met the eye of the worshipper in the fine linen hangings of the outer court, and in the blue, and purple, and scarlet, and fine-twined linen of the veils, and sacerdotal vestments, was none other than this, "Ye shall be holy, for I the Lord your God am holy." (*E. F. Willis, M.A.*) *Goats' hair:*—Goats' hair formed part of the free-will offerings of the Israelites (chap. xxxv. 23). Many of the goats of the East have black hair, of which cloth is made for tent coverings, but there are some species of goats which have fine white silky hair, among which is the Angora goat, and not a few writers are of opinion that it was hair of this sort with which the tent of the Tabernacle was made. (*W. Brown.*) *Rams' skins.*—The Israelites, being rich in flocks and herds, would have no difficulty in supplying rams' skins. Those brought by the Israelites (chap. xxxv. 23) were dyed, and probably tanned. "Leather of this very description (says Dr. Thomson) is still sold in Syrian towns. From time out of mind the southern part of Syria and Palestine has been supplied with mutton from the great plains and deserts in the north, east, and south; and the shepherds do not ordinarily bring the females to market. The vast flocks which annually come from Armenia and northern Syria are nearly all males. The leather, therefore, is literally 'rams' skins dyed red.'" (*Ibid.*) *Badgers' skins:*—The Hebrews brought badgers' (tachash) as well as rams' skins. It is generally admitted that "badger" is a wrong interpretation of the Hebrew word "tachash," but the learned are not agreed as to what animal is intended. Some are of opinion that it was a fish, and others that it was a quadruped; but whether it swam the ocean or ranged the forest, it was likely a large and powerful creature, since its skin was used for the sacred tent's outer covering, which doubtless required to be of a tough and strong nature. This would not, however, prevent the skins from being made suitable for ornamental purposes. Sandals formed of these skins appear to have been worn by ladies when dressed in the most costly and splendid attire, and decked with the most precious ornaments; "I have shod thee with badgers' skins" (Ezek. xvi. 10); so there can be little doubt that the outer covering or roof of the Tabernacle was not only strong, but also beautiful and ornamental. It is not improbable that the shoes or sandals of the Israelites were also made of this material; and if they were, it was as effectual in defending their feet as it was in preserving the Tabernacle from those influences that might have been hurtful to it. "Thy foot did not swell these forty years." (*Ibid.*)

Vers. 10–16. **Make an ark.**—*The ark:*—I. THE VEIL, BY WHICH THE ARK WAS HIDDEN FROM VIEW. This veil of the Tabernacle was the same as that which subsequently hung in the Temple, and was rent in twain when our Lord expired on the Cross. We may look at it from two points of view, considering what it symbolized when it was an unrent veil, and what the rending of it signifies. The unrent veil was a symbol of darkness and difficulty. To the Jew, it shut out his view of heavenly things, and obstructed his way of approach to them. That veil was a concealing thing. All that stood behind it was effectually hidden from sight. But that Most Holy Place represented heaven. And thus, by the unrent veil, as St. Paul says: "The Holy Ghost thus signified, that the way into the Holiest of all was not yet made manifest" (Heb. ix. 8). That unrent veil was a darkening thing. It was at the same time an obstructing thing. It barred the entrance to the heavenly place. The holiest and best of God's people could not pass within that veil. The high-priest alone might enter, and he but once a year. But what does the rent veil signify? of course the opposite of that which the unrent veil represented. Jesus, we know, came as "the light of the world." He is the revealer of secrets; the unraveller of mysteries. II. The place in which the ark stood. The dimensions of this part of the Tabernacle were those of a cube. The measure of its sides, its ceiling, and its floor was all the same. The cube is the most perfect of all forms, the natural emblem of perfection. And as the form of this place denoted its perfection, so did the material of which it was composed. Gold, pure gold was the material. This met the eye on every side. Gold is the purest and most precious of the metals. In its way, too, gold stands as the symbol of perfection. When we say of a thing that it reaches the golden stage, we say that which expresses the highest idea of its development. And then the furniture of this hallowed place spoke the same language. This told of perfection too. And what was this? One object alone met the eye here. This was that great central object of interest in this whole sacred structure—that keystone of this arch—that sun in the midst of this grand system—that gem in the heaven-formed ring of these hallowed services —the ark of the covenant. III. The structure of the ark. This ark was a symbol of Christ. The constituent parts of it seemed to represent the two natures of our Saviour. The wood of the ark aptly emblemized the human nature of Christ. The tree from which this wood was obtained had its growth in the wilderness. And so in the development of His humanity, it was declared of Christ that "He should grow up like a root out of a dry ground." The acacia wood was incorruptible. It was not subject to decay. And it is just so with the humanity of Christ. That humanity experienced no decay in life; it was the subject of none in death. He saw no corruption in the grave. He will see none for ever. And in like manner the gold of the ark represented Christ's Divinity. IV. The contents of the ark. The two tables of the law were preserved in the ark. This was a very significant fact. It illustrates two important truths. It proclaims the perfect righteousness and the absolute security of the children of the covenant. In conclusion: How striking are some of the points of contrast between the Jewish and the Christian ark. The one was composed of created materials. The time had been when the wood and the gold, wrought up into the form of the ark, had no existence. The other, as to the most important part of His being, at least, was constituted "from everlasting, from the beginning, or ever the world was." (*R. Newton, D.D.*) *The ark of the testimony: the transient symbol of an eternal truth:*—I. The ark may be taken AS SYMBOLICAL OF THE DIVINE PRESENCE, OR THE DIVINE PLAN IN HUMAN LIFE. It was a visible form of an invisible power. 1. In the ark, for example, you find law. See, too, the peculiar place occupied by law: the ark is in the Tabernacle; not only in the Tabernacle, but in the most sacred part of that sacred place; not only in the holiest part of the holy house, but actually in the midst of the ark is found the immutable law of God. Thus we have law at the very centre and heart of things! That which is at the heart of things is right: not something fickle, eccentric, tantalizing; but law, righteousness, God! 2. But, happily, the ark represents something more than law; and every reflective man will acknowledge that in the system within which we live, there is a mystery for which some gentler name than law must be found. The lid of the ark was the seat of mercy. It signified propitiation, favour, mediation, ground and medium of communion with God. Study that tender symbol a moment, if you please. Law, in coming up from the centre, comes through the lid or covering of mercy; it is, so to speak, attempered, or it would come like a sword, or a fire, or a judgment terrible in righteousness. On the other hand, starting the movement from the outside, in our appeal to law we go through the medium of mercy. We do not, dare not, challenge the law in its own name or on its own merits. "By the deeds of the law shall no flesh living be justified." Our approach is through mercy, and our daily prayer is, "God be merciful unto me a sinner." II. We now pass onward to notice A FEW REMARKABLE POINTS IN THE HISTORY OF THE ARK. In doing this, we shall be more careful about the spiritual teaching than about the mere chronology of that history, and thus we shall secure closer continuity of doctrine and illustration. 1. As our song is to be of mercy and judgment, it will be grateful to us first to see how the mercy of the

Lord was revealed amongst His people (see Num. x.). Unquestionably there is a law of movement. We must go forward. How? Into darkness? Into danger? Into thickening mysteries that bring with them sevenfold darkness, and trouble that makes the soul afraid? No; we are offered guidance, defence, and rest! 2. As we have thus seen the goodness of the Lord, we may now behold also His severity, as shown here and there in the history of the ark. Fall of Jericho, Dagon, Bethshemesh, Uzza. Will man attempt to eke out the failing strength of Omnipotence? Doth it become us to watch the stars lest they fall, or to open the clouds at dawn lest the sun should miss his way? Shall we appoint ourselves the special guardians of the truth, and surround it with our defences, lest God should have no foothold on His own earth? III. We now come still more closely to PRACTICAL APPLICATIONS. Here and there in the course of the study we have indicated one or two modern bearings of the subject, which admit of obvious amplification. Let us look at one or two others. The Israelites had a visible symbol of the Divine presence so long as they retained the ark in their midst. It was something to look at— something for the heart to stay itself upon in the time of fear and trouble. But look at our own case. Are we not left without a centre that can be seen, and without a locality sanctified above all other places? Have we not fallen on mean times —all poetry dead and gone, all music hushed for ever? To such questionings the Scriptures give a distinct reply. They tell us that ours are the brightest and noblest of all the days of time (see 2 Cor. iii. 7, 8; Jer. iii. 16). The local has become the universal, and all things are inscribed—"Holy unto the Lord." That law and mercy are still at the heart of things is a truth which is acknowledged in some form even by others than Christian believers; but by Christian believers it ought to be ardently and gratefully maintained as at once the glory and the security of life. And yet we are not left without a visible sign of God's presence. So long as we have the Bible we have the ark of the covenant. (*J. Parker, D.D.*)

The ark :—Of all the appurtenances of the Tabernacle, the highest in the estimation of the Hebrews was a chest of acacia wood three feet and nine inches in length, two feet and three inches both in width and in height, plated within and without with gold, which they called the ark. Around it was a band of gold called a crown. This name would seem to indicate that the band was wrought in imitation of leaves and flowers, a crown having originally consisted of such materials, and having retained the semblance of them when the perishable chaplet gave place to the unfading gold. The specifications do not state how far from the base of the ark this crown was attached; and some have assumed that, *as a crown,* it must necessarily have been placed at the top. It may however have been merely an ornamental band of gold, wrought in imitation of leaves and flowers, and attached just above the rings and staves, by means of which the ark was borne from place to place. The rings just mentioned were of solid metal, like the ornamental cincture, and four in number, one at each corner. They held in place two staves of acacia wood overlaid with gold, by means of which the Levites might bear the ark on their shoulders. The lid of the ark was of pure, solid gold; and two cherubs of the same material stood upon it, one at each end, face to face, and stretching forth their wings over the ark. The position and attitude of these figures make it necessary to infer that they were of small size; but their exact measure is not known. This golden cover was called the mercy-seat, or throne of grace; and is sometimes mentioned by this name, as if it were something independent of the ark. More frequently, however, it is in some way connected with the sacred coffer beneath. It was in particular what the whole Tabernacle was, the dwelling-place of Jehovah, the place where He would meet His people; it was the point in which the significance of the whole institution centred. Within the ark were deposited, according to the direction given to Moses, the two tablets of stone on which Jehovah had written with His own finger the words of the Ten Commandments. There has been a difference of opinion on the question whether the ark contained anything more than the two tablets of stone. From statements in chap. xvi. 33, 34 and Num. xvii. 6–10, it appears that Aaron's rod and the pot of manna were deposited near, but not within, the ark. But this does not forbid the supposition that afterward (see Heb. ix. 4, 5) they were kept within the ark, till, in some way unknown to us, they were lost. On such an hypothesis, the passage in 1 Kings viii. 9, which testifies of what was the case on the day when the ark was deposited in the Temple, has a deeper significance than if the ark had never contained anything but the tablets of stone. The appointed place for the ark of the covenant was in the holy of holies; where it probably stood in the middle of the chamber, with the longer sides toward the east and the west respectively, and the cherubs looking northward and southward toward each other. (*E. E. Atwater.*) *The ark :*—Was the ark a treasure chest? In Christ dwelleth all the fulness of the Godhead. Was it a small chest? Christ made Himself of no reputation, and took upon Him the form of a servant. Was it made after a heavenly pattern? Christ came down from heaven. Was it made of wood? Behold the Man! Was it made of incorruptible wood? Behold the purity of His character! Was it over-laid within and without with gold? Behold your God! God was in Christ. The Spirit of the Lord was upon Him. Had it a crown of gold round about? Behold your King! Had it rings and staves that it might be moved from place to place? "I will give to Jerusalem one that bringeth good tidings." Were the staves always to be in the rings? Christ is always ready to bless and to save. "The Lord was ready to save me." The staves in the rings give a warning to the careless. Privileges despised may soon be removed. (*R. E. Sears.*) **And shalt make upon it a crown of gold round about.**—*The crowns of gold around the holy vessels of the tabernacle :*—There is nothing insignificant in God's universe. Everything that He has made has a meaning and a purpose. There is not a curl in a cloud, or a curve in a leaf, or a tint on a blossom, but has a reason for it, and speaks of its origin. We may be sure that the Jews at the time read in these objects moral and spiritual truths that had a direct practical bearing upon their daily religious life. I wish to deal in this manner with one of the details in the construction of the Tabernacle, to which attention is not usually directed, because it seems a very insignificant and unimportant feature. You place under the microscope a single hair of cotton-wool, which to the naked eye is so fine as to be little more than visible. In this magnified fibre you see a peculiar twist, produced by its mode of growth in the cotton-pod. You would think that twist of no consequence or meaning, and yet it is by means of this peculiarity that the fibre can unite with other fibres, and form together a thread strong enough to be woven. Without this apparently accidental irregularity on the surface of a hair, it would be impossible to spin cotton thread or to weave cotton cloth; and thus one of the staple manu-factures of one of the greatest nations in the world would not have come into existence, and mankind would have lacked the principal material of their clothing. You see about the end of June, hanging out of the ears of the green corn when it is in flower, slender white filaments tipped with a powdery substance. These are the vital organs by which the grains of corn are formed and filled; and without their agency, the whole produce of the fields would fail, and there would be no bread for man. As it is with these details of nature that seem so insignificant, and yet in reality are so important, so it is with the crown of gold that was round about the ark, and the table of shewbread and the altar of incense, which seems at first an insignificant detail. It was purposely designed by God, and is full of meaning to us. Now what did this feature mean? The word translated "crown" in the text occurs only in connection with the holy vessels of the tabernacle. It means literally a border or rim of wreathed work; and it comes from a root which signifies to bind together. This border or rim was put upon the top of the ark, and of the table of shewbread, and of the altar of incense, projecting a little beyond the sides of these vessels, in order that the objects placed upon them might not slip off. Usually there was no danger of this when the vessels remained in their appointed places in the stationary Tabernacle. But from time to time the Tabernacle had to be taken down when the Israelites required to remove their camp and journey to another place in the wilderness. These vessels had therefore to be transported along with them. But there was this significant distinction between them and the rest of the furniture and frame work of the Tabernacle—that while the other articles were removed in waggons by means of oxen, the holy vessels had to be carried by the hands of man. For this purpose they were furnished with rings at their sides, through which staves were passed, by the help of which the Levites bore them in front of the cavalcade, without daring to touch them. It may be asked why was it of so much consequence that the objects belonging to the sacred vessels should be kept unmoved in their proper places? Look first at the mercy-seat or lid of the ark—why must it not be displaced in the slightest degree? The ark, we know, contained the two tables of stone, on which was inscribed the law which promised life on condition of obedience, but threatened death without mercy against transgression. At Sinai the Israelites entered into a solemn covenant with God which bound them to obedience, and bound God to punish disobedience. But, as we all know, the covenant was speedily broken. The Israelites who, in their ignorant self-confidence, had resolved that "all that the Lord hath said will we do," almost immediately sinned grievously against the Lord, so that Moses broke the first tables of the law, and the law, as the Apostle Paul said, "was found unto death." It ended in the ministration of condemnation. But while the Israelites thus bound judgment upon themselves, God devised an expedient by which the failure and ruin might be remedied. In the midst of wrath He remembered mercy : He commanded the ark to be formed in order that the tables of the law might be put into it, and it might thus shut out of sight the ministration of death. The law was to be carefully preserved, but it was to be no less carefully concealed, so that its ministration of death should not break out in vengeance. The cover of the mercy-seat was put over the ark, so as exactly to fit it. By this expressive symbol it was indicated that mercy triumphed over judgment—that mercy is the deepest element in every judgment, and the end for which it is graciously designed ; the first sentence against our fallen first parents being the key to all other judgments. God, while inflexibly just, could still pardon the sinner. But if by accident or intention the lid of the mercy-seat were to be displaced, the law would have no cover or concealment ; it would break forth and carry out without hindrance the threatened punishment of sin, and all Israel would be destroyed, for they had all sinned, and broken God's commandments. We are told that on one occasion the inhabitants of Bethshemesh looked into the ark while it rested on a great stone in their fields, and many of them were smitten to death in consequence of their unhallowed curiosity. They had removed the mercy-seat and so let loose the law to carry out its threatened vengeance against sin without restraint. Equally important was the use of the crown of gold round about the table of shewbread. That table symbolized the provision which God made for the spiritual wants of His people. The twelve loaves upon it indicated that each tribe had its own portion prepared for it before the Lord, of the same weight and of the same size. The bread was changed from week to week ; for, after remaining during that period in the presence of the Lord, it was afterwards partaken of by the priests, who were thus specially strengthened and refreshed for their service in the Tabernacle. But it was ever the same bread. It was called the "continual" shewbread, because it was always before the Lord. And the object of the golden crown or raised rim round about it, was to keep the shewbread securely in its position on the table, so that it might not fall to the ground, or have its place—which was carefully arranged—altered in the least degree, through the stumbling of the Levites who bore it on their shoulders in their journeys through the wilderness. Unchanged by the wanderings of His people, unhindered by their frequent murmurings and backslidings—the crown of gold around the table of the shewbread kept the bread securely in its place. The mercy-seat kept on the ark by its golden crown indicated God's unchanging mercy ; and the shewbread, kept in its place by the golden crown of its table, indicated God's unvarying care for His people. The crown of gold around the altar of incense was also most significant. The altar of incense was not for sacrifice, for no victim was offered upon it ; it was ordained in order that the fragrance of sweet spices might constantly ascend from it to God. It indicated not atonement for sin, but the cleansing of the sinner from sin, and his acceptance before God. It was ministered to by the priests only. But it was most closely connected with the brazen altar of burnt-offering outside, to which all Israel had access ; for it was through the death of the victim that the sinner was accepted, and through the blood of atonement that he had communion with God. The coals of fire that were put on the incense altar to burn the fragrant spices, were previously taken from the altar of burnt-offering on which the victim had been reduced to ashes. The golden vessel was, therefore, of especial importance, because it indicated the highest priestly ministration. The crown of gold which encircled it at the top was meant to keep the coals of fire and the holy spices on it from being scattered or displaced. Morning and evening and all the night long the priests had to burn incense before the Lord. During the journeys of the Israelites the coals were to remain burning, and the spices were not to be removed. The incense offering was to be continuous and uninterrupted even while the altar was being carried by the Levites from one place to another. There was to be no cessation of the service during the transit. From its top a cloud of fragrance was to rise up constantly to heaven, typifying an ever active unceasing ministry in God's presence. The office of the golden crown was, therefore, to enable the altar to fulfil this important function, to keep the materials of the offering in their proper position while the altar was stationary, or while it was being carried on the shoulders of the Kohathites. Were the live coals to be extinguished, or to fall off the altar, were the cloud of incense to cease travelling onwards with the host of Israel, then there would be no Divine intercession on their behalf. Their murmurings because of the difficulties and privations of the way would have nothing to screen them from the judgment of heaven. The crown of gold around the holy vessels might seem of no use when the Tabernacle was stationary and all its furniture fixed. And yet its very existence testified silently of the faithfulness of God. Looking upon this interesting and significant feature of all the holy vessels, the priests realized that God was not a capricious Being, moved by impulse in regard to the provision which He made for the wants of His people, but was the same yesterday, to-day, and for ever; that the qualities of grace in Him were eternal qualities, and not merely assumed for the occasion. His provision of grace was not one called forth by the necessity of the time, but was pre-ordained and pre-arranged from all eternity. But it was on the march that the active use of the golden crown was called forth. When the vessels were in transit, the crown was indispensable to keep their contents in their places. It was when they were journeying from place to place that the Israelites required most to realize the uninterrupted grace of God, for it was then that they were most inclined to stumble and fail, because of the difficulties and privations of the wilderness. Now, what is the use to us who live under the Christian dispensation of this interesting feature of the Old Testament ritual? It means to us now that God remains true to His original purpose of grace; and that His idea in the creation and redemption of man will yet be realized. God never forsakes the work of His own hands. The Christian Church corrupted its ways and went to awful lengths of worldliness and ungodliness, but still His long-suffering faithfulness opened a vision of hope in the darkest days. Around all the symbols and tokens of His grace is the golden crown of His faithfulness to the primeval promise that the seed of the woman shall bruise the head of the serpent; and He looks forward steadfastly to a time, far over the gulf of ages, when a great salvation shall compensate for all the misery of the world, and Christ shall see of the travail of His soul and be satisfied. And to the individual believer is it not an inspiring thought that the golden crown is still around the mercy-seat; that it is kept ever unshaken amid all his stumblings and backslidings by God's unchanging purpose of love? Mercy that endureth for ever has been established on the ground of everlasting righteousness. You who believe in Christ are not under the law, but under grace; and God is not merely pitiful and merciful, but faithful and just to forgive all your iniquities. How comforting, too, is the thought that the golden crown is ever around the table of shewbread, securing and maintaining unshaken all your blessings in Christ! Having given you His own Son, God with Him will freely give you all things. And lastly, how comforting is the thought that around the altar of incense is ever the golden crown; assuring you that the sweet savour of Christ's name, and the very person of the once crucified but now glorified Redeemer, are ever a fragrant memorial on your behalf in the presence of God! Jesus Christ ever liveth to make intercession for you. (*H. Macmillan, D.D.*)

Vers. 17–22. **Put the mercy-seat above upon the ark.**—*The ark and the mercy-seat :*—It was a leading and distinctive feature of Jewish worship that no image was to represent Jehovah, and yet the Jews were taught that the omnipotent God resided specially in the Tabernacle, or Temple, of their nation, and special rites and prohibitions guarded it, as if the great King were indeed there. 1. The Jewish holy of holies was empty of any image of Deity, and was entered by the high-priest alone, and by him only once a year. The centre of interest in the room was the ark of God, a chest of acacia wood, about four feet long and two feet six inches broad and deep. It contained the tables of testimony, the written agreement or covenant between God and the people of Israel. 2. That was not all. The lesson taught at Sinai was not all that the Jewish ark taught, for the ark had a lid or covering known as the "mercy-seat." Inside the ark and below was the law; above and upon the ark was that vacant space associated, through the sprinkling of blood, with the covering or forgiving of the people's transgressions; and with this seat of mercy and pardon above, rather than with the seat of law below, the presence of God was associated. The material arrangements taught the Jews great spiritual lessons: (1) That the law had been broken. (2) That mercy prevails over law. (3) That the mercy-seat needed to be sprinkled with blood. (*T. M.*

Herbert.)   *The mercy-seat; its symbolic substance :*—Although there is but one piece of beaten—or very pure and malleable gold—yet the plate, or lid of the chest, is obviously distinguished from the cherubim; and therefore let us treat them severally. I. It is obvious that the deposit of the tables in the body of the ark is no guaranty of their protection and safety, so long as there is no cover to it. The precious contents are still exposed, though nearly surrounded with golden walls. But place on it this plate of solid gold, of adequate thickness, and of length and breadth fully commensurate with the chest itself, and of course with the tables within, and you complete the idea of protection and safety. What then does this shield of protection physical represent in the typical or symbolical substance ? The answer cannot be mistaken ; Jesus Christ is the Protector and Fulfiller of law. He only does all things well. Thus it becometh us to fulfil all righteousness. He is the Lord our Righteousness. 1. The law prohibits certain things from being done ; and it must be specially noted, that the Decalogue presents law to us in the negative form chiefly ; eight of the Ten Commandments are formal negations, yet involving substantial affirmatives. A ninth also, viz., the Fourth Commandment, is largely a negation. The Fifth alone is purely affirmative. In this form our Redeemer fulfilled all law ; He did no evil, nor was guile found in His mouth. 2. But the Divine law is not a mere negation. Law is positive. It requires active exercise of all the talents bestowed, and it exhibits positive benefits as the rewards of active obedience. Thus did our Redeemer fulfil law. The only positive word of the ten, He observed rigidly—He was obedient to His parents until He began to be about thirty years of age. Equally full and complete was His compliance with all positive requirements of law. As is the mercy-seat to the material substance of the tables, so is Christ to the moral and spiritual substance of the inscribed law. II. We proceed with the cherubim. "The generic meaning of the Hebrew word cherub, the plural of which is cherubim, is not settled with certainty. Some critics refer it to an Arabic source, and infer the meaning to be nearness, contiguity—hence, a minister or servant ; and thus cherubim are the servants of God. Others deduce it from two Arabic words which signify 'as' or 'like to a boy.' " They are most probably correct who form the word from a Hebrew term that means to ride (raukab) by an interchange of two of the letters. We have the original and the derived word brought into immediate connection in Psa. xviii. 10 : " The Jehovah rode upon a cherub, and did fly." With a very slight modification, the word here translated, rode, is used to signify the car or vehicle of the cherub, in 1 Chron. xxviii. 18. What then are the Mosaic or Sinaitic cherubim designed and adapted to set forth ? 1. They spring from the mercy-seat, are a unit with it, and are upheld by it. Here are symbolized—(1) The issuance of the messengers of salvation from the Saviour Himself. (2) They are of the same piece of gold ; this teaches the official unity of Christ and His ministry. (3) Permanent and constant dependence ; as the cherubim rest their weight on the mercy-seat, so ministers of the gospel depend upon Christ. 2. They have the human form and face. These proclaim the intelligence and kindly sympathies of the men who minister in holy things. 3. They have the lion-face—the courage necessary to meet and defy danger and death. 4. They have the ox-face—patient endurance of labour and toil. 5. They have the eagle-face—symbol of intelligence and lofty aims. 6. They have the wings, which spread out over the mercy-seat, and betoken their readiness and ability to waft to all the world the glad tidings, that the law has been fulfilled and justification secured to all who believe in their jewel-crowned King. 7. They have their faces turned downward to the mercy-seat and the law it covers. This indicates their chief study of these things, into which the angels desire to look. 8. Their faces are turned inward, which teaches the restrictions and limitations of that dispensation ; whereas those of Ezekiel and John turn outward and in all directions ; because the times referred to by their ministry are aggressive; the Sinai restrictions of the Abrahamic covenant—that middle wall of partition is broken down and the Abrahamic covenant goes forth to make Abraham the father of many nations, the heir of the world. *(George Junkin, D.D.)*   *The gospel under the law :*—I. WE HAVE HERE THE VERY CORE OF THE SYMBOLICAL ORDINANCES OF THE JEWISH CHURCH. At this point all the interest of the dispensation is concentrated. The days of that people's life as a spiritual community all array themselves around that day, when their high-priest, their daysman—who represented their nation in shadow, as Christ, in substance, represents the world—entered that inner sanctuary with the incense of his people's prayers and the blood of his people's sacrifice, and received commission from the Lord God who dwelt between the cherubim, to lay the sins of the nation on a victim, who should bear them into the wilderness away. Here, then, is the focus of the spiritual power of the dispensation, I mean its power to order man's spiritual relations with all things and with God. And hither, to this mercy-seat above the ark, we are to look—if my principle, that this is a typical people, typical of you and me, be a right one—for those elements of the good word of God to the men of that dispensation, which relate it to the universal gospel of God to man and to all worlds—God's method of "reconciling all things to Himself." II. LET US PASS WITHIN THE SHRINE, AND BEHOLD WHAT IT HAS TO REVEAL. 1. What is the supreme symbol here? The last, the highest, the crown of the whole, is the mercy-seat. And this appears to me to mean more, infinitely more, than a promise of forgiveness, upon certain terms. The fact that with the mercy-seat God completed and crowned the symbolism of the Jewish dispensation; that He only felt it fit to be His habitation and organ of expression when that mercy-seat was set there over the ark; that till then it was a mere shell of a dispensation—as Adam's body was a mere shell of a man until God had breathed into his nostrils the breath of life— but that when the mercy-seat was set, it became capable of entertaining the Divine glory, and became, in fact, inspired; this fact, I say, is the broad, grand declaration to Judaism of the essential nature of God. It was the utterance to that age, of the word which by ten thousand half-articulate voices has been uttering itself to man since the first days of the creation, and has now become fully articulate in Christ— God is love. The truth is the same for them and for us; the substance of the proclamation is the same; the difference lies here, they heard the word, and saw the glory, but "Hereby know we the love of God, because He laid down His life for us." 2. Beneath the mercy-seat, within its bosom, as it were, was the ark of the testimony, and in it the word of the law. The image here reveals a harmony—the tables of stone in the ark, the mercy-seat above it, crowning it, and the glory of the Lord enveloping the whole. The two ideas are inseparable—mercy and righteousness—when we connect them with the Divine name. "Mercy and truth have met together, righteousness and peace have kissed each other," in every manifestation of the love of God to man. 3. The third lesson of the symbol, perhaps the highest, is to be gathered from the contemplation of its unity. We have considered it in its parts, but it is essentially one. An ark, with a mercy-seat above it, the cherubim shadowing both, and the Divine glory, the light which was the sign of God's personal presence, bathing the whole. It tells us that mercy only crowns us fully with its benediction, when the Divine testimonies are hidden within the heart. Man is the true Shekinah. The glory shines from him when the Word is enshrined within him. "Christ is the end of the law for righteousness to every one that believeth." In Him it is no law of words addressed sternly to the understanding, but a law of life shrined lovingly within the soul. (*J. B. Brown, B.A.*) *The mercy-seat :*—There was no seat in the Tabernacle for the priests, because their work was never done. They stood to minister in the holy place. "And every priest standeth daily ministering, and offering oftentimes the same sacrifices, which can never take away sins. But this Man (Christ), after He had offered one sacrifice for sins for ever, sat down on the right hand of God" (Heb. x. 11, 12). The only seat there was belonging to the Tabernacle was the mercy-seat, the throne of God really, where mercy reigned. Mercy signifies goodness bestowed on the unworthy and undeserving. The mercy-seat represented Jesus Christ, "whom God hath set forth to be a propitiation" or mercy-seat, "through faith in His blood, to declare His righteousness for the remission of sins" (Rom. iii. 25). Jesus is the true mercy-seat or throne of grace, where "grace reigns through righteousness unto eternal life" (Rom. v. 21). This is the throne we are urged to approach boldly, that we may obtain mercy and find grace to help in time of need (Heb. iv. 16). God has two thrones, a throne of mercy and a throne of judgment. He now sits on the throne of mercy, dispensing mercy and grace to every one that comes to Him. That seat will soon be removed, and the judgment seat will be put in its place, and God will sit upon it to judge all men according to their works. (*G. Rodgers.*) *The mercy-seat :*—Our mercy-seat, our reconciliation-residence is Jesus, the Divine Saviour, the God-man mediator. And all the typical teachings of this branch of our subject may be drawn out in the attempt to answer one question, viz.: What sort of a mercy-seat have we in Christ? I. In replying to this inquiry, I desire to show that we have in Christ, in the first place, AN AUTHORIZED MERCY-SEAT. He who occupies this mercy-seat is "a just God and a Saviour." No violence is done to any principle of honour, or of justice in the government of the universe by the dispensing of grace from this mercy-seat. The Divine law is magnified and made honourable. Every attribute of the Divine character is vindicated. II. But I observe secondly of the mercy-seat which we are bidden to approach in Christ that it is an ENCOURAGING MERCY-SEAT. Christ, in the glory of His finished righteousness, is the medium through which God looks at all His believing children. He sees them only " in the face of His anointed." Hence it is said of believers in Christ that " they are righteous " in God's sight, " even as He," *i.e.*, Christ " is righteous." III. But thirdly I observe respecting this mercy-seat that it is FULL OF PRIVILEGE FOR THE PRESENT. Suppose you were travelling in a foreign land. You are cut off from intercourse with all whom you most love on earth. There is only one channel through which you can hear from home, and obtain the supply of all that is necessary to meet your daily wants. How precious that channel of communication would be to you! How you would prize it! How anxious and careful you would be to keep it open! The thought of having it interrupted, or cut off, would be insupportable to you. Yet this is but a faint image of the Christian's position here in the world, and of the relation of the mercy-seat to Him. IV. There is only one other point of view from which we may glance at the mercy-seat, and thus contemplated it shines before us as BRIGHT WITH HOPE FOR THE FUTURE. Hith rto it has always been true of Jehovah that, "verily He is a God that hideth Himself." But the time cometh, when of all that pertains to the character and work of God, it may be said, " There hath been nothing hid that will not be made manifest." " What we know not now we shall know hereafter." The true Shekinah upon the mercy-seat will have no single dark point connected with it. Over all its outspread surface the cloud will be lighted up with the splendours of Divinity. You have often seen a mass of clouds in the western sky, unillumined by the sun's rays, as the day was drawing to a close. You know how dark and unattractive that mass appeared. But presently you see the sun pass behind it, and what a wondrous transformation is wrought in its appearance! How radiant the whole mass becomes! How every point in it glows and sparkles with the splendours of the sun that shines through it! So will it be with the cloud upon our mercy-seat. When Jesus was on earth the coarse garments of humanity were upon Him. Then the shekinah cloud was dark. But the redeemed shall look upon that cloud again amidst the glory of the heavenly kingdom. Then all darkness will have passed away. The sun of uncreated Deity will be pouring all its brightness through it. (*R. Newton, D.D.*) *The mercy-seat :*—I. THE DESIGN OF THE APPOINTMENT. " And there I will meet with thee." Meeting with God—communion with God ; and instruction from God—these are in the text the declared purposes of the solemnities observed before the ark, and they are also the great objects to be always associated with the public assemblies of the Christian Church. II. SOME OF THE PECULIARITIES OF THIS INSTITUTION.—1. It was altogether of Divine appointment. 2. Another significant fact is that the name " mercy-seat " is manifold in its meaning. By St. Paul, in Romans iii. 25, the mercy-seat is called a propitiation. The mercy-seat is the place of propitiation, whither the sacrificial blood was carried, and the red showers were cast around by God's high priest. " There I will meet with thee," saith the Divine word. Only through a sacrifice can God be approached. The mercy-seat is also called a " covering," because, as it concealed in the thick darkness the contents of the ark, it so became an emblem of the completeness of the process of Divine forgiveness (Psalm xxxii. 1). The Hebrew word for the mercy-seat is Capporeth, derived from Caphar, a covering, the word which, in Genesis vi. 14, represents God as directing Noah to pitch the ark within and without. About eighty times the word is used in the Old Testament, and is rendered in our version atone, or atonement. Thus early, even, as the ministry of Noah, the doctrine of shelter through substitution was preached to the world. The position occupied by the mercy-seat is equally significant ; it was "upon the ark," within which was contained the handwriting of God —the covenant; the promises of God, and His requirements. III. THE SPIRITUAL BLESSINGS WHICH WERE TYPIFIED BY THE MERCY-SEAT. 1. To the mercy-seat we must resort to obtain the assurance of the forgiveness of sin. 2. To the mercy-seat we repair in all times of trial and distress. So long as communion with God is unimpaired we have a specific for all human woe. 3. Thither also we repair for renewed supplies of grace and strength. We can only rightly perform our work for the Lord, as we obtain from Him fresh impartations of heavenly power. 4. It is thither that we must by faith bear the wants of the Church and the world. (*W. G. Lewis.*) *The mercy-seat :*—I. CONSIDER THE TYPICAL PROPERTIES OF THE MERCY-SEAT. 1. It was intended as a covering to the ark, the latter being overlaid, and the former made of pure gold. In the ark, covered with the mercy-seat, were deposited the two tables of the law, given to Moses at Mount Sinai. This rich and splendid symbol afforded a striking representation of the incomparable worth and excellence of the Saviour, who in due time should become the true propitiatory. The way of salvation by the cross of Christ, agrees with the strictest principles of justice ; and to justice and equity it is frequently ascribed, as well as to the richest grace (Psa. l. 5, 6 ; Isa. i. 27 ; Rom. iii. 25). 2. As the mercy-seat covered the ark, so the cherubims of glory covered, or as the apostle expresses it, overshadowed the mercy-seat. To this the apostle Peter seems to allude, when he speaks of the angels as looking with eager expectation into the wonders of human redemption (1 Pet. i. 12). The holy angels love the Redeemer, worship Him, and rejoice in the reconciliation of sinners to God through Him. 3. The mercy-seat, and cherubims overshadowing it, formed a glorious throne, in which the Shekinah or visible presence of the Deity resided ; and hence the Lord is said to dwell between the cherubims (Psa. lxxx. 1 ; Isa. xxxvii. 16). Thus all the gracious manifestations of the Divine nature are through the Redeemer. 4. The most solemn acts of worship, under the Levitical dispensation, had a more immediate reference to the mercy-seat. All of which prefigured the substitution of Christ in the sinner's stead, the necessity of His atonement, and the bearing away of the sins of His people which were laid upon Him. 5. The mercy-seat was the fountain of all good to Israel ; from hence proceeded their choicest blessings. There it was that God gave an audience to His people, and a favourable answer to their prayers, through the medium of an intercessor ; and though they were not permitted personally to approach, yet all their supplications were directed towards it. Nor can a word of mercy or of peace be heard, or any prayers be answered, but through Christ, who is our mercy-seat. II. THE PRIVILEGES CONNECTED WITH THE MERCY-SEAT, AS THE MEDIUM OF APPROACH TO GOD : " There will I meet with thee, and I will commune with thee." 1. " I will meet with thee," saith the Lord. Not as He once met Moses at the inn, and sought to slay him ; nor as the angel met Balaam, with a drawn sword in his hand ; nor as the Lord once threatened to meet with Ephraim, as a bear bereaved of her whelps. But as an affectionate parent or tender friend, which implies a drawing nigh on one part, and sensible manifestation on the other. 2. " I will commune with thee." Communion generally denotes that tender intercourse which one person has with another ; and here it is expressive of that sacred fellowship which subsists between God and His people. This puts the greatest honour upon the creature, and discovers the most amazing condescension on the part of God. (*B. Beddome, M.A.*) *Lessons :*—1. Is there a mercy-seat ? and may we bring our sins, our wants, and sorrows to it ? Oh, let us avail ourselves of the inestimable privilege. A seat of mercy in a fallen world ! how does this bespeak the character and benignity of God ! Why will ye die ? 2. Is it possible to realize communion with the Holy One in our present lapsed and miserable condition ? There will I commune with thee, is the promise of His grace. Let then the children of God seek the closest intimacy with the Father of their spirits. The glorious brightness of the eternal Godhead is attempered to our enfeebled powers in the human sympathies of the man Christ Jesus. His bosom is the bosom of a friend. 3. Will the Lord open unto us His word, and reveal unto us the purposes of His love ? Yes ; He will do so, if ye will wait in meditative and prayerful expectation upon Him (Psa. lxii. 5). 4. Amidst the painful bereavements and separations we are often called to experience here, may we entertain a well-grounded confidence of a blessed re-union in eternity ? Assuredly we may. All Israel had but one seat of mercy : God in Christ is also the sinner's friend and the mourner's comforter. In meeting Him, we meet each other in Him. All the sun's bright rays of light centre in a common focus : all believers are but the several radiations of a single Saviour, and all will converge to that central Lord again. (*W. Mudge.*) *The cherubim :*—The etymology of the word *cherub* being lost, the name renders us no assistance in the interpretation of the symbol. It is noteworthy, however, that Ezekiel applies to similar composite figures the appellation "living creatures"; and St. John a similar designation, unfortunately translated "beasts." Following this clue, we inquire if there is anything in the composite form itself to carry us onward in this line of interpretation. The cherubs of the Tabernacle are not described in the specifications, but mentioned as if the form were already so well known as to need no delineation for the sake of the general reader. Doubtless the artists were furnished with minute directions. The living creatures seen by Ezekiel are described by him with considerable amplification (chap. i. 5-25). They were compounded of four animals—ox, lion, eagle, man,—each excelling in some one life-power. The combination suggests a being, real or ideal, uniting in himself the qualities in which these four different manifestations of life are severally eminent. The human form is the ground-work of the composition; and the additions to it are suggestive of an improvement on man by adding to his faculties those in which other animals are his superiors; as, *e.g.*, the power of vision and motion peculiar to the eagle, the strength of the lion, and the submission of the ox. The cherubs seen by St. John in the Apocalypse were different in appearance from those described by Ezekiel, each having for its ground-form one of the four animals already mentioned; but the recurrence of these four, notwithstanding this diversity, confirms the deductions already stated. The idealization of earthly creatural life by the combination of its highest manifestations was projected into shape as a composite animal figure, not constant in form, but varying as one element or another prevailed in the ideal conception. The presence of all these four animal forms in the visions both of Ezekiel and of John, renders it probable that the four were wholly, or in part, contained in the cherubic figures of the Tabernacle. Was, then, this idealization of life designed to represent beings actually existing in the high grade of life, or did it point backward to what man was before the fall, and forward to what he is to be in the restored paradise? There is no passage of Scripture which indisputably teaches the actual existence of beings represented by these composite animal figures. In most cases, cherubs appear in scenes which are plainly symbolic or poetic. The passage in Genesis iii. 24, properly understood, affirms of the cherubs only that they were placed in the east of the garden, or near its entrance, for doubtless Eden, like the Tabernacle in the wilderness, fronted the rising sun. The inference is that they were placed there to have the same significance as they had in the Tabernacle, in the Temple and in the Apocalyptic vision of heaven. If, under the Mosaic and Christian dispensations, these composite figures symbolized humanity redeemed, sanctified, and glorified, probably they had a parallel meaning when employed in the symbolism of earlier times. What they signified in the Tabernacle and in the Temple being the very point to be illuminated, we pass at once from the first scene in the history of redemption where they appear, to the vision of heaven in which a Christian Hebrew beheld these symbolic beings before and around the throne of God (see Rev. v. 9, 10). What clearer evidence than this do we need that the composite animal figures of Hebrew symbolism represented humanity raised from its death in Adam to fulness of life in Christ? They were "living ones" because Christ having died for them, and risen again, had made them partakers of His life. (*E. E. Atwater.*)　　*The cherubim:*—That it cannot be the angels, who are intended by these mysterious representations, is rendered perfectly clear when you consider that they were part and parcel of the ark itself. They were not something placed upon it, or added to it, but they were something made of it, or for it. They were beaten out of the very materials of the ark itself. The same gold which covered the mercy-seat was wrought out into the form of the cherubim. This could have no significancy as applied to the angels. They are indeed "ministering spirits unto the heirs of salvation," but they stand in no such intimate relation to the covenant of redemption as is indicated by the position which the cherubim occupied. There can be no question on this point. It is not the angels who are represented by the cherubim. To whom then, or to what do they refer? They are doubtless to be regarded, not perhaps as actual existences at all, but as symbols of the glorious qualities or attributes of Christ our Saviour, in carrying on the great work of our redemption, and of attributes or qualities which His ransomed people shall share with Him in the glory of His heavenly kingdom. Let us look then at the qualities indicated by the four-fold faces of the cherubim. 1. The first is the face of a man. This stands before us as the natural, and admitted index of knowledge, or intelligence. And this we know is a quality or attribute which Christ, in His position as our Redeemer, the crowning glory of our ark of the covenant, possesses in the fullest measure. "In Him are hid all the treasures of wisdom and knowledge." 2. But the cherubim are representative of our humanity in its glorified state. And looking at it from this point of view we may gaze upon the "face of a man" in this mysterious symbol till it seems to have a voice and utterance, and to speak to us in eloquent terms of the grand disclosures, the marvellous unfoldings, of what are now hidden things, awaiting us in that bright world to which we are hastening. 3. The second face which the cherubim bore was "the face of a lion." Two qualities are here indicated, viz., courage and majesty. Now the great Captain of our salvation, in the campaign which He undertook, when He resolved to put down the rebellion which had broken out in this province of His Father's dominions, afforded the grandest exhibition of this noble quality which the world or the universe has ever witnessed. And this quality is a characteristic of redeemed humanity as well as of Him who redeemed it. It applies to true Christians even now. "The righteous are bold as a lion," says the wise man. But it will apply to them much more truly hereafter. It is said of them that—"they shall have boldness in the day of judgment." But "the face of the lion" was indicative of majesty as well as courage. This is the halo round Christ's character—the radiance formed by this shining forth of His own glory. He is "the brightness of the Father's glory, and the express image of His person." But this is a quality, too, which will mark the condition of the redeemed, in the glory of their future state. True, with them it will not be an inherited, but an imparted quality. In themselves, of their own, they have nothing attractive, or majestic. But they do have that imparted to them, by their glorious Lord, which makes them so. 4. The third face which the cherubim bore was "the face of an ox." The quality which this represents is, manifestly, that of strength for service. This, we know, is a glorious attribute of our Divine Redeemer. It is one which He possesses, too, in absolute perfection. But it symbolized the same quality as marking the condition of His people in that glorious kingdom to which it is His gracious purpose eventually to bring them. It is the covenant privilege of the redeemed, even now, in the imperfection of this fallen state, to be "strong in the Lord, and in the power of His might." They "take hold of His strength," and this enables them to mount up with wings as eagles, to "run and not be weary, to walk and not faint." But the ark, and the cherubim upon it, point us onward to the heavenly world. It is a quality, or property, of redeemed humanity in the glory of the resurrection state to which the symbol now before us refers. There will then be bliss in every service, and rest in every motion. 5. The last face associated with this mysterious symbol was "the face of an eagle." Now, one of the things for which an eagle is remarkable, is its keenness of vision. And all the power, or quickness of vision, which the eagle possesses is but a symbol of a corresponding attribute of character pertaining to Christ. His eyes are in every place. "He seeth the end from the beginning." He knoweth our necessities before we ask. 6. But how does this apply to the redeemed in the glory of their future state (see Heb. vi. 5)? which certainly refers to faculties, attributes, or qualities, mental, moral, or physical, to be possessed by the redeemed of Christ amidst the glory and blessedness of the world to come. Again, when I read Isaiah xxxiii. 17, I feel that, if I am a believer in Jesus, I have here a promise, in symbol, of such an enlargement of perceptive faculty and power of vision as quite passes my capacity at present to comprehend. 7. But quickness of motion, or speed of flight is another characteristic quality of the eagle. And this we know is a quality which strikingly marks the character of Christ in carrying on the work of our redemption. It was so when He was on earth. What He did for those who sought His gracious intervention, He did quickly. This quality marks His character still. It is only by the practical development of it that He can make good His word when He engages in one place to be to all His people "a very present help in trouble"; and in another to be always "a God at hand, and not afar off"; or when, in still another place, His promise runs—"Before they call I will answer, and while they are yet speaking I will hear." It is clearly manifest how "the face of the eagle" upon the cherubim points to this feature of our Lord's character. 8. But what bearing has this on the position of the redeemed in glory? I answer, a very natural and necessary bearing. It teaches us that quickness of motion, or speed of flight, will be a characteristic of that state. (*R. Newton, D.D.*)   *The cherubim :—*It is very instructive to observe that the first time we read about the cherubim is in Gen. iii. 24, where they are seen with flaming swords guarding the way to the tree of life, and ready to destroy any man who might be bold enough to try and force his way through to that tree; and the next time we read of them is in (Exod. xxv.), where they are guarding the throne of mercy; and here, blessed be God, they hold no flaming swords in their hands, but they are bending over the mercy-seat, and looking at the blood sprinkled there. They are not looking under the mercy-seat; there was the law, the ministration of death. They do not turn their faces eastward and look out at the people; had they done so, they would have beheld a multitude of sinners : but they look at that which conceals and covers up the ministration of death. Their eyes are fixed on the propitiation for sin—on that which is an atonement for sin. They are looking at Jesus; there they find their joy and rest. And I would look where they look: my mind would be occupied with that which gives joy to the highest rank of angels, the ministers who stand nearer to the throne of God than any other beings in the universe. (*G. Rodgers.*) **There I will meet with thee.**—*Meeting with God :*—I. To the Jews, GOD SET APART ONE SPECIAL PLACE FOR SACRIFICE, ONE SPECIAL PLACE FOR CLOSEST COMMUNION, AND HE WHO WANTED SOME DIRECT ORACLE FROM GOD MUST GO TO THAT SPOT TO GET HIS ANSWER. The oneness continues, but now it is not oneness of spot, but it is oneness of path. And there the spot lies, at the end of the path—it is one path. All the oneness of the types of the Mosaic law go to make the oneness of the Lord Jesus Christ. And as on that one grand spot, "between those cherubims," God declared He would meet and commune with Israel, so now, at that one spot, Christ, God covenants that He will meet with you, and commune with you. Christ is God's mercy-seat. Christ is the gold of His Deity, and the wood of His humanity, and all to enshrine, to keep the law, the law for man. In after times, two other things were placed in the ark, of which we will not speak now—the rod of Aaron, emblem of the eternal priesthood of Christ, and the pot of manna, showing that Christ is the bread and the nourishment, the sustenance of His people in the journey of life. II. IT WAS UPON SUCH A MERCY-SEAT, GOD SAID, "I WILL MEET WITH THEE, AND COMMUNE WITH THEE." You see, then, that your interviews with God, your holy communings, depend upon the Lord Jesus Christ. According to your views of Christ, according to your nearness to Christ, so will be your experience here in private of communion with God. Accustom yourself to lay out in order the ark, and all that went to make that mercy-seat, and that glory, and those communings. And the more you lay out in order before your mind the attributes, and the glory, and the work of Jesus, the more you will hear still small voices, the more you will enjoy those "times of refreshing," the more God will reveal Himself to you as He does not to the world, the more you will "acquaint yourself with Him, and be at peace." If you have not real communion with God, the reason lies simply there—Christ is not in His place —the ark is not set up—you are not honouring Christ—you have low views of Christ—you have been looking at wrong things—you are expecting communion apart from your Saviour. III. THERE COULD BE NO TRUE THRONE OF GOD IN THE WORLD, IF MERCY WERE SEPARATED FROM JUSTICE. But now it is just in God to be merciful, because of the deep things that that ark tells us. Therefore if any of you are worshipping God in fear, if there are any downcast and depressed, any who think they hear condemning sounds, any to whom God presents Himself in the light of a Master, One whom they fear, remember, God sits upon a mercy-seat. It is in mercy He communes with you. He has no word but mercy. Judgment is a strange word. He loveth mercy—mercy dwells with God—it is all mercy. Go to Him for mercy, let it be a poor sinner communing with his God upon a mercy-seat. (*J. Vaughan, M.A.*) *Community between God and man :*—I. That in Christ we meet with God as a Being of IMMUTABLE RECTITUDE. In Christ the moral law was— 1. Perfectly embodied ; 2. Powerfully enforced. II. That in Christ we meet with God as a Being disposed to EXERCISE CLEMENCY. 1. Christ is the highest expression of God's mercy. 2. Christ is the greatest demonstration of God's mercy. 3. Christ is the mightiest agent of God's mercy. The messenger of infinite love. III. That in Christ we meet with God as THE LORD OF ANGELIC INTELLIGENCES. (*Homilist.*) *The mercy-seat :*—I. In the mercy-seat, or in Christ, we meet the LAW OF GOD. 1. Christ gives a new view of law. 2. Christ introduces a new relation in reference to law. 3. Christ creates in His people an affection for the law. II. In the mercy-seat, or in Christ, we meet the MERCY OF GOD. 1. The atonement of Christ is the medium for the exercise of mercy. 2. The atonement of Christ is the evidence of the value of mercy. III. In the mercy-seat, or in Christ, we meet the GLORY OF GOD. 1. This may be applied to the very essence of God. 2. Christ in the Scriptures is represented as reflecting the moral attributes of God. IV. In the mercy-seat, or in Christ, we meet the ANGELS OF GOD. (*Caleb Morris.*) *Condition of communion with God :*—Birds cannot converse with men unless they had a rational nature put into them, nor can men converse with God unless, being made new creatures, they partake of the Divine nature. Communion with God is a mystery to most ; every one that hangs about the court doth not speak with the king ; all that meddle with holy duties and, as it were, hang about the court of heaven, hath not communion with God ; it is only the new creature enjoys God's presence in ordinances, and sweetly converses with Him, as a child with a father. (*T. Watson.*)

Vers. 23–30. **Set upon the table shewbread.**—*The table of shewbread :*—I. The first lesson we learn here is taught us by THE NATURE OF THE BREAD UPON THE TABLE

This we know, on the very best authority, was a symbol of Christ. Jesus taught us this distinctly and clearly when He said, "I am the Bread of Life." That bread upon the table points to Jesus. How apt a type, or emblem of Him, it was! The bread was a prepared substance. A compound substance. A necessary substance. As suitable as necessary. II. Our second lesson is furnished by observing THE WAY IN WHICH THIS BREAD WAS MANIFESTED. Two things were required to this end, viz., the light which shone from the golden candlestick, and the table to lift up, or elevate the bread so that it could be distinctly seen. If the candlestick were not lighted, and casting forth its illuminating beams, the bread might be upon the table, but darkness would envelope it. The officiating priest could never see it. And so it is only the light of revelation, the illuminating influence of the Holy Ghost, which can make manifest Christ, the true bread from heaven, to the souls of famishing sinners. III. The third lesson it teaches us is suggested by THE ABUNDANCE OF THE SUPPLY placed upon it. The table bore twelve loaves. There was one for each of the tribes. No part of God's family was overlooked, or neglected, in the symbolical provision thus made for their necessities. And what was true, in this respect, of the symbol, is equally true of the thing symbolized. Jesus, whom the bread upon the golden table represented, is an infinite Saviour. The resources of His sufficiency are exhaustless. IV. We are taught a lesson by the TIME FOR THE RENEWING of the bread upon it. By an ordinance of God this was always to be done upon the Sabbath. Thus God would put honour upon the Sabbath, and associate it, in the minds of His people, with the thought of obtaining the supply of their spiritual necessities. V. We learn a lesson from the continual FRESHNESS of the bread set out upon it. Christ never grows old. His people are often weary of other things; they grow weary of themselves—weary of their sins and sorrows, and weary of the world and its vanities—but they never, never grow weary of Jesus. Having once eaten of the bread which He gives, which He constitutes, it is literally true that they "never hunger" for the husks the world can offer. VI. We gather our sixth and last lesson from THE COVERING OF FRANKINCENSE WHICH WE SEE SPREAD OUT OVER THE TOP OF THE BREAD. When we remember that these loaves were a figure of Christ, and that frankincense is a token of that which is pleasing, or grateful, we seem to have exhibited, in beautiful symbol before us, the acceptableness of Christ and His work to the Father. (*R. Newton, D.D.*)   *The table in God's house:*—"Table," gives us the idea of fellowship, social intercourse, friendship, satisfaction; all which we find in the house of God. "Truly our fellowship is with the Father, and with His Son Jesus Christ." What a sacred privilege it is to eat bread in the presence of God. And not only to eat in His presence, but to eat the "Presence Bread." "He shall eat the bread of his God, both of the most holy and of the holy." At God's table there is social intercourse. The saints commune one with another and all commune with God. "We are all partakers of that one bread." Sweet is the intercourse of God with His people at the table of His grace. It is a proof of friendship. "I have eaten my honeycomb with my honey; I have drunk my wine with my milk: eat O friends; drink, yea, drink abundantly, O beloved." Here we find sacred satisfaction. "I will abundantly bless her provision. I will satisfy her poor with bread." "They shall be abundantly satisfied with the fatness of Thy house." "The meek shall eat and be satisfied." "Thou preparest a table before me in the presence of mine enemies: Thou anointest my head with oil, my cup runneth over." There is no stint where God is the host. In His house there is bread enough and to spare. He fills our cup to overflowing with consolation, and with joy. Those who dwell in God's house will never come to an empty table, nor find God absent from His throne of mercy. "Surely goodness"—to supply my wants—"and mercy,"—to pardon my sins—"shall follow me all the days of my life: and I will dwell in the house of the Lord for ever." (*R. E. Sears.*)   *The tables of grace and glory:*—The incorruptible wood may be an emblem of grace, the gold an emblem of glory. God's table on earth is the table of His grace. His table in the heavenly world is the table of His glory. If we are guests at the table of grace, we shall be entertained at the table of glory. Grace is glory begun. Glory is grace perfected. Grace is the earnest of our inheritance. Glory is the possession of the estate. By grace we are prepared for glory. When the work of grace is completed, we shall hear the welcome, "Come up higher." By faith we sit at the table of grace. At the table of glory faith will be changed to sight. Both tables are furnished with the same provision. Christ the true Bread of Life is the spiritual food of the believer on earth : and in heaven we shall eat the same Divine celestial Bread. "The Bread of God" is the nourishment of the spiritual life ; and it is the joy of the eternal life. (*Ibid.*)　*The table of shewbread :*—Made of acacia wood, and plated with gold, it was three feet long, one foot and six inches wide, two feet and three inches high. Around its verge was an ornamental cincture of solid gold, similar to that which adorned the ark. Beneath this was a border of wood four inches and a half wide, plated, of course, with gold, and adorned with another crown of gold. The table was furnished with golden rings at the corners, and with staves which were put through these rings when the table was to be carried on the shoulders of the Levites, but removed when the tabernacle had been erected in a new encampment, and the bearers had deposited their burden in its appointed position. The rings were attached at the same height as the wooden border; but the specifications do not intimate how far above the ground this was affixed. (*E. E. Atwater.*)　*The shewbread, &c. :*—The table was furnished with two dishes for bread, two for frankincense, and probably two for wine. Twelve flat loaves of bread in two piles, constantly stood on it, fresh loaves being brought every Sabbath, and the loaves which were removed being eaten by the priests only. The number of the loaves doubtless indicates that the whole covenant people, the twelve tribes of Israel, were to participate in this offering to their covenant God. On the top of each pile was a dish of frankincense, and near by were cups of wine, as seems probable from the description of the dishes as suitable to pour with (ver. 29 margin). The Septuagint calls them bowls and cups; and the Jewish tradition is, that they contained wine for a libation or drink-offering, such as accompanied every food-offering at the altar in the court. The table of shewbread was in some sense an altar, being the appointed place where certain offerings to Jehovah were to be placed before Him. The materials of these sacrifices were the same as those of the food-offerings and drink-offerings in the court. Corn and wine, or bread and wine, being the product of the life-work of the Hebrews, represented, in the symbolism of the Tabernacle, the fruit of work in the higher sphere where one labours not for perishable food, but for that which endureth unto everlasting life. This is the true bread from heaven of which wheat, manna, and other kinds of food, are figures; it is not only the life-product of those who have been born again, but their chief enjoyment, the sufficient reward of all their labour. Knowing, however, that God has even more desire for the sanctification of His people than they themselves have, they wish Him to enjoy with them the fruits of this spiritual husbandry. It is this fellowship of God with His people in the enjoyment of their sanctification which the shewbread represents. (*Ibid.*)　*Significance of the golden table :*—May not the golden table point to the abundant supply of good things prepared in the heavenly temple, for all those whom Christ will make kings and priests unto God for ever? There a table is spread before His face, that is continually furnished with new wine and heavenly manna, with which the ransomed of the Lord will be refreshed, and made glad : "In Thy presence is fulness of joy ; at Thy right hand there are pleasures for evermore." (*W. Brown.*)　*The shewbread :*—The bread was made of fine flour (Lev. xxiv. 5–9), and was unleavened. Twelve cakes, in piles of six each, always stood on the table ; hence it was called the perpetual bread. It was also named the bread arranged in order, the meaning of which is obvious. Its more significant name we will notice presently. On the top of each pile was placed frankincense, probably in the cups we have spoken of. It is thought by some that this frankincense was burned once a week, when the bread was being renewed ; and by others that it was ever burning, which does not appear very likely, as the quantity consumed would be very great ; but there may have been some means by which it was very slowly consumed, and kept always burning ; in that case the holy place would be ever fragrant. The bread was called the " shewbread " (Hebrew, " bread of faces," or " presence bread ") because it was before the symbol of God's presence—the veil only intervening. The bread was renewed every Sabbath by fresh loaves ; those which were removed belonged to the priests, and could be eaten only by them, and in the holy place and nowhere else. All thank-offerings were holy—this one was peculiarly so : "It is most holy unto Him of the offerings made by fire ", (Lev. xxiv. 9). Only the shewbread and the incense offerings were presented in the holy place ; all the other offerings were brought to the brazen altar in the court. The ceremonies connected with all the sacrifices were soon over, except in the case of the shewbread, which was a ceaseless offering. The bread was ever on the table before the Lord. (*Ibid.*)　*The shewbread :*—This bread was made of fine flour. Fine flour is bread-corn which has been bruised until it is smooth and even. Christ is the bread-corn bruised, and in Him there is no roughness or unevenness. In us there is much unevenness ; we are soft and smooth one day, and changed and rough the next. But it was not so with Christ. The circumstances in which He was placed were ever changing, yet He remained always the same—unchanged and unchangeable. Leaven is the emblem of evil: it is a corrupt and a corrupting thing (Matt. xvi. 6–12; Mark viii. 15; Luke xii. 1; 1 Cor. v. 6–8; Gal. v. 9). Christ was before God during the whole of His life, as the bread was before God in the Tabernacle seven days. The number seven is the symbol of perfection; it is a complete period. And as God discovered no leaven in the bread during the time it was before Him on the table, so He found no evil in Jesus during His life on earth; and as the bread was taken from the table and given to the priests, so Christ is given to the saints, the spiritual priests, that they may live on Him. He is our food, our daily bread. And as we must have bread every day on our tables, whatever else of sweet or savoury food we may have beside, so we must have Christ to feed upon every day. We may have many other things and many other friends, but we cannot do without Christ. No one can be healthy and strong who does not get good food; and no soul can be truly healthy that does not feed on Jesus Christ. To eat a book is to consider it well, and to eat the flesh and to drink the blood of Christ is to consider Him with faith and love; it is to receive Him into the heart. This is the soul-refreshing, soul-satisfying, and imperishable food of the Father's house. Feeding on this blessed food will keep us from longing after the husks that swine feed on. In Christ God has provided a feast for fainting and famishing souls; and hungry souls thankfully receive Him, but others turn away. None but priests could feed on this bread (Matt. xii. 4; Mark ii. 26). And a man must now be a priest before he can enter into the true Tabernacle and eat the food of the Father's house. Not even the priests could eat the shewbread outside of the Tabernacle: they must eat it in the holy place (Lev. xxiv. 9). So a man must be holy to find full enjoyment in Christ. Happiness and holiness are twin sisters, and they travel side by side: they are never separated, so you cannot have one without the other. The more we feast on this heavenly bread, the holier and happier we must become. Eating and drinking are acts which one cannot perform for another. The food may be very good, but it does not minister strength and nourishment to my body till I eat it; by this act I make it my own. So we must receive Christ by faith, receive Him for ourselves. (*G. Rodgers.*)

Vers. 31–37. **A candlestick of pure gold.**—*The golden candlestick:*—I. This LIGHT SHINES BECAUSE IT IS LIGHT, WITHOUT EFFORT, SPONTANEOUSLY. If the lamp is kindled it will shine; and so this emblem has its beautiful felicity in that it points, as the highest definition of all Christian men, to the effortless, spontaneous irradiation and streaming out from themselves of the fire that lies within them. Like a light in an alabaster vase, that shines through its transparency and reveals the lovely veining of the stone, so the grace of God in a man's heart will shine through him, turning even the opacity of his earthly nature into a medium for veiling perhaps, but also in another aspect for making visible the light that is in him. II. THE LIGHT WAS DERIVED LIGHT; AND IT WAS FED. We have a priest who walks in His temple and trims the lamps. The condition of the light is keeping close to Christ, and it is because there is such a gap between you and Him that there is so little brightness in you. The candlestick was really a lamp fed by oil; that symbol, as Zechariah tells us, stands for the Divine influence of God's quickening Spirit. III. THE LIGHT WAS CLUSTERED LIGHT. The seven-branched candlestick represented the rigid, formal unity of the Jewish Church. In the New Testament we have the seven candlesticks diverse, but made one because Jesus Christ is in the midst of them. In this slight diversity of emblem we get the whole difference between the hard external unity of the ancient Jewish polity and the free variety in unity and diversity of the Christian Church, with its individual development as well as with its binding association. (*A. Maclaren, D.D.*) *The candlestick:*—Look at the text as typical of Christ and His Church. I. PERFECTION OF LIGHT. He was "the true Light," &c. (John i. 9). He came to shed light on every important subject; to let us know—1. What God is, "in the face of Jesus Christ." To let us know—2. What man is—in his sin, his spiritual relations, his wants, his destiny, &c. To let us know—3. The future—to bring to light life and immortality. II. PERFECTION OF UNION. Branches united to one stem, and both of same material. (*The Study.*) *The candlestick:*—It was composed of a main shaft, with its connecting branches. 1. If these branches represent the Church of Christ, the central shaft may well be regarded as representing Christ Himself. From Christ the Church springs, and by Him it is supported, as the outspreading arms of the candlestick are by its central shaft. The Church is united to Him, and sustained by Him. 2. Notice next the branches of the candlestick. These sprang from the central shaft, and were of the same material with each other, and with it. So it is with Christ and His people. " He who sanctifieth, and they who are sanctified are all of one." 3. Notice next the ornaments upon the candlestick. (1) There were " bowls like almonds " wrought upon it. In these the branches terminated, forming appropriate receptacles for the lamps of the candlestick. The almond, being the first tree to bud in the spring, was a fit type of Him who is " the First-born from the dead." (2) The next ornament was the *knops*. These may have been swelling buds, from which the branches of the candlestick sprang, expressing the idea that these spreading arms owed both their existence and fruitfulness to the parent stem. (3) The other ornaments were the flowers. Natural emblems of beauty, representing spiritual loveliness of Christ's people. Lessons: 1. The necessity of a Divine revelation. Without the light of the candlestick, darkness, the most profound, must have filled the Tabernacle. And just such would have been our condition, spiritually considered, without the light of Divine revelation. Reason, the natural sun in the mental world, can shed no light upon the soul's concerns. There is no window in the soul through which the light of this natural luminary can shine. The priest in the sanctuary could only see his way and discharge his duties by the help of light from the candlestick, and this was light from heaven, a Divine revelation. And it is only by the aid of such a revelation that we can see our way in reference to spiritual things. 2. The benefits of such a revelation. We perceive this the moment we look around us, in the holy place, and observe what the light of the candlestick discloses to our view. See, over against it stands the golden table with its shewbread. The candlestick, with its heavenly light, enabled the priest, as he entered the holy place, to see where to find this bread. He could not have seen it without this light. And so it is only the light of Divine revelation which reveals Christ, the heavenly bread, to souls that are hungering and perishing for the want of it. 3. The perfection of this revelation. Seven lamps. (*R. Newton, D.D.*) *The golden candlestick :*—The candlestick of the Tabernacle was to burn continually in the holy place (Lev. xxiv. 2); continually let us question ourselves with respect to our attainments, state, and prospects. In individuality of character let each one ask—1. Have I seriously and deliberately sought the illumination of my understanding in the things of God from above ? I read, " If thou criest after knowledge, and liftest up thy voice for understanding ; if thou seekest her as silver, and searchest for her as for hid treasures ; then shalt thou understand the fear of the Lord and find the knowledge of God " (Prov. ii. 3–5). Do I thus cry and lift up my voice in supplication for heavenly wisdom ? And is God's Law really better to me than thousands of gold or silver ? The blessing is annexed to the precept; can I expect the one without a compliance with the other ? 2. Am I walking in the light and comfort of the Holy Ghost ? As both a Teacher and a Comforter is the Spirit given. Does He lead me in the way everlasting (Psa. cxxxix. 24), and cheer me with tokens of good (Psa. lxxxvi. 17) ? 3. Do I realize the constant inspection of the Son of Man amidst the congregations of His people ? He walks among the golden candlesticks. Is the preacher free from all unbecoming fear of his fellow-mortals on the one hand, and is there no lurking latent aiming after worldly popularity on the other ? Does the hearer listen as for life, cultivating a child-like spirit before the Lord, and cherishing no needless or refined fastidiousness about voice or manner in the teacher ? (*W. Mudge.*) *Of the golden candlestick :*—The pure gold signified how excellent the Word of God is: " More to be desired are they than gold, yea, than much fine gold (Psa. xix. 10). We are not curiously here to seek the difference of the knops, branches, and flowers, but only to rest in the general—that the candlestick signified the Word. The candlestick had seven branches; it signified the divers gifts bestowed upon His Church by the Word, and John alludeth to the seven branches of this candlestick : " And in the midst of the seven candlesticks one like the Son of Man clothed with a garment " (Rev. i. 13). This was but *typus arbitrarius*, or an allusion ; for the golden candlestick was not made to be a type of the seven Churches of Asia, but it is only an allusion to it. So " the fruit of the righteous is a tree of life " (Prov. xi. 30), here is an allusion only, that it is like to the tree of life. The oil which was in this candlestick was pure oil. " Command the children of Israel that they bring unto thee pure oil olive, beaten for the light, to cause the lamps to burn continually " (Lev. xxiv. 2). This pure oil is called golden oil, or gold for the purity of it, because the oil was bright, clear, and glistering, like gold

(Zech. iv. 12). So "Gold cometh out of the north" (Job xxxvii. 22); that is, fair and clear weather. It was beaten oil, to signify with what pain and travail the Word is prepared, and with patience preached and made to shine in His Church. The Lord commanded to make snuffers of pure gold for the snuffing of the lamps, and snuff-dishes to receive the snuff. He would have the snuff taken from the light, to signify that He would have the Word kept in sincerity and purity; and He would have the snuffers of gold, to teach them to be blameless and holy who are censurers and correctors of others; and He would have the snuff-dishes of gold, to teach them that the covering of the offences of their brethren was a most excellent thing. Lastly, in what manner the priests dressed the lamps. When the lamp was out he lighted it, and when it was not out he dressed it. When the middlemost lamp was out he lighted it from the altar; but the rest of the lamps every one he lighted from the lamp that was next; and he lighted one after another, to signify that one Scripture giveth light to another; and they say in the Talmud that the cleansing of the innermost altar was before the trimming of the five lamps; and the trimming of the five lamps before the blood of the daily sacrifice; and the blood of the daily sacrifice before the trimming of the two lamps; and the trimming of the two lamps before the burning of incense. That the priests should order and trim the lamps signifieth how Christ and His ministers should continually look unto the purity of doctrine and preaching of the light of the gospel from evening to morning in the dark place of this world, "until the day dawn, and the day star arise in our hearts" (Rev. i. 13; 2 Pet. i. 19). (*John Weemes.*) *The candlestick a type of Christ:*—I. IT WAS THE ONLY THING THAT HELD THE LIGHT WHICH ENLIGHTENED THE SANCTUARY! From Christ all the light of grace comes for the benefit of His Church. II. IT HAD SEVEN LAMPS (ver. 37), to signify that perfection of light that is in Christ. III. IT WAS PLACED IN THE SANCTUARY. So is Christ as a glorious light placed in His Church. IV. It had an upright stem, which bore the many branches issuing from it. V. THE BRANCHES WERE ADORNED WITH BOWLS, KNOBS, FLOWERS, &c. So are Christ's ministers adorned with many graces. VI. AARON DRESSED THOSE LAMPS AND RENEWED THEIR OIL DAILY. So our High Priest is the only enlightener of His faithful ministers. VII. THE CANDLE-STICK HAD SNUFFERS AND SNUFF-DISHES OF PURE GOLD; which might figure forth the good and godly discipline of the Church whereby evil persons who hinder its glory are taken away. (*B. Keach.*) *The golden chandelier:*—This consisted of a main shaft with three branches diverging from it on each side. It was made wholly of gold. If hollow, it could hardly have been beaten into shape with the hammer, but must have been cast, perhaps in separate pieces, and afterwards soldered together. The weight of it, including the lamps and a few small utensils used in trimming them, was a Hebrew talent, or about one hundred and thirteen pounds troy; which in gold coin would be equivalent to £5,500. There was a threefold ornamentation in the chandelier, repeated four times in the main shaft, and thrice in each of the branches, described as a bowl, a knob, and a flower, and by some supposed to represent the cup-shaped calyx, the round fruit, and the open blossom of an almond tree. The word translated "flower" signifies, however, a stem; and the order in which the triad is arranged indicates that the first was the flower, the second the fruit, and the third the stem. The three pairs of branches came out of the main stem at the three places of junction between its four sections of calyx, fruit, and stem. On the upper extremities of the chandelier were seven eye-shaped, or almond-shaped lamps; the wick of the middle lamp projecting from its west end, and the wicks of the others from the end of the lamp nearest to the main shaft. These lamps were not fastened to the chandelier, but so placed upon it that the priest could remove them when he came in the morning to extinguish and trim them, and in the evening to light them for the night. But, though not fastened to the stand as a part of it, they had each its appointed place in the row, and never exchanged places. It seems so natural that the row of lamps should have been parallel with the south wall of the Tabernacle, near which it stood, that almost all writers have passed over the testimony of Josephus to the contrary; who is careful to state that "the lamps looked to the east and to the south, the candlestick being placed obliquely." (*E. E. Atwater.*) *Significance of the lamp-stand:*—The light emitted by the lamps may have been sometimes useful to the priests in their ministrations; but their aggregation on one stand, and the significant seven by which the number of them is determined, indicate that they were placed here to assist in the representation of religious thought. Their position with reference to the table suggests the possibility that the light was, in its symbolism, the complement of the shewbread. With this hint in mind, we ask, What is it of which light is the natural emblem? Sometimes it is used for knowledge, and especially for the knowledge of God and His relations to man. Knowledge is light ; and to impart knowledge is to enlighten. But the import of light in Scripture extends beyond the sphere of the intellect into that of the con-science, covering the domain of duty as well as of verity. The children of light are those who obey, as well as perceive, the reality of the invisible and eternal. Hence those who are the light of the world not only impart knowledge to the ignorant, but reproof to the erring. In short, light in Hebrew symbolism, includes holiness, as well as knowledge. The offering of light which the covenant people brought as an accompaniment to the fruit of their life-work was the symbol of sanctified character. The two symbols are mutually complementary. The prayers and the alms of a good man come up as a memorial before God ; and his example, by holding forth the word of life, diffuses an assimilating influence. But this light of holiness man is as unable to produce of himself as is a lamp to shine without oil, and oil is the symbol of the Holy Spirit ; so that the oblation of light which the covenant people presented to Jehovah in the Tabernacle contained in itself a declaration that they were sanctified by the indwelling Spirit of God. The same idea was again brought to view in the number of the lamps ; seven representing a transaction between God and man, and therefore in Mosaism standing for the covenant itself. The illumina-tion was effected by the co-operation of the infinite and the finite ; and the lamps were seven because that is the sum of the numerical signatures of the two parties united in producing the light. The lamp-stand served not merely to bear the lamps, but to assist in the symbolism. It represents the covenant people, the organized community, who by the example of their obedience shine for the illumination of the world. The seven branches indicate that it is not a merely human institution, but that God is in the midst of it. (*Ibid.*) *The light of Christ :*—" A friend told me that the electric light was so much under control that a gentleman had it in his scarf-pin at a meeting to discuss the utility of the new light. When he stepped on to the platform, the gas was lowered ; he then touched two little springs placed on each side of his body, and the brilliant light shone out under his chin, giving light to all around. In a similarly brilliant manner the light of Christ should radiate from every part of living Christians ; their eyes should shine with it, their tongues sparkle with it, their hands should be gentle, and their feet should be swift to let others know about Jesus, the Light of the world." *Increas-ing luminousness the duty of Christ's Church :*—It should grow as rapidly in this grace as it does in any other. The world has advanced in nothing, perhaps, more marvellously than in the betterment of its light-producing contrivances. The improvement made during the last century is very marked. Mankind's lamp one hundred years ago smoked almost as much as it shone. Its wick, being round and bulky, brought up more oil than could be consumed. The first change was to a flat thin wick. This gave a wider surface for the air to act upon. Those particles of carbon which had previously passed off as soot were changed from smoke to flame. The lamp became still more brilliant when the Argand burner was invented. This is cylindrical and hollow. Through its centre rushes a current of air. The flame is thus both enlarged and intensified. The chimney, afterwards added, caused a stronger draught and a fiercer combustion. Mr. Gurney went a step further when he arranged to substitute a current of pure oxygen for common air. The light pro-duced resembled sunshine, and when introduced to the House of Commons, super-seding the two hundred and forty wax candles previously used, rendered it unprecedently bright. Then came coal-gas, and now, last of all, has blazed upon us the electric light, which is veritable lightning. (*J. Brekenridge.*) *A blended radiance :*—The seven-branched candlestick of the ancient Tabernacle and Temple represented the rigid, formal unity of the Jewish Church. We go to the New Testament, and instead of one hard, external unity, represented by that upright stem, and its three arms on each side, we have the seven candlesticks, diverse, but made one because Jesus Christ is in the midst of them. And in that slight diversity of emblem we get the whole difference between the hard, external unity of the ancient Jewish polity and the free variety in unity and diversity of the Christian Church, with its individual development as well as with its binding association. But for all that, the Church is one light. The rings of light in our gas-stands are pierced with a great number of little holes round each circle, but when you light each tiny jet they all run into one. So the highest form of Christian witness is not when a man starts off from his brethren and sets himself alone in a corner, but when he is content to blend his radiance with his brethren's radiance, and not to mind about his own prominence so long as he contributes to the general light of all. (*A. Maclaren, D.D.*) *The golden candlestick* :—Christ and the Church are both seen here. The base and stock, or main pillar, represent Christ. The branches represent the Church of Christ. Jesus was bruised, and His people are bruised. Christ was made "perfect through suffering" (Heb. ii. 10). And the people of God have to be bruised (Phil. iii. 10). It was the duty of the high priest to trim the lamps twice every day, when he came with his golden snuffers and removed any dead material which hindered the light from shining. So Christ, our High Priest, walks among His golden candlesticks, and He has often to apply the snuffers, and to cut off something which hinders the lamp from sending forth its light as it did in times past. When the high priest came with his snuffers he brought the oil-vessel at the same time ; so when Christ removes a something which we love, but which hinders us from giving forth that light which ought to shine out from us, He gives us more of the oil of the Holy Spirit's power and grace, so that our afflictions may really make us brighter and better Christians. We read about snuffers and snuff-dishes in connection with the candlestick, but not a word is said about an extinguisher. No extinguisher was needed, because the light was never to go out. Our High Priest never comes to us to put out our light ; He would have it burn on all the time we remain in the wilderness. Let the Christian remember this, and never mistake the snuffers for the extinguisher. As the candlestick faced the table of shewbread, and so enabled the priests to find their food, it may represent the light of the Holy Ghost which shines on Christ, the true bread. The table is prepared, the food is there, but without the light of the Spirit we shall never find it. We should thank God as much for the Spirit as for the Son, for one will be of no use to us without the other. (*G. Rodgers.*)

Ver. 40. **Their pattern, which was shewed thee in the mount.**—*Heaven's teaching on earth's duties* :—I. That nothing is too trivial for God to notice. II. That we should speak to God about ordinary work, even in our seasons of highest spiritual communion. III. That even slight deviations from God's directions are forbidden. IV. That what we are called upon to do has far more depending upon it than we suppose. (*A. Rowland, LL.B.*) *Purpose in life ; a lesson to the young* :—I. The necessity of a deliberate purpose in life. When an architect, or builder, or engineer, undertakes the construction of a house, the first thing he does is to get perfect his plans, and to be sure they are correct, so that he knows well what the future house, or bridge, or railway, will be like. If he went at his work in a haphazard manner, it would end in failure and disappointment. So with life. II. This purpose of life should be formed on the model shown us by God. 1. The highest life is the holiest life, for it is nearest to the model set us by God. 2. The plan by which we are to mould our temporal concerns is already given us. Look at Mount Sinai for laws to obey; at the Mount of Olives for loving directions : at the Mount of Transfiguration for anticipation, hope of glory; at Mount Calvary for forgiven sin. (*Homilist.*) *The pattern in the mount* :—I. Moses did his work from a plan, and did not get his plan from his work. Reality is prior to the show of itself. There are no planless seeds. A far-reaching plan is the best one. Calculation is better than caprice. We are wiser in the long reach of thought than in the short reach. We are lost in the woods because we have no room for a long look. You say life is short. Better live on the short arc of a long circle than describe a little circle with the same line. Immediate results are meagre results. Plan solidifies. Power is measurable by purpose. Shiftlessness is a name for aimlessness. To-morrow depends on to-day, but to-day depends on to-morrow also. Past and present sustain each other. Plan gives moral safeguard. Adam fell because he had nothing to do, and the first act in the redemptive scheme was to set him to work. Satan recruits his ranks from the vagrants. The apostles were working men. The drifting boat drifts down stream. Young aimlessness is the beginning of old iniquity. Employment is a subsidiary means of conversion. Character, purpose and apprenticeship are not far apart. II. Moses brought down his pattern from the mount. There is a celestial way of doing earthly things. Earthly success is a quotation from overhead. Our ideals are from patterns in the mount. There is something in them we never put into them. Whence are our ideals? We have never seen a perfect thing. What do we mean by using the word? We must go with Moses to the mount for the answer. In nothing do men have so much faith as in their ideals, and there is nothing which it is so hard to explain. We do not make laws, but find them. We cannot enact truth any more than gravity. There may be a myth about Sinai, but it is one we were bound to invent if it never was reality. The problem of life is to make the ideal real. Once it was done in Galilee. The two meet in Jesus. (*C. H. Parkhurst, D.D.*)

CHAPTER XXVI.

VERS. 1–14. **Curtains.**—*The curtains of the Tabernacle:*—I. THAT THE GLORY OF GOD IS HIDDEN TO ALL WHO STAND OUTSIDE JESUS CHRIST. Man cannot surprise God and penetrate His secrets. II. THAT IN CHRIST THE GLORY OF GOD IS MOST BRIGHTLY REVEALED. 1. There is such a thing as regarding Christ from the outside; and then, as the Jews, we see no beauty in Him. 2. There is such a thing as knowing Christ as a great Teacher, a great Example; "the goats' hair curtains hooked with brass." 3. But it is only when we believe in Christ as the Son of God, and rest in Him as such, that we behold the fulness of His glory. The colours are the symbols of the different names of God; blue signifies the special revelation of God, being the colour of heaven and ether; red denotes the highest dignity, majesty, and royal power; crimson is that which fire and blood have in common, and symbolizes, therefore, life in its full extent. In Christ, the love, the life, the beauty, the majesty of God are most brightly expressed. III. THAT IN CHRIST IS EVERLASTING SECURITY AND BLESSEDNESS. (*W. L. Watkinson.*) *The curtains and the coverings:*—I. LET US LOOK AT THE BEAUTIFUL CURTAINS THAT FORMED THE TABERNACLE. 1. If we view the Tabernacle as an emblem of Christ in His incarnation, the beautiful curtains of cunning work were emblematical of the attributes and perfections of Jehovah, "In Him dwelleth all the fulness of the Godhead bodily." Here every perfection meets and shines. 2. These beautifully-wrought curtains were emblems of the perfect graces which adorned the human nature of Jesus. 3. May we not see in this beautiful piece of tapestry the various characters of Christ? Here by faith we behold the Priest and His sacrifice, the King and His golden crown, the Prophet and His teaching, the Mediator and His fulness. Here by faith we behold the Shepherd and His watchful care, the Husband and His everlasting love, the Friend and His faithful counsel. Here in a mystery of grace we may discover the Root and the tree, the Vine and the branches, the Head and the members. 4. The curtains were the same in the holiest as in the holy place. The Church triumphant and the Church militant have the same Christ. 5. These curtains were fastened together by blue loops and taches of gold so as to form one Tabernacle. The loops and taches were exactly over the vail (ver. 33). This may teach us the connection between Christ's work in heaven and His work on earth. 6. These curtains were full of cherubim. May not these cherubim be emblems of believers who are Christ's mystical body? Christ and His members are one. 7. These curtains are emblems of the Churches of Christ adorned with the graces of the Holy Spirit. 8. The loops and golden clasps which united the curtains together show us the place for little deeds of kindness and little deeds of love. Kind words fitly spoken are golden clasps. There is far more power in kind words than some people think. Kind words are very uniting. 9. The Tabernacle was divided into two parts, but it was only one Tabernacle. The saints in heaven and the saints on earth make but one Church. II. WE MAY NOW LOOK AT THE TENT OF GOATS' HAIR, WHICH FORMED A COVERING FOR THE TABERNACLE. The curtains of goats' hair were emblematical of the righteousness of Christ, which is the justification of the Church. These curtains were joined together by clasps of brass. "And he made fifty taches of brass to couple the tent together, that it might be one." Brass is an emblem of strength. "In the Lord shall one say, have I righteousness and strength." "In the Lord Jehovah"—Jehovah Tsidkenu—"is everlasting strength." May we not have an emblem in these two large goats' hair curtains, of righteousness in its twofold aspect? Christ's righteousness imputed is our justification. Christ's righteousness imparted is our sanctification. We cannot have one without the other; they must be in our experience "coupled together." Jesus Christ is our Righteousness and our Sanctification (1 Cor. i. 30). Christ *for* us is our perfect righteousness. Christ *in* us is our perfect sanctification. III. OVER THE TENT WAS A COVERING OF RAMS' SKINS DYED RED. Beautiful emblem of the protecting blood of Christ. IV. ABOVE THE COVERING OF RAMS' SKINS DYED

RED WAS A COVERING OF BADGERS' SKINS. These skins were probably dyed blue. Perhaps a part were dyed purple. If so there would be seen on the outside, as well as the inside, "the blue, purple, and scarlet." This outside covering teaches us that the Church is under the protection of heaven. The blue skins were over the red skins. Heaven only protects the blood marked. "Kept by the power of God." (*R. E. Sears.*) *The beauty of holiness within :*—Observe: 1. As the outside of the Tabernacle was coarse and rough, the beauty all lying within, so those in whom God dwells must labour to be better than they seem to be. Hypocrites put the best side outward, like whited sepulchres, but "the king's daughter is all glorious within" (Psa. xlv. 13); in the eye of the world black as the tents of Kedar, but in the eye of God comely as the curtains of Solomon (Cant. i. 5). Let our adorning be that of the hidden man of the heart which God values (1 Pet. iii. 4). 2. Where God places His glory, He will create a defence; even on the habitations of the righteous there shall be a covert (Isa. vi. 5, 6). The protection of Providence shall always be upon the beauty of holiness (Psa. xxvii. 5). (*A. Nevin, D.D.*) *The curtains :*—The materials used in the manufacture of this fabric were precisely the same as those which formed the vail; a different arrangement, however, is adopted as to the "fine linen." In the vail, the blue first meets the eye; and the fine linen is last in the series. In these curtains, the fine linen stands first, succeeded by the blue and the other colours. The vail, we know from Heb. x. 20, was a type of the Lord Jesus in the days of His flesh, and was rent when He yielded up the ghost. The curtains, fastened together by golden taches, seem to foreshadow Christ in resurrection. The same glorious display of God and man, wondrously united, meets the eye of faith, whether the blessed Lord be contemplated when sojourning on this earth or raised to the right hand of the Majesty on high. Resurrection added to Him no new perfections; for He was, while on earth, the Resurrection and the Life. He was ever perfect. (*H. W. Soltau.*) *Analogies :*— The beautiful and costly cherub-curtained habitation bears some analogy to the believer, to the Church, to Christ, and to heaven. I. To THE BELIEVER. God, who dwelt within these curtains, condescends to dwell graciously in the heart of every true Israelite—"saints are an habitation of God through the Spirit." As the Tabernacle was more beautiful within than without, so are God's children. They are clothed with the spotless robe of Emmanuel's righteousness, and adorned with humility, love, holiness, and heavenly-mindedness. II. To THE CHURCH. Believers, of whom the Church is composed, although scattered among many sects of professing Christians, are yet all one in Christ Jesus. As the curtains though woven separately were afterwards sewed together and formed two great curtains, which, when hung, were united into one by means of loops of blue and clasps of gold, so God's children are knit together by the silver ties of affection and bound together by the golden clasps of love. III. To CHRIST. He was the true Tabernacle, which "the Lord pitched and not man." IV. To HEAVEN. There angels and saints behold God shining, not by a mere symbol as He did within the cherub-curtains, but in the "face of Jesus Christ!" There are those glorious beings who are mighty in strength (and whose perfections probably were shadowed forth in the cherubs that stood upon the mercy-seat and adorned roof and walls), even thousands and tens of thousands of holy angels, guardians of the saints while on earth, and their companions and fellow-worshippers for ever in the heavenly temple. (*W. Brown.*) *The golden and brazen taches :*—Fifty taches, or clasps of gold, linked together the innermost or beautiful curtains of the tabernacle. Fifty taches of brass coupled the goats'-hair curtains. By the former one tabernacle—by the latter one tent was made. The vail, which divided the interior into two unequal portions, was hung up under the taches. As long as that vail remained entire, there might be said to be two tabernacles. At the same time, there was an intimation that the whole interior was but one holy place, in the fact of the curtains that covered, being connected by the taches, and forming one tabernacle, and one tent above it. All priestly service is now conducted in the holiest. Heaven itself is the place where Christ appears in the presence of God for us. The fifty taches of gold may be so many distinct presentations of the glories of Christ, expressed in His various names and titles, as seen crowned with glory and honour upon the throne of God. The taches of brass may exhibit the same names and titles as appertaining to Him when He was on earth, the Second Man, the Lord from heaven; as it will be found that the brass is used as a type of the Lord on earth in suffering and trial; while the gold has a resurrection aspect of the same glorious One. He has, as risen from the dead, retaken His own glorious titles; having, for the joy set before Him, endured the cross. The brazen taches seem appropriately to knit together the curtains of goats' hair, which proclaim to us His sorrows and sufferings on the tree; while the golden taches, as appropriately coupled together the beautiful curtains, which manifest Him as received up in glory, because of the perfection of His labour and service in suffering on earth.   (*H. W. Soltau*.)   *The coverings of the Tabernacle* :—The coverings of the Tabernacle were four in number, viz., badgers' skins, rams' skins dyed red, goats' hair, and the embroidered covering.   Much difficulty has been felt, and is still felt, as to the animal which in our translation is called a badger.   Some think it was a seal, and that the entire Tabernacle, excepting the east end where the door was placed, was covered with seals' skin.   Others think that this covering was made of the skins of a species of stag goat; but be this as it may, it is clear that the outer covering was made of some hard and durable substance; so hard was it that shoes were sometimes made of the same material (Ezek. xvi. 10).   In this covering there was nothing beautiful or attractive.   I can suppose a man to have stood at the top of some high hill, and to have looked down on the long, dark, coffin-like structure, and to have said, "Well, I have heard much about the Tabernacle as being a very costly building, but I see no beauty at all in this long, dark tent"; but the priests who had been within could tell of gold, and silver, and the richest embroidery to be seen there.   It was all glorious within, but rough and unsightly without.   This badger skin covering sets forth the humility of Christ when on earth among men, who, judging of Him according to the outward appearance, said, " He hath no form nor comeliness; there is no beauty in Him that we should desire Him "; so they despised and rejected Him (Isa. liii. 2, 3).   But we know there was much in Christ which did not meet the eye of men generally; and those who, taught of the Father, knew Him as the Christ the Son of the living God (Matt. xvi. 16, 17) were attracted to Him, for He was to them the " chiefest among ten thousand and altogether lovely" (Song of Sol. v. 10, 16). The rough badger skin outside was as needful as was the beautiful covering underneath; and the humility of Christ was as needful for us, and for the glory of God, as was His exaltation.   This covering of badgers' skins was thick enough and hard enough to be an effectual protection from the rain, dew, and fine sand of the desert, and nothing could get through it to stain the fine linen or to dim the gold within.   This shadows forth to us the holy determination of Christ to stand as a faithful and true witness for God on earth: the truth was in Him, and He kept it to the end.   (*G. Rodgers*.)   *The rams' skins dyed red* :—This red covering was probably made of the skins of rams which had been devoted to God, and had suffered death as burnt-offerings—not as sin-offerings.   The skin of the sin-offering was burnt to ashes outside the camp (Lev. iv. 11, 12), but the skin of the burnt-offering belonged to the priest who offered it to God (Lev. vii. 8).   If the badger-skin covering sets forth the humility of Christ, this covering dyed red sets forth the depth of His humility.   This blood-red skin reminds me of Him who when pressed, crushed, and distressed in the garden of Gethsemane, did "sweat as it were great drops of blood." (*Ibid.*)   *The goats'-hair covering* :—This was the only covering that was permitted to hang over any part of the east end of the Tabernacle.   The eleventh breadth, hanging over the door, would meet the eye of the worshipper the moment he came within the gate of the court.   The spiritual teaching of this I think to be of the greatest importance, as we shall see when we understand what particular aspect of our blessed Jesus this covering was designed to teach.   Observe, first of all, that the sin-offering whose blood was carried into the holy of holies, and sprinkled on the mercy-seat, and before the mercy-seat, to make an atonement for the people of Israel, was a goat (Lev. xvi. 15, 16).   This was " the blood of sprinkling," of which we read so much in the Bible.   With this blood in his hand, the high priest entered once a year, and stood in the presence of God.   This was the blood which he offered for the errors of the people, and which made atonement for them.   This was the blood at which God looked, and with which He was satisfied; it had a voice, and spoke better things than the blood of Abel.   When it was sprinkled on the mercy-seat, which covered up the tables of the law, it seemed to speak to God of punishment which had been borne and of a life which had been given up.   Observe again, the animal that bore away the sins of the people into the wilderness, where they were found no more, was a goat.   I refer to the scapegoat, of which we read in Lev. xvi.   This goat going away with the people's sins would show those outside of the Tabernacle what the blood of the slain goat had done within the vail, viz., that it had put away sin and had set them free; and as they gazed on the folded part of goats'-hair cloth, as it hung over the east end of the Tabernacle, it would seem to preach the gospel to them by reminding them how their sin was put away on the tenth day of the seventh month. It would speak of abounding grace, telling them that they had received double for all their sins. The first covering told us of the humility of Christ; the next told us of the depth of His humility; this tells us of the blessed results of His suffering and death, viz., that the sins of the Lord's people are put away, for ever put away. (*Ibid.*)

Vers. 15–30.—**Boards for the Tabernacle.**—*The Tabernacle boards and bars:*—I. THAT INVINCIBLE STRENGTH UNDERLIES THE APPARENT WEAKNESS OF THE GOSPEL. II. THAT THE GOSPEL, DESPITE ALL ITS NATURAL AND HUMAN ASPECTS, HAS A DIVINE CHARACTER AND BASIS. Our faith rests in the power of God. III. THAT OUT OF THE STRENGTH OF CHRIST SPRING THE HIGHEST GLORY AND JOY (ver. 29). Let the Church seek to realize its full privilege in Christ. In character, we are often satisfied with the bare boards of mere honesty and uprightness; in experience, we are content with the boards and bars, a mere sense of safety; in hope, we rest content with the bare expectation of pulling through in the judgment. The gilded boards of the Tabernacle are eloquent illustrations of the New Testament doctrine that in Christ we must rise to beauty, to brightness, to bliss. IV. THAT CHRIST IS AN EVERLASTING DWELLING-PLACE TO HIS PEOPLE. Tabernacle built of boards of acacia, a wood so durable it does not rot even in water. The strength of Christ is everlasting. (*W. L. Watkinson.*) *The boards and bars.*—Each board of shittimwood, overlaid with gold, seems to pourtray the Lord Jesus Himself, the Son of God, the Son of Man. The shittim wood, incorruptible wood, being a shadow of that great truth, that He "partook of flesh and blood"; "the seed of the woman": "the Second Man"; "from heaven"; yet "the Son of David"; "of the fruit of His loins"; and at the same time "the Son of the Highest"; born of the Virgin, "the Man Christ Jesus"; made "in the likeness of sinful flesh"; though, unlike any other man that ever lived on earth, incorrupt and incorruptible; having a body prepared for Him by God, in order that He might die; but without taint of mortality or death in Him. The gold also presents the other great truth, that He is "the mighty God"; "the brightness of God's glory"; "the only begotten of the Father"; "the Son" from everlasting, and to everlasting. The boards are like the ribs of truth, the massive framework, without which no dwelling-place of God could be created; no meeting-place between God and man provided. If the wood could corrupt, or if the fine gold could become dim, if the taint of mortality, or mouldering flesh, be connected, by human theory or speculation, with the glorious Emmanuel, the Tabernacle of God must tremble and totter; the great truths of salvation are shaken, and a mis-shapen mass of ruin takes the place of the divinely-ordered palace of the Most High. The massive framework of the golden boards and bars formed a compact structure, over which the curtains and coverings were suspended. They were to the curtains what the poles are to a tent. They upheld and sustained the glorious display of the blue, purple, scarlet, and fine linen cherubim, as also the goats'-hair curtains. Thus what the Lord Jesus Himself was and is, viz., Son of God, Son of Man—*that* He has made manifest in His life, and above all, in His death; and His blessed work there derives all its unspeakable value and eternal efficacy from Himself. It is faith in Him that is salvation. (*H. W. Soltau.*) *The boards of the Tabernacle:*—The Church of Christ is here seen in type as the dwelling-place of God. It was set upon the earth and God dwelt in it. The Church of Christ is composed of many persons separated from the world, and built upon the sure foundation, which is Christ. And as those boards were covered with gold, so the people of God are made partakers of the Divine nature (2 Peter i. 4); as they had been separated, cut off from the place in which nature had placed them, so the members of the true Church of Christ have been cut off from the place in which they stood by nature, which was one of guilt and condemnation, and they have been joined by living faith to the living Jesus. Nature provided no foundation on which to build the Tabernacle, and nature has provided no foundation on which the sinner can build his hope; but as God provided a foundation for the Tabernacle in the redemption-money of the people, so now He has provided a foundation for His people in the redemption which is in Christ Jesus. And as no board could be a part of the Tabernacle without being built upon the silver foundation, so no person can be any part of the true Church of God if he be not built by faith upon Christ. (*G. Rodgers.*) *Believers typified by the boards:*—Were they golden boards? Every believer is a partaker of the Divine nature (2 Peter i. 4). They are born from above, and they are heavenly minded. Their affection is set on things above. God's people are a holy people. "The beauty of holiness" is the gold with which God will beautify and adorn His people. The knots and grains of the wood were all hidden from view beneath plates of pure gold. God hides all our imperfections from view beneath the gold of His perfect righteousness. (*R. E. Sears.*) **Sockets of silver.**—*The sockets :*—It is perhaps worthy of notice here that the whole of the redemption money, amounting to 100 talents and 1775 shekels, was identified with the supporting or bearing up of different parts of the Tabernacle. The 100 talents formed the foundations and supported the walls of gilded boards which were the stay of the two sets of curtains and the two-fold skin roof; and the 1775 shekels (little more than half a talent) were used up in making silver hooks for the court pillars, and in overlaying the capitals of these pillars and their connecting rods (fillets) which rested on them, and from which the court hangings were suspended. These odd shekels bore up the linen court walls, and the 100 talents bore up the sanctuary. The hundred ransom silver sockets being worth £40,000 sterling, constituted a very costly basis, from which, whether it had a typical import or not, our thoughts not unnaturally rise to an infinitely more valuable one, even to Him" who gave Himself a ransom for all." Prophets and apostles alike testify that He is that sure foundation on which the spiritual edifice rests. Had the sockets not been made of the atonement money as commanded (chap. xxx. 16, xxxviii. 27), but of some other material, God certainly would not have acknowledged the Tabernacle which rested on them as His palace-temple. He never would have enthroned Himself in visible symbol on the mercy-seat. In like manner, those who substitute their own good works, or anything else in the room of the Redeemer, on which to build their hope of salvation, are building on the sand, and cannot form a part of that building which is an "habitation of God through the Spirit," for "other foundation can no man lay than is laid, which is Christ Jesus." (*W. Brown.*) **Tenons.**—*Tenons :*—Although thousands and tens of thousands are resting on the Rock laid in Zion, it is able to bear the weight of countless millions more, and can never by any possibility be overburdened. Those, however, who would build on it, must do so in the way pointed out in the Scripture, or it will not avail them. It was by means of the tenons (Hebrew "hands") that the boards took hold of, and rested on the silver bases. Faith is the hand by means of which sinners lay hold of and rest on the Redeemer. Remember that the boards required to be not merely *on*, but *in* their respective sockets, or they would not have been upheld. In like manner sinners, in order to be saved, must not only be on, but in the spiritual foundation. Unless they are by faith rooted in Christ Jesus, as the boards by their tenons were rooted in the ransom 'money, they cannot stand. (*Ibid.*) **Bars.**—*The bars :*—The bars were all overlaid with gold. One of the bars passed through the centre of the boards from end to end; holes being made, no doubt for that purpose. Thus the boards became one solid wall. But that they might be more firmly united, each board had four gold rings fastened to it, and through these rings the other four bars were passed. 1. There was a sevenfold bond of union. The five bars, the silver sockets, and the corner boards. Paul gives us the gospel meaning of this in his Epistle to the Ephesians (iv. 4-6). 2. The centre bar which passed through the boards from one end to the other, was a lively type of the indwelling of the Godhead in all believers. All the Three Persons of the Trinity are spoken of as dwelling in the renewed heart. "Christ in you the hope of glory." "Jesus answered and said unto him, if a man love Me, he will keep My words; and My Father will love him, and We will come unto him, and make Our abode with him." "What! know ye not that your body is the temple of the Holy Ghost which is in you, which ye have of God, and ye are not your own." What a glorious bond of union is this! Christians of all denominations are one here; for without the love of the Father, the grace of the Son, and power of the Holy Ghost, no man can be a Christian. 3. These bars remind us of the encircling arms of love and mercy. "Underneath are the everlasting arms." "As the mountains are round about Jerusalem, so the Lord is round about His people from henceforth even for ever." All Christians are one in the Divine protection. "All His saints are in thy hand." 4. All Christians are one in love to God. 5. Another bond of union is reverence for the Word of God. Christians may differ in their interpretations of the Word. All may not have the same measure of wisdom to understand its mysteries; but all Christians are one in their esteem and love for the grand old Book! Is it not the one revelation of the Divine will? (*R. E. Sears.*)

Vers. 31–37. And thou shalt make a vail.—*The Tabernacle vails :*—I. THESE VAILS SIGNIFY THAT THE HIGHEST VISION AND FELLOWSHIP OF GOD ARE AS YET DENIED TO MAN. God's presence is fenced about from sinful man. II. WHILST THESE VAILS REMOVE GOD FROM THE APPROACH OF MAN, THEY GIVE THE PROMISE OF A FULLER REVELATION. The God of mercy, and love, and life, shines through the obscuration. III. THAT THESE VAILS ARE TAKEN AWAY IN CHRIST (Mark xv. 38). In Christ we stand "within the vail." In Him we realize the presence and joy of God. (*W. L. Watkinson.*) *The vail of the holiest :*—1. It was glorious, of embroidered work : this faith guild signified the body of Christ, filled with the fulness of God, or beautified with all the most excellent graces of the Spirit. 2. It was replenished and wrought full of cherubim, noting thereby that serviceable and ready attendance of the angels on Christ's natural and mystical body. 3. It was borne up by costly pillars, to show that the humanity of Christ, especially in His sufferings, should be borne up by His Deity. 4. By the vail only, there was entry into the holiest place of all : so by the vail, *i.e.* the flesh of Christ, which was rent, as it were, upon the cross, a new and living way is made for us to the Father. (*B. Keach.*) *The cherubims on the vail :*—The Tabernacle in the wilderness was divided into two compartments—the holy place and the holy of holies—by a vail. That vail was stretched upon four pillars of wood overlaid with gold. It consisted of one huge screen of fine-twined linen, reaching from the roof to the floor, and from one side to the other. On the ground-work of linen were spread, in various ornamental patterns, the simple colours known to the ancients—blue, purple, and scarlet. The holy of holies was shut in by this vail from every human eye. No worship was carried on there. When first seen on earth, the cherubims were placed at the gate of the Garden of Eden, to keep the way of the tree of life. The flaming sword with which they were associated, which turned in every direction, was the symbol of God's judgment, the witness of the terrible majesty of God's holiness which had been insulted by man's sin, telling our fallen first parents that so long as the sin continued, the flaming sword would shut up every avenue against their return to their original happy state. The cherubims, on the contrary, were placed there as an image of mercy and hope, to signify that for the creation that had become alienated from God was destined a happy reconciliation. The same great truth was signified by the golden cherubims that covered the mercy-seat with their wings, and between which God met and communed with the high priest. Now, what I want to draw particular attention to is the fact that, secluded as was the holy of holies of the Tabernacle, and guarded by the most solemn prohibitions, its mystery was not left altogether unknown. The most conspicuous feature of the vail—that which at once arrested every eye— was the cherubims embroidered over its whole surface, in such a way that it seemed to have been fashioned of nothing else. Thus on the vail that concealed the awful shrine of Jehovah from mortal eye was revealed one of the most characteristic and significant objects of that shrine. In this way the priests, who were not permitted to enter the holy of holies, could have some conception of what was within it. The cherubims pourtrayed on the vail and on the curtains were no doubt faint and inadequate pictures of the originals on the mercy-seat. They could not have been otherwise. They were a flat representation of objects that stood out in the sacred shrine in the clearest and fullest relief. They were an embroidery in perishing materials, at comparatively slight cost of labour, of a work of the highest art, beaten out in the purest gold, with the most unwearied industry and the most consummate skill. But with all these necessary imperfections, the needlework of the vail and of the curtains gave a fair idea of the cherubims which stood in the most holy place, in their invisible and unapproachable glory. The Jewish priests and worshippers were not left in complete ignorance. There were witnesses to picture to them that which they could not see. They had shadows of the realities behind the vail. Their faith had elements of sight to support it. I wish to make use of this most interesting fact as a graphic illustration of the great truth, which is true throughout the universe, that things concealed from us have their shadows manifested in the things we see. The universe is a great tabernacle divided by a vail and curtains into an outer and inner compartment, as it were. From the inner we are shut out, and we cannot see with our bodily eyes the things that are contained in it. And yet we have representations of these hidden mysteries before our eyes every day, which give us a more or less satisfactory idea of them. Here we see in part, and prophecy in part. The horizon, for instance, is a vail that comes down to conceal from us what is beyond. Many of us will never be able to visit foreign countries, and ascertain with our own eyes what the nature of these countries and the mode of life in them may be ; and yet, within the horizon in which we spend our life we have shadowy intimations of the most distant regions of the earth. Ships come to us with their produce ; our houses are full of objects brought from them ; books describe them to us ; and letters from friends make us partakers of their larger experience. Even the scenery around our homes is not so dissimilar to that of foreign lands as we might suppose. Between us and the lofty summits of a great mountain range there is a vail often woven of cloud and mist. Elevated far above the busy common-place haunts of man, these sublime peaks seem to dwell apart, to retire into a more awful solitude than exists on the surface of the earth. And yet the lofty summit of the mountain sends down into the valley by the streams that channel its flanks waifs of brilliant Alpine flowers, which take root and grow among the common lowland plants: and thus the dweller at the foot of the mountain knows what kind of vegetation abounds in the upper regions as truly as if he had actually scaled the heights. Many who live far inland have a vail of mountain ranges between them and the great ocean. They may never be able to stand on its shore, gaze on its foaming billows, or listen to the beating of its mighty pulse. And yet, up the reaches of the quiet inland river, into the heart of the mountains, into the midst of shady woods, the ocean sends its tidal waters, its fresh invigorating breezes, and its white-winged sea-birds, so that the inland inhabitants may have some idea of the vast world of waters that extends far beyond their horizon. The vail of daylight hides from us the other worlds in space ; and the darkness of night which brings out the stars only increases their mystery. But the vail which conceals also reveals. Spectrum analysis has made known to us the chemistry of the sun and stars, the physical constitution of the most distant worlds. This wonderful science shows to us that the substances of the stars are identical with those of our own earth. Not a single new or unknown element has been discovered in the remotest stellar ray subjected to its scrutiny. Upon the very vails that separate us from the inmost and remotest sanctuaries of nature we see impressed the images of the objects which they hide from our view. But it is not only natural things that thus reveal themselves by that which conceals them ; the realities of the spiritual world are also manifested to us on the vail of earthly things. We have numberless analogies in nature which make plain to our understandings the mysteries of grace. Our Lord revealed to His disciples and to the multitude what the Kingdom of Heaven was like by showing to them its shadows on the vail of common objects and common processes, in His parables. The Kingdom of Heaven is like everything we see and deal with. The youngest person can see the meaning of the great truths of salvation in some degree and measure by the help of the figure of them which his own experience presents to him. The doctrine of the atonement is in remarkable keeping with the sympathetic nature which God has imparted to children, by which they feel for others, and can therefore understand how one person may carry his loving-kindness to such an extent as to give up his life for his friend. The forgiveness of God has a shadow of it in the sorrow which all truly sensitive minds feel when they have offended one dear to them, and in the joy which the sense of being reconciled and accepted by the one from whom their faults had estranged them imparts. There is thus not a mystery of the holy of holies of Divine truth but may be seen in dim yet true shape, embroidered, as it were, upon the vail of natural objects around us, and of our own common instincts and experiences. But I go on further to show that the realities of the eternal world are manifested to us by the things of time. The vail of death, which no human hand can lift, hides the scenes beyond from our view. The Bible speaks to us of the existence of that happy land, and discloses its glory in forms which far transcend our earthly imagination. It calls our future home a new heaven and a new earth. The ascension of our Lord to heaven, with all the attributes of perfect man, the resurrection of man in a body strictly identical with his present body, prove beyond doubt that the scene of our translation, with all its circumstances, must be accommodated to the nature of man. From the very constitution of our nature, we form our anticipations of the future from our past experiences. The objects and experiences of earth are preparations for those which await us above. On the vail that hides our future home from us, we see pictured the cherubims of glory. Yes ; the cherubims of heaven are seen on the vail of earth. Heaven is filled with objects long endeared to us, and with pleasure which we have already enjoyed in part, and learned from the foretaste to long for the full fruition. We have now the earnest of the purchased possession—the first-fruits of the great harvest. Now, what is the practical outcome of thoughts like these? Does it not teach us that we have no excuse for sinful ignorance, seeing that God has brought within the range of our touch and vision in earthly images His perfect heavenly things, and placed us so that we can understand the things that belong to our spiritual life by the things that belong to our daily life? Do not these glimpses and foreshadowings of unseen and eternal things also inspire us with a deeper interest in them? And more than all, does not the fact of the cherubims upon the vail being the same as those in the shrine show to us that our life is continuous here and hereafter—that it is one history and one development? If you are to behold and enjoy the glorious cherubims of the heavenly world, you must have them represented, as it were, upon the vail of your earthly tabernacle. Your hearts must be turned now to the heavenly harmonies. When certain conditions of light are present, if you look through a window at a particular angle into the street, you see a flame apparently outside, flickering strangely in the air. It is only the reflection of the fire in the room on the window-pane. Is not the heaven you see beyond the window of this life, the projected reflection of your present experience? What you are now determines your future; and the heaven of each man is just what he himself makes it, according as the fire of love and holiness burns more or less brightly on the hearth of his heart. (*H. Macmillan, D.D.*)   *Significance of the cherubim in Exodus:*—Many have supposed that the Church is symbolized by the cherubim in Exodus. But the fact of their forming the vail seems to preclude this interpretation. As the vail shadows forth Christ in the flesh, we cannot suppose that any type would be given representing the union of the Church with Him then; as, before death, the corn of wheat abode alone: it must die, in order to bring forth fruit. The union of the believer with Christ is in life, quickened together with Him: seated in heavenly places in Him. He was the Substitute in death; but He is the last Adam, the head of the new family, and source of its existence in resurrection. The lion (one of the four faces of the cherubim) is classed with the king, against whom there is no rising up, in Prov. xxx. 30, 31; and is also described as going well, and being comely in going; and as strongest among beasts, turning not away from any. Majesty, strength, and courage are therefore here typified. The ox, in addition to its well-known character for patient enduring labour, is also recognized in Scripture as knowing its owner; herein it may prefigure the persevering resolution of Him who unflinchingly set His shoulder to the arduous work committed to Him by His Father, and who always recognized His Father's will, and delighted to do it. The way of an eagle in the air is alluded to in Prov. xxx. 19, as too wonderful to be known: referring probably to the astonishing extent and accuracy of its vision as to things of earth, when poised aloft, and to its swiftness of flight when the object of its search is discovered. Fit emblem this of Him, whose eyes search the depths of the heart, and who is as rapid in discovering where the lawful prey is, as in delivering it from the power of the destroyer. These three faces, combined with the human face and form, completed the cherubim: for all this power, labour, activity, and quickness of perception, were put forth under the control and guidance of perfect wisdom and sympathy. Wings were also spread abroad over the surface of the vail, proceeding from the cherubim; denoting the heavenly origin and unearthly ways of the Son of Man, who was "from above," and who could say, even while here, "The Son of Man, who is in heaven." (*H. W. Soltau.*)   *The pillars of the vail:*—The pillars of the vail were four in number. Unlike those on which hung the curtain for the Tabernacle door, they had no capitals; thus they lacked the ordinary completeness of a pillar. May not our thoughts be directed by this, to the contemplation of those Scriptures, which speak of the Lord as *cut off*? (see Isa. liii. 8; Psa. cii. 23, 24). And yet the very fact of this seemingly abrupt termination of the life of the Lord Jesus, in the days of His flesh, has made Him to be unto us "wisdom, righteousness, sanctification, and redemption"; a fourfold perfection, meeting our fourfold need; to which possibly the number of vail-pillars may allude. (*Ibid.*)   **The door of the tent.**—*The door of the Tabernacle:*—1. This was the only door of the Tabernacle; it must therefore have been an emblem of Jesus Christ (John x. 9). There was only one entrance into the court, only one door into the holy place, and only one way into the holy of holies. Jesus is the Way, the Truth, and the Life. No man cometh unto the Father, but by Him. The curtain at the door of the Tabernacle was made of blue, and purple, and scarlet. Here we have an emblem of the Saviour's threefold Name. Lord—Jesus—Christ. He is Lord of all power, majesty, dominion, and glory. May not the "blue, and the purple, and the scarlet," be figurative of Jesus in His threefold office, as Priest, King, and Prophet? The scarlet shows His priestly sacrifice. The purple His kingly dignity. The blue His heavenly teaching as the prophet. It is only as we see Jesus in His threefold office, that He is the Door. As the Priest, He is the sacrificial Way. As the Prophet, He is the Truth. As the King, He reigns to give Life. As Jesus, He is our saving Priest; as Christ, He is our anointed, instructing Prophet; and as Lord, He is our ruling King. In Him these offices are united. We may distinguish between them, but we must not separate them. 2. May not the five pillars which held up the curtains at the Door, be emblems of gospel ministers, whose work it is to hold up Christ before the people? 3. These pillars had sockets of brass. Brass being in Scripture an emblem of strength, we may here see the servants of God strengthened for their work. May we not see Jesus Himself in the sockets of brass? "His feet are like fine brass." Jesus upholds His servants with His own strength. "Lo, I am with you alway, even unto the end of the world." He who holds the stars in His right hand, upholds His servants as pillars in the house of God. Were the pillars beautiful? So are ministers abounding in their work (Isa. liii. 7). (*R. E. Sears.*) *The door of the Tabernacle :*—The hanging, which formed the door, was made of the same materials as the vail; the only difference being that in the former the colours were skilfully intermixed, whereas in the latter a pattern of cherubim was cunningly or ingeniously embroidered. The priests, who entered within the door of the Tabernacle, alone beheld the cherubim of glory worked into the vail and roof, whilst the worshippers in the court saw the same colours intermingled in the door-curtain. May not this be intended to teach us, that every worshipper of God recognizes the beauty and perfection of Christ, God manifest in the flesh, as his eye rests upon the door-curtain. But the nearer we approach to God as His priests, the more intimate our fellowship with Him in heavenly places, the more shall we discern the glories of Jesus, and realize His power, majesty, and strength. He will be the one object that fills our soul, and under the shadow of His wings shall we abide. (*H. W. Soltau.*)

CHAPTER XXVII.

VERS. 1–8. **An altar of shittim wood.**—*The altar of burnt-offering :*—I. The altar of burnt-offering was made partly of WOOD, and partly of BRASS. The wood was incorruptible; and was therefore a lively type of the incorruptible humanity of Jesus. II. The altar of burnt-offering, was not a golden altar; but A BRAZEN ALTAR. Brass is a durable metal, and an emblem of strength. Christ was equal to His mighty work. "I have laid help upon one that is mighty." He is "mighty to save," and strong to plead the cause of His people. III. The altar was FOURSQUARE. There were firmness, stability and strength. The purposes of Divine love cannot be overturned. The atonement Christ has made is perfect and complete. Our altar presents a bold front to the enemy. It is a solid mass of strength. IV. It was A HORNED ALTAR. In Christ we have sovereignty, protection, dignity and glory. Horns in Scripture are almost invariably emblems of power—regal power. Christ is King of kings and Lord of lords. V. It was AN ANOINTED ALTAR. The holy anointing oil was poured upon it, and thus it was sanctified, and became most holy. Christ was anointed with the oil of gladness above His fellows. The fulness of the Spirit was upon Him. VI. THE SANCTIFIED ALTAR SANCTIFIED ALL THAT WAS LAID UPON IT. "Whatsoever toucheth the altar shall be holy." The altar was therefore greater than the sacrifice. It is the altar that sanctifieth the gift. The Divine nature of Christ sustained His human nature, and gave efficacy to His sacrifice. Christ's glorious Person is the only Altar on which we can offer acceptable sacrifices to God. VII. Christ is A SPIRITUAL ALTAR, and on it we may offer spiritual sacrifices. To this Altar we must bring our prayers. If we pray in the name of Jesus, we give wings to our feeble breathings. To this Altar we must bring our praise. "By Him therefore let us offer the sacrifice of praise to God continually, that is, the fruit of our lips giving thanks to His name." No service of song can be acceptable to God apart from Jesus Christ. VIII. IT WAS A SACRIFICIAL ALTAR. On this altar was offered the daily sacrifice—a lamb every morning, and a lamb every evening. "Behold the Lamb of God!" Christ is the Lamb of God's providing. IX. It was a BURNING ALTAR. On the altar sacrifices were continually burning. The fire was never to go out. Perfection was not to be found under the old dispensation. Christ's sacrifice was one; and it was offered but once. "Christ was once offered to bear the sins of many." "By one offering He hath perfected for ever them that are sanctified." At the Jewish altar the fire consumed the sacrifices; but the sacrifice Christ offered consumed the fire. "It is finished." X. The altar of burnt-offering was GOD'S ALTAR (Psa. xliii. 3, 4). Jesus is the Christ of God. He is God's beloved Son. In coming to Christ we come to the altar of God's providing; we come to the altar of God's appointment. XI. It is the SINNER'S ALTAR. The altar was erected on purpose for the guilty; and Christ came into the world to save sinners. XII. It is A BLOOD-STAINED ALTAR. Where the blood is, it is safe for the sinner to go. Being sprinkled with blood, it is A PROTECTING ALTAR. XIII. The altar of brass was A NOURISHING ALTAR. The priests had a portion of the sacrifices for their food (1 Cor. ix. 13). "We have an altar"—the glorious Person of Christ—"whereof they have no right to eat which serve the Tabernacle." The old dispensation has passed away. The present dispensation is spiritual. Having " the heavenly things themselves," we have no need of "the patterns." In Christ we have all the "good things," of which the Tabernacle and its services were "shadows." All believers are priests. All wait at the altar. All live on Christ. XIV. It was A CONSPICUOUS ALTAR. No one could enter the court of the Tabernacle without seeing the brazen altar. Christ must be the preacher's theme. Christ is the only object of saving faith, and Jesus only must be the subject of our ministry. (*R. E. Sears.*) *The size of the altar :*—It is observable in Scripture that Moses' altar was but five cubits in length, and five in breadth, and three in height (ver. 1); but Solomon's altar was much larger (2 Chron. iv. 1). Now the reason hereof seems to be this, because Moses was in a warfare, in an unsettled condition, in the wilderness, in continual travel, full of troubles, and could not conveniently carry about an altar of that bigness; but Solomon was on his throne in a tranquil state, settled in quiet possession of his kingdom, and as his name was, so was he a true Solomon, that is, peaceable. Thus it ought to be with all good men, that when they have more peace and prosperity than others, their service of God should be proportionable. Solomon's Temple must outstrip Moses' Tabernacle in beauty and glory, and Solomon's altar must exceed the bigness of Moses' altar. In their peace and plenty, their holiness should outshine others that are in want and misery, when God lays not so much sorrow upon them as upon others, they should lay the more duty upon themselves. If God send them fewer crosses and more comforts, they are to return more service and commit less evils. (*J. Spencer.*) *The altar of brass :*—The altar was four-square, and it had four horns. The animals offered in sacrifice were horned animals, and were doubtless bound by their horns to the horns of the altar, and then slain (Psa. cxviii. 27), so that the ground round about the altar would be always red and wet with blood. Life is in the blood; to shed the blood is to sacrifice the life; and the first thing that meets our eye as we enter the gate of the court, and look at the earth on which we are walking, is blood—sacrificed life. To this altar the sinner came leading his sin-offering. Here he stood before God, and his sins were confessed, and transferred or imputed to the unblemished and innocent animal, which had then to suffer and to die for sin, but not for its own sin. The innocent one died for the guilty one. These sacrifices were typical of Christ's sacrifice. He suffered, the Just for the unjust: on Him our sins were laid; He bore them in His body on the tree. He was made sin, or a sin-offering, for us, and by His stripes we are healed. His blood was shed for the remission of sins, and now it cleanseth us from all sin (1 Pet. iii. 18; Isa. liii. 5, 6; 1 Pet. ii. 24; 2 Cor. v. 21; Matt xxvi. 28; 1 John i. 7). Christ is our Altar, our Sacrifice, and our Priest. He offered Himself for us. And having met most fully all God's claims, He now meets and supplies all the penitent believing sinner's need. Every saved sinner has come to this spot—has seen Jesus as the Lamb of God which taketh away the sin of the world (John i. 29). We have seen Christ as the Redeemer, and as the Gate or Way to God, and now we see Him as the Altar, Priest, and Sacrifice. Here we stand with our hand of faith on His head, and we feel that as our Sin-offering He has suffered for our sin, and has put it away. Our life was forfeited, but Christ who loved us, and gave Himself for us, has sacrificed His own life to save us from eternal death (Eph. v. 25; John x. 11, 15). (*G. Rodgers.*) *Significance of the altar of burnt-offering :*—In other cases an altar was said to be built, or elevated; but the portable structure used as such in the Tabernacle is spoken of as made, or constructed, because it had a frame of wood overlaid with copper. This frame was probably filled with earth to answer the requirements of the general statute. There is no intimation of this, indeed, in the writings of Moses; but neither does he mention any other expedient for holding the fire in place. Copper as dug out of the ground, similar to it in colour, and inferior to that metal which among metals represented celestial glory, was appropriately associated with earth in an altar belonging to a permanent and yet portable institution. By the affinity of the copper with the earth, this frame of an altar, which could be carried from place to place, fulfilled the same end in the expression of thought, as an altar of earth. The wood being, in the first place, designed for a frame on which the copper might be fastened so as to give sufficient size and strength without too great weight, was of acacia for the same reason which required this particular species of timber in the planks of the house, and the pillars of the court. The Tabernacle being a place of life, acacia wood, on account of its superiority to decay, was sought for every purpose which was to be answered with wood, whether in the edifice or its furniture. Not only the frame, or wall of the altar, was of acacia covered with copper, but also the horns; and this fact may help to determine the significance of these projections. The horn is, in cornute animals, the instrument of power, and thence becomes an emblem of strength, and as such is congruous with all the other elements combined in the altar as a symbol. It has, accordingly, been commonly understood that the horns of the altar represented the power of its ministrations. But recently it has been suggested that among the metaphorical significations of the horn, height was no less appropriate than strength as an attribute of an altar. The horn is the highest part of the animal, carried aloft as a badge of power and the honour consequent on power, and therefore used as a sign of elevation. To lift up the horn is to exalt, either in the physical or in a figurative sense. The horns of an altar may be intended, therefore, to symbolize still more emphatically the elevation of the earth on which the sacrifice is offered toward heaven, the residence of the Being to whom it is presented. The copper with which the horns were overlaid seems to countenance this interpretation. May not both shades of meaning be comprehended in one and the same emblem? The horns elevating the place of sacrifice nearer to heaven, the efficacy of the altar was especially conspicuous in these symbols of elevation. (*E. E. Atwater.*) *The brazen altar:*—This altar of burnt-sacrifice, with the offerings presented upon it, stands before us as a type of Christ and His cross. And the materials of which the altar was composed point strikingly to His twofold nature. His humanity, if found alone, would have been consumed by the fire of Divine justice, which blazed forth against Him when He stood as our substitute and bore our sins in His own body on the tree. And then, on the other hand, His Divinity, if found alone, like the altar, if all of brass, would have been too oppressive for us. It would have made us afraid by its excellency, and would have overwhelmed us by its majesty. But blended with the humanity, and tempered and softened by its transmission through the vail of flesh, it meets our necessities in every respect, and furnishes us with just the help and comfort that we need. (*R. Newton, D.D.*)   *Lessons:*—I. Look now at the POSITION which God assigned to the altar of sacrifice in the Jewish Tabernacle, that heaven-sketched symbol of the Church. Behold one of the marks of a true Church. It will give great prominence to the altar, the cross of Christ, or the doctrine of His atoning sacrifice. II. THE RELATION WHICH IT BORE TO EVERY OTHER PART OF THE TABERNACLE. It was the most important part of the whole Tabernacle. Like the root to the tree, like the foundation to the building, like the fountain to the stream, like the mainspring to the watch, like the heart to the body, it was that, on which every other part of the sacred structure depended, and from which it derived all its value. This altar represents the cross of Christ. As we look at it from this point of view, we seem to see written on it as with a sunbeam, the great practical truth, that the way to heaven—the only way by which any of our ruined race can enter there—lies over Calvary. There is no pardon, no renewal, no acceptance, no righteousness, no peace, no grace, no blessing, no salvation to any of Adam's children, but through the sacrifice once offered upon the cross. And this is true not of our persons only, but of our services also. "Accepted in the beloved," is the great underlying doctrine of the gospel. Our prayers, our praises, our sighs, our tears, our repentance, our faith, our words, our actions, our labours, our sufferings, our vows, our alms-givings, our sermons, our sacraments—all things that may be crowded into the entire circle of our services—have worth, or merit, not in themselves, but only as they stand connected with the sacrifice which Jesus offered on the cross, and are sprinkled with His atoning blood, in all its prevailing efficacy. III. Our third lesson from this altar is suggested by the CONTINUITY of the offerings presented upon it. There was to be no cessation, no suspension, or interruption of the service here rendered. The sacrifice on the Jewish altar was an imperfect sacrifice, and hence the necessity for its repetition. They were "sacrifices," as St. Paul says, "offered year by year continually, which could never make the comers thereunto perfect." Our sacrifice, offered upon the cross, is a perfect sacrifice, and therefore it needs no repetition. It was offered "once for all"; and by this one offering, Jesus, our great High Priest, "perfects for ever them that are sanctified"; *i.e.*, all His believing people. The offering was once made, but the merits, the influence, the efficacy of the offering, abide continually. And because it thus abides, there needs no repetition of it. IV. Our fourth lesson is taught us, when we consider the EFFICACY OF THE OFFERINGS presented on the brazen altar. You may say, indeed, that we have just spoken of their imperfection, and that is true. They were not intended to do for the Jews what the sacrifice of Christ does for us. They were only types, or shadows of that sacrifice. Of course they could only have a typical, or shadowy efficacy. This, however, they had in perfection. And here the brazen altar points significantly to the cross of Christ. It speaks to us, in eloquent tones, of the thorough efficacy, the absolute perfection of the sacrifice He offered. V. The fifth and last lesson taught us by this altar is seen, when we observe the EXTENT OF ITS BENEFITS. It was open to all. (*Ibid.*) *The brazen altar of burnt-offering :*—In this we have a significant type of our Lord, regarded more particularly in His Divine nature. This view "is supported by our Lord Himself, when He says that the altar is greater than the sacrifice (Matt. xxiii. 19). Both sacrifice and altar were but shadows, and derived their importance wholly from the reality to which they referred. But as a shadow of Christ's sacrifice, the importance of the legal victims was immeasurable ; and yet our Lord says the greatness to which the altar pointed transcends it. Then lies not the thought very near, that the altar pointed to His Divinity ? And still further is this conclusion justifiable by the additional saying of our Lord, that the altar sanctifies the sacrifice ; for was it not the union of His Divine with His human nature which imparted to the latter its majesty inconceivable, and to His sacrifice its miraculous and eternal efficacy ? " A remarkable confirmation of this view is found in the fact that the altar, during removal, was covered with a *purple* cloth, which colour symbolized the hypostatic union. The construction of the altar pointed another lesson. The outer covering of brass concealed and protected an interior of wood. In fact, the altar was said to be made of wood. Now in Hebrew, wood and tree are synonymous, and trees are frequently spoken of in the Bible as emblematic of God's saints. By the wood of the altar was signified the members of Christ : " It was a visible parable of the mystical union between Christ and His people. As the wood was hidden within the altar, so in God's eye were they hid in Him." And the lesson thus taught by the altar was this : Rom. viii. 1. " The altar was surmounted by four horns, the well-known emblems of power ; and these horns were deeply marked with sacrificial blood ; and it fell from them as it fell from Him whom the altar typified in the garden and on the cross. These horns were, therefore, at once symbols of might and reconciliation, and were outstretched to the four corners of the earth, to call men to flee unto Christ to be saved." (*E. F. Willis, M.A., with quotations from H. Douglas, M.A.*) *The altar of burnt-offering :*—This altar was the foundation of all the Tabernacle worship. The priests could not enter into the holy place except on the ground of sacrifice presented on the brazen altar. Nor could the high priest on the great atonement day enter the holy of holies without having first offered not only the ordinary sacrifice, but an additional sin-offering on the altar in the court. Not only was the Shekinah glory within the vail impossible of access, but the bread of the presence, the light of the lamps, the privileges of the altar of incense, were all closed until a sacrifice had been offered upon the altar. Thus were the children of Israel taught, and thus, too are we taught, that the first thing for the sinner to do, before he can taste the heavenly bread, before he can see the heavenly light, before he can even pray with acceptance, is to avail himself of the atonement which God has provided. The altar was the people's place of meeting with God. It was free to all. The call was addressed to every child of Israel : " Come into His courts and bring an offering with you." The atonement which God provides is free to all without exception, and without distinction. (*J. M. Gibson, D.D.*)

Vers. 9–19. **The court of the Tabernacle.**—*The court of the Tabernacle :*—I. This court may be AN EMBLEM OF THAT SACRED ENCLOSURE WHICH ALWAYS SURROUNDS THE

CHURCH. "A garden enclosed is my sister, my spouse." God Himself, with all His infinite perfections and attributes, is round about His people. Every attribute of God is a pillar in our protecting wall, power, sovereignty, justice, righteousness, truth and faithfulness, appear in perfect harmony with love, benevolence, mercy, tenderness, compassion and goodness. All unite to uphold the separating wall between the Church and the world. II. We may look upon this court as emblematical of THE LIFE AND MINISTRY OF CHRIST. Only the true Christian can enter into Christ, but a sinner may read His life. As the court led to the Tabernacle, so the reading of the life of Christ has often been the means of the soul believing in Jesus. In the life of Christ we have a perfect model for the Christian's imitation. Christ has left us an example that we should follow His steps. III. We may view the court of the Tabernacle as AN EMBLEM OF THE HOLY SCRIPTURES. We cannot come to God without entering the court of revelation. He that loves the Bible has entered the outer court of the Tabernacle. Reverence for the Word of God is a good sign. IV. The court of the Tabernacle was A PLACE OF WORSHIP. Here the Israelites came with their various sacrifices; and here God accepted them. If we would be accepted by God, we must observe God's order, and come to the place He has appointed. We must also come in a right spirit. V. In the court of the Tabernacle we have A FIGURE OF THE PROFESSING CHURCH. 1. Not all who entered the court entered the Tabernacle. Not all who make a profession of religion possess it. The heart, as well as the lip, must be right. The court was the way to the Tabernacle. There is no evidence that a man possesses grace while he neglects the means of grace. If a man has no love to God's house, he can have no love to God. If we have no desire to be numbered with God's people, there cannot be much desire after God Himself. (*R. E. Sears.*) *Hangings of the court:*—It is likely that those hangings would be of open work, and that the people would be able to look through this linen fence, and see what was being done inside. This would set forth the guilelessness of Christ's character. He was no deceiver; there was no guile in His lips. He lived in a very hollow age, when deceit was the order of the day; but He was a transparent Man, an unselfish Man, a perfect Man. At the east end was a hanging called the gate. The basis of this gate would be the same as the fine linen in other parts of the court, and the meshes would be nearly filled up with blue, purple, and scarlet wools. This gate is Christ, the one gate, the one only door to God and to happiness in this life, or in the life which is to come. Those white hangings were suspended from upright pillars, standing in blocks of brass. The pillars were strong enough to sustain the weight of the hangings, and they were high enough to keep the fine linen from touching the ground, or contracting defilement in any part. So our Lord Jesus was sustained in His holy conduct in every part of His life by those upright principles which He had in His holy nature. (*G. Rodgers.*) *Fine linen:*—The fine linen was a thing of the earth. It had grown from seed which had been cast into the ground, and had died there, after which life came up out of death; there was death and resurrection. After this it went through many processes before it was seen about the dwelling-place of God. So the Christian has to learn death and resurrection. We have to die, and to be quickened to life, and we have to pass through some painful processes. Satan himself is sometimes permitted to sift us and to twist us, and he handles the soul roughly; but it is all needed to make us the fine-twined linen such as God would have us be. All things do indeed work together for our good, if they help to conform us to the image of Christ (Rom. viii. 28, 29). (*Ibid.*) *The gate of the court:*—The word "hanging" is in the Hebrew exclusively used for the vail, the door of the Tabernacle, and the gate of the court; and serves, therefore, to connect together these three in type. Each of these hangings covered or hid the interior from the eyes of one approaching from the outside. Each had the character of a door. All three were made of the same materials arranged in precisely the same order; and all three were of the same dimensions as regards their area. The same truth seems, therefore, to be embodied in each of these typical curtains. The same Jesus, God manifest in the flesh, is pourtrayed in each. There could be no access to God of any kind, whether of comparatively distant worship or of closest intimacy, but through the one door, the Lord Jesus (John x. 7). Cain was the first who tried another path; and instead of being able to draw near, his very attempt ended in his going out from the presence of God into the land of banishment. Thousands follow in his footsteps, and think to worship and to offer without passing through the door. (*H. W. Soltau.*) *The hanging of fine linen:*—The court itself, with the exception of the gate, was closed by a hanging of fine-twined linen, five cubits high.

Fine linen seems to be used in Scripture as a type of righteousness—a righteousness equal to all the demands of God—enabling him who possesses it to stand in God's glory; in contrast with sin, by reason of which, all come short of the glory of God. The Israelite, who entered through the gate of the court, would be encompassed, shut in, and protected by this hanging of fine-twined linen. Though in a wilderness, he stood on holy ground; and the fine linen by which he was surrounded shut out from his eye the dreary barren prospect, through which he was wending his way. The lovely Tabernacle of God stood partially revealed to his gaze. The courts of the Lord's house, overshadowed by the cloud of glory, were before him. The altar, with its lamb for the burnt-offering, sent up an odour of a sweet savour on his behalf. The laver, filled with water, told him of a fountain filled with life and purity, which would cleanse away even the ordinary defilement contracted whilst passing through a wilderness of death. He had entered through the gate of the court, the appointed doorway; within, every object proclaimed life, peace, righteousness, acceptance, and nearness to God. Moreover, no deadly foe could enter these precincts. Thus the court presented a place of security, of holiness, and of intercourse with God. Jerusalem on earth will hereafter afford some such place of refuge for the nations of the earth. (*Ibid.*)   *The pins :*—By means of these pins of brass, the Tabernacle and the court were securely fastened to the desert ground, so that no storm or flood of waters could sweep away this structure, although many of the materials were such as to be easily affected by the wind or rain. May we not be reminded by this type, of the stedfast purpose of Christ, to pursue the path marked out for Him by the counsels of God, even though that path ended in the storm of judgment and in the billows of wrath. What a wondrous object of contemplation is the blessed Lord, as revealed to us in the Scriptures of truth. Weak, yet immovably firm. Himself the mighty God, yet dependent for everything on God His Father. Oh! the wondrous power of that weakness. Oh! the marvellous victory of that death. Oh! the eternal stability of Him laid low in the depths of the grave. (*Ibid.*)

Vers. 20, 21. **Pure oil olive beaten for the light.**—*Symbolic references :*—I. The purity of the light (Psa. xxvi. 9). II. The perfection of the light. III. The perpetuity of the light. Christ can never be superseded. (*J. S. Exell, M.A.*)   *Oil for the light :*—1. The source whence the oil was obtained—the "olive." Thus is grace, free and full, obtained from Christ, the "Plant of renown." 2. The qualification it was to possess—it was to be "pure." All the grace which comes from Christ is pure and unalloyed. 3. The instruments of its dispensation—"the children of Israel." The children of God are now the recipients and dispensers of Christ's grace. 4. The uses to which it was put—it caused "the lamp to burn always." Grace causes the life of each Christian to shine with a brighter glow. (*S. Thomas.*)   *Lamps burning always :*—It is difficult to understand from the various passages bearing on the subject, whether the lamps burned both day and night, or only during the night—some passages apparently favouring the one view, and some the other; thus, "To cause the lamp to burn always" (ver. 20); and, "Command the children of Israel, that they bring unto thee pure olive oil, beaten for the light, to cause the lamps to burn continually" (Lev. xxiv. 2). These passages seem to teach that the lamps burned both day and night. If they do not teach that, the meaning must be that "continual" and "always" signify at regular intervals, as in the case of some ordinances and offerings which are called perpetual, though occurring only at intervals. The other view, that they burned only during the night, seems to be supported by, "Aaron and his sons shall order it from evening to morning" (ver. 21); "And Aaron shall burn thereon (the golden altar) sweet incense every morning, when he dresseth the lamps" (chap. xxx. 7, 8). From these texts it would appear that the lamps burned only during the night. If they were not intended to teach that, the meaning must be that the lamps were dressed in the morning, probably one after another, not necessitating more than one being extinguished at a time, and after being dressed and lighted, burned during the day, the lamps receiving such further attention in the evening as admitted of their burning till the morning. As there were no windows in the Tabernacle, and the priests had duties to perform during the day in the holy place, it is almost certain that the lamps burned always. (*W. Brown.*)   *Light symbolism :*—As the first apartment in the Tabernacle was illuminated by the sevenfold light of the candlestick, and as the Church, composed of all genuine believers on earth in every age, is enlightened by the Holy Spirit, so will the

Church triumphant in heaven, that great temple not made with hands, be a place of glorious light; and the light shall never go out, it will burn always; so that there shall be no night there, nor sun, nor moon, nor stars shall shine in that happy place, for the glory of God and the Lamb is the light thereof. (*Ibid.*) *Burning with pure oil :*—It is related in the biography of one who lived to become a devoted Christian man, that while he was yet a little boy, the passage read from the Bible in the family on a certain occasion was ver. 20, describing the oil used in the vessels of the Tabernacle. The meaning and application of the verse was explained by other passages from the New Testament. This boy was then but five years old, and it was not supposed that he could understand or feel the slightest interest in a subject considered far beyond his age. The older children left the room after family worship, but the little boy was detained, as usual, to be taught some simple verses of the Bible by his mother, and to pray with her. He kneeled down at length to pray, and in the midst of his prayer he paused, and exclaimed, earnestly, "O my God, make me to burn this day with pure oil!" The morning lesson had not been lost upon him; he had understood its import. "Most evidently," says his biographer, "was this prayer heard and answered throughout the day of his life." How appropriate is this petition for the morning offering of every Christian, "Make me to burn this day with pure oil"! If He who hath all hearts in His keeping vouchsafe a gracious answer to that prayer, the example of the disciple must be one that will glorify the name of Jesus. Such a man will walk with God. No unhallowed fires will be lighted in his bosom. Neither revenge nor hate can burn there. The peace and joy of the believer will fill his soul.

CHAPTER XXVIII.

VER. 1. **The priest's office.**—*Interpretation of the priesthood :*—The Hebrew priesthood was instituted because the people were not qualified to draw near to God in person. By virtue of their election, the people of Jehovah were entitled to dwell in His habitation, but their consciousness of sin made them afraid of Him: therefore, in condescension to their inability to understand the greatness of His love, He provided a class of persons who, as the representatives of His elect, might in their stead enter the Tabernacle. To draw near to God, and to be a priest, are equivalent expressions. Aaron drew near in behalf of those who were elected to have spiritual communion with God, but were not yet delivered from bondage to fear; and his admission within the habitation signified that they were entitled to a corresponding access in spirit, that they were called a kingdom of priests for the reason that they might thus draw near to God in spiritual fellowship. By his office he was qualified to do outwardly and symbolically what all might do in spirit and in truth. But, before Aaron could enter the holy habitation in behalf of the people, he must officiate at the altar of sacrifice, and expiate sin; for his constituents were sinful, and the representation of their approach to God as members of His household must be preceded by signs that their sin was taken away: otherwise it might be inferred that Jehovah was indifferent whether His people were holy or unholy. The Hebrew priesthood therefore symbolized in general, the expiation of sin, and the admission to filial intercourse with God effected thereby. (*E. E. Atwater.*) *The priests :*—I. QUALIFICATIONS. Every applicant for the priesthood had to prove his descent from Aaron, and had to be free from bodily defect or blemish (see Lev. xxi.). This restriction pointed to the dignity and holy character of the position occupied by a priest, and to the inward purity requisite for the proper discharge of his sacred duties. II. DUTIES. The chief duty of the priests was to offer or present offerings and sacrifices to God. They had sometimes to kill the victims (Lev. xvi.) and always to sprinkle and pour out their blood, and also to burn their carcases, or part of them, on the altar. They had the charge of the altar and the sanctuary; they had to see that the fire was ever burning on the altar; they made loaves of shewbread, trimmed and lighted the lamps of the golden candlestick, and evening and morning burned incense on the golden altar, and, in general, conducted the sacred services of the Tabernacle worship. Their duties were not, however, confined to the performance of the rites and ceremonies of that worship; for the law being committed to their custody, they, with the Levites, were intrusted with the religious instruction of the nation (Deut. xxxiii. 10) ; and the people were exhorted to seek knowledge at the priests' lips. III. MAINTENANCE. The priests were not permitted to follow any secular calling. Their time was entirely devoted to their sacred work; hence it was necessary and just that their maintenance should be provided for at the expense of those for whose spiritual and temporal welfare they ministered. The remuneration consisted principally of the redemption money paid for the first-born Israelites, the first-fruits of the field, the fruit of trees in the fourth year, parts of various of the offerings, and a tenth of the tithes which fell to the Levites. They were not able, of course, to reap all these dues till they reached the promised land. (*W. Brown.*) *The priest-hood :*—Previous to this time, there was probably no separate order of priesthood in the Church of God; but every father was the priest of his family, as in killing the lamb of the passover and sprinkling the blood, or each worshipper had been at liberty to transact the business of sacrifice as he pleased. So far, in the history of Israel as redeemed from Egypt, Moses seems to have officiated occasionally as priest, as in the case of offering the sacrifice and sprinkling the blood of the covenant ; or he selected young men as temporary priests. But the erection of a special place of worship, most notably carried with it the setting up an order of priesthood, with ritual of worship. The very name " cohen," which we translate " priest," is supposed to denote the idea of a familiar friend of God. The distinc-tive function of the office was to receive and present to God, as His nearest friend and associate, that which belonged to Him. The three great elements entering into the idea of their position and office were: 1. That they are chosen by Jehovah Himself to be His. 2. That they are officially holy in a pre-eminent sense. 3. That they have, by reason of their election and holiness, the privilege of drawing near to God, as holding a position intermediate between man and God, and there-fore of mediators. (*S. Robinson, D.D.*)

Ver. 2. **Holy garments for Aaron.**—*The vestments of our High Priest :*—The vestments appointed by God for the high priest when he went into the holy place were, besides those which he wore in common with the other priests, four : the ephod, with its "curious girdle " ; the breastplate; the robe of the ephod ; and the mitre. 1. And speaking of these garments generally, you will notice that it was God's especial command that they should all be made of linen, which, being a material of a very simple and natural kind, has always been understood by the Church to be typical of that human nature which Christ wears still in His glorified state, and in which, as man, we are distinctly to understand that He now executes, as our Representative, all the services of His exalted Priesthood. 2. And, further, it is to be observed generally, that all the garments were carefully fastened together so as to be one. The girdle binding the ephod, and the ephod the robe, and the breastplate carefully joined to the ephod by chains of gold ; signifying, again, the complete unity which there is in all Christ's work for His people, so that it cannot be divided ; for if we have Him in one of His offices so, necessarily, we hold Him in all. A blessed truth ! there is no such thing as anything partial in the work of Jesus; no partial pardon; no partial peace! If you have one promise, you have every promise ! 3. And yet, once more, generally, you will see that (unlike the description of our Saviour's garments in the 59th chapter of Isaiah, and unlike that which is provided for the believer in the 6th chapter of Ephesians) all these are robes, not of war, but of peace. Indicating that the warfare is now accomplished, and that our Saviour, having triumphed over His enemies and ours, is now set down in the calm and quiet of His holy, peaceful functions. A thought which should be one of unselfish joy to the Christian. 4. The robe of ephod repre-sents the perfect robe of the obedience of the Lord Jesus Christ, which He wore as man, and which He will always present to the Father for our sakes. Its seamless fabric denotes the perfectness and the unity of the righteousness which He has wrought. 5. The ephod itself was a closer vestment—long behind, and short in front—which was worn over the robe, and fastened by clasps, or " ouches," over the shoulders ; it was also " for beauty and for glory "—" of gold, of blue, and of purple, of scarlet, and fine-twined linen, with cunning work," costly and magnificent. Upon each shoulder, in the " ouches," was placed an onyx stone, and on either onyx stone were engraven the names of six of the tribes of the children of Israel, placed according to their seniority. Concerning this engraving, God was very express : " With the work of an engraver in stone, like the engravings of a signet," that is, very accurately, very deeply, very beautifully, "shalt thou engrave the two stones with the names of the children of Israel: thou shalt make them to be set in ouches of gold. And thou shalt put the two stones upon the shoulders of the ephod for stones of memorial unto the children of Israel: and Aaron shall bear their names before the Lord upon his two shoulders for a memorial." And, then, the ephod was girt about with a girdle of the same kind. Here, then, we have our great High Priest continually standing in heaven, and always of necessity bearing, as part of His own glory, the names of all His people in holy remembrance before God. He both remembers us, and causes us to be remembered. We are held in perpetual remembrance. The weakest and the strongest—the greatest saint with the unworthiest and guiltiest sinner—we are all remembered: everything which goes to make our name is there: the smallest work, the secret sorrow that the world knows nothing of: it is all in the memorial: our prayers, and tears, and sighs—they are all gone there! they are all rivetted there! There they are! They are knit into the dignity of Jesus, into the glory and the excellency of Jesus! 6. The breastplate teaches that Christ not only bears His people on His shoulders for strength, but lays them separately on His heart for love. He identifies His interest with ours. It becomes a dear and fond thing to Him to have us upon His breast, that He may save us and magnify us for ever! We live always in His love, and God sees us there; in that love, loves us—unloveable though we be—for the love He has to us. And, living on His heart, each one in his own proper place and order, we hold in Him safe and privileged intercourse. 7. The high priest wore a mitre of linen, with this inscription, "Holiness to the Lord." Now observe the comfort of this thought. Here we all are assembled, in our holy devotions before the mercy seat of God, but every prayer we have put up this day is stained, and every service is unclean before Him "who chargeth His angels with folly"! Presently, your petitions will go up in your own bedroom; and the very supplication, in which you ask for pardon, only goes to increase the amount of the guilt that has to be pardoned. It is all unclean! The brand of sin, the degradation of sin, is everywhere! But He, in His very character and being, as our Representative, is standing before God; and high emblazoned upon His front is His own proper righteous title, "HOLINESS TO THE LORD"—not for Himself, He needs it not, but for us! He "bears the iniquity of our holy things"—what a thought! even as if we were the holy, we poor worms—as if we were the holy—we stand before God: "Holiness to the Lord." A poor sinner, incapable of one pure thought, lifts himself up in Christ, and looks in the face of God, and stands there, in his High Priest—"Holiness to the Lord";—and God recognizes His own eternal counsel, and acknowledges the unworthiest services of the poorest sinner to be—"Holiness to the Lord." (*J. Vaughan, M.A.*) *The priestly garments:*—They signified—1. The function to be glorious and excellent. 2. The fitness of their persons to that office. 3. The glory of the true High Priest, Jesus Christ, of whom Aaron was but a figure. For all the glistering show of these priestly garments set forth the more angelical brightness of all the virtues which should shine in Jesus Christ. The priestly garments appointed by God were ten in number; of which four belonged to the inferior priests (vers. 40, 42). 1. A linen garment. Which signified the white garment of Christ's righteousness and innocency; which they were to appear in before the Lord, if they would be acceptable in their persons and duties. Noting to us by the way, that every godly minister wears a white linen garment, not woven and made by men, but by God; not without him, but within him; not a shadow or ceremony, but the substance and truth, to which all shadows give place. Nay, there is no private man that is godly, but he must wear this white linen garment, having put it on in the laver of regeneration: as Gal. 3, 27. 2. A girdle (ver. 40). Which signifies constancy and stability in the truth, both in our High Priest, Jesus Christ, who was not a reed shaken, but a firm rock: as also in His members, who are commanded to stand fast, their loins girt with verity (Eph. vi. 14). Hence follows, that the minister's word must be yea and nay; his course must be constantly gracious and watchful. And for private Christians (Heb. xiii. 9). 3. A bonnet (ver. 40). A symbol and sign to them of God's protection still covering them in their faithful service: signifying to us the Lord's cover and faithful protection both over our head, and over His members for His sake. 4. The breeches (ver. 42). Putting more comeliness upon the uncomely parts. Signifying to them and us—(1) What reverence we ought to use in the service of God; far removing thence every uncomely thing. (2) Shadowing out the true and perfect holiness, with which Christ's humanity was clothed; and not only with that, but with the majesty of His Deity, which highly graced and honoured the despised and frail humanity, which had no form nor beauty (Isa. liii. 2). (3) Not darkly representing that care and respect which our Lord and Saviour Christ hath of His inferior, base, and despised both ministers and members through the world (Isa. xli. 14). To the high priest belonged six peculiar garments: I. First the EPHOD (ver. 4), in which—1. The matter. It was not wool or silk, but linen, which riseth out of the earth (Ezek. xliv. 17). Signifying that holy flesh of Christ which veiled His Deity as a garment; and that it was taken not from heaven, but from His mother on earth, as the matter of that garment grew immediately out of earth. 2. The form. It was a long white garment: signifying the long white garment of Christ's absolute righteousness; white, innocent and unspotted; and long, to cover all our nakedness, without patching of merits. 3. The ornament of it. In it were set two onyx stones, and in them the names of the twelve tribes of Israel engraven, which Aaron carried upon his shoulders; signifying—(1) That the names of the godly are not lightly written, but fast engraven in the love and memory of Christ. as those names were engraven in very hard stones. (2) That Christ doth still carry His Church on His shoulders; lifting them up out of dust and misery, and bearing them upon the shoulders of His power and providence, as on eagles' wings (Isa. xl. 31). II. The second garment peculiar to the high priest was called THE BREASTPLATE OF JUDGMENT (ver. 15), the most precious part of all his garments. 1. In respect of the twelve costly and glittering stones, which were set in four rows, according to the number of the tribes (ver. 17–22). In which—(1) The shining of these stones signified the shining purity and innocency of Jesus Christ, both in Himself and in His members. If they be pure as the sun, fair as the moon, what is He? (2) Their price of great value and worth signified what a price the Lord Jesus valued His Church at. (3) Their place or situation. They are set in the pectoral, and Aaron must carry them on his heart: signifying that Christ hath as much care of His Church, as if it were enclosed in His heart; lets out His blood to make room in His heart for them. (4) Their number; twelve, according to all the tribes: noting that there is room in the heart of Christ for every one of the elect. None can anticipate or prevent the other. With Him is plentiful redemption. The former without the latter shall not be perfected (Heb. xi. 40). (5) Their order. They stand in four rows in a comely quadrangle: signifying the comely order that Christ hath established in the Church: some in higher places, some in lower, some in one rank and office, and some in another, as those stones, but all stand seemly and fitly. And this order we must maintain, keeping our ranks as they did. (6) The figure. The foursquare (ver. 16), signifying the stability and firmness of the Church, as a foursquare, turn it any way 'tis firm. Satan and all deceivers shall not pick one stone out of Christ's pectoral. The gates of hell shall not prevail against him that is fixed in that rock and stone of Israel. (7) Their use. That Aaron, who before bare the names of Israel on his shoulders before the Lord, might now bear them on his heart continually for a remembrance before the Lord, when he goeth into the holy place (ver. 29). Signifying—(*a*) The ardent love of Jesus Christ towards His Church, who bears it not only on His shoulders as a shepherd, or only in His arms as a nurse; but upon His heart, and in His heart, never to forget our good. (*b*) Bearing of the names continually before the Lord on His heart signifieth the continual mindfulness and intercession of Jesus Christ for His Church in that heavenly sanctuary (Heb. vii. 25). By virtue of which all our prayers get audience and acceptance. (8) The quantity. As all the names of Israel were gathered into a narrow compass: so Jesus Christ our Mediator shall gather together into one all the dispersed sons of God, and present them before God as the most beautiful and precious parts of the world (John xi. 52). (*T. Taylor, D.D.*) *The garments of the priesthood, and their significance:*—In almost every modern nation there are some remnants of the ancient custom of representing office by garments of peculiar material, shape, and colour. History registers the decline of the custom, but not its birth and growth; for it was as powerful as ever in the earliest age which has transmitted to us its records. In the time of Moses, both kings and priests in every country were clothed in a garb not only distinctive but emblematic. In interpreting the significance conveyed by the garments of the Levitical priesthood, it will be convenient to treat first of the four pieces worn by priests of ordinary rank, and then of those peculiar to their chief. Is there, then, no significance in the fact that this official costume consisted of four pieces? As four limits the colours of the tapestry, the ingredients of the incense, the spices of the holy anointing oil, the composite parts of the cherubs, we conclude that the same signature of the kingdom of God was designedly impressed on the official costume of those who were elected to draw near to Jehovah. This judgment is confirmed by the recurrence of four as the number of pieces additional to the dress of the ordinary priests which the head of the order was required to wear in the performance of official duty. The numerical signature of the Tabernacle was thus impressed on the official garments of its priesthood. The garments of the priests of ordinary rank were all of pure white except the girdle. The drawers, the coat, and the bonnet were of *shesh*, bleached, but not dyed. White raiment was emblematic of ethical purity. It was "the righteousness of the saints." As worn by the priest, it signified that those who were admitted to intimacy with the Holy One of Israel must be pure in heart and life. The material also contributed something to the significance of the dress. The garments must all be of linen; and in the vision of Ezekiel the directions given for the official raiment of the priests add to the requirement of linen the express prohibition of anything woollen. The reason of the requirement lies, doubtless, in the greater cleanliness possible in a warm climate to one whose garments are exclusively of this material. Not only was the costume of a priest significant in its material, colour, and number of pieces, but each of the four garments of which it was composed contributed an element peculiar to itself. The coat, or tunic, was first in importance, as it was in size. Reaching from the neck to the ankles, it was merely coincident, as a covering of the person, with the whole costume; so that the other three garments were supplements to this, rather than its equals. Its import, as might be expected, is also nearly the same as that of the whole dress. As the entire costume of four pieces, by means of its material and its dominant colour, was suggestive of holiness, so was the coat in particular, as it invested the person from the neck to the ankles with linen white and shining as light. Moreover, this garment was woven in one piece to represent, by this sort of integrity, moral wholeness or holiness. The tunic of the priest was also woven so as to exhibit checks like the pattern called damask; for such is the meaning of the descriptive adjective which the English translators incorrectly regarded as equivalent to "broidered." The coat was therefore covered throughout with four-sided figures of small size. Bähr thinks that these were symbols of like import with the precious stones in the breastplate of the high priest; as if every member of the sacerdotal family bore on his person visible signs that as a priest he was the representative of the tribes of Israel, these symbols designedly having, in the case of the subordinate priests, only a reflection of the glory and beauty of those which distinguished the head of the order. A girdle of some kind was in ancient times, as it is even now, essential to the completeness of an oriental costume; and, by means of diversity in material, size, shape, and ornamentation, was easily made a badge of office. The girdle of the Hebrew priest seems to have been, more than any other article of his attire, an official badge. According to the traditional law of the Hebrews, the priest must remove his girdle when he ceased to officiate, but might, if more convenient, continue to wear the other official garments through the day. How the girdle of the priest symbolized his office as an *attaché* of the Tabernacle, is evident when we consider its peculiar ornamentation. Like the other garments it was of white linen; but, unlike them, it was interwoven with threads of blue, purple, and crimson. The four colours of the Tabernacle signified that the wearer belonged to the institution. This badge of office certified that he had a right to enter the habitation where these significant colours were dominant. The Arab wears on his head a cap similar to the Turkish *fez*, which he calls a *tarbush*. The Bedouin spreads over it a handkerchief folded so that three of the four corners hang down on the back and shoulders, and binds it in place with a twisted rope of goat's hair or camel's hair, reaching around his head. The Syrian Arab, if he wishes any addition to his *tarbush*, ties a handkerchief over it, or winds around it a shawl of wool, silk, or cotton, so as to form a turban. The oriental turban has exhibited both in modern times and in the remotest antiquity, a great variety of form, material, and colour. By means of this diversity it has served to distinguish between men of different nations, and of different classes in the same nation. As an ancient Assyrian king was distinguished by a head-dress of a peculiar shape and ornamentation, as a descendant of Mohammed is known by the colour of his turban, so the dignity of the Hebrew priest, as an attendant on Jehovah in His holy habitation, was symbolized by a turban peculiar to his order in its material, its colour, and perhaps its shape. The priests must wear drawers while officiating, to cover their nakedness; and neglect to do so was to be punished with death, even if no exposure of the person resulted. The covering was therefore symbolic. It was a removal from the significant tableau in which the priest was engaged, of those parts of his person which, as excretory, were especially representative of defilement. The significance of the costume of the Hebrew priest cannot be fully seen by one who overlooks the fact that it left his feet uncovered. An oriental does not wear a shoe or sandal for protection from cold, but from filth, and lays aside at least the outermost covering of his feet when he enters a house, because he will not need such protection in such a place, and because his shoe might bring filth into the house. The costume of the high priest consisted of the four pieces worn by his subordinates, and of four others peculiar to him as the head of the order. Over the tunic he wore the robe of the ephod, the significance of which resulted from its blue colour and the ornamental fringe which hung from its border at the bottom. To understand the meaning of this fringe see Num. xv. 38, 39. The ornaments were intended to remind the wearer of the commandments of Jehovah, and were connected with his garment, whatever its colour, by a cord or ribbon of blue, to signify the heavenly origin of that which he was to keep in remembrance. But this fringe, in the case of the high priest, consisted of tassels in the shape of pomegranates, alternated with little golden bells. If, as seems probable, the pomegranates symbolized the law in its totality as including every specific requirement, it is at least a plausible conjecture that the bells with which they alternated signified that the high priest, or rather the covenant people whom he represented, were not only to remember the commandments of Jehovah, but by obeying to proclaim them. So far as they remembered and obeyed it, the Word of the Lord sounded out from them. The specifications for the ephod make its shoulder-pieces so prominent that the Greek and Latin versions give it names in those languages which characterize it as a shoulder-garment. But the shoulder as the seat of strength was, in the early times, when the strongest ruled, the seat of authority, and the most appropriate position for an emblem of government. We infer, then, that the ephod was a symbol of rank; and from the materials of which it was made, that it invested the wearer as a badge of royalty. This garment was provided for the high priest as the representative of the holy nation, that the jewels on its shoulders, and the threads of beaten gold woven into it throughout, might signify that they were kings as well as priests. The breastplate of judgment was closely connected in significance with the ephod, indicating that the wearer was a ruler endowed with wisdom for the decision of important questions relating to the public welfare. He wore it on his heart because the heart was regarded as the seat of wisdom. The head-dress of the high priest was distinguished from that of his subordinates not only by its shape, but by its plate of gold bearing the inscription, "Holiness to Jehovah." This plate, peculiar to him as the head of the priesthood, and of the nation as a kingdom of priests, was another badge of rank, and equivalent in meaning to a crown. The inscription, peculiarly important from its position on the forehead, proclaimed that the high priest, through his election, his physical faultlessness, his separation from common life, his investment with the robes of office, and his consecration, was so holy that he might not only approach Jehovah, but could take away the sins of his people (ver. 38). Their iniquity was taken away, and they were accounted holy because their representative was holy. (*E. E. Atwater.*)   *The robes of glory and beauty :*—Aaron had not in himself the proper qualifications for shadowing forth the Lord Jesus, the great High Priest; so the requisite beauty and glory were put on him symbolically. Arrayed in those beautiful, costly, and Divinely-appointed garments, he was symbolically what Jesus Christ is in reality, and he could minister about the Tabernacle as a type of Him who is the true Minister and the ever-living Saviour. These garments were said to be "for glory and for beauty " (ver. 2). They were very costly and very beautiful, and everything belonging to them was significant in some way of the manifold excellencies and glories of the blessed Jesus. They are so many glasses which God has given to us, by which we may see Jesus in various aspects, as manifested to us in all His moral comeliness, and beauty, and spiritual excellences. I love to see Jesus as set forth here, because He is so lovely. "He is altogether lovely " (Song of Sol. v. 16). And yet even here we do but see through a glass darkly ; we only know Him in part ; we do not see Him face to face (1 Cor. xiii. 12). He is here looking forth at the windows, and showing Himself through the lattice (Song of Sol. ii. 9), and it is very blessed to see Him thus ; but it will be much better to see Him as He is, with no window or lattice between Him and ourselves (Phil. i. 23 ; 1 John iii. 2).   (*G. Rodgers.*)

Vers. 6–14. **The ephod.**—*The ephod :*—The ephod, with its " curious girdle ' and the oynx stones upon its shoulder-pieces, was the distinctive priestly garment. It hung upon the shoulders down to the waist, and was formed of the most costly and beautiful materials, corresponding exactly to those employed in the interior decoration of the holy place. The girdle was made of the same materials, with the same combination of colours. As garments were associated in the Hebrew mind with character, and the girdle with energy in work, we find in the correspondence of both with the interior of the holy place, a memorial of the necessity that those who enter the house of the Lord must be themselves holy and beautiful in character, and be engaged in high and holy service. But the most important parts of the ephod were the shoulder-pieces, on which were set two oynx stones, with the names of the tribes engraven on them (see ver. 12). Here we have the idea of representation clearly and beautifully symbolized. The shoulders, to a Hebrew mind, were the symbol of strength; and the idea was, that when the high priest entered the holy place he did not go alone, but carried with him on his strong shoulders the children of Israel whom he represented ; and the estimation in which the people were held was expressed in the value of the precious stones on which the names were engraved, and the setting of pure gold with which they were surrounded. (*J. M. Gibson, D.D.*) *The ephod :*—The ephod, with the breastplate and girdle fastened to it, and put upon the person of Aaron, constituted him a worshipper ; adorned with this he could draw near and worship in the holy place. It was put on over the blue robe, and is supposed to have been much shorter than that garment, reaching a little below the knees, whilst the blue robe reached down to the feet. It fitted closely to the person, and was kept in its place by the girdle. It was made of gold, blue, purple, scarlet, and fine linen. These materials represent the purity, loveliness, and glory of Christ as the Man Jesus Christ and the mighty God. It would spangle with gold, and the colours would be so blended as to display their richness and beauty in the best possible way. The four materials were the same as the vail was made of, viz., fine linen, blue, purple, and scarlet, which represent the manhood of Christ in all its perfection as such (Heb. x. 19, 20) ; but in the gold thread with which that cloth was embroidered (chap. xxxix. 3), I see the Godhead of the Lord, and the two are so joined together that you cannot have one without the other. The back and front parts of the ephod were joined at the shoulders, by means of the shoulder-pieces from which it was suspended. In each shoulder-piece was a precious stone set in gold—an oynx stone, a beautiful white and half-transparent stone. In these precious stones the names of the twelve tribes of Israel were engraven. Aaron carried the names of his people upon his shoulders. He presented them thus before the Lord, and when God looked down upon Aaron, He saw the names of His people indelibly engraven in white stones. The shoulder is the place of strength. The omnipotent strength of Christ is ours. He carries His people's burdens and themselves too (Isa. lxiii. 9, xl. 11, xlvi. 4; Psa. lv. 22). The government is upon His shoulder, and the crown is upon His head. (*G. Rodgers.*)

Vers. 15–30. **The breastplate of judgment.**—*The breastplate :*—A full description of the breastplate is given twice over in the Book of Exodus, and from it we may gather certain useful lessons as to the Church in all ages. I. There were twelve stones in the breastplate, EACH OF THEM DIFFERENT, AND EACH BEARING A DIFFERENT NAME. This shows what variety there is among believers. So long as the human race differs so much in mental structure, we shall not be able to think alike, even in those things that are spoken of in Holy Writ. There are differences with regard to worship, differences in religious feelings and experiences; the stones are not alike, yet they are all on the same breastplate. II. This brings us to another truth—THE UNITY OF THE CHURCH, ALL DIFFERING, YET ALL ON THE HEART OF CHRIST. The enemy has only to show himself, and men who differ amongst themselves agree to drive him back. III. They were all precious stones ; NOT ONE WAS MEAN OR CONTEMPTIBLE. God's Church has ever been costly. No jewel is what it afterwards becomes when first found. Let not the stone which sparkles in its setting sneer at that which only looks like a pebble. The Master has chosen it ; He knows that He has put within its rude exterior that which only needs time and skill to make it "shine as the stars for ever and ever." IV. Why were those precious stones put upon the breastplate? They were not on the mitre ; THEY WERE UPON THE HEART, TEACHING US THAT THE CHURCH IS BELOVED. Every believer is on the heart of God. V. GREAT PAINS WERE TAKEN TO KEEP THE

BREASTPLATE FROM BEING LOST. It was not only fastened to the shoulders by chains, but the bottom part of the breastplate was fastened by two rings lashed to the two rings in the ephod. This tells us of the Church's security. (*T. Champness.*) *The breastplate :*—As the heart is the place of affection, and the shoulder the place of strength, Aaron had to carry the names of his people on his heart, to show that he loved them, and on his shoulder, to show that he was ever ready to serve them. The typical and spiritual meaning of this is very sweet. Jesus Christ is our great High Priest, and the names of all His people are not upon, but in, His heart. His omnipotent strength and His infinite love are ours—ours for ever. He never forgets one of His people, nor fails to love them. They are His jewels, His special treasures, His Father's love-gifts, and He values them because His Father gave them to Him. The time is coming when He will count up His jewels, and it will then be found that not one soul given to Christ by the Father will be missing. As every ray of light that fell upon Aaron would fall upon the names of Aaron's people, so every smile that God gives to Christ is given also to the people of Christ; for Christ and His people are one, and God never looks upon Christ without seeing His people—all His people, for they are in Him—loved as He is loved. (*G. Rodgers.*) *The topaz :*—The topaz is a beautiful jewel, of a bright orange or golden colour, though they are sometimes found green, blue, and red. It is very hard, being next to the ruby in this respect. I saw lately an account of a fine old topaz seal among the curiosities in a museum in England. What is called the field of the seal was blue. On this there were three arrows. On the top or crest of the seal was the head of a dragon on a crown. And round the seal was this inscription or motto— "*Sola bona quæ honesta.*" The meaning of this is "Honesty, which is the only good thing." And this, according to the old proverb, might be rendered, "Honesty is the best policy." The topaz is considered to represent honesty. Most people think that if they don't cheat when they get a chance, and don't steal from those about them, they are honest. True honesty means to give to all persons whatever belongs to them. I want to speak of four different kinds of temptations, and to show how this precious jewel, the Bible topaz, will be a safeguard to you against them all. I. The first kind of temptation in which this jewel will be a safeguard to us are TEMPTATIONS FOR THE EYE. You know when an army is besieging a walled city or fortress how very careful those inside of it are to protect the gates. But our souls are like walled cities or fortresses. Satan is the enemy trying to get in. And the eye is one of the gates of entrance. We must guard this gate well if we want to keep our souls safe. Job said he had "made a covenant with his eyes" not to look on anything that it was not right to look at. David used to pray—"Turn away mine eyes from beholding vanity." And if we keep this precious Bible jewel, the topaz of true honesty, about us, it will be a safeguard to us in temptations. The first temptations from which it will save us are temptations for the eye. II. The second kind of temptations in which this Bible jewel, the topaz of true honesty, will be a safeguard to us are TEMPTATIONS FOR THE EAR. This is another of the principal gates of entrance to the soul. And it is a very important gate. It ought to be most carefully guarded. We receive a great deal of good, and a great deal of harm, through the ear. If our souls are saved at last, they will be saved by what we hear ; and if our souls are lost at last, they will be lost by what we hear. III. The third kind of temptations from which this jewel will save us are TEMPTATIONS FOR THE TONGUE. Oh, how much sin people commit by means of the tongue! If we could keep from saying what is wrong, how nicely we should get along ! Well, if we carry this Bible jewel, the topaz of true honesty, about us all the time, it will keep us safe from these temptations. IV. The fourth and last kind of temptations we are to speak of from which this jewel keeps us are TEMPTATIONS FOR THE HAND. I mean by this, the temptation to take or to keep what does not belong to us. If we keep this jewel about us—that is, if we remember God's presence and try honestly to please Him—it will save us from ever taking or keeping what does not belong to us. If you want to keep this jewel about you all the time, so as to be kept from temptation, there is one text you must always remember. It is this, "Thou, God, seest me." Oh ! pray God to write that text on your memory. (*R. Newton, D.D.*) *The emerald :*—The emerald is a jewel of a beautiful, soft, rich green colour. Ireland is called the "Emerald Isle" because the grass which covers its hills and valleys is such a beautiful green. When you look at this island from the deck of a vessel far off at sea, it looks like a great jewel—a great emerald rising out of the ocean. The emerald stands, in value among jewellers, next to the ruby. It is spoken of several times in the Bible. In old times people used to think that the emerald had certain wonderful or magical powers. It was not true that it had any such powers. But hope, which is the Bible jewel represented by the emerald, does have them. I wish to speak of three of these powers. This will give us three reasons why hope may be compared to an emerald. I. And the first reason why hope may be compared to an emerald is because it makes us INDUSTRIOUS. People used to think that the emerald had the power of curing idleness or of making men industrious. If it only had this power the emerald would be the most valuable of all jewels. Then, when boys and girls were put to school, it would only be necessary to hang an emerald round each one's neck, and there would be no lazy scholars. The owners of all our workshops and factories would want to have a good supply of emeralds. I need not tell you, however, that the emerald never had any such power as this. But hope, the beautiful Bible jewel, that which the emerald represents, does have this power. If people hope to get rich they know that they must be industrious and work hard. II. Again, people used to think that the emerald had the power of taking away fear. And this leads us to speak of the second reason why hope may be compared to an emerald, because IT MAKES US COURAGEOUS. The Bible tells us that " hope maketh not ashamed " (Rom. v. 5). In one place in the Bible hope is compared to a helmet. And a soldier who had his head covered with a good helmet would be very bold and courageous. He would not be afraid when the arrows were flying thick around him. In another place in the Bible hope is compared to an anchor (Heb. vi. 19). Suppose that you and I are at sea on board a vessel. A storm is driving our vessel right on towards a rocky and dangerous coast. If we have no anchor on board we may well be afraid, for pretty soon we shall be dashed against the rocks and perish. But suppose we have a good anchor, and a strong cable to hold it by on board our vessel. We drop our anchor in the sea. It sinks to the bottom and is buried in the mud and sand, or takes hold of the rocks there. It keeps the vessel from drifting towards the shore. We are safe. Our fear is gone. Let the winds blow, and the waves roar ever so much, they can't hurt us. The anchor gives us hope, and this hope makes us bold or courageous. And it is just so when we become Christians. Then we love Jesus. We have hope in Him. That hope is to our souls just like what the anchor is to the sailor. It keeps us from being afraid. III. Another strange power, which it used to be supposed the emerald had, was that of taking away gloom and sadness from the minds of people. Of course this was a mistake. It never had any such power. But this points out to us a third reason why hope may be compared to an emerald. It is because it makes us CHEERFUL. Hope is a bright, sunshiny thing. You know how beautiful the rainbow is! Hope is sometimes compared to the rainbow. And it may very properly be so compared, because it seems to paint in bright colours the things it leads us to look for, and to put rainbows all about them. There is a steam ferry-boat on the river Mersey in England. It runs from Liverpool to Birkenhead and back. Several years ago passengers on that ferry-boat would sometimes see on a warm bright day a poor crippled boy. His body was grown almost to a man's size, but his limbs were withered and helpless, and not bigger than the limbs of a child. He used to wheel himself about in a small carriage, like those that boys use in their play. He had a little musical instrument called a concertina, and on this he used to play some sweet simple tunes. He never asked for anything, but yet very few of the passengers could hear his touching music, or look at his honest, cheerful face, without dropping a penny or two into his carriage. One day a lady was standing near, looking at him with great pity. She thought how sad and lonely he must feel, unable to help himself, and with no prospect of ever being any better in this world. She said to a lady who was with her, but not intending that he should hear it—" Poor boy! what a sad life he has to lead; and nothing in all the future to look forward to!" But he did hear it. And in stepping out of the boat that lady saw a tear in his eye and a bright smile on his face trying to chase the tear away, as he said—"I'm expecting to have wings some day, lady." (*Ibid.*) *The sapphire :*—I want to find out what this jewel stands for or represents. Well, when I come to read about the sapphire, I find that in old times people used to think that if you carried one of these jewels on your heart, or in your bosom, it would have the effect of making you strong. And then we have only to ask ourselves which of the Bible jewels, or Christian graces, is it which has the greatest power to make people strong? We see in a moment that it is faith. And so we feel safe in saying that the sapphire stands for faith or trust in God:

Faith may be compared to the sapphire because it makes us strong: I wish to speak of two things for which faith makes us strong. I. In the first place, faith makes us STRONG TO SUFFER. II. The second reason why faith may be compared to the sapphire is because it makes us STRONG TO SERVE. Now, my dear children, if you want to have this Bible jewel, you must ask Jesus to give it to you. You can't find it. You can't buy it. Your parents, or teachers, or friends, can't get it for you, or give it to you. Nobody but Jesus can give it to you. It is only His grace that can put it in your hearts. If you pray earnestly to Jesus to give you a believing, trusting heart, He will give it to you. This precious jewel, trust in Jesus, is all we need to make us comfortable and happy here, and all we need to save our souls and take us to heaven at last. It is faith, simple faith, or trust in Jesus, that saves us. (*Ibid.*) *The diamond :*—Every true Christian is a spiritual diamond, one of God's jewels. Let us look at this diamond and see what there is about it on account of which a Christian may be compared to it. I. ITS HARDNESS. It is one of the hardest things in the world. 1. It will bear a great deal of rough handling without being scratched or injured at all. And Christians are just like diamonds on this account. They can bear trial or hard treatment without being injured by it. 2. It can make marks that cannot be rubbed out. When we become Christians, we are like diamonds in this respect. One day the superintendent of a Sunday school in this city was going along near Third and Dock Streets. He saw one of the large boys belonging to his school coming out of a drinking-saloon. The boy's name was George Simpson. As the superintendent passed by he raised his finger, and shaking it gently, he said, in a kind, but serious way, " Take care, George, take care." Some ten or twelve years passed away. He had forgotten all about it. But one day a very genteel-looking man came up to him in the street, and, bowing to him, said, " I think, sir, this is Mr. P., who used to be superintendent of such a Sunday school?" " That is my name, sir, but I don't remember you." " Don't you remember a boy named George Simpson who used to belong to your school?" " No, I can't recollect the name." " Well, sir, don't you remember meeting him one day coming out of a drinking-place near the corner of Third and Dock Streets, when you shook your finger at him, and said, 'Take care, George'?" " Oh, yes, I remember that." " Well, sir," said the young man, " I am George Simpson, and I want to thank you for what you did and said that day. It was a little thing, but it saved me from ruin. I was just beginning to go in the drunkard's ways. But something in your words and manner made a great impression on me. I gave up drinking. Not long after, I joined the Church. Now I am living in the West, and am quite well off ; but, my dear sir, I owe it all to you." Here you see how the superintendent was like a diamond, making a mark that never can be rubbed out. II. ITS BRIGHTNESS. The most brilliant of all jewels. It gives up freely the rays of light that God freely bestows upon it. And this is what makes it look so bright and beautiful. And so you see that when Jesus said, " Freely ye have received, freely give," it is about the same as if He had said, " Be like the diamond, which gives back again so freely the light which it receives." A piece of coal does not reflect any light. All the light that falls on it is swallowed up and kept to itself. This is what makes it look so black, so dark, and disagreeable. Selfish, miserly people are like coal in this respect. They don't reflect or scatter about them anything they receive. Whatever God gives them they swallow up and keep to themselves. III. But there is a third thing connected with diamonds, on account of which Christians may be compared to them, and that is THE WAY TO FIND OUT COUNTERFEITS. There are many counterfeit diamonds. Men can make imitation diamonds. And these often look so very much like the real that it is difficult to tell one from the other. And then God sometimes makes stones that appear so much like diamonds that hardly one person out of twenty can tell the difference between them. Sometimes even the merchants who are engaged in buying and selling diamonds can hardly tell a real jewel from an imitation. There are one or two tests, however. A real diamond can't be scratched. Another way is by putting it beside a true diamond and comparing them together. And so, if you wish to tell if a person is a true Christian, you must compare him with Jesus, and see if he is like Him. Jesus was gentle, loving, and kind. And the Bible says that " unless the same mind be in us that was in Christ Jesus, we are none of His." This means that unless we are like Him we are not true Christians. And then there is another way by which you can tell a real diamond from a counterfeit. If you put them in water, the diamond will still look bright and shine ; the counterfeit, instead of shining, will look dark and dull. The Bible compares affliction or trial to water; and you can easily tell a true Christian from a counterfeit by seeing how he acts when affliction comes upon him. (*Ibid.*) *The agate:*—In old times people used to think that this jewel had the power of securing success. It was supposed that if persons only had an agate with them they would be sure to get the victory over their enemies. The agate was considered as the conqueror's jewel. And now what is the Bible jewel that will always give us the victory—that will make us "more than conquerors through Him that hath loved us"? It is the grace of God. This is the Bible jewel that we may compare to the agate. And there are two things over which this jewel, the grace of God, will make us conquerors, if we have it in our hearts. Each of these things begins with the letter S. I. The first thing over which this Bible jewel, the grace of God, will make us conquerors is SIN. The Bible tells us that we are born in sin. Our hearts are full of sin. Unless we get this sin driven out, and overcome, we never can be happy, either in this world or in the world to come. We read a great deal in the Bible about the wrestling, and struggling, and fighting, that Christians have to do. And the thing they have to fight against all the time is sin. When two people are fighting, it generally happens that they keep on at it till either one or the other of them gets the victory. And so it is in the great battle we have to fight with sin. Either we must conquer it, or it will conquer us. But we never can conquer sin ourselves. And there is nothing that will give us the victory over it but the grace of God. This is the real agate, the Bible jewel, that will give us the victory. II. The second thing over which this jewel will make us conquerors is SATAN. This is the next S. Satan is the great tempter. The Bible tells us that he "goeth about as a roaring lion, seeking whom he may devour" or destroy. The only way in which Satan can destroy us, or do us any harm, is by tempting us to sin. And he cannot hurt us, even in this way, unless we yield to the temptation. If we only have this Bible jewel, the grace of God, with us, it will make us conquerors over Satan. And then, although he is so powerful and so wicked, and although he tries so hard to injure us and keep us from getting to heaven, he won't be able to do us any harm. (*Ibid.*)   *The conqueror's jewel:*—The greatest enemy with which we have to fight is sin. This enemy meets us in many forms. But the form in which it gives us more trouble than any other is perhaps that of selfishness. This is an evil that is very hard to conquer. Suppose we are walking in the country, and meet a snake in the path; with the cane in our hand we strike it again and again, till it lies still and motionless. We leave it, and go on our way, feeling sure that we have killed the snake. But when we have finished our walk, and come back to the place where we left the snake, we find it still alive and active. Then we say to ourselves, "Snakes are hard to kill." And it is just so with selfishness. It is a very difficult thing to conquer it. If we wish to subdue it, and get the victory over it, we must be sure to have this conqueror's jewel, the grace of God. And there are three things that this jewel will lead us to do in fighting against selfishness. I. In the first place, it will lead us TO PRAY AGAINST IT. Prayer is necessary to our success in everything we do. Jesus said to His disciples, "Without Me ye can do nothing." And this is as true now as it was then. It is as true of us as it was of the disciples. And it is particularly true of the thing we are now considering. If we want to get the victory over the selfishness of our own hearts, it is especially necessary for us to pray to Jesus to help us. II. The second thing that this conqueror's jewel will lead us to do in getting the victory over selfishness is TO STRUGGLE AGAINST IT. We must not think that praying is to take the place of striving. God only helps those who strive to help themselves. Suppose that you and I have to climb up a high mountain. We kneel down at the foot of the mountain, and pray God to help us get up to the top of it. And then suppose we should sit down and wait for God to send an angel to take us in his arms and carry us up to the top of the mountain. Have we any right to expect that God would help us in that way? Not at all. We might wait all our lives, but we never should get any help. If we want to get up the mountain, we must begin to climb, and we must keep on climbing till we get to the top, and while we are doing this God will help us. No soldier ever expects to gain the victory over his enemies without a hard struggle. We have all read about the great victory which the Duke of Wellington obtained over the Emperor Napoleon at the battle of Waterloo. But he had to fight hard all day before he gained that victory. And so, if we want to get the victory over our selfishness, we must struggle hard against it. III. The third thing that this conqueror's jewel will lead us to do in getting the victory over selfishness is TO REMEMBER THE EXAMPLE OF JESUS. Jesus came down from heaven to do three things for us. The first was to fulfil God's law for us. The second was to die for our sins. The third was to show us how to live. The Bible tells us that "He left us an example that we should follow His steps." You know, when we are learning to write, our teacher sets us a copy. Then we take the word or sentence that has been written for us, letter by letter, and try to make others like them. And just in the same way the life of Jesus is set before us as our copy. We are to keep it before us, and try to make our own lives like His. Being a Christian means being like Jesus. Now it is said of Jesus that "He pleased not Himself." (*Ibid.*) *The amethyst :*—The amethyst is a very precious jewel and very much admired. Its colour is a mixture of blue and red. It is a rich purple, very much like the appearance of a bunch of ripe, dark-coloured grapes. The name of this jewel comes from the Greek language, and it means not to intoxicate, or not to make drunk. The amethyst is the temperance jewel. The boys and girls, and men and women, who make clear, cold, sparkling water their principal drink, should take the amethyst as their favourite jewel. In old times people used to think that if they only had a cup made out of an amethyst to drink from, they never would get intoxicated. And if they only carried one of these jewels about them it would have the same effect. They thought the amethyst was a charm against intemperance, and a cure for it when men fell into this dreadful habit. What a blessed thing it would be if this were so! Then this jewel would be worth its weight in gold, and ten times more than that. But it cannot do this. It is only the Bible jewel, which the amethyst stands for, that can do this. And what is the Bible jewel that may be compared to the amethyst ? It is the fear of God. This is the real temperance jewel. I wish to speak of three ways in which this Bible jewel—the true amethyst—the fear of God—will be a temperance jewel to us. I. In the first place it will KEEP US FROM LEARNING TO DRINK. You know what a dreadful thing it is to be plunged over the Falls of Niagara. Nobody can go over there without being killed. And if, when you are visiting the falls, you should see a person sailing in a boat on the river above the falls, to see how near he could go without being drawn over, you would think that a very dangerous position to be in. And so it would be. So long as a person is on the river above Niagara he is always in danger of being drawn over. But if he keep out of the river, he is free from danger. Now, to fall into intemperance is worse than going over Niagara. And learning to drink intoxicating liquor is like sailing on the river above Niagara. You are in danger at any time of being drawn over. This Bible gem, the fear of God, is the true amethyst—the temperance jewel—in the first place, because it will keep us from learning to drink. II. It is so, in the second place, because it will KEEP US FROM TEMPTING OTHERS TO DRINK. It is impossible to tell how much harm is done in this way. God has tried to stop this evil by speaking about it in the Bible. He says in one place, "Woe unto him that giveth his neighbour drink, that putteth the bottle to him" (Hab. ii. 15). III. And then there is another reason why this Bible jewel, the fear of God, may be compared to the amethyst— the true temperance jewel—and that is, IT WILL LEAD US TO STOP DRINKING even when we have got into the habit of doing so. When the habit of drinking is once formed it becomes very strong. Nothing but this temperance jewel will enable any one to break off from the habit of drinking. My dear young friends, you know that in Switzerland there are great mountains, very high and very steep. Many of them have there tops covered with ice and snow. Sometimes great masses of this ice and snow will get loose and fall. In their fall they go rushing down the sides of the mountains with a noise like thunder. These masses of falling ice and snow are called avalanches. If travellers, or cottages, or even villages are in their path, they are swept away into instant destruction. When an avalanche is once started, it never can be stopped till it gets to the bottom of the mountain. Sometimes a very little is enough to start an avalanche. The stepping of your foot upon it; the taking away of a loose stone; or even the jarring of the air may do it. What a dangerous thing it is to loosen an avalanche and send it down the mountain side, breaking and crushing everything before it! But drunkenness is worse than an avalanche. And when any one gets into the habit of drinking he is loosening an avalanche over his head which may at any time rush down upon him and kill him. Be very careful how you do this. Don't get into the habit of drinking, and then you will be sure never to become a drunkard. (*Ibid.*)

Ver. 29. **Aaron shall bear the names.**—I. THE PERSON TYPIFIED BY AARON. 1. Christ (Heb. v. 4, 5). 2. His Divine call to the priesthood (Heb. v. 10). 3. The destruction of His enemies (1 John iii. 8). 4. The leader of His people (John x. 3). 5. The averter of God's vengeance (1 Tim. ii. 5). II. THE PERSONS REPRESENTED BY THE TERM "ISRAEL." Ancient Israel, as an elect nation, was a typical people, representing the collective body of Christ's Church. For which compare Deut. vii. 6–8 with Rom. viii. 28–30. 1. All true believers are called Israel (Gal. vi. 16). 2. They are circumcised, as was Israel (Rom. ii. 28, 29). 3. They are a peculiar people, as was Israel (Tit. ii. 14). III. WHAT IS MEANT BY AARON'S BEARING THEM ON HIS HEART. 1. Christ's affection for us (1 John iii. 16). 2. His great pity towards us (Isa. lxiii. 9). 3. His interest in us (John xvii. 9, 10, 24). IV. WHAT WE ARE TO UNDERSTAND BY AARON'S GOING INTO THE HOLY PLACE. Eternal exclusion from God's glory would have been our unchanging portion, had not the blessed Saviour opened a way for our admission. See it literally explained in Lev. xvi. 1. It shows Christ's entrance into heaven for us (Heb. ix. 24). 2. To present His perfect offering for us (Heb. ix. 12). 3. His continual intercession (Heb. vii. 25). V. HERE I SHALL EXPLAIN THIS " CONTINUAL MEMORIAL," EVER BEFORE THE LORD : It may signify—1. The constant efficacy of His blood. 2. The perfection of His everlasting righteousness. 3. The daily outpouring of His Spirit. 4. The gracious preservation of His people in holiness. 5. It represents the place which Christ's Church occupies in His heart, in glory. 6. And ensures our everlasting enjoyment after this time-state is passed away. (*T. B. Baker.*) *The connection between priest and people :*—That the connection between the priest and the people might be made more plain, God not only placed on his breast the memorials of the twelve tribes, but also engraved their names on his shoulders. Thus the people would understand that this one man was not separated from the others for the sake of private advantage, but that in his one person they were all a kingdom of priests (see 1 Pet. ii. 5 ; Isa. lxvi. 21 ; Rev. i. 6). Hence arises our confidence of ascending to heaven because Christ raises us up with Him ; we "sit together in heavenly places in Christ Jesus" ; however weak we may be in ourselves, herein is all our strength that we are His burden. (*J. Calvin.*) *Shoulder and heart ministry :*—History shall not be forgotten, deliverances shall be held in perpetual remembrance ; marvels of the Lord wrought yesterday shall be as the marvels wrought in the present hour. Then there shall be a tenderer representation—the names shall be upon the heart. There shall be a ministry of love, a pleading of sympathy, an identification of the spirit of the man with all the difficulties and distresses of the people. Shoulder work : representing publicity, courage, strength, leadership—shoulders to which men may look as to strong towers ; and then the delicate heart-work ; the sweet sympathy, the paternal or fraternal interest in all that concerns the development, and culture, and completion of poor, shattered, struggling human life. It is nothing to bear upon the shoulder—that is a kind of burden-carrying, and there is a kind of applause immediately following the completion of any athletic task—but who can tell the heart-work of the true mediator or minister of the new covenant ? A man who enters into this work with his whole soul must live a life of singular tension and agony, otherwise he is but a shatterer of words ; only his shoulder engaged in the function ; his heart is at liberty to run after any vanity and court the applause of any foolish idolatry. We must look at ideals ; we must fasten our attention upon the thing as God meant it to be, and taking the Divine meaning of the priesthood in the olden time and of the ministry of to-day, we have amongst us men who care for us, men with strong shoulders, tower-like men ; sturdy, visible, valiant, dauntless men ; men who can speak in the darkness and make their voices heard in the storm ; men who know not the cloud of fear and who heed not the tempest of opposition. But we need in the same men other qualities, tenderer elements, more gracious and insinuating forces that find their way into our inmost experience, into our heart's aching and sore necessity—men who are taught of Heaven to speak a word in season to him that is weary ; men who have the gift of consolation, who can lower the voice into a tender and helpful whisper, and who can bring all God's gospel to bear in gracious and healing application upon the wound which makes the heart sore. This is the ideal. That we do not rise to it may be a rebuke to ourselves, but it is no just criticism upon the Divine purpose. It is an ideal we should do much to sustain. We cannot tell what we owe to the men who teach us great doctrines, who pray off many a burden that strains our strength ; who speak to us, even between the lines of their eloquence, things that help us to bear life's misery with a more cheerful courage. We do not know what is being done by ministry of a truly Christian type, whether in the pulpit, or in the school, or in the family, or in the market-place. No man can measure the full issue and outgoing of influence connected with the profound agonistic service on behalf of truth and humanity. (*J. Parker, D.D.*)

Ver. 30. **The Urim and the Thummim.**—*The Urim and Thummim:*—A very great mystery hangs over those two words—" the Urim and the Thummim "—commonly translated " light and perfection "—in the Septuagint version, " manifestation and truth,"—and in the Vulgate, " doctrine and truth." But until there shall stand up a priest with Urim and Thummim, we are told, both in Ezra and Nehemiah, it will remain a mystery. And as a mystery we must view it. I. THE STONES REPRESENTING THE CHURCH, THAT WERE BORNE UPON THE HIGH PRIEST'S BREAST AND THE HIGH PRIEST'S SHOULDERS, CONNECT THEMSELVES WITH THE URIM AND THE THUMMIM. In some way or other, it is quite clear that God was pleased to reveal His will in connection with these twelve stones. In what way it is very difficult to determine. There are these possible interpretations. It may be that it pleased God at certain times to throw a miraculous light upon these twelve different coloured stones, which did in some way write His mind; either by the initiatory letters, or by some signs which were familiar to the high priest, God did, by the means of these twelve precious stones, representing the twelve tribes, convey His will to the high priest—that he might again convey it to the people. But the closest investigation that has been given to the subject does not lead to that conclusion—and those who are the most competent to speak do not adopt that interpretation. It has been rather supposed that these stones were not made themselves the channels or the mediums by which God conveyed His will, but that they accredited, as it were, and empowered the high priest, when he was before God, authenticated the high priest, that then God seeing him in the fulness of his priesthood, was pleased to convey spiritually and not materially by these stones to his mind what God had in His own mind upon the subject that was transferred to him for consultation. II. Consider now practically WHAT IS THAT WHICH IS TO US THE URIM AND THUMMIM?—AND HOW SHOULD WE CONSULT GOD, AND OBTAIN OUR ANSWERS? 1. And here let me speak to you of the very great importance of going to God very often consultingly. In prayer, pray consultingly—in reading, read consultingly. Always consult God first, before you ask any man—if possible, before you ask yourself. Before you go to a thought, if possible, ask God to take the initiative—ask God first to speak even before your own heart speaks. 2. You must be very careful, whenever you go to consult God, that there are two conditions. (1) That your mind is not pre-occupied, that you be free, that you do not bring pre-conceived and settled ideas, and then ask God to fall in with your view. You will be surprised, if you examine your own hearts, how very generally you do that. You have settled what you wish, and then you go to God to persuade God, as it were, to follow your design. Try to go to God as the blank sheet, that God will write there, upon a mind quite free, His own entire will. (2) And again, it is quite essential, if you will have answers to your consultings of God, that you should have thoroughly and honestly made up your mind to follow whatever you find to be, believe to be God's guidance. If you do not go to God with that true determination, you will consult him in vain. (3) If we are to attain Urim and Thummim in our consultations with God, we must do it through priesthood—in the recognition of the priesthood of the Lord Jesus Christ. III. THERE ARE MANY WAYS IN WHICH GOD MAY GIVE US THE URIM AND THUMMIM TO DIRECT OUR STEPS. 1. By a light breaking on some passage of the Bible. 2. By the Spirit of God illuminating our own minds. (*J. Vaughan, M.A.*) *The Urim and Thummim:*—We lean to the opinion that the precious stones constituted the Urim and Thummim, but not by reason of any supernatural illumination of the letters, and that the stones rendered the breastplate the ornament or badge which qualified the high priest for making inquiries of Jehovah: " They shall be upon Aaron's heart when he goeth in before the Lord." The precious stones may have received the collective name of Urim and Thummim: 1. On their own account. Of all earthly objects, these precious stones are the most lustrous, and emit light of themselves. Like the stars they shine in the darkest night, and for that reason they have been called the " stars of earth." Are they not, then, well called lights? Thummim signifies perfection. The stones, from their brilliancy, purity, and uncommon beauty, are perhaps the most striking emblems which earthly objects furnish of truth or perfection, and are therefore not inappropriately named " Thummim." 2. On account of their being the badge or ornament which it was necessary for the high priest to wear when he consulted Jehovah. The object of the high priest was to get light on some dark subject, or to arrive at the truth on some matter he could not discover otherwise, or to give a righteous decision in cases in which his knowledge or wisdom was deficient, and such as would accord with innocence and justice. For these reasons the gems seem to be appropriately called " Urim and Thummim." 3. On account of their representing the children of Israel. The names of all the tribes being on the stones—one name on each—the Israelites might see in these stones an emblem of what it was designed they should become, before they were meet for being worshippers in the heavenly temple ; and the high priest might be reminded by them that his mission was to bring the pious Israelite into that state of perfection. Like these gems, man by nature is of the earth earthy. Both have their origin in mother earth. Yet both, when polished, may shine like the stars of the firmament. (*W. Brown.*) *The Urim and the Thummim :*—As to the Urim and the Thummim, whether they were precious stones bearing those significant names, or what they were, no one is able at present to decide. Urim means " Lights " ; Thummim, " Perfections." These mysterious contents of the breastplate seem to direct our thoughts to the heart of the Lord Jesus, as containing all lights and perfections, all grace and truth, all mercies and righteousness. In Him was light : and He manifested forth that light ; He declared the Father. He is the light of the glory of God : all fulness of light dwells in Him. The Septuagint translation " Manifestation," is not an inappropriate expression, though rather a paraphrase than a translation. We are told in Eph. v. 13, " Whatsoever doth make manifest is light." The high priest, with the Urim in his breastplate, became the channel by which God made manifest His counsels. The Lord Jesus, as the great High Priest, makes known the counsels and purposes of God. He is light; and in Him is no darkness at all ; so that the mind and will of God can be perfectly revealed to Him, and can by Him be communicated to His saints. He is the brightness or shining forth of God's glory, the irradiation of God. The Thummim also, or all perfections of truth and holiness, dwell in Him. Light and truth, love and holiness, grace and righteousness are inseparable. Sometimes we find the Urim mentioned, without the Thummim (Num. xxvii. 21 ; 1 Sam. xxviii. 6). From these two passages it is clear that by means of the Urim, or lights, in the breastplate of the high priest, the counsel, judgment, and prophetic guidance of Jehovah were revealed. In three other passages (Deut. xxxiii. 8 ; Ezra ii. 63 ; Neh. vii. 65), the Urim and Thummim are mentioned together. " Urim " is also translated " fire " and fires (Isa. xxiv. 15, xxxi. 9, xliv. 16, xlvii. 14, l. 11 ; Ezek. v. 2). In the vision of the Son of Man (Rev. i. 12–16), the eyes of the High Priest, in the midst of the seven golden candlesticks, were as a flame of fire. The lights and perfections of God searched into the ways of the seven Churches ; and the Priest of the Most High could say, as He addressed each separately, " I know thy works," and could give a word of encouragement or of rebuke, according as it was needed. (*H. W. Soltau.*)

Vers. 31–35. The robe of the ephod.—*The robe of the ephod :*—The third peculiar garment of the high priest was the robe of the ephod (vers. 5, 31). On the skirts of which were fastened—1. The pomegranates of blue silk, and purple, and scarlet round about. This fruit hath a most pleasant smell, sweet in itself, and sweetening other things round about it ; and is full of precious juice and liquor. 2. Bells of gold between them round about, a golden bell and a pomegranate ; the use of which was, that his sound might be heard round about when he went into the sanctuary and holy of holies. The whole garment signified the righteousness of Christ's human nature, which is—(1) Most sweet itself, having a most pleasant savour as the pomegranate. (2) Full of most precious juice and virtue, to qualify and abate the raging heat of God's displeasure, as the juice of pomegranates doth allay the burning heat of an ague that would shake the body to pieces. (3) Casts upon us a sweet savour being wrapped in it. For we, by nature, stinking in our sins and rottenness, are loathsome to the Lord ; but once covered with this mantle, we are a sweet savour to God. 3. This garment hath a sweet sound, as of golden bells, which to hear were most delectable, because the garment of Christ's righteousness brings grace to us no otherwise than by the sound of the gospel. For faith, by which we put on Christ, is wrought by hearing the sweet sound and golden bell of the gospel. Whence some have thought, that by this part of the priest's attire, is shadowed the prophetical office of Christ. Sweet is the proclamation of the gospel of peace ! 4. The use. That by these bells the priests must be heard when he goeth into the sanctuary ; signifying the power of Christ, our High Priest's, perpetual intercession (being entered into the sanctuary of heaven) for His elect and chosen. (*T.*

Taylor, D.D.) *The blue robe :*—The robe was of one piece, and was all of blue. This colour sets forth that which was pre-eminently heavenly in the character of Christ, and it reminds us of that perfect, seamless robe of Christ's righteousness, which is " unto all and upon all them that believe " (Rom. iii. 22). The bottom of this long robe was ornamented with golden bells and pomegranates. Here were sound and fruit, and as much fruit as sound. As he moved about in the court or in the tabernacle, every step sent forth a sweet golden sound from each of the many little bells hanging about his feet, and Aaron would seem to say by this sound, " I am ready to serve you, and to bless you." The pomegranates would often remind him that a priest must do more than make a sound ; he must work as well as talk ; he must produce both sound and fruit, and both must be good. These bells and pomegranates were about the feet—the walk of the high priest; reminding us of the loveliness of Christ's walk, and of the sweetness and pleasantness of His conversation. The sound of these bells would not be heard in the camp, and but faintly, if they could be heard at all, outside the court. To hear this sweet sound distinctly, a man must have come as far as to the brazen altar ; but he could not come there without an offering. And as the first offering he was required to bring was a sin-offering, if a man stood at the altar of brass and listened to the sweet and joyful sound of the golden bells about the hem of the priest's blue robe, we are quite sure that he had come, first of all, as a sinner to be pardoned and saved. So now a man must feel himself a sinner, and in need of a sin-offering: he must come out from the world ; must draw near to Him who is both the altar and the sacrifice ; must lay his hand by faith on the head of Christ. (*G. Rodgers.*) *The robe of the ephod :*—This robe embodied the colour of the heavens ; it was all of blue. It seems to have typified the especial glory of the true High Priest, whose name is " Prince of Peace," the " Lord of Peace " ; and who wears His princely robes as King of Righteousness, and King of Peace, upon the ground of having made full, perfect, and eternal peace through the blood of His cross. God, known as love, is the God of peace : and He has brought again from the dead our Lord Jesus, that Great Shepherd of the sheep, through the blood of the eternal covenant. That title, " the Great Shepherd of the sheep," seems to sum up in one name the whole of the priesthood of Christ, as described in the Epistle to the Hebrews. He is the Great Shepherd ; for He is King as well as Priest. He has royal power ; a royal heart ; royal glory ; and His dominions are righteousness and peace ; and He is the Shepherd, having proved His love and care for the sheep, in laying down His life for them ; and all His priestly service on their behalf is conducted with the heart of a good Shepherd, who loves His own, and whose own the sheep are. This is, therefore, a princely, priestly, shepherd robe. It displays the love of God as seen in the gift of His Son and as manifested by the Son Himself, in laying down His life, and so making peace. It was a robe which covered the high priest from head to foot, and showed the great object of His priesthood, namely, to maintain, on the behalf of His own, that peace with God which He had procured at the cost of His own blood, and which the God of peace had sealed and established, by raising Him from the dead through the blood of the everlasting covenant. This robe was all of one piece, woven from the top throughout, and a provision was made by means of a binding of woven work round about the hole in the top of it, that it should not rend or be rent. Is not this very significant of the unchanging love of Christ? (*H. W. Soltau.*) **A golden bell and a pomegranate.**—*Golden bells :*—I am glad that the first use of bells was a religious use ; and hereafter the gospel of God to me shall be a chime of bells ; and whether I hear them in the garments of the high priest, or in the cathedral tower, they shall suggest to me the gladness, the warning, and the triumph of the gospel. 1. These gospel bells, like those that adorned the high priest's robe, are golden bells. Other bells are made of coarser materials—zinc, and lead, and tin, and copper ; but these gospel bells are bells of gold. There is one bell in Europe that cost three hundred thousand dollars. It was at vast expense that metallic voices were given to the towers of York, and Vienna, and Oxford. But all the wealth of heaven was thrown into this gospel bell. No angel can count its value. Eternity cannot demonstrate its cost. When the bell of the Russian Kremlin was being fused, the lords came and threw their gold into the molten mass ; but when this Gospel bell was to be constructed, the kings of heaven, the hierarchs of eternity, threw into it their crowns and their sceptres. It is a golden bell. Do you believe it ? Hear it ring ! " God so loved the world that He gave His only begotten Son, that whosoever believeth in Him should not perish, but have everlasting life." " Him hath God exalted to be a Prince and a Saviour, to give repentance unto Israel, and forgiveness of sins." 2. I remark, further, that these gospel bells, like those around the high priest's garment, are bells of invitation. When the Jews heard the clash of those bells in the hem of the priest's robe they knew it was an invitation to worship. That is the meaning of every church tower from San Francisco to New York, and from London to St. Petersburgh. It is, "Come—come." 3. I remark, further, that the gospel bells, like those on the high priest's robe, are bells of warning. When the Jews heard the clash and ring of these bells, it was a warning for them to worship, lest their God be offended. On Bell Rock, in the German Ocean, there is a lighthouse, and there are two bells, that every half-minute ring out through the fog, through the darkness, through the storm, and over the sea. Beware! Beware! The helmsman on the ship, hearing the warning, turns the wheel and steers off. It is a startling thing, at midnight, to hear the heavy clang of a fire bell, if you live in the third ward, and the tongue of the bell strike one, two, three! If a city is besieged, and the flash of the musketry is seen on the hill-tops, and the cavalry horses are dashing up and down, and the batteries are being unlimbered, all the bells of the city call, to arms! to arms! So this gospel bell is a bell of alarm. 4. I remark, further, that the bells on the high priest's robe were bells of joy. When the Jews heard the chiming of those bells on the priest's robe, it announced to them the possibility of pardon for their sins, and of deliverance. "Behold! I bring you good tidings of great joy, that shall be to all people." There have been bells rung on days of victory. The bell of London rang after Waterloo. The bells in many of our cities rang after the settlement of our national strife. The great bells of York, and Oxford, and Vienna, at some time, have sounded the victory. 5. These gospel bells, of which I speak, are bells of triumph. Aye! they are ringing now: "All flesh shall see the salvation of God." "And He shall reign for ever and for ever!" The Bishop of Malta, in superstition, had all the bells of the city rung, in the hope that the storm that was raging in the city might be quieted. That was superstition: but I think it is faith in God that leads us to believe that the ringing of these gospel bells will yet silence all the storms of this world's sin, and all the storms of this world's trouble. Oh! when Jesus, our Great High Priest, in full robes shall enter into His glory, the bells on the hem of His garments will ring with the music of an eternal merriment. 6. But we shall have no share in that joy unless now we listen to the gospel tiding. There is a bell on the other side of the waters, weighing two hundred and eight thousand pounds; and it takes twenty-four men to ring it. But to bring out all the sweetness of this gospel bell would take all the consecrated spirits of earth—seraphim and archangel. Who in this august assembly will listen? Who will listen now? In New England they have what they call a passing bell; that is, when some one dies in a village, word is sent to the sexton, and he sounds the bell just as often as the man lived years: and when the sound is in the tower, the people are solemn, and they say, "Some one is dead—who is it?" For us the passing bell will soon sound. Gone from the family. Gone from the church. Gone from the last opportunity of salvation. (*T. De Witt Talmage.*)   *Lessons:*—As the priests must have in their skirts both bells and pomegranates: so must every evangelical minister. 1. The bells allow them not to be dumb dogs (Isa. lvi. 10), but the sound of the law and gospel must clearly sound in their mouths, to be heard afar off. 2. These bells must be of gold, to put ministers in mind that their doctrine be pure; not corrupt, not savouring of popish liberty, or self-respect. 3. They must never come into the congregation without these bells; for ministers must still be furnished with some sound matter of instruction and edification. How is it then that many come into the congregation and never bring bells? Many are afraid lest the sound of their bells should be heard too much, and that it would disgrace them to be counted diligent preachers. And many scorn others that their bells sound so often. 4. To the bells, ministers must join pomegranates: with the wholesome word, join good works and holy life. He carries the bell, a minister whose life is agreeable with the holy doctrine (Matt. v. 19). He that keepeth the commandments, and teacheth others so to do, shall be great in the kingdom of God. John Baptist had both bells (being a burning light in himself), and pomegranates; being a shining light unto others. And as the pomegranates smelled sweet; so must ministers labour to leave a sweet smell behind them everywhere. (*T. Taylor, D.D.*)   *The church-going bells:*—In considering the usefulness of church bells, it may be proper to say: First, that they render a worthy claim for their existence in promoting the temporal welfare of communities where their voice is heard. But, secondly, the worth of a bell is perhaps still more evident when we consider its use for religious purposes. The ways of its usefulness, when calling the people together for worship, are easily seen. I. IT CALLS ATTENTION TO THE CLAIMS OF GOD FOR LOVE AND SERVICE. NOTHING IS MORE MANIFEST THAN THAT MEN ARE APT TO BECOME CARELESS IN RESPECT TO THESE CLAIMS. II. IT IS USEFUL IN PROMOTING A LARGER ATTENDANCE UPON THE SERVICES OF THE SANCTUARY, THAN WOULD BE SECURED BUT FOR ITS INFLUENCE. III. ADDED TO AN INCREASE OF ATTENDANTS, THE BELL PRO-MOTES PUNCTUALITY. IV. THE BELL IS USEFUL IN THE INFLUENCE IT HAS IN PREPAR-ING THE MIND OF THOSE WHO OBEY ITS CALL FOR WORSHIP. V. THE BELL IS USEFUL BECAUSE OF THE SACRED ASSOCIATIONS CONNECTED WITH ITS SOUND, AND THE HALLOWED MEMORIES ITS NOTES INSPIRE. (*G. L. Foster.*) *The dumb bell :*—Mr. Gatty, in his book on " Bells," gives the following anecdote, on the credit of Cardinal Baronius : " When Charles II., king of France, A.D. 615, was at Sens, in Burgundy, he heard a bell in the church of St. Stephen, the sound of which pleased him so much that he ordered it to be transported to Paris. The Bishop of Sens, however, was greatly displeased at this, and the bell so sympathized with him that it turned dumb on the road and lost all its sound. When the king heard of this he commanded that the bell should be carried back to its old quarters, when, strange to relate, as it approached the town, it recovered its original tone, and began to ring so as to be heard at Sens, whilst yet about four leagues distant from it." The true preacher grows silent if forced to any other service than his Lord's. If he attempts to speak on any other topic than that which concerns his Lord and the gospel, he misses his former force ; he is not at home, he is glad to end his speech and sit down. Our bell is dumb if it does not ring out for Jesus. The world would soon dismiss us if it had hired us to be its orator, for our heart is elsewhere, and only upon the one dear, familiar theme can be eloquent. (*C. H. Spurgeon.*)

Vers. 36–38. Holiness to the Lord.—*Holiness to the Lord :*—This plate of pure gold was fastened by blue lace to the mitre, or turban, or tiara, or linen, which was upon the head of the high priest. He put it on with the robe of the ephod, the robe under the breastplate and the ephod—the robe of the ephod, which had, round the bottom, a bell and a pomegranate alternately—fruitfulness and music—showing the fruitfulness of the priesthood and the music of the priesthood before God, without which emblems the high priest might never enter into the holy of holies, lest he die. To teach man that no creature can ever stand before God but through priest-hood, lest he die. Were we to stand before God but in the fruitfulness and music of the priesthood of Jesus Christ, we should die. The plate of pure gold upon his forehead, he went in before God to present the inscription graven there like the engraving of a signet, " Holiness to the Lord," to take away the iniquity of the holy things of Israel, and to make those holy things, purged from their iniquity, acceptable to God. Consider the subject of holiness. I. THE WORD IS USED IN THREE SENSES IN THE BIBLE. 1. Sometimes the word " holy " means that which is set apart, consecrated. In that sense the vessels of the Temple were holy. 2. Sometimes the word signifies the indwelling of the Spirit, with His gradually sanc-tifying processes. In this sense the church is holy. 3. There is a still higher sense in which man is perfectly holy. Christ perfects them that are sanctified. II. THE TRUE DEFINITION OF HOLINESS IS THE LIKENESS OF GOD. But we cannot conceive of the likeness of God but through a medium, and that medium must be the Lord Jesus Christ. Whatever traits we find characterizing the life of Jesus, these make up holiness. 1. The life of Christ was a separate life. 2. He always carried about an inner sanctuary in His own soul. 3. The life of Christ had a subdued tone. 4. It was a life consecrated to an object. 5. It was a life of praise. III. LOOK UPON HOLINESS AS AN END TO BE OBTAINED. Do not seek holiness as a means to happiness, but happiness as a means to holiness. Be more careful about the holiness of little things than of great things. (*J. Vaughan, M.A.*) *Christ our High Priest, bearing the iniquity of our holy things :*—The first thing that strikes us here is, that it is the head of the high priest that is thus adorned, the most honourable member of the body, the seat of the indwelling soul. Then, again, it is the forehead that is selected, which is the comeliness and glory of the head—the place on which the eye of the observer rests, and on which the eye of God would rest when meeting with the priest or the worshipper. On the forehead of the high priest, on " the forefront of his mitre," was the ornament to be fastened. It con-sisted of a plate of pure gold, the purest and costliest of metals, to signify the purity that God demanded. On it there was to be engraved, like the engravings of a signet, distinct and deep, " Holiness to the Lord,"—still farther foreshadowing the-awful holiness of God, and the no less awful holiness which He required in the sin-bearer. Forming thus the most prominent part of his dress, and placed upon his forehead, it would be that on which the eye of God might be said first to rest, whether at the brazen altar, or the altar of incense, or the mercy-seat, in all parts of his holy service. When standing before God, it was this peculiar adorning that presented itself, with its inscription, "Holiness to the Lord." Thus, then, there was proclaimed to Israel a free forgiveness for the iniquities of their holy things. It was forgiveness through the holiness of another, as if God would teach them that while He required holiness in him who was to bear any sin, yet especial holiness was required when bearing the sins of our holy things. And then there was not merely the bare forgiveness, but there was the acceptance thus provided, both for themselves and their services, before the Lord. All this was to Israel the shadow of " good things to come." The law, indeed, made nothing perfect, but it was the bringing in of the better hope, by which we draw nigh to God (Heb. vii. 19). This better hope has now been brought in. What was thus foreshadowed afar off by Aaron, as Israel's high priest, has been fulfilled to us in Jesus of Nazareth, God's own anointed Priest. I. WE LEARN HOW COMPLETE IS THE PROVISION MADE BY GOD FOR A SINNER'S ACCEPTANCE. This provision is entirely in Him who is our great High Priest. It is not in ourselves at all, but in Him alone. " It pleased the Father that in Him should all fulness dwell." He is the Father's infinite trea-sure-house of all blessing, secured for, and set open to sinners. Nothing that a guilty soul can require, is awanting in Him. Out of Him, there is nothing; in Him, there is everything. " He, of God, is made unto us wisdom, and righteous-ness, and sanctification, and redemption." In our text, however, the allusion is not to His fulness in general, but to His priesthood alone, as making provision for a sinner's pardon and acceptance : and this in reference to the sins of our holy things—the sins committed in our more direct transactions with God. For every sin, and for every kind of sin, there is provision in Him on whom our sins were laid. For all these there is a special way of pardon ordained by God, and certain sins are minutely specified, in order to show us that no case has been overlooked or left without a special remedy. II. LET US LEARN HOW PERPETUAL AND UNCHANGEABLE THIS PROVISION IS. It is written here, concerning the high priest on earth, "It shall be always upon his forehead, that they may be accepted before the Lord." In this we have a vivid type of Him, who is " the same yesterday, to-day, and for ever " ; who hath " an unchangeable priesthood " ; who " ever liveth to make intercession for us." He who bears the iniquity of our holy things, is one who changes not ; who is ever the same holy High Priest, and ever glorious in the Father's eyes. We vary, but He varies not. Our feelings change, His alter not. Our soul fluctuates, ever rising and falling, ever ebbing and flowing, but He remaineth steadfast and true. We grow cold and faithless, He abideth faithful, He cannot deny Himself. His is a priesthood which endureth for ever, which never loses aught of its efficacy and value. III. LEARN HOW GLORIOUS AND CERTAIN IS THIS PROVISION. It depends upon the holiness of the high priest. Not upon his grace, or mercy, or compassion, but upon his holiness. It is because there is such holi-ness in him to meet and satisfy the holiness of God that our forgiveness is so secure, and the way of our obtaining it so glorious. What an ample pardon, what a secure acceptance, must that be which is secured to us by the holiness of our great High Priest ! for His holiness cannot change, neither can it pass away. His mercy might be worn out by our sins, and He might forget to be gracious, but He cannot cease to be holy. IV. LEARN HOW ACCESSIBLE AND FREE IS THIS PROVISION. It is set open to all. Its benefits are wide and unrestricted " Look unto Me and be ye saved, all the ends of the earth." (*H. Bonar, D.D.*) *The mitre :*—1. Made of blue silk and fine linen (ver. 39), like (as it seems) to an half-coronet. 2. Beautified with a golden plate, on which was written " Holiness to the Lord." 3. The use. Aaron must ever have it on his forehead while he bears the iniquity of their offerings, to make the people acceptable before the Lord (ver. 38). I. THE MITRE AND CROWN ON THE PRIEST'S HEAD SIGNIFIED—1. The Deity of Christ our head, which as a crown or circle wants beginning and end. 2. The kingly office of Christ, with all that honour and crown of glory set on the head of our Redeemer, to whom all power is given in heaven and in earth. II. THE GOLDEN PLATE IN WHICH WAS WRITTEN " HOLINESS TO THE LORD," DID NOT ONLY DISTINGUISH IT FROM THE MITRES OF THE ORDINARY PRIESTS, WHICH WANTED SUCH A PLATE : BUT SPECIALLY TYPIFIED JESUS CHRIST OUR HEAD, in whom was most conspicuous (as in a man's forehead), a most Divine and perfect holiness purer than the gold of that plate. III.

THE USE WAS SIGNIFICANT, that as the high priest, having on this plate, with this inscription, got the iniquities of the people pardoned, which he bare before the Lord : So our High Priest, Jesus Christ, presenting before His Father, His most absolute holiness, gets a pardon for all our sins, which He bears upon Himself. And as their sins were pardoned in respect of the high priest, who represented Christ : So both theirs and ours are indeed and in truth pardoned, for the true and eternal High Priest, who is Christ Himself. (*T. Taylor, D.D.*) *Holiness to the Lord :*—Holiness to the Lord! Where is that inscription to be stamped now ? The Jewish Tabernacle has expanded into that world-wide brotherhood, where whoso-ever doeth righteousness is accepted. Morning has risen into day. The ministry of Aaron is ended. All the outward glory and beauty of that Hebrew worship which the Lord commanded Moses has vanished into the eternal splendour of the gospel, and been fulfilled in Christ. What teaching has it left? What other than this ?— that we are to engrave *our* " Holiness to the Lord " first on the heart, and then on all that the heart goes out into, through the brain and the hand; on the plates of gold our age of enterprise is drawing up from mines and beating into currency ; on bales of merchandise and books of account ; on the tools and bench of every handicraft ; on your weights and measures ; on pen and plough and pulpit ; on the door-posts of your houses, and the utensils of your tables, and the walls of your chambers ; on cradle and playthings and schoolbooks ; on the locomotives of enter-prise, and the bells of the horses, and the ships of navigation ; on music-halls and libraries ; on galleries of art, and the lyceum desk ; on all of man's inventing and building, all of his using and enjoying, for all these are trusts in a stewardship, for which the Lord of the servants reckoneth. (*Bp. F. D. Huntington.*) *Material and shape of mitre :*—Elsewhere this ornament is called " nezer," from a verb signifying to separate ; and hence denoting a crown as a mark of separation or dis-tinction. The same word is applied to the diadem of kings. Indeed, such turbans of fine linen, with an encircling or front ornament of gold or precious stones, seem to have been the usual diadems of ancient kings. Justin says that Alexander the Great took his diadem from his head to bind up the wounds of Lysimachus. This shows clearly that it was of linen. Probably, it had some distinguishing ornament like that of the high priest here. 1. Jahn says curiously enough that, in the time of Josephus, the shape of the mitre had become somewhat altered. It was circular, was covered with a piece of fine linen, and sat so closely on the upper part of the head that it would not fall off when the body was bent down : apparently it did not cover the whole of the head. It may be that there is mystical reference to the crown of gold worn by each of those who exulted before God in the acknowledg-ment that He had made them prince-priests unto Himself. Each cast his mitre-coronet down before Him, who sat upon the throne, singing—

> "I bless Thee, gracious Father, for Thy pleasant gift to me,
> And earnestly I ask Thee, that it may always be
> In perfect consecration laid at Thy glorious feet,
> Touched with Thine altar-fire, and made an offering pure and sweet."

On the cultivation of holiness :—Let me say a few words concerning the cultivation of holiness. Look upon holiness as an end to be obtained. Do not seek holiness as a means to happiness—but happiness as a means to holiness. In heaven itself, the bliss of that world of glory is to be most prized because the happiness of that world will be the attainment of spotless sanctity. Be sure you take your forgive-ness—accept the peace which God freely offers—believe in the love of God ; receive gladly and gratefully every token of that love ; if it be only for this, that it is the means to holiness ; it will make you holy. And you may argue it with God so ; " Lord, give me happiness that I may be holy, for I find that without happiness I cannot glorify Thee by holiness, make me happy that I may be holy." Another suggestion which I would make to you in the cultivation of holiness, is to be more careful about the holiness of little things than of great things. It is so easy to go to church, and have a very devout manner, and even at the time to feel devoutly, and then to go away into life, and to have so very little holiness ; rather, such un-holiness, in the common affairs of our common life. Now that which characterizes the dispensation on which we are entered, and will characterize it infinitely presently, is this—that there shall be holiness to the Lord, not in the sanctuary, but in the common-places of every-day life, out of doors and in doors ; out of doors on that most familiar thing in the East, " the bells on horses "—the very harness of the horses is to be holiness; and in doors (the same passage in the last chapter of Zechariah), in doors, upon the most ordinary vessels that are used for domestic uses, the commonest thing that is in the house is to be " Holiness to the Lord ! "— the very culinary vessels are to be " Holiness to the Lord." (*J. Vaughan, M.A.*) *The mitre :*—The white linen is the emblem of purity ; the head is the seat of thought and of intellect. Christ had a pure mind ; all His thoughts were holy thoughts. And because He is so holy, He can bear His people's sins (Isa. liii. 4). He who is our Great High Priest before God is pure without a stain. God sees Him as such, and He stands for us who are His people, and we are accepted in Him. His holiness is ours by imputation. Standing in Him we are, in the sight of God, holy as Christ is holy, and pure as Christ is pure. (*G. Rodgers.*) *Holiness to the Lord in common things :*—In an old book I was reading the other day the writer laughed at some commoner who had just been made a peer, because he had his coat of arms burned and painted even upon his shovels and wheelbarrows. Now, in my reckoning, that was a very fine action and full of significance. If a man is a true man he is a man of God, a prince of God ; and he ought to put the stamp of his nobility on the commonest things with which he has to do. (*Christian Journal.*)   *Holiness unto the Lord :*—

> Write on our garnered treasures,
> Write on our choicest pleasures,
> Upon things new and old,
> The precious stone and gold—
> Wife, husband, children, friends—
> On all that goodness lends ;
> Go write on your good name—
> Upon your cherished fame—
> On every pleasant thing—
> On stores that Heaven doth fling
> Into your basket—write !
> Upon the smile of God,
> Upon His scourging rod—
> Write on your inmost heart,
> Write upon every part—
> To Him who claims the whole,
> Time, talent, body, soul—
> HOLINESS UNTO THE LORD !

That Aaron may bear the iniquity of the holy things.— *The iniquity of our holy things :*—I. A SAD SUBJECT. "The iniquity of the holy things which the children of Israel shall hallow." 1. They were " holy things." Despite the iniquity, their offerings were hallowed and holy. This is a precious saving clause. Our prayers, our praises, our service of God, these are holy things, albeit that iniquity attaches to them. They are holy as to God's ordinance, for He has ordained them for His glory. "Whoso offereth praise glorifieth Me." When we do what God bids us, the act is holy, because done in obedience to the Divine ordinance. Such deeds are holy as to the Divine design : for the sacrifices which the Israelites brought were meant to set forth Christ and His glorious work, and therefore they were holy. The great Father teaches us much precious truth by every institution of the Tabernacle and the Temple, and the gospel Church, and therefore obedience to each ordinance is holy. These deeds were often holy in the intent of the worshipper. 2. But although "holy things," there was iniquity upon all of them ; and did we ever do anything yet that had not some spot of iniquity upon it ? Is not our repentance, after all, but poor stuff compared with what it ought to be ? Is not unbelief mixed with our faith ? Hath not our love a measure of lukewarmness in it ? No act of consecration, no act of self-sacrifice, no rapture of fellowship, no height of spirituality has been without its imperfection. 3. Furthermore, some of these sins are apparent : indeed, many of them are painfully before our own eyes. If the Lord sees iniquity in our holy things, what iniquities there must be in our unholy things ! I have to complain that wandering thoughts will intrude in my prayers, my study of the Word, my sacred song, my choice meditation ; indeed, even in ministering the Word among you, I find my mind roaming. I have to complain also—and I fear many here would have to complain even more than I do —of want of faith in prayer. 4. These are only a few of the iniquities of our holy

things which we can see ; but beside these there are many imperfections of our service which we do not notice because we are not spiritual enough to discern them ;
but God sees them. Bring me that microscope! I have just now put the wing of a
butterfly under it. That is God's work, and, as I enlarge it, I discover no imperfection, but more and more of marvellous beauty. That butterfly's wing under
the microscope becomes most wonderful, and I worship God as I gaze upon His
handiwork. Take the butterfly away now and put your needle in its place. What?
Why this is a rough bar of iron which has never been smoothed or polished. This
is wretched workmanship. It does not seem fitted for delicate work. Such is man's
manufacture, the best of it. When God puts your prayers and my sermons under
His microscopic eye, they are not at all what we thought they were, but quite the
reverse. This ought to humble us as we come before the presence of the All-seeing
One. 5. These imperfections in our holy things are so grievous that they would
prevent any one of our works, or offerings, or prayers being accepted before the
thrice-holy God. II. A GLAD SUBJECT. What was done in type has also been done
in reality. 1. Consider, then, that God provided the high priest. It was ordained
that he should be a man perfect in his person. In our Lord Jesus there is no defect
open or secret. He is perfect, and so He can be high priest unto God. The man
had to be chosen of God. Aaron was so. Christ is ordained of God, and by
Divine authority He stands as high priest for us. This man had to be anointed
for his work. Aaron was anointed with oil ; but our Lord was anointed with the
Holy Spirit. 2. This high priest was altogether given up to his people. He has
a heart ; his people's names are on the breast-plate which covers it. He has
shoulders : his people's names are written on his shoulder-pieces, and thus he lends
them his power. Thus Christ has given up His thought, His judgment, His mind,
His every faculty to His people. He is all ours. The high priest reserved nothing
of himself ; he gave all of himself to all his people. 3. The high priest bore "the
iniquity of the holy things." All the iniquity of our holy things our Lord Jesus
has borne, and it is no longer imputed unto us. As He stood before God, though
He bore the iniquity of the people, yet He exhibited to God no iniquity, but
on His forehead was written, "Holiness to Jehovah." Notice that He bore before
God a holiness most precious ; in token whereof, in type, the engraving was inscribed
upon a plate of pure gold. The righteousness of Christ is more precious to God
than all the mines of gold in the whole world. There was no iniquity in His holy
things ; His holiness was conspicuous and undeniable, it shone on the forefront of
His mitre. That holiness of His was permanent. One thing more I want you to
notice, and that is, that he always wore it, "And it shall always be upon his forehead." Jesus is always "Holiness to God" on our behalf. Our holy work is now viewed
with Divine favour. Will you not offer more and more of these holy things, since they
are in very deed accepted in Christ? Now I have taught you the main doctrine of
the type, I desire to bring forth one or two lessons. 1. The first is, see here a
lesson of humility. Our good works, if we lay them up in store, and value them as
jewels, will, like the manna in the wilderness, very soon breed worms and stink.
There is enough rottenness in our best performances to make them offensive to an
enlightened conscience. Oh, that this fact, that even our holy things are tainted, may
be the death-warrant of our pride! 2. In the next place, learn the awful hazard
of going unto God without our High Priest. 3. Learn how you must be dressed
as a royal priesthood unto the Lord. 4. Lastly, let sinners gain a store of comfort
here. If God's own people have iniquity in their holy things, and yet they have
Christ to bear it for them, how patient must He be who is our High Priest. (*C. H.
Spurgeon.*)

Ver. 39. **The coat of fine linen.**—*The embroidered coat :*—The portion of the high
priest's dress called the coat was more properly a tunic. It was the innermost garment worn by the high priest, being placed first upon him after he was washed (Lev.
viii. 7). It seems to be derived from a verb meaning "to cover, or hide." It seems to
have been interwoven, like net or chequer work, so as to present what in modern
days we should call a "damask" appearance, combining weaving with a species of
embroidery. The blue robe, and gorgeous ephod with its cluster of brilliant
precious stones on the shoulders and breastplate, would entirely conceal from the
eye of an observer this fine linen coat. Beneath, therefore, the splendid dress of the
high priest there was a more humble attire of pure white, though it was still a
"garment for glory and beauty." The outer garments were distinctly of a representative character ; that is, they bore the names of Israel before the Lord. But in

this under tunic there was no apparent connection with that people. It was rather the personal clothing of the high priest, manifesting him, beneath all his official glory, as one who could minister before the Lord in a perfect righteousness of his own. A glory and beauty no less costly and precious than was displayed by the other garments, though to the eye of sense not so striking in appearance. In fact, the high priest could not have worn his magnificent apparel unless he could previously exhibit a spotless purity, diversified in every possible way like the embroidered fine linen coat. The Lord Jesus, in the days of His flesh, passed through an ordeal of temptation and suffering, throughout which He evinced His complete fitness to be the Great High Priest in resurrection, showing forth a righteousness and holiness, as well as grace, sympathy, and tenderness which proved Him perfectly suited for this high dignity and responsibility. (*H. W. Soltau.*) *The embroidered coat:*—This garment was most proper to our High Priest of the New Testament, Jesus Christ, who is by it described (Rev. i. 13), "clothed in a garment down to the feet." Noting—1. The excellency of His person, who is "Prince of Peace " (Isa. ix. 6), for such long white garments ever betoken peace, both within the church and without. 2. That He excelled in wisdom and counsel, being the Great Counsellor and the "Spirit of counsel and understanding resting in His breast " (Isa. xi. 2), for to such also the garments belonged (Dan. v. 7, 16). 3. The lovely and beautiful connection and conjunction of His prophetical, priestly, and princely offices; sincerely and perfectly fulfilling them and appearing before God in them as in a most costly embroidered garment consisting of many pieces and many colours fitly couched and laid together. And this garment He wore, not only on earth (as the priests did), but now after His ascension, He continues to perform the office of the High Priest for His Church, in the same embroidered garment, presenting before God the merit of His only sacrifice and making intercession to the Father for it. (*T. Taylor, D.D.*)　　**The girdle.**—*The girdle:*— This was worn by the Hebrews as an ornament and as a strengthener. It was put on Aaron, but our Jesus has in Himself everything that was symbolized by this, and everything else that was put on Aaron. I like to look at the girdle as the symbol of service, and at Jesus Christ as our girded High Priest, ever ready to go to God on His people's errands. Jesus is ever ready for any service His people may need. He will present their prayers to God and obtain answers for His beloved disciples, or He will stoop to wash their feet. (*G. Rodgers.*)　　*The girdle:*—This girdle was made of the same materials as the vail; but the order of their arrangement was that of the innermost curtains of the Tabernacle, viz., "fine linen, blue, purple, scarlet." The fine linen, type of righteousness, comes first, answering to that beautiful passage in Isa. xi. 5. Righteousness and faithfulness which the Lord Jesus has made perfectly manifest and proved to the utmost in His death upon the Cross. The object of the girdle was to strengthen the loins for service. And the high priest, beneath garments of majesty, glory, brilliancy, and power, still preserved his place as the girded righteous servant of the Lord. So the Lord Jesus upon the throne of glory, having all power in heaven and in earth, and with the name above every name, yet delights to maintain His place as God's servant, fulfilling the Father's counsels and accomplishing His will in the salvation and ultimate perfection of those that are His. We have in John xiii. a striking illustration of our blessed Lord's holy service; deeply instructive to us in two ways: first, as teaching us what His present occupations are in our behalf, and next, as giving us an example which we have to follow if we would taste of His happiness and joy. One way in which we may wash one another's feet is by prayer and intercession for one another; and another mode is by seeking to deliver any of the Lord's people that may be ensnared, from the entanglements into which they have fallen. (*H. W. Soltau.*)　　*The girdle:*—The sixth garment is the girdle of needlework (ver. 39). Of divers matter, linen, blue silk, purple and scarlet, and of divers colours (chap. xxxix. 29). The use of it was to fasten the priest's garment unto him, that they may not hang loose upon him in his ministration; and specially points out unto us our High Priest, Jesus Christ, described after His ascension (Rev. i. 13), "And girt about the paps with a golden girdle." Noting in Christ four things. 1. The truth and constancy in accomplishing all the gracious promises of the gospel, seeing our High Priest is girt about with a girdle of verity. 2. His justice, integrity, pure and uncorrupt judgment, as gold (Isa. xi. 5), "Righteousness shall be the girdle of His loins and faithfulness the girdle of His reins." 3. His readiness to do the office of a Mediator. 4. His mindfulness and care in performing His office. For as not girding is a sign of carelessness and negligence, so girding of care and industry. So our Lord and High Priest never carelessly cast off any poor and penitent sinner; but in the days of His flesh minded their misery; and now in heaven keeps on His girdle, casts not off the care of His Church, but perpetually accomplisheth whatsoever is needful for her salvation. (*T. Taylor, D.D.*)

CHAPTER XXIX.

Vers. 1–37. **To minister unto Me in the priest's office.**—*The consecration of priests :*—I. The priests were washed first. 1. Regeneration. 2. Remission of sin. II. After being washed, the priests were clothed. We must have the fine linen of an inward sanctification, and the outer garment for glory and for beauty, of the imputed righteousness of Christ. 1. These garments were provided for them. 2. These garments formed a complete apparel. 3. These garments were very comely to look upon. 4. The dress provided was absolutely necessary to be worn. III. These priests were anointed. Be filled with the Spirit. A man in Christ is fragrant with a holy perfume before the Lord, but out of Christ he is an unclean thing, and cannot approach the altar. IV. They had next to share in the sin-offering. Lift your eyes to Jesus, your ransom and substitute. V. After the sin-offering the consecrated ones went on to take their share in the burnt-offering. The sin-offering indicated Christ as bearing our sin, but the burnt-offering sets Him forth as presenting an acceptable offering unto the Lord. VI. After the priests had seen for themselves the sin-offering and the burnt-offering, it was needful that they should partake of a third sacrifice, which was a peace-offering. This was shared between the Lord and the priest or offerer. Thus it was an open declaration of the communion which had been established between God and man, so that they ate together, rejoicing in the same offering. Conclusion: 1. Do you and I offer sacrifice continually? Do we every day feel that our whole being is "Holiness unto the Lord"? 2. What have you to offer now? Bring continually of your—(1) Substance. (2) Talent. (3) Influence. (*C. H. Spurgeon.*)

Ver. 10. **The Tabernacle of the congregation.**—*The tent of meeting :*—The Tabernacle of the congregation—or, rather, tent of meeting—was the place where God's presence was manifested. This was granted to the people of Israel, first in the pillar of fire and cloud, then in the Tabernacle and Temple. And now for us in Jesus Christ there is "God manifested in the flesh." I. In and through Christ God is revealed. II. Through Him and by Him the Lord God is approached. 1. We have the right of approach through Jesus Christ. His life embodied a perfect righteousness. His death is the accepted sacrifice. 2. We have not only the right of approach, but also the power to approach, sharing the Spirit of the Divine Redeemer; for the final result and crowning proof of our Lord's exaltation was this—He sent the Comforter. (*J. Aldis.*)

Vers. 26–28. **Which is waved, and which is heaved up.**—*The wave-offerings and heave-offerings :*—1. As illustrating the state of the heart in those who truly offer themselves up to God, there is something impressive and beautiful in the ancient wave-offerings and heave-offerings. Waving is one of nature's universal laws. The whole creation, with its myriads of planets, suns and heavens, lives because it waves to and fro the central life. The life of God waves to and fro between our spirits and Him. 2. In prayer our souls are heaved up towards the eternal Soul of our souls. Nothing heaves up the soul like a perfect love. Our daily heave-offering is a labour that has a great reward. Our aspirations, our inner heavings and upliftings, are the works which will follow us into the eternal world. They will follow us by being actually constituent elements of our future body. 3. Some persons think it strange that we should be exhorted to hasten the coming of the kingdom of God. But all who have a thrilling expectation of it may be sure that the vital element of the new coming is waving in upon them, and that as they heave up their souls and expand with desire to draw down the heavenly fire they are unconsciously hastening the coming of the day of God. (*J. Pulsford, D.D.*) *The peace-offering :*—This was the most important sacrifice of all. It consisted of a ram, called "The Ram of Consecration," or more literally, the "Ram of the Fillings," because the hands of the consecrated persons were *filled* by portions of it being placed upon them. Of this ram of consecration, after Aaron and his sons had imposed hands upon it, and it had been slain, some of the blood was placed upon the tip of Aaron's right ear, and upon the thumb of his right hand, and upon the great toe of his right foot, and similarly upon the same three members of his sons, the remainder of the blood being sprinkled upon the altar round about (vers. 19, 20; Lev. viii. 22–24). This represented the consecration to God of such members of the body as would be more especially called into exercise by the duties of the priestly vocation The ear was consecrated to listen to the voice of God, the hand to do His will, the foot to walk in His ways. Secondly, those parts of the peace-offering, which hereafter, in the exercise of their priestly office, it would be their duty to receive of the offerer and burn upon the altar, were laid upon the hands of Aaron and his sons, together with a meat-offering, and waved as a wave-offering before the Lord (vers. 22–24; Lev. viii. 25–27), and then burnt upon the altar (ver. 25; Lev. viii. 28). This ceremony was called *the filling of the hands*, and so essential a part of the consecration ceremony was it, that the expression to "fill the hand" became equivalent to "consecrate to the priesthood." The sacrifice itself was called the ram of consecration, or the ram of fillings. The intention of this action was to deliver to the ordained persons the sacrifices which they were in future to offer to God; it was a formal initiation into the sacrificial duties of their office. It indicated that from that time forward, the right and duty of officiating at the altar, and of superintending the burning of the sacrifices, would be theirs. Similarly, in the early ordinals of the Greek Church, a portion of the "sacrifice," *i.e.*, of the consecrated elements, was placed in the hands of the person who was ordained priest: a tradition still observed in the Eastern Church, and which, in a remarkable manner, links together the priesthoods of the Jewish and Christian Churches. The next part of the ceremony connected with the ram of consecration, was the sprinkling of Aaron and his sons and their vestments with its blood, mingled with anointing oil (Lev. viii. 30). Hence it could be said that the sons of Aaron were anointed as their father was anointed (chap. xl. 15); they, like him, were sprinkled with oil, but he alone, as high priest, had the oil *poured* upon his head, and could thus be called, in contradistinction to the other priests, pre-eminently "the anointed priest." In this secondary anointing, it is to be observed, that the clothes were sprinkled and consecrated *upon* and *with* the persons. The clothes represented the office filled by the person. The person and the clothes together represented the priest; therefore the consecration was performed on both together. Lastly came the sacrificial meal: the solemn eating of the body of the consecrating peace-offering by Aaron and his sons within the precincts of the Tabernacle (Lev. viii. 31). It is interesting to observe that the apostles were consecrated to their priestly office by a like "filling of the hands," and by a like sacrificial meal, when our Lord placed *in their hands* the broken bread with the words, "Take, eat, this is My body." (*E. F. Willis, M.A.*)

Vers. 38–46. **I will dwell among the children of Israel.**—*The Divine presence in the Church:*—I. The CONDITION OF THE DIVINE PRESENCE, moral and spiritual condition: everything must be holy. Entirely, daily, permanently, must we yield ourselves to God. II. The BLESSEDNESS OF THE DIVINE PRESENCE. 1. Enlightening (vers. 42). 2. Glorifying (vers. 43, 44). 3. Redeeming (ver. 46). 4. Abiding. "Dwell." "Pleasures for evermore." (*J. S. Exell, M.A.*)

CHAPTER XXX.

Ver. 8. **Burn incense upon it.**—*Incense:*—All religious ceremony and ritual is a picture, in external and material form, and upon a lower platform, of something higher, properly religious. Now this altar of incense had a very distinct meaning. I. The first thing that I want to point out is WHAT A LOVELY, SIGNIFICANT, AND INSTRUCTIVE SYMBOL OF PRAYER THE INCENSE IS. Now what were the aspects of prayer suggested by the symbolism? 1. First of all, I suppose that the essence of it is the ascent of a man's soul to God. "To enter into thyself is to ascend to God."

To go deep down into thine own heart is to go straight up to the Father in heaven. Incense is prayer, because incense surely wreathes itself upwards to God. 2. Let us learn another lesson from the incense, and that is that the prayer which ascends must be the prayer that comes from a fire. The incense only climbs when it is hot. 3. The kindled incense gave forth fragrant odours. When we present our prayers, they rise up acceptable to God in curling wreaths of fragrance that He accepts. II. Notice THE POSITION OF THE ALTAR OF INCENSE IN RELATION TO THE REST OF THE SANCTUARY. It stood in the holy place, midway between the outer court, where the whole assembly of worshippers were in the habit of meeting, and the holiest of all. It stood in a right line betwixt the outer court and the mercy-seat, where the symbolical presence of God was visible in the Shekinah : and whosoever approached the altar of incense had to pass by the altar of sacrifice : and whosoever was on his way to the holiest of all had to pass by the altar of incense. All prayer must be preceded by the perfect sacrifice; and my prayer must be offered on the footing of that perfect Sacrifice which Christ Himself has offered. And so you and I remember the Altar of Sacrifice whenever we say, "For Christ's sake.—Amen." And if we mean anything by these words except the mere empty formula, we mean this :—"I stand here, and venture to put my grains of incense upon the altar, because He died yonder upon the Cross, that I might pass into the Holy Place." The prayer that goes another way round, and does not pass by the Altar of Sacrifice, is not the prayer that God desires and accepts. And, still further, let me remind you that, as I said, whosoever was on his road into the holiest of all had to pass by the altar of incense. That is to say, there is no true communion of spirit with God, except on condition of habitual prayer, and they that are strangers to the one, are strangers to the other. III. THE PERPETUITY OF THIS OFFERING. Morning and evening the incense was piled up and blown into a flame, and all the day and night it smouldered quietly on the altar ; that is to say, special seasons and continual devotion, morning and evening kindled, heaped up, and all the day and night glowing. And dim lives may still, like the priests in this ritual, pile up the incense on the altar at fixed seasons, sure that if we do, it will glow there all the day long. But only remember, there is not much chance of a man's devotion being continuous unless he has, and sticks to, his fixed seasons for formal and verbal supplication. IV. This altar that bore the perpetual incense, ONCE A YEAR AARON HAD TO OFFER A SACRIFICE OF EXPIATION FOR IT. It was never used for anything except the laying upon it of the fragrant incense, and yet yearly this sacrifice to cleanse it from defilement was duly presented. Now why was that? Was it not in order to express the profound feeling that the purest worship is stained, and that howsoever clear and exclusive may be the occupation and the use of this altar for the one solemn purpose, the iniquities of the offerers had defiled it. Let us be thankful that we have a great High Priest who truly cleanses us from the infirmities of our worship, and bears the iniquities of our natures, and is ever ready to aid our prayers with the incense of His own sacrifice, that all their imperfections may be washed away, and they and we received and made acceptable in His sight. (*A. Maclaren, D.D.*) *The altar of incense :*—The altar of incense was made of acacia wood, and stood about a yard high and eighteen inches square. The altar and incense were symbolic—I. OF THE PRAYERS OF GOD'S PEOPLE. 1. In prayer we speak to God and tell Him the thoughts of our minds, the feelings of our hearts, the desires of our spirits. The incense smoke ascended, arrow-like, in a straight and most direct column to heaven. Our prayers ascend immediately and in the directest way to the heart and ear of God. 2. In prayer we stand very near God. The altar of incense was placed "before the mercy-seat." 3. The pleasant odour of the incense is symbolic of the acceptableness of prayer. II. OF INTELLIGENT, UNCEASING, AND REVERENT PRAYER. 1. The burning of incense is intelligent prayer. It took place in the light ; and our prayers should be presented to God intelligently. 2. Unceasing prayer. It was a perpetual incense before the Lord. 3. Reverent prayer (ver. 9.) III. OF PRAYER OFFERED IN CHRIST'S NAME. Aaron sprinkled the golden horns with the blood of atonement. This act is typical of the offering of prayer in the name of Christ. IV. OF THE POWER OF PRAYER. The horns of the altar symbolize power. "The effectual fervent prayer of a righteous man availeth much." (*D. R. Jenkins.*) *The altar of incense :*—I. We gather our first lesson from THE SHAPE AND POSITION OF THIS ALTAR. The altar was four-square. The same measure and estimate were thus presented every way, whether towards God, or towards man. But the squareness of the altar also denoted the stability of the service connected with it. Prayer and praise are not temporary things. Prayer indeed will be confined to earth, for it is the language of want. But "praise waiteth for God" in the heavenly, as well as in the earthly Zion. II. Our second lesson from the golden altar is taught us by THE CONDITION NECESSARY TO THE OFFERING OF ITS INCENSE, viz., that there be a fire burning on it. 1. This incense on the altar typified the intercession of Christ. But the fragrance of the incense could not be brought out, nor its efficacy put forth till the action of fire was employed. And these burning coals on the golden altar, to what do they point us in this view of our subject but the sufferings of Christ? "It behoved Christ to suffer." 2. The golden censer on this altar, with the incense rising from it, denotes, we know, the prayers of God's people (see Rev. viii. 3, 4). Here again we see that the incense could yield no fragrance without fire. The priest put it on the live coals, and then the odorous clouds went fuming up, a sweet savour, acceptable to God. And here we are taught in a most significant way, the necessity of heartiness in our worship if we would have it well-pleasing to God. III. Our third lesson from this altar is taught us by the CONTINUOUSNESS OF THE INCENSE upon it. How beautifully this points us to Jesus, His offering, once made upon the brazen altar, was never repeated; and so the incense of His merits, once thrown upon the fire on the golden altar, never needs to be repeated. The intercession of Christ is uninterrupted. IV. Our fourth lesson from this subject is furnished by observing THE CONNECTION OF THE ALTAR OF INCENSE WITH BOTH THE OUTER AND INNER SANCTUARY. Now we know that the outer part of the sanctuary, or the holy place, represented the Church on earth; while the inner part, or the most holy place, represented the Church in heaven. The lesson taught us by the part of the subject now before us is, that the golden altar, with its incense, belongs alike to both these departments of the Church of Christ. All the service performed, and all the joy experienced by the redeemed in the Church on earth is based upon the sacrifice of Christ, and connected with the incense of His merits. And the same will be true of the redeemed in the Church in heaven. V. Our fifth and last lesson from this subject is gathered from THE NATURE AND COMPOSITION OF THE INCENSE offered upon the golden altar. Now, observe this incense was composed of four substances. Three of these, onycha, stacte, and galbanum, were substances entirely unknown to us. These may point to the divinity of Christ, in the mysteriousness of its connection with His death and sacrifice. The frankincense was a substance with which we are acquainted. It may represent the humanity of Christ. This we know and understand, for it was like our own, in all respects, save that it was free from sin. The elements composing this incense were mingled together in equal parts. This seems to point significantly to the entire and perfect harmony of character which distinguished our glorious Saviour. There was nothing out of place in Him. Again, the materials of which the incense was composed had to be beaten into small particles, or reduced to powder before it was prepared to give out its rich fragrance. And so Jesus, our glorious Saviour, had to be brought very low, and stoop to the most wondrous humiliation, before the golden censer of His merits could yield those sweet odours which are so refreshing to the souls of His people, and at the same time so well pleasing to God, and so efficacious to secure our acceptance before Him. (*R. Newton, D.D.*) *Incense and light:*—I desire to call your attention to the conjunction which was established by the Divine law between the burning of the incense and the lighting of the lamps; these two things, being both of daily observance, were attended to at the same moment for reasons worthy of our study. I. And first I call your attention to THE WONDERFUL CO-OPERATION BETWEEN THE INTERCESSION OF CHRIST FOR US, AND THE WORK OF THE HOLY SPIRIT IN US. 1. Note, that we have these both revealed in their fulness at the same time. When our Lord ascended on high to plead before the throne, the Spirit descended to abide in the Church. After the Lord was taken up the disciples received the promise of the Father and were illuminated by the Holy Ghost. 2. Now, as they were connected historically, so are they continually connected as a matter of fact. Herein lies our hope for our own eternal salvation, in the ceaseless plea and the quenchless light. 3. Furthermore, this conjunction, as it is a matter of history, and as it is continuous, will always be seen by us personally when our prayer is the effectual fervent prayer of a righteous man that availeth much. 4. That in God's drawing near to man there is the same conjunction of incense and light. If the glory of God were to come forth from between the cherubim, if it should come past the veil to be revealed throughout the world, that glory would pass by these two, the golden altar of incense and the golden lamp of light. I mean this: God can have no dealing with men at all except through the merit of Christ and the light of the Spirit. II. Secondly, our text seems to teach

THE CONNECTION BETWEEN PRAYER AND KNOWLEDGE. The golden altar represents intercession offered by Christ, and also the prayers of all the saints, which are accepted through His intercession; and as the candlestick stood side by side with it, and represented the light of the Spirit of truth, so must true prayer and true knowledge never be separated. 1. So I gather, first, that prayer should be attended with knowledge. It is ill when men worship they know not what. God is light, and He will not have His people worship Him in the dark. When they burn the incense they must also light the lamp. 2. But now turn the thought round the other way—knowledge should always be accompanied by prayer. Revealed truth is as a church-bell summoning us to come into the presence of the Lord, and bow the knee before Him. III. I desire, in the third place, to show SOME SPECIAL PRACTICAL CONNECTION BETWEEN THE INCENSE AND THE LAMP. "And Aaron shall burn thereon sweet incense every morning: when he dresseth the lamps, he shall burn incense upon it." So, then, there should be prayer especially at the dressing of the lamps: that is to say, when preparing our minds for that ministry by which we enlighten the people among whom we dwell we should be specially earnest in prayer. Dr. Adam Clarke used to say to young ministers, "Study yourselves dead, and then pray yourselves alive again"; and that is an excellent rule. One thing more, this burning of the incense was not only at the dressing of the lamps, but also at the kindling of the lamps, when they began to shine. I want to plead very heartily with you that when it is my privilege to come here this week and at all other times to light the lamps, you who are my beloved helpers will take care to burn the incense at the same time. We need the incense of prayer more than ever in these latter days. (*C. H. Spurgeon.*)　　*The altar of incense:*—This altar of incense may remind us of many things concerning prayer. I. ITS SIZE : not very large, the smallest altar. A good prayer need not be long. God knows what we have need of. Like the Lord's Prayer, it may include much. II. ITS DESIGN : symmetrical. Prayers should not be one-sided, but well-proportioned. Not all about one thing, or too many things. There was a simple beauty about the altar. Four-square, crown of gold. III. ITS MATERIAL : choice, the best wood and metal. In prayer there may be the word of human infirmity and need; but there must be the fine gold of truth, &c. IV. ITS PLACE : in the holy place, in front of the vail that concealed the most holy. There should be prayer before entering God's house, as well as inside the house. V. ITS USE : to burn incense, offering to God of holy desire, thanksgiving, praise. Note—1. This incense, carefully compounded of the most precious ingredients. Not to be used for ordinary purposes. Prayer is holy to the Lord. 2. The lamp was lighted opposite when the incense was kindled. Prayer needs Divine illumination: should bear the light as being without hypocrisy. 3. The incense was burnt morning and evening. Our days should begin and end with prayer. (*Biblical Museum*).　　*The altar of incense:*—Consider this as—I. A TYPICAL INSTITUTION. Notice here—1. Its daily use. 2. Its annual expiation. II. AN EMBLEMATIC RITE. In this view it marks—1. The privilege of Christians. 2. The ground of their acceptance. Application: (1) How highly we are privileged under the Christian dispensation. (2) What a holy people we should be unto the Lord. (*C. Simeon, M.A.*)　　*The altar of incense:*—At the west end of the outer apartment, in front of the curtain which separated it from the holy of holies, stood the altar of incense, three feet high, with four equal sides, each one foot and six inches in horizontal measure. It consisted of a frame of acacia wood, with horns of the same material at the four upper corners, plated over all the external surface with gold. It was not left open at the top, like the great altar of burnt-offering, but covered with a board of acacia wood, overlaid with gold like the four vertical sides; and this cover is designated by the word which signifies the roof of a house. Like the ark and the table, it had rings for convenience in transporting it, and a pair of gilded staves, which, however, did not remain in the rings when the altar was in place. Just above the rings was a crown, or cincture, of the kind affixed to the ark and the table. The incense was probably burned in a censer placed on the top of the altar; the ashes remaining in, and being carried away with, the censer. (*E. E. Atwater.*)

Ver. 12. **A ransom for his soul.**—*The ransom for the life:*—The word which is here rendered "ransom" is afterwards rendered "atonement." The atonement covered or removed what displeased God, and thus sanctified for His service. Our notion of atonement under the law should ordinarily be limited to the removal of the temporal consequences of moral or ceremonial defilement. The sum of half a shekel was the tax that every man had to pay as his ransom, and as this is the single instance in the Jewish law in which an offering of money is commanded, it seems highly probable that it was not a ransom for the soul so much as a ransom for the life which the Israelite made when he paid his half-shekel. On all occasions in which the soul, the immortal principle, is undeniably concerned, the appointed offerings are strictly sacrificial. Consider: I. THE RANSOM FOR THE LIFE. Our human lives are forfeited to God; we have not accomplished the great end of our being, and therefore we deserve every moment to die. The Israelites paid their tax as a confession that life had been forfeited, and as an acknowledgment that its continuance depended wholly on God. We cannot give the half-shekel payment, but we should have before us the practical remembrance that in God's hand is the soul of every living thing. II. THE RICH AND THE POOR WERE TO PAY JUST THE SAME SUM. This was a clear and unqualified declaration that in the sight of God the distinctions of rank and estate are altogether as nothing; that, whilst He gathers the whole human race under His guardianship, there is no difference in the watchfulness which extends itself to the several individuals. III. If we understand the word "soul" in the ordinary sense, the text is a clear indication THAT GOD VALUES AT THE SAME RATE THE SOULS OF ALL HUMAN BEINGS. Every soul has been redeemed at the price of the blood of God's Son. Rich and poor must offer the same atonement for the soul. (*H. Melvill, B.D.*) *The soul-ransom :*—I. DIVINELY APPOINTED. "The Lord spake," &c. Who else had a right to speak on this matter? How would it have been had man spoken? God mercifully prevents confusion by Himself speaking. So, in our case. "I have found a ransom." II. UNIVERSALLY ENFORCED. "They shall give every man a ransom for his soul." No moral man shall, in the pride of his self-righteousness, conclude that he needs no ransom; nor shall any vile sinner, in utter despair, conclude that a ransom will in his case be useless. "He gave Himself a Ransom for all." How if we "neglect so great salvation"? III. EQUALLY DISTRIBUTED. "The rich shall not give more, and the poor shall not give less." There should be no excuse for misrepresenting their circumstances. They were taught that the soul, and not wealth, was the thing considered. Men spiritually on one level (Lev. xix. 15). The rich and the poor might be sundered by circumstances in the tent, but were on an equality in the Tabernacle. In the house of God the rich and the poor meet together, &c. Each went with his half-shekel to Him who respecteth not the person of any man. IV. MERCIFULLY MEASURED. "An half-shekel shall be the offering of the Lord." In other matters there was a difference (see Lev. v. 7; see marg.; Lev. xii. 8; xiv. 21, 22, 30, 31). The poor were always treated with special consideration. It was a mercy to the rich to humble him, and to the poor to inculcate proper self-respect. A mercy to all, to inculcate the habit of giving as a "means of grace." Learn—1. That in soul matters men are equal before God. 2. That our ransom is paid for us. 3. That we are not redeemed with corruptible things, &c. (*J. C. Gray.*) *Silver sockets : or, redemption the foundation :*—1. Observe that this redemption, without which no man might rightly be numbered among the children of Israel lest a plague should break out among them, must be personal and individual. You must each one bring Christ unto the Father, taking Him into your hands by simple faith. No other price must be there; but that price must be brought by every individual, or else there is no acceptable coming to God. 2. It was absolutely essential that each one should bring the half-shekel of redemption money; for redemption is the only way in which you and I can be accepted of God. There were many, no doubt, in the camp of Israel who were men of station and substance; but they must bring the ransom money, or die amid their wealth. Others were wise-hearted and skilful in the arts, yet must they be redeemed or die. Rank could not save the princes, nor office spare the elders: every man of Israel must be redeemed; and no man could pass the muster-roll without his half-shekel, whatever he might say, or do, or be. 3. Note well that every Israelitish man must be alike redeemed, and redeemed with the like, nay, with the same redemption. "The rich shall not give more, and the poor shall not give less than half a shekel." 4. And it must be a redemption that meets the Divine demand, because, you see, the Lord not only says that they must each bring half a shekel, no more, no less, but it must be "the shekel of the sanctuary"—not the shekel of commerce, which might be debased in quality or diminished by wear and tear, but the coin must be according to the standard shekel laid up in the holy place. I. I want you to view this illustration as teaching us something about GOD IN RELATION TO MAN. The tent in the wilderness was typical of God's coming down to man to hold intercourse with him. The Lord seems to teach us, in relation to His dealing with men, that He will meet man in the way of grace only on the footing of redemption. He treats with man concerning love and grace within His holy shrine; but the basis of that shrine must be atonement. II. I think we may apply this illustration to CHRIST IN HIS DIVINE PERSON. The Tabernacle was the type of our Lord Jesus Christ, for God dwells among men in Christ. "He tabernacled among us, and we beheld His glory," "In whom dwelleth all the fulness of the Godhead bodily." Our Lord is thus the Tabernacle which the Lord hath pitched and not man; and our first and fundamental idea of Him must be in His character as Redeemer. Our Lord does come to us in other characters, and in them all He is right glorious; but unless we receive Him as Redeemer we have missed the essence of His character, the foundation idea of Him. III. The Tabernacle was a type of THE CHURCH OF GOD AS THE PLACE OF DIVINE INDWELLING. What and where is the Church of God? The true Church is founded upon redemption. 1. Christ is a sure Foundation. 2. An invariable Foundation. IV. I think this Tabernacle in the wilderness may be viewed as a type of THE GOSPEL, for the gospel is the revelation of God to man. Now, as that old gospel in the wilderness was, such must ours be, and I want to say just two or three things very plainly, and have done. Redemption must be the foundation of our theology—doctrinal, practical, and experimental. Ah, and not only our theology but our personal hope. The only gospel that I have to preach is that which I have to rest upon myself—"Who His own self bare our sins in His own body on the tree." This is henceforth the burden of our service, and the glory of our life. Those silver sockets were very precious, but very weighty. I dare say the men who had to move them sometimes thought so. Four tons and more of silver make up a great load. O blessed, blissful draught, to have to put the shoulder to the collar to draw the burden of the Lord—the glorious weight of redemption. (*C. H. Spurgeon.*)   *The atonement money :*—The atonement money preached a very clear and blessed gospel. It told out the great truth, that birth in the flesh availed nothing. Every man must give a ransom for his soul. The price was fixed by God Himself. Each man, whether poor or rich, must bring the same. One could not pay for another. Each person was estimated by God at the same price. Salvation must be an individual, personal matter, between the soul and God. Every man has to bring his own half-shekel. The half-shekel was to be of silver; the unalloyed, unadulterated metal. Three things are probably here presented in type : the Lord Jesus as God—as the pure and spotless One—and as giving His life a ransom for many. The silver, being a solid, imperishable, precious metal, may have this first aspect; its chaste whiteness representing the second; and its being ordinarily employed as money or price may point out its fitness as a type of the third. (*H. W. Soltau.*)   *Universal equality :*—Why, under these circumstances, the ransom of half a shekel? Everybody when he went over to the official group was called specifically as a man of twenty years of age and upward. Let us see. Strip away wealth. Strip away learning. Strip away rank. Strip away fame. Reduce us to our natural nakedness. What is left? Nothing but a sinful man. There are four moments in our ecclesiastical life when we are all reduced to this naked simplicity, to this fundamental similarity. At the moment of our baptism. The minister receives into his arms, literally following the example of our Lord—"this child," not this prince or this peasant. Again, at the moment of our marriage. I remember that many years ago, when the Prince of Wales was married, and I was a mere boy, I was struck by the fact that the Archbishop of Canterbury turned to the Prince of Wales and said, "Wilt thou have this woman to be thy wedded wife?" not "this Princess of Denmark." And then to the woman he said in effect, we know nothing of the heir to the British throne in the house of God,—wilt thou have "this man" to be thy wedded husband? I was struck even then at the way in which the most exalted were reduced to their simple humanity. Then, again, at the Holy Communion, all men are absolutely equal. One table for rich and poor. I remember a beautiful incident in the life of the Duke of Wellington when he was Lord Warden of the Cinque Ports, a position held by the late Earl Granville, whose death we all so much lament. The Iron Duke was in church, and was going to receive the Lord's Supper, when a peasant, who had not noticed the duke, kneeled by his side. Discovering who he was, and being much terrified, he was getting up, when the duke put his hand on his shoulder, and said, "Don't move, we are all equal here." Wisely said, profoundly true. There is one other moment when we are all equal—at the moment of death. If any mighty monarch is fortunate enough to be a Christian, the utmost the Christian minister will say at his burial is this, " We commit the body of our dear brother to the dust." Our brother, nothing more. As there are four moments in our ecclesiastical history when we are reduced to our common humanity and to our absolute similarity, so there is one moment in our civic history, and that moment is to-night, perhaps the only time in your life when you will be absolutely on an equal with the greatest in the land. This is why in that old theocracy every man who was numbered in the census had to pay a tribute to the Tabernacle. When nothing is left except our common humanity surely then we must make our common confession, " All we like sheep have gone astray; we have turned every one to his own way; and the Lord hath laid on Him the iniquity of us all." You may be a duke. You may be an Oxford graduate. You may be a millionaire. But all these are superficial distinctions. At bottom you are a sinful man needing the mercy of God as much as the rest of us. Therefore, when for one moment all social, artificial distinctions ceased, each man paid his half-shekel to the Tabernacle as an acknowledgment of his obligation to sue for the mercy of heaven and to do the will of God. (*Hugh Price Hughes, M.A.*)

Vers. 17–21. **A laver of brass.**—*The true washing:*—I. DIVINE (John xiii. 8). II. SPIRITUAL (Jer. iv. 14). Rest not in a mere social or ecclesiastical purity. III. ESSENTIAL. " That they die not" (Rev. vii. 13–15). (*J. S. Exell, M.A.*) *The laver:*—1. This laver teaches us, among other things, that those who would come to God must approach Him with clean hands (see Psa. xxvi. 6 ; xxiv. 2–4 ; cxix. 9). I think these texts show that those who profess to serve God must cultivate holiness of heart and life, and that whilst the blood of Christ cleanses us from all sin, we are to cleanse ourselves by coming constantly under the power of the Word. 2. None but priests were permitted to wash in this laver, and none were consecrated to the office of priests besides those who were born into the priestly family. All the Lord's people are priests, and as such they are called to offer spiritual sacrifices to God (Rom. xii. 1; Heb. xiii. 15, 16 ; 1 Pet. ii. 5, 9). They enter the priestly family when born again, and none but those who are " twice born" can offer any sacrifice to God which He will accept. At their ordination the priests were washed all over: this they did not do for themselves; it was done for them by Moses, and answered to the washing of regeneration, which God does for us when He brings us into His house and makes us His servants. Afterwards there was the daily washing of the hands and feet: this Moses did not do for them ; they did it themselves, did it every day, and the neglect of it was punished with death (Lev. viii. 6 ; Exod. xxx. 18–21). God has made all His people clean. As He sees them, there is no sin on them ; but as to their daily walk, they need to be constantly judging themselves by the Word. And as the action of water will remove any defilement of the hands or feet, so the action of the Word, when we come properly under its power, will correct our wrong habits, will purify our thoughts, and make us clean. (*G. Rodgers.*) *The laver:*—There are three principal points with which the lessons taught us by the laver may be connected. I. In the first place, let us consider what we are taught by THE LAVER WITH ITS SUPPLY OF CLEANSING WATER. The laver, with its abundant supply of pure cleansing water, points to the Spirit of God, and the truth through which that Spirit acts, as the great appointed instruments for carrying on the work of sanctification in the souls of believers. II. But, secondly, let us inquire what lessons we are taught by THE PERSONS WHO USED THE LAVER. It was only the priests who had access to the laver. We see here the true character of God's people ; the high privilege accorded them ; and the nature of the service required of them. III. But there is a third and last point of view from which to contemplate this laver, and gather instruction from it, and that is THE POSITION IT OCCUPIED. This is very significant. The direction given to Moses, on this point, was most explicit : " Thou shalt put it between the tent of the congregation and the altar." " The tent of the congregation " means the Tabernacle. Thus the laver stood, by Divine direction, midway between the brazen altar and the Tabernacle. The Jew was required to come first to the brazen altar, with its propitiatory sacrifice, and then to the laver, with its cleansing water. Not the washing first, and then forgiveness, but forgiveness first, and then the washing. (*R. Newton, D.D.*)

Vers. 22-33. **An holy anointing oil.**—*The anointing oil:*—I. THE UNIVERSAL NEED THERE IS OF THE HOLY SPIRIT'S INFLUENCE. 1. There was nothing under the law so holy, but that it needed this Divine unction. 2. Nor is there anything under the gospel which does not need it. II. HIS SUFFICIENCY FOR ALL TO WHOM THAT INFLUENCE IS APPLIED. This appears—1. From the preciousness of the ointment which was used. 2. From the virtue infused into everything anointed with it. Application—(1) Seek the Holy Spirit for your own souls. (2) Guard against everything that may reflect dishonour upon Him. (*C. Simeon, M.A.*) *The use of oil in daily life and in the symbolism of worship:*—I. The use of oil IN DAILY LIFE may be described as threefold. 1. In the first place, it was used for the anointing of the body, by which the skin was rendered soft and smooth; refreshed and invigorated. Orientals ascribed a virtue to it which penetrated even to the bones. Coincident with this was the use of oil in sickness, as a means of lulling pain and restoring health. 2. The second use of oil in the preparation of food is to be looked at from the same point of view. Here also the object was, so to speak, to anoint the food, so as to make it soft and palatable. 3. And thirdly, not less frequent and important was the use of oil for burning and giving light, surely also an anointing for the purpose of enlivening and invigorating. The thing to be anointed was the wick of the lamp. The wick would burn without oil, but only with a weak and miserable light, and very speedily it would become extinguished. II. All these modes of using oil are transferred to the SYMBOLISM OF WORSHIP. 1. The first we see at once is the anointing of the Tabernacle, its vessels, and the priests themselves. 2. The second is seen in the *minchah*, or meat-offering, not "meat" at all in our modern acceptation, but composed of wheat, commingled with oil (Lev. ii. 1-8). 3. The third in correspondence is obviously the ever-burning sacred lamp of the holy place. (*J. H. Kurtz, D.D.*) *The holy anointing oil:*—Moses being commanded of God to make an holy anointing oil (ver. 23), was to take a certain quantity of some principal spices, such as myrrh, cinnamon, calamus, and cassia, then to compound them after the art of the apothecary. And thus it is, that the oil of our charity must be rightly ordered; every Christian alms-giver must be a kind of spiritual apothecary. First, his alms must be like myrrh, which distils from the tree without cutting or the least incision, so his charity to be free without the least compulsion. Secondly, cinnamon, hot in taste and hot in operation, so his alms, neither stone-cold as Nabal, nor lukewarm as Laodicea, but hot; as it was said of Dorcas, that she was full of good works. Thirdly, cassia, as sweet as the former, but growing low, the emblem of humility, so giving, but not vain-gloriously. Lastly, calamus, an odoriferous powder, but of a fragile reed; so giving, but acknowledging his weakness, thinking it no way meritorious; for, saith St. Bernard, "Dangerous is the state of that house which thinks to win heaven by keeping house," &c. (*J. Spencer.*) *The holy anointing oil:*—This is to be composed of five ingredients: 500 shekels of pure myrrh, 250 of sweet cinnamon, 250 of sweet calamus, and 500 of cassia, and a hin, about three quarts, of olive oil. It is said to be compounded after the art of the perfumer. It is probable, therefore, as the Rabbins suppose, that the three spices were soaked in water, and boiled, and their essence extracted and mingled with the myrrh and oil (vers. 26-30). With the anointing oil are to be anointed the tent of meeting, the ark of the testimony, the table, the candlestick, and the altar of incense, the altar of burnt-offering, the laver, and all their appurtenances. Being thus anointed, they are hallowed, and are accounted most holy (ver. 10). Aaron and his sons are to be anointed and consecrated to their priestly office (vers. 31-33). This is to be a standing oil for anointing, not to be used for common purposes, not to be imitated in ordinary compounds, on pain of excommunication (Gen. xvii. 14). The anointing oil is an impressive symbol of sanctifying grace. It is analogous to the water of the laver, which cleanses. The latter points to the quality required; the former to the end contemplated. That which is dedicated to God must be cleansed from stain. (*J. G. Murphy, LL.D.*)

Vers. 34-38. **Sweet spices.**—*The incense:*—The incense employed in the service of the Tabernacle was compounded of four ingredients: stacte, onycha, galbanum, and frankincense. It might only be used in the worship of God. The penalty of death was affixed to the making or using of it for profane purposes (vers. 37, 38). It is called "holy of holies" (ver. 36), or "most holy." This incense was burnt morning and evening upon the golden altar of incense, which stood in the holy place (vers. 7, 8). We see, here, that in the original institution the burning of

incense was the special work of the *high* priest; the duty is as
himself, not to his sons. Like the shewbread, and the daily sacrih
also is called "perpetual" (ver. 8). Besides the daily incense, th
incense in the Holy of Holies by the high priest on the Day of Atonem
a very solemn and important part of the ceremonies of that day. But for
of incense covering the mercy-seat, the high priest would have died on ente.
holiest place (Lev. xvi. 13). Incense was a symbol, not only of prayer gen.
but more especially of *intercessory* prayer. On one remarkable occasion we
even the power of *atoning* ascribed to the offering of incense (Numb. xvi. 46–4
Here the rehearsal, as it were, of the incense-offering of the day of atonement,
exercised a similar intercessory and atoning power, even without any accompanying
sacrifice or shedding of blood. A wonderful foreshadowing of the more powerful
incense-offering of a greater High Priest who "ever liveth," &c. (*E. F. Willis,
M.A.*)

CHAPTER XXXI.

Ver. 6. **In the hearts of all that are wise hearted I have put wisdom.**—*The
danger of accomplishments :*—There are persons who doubt whether what are called
"accomplishments," whether in literature or in the fine arts, can be consistent
with deep and practical seriousness of mind. I am not speaking of human learning; this also many men think inconsistent with simple uncorrupted faith. They
suppose that learning must make a man proud. This is of course a great mistake;
but of it I am not speaking, but of an over-jealousy of accomplishments, the
elegant arts and studies, such as poetry, literary composition, painting, music,
and the like; which are considered, not indeed to make a man proud, but to make
him trifling. Of this opinion, how far it is true and how far not true, I am going
to speak. Now, that the accomplishments I speak of have a tendency to make us
trifling and unmanly, and therefore are to be viewed by each of us with suspicion
as far as regards himself, I am ready to admit, and shall presently make clear. I
allow that in matter of fact, refinement and luxury, elegance and effeminacy, go
together. Antioch, the most polished, was the most voluptuous city of Asia. But
the abuse of good things is no argument against the things themselves; mental
cultivation may be a Divine gift, though it is abused. An acquaintance with the
elegant arts may be a gift and a good, and intended to be an instrument of God's
glory, though numbers who have it are rendered thereby indolent, luxurious, and
feeble-minded. But the account of the building of the Tabernacle in the wilderness, from which the text is taken, is decisive on this point. How, then, is it that
what in itself is of so excellent, and, I may say, Divine a nature, is yet so commonly
perverted? Now the danger of an elegant and polite education is that it separates
feeling and acting; it teaches us to think, speak, and be affected aright, without
forcing us to practise what is right. I will take an illustration of this from the
effect produced upon the mind by reading what is commonly called a romance or
novel. Such works contain many good sentiments (I am taking the better sort of
them); characters, too, are introduced, virtuous, noble, patient under suffering,
and triumphing at length over misfortune. But it is all fiction; it does not exist
out of a book which contains the beginning and end of it. We have nothing to
do; we read, are affected, softened, or roused, and that is all; we cool again—
nothing comes of it. Now observe the effect of this. God has made us feel in
order that we may go on to act in consequence of feeling; if, then, we allow our
feelings to be excited without acting upon them, we do mischief to the moral
system within us, just as we might spoil a watch, or other piece of mechanism, by
playing with the wheels of it. We weaken its springs, and they cease to act truly.
For instance, we will say we have read again and again of the heroism of facing
danger, and we have glowed with the thought of its nobleness. Now, suppose at
length we actually come into trial, and, let us say, our feelings become roused, as
often before, at the thought of boldly resisting temptations to cowardice, shall we
therefore do our duty, quitting ourselves like men? rather, we are likely to talk
loudly, and then run from the danger. And what is here instanced of fortitude is
true in all cases of duty. The refinement which literature gives is that of thinking,
feeling, knowing and speaking right, not of acting right; and thus, while it makes

...ae manners amiable, and the conversation decorous and agreeable, it has no tendency to make the conduct, the practice of the man virtuous. The case is the same with the arts last alluded to—poetry and music. These are especially likely to make us unmanly, if we are not on our guard, as exciting emotions without insuring correspondent practice, and so destroying the connection between feeling and acting; for I here mean by unmanliness the inability to do with ourselves what we wish—the saying fine things and yet lying slothfully on our couch, as if we could not get up, though we ever so much wished it. And here I must notice something besides in elegant accomplishments, which goes to make us over-refined and fastidious, and falsely delicate. In books everything is made beautiful in its way. Pictures are drawn of complete virtue; little is said about failures, and little or nothing of the drudgery of ordinary, every-day obedience, which is neither poetical nor interesting. True faith teaches us to do numberless disagreeable things for Christ's sake, to bear petty annoyances, which we find written down in no book. And further still, it must be observed, that the art of composing, which is a chief accomplishment, has in itself a tendency to make us artificial and insincere. For to be ever attending to the fitness and propriety of our words, is (or at least there is the risk of its being) a kind of acting; and knowing what can be said on both sides of a subject is a main step towards thinking the one side as good as the other. With these thoughts before us, it is necessary to look back to the Scripture instances which I began by adducing, to avoid the conclusion that accomplishments are positively dangerous and unworthy a Christian. But St. Luke and St. Paul show us that we may be sturdy workers in the Lord's service, and bear our cross manfully, though we be adorned with all the learning of the Egyptians; or, rather, that the resources of literature and the graces of a cultivated mind may be made both a lawful source of enjoyment to the possessor, and a means of introducing and recommending the truth to others; while the history of the Tabernacle shows that all the cunning arts and precious possessions of this world may be consecrated to a religious service, and be made to speak of the world to come. I conclude, then, with the following cautions, to which the foregoing remarks lead. First, we must avoid giving too much time to lighter occupations; and next, we must never allow ourselves to read works of fiction or poetry, or to interest ourselves in the fine arts for the mere sake of the things themselves; but keep in mind all along that we are Christians and accountable beings, who have fixed principles of right and wrong, by which all things must be tried, and have religious habits to be matured within them, towards which all things are to be made subservient. If we are in earnest we shall let nothing lightly pass by which may do us good, nor shall we dare to trifle with such sacred subjects as morality and religious duty. We shall apply all we read to ourselves; and this almost without intending to do so, from the mere sincerity and honesty of our desire to please God. We shall be suspicious of all such good thoughts and wishes, and we shall shrink from all such exhibitions of our principles as fall short of action. Of all such as abuse the decencies and elegancies of moral truth into a means of luxurious enjoyment, what would a prophet of God say? (Ezek. xxxiii. 30-32; 2 Tim. iv. 2-4; 1 Cor. xvi. 13). (*J. H. Newman, D.D.*) *The wise hearted ones :*—Who are the wise hearted ones? 1. They are those who prove themselves as having ability to do useful work. Work done, and well done, though it be in itself of trifling value, is the determination of wisdom. 2. The wise hearted are they who reach beyond present ability to perform. No true workman is satisfied to simply repeat his last job. 3. The wise hearted are they who, at Christ's call, enter His kingdom, there to labour under the influence of the purest, strongest motives. (*C. R. Seymour.*) *Grace and genius :*—I. NATURAL GIFTS ARE OFTEN DISCOVERED BY GRACE. II. NATURAL GIFTS ARE DIRECTED BY GRACE. III. NATURAL GIFTS ARE HEIGHTENED BY GRACE. IV. NATURAL GIFTS ARE SANCTIFIED BY GRACE. (*J. S. Exell, M.A.*) *The method of Providence :*—God would have everything built beautifully. What an image of beauty have we seen this Tabernacle to be through and through, flushed with colours we have never seen, and bright with lights that could not show themselves fully in the murkiness of this air! He would make us more beautiful than our dwelling-place. He would not have the house more valuable than the tenant. He did not mean the worshipper to be less than the Tabernacle which He set up for worship. Are we living the beautiful life—the life solemn with sweet harmonies, broad in its generous purpose, noble in the sublimity of its prayer, like God in the perpetual sacrifice of its life? Not only will God build everything beautifully; His purpose is to have everything built for religious uses. His meaning is that the form shall help the thought, that images appealing to the eye shall also touch the imagination and graciously affect the whole spirit, and subdue into tender obedience and worship the soul and heart of man. What is the Tabernacle for? For worship. What is the meaning of it? It is a gate opening upon heaven. Why was it set up? To lift us nearer God. If we fail to seize these purposes, if we fail of magnifying and glorifying them so as to ennoble our own life in the process, we have never seen the Tabernacle. Herein is it for ever true that we may have a Bible but no revelation; a sermon but no Gospel; we may be in the church, yet not in the sanctuary; we may admire beauty, and yet live the life of the drunkard and the debauchee. In all His building—and God is always building—He qualifies every man for a particular work in connection with the edifice. The one man wants the other man. The work stands still till that other man comes in. (*J. Parker, D.D.*) *Various kinds of inspiration:*—Who can read these words as they ought to be read? How it makes ministers of God by the thousand! We have thought that Aaron was a religious man because of his clothing and because of many peculiarities which separated him from other men; but the Lord distinctly claims the artificer as another kind of Aaron. Who divides life into sacred and profane? Who introduces the element of meanness into human occupation and service? God claims all things for Himself. Who will say that the preacher is a religious man, but the artificer is a secular worker? But let us claim all true workers as inspired men. We know that there is an inspired art. The world knows it; instinctively, unconsciously, the world uncovers before it. There is an inspired poetry, make it of what measure you will. The great common heart knows it, says, "That is the true verse; how it rises, falls, plashes like a fountain, flows like a stream, breathes like a summer wind, speaks the thoughts we have long understood, but could never articulate!" The great human heart says, "That is the voice Divine; that is the appeal of heaven." Why should we say that inspiration is not given to all true workers, whether in gold or in thought, whether in song or in prayer, whether in the type or in the magic eloquence of the burning tongue? Let us enlarge life, and enlarge Providence, rather than contract it, and not, whilst praying to a God in the heavens, have no God in the heart. You would work better if you realized that God is the Teacher of the fingers, and the Guide of the hand. Labour is churched and glorified. Art turns its chiselled and flushed features towards its native heaven. (*Ibid.*) *Gifts from God as well as graces:*— God gave the plan clearly, graphically, distinctly, to Moses; but it needed men raised up specially by the Spirit of God to execute the plan, and to give it practical development. And we learn from this fact that a gifted intellect is as much the creation of the Spirit of God as a regenerate heart. Gifts are from God as truly as graces; it needs the guidance of God's good Spirit to enable a man " to work in gold, and in silver, and in brass, and in cutting of stones, to set them; and in carving of timber, to work in all manner of workmanship "; just as it does to do justly, and to love mercy, and to walk humbly with God. We thus see that God gives light to the intellect as well as grace to the heart; and we may, perhaps, from this learn a very humbling, but a very blessed truth—that the man with a gifted intellect is as much summoned to bow the knee, and to thank the Fountain and the Author of it, as the man that has a sanctified heart feels it his privilege to bow his knee, and to bless the Holy Spirit that gave it, for this his distinguishing grace and mercy. (*J. Cumming, D.D.*) *Spiritual gifts:*—1. Prize them inestimably. 2. Covet them earnestly. 3. Seek for them diligently. 4. Ponder them frequently. 5. Wait for them patiently. 6. Expect them hopefully. 7. Receive them joyfully. 8. Enjoy them thankfully. 9. Improve them carefully. 10. Retain them watchfully. 11. Plead for them manfully. 12. Hold them dependently. 13. Grasp them eternally. (*BiblicalMuseum.*) *Genius and industry:*—A friend of Charles Dickens, a man who had given promise of a noble career as an author, but who, through indolence, had failed in doing any permanent work, called upon him one morning, and, after bewailing his ill-success, ended by sighing, "Ah, if I only were gifted with your genius!" Dickens, who had listened patiently to the complaint, exclaimed at once in answer, "Genius, sir! I do not know what you mean. I had no genius save the genius for hard work!" However his enthusiastic admirers may dispute this, certain it is that Dickens trusted to no such uncertain light as the fire of genius. Day in and day out, by hard work, he elaborated the plot, characters, and dialogue of his imperishable stories. Whole days he would spend to discover suitable localities, and then be able to give vividness to his description of them, while, sentence by sentence, his work, after apparent completion, was retouched and revised. The great law of labour makes no exception of the gifted or ignorant. Whatever the work may be, there can be no success in it without diligent, unceasing, persevering labour.

Ver. 18. **Written with the finger of God.**—*God's writing :*—It is said of these tables that they " were the work of God, and the writing was the writing of God, graven upon the tables." Some infidels have carped at this; and I must say it does seem to me as if it were not human finger, or human *stylus*, or pen, but God Himself that engraved it; but why should it be thought impossible for God to engrave upon stone? Have we not discovered that the lightning can carry our messages—that the lightning let go at London can print at Dover, as has been more recently shown—is it not found that the very rays of light themselves can engrave the most exquisite and intricate imagery; and should it be thought strange, then, that God should Himself engrave upon stone the Ten Commandments? The fact is, the higher we rise in scientific knowledge, the more we see how true this Book is, how worthy of God to write it, how dutiful in man to believe, and bless Him and rejoice in Him. (*J. Cumming, D.D.*)

CHAPTER XXXII.

Vers. 1-6. **Up, make us gods.**—*Idolatry :*—I. THE VERY ESSENCE OF IDOLATRY IS NOT SPIRITUAL IGNORANCE AND OBTUSENESS, BUT A WILFUL TURNING AWAY FROM THE SPIRITUAL KNOWLEDGE AND WORSHIP OF GOD. 1. This act of idolatry was in the very front of the majesty and splendour of Jehovah revealed on Sinai. 2. With the idol before him, the priest proclaimed a feast unto the Lord; and the people pleased themselves with the thought that they were " fearing the Lord, while they served their own gods." The real heart of idolatry is here laid bare. It is, in plain terms, an effort to bring God within reach; to escape the trouble, pain, ahd weariness of spiritual effort, and substitute the effect of the eye, hand, and tongue for the labour of the soul. 3. In God's sight—*i.e.*, in reality—this is a turning away from Him. They meant this bull to be an image of God their leader. God saw that it was an image of their own idolatrous and sensual hearts. II. THE CONTRAST BETWEEN THE PROPHET AND THE PRIEST. III. THE CENTRAL PRINCIPLE OF IDOLATRY IS THE SHRINKING OF THE SPIRIT FROM THE INVISIBLE GOD. It is the glory of the Incarnation that it presents that image of the invisible God which is not an idol, that it gives into the arms of the yearning spirit a Man, a Brother, and declares that Jesus Christ is the God of heaven. (*J. B. Brown, B.A.*) *Lessons from the worship of the calf :*—I. THE DIFFICULTY TO HUMAN NATURE OF FAITH IN THE UNSEEN. II. THE IMPATIENCE OF MAN AT GOD'S METHOD OF WORKING. Moses delayed in the mount. The people would not wait for the man with God's Word. III. THAT MAN WILL HAVE A GOD. Up, make us gods. They are often manufactured gods. The man who would be popular must make gods to go before the people. It is the very height of folly when men of science, art, or manufactures, say of their own works, " These be thy gods, O Israel." IV. THE EFFECT OF SLAVISH ADHERENCE TO OLD IDEAS. In one sense, at least, they were not out of Egypt—The sacred ox. See the importance of keeping the young from early impressions of error. Let none expose themselves to false teaching, it may bring them into bondage. V. THEIR EXTRAVAGANT EXPENDITURE FOR THE GRATIFICATION OF A FANCY (ver. 2, 3). People often spend more in superstition than Christians for the truth. Christians spend far more for luxury, pleasure, fancy, than for Christ. Who amongst us is willing to do as much for Jesus as these people did to procure a golden calf? VI. HOW ART IS DESECRATED TO SINFUL PURPOSES (ver. 4). So in building at Babel; in worship at Babylon, and Ephesus, and Athens. Abundant proof in our picture galleries and museums, and also in our modern theatres, gin palaces, &c., &c. VII. THAT IF GOD IS DISHONOURED, MAN IS MISLED, HUMILIATED, RUINED. (*W. Whale.*) *The golden calf of Aaron and the Lamb of God—an infinite contrast :*—1. The calf of gold was made of earth's choicest valuables. The Lamb of God was heaven's greatest treasure. 2. The calf of gold was made to make God visible. Christ was God manifest in the flesh. 3. The calf of gold was made to meet a seeming extremity. Christ came when man was lost beyond hope. 4. The calf of gold was made to go before the children of Israel to the land of promise. Christ is the way from sin and bondage to a land glorious beyond the imagination of men to conceive. (*Homiletic Monthly.*)   *The golden calf:*—I. The first fact that asserts itself in these lines is this—THAT THE GREATEST MANIFESTATIONS OF GOD'S PRESENCE AND POWER DO NOT NECESSARILY KEEP US FROM SIN. We must rely on Christian principle ; or, if we say it in other terms, we must walk by faith, not by sight. II. Another lesson which comes out of this painful history is THE UNCERTAINTY OF POPULAR MOVEMENTS IN RELIGION. They are very deceptive, and never more so than to-day, when the democratic idea is carried over into the realm of Christian faith and made to do duty where it has no place. The work of the tempter is seen not only on individuals, but on whole communities, swaying them from the severe standard of purity and truth. With the children of Israel the rule was the Ten Commandments which they had just accepted from Jehovah and which left them no excuse for idolatry. With us the standard is the whole Word of God. III. PERHAPS THE MOST PITIABLE FIGURE IN THE WORLD IS A PRIEST LIKE AARON WHO WEAKLY SUCCUMBS TO THE POPULAR WILL AND ATTEMPTS TO LOWER THE UNCHANGING AND THE SPIRITUAL LAWS OF GOD. It was convenient for the turbulent and idolatrous crowd at the foot of the mountain to have an Aaron to do their wicked work. It made it look better and soothed the outcries of conscience. It has often been convenient for godless and cruel monarchs, like Henry the Eighth, to have a Wolsey to sanction their wickedness. IV. Lastly, we see THAT THE COVENANT WAS BROKEN, BUT NOT ANNIHILATED, BECAUSE THERE IS FORGIVENESS WITH GOD OUR FATHER. The two tables were shivered to atoms, but the law that was written on them by God's finger is still in power. (*E. N. Packard.*)   *Makeshifts:*—It was then a period of ignorance and superstition ; but even now the greater portion of humanity worship tangible gods. The cry is for something which can be touched ; and though men believe in an invisible God, yet they seek to gather comfort from makeshift idols. Men see that gold will enable them to obtain the comforts of life, and thinking that such comforts will give joy to the soul, they say, "Oh, that we could get gold !" They work and slave, and bow down, and sacrifice themselves for gold, as if it were a god. The fountain of pure joy and rest can be given only by a *living* God ; gold is a dead thing, which does not know us and cannot sympathize with us. Men have an instinct for religious worship and for holy conduct, and if they do not exercise this sacred instinct in its true channels, they must have a makeshift to satisfy them for the time being. Let us describe some of the makeshifts on which men try to lean for comfort. 1. Some people make their intention to serve God to-morrow a makeshift for goodness to-day. You use this intention as a makeshift for true piety, and try to persuade your conscience to be content with it instead of the genuine article. 2. Many people seek worldly satisfactions as makeshifts for spiritual realities. Men say, "If I had this wealth, or that friendship, or his love, or her affection, I should have a happy soul." They think that earthly satisfactions will be good makeshifts for blessings which none but God can bestow. 3. Others seek in the approval of men a makeshift for the approval of God. 4. Is it not true that many people consider the pleasures of sin a makeshift for the joys of holiness? Can you find any of the men who have given themselves to sin and profligacy who can truly say that they have enjoyed life? 5. Perhaps you have given up some sins, and make that fact a makeshift for perfect cleansing. As a child is content with washing a part of her face, leaving the crevices of the eyes and ears untouched, so you have put away some of your sins, but have left your heart as it was. 6. Some people make attendance at church a makeshift for Divine service. (*W. Birch.*)   *Aaron's sin :*—Aaron, formerly so courageous; fearlessly speaking to Pharaoh ; who was a mouth unto Moses his brother; called the saint of the Lord. Aaron, so prompt in obedience to the will of God, listens to the people, and actually leads them on in the way to destruction! In all probability he was afraid of offending the people, who were assembled in numbers, and he had not courage to resist their sinful desires. We have other instances in Scripture in which the servants of God failed in that very grace for which they were most remarkable. Simon Peter could declare his determination to go with his Master to prison and to death ; yet within a short time he cursed and swore, saying, "I know not the man." Elijah, who cut off four hundred and fifty of the prophets of Baal, was intimidated by the threats of Jezebel, fled from his post of duty and usefulness, and wished for himself that he might die. We may remark from this that no sacredness of office or of character will keep man from sin. It is only grace that can effect this for us. It is imagined by many that Aaron did not intend to promote idolatry; that he merely gave the advice which he did give to get rid of the difficulty, and that he did not expect the people would make the sacrifice which he demanded, knowing their love for their ornaments and jewels. But how unwise and unholy was such conduct : he was at any rate appearing to sanction what he knew to be wrong ; he was putting the most important interests in jeopardy, and descending from the only ground which a child of God ought to occupy in moral questions. But Aaron's manner of defending himself with Moses afterwards proves that he had given way in opposition to his conscience (ver. 24). What need have we to pray that ministers especially be not left to themselves! we are men, not angels ; we are compassed with infirmities, and subject to like passions with others; we have need constantly to watch and pray, that *your* desires may not lead *us* to say or do what would be injurious to your best interests. (*George Breay, B.A.*) *Aaron's flexible disposition* :—Of ready and eloquent utterance, he seems, like many who have been similarly gifted, to have been of a pliant and flexible disposition. He bent, like the sapling, to almost every breeze ; his nature was receptive rather than creative ; he took impressions from others, but made little or no impression on them in return ; he floated on the current which others formed, but he rarely, if ever, made a torrent which swept all opposition before it. He had little of that formative power which is always the indication of the possession of the highest greatness, and by which the individual moulds and fashions all who come within the range of his influence. He had more of the soft impressiveness of the melted wax than of the hardness of the die that stamps it. Hence he was well enough in time of peace, and when everything was going smoothly ; but when a sudden emergency arose, when a mutiny was to be quelled, or, as in the present instance, a fit of idolatrous madness was to be repressed, he proved unequal to the occasion, and was found yielding, against his better judgment, to the demand of the multi- tude. From a timid and pusillanimous regard to his own safety, he would not oppose the wishes of the people ; and so it happened that the spark, which a moment's firmness might have trodden out, became at length a mighty conflagra- tion, in the flames of which some thousands were consumed. It was in his power, had he resisted the demand at the first, to have prevented all this evil; and even if he could not have put down the idolatrous revolt, it was still his duty to have offered to it the most uncompromising opposition. Hence his conduct was not only condemned by Moses, but also in the highest degree displeasing to God (Deut. ix. 20). 1. It is always wrong to do wrong. Aaron does not think for a moment of denying that idolatry is a sin ; but the whole drift of his reply to Moses is, that his making of the golden calf was, as far as he was concerned, a thing which he could not get rid of. The man who came home intoxicated last night, saying that he could not help it, because he met some friends who insisted on his going with them, and he could not get away ; the family who are ruined by reckless extrava- gance, and declare that they were under the necessity of keeping up appearances ; the merchant who, on the eve of bankruptcy, has recourse to dishonourable expedients ; the youth who helps himself to his employer's money, because he had to do something to pay his debts—all are in the same category with Aaron. (1) In settling what is your duty you have nothing to do with consequences. The moment you begin to trouble yourself about what will be the issue, you admit the tempter to a parley ; and it will be well if in the end he do not bring you over to his views. (2) We must remember that no one can compel us to sin. We cannot do wrong until we choose to do it, and the choosing is a free act of our own. 2. The difficulty of doing right is always exaggerated by the timid. The world's own maxim is, "Grasp the nettle firmly, and it will not sting " ; and a deep knowledge of your own heart, or a large experience of the ways of men, will convince you that, if with spirit and energy you do the right thing at the right time, opposition will fall away from before you, and they who threatened to persecute will in the end approve. Nor ought we to forget that God has promised to be with those who stand up bravely for His cause. The stern eye of an unflinching man will hold— so it is said—even the lion spell-bound ; and courage in the service of God, turning an unyielding eye on Satan, will send him away from us for a season. 3. The consequences of wrong-doing are always more serious than the wrong-doer at first supposed. I can imagine Aaron bitterly upbraiding himself for his weakness when he saw the fatal fruits of it, but then it was too late to repair the wrong. You can- not stay the shell midway in its flight; after it has left the mortar it goes on to its mark, and there explodes, dealing destruction all around. Just as little can you arrest the consequences of a sin after it has been committed. You may repent of it, you may even be forgiven for it, but still it goes on its deadly and desolating way. (*W. M. Taylor, D.D.*)   *That most men have their weaknesses, by which they may be taken:*—I have never read of any island so impregnable but nature has left in it some place or other by which it might be vanquishable; nor have I ever met with any person so well armed, at all points, as not to leave some way whereby he might be sometime surprised: this passion, that affection, this friend or that kinsman, this or that delight or inclination. He is the strongest who has the fewest accesses. As those places are the weakest which lie open to every invader, so, certainly, he is the most subject to be overcome whose easiness exposes him to be prevailed upon by every feeble attempt. And however fertile he may be by nature, and of a good soil, yet, if he lies unsurrounded, he shall be°sure to be always low. At least he ought to have a fence and a gate, and not let every beast that has but craft or impudence to graze or dung upon him. (*Owen Felltham.*)   *Lack of decision of character:*—" A man without decision," writes John Foster, " can never be said to belong to himself; since, if he dared to assert that he did, the puny force of some cause about as powerful, you would have supposed, as a spider, may make a seizure of the hapless boaster the very next moment, and contemptuously exhibit the futility of the determination by which he was to have proved the independence of his understanding and his will. He belongs to whatever can make capture of him; and one thing after another vindicates its right to him by arresting him when he is trying to go on, as twigs and chips floating near the edge of a river are intercepted by every weed and whirled in every little eddy. Having concluded on a design, he may pledge himself to accomplish it, if the hundred diversities of feeling which may come within the week may let him. His character precluding all foresight of his conduct, he may sit and wonder what form and direction his views and actions are destined to take to-morrow; as a farmer has often to acknowledge that next day's proceedings are at the disposal of its winds and clouds. This man's notions and determinations always depend very much on other human beings; and what chance for consistency and stability while the persons with whom he may converse or transact are so various? A succession of persons whose faculties were stronger than his own might, in spite of his irresolute reaction, take him and dispose of him as they pleased. Such infirmity of spirit practically confesses him made for subjection; and he passes like a slave from owner to owner."   *A disappointing development of character:*—How surprised sometimes is the naturalist who, after carefully preserving a chrysalis, and awaiting day by day the appearance of the beautiful butterfly, of which it is the coarse and mysterious envelope, sees a crowd of flies emerge in place of it! This is through the work of the echinomyia, a genus of insects which derive their nourishment from flowers. They deposit their eggs on caterpillars, and the young larvæ on hatching penetrate their bodies and feed on their viscera. How surprised sometimes is the kind father of a family who, after carefully watching the growth of a child, and anticipating the development of a noble character, sees to his dismay an exhibition of all the gross and common vices instead of it. This is the work of various bad associates, such as servants, tutors, or others who, whilst deriving their livelihood from tending children, have deposited in their minds—perhaps unintentionally, but nevertheless effectually—vicious ideas which have only waited the opportunity for a horrible unfolding. The victory of these vicious ideas is so insidious that forethought is disarmed. The embryo is placed where even ingenuity might search in vain. When those ideas develop they are as certain to destroy a beautiful character as the echinomyia are to destroy the most lovely butterfly. (*Scientific Illustrations, &c.*)   *We must not be persuaded to sin:*—Then there was John Bunyan, who, under the despotic and profligate reign of Charles II., was sent to the Bedford gaol. True, they offered to release him, and allow him to go back to his wife and four children (one of them blind), but it was at the sacrifice of his convictions, and he scorned that. He was a man every inch of him, and in reply to the offer he said, " Before I will do that, I will stay in the gaol until the moss has grown around my eyebrows." Brave John Bunyan! **Sat down to eat and to drink.**— *Epicurism described and disgraced:*—I. WHO DID THIS? The people; who had impiously presumed to set up a worship against God. Whence note that feastings and idleness are the undivided companions of idolatry. The counsel, then, of the apostle, upon this ground, is not unseasonable (1 Cor. x. 7). Be not idolaters, as they were. But we are the people of God, and baptized in the name of Christ; there is no fear we should be idolaters. The Jews were God's people, yet set up the golden calf. II. WHEN THEY DID THIS. Even when their case was most miserable, then were they most insensible; for—1. They had robbed themselves and made themselves poor, in that the ear-rings and jewels which God had given them from the Egyptians they bestowed upon an idol. 2. They had committed an horrible sin, aggravated sundry ways. They had turned the glory of an incorruptible God into the similitude of a calf that eateth hay. 3. For this fearful sin they lie under a heavy punishment: they were now naked, and God was coming to revenge upon them; and after He was entreated, at the instance of Moses, to spare them, yet, for example, three thousand of them were presently slain. III. But is it not lawful to eat and drink? Yes, it is not lawful only, but necessary to nourish our life, to repair strength decayed, and enable us to our duties and callings. Nay, more: we may use the creatures, not only for necessity, but for delight. God hath given us leave liberally to use His mercies, and furnished us with variety far beyond necessity. He hath not given bread only to strengthen the heart, but oil to make the face shine. What, then, did this people other? They failed in many things. 1. Whereas the chief end of eating and drinking is to glorify God (1 Cor. x. 31), the end of this eating and drinking was to dishonour God and honour the calf. 2. Whereas eating and drinking should fit us to our duties and callings, both general and special, they by eating and drinking made themselves fit for nothing but play and wantonness. 3. Whereas men ought to eat and drink according to the call of nature, in sobriety and moderation, the text noteth an intemperate waste both of time and creatures, addicting themselves to the creature and nothing else. 4. Whereas feastings are seasonable in times of joy and gladness, these feast in a time when God's judgments are coming on them for their sin, and so the deepest sorrow would better beseem them, as also did they in Noah's time. They ate and drank, &c. (and Isa. v. 12), not considering the work of God. (*T. Taylor, D.D.*)　　**Rose up to play.**—*On recreation*:—If we be ruled by God in our sports and rejoicings, we must listen to His directions. I. First, our choice must be of sports in themselves lawful. We may not play with holy things, suppose Scripture phrases; we must fear the holy name of Jehovah, not play with it. Neither on the other side may we play with sin, or things evil in themselves, viz., to make one drunk or swear, or to laugh at such persons. It is a matter of sorrow to see God's image so defaced. So in other sinful merriments. Or if we have not warrant for them, by general rules of the Word, if the laws of the land prohibit them as unlawful. Here pause on that rule (Phil. iv. 8). And Christian wisdom will also guide us to the choice of the best sports. A spiritual mind will choose spiritual recreations, as a carnal mind will use carnal. II. Secondly, when we have chosen warrantable sports, we must beware we sin not in the use of them. And to keep us from sin in our recreations we must look to our neighbour, to ourselves. 1. For our neighbour two rules must be observed: one of wisdom, the other of justice. (1) For wisdom: we must wisely sort ourselves in our sports with the most sober, godly, and wise of our degree, condition, and sort of life, that may rather watch over us that we offend not in them than anyway draw and provoke us so to do. No pestilential air so contagious as where swearers and riotous gamesters are met. (2) For justice: the rule is that we must not use gaming as a colour to purchase our neighbour's money, or to help ourselves by the hindrance of his estate. 2. We must look carefully to ourselves. First, for our affection, that it be moderate. We may use lawful sports, but not love them. Secondly, for our ends. Our ends must not be to pass the time, which passeth whether we will or no, and we ought to redeem our time, and not let it pass without gaining something better than itself; nor yet to maintain idleness as men that cannot tell what to do with themselves else. Again, the end of sport is preservation of our health, both of soul and body, and not to impair the health of either, as many by watching at play, and forgetting or foregoing their diet and rest for play, destroy their health and call in numbers of diseases on themselves, and oftentimes untimely death. Lastly, seeing nothing can be lawful wherein some glory accrues not to God, therefore, if the end of our sports be not to enable us with cheerfulness in duties of religion and Christianity, it will all be returned as sin in this reckoning. (*Ibid.*)　　*The right use of amusements*:— Remember our amusements and recreations are merely intended to fit us for usefulness. I hope that none of you have fallen into the delusion that your mission in life is to enjoy yourselves. Pepper and salt and sugar and cinnamon are very important, but that would be a very unhealthy repast that had nothing else on the table. Amusements and recreations are the spice and the condiment of the great banquet. But some of you over-pleasuring people are feeding the body and soul on condiments. We are to make these recreations of life preparations for practical usefulness. We must make our amusements a reinforcement of our capacity. Living is a tremendous affair, and alas! for the man who makes recreation a depletion instead of an augmentation. Once when the city of Rome was besieged by Hannibal's army there was a great shout of laughter inside the walls, and it strangely frightened the besieging army, and they fled in wild precipitation. That is a matter of history. But no guffaw of laughter will ever scatter our foes, or lift our besiegement, or gain our victory. It must be face to face, foot to foot, battle-axe to battle-axe, if we achieve anything worthy. Can you imagine any predicament worse than that which I now sketch? Time has passed, and we come up to judgment to give our account for what we have been doing. The angel of the judgment says to us: "You came up from a world where there were millions in sin, millions in poverty, millions in wretchedness, and there were a great many people, philanthropists and Christians, who toiled themselves into the grave trying to help others. What did you do?" And then the angel of the resurrection, the angel of the judgment will say: "Those are the women who consecrated their needle to God and made garments for the poor." The angel of the resurrection, the angel of the judgment facing the group of pleasurists: "What did you do?" " Well," says one of them, " I was very fond of the drama, and spent my evenings looking at it." May the Almighty God forbid that you and I should make the terrific mistake of substituting merriment for duty! Pliny says that the mermaids danced on the green grass, but all around them were dead men's bones. Neither bat nor ball, nor lawn tennis racquet, nor croquet mallet, nor boat, nor skate— although they all have their uses—can make death, life, and eternity happy. (*T. De Witt Talmage, D.D.*)   *A sermon on play :*—Play is neither idleness nor folly. It is one of the many good things which have come into your life from heaven. It is a gift from God. It is a part of your life as truly as prayer is, as truly as the soul itself is. And it is part of the life of children all the world over. 1. Now, the first thing I want you to see is that this playing of you boys and girls is a pleasure to God. He is a God so kind and loving that He delights in everything innocent that is a delight to you. Just as He delights in the songs of birds and in the colour and fragrance of flowers, He delights in the play of childhood. 2. God has made play a part of your life, because He wants you to be strong. He has work waiting in the years to come for every boy and girl on the earth. And although it is not all the same kind of work, all of it is work which will want strength for the doing. Therefore He will not have you always at tasks. He has divided the time for tasks with the time for play. He will have you out in the open air. By your games He will have your body in endless motion. You shall run and not be weary. 3. For another thing God wants you to have a happy gateway into life. Nobody can tell beforehand whether your after-life will be happy. In games you are joined together, just as we who are old are in our toils. The playground is a little world. You cannot have any pleasure in any of its games unless you try to have the others playing with you as happy as yourself. To be unkind, unjust, unfair, or ungenerous in a game is to spoil it or bring it to an end. Surely this is a new, rich addition to our knowledge of God when we discover that the same kind Father, who gave His Son to die for us, that He might deliver us from sin and death, made the joy and play of boys and girls in the streets and in the house. May you carry something of the joy of it through life with you, and may you remember that God has been so good to you that He has set your life between two worlds of joy—the world of your happy childhood and the world that awaits you in heaven! (*A. Macleod, D.D.*)

Vers. 11–14. **Moses besought the Lord.**—*The intercession :*—We find him in succession—1. Highly privileged. 2. Deeply grieved. 3. Raised to a holy frame of mind. 4. Visibly answered. 5. Abundantly strengthened. I. Many events have taken place since Moses, at the Lord's command, drove back the waters of the Red Sea, and the song of deliverance voiced forth from heart and mouth of many myriads. Amidst the sound of thunder and of trumpets, heaven has already spoken to the earth, and Israel's camp has now for weeks been gathered round Mount Sinai, waiting patiently till Moses shall return. Return! Where is he, then, you ask, and where can Amram's son remain with more advantage than amidst the people, who, as is already fully evident, cannot remain without his help and guidance for another single day? Where? As if Moses could have been himself had he been always living in the abject sphere in which this Israel moved;

as if a man to whom the Lord Almighty has vouchsafed a look into celestial mysteries should hasten back to earth again! The story of those forty days is written in heaven's register; and if Moses were himself still here to give his witness as to what occurred, perhaps he would repeat the words of Paul regarding the most blessed hour of his experience, "Whether it took place in the body, or out of the body, I cannot tell—God knoweth." It is enough for us that he receives the law there through the medium of angels; that at this time he may have had withdrawn from him the cloud, which hitherto had quite concealed from human eyes God's counsel in its grand development, as now revealed in these last times; that there is now made known to him, not merely the grand principles of law to regulate the Jewish commonwealth, but God's express appointments as to everything relating to the life, both civil and religious, of the chosen nation, even to minute details; that he is now allowed (and this, the greatest privilege of all, I mention last) to pray in such a way that he most truly lives in close communion with the Infinite. Oh, happy Moses! who shall tell in what a stream of deep enjoyment you must then have bathed; how much refreshment your soul must have drawn from the full cup of God's delights; and how oblivious you must have now become of all the troubles which so often, like a leaden weight, oppressed your soul on earth? How high stands this great man of God above the carnal Israelites, who long for nothing so incessantly as for Egyptian flesh! Among those born of women, there has not been one, belonging to the days of the Old Covenant, that stood in such an intimate relation to Jehovah, except, it may be, Abraham alone: in this respect, then, we look upon Moses as a happy man. But the greatest privilege which Moses had at Sinai—confidential intercourse with God—is granted to each one of us who know Him in His Son. II. Yet do not think that such a privilege exempts you from a multitude of struggles on this earth; rather, when you but look at Moses' case, and find how deeply grieved he was, the contrary seems true. He is still standing in God's holy presence, raised above the dust of earth, when suddenly he hears the words addressed to him, "Go, get thee down; for thy people, which thou broughtest out of the land of Egypt, have corrupted themselves." "Thy people": these are bitter, cutting words. Is it not just as if Jehovah meant to say, "A people such as this can no more be accounted Mine"? What has occurred to rouse the Holy One to wrath? "These be thy gods, O Israel, which brought thee up out of the land of Egypt." Oh, wretched nation, thus, when not much more than called to liberty, to stretch their hands out for the fetters of unrighteousness, and, as it were, before the eyes of that Jehovah who touched yonder mountain-top and made it tremble, thus so quickly to transgress the first requirement of His holy laws! But we may also readily imagine what unutterable grief it was to Moses in particular, that even while in the immediate presence of his God, a dark cloud rises on His face. Is this, then, the reward for all the faithfulness with which he has devoted his whole energies to such an arduous work as Israel's deliverance? Is this the seal confirming what the people, scarcely forty days before, declared, "All that the Lord hath spoken we will do"? Where are the songs of thanksgiving that echoed all along the shores of the Red Sea? They now are changed into the shouts of a rebellious mob. Where is the spoil that the dismayed Egyptians gave up? It has been spent on the adorning of an idol. Where is the prospect now of national prosperity to be enjoyed if men observed the ordinances of the Lord? "I have seen this people, and behold it is a stiff-necked people; now, therefore, let Me alone, that My wrath may wax hot against them, and that I may consume them." "Let Me alone!" How well we recognize in these few words the living God, who glories in omnipotence combined with faithfulness, and who will not even let His anger burn without forewarning this His faithful servant of the dreadful work He is about to do. But ye should be in something like a proper state to understand the depth of this man's sorrow—ye who had saved your dearest child from certain death, and who, just at the very moment when you fancied all was safe, beheld the one whom you had rescued rushing wilfully into the jaws of death. But which of us, my fellow Christians, has not at some time had experience like Moses' in that memorable hour? We may have deemed ourselves blest in our fellowship with God, when suddenly the harsh, discordant sound of sin was heard—the clash of weapons in the struggle of this life. For the disciple always finds even yet, as did his Lord of old, that the desert where he undergoes temptation immediately adjoins the Jordan of self-dedication; yea, just in proportion as, like Moses, we are placed in higher station, and more privileged than other men, we often find our trials too are heavier. Like Moses, too, we often see our noblest efforts for the good of men in general rewarded with most base ingratitude; or, in a few brief hours, what we have raised by dint of sweat and toil, continued through successive years and months, is broken down through careless weakness on another's part. In utter disappointment, we pour out our grief before the ruins of the edifice we reared so carefully; and when we would continue to rejoice in hope that God will yet fulfil His promises, it seems as if God hid His face from us, and we are terrified. III. Would that we all were but of such a holy frame of mind as was the servant of the Lord, whose utter disappointment you have hitherto been witnessing. Does not the simple fact that Moses, at a moment such as this, betakes himself to prayer say very much for him? But which of us that suddenly perceives what deeply grieves us is at once inclined to pray, and not, instead, disposed to cry out in despair, but most of all disposed to silence and to utter inactivity? Now, it is well for him that he still lingers at the top, not at the foot, of Sinai, for he is near that God to whom he never called in vain. Moses pours out his supplications in the quiet solitude—for whom? Is it for himself, that God may give him strength to bear the burden of such oft rejection by the people? But wherefore should he think about himself, when his heart is filled with the thought of Israel's salvation? Why should he think of men in their rejection of himself, when they so shamefully provoked the Lord? Nay, here the lawgiver becomes a mediator, interceding for his people in their sins, with but his prayers for an offering; words fail me in attempting to describe his true nobility of soul, which comes out in his prayers and pleadings here. Does it not seem as if love were exhausting all its energies in trying to find out, not some slight palliations of the shameful conduct which must be pronounced quite inexcusable, but some good grounds for not requiring, in this case, full satisfaction for the vast amount of guilt incurred? Now he reminds Jehovah of the great deliverance He has already wrought for Israel, and asks Him if He really intends to bring destruction upon His own handiwork. Then He points out to Him what the Egyptians and the other nations well might say when they would learn that the object of their hatred was destroyed. Again, he lays before Jehovah His own promise made to Abraham, Isaac, and Jacob; and he asks what must become of that, if He do not turn from His wrath in time. And, finally, he earnestly entreats the Lord, if it must even be so, to take away his life, if Israel's life, now forfeited, cannot be bought at any other price. In the full strength of interceding love he can be quite oblivious of everything except the sinful Israel; nor does he leave the mountain-top till he brings down with him the promise that the sentence, merited even though it is, shall be delayed at least, if not repealed. Does not a holy rapture seize you when you listen to a prayer like this? Here, we deliberately say, there is one greater even than Abraham when pleading in behalf of the guilty Sodom; for those wicked men had not rejected Abraham, at least in person, and the patriarch did not express his readiness to give his own life as an offering for sin. Who does not feel that prayer like this truly deserves the name; while, on the other hand, so much of what bears that fair name is little more than a mere mumbling over of some forms, and that, too, in a way the most mechanical—if it be not, indeed, but covert sin? Nay, it is not enough that you should cry to God for help whenever your own want and misery oppress your soul; Moses calls loudly, "Pray for others too"—and the more earnestly for them, as they are more unfortunate, more sinful than yourselves, and more unthankful and unkind to you! Neither is it enough that you present to Him your own and others' miseries; for Moses says again, "God's honour must be made the one great object in your prayer"; woe to the man whose prayer is but self-seeking, who does not endeavour to extol God's majesty! Nor yet, again, is it enough that you should raise your heart at special times in prayer, but soon abate your zeal; Moses cries out to every one who strives on earth, "Continue, persevere in prayer; the faithful friends of God are the best friends of men!" IV. But does not this still further and more plainly show itself when you perceive how Moses was heard in prayer? There is (may I express it so?) something beyond description, human or Divine, in these words found in ver. 14: "Then the Lord repented of the evil which He thought to do unto His people." Nay, what man could expect by prayer to make God alter His decree? what godly man could wish to have such power? God has determined at all times to show His grace to sinful men, but He is gracious only to the humble prayer; and now, when Israel themselves neglect to pray that He may take away impending judgments, Moses puts himself in the position of the sinners; and no sooner does he venture on his intercession than he obtains God's pardon for them all.

Moses has prayed for grace, but grace does not in every case mean quite the same thing as impunity; and Moses himself is fully conscious that the nation must atone for its own sins, even when it is not visited according to its sins. "Thou wast a God that forgavest them, though Thou tookest vengeance of their inventions." These words, penned by the Psalmist, form the motto of God's dealings with Israel. When God exterminates some hundreds, He acts like the surgeon, sparing not the knife though it inflicts much pain, nor hesitating to remove most precious, yea, important, members, that the body may itself be saved from otherwise inevitable death. Yea, what is it that prayer cannot do—humble, believing, fervent, persevering prayer? It opens up the treasures hid in God's paternal heart, and shuts the flood-gates of His penal judgments; it brings blessings down upon the head already laden with the curse of sin; nor has it lost its power, although the mouth of him who offered it is long since silent in the dust of death. And is the history of the Israel of the New Covenant less rich in illustrations of the truth that God desires to have entreaty made to Him, not merely by, but also for, His people, so that He may pity them? Run over, then, yourselves the annals of Christ's reign, and ponder specially the record made of your own history. What keeps the sword from Peter's head when that of James already is removed? The Church sends up in his behalf a constant prayer that keeps the rock from falling down. What has the Christian Church to thank for her great teacher, Augustine? The prayer of Monica; because a child for whom so many tears were shed could not by any possibility be lost. Christians! if you most truly seek your brother's and your own salvation, persevere in prayer! V. "Your own salvation"—yes; it is just here that our own interest, which we so fully understand, combines most beautifully with our brother's too. Come, look at Moses, in the last place, fully strengthened after prayer. Let us once more look to the sequel of the history. When you behold the man of more than eighty years descending from the mountain of the Lord with all the fire of youth still full in him, do you not recognize in that the power of fellowship with God in heaven? What calmness in his eye, what firmness in his gait, what firm decision in his actions, and what strength combined with moderation, as this very page can testify! Surely you do not disapprove of what he did, when, in a boiling rage, he cast away the tables made of stone, so breaking them, and strewed the dust obtained by pounding down the golden calf upon the water used to quench the thirst of Israel? "See my zeal for the Lord!" So Moses might have said with better right than Jehu did in later times, for his was anger without sin. And we confess that we would scarce have looked on him as Moses—yea, would almost have despised him—had he not on this occasion cast a single glance of deepest anger upon the abomination now committed by the Israelites. What would have been the meaning of such intercession for a race of sinners if the intercessor had esteemed the sin itself as trivial? Then, even though the world be all opposed to us, the Lord, in His eternal faithfulness, remains upon our side; though even our dearest friends may fall, the Friend who cannot die still watches us; although the head may bend through weariness, the heart that still can pray renews its youth. Behold in this the explanation of the mystery why two men, both engaged in the selfsame life-struggle, may yet fight in ways so utterly dissimilar, that while the one sinks under wounds he has received, the other issues from the fight victorious; the one required to carry on the war at his own charges, while the other had Omnipotence itself upon his side. On Sinai Moses prays for a rebellious nation; on Golgotha you hear Jesus pleading for His executioners when He was being crucified. Moses invokes God for His grace towards Israel only; Jesus for that same grace to sinners of all tribes and tongues, peoples and nations—yea, even towards you and me, in all our guilt. Moses but offers to make his own life a sacrifice for sin, while Jesus actually gives His life as a ransom for many. Moses obtains for Israel no more than mitigation of the penalty, not full forgiveness; Jesus can bestow a full salvation on all those who come to God by Him. Moses expires when he has watched and prayed for forty years, seeking the good of Israel; but Jesus ever lives, appearing in God's presence for our interest. Nay, Israel, we do not envy you of this your prayerful mediator; we thank God that we look unto a higher One. (*J. J. Van Oosterzee, D.D.*)

Ver. 24. **There came out this calf.**—*Aaron's excuse:*—I. There never was a speech more true to one disposition of our human nature than this of Aaron. WE ARE ALL READY TO LAY THE BLAME ON THE FURNACES. "The fire did it," we are all of us ready enough to say. "In better times we might have been better, broader men, but now, behold, God puts us into the fire, and we came out thus." Our age, our society, is what, with this figure taken out of the old story of Exodus, we have been calling it. It is the furnace. Its fire can set, and fix, and fasten what the man puts into it. But, properly speaking, it can create no character. It can make no truly faithful soul a doubter. It never did. It never can. II. THE SUBTLETY AND ATTRACTIVENESS OF THIS EXCUSE EXTENDS NOT ONLY TO THE RESULTS WHICH WE SEE COMING FORTH IN OURSELVES ; IT COVERS ALSO THE FORTUNES OF THOSE FOR WHOM WE ARE RESPONSIBLE. Everywhere there is this cowardly casting off of responsibilities upon the dead circumstances around us. It is a very hard treatment of the poor, dumb, helpless world which cannot answer to defend itself. It takes us as we give ourselves to it. It is our minister, fulfilling our commissions for us upon our own souls. III. THERE IS DELUSION AND SELF-DECEPTION IN THIS EXCUSE. Very rarely indeed does a man excuse himself to other men and yet remain absolutely unexcused in his own eyes. Often the very way to help ourselves most to a result which we have set before ourselves is just to put ourselves into a current which is sweeping on that way, and then lie still, and let the current do the rest, and in all such cases it is so easy to ignore or to forget the first step, and so to say that it is only the drift of the current which is to blame for the dreary shore on which at last our lives are cast up by the stream. IV. If the world is thus full of the Aaron spirit, WHERE ARE WE TO FIND ITS CURE ? Its source is a vague and defective sense of personality. I cannot look for its cure anywhere short of that great assertion of the human personality which is made when a man personally enters into the power of Jesus Christ. (*Bp. Phillips Brooks.*) *Shifting responsibility* :—I. AARON BLAMED SOCIETY. Thus is it with men now. Yielding to the pressure of society, we do not live out our highest convictions. 1. We defer to public opinion. Great is the tyranny of public opinion, and many dare not brave it. Aaron dare not in the text, and thousands still are overawed by it. We like to be talked about, but not against. We stay short of being what we ought to be, of doing what we ought to do, for fear of the adverse criticism of our neighbours, work-fellows, countrymen. 2. We defer to public custom. The Jewish rabble wanted images, such as were in Egypt, and Aaron had not courage to resist the demand. So we often bow to the questionable customs of society. Our convictions are otherwise, but we have not the bravery to be singular—we cast a grain of incense on the world's altar when we ought to hurl a stone at its gods. 3. We defer to public violence. " They gathered themselves together unto " (ver. 1)—rather " against "—Aaron in a tumultuous manner, to compel him to do what they wished. And Aaron was coerced by them. So we often fear the anger, menace, violence of those around us, and act a consciously unworthy part. Aaron in the text blaming " the people " is a picture of thousands of us to-day ! We do not wish to act thus and thus, but we are the victims of our social surroundings. It is not I, but the people. We, none of us, are guilty ; it is the crowd behind which pushes us. II. HE BLAMED NATURE. " I cast it into the fire, and there came out this calf." As if it were not his fault, but nature's. He says nothing about the mould that he made ; nothing about the graving tool that he used (ver. 4) ; but nature has done it—it has done itself. So do we reason still. 1. We blame nature for our sins. We ignore the fact that we failed to interpose our will ; that we fed the fires of passion ; that in making preparation for the flesh, to fulfil the lusts thereof, we constructed the mould. 2. We blame nature for our miseries. Lessons : 1. The childishness of this method of shifting responsibility. 2. The foolishness of it. 3. The uselessness of it. (*W. L. Watkinson.*) *Aaron's apology* :—Aaron's excuse is the standing excuse of at least one large class among us. Servants use it every day. Who has not heard them plead ? " Please, ma'am, I couldn't help it ; it broke in my hands." As if it were not they, but the wilful jug or dish which was responsible for the fracture, or some malign fate which mocks at human endeavour and care. " It was an accident " has been their sigh ever since domestic service became an institution among us. But is the plea confined to them ? Do you not also hear it from the lips of every child ? " I didn't do it "—they are all quite sure of that ; though, if they did not do it, it would be hard indeed to say who did. Here are two large classes, then, to whom Aaron's excuse is familiar ; and to one of these classes we all belonged in our time. But are there no more ? Most of you will remember that inimitable scene in " Adam Bede " in which Mrs. Poyser, while rating the clumsy Molly for her broken jug of beer, herself drops a still more precious jug from her angry fingers, and exclaims : " Did anybody ever see the like ? The jugs are bewitched, I think." You will remember how she proceeds to argue that " there's times when the crockery seems alive, an' flies out o' your hand like a bird," and concludes, philosophically enough, that "what is to be broke will be broke." Possibly most of us have known mistresses who, while indignantly repudiating the common excuse of their maids, have nevertheless condescended to employ it in their own behalf. And what bankrupt tradesman, or broken merchant, or fraudulent banker is there who does not plead the same, or a similar, excuse? It is hardly ever their fault that they cannot pay twenty shillings in the pound; it is their misfortune. "Things have gone against them." "Circumstances over which they have no control have been their ruin"—not their own rashness, or dishonest discounts, or risky speculations. They put their capital into that shop, that firm, that bank, and, lo, there came out this ugly calf of bankruptcy! But you must not blame them; it is the furnace that was in fault. And if mistresses no less than their maids, and men of business no less than their wives, attribute to accident, mischance, or a malignant and mysterious fate, results of which the cause might be found much nearer home, scholars no less than men of business, men of science no less than scholars, Christian commentators no less than men of science, too often betake themselves to the same egregious line of argument and excuse. There are illustrations and repetitions and modifications of Aaron's apology which touch us closer home. The man who is a sinner—as which of us is not?—has it perpetually on his lips. How often, when arraigned at the bar of Conscience or taken to task by Authority, have we urged that we really could not help ourselves; that, to use Mrs. Poyser's word, we were "bewitched" by some evil and malignant power; that it was impossible to keep the law we had transgressed, and that "what is to be broken" will and must be broken? "A hot temper leaps o'er a cold decree." With passions so fierce and strong as mine, with a natural and hereditary bias to evil, exposed to temptations so numerous and so nicely adjusted to my temperament, why should I be blamed, why should I overmuch blame myself, if now and then I have overleaped the cold and strict requirements of the law? Such as I am, in such a world as this, with a passionate craving for immediate enjoyment, exposed to forces so powerful and so constant in their operation, hampered by conditions so inauspicious, how could I do otherwise than I have done? Is it my fault that, with desire and opportunity conspiring against me, I have sometimes been overmastered or betrayed by them, and broken a commandment which no man has always kept? . . . Well, Aaron's excuse for himself has reminded us of a good many excuses as irrational and absurd as his which men make to this day. And we have seen and acknowledged that there is some element of truth in them; that what we call accident does play a certain part in our life and the lives of our fellows. But though, in the abstract, we cannot define this mysterious power, or determine exactly how far we are subject to it, in conduct and practice we have no great difficulty in dealing with it. We make allowance for our servants; we admit that even the most careful must meet with an accident sometimes, and that there are times even when a small series of such accidents are almost certain to tread on each other's heels. Nevertheless, if, after due trial, we find that a servant has contracted a constant and incorrigible habit of breaking whatever is breakable, we promptly dismiss her as too unfortunate for us, or as abnormally clumsy, or as wilfully negligent. We make allowance, too, for the accidents of commerce; we confess that now and then a man may fail honourably because he fails through no fault of his own. But if we meet with a man who has failed in almost everything he has undertaken, and who has spent half his time in the Court of Insolvency and its purlieus, we are in no hurry to associate ourselves with him or to assist him; nay, unless he can bring surprisingly good evidence to the contrary, we set him down as a lazy vagabond or an unscrupulous rogue. Just so we make, or ought to make, allowance for a man who is "overtaken by a sin." And for ourselves, my brethren, let us have done with this poor subterfuge, which we know to be, for us at least, a mere refuge of lies even as we run into it. (*S. Cox, D.D.*) *Excuses for sin:*—Here is a man all gross and sensual, a man still young who has already lost the freshness, glory, and purity of youth. Suppose you question him about his life. You expect him to be ashamed, repentant. There is not a sign of anything like that! He says: "I am the victim of circumstances. What a corrupt, licentious, profane age this is in which we live! When I was in college I got into a bad set. When I went into business I was surrounded by bad influences. When I grew rich, men flattered me. When I grew poor, men bullied me. The world has made me what I am, this fiery, passionate, wicked world. I had in my hands the gold of my boyhood which God gave me. Then I cast it into the fire, and there came out this calf." Another man is not a profligate, but is a miser, or a mere business machine. "What can you ask of me?" he says; "this is a mercantile community. The business man who does not attend to his business goes to the wall. I am what this intense commercial life has made me. I put my life in there, and it came out this." And then he gazes fondly at his golden calf, and his knees bend under him with the old long habit of worshipping it, and he loves it still, even while he abuses and disowns it. And so with the woman of society. "The fire made me this," she says of her frivolity and pride. And so of the politician and his selfishness and partisanship. "I put my principles into the furnace, and this came out." And so of the bigot and his bigotry, the one-sided Conservative with his stubborn resistance to all progress, the one-sided Radical with his ruthless iconoclasm. So of all partial and fanatical men. "The furnace made us," are ready to declare. Remember that the subtlety and attractive-ness of this excuse, this plausible attributing of power to inanimate things and exterior conditions to create what only man can make, extends not only to the results which we see coming forth in ourselves; it covers also the fortunes of those for whom we are responsible. The father says of his profligate son, for whom he has never done one wise or vigorous thing to make a noble and pure-minded man: "I cannot tell how it has come. It has not been my fault. I put him into the world, and this came out." The father whose faith has been mean and selfish says the same of his boy who is a sceptic. Everywhere there is this cowardly casting off of responsibilities upon the dead circumstances around us. It is a very hard treat-ment of the poor, dumb, helpless world which cannot answer to defend itself. It takes us as we give ourselves to it. It is our minister fulfilling our commissions for us upon our own souls. If we say to it, "Make us noble," it does make us noble. If we say to it, "Make us mean," it does make us mean. And then we take the nobility and say, "Behold, how noble I have made myself." And we take the meanness and say, "See how mean the world has made me." . . . The only hope for any of us is in a perfectly honest manliness to claim our sins. "I did it, I did it," let me say of all my wickedness. Let me refuse to listen for one moment to any voice which would make my sins less mine. It is the only honest and the only hopeful way, the only way to know and be ourselves. When we have done that, then we are ready for the gospel, ready for all that Christ wants to show us that we may become, and for all the powerful grace by which He wants to make us be it perfectly. (*Bp. Phillips Brooks.*)

Ver. 26. **Who is on the Lord's side ?**—*Who is on the Lord's side ?*—I. THE CONFLICT, AND WHICH IS THE LORD'S SIDE. The commands of God *versus* self-pleasing. Holiness and right, against sin and oppression. II. THE LORD'S FRIENDS, AND WHAT THEY MUST DO. 1. They must own their allegiance openly (ver. 29). 2. They should come out and rally to the standard. We do this by open union with the Church, by boldly rebuking sin, by testifying for truth, by not conforming to the world, and by conforming to Christ our Lord (2 Cor. viii. 5). 3. They must be willing to be in a minority. 4. They must become aggressive (ver. 27). 5. Their zeal must overcome nature's ties (Deut. xxxiii. 9). 6. They must do what they are bidden (ver. 28). III. THE LORD'S HOST AND ITS ENCOURAGEMENTS. 1. Their cause is that of right and truth. 2. It is God's cause. 3. Christ Himself is our Captain. 4. The angels are with us. 5. Thousands of the best of men have been on this side (Heb. xii. 1). 6. It is the side of conscience and of a clean heart. 7. It is that side of the warfare which ends in heaven and victory. IV. THE QUESTION OF THE TEXT, AND PROPOSALS FOR ENLISTMENT. (*C. H. Spurgeon.*) *Who is on the Lord's side ?*—I. This is a DIVINE question. "If any man love not the Lord Jesus," &c. II. A SPIRITUAL question. Are we new men in Christ Jesus by the new birth? III. A CRISIS question. Truth cannot be divided; conduct cannot have two hearts. IV. A VITAL question. Treason is in God's government, what it is everywhere, a capital crime. V. A DETERMINATE question. Ithuriel's spear disclosed whatever it touched. This inquiry settles fixedly the state of each man for the eternity he is to enter. VI. An EXPERIMENTAL question. 1. There are only two sides ever to be found. 2. There is great comfort in being on the right side. 3. It is unsatis-factory, profitless, and perilous to be upon the wrong side. The soul will rest nowhere there. There will come no possible advantage from rebellion; danger and destruction are directly in the path of one who lifts himself against God. 4. Any one can know which side he is on, if he truly desires it. (*C. S. Robinson, D.D.*) *On which side are you ?*—I. DECISION. 1. It is a decision upon the most sublime and important theme which can ever come under a man's notice. God and Satan, truth and falsehood, holiness and sin. 2. This decision, so important and weighty, should be made as early as possible. When Agesilaus came to the borders of Macedon he sent the laconic message, " As friends or as enemies ? " The answer was, " We must stop awhile, and take advice." His reply was, " While you advise, we march." Wait not. Every hour renders it more likely that you will make a foolish choice. 3. This is a decision of the greatest importance, for it will influence every subsequent decision throughout life. True religion gives a tincture to everything with which the man comes in contact. 4. As to this decision there ought to be no possible difficulty. A man should decide for God, since He is his Creator, Redeemer, Preserver. 5. This decision involves but one alternative. There is no synagogue of the undecided on earth, and no purgatory of middle men in the unseen world. II. THE AVOWAL. "Let him come unto me." "For God—to me." 1. A coming out from amongst the idolaters. Do not conceal your religion. 2. They were to come to the leader. Follow the Lamb whithersoever He goeth. 3. Those who were to come to Moses were, of course, to come to one another. Do not birds of a feather flock together? If God has made you birds of paradise, hasten to fly like doves to your windows. III. CONSECRATION. 1. Obey God's will. 2. Serve God actively and energetically. 3. Do this at all hazards and costs. (*C. H. Spurgeon.*) *Only two sides :*—1. To be on the Lord's side is, in the first place, to put your whole weight on Christ Jesus as your personal Saviour. 2. To be on the Lord's side is publicly to profess Him. 3. To be on the Lord's side you must consecrate your life to Him. 4. Reasons for being on the Lord's side. (1) It is the happy side. (2) It is the safe side. (*T. De Witt Talmage.*) *Religious decision :*— We would enforce upon you the importance of coming to a determinate and decided judgment on the great business of religion. Examine its claims : if they be spurious or unfounded, then reject them; but if they be true, if they agree with certain powers and feelings of your mind, then give to religion the attention its importance demands. Do not play with so keen a weapon ; do not trifle on the most solemn of all subjects. Decision of character is a highly valuable quality of mind. It gives to its possessor great advantages over others in the ordinary affairs of life. This quality of mind is needed in proportion to the difficulties which obstruct the attainment of any end. I. WE ADDRESS OURSELVES TO THOSE WHO VACILLATE BETWEEN GOD AND THE WORLD, BETWEEN RELIGION AND IRRELIGION. There is a class, and a numerous class of men, especially in our own enlightened country, who may be considered in this condition. II. TO THOSE WHO ENTERTAIN A SCRIPTURAL HOPE OF SALVATION, BUT HAVE NOT MADE A PUBLIC AVOWAL OF THEIR FAITH. This backwardness to associate with the professing people of God results from various causes. In some it is the effect of mistaken views of what is required in order to the fellowship of the Church. In other men, this backwardness publicly to acknowledge the Saviour is the effect of a very lax and unscriptural view of what religion requires. They suppose that if their hearts are right with God it is not at all necessary that they should make a public profession. III. THE LANGUAGE OF MOSES IS APPLICABLE TO THOSE WHO HAVE MADE A PROFESSION OF RELIGION. That many Christians are open to a charge of compromising their principles cannot be doubted by any who are conversant with the transactions of daily life. (*S. Summers.*) *Duty of being on the Lord's side :*—I. WHAT IS IMPLIED BY BEING ON THE LORD'S SIDE. 1. On the side of His truth. 2. On the side of His character. 3. On the side of His gospel. 4. On the side of His law. 5. On the side of His honour. II. WHY WE OUGHT ALL TO BE ON THE LORD'S SIDE. 1. The first reason which I shall offer why we ought all to be on the Lord's side is, that it is the side of truth and righteousness. 2. As another reason why you ought to be on the Lord's side, let me beseech you to consider seriously on what side you are if you are not on His. 3. Consider, further, why you ought to be on the Lord's side, how much the Lord has done for you. 4. Another reason why we ought to be on the Lord's side is, that it is the side of happiness. 5. Further : let me entreat those who are not yet on the Lord's side to consider that they have not one reasonable plea for being on the side of Satan. (*Preacher's Treasury.*) *Decision of character :*—I. The text clearly implies a solemn fact, that THERE IS A SIDE IN ANTAGONISM TO THE LORD'S—that there are interests, that there are opinions, that there are principles, that there are lives that are in diametrical opposition to the side of God, and truth, and of righteousness. No reflective mind can survey our humanity without coming to this conviction : Surely all this unrighteousness, all this living for self, all this oppression, this worldliness, cannot be on the side of God's moral government. There are questions of science, and of politics, and of literature on which a man may assume a neutral position ; but in the great matter of your salvation, God's claim to your love, there is and there can be no neutrality. It is not a matter optional with you whether you repent or not, whether you believe or not, whether you are the follower and disciple of Christ or not. It is not a matter to you of utter indifference whether or not you are known in this world to be a child of God and an heir of glory. II. WHAT IS IT TRULY TO BE ON THE LORD'S SIDE ? 1. Let me remark, simply and emphatically, that to be on the Lord's side is to love Him. Love and hate to one and the selfsame being are emotions not only incongruous, but impossible in the human breast. There are no two properties in chemistry more opposite to each other in their nature and in their operations than are these two emotions—love and hate. 2. To be on the Lord's side is to be on the side of His truth. The truth of God, next to His beloved Son, is the most precious thing that He possesses. Declare yourself on the side of the gospel and on the side of God's truth ; let there be no compromise ; let there be no doubt whatever as to the firmness and sincerity with which you hold it. 3. To be on the Lord's side is, then, to be on the side of the Lord's people. If you are on the side of the Lord, you will not be ashamed of the Lord's people. You may find many of them in lowly life, you may find many of them battling and struggling with its difficulties, you may find many of them unlearned and ignorant as touching the lore of this world. 4. But to be on the side of holiness it is essential to be on the side of the Lord. The Lord's side is holiness in conflict with sin, righteousness in antagonism with unholiness. III. " WHO IS ON THE LORD'S SIDE ? " There are many considerations with which one might enforce the challenge, and press it upon your personal and solemn consideration. Let these suffice—1. It is the only right side. 2. I remark, in addition to this, that it is the only winning side. (*O. Winslow.*) *Who is on the Lord's side ?*—I. THE TEXT IMPLIES AN OPPOSITION. II. THE TEXT ADVOCATES A DUTY. It is the duty of being on the Lord's side. 1. To be on the Lord's side is to acknowledge Him as the only Lord. 2. To be on the Lord's side is to render from the heart actually to Him emotions of reverence, of admiration, and of gratitude, which are permanent and supreme. 3. To be on the Lord's side is to abandon and repudiate all refuges which are false, in connection with the great principle of acceptance before Him, and to rest entirely and implicitly upon the one method which He has been pleased to propound, and which is found in the expiation and in the imputed righteousness of His Son. 4. To be on the Lord's side is to become practically conformed to His commandments. 5. To be on the Lord's side is to be diligent in the advancement of His glory. Again : you are to observe what are the inducements to be on the Lord's side. 1. You should be on the Lord's side because He possesses an unimpeachable and absolute right to you. (1) He has the right of a Creator. (2) The right of a benefactor. (3) In order to save you from that wrath, He has rendered His most precious and incomparable gift : He gave His own Son. (4) Because you will be made partakers of vast and incomparable blessings. (5) Because by not being so you are exposed to overwhelming punishment and sorrow. III. THE TEXT DEMANDS A DECLARATION. " Moses stood in the gate of the camp, and said, Who is on the Lord's side ? let him come unto me." God will not have His servants to live in secret and in retirement ; they are to proclaim and publish the fact that they are for Him. 1. This declaration should be made by verbal announcement in the intercourse of social life : " With the mouth confession is made unto salvation." 2. This declaration is also to be made by union with the people of God in the Church of His Son. 3. This declaration also is to be made by active and devoted diligence in promoting the cause of God among the apostate and the rebellious of your race. (*J. Parsons.*) *The Lord's side :*—I. WHAT IS IMPLIED IN BEING " ON THE LORD'S SIDE." It implies—1. A decided renunciation of the cause of sin. 2. Believingly to choose God as our portion. 3. Cheerful obedience to His commands. 4. An undaunted profession of His religion. 5. A consecration of all we possess to His honour and glory. II. THE ADVANTAGES ARISING FROM BEING ON THE LORD'S SIDE. 1. It is the most honourable side. 2. It is the most happy side. 3. It is the most useful side. 4. It is the most safe side. Application : 1. Congratulate those on the Lord's side. Exhort them to steadfastness and perseverance. 2. Invite poor ruined sinners to throw down their weapons and sue for mercy. 3. Plead with the miserable backslider, that he may return to the Shepherd and Bishop of his soul. " I will heal his backslidings," &c., " saith the Lord." (*J. Burns, D.D.*) *On decision in religion :*—I. THERE ARE TWO GREAT INTERESTS IN THE WORLD—God and Satan. No neutrality. II. SOME

ARE UNDECIDED ABOUT SERVING GOD. They wish to become Christians, and yet will not give up their beloved sins. They have too much knowledge to enjoy the world, and too great a love of the world to enjoy religion; and thus they halt between two opinions. III. ALL OUGHT TO DECIDE FOR GOD. IV. THE SIN AND DANGER OF REMAINING UNDECIDED. It is base ingratitude and the most presumptuous rebellion. V. WE PRESS IMMEDIATE DECISION. It is your duty to God, to yourself, and to the Church of Christ; it is your privilege, and will be both to your honour and advantage. VI. THE WAY TO SHOW YOUR DECISION. (*Evangelical Preacher.*) *The right position :*—I. GREAT DANGER OF DELUSION HERE. 1. Think not that you are on the Lord's side because you have been baptized and confirmed. You may have broken the covenant and trampled upon its mercies. 2. Think not that you are on the Lord's side because you attend the Holy Communion. It cannot make a saint of a hypocrite. 3. Think not that you are on the Lord's side because you take pleasure in religious services. Herod heard John gladly, but would not abandon his vicious course of life. 4. Think not that you are on the Lord's side because you are conscious of no hostility to Him. Few men, however depraved and guilty, really believe themselves the enemies of Christ. Nothing special has occurred to call forth their opposition. 5. Think not that you are on the Lord's side because you meditate with delight upon His character. Such is the constitution of the human mind, that it cannot help admiring a high degree of virtue. No doubt the conscience of hell itself is with God. 6. Think not that you are on the Lord's side because you faultlessly perform all your social duties. The young ruler. 7. Think not that you are on the Lord's side because you sometimes experience slight compunctions for sin. Felix, Agrippa. 8. Think not that you are on the Lord's side because you cherish in your heart an ardent desire of salvation. Who has not had such desires? Who would not die the death of the righteous? 9. Think not that you are on the Lord's side because you show a commendable zeal in the propagation of your religious opinions. The Jesuit is more zealous than you. So are the Hindoo, Mussulman, Mormon. 10. Think not that you are on the Lord's side because you are successful in your efforts to promote Christianity around you. Have you ever equalled the success of the Arabian impostor or of the profligate saints of Utah? 11. Think not that you are on the Lord's side because your fair exterior makes others regard you as a true servant of God. II. What is it, then, to be on the Lord's side, and HOW ARE YOU TO ASCERTAIN YOUR TRUE POSITION? What is implied in loyalty to God and an alliance with Jesus Christ? It implies baptism, for this is the entrance into the Christian covenant. It implies confirmation, for this is the public recognition and ratification of that sacred compact with the Lord. It implies Holy Communion, for this is the formal and frequent repetition of the believer's oath of allegiance to his King, the Captain of his salvation. But it implies much more, which is involved in all these, and without which all these can make no man a thorough Christian. If you are on the Lord's side, you are for His Church, against all schism; for His truth, against all heresy; for the faith of His saints, against all human theories and speculations. (*J. Cross, D.D.*) *The Lord's side :*—I. In outward profession they are on the Lord's side WHO HAVE BECOME PARTAKERS OF THE PECULIAR ORDINANCES WHICH THE SAVIOUR HAS ESTABLISHED FOR HIS CHURCH. These ordinances He has made imperative. II. There is another standard which looks far beyond all outward professions in a determination of this question. THERE IS A CHARACTER WHICH THE POWER OF MAN CANNOT FEIGN, AND WHICH ACCURATELY MARKS THOSE WHO HAVE ENLISTED THEMSELVES UNDER THE BANNER OF THE KING OF SAINTS. These evidences are to be presented, not as the marks by which we may form an opinion of others, but as the testimony by which we may examine ourselves. 1. They who are on the Lord's side have been converted by the power of the Holy Ghost from their natural state of blindness and enmity to God. 2. They who are on the Lord's side in this division of the world make it their object to live by faith in His promises and power, and as pilgrims on the earth, to become prepared for a better country—that is, an heavenly. 3. They who are on the Lord's side experience a daily conflict with the principles of sin. While men are unconverted, this contest is unknown. 4. They who are on the Lord's side are going on from grace to grace. The mind of Christ is forming within them. (*S. H. Tyng, D.D.*) *The challenge of Moses :*— I. THE TRUTHS WHICH THE TEXT TEACHES. 1. That there are two great interests in the world—a good one and a bad one—God, the great eternal, on the one side, and Satan, the prince of darkness, on the other. I should not say too much, I presume, if I venture to affirm all belong to God by right. But Satan has usurped a dominion.

All are on one side or the other. 2. Some are undecided about serving God. Not from the want of conviction; their consciences speak for God, but their wills rebel. II THAT IT IS OF THE UTMOST IMPORTANCE FOR US TO ASCERTAIN TO WHICH CLASS WE BELONG. What is implied in being on the Lord's side ? 1. Enlightenment of mind. It is necessary for us to see both the error and danger there is in being on the side of Satan and sin, and to discover the excellency and superiority of Christ's cause and gospel. 2. It is believingly to choose Christ for our portion. 3. It includes obedience to His truth. If we are on the Lord's side, we shall delight in His law. 4. It includes a determination of mind to sacrifice everything for Him. III. Point out some of the ADVANTAGES OF BEING ON THE LORD'S SIDE. 1. It is the most honourable side. It is not the side of the despot or tyrant, but it is the cause and service of the God of love. It is not the service of sin, but of purity. 2. It is the strongest side. And it is astonishing to see how fond some persons are of being on the strongest side. 3. It is the most happy side. This cannot be confuted. For while there is no peace for the wicked, the Christian hath peace with God—an inward tranquillity, to which the world are strangers ; the retrospect, and their present experience as well as their future prospects, are fraught with happiness and joy. 4. It is the most useful side. Sin injures others as well as ourselves. 5. It is the most safe side. In fact, no other state is safe. Learn—1. The important question, " Who is on the Lord's side ? " We congratulate those who are, and would say to them, "Be steadfast, unmovable " (1 Cor. xv. 58). 2. The sin and danger of remaining undecided. It deprives you of present happiness, and, if grace prevent not, it will shut you out of heaven at last. 3. That the way to show your decision is to come out from the world and be separate. (*W. Rose.*) *Holding up the colours :*—I remember a story of the Crimean war, of that terrible day at Inkerman in which our little wasted and dispirited army was suddenly overwhelmed, in the mist and in the darkness of a thick November morning, by vast masses of Russians. The men had to fight their way out as best they could. There was one little company surrounded and hemmed in on every side by the enemy, but there were a few gallant and brave men in their midst fighting their way through hosts of foes that hedged them in on every side. There was a voice heard by a spectator at a distance, " Hold up the colours " ; and still as they pressed on, and still as one and another fell, and still as that little company became smaller, still the cry went up, " Hold up the colours." Holding up the colours, they fought their way through to life and liberty and victory. Oh, it is a lesson to us ; whatever else we do, hold up the colours. Let men know what we are; let them know that we are Christ's. On our colours is engraven, " Christ and His salvation." Hold fast the colours— there is no fear of the victory. (*G. Rogers.*)   *Are we on the Lord's side ?*—" We trust the Lord is on our. side, Mr. Lincoln," said the speaker of a delegation of Christian people to that good man, during one of the darkest days of the American Civil War. " I do not regard that as so essential as something else," replied Mr. Lincoln. The worthy visitors looked horror-struck, until the President added: " I am most concerned to know that we are on the Lord's side." The right side is not my side or your side. The Lord's side is the place to which every one of us should rally. His banner has right, truth, love, and holiness written on it. Be sure you stand up for God's banner, even if you stand alone. (*C. H. Spurgeon.*)   *The choice to be made :*—Guizot, in his life of St. Louis of France, says that the latter had many vassals who were also vassals of the King of England, and that many subtle and difficult questions arose as to the extent of the service which they owed to these kings. At length the French king commanded all those nobles who held lands in English territory to appear before him, and then he said to them : " As it is impossible for any man living in my kingdom and having possessions in England rightly to serve two masters, you must either attach yourselves altogether to me or inseparably to the King of England." After saying this, he gave them a certain day by which to make their choice.   *Out and out for Christ :*—An Irish gentleman, pointing to a young man, once said: " Is he an O. O. ? " " What do you mean by O. O. ? " " I mean," was the reply, " is he out and out for Christ ? " This is what all ought to be who bear Christ's name. " When all who belong to the Lord," one says, " are willing to speak for Him, willing to work for Him, willing to die for Him, then Christianity will advance, and we shall see the work of the Lord prosper."

Ver. 27. **Slay every man his brother.**—*Idolatry punished :*—THE ACTORS IN THIS IDOLATROUS SCENE. 1. Their historical character. 2. The recent experiences through which they had passed. 3. In view of these facts what a revelation of human nature we have here! (1) Of its fickleness. (2) Of the difficulty of making deep religious impressions. (3) Of the imperiousness of the religious nature (ver. 1). (4) Of the depraved tendency of man's natural religious instincts (ver. 6). (5) Of the ingratitude of human nature. (6) Of the weakness of their present leader, Aaron. II. THE PUNISHMENT. 1. The opportunity to repent before the punishment was meted out (ver. 26). 2. The fidelity of the sons of Levi. 3. The terrible slaughter (vers. 27, 28). 4. The condition of forgiveness (vers. 29, 30). 5. The tender-hearted intercessor (vers. 31, 32). 6. The result of the intercession (vers. 33–35). Lessons : 1. The plausible grounds on which men justify themselves in following their inclinations. (1) Doubtless the leaders in this idolatry were those who had been corrupted in Egypt, and were longing to have a taste of Egyptian religion. (2) Their excuse was the delay of Moses in coming down from the mount. 2. The ease with which some leaders will fall in with a popular cry. 3. False leaders will lie to justify themselves. 4. What a power for good or evil is a great popular enthusiasm! 5. The contrast between the religion of man and the religion of God. 6. Sin is no less odious in God's sight because it is committed in the name of religion. God is ever ready to forgive the truly penitent. (*D. C. Hughes, M.A.*)   *Penalty a veiled blessing :*—When a thunderstorm is in progress, and torrents of rain are falling, one might wonder why God allowed such a seemingly evil thing to happen. But the farmer, who has been watching for weeks for some sign of rain, knows that this sudden storm and downpour is a blessing in disguise. So the penalties by which God preserved the Israelites from complete self-destruction were veiled blessings. Frowning fortresses, heavy artillery, and iron-clad ships are sometimes God's best instruments in His sharp surgery of the nations. It is hard to see how the visitation of a penalty is often an act of mercy ; but when Moses for his sin was denied an entrance into the Holy Land, was it, after all, a great hardship that he was taken into God's Paradise instead? (*S. S. Times.*)

Ver. 29. **Consecrate yourselves to-day to the Lord.**—*Immediate devotedness to God :*—I. THE NATURE OF THIS CONSECRATION. 1. We must recognize the claims of Jehovah. 2. We must concur as to the manner of our consecration. 3. We must be deeply anxious respecting this consecration. 4. We must earnestly and believingly give ourselves up to the Lord. 5. This act of consecration must be entire and for ever. 6. This act must be our own individual act. 7. This act must be effected and sustained by Divine grace. 8. This act must be immediate. " To-day " we have life, means, promises. To-morrow all may be lost, and for ever. Now, let us urge you to this immediate consecration—II. BY SEVERAL IMPORTANT CONSIDERATIONS AND MOTIVES. 1. It is rational. 2. It is improving. 3. It is felicitous. 4. It is consolatory. 5. It is saving. Application : 1. Let me urge the text on all classes—the young especially. 2. Let me urge all *now*. 3. I urge by a countless number of considerations. By the majesty and glory of the God who seeks your salvation, and not death. By the Spirit within you. By the flight of time. (*J. Burns, D.D.*)   *Consecrate yourselves to the Lord :*—If you say you are on the Lord's side, prove it. If you are His in one thing, be His in all things. There are a great many who call themselves on the Lord's side when they want daily bread or daily protection, who hesitate to stand out against brother and neighbour when the time of trying division for conscience' sake comes. The reason why so many of us accomplish so little for the Lord is, that we are only partially consecrated to the Lord. We are His for Sunday and Wednesday evenings; or for Him in one line or another of thought or conduct ; or for Him in all lines but one. Mr. Moody has said that " the world has yet to see the power of one man wholly consecrated to God." Uncle Johnny Vassar, or David Livingstone, or Martin Luther, or some such man as that, gives us a glimpse of the possibilities of one who is consecrated to the Lord. What a pity that such illustrations are so exceptional ! " Consecrate yourselves to-day to the Lord, that He may bestow upon you a blessing ! " (*H. C. Trumbull.*)

Vers. 31, 32. **If Thou wilt forgive their sin.**—*Moses interceding for the people :*— It was a very happy thing for Israel that they had an intercessor. It is not that God needs it. God does not need the intercession of Jesus Christ—Christ told us so. " I say not that I will pray the Father for you, for the Father Himself loveth you." And we believe that as the death of Jesus Christ availed for the believers in the Old Testament, so did His intercession—that there was an anticipation of the intercession of Christ when Abraham interceded, or Moses. I. And first let me give you THREE REASONS WHY INTERCESSION IS A VERY HIGH DUTY. 1. It is a power given to every man to wield—a power of love, a mighty instrument for which we are responsible. 2. St. Paul puts it very prominently. You will remember that, writing to Timothy, he says, " I exhort that first of all supplications, prayers, intercessions, giving of thanks be made for all men." What would we give for love that does not speak in prayer ? 3. And you are never so exactly a copy of Christ as when you are praying for a fellow-creature. II. THE PRIVILEGE OF IT IS EXCEEDING GREAT. Let me mention one or two of the privileges. 1. It is such a beautiful way of giving expression to love. 2. It revives the spirit of prayer in ourselves. III. LET ME GIVE YOU ONE OR TWO WORDS OF PRACTICAL ADVICE RESPECTING INTERCESSORY PRAYER. 1. Like other prayer, it must have intensity. 2. It should be accompanied with thanksgiving. 3. Let me also suggest to you that without which no duty is ever well performed—your method with your intercessory prayer. Of course it must be left to every one's own judgment how to do it. Only, have method, and have a period of the day, one of your stated prayers, which shall be, if not entirely, yet to a great extent, given to intercession. The method will be helpful, and it will give strength to the action, for what we do with design and plan we do always better than that which is left to the feelings of the moment. And amongst the arrangements of prayer it will be well to settle with yourselves when, and where, and how much shall be given to intercession. (*J. Vaughan, M.A.*) *The forlorn hope :*—Moses was one of those who had greatness forced upon him, not being capable of pursuing it—the meekest and most retiring of men by nature, while appointed the leader of a rebellious multitude. Immovable as a rock, courageous .as David, where the honour of God was concerned, his own honour, in the ordinary sense, was not his care, and for it he seemed to have no sensibility. Happy those who learn to forget themselves, and to have God only in their eye ! And shall not God acknowledge and recompense the grace which, flowing from Himself, turns its streams to Him again ? Is it not fit that He should distinguish those who withhold nothing from Him ; who achieve no honour that they do not cast forthwith at His feet ? 2. Look at another attribute of a heaven-formed character. Where among us are the men that have the gift of intercessory prayer in any measure like the Lord's servant Moses? Who are they, in a day of general defection and rebuke, that, like Moses, uncontaminated with the sins, unseduced by the errors of their generation, find it their part to ascend alone into the mount, if peradventure they may make an atonement? 3. It has been conjectured by some that Moses here uses the language of desperation, and invokes upon himself the irremediable sentence of final perdition. But when we consider all that this includes in it, of eternal separation from the Fountain of happiness, of alienation matured into enmity, of abandoned association with the cursed and blaspheming spirits of the infernal world, it is impossible that so revolting a wish entered his soul, or that his heavenly spirit, held in the bonds of unchanging love, was violated by the intrusion of so cruel and abhorred a sentiment. It is probable he refers to the declaration made above, that in rejecting Israel God would make of him a great nation. This interpretation is quite natural, for how could his heart sustain the alternative? Could he, so true, so loyal an Israelite, separate his lot from that of Israel ? Could he, bereft and bespoiled of the fruit of years of anxious toil, and of faith founded on inviolable promises, accept of this as an indemnification for his loss, or consent to console himself with new projects of happiness, or erect his name and found his greatness on the ruins of forgotten Israel? No ; rather let the grave yield him a refuge from such parricidal honours. Life had cost him already too many pangs to leave him energy to commence it anew. It was enough now to be allowed to share the common desolation, and having sustained for a moment the dreaded consummation of his woes, that his life and hopes should be extinguished together. Faithful Moses ! Thy interests as well as thy wishes were safe, left for decision at the righteous tribunal of the heart-searching God. (*H. Grey, D.D.*) *The training of the missionary spirit :*— I. THE CHURCH CONTEMPLATIVE. Consider the communion of Moses on the mountain with God. No wonder that Moses should delay to come down. When the sublime truths of the Godhead find a lodgment and settled home in our hearts, so that we can treat them as the familiar things of our faith, and not as passing imaginations, we have great confidence towards God. Selfishness is purged out from us, and with selfishness goes fear. The pure in heart see the Holy One ; the unselfish see the Eternal Son. II. THE CHURCH MILITANT. The spiritual life is vast and varied ;

quietism alone cannot express it, even though it be the fellowship of God's own peace. The change which is wrought in Moses is immediate and startling. He who, alone with God, can venture on remonstrances with God, in the assurance that his pleadings will be accepted; when he sees the turbulent levity of the people, and hears their licentious singing, is transported with indignation. The degradation of idolatry is illustrated in Israel's transgression. 1. It is, first, a revelation of the profound unbelief of the people. Moses was unto them instead of God. " Speak thou with us, and we will hear," they had said, amid the lightnings of Sinai; " but let not God speak with us, lest we die." Here was their first declining, and from this point the descent was facile. Moses instead of God, and a calf instead of Moses. 2. Next, the fatuity of the people is exposed. Ignominious as is their worship, still more ignominious is Aaron's stupid account of it. 3. And then there is the people's permanent demoralization. They are unconvicted by the remonstrances of Moses, unmoved by his earnestness; fear and the darkness of night alone could quiet them. " Even as they refused to have God in their knowledge, God gave them up unto a reprobate mind, to do those things which are not fitting." How different is the sight of sin from our hearing of it: sin as it affects God seems so easily condoned; sin, when it affects ourselves, appears so heinous. III. The CHURCH SACRIFICIAL. The next day displays a new composure in Moses. A graver, wiser man, his conflicting emotions steadied under the constraint of a solemn purpose. He goes to commune with the Lord. The words declare his sense of the wickedness of the people, his feeling that nothing can be said to abate the heinousness of their transgressions. Submission is the only offering which their intercessor can present, and out of the submission comes a trembling hope. There is here the utmost tenderness of a human heart; there is also an absolute resignation to the will of God. They are truly sacrificial words, sacrificial in the self-devotion they bespeak, sacrificial in the force of their appeal to heaven. Some sort of premonition that his sacrificial purpose would not be ratified by God appears in Moses' language. It does not mar the sincerity of his self-offering, but the words halt upon his lips in which a simple faith that he could be in the room of Israel would have been expressed. " If Thou wilt forgive their sins—; and if not "— what? Not, blot me, instead, out of Thy book which Thou hast written!—but, " blot me—that is blot me with my people—let me share their forfeiture; I ask no destiny but theirs." It seems to me that one of the hardest lessons which saintly souls have to learn to-day is that they cannot sacrifice themselves for the sins of the world. It is hard, because the sympathy which impels them is so pure and deep; it has so much of the spirit of Christ in it. To the sacrificial Church God is able to reveal the true atonement, to makes us preachers of Him, in whom, " according to the riches of His grace," the world may have " redemption through His blood, the forgiveness of sins." IV. The MYSTERY OF THE DIVINE SACRIFICE. He that is willing," says Christ, " to lose his life for My sake shall find it." Moses was accepted for the people in a deeper sense than he had thought of. He was reinstated in his post as leader, his passion of self-devotedness transformed into faith and patience. The qualified blessing of " an angel to go before him " was changed— as Moses, in his pleading for the people, revealed his undaunted confidence in God's fidelity, and his quenchless affection for the people—into a larger promise: " My presence shall go with thee; and I will give thee rest." And when, emboldened by all the love from God, he goes on to ask for more, there is more vouchsafed him. The Lord declared that He would make all His goodness pass before His servant; and intimated to him that beyond even this was a deep, unutterable secret, which none might rend, but of which, if we could but rend it, we should see the burden to be grace. To such surpassing heights of human efficiency do those attain who are willing to give themselves away. The reward of the Church sacrificial will be victory over the powers of evil. (*A. Mackennal, D.D.*) *The prayer of Moses:—* I. We are to inquire TO WHAT BOOK MOSES REFERS IN THE TEXT. He says to God, " Blot me, I pray Thee, out of Thy book which Thou hast written." I would observe that Moses could not mean the book of God's remembrance. The prophet Malachi speaks of such a book. Moses must have known that there was not only a moral, but a natural impossibility of God's blotting his name out of the book of His remembrance. God cannot cease to remember any more than He can cease to exist. And there is another book of God, often mentioned in Scripture, which is called the book of life, and contains the names of all whom He designs to save from the wrath to come, and admit to heaven. It plainly appears by God's answer to Moses, that this is the book he meant. II. WHAT WAS THE IMPORT OF HIS

REQUEST, WHEN HE SAID TO GOD, " Yet now, if Thou wilt, forgive their sin ; and if not, blot me, I pray Thee, out of Thy book which Thou hast written." Here are two things requested, and both conditionally. Moses prays, if it were consistent with the will of God, that He would pardon the sin of His people in making the golden calf. "Now if Thou wilt, forgive their sin." He prayed for the exercise of pardoning mercy towards the people conditionally, because God had seemed to intimate that He intended to destroy them, by saying, "Let Me alone, that My wrath may wax hot against them." Moses had reason to fear that God would, at all events, withhold His pardoning mercy. And therefore to render his intercession more prevalent, and to express his most ardent desire for their forgiveness, he prays again conditionally : "And if not, blot me, I pray Thee, out of Thy book which Thou hast written." This was implicitly saying, " O Lord, since Thou hast proposed to spare me and destroy Thy people, I pray that Thou wouldest rather blot me out of the book of life, and spare them. If Thy glory require that either they or I must be destroyed, I pray Thee spare them and destroy me. Their salvation is unspeakably more important than mine ; and I am willing to give up my salvation, if it might be a means, or occasion, of preventing their final ruin." III. WHETHER THIS PETITION OF MOSES, TAKEN IN THE SENSE IN WHICH IT HAS BEEN EXPLAINED, IS A PROPER ONE. 1. It appears to have been perfectly acceptable to God. He did not rebuke him for a rash request, but, on the other hand, plainly intimated that He was highly pleased with his noble, disinterested desire. And since God did not condemn it, we may safely conclude that it was highly acceptable in His sight. 2. It was perfectly agreeable to the dictates of reason and conscience, that Moses should have been willing to give up all his own personal interests, to promote the glory of God and the future and eternal good of his nation. He supposed that the glory of God was greatly concerned in the preservation of His people from deserved destruction ; and he plead this as the most powerful argument to move God to forgive and spare them. 3. The petition of Moses was agreeable to the very law of love. God requires all men to love Him with all their heart, and their neighbour as themselves. 4. The request of Moses was perfectly agreeable to the spirit which Christ uniformly expressed through the whole course of His life on earth. He always gave up a less good of His own for a greater good of others. 5. That the prayer of Moses was proper, because it was agreeable to the prayers and practice of other good men. Paul said, " My heart's desire and prayer to God for Israel is that they might be saved." Yea, he did solemnly declare, "I could wish that myself were accursed from Christ for my brethren, my kinsmen according to the flesh." Improvement : 1. If the prayer of Moses in the text was proper and acceptable to God, then true love to God and man is, strictly speaking, disinterested love. Moses expressed a love which was not only without interest but contrary to interest. 2. If the conditional prayer of Moses was proper, then it is impossible to carry the duty of disinterested benevolence too far. 3. If the prayer of Moses was proper, then none ought to be willing to be lost, only conditionally. 4. If the prayer of Moses was proper and sincere, then those who possess his spirit are the best friends of sinners. 5. If the prayer of Moses was proper and sincere, then none can pray sincerely for any good without being willing to do whatever is necessary on their part to obtain it. 6. If the conditional prayer of Moses was proper and acceptable to God, then the prayers of the people of God are always heard and answered. It is their wisdom as well as their duty always to pray conditionally and submissively ; for then they may be assured that their prayers will be graciously answered. 7. If the conditional prayer of Moses was acceptable to God, then the prayers of sinners are always sinful and unacceptable to God. They are not willing to be denied on account of God's glory. (*N. Emmons, D.D.*) *The broken sentence :*—I. THE PROBLEM WITH WHICH HE HAD TO DEAL. 1. Their idolatry. The great lawgiver and leader, acting on their request, thereupon withdrew himself into the Divine pavilion, and was absent for about six weeks. At first, without doubt, the people were well content. Better to be temporarily deprived of their leader, than be exposed to those terrible thunderings. But, after a while, they became uneasy and restless. From one to another the word passed, " Where is he ? He did not take food enough with him to sustain him for so long." And then turning to Aaron, the man of words, sure that neither he nor twenty like him could fill the gap which the loss of Moses had caused, they cried, " Up, make us gods, which shall go before us." We may notice, as we pass, the essential nature of idolatry. For in this marvellous chapter we have its entire history, from the first cry of the soul, which betrays a mighty yearning for an idol, to the draining of the last bitter dregs, with which, when ground to powder, the idolater has to drink its very dust. It is an attempt on the part of the human spirit which shrinks from the effort of communion with the unseen and spiritual, to associate God with what it can own and handle, so as to have a constant and evident token of the presence and favour of God. This was the case of Israel. It was only three months since they had stood by the Red Sea, and seen its waters roll in pride over the hosts of Pharaoh. Every day since then God's love had followed them. But notwithstanding all, they had been carried away before that imperious craving of the human heart which cries out for a sensible image of its worship. Their idolatry, then, was a violation, not of the First, but of the Second, Commandment. They did not propose to renounce Jehovah—that was left for the days of Ahab ; but they desired to worship Jehovah under the form of a calf, and in distinct violation of the emphatic prohibition which said, "Thou shalt not make unto thee any graven image, or the likeness of any form that is in heaven above, or the earth beneath ; thou shalt not bow down thyself to them nor serve them." This was the sin also of Jeroboam. 2. Their degradation. There can be no doubt that the worship of the calf was accompanied with the licentious orgies which were a recognized part of Egyptian idolatry. As much as this is implied in the narrative. " The people sat down to eat and to drink, and rose up to play." It is an awful thing when a single man throws the reins on the neck of inordinate desire, but how passing terrible it must have been when a whole nation did it. 3. The claims of God. There was every reason to believe that God would exact the full amount of penalty, not because He was vindictive, but because the maintenance of His authority seemed to demand it. How could God maintain His character with His own people without imperilling it with the Egyptians ? If He spared the people they would begin to think that neither His threats nor His promises were worth their heed. And if He destroyed them, His glory would be dimmed, and He might seem to have become unmindful of the oath which He swore by Himself to His servants, Abraham, Isaac, and Israel. It would almost seem as if this proposal was like the suggestion made to Abraham that he should offer up his only son Isaac. In each case God tried or tested His servant. But there is this great difference between the temptations of the devil and of God. The former seeks to bring out all the evil, and to make it permanent, as the streams of lava poured from the heart of a volcano ; the latter seeks to bring out all the good, and to make it ours ; for moral qualities never become ours till we have put them into practice. II. THE EMOTIONS WITH WHICH HIS SOUL WAS STIRRED. In the mount he acted as intercessor. It was not against the people, but against their sin, that his anger flamed out. " Moses' anger waxed hot, and he cast the tables out of his hands, and brake them beneath the mount." Those splintered bits leaping from crag to crag are an apt symbol of man's inability to keep intact the holy law of God. When he reached the camp he seems to have strode into the astonished throng and broke up their revelry, overturned their calf, ordering it to be destroyed, and the fragments mingled with the water they drank. But as it would seem that this did not avail to stay the inveterate evil, he was compelled to use more drastic measures, and by the sword of Levi to extinguish the evil with the life-blood of three thousand men. Then when the next day came, when the camp was filled with mourning over those new-made graves, when the awful reaction had set in on the people and himself, the tide seems to have turned. His indignation was succeeded by bitter sorrow and pity. "Ye have sinned a great sin, and now I will go up unto the Lord, peradventure I shall make atonement for your sin"; but he did not tell them the purpose which was in his heart, nor the price which he was purposing to pay. III. THE OFFER THAT HE MADE. He went quietly and thoughtfully back to the presence-chamber of God, as the people stood beholding. "Peradventure," he had said. He was not sure. He felt that the sin was very great. He could not see how God could go back from His solemn threatenings. He was convinced that if the merited judgments were averted, it must be in consequence of an atonement. Yet, what atonement could there be ? Animals could not avail, though they were offered in hecatombs. There was only one thing he could suggest—he could offer himself. And it was this which made him say, "Peradventure." He could not be sure that the ransom price would be large enough. It may be asked how came he to think of atonement ? But we must remember that probably there had already been much talk between God and himself about the sacrifices which the people were to offer. And Moses confessed his people's sin to God, and added : "Yet now, if Thou wilt forgive their sin ——" He would not finish that sentence. He could not trust himself to depict the blessed consequences that would ensue, if only God would forgive. But the dark fear oppressed him that free pardon was too much to expect. Ah! how little did he realize the love of God in Jesus Christ our Lord. Of course, the offer was not accepted. No one can atone for his own sin, much less for the sins of others. Yet the people were spared. The passing by of their transgression was rendered possible by the propitiation which was to be offered in the course of the ages on the cross (Rom. iii. 25). (*F. B. Meyer, B.A.*) *Moses intercedes for Israel :*—Notice—I. THE SIN OF ISRAEL. This was a dreadful compound of ingratitude, folly, and impiety. Its greatness will be easily imagined from the indignation which both God and Moses expressed against it. II. THE INTERCESSION OF MOSES. 1. He reminds God of His relation to them. 2. He reminds Him also of His promise to their fathers. 3. He expresses his concern respecting God's honour among the heathen. 4. He humbly confesses the greatness of their sin. 5. He wishes to be punished in their stead. III. THE REPLY OF GOD. He remits their punishment. (*C. Simeon, M.A.*) *The godliness of Moses :*—The indication of an impetuous, fiery spirit in Moses, only reveals the beauty of the meek patience which marked his life. I. IN THE STORY OF THE GOLDEN CALF WE SEE—1. Man's natural tendency to worship. 2. The Israelites employing the very tokens of their deliverance to build a god for themselves. The very gifts of heaven—wealth, intellect, power—men turn into idols. 2. In worshipping a golden calf the Israelites utterly degraded themselves. II. THE GODLINESS OF MOSES MANIFESTED ITSELF IN SELF-SACRIFICING SYMPATHY. Fronting death and its mystery, he stood sublimely willing even to be cut off from God if the sin of the people might thereby be forgiven. 1. His revulsion from their sin mingled with his own love for the people. The holiest men ever feel most deeply the sin of their fellows—they see its seeds in themselves ; they find its shadow falling across their heaven. 2. He felt the promise of his people's future. In them lay the germ of the world's history ; through them might be unfolded the glory of Jehovah before the face of all nations. Gathering these feelings together, we understand his prayers. (*E. L. Hull, B.A.*) *"Blot me, I pray Thee, out of Thy book" :*—There are various ways in which this passage may be understood. You may take it quite literally, and say that Moses really would sacrifice himself for a time, or fatally, but not sacrifice himself for ever. Christ made Himself a curse, but not for ever. If it would be possible to make myself a curse for a season for others, I should be within the pattern of Christ—for He made Himself for a season a curse. But I should transgress the boundary, I should go out into a sinful extravagance, if I wished to be accursed for ever—for after all I am not to love another soul more than mine— that is never commanded. And there is to be high measure of right self-love, because the love of a fellow-creature is to be proportioned to the self-love, and if I have no great self-love, I cannot have love to a fellow-creature. Therefore, I must love myself greatly—in the right way. How, then, are we to understand it? When Moses prayed that God would blot his name out of the book, it may have been out of the register of those who were to inhabit the earthly Canaan—that he would give up all the enjoyments of the land flowing with milk and honey, all the promised blessings of Palestine, for the sake of the forgiveness of the guilty Israelites. And if that was it—for securing their eternal happiness he was willing to give up all happiness here, I suppose he would not have been sinful. And I suppose our earnestness should go to that point—that I would give up all earthly happiness so that my child, my friend, my enemy, might be saved. Or, again, it may simply be the language of intensity—the expression of exceeding feeling. But, whichever it be—if you would intercede, it must not be in a light way, it must not be in commonplaces, it must not be superficial and cold. (*J. Vaughan, M.A.*) *Intercession for others :*—Never think lightly of this matter of intercession. There is a very light way in which people say, "Pray for me," and a very light way in which people answer, "Yes, I will." Be careful as to asking the favour, or promising to grant it. You may find it a good rule to promise, indeed, whenever you are asked by any one to pray for them, but to promise with this limitation—"I will do it once, I will do it the next time that I am on my knees before God, I will remember to pray for you." That you will be able to do. But to undertake always to pray for all who ask it is a burden of the conscience—a thing impossible. You will have those for whom, doubtless, you do pray continually, and many ; but as respects the ordinary request that you will pray, I would suggest to you not to withhold the promise, but with the limitation that you will pray once. For it is a blessed thing to have intercessors. And how blessed a thing it is God seems to teach us in that He has revealed to us that we have the Holy Ghost an intercessor, and the Lord Jesus Christ an intercessor. We have an intercessor always within us, and one always above us. " The Spirit maketh intercession for us [and in us] with groanings which cannot be uttered." And here is the comfort—that " He that searcheth the heart," God in heaven, " knows the mind of the Spirit " in the man. The Holy Ghost in the man asks everything that is according to the will of God. (*Ibid.*) *Effective intercession :*—Amongst the many touching and interesting incidents that occurred in Stanley's last journey, there are but few to equal the following :—Stanley had much trouble with his men on account of their current propensity to steal, the results of which brought upon the expedition much actual disaster. At last he doomed the next man caught stealing to death. His grief and distress were unbounded when the next thief was found to be Uledi, the bravest, truest, noblest of his dusky followers. Uledi had saved a hundred lives, his own among the number. He had performed acts of the most brilliant daring, always successful, always faithful, always kind. Must Uledi die ? He called all his men around him in a council. He explained to them the gravity of Uledi's crime. He reminded them of his stern decree, but said he was not hard enough to enforce it against Uledi. His arm was not strong enough to kill Uledi; some other punishment, and a hard one, must be meted out. What should it be ? The council must decide. They took a vote. Uledi must be flogged. When the decision was reached, Stanley standing, Uledi crouching at his feet, and the solemn circle drawn closely around them, one man whose life Uledi had saved under circumstances of frightful peril, stood forth and said : " Give me half the blows, master." Then another said, in the faintest accent, while tears fell from his eyes, " Will the master give his slave leave to speak ?" " Yes," said Stanley. The Arab came forward and knelt by Uledi's side. His words came slowly, and now and then a sob broke them. " The master is wise," he said. " He knows all that has been, for he writes them in a book. Let your slave fetch the book, master, and turn its leaves. Maybe there is something that tells how Uledi saved Zaidi from the white waters of the cataract ; how he saved many men—how many I forget —Bin Ali, Mabruki, Koni Kusi, others too ; how he is worthier than any three of us ; how he always listens when the master speaks, and flies forth at his word. Look, master, at the book. Then, if the blows must be struck, Shumari will take half and I the other half." Saywa's speech deserves to live for ever. Stanley threw away his whip. " Uledi is free," he said. " Shumari and Saywa are pardoned." *Self-sacrificing devotion :*—An extraordinary act of devotion is described in the " Spirit of Missions," as it was related by Bishop Boone, while on a visit to this country. He said : " I had a very valuable Chinese servant in my employ, upon whom I leaned with implicit confidence, and one day he came to me and said : ' I shall be obliged to ask you to find some one to take my place, as in the course of a few weeks I am to be executed in place of a rich gentleman, who is to pay me very liberally for becoming his substitute'—such a mode of exchange, as the reader may know, being in accordance with the law of the empire. I then inquired what possible inducement there could be for him to forfeit his life for any amount of money, when he replied : ' I have an aged father and mother, who are very poor, and unable to work, and the money that I am to receive will make them comfortable as long as they live. I think, therefore, it is my duty to give up my life for the sake of accomplishing this.' " *Pardoned, yet punished :*—The Lord may grant pardon, and yet there is a sense in which He will still " plague the people " for their sin. The drunkard may give up his sin and become a Christian, and yet come to a premature grave because of his former evil course. The man who has squandered vast estates in evil-doing may repent, but his repentance will not bring back that which he has lost. The boy who spends foolishly the time in which he should be gaining knowledge and virtue will feel the effects of that misspent time all his life. Some opportunities which we have carelessly allowed to slip by unimproved will never come again to us to all eternity. In that sense each of us must bear his own iniquity. (*S. S. Times.*) *An example of intercession :*—Said a servant to President Bacchus, " The physician said, sir, that you cannot live to exceed half an hour." " Is it so ? Then take me out of my bed, and place me upon my knees ; let me spend that time in calling upon God for the salvation of the world." It was done. He died upon his knees, praying for the salvation of sinners.

CHAPTER XXXIII.

Vers. 1-3. **Without the camp.**—*The Tabernacle without the camp :*—I. First, then, they that seek the Lord must go without the camp. 1. It is scarcely necessary for me to say that no man can be a true seeker of God who has anything to do with the camp of the profane. We must take care that our garments are entirely clean from those lusts of the flesh, and those blasphemies of the ungodly. 2. Again, we must as much come out from the camp of the careless as from the camp of the profane. The largest company in the world is not that of the profane, but of the thoughtless—not those who oppose, but who neglect the great salvation. 3. But we must go further than this : if a man would have fellowship with God he must go even out of the camp of the merely steady, sedate, and thoughtful; for there be multitudes whose thoughts are not God's thoughts, and whose ways are not His ways, who are in every respect conformed outwardly to the laws of God, and who rigidly observe the customs of upright society—who think, and therefore abhor the trifles of the world —but who, notwithstanding, have never learned to set their affections on things above. It is not enough to leave the Amalekites; thou must leave even the hosts of Moab, brother though Moab may seem to be to the Israel of God. 4. He that would know anything of God aright must even come out of the camp of the merely religious. Oh, it is one thing to attend to religion, but another thing to be in Christ Jesus; it is one thing to have the name upon the church book, but quite another thing to have it written in the Lamb's book of life. II. This going out of the camp will involve much inconvenience. 1. You will find that your diffidence and your modesty will sometimes shrink from the performance of duty's stern commands. If Christ be worth anything, He is worth avowing before the world, before men, before angels, and before devils. 2. Peradventure when you go without the camp you will lose some of your best friends. You will find that many a tie has to be cut when your soul is bound with cords to the horns of the altar. Can you do it? As Christ left His Father for you, can you leave all for Him? 3. You will find, too, when you go without the camp, you will have some even professedly godly people against you. "Ah!" they will say, when you are filled with the Spirit, and are anxious to serve God as Caleb did, with all your heart—" Ah! young man, that is fanaticism, and it will grow cool by and by." 4. Another inconvenience to which you will be exposed is that you will be charged falsely. So was your Master, remember. Endure, as He did. 5. Again, you must expect to be watched. If you profess to go without the camp, others will look for something extra in you—mind that they are not disappointed. I have heard some say, " I do not like to join the Church because then there would be so much expected of me." Just so, and that is the very reason why you should, because their expectation will be a sort of sacred clog to you when you are tempted, and may help to give impetus to your character and carefulness to your walk, when you know that you are looked upon by the eyes of men. III. Now I come to use certain arguments, by which I desire earnestly to persuade each Christian here to go without the camp ; to be exact in his obedience ; and to be precise in his following the Lamb withersoever He goeth. 1. I use first a selfish argument, it is to do it for your own comfort's sake. If a Christian can be saved while he conforms to this world, at any rate he will be saved so as by fire. Would you like to go to heaven in the dark, and enter there as a shipwrecked mariner climbs the rocks of his native country? 2. But I have a better reason than that, and it is, for your own growth in grace do it. If you would have much faith, you cannot have much faith while you are mixed with sinners. If you would have much love, your love cannot grow while you mingle with the ungodly. 3. I beseech you, Christian men and women, come right out and be your Master's soldiers wholly for the Church's sake. It is the few men in the Church, and those who have been distinct from her, who have saved the Church in all times. 4. And for the world's sake, let me beg you to do thus. The Church itself can never be the salt of the world, unless there be some particular men who are the salt of the Church. 5. And now lastly, for your Master's sake. What have you and I to do in the camp when He was driven from it? What have we to do with hosannas when He was followed with hootings, "Crucify Him, crucify Him"? What have I to do in the tent while my Captain lies in the open battle-field? (*C. H. Spurgeon.*)

Vers. 4-8. **Put off thy ornaments from thee, that I may know what to do unto thee.**

—The work of Lent:—Lent is a season with a likeness to Jewish ordinances, because man in his nature and wants is ever the same; it is a Christian season, because its one object is to make us know more of the nearness of God to man, which is the great fact of Christianity. In the text we have one of God's most explicit statements of the need of such observance; and we ask the meaning of that reason which He assigns for a season of special penitence and humiliation. 1. God wishes to know what to do with us. If the putting aside of ornaments, no matter how valuable or brilliant, is the condition of that process, it ought to be done; for God's action must be full of power and love; and to be told that His hand is to be felt in our life, must imply that a blessing is to be bestowed upon us far beyond anything that can come from any other addition. 2. Never at any stage of His revelation has God ceased, in one form or other, to prescribe temporary and voluntary relinquishments, in order that He may enter. The ornaments, or God's voice—that is the simple form of choice. 3. The object of God's dealings with men is, that He may destroy their sin. And there is no more fruitful source of sin than those ornaments which He tells us to put away. The things which gather about our lives are causes of separation from our brother. The innocence or the desirability of the ornament may make no difference in the result. Learning, applause, and culture may make us just as forgetful, or unsympathetic, or even cruel towards others, as the more material possessions of life. 4. We can see, therefore, that this command is like the call of a John Baptist: Make the way plain, the path straight and level, for the coming of the Lord; remove the stumbling-block which has been in thy own or thy brother's path. Men must learn to see their oneness as brothers, before sin can be done away; lives very different from each other must be placed side by side, and then new modes of thought and comparison will at once enter. How often one word, which gives us a glimpse into the real condition of another's heart, makes us ashamed of some feeling which we have been cherishing toward him! 5. But the sins against our brethren are not the only evil that our ornaments work, and do not constitute the only reason why they must be abandoned before God can do His work for us. Those very sins spring from a deeper injury which has been done to our souls. These things that have attached themselves to life come to be regarded as its substance, and to regulate its whole movement. What the text says to us, then, is this: Cease to depend upon the present condition and surroundings of life. Think of yourself as an immortal soul. Try to imagine yourself as cut off from all these pursuits and surroundings, for so, in fact, you must be at some time; then count over the treasures of your life, and see whether there is enough to support an immortal soul. 6. The Lenten call is a call to greater moderation in the use of the things of this life, so that they shall not become our masters; it is a call to exalt the true Master of our life, so that every ornament of our being shall be discarded for ever, which is not worthy to minister to His glory, or which attempts to fight against His supremacy, so that all which remains shall be used in obedience to His commands, and in subservience to His purposes. It is by this test that innocent and sinful indulgence in the things of this life is to be discriminated, that the line of the too much and the too little is to be drawn, and that we are to be made men and women worthy and fit to use the world rightly. 7. But why does God need that the ornaments of men's lives should be put off before He shall know what to do unto them? Is it not limiting His power to say that He cannot deal with us as we are, with all our ornaments upon us? The work which God is to do for us has for its greatest mark that it is dependent upon what we are. It is the work of overcoming sin. God, when He made man, gave him all he needed for full development and growth. His course was forward and upward, ever increasing in power and glory, while obedience and dependence upon God ruled his action. No redemption would be necessary for such a being. Man's sin, his desire after the things of this world, his willingness to build up his life with those, created the great necessity. The self-will of man called upon God for new action—action which His Divine wisdom could alone create, and which His Divine power could alone execute. That He may know what it shall be, He asks some indication of man's desire. There is nothing to do but to punish, to let the life which persistently holds to what has been its destruction, go its own sad way of separation from God, if there is no relaxing of the nervous grasp on earthly good and ornament. But at the very first sign of a willingness to put such things away, to bridle life's passion, and to restrain life's desire, the way of redeeming love is open. Man is ready; and God knows what to do, and He is able to make him His child once more. 8. Let us, then, rejoice at this season for putting away the

mere ornaments of life, and in it open our ear anxiously, constantly, eagerly, to hear the word of His gracious intention. God's treasury is full of the true ornaments of life. He readily offers them to us. Receive them as readily, and the world's ornaments will lose their false glitter ; our hearts will cease to desire them with that eager covetousness which conceals all the better impulses of the soul, and God will be able to do for us all the deep purposes of His wisdom and His love. (*Arthur Brooks.*)   *Repentance of the Israelites :—*I. GOD IS NOT ABLE TO EXERCISE MERCY TOWARDS AN IMPENITENT TRANSGRESSOR. He cannot do this, because it would —1. Be inconsistent with His own perfections. 2. Be ineffectual for the happiness of the persons themselves. 3. Introduce disorder into the whole universe. II. WHERE HUMILIATION IS MANIFESTED, MERCY MAY BE EXPECTED. This appears from— 1. The very mode in which repentance is here enjoined. 2. The experience of penitents in all ages. Application : 1. Consider what obstructions you have laid in the way of your own happiness. 2. Endeavour instantly to remove them. (*C. Simon, M.A.*)   *A fashionable sin :—*The house of prayer is a poor place to exhibit beads, ribbons, ruffles, gewgaws, and trinkets. The evils of such extravagance are many. It keeps people from worship, when they have not apparel as gorgeous as their neighbours. It loads the poor with burdens too heavy to be borne to procure fashionable clothing. It leads many into temptations, debt, dishonesty, and sin. It causes many a poor shop girl to work nearly all Saturday night, that some customer's fine clothes may be ready for the Sunday show. It keeps people at home in cloudy or stormy weather, when, if they wore plain clothing, they could defy clouds and storms. It consumes the hours in dressing, crimping, and fussing, keeping people from church, and wasting time, hindering the reading of the Scripture, and making Sunday a day of folly. It makes the poor emulous, malicious, and envious, and plants many a bitter thought in the minds of children and others, when they see their neighbours decked in finery—often unpaid for—and feel that people are respected, not for their integrity of character, but for the fashion of their clothes. It is forbidden in God's Word. And yet we seldom find a minister that dare open his mouth against this fashionable sin. Christian people should dress plainly before the Lord, for example's sake at home and abroad, for decency's sake, and for the sake of Christ. (*Christian Age.*)

Vers. 9–11. **The Lord talked with Moses.**—*Speaking to God :—*In the minds of many prayer seems to differ widely from other forms of communication. Not perceiving any tangible object of address, they feel as if to pray were to talk with nothing. "How can you pray with vigour into the empty air ? " asked a candid doubter. Even Christians sometimes lack the sense of communion, and then prayer is scarcely more than soliloquy in the form of petition. And yet speaking to God is really very much like speaking to men. Since God is a person, address to Him must conform to the general principles of personal address. I. In speaking to God, as in speaking to men, WE MUST ADDRESS THE INVISIBLE. Converse is mental, not physical. The form you see is not the man you talk with. We speak not to the ears which catch the words, but to the mind which perceives the thought. A mere lump of organized clay cannot be a party to conversation. If, then, one asks, How can you pray into empty air ? we may reply by asking : How can you talk to a clod of clay ? In every case, whatever direction be given to words or other signals of communion, the real address is to mind. One using an acoustic tube apparently speaks to the mouth-piece in the wall. But he really addresses a person in another room. Words are usually directed towards eyes and ears because through these mind is reached. So prayer seems to the prayerless as speech thrown into void space. It is really a direct address to the Infinite Mind which pervades all space. II. In speaking to God, as in speaking to men, we not only address the invisible, but THE PRESENCE OF A VISIBLE FORM, OR SYMBOL OF PERSONALITY, IS UNNECESSARY. The blind communicate without seeing a form, and the deaf without hearing a voice. We may speak to a person behind a wall or screen if only assured that he is within call. By letter we address friends hundreds of miles distant. Thus it is evident that prayer to God is only one of many forms of address to mind with no visible form present. We only need to know that the mind addressed is within reach by any means of communication. III. In speaking to God, as in speaking to men, THE ENJOYMENT OF COMMUNION IS VARIABLE, AND INCREASES WITH CUSTOM AND ACQUAINTANCE. Many people have heard of God, but are not acquainted with Him. They know Him only by reputation. They are not on speaking terms with Him. Hence they have not learned to enjoy His company. They do not love to pray. But let them reverently and sincerely cultivate an acquaintance with God, so as really to know Him, and they will delight in holy communion. (*The Study.*) *Friendship with God:*—Mr. Toller, of Kettering, invited a company to meet Robert Hall. Among the guests was Andrew Fuller, who, with Toller, had previously accompani·d Hall in a forenoon walk in the country. They returned together at the dinner-hour; and Hall immediately went up alone to his own chamber. The company waited for some time, but he did not appear. At length a messenger was sent to say that dinner was ready. But as the servant approached the chamber, she paused and listened, for Hall was on his knees pleading with God in prayer. When this was repeated to the company, Fuller exclaimed: "Don't disturb him; he is with his best Friend." *Friendship with God:*—Augustine, in his "Confessions," te'ls a story, which he heard from his friend Pontitianus, to the following effect. Two courtiers in attendance on the emperor, who was then witnessing the public games, strolled into some gardens, and entering a neighbouring house, which happened to belong to a Christian, were attracted by a manuscript life of the hermit Anthony. As pastime, one of them began to read it, but his curiosity soon grew into a deep conviction, which made him cry out to his friend: "What attainment do we propose to ourselves so great as to be the intimate friends of the emperor? and even when arrived at, how unstable and full of peril is the position? But here, if I wish to be the friend of God, He will receive me immediately!" *Communion with God:*—There was each morning during his first sojourn in the Soudan one half-hour during which there lay outside Charles George Gordon's tent a handkerchief, and the whole camp knew the full significance of that small token, and most religiously was it respected by all there, whatever was their colour, creed, or business. No foot dared to enter the tent so guarded. No message, however pressing, was carried in. Whatever it was, of life or death, it had to wait until the guardian signal was removed. Every one knew that God and Gordon were alone in there together.

Ver. 14. My presence shall go with thee, and I will give thee rest.—*God's presence giving rest:*—This is a word in season to every one who is weary. I. In what sense has God said, "My presence shall go with thee"? He is present to the believer as a Friend whose love has been accepted, and whose conversation is understood with all the intelligence of a kindred nature. II. In what sense does the presence of God give rest? 1. It tends to give rest from the terror incident to a state of condemnation. 2. It gives rest from the anguish which springs from a discordant nature. 3. It gives rest from the cravings of an unsatisfied spirit. 4. It gives rest from the distraction felt amidst uncongenial scenes and associations. 5. It gives rest from the disquietude which results from want of human sympathy. 6. It gives rest from apprehensions regarding the future. 7. The presence of God with us now is the pledge of perfect rest in the next life. (*C. Stanford, D.D.*) *The pilgrimage of a true life:*—I. The path of a true life. 1. From captivity to freedom. 2. From scarcity to plenty. II. The companion of a true life. God's guiding, succouring, and protecting superintendence. III. The destiny of a true life. "Rest." Not inactivity. Harmonious activity is the destiny of the good; activity in harmony with all our powers, with the order of the universe, and with the will of God. (*Homilist.*) *A gracious promise:*—I. "My presence shall go with thee." 1. By the presence of God, we are sometimes to understand His essential presence or ubiquity, which pervades all matter and space, and without which nothing could exist. 2. There is also the providential presence of God, by which He sees the wants, and provides for the necessities of His numerous family. 3. By the presence of God here is meant His gracious presence which He mercifully condescends to manifest in His house, and to reveal to His people. 4. The gracious presence of God is essentially necessary to His people, in order to show them the right way and enable them to walk therein. 5. The gracious presence of God is indispensable to His people to purify them, and make them ready for the heavenly Canaan. If ever we be made "meet to be partakers of the inheritance of the saints in light," it must be "through sanctification of the Spirit, and belief of the truth." II. "I will give thee rest." 1. The rest here mentioned has, undoubtedly, a primary reference to the land of Canaan, in which the people of Israel rested, after the toils, dangers, and fatigue of the wilderness. But then, there is something more implied in the word than this. 2. The people of God enjoy a comparative rest in this present world, inasmuch as they are delivered from the power and pollution of sin, and possess that kingdom of grace which consists of righteousness, peace, and joy in the Holy Ghost. 3.

But there still remaineth a rest for them beyond the confines of the grave, in the participation of that felicity which is at the right hand of the Most High. (*B. Bailey*.)   *God's presence and rest:*—I. The journey. The people were in a journeying condition. 1. They had come from Egypt. A land of toil and oppression and misery. 2. They were journeying in the wilderness. A land of drought, sterility, and dangers. They had many trials and enemies. A true picture of the world through which believers are travelling. 3. They were travelling to Canaan. A land promised to their fathers; a land of freedom and rest, of plenty and happiness. II. The presence. "My presence shall go with thee." This presence was—1. Divine. 2. Visible. Pillar of cloud by day and pillar of fire by night. 3. Efficient. Not merely Divine recognition and observation, but with them to do all for them they required. 4. Continued. "When flesh and heart fail," &c. "This God is our God for ever and ever," &c. III. The rest. "And I will give thee rest." 1. The rest of triumph after the conflicts of life. 2. A rest from the toils of wilderness journeyings. 3. A rest from the fears and dangers of the way. 4. A rest from the sufferings and afflictions of life. 5. A rest of eternal and heavenly glory. (*J. Burns, D.D.*)   *God's gracious presence with His people:* —I. The nature of the presence. God's gracious presence with His people is more than His natural attribute of omnipresence. II. While, however, God is constantly present with His own people, there are certain times in which His presence is specially manifest. III. The mental states which precede the gift of God's presence. 1. Earnest prayer. 2. The spirit of mourning and humiliation. (*D. Macaulay, M.A.*)   *God's presence promised:*—I. The need of refuge in God from the lives of others. Even in human society at its best the heart has no safe refuge. II. The prayer of Moses suggests the need of one worn by well-doing. That well-doing brings exhaustion and despondency and so specially needs God's aid is a fact which we sometimes forget. III. The prayer of Moses expressed the need of one weighted by the sense of responsibility. He had a great work to do. He who feels little need of God has a low sense of personal responsibility. But he who faces all responsibility and tries to see his life as he will see it when the end of all things has come, has great need of God. To him life becomes a serious thing. For help he will often "lift up his eyes unto the hills," and will take help from no lower source. IV. This prayer of Moses received a gracious answer. It was the vision of God. (*Willard G. Sperry.*)   *God's special presence distinguishes His own people:*—I. The promised presence of God with His people will, so long as they are favoured with it, produce a wide difference and separation between them and all other men. When God comes to dwell in the soul, He imparts to it a portion, not only of His own views, but of His own feelings. He not only illuminates the understanding with His own light, but, as an apostle expresses it, sheds abroad His love in the heart. II. That in proportion as God withdraws the manifestations of His presence from His people, this difference and separation between them and other men will diminish. God is the Sun of the soul. When He favours it with His presence and exerts upon it His influence, it is enlivened and enlightened, and made to glow with love, and hope, and joy, and gratitude. But when He withdraws and suspends His influences, spiritual darkness and coldness are the consequence. Then it is night, it is winter with the soul. In proportion as He thus withdraws from His people, they cease to view Him as a present reality; they cease to have those views, and to exercise those affections, which constitute the grand essential difference between them and other men. Nor is this all. As holy affections decline, sinful affections revive. It remains only to make a suitable improvement of the subject. 1. With this view, permit me, in the first place, to say to each individual in this assembly, Do you know experimentally the difference between the presence and the absence of God? 2. Let me improve this subject, by inquiring whether this Church now enjoys the peculiar presence of God, as it once appeared to do? (*E. Payson, D.D.*) *God's presence realized:*—Since God is everywhere, in what sacred and peculiar sense is He present to the believing heart? "Lord, how is it that Thou dost manifest Thyself to us, as Thou dost not unto the world?" The principle on which He does so is illustrated by some of the common facts of life. A man is present to his friend, as he is not to a stranger, though he may be at the same moment speaking to both. The light which floods the landscape with a deluge of beauty is present to him who sees it, as it is not to the blind man walking at his side. Music, though it may ripple round the deafened ear, is only present to him who hears it. The discourse of the naturalist on his experiments, of the scholar on his books, of the mathematician who is talking with raptures on the beauties of a theorem, will bring things into the presence of initiated listeners, which are still remote from the minds of those in the very same company who have no sympathy with the theme. So, "two women may be grinding at a mill "; "two men may be in the field "; one a believer, the other an unbeliever; and although the Great Spirit is near to them both, there is a sense in which He is present to the one as He is not to the other; for, in the case of the believer, the causes of estrangement have been taken away, a new relation exists, a new life has been born, and God is present as a Friend, whose love has been accepted, and whose conversation is understood with all the intelligence of a kindred nature. Everything we need to secure that peace which the world cannot give is secured by the promise, " My presence shall go with thee," for that tranquil presence does not merely attend us, it enters the very soul, and sheds its benediction there. Plato seemed to have a glimpse of this glorious truth when he said, "God is more inward to us than we are to ourselves." What was to Him a beautiful speculation is to us an inspiring reality ; for we are the "temples of the Holy Ghost." He dwells within us as a pitying, purifying friend, to kindle celestial light in our darkness, and by removing the cause of discord, and restoring the equilibrium of the soul, to give us peace at the very seat of life. Ignatius, from his eminent devotion, was called by his companions " The Godbearer "; and when Trajan said to him, " Dost thou then bear the Crucified One in thy heart?" his reply was, "Even so ; for it is written, ' I will dwell in them, and walk in them, and I will be their God, and they shall be My people.' " This honour have all the saints, yet all do not seem to be fully conscious of it. Only let us feel it ; only let us own that inward authority, and listen to that inward voice ; only let us act in obedience to the suggestions of that " Power that worketh within us to will and to do of His good pleasure," and we shall find that in proportion as we are actuated by the life of God within us, shall we feel "His peace." (*C. Stanford, D.D.*) *Choice food for pilgrims to Canaan:*— I. WHAT ARE THE BENEFITS OF THE DIVINE PRESENCE WHICH IS HERE PROMISED ? 1. The acknowledgment of the people as being peculiarly the Lord's. 2. Preservation and protection. 3. Direction and guidance. 4. Real worship in the wilderness. What is bread, what is wine, and what is the table, if the King Himself be not there ? 5. Communion with God. He is always ready for fellowship with His people. II. WHAT ARE THE DEMANDS OF THIS PRESENCE ? 1. That we rely upon it. Away with fear and melancholy. Treat it as a matter of fact, and be filled with rest. 2. That we use it. Exercise faith in God. 3. Do not lose it. Oh, how reverently, cautiously, jealously, and holily ought we to behave ourselves in the presence of God ! 4. Glorify Him all that you possibly can. Seek out those who have lost His company, and go and cheer them. III. WHAT IS THE CHOICE BLESSING WHICH IS APPENDED TO THIS PRESENCE. " Rest "—both now and hereafter. (*C. H. Spurgeon.*) *Alone: yet not alone:*—I cannot see that this choice of Moses, to walk in God's way, if but assured of God's presence, differs in anywise from the choice which that people was called on to make at that moment, and which God is ever pressing upon us all. In considering it in its broad human aspect, I observe —I. HERE ARE TWO WAYS ON WHICH THE CHOICE IS TO BE EXERCISED—TWO PATHS, WHICH VERY PLAINLY DIVERGE. It is the old, old choice—worldliness, godliness— duty, pleasure—God's will, self-will—the passions and appetites of the flesh or of the mind, the convictions of conscience and the Word of God. II. THE CRY OF THE HUMAN SPIRIT FOR REST. The longing of man's spirit amid all these strifes, discords, and confusions, is for rest. Nothing can eradicate man's conviction that strife and discord have no right in the universe ; that they are abnormal ; that the normal condition of things and beings is harmony, and that harmony is the music of rest. God must rest—rest even in working ; and all that is of God and from God has the longing and the tending to rest. III. THE DIVINE ASSURANCE WHICH WAS TO MOSES, AND SHOULD BE TO US, AN ALL-SUFFICIENT WARRANT TO LEAVE THE WORLD AND THE PLEASURES OF SIN AND COMMIT OURSELVES TO THE DESERT UNDER GOD'S GUIDANCE, AS THE PATH TO THE HEAVENLY REST. (*J. B. Brown, B.A.*) *Two kinds of rest :*—There are two kinds of rest, or rather what goes by the name of rest, within reach of man. The secret of the one is, escape from trouble ; the secret of the other is, entering into life. Life is the harmonious balance of conflicting forces, the calm control of all opposite powers. Escape from trouble is not permitted to man, though he thinks it is. It is a wonderful feature in man's constitution that he can find rest only in his highest, in the full culture and activity of all his powers. He tries to rest in a luxurious home, in a feverish orgy, on a wanton's breast. But who shall paint the anguish of the rest of the wicked? How many a man has gone out from a scene of uproarious merriment, to blow out his brains, in blank despair! There is no rest but in God. Man rests only in the fulness of his existence, in the completeness of his life. Moses found no rest in communion with earthly natures, but there was rest for him—it bathed his soul like the dewy moonlight the flowers —when he entered into that which is within the veil, and talked "of things unspeakable" with God. Having faith in the Saviour's power and love, the spirit rests amid the severities of discipline, yea, sleeps sometimes, as Jesus did while the storm was highest; for ever when the danger is imminent, and the foaming surges are parting to engulf their prey, the Divine presence within shines forth around, and immediately there is a great calm, and the spirit rests still. (*Ibid.*) *The Divine presence :*—I. HELP COMES WHEN MOST NEEDED. The idolatry of Israel discouraged Moses. So the trials which bring us to God in dependence and prayer, bring the Divine presence and blessing to our aid. II. THE DESIRE OF THE SPIRITUAL MIND IS THE PRESENCE OF GOD. "If Thy presence go not with me, carry us not up hither." "Leave me not, neither forsake me, O God of my salvation." III. GOD SUPPLIES THIS WANT. "His name shall be called 'God with us.'" "Lo, I am with you alway, even unto the end of the world." "He shall give you another Comforter that He may abide with you for ever." The experience of this presence is a joy to be sought and found only in fidelity to God. It restrains from evil and inspires to good works. It gives rest from the uncertainties suggested by unbelief and doubt. It supplies the happiness of assurance and the calmness of peace. (*E. W. Warren, D.D.*)   *God's presence our rest :*—Rest must be sought deeper down than in circumstances. It must begin at the centre of our being, and in its accord with the being of God. His presence must be welcome to us and accompany us, or rest is a vain dream. I. THE CIRCUMSTANCES BY WHICH THIS ASSURANCE WAS CALLED FORTH. 1. Moses was a very lonely man. Perhaps more lonely in the midst of the two millions of people whom he was leading as a flock than he had been amid the solitudes of the desert tending the flock of Jethro. The very contrast between his lofty enjoyment of Divine communion and the people, always set on sensual pleasure, must have lent intensity to the isolation of his spirit, which reared itself amid their sensual longings, as the peak of Susafeh above the lower ranges of Sinai. In this his loneliness he has been compared to Elijah at Cherith or on Carmel; to Paul standing aged and friendless before the tribunal of Nero; to Alfred when, in the words of the old chronicler, he "lived an unquiet life in the woodlands of Somerset"; to Columbus when, with his great secret locked in his heart, he still prosecuted his quest over the weary waste of waters. Jesus was the most lonely man that ever lived. He drank the cup of loneliness to its dregs. And Moses said unto the Lord, "See, Thou sayest unto me, Bring up this people: and Thou has not let me know whom Thou wilt send with me." Note that last clause, "whom Thou wilt send with me." Do they not contain a sigh for a comrade, a companion, a friend in whose sympathy and judgment he might confide. In the physical world we are told that in the most solid bodies the atoms do not touch; and how often, though the crowd throngs us, we are not conscious that any one has touched us. It is to that state of mind that the assurance of the text is given. 2. In addition to this, the hosts were soon to leave the mountain region of Sinai, with which Moses had been familiar during his shepherd life, in order to take the onward road through unknown deserts, infested by daring and experienced foes. Such a summons to arise and depart is often sounding with its bugle-call in our ears. We are not like those who travel by the metal track of the railroad, on which they have been to and fro every day for years, and are able to tell exactly the names and order of the stations; but like an exploring expedition in an absolutely unknown district, and even the leader, as he leaves his hammock in the morning, does not know where it will be slung at night. 3. Still further difficulties had lately arisen in connection with the people's transgression. From a careful study of the passage it would seem that a change was proposed by their Almighty Friend. Hitherto He had gone in the midst of them. Now He avowed His intention of substituting an angel for Himself, lest He should suddenly consume the people because of their stiff-neckedness (chap. xxxiii. 3). But now it seemed likely some sensible diminution of the evidence of the Divine presence and favour was about to take place; and the fear of this stirred the soul of the great leader to its depths. Are there not times with many of us when we have reason to fear that, in consequence of some sad failure or sin on our part, the Lord may be obliged to withdraw the conscious enjoyment of His love? Supposing He should be compelled to leave me to myself, to withdraw His tender mercies, to shut up His compassions. Supposing that I should be like a sledge abandoned in Arctic snows, or a ship abandoned by its crew in mid-ocean. II. THE PLACE WHERE THIS ASSURANCE WAS GIVEN. The earlier intercourse between the servant, faithful in all his house, and Him who had appointed him seems to have been on the mountain summit. But after the outburst of the people's sin a change was made which did not necessitate such prolonged or distant absences from the camp. Indeed, he was absent for only one other period of forty days till the time of his death, some thirty-eight years afterwards (chap. xxxiv. 28). During the prolonged interview which he had been permitted to enjoy, God had spoken to him much of the Tabernacle which was shortly to be reared. He at once saw the blessedness of this proximity of the shrine for worship and fellowship, and his ardent soul seems to have been unable to brook delay. It was no longer necessary for him to climb to the mountain summit, entrusted with errands on behalf of the people, or eager for advice in difficult problems. He was able to transact all necessary business by going out to the tent. Thus the Lord spake with Moses face to face, as a man speaketh unto his friend; and Moses spake to his Father, who is in secret, with the freedom of a child. And as the people beheld that wondrous sight of God stooping to commune with man, they rose up and worshipped, every man at his tent door. It was as if he said, Wilt Thou Thyself be my Comrade and Companion, my Referee in difficulty, my Adviser in perplexity, my Friend in solitude? Thine angels are strong and fair and good, but none of them will suffice me, nothing short of Thyself. Without Thee, it were better for me to relinquish my task and die; but with Thee, no difficulty can baffle, no fear alarm, no obstacle deter. And God's answer came back on his spirit with music and balm, " My presence shall go with thee, and I will give thee rest." Nothing was said as to the people. But faith gets bolder as it mounts. Each answer to its claims makes it claim more. We may seriously question whether our faith is of the right quality if it is unable to compass more in its hand to-day than it did a year ago. And, therefore, Moses not only took the assurance of the Divine presence for himself, but asked that it be extended to include the people. "Wherein now shall it be known that I have found grace in Thy sight, I and Thy people? Is it not that Thou goest with us, so that we be separated, I and Thy people, from all the people that are upon the face of the earth." In this respect also he was successful. And the Lord said unto Moses, I will do this thing also that thou hast spoken, for thou hast found grace in My sight. There are moments of holy intercourse with God, rapturous, golden moments, in the lives of all His servants; when next they visit us, and we would make the most of their brief, bright, rapturous glow, let us plead, not only for ourselves, but for others, asking for them an equal blessedness. III. THE BLESSEDNESS WHICH THIS ASSURANCE GUARANTEED. There was, first, the Divine presence; and there was, secondly, the promised rest; not the rest of Canaan, for this Moses never saw, but a deeper and more blessed inheritance, which may be the portion of all faithful souls. But at their heart these two are one. The Divine presence is rest. Of course the conscious presence of God with us is only possible on three conditions. Firstly, we must walk in the light, as He is in the light, for He will have no fellowship with the unfruitful works of darkness, or turn aside to go with us on any crooked path of our own choosing. Secondly, we must recognize that the blood of Jesus Christ His Son goes on cleansing us from all sin, not only that which we judge and confess, but that also which is only seen by His prue and holy eyes. Thirdly, we must claim the gracious aid of the Holy Spirit to make real that presence, which is too subtle for the eye of man, unless it be specially enlightened. And, above all, we must remember that for us, at least, that presence is localized in the man Christ Jesus. For us there is no attenuated mist of presence, though a mist of light, but a Person in whom that presence is made real and touches us. 1. God's presence is rest from the conscience of sin. " I will remember their sins no more." 2. God's presence is rest from anxiety. The future is dim, and we are apt to strain our eyes as we peer into its depths. Now we are elate with building castles of light, and again we are immured in dungeons of foreboding. We cannot rest tossed to and fro like this, but when we can look from the mist to the face of our Guide, who goes with us, such wisdom and kindness mingle there that we are at rest. 3. God's presence gives rest to our intellect. The mind of man turns sick before the trifles and frivolities with which men, for the most part, seek to satisfy its insatiable appetite, and craves eternal truth, and this alone can be found in God. 4. God's presence is rest to our judgment. This regal faculty is con-

stantly being called into play to select out of one or two paths which offer themselves that which we should follow. It is left for Him to choose, and to make
known His choice, whilst the soul waits, exercising careful thought indeed, but
concentrating its whole power in seeking to know the Divine will. 5. God's pre
sence is rest to our will. The will of the self-life, which chafes like an unquiet
sea, can only come to rest in the will of God, compelled by the powerful attraction
of His near presence, just as we might conceive of a body passing from the earth to
the sun, increasingly losing the attraction of the planet as it feels the pull of the
mighty orb of day. 6. God's presence is rest from weariness. There is in each of
us a fund of natural energy, determined largely by health or temperament, or
favourable circumstances. But at times this is crushed by disappointment and
failure, and the sense of its inadequacy for some great task. But when God is
near it falls back on Him like a tired child on a father's strength, and is at rest.
7. God's presence is rest to our heart. Who is there that does not pine for love?
But to know God, to love God, to be loved by God, to delight in God's perpetual
presence—this is rest. I have a vision of a woodland glade. A group of tired,
frightened children are cowering around the bole of an old tree, dropping the
fragile, withered flowers from their hands and pinafores, as the first great drops of
the thunder shower, which had been darkening the sky, begin to fall. They have
lost their way, they sob bitterly, and crowd together. Suddenly through the wood
there comes a quick step, beneath which the twigs crackle and break—father has
come, and as he carries some in his strong arms through the storm on the nearest
track for home, and the others run at his side, they have learnt that there is a
presence which is rest. (*F. B. Meyer, B.A.*)

Vers. 15–17. **If Thy presence go not with me, carry us not up hence.**—*The withdrawal of God's presence deprecated:*—What was the special grace desired by Moses
in these memorable words? What withdrawal of honour and privilege was threatened? If we had only this chapter, we might infer that the difference in God's future
dealings with Israel would be, that He would henceforth commit them to the care of
an angel—some messenger of His providence less holy than Himself—and that the
honour and privilege which His personal presence implied would be withdrawn
(vers. 1–3). Apart, however, from the fact that it is difficult to conceive of any real
difference between God's personal and instrumental superintendence, we no sooner
turn our attention to the account of His proposed dealings with Israel before they
fell into the idolatry of the golden calf, than we find that the handing over of the
command of their hosts to an angel could not have been the change of treatment
that filled Moses with such dismay. There is no warrant for the supposition that
the angel of this chapter is an inferior being to the angel of the Divine presence
spoken of in chap. xxxiii. Indeed, there can be no reasonable doubt that when God
says, "Must My presence [literally, My face] go with thee, that I may give thee
rest?" the reference is to the angel in whom God's name was, and whose visible
symbol was the pillar of cloud and of fire. And of course the reference will be the
same in Moses' reply: "If Thy presence go not," &c. What, then, was the grace
which God proposed to withdraw from Israel? By their shameful apostasy after
the manifestation of the Divine glory at Sinai, they had shown that the grandest
and most awful signs of the Divine Majesty could easily be forgotten; and it really
seemed that the presence of the pillar of cloud and of fire in their midst would not,
when once it should become familiar, deter them from rebellion. It would be better
not to give them the opportunity of openly insulting the Divine Majesty. A grace
which failed to inspire awe would inevitably harden. God intimated, therefore, that
the angel of His face, instead of having His holy tent in the midst of the tents of the
congregation, should simply go before them to prepare their way. If, now, we look at
chap. xxix. 42–45, we shall see of what they would be deprived by the threatened
change in God's dealings. Evidently they would lose the sanctuary which was to
be their peculiar glory. To the nations they would appear a people that not only
had no visible God, but no public religious rites. Moses, their leader, instead of
being able to commune with God and ask counsel of Him, would be left to the
guidance of his own sagacity. The Children of Israel could not come to inquire of
God; no atonement could be carried into the presence of His mercy-seat; and no
blessing could be spoken by the priests, conveying peace to the hearts of the thousands of Israel. They were to be left to follow their own desires and the counsels
of their own hearts. God would fill them with their own ways. Only His providence engaged to direct their path and prepare their way to enter the Promised

Land. The effect of this terrible reservation in the conditions on which God pardoned their apostasy, would have resembled the effect of a papal interdict in mediæval times, when nations were denied the public offices of religion and shut up to a life almost without God in the world. It was this terrible prospect that called forth Moses' passionate entreaty, "If Thy presence go not *with* us, carry us not up hence." Better that we should remain in the wilderness, better that we should die where we are, than live under such perpetual discouragement, so manifestly forsaken of God! The lesson God desired to teach was conveyed by the mere threatening, and, in answer to the intercession of Moses, He consents to the construction and erection of the Sanctuary. When completed, He solemnly took possession of it, and Jehovah's sacred tent became the visible centre of the camp of Israel (chap. xl. 34–38). The application of this incident is obvious, though, since we live under a new and better covenant, we are in a somewhat different case from the children of Israel. The Shekinah has been set up in the family of man, and can never be removed. Immanuel, God with us, is the imperishable possession of the human family. Atonement for the sins of mankind has been made; Divine forgiveness has been pronounced; God and man are reconciled. The question for us is, Are we content to live without a personal sense of the Divine presence, without tasting for ourselves that the Lord is gracious, without seeking counsel and guidance from the oracles of God and obtaining answers of peace to our prayers? Does a life of practical atheism seem to us something too terrible to be endured? Would an interdict of our sanctuary services, a prohibition laid upon private prayer, a withdrawal of Divine promises, fill us with heart-felt dismay? (*E. W. Shalders, B.A.*)

Ver. 18. **Show me Thy Glory.**—*Moses' aspiration:*—It was a fine aspiration, worthy of the man who uttered it, and the occasion on which he spoke it—"Show me Thy glory." It was the reaching out of a darker dispensation after gospel light —the reflections wishing to lose themselves in the great original. It was a man who had had great things given him, and therefore asked more. He had had law; he had had presence. And now from presence he mounts up to the only thing above it—glory, which is above presence. That is always a right field of aspiration—something beyond the present attainment, taking the mercy given as stepping-stones up higher. Do not be afraid of high spiritual ambition. Cultivate aspirations—they are little different from prayer—they are very elevating. I. Let us see to what Moses aspired. What are we to understand by "glory"? Evidently it was more than law. There are three kinds of glory. 1. There is the glory of circumstances that addresses itself to the senses—the glory, to the Christian, of gold and of pearl, the glory of surrounding angels, the glory of beautiful ministrations, the glory of light. 2. Then there is moral glory—such as that of the Lord Jesus Christ upon earth (John i. 14). 3. The glory of the sense or consciousness that everything goes back to the Creator, encircling Him with His own proper perfections, the living of God in the adoration, gratitude, and service of His creatures. Moses saw all three. His prayer had an answer on the Mount of Transfiguration. II. It was a very remarkable answer that God made to him. "I will make My kindness"—goodness, kindness, they are the same—"My kindness pass before thee." Kindness is glory. For example, glory is a covenanted thing, but the only covenanted thing is love. I do not read of other things covenanted; but God's glory must be in His covenant, therefore it is God's kindness. The glory of God was in Jesus Christ. That was the manifestation of the glory of God—that is kindness. The glory of God is Himself. Now God is love—He has many attributes, but they meet to make love. And take this lesson. Kindness is greatness, goodness is glory. Really, it is no greatness, it is no glory to see faults. It is so easy, and it is so poor, and it is so mean to see faults, and talk of faults. But it is great, really great, intellectually great, morally great, to see excellencies. Kindness is glory—it is a heavenly truth —the kindness of God is His glory. And every one among us is really glorious in proportion as he is kind. And the one of kindest judgments and kindest words has the most glory because he is nearest to the likeness of God. (*J. Vaughan, M.A.*) *The influence on the human mind of the manifestation of God's glory:*—Correct views of the Divine character lie at the foundation of true religion. The attributes with which the Divine character is invested have also a powerful influence on the mind. Carrying forward the same train of thought, we shall find that even under the full light of the system of Christianity, the peculiar aspect in which the Divine character is viewed will greatly modify Christian conduct and enjoyment. Thus, upon one may rest a sense of the terrible majesty of God. On another may rest a sense of awe and veneration, and the still small voice seem ever to sound in his ears, "Be still, and know that I am God." To a third is presented most vividly the idea of holiness; and to a fourth, the idea, the triumphant thought, is, "God is love." These various views must greatly modify our mode of approach before God. I. First, then, LET US CONSIDER THE DESIRE OF MOSES. 1. Did he desire to behold some grand and glorious manifestation of the Deity; some outward form or shape to represent the great Jehovah? Why should such be his desire? In the first place, he must have had correct views of the Deity—he must have known that "God is a Spirit." Our tendency to attach form to the Deity arises from the limited nature of our faculties. We are principally influenced by external qualities; we judge by them; and though we know a spirit has not the ordinary qualities of matter, yet we can form no distinct conception without associating some of them. But, in the second place, why should he desire to behold such external displays of glory and power? He had worshipped at the burning bush. The sea had divided at his approach; the Divine presence, as a pillar of cloud by day and of fire by night, had been his guide and protection; and, lastly, he had stood amidst the terrific scenes of Sinai until he exclaimed, "I do exceedingly fear and quake." 2. May he have used the expression in the sense of the Psalmist where he says, "The heavens declare the glory of God"; desiring to understand more of creative power and skill? There can be doubt that he earnestly desired to know all that could be known in reference to the great work of creation. 3. Is it probable that he desired to behold the glory of God as manifested in his past government of the world? In this he had already been instructed. 4. Since, then, his prayer could not refer to external exhibitions of the glory of the Deity, or to His creative power, or past government of the world, it only remains for us to turn toward the future. And if we view the circumstances surrounding him, we shall see that by his prayer, "I beseech Thee, show me Thy glory," he desired to understand the merciful purposes of God toward the Israelites, and through them to the world. That the Almighty had great designs in view in reference to the Israelites, he had a right to infer, from what had already been done for them. As when an architect collects in one place a vast quantity of materials, we have a right to expect the erection of some magnificent edifice; so, from previous and vast preparation on the part of the Deity, some event of momentous importance might be inferred. Abraham had been called from his native land and from among his kindred; his sons had been trained under peculiar circumstances. What connection this had with the hope of a Messiah! Again, the circumstance through which he had just passed were of a most singular character. He had been upon the sacred mount. Israel had said, "Let not God speak with us"; and Moses had stood as their representative for forty days. But this very people who had heard the voice of God had turned to idolatry at the foot of the mount. What can be the measure of that mercy which is preceded by the preparatory act of the pardon of two millions and a half of people? His longing soul desires to know all the purposes of God. The act of mercy, just witnessed, kindled within him a greater love for God, a more earnest wish to fathom the depths of His goodness; and, with the vehemence of intense desire, he cries out, "I beseech Thee, show me Thy glory"—grant me a full exhibition of Thy mercy and Thy love. II. Let us next consider HOW FAR THIS DESIRE WAS SATISFIED. In answer to this earnest prayer, the Deity replies, "I will make all My goodness pass before thee," &c. (chap. v. 19). Again in verses 21-23, "Behold there is a place by Me, and thou shalt stand upon a rock," &c. And again it is said in chap. xxxiv. 5-7, "And the Lord descended in the cloud, and stood with him there, and proclaimed the name of the Lord." In this manifestation of the Divine character to Moses, a few particulars may be noticed. 1. He proclaimed the name of the Lord before him. This probably refers to such a general view of the Divine administration as exhibits the benevolence, holiness, and justice of God, intimately blended in the government of man. 2. He made all His goodness pass before him. This was probably a prophetic view of His mercy to the Israelites as a nation. 3. He showed him His administration as a sovereign: "I will be gracious to whom I will be gracious, and I will show mercy on whom I will show mercy." Here was explained the difference of the treatment of Israel and Canaan. 4. He gave him a prophetic view of the mission of Christ. This is indicated in the expression, "Thou shalt see My back parts." The Hebrew word in this place translated "back parts," refers to time as as well as to position. And many able commentators and critics have referred this passage to the incarnation of Christ. The revelation appears to have been given to Moses to strengthen his own faith, and to fit him for those arduous duties required of the leader of such a people. He is placed in the "cleft of the rock," and before him passes, as though spread out on an immense canvass, the representations of the future. III. We can now inquire WHY HIS PETITION WAS NOT FULLY GRANTED. 1. From what has been already expressed, we are prepared to assume that it was not because in any manifestation there would be such terrific grandeur as should destroy human existence. For, first, Moses, we think, did not pray for external manifestations. These could be but symbols; and, however vast and magnificent the symbols might be, they never could adequately represent the Divine character. But, secondly, there is no intimation made, as we think, that if an exhibition were given, it would be one of terrific majesty. 2. The language employed in the text, "Thou canst not see My face; for there shall no man see Me and live," does not express any reason why man is unable to bear a view of the Deity. It simply declares the fact that man cannot see the face of God. 3. The reason why man could not behold this and live, would not be because of its terror or majesty; but because the view of the riches of His grace, His compassion and benevolence would excite emotions of reverence, of admiration, of love, and of joy, too overwhelming for humanity to bear. Each manifestation of the benevolence of God called forth songs of joy and ascriptions of praise from those who beheld them in ancient times. "Lord, now lettest Thou Thy servant depart in peace, according to Thy word; for mine eyes have seen Thy salvation." Now if, in these cases, a single view had such an effect, what would be the result if all the mercy and compassion of God, in its unbounded immensity and inexhaustible fulness, could, at one moment, be revealed to the human mind? Humanity could not bear the vision. To support this view we may reflect, that things exciting emotions, even of a pleasurable character, may extend so far as to become destructive, and that emotions of joy may in themselves destroy life. Light is pleasant, it spreads a halo of beauty and glory around the face of nature. The eye is never satisfied with the revelations which are made through its medium. Yet let that light, which thus spreads beauty around, fall upon the eye in the concentrated form of a ray from the meridian sun, and the power of vision is impaired, if not totally destroyed. The same is true of mental emotion. How the mind operates upon the body we cannot tell. But that the emotions of the mind do affect the body is universally admitted. Death from surprise, from fright, from terror, from all the depressing passions, has been by no means uncommon. In the every-day walks of life, who has not known of a case like this? A beloved son has left the home of fond parents to engage in commercial pursuits, or visit some distant place. By various causes his stay is prolonged, until at last the tidings reach his parents that he was wrecked off some rocky coast; or, that he perished in a fatal epidemic. They mourn for him as one that is lost; and they think of him only as in the spirit world. Years pass away, and though strangely preserved, his parents are not aware of his existence. He starts for home. Already he stands upon the hill that overlooks the scenes of his boyhood; the house, and trees, and shrubs, all stand as when he left; his heart exults at the thought of embracing his parents, and, thoughtless as to consequences, he hastily approaches. He opens the door. His mother gazes at him but a moment, cries, "My son, my son," throws her arms fondly around his neck, and swoons away in his arms. And instances have occurred, in which, from that swoon, there has been no recovery. History informs us that, in the time of the great South Sea speculation in England, many, overjoyed by their success, became insane. At the restoration of Charles II., a number of the nobility were so affected by the recovery of their titles and estates, that they became diseased, and in a short time died. Leo X., one of the most renowned occupants of the Papal chair, was so rejoiced by a victory somewhat unexpectedly gained over his enemies, that he sunk beneath the excitement. The heir of Leibnitz, the celebrated mathematician, on finding that a chest, filled as he supposed with paper, contained a large quantity of gold, became so excited by the discovery, that he was seized with a fatal disease of the heart. If such, then, be the influence of joyful emotions, when arising from temporal subjects, will the effect be diminished by adding the revelation of the unseen and eternal? Can emotions excited by the view of the majesty, holiness, wisdom, and compassion of the eternal Jehovah be less strong than those excited by considering a small portion of the work of His hands? As a general inference from this subject, we may notice what a sublime view is thus presented of the revelation contained in the Word of God. 1. It is a system of truth, in which, directly or indirectly, each separate truth leads to the great commanding truth of the being and attributes of God. This is the substance of revelation; God displayed in creation, in government, and in mercy to man. All other statements are but as secondaries revolving around their primary. The greatest minds may here be for ever engaged; but, like the parallel lines of the mathematician, there may be eternal approximation without perfect attainment. 2. But revelation is not merely a system of sublime truth. It is truth so presented as to affect our sensitive nature. It is not abstract speculation alone that is employed; our affections, our sympathies, are all enlisted. It is a system intended to operate upon man. (1) It operates by presenting the grand, the lofty, the majestic attributes of the Divine character. (2) It operates by inspiring man with what is termed, technically, the sympathic emotion of virtue. The performance of a brave, a noble, a patriotic, or a virtuous act, makes us desire to do the same. And when God reveals Himself as a God of mercy, employing His omnipotence in acts of compassion, there is a voice that whispers to the heart through every such manifestation, "Be ye merciful, even as I am merciful." (3) It operates by exciting gratitude and joy for personal salvation—for pardon, for regeneration, and for adoption into the family of the Most High. The grateful soul is ready to exclaim, "What shall I render unto the Lord for all His benefits toward me!" "What am I, and what is my Father's house," that I should thus be the subject of Divine love! (4) A fourth effect of such revelation is, that the soul desires to dwell constantly as in the presence of God. In Him is all fulness—the treasures of wisdom and knowledge for the intellect, of grace and mercy for the soul. The world diminishes in value; eternity, with all its spiritual blessedness, gradually unfolds before the moral vision. 3. That such are the effects of the manifestation of God's mercy, we are further warranted in believing from the history of distinguished individuals. Moses, when the name of the Lord was proclaimed before him, and His goodness passed before him, "made haste and bowed his head toward the earth and worshipped." He adored and reverenced. And such was the influence of the manifestations he received, that his face shone with such glory that the people could not look upon him unveiled; or, in other words, the manifestations of goodness and of glory were carried to the utmost possible point at which his usefulness to the people of Israel could remain. When Daniel was showed in prophetic vision the return of the captive Jews, and when the succession of empire was revealed, and things that should happen in the latter days, he says, "There remained no strength in me"; and before he was able to hear the whole prediction the angel touched him to strengthen him. On the mount of transfiguration the disciples were so overwhelmed that "they knew not what they said," or did not fully see the impropriety of their request, and yet were so enchanted that they said, "Master, it is good for us to be here." 4. What an unfailing source of comfort and joy is opened for the Christian in the revelation which God hath given! His joy is not of this world, it is in God. The world may change, but God changeth not. God's glory never faileth—the Christian's spring of happiness never runs dry. It is a river of mercy, a river of grace, and he that drinketh of its water needs never thirst again for the turbid streams of earthly joy. 5. If then the effect of the manifestation of God's mercy and love be to elevate, to ennoble, and to rejoice the heart of man, why should not our minds dwell upon the Divine character? Christianity alone offers man knowledge and joy which can perfectly fill his expansive capacity, and for that knowledge and that grace unceasing effort should be made, and ceaseless prayer offered to the Most High. For this we may come boldly to the throne of grace. 6. And if the limit of manifestation of mercy is found in the circumstances of the creature and not in God, who shall attempt to say what glorious enjoyment awaits the celestial citizen? 7. Does it seem unreasonable that when life is about to be over, the Deity should withdraw His hand, and let such a view of His glory upon the mind, that the physical frame shall fall, and the unfettered spirit rise to the full enjoyment of beatific love? (*M. Simpson, D.D.*) *Moses' sight of God:*—I. THE REQUEST OF MAN. 1. That man, as man, naturally looks for some special display of the Divine presence and attributes. 2. That man, as a sinner, needs an expression of God's readiness to forgive. II. THE RESPONSE OF GOD. 1. That there are limitations to a full revelation of His glory. (1) Human capacity and preparation. (*a*) The bodily senses. (*b*) The mind. (2) The Divine pleasure. 2. That within these limitations there is given an abundant revelation. 3. That the brightest feature of the revelation is Divine love. 4. That from what we now behold, we are led to expect a still more glorious revelation hereafter. (*B. Dale, M.A.*) "*Show me Thy glory*":—1. That God raises human society by the ministry of individual men. 2. That the individual man by whom He raises society, He qualifies by a close fellowship with Himself. I. THE PROFOUNDEST CRAVINGS OF THE SOUL. "Show me Thy glory." 1. This craving explains the existence of polytheism. 2. This craving implies a supreme existence. 3. This craving renders the prevalence of atheism impossible. 4. This craving reveals the grand distinction of human nature. II. THE GRANDEST REVELATIONS OF GOD. "I will proclaim the name of the Lord before thee." 1. The revelation of moral character. 2. The revelation of the sublimest moral character. (1) Absolute love. (2) Compassionate love. (3) Sovereign love. III. THE NECESSARY IGNORANCE OF MAN. "Thou canst not see My face," &c. (*Homilist.*) *The sublime prayer of Moses:*—I. THE IMMEDIATE CIRCUMSTANCES WHICH PRECEDED THE PRAYER. II. THE PRAYER ITSELF. "Show me Thy glory." It is clear from the context that he meant, Unveil Thyself to my vision; let me see Thy essential majesty and splendour; remove all obscurity from my vision. We have to observe here—1. The imperfection of the best saints. Imperfect in knowledge and judgment; fallible in our desires and devotions. 2. The beneficence and care of God for His people. Not only in giving, but in withholding. How important to ask according to His will. To refer all to His wisdom and love, and in everything to be able to say, "He hath done all things well." III. THE ANSWER RETURNED. 1. The literal request was mercifully refused. 2. The spirit of the prayer was graciously answered. Application: 1. Learn the lofty eminence to which true piety exalts a man. Intercourse with heaven. 2. The true breathings of the devout soul. "Show me Thy glory." Everything else is tinsel. 3. A perfect acquaintance with God's goodness is offered us in the gospel. "Oh, taste and see," &c. (*J. Burns, D.D.*) *The Christian's desire to see God's glory:*—I. WHAT IS MEANT BY GOD'S GLORY, WHICH THE CHRISTIAN DESIRES TO SEE? 1. It is glory, in His gracious conduct to sinners, in and through His Son. 2. It is His glory, as manifested to the soul in pardoning mercy and love. 3. It is His glory, as manifested to the soul, making him a partaker of the Divine nature (2 Pet. i. 4). II. WHERE DOES THE REAL CHRISTIAN WISH TO SEE THE GLORY OF GOD? 1. In all His ordinances in this world, especially in the assembly of the saints. 2. Much of God's glory is here to be seen. The glory of His wisdom, in devising the scheme of redemption, &c. 3. How glorious is the discovery here made of His justice and holiness, in the satisfaction made for sin by the death of His Son. 4. Here Divine grace is to be seen in its brightest lustre. In its (1) freeness, (2) condescension, (3) sovereignty, (4) riches. 5. Here is displayed the glory of God's faithfulness to His promises. 6. The Christian desires to see the glory of God above (Phil. i. 23; 2 Cor. v. 1, 2). III. WHY DOES THE CHRISTIAN DESIRE TO SEE HIS GLORY? 1. He desires to see it in His ordinances here because (1) The glory of God is transforming. (2) It is reviving. 2. He wishes to see this glory in heaven, because it will there be (1) most clear and full; (2) most satisfying; (3) permanent and everlasting. (*Theological Sketchbook.*) *The presence of Christ:*—I. THAT THE DESIRES OF RELIGION INTENSIFY WITH ITS GROWTH. 1. The more grace Moses found, the more he sought. 2. To surfeit, not to satisfy, is the nature of earthly good. 3. But here is satisfaction without surfeit. II. THAT CHRIST IS THE MEDIUM OF DIVINE MANIFESTATION. 1. The rock was an emblem of Christ. 2. Here God revealed Himself to Moses. 3. Man in Christ sees God and lives. III. THAT DIVINE VISIONS ARE ATTENDED WITH GRACIOUS EFFECTS. 1. Life is imparted by them. 2. Devotion is kindled by them. 3. Spiritual vigour is imparted by them. 4. Moral influence is gained in them. (*J. A. Macdonald, M.A.*) *Moses' request, and God's gracious promise:*—I. AND WHAT DID MOSES ASK FOR? What was the desire of his heart? His prayer was, "I beseech Thee, show me Thy glory." But, it may be said, had not Moses, on various occasions, seen the glory of God? The more of these heavenly treasures we possess, the more highly do we prize them, and the more eagerly do we seek for an increase. These are things that never deceive, never disappoint, never cloy. Our experience of them convinces us that they are solid, substantial, satisfactory. The capacity of the soul is expanded, and we are prepared for larger communications of purity and love. And they who have made the highest attainments in the Christian life, and have experienced most largely the efficacy of the Redeemer's all purifying blood, will be found to be most anxious to rise still higher in spiritual blessings. II. GOD'S REPLY TO THE REQUEST PREFERRED BY MOSES. III. BUT WE HAVE TO OBSERVE, THAT THE DISPLAYS OF THE DIVINE GOODNESS ARE MADE ONLY ACCORDING TO GOD'S OWN WILL. And what is the character of those to whom the mercy of Jehovah will be extended? The penitent, the humble, the meek, the lowly. IV. WE OBSERVE, THAT THERE ARE CERTAIN DISPLAYS OF THE DIVINE GLORY, WHICH ARE GRANTED

TO GOD'S BELIEVING PEOPLE HERE BELOW, ON EARTH. A partial, indistinct, and necessarily defective view—a glimpse at the heavenly glory—a transient exhibition of the Divine excellence. And even before this was granted to Moses, a certain process was necessary: he must be duly prepared. V. STILL IT MUST BE GRANTED, THAT THE MOST EMINENT AND MOST DELIGHTFUL DISPLAYS OF THE DIVINE GLORY ARE RESERVED FOR THE HEAVENLY WORLD. The eye of the disembodied spirit will be strengthened and fitted to gaze, with a steady and direct view, on the uncreated Sun. (*W. P. Burgess, D.D.*) *The object of a Christian's desire in religious worship*:—I. WHEN CHRISTIANS, THEN, DESIRE TO SEE THE GLORY OF GOD, IT SEEMS CHIEFLY TO IMPLY THE FOLLOWING THINGS. 1. They desire to see the glory of an eternal independent God; they desire to see the only living and true God in His own inherent excellence and infinite perfection. (1) That there is in the fulness of the Godhead an infinite and endless variety even for the employment of our intellectual powers. (2) That the real and proper knowledge of the glory of God is by inward and spiritual illumination. 2. That the believer desires to see the glory of a gracious and reconciled God, not only infinitely glorious in Himself, but infinitely merciful to him. This view ought never to be separated from the former. Take away the Divine mercy, and the lustre of His other perfections is too strong for us to behold. 3. The believer desires to see the glory of God as an all-sufficient God. (1) When the believer sees the fulness of God, then his anxiety, and distressing fears of every kind, are at an end. Does he want provision? "The earth is the Lord's, and the fulness thereof." Does he want friends? God is able to make his enemies to be at peace with him. (2) I shall only add that the Divine all-sufficiency is to be considered as regarding our sanctification as well as comfort. And what courage does he derive from the fulness of Divine protection, the greatness of Divine power, and the faithfulness of the Divine promise! II. I proceed NOW TO MAKE SOME PRACTICAL IMPROVEMENT OF WHAT HATH BEEN SAID. And—1. Let us admire the Divine condescension in admitting His saints to a discovery of His glory. 2. Let me beseech you to try yourselves whether this ever hath been your attainment, and whether it is your sincere desire. 3. I exhort you, in the most earnest manner, to diligence in seeking after real communion with God in His instituted worship. How highly are we favoured with light and liberty! How little are many sensible of their privileges! III. I conclude by offering to those who would see the glory of God A FEW DIRECTIONS AS TO THE BEST PREPARATION FOR SUCH A DISCOVERY. 1. If you would see the glory of God in His sanctuary, be serious in self-examination and the renunciation of all known sin. Holiness is an essential attribute of the Divine nature; and, therefore, He must be worshipped in the beauty of holiness. 2. In order to see the glory of God you must be clothed with humility (Isa. lxvi. 2). 3. In the last place; if you desire to see the glory of God, be fervent in preparatory prayer: if there is any blessing that requires importunity and wrestling with God, surely this high and happy privilege of communion with Him in His house must be of that kind. (*J. Witherspoon.*) *The desire to see God's glory*:—I. WHAT A CHILD OF GOD MAY HAVE HIS EYE TO WHEN DESIRING TO SEE GOD'S GLORY. II. WHERE WOULD A SAINT SEE THE GLORY OF GOD OR HAVE IT SHOWN TO HIM? 1. In many ordinances here. Where God records His name (chap. xx. 24). (1) The glory of His wisdom in contriving a way how heaven and earth might be reconciled, notwithstanding the wide breach made by sin; and how the seeming contrary pleas of God's attributes might be adjusted. (2) Here Divine grace is to be seen in its brightest lustre: in its freeness, pitying us without merit or motive, and against the highest provocation: in its condescension, pitching upon us, and resolving to save us, how unworthy soever: in its sovereignty, passing by angels, and providing a Saviour for men: in its riches. (3) Here is displayed the glory of God's faithfulness to His promises, and willingness to promote His people's comfort. 2. A saint desires to see the glory of God in the state above, and without need of these present ordinances, even in heaven. III. WHY THEY DESIRE THIS. 1. In ordinances here they desire this. (1) Because the glory of God is transforming. (2) The glory of God thus shown to His people is most reviving. 2. And as to heaven, the people of God desire, He would there show them His glory, and eminently—(1) Because it will be most clear and full. (2) The glory to be revealed above will be most satisfying. (3) The manifestation there made will be permanent and everlasting. IV. THIS DESIRE THEY ARE TO OFFER UP IN PRAYER TO GOD. Desire is the life of prayer, and this is to be made known by way of request to God. 1. To testify our value for it. They that esteem it a favour to see God's glory, are to show this by seeking after it.   2

'Tis God only that can show us His glory, and make us to see it; that can fit us for the favour, and then vouchsafe it to us. Is this glory wont to be revealed and displayed in ordinances? make this your end in attending upon them to see it. (1) Get into a state of peace and reconciliation with God through Jesus Christ; such only as are so are capable of beholding His glory. (2) Desire and pray for some sight of this glory. (*D. Wilcox.*)   *The glory of God*:—I. Consider, first, His NATURAL attributes. 1. God is self-existent. All other beings are created, and created by Him. He is the great Parent of existence. 2. Reflect next upon His omnipresence. He fills heaven and earth. 3. Survey His power. He is almighty and can do everything. He can act without agents or instruments. All other beings, animate or inanimate, are but His instruments to fulfil His will. 4. View, lastly, the immeasurable extent of His bounty. All creatures in earth and heaven are replenished out of the storehouse of His beneficence. II. But the glory of God derived from what may be termed, by way of distinction, His natural attributes, is NOT THE HIGHEST DESCRIPTION OF HIS GLORY, or even that in which it properly consists. 1. His goodness. The goodness of God is that attribute by which all His other perfections are directed to the best possible end. It is that which renders His wisdom, power, and presence, not only not dangerous, but in a supreme degree beneficial, to the whole creation. 2. But the holiness of God forms another principal feature in His glory. He "will by no means clear the guilty." 3. But is justice also a modification of goodness? Justice towards some is the security of all. Were an indiscriminate mercy to be shown to all, sin would prevail, and soon prostrate the mercy of God, and efface from the universe every trace of His goodness. (*J. Venn, M.A.*)   *The glory of God illustrated*:—I. Let us consider WHAT WE ARE TO UNDERSTAND BY THE GLORY OF GOD. The glory of any moral agent is that intrinsic moral excellence which renders him worthy of approbation and esteem. This is never seated in the understanding, but in the heart. As a man thinketh in his heart, so is he; and as God thinketh in His heart, so is He. God is love. And in this consists His real, intrinsic, supreme, moral excellence and glory. II. To consider WHAT IS TO BE UNDERSTOOD BY GOD'S DISPLAYING ALL HIS GOODNESS. His promise to Moses is very singular and very significant. "I will make all My goodness pass before thee." That God may display all His goodness, He must do two things. 1. He must display His goodness to as high a degree as possible. 2. God's displaying all His goodness farther implies His displaying it in all its branches, and agreeably to the various natures and characters of His dependent creatures. In particular—(1) It implies displaying His benevolence towards all sensitive natures. (2) In order to display all His goodness, God must display His complacency towards all holy beings. The goodness of the Deity naturally and necessarily inclines Him to love goodness, wherever He sees it. (3) Another branch of Divine goodness is grace towards the guilty and ill-deserving. Such a display of Divine grace is absolutely necessary, in order to give a full display of Divine goodness. It must be observed—(4) That another branch of God's goodness is distributive justice, or a disposition to punish impenitent sinners according to their deeds. III. THAT GOD, BY THUS DISPLAYING ALL HIS GOODNESS, NECESSARILY DISPLAYS ALL HIS GLORY. But the truth of this will more fully appear if we consider—1. That when God displays all His goodness, He displays all His moral character. The Supreme Being has no moral excellence but what is included in His goodness. God is love; all His goodness consists in love; all His love lies in His heart; and His heart is the seat of all His moral excellence. 2. When God displays all His goodness, He necessarily displays all His natural as well as moral excellence. But all these natural attributes derive their real glory from His goodness, without which they would be a blemish rather than a beauty in His character. Inferences: 1. If God be a being who possesses and displays perfect goodness, then the religion which He has required of mankind is a reasonable service. 2. If God must display His goodness in order to display His glory, then by seeking His own glory He must necessarily seek the good of His creatures. 3. If God cannot display all His glory without displaying all His goodness, then the glory of God required the existence of natural and moral evil. All the goodness of God in all its branches could not have been displayed if natural and moral evil had not existed. 4. If the supreme glory of God consists in His goodness, then those who love any part of His character must necessarily love the whole. 5. If the supreme glory of God consists in His goodness, then those who dislike any part of the Divine character must necessarily dislike the whole. 6. If the goodness of God forms His whole moral character, then those who do not love Him supremely must necessarily hate Him supremely. 7. Does the glory of

God consist in His goodness, or in His feeling properly towards all His creatures of every character? 8. If the glory of God consists in His goodness, then a clear view of His goodness would destroy all the false hopes of sinners respecting their good estate. 9. If the glory of God consists in His goodness, then we learn why sinners are represented as blind to His glory. They must feel as He does, in order to have a moral view of His moral excellence. 10. If God's glory essentially consists in His goodness, then those who have seen His real glory in the least degree will desire to see more and more of it. This appears from the nature of spiritual discoveries, which afford peculiar satisfaction to those to whom they are made. (*N. Emmons, D.D.*) *The glory not to be revealed :*—I. THAT THERE IS IN THE DIVINE NATURE AN INTERIOR AND HIDDEN GLORY WHICH CANNOT BE REVEALED. The word glory is a large and comprehensive term, including all that is ineffably great and lovely in the Divine essence. This glory is everywhere revealed. The glory of God is not to be looked upon as something separate and distinct from His nature; but rather that nature in the sum and fulness of its perfection. And as His being is past finding out, so is His glory above the heavens. II. THAT THE SUBLIMEST MANIFESTATION WHICH GOD HAS MADE OF HIS GLORY IS IN CONNECTION WITH THE GREAT REMEDIAL SCHEME OF MAN'S REDEMPTION. It matters little whether we conceive of God as light, or life, or love. It is the light which reveals the life, and it is the life which expresses itself in the love. If God be love, then the highest manifestation of this love must be regarded as the highest revelation of His glory. It is the infinite and ineffable benignity of the Divine nature which renders its glory so engaging and attractive. Light is blended with love—greatness is inseparable from goodness—majesty is mellowed and modified by mercy. The Cross exhibits the only ground on which God and man can ever meet. If the Divinity has never inhabited humanity, man can never rise into communion with God. If the necessary and all-effective means do not exist for impressing His image upon us while we are on the earth, we can never see His face in heaven. To behold His glory we must partake His purity. III. THAT NOTWITHSTANDING THIS REVELATION WHICH GOD HAS MADE OF HIMSELF, THEY ARE THE PURER AND THE LOFTIER SPIRITS AMONGST US WHICH ARE FAVOURED WITH THE MORE SPECIAL MANIFESTATIONS OF DIVINE GLORY. We assert it without fear of contradiction, that even Nature herself will withhold all her higher and more glorious revelations unless there be a correspondence or likeness between her own spirit and the spirit of those who would commune with her. So in the intercourse between mind and mind. In like manner God never reveals Himself in the depth of His glory to any man, till the man has first yielded his whole nature to the purifying and transforming power of the Spirit, and has thus taken on higher degrees of moral purity and perfection. It is only the pure in heart that can see God. As the Jew had his outward ceremonial ablutions, the Christian should have his inward spiritual purifications. An external reformation does not necessarily imply an internal renovation; but if the inner man is renewed and sanctified, the outer man must exhibit the effects of the change. We must be cleansed both in the flesh and in the spirit. IV. THAT THESE DEEPER MANIFESTATIONS OF DIVINE GLORY ARE NOT GIVEN AS MERE FRUITLESS EXHIBITIONS, BUT TO QUICKEN THE LOVE AND TO INCREASE THE DEVOTEDNESS OF THOSE TO WHOM THEY ARE IMPARTED. The heart-throbs of piety have their expression in a life of enlightened and cheerful activity. We have each a work to do in the world, and for God; and to do it as the work of God ought to be done, we need not only the symbols of His presence and love, but the baptism of His Spirit—the plenitude of light and the fulness of grace. V. THAT THE REVELATION OF THIS GLORY IN THE WORLD TO COME WILL FOR EVER FIX THE ATTENTION, AND HEIGHTEN THE RAPTURE, AND ENERGIZE THE ACTIVITY OF THE INHABITANTS OF THAT BLESSED STATE. The brighter and the fuller the revelation, the more profound and fixed will be our attention. Every thought will be captivated, every emotion will be stirred, and the joy of the soul will rise into rapture, heightened and perpetuated for ever. (*R. Ferguson, LL.D.*) *The festive time :*—Come, and behold in this communication, asked for and obtained by Moses—1. The crown of the Old Covenant. 2. The mirror of the New. 3. The promise and prediction that God's glory, in its fulness, would in future be revealed. 1. The festive shouts that Israel raised in honour of the idol they first made are silent now, and the avenging sword, at Moses' prayer, is now averted from the nation's head. Only three thousand sinners have endured the righteous punishment deserved by many more—by nearly all. Moses feels himself, at last, no longer able to restrain his wish for further light: he prays the Lord to show whom He will send, and what He means to do with a nation that is still His own. Moses further states, most positively, that he would prefer to go no farther, than remain without the guidance of the Lord Himself ; then, filled with joy and with astonishment, the man of God essays to take one further step, and gives expression to his heart's wish in the prayer, " Show me now Thy glory." Who shall determine what it was that Moses understood, and felt, and wished, when he employed these words? We know, of course, that ere this time he had seen much more of God's glory than all other men. The bush that burned, and yet was not consumed ; the Red Sea moved out from its bed ; the manna rained down from above ; the arid rock changed to a source of living streams ! Alone, upon the top of Sinai, and amidst most dreadful signs, he had received the law of God ; moreover, with the elders of the Israelites, he had beheld the pavement which the King of Israel laid for the palace where He sits enthroned—what seemed transparent sapphire-stone (chap. xxiv. 9, 10). What more is it that this insatiable, this high-minded servant of the Lord desires ? The Lord Himself gives answer to the question, when He (ver. 20) in so many words declares, "My face cannot be seen." That is to say, Moses has hitherto but heard the voice of Him that spake out of the cloud ; now he beseeches that the veil of mystery shall be removed, and that he may be shown the face of God, beaming with heavenly light. Say not that this request comes from a narrow mind ; above all, do not say that it is unbecoming and irreverent. It was the very multitude of promises which he had just received that gave him all the greater boldness to ask more, and to express a bold desire that long had slumbered in his pious soul. Up till this time the angels had been called to mediate between him and the Lord ; but now he would approach the Lord directly and immediately. One aspect of that nature Moses has already looked upon, when he received the law ; but he thinks there are still other aspects, hitherto concealed from him, and his spirit cannot rest till he has also looked on these. It certainly may be impossible to gratify the wish of Moses to the full. What mortal would be able to behold the face of God, and yet not be immediately consumed by the intensity of glory there revealed ? Nevertheless, as far as possible, at least the spirit of this pious prayer shall be observed, though Moses shall not find it literally fulfilled. Not God's face in itself, but only the last fold seen in His royal mantle—such is the most, the only thing that He can show to any creature upon whom He will confer the highest privilege ! Thus there is pointed out once more, not merely the unlawfulness, but also the absurdity of the idolatry of which the Israelites had just been guilty. The Lord Himself, by His free grace, seeks to restore the broken covenant, and to reveal Himself towards the mediator of the Old Covenant not merely as the Great Invisible, but as a God in whom compassion flows. Imagine the emotion of the man of God, and how he must have watched throughout the sleepless night for the expected hour ! On Sinai, at the bush, Moses was taught to view Jehovah as the Infinite ; at the giving of the Law, as the God of spotless holiness ; but here, moreover, as the God of everlasting mercy. This revelation forms the bond by which God joins Himself once more to Israel ; and unto Moses, as a compensation for the fact that his most earnest prayer has not been answered to the letter, there is promised the fulfilment of his earlier request— that the Lord Himself will go with the nation. Moses desires to see ; but God desires, above all things, to make him hear and follow Him. But what he now hears is the grandest revelation ever made by God under the Old Economy. Truly, there is no wonder, then, that Moses tarries other forty days upon the mountain-top in heavenly ecstasy ; and that his countenance beams forth with heavenly glory, when, bearing in his hands two tables made of stone, the pledge of the renewal of God's promises, he leaves the consecrated ground. Happy Moses, unto whom, at least on one occasion, it was granted, even on this side of the grave, to contemplate to such a large extent the glory of the Lord ! 2. Happy Moses: are these words found on your lips too? Then surely you will joy when you remember that the privilege, accorded in those days to him, is equally attainable by every Christian now. Come, give us your attention still, while, in the revelation, viewed already as the crown and glory of the Old Economy, we also let you see the mirror of the blessings of the New. The glory of the Lord is shown us in another way, but with no less of clearness than before. Is this too strong a statement? Only look to the person of the Redeemer, the work of redemption, the guidance of the redeemed ; and then see whether you have any ground for feeling envy towards Moses in his privilege. " Show me Thy glory ! " It was more than a mere personal want to which Moses gave expression in this prayer. It was the wish that lived, consciously or unconsciously, within the heart of multitudes, in whose eyes this whole earth, with all its glory, was too poor and small to satisfy the deepest wish felt by the longing heart. Men felt that God—yes, God Himself—must needs appear on earth, if earth were to become a gate of heaven. "Oh that Thou wouldst rend the heavens, that Thou wouldst come down, that the mountains might flow at Thy presence!"—such was the strong expression of the feeling in the prophet's heart (Isa. lxiv. 1). And lo! the heavens did open when the fulness of the time had come: "The Word was made flesh and dwelt among us; and we beheld His glory, the glory as of the Only-begotten of the Father" (John i. 14). He who is very God was manifested in our human flesh: but what is here shown to Moses, viz., that God is a Spirit, God is Light, God is Love—how plainly may we read this in the Gospel, as if written there in heavenly characters, when we look to the revelation of God's glory in the Son of His love! "No man hath seen God at any time: the only-begotten Son, which is in the bosom of the Father, He hath declared Him" (John i. 18). How God's unspotted holiness beams towards you, in Him who well can ask a friend and foe, "Which of you convinceth me of sin?" (John viii. 46) who always sees the Father, just because He ever does what is well-pleasing in His eyes; who prays without ceasing, but in no case for the forgiveness of His own sins; and who awaits His being glorified, not as a favour, but an undisputed right! And the love of God:—but where shall I find words with which I may describe the love of Christ, Divine in origin and splendour, but a splendour which is tempered by its covering—a lowly, human form? But that glory does not shine forth from His works alone, nor does it merely manifest itself in what He says; it beams upon us from the splendour seen in His whole mien. And that appearance, too, exhibits as calm majesty as God does when He shows Himself to Moses here: He does not cry, nor raise His voice, nor cause it to be heard in the streets; but when we look on Him, we feel like Moses when the cloud passed by before his eyes; surely we see in Him more than the hinder portion of the royal train—we see God's greatness in the face of Him who was God of God and Light of Light, whereunto no man can approach, but who has yet come near and lived in humble servant-guise. If here the revelation given by God is made to Moses only, it is now, in Christ, bestowed upon the poorest whom the Holy Ghost has taught to see the Father in the Son. If here, through Moses, God reveals His nature to one single people, now the light arises over all the nations that but sat in the darkness heretofore; for here, "there is neither Greek nor Jew, circumcision nor uncircumcision, barbarian nor Scythian, bond nor free, but Christ is all and in all" (Col. iii. 11). And how much more impressively that voice sounds when we venture on a second step, and meditate on God's redeeming work! What is the sin which, in God's eyes, polluted Israel, compared with the abominable sins which stand against a whole lost world—against you and me—before the God of unspotted holiness? We all deserved that God should turn away His friendly countenance from us, as from that people; and that He should not guide us by an angel, but, instead, give us the portion of the fallen ones. And yet, what is even the assurance of God's pity and His grace that Moses learned, when we compare it with the matchless fact that the Beloved of the Father dies for His worst enemies, and that God in Him not merely shows us heaven opened, but unlocks to us the heaven we forfeited? It is just here especially that we, no less than Moses, fail in finding words with which we can express our thoughts; but this we feel, that, louder far than anywhere besides on earth, the voice out of the cloud is found re-echoed from the cross. Now let us take one other look at the guidance of the redeemed, who, like Moses, found favour in the sight of God. Does it need much to show that, in this too, the glory of the Lord is seen almost at every step? But ye who are the Lord's redeemed have an experience that speaks more strongly still; for not merely do ye live by His long-suffering, but ye continue in His favour and in fellowship with Him; and ye learn by experience, like Moses, that He never puts to shame or pours contempt upon the humble prayer of faith. And surely you, too, know full many a spot, as Moses did the crevice in the rock, where you sit gladly down, there to review the way by which the Lord, in His eternal faithfulness, has thus far been conducting you? I hear you say already that the sum of your inquiries is comprised in this: the voice out of the cloud has been the voice addressed to me through all my life on earth! 3. The festive time of Moses' life becomes, lastly, to us a prophecy of the future revelation of God's eternal glory. When you, like Moses, must depart, you should not fail in making the acknowledgment that you have seen, at least in some degree, the glory of the Lord. But that something, though we had the power to multiply it even a thousand-fold, what is it when compared with the far greater, tho

entire amount of what believing hearts desire?   Our deepest need, our highest
blessedness is, not to hear the voice of God, but to behold the Lord Himself; but
that is just the very wish denied us here on earth, even as in Moses' case.   Nay,
more; we do not even stand, like Moses, on the top; we dwell, like Israel, scattered
in tents at the foot of the mount of God's glory.   "We walk by faith, not by sight":
such is the motto of the New as well as of the Old Economy; and it is well for us
that this grand principle is never modified.   How should we ever be prepared for
heaven if, in this life, the school of faith were now already closed?   And what
surprise of pleasure could the future bring us, if this day or yesterday beheld each
enigma sufficiently explained?   "How very little after all is it that I have seen!"
must Moses frequently have said when he looked back upon that morning.   We
hope for the salvation of the Lord, but how wide the difference between the living
hope and the desired enjoyment!   We have moments of presentiment, of spiritual
intercourse, of (I might almost say) immediate contact between the Eternal Spirit
and our own; and at such times a voice comes whispering, "Thus shalt thou see
hereafter."   Yet something always intervenes between this heart of ours and God;
He lays a covering hand upon the eyes of His most faithful worshippers, that they
may not yet fully see the truth; nevertheless, they make their own conjectures with
regard to it, they constantly draw nearer it, and almost seem to grasp it with their
hands while they engage in prayer.   So is it here; so must it be on earth; but so
it will not always be.   With God's hand laid upon our eyes, we grope along for
days or years in deepest gloom until we reach death's vale, . . . then the Lord
passes by before us, while the chilly breath of him who is the King of Terrors blows
upon our face.   "Show me now Thy glory": thus faith entreats with almost
faltering lips; and never, God be thanked, did Heaven continue silent at the last
prayer breathed on earth.   The Lord, as it were, makes all His goodness pass once
more before His dying friends, since "He is truly gracious towards those to whom
He is gracious."   More closely than at any time before does He approach, while He
proclaims His name before us, . . . then He lifts His covering hand from off our
eyes, and lo, we see!   Come, follow me a little longer, while, in closing, we
address three questions to your heart and conscience.   1. Have you, too, ever
yet desired what Moses sought so eagerly?   Ah! if each one of you were plainly
asked, What is your chief desire? how many, nay, how few, Lord, could lay
their hand upon their heart and say, I desire nothing more earnestly than living,
personal communion with God!   Perhaps, indeed, an evanescent wish for something
higher, better, may not be unknown to many here, especially when earthly things
bring disappointment, and the future is concealed from sight.   And when sometimes—although, of course, we are unwilling to believe this true of every one of
you—the soul's necessities assert themselves, and that soul has begun to cry for
God, oh, what a constant tendency there is to seek peace where it cannot possibly
be found; how every kind of artifice is tried to smother heart and conscience when
they cry; how frequently, like Israel at the foot of Sinai, we sit down smitten,
chastised, and stripped of all that formerly adorned us, but without true
penitence, without true longing after God!   2. Have you, too, already seen
what Moses saw?   There is no doubt of that, if you have really, by faith,
beheld the Christ of God; but, on the other hand, how many are there here
at whom the Lord can ask, as once at Philip, "Have I been so long time with
you, and yet hast thou not known Me?"   Or are there not those who are carried
off by a most fatal spirit of the times, and who will not believe what they do not
first understand?   If you indeed desire that such a witness shall apply at least to
you, do not forget that you, like Moses, must especially concern yourself with these
three things—a clear eye, a pure heart, and constant prayer.   The eye of faith is
the organ of the soul, by which we see the glory of the Lord in Christ; and He
Himself must open that for us.   One little speck of dust may cause such floods of
tears as to conceal the sun from you; the dust of earth but hurts the eye that would
behold the glory of the Lord!   Oh, how much of the carnal still remains in us to
be destroyed, in order that the spirit may be truly fit for even the least amount of
living fellowship with God!   Like Moses, keep that festive season of your inner life
in constant memory; and if Heaven hears your thanksgiving, let earth enjoy its
fruits!   3. Have you already done what Moses did?   The sequel of the history
informs you of the earlier, but also of the later influence of what was now revealed.
Bowing in deepest reverence, and well assured that he has found grace in the sight
of God, the mediator of the Old Covenant repeats the prayer, "Let the Lord, I
beseech thee, go among us, for this is a stiff-necked people; and pardon our iniquity

and our sin, and take us for Thine inheritance" (chap. xxxiv. 9). Oh, What a glorious, but also blessed, calling to be like the man of God in this point too! Does it not strike you how, in pleading here for Israel, he does not speak of *their* sins, but of *ours*, and puts himself upon a level with those rebels? Now, it is true, we must, like him, descend the mount and enter the dark vale; but what is it that we can need, if but we have the Lord with us, and our whole nature, like His shining face, gives evidence of our close, friendly intercourse with God? Even as He veiled that strange, mysterious lustre from the eyes of Israel, we too must often hide, from an unholy world, the blessed mystery of our own inner life; but when we go into the solitude, and there approach God's throne of grace, how priceless is this privilege, that we believers may, like Moses, cast off every covering, and then find our refreshing in His kindly light. (*J. J. Van Oosterzee, D.D.*) *A daring prayer:*—It was a daring prayer offered by Augustine when he said, "Lord, hast Thou declared that no man shall see Thy face and live?—then let me die, that I may see Thee!"

Ver. 19. **I will be gracious.**—*Election no discouragement to seeking souls :*—Because God is the Maker, and Creator, and Sustainer of all things, He has a right to do as He wills with all His works. I. Let us begin with this assertion, which we are absolutely sure is correct : THIS DOCTRINE DOES NOT OPPOSE ANY COMFORT DERIVED FROM OTHER SCRIPTURAL TRUTHS. There is not the slightest shadow of a conflict between God's sovereignty and God's goodness. He may be a sovereign, and yet it may be absolutely certain that He will always act in the way of goodness and love. It is true that He will do as He wills; and yet it is quite certain that He always wills to do that which, in the widest view of it, is good and gracious. II. That THIS DOCTRINE HAS A MOST SALUTARY EFFECT UPON SINNERS. To the awakened sinner, next to the doctrine of the Cross, the doctrine of distinguishing grace is perhaps the most fraught with blessings and comfort. 1. In the first place, the doctrine of election, applied by the Holy Ghost, strikes dead for ever all the efforts of the flesh. 2. Again, this doctrine gives the greatest hope to the really awakened sinner. 3 Moreover, do not you see how the doctrine of election comforts the sinner in the matter of power. His complaint is, "I find I have no power to believe; I have no spiritual power of any kind." Election stoops down and whispers in his ear—"But if God wills to save you, He gives the power, gives the life, and gives the grace; and therefore since He has given that power and might to others as weak as you, why not to you? Have courage, look to the Cross of Christ and live." And oh! what emotions of gratitude, what throbbings of love does this doctrine cause in human hearts. I wanted to have said a word as to the effect of this gospel upon incorrigible sinners. If you are ever to be pardoned, God must do it. (*C. H. Spurgeon.*) *Moral glory :*—How precious is the thought suggested by this—that when God is seen to be most good to His creatures, He is then seen to be most glorious in the universe; that the glory and the goodness of God are so connected together that where the one is most revealed, the other shines in its richest splendour. Not power in creating, not justice in punishing, but goodness in saving, sets forth most the glory of God. Creation is the mirror of His power; Sinai is the pedestal of His justice; but Calvary is the scene of His goodness, and therefore of His great glory. And we all know that great genius may make us wonder, great riches may make us envy, great strength may startle us; but great goodness rises upon the soul with an influence like the sun in his shining light, making us love as well as admire, and reverence, and esteem. Lost as man is, goodness is still most impressive on the heart of the very worst. Even with all our depravity, who does not admire Howard, the philanthropist, vastly more than Byron, the poet? There may have been little genius in Howard, as the world calls genius, but there was a beneficence that went into the retreats of fever, into the lairs of vice, shut its eyes to monumental remains of ancient days, and opened his heart only to the cry of them that were appointed to die. And when one hears what he did, and what he dared under the inspiration of goodness, one is not awed, but charmed and delighted, with the character of Howard. But when we see, on the other hand, great genius—and one cannot but admire such a genius as that gifted nobleman had—we wonder at the greatness and the versatility of intellect; but when that intellect was used only to scathe, and to wither, and to blast, we look upon it in the same way as upon the sirocco in the desert, we are rather terrified at it, or retreat from it, or would rather wish we should not see it at all. But how complete is the contrast between goodness in a Howard, and mere power in a Byron! And is there one in this assembly that would not infinitely rather take the example of Howard as his model, than wish the power of Byron to be his possession? But this is in the human, and I quote it in the human only to show you more clearly the truth I am trying to teach; that not the manifestation of power, not the manifestation of justice, but the manifestation of goodness, is the most impressive on the heart. (*J. Cumming, D.D.*)

Vers. 20–23. **My face shall not be seen.**—*God's glory must be veiled from human sight:*—If God had revealed all His glory—if He had not put the shadow of His hand upon Moses, if He had not revealed merely His skirts, as it were, as He passed by—Moses would have been overwhelmed. And this explains to you what is often said in Scripture, "No man can see God and live,"—not because God would destroy the man, but because the glory would be so intense that it would overwhelm him. Moral grandeur may be overpowering, and we learn in history that there have been cases where mental emotion has struck dead the physical economy. A celebrated American astronomer was watching the transit of Venus over the sun's disk; he believed that that transit would take place at a specified moment; and when he saw the shadow of the planet appear on the disk of the sun, such was his excitement or gratification, that he fainted away from excess of joy. Sir Isaac Newton was so overcome by the sense of the magnitude of his discoveries, or of the extent of what he saw in consequence of the great principle he had laid down, that from excess of feeling he was unable to carry out his own grand calculations, and others had to do it for him. Now, if excess of knowledge, of joy, or prosperity, have these powerful effects upon the human frame, we can conceive that too grand an apocalypse of God would be unbearable now; just as the eyeball would be blinded by excess of light. But you can conceive what a splendour and majesty we shall behold when we see God, not through a glass darkly—the smoked glass or lens through which we look at great brightness—but we shall see Him face to face. And what a change will have passed upon us when we can bear to look upon Deity and not shrink! (*J. Cumming, D.D.*) **There is a place by Me, and thou shalt stand upon a rock.**—*The believer's standing place:*—To those who like typical texts, there is a peculiar charm in such as this: "a place by Me," and "a rock" for a standing place. What suggestions—1. Of the believer's firm foundation—the "Rock." 2. Of the believer's fellowship with God—"a place by Me." 3. Of the believer's favour with God—a vision of His glory. (*A. T. Pierson, D.D.*) *The place by God, or the right standpoint:*—The guide-books name the time when rainbows may be seen on some of the many waterfalls which abound in Switzerland. One day, when I was at Lauterbrunnen, I went to the famous Staulbach Fall (980 feet), and sat down by the flagstaff, and waited and watched. Others did the same, and we all went away disappointed. Next day one of my friends said he would show us how to find the rainbow. So I went again, and saw a most lovely one, and stood almost in the centre of it. Then I found that not only were sunshine and spray necessary to produce a rainbow, but also that those who would see it must stand between it and the sun, *i.e.*, it could be seen only at a given point. Then I perceived that those who would see the glory of God could see it only in the face of Jesus Christ, and that the reason why so many fail in this respect is because they do not take the right standpoint. (*Gavin Kirkham.*) *The standpoint of the Cross:*—I was talking about Christ to an impenitent neighbour the other day. He said: "Why can't I feel about Him as you do? I have read the Bible a good deal. I have heard a good deal of preaching. Yet I can't get up any enthusiasm in regard to this Saviour that you talk so much about." I said to him: "You make me think of my visit to the White Mountains some years ago. We were told that there was a wonderful piece of natural statuary there—a man's face, chiselled, as it were, out of a granite cliff. We went to see it. We found what we supposed was the cliff, but there was no appearance of human features—no form or comeliness such as we had been told of. We were about to turn away disappointed, when a guide came along, and said, 'You are not looking from the right point.' He led us up the road a few rods, and then said, 'Now turn, and look.' We did so, and there was the face as distinct as any of ours, though of gigantic size. Until we reached the right spot we could see only a jagged rock, and not a symmetrical face. The vision of the form and comeliness depended upon the angle of observation. And it is so with you, my friend. Come with me under the shadow of the Cross. Come there as a penitent sinner. Look there upon that 'visage so marred more than any man.' Realize that the mangled, thorn-crowned Sufferer is dying for you, and you will see in Him a beauty that will ravish your soul." (*T. L. Cuyler.*)

CHAPTER XXXIV.

VER. 1. **Hew thee two tables of stone.**—*The renewal of the two tables :*—I. THAT THE MORAL LAW IS PERPETUALLY BINDING. Having been broken, it must be renewed. II. THAT THE RENEWAL OF THE MORAL LAW WHEN BROKEN ENTAILS DUTIES UNKNOWN BEFORE. " Hew thee two tables of stone "; " and he hewed two tables of stone." This fact is very typical and suggestive. 1. In the first inscription of the moral law upon man's heart, the preparation and the writing were exclusively the work of God. When our first parents awoke to consciousness, the " fleshy tables " were found covered with the " oracles of God." 2. When those tables were defaced and those oracles transgressed, the work of preparation fell largely upon man. Ever afterwards man had to prepare himself by acts of penitence and faith—not excluding Divine help, of course—but nevertheless those acts are acts of man. 3. But this renewal of the Divine law is accomplished in such a way as to deprive man of all ground of glorying, and so as to ascribe all the glory to God. The tables were of plain stone, all their embellishments were by the Divine hand. III. THAT WHEN THE MORAL LAW IS BROKEN, GOD GRACIOUSLY OFFERS TO RENEW IT UPON MAN'S COMPLIANCE WITH THE REVEALED CONDITION. So when man by repentance and faith " puts off the old man and puts on the new," he is renewed in the image of Him that created him, on which the moral law is inscribed (Col. iii. 9–16). IV. THAT THESE CONDITIONS SHOULD BE COMPLIED WITH—1. Speedily. " Early in the morning." 2. Personally. This great work is a transaction between God and the individual particularly concerned. 3. Patiently. Moses waited again forty days and forty nights. (1) Do not hurry the work over. What is being done is being done for eternity. (2) Don't despond if the work is not progressing as rapidly as you might wish. If God is writing on your heart, let that be your comfort, and let God use His own time. Learn—1. The value of the moral law. 2. The importance of having that law not only on stone or paper, but in the heart. 3. The necessity of a public and practical exhibition and interpretation of that law in the life. (*J. W. Burn.*)   *God re-writing the law :*—Can you think of a course more merciful than this ? " Bring two tables of stone just like the first, and I will write it over again ; I, God, will write over again the very words that were on the first tables that thou brakest in pieces." There is no mercy like the mercy of the Lord ; I never find any tenderness like His tenderness. You remember some years ago George Peabody gave half a million of money to the London poor ; and I think some eighteen thousand people are sheltered in the houses that have sprung out of that splendid charity. I remember that when Peabody's charity had awakened England to a sense of his goodness, the Queen of England rose equal to the occasion, and she offered this plain American citizen some title, and he declined the honour. And then she, with a woman's delicacy of insight, and with more than queenly dignity, inquired if there was anything that Peabody would accept ; and he said, Yes, there was, if the Queen would only write him a letter with her own hand ; he was going to pay a last visit to his native land across the Atlantic, and he should like to take it to his birthplace, so that at any time, if bitterness should arise between these two nations, his countrymen could come and see that letter, and they would remember that England's Queen had written it to a plain American citizen. The Queen of England said she would write him a letter, and she would do more than that—she would sit for her portrait to be painted, and he should take that with the letter ; and she put on the Marie Stuart cap which, I think, she had only worn, perhaps, twice since the death of the Prince Consort, and she sat day after day in her robes of state, and the painter painted one of the finest portraits of the Queen that has ever been executed. When it was finished she presented it to Mr. Peabody, and he took it, with the Queen's letter, away to his birthplace yonder. Now, suppose George Peabody, in some fit of forgetfulness, had torn the Queen's letter up, and flung it into the fire, and dashed the portrait down and broken it to fragments ; and suppose that, after that, somebody had told her Majesty that George Peabody was penitent, do you think she would have written him the letter over again ? do you think she would have sat again for another portrait to be painted, just like the first one ? Who can tell ? Yet our Father in heaven, if you have broken the tables of your covenant with Him, bring your broken heart back again to His feet, and He will renew the covenant. (*T. Guttery.*)

Vers. 2, 3. **Come up in the morning.**—*Be ready in the morning : an address for*

New Year's eve:—I. Be ready for a CONSCIOUS CONTACT WITH GOD in the future. 1. As a duty. 2. As a privilege. "In Thy presence is fulness of joy." 3. As a calamity. The hell of the guilty. II. Be ready for a CONSCIOUS ISOLATION OF YOUR BEING in the future. "No man shall come up with thee." 1. There are events which will give us a profound consciousness of isolation. (1) Bereavements. (2) Personal affliction. (3) Death. 2. There are mental operations that will give us a profound consciousness of isolation. Remembrance of past sins, &c. (*Homilist.*) *Morning on the mount:*—I. GOD WISHES ME TO BE ALONE WITH HIM. How solemn will the meeting be! Father and child; Sovereign and subject; Creator and creature! The distance between us will be infinite, unless He shorten it by His mercy! Oh, my poor broken and weary heart, think of it and be glad. He will shed His light upon thy tears, and make them shine like jewels; He will make thee young again. II. HOW SHALL I GO BEFORE GOD? In what robe shall I dress myself? "All the fitness He requires is to feel my need of Him." But when I think of Him the thought of my great sin comes at the same time, and it is like a black cloud spread between me and the sun. When I think of anything else, I am happy for the moment; but when I think of God, I burn with shame and tremble with fear. This morning I must meet Him on the mount—meet Him alone! Alone! Surely He need not have said expressly so; for to be with God is to be in solitude, though the mountain be alive with countless travellers. III. God asks me to meet Him in the TOP OF THE MOUNT. I am called to climb as far away from the world as I can. For many a day I have not seen the top of the mount. I have stood on the plain, or I have gone to the first cleft, or have tried a short way up the steep. I have not risen above the smoke of my own house, or the noise of my daily business. Oh, that I might urge my way to the very top of the hill chosen of God! "What must it be to be there?" The wind will be music. Earth and time will be seen as they are, in their littleness and their meanness. IV. The MORNING is the time fixed for my meeting the Lord. What meaning there is in the time as well as in the place! This very word morning is as a cluster of rich grapes. Let me crush them, and drink the sacred wine. In the morning—then God means me to be at my best in strength and hope; I have not to climb in my weakness; in the night I have buried yesterday's fatigue, and in the morning I take a new lease of energy. Give God thy strength—all thy strength; He asks only what He first gave. In the morning—then He may mean to keep me long that He may make me rich! Blessed is the day whose morning is sanctified. Successful is the day whose first victory was won in prayer. Health is established in the morning. Wealth is won in the morning. (*J. Parker, D.D.*) *Rising early for prayer:*—We have a saying among us, that "the morning is a friend to the muses"; that is, the morning is a good studying time. I am sure it is as true that the morning is a great friend to the graces; the morning is the best praying time. (*J. Caryl.*) *Rising early for devotional exercises:*—It is told in Sir Henry Havelock's "Life," how he always secured two hours for devotion before the business of the day began, even in his busiest time, by rising at five or four, as required. . . . Colonel Gardiner had the same habit. Early rising for the objects of this world is usual enough, and much to be commended; but the same industry that will advance a man's temporal interests will make him spiritually rich, and give him great treasure in heaven, if it be used towards God. . . . On the contrary, late rising in the morning, rapid dressing, curtailing even the few moments allotted to thanksgiving and prayer, before the plunge into the world's affairs, deafens our ears and hearts to things spiritual; we exchange an interview with our God, who can give us all good, for the miserable gratification of our indolence. *Morning prayer:*—Let the day have a blessed baptism by giving your first waking thoughts into the bosom of God. The first hour of the morning is the rudder of the day. (*H. W. Beecher.*)

Vers. 6, 7. **The Lord, the Lord God, merciful and gracious.**—*The name of the Lord:*—I. "THE LORD." There we lay our basis. Unless you are prepared to admit the perfect sovereignty of God, you can go no further—you will see no more. II. Then we put it in combination—"the Lord GOD." And oh! what a combination! We put all sovereignty with all the mystery of the Godhead —God, that unfathomable word. But amongst all those wondrous attributes which go to make the word God, there is one stands out—that name leads us to it. The root of the word is kindness—God, the good. The Lord the good; the Lord— love; God. We put the infinitude of His sovereignty in combination with the boundlessness of His affection, and we say, "The Lord, the Lord God." III. But now we come to the goings forth of that wonderful mystery of Godhead to man—MERCY. You know that the strict meaning of the word mercy is—a heart for misery. Therefore the first thought is—the great Lord God stooping to the wretched, going forth to the miserable. IV. And why merciful? Because GRACIOUS. Grace is the free flowing of undeserved favour. V. "LONG-SUFFERING!" It is the most marvellous part of the character of God—His patience—it is so contrasting with the impetuosity, the haste, the impulsiveness of man. He is provoked every day, but He continues patient. VI. Now it rises—"ABUNDANT IN GOODNESS AND TRUTH." Abundant is enough and something over—a cup so full that it mantles—abundant, "abundant in"—VII. "GOODNESS," and—VIII. "TRUTH." IX. "KEEPING MERCY FOR THOUSANDS." There are thousands who do not yet see or feel their mercy, for whom God is now keeping it in reserve—say, persons not yet converted. X. FORGIVING INIQUITY AND TRANSGRESSION AND SIN." We are getting all the more now into the work of Christ. And what distinction shall we make between "iniquity, transgression, and sin?" Is "iniquity" acts of injustice to a fellow-creature—and "transgression" acts of injustice towards God—and "sin," the deep root of all in the human heart? Or is it thus? Is "iniquity" that principle of all wrongness, the want of uprightness, the acting unfairly by God or man;—and then "transgression" the act, whether it be to God or man, to God through man, "transgression,"—and then "sin" again the inner nature from which that transgression, which makes that iniquity, springs. I think that is the true intention—iniquity, transgression, sin. But He pardons all. XI. "BY NO MEANS CLEAR THE GUILTY." The word "guilty" is not in the original—"by no means clear." Whom? He will not clear any one whom He has not pardoned. "Guilty" means a man still subject to wrath. If a man does not accept Christ, he is still subject to wrath—that man God will never clear. XII. And then comes that very difficult part—THAT HE "VISITS THE INIQUITY OF THE FATHERS UPON THE CHILDREN, AND UPON THE CHILDREN'S CHILDREN, UNTO THE THIRD AND TO THE FOURTH GENERATION." It seems to me to be an ever-standing visible proof and monument of God's holiness and justice. He visits sin from generation to generation. There are inherited dispensations, inherited calamities. Is it unjust? It is the principle of the greatest justice that we read of in the history of this world. For the atonement all depends upon that principle. If God does visit the sin of one in the sufferings of another, has not He also laid it down that He visits the righteousness of one in the happiness and the eternal salvation of another? And did we so do away with that principle, where would be our hope? (*J. Vaughan, M.A.*)   *God's mercy :*—I. WHAT THE MERCY OF GOD IS. 1. That perfection whereby He assists His creatures in misery (Lam. iii. 22). 2. His mercy is infinitely great (Psa. cxlv. 8). 3. He is the Fountain and Father of mercy (2 Cor. i. 3). II. TO WHOM GOD IS GENERALLY AND ESPECIALLY MERCIFUL. 1. To mankind in general (Psa. cxlv. 9). 2. He continues life notwithstanding our sins (Psa. lxxxvi. 13). 3. In delivering out of troubles (Psa. cvii. 13). 4. In granting all the necessaries of life (Matt. v. 45). 5. Especially is He merciful to His people (Deut. xxxii. 43). 6. In pardoning all their sins (Heb. viii. 12). 7. In quickening them to newness of life (Eph. ii. 4, 5). 8. In assisting us to exercise all true grace (1 Cor. vii. 25). 9. Support under spiritual troubles (Psa. xciv. 17–19). 10. Blessing troubles for our good (Heb. xii. 10). 11. Bringing to heaven at last (Titus iii. 8). III. THE USES THAT ARE TO BE MADE OF GOD'S MERCY. 1. Not to abuse it to licentiousness (Rom. vi. 1, 2). 2. We should be merciful to others (Luke vi. 36). 3. Pardoning their injuries, pitying their miseries, and relieving their necessities (Gal. vi. 10). 4. We must attribute all our blessings to the mercy of God towards us (Psa. cxv. 1). 5. This should teach us to love Him (Psa. cvi. 1). 6. Cause us to fear Him (Psa. ciii. 11). 7. And induce us to praise Him (Psa. ciii. 2, 3, 4). 8. God's mercies are greater than our miseries (1 John iv. 4). 9. They are sealed to us by Christ's blood (Heb. xii. 24). 10. His mercy is only known by the influence of the Holy Spirit (Eph. i. 13, 14). (*T. B. Baker.*)   *The unveiled mystery of God :*—There is in man a yearning after the unseen. Every one feels, even if he will not confess it, that another world lies, after all, behind this one. But the world of spirits is twofold—the kingdom of the powers of darkness below, and the kingdom of light in heaven. In man there is by nature a secret drawing to that which is below. There is the dark point of sin in us which draws us downward. Whoever follows this drawing goes to destruction. But there is in man another drawing—a drawing to light, a drawing to God. For we were made for Him. But although we have separated ourselves from Him, He has not altogether given up His connection with us. He who would paint God, must paint love—a fire of love which fills heaven and earth. But who can comprehend and describe this boundless and endless love? It has collected itself, and given itself a bodily form, in order to reveal itself to us. The heart of God has opened itself up to us—eternal love has revealed itself to us in Christ Jesus. But it is not in the New Testament that this is revealed for the first time. It is as old as the revelation of God's eternal counsel of love. Even in the Old Testament Christ is contained, although in type and prophecy. There is darkness round about God, He is veiled in mystery, no mortal man beholds His countenance and lives; the eyes of Moses are holden by Jehovah, whilst He passes by him. But a word falls upon his ear: in this word God pronounces His nature, and this word runs thus—"God is love." That is the unveiled mystery of God. Let us then consider this unveiled mystery in the threefold way in which our text sets it before our eyes. I. IN THE DIRECTION OF LIFE. God orders the vast and disposes of the most isolated object. That is just His greatness—attention in what is little. But how often are our ways and God's direction of our life a mystery to us! That He leads us happily and blessedly, we believe, although what we see often appears to us to be strange. Yet we shall one day stand upon the heights of light and look back upon our dark paths in the valley, and they will be light, and our understanding will give its judgment in the praise of love. That is the unveiled mystery of God in the direction of life. II. We will consider this unveiled mystery IN THE FORGIVENESS OF SIN. For our life is full of sins and guilt. The termination of our life is the seal of the forgiveness of sins. We bear the law of God written on our hearts. But our sin has broken it. We are sorry; we should like to be pious and holy. Hence we come and present ourselves before God with new resolutions: from henceforth it shall be otherwise with us. But how long does it continue till it is as before? It will not come to a really new life. We amend there and then; but our moral life remains at all times a wearying work, and never becomes a free, joyful matter, which is understood of itself—which gushes and streams fresh and gladly out of the heart. Whence is this? The failing is in the foundation. God must make such an impression upon us as to win our hearts, and to make it impossible for us to do other than love Him. By what means does God make such an impression upon us? Not by His infinite greatness and majesty, but by His gracious love. "We love Him because He has first loved us" (1 John iv. 19). And what love is that? It is God's pardoning love: not the love manifested in the displays of His goodness, in His anxiety for our earthly life. This humbles us, but it does not yet touch our innermost being. The innermost point in us, where we are connected with God, is the conscience. And just here we feel ourselves separated from God. Here we must experience the love of God: that is His forgiving love. But this is the right foundation of all moral work. III. We will consider this unveiled mystery IN COVENANT FELLOWSHIP. The covenant of God with Israel rests on the forgiveness of sins. God dwells in the midst of them, He is their God and they are His people, and He leads them on their way, and He brings them to the goal. He thus reveals Himself to them as a covenant God. But all this is only a prophecy of the covenant of God with us in Christ Jesus. This rests on the true, real forgiveness of sins. But all this is but the commencement of the completion. We wait for the fulfilment of the promise. In hope, the abode yonder is already here. But we are not yet yonder. We are still on our pilgrimage to the hall of blessedness. There for the first time will there be the right celebration of the covenant. (*J. C. Luthardt, D.D.*) *The moral nature of God:*—I. THE FORM IN WHICH THE REVELATION IS MADE. 1. In the first place, it is given, not in the cold and formal terms of a merely ethical and philosophical system, but in its warm and sympathetic application to the needs of man's life. The profoundest truth is here implied. But the form of the declaration is simple, couched in the every-day speech of men, such as all men, in any and every condition, could easily and readily apprehend. 2. It is not only addressed to man upon the simplest side of his nature, but it sets in the very foreground of the Divine qualities those which have regard to man's sinfulness, and the need in which he stands, of tenderness, pity, and grace. What a recognition is this of the true state of the human heart! God's revelation is no philosophy of the "might have been," of the "ought to be"—dreamy, vague, hypothetic, and useless. But it is a practical dealing with what is. It takes man just as it finds him. II. Now, let us inquire, WHAT IS THE REVELATION which is thus made in so human and so gracious a form? God declares Himself to be "merciful and gracious." By the first quality we understand pitifulness, a tenderness towards the weak and helpless, with an added sense of gentleness and forgiveness towards those that are not only weak but wicked, sinful as well as sad. And while God is this, it is all of favour, free and unmerited. He is gracious as well as merciful. But there are added qualities of mercy and grace beyond the mere broad and general fact of their possession. These might be of the Divine nature, and yet their exercise might be restrained within narrow and brief limits of occasion and duration. But God is " longsuffering and abundant in goodness and truth." We must not forget that these qualities of God's moral being are related, as we have said, to human conditions, especially that of sin, and in respect of that He is " longsuffering." For man is not merely a sinner, but he perpetuates the sin, he continues sinning; he is alienated from God, and remains an alien, with hard and ever harder heart, going farther away, being less accessible, increasing his rebellion ever. And yet God's mercy does not cease. He loses no patience. He waits and watches. And of this mercy and clemency no one need doubt the power or the sufficiency. God is declared further to be " abundant in goodness and truth." Goodness is perhaps an attribute of wider reach than mercy, embracing mercy for the sinner and the wretched in the beneficent relation towards all whose welfare and happiness God ever seeks. Truth is that harmony of being upon which we may ever depend. It is order and peace, it is fidelity and changelessness—everything that renders trust in the truthful God a certain thing, not liable to disappointment, change, and decay. The emphasis, perhaps, is to be placed upon the word "abundant." God has enough and to spare. Then, these are by no means quiescent, inoperative attributes of the Divine nature. Men often lose themselves and the clearness of their thoughts in mere abstract statements of the qualities of God, but in this declaration of Himself, Jehovah shows how practical is the revelation which He gives. " Keeping mercy for thousands forgiving iniquity and transgression and sin." The phrase " keeping mercy for thousands" is a striking one. The term thousands is indefinite, signifying a very large number. It may be used in contrast with the "third and fourth generation" of the following clause, and if so, it indicates that the mercy of God is preserved through all the ages of mankind, and remains perpetual and ceaseless, for the universal race for ever. The forgiveness, too, how full is this! It is not merely the single sin that is pardoned. The continued habit of sin, the formed and indurated character of evil, the strong and defiant wickedness, even these may find mercy and have experience of God's pardoning grace. It is His prerogative. It is His nature. All this is based upon the most absolute justice and integrity of righteousness. " He will by no means clear the guilty." The eternal claim of moral order must be recognized, and until guilt is purged and sin is destroyed, the sinner cannot be cleared. Let us, now, gather up the great truths of this sublime passage, and lay their meaning and their power to our hearts. 1. The revelation which God grants of Himself is in the sphere of moral being. 2. This moral aspect of Deity is in complete harmony with every other side of the Divine nature. 3. The moral being of God, as it is revealed, necessarily provides a satisfaction of its claims of justice and rectitude. 4. In this completeness of revelation there is an abundance of grace and mercy which is offered to all men. This, then, is the final truth which appears in the revelation of God. Let no man despair. (*L. D. Bevan, D.D.*) *God's great goodness :—*I. THE GLORY OF GOD IS HIS GOODNESS. When Moses said, " I beseech Thee, show me Thy glory," the Lord answered, " I will make all My goodness pass before thee " (chap. xxxiii. 18, 19, xxxiv. 6). 1. We see it in nature (Psa. xxxiii. 5, cxlv. 9, lxv. 11). 2. We see it in providence (1 Kings viii. 66; Psa. xxxi. 19; Zech. ix. 16, 17). 3. We see it in grace (Eph. i. 7; Psa. xxiii. 6; Jer. xxxi. 14). II. THE EFFECT OF GOD'S GOODNESS UPON THE HEART OF MAN IS MEANT TO BE—1. Sorrow at having offended God (Rom. ii. 4; Job xlii. 5, 6; Hosea iii. 5), 2. Delight in praising God (Psa. cvii. 8; Isa. lxiii. 7). 3. Desire to receive God's blessings (Numb. vi. 24, 26; Mic. vii. 18, 19). 4. A disposition to imitate God's character (Luke vi. 36; Eph. v. 2; 1 John vi. 11). (*Clergyman's Magazine.*) *God's goodness :—*The late Dr. Samuel Martin, in a letter to a friend after Dr. Davidson's death, thus speaks of that pious and devoted man, whose memory is hallowed in the minds of all who knew him :—" He studied divinity at Glasgow College. Thomas and I lived together, companions and fellow-students ; and I, being some years older, was considered as a kind of guardian. On looking back to that period, in reviewing fully sixty years' intercourse and friendship, I ever found in him, from first to last, genuine and unaffected piety, affection, benevolence, regular, exemplary, amiable deportment. I recollect, with pleasure, the family devotions of our little society. I well remember an exclamation, on one occasion, to me, after rising from prayer—a striking proof of his characteristic humility, gratitude, and tenderness of conscience, 'Oh, Martin, it is the Divine goodness, of all things, that humbles me most!'" *God's forgiving mercy :*—I once visited the ruins of a noble city that had been built on a desert oasis. Mighty columns of roofless temples still stood in unbroken file. Halls in which kings and satraps had feasted two thousand years ago were represented by solitary walls. Gateways of richly carven stone led to a paradise of bats and owls. All was ruin! But past the dismantled city, brooks, which had once flowed through gorgeous flower-gardens, and at the foot of marble halls, still swept on in undying music and unwasted freshness. The waters were just as sweet as when queens quaffed them two thousand years ago. A few hours before they had been melted from the snows of the distant mountains. And so God's forgiving love flows in ever-renewed form through the wreck of the past. Past vows and past covenants and noble purposes may be represented by solitary columns and broken arches and scattered foundations that are crumbling into dust, yet through the scene of ruin fresh grace is ever flowing from His great heart on high. (*T. G. Selby.*) **That will by no means clear the guilty.**—*God justified in man's salvation :*—I. MAN THINKS OF GOD AS IF GOD WERE SOMETHING LIKE HIMSELF: and hence he would make God a changeable and capricious Being; he would make Him connive at sin and make light of transgression, accepting a few tears, or a few resolutions, or a few alms, as satisfaction enough for him to receive pardon. All such ideas of God are base and unwarrantable, and will cover those who entertain them with everlasting confusion. The nature of God makes it impossible for Him to clear the guilty. If the positive be true, that God loves holiness, the negative must be true, that He hates iniquity. II. And now some will probably say, "WHY, THIS IS CONTRAVENING THE VERY GOSPEL; IT IS SURELY FAVOURING THE NOTION THAT NONE CAN BE SAVED; for who can be saved, when there is no guiltless man? And if God will not clear guilty men, how is any one to meet his Maker in peace?" The view I have of it is this—that God does not clear the guilty; no, but I will tell you what He does, which is infinitely more to His glory, and of necessity more for our peace—He makes the guilty guiltless, and He makes the unrighteous perfect in righteousness. He does this in virtue of the life laid down for the guilty, for all who in Him have believed; in Him all have paid the penalty, all have satisfied God's justice, and all have perfect righteousness. (*H. Stowell, M.A.*) *The guilty "by no means cleared" :*—I. WHAT IS TO BE UNDERSTOOD BY THE LORD "NOT CLEARING THE GUILTY"? When He pronounces the sentence of acquittal, it will be in full accordance with justice. And yet the basis of this world's religion is nothing more than a belief that God will "clear the guilty." What are all the delusions of self-righteous workings? what are all the endeavours to put off till a more convenient season comes? what is all the resting in ordinances, forms, and external things? Just a forgetfulness that God is a heart-searching God. II. But now observe, WHY is it true that God "will by no means clear the guilty"? Everything in God forbids it. His very faithfulness renders it impossible. Now, faithfulness is part of the Divine goodness. What forms the real substance of our hope? that through God's grace we shall be at last in heaven? God tells me, that "he that believeth shall be saved"; He tells me, that the "blood of Jesus Christ cleanses from all sin." What gives us confidence? Simply, God's faithfulness—I believe it, because God says it. Take that away, and where is His goodness? It is no more. Now bear this in mind, that what gives stability to the promise gives stability to the threatening. The love of God is a holy love. Now the great cause of all misery is sin; and that which forbids sin is a holy love. Yes, and one may even say that the penalty, awful and fearful as it is, is one of the great unfoldings of His love. Conclusion: 1. The subject has a very awful look, as it regards the sinner hardened in his trespasses. "He will by no means clear the guilty ones." 2. The words are full of encouragement to the poor penitent spirit—"He will by no means clear the guilty." "Ah!" you are ready to say, "how can He clear me? I am all guilt." Thou never hadst any due conception of thine own guiltiness, and of what thy guiltiness is before God. Yet none at all hast thou. Why? Because it has all been transferred to Jesus. Because He has taken it and borne it away. He has endured it. He was "not cleared," He endured the penalty. 3. How this truth should lead to—(1) Confession of sin; (2) holy service. (*J. H. Evans, M.A.*) *Union of justice and grace in God :*—"Behold the goodness and severity of God," says the Apostle Paul. In most cases the goodness is illustrated by one kind of events and the severity by another, but in Christ's work the same event of His death displayed the two sides of God's character alike and at once, and thus pardon was never offered to the guilty without a loud protest against sin. Now the pains taken to inculcate both these qualities through the entire Scriptures seem to point at something in man, some conception of character which he needs to have impressed upon him and which he ought to realize in his own life. I. And in pursuing this subject we remark, first, THAT AMONG MEN HE WHO IS CAPABLE OF EXERCISING ONLY HARD, UNRELENTING JUSTICE IS HELD TO BE FAR FROM PERFECTION, AND CANNOT BE LOVED ; WHILE, ON THE OTHER HAND, A CHARACTER IN WHICH BARE KINDNESS OR GOODNESS IS THE ONLY NOTICEABLE TRAIT SECURES NO RESPECT.   Only where we see the two qualities united can we feel decided confidence and attachment. They do not check each other, as might be supposed, but add to each other's power. The indiscriminately kind man is felt to be weak ; the harsh rigorous nature may have intellect in abundance, but fails to warm the souls of men. When united they form character, a character in which there is depth, the depth of intellect resting below temper and impulse on a foundation of wisdom and true excellence of heart. There can be no moral government among men without wisdom, for he who makes men good must look not at immediate impressions, but at results : he must take long stretches of time into view, and long series and interactions of causes shaping character. When did instinctive benevolence ever fail to thwart its own wishes and to corrupt its beneficiaries? The union of these opposites, where alone wisdom can be found, ensures the best government, and as every one must be in some way a governor, of a family, or a workshop, if not of a town or state, the whole of the vast interests of mankind depend on this union. II. IF GOD IS TO BE HONOURED AND LOVED BY HUMAN BEINGS, HE MUST PRESENT HIMSELF TO OUR MINDS UNDER THE SAME TWOFOLD ASPECT. He must be seen in the light of those qualities which we may call by the name of justice, and of those to which we give the names of goodness, kindness, tenderness, or mercy. Sinners are recovered and reclaimed first by a sense of sin, and then by a perception of Divine love, and without the latter they would not think of their sins, or grow into that filial fear, that holy worship which the Psalmist intends. Only under this twofold aspect of God is true religion, the religion of the soul, possible. III. We add thirdly, THAT IT INVOLVES A VERY HIGH DEGREE OF WISDOM TO KNOW WHEN TO BE JUST OR SEVERE, AND WHEN TO EXERCISE GOODNESS OR GRACE. It is a great problem to govern a nation ; it is a greater to govern a virtuous universe ; but a greater still is presented when the element of evil is thrown into the question, and the interests of the many come into conflict with the happiness of the sinful few. Especially when we look on God as training His creatures up for a higher condition ; enlarging their powers, helping the strong to grow stronger, pitying the weak and revealing Himself as their forgiving God ; then above all does it appear that the balances of the moral universe are exceedingly delicate, and that there is need of a hand, firm and wise beyond our thought, to hold them. No solution of the intricacies of things has been offered to man deserving of notice but that which Christ has made. The reconciliation of holiness and love in His work, its just, well-balanced training of the whole moral nature challenge our respect, our admiration, even if we will stand aloof from Christ. He is made of God unto us wisdom and righteousness and sanctification and redemption. IV. And now, having brought your minds to Christ, I close with the remark that HE UNITED THE TWO SIDES OF CHARACTER WHICH WE HAVE SPOKEN OF, IN THEIR DUE MIXTURE, IN HIS ONE PERSON. And it is well worthy of being remarked that their union proves their genuineness and their depth.   He who could love so and forgive so, notwithstanding His deep sense of the sin, what strength of character must He have had, what a depth and truth of love, what a power of loving, what an inexhaustible richness of soul! And He who could rebuke so and show such strong displeasure against evil doing, how hard, humanly speaking, must it have been for Him to love objects so far from loveliness ; and if He loved them as He did, must not His love have been of another kind than ours, one superior to personal slights and injuries, wholly unlike instinctive kindness of temper, partaking of a quality of lofty wisdom!   (*T. D. Woolsey.*)   *Universal redemption subversive of the assurance of salvation :*—Draw near and contemplate this Christian paradox ; come, behold with us, for a time, this Christian mystery, the certainty that the guilty cannot be cleared—that God cannot do it—is the safeguard of redemption, the guarantee of the offered atonement. I. It is true that this declaration of God's character—of the impossibility of His clearing the guilty— SHUTS MANY LARGE AND WIDE DOORS OF HOPE. The hearts of sinners are full of devices for salvation. They have many entrance-ways to pardon and favour. 1. There is the placability and compassion of God upon which they largely draw. The Divine anger is thus, in their imagination, a bugbear, well got up to scare transgressors, to keep them in check, but, as to any ultimate and eternal condemnation resulting from it, all is set aside by their convenient doctrine of His easy and overwhelming compassion. 2. Again, there is the tempter's suggestion of the changeableness of God, " ye shall not surely die," opening to many a wide door. It is not that the veracity of God is actually questioned. But then He may take back or change His word. These deceitful hopes are met, and the door they open for ever shut, by the one decisive passage—" and I will by no means clear the guilty." II. Whilst this passage shuts with so decisive a hand every false door of hope, and announces in characters of light, that guilt cannot go unpunished, IT YET OPENS A DOOR OF HOPE THAT NEVER CAN BE SHUT, and is an immovable anchor to every soul that has fled for refuge to the great propitiation. He can by no means clear the guilty, therefore am I assured He can by no means punish the innocent. In Christ I am innocent; guilt is no longer attachable to me; my soul is justified; justice, with its sword, has no claim upon me—it is satisfied; the law, with its penalties, has no demand against me; every jot and tittle of it is fulfilled. " Who is he that condemneth? it is Christ that died." III. We observe that the strong consolation drawn from this passage is WARRANTED ONLY ON THE SUPPOSITION THAT, IN DYING, CHRIST DIED AS A TRUE AND REAL SUBSTITUTE IN THE ROOM AND STEAD OF HIS PEOPLE, AND FOR THEM ALONE. (*J. Lewis.*)   *Justice and mercy not antagonistic :*—Now, there is no greater mistake than to suppose that the Divine Being, as a God of justice, and a God of mercy, stands in antagonism to Himself. Observe, I pray you, that it is not mercy, but injustice, which is irreconcilable with justice, and that it is cruelty, not justice, that stands opposed to mercy. These attributes of Jehovah are not contrary the one to the other, as are light and darkness, fire and water, truth and falsehood, right and wrong. No. Like two separate streams which unite their waters to form a common river, justice and mercy are combined in the covenant of redemption. Like the two cherubims whose outstretched wings met above the ark, or like the two devout and holy men who drew the nails from Christ's body, and bore the sacred burden to the grave, or like the two angels who received it in charge, and, seated like mourners within the sepulchre, the one at the head, the other at the feet, kept silent watch over the precious treasure, justice and mercy are associated in the work of Christ. They are the supporters of the shield on which the cross is emblazoned. They sustain the arms of our heavenly Advocate. They form the two solid, immovable, and eternal pillars of the Mediator's throne. On Calvary, mercy and truth meet together, righteousness and peace kiss each other. (*T. Guthrie, D.D.*)   **Visiting the iniquity of the fathers.**—*The law of heredity :*—We are born into a life where we cannot determine the nature of the influences which we exert. We can repress some, modify others, and develop still others; but we cannot determine the effect, nor change it. A certain influence we must exert one upon another. I. First, we will mention VOLUNTARY INFLUENCE, or the capacity which we have gained of influencing our fellow-men by bringing power, or the causes of power, to bear upon them on purpose. This is the more familiar form of influence. It is the foundation of all instruction. The parent influences the child on purpose. The teacher purposely influences all the minds that are brought under his care. Friends influence friends. We draw men to our way of thinking, and to our way of acting. We persuade; we dissuade; we urge; we enforce our agency; and in a thousand ways we voluntarily draw men to and fro. II. Then, besides all this, besides what we do on purpose, there is the other ELEMENT OF UNCONSCIOUS influence which men exert—that which our nature throws out without our volition. For I hold that it is with us as it is with the sun. I do not suppose that the sun ever thinks of raising the thermometer; but it does raise it. Wherever the sun shines warmly, the mercury goes up, although the sun and the instrument are both unconscious. And we are incessantly emitting influences good, bad, or negative. We are perpetually, by the force of life, throwing out from ourselves imperceptible influences. And yet the sum of these influences is of the utmost weight and importance in life. A single word spoken, you know not what it falls upon. You know not on what soul it rests. In some moods, words fall off from us, and are of no account. But there are other moods in which a word of hope, a word of cheer, a word of sympathy, is as balm. It changes the sequence of thought, and the whole order and direction of the mind. Single words have often switched men off from bad courses, or off from good ones, as the case may be. A simple example, silent, unspeaking by vocalization, but characterized by purity, by simplicity, crystalline and heavenly, has sweetened whole neighbourhoods. Fidelity, disinterestedness in love, pure peacefulness, love of God, and faith in invisible things, cannot exist in a man without having their effect upon his fellow-men. It is impossible that one should stand up in the midst of a community and simply be good, and not diffuse the influence of that goodness on every side. That which is true of goodness is true also of evil. Men who are under the influence of the malign passions are sowing the seeds of these passions. Sparks fly out from them as from the chimney of a forge. It is the inherent necessity of wickedness to breed wickedness and distribute it. A man is responsible, not only for what he does on purpose, but what he unconsciously does. And the load of responsibility grows as you take in these widening circles. More than this, the greater the nature, and the more ample the endowment, the more influence does a man exert both for good and for evil. The moral tone of our literature in this respect is exceedingly bad. There is almost a maxim that genius has a right to be lawless as to its method of doing right things. Every man is responsible for duty; and duty, and responsibility for it, augment in the proportion of being. III. Our influence is not merely voluntary, or involuntary and unconscious, BUT IT BECOMES COMPLEX, BECAUSE IT IS COMPOUNDED WITH THE LIVES AND THE ADDED INFLUENCE OF OTHERS. We are social. We come into relations with men. Our freedom touches theirs. We inspire them. But we do not change their nature. We, as it were, sow germs in their soil. These germs go on and become forces in their hands. So that that which we do to single ones, they propagate. But men's influence is not limited to their voluntary action, nor to the complex social relations which they sustain, and by which their influence is propagated indirectly. IV. In some respects MEN HOLD IN THEIR HANDS THE HISTORY OF THE FUTURE. The very solemn declaration of our text—"Visiting the iniquities of the fathers upon the children, and upon the children's children, unto the third and to the fourth generation "—this is the mystery of ages. If it were but on the one side; if men, having the power of beneficence, had the power to perpetuate it, we should admire that; but if it is a fact that men have the power of transmitting corruption, and so of influencing after times, who can fail to marvel at that? If that is a law, men may well stand appalled in the presence of such results as must fall out under it. And it is a law, it is a fact. We must learn this great hereditary law, and we must include in our purposes of benevolence the wise selection, the perpetuity and the improvement of the race, by the observance of this great law of hereditary transmission. The malignity of sin is a terrible malignity, as it is revealed by this great law of the transmission of influence to posterity, either directly and voluntarily, or indirectly and unconsciously. There are multitudes of men that are careless of themselves. They are said to be their own worst enemies. They are men that are free and easy; that squander their money; that pervert their disposition. And because they are good-natured and genial, people say of them, " They are clever fellows; they are kind men; they do no harm; at any rate they are their own worst enemies." Now, a man that is spending his whole life to destroy himself, cannot stop with himself. And the better fellow he is, the more likely is he to exert an influence. More than that, it is not himself alone that is destroyed. The babe in the cradle is cursed. The daughter unborn is cursed. The heir and sequent children are cursed. V. I will add but a single consideration more: AND THAT IS A CAUTION AND A WARNING TO ALL THOSE WHO ARE CONSCIOUSLY BEARING IN THEMSELVES THE SEED OF TRANSMISSIBLE DISEASE. I think there is no crime and no misdemeanour, to those that are instructed, greater than that of forming marriage connections under such circumstances. (*H. W. Beecher.*)   *The organic unity of the race :*—I. Let us, in the first place, observe the natural fact we may almost call it, of THE UNITY AND SOLIDARITY OF THE RACE. The method of the preservation and reproduction of the species, which God has appointed, is that of parentage and off-spring. The relations of the different parts of this prolonged species are such, as to involve a certain unity. Birth and nurture, the family relation, the law of similarity, the limits of variation, by which the children cannot diverge from the parental type beyond a certain mark of liberty, all these are what we may call physical and bodily elements of unity in the race. This unity is found, as we rise to the human race, to involve the descendant in the conditions of the parent, to a degree that is much more striking than in lower species. The human infant remains longer in dependence upon the parent; the years of education extend farther; the conditions of life for the offspring, in proportion as civilization and culture make life more complicated, and more deeply affected by the parent. That this unity of the race is taught by Scripture, no one can doubt. It is further illustrated by the Divine treatment of individual cases, and by the development of the Divine purpose throughout the sacred history. . . . If there be lessons in history, this lesson at least is clear. God has bound men into the unity of their descent, and deals with man along the lines of his generation. II. Our text does more than merely reveal the truth which we have stated and illustrated; it further shows us that this organic unity of the race IS OF A MORAL QUALITY AND INVOLVES MORAL DISCIPLINE. God declares that He visits the iniquity of the fathers upon the children, and upon the children's children, unto the third and unto the fourth generation. We are not bound by the mere number of the descents to which the visitation will be applied. The very form of the phrase suggests indefiniteness. It may be that, as a matter of fact, only one generation shall suffer, or, on the other hand, the dread judgment may descend beyond the third and fourth line of the posterity. The law is one of the generalities of human life, not to be measured by the accuracies of arithmetic. Man needs not to be exalted to presumption, nor cast down to hopelessness, by the words of this revelation. And, as we interpret the duration of the penalty in the general sense, so we may find, in the words of judgment, something more than the mere formula of doom. If there be a visitation of the father's sin, there surely must be also a benediction from the father's virtue. These words therefore reveal to us the moral quality of the race's organic unity. That which is involved in the descent of child from parent is not by way of mere natural cause and effect. It is indeed part of the material conditioning of the universe. But it is superintended by the God who governs, and governs not only by physical law, but also with moral and spiritual ends. He reveals Himself as administering it, and we know therefore that if it be a Divine visitation, it is done with wisdom and regulative grace, it is done for the higher purposes of character, for the evolution of good, and for the final extinction of evil, and therefore, it must hold, blended with it, not only the designs of moral law and the vindication of justice, but also the sublime issues of grace and salvation, inasmuch as God is a Father as well as a Ruler, a Saviour as well as a Judge. It is, then, not a doom, but a discipline. It is not to work itself out like some physical mechanical law, catching you as a machine catches the unwary or the blundering operative, and then never letting him go, until it has dragged him through all its terrible course of wheels and rollers, cogs and crushing pistons, to throw him out, at length, a torn and mangled' dismembered, slaughtered travesty of life and power. This is your philosophic view of human descent, but this is not the Divine. God "visits the sins of the fathers on the children." We know then that He does it to discipline the race' "My Father is a husbandman," said Jesus, teaching us the same blessed lesson under a beautiful figure. What, may we now ask, is the practical outcome of all this truth, man's organic relation, this relation divinely regulated and applied to the discipline of the race? 1. In the first place, will it not give us a fresh sense of the responsibility of life? We are links in the chain of human life. We receive the influences of our fathers, we hand these on to our children. 2. Shall we then not deeply consider the tremendous responsibility with which we are freighted? We may involve a long line of descendants in the result of our living. 3. The import of this lesson becomes all the greater when we consider it as it bears upon family life, and the relations which subsist between the parent and the child. What a sanctity has not God given to the family! Nothing must break the bond which binds society into its essential and formative elements—the circles of home. 4. Let us, then, seek to render this Divine law of great potency in the building of our Church and the furtherance of the kingdom of Christ as it is given to us. "To you and to your children" is the promise. 5. And finally, let me ask you to reflect upon your relation to Jesus Christ in the light of this organic unity of the race. (*L. D. Bevan, D.D.*) *The iniquity of the fathers visited upon their children:*—1. That this passage has no reference whatsoever to God's treatment of mankind in a future state. It does not mean that God will punish children in a future state for the sins of their parents; but the visitation which it threatens is exclusively temporal (see Ezek. xviii. 20). 2. That God never visits children even with temporal judgments for the sins of their parents, unless they imitate, and thus justify their parents' offences. Hezekiah, Josiah, and many other pious men were the children of exceedingly wicked parents; but as they shunned the sins of their fathers, and were supremely devoted to God, they enjoyed His favour in a very high degree, and were visited with no marks of displeasure on account of their progenitors. There is, however, one apparent exception to these remarks, which must be noticed. It is evident from facts, that even pious children often suffer in consequence of the wicked conduct of their parents. If a father be idle, or extravagant, his children, and perhaps his children's children, may suffer in consequence; nor will any degree of piety always shield them from such sufferings. It must, however, be added, that the sinful example and conduct of wicked parents has a most powerful tendency to prevent their children from becoming pious, to induce them to pursue vicious courses, and thus to bring upon them Divine judgments. 3. That our text describes God's method of proceeding with nations, and civil or ecclesiastical communities, rather than with individuals. I do not say that it has no reference to individuals, but that it refers principally to nations, states, and churches. That we may perceive the justice, wisdom, and propriety of this method of proceeding, it is necessary to consider the following things. It is indispensably necessary to the perfection of God's moral government that it should extend to nations and communities as well as to individuals. This, I conceive, is too evident to require proof; for how could God be considered as the moral governor of the world if nations and communities were exempt from His government? Again, if God is to exercise a moral government over nations and communities by rewarding or punishing them according to their works, the rewards and punishments must evidently be dispensed in this world; for nations and communities will not exist, as such, in the world to come. In that world God must deal with men, considered simply as individuals. Further, it seems evidently proper that communities as well as individuals should have a time of trial and probation allowed them; that if the first generation prove sinful, the community should not be immediately destroyed, but that the punishment should be suspended, till it be seen whether the nation will prove incorrigible, or whether some succeeding generation will not repent of the national sins, and thus avert national judgments. Now it is evident that if God thus waits upon nations, as He does upon individuals, and allows them a season of probation, a space for repentance, He cannot destroy them until many generations of sinners are laid in their graves. Besides, by thus suspending the rod or the sword over a nation, He presents to it powerful inducements to reform. He appeals to parental feelings, to men's affection for their posterity, and endeavours to deter them from sin by the assurance that their posterity will suffer for it. (*E. Payson, D.D.*)

Vers. 21–26. **Thou shalt rest.**—*Sabbath rest in harvest:*—"Six days thou shalt work, but on the seventh day thou shalt rest: in earing time and in harvest thou shalt rest"; that is, you shall not violate the Sabbath-day because it is harvest. I have heard persons say, It has been six days very wet; the corn is standing, and Sunday happens to be a bright sunny day; and they say, We ought to go and cut down the corn on the Sabbath-day. Here is a provision for this very possibility. God says, Even in harvest and earing time you shall still keep the Sabbath sacred to God. And I have noticed, although I admit my observation has been very limited, that that man who has cut down his corn on the Sunday in order to get it in well, did not succeed one whit better in the long run than he that observed the Sabbath as holy, and waited for sunny week-days in order to do his week-day work. I admit that there are works of necessity and mercy that are proper to be done on the Sabbath-day; and I can conceive the possibility that a time may come—an autumn may come—when, even upon the Sabbath-day, you should be obliged to cut down the corn in consequence of unfavourable weather on the week-days; but you should first be well satisfied that there is no prospect of sunshine during the six days that are to follow. Do not forget that God said—not as ceremony but morality—that in earing time, and in harvest even, thou shalt rest, or sabbatize, or keep the Lord's day. (*J. Cumming, D.D.*)　　*Exemplary Sabbath-keeping :—* I remember one time, many years ago, I was standing out for Sunday, but the owners could not bear the thought of the smacks laying to for the Sabbath. Well, the owner I sailed for wanted me to work on Sunday. I felt I could not, so I had to leave my berth. I walked about eight weeks after that in search of employment. Several owners asked me whether I wanted a situation. I asked them whether they wished me to fish on the Lord's day. They said, yes. I had to decline. Well, the money was getting short, and I used to go in the dark places on the sands to lift up my heart to God to help me to stand against this fierce temptation. I had no help at home. My wife, not loving my Saviour, could not understand my objection, and I have often seen her crying to think that she and the two little children would have no bread to eat. My faith told me that my Father in heaven would not let them be without bread and water—that would be sure. At length the time came when I had to take my watch to pledge to get bread. I started with a heavy heart, and when I got to the shop I could not gain

courage to go in for a long time. I walked up and down praying to God to keep me
strong and faithful and able to part with everything rather than to betray my trust.
At last I went in, and there stood one of our Church helpers behind the counter.
' Hullo,' says he, ' Wilkinson, has it come to this ? ' He was a dear young Christian, and has been a minister of the gospel for many years now. He asked me what
I wanted there. Then I told him I had come to pledge my watch to get bread for
wife and children. The tears stood in both our eyes. At last he asked, ' How
much do you want on it ? ' I said, ' I don't know; give me enough to get something to eat to-day ; and to-morrow, perhaps, God may see fit to give me something to do where I can still serve Him.' Well, he gave me some money, and he
shook hands with me, and said, ' Have faith and courage ; keep trusting in the
Lord, and He will bring you through.' And so He did. The next week three
smacks had to be sold, and a Christian man bought one. He asked me to go as
skipper of her. He told me, before I went to sea, not to do anything on Sundays
if I could help it. That is twenty-six years ago, and that is how the Lord brought
me through. (*Captain Wilkinson*, Mission Smack "Ed. Birkbeck.") **Observe the
feast.**—*God's provision for His people's enjoyment:*—I. THAT SEASONS FOR REJOICING
WERE COMMANDED. Let those who think that the Old Dispensation was gloomy remember
that there was Divine injunction for joy and feasting three times a year. II. That
these seasons for rejoicing WERE CONVENIENTLY APPOINTED. Not in winter, but—1. In
spring, Passover. 2. Summer, First-fruits. 3. Autumn, Ingathering. III. That
these seasons for rejoicing HAD A RELIGIOUS BASIS. 1. The feasts were "unto
God." 2. Were in remembrance of Divine services which made rejoicing possible.
IV. That these seasons for rejoicing WERE CONNECTED WITH RELIGIOUS ACTS (vers.
17–19). 1. Personal dedication. 2. Sacrifices. V. That seasons of rejoicing
must NOT ENGENDER SLOVENLINESS AND UNCLEANNESS (ver. 18). VI. That seasons of
rejoicing MUST NOT BE DESECRATED BY UNNATURAL OR SUPERSTITIOUS CEREMONIES.
"Thou shalt not seethe a kid in his mother's milk"; an outrage on nature and
connected with witchcraft. In conclusion, if Judaism was a religion of joy,
much more so is Christianity. The latter—1. Was inaugurated as "glad tidings
of great joy." 2. Its leading fact and doctrines are grounds of joy (1 John i. 1–4).
3. Its great central and fundamental principle is an occasion of joy (Rom. v. 11).
4. The "fruit of the Spirit is joy." 5. It provides an eternity of joy. 6. But
remember the joy of the Lord is your strength, and it is only "in the Lord" that
we can rejoice evermore (Phil. iv. 4). (*J. W. Burn.*) **Thrice in the year.**—*The
three yearly feasts at Jerusalem:*—We will—I. Draw your attention to THE INSTITU-
TION RECORDED IN THE TEXT. Consider—1. Of what nature this appointment was :
partly political, and partly religious. 2. What care God took to guard against the
objections to which it was liable. II. SUGGEST SOME OBSERVATIONS FOUNDED UPON
IT. 1. The service of God is of paramount obligation. 2. They who serve the
Lord shall be saved by Him. (*C. Simeon, M.A.*)

Vers. 27, 28. **He wrote upon the tables.**—*The second tables:*—The Ten Commandments were twice written by the finger of God Himself (see Deut. x. 1–3),
and upon enduring tables of stone, to show how deeply and permanently they were
to be engraven upon the heart of man. Twice written, once upon a broken and
once upon an unbroken tablet, symbolically setting forth the truth that they were
once written upon the nature before the Fall, and are to be inscribed a second time
upon that nature, which inscription is made at his regeneration. Also, as they
were once written upon stone, they were to be engraved a second time upon the
heart, as the prophet Jeremiah predicted would be, and as the apostle asserted had
been done (Heb. viii. 10). Then by special command they were afterwards
deposited for safe keeping in the ark of the covenant, upon which rested the
Shekinah of the Lord, the most inviolably sacred place outside the courts of
heaven, and by special designation were ever afterward known as the "Tables of
the Testimony." (*Jas. Stacy, D.D.*)

Vers. 29–35. **The skin of his face shone.**—*Moses transfigured:*—This was the
transfiguration of Moses. Let us consider the narrative as a spiritual parable, and
try to read in it some of the conditions and privileges of exalted communion with
God. Communion with God is the highest prerogative of spiritual beings. It is
the instinctive craving of human souls; it is the supreme privilege and joy of the
religious life ; it is the inspiration and strength of all great service. God redeems
us and saves us by drawing us to Himself. By mysterious voices He solicits us;

by irrepressible instincts He impels us; by subtle affinities He holds us; by ineffable satisfactions He makes us feel His nearness and fills us with rest and joy. I. WE ARE ADMITTED TO FELLOWSHIP WITH GOD ONLY THROUGH PROPITIATORY SACRIFICE. Moses builds an altar under the hill, offers sacrifices upon it, and sprinkles the blood thereof before he ascends the holy mount to commune with God. <u>We must seek fellowship with God through the one propitiatory sacrifice of Jesus Christ.</u> Not only is the sacrifice of Christ the medium through which the forgiving love of God becomes possible; it is the supreme expression of it. II. WE ARE QUALIFIED FOR OUR HIGHEST INTERCOURSE WITH GOD BY THE SPIRITUAL GRACE OF OUR OWN SOULS; Moses was qualified for this revelation of the supreme glory of God by his peculiar magnanimity and self-sacrifice. When God admits us to intercourse with Himself, what we see will depend upon our capability of seeing. <u>Only the pure in heart can see God.</u> III. WE ARE ADMITTED TO VISIONS OF THE HIGHER GLORY OF GOD ONLY WHEN WE SEEK THEM FOR THE USES OF PRACTICAL RELIGIOUS DUTY. If selfishness be a disqualification, so is mere sentiment. A man who seeks God for his own religious gratification merely may see God, but he will not see God's supreme glory. <u>Our chief reason for desiring to know God must be that we may glorify Him in serving others.</u> IV. THE MOST SPIRITUAL VISIONS OF GOD, THE CLOSEST COMMUNION WITH GOD, ARE TO BE REALIZED ONLY WHEN WE SEEK HIM ALONE. In our greatest emotions we seek solitude instinctively. Human presence is intolerable to the intensest moods of the soul. No man can be eminent either in holiness or service who does not often ascend to the mountain-top, that he may be alone with God and behold His glory. V. THE SUPREME REVELATION OF GOD TO WHICH WE ATTAIN THROUGH SUCH FELLOWSHIP WITH HIM IS THE REVELATION OF HIS GRACE AND LOVE. When a man sees this, the glory of God has passed before him. VI. THE REVELATION OF GOD'S GLORIOUS GOODNESS TRANSFIGURES THE MAN WHO BEHOLDS IT. (*H. Allon, D.D.*) *Unconscious beauty:* — "<u>He</u> wist not that the skin of his face shone." Few and simple as these words are, there could be none grander written to the memory of a hero. The noblest and loftiest character is assuredly that of the man who is so absorbed in the Divine nature of his calling, and so conscious of the need of those for whom he labours, that he becomes forgetful of the beauty in his character which others recognize, and almost unconscious that he is himself the worker. I. THERE ARE MANY UNCONSCIOUS BELIEVERS AND WORKERS IN THE WORLD STILL, WHO MAY GATHER HELPFUL THOUGHTS FROM THIS FACT CONCERNING MOSES. Much time and ability has been devoted to discussing the question of "Christian assurance." To say that if we do not *feel* that we are saved, we *are* not saved, is to lose sight of what salvation really means. It is nowhere stated in Scripture that an assurance of that salvation which is a gradual matter, a day-by-day struggle and deliverance, is either universal or necessary. God may think it best that some of us should not have assurance, as on that great day He kept Moses unconscious that the skin of his face shone. II. Perhaps some of us may feel that THERE WERE MOMENTS OF SUCH BRIGHT AND HOPEFUL EXPERIENCE ONCE, BUT THEY ARE PAST NOW, and that seems to us the saddest thought of all. Still we need not despair. We should go back as Moses did to the mount where God had spoken to him, to the source of the old enthusiasm and the former faith. If we go back and stand face to face with the crucified Christ, our life will glow anew with the radiance of His love, even though we ourselves are unconscious of it. III. THIS HOLDS GOOD ALSO REGARDING OUR WORK FOR GOD. Many a splendid silent work is done on earth, and the doer is perhaps unconscious of it, and may remain unconscious till the great day of the Lord shall reveal it. (*T. T. Shore, M.A.*) *Moses' face shining : a picture of true glory* :—1. Man has an instinct for glory. 2. Man has sadly perverted this instinct. 3. The Bible rightly directs it. I. THE TRUE GLORY OF MAN INVOLVES FELLOWSHIP WITH THE ETERNAL. The human character is formed on the principle of imitation. To get a perfect character implies—1. The existence of a perfect model. 2. The love of a perfect model. 3. The knowledge of a perfect model. II. THE TRUE GLORY OF MAN HAS AN EXTERNAL MANIFESTATION. 1. True glory will show itself in the "face" of our person. 2. Language. 3. Life. III. TRUE GLORY IS NEVER SELF-CONSCIOUS. "Moses wist not." There are several things that necessitate self-obliviousness in a truly great soul. 1. His standard of judgment. 2. His circle of life. He who stands before God feels his nothingness. 3. His spirit of life. Love is a passion that drowns the lover in the loved. "I live, yet not I." IV. TRUE GLORY WILL COMMAND THE REVERENCE OF SOCIETY. 1. The law of conscience will ensure universal respect for it. 2. The law of guilt will ensure

No!

trembling homage for it. (*Homilist.*)   *The shining face:*—I. THE SHINING FACE THE RESULT OF HIS LONG AND CLOSE COMMUNION WITH GOD. The heavenly light within will shine out. II. THE SHINING FACE WAS BEHELD BY THE PEOPLE. The good man's walk and conversation are known of all. III. THE SHINING FACE AWED ALL WHO BEHELD IT. The consciousness of sin makes the wicked fear pious friends, whose presence rebukes them. IV. MOSES KNEW NOT THAT HIS FACE SHONE. The more grace we have the less self-consciousness. The more good others see in us, the less do we see ourselves. Application : 1. If you cannot do anything else for God, you can exhibit a shining face. 2. Do not be discouraged because you are not conscious of any good influence you exert. (*J. L. Elderdice.*)   *Communion with God:*—I. THE DISTINGUISHING CHARACTERISTICS OF COMMUNION WITH GOD. 1. It is mediatory. 2. It is individual. 3. It is protracted. 4. It is self-denying. II. THE IRRADIATING POWER OF COMMUNION WITH GOD. 1. Its manifestation. 2. Its unconsciousness. 3. Its effect. (1) Awe-inspiring. (2) Heart-attracting. (*T. Baron.*)   *The Divine glory and its effects:*—We learn here three things with regard to the beauty of a sanctified character. I. THE NATURE OF THIS BEAUTY,—it is that which shines. 1. Its self-manifestation may be often a passive thing. It was Moses' face that was the index of his mood at the time,—not his tongue nor his hands. So with the child of God ; the beauty that bathes him is a matter that exists independent of any definite words spoken, or any outward deeds done. The beauty of the believer is the beauty of joy ; and joy does not always need speech to express itself, or the word to others, "I am glad." 2. Then, too, we learn that spiritual beauty is often an unwitnessed thing. It is by no means conditioned by the position a man occupies, or the numbers that are there to see. For the glory on Moses' face was not brought there just that others might watch and admire. His features would have glowed all the same, had there been no one to watch and to marvel in all the plain ; and heaven's own light would have glanced and flickered from his face among the bare dead sands and unconscious stones where he trod, making the solitude around him luminous. So again with the child of God. His shining does not need the stimulus of spectators. II. THE SECRET OF THIS BEAUTY. Communion with God,—that is the source it must spring from, lending sanctity to the character, and beauty to the very face. To see God's face is to shine ; to keep seeing it is to keep shining. It is thus that the marvel of the story is repeated, and God's praying saints come forth from this privacy with their faces aglow; and the dying grow luminous on their beds, till the watchers wonder. Why, where is there brightness like the brightness of heaven? They are all lustrous there! Uncover yourselves therefore to the light; keep yourselves up where the light is shining. The struggle will be to do that, and will be over when you have done it. So and so only will you shine yourselves. The manner of this shining is reflection. and the secret of it is communion with God. III. THE CHARACTERISTIC BY WHICH IT IS MARKED. That characteristic is unconsciousness. "Moses," we are told, "wist not that his face shone." It is always most real when it radiates unawares. Is it not the case that many an act which would otherwise have affected us favourably, attracted our admiration, won our esteem, is shorn of its grace and becomes worthless or worse for us, just because vitiated by self-consciousness? For instance, I may be glad to receive a kindness ; but if the man who professes to show it me betrays so plainly that he thinks it a kindness, and imposes a debt on myself while he does it, then I refuse to have the favour at his hands, or I grudge the necessity that compels me. Or I may feel that I stand in need of forgiveness; but if the brother at whose door I am suing for it makes it clear, while he gives me his hand, that he counts his act a magnanimous one, his forgiveness is emptied of its grace. Why, there are books one could point to, as well as people, in whose case the principle holds true. In language and in sentiment they are otherwise unexceptional. They treat of moral and religious truth with a freshness of view and a beauty of utterance which in themselves would arrest and stimulate. But you cannot help feeling throughout them the presence of an evil underflavour the while—the taint of the writer's self-consciousness in it all, that maims and defiles his message—the traces of a spiritual ostentation through the whole, that makes you recognize while you read that the question is being asked you—not, "What think ye of the truth merely?" but, "What think ye of me who am saying it?" Nor is this unconsciousness without its directer proofs. Two at least will invariably be found with it—appreciation of others, depreciation of self. Nor is the reason of all this far to seek. This unconsciousness of grace that we speak of, issuing not only in appreciation of others, but in depreciation of self, may be accounted for by converse with a high ideal. For the greater an artist's success, the greater his sense of imperfection. The more that he strives to attain, the further will his standard recede from him, the more unsatisfactory will his attainments appear in the light of it. What, then, must the case be when the standard is an infinite one, and the mark we reach forth to is the perfection of a God! (*W. A. Gray.*) *The element of unconsciousness in character* :—See also Judges xvi. 20. I. Let us note, in the first place, THAT THIS QUALITY OF UNCONSCIOUSNESS IS INVARIABLY CONNECTED WITH A PECULIAR ANTECEDENT HISTORY. The facts stated regarding Moses and Samson do not stand out in isolation in their biographies. They are in immediate relation to the preceding incidents in their careers. The new man can form good habits, just as the old man formed evil ones, and in proportion as these habits gain strength, the consciousness of effort after the things which they lead us to do begins to diminish in us. Hence in the details of daily life the character of the believer, as he grows in holiness, shines with a radiance of which he is largely unaware. Now this truth has another side, for it comes in also with fearfully dangerous influence in the continued commission of sin. The more one practises iniquity, the greater facility he acquires in committing it, the stronger becomes the tendency to indulge in it, and the weaker ever is his sense of its enormity. In a manufacturing town in England, some years ago, it became necessary to do some repairs at the top of one of the tallest smoke-stacks in the principal factory, and an expert was engaged for the purpose. He flew his kite over it, and fixed his tackle so that he could hoist himself up. But when he reached the summit, through some accident, the whole tackling fell, and there he stood without any means of coming down again. Every plan was tried to get a rope to him without success. A great crowd collected at the base of the chimney, and among these was the wife of the unfortunate man. A happy thought struck her, in her earnestness for her husband's safety. She knew that he wore at the moment stockings which her own hands had just knitted. So, at her suggestion, they called him to undo the yarn of which they were composed, and by and by a tiny thread came fluttering down on the breeze. When it reached the earth, they tied it to a piece of twine, which he drew up with the yarn. To the twine again they tied a thicker string, and then to that a cord, and to that again a cable, and so he was saved. That was a work of deliverance. But there is a similar gradation in the cord of evil habit by which a sinner is bound. It is first a brittle yarn, then a tiny twine, with which a child might play. II. But I advance another step in the prosecution of my theme, and remark, in the second place, THAT THIS QUALITY OF UNCONSCIOUSNESS MARKS THE CULMINATION OF CHARACTER EITHER IN GOOD OR EVIL. The highest greatness is that which is unconscious of itself. The very forthputting of an effort to be great in any direction indicates that we lack that greatness. So long as we are conscious of an effort to be something, we are not fully that something, therefore we ought to redouble our exertions. When a venerable minister was called upon once unexpectedly to preach, he delivered extempore a sermon of great power. It seemed to come perfectly natural to him. There was no appearance of effort; and one hearer, amazed at the character of the discourse, asked, "How long did it take you to make that sermon?" "Forty years," was the reply. And there was deep philosophy in the answer, for had "the old man eloquent" not given these forty years to diligent study and laborious effort, he could not then have preached so easily. Now, in the same way, our conscious endeavours after the Christian life will, if faithfully prosecuted, lead up to a time when, in some emergency, we shall meet it with the most perfect ease, and be hardly aware of any exertion. Let this thought stimulate us to perseverance in our great Christian life-work of building character. The longer we labour the less arduous will our labour become, until by and by we shall lose the sense of labour in the joy and liberty of our happy experience. But note again at the other end of the scale that the deepest degradation is that which is unconscious of its dishonour. Hence, however degraded a man may be there is hope of his recovery if he only knows his condition. That is the handle by which yet, through the grace of God, you may raise him, and you will succeed in lifting the fallen from their defilement only by awakening in them that consciousness. Their fall has stunned them into insensibility, and the first thing you have to do with them is to restore them to consciousness. (*W. M. Taylor, D.D.*) *Communion with God, and its results* :— I. First, THE CONVERSE WHICH MOSES HAD WITH GOD ON THE TOP OF THE MOUNTAIN WAS THE CAUSE OF THAT GLORY WHICH RESTED ON HIS COUNTENANCE. There is, no doubt, a great deal of what is miraculous in connection with this transaction; but though we are not to look in our own particular case for anything analogous to it, yet we are to expect something spiritually correspondent with it. 1. The first remark that I offer to your attention is, that on ascending the mountain to hold intercourse with God, Moses observed the rites of the religious dispensation under which he lived. A devotional spirit must be cherished and cultivated ; and it is promised, on the part of the Saviour, that what we ask in prayer, believing, that we shall receive. But in addition to this, God must lift the veil from His own throne. He must give utterance to the voice of mercy and love. He must display reasons to the humble waiting spirit, and must manifest Himself in some clear manner, before we can be made conscious of communion with Him. 2. Moses ascended the mountain alone. This opens to us another principle of religion. It is this— that in all respects it is personal. Our devotional exercises are of this nature. It is true, indeed, that we meet in public fellowship; but there is a sense in which the soul sits solitary and alone in the midst of a mighty multitude. Here I stand, and there you sit ; but one character, one faith, one love, one hope, one joy. And our several emotions are all personal, and belong to ourselves. You know not my feelings ; I know not yours. 3. As Moses drew a pattern from God on the mountain, so must we derive grace to fill it up from the same source. Now as far as we are employed in building the internal temple of Christianity, we must derive grace and strength from intercourse with God for the discharge of this great duty ; and as Moses received the law from God, so we must receive grace and power to obey it from the same source. This remark is applicable both to our personal and public duties. II. The second general observation to be made RELATES TO THE NATURE OF THAT LIGHT, AND BEAUTY, AND GLORY, WHICH RESTED ON THE FACE OF MOSES. I should here remark, that there is a great mystery in this, but that it was intended to be symbolical of a better glory. That intercourse with God will make or cause His beauty to rest upon the soul. There may be no external glory, such as beamed on the face of Moses, but a spiritual glory beaming forth, instead, upon the mind. 1. There must be, for instance, rapturous joy. How can it be otherwise? The impulses of religion, when they exist in the mind, as they should do, by constant fellowship with the eternal Trinity, must be transporting and animating in the highest degree. 2. Intercourse with God must have the effect of expanding the capacity and enlarging the soul. 3. I may also add, that intercourse with God will produce, if not external or physical beauty, yet a beauty of character. Internal purity will be corroborated by outward conduct. III. The final remark which I offer for your attention, relates to THE VAIL WHICH MOSES PUT ON HIS FACE WHEN HE DESCENDED FROM THE MOUNTAIN TO HOLD FELLOWSHIP WITH THE PEOPLE. There is a mystery in this; but the mystery we shall not attempt to unravel. Allow me here to say generally, that religion in its beauty and glory is often in the present life veiled beneath circumstances which obscure its grandeur. (*J. Dixon.*) *A transfigured soul :*—You have heard of the marks on the bodies of Roman Catholic devotees which go by the name of stigmatization. There appear on the hands and feet of the rapt saint wounds similar to those inflicted on the crucified Saviour. It is alleged that the intense brooding of their sympathetic and ravished souls on the Redeemer's agonies have led to their bearing about, in a literal sense, on their bodies the marks of the Lord Jesus. We shall leave physiologists to explain the alleged phenomena, or to expose the possible imposture, and go on to say that this physical stigmatization has a moral counterpart ; that though the wounds inflicted on the Saviour's flesh may not be reproduced on the bodies of His saints, the moral glory of His nature may be republished in their souls, and through their faces may be radiated into the world, as His own glory, usually veiled, once was allowed to burst through the environing flesh on the Mount of Transfiguration. In meditating on this incident in the history of Moses I suggest to you—1. That the effulgence of his face was the result of his eighty days' fellowship with God. I have read somewhere that people who live together through long-wedded years at last grow like each other, not only in their ways of thinking, of looking at things—in their moods and habitudes of mind—but even in their cast of face and feature. Such power, it is said, has long and constant fellowship to make people variously constituted of like temper, and even appearance. I can understand it in the case of the moral and mental dispositions. The stronger nature makes the weaker surrender its own personality and qualities, and borrow from that by which it is swayed. It is, indeed, by the working of this mysterious law of spirit that the Christian believer is renewed into Christ. If, therefore, the face of the sage and seer shone with unwonted lustre, it must have been because of a corresponding purification of his moral nature. It is to this condition alone that a glimpse of the beatific vision and an insight into Divine things are given. " Blessed are the pure in heart, for they shall see God," and discern truth. 2. Did the translucency fade away, as the golden glory fades from the hill-tops when the sun has set; or did it last till the day of his death? Had he ever after kept his spirit up to the moral elevation to which it rose on Sinai's height, the splendour of his visage would have been subject to no eclipse or wane; it would have shone not only with an undiminishing, but with an ever-increasing light. 3. Though the face of Moses shone, he was quite unconscious that there was anything unusual about him; " he wist not that the skin of his face shone when he talked "; he had no knowledge of the marvellous external results which his eighty days' companionship with God had wrought in his appearance. There is a beautiful unconsciousness about the Christian. All the world is applauding and reverencing him; blessing him for the vision of excellence with which he refreshes it; acknowledging that his very existence fertilizes the field of life; but were you to overhear his own estimate of himself, you would find it other and different. Did you listen to his prayers, you would find them full of heart-breaking confessions of unworthiness. (*J. Forfar.*) *The law a light:*—1. First, it was signified that the law proceeded from a higher world of light, of knowledge, and of holiness, since its very gleams were to be seen outwardly on the minister of the law. 2. Since the people could not bear the shining of the light, it represented how fearful, condemnatory, and fatal the law was for a sinful people. (*Otto von Gerlach, D.D.*)   *The highest excellence is that which is least conscious of itself:*—The greatest achievements made by the sculptor or the painter have been those in the production of which he has been fullest of his conception, and had least thought of himself. I do not mean to say that the noblest artists have not been indefatigable workers; on the contrary, they have laboured with such persevering effort that at last they can produce, almost without the consciousness of exertion, something that will never be forgotten; and their supreme work is that which seems almost to have come to them of itself, so that they were more passive than active in its transmission to their fellows. The best sermons write themselves, and are given to the preacher before they are given by him, so that he cannot think of them as wholly his own. But it is the same in spiritual things. If I am conscious of an effort to be humble, very clearly I have not yet attained to humility; while, on the other hand, the very moment I become conscious that I am humble, I have become proud. And so with every other grace. What a discount you take from a man's character when, after you have said of him, he is this, or that, or the other thing that is good, you add, " but he knows it." You might almost as well have taken a sponge and wiped out all that went before. So if you know your excellence, you have not reached the highest excellence; there remaineth yet the loftiest and the hardest peak of the mountain to be climbed by you, and that is humility. (*W. M. Taylor, D.D.*)   *Light through converse with spiritual things:*—There is one kind of diamond which, after it has been exposed for some minutes to the light of the sun, when taken into a dark room will emit light for some time. The marvellous property of retaining light, and thereby becoming the source of light on a small scale, shows how analogous to light its very nature must be. Those who touched the Saviour became sources of virtue to others. As Moses' face shone when he came from the mount, so converse with spiritual things makes Christians the light which shines in the dark places of the earth. "Let your light so shine before men." (*Weekly Pulpit.*)   *Moral illumination:*—The spaces between the windows of one of the rooms of a famous palace are hung with mirrors, and by this device the walls are made just as luminous as the windows, through which the sunshine streams. Every square inch of surface seems to reflect the light. Let your natures be like that—no point of darkness anywhere, the whole realm of the inward life an unchequered blaze of moral illumination. (*T. G. Selby.*)   *The outshining of a joyful heart:*—Moses came down from the mount, when, like the bush of Horeb, he had been in the midst of the fire and was not consumed, and as he came, the light of his soul transfigured his face, " the beauty of the Lord our God was upon him," and the ninetieth Psalm seemed to be shining through it. As the brightly-coloured soil of volcanic Sicily makes flowers of the brightest tints, so there was a garden in the prophet's face, glorified by the outshining of his joyful heart. (*Christian Age.*) *The after-glow of devotion:*—One of the most solemn and delightful privileges of the traveller is to watch the after-glow upon the mountains when the sun has disappeared. This was accorded to us on several occasions, but was never more impressive than in the valley of Chamounix. To see the hoary head of Mont Blanc, and even the pointed aguiles of the locality, too steep to allow the snow to settle on them, all aglow with rosy tints, made us feel as though by some transformation scene we were inhabitants of another world, or as though heaven had come down to earth, and the tabernacle of God had been pitched among men. (*G. Kirkham.*) *Light reflected from the cross :*—With much pathos Mr. Varley once told the story of Sybil, a negress slave, whose mistress said to her : " When I heard you singing on the house-top I thought you fanatical, but when I saw your beaming face I could not help feeling how different you were to me." Sybil answered, " Ah, missus, the light you saw in my face was not from me, it all came 'flected from de cross, and there is heaps more for every poor sinner who will come near enough to cotch de rays." *Exhortation to humility :*—I charge you, be clothed with humility, or you will yet be a wandering star, for whom is reserved the blackness of darkness for ever. Let Christ increase, let man decrease. Remember, " Moses wist not that the skin of his face shone." Looking at our own shining face is the bane of the spiritual life, and of the ministry. Oh ! for closest communion with God, till soul and body, head and heart, shine with Divine brilliancy ! But oh ! for a holy ignorance of their shining ! (*R. McCheyne.*) *The absence of self-consciousness :*—Near the close of the summer season, in a pleasant summer retreat, a new-comer found the entire company of the little hotel preparing to give a fête in honour of a young lady who was about to leave them. The young men had hired a band, marquees were erected on the lawn, the house was wreathed with flowers ; everybody had some little farewell gift ready for " Miss Betty." The stranger was curious. " This Miss Betty is very beautiful ? " he asked. " No, I think not ; it never occurred to me before, but I believe she is homely." " A great heiress, then ? " " On the contrary, a poor artist." " Brilliant? Witty? Highly intellectual ? " " No, indeed ; she never said a fine thing in her life. But she is the best listener I ever knew. Neither is she learned or clever or fascinating; but she is the most lovable girl in the world." " What is the charm, then ? " Betty's friend looked perplexed. " I do not know," he hesitated, " unless it is that she never thinks of herself." The charm of this woman was an absolute absence of all self-consciousness. She was neither vain nor modest. She simply forgot that there was such a person as Betty Gordon, and with her warm heart and quick sympathies threw herself into the lives of others. It was a peculiar, powerful attraction, and brought the little world about her to her feet. **He put a vail on his face.**—*The vailed face :*—It appears to be a law of our being, and the being of all material things, that everything grows like to that with which it is conversant and familiar. It is a law ruling all creation. We find it in the Arctic regions and we find it in the tropics—namely, life assimilates itself to the nature which is around it. Friendship, the intercourse of common friendship, will affect the countenance. When we go to moral life, there is its evil and its blessed application. Those who frequent the good gather the image of their goodness; and those who deal much with God, they grow God-like. I. WHAT WAS THE GLORY ON MOSES' FACE ? St. Paul gives us a remarkable answer to this question. He says, " They could not look steadfastly to the end of that which is abolished." " That which is abolished " is the law, and the end of the law is Christ; therefore the glory upon Moses' face was the Lord Jesus Christ. II. IT WAS NOT IN COMPASSION FOR THE WEAKNESS OF THE ISRAELITES THAT MOSES PUT A VAIL UPON HIS FACE. The Jews had lost the power to see the end of that which is abolished, to see the glory of God in Jesus Christ reflected in the law. The vail was judicial, the consequence of sin ; it was interposed between them and the beauty, the lustre, of the mighty glory of God in the person of Jesus Christ. III. THERE ARE VAILED HEARTS AMONG US NOW ; AND THE REASON OF THE VAIL IS SIN. Do you think that like those Israelites you have committed some sins under the mount ? It will quite account for the vail, and the vail will be proportioned to that state of life. Every wilful disobedience of conscience, every going against a conviction, will thicken your vail. It will be God's retribution to you—the intellect dulled, the mind warped, the heart hardened, the Spirit hindered, by the sin. What is the remedy ? " When it shall turn to the Lord, the vail shall be taken away." Then Christ is the remedy. (*J. Vaughan, M.A.*) *Moses' vail :*— The vail which Moses put on his face, when he perceived that it shone—1. Teaches us a lesson of modesty and humility : we must be content to have our excellences obscured. 2. It teaches ministers to accommodate themselves to the capacities of the people, and to preach to them as they are able to bear it. 3. The vail

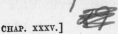

signified the darkness of that dispensation in which there were only "shadows of good things to come." (*A. Nevin, D.D.*) *The vail on Moses' face :*—St. Paul, in the New Testament, makes large use of this narrative of the glory that shone on Moses' face as he came down with the renewed covenant. Thus he employs it as in a typical sense an emblem of the relative glories of the old legal and the new evangelical dispensation (2 Cor. iii. 10–18). Even as a rhetorical figure, how beautiful is this application of the narrative of Moses to the purpose of setting before Jewish Christians the relation of the new to the old dispensation. Moses, with his vail, stands as a symbol of his own dispensation, which was, in fact, the gospel under a vail. And the symbol is represented as having a threefold significancy, when contemplated in its different parts. First, the symbol points out the intrinsic excellence and glory of the old dispensation, even though far less glorious than the new. But as the glory of Moses' face was absorbed and lost when he entered "the tent of meeting," to commune with God, so the brightness of the old dispensation of Moses is eclipsed in the transcendent brightness of the gospel. Again, the narration of the veiled Moses, in the apostle's view, symbolizes the comparative obscurity of the old exhibition of the way of salvation. The vail represents the indistinct view which the Israelites had through the ritual teachings of the law ; the brightness of the gospel light was covered up by rites that their minds did not penetrate. Nor will many of them now lift the vail, as the new dispensation invites them to do. Hence, again, this vail typified the blindness and ignorance under which the Jewish mind laboured, even in the time of the apostle. They had so long looked at Moses vailed that they now seemed to think the very vail an essential part of the system of salvation. (*S. Robinson, D.D.*)

CHAPTER XXXV.

VER. 3. **Ye shall kindle no fire.**—*The unkindled fire :*—In the old time it was a law that each night, at a prescribed hour, a bell should be rung, on hearing which the people were to put out their fires. This a law not about putting fires out each day, but against lighting a fire on one particular day. Why this law ? I. To SHOW THAT ON THE SABBATH, ESPECIALLY, MEN SHOULD ATTEND TO THE INTERESTS OF THE SOUL RATHER THAN TO THE COMFORTS OF THE BODY. II. To REMOVE FRIVOLOUS EXCUSES FOR NON-ATTENDANCE ON RELIGIOUS WORSHIP. III. To GUARD THE TIME OF FEMALES OR SERVANTS FROM UNRIGHTEOUS INVASION; and teach men that women had religious rights and duties equally with themselves. IV. To INCULCATE IN ALL THE DUTY OF SELF-SACRIFICE IN MATTERS RELATING TO THE SOUL AND GOD. (*Biblical Museum.*) *The rest of plants :*—All creation seems to possess the instinct of rest. We well know how eagerly the human heart sighs for rest. But it is not so well known that even plants sleep. Their strange sleep, says Figuier, vaguely recalls to us the sleep of animals. In its sleep the leaf seems by its disposition to approach the age of infancy. It folds itself up, nearly as it lay folded in the bud before it opened, when it slept the lethargic sleep of winter, sheltered under the robust and hardy scales, or shut up in its warm down. We may say that the plant seeks every night to resume the position which it occupied in its early days, just as the animal rolls itself up, lying as if it lay in its mother's bosom. All the world seems to express the sentiment contained in the words uttered by one of old, who desired the wings of a dove in order to seek and obtain rest. (*Scientific Illustrations.*) *Sabbath breaking condemned :*—Dr. Beecher was seen one Monday morning leaving his house with a basket in his hand which he was carrying to the fish-market, and in which he intended to carry home a fish for the family table. Unknown to him, a young man of undecided religious principles was following and watching him. The minister soon came to the fish-market. Here Dr. Beecher picked up a fine-looking fish, and asked the fisherman if it was fresh and sweet. "Certainly," replied the man, "for I caught it myself yesterday," which was the Sabbath. Dr. Beecher at once dropped the fish, saying, "Then I don't want it," and went on without another word. We are not informed whether the preacher obtained his fish, but when the young man who was following him that morning related his experience some time afterwards on his admission to the Christian Church, he stated that Dr. Beecher's consistency evinced in the fish-market had been the turning-point in his career. It convinced him of the power of religion in life, had induced him to attend the ministry of the man who had won his respect, and he was converted.

Ver. 29. **A willing offering.**—*The willing offering :*—Remember that at this time there was no legislation to Israel about giving. A little while after there were strict laws how much they were to give—and every Israelite was by law presently compelled to give no less than two-tenths—first one-tenth and then another tenth —one-fifth of all his property to God; but now that legislation had not taken place, and they gave in the freeness of their own willing hearts. But God has withdrawn legislation again with respect to His Church's gifts to Him. Only He has laid down broad principles—and we act upon those broad principles in the free-dom of the gospel. And here is our opportunity of testing our great love to God— that we are ourselves to be a law to ourselves, that we should give as the Spirit of God moves us. Now let us see, a little more carefully, some rules for giving. We cannot give before we have received. We can only give Him of His own; and, therefore, he who would be a good giver must be careful first to be a good receiver. I. Having received largely and freely, then, to give is first to GIVE ONE'S SELF. And I would advise you, before you make any gift whatsoever, to go through an express act of surrender of yourself to God. That done, then make your gift, whatever it be, that you have in your heart to give—make it a solemn, consecrated gift. By some special acts of prayer, dedicate it to God. Then make your act of charity, to the Church or to your fellow-men. II. And now the practical question comes— How MUCH OUGHT WE TO GIVE ? A question which, in the freeness of the* gospel, it is impossible to answer. The answer would vary according to many circum-stances, so that it would be impossible to lay down one abstract law. The line has too often, perhaps, been drawn, that it becomes a Christian to give one-tenth of his income to God. But if a man with small means ought to give one-tenth, then a man with double the means ought to give a fifth ; because the rate of giving ought to rise in proportion to the income. And, again, the rate of the giving must be accord-ing to the demands and the claims which are upon the Christian. So that those who have families—wives and children—depending upon them, ought not to give in the same proportion to their income as those who have none. So that should it be that any person, either of his own fault or other's fault, is involved in debt, then that person should consider first the justice of paying the debt, and then go on to the luxury of giving to God or to the Church. I do not say that a person who is in debt should be deprived altogether of the privilege of giving to God. Because, if he make his gift to God a thing taken out of that which he would certainly other-wise have spent upon himself, then he is not injuring his creditors, though he gives part of his income, and though he be in debt, to God. But then he must be careful that by that gift he does not defraud his creditors, because there must be perfect justice before charity. (*J. Vaughan, M.A.*) *The blessings of giving :*—There is nothing so like God—because the essence of God is He is always emitting. "He opens His hand, and fills all things living with plenteousness" : and all things are His. And the more expansive our minds, the more open our hearts, the more we give, the more we grow into the likeness of the great giving God. And it is such a sweet feeling one almost fears that we may be led to do it for the very sweetness there is in the act. But it is the happiness of giving when it is done to express our own feelings of love to Jesus. And though there is no merit in any gift that any man can ever give, yet there is " a good foundation for the time to come." And this is the way it is a foundation. It is an evidence. In the great day of judg-ment, the thing examined will be, "Did you love Christ ? " For witness there will stand out your acts, to prove whether you did or did not love Christ—that is, whether you had accepted His salvation, and had loved Him in return. And your acts will stand out in testimony, to prove or disprove your love to Christ. And not only so. This world is a failing world, and everything around us will be bank-rupt. Therefore, do you so use "the mammon of unrighteousness," the spoils of Egypt—money—do you so use " the mammon of unrighteousness " that it will be a " friend " to you—not an enemy, to rise up against you as a witness to your selfishness, and your pride, and your worldliness, but a friend to speak for you. (*Ibid.*) *Free giving :*—I. THE LORD'S OFFERING SHOULD BE IMMEDIATE. The people in this instance were sufficiently informed of the need. They had time to learn how far they could individually meet it, and then they returned with their presents. A simple, practical reply this, to the Divine call. " He gives twice that gives quickly." Emergencies are not continuous. II. THE LORD'S OFFERING MUST

BE VOLUNTARY. III. THE LORD'S OFFERING IS TO BE OF SUCH AS WE HAVE. Good wishes and approving words bring down no scales which turn with deeds. " Most men," said Sydney Smith, "are ready to act the good Samaritan *without* the oil and the two pence." IV. THE LORD'S OFFERING MAY BE COMPLETE (chap. xxxvi. 5, 6). (*De Witt S. Clarke.*) *A great demand, and the gracious response:*—I. A GREAT DEMAND. 1. God sometimes makes demands upon His people. Sometimes by providential calls for help. Our brother dies suddenly and leaves his orphan children dependent on our care. In these children God comes to us and says—Give! 2. The demands which God makes upon His people are sometimes apparently harsh and unreasonable. Here, from these newly-escaped slaves, He demands a Tabernacle which cost, it is computed, at least £250,000. 3. God sometimes makes demands upon His people which cannot be met without real self-sacrifice. 4. He demands that these sacrifices shall be made with good will (chap. xxv. 2, xxxv. 5 ; 1 Cor. viii. 12, ix. 7). God makes such demands upon His people—(1) Not because He needs anything at their hand (Psa. l. 9–12). (2) But solely for their welfare. (*a*) They need to be saved from covetousness, which is idolatry. (*b*) They need to have their character ennobled, and this can be accomplished only by the exercise of self-denial. (*c*) They need channels for the expression of gratitude and joy. By those who truly love God, opportunities by which they may honour Him are welcomed with eager joy. II. A GLORIOUS RESPONSE. The demand for contributions for the erection of the Tabernacle was more than met (chap. xxxvi. 5–7). How did this come to pass ? 1. A spirit of holy enthusiasm possessed the people. 2. This spirit of holy enthusiasm possessed not a few wealthy men only, but the whole people (vers. 21, 29). 3. This spirit of holy enthusiasm moved them to give not only of their superfluity, but also things needful to them in daily life (vers. 22–24); and not only to give, but also to labour (ver. 25). 4. This spirit of holy enthusiasm transformed every sacrifice that was made for God into an occasion and cause of great joy. So, again, was it at the erection of the Temple (1 Chron. xxix. 9). Finally, this glorious response on the part of the people was gloriously acknowledged by the Most High (chap. xl. 34, 35). (*The Preacher's Monthly.*) *An old subscription list :*—There was plenty of compulsory work, of statutory contribution, in the Old Testament system of worship. Sacrifices and tithes and other things were imperative, but the Tabernacle was constructed by means of undemanded offerings, and there were parts of the standing ritual which were left to the promptings of the worshipper's own spirit. There was always a door through which the impulses of devout hearts could come in, to animate what else would have become dead, mechanical compliance with prescribed obligations. I. We have set forth here THE TRUE MOTIVE OF ACCEPTABLE SERVICE. "They came, every one whose heart stirred him up, and every one whom his spirit made willing." There is a striking metaphor in that last word. Wherever the spirit is touched with the sweet influences of God's love, and loves and gives back again, that spirit is buoyant, lifted, raised above the low, flat levels where selfishness feeds fat and then rots. The spirit is raised by any great and unselfish emotion. Continual contact with Jesus Christ, and realization of what He has done for us, is sure to open the deep fountains of the heart, and to secure abundant streams. If we can tap these perennial reservoirs, they will yield like artesian wells, and need no creaking machinery to pump a scanty and intermittent supply. We cannot trust this deepest motive too much, nor appeal to it too exclusively. Let me remind you, too, that Christ's appeal to this motive leaves no loophole for selfishness or laziness. Responsibility is all the greater because we are left to assess ourselves. The blank form is sent to us, and He leaves it to our honour to fill it up. Do not tamper with the paper, for remember there is a Returning Officer that will examine your schedule who knows all about your possessions. II. We get here THE MEASURE OF ACCEPTABLE WORK. We have a long catalogue, very interesting in many respects, of the various things that the people brought. Such sentences as these occur over and over again—" And every man with whom was found " so-and-so " brought it "; " And all the women did spin with their hands, and brought that which they had spun "; " And the rulers brought " so-and-so. Such statements embody the very plain truism that what we have settles what we are bound to give. Or, to put it into grander words, the capacity is the measure of duty. Our work is cut out for us by the faculties and opportunities that God has given us. The form as well as the measure of our service is determined thereby. " She hath done what she could," said Jesus Christ about Mary. We often read that, as if it were a kind of apology for a sentimental and useless gift, because it was the best that she could bestow. I do not hear that tone in the words at all. I hear, rather, this: that duty is settled by faculty, and that nobody else has any business to interfere with that which a Christian soul, all aflame with the love of God, finds to be the spontaneous and natural expression of its devotion to the Master. The words are the vindication of the form of loving service; but let us not forget that they are also a very stringent requirement as to its measure, if it is to please Christ. "What she could." The engine must be worked up to the last ounce of pressure that it will stand. All must be got out of it that can be got out of it. III. Notice, again, how in this list of offerings there comes out the great thought of THE INFINITE VARIETY OF FORMS OF SERVICE AND OFFERING, WHICH ARE ALL EQUALLY NEEDFUL AND EQUALLY ACCEPT- ABLE. The list begins with "bracelets, and ear-rings, and rings, and tablets, all jewels of gold." And then it goes on to "blue, and purple, and scarlet, and fine linen, and red skins of rams, and badgers' skins, and shittim wood." And then we read that the women did spin with their hands, and brought that which they had spun—namely, the same things as have been already catalogued, the blue, and purple, and scarlet, and fine linen. That looks as if the richer gave the raw material, and the women gave the labour. Poor women, they could not give, but they could spin. They had no stores, but they had ten fingers and a distaff; and if some neighbour found the stuff, the ten fingers joyfully set the distaff twirling, and spun the yarn for the weavers. Then there were others who willingly undertook the rougher work of spinning, not dainty thread for the rich soft stuffs whose colours were to glow in the sanctuary, but the coarse black goats' hair which was to be made into the heavy covering of the roof of the Tabernacle. No doubt it was less pleasant labour than the other, but it got done by willing hands. And then, at the end of the whole enumeration, there comes—"And the rulers brought pre- cious stones, and spices, and oil," and all the expensive things that were needed. The big subscriptions are at the bottom of the list, and the smaller ones are in the place of honour. All this just teaches us this—what a host of things of all degrees of preciousness in men's eyes go to make God's great building! All the things that are given, and the works that are done from the same motive, because of the will- ing heart, stand upon the same level of acceptance and preciousness in His eyes, whatever may be their value in the market-place. (*A. Maclaren, D.D.*) *Free giving:*—I. CO-OPERATION IN FREE GIVING. 1. The men brought their gifts (vers. 23, 24). 2. The women brought their gifts (vers. 25, 26). 3. The rulers brought their gifts (vers. 27, 28). II. GIVING BASED ON AN ACCEPTABLE PRINCIPLE. 1. Its motive was right (ver. 29). 2. Its judgment was correct. (1) The givers did what they could in their respective lines. (2) The character and variety in the gifts noticeable. III. FREE GIVING, IN ITS INFLUENCE UPON GOD (vers. 30–35). 1. If the gifts had not been forthcoming, the special skill would not have been brought into requisition. 2. The gifts, without the skill to use them, would have been of no account. 3. A Divine law is here discovered—God ever imparts to a willing people every needed grace for complete success. Lessons: 1. The contrast between the child- ren of Israel bowing before the calves of gold and bearing cheerful offerings for God's sanctuary, is marked and suggestive. (1) It suggests the power of a sentiment for good or evil. (2) It suggests the responsibility of leaders of the people. The few create the sentiment, the many adopt it. 2. The contrast between the feelings of their covenant God toward them in these opposite attitudes. (1) Toward His sinning people He is angry. (2) Toward His obedient people He is full of grace and blessing. 3. Suggestive also is the contrast between the joy and peace of a disobedient and an obedient people. 4. We have here an instructive example of how much can be accomplished by a willing and united people in a short time. (1) Consider the costliness of the Tabernacle. (2) Consider the skill required. (*D. C. Hughes, M.A.*) *Free gifts for the Tabernacle:*—I. ART SHOULD BE CONSECRATED TO THE SERVICE AND WORSHIP OF GOD. Emptiness and gloom do not honour Him whose are the silver and the gold, and whose handiwork is manifest in star and crystal, flower and feather. We cannot go far wrong when the Word of God encourages us in chaste use of symbols, making art the handmaid of religion, and every avenue to the soul a highway to God. II. THE ARTIZAN'S CALLING IS HONOURED OF GOD AND HIS LAWGIVER. He who is diligent in business and fervent in spirit serves the Lord, and even in our manual occupations we may be fellow-workers with God. He who works rightly is so far God-like. III. GIVING, WHEN RIGHTLY DONE, IS AN ACT OF WORSHIP. To hear the Word without an offering is to be a hearer of it and not a doer. Stinginess in a Christian contradicts the cross and its lesson. We are to give promptly and regularly. Zeal cools by delay. Ideas shrink and vision shortens when the heart is not roused. Like the willing people before Moses, let us give now and see the good of our gifts while we live. Better be our own executors, writing our wills on living human hearts rather than on the skins of dead sheep or lawyers' foolscap. IV. IMPULSIVE GENEROSITY IS NOT TO BE CONTEMNED. Sentiment is more powerful than logic, and every minister of Christ and leader of men should imitate Moses, who proved himself, under God, a heart-rousing, pocket-compelling preacher. To thrill the money-nerve unto good ends is a noble achievement. Then the maid forgets her ornaments. The lady's jewels are cast into the molten mass that is to make a church bell, supply the needs of the battle-field, the hospital, or the famine-stricken land. V. THE PATH OF SAC-RIFICE LEADS US TO CHRIST AND HIS CROSS. The heart that prompts the offer of the cup of cold water, when cultivated by Divine grace to highest possibilities, rests only under the cross of Calvary. (*William E. Griffis.*) *Materials and offerings :* —I. THE MATERIALS OF WHICH THE TABERNACLE WAS MADE. 1. Various. Nothing is too good for God's service. Common things are useful, and not to be despised. The meanest things may be sanctified to God's service. In the Church of Christ we find persons of all nations and stations. Sinners of every degree, colour, character, and size; redeemed, called, sanctified, and blessed, are the materials with which God builds His spiritual house. 2. Suitable. We cannot improve on God's choice, nor conceive of a better plan. So in the Church of God perfect wisdom is seen. His glory is great in our salvation. Christ will have a revenue of praise from every soul He rescues from hell. Great sinners are just suitable for a great Saviour. 3. Very costly. Who can tell the value of one soul? 4. Mostly from Egypt. God gathers all the materials for His sanctuary out of the house of bondage. 5. Beautiful. 6. Durable. II. THE WILLING PEOPLE WHO BROUGHT THE MATERIALS. A beautiful illustration of the fruit and effect of God's forgiving love. Having willing hearts, the people brought willing offerings. All classes had a share in the giving—poor as well as rich—and all their gifts were accepted. III. THE SKILFUL WORKMEN WHO BROUGHT THE MATERIALS INTO BEAUTEOUS FORM. (*R. E. Sears.*) *Voluntary contributions for Church work :*—I. LET US COMPARE THEIR DESIGN IN ERECTING THE TABERNACLE WITH OURS. It was to establish a religion which, when we consider, we cannot but rejoice that we live in brighter days. Not that we would speak disrespectfully of a system which God Himself instituted; but we may safely say that it was inferior to ours. When the Jews laboured to build the Tabernacle they laboured to establish a religion that was—1. Obscure. There was some light, but it was mingled with much darkness. The truths taught were enveloped in obscurity. 2. Their system was contracted. When they sought to build a Tabernacle, it was only for the use of a million or a million and a half of people. Theirs was a spirit of sectarianism. It was wisely appointed, indeed, to keep them from mingling with the heathen around them. But we cannot help rejoicing that we are not thus shut up. The gospel is designed for all nations, tongues, and people. 3. Their system was burdensome. Their observances were pompous, their rites were numerous and costly. But our yoke, in this respect, is easy, our burden is light. Here are but few institutions, and those are simple and efficient. 4. Their system was temporary. It was only suited to the Jewish meridian, it was only adapted to the service of the Tabernacle. Whereas the Christian system is adapted to every government, for it interferes with none ; to every climate, for it is not regulated by the usages of country ; to all people, for it is alike friendly to all. II. LET US COMPARE THE EXERTIONS OF THE JEWS WITH OURS, IN REFERENCE TO THESE RESPECTIVE SYSTEMS. 1. Their exertions were prompt. 2. General. 3. Proportionate. All seemed to ask, " What talent have I by which I may promote this cause? " If our Churches were possessed of this spirit, how much more would be done : ministers can preach and speak, but there must be collectors also, distributors of reports, &c. Those who have not a ready tongue, may have a flowing pen. III. LET US CONSIDER THE OBLIGATIONS UNDER WHICH THEY WERE LAID, AND UNDER WHICH WE ALSO ARE LAID. 1. They had received a revelation from heaven. If they who received a revelation under the influence of terror did so much, we ought surely to do more! If they did so much under the smoke of Sinai, ought not the droppings of the cross to influence us? Oh, let us feel ashamed that we have made so few exertions. 2. They had experienced merciful deliverances from heaven. 3. They had enjoyed merciful supplies from heaven. (*J. Blackburn.*) *The popular response :*—1. The answer of the people was marked by the spirit of willinghood. Some form of the word willing occurs again and again : " Every one whom his spirit made willing "; " As many as were willing-hearted." God will have nothing out of the reluctant hand. We may throw an offering down, but it is not taken up by heaven. It evaporates downwards; it is not received by the condescending and sympathetic sun. 2. The answer was the deepest and truest cure of all murmuring. The people had been murmuring again and again, but the moment they began to work they ceased to complain. You would murmur less if you worked more. An evil thing is idleness. It must always sit with coldness, and the two must keep one another in evil countenance. The one thing to be feared is stagnation. Hear heaven's sweet appeal for service, for sacrifice, and know that the appeal is not the demand of exaggeration, but that it is inspired by the very spirit of consideration for human feeling, and expresses the very philosophy of human spiritual education. (*J. Parker, D.D.*) *Gifts to the Lord:*—I. The spirit of the people was thoroughly DEVOTIONAL. It will result in no success whatsoever to attempt to manage the Lord's interests in a merely mercenary and marketable way. Any Church enterprise will fail if it only seeks to please a crowd, to fire the ambition of a denomination, or become a monument of personal pride. For this is not its end; its purpose is salvation of lost souls, and anything short of that is simply waste of money and zeal. We have heard it said that once the venerable keeper of the Eddystone lighthouse was completely prostrated by the wild conflict of the ocean during a violent storm which threatened to destroy the slender shaft of stone out in the midst of the waves. He joined the small company of his helpers in guarding the windows, defending the doors, saving the boats, fastening the broken chains, till he used up his infirm strength completely. They laid him down in one of the little chambers to die, for no one could be spared to watch. After a while they came to tell him the storm was abating; but, left for a moment, he had crept up the stairs to the lantern, and was there feebly trimming the lamps. "I was afraid some vessel might miss the light," he said in explanation. They told him, a little petulantly, that he might have spared his strength to help preserve the building. "No, no," he answered, with an anxious look out over the offing; "I was not put out here to save lighthouses, but to save ships!" II. The spirit of the people was universally INDUSTRIOUS. Personal labour is more valuable often than money in the Lord's service, for it more surely carries the heart with it. There is an exquisite little story told us in the classics, of one Cressinus, whom the Romans arrested for witchcraft because he grew opulent on so small a farm. But he came to the judgment producing his tools, and displaying his hardened hands: "These are my sorceries," he exclaimed; "these implements of honest toil are all the witcheries I know of!" And they freed him on the plea. The eight fingers and two thumbs of Christians are the best ten friends that any congregation in difficulties ever has found under God. III. The spirit of the people was self-sacrificingly LIBERAL. There was once a man who was prospered in business and grew wealthy. Then he lavished his fortune in house and equipage, and in all personal indulgence of self. He suddenly failed, and in shame and sorrow stood by while his furniture and pictures, his horses and plate, were scattered among strangers by the glib auctioneer. Some days afterwards he happened to be present at the dedication of a mission chapel for the poor, which a Christian friend had just erected. "Ah, how I wish," said he, as his memory told him of his improvident excesses in former times—"how I wish now that some of the wealth I wasted was invested here with yours in this building, which will be doing God's service long after I am forgotten!" IV. The spirit of the people was prayerfully INGENIOUS. The principle of division of labour was carried into use among the people so that every sort of fitness should be put into service. Really, the rule appears to have been that every one should do the exact thing he could do the best, and give all he was able to offer in the line of unobtrusive contribution. There was certainly something for each man and each woman to do; and they all became alert to find out their vocation. It is remarkable to see how unconscious they are of any claim to special praise. There is no clapping of hands for each other; there is no plaudit from the skies. The famous statue of Phidias, called the Olympian Jove, was reckoned one of the wonders of the world; and the Grecian orators used to declare that on its completion Jove himself struck the pavement in front of it with glorious lightning in token of his approbation. This will do very well as a tale for a superstitious and self-seeking multitude. But our God never compliments human industry, nor flatters his creatures for simply doing their duty. They must be content to wait with the approval of their own consciences, and watch the rising of each fair enterprise like a tabernacle for God's dwelling. V. The spirit of the people was enthusiastically AFFECTIONATE. Over and over again we are reminded that their hearts were in every case " stirred up," and their spirits were made " willing-hearted." It is not even worth while to delay in illustrating this point; for the whole after history shows that their success in such a vast undertaking came from the same temper as that which actuated the nation in after times when building the Temple : " The people had a mind to work." Therein is our very best lesson for modern endeavour. (*C. S. Robinson, D.D.*)   *Willinghood :*—I. DESCRIBE THE WILLING OFFERER. He is one who gives—1. As much as he can. 2. Of the best he has. 3. Cheerfully, as to the Lord. II. OFFER SOME REASONS FOR WILLINGNESS IN THE SERVICE OF GOD. 1. The Lord loves a cheerful giver. 2. The value of what is given in enhanced by the manner of the bestowment. 3. The willingness of one stirs the liberality of others. 4. Good works are often delayed, fatally, by the slowness of giving. 5. We are not our own, and all we have is God's. 6. God gave " this unspeakable gift " willingly. (*Biblical Museum.*)   *Strange offerings :*—About nine o'clock in the morning the people gathered together in the church. Fully five hundred natives were present, and the building seemed to be well filled. It is hard to say how many the Port Moresby church will hold. The people sit on the floor. They have a way of folding up their legs and then sitting on them, and this saves space by doing away with all need for chairs. They can stay seated in this cramped position for an hour or two. Upon this occasion the floor was almost entirely covered with people who listened well to what was said. I have never faced such a congregation before. Towards the front the people were simply but decently dressed. Many of them were young men and women who are being trained for native teachers in the Mission School. You had only to look a few yards behind them to see the naked savage sitting almost motionless, and looking just a little hideous in his grotesque ornamentation. To look from one man to another was to see what has been done, and what can be done for these people by the gospel of Christ. The collection was a very strange one. Very few of the people have any money, so, instead of silver and gold, they brought such as they have—viz., 325 spears, 65 shell armlets, 92 bows, 180 arrows, besides shields, drums, shell necklaces, feather and other ornaments. Altogether, counting money given by the missionaries and the native teachers, the collection was worth £30 1s. 6d. (*Lewis, Missionary in New Guinea.*) *Self-denying offerings of women :*—General Longstreet, speaking of the struggle at Centreville, says : " The Federals had been using balloons in examining our positions, and we watched with envious eyes their beautiful observations, as they floated high up in the air, and well out of the range of our guns. We longed for the balloon that poverty denied us. A genius arose for the occasion and suggested that we send out and gather together all the silk dresses in the Confederacy and make a balloon. It was done, and soon we had a great patchwork ship of many and varied hues." (*H. O. Mackey.*)   *Consecrated jewels :*—A few months before the death of Miss Frances Ridley Havergal, the sweet and accomplished missionary poetess, she sent to the Church Missionary Society her jewels, value £50. Had she been strong enough, she herself would have gone to India. *Consecrated plate :*—Lord Shaftesbury, on one occasion, said to me, " I am going to build a schoolroom in your parish." I knew that he had a good many claims on him, and I said " Let me help you to collect the funds." But he would not, and he built schoolrooms in two of the parishes on the estate. Afterwards he said to me, " You asked me to allow you to help me in collecting funds, but I thought it was not my duty to do so. Do you know how I got the money ? " I said, " No, of course I do not." " Well," he said, " I found I had so much more plate left me by my father than I wanted, that I thought I would sell enough to build these two schoolrooms." (*Bp. Bickersteth.*) *The motive to liberality :*—Diodorus Siculus relates that the forest of the Pyrenean Mountains being set on fire, and the heat penetrating to the soil, a pure stream of silver gushed forth from the bosom of the earth and revealed for the first time the existence of those rich lodes afterwards so celebrated. Let the melting influence of the cross be felt, let the fire of the gospel be kindled in the Church, and its ample stores shall be seen flowing from their hidden recesses and becoming "the fine gold of the sanctuary. (*J. Harris.*)   *Offerings of devotion :*—The Rev. Dr. D. Fraser tells the following :—After a sermon preached by him at the opening of a church elsewhere, a lady of fashionable position in society came to him. " Why should I have two watches while the house of God remains unpaid for ? " He replied, " Really, I cannot tell why." She then said, " Well, I will give the better watch of the two toward the cost of the church." She did so, and a jeweller paid £25 for it, which was a sensible addition to the fund. Dr. Fraser added that at another collection, on the previous Sunday, a lady who had not a piece of gold, and who did not care to give silver, took the chain off her neck and put it on the plate. She would lose nothing by that. They might say that these were impulsive women. Well, impulsive women might rise up to condemn illiberal men in the day of the Lord. *Variety of offerings in God's treasury :*—I remember once being in the treasury of a royal palace. There was a long gallery in which the Crown valuables were stored. In one compartment there was a great display of emeralds, and diamonds, and rubies, and I know not what, that had been looted from some Indian rajah or other. And in the next case there lay a common quill pen, and beside it a little bit of discoloured coarse serge. The pen had signed some important treaty, and the serge was a fragment of a flag that had been borne triumphant from a field where a nation's destinies had been sealed. The two together were worth a farthing at the outside, but they held their own among the jewels, because they spoke of brain-work and bloodshed in the service of the king. Many strangely conjoined things lie side by side in God's jewel-cases. Things which people vulgarly call large and valuable, and what people still more vulgarly call small and worthless, have a way of getting together there. For in that place the arrangement is not in order of what the thing will fetch if it is sold, but what was the thought in the mind and the emotion in the heart which gave it. Jewels and camel's hair, yarn and gold and silver, are all massed together. Wood is wanted for the temple quite as much as gold and silver and precious stones. So, whatever we have, let us bring that; and whatever we are, let us bring that. If we be poor and our work small, and our natures limited, and our faculties confined, it does not matter. A man is accepted "according to that he hath, and not according to that he hath not." He gives much who gives all, though his all be little; he gives little who gives a part, though the part be much. The motive sanctifies the act, and the completeness of the consecration magnifies it. Great and small are not words for God's kingdom, in which the standard is not quantity but quality, and quality is settled by the purity of the love which prompts the deed, and the consequent thoroughness of self-surrender which it expresses. Whoever serves God with a whole heart will render to Him a whole strength, and will thus bring Him the gifts which He most desires. (*A. Maclaren, D.D.*) *Willing offerings acceptable to God :*—There was once a missionary meeting held in the West Indies among the negroes, at which these three resolutions were agreed upon—1. We will all give something. 2. We will give as God has prospered us. 3. We will all give willingly. As soon as the meeting was over, a leading negro took his seat at the table, with pen and ink, to put down what each came to give. Many came forward to give, some more and some less. Amongst those that came was a rich old negro, almost as rich as all the others put together, and threw down upon the table a small silver coin. "Take dat back again," said the negro that received the money; "dat may be according to de first resolution, but it not according to de second." The rich man accordingly took it up, and hobbled back to his seat in a great rage. One after another came forward, and as almost all gave more than himself, he was fairly ashamed of himself, and again threw down a piece of money on the table, saying, "Dare! take that!" It was a valuable piece of money: but it was given so ill-temperedly, that the negro answered again, "No! dat won't do yet! It may be according to de first and second resolutions, but it is not according to de last"; and he was obliged to take up his coin again. Still angry at himself and all the rest, he sat a long time, till nearly all were gone, and then came up to the table, and with a smile on his face, and very willingly, gave a large sum to the treasurer. "Very well," said the negro, "dat will do; dat according to all de resolutions." Whatever we do for the worship and service of God, we should do it freely, cheer-fully, and cordially. "God loveth a cheerful giver." If cheerful giving to God's cause was required under the old dispensation, how much more is it required under the new! *I must give before I can pray :*—The venerable Dr. Sewall, of Maine, once entered a meeting in behalf of foreign missions, just as the collectors of the contribu-tions were resuming their seats. The chairman of the meeting requested him to lead in prayer. The old gentleman stood hesitatingly, as if he had not heard the request. It was repeated in a louder voice, but there was no response. It was observed, however, that Dr. Sewall was fumbling in his pockets, and presently he produced a piece of money, which he deposited in the contribution box. The chairman, think-ing he had not been understood, said loudly, "I didn't ask you to give, Dr. Sewall, I asked you to pray." "Oh, yes," he replied, "I heard you, but I can't pray till I have given something." *The worth of youthful giving :*—The Rev. Dr. Dickson, of Baltimore, in an address at the Maryland State Sabbath-school Convention, spoke of the need of cultivating " the grace of giving " in early life. Twenty years ago, he said, he proposed to his Sabbath-school superintendent to take up a collection every Sabbath morning from the children. " Why, my dear pastor," exclaimed the superintendent, " you shear the sheep pretty often, and this looks really like wanting to shear the tender lambs ! " The thought startled the speaker. A few days after, however, he was in the store of one of his parishioners, purchasing stockings. He had selected a good article, as he thought, when the merchant inquired, " Why do you not select the lambs' wool ? " " Lambs' wool ! why, are they better ? " " Yes, they are a world softer, far more pliable, and I believe wear longer than those made from old sheep's wool." He did not remember, and needed not to inform the hearers, whether he took the stockings ; but he knew that he took the fact to his superintendent, telling him that " lambs' wool was the best wool, and he meant to try it ! " The many early traits of selfishness, avarice, covetousness, subdued by the earlier formed habits of giving in children who could tell !

Vers. 30–34. **To devise curious works.**—*Bezaleel ; or, invention, art, and religion :*—Religion may not despise art and inventive power. It should absorb everything that can give pure joy and assist devotion. The best art generally has a Godward look. I. ART AND CHRISTIANITY BOTH IMPLY WORK. Indolence is disgrace. Work is honourable, whether it be the work of the horny hand, the skilful touch, or the busy brain. There is no curse upon work, unless when poorly paid. Indeed, the world would be accursed if there were no work, no art, no skill. II. ART AND SCIENCE, LIKE RELIGION, STIMULATE THOUGHT. Man, weak in bodily frame, is to be strong by the exercise of mind. Thought is to overcome force, and ingenuity inertness. We believe that Christianity will flourish best where there is truest art culture and deepest reverence arising from contemplation of God's works. III. ART, SCIENCE, AND CHRISTIANITY ALIKE TEACH US THAT WE ARE MUTUALLY DEPENDENT. The comforts and joys, as well as the necessaries of life, are the result of much thought and care on the part of others. IV. ART AND SCIENCE, LIKE CHRISTIANITY, ARE USEFUL IN FOSTERING PURER AND HIGHER TASTES. God intended that we should be educated in this way to appreciate something higher in the better world. (*F. Hastings.*) *The true design of work :*—We are accustomed to limit the inspiration of God's Spirit to thoughts and words. For this. however, we have no warrant in Scripture. The sevenfold Spirit has differences of administration and operation. The body as well as the soul experiences His sanctifying influence. He enters the sphere of man's labour as well as of his thought, and inspires the work of his hands as well as the meditations of his mind. The same Spirit that inspired the eloquence of Isaiah, and the melodies of the chief musician Asaph, also imparted to Samson that marvellous bodily strength which he displayed in Herculean labours, and tremendous feats against the Philistines ; and to Bezaleel and Aholiab that fine æsthetic taste and mechanical skill, by which they were enabled to construct the Tabernacle after the pattern shown on the mount. What is the lesson conveyed to us by the Theocratic government of Israel, whose affairs, secular and religious, national and individual, were regulated directly by God Himself ? Is it not that the whole of life is one ; that true religion is the proper use of man's whole being, and of the universe around him ? What does the ascension of our Lord teach us ? Is it not the unity of life ; the oneness of the natural and the religious life ? Godliness is now profitable unto all things. It is not the setting up of an estrangement between man and the outer world, but the working out of a true harmony between them ; not the elimination of any of the elements of man's life, but the proper blending of the whole—the sanctification of body, soul, and spirit ; the doing all, whether we eat or drink, or whatsoever we do, to the glory of God. Bearing in mind this solemn truth of the unity of all life, let me proceed to consider the significance of the inspiration of Bezaleel and Aholiab. This fact is not of individual but of general application. It is not unique, but representative. The Tabernacle of the wilderness was a miniature model of the whole earth, just as the people of Israel were the miniature pattern of all nations. Every man has a part assigned to him in the erection and adorning of this wonderful Tabernacle, whose floor is the green fields, whose walls are the rocks and mountains, and whose roof is the ever-changing sky. Every man who does a day's work is a fellow-worker with God, in carrying out His great design in creation, in improving the face of nature, changing the wilderness into a garden, in making the world fairer and richer, and better fitted to be the home of redeemed man, and the shrine of the Most High God. Toil is the first stage of the process of redemption—" the condition of man's elevation out of the state of a sinful, suffering, degraded creature, to the friendship, fellowship, and likeness of God.' In the Pacific Ocean there are lovely islands built entirely by coral zoophytes, out of the profound depths of the ocean. Raised above the waves, floating germs of vegetation alight on them, and speedily cover them with a fair clothing of verdure. Man comes and takes up his abode on these Edens, and makes their resources subservient to the purposes of human life. By and by the missionary appears, and by the preaching of the gospel changes the moral wilderness into a garden of the Lord. The last great result is thus but the completion of a process begun by the mere natural instinct of a creature in the depths of the ocean. The work of the missionary rests upon, and is closely connected with, the work of the polyp. So is it with human toil. It may be a mere instinctive process carried on in the depths of spiritual ignorance; a blind, aimless motion, having no higher object than the mere satisfying of natural wants. Man may be induced to work purely by physical necessity, because he cannot otherwise get his bread ; and yet toil is absolutely necessary as the foundation upon which the spiritual structure of our soul's salvation is laid. The effects of the fall began indeed in the soul; and it is in the soul that they must first be counteracted. The work of grace is radical. It begins in the heart, and spreads outwardly through the life. But work is the fulcrum by which its blessed leverage is exerted, the discipline through which it is carried out. Toil, first of all, teaches man his utter poverty. He forfeited life and all the means of life by his sin. As an outlaw under sentence of outlawry, he can hold no possessions whatever; he has no right even to his daily bread. But further, toil makes man subject to the law which he has broken. He sought to escape from law by his transgression. Striving to escape from the beneficent law of God, he fell under the cruel law of poverty, hunger, and death. He must become, as Mr. Brown says, the servant of the laws by which God maintains the order and life of the world, if he would earn the smallest blessing from their co-operation. Only by falling in with the Divine rule in every work can any man hope to succeed in it. Those who conquer nature are those who comprehend and obey her. But further still, toil opens the door into the sphere of duty, and is the hinge on which the deepest relationships and richest experiences of life turn. Not for himself does any man toil. Wife and children have to be provided for. But the highest ministry which our toil performs is to bring us into communion and fellowship with God our Redeemer, to make us fellow-workers with God. We enter into His purposes, comprehend His plans, and sympathize with His feelings. The patience which the husbandman exercises in waiting through the long summer months for the fruit of what he sows, and which the artist and mechanic display in slowly developing their special work, enables us in some measure to understand the patience of God in His work of providence and redemption. The disappointments and failures to which all kinds of work are exposed, prepare us for sympathizing with God's grief over the ruins of the world which He had made all very good, and over the disappointments which He meets in His redemption work. The courage, the faith, the devotion, the perseverance, the self-denial which our daily work calls forth, are closely related to our higher moral and spiritual discipline, and have the most important effect in redeeming us from the consequences of the fall. We need the inspiration of God's Spirit—the inspiration which Bezaleel and Aholiab had—to rescue our work from the degradation into which it so easily slides, and make it what God meant it to be. The very labour of our hands sinks down into depraved methods, unless kept up by the ennobling influence of God's Spirit. The inspiration of the Spirit does not indeed impart gifts—does not stand in place of natural abilities and attainments. Men have different talents naturally; and a Christian may have only one talent, while a thoroughly worldly man may have ten. And yet it is marvellous what the inspiration of the Spirit can do, even in the absence or deficiency of natural attainments. The entrance of God's Word gives light, and makes the simple wise. Conversion is itself an education. Religion exalts and ennobles the whole man. It quickens and elevates all his powers, and makes itself felt in everything with which he has to do. We see the marvellous influence of the Christian religion, even although mixed with much superstition, in the art of the Middle Ages—in those paintings of sacred subjects, and those abbeys and cathedrals which are the admiration of our age. There is nothing in Christianity that forbids, but, on the contrary, everything that favours the widest expansion, the loftiest achievement of the human mind, and the most skilful production of the human hand. It behoves all who are Christians, then, to show what Christianity can do in the way of purifying and ennobling common every-day work. Let us seek to make our work an essential part of our religion. The labour of Bezaleel, from a worldly point of view, was evanescent. The Tabernacle which he constructed with such rare skill, passed away; all its precious materials and workmanship disappeared like a beautiful dream of the morning, and not a trace of them now remains on the face of the earth. And yet, notwithstanding this, the work of Bezaleel was abiding in its spiritual results. Israel reaped the benefit of it through all their generations. We ourselves are the better for it to-day. (*H. Macmillan, D.D.*) *Inspiration for handicraft:*—No nobler thought of God, no more welcome gospel, after an assurance of purifying grace, has been uttered than this which these verses hold. Fallacious and fatal is the thought that a man can live a divided life. Hopeless is his struggle to " serve two masters." And surely few heresies have done so much damage to religion as that which would lead a man to think that the things which necessarily occupy a large proportion of his time and energy are matters of no concern to the God who claims his worship, and that to Him the toil of the industrious, the genius of the skilful, the patience of the earnest, with all the products of such life's endeavour, are things of no moment, lying outside the region of His care and cognizance. Honour to the soul that rises in revolt against an injustice to God and man ! I meet with men who are troubled by this misconception ; men who need, as we all need, help from God day by day, and all day long ; men who, if their industry cannot be brought within the sphere of their religion, feel that they must be irreligious, or at all events unreligious for the greater part of their life. Let me try to win such men from their mistake by setting before them this truth of God. Do you not feel how full-charged this truth is with the power of quickening and redeeming grace ? Do you not feel how all-inclusive this truth is, how it touches every man, and makes his whole self worthy, how it touches the whole of the man, and leaves nothing of him outside of Divine help, nothing of him undignified by Divine overruling ? Let us put the truth into plain words, and look it straight in the face—power of hand and brain is of God and for God. It has a comely aspect, significant of hope, voiceful with strenuous incentive, calm with conscious triumph. We are brought just back to this simple, ancient way of putting the fact, after all the revelations and imaginations concerning species and development, which have been given to the world. Genius may be largely hereditary, special capacities may be cultured and developed. But who planned the conditions and the laws? It is interesting to discover method; but method is not cause. Knowledge of the means through which anything is done is not the same as a knowledge of that *by* which the thing is done. I don't know, I don't believe that any one wants to try to prove atheism. But we might almost as well doubt the very existence of our God as fail to reap the great harvest of privilege which springs from this great seed-truth, " in Him we live and move and have our being." Oh, if all the thinkers and workers in the world, our fellows and associates in the office and the warehouse, in the factory and in the foundry, could be brought to feel this, what a power for good would grow ! If men and women went into each day's toil with not a vague, shadowy idea, but a great and vivid conviction that the strength, the skill, the ingenuity, power of adroit and delicate touch, power of fanciful and beautiful designing, strength to sling the hammer and make the anvil ring, delicacy, deftness, knack, that indescribable way of doing just the right thing at the right time, which is so marvellous to watch—that all this is a Divine gift bearing the seal of the Most High God, the pledge of His thought and care and love, a holy trust to be used for Him—would not such a conviction be as good as it was great, as redemptive as it was real ? It makes all the difference between drudgery and duty, between toil and work. It changes hard labour, recompensed by coin of the realm by which a man's debts are paid and his needs met, into an exultant exercise of power, recompensed by the approval of a conscience void of offence, recompensed more gloriously by the approval of the Master who was once Himself a workman and is eternally a worker: " Well done, good and faithful servant : enter thou into the joy of thy Lord." I appeal to those who listen to me to get rid of the fallacy and to get hold of the fact. The call to labour is a summons to high privilege. The inspiration to true labour has its origin in God. Take the truth with you to-morrow, friend, and it will lift your life out of its monotony and rid it of any aspect of dreariness. It will put a soul into what has, perhaps, been a lifeless thing. It will send a glow to you through what, perhaps, hitherto has chilled your very heart.

It was the Lord God who put wisdom and understanding into every wise-hearted man " to know how to work all manner of work for the service of the sanctuary," and He, the Lord, is " the same yesterday, and to-day, and for ever." This brings me naturally to the emphasizing of another point illustrated here : that the power, the disposition to use the skill is also a Divine gift. I say use, for misuse and abuse are of a man's own selfishness. Often do we hear the question, " What will he do with it ? " Now I imagine that a man who has felt the pressure of the solemn fact of which I have spoken, namely, that power of hand and brain is of and for God, will be found looking for this second fact—that power to use the skill is also a gift from Him. If I discover that I am in possession of some precious thing which has come to me from God, the natural and immediate impulse will be to look to Him for guidance and power in the use of it. I am anxious not to misuse it. I fear to make a mistake. A man makes a sorry bargain who sells himself for money or for the passing gratification of his senses. Yet men have been tempted to abuse their skill, intelligence, strength, by the doing of a deed, one result of which was the enabling them to say, " That pile of gold is mine," a saying which could only be true for a time, and another result of which was the withering and maiming of their very soul. I believe in the possibility of consecrating all endeavour. I believe that daily labour in any man's lawful calling may be ennobled with the grandeur of Divine service. If, then, you and I feel gracious influences and powers leading and qualifying us to use our force and skill in this highest way, " not with eye-service as men-pleasers," but with " singleness of heart " as reverencing God, thankfully may we recognize the influence as His influence, the power as His power, the grace as His grace. Mental endowment and power of speech, physical endowment and power of handicraft, are high gifts, and the generosity is meant for good. (*D. Jones Hamer.*)   *Consecrated ability :*—There was, of course, a special Divine influence on these two artists ; but in a very real sense, it is true of every man of genius that his excellence has been given him by God, and he should seek to consecrate it to God's service. Let us be just, also, and add that, in a large proportion of instances, they have done so. Take the noblest things in poetry, music, architecture, and painting, and you will find that they have been done in the service of God, and have a religious significance. The grandest epic in our language is on a religious theme ; and some of our grandest lyrics have come from the harp of a pious heart, swept by the breeze of a holy influence. What are the oratorios of Handel but the consecration of his genius to Jehovah? and the finest specimens of architecture which Europe has to show are its venerable cathedrals, every one of which, in the ideal of its designer, was a sermon in stone. The greatest triumphs of the painter have been in the delineations of sacred subjects ; and many among them who have become famous have, like the Fra Angelico, done their work upon their knees. . . . Every true product of art, no matter in what department, is a poem ; and if we can adopt the lyrics of the singer into our hymnology, why should we not encourage our artists to preach on the canvas and in the marble ? Never minister gave a more eloquent sermon than that painted by Holman Hunt in " The Light of the World." And the advantage is on the painter's side in more ways than one, for, while the sermon dies out of recollection, the picture lives. So let us encourage men of genius to consecrate their abilities to God's service ; and then, perhaps, the time will come when, in the highest of all senses, " the day of the Lord shall be upon all pleasant pictures." (*W. M. Taylor, D.D.*)   *Art inspiration :*—Few minds are sunlike, sources of light to themselves and to others. Most are moons, which shine with a derivative and reflected light. Bezaleel and Aholiab drew their skill from Divine inspiration. Indeed, it has been said by Cicero that all great men are in some degree inspired. They are Divinely qualified for their respective missions. Was not Gutenburg inspired to invent printing, with the view to a world-wide diffusion of the Word of God ? The history of nations and of the Church afford numerous illustrations of this species of inspiration in the raising up of special men to certain works when such needed to be done. *Artistic education of Israelites in Egypt :*—Under Jehovah's merciful providence even the captivity of Israel had a sunny side. Egypt, then at the noon of her civilization, was pre-eminently the home of science, art, and culture. For both rede-craft and hand-craft her children were world-famed. The Israelites were educated in a school of fine arts as well as in brickyards. Not all their sons and daughters toiled in clay, or ate only cheapest bread and onions. Many were house and body servants to Egyptian ladies and gentlemen. The brighter and more dexterous learned trades ; and though slaves, served their masters as skilled mechanics or workers in

1

art products. Not a few secured first-class knowledge in stamping, chasing, and various branches of metal-work, in the lapidary and glyptic art, as well as in weaving, dyeing, carpentry, and leather-dressing. In addition to their theoretical knowledge and practical handicraft, they had pretty full sets of models and master-pieces of mechanism. The keepsakes and souvenirs borrowed from the Egyptians were easily copied and manufactured, when raw material from mine and flock, sea and soil, in the Sinaitic peninsula were put to account. It was not entirely a " horde of slaves " that went up out of Egypt. Between the mob of ignorant freedmen and the princes, statesmen, and leaders inspired of God, stood another class of men : these were metallurgists, jewellers, engravers, architects, and weavers pos-sessing that skill, born of hand and brain working in harmony, without which a high civilization and the order of cities are impossible. (*W. E. Griffis.*) *Prayer for artistic skill answered :*—A young painter was directed by his master to complete a picture on which the master had been obliged to suspend his labours on account of his growing infirmities. "I commission thee, my son," said the aged artist, " to do thy best upon this work. Do thy best." The young man had such rever-ence for his master's skill, that he felt incompetent to touch canvas that bore the mark of that renowned hand. But " Do thy best " was the old man's calm reply; and again, to repeated solicitations, he answered, " Do thy best." The youth tremblingly seized the brush, and kneeling before his appointed work, he prayed: "It is for the sake of my beloved master that I implore skill and power to do this deed." His hand grew steady as he painted. Slumbering genius awoke in his eye. Enthusiasm took the place of fear. Forgetfulness of himself supplanted his self-distrust, and with a calm joy he finished his labour. The " beloved master " was borne on his couch into the studio, to pass judgment on the result. As his eye fell upon the triumph of art before him, he burst into tears, and throwing his enfeebled arms around the young artist, he exclaimed, "My son, I paint no more!" That youth, Leonardo da Vinci, became the painter of " The Last Supper," the ruins of which, after the lapse of three hundred years, still attract large numbers annually to the refectory of an obscure convent in Milan. (*Christian Journal.*) *Wisdom a Divine gift :*—A touching story is related of Thomas Telford, the Scottish mason who became one of the greatest of British engineers. His great scheme of a suspension bridge over the Menai Strait, connecting Carnarvonshire with the Isle of Anglesea, had passed through many stages of difficulty and doubt. Will and genius had battled with, and overcome the obstacles, and the bridge was a fact. An experiment had been made, and all went well. Enthusiastic friends missed the designer. They went to seek him, and to tell him how thoroughly his plans appeared to be justified, and how reward had come for labour and anxiety. Telford was found on his knees, lifting up his heart to God in adoration and prayer. He recognized that all wisdom and all power was a Divine trust, and that God was the Giver of all his good. This is the right way to take success. Such men do not lose in soul-stature through their prosperity.

CHAPTER XXXVI.

VERS. 1-38. **Every wise-hearted man in whom the Lord put wisdom and under-standing to know how to work.**—*Consecrated art :*—Dannecker, the German sculptor, occupied eight years upon a marble statue of Christ. He believed then, and ever afterward, that he had been inspired of God to do that thing. He thought that he had seen a vision of Christ in his solitary vigils. He had but transferred to the marble the image that the Lord had shown to him. His rising fame attracted the attention of Napoleon, and he was requested to make a statue of Venus similar to Ariadne, for the gallery of the Louvre. He refused, saying, " A man who has seen Christ would commit sacrilege if he should employ his art in the carving of a pagan goddess. My art is therefore a consecrated thing." Is there not an experience of communion with God in Christ, not uncommon with mature believers, which is equivalent to a vision of the Lord, and which renders life and life work, even its humblest occupations, sacred ? The lowliest not less than the loftiest life may have this element of an infinite dignity. *Indolence in the Church :*—A North American Indian convert, being catechised upon " original sin," stated that he rather thought that in *his* case it was laziness. Original sin certainly seems to take this form in the case of many members of our Churches. What is the proportion of Christian workers in any Church? Are they not invariably a small minority? Why so? What exemption can the majority plead? It is said the working bees cast out the drones from the hive. Were we to proceed upon this principle, what terrible depletion would our Churches suffer! (*J. Halsey.*) *False estimates of Church-workers :* —We sometimes form a too favourable estimate of the number of workers in our Churches, erroneously judging from the number of departments of service, and imagining that each department has its own distinct staff; whereas, as a rule, it is the individuals who are active in one sphere who display the same activity in another. I believe that in dramatic exhibitions the impression of a large army is sometimes produced upon the spectators by the device of marching the same band of persons over and over again across the stage. We get our impressions of the noble army of Christian workers very much in the same way. (*Ibid.*)

CHAPTER XXXVII.

See ch. xxv. 10–40; ch. xxx. 1–6, 23–38.

CHAPTER XXXVIII.

VER. 8. **The looking-glasses of the women.**—*The looking-glass and the laver :*— Unlike our looking-glasses made of silvered glass, which did not come into use till the thirteenth century, these primitive looking-glasses were made chiefly of an alloy of copper, tin, and lead, wrought with such admirable skill that it was capable of receiving the highest and most enduring polish. The mirror itself was a round or pear-shaped plate, often encircled with a wreath of leaves, or adorned with figures engraved upon the rim; and it was attached to a handle often carved with some elegant form of life. Numerous *specchi* of this kind have been found in Etruscan tombs, retaining their polish so brightly as sometimes to fit them for their original purpose; and having on their disks scenes of Etruscan life and manners, and representations or symbols of the national faith, illustrated by inscriptions in the native character, they have been well called by Bunsen "a figurative dictionary," eminently useful to the archæologist for the light they throw upon the creed and history of this ancient and most mysterious race. In Japan certain metal mirrors have acquired a magic fame, and are brought to this country as curiosities, on account of the figures which shine through them when seen in a certain light, while directly viewed they reflect only on their polished surface the face that looks into them. The specula of the Hebrew women were brought with them from Egypt, and doubtless formed part of the spoil which the Israelites took from the Egyptians at the time of the Exodus. In that country they were used not only in domestic economy, but also in the idolatrous worship of the temples; and probably the Hebrew women who assembled at the door of the Tabernacle of the congregation had adopted this custom, and worshipped the God of Israel as the Egyptian women worshipped Isis or Anubis, dressed in linen garments, holding a sistrum in their right hand and a mirror in their left. It is not without deep significance that this holy vessel, typical of spiritual cleansing, should have been formed of such materials. The whole transaction is a most beautiful and expressive symbol of the vast difference between the beauty which man sees in himself, and the beauty which God induces in him by the means of grace. In fact, the whole gospel scheme might be represented to the eye pictorially by these two emblematical objects—the looking-glass and the laver; for it shows us to ourselves, and it cleanses us from our impurity. 1. Let us look, in the first place, at the gospel as a mirror showing us to ourselves. Contemplating the features of our character in our own natural looking-glass, we are satisfied with the image that is reflected there. Comparing ourselves with ourselves we have no sense of contrast; we come up to our own ideal; we realize our own standard of goodness. Comparing ourselves with others we are raised in our own estimation ; we see many guilty of meannesses and follies which we should scorn. We feel like the self-righteous Pharisee in the temple, and thank God that we are not as other men, or as the publican beside us. But the gospel is the true mirror in which we see our true image reflected. The holiness of God, as it is revealed to us in the face of His Son Jesus Christ, is the best mirror in which to see reflected our own sinful image. That holiness is the part of the Divine image which we have completely lost in our fallen state. When the pure searching light of His law shines into our hearts, how defiled and unworthy do many things appear which before were regarded as clean and good ! What secret unsuspected sins are made manifest like the myriad motes which float in the sunbeams that enter a dark room ! How true it is, that those who are ignorant of God are ignorant of themselves ! The mirror must lead to the laver. Having learned what our true condition is, we must cease to look at ourselves, and have recourse to the cleansing bath which God has provided in the gospel for the sinner conscious of his sin. The fact that the laver was made of the looking-glasses teaches this practical lesson to us. We see our impurity in order that we may apply for cleansing. Our uncomeliness is revealed to us for the very purpose of causing us to seek for the beauty of holiness. 2. The laver made of the looking-glasses of the women stood in the court of the Tabernacle between the altar of burnt-offering and the door of the holy place. As the altar removed the legal obstacle that lay in the way of a sinner's access to God, so the laver removed the moral. The one by the atonement which it presented opened up the way to God ; the other by the purification which it effected qualified the believer for coming into God's presence. And viewed in this light, what an expressive symbol is it of the spiritual fountain opened in the house of David for sin and uncleanness ! The laver in which we are washed becomes the mirror in which we see our own reflection ; and the mirror of self-complacency, in which hitherto we sought to see visions of our own comeliness whereof to glory in the flesh, is converted into the fountain of life in which the discovery of our own vileness is overborne by the discovery of the surpassing, all-compensating loveliness of Him in whom God sees no iniquity in Jacob, and no perverseness in Israel. (*H. Macmillan, D.D.*)   *The laver and looking-glasses :*—I shall take that laver of looking-glasses, spoken of in the text, as all-suggestive of the gospel, which first shows us our sins as in a mirror, and then washes them away by Divine ablution. 1. Now, I have to say that this is the only looking-glass in which a man can see himself as he is. There are some mirrors that flatter the features, and make you look better than you are. Then there are other mirrors that distort your features, and make you look worse than you are ; but I want to tell you that this looking-glass of the gospel shows a man just as he is. When the priests entered the ancient Tabernacle, one glance at the burnished side of this laver showed them their need of cleansing. So this gospel shows the soul its need of Divine washing. " All have sinned, and come short of the glory of God." That is one showing. " All we, like sheep, have gone astray." That is another showing. In Hampton Court I saw a room where the four walls were covered with looking-glasses, and it made no difference which way you looked, you saw yourself. And so it is in this gospel of Christ. If you once step within its full precincts you will find your whole character reflected—every feature of moral deformity—every spot of moral taint. 2. I want you to notice that this laver in which the priests washed was filled with fresh water every morning. So it is with the gospel of Jesus Christ ; it has a fresh salvation every day. Come this morning and take the glittering robe of Christ's righteousness from the Saviour's hand. You were plunged in the fountain of the Saviour's mercy a quarter of a century ago. That is nothing to me ; I tell you to wash now in this laver of looking-glasses, and have your soul made clean. 3. I notice, also, in regard to this laver of looking-glasses spoken of in the text, that the priests always washed both hands and feet. The water came down in spouts, so that without leaving any filth in the basin, the priests washed both hands and feet. So the gospel of Jesus Christ must touch the very extremities of our moral nature. 4. I remark, further, that the laver of looking-glasses spoken of in the text, was a very large laver. I always thought from the fact that so many washed there, and also from the fact that Solomon afterwards, when he copied that laver in the temple, built it on a very large scale, that it was large, and so suggestive of the gospel of Jesus Christ and salvation by Him—vast in its provisions. The whole world may come and wash in this laver and be clean. 5. But I notice, also, in regard to this laver of looking-glasses spoken of in the text, that the washing in it was imperative and not optional. When the priests came into the Tabernacle (you will find this in the 30th chapter of Exodus), God tells them they must wash in that laver or die. The priests might have said : " Can't I wash elsewhere? I washed in the laver at home, and now you want me to wash here." God says, " No matter whether you have washed before. Wash in this laver or die." " But," says the priest, " there is water just as clean as this, why won't that do ? " " Wash here," says God, " or die." So it is with the gospel of Christ—it is imperative. There is only this alternative : keep our sins and perish, or wash them away and live. (*Dr. Talmage.*) *Old things turned to new uses :*—In many ancient religions women took a leading part in some of the ceremonies. This was so in Egypt. Each woman had a looking-glass made of polished brass, and that mirror was used in some way in connection with idolatrous practices. When the Tabernacle was being built the women gave up their mirrors and so contributed to the formation of the laver, which was made of brass, and the foot of it of brass. Thus we have old things turned to new uses, and it is for us to say whether we shall regard this incident as a piece of ancient history, or whether we shall enter into the spirit of it and realize the action in our own day and on a broader scale. How came the women to give up their looking-glasses to assist in constructing the laver ? Because a superior spirit had taken possession of them. That is the philosophy and that the explanation of the case. What then is the spirit that is to enter into us? None other than the spirit of Christ. We might use many words in describing the spirit, but all the words would focalize themselves at last in this sublime expression—" For Christ's sake." The highest personality is Christ. We follow Him, and in proportion as we follow Him all things we possess are His. There is room in the sanctuary for everything. This is the point we have so often missed in our Christian teaching. No punishment is burning enough for the men who would belittle God's house. What have you ? You have nothing that cannot be used in the building of God's house and kingdom. Have you nothing but the little looking-glass ? It can be used. Is yours, on the other hand, but one small flower which a child could pluck ? It was God's flower before it was yours, and He will never consent to lose a flower ; it cost Him thought and care and love ; He dressed the flower as Solomon never could dress himself. Blessed will be the day when the breweries of the country are turned into mechanics' institutes, great sanitary establishments for the washing and cleansing of the people. Blessed will be the day when the rich man's saloons shall be thrown open to the poorest neighbours he has who will come to look at his articles of *vertu,*—who will turn over his curiosities and examine them with honest fingers, and so admire them as to be touched into desire for broader life. Blessed—bright will be the day when in that sense we shall have all things common ; when the strong man's strength shall be the weak man's refuge ; when the homeless shall have a large home in the charity and love of his richer brother ; when the one object of every heart will be to extend the happiness of mankind—the one question in the morning being, What good can be done to-day ? and the one question at eventide, What good has been accomplished ? My persuasion is that if ever that time is to be brought about, it can only be by the extension of the spirit of Jesus Christ. Taking the Christian view, all becomes larger still and brighter, and the hope is given that one day everybody will be in the kingdom, and every man, woman, and child, will be doing their very best to make that kingdom what God means it to be. The great men, by heroic strength, by dauntless valour, will carry on their sublime occupation ; the patient women—gentle souls, having the genius of sympathy and the faculty of interpreting by suffering—will contribute their important, their ineffably valuable share ; and little children will make up the sum total of the consecration. (*J. Parker, D.D.*)

CHAPTER XXXIX.

Vers. 32–43. **They brought the Tabernacle unto Moses.**--*The delivery of the work to Moses :*—I. The presentation of the work : " They brought the Tabernacle unto Moses." So, whatever work or service is done in connection with the Christian Church should be solemnly presented to Christ, who is the Chief Builder of the Christian Temple. II. The inspection of the work : " Moses did look upon all the work " ; and so does Christ inspect every offering that is brought to Him. Paul tells us in 1 Cor. iii. 13, that a day is coming in which every man's work will be tried of what sort it is—tried by fire—tried with the most terrible exactness. III. THE APPROBATION OF THE WORK : "Behold, they had done it as the Lord had commanded." So in Christian service nothing can be accepted that is not minutely in accordance with the Divine specification. IV. THE REMUNERATION OF THE WORK: "And Moses blessed them." So is all faithful service done to Christ rewarded even here with spiritual blessing. So will it be in the end (1 Cor. iii. 14). Lessons: 1. The dignity of Christian work as presented to Christ. 2. The duty of fidelity in Christian work, considering it must be inspected by Christ. 3. The grand aim in Christian work, to be accepted by Christ. *Cf.* 2 Cor. v. 9. 4. The high stimulus in Christian work, the certainty of being rewarded by Christ. (*J. S. Exell, M.A.*) *The Tabernacle itself :*—The Tabernacle held an important position in the divinely-appointed worship of the Jewish Church. No less than thirteen chapters in the Book of Exodus (xxv.–xxxi. ; xxxv.–xl.) are devoted to the account of it; an account twice repeated, extending to the minutest details of shape, size, material, colour, and workmanship. Special stress is laid upon the fact that it was made after a heavenly design exhibited to Moses during the forty days of his mysterious communing with Jehovah on Mount Sinai (xxix. 9, 40; xxvi. 30). The smallest details are included in this heavenly pattern (xxvii. 8; Numb. viii. 4). This heavenly pattern of the Tabernacle is twice referred to in the New Testament (Acts vii. 44; Heb. viii. 5). Not only was the Tabernacle made after a heavenly pattern, but divinely-inspired artificers carried the design into execution (xxxi. 1–6; xxxv. 30–35 ; xxxvi. 1). We see from these passages that, in matters which concern the worship of God, the minutest details as to the colour, shape, material, and make of the ornaments of Divine service, and of the ministers of it, are not thought unworthy of a special Divine revelation as to their design, and of a special Divine inspiration for the carrying of that design into effect. At the close of the work we are told, in words that carry our thoughts back to the blessing bestowed upon the first creation (Gen. i. 30), that Moses recognized its exact accordance with the heavenly pattern which he had seen (xxxix. 43). (*E. F. Willis, M.A.*) *Names of the Tabernacle :*—It is called the House of Jehovah (Exod. xxiii. 19; Josh. vi. 24 ; 1 Sam. iii. 15); the Temple of Jehovah (1 Sam. iii. 3); the Sanctuary (Exod. xxv. 8; Lev. xii. 4 ; xvi. 33 ; xix. 30; xx. 3; xxi. 12; Numb. iii. 38, &c.) ; or simply, the Tabernacle (Exod. xxv. 9; xxvi. 16 ; xxvii. 9, 19, &c.); or Dwelling, *i.e.*, of God. The two most characteristic names, however, are, the Tent or Tabernacle of the Testimony (Numb. ix. 15; xvii. 22, &c.), and the Tent or Tabernacle of Meeting (Exod. xxvii. 21 ; xxxix. 32, 40; xl. 7, 34, 35, &c.). The name Tent or Tabernacle of the Testimony had reference to that which was one of the two chief objects of the Tabernacle, viz., to serve as a shrine for " the Testimony " —the two tables of stone on which were engraved the ten words of the Divine Law. The other characteristic name, that of Tabernacle or Tent of Meeting, speaks of the other chief end for which the Tabernacle existed, viz., to be a place of meeting between God and His people (Exod. xxv. 8, 22; xxix. 42–45 ; xxx. 6, 36). (*Ibid.*) *Completed labour :*—I. THE WORK WAS COMPLETED ACCORDING TO PLAN. II. It was completed IN A SHORT TIME. III. It was completed WITH GREAT JOY. The joy of—1. Knowing that each had done something, and that something his best. 2. Anticipation. IV. The completed work may remind us of the WORDS OF HIM WHO SAID, "I have finished the work Thou gavest Me to do." V. As the house in the wilderness was finished down to the last pin, so THE CHURCH IN THE WORLD, of which it was a type, shall be perfected down to the last and meanest member. *The Jewish Tabernacle :*—1. It was a school of object-lessons, designed to teach the ignorant and sensual Israelites the truths of the invisible and eternal kingdom of God. It was a small model of heavenly realities—a pattern of sight in the heavens (Heb. ix. 23). It was, in the realm of religious truth, something like the planetarium used in a recitation room in teaching astronomy. 2. The principal lessons it taught were—(1) The holiness of God. (2) The sinfulness of man. (3) The distance between God and man. (4) The fact that God will abide with man. (5) The Divine plan for bringing God and man into union.

CHAPTER XL.

VERS. 1–38. Set up the Tabernacle.—*The primary and universal obligation to the worship of Jehovah; the proper means to its right performance, with their evidences and fruits:*—I. WHAT IS IMPLIED IN THE INJUNCTION IN THE TEXT? 1. The worship of Jehovah, at whose command the Tabernacle was erected. 2. The setting up of the Tabernacle, at God's command, implied that He required a specific worship; and the doing this at the seasons expressed in the text, that He called for especial homage at particular times, and in an express manner; and a compliance with the direction was an evidence of obedience to the will of Jehovah. 3. But further, this setting up of the Tabernacle at God's command implied His sovereign rule and authority among the Jews. 4. Again, as the setting up of the Tabernacle at God's command implied His sovereignty, so a compliance with the injunction or direction implied a disposition to serve Him. II. HOW IT MAY BE CARRIED INTO EFFECT BY US. 1. It may be done by our punctual and devout attendance on Divine worship. 2. If we would carry the injunction in the text into effect suitably, we must duly observe and keep all the ordinances of God's house. 3. I observe that the spirit of the commandment before us will be carried into effect in a more especial manner by us if we make Christ the Alpha and Omega—the beginning and the ending of all our religious worship—the great object of faith and adoration in all our ceremonial observances. 4. Lastly, that your services may be suitable, acceptable, and efficient, seek the teaching and direction of the Holy Spirit. III. THE EVIDENCES WHICH WILL PROVE THAT IT HAS BEEN DONE. 1. In the first place, if you have set up your Tabernacle; if you are resolved that, whatever others do, as for you and your household ye will serve the Lord; and if you are enabled to approach Him in a suitable disposition, and by a right faith; then you will enjoy in your own souls all the blessings of His house, and the blessedness of those whom He causes to come near unto Him. 2. If you have set up your Tabernacle, and are led by the Spirit to serve God with your spirit, then you will bring forth the fruits of the Spirit (Ephes. v. 9; Gal. v. 22, 23; 1 Pet. iv. 11). 3. If we have set up our Tabernacle, and serve God in His Son, are led by His Spirit, and bring forth the fruits of the Spirit, then we shall be prepared for the rewards of the righteous, and to stand before the Son of man "at His appearing and His kingdom." Lessons: 1. As the command for the erection of the Tabernacle is given us by God, and every direction respecting it comes from Him, what presumption is it in any man to go about the formation of a different Tabernacle after his own fancy! 2. As the setting up of the Tabernacle was to be done forthwith at God's commandment, and for the whole congregation, what madness for any to think of postponing the duty to a more convenient season! 3. As the Tabernacle is erected for God's service, was to be resorted to at stated times, and attendance upon it is designed for our greatest good—as a Bethel, a house of mercy, a Bethesda, from which we may derive healing, how should we prize seasons, and means, and opportunities, of attending it! (*J. Allport.*)　　*The setting up of the Tabernacle on New Year's Day:*—Out of materials specially provided by Him who holds in His hands the springs of action in men, and by artizans inspired by an extraordinary skill, and according to the pattern given to Moses, the Tabernacle was prepared, every part made ready and stored up for the day of erection. But God named that day Himself, and Moses waited for it. I. And now I would have you notice THE SPECIAL DAY WHICH GOD SELECTED. It was the first day of the first month—that is, New Year's Day; and the reason of this choice is of course to be looked for in a benevolent regard to the religious good of the Jewish people. It would fix a suitable season for a commemorative festival of the great blessing vouchsafed to Israel by a Tabernacle for the Divine presence among them—a festival, be it remarked, that was not forgotten by them in after times, for we read that, in the revival of religion under Hezekiah, it was on the first day of the first month that the House of God was sanctified for the pious and pure worship of the Lord. Moreover, this selection would, I suppose, make New Year's Day, in the Jewish calendar, a day of religious observance. Consider, first, that the Christian's body and the Christian's spirit are together the Tabernacle of God. He is "an habitation of God through the Spirit." "Know ye not," saith the apostle to the Corinthian Christians, "that ye are the temples of the Holy Ghost?" "He that dwelleth in love," writes John, "dwelleth in God, and God in him." And wherever this indwelling of God is, there and there only is there a Christian man or a Christian woman; wherever there is this indwelling of God, there and there only is the true antitype of the beautiful Tabernacle which was set up on the first day of the first month in the Jewish calendar. This is the true Tabernacle, too, in which God rests for ever, because He delights therein. Now mark: such a wonderful Tabernacle like that which was put up by Moses on the first day of the first month can only be made of materials which God has selected, and which God has gathered together for that work; for the light and the elements and the features and graces of the Christian character are His gift, such as holy trust, humble desire, love, meekness, gratefulness, praise, prayer, and joy in Christ. And again, those materials must be wrought up and combined according to the pattern which has been shown to us in the mount. Marvellous pattern! the living model of the character of Jesus, the true Tabernacle of the Father. II. ISRAEL'S OBEDIENCE IS EXEMPLARY TO THOSE WHO ARE ALREADY CHRISTIAN MEN. There is some new work now for God to be done, or some old work for God to be done in a new spirit. For instance, responsibility of time to be more felt, and its management and use arranged with an increased Christian conscientiousness. The dedication of self to the Saviour has to be renewed, and everywhere and always remembered. Does not our work for Him who died for us want to be done secretly in the heart, openly in the family, and in the church, and in the world, with a new love, a new spirit, a new resoluteness, and a new will? Ah! a new year summons a Christian in a new manner of spirit unto obedience to his Divine Master. Let us, on such an occasion, listen to our Father's voice, and on the first day of the first month set up our Tabernacle; and then be assured that through all the journeyings of the year, as upon the Tabernacle of Israel, shall the tokens of the Divine presence rest upon us. III. For notice, in the next place, THAT ON THE FIRST DAY OF THE FIRST MONTH, IMMEDIATELY THE TABERNACLE WAS SET, THE CLOUD OF THE LORD WAS UPON IT BY DAY, AND THE FIRE OF THE LORD WAS UPON IT BY NIGHT, AND BOTH CONTINUED TO REST THERE THROUGH THE JOURNEYINGS OF THE PEOPLE. Oh! it must have been a marvellous phenomenon, that under which the Almighty God thus certified His protection and guidance to the people. And it was a necessary phenomenon, too, under their novel circumstances. The desert was pathless, and they had no guide, and so by this they were conducted in their journeyings. It was adapted, too, to meet their wants: it was "the pillar of cloud by day" to screen them from the fierce sun, and it was "the pillar of fire by night" to light up the encampment and warm the chill air. And is not Christian life a pilgrimage? Are we not strangers upon earth, seeking a better, a heavenly Temple? Could we reach it without a Divine Guide? And though we have not the same sensible proofs of God's presence which were granted to Israel, is it not most assuredly with us just as it was with them? (*C. P. Eyre, M.A.*) *Tabernacle foreshadowings:*—The Tabernacle, as a whole, is a finger-post directing me to that mystic Person in whom "God in very deed dwelt with man upon the earth." Its white-robed priest is the shadow of Him who was "holy, harmless, undefiled," and whom I recognize as my true High Priest. Its bleeding lamb laid upon the altar is the likeness of that Lamb of God by whose precious blood I have been redeemed from all iniquity; its innermost sanctuary is the type of that heaven into which He has entered to make atonement for my sin; and its outer apartment is the analogue of the present world, in which we are to serve Him with the incense of our devotions, the light of our characters, and the fruit of our lives. The incarnation in the person of Christ, the mediation and expiation of His priestly work, and the consequent obligation under which His redeemed people lie to honour Him with unceasing service and shining holiness—or, putting it all into four words, incarnation, mediation, expiation, consecration—these are the things of which the Tabernacle, with its furniture, services, and attendants, were the special types; and as thus we condense its teachings into their essence, we come to a larger and more comprehensive view of the doctrines of the gospel itself, and discover that we have been studying the same truths, only under a different form. (*W. M. Taylor, D.D.*)